Contents at a glance

Programming Windows, Sixth Edition

Charles Petzold

PUBLISHED BY
Microsoft Press
A Division of Microsoft Corporation
One Microsoft Way
Redmond, Washington 98052-6399

Library of Congress Control Number: 2012955549
ISBN: 978-0-7356-7176-8

Printed and bound in the United States of America.

Second Printing

Microsoft Press books are available through booksellers and distributors worldwide. If you need support related to this book, email Microsoft Press Book Support at mspinput@microsoft.com. Please tell us what you think of this book at http://www.microsoft.com/learning/booksurvey.

Microsoft and the trademarks listed at http://www.microsoft.com/about/legal/en/us/IntellectualProperty/Trademarks/EN-US.aspx are trademarks of the Microsoft group of companies. All other marks are property of their respective owners.

The example companies, organizations, products, domain names, email addresses, logos, people, places, and events depicted herein are fictitious. No association with any real company, organization, product, domain name, email address, logo, person, place, or event is intended or should be inferred.

This book expresses the author's views and opinions. The information contained in this book is provided without any express, statutory, or implied warranties. Neither the authors, Microsoft Corporation, nor its resellers, or distributors will be held liable for any damages caused or alleged to be caused either directly or indirectly by this book.

Acquisitions Editor: Devon Musgrave
Developmental Editor: Devon Musgrave
Project Editor: Devon Musgrave
Editorial Production: Waypoint Press
Technical Reviewer: Marc Young
Indexer: Christina Yeager
Cover: Twist Creative • Seattle and Joel Panchot

Table of Contents

What do you think of this book? We want to hear from you!

Microsoft is interested in hearing your feedback so we can continually improve our books and learning
resources for you. To participate in a brief online survey, please visit:

microsoft.com/learning/booksurvey

What do you think of this book? We want to hear from you!

Microsoft is interested in hearing your feedback so we can continually improve our books and learning resources for you. To participate in a brief online survey, please visit:

microsoft.com/learning/booksurvey

Introduction

This book—the 6th edition of *Programming Windows*—is a guide to writing applications that run under Microsoft Windows 8.

To use this book, you'll need a computer running Windows 8, on which you can install the Windows 8 development tools and software development kit (SDK), most conveniently in the form of the free download of Microsoft Visual Studio Express 2012 for Windows 8. That download is accessible from the Windows 8 developer portal:

http://msdn.microsoft.com/windows/apps

To install Visual Studio, follow the "Downloads for developers" link on that page and then the "Download the tools and SDK" link on the following page. This page also provides information on obtaining a Windows 8 developer account that lets you upload new applications to the Windows Store.

The Versions of Windows 8

For the most part, Windows 8 is intended to run on the same class of personal computers as Windows 7, which are machines built around the 32-bit or 64-bit Intel x86 microprocessor family. Windows 8 is available in a regular edition called simply Windows 8 and also a Windows 8 Pro edition with additional features that appeal to tech enthusiasts and professionals.

Both Windows 8 and Windows 8 Pro run two types of programs:

- Desktop applications

- New Windows 8 applications, often called Windows Store applications

Desktop applications are traditional Windows programs that currently run under Windows 7 and that interact with the operating system through the Windows application programming interface, known familiarly as the Win32 API. To run these desktop applications, Windows 8 includes a familiar Windows desktop screen.

The new Windows Store applications represent a radical break with traditional Windows. The programs generally run in a full-screen mode—although two programs can share the screen in a "snap" mode—and many of these programs will probably be optimized for touch and tablet use. These applications are purchasable and installable only from the application store run by Microsoft. (As a developer, you can deploy and test applications directly from Visual Studio.)

In addition to the versions of Windows 8 that run on x86 processors, there is also a version of Windows 8 that runs on ARM processors, most commonly found in low-cost tablets and other mobile devices. This version of Windows 8 is called Windows RT, and it only comes preinstalled on these machines. One of the first computers running Windows RT is the initial release of the Microsoft Surface.

Aside from some preinstalled desktop applications, Windows RT runs new Windows Store applications only. You cannot run existing Windows 7 applications under Windows RT. You cannot run Visual Studio under Windows RT, and you cannot develop Windows 8 applications under Windows RT.

The Windows 8 user interface incorporates a new design paradigm that is likely to be reflected in Windows Store applications. Somewhat inspired by signage in urban environments, this design paradigm emphasizes content over program "chrome" and is characterized by the use of unadorned fonts, clean open styling, a tile-based interface, and transitional animations.

Many developers were first introduced to the Windows 8 design paradigm with Windows Phone 7, so it's interesting to see how Microsoft's thinking concerning large and small computers has evolved. In years gone by, Microsoft attempted to adapt the design of the traditional Windows desktop to smaller devices such as hand-held computers and phones. Now a user-interface design for the phone is being moved up to tablets and the desktop.

One important characteristic of this new environment is an emphasis on multitouch, which has dramatically changed the relationship between human and computer. In fact, the term "multitouch" is now outmoded because virtually all new touch devices respond to multiple fingers. The simple word "touch" is now sufficient. Part of the new programming interface for Windows 8 applications treats touch, mouse, and pen input in a unified manner so that applications are automatically usable with all three input devices.

The Focus of This Book

This book focuses exclusively on writing Windows Store applications. Plenty of other books already exist for writing Win32 desktop applications, including the 5th edition of *Programming Windows*. I'll occasionally make reference to Win32 API and desktop applications, but this book is really all about writing new Windows 8 applications.

For writing these applications, a new object-oriented API has been introduced called the Windows Runtime or WinRT (not to be confused with the version of Windows 8 that runs on ARM processors, called Windows RT). Internally, the Windows Runtime is based on COM (Component Object Model) with interfaces exposed through metadata files with the extension .winmd located in the */Windows/System32/WinMetadata* directory. Externally, it is very object-oriented.

From the application programmer's perspective, the Windows Runtime resembles Silverlight, although internally it is not a managed API. For Silverlight programmers, perhaps the most immediate difference involves namespace names: the Silverlight namespaces beginning with *System.Windows* have been replaced with namespaces beginning with *Windows.UI.Xaml*.

Most Windows 8 applications will be built not only from code but also markup, either the industry-standard HyperText Markup Language (HTML) or Microsoft's eXtensible Application Markup Language (XAML). One advantage of splitting an application between code and markup is potentially splitting the development of the application between programmers and designers.

Currently there are three main options for writing Windows 8 applications, each of which involves a programming language and a markup language:

- C++ with XAML

- C# or Visual Basic with XAML

- JavaScript with HTML5

The Windows Runtime is common to all these options, but the Windows Runtime is also supplemented by another programming interface appropriate for the particular language. Although you can't mix languages within a single application, you can create libraries (called Windows Runtime Components) with their own .winmd files that can be accessed from any other Windows 8 language.

The C++ programmer uses a dialect of C++ called C++ with Component Extensions, or C++/CX, that allows the language to make better use of WinRT. The C++ programmer also has direct access to a subset of the Win32 and COM APIs, as well as DirectX. C++ programs are compiled to native machine code.

Programmers who use the managed languages C# or Visual Basic .NET will find WinRT to be very familiar territory. Windows 8 applications written in these languages can't access Win32, COM, or DirectX APIs with as much ease as the C++ programmer, but it is possible to do so, and some sample programs in Chapter 15, "Going Native," show how. A stripped-down version of .NET is also available for performing low-level tasks.

For JavaScript, the Windows Runtime is supplemented by a Windows Library for JavaScript, or WinJS, which provides a number of system-level features for Windows 8 apps.

After much consideration (and some anguish), I decided that this book would focus almost exclusively on the C# and XAML option. For at least a decade I have been convinced of the advantages of managed languages for development and debugging, and for me C# is the language that has the closest fit to the Windows Runtime. I hope C++ programmers find C# code easy enough to read to derive some benefit from this book.

I also believe that a book focusing on one language option is more valuable than one that tries for equal coverage among several languages. There will undoubtedly be plenty of other Windows 8 books that show how to write Windows 8 applications using the other options.

With that said, I have greatly enjoyed the renewed debate about the advantages of C++ and native code in crafting high-performance applications. No single tool is best for every problem, and I will be exploring C++ and DirectX development for Windows 8 more in the future, both in my blog and the pages of *MSDN Magazine*. As a modest start, the companion content for this book includes all the program samples converted to C++.

The Approach

In writing this book, I've made a couple assumptions about *you*, the reader. I assume that you are comfortable with C#. If not, you might want to supplement this book with a C# tutorial. If you are coming to C# from a C or C++ background, my free online book *.NET Book Zero: What the C or C++ Programmer Needs to Know About C# and the .NET Framework* might be adequate. This book is available in PDF or XPS format at *www.charlespetzold.com/dotnet*.

I also assume that you know the rudimentary syntax of XML (eXtensible Markup Language) because XAML is based on XML. But I assume no familiarity with XAML or any XAML-based programming interface.

This is an API book rather than a tools book. The only programming tool I use in this book is Microsoft Visual Studio Express 2012 for Windows 8 (which I'll generally simply refer to as Visual Studio).

Markup languages are generally much more toolable than programming code. Indeed, some programmers even believe that markup such as XAML should be entirely machine-generated. Visual Studio has a built-in interactive XAML designer that involves dragging controls to a page, and many programmers have come to know and love Microsoft Expression Blend for generating complex XAML for their applications. (Expression Blend is included among the free download of the development tools and SDK I mentioned earlier.)

While such design tools are great for experienced programmers, I think that the programmer new to the environment is better served by learning how to write XAML by hand. That's how I'll approach XAML in this book. The XAML Cruncher tool featured in Chapter 8, "App Bars and Popups," is very much in keeping with this philosophy: it lets you type in XAML and interactively see the objects that are generated, but it does not try to write XAML for you.

On the other hand, some programmers become so skilled at working with XAML that they forget how to create and initialize certain objects in code! I think both skills are important, and consequently I often show how to do similar tasks in both code and markup.

As I began working on this book, I contemplated different approaches to how a tutorial about the Windows Runtime can be structured. One approach is to start with rather low-level graphics and user input, demonstrate how controls can be built, and then describe the controls that have already been built for you.

I have instead chosen to focus initially on those skills I think are most important for most mainstream programmers: assembling the predefined controls in an application and linking them with code and data. This is the focus of the 12 chapters of the book's Part I, "Elementals." One of my goals in Part I is to make comprehensible all the code and markup that Visual Studio generates in the various project templates it supports.

Part II, "Specialities," covers more low-level and esoteric tasks, such as touch, bitmap graphics, rich text, printing, and working with the orientation and GPS sensors.

Source Code

Learning a new API is similar to learning how to play basketball or the oboe: You don't get the full benefit by watching someone else do it. Your own fingers must get involved. The source code in these pages is downloadable via the "Companion Content" link here:

http://shop.oreilly.com/product/0790145369079.do

But you'll learn better by actually typing in the code yourself.

My Setup

For writing this book, I used the special version of the Samsung 700T tablet that was distributed to attendees of the Microsoft Build Conference in September 2011. (For that reason, it's sometimes called the Build Tablet.) This machine has an Intel Core i5 processor running at 1.6 GHz with 4 GB of RAM and a 64-GB hard drive. The screen (from which most of the screenshots in the book were taken) has 8 touch points and a resolution of 1366 × 768 pixels, which is the lowest resolution for which snap views are supported.

Although the Build Tablets were originally distributed with the Windows 8 Developer Preview installed, I progressively replaced that with the Consumer Preview (build 8250) in March 2012 and the Release Preview (build 8400) in June 2012, and eventually the official release of Windows 8 Pro. Except when testing orientation sensors, I generally used the tablet in the docking port with an external 1920×1080 HDMI monitor, and an external keyboard and mouse.

When the Microsoft Surface first became available, I purchased one for testing my applications. For deploying and debugging applications on the Surface, I used the technique discussed by Tim Heuer in his blog entry:

http://timheuer.com/blog/archive/2012/10/26/remote-debugging-windows-store-apps-on-surface-arm-devices.aspx

This technique is more formally described in the documentation topic "Running Windows Store apps on a remote machine":

http://msdn.microsoft.com/en-us/library/hh441469.aspx

The Surface became particularly vital for testing programs that access the orientation sensors.

For the most part, however, I'm still using the Build Tablet in the docking station. The external keyboard, mouse, and monitor lets me run Visual Studio and Microsoft Word as I'm accustomed to, while my Windows 8 programs run on the tablet's touch screen. This is a fine development environment, particularly compared with the setup I used to write the first edition of *Programming Windows*.

But that was 25 years ago.

The *Programming Windows* Heritage

This is the 6th edition of *Programming Windows*, a book that was first conceived by Microsoft Press in the fall of 1986. The project came to involve me because at the time I was writing articles about Windows programming for *Microsoft Systems Journal* (the predecessor to *MSDN Magazine*).

I still get a thrill when I look at my very first book contract:

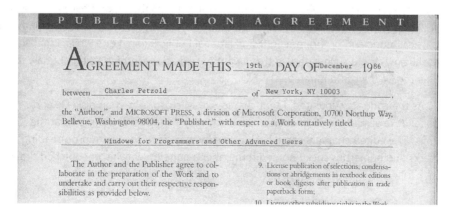

Perhaps the most amusing part of this contract occurs further down the first page:

> **II MANUSCRIPT**
>
> The Author agrees to prepare and submit one (1) clean copy and one (I) ASCII readable diskette of the final manuscript of the Work, equivalent to approximately 100,000 words, not later than April 30, 1987
>
> the due date. (A full manuscript page of text consists of approximately 250 words.) The Author's final manuscript shall be in double-spaced typescript or its equivalent, satisfactory to the Publisher in organization, form, content, and style and accompanied by appropriate illustrative material, table of contents, tables, bibliography, and instructional aids ready for reproduction.

The reference to "typescript" means that the pages must as least resemble something that came out of a typewriter. A double-spaced manuscript page with a fixed-pitch font has about 250 words, as the description indicates. A book page is more in the region of 400 words, so Microsoft Press obviously wasn't expecting a very long book.

For writing the book I used an IBM PC/AT with an 80286 microprocessor running at 8 MHz with 512 KB of memory and two 30 MB hard drives. The display was an IBM Enhanced Graphics Adapter, with a maximum resolution of 640×350 with 16 simultaneous colors. I wrote some of the early chapters using Windows 1 (introduced over a year earlier in November 1985), but beta versions of Windows 2 soon became available.

In those years, editing and compiling a Windows program occurred outside of Windows in MS-DOS. For editing source code, I used WordStar 3.3, the same word processor I used for writing the chapters. From the MS-DOS command line, you would run the Microsoft C compiler and then launch Windows with your program to test it out. It was necessary to exit Windows and return to MS-DOS for the next edit-compile-run cycle.

As I got deeper into writing the book over the course of 1987, much of the rest of my life faded away. I stayed up later and later into the night. I didn't have a television at the time, but the local public radio station, WNYC-FM, was on almost constantly with classical music and programming from National Public Radio. For a while, I managed to shift my day to such a degree that I went to bed after *Morning Edition* but awoke in time for *All Things Considered*.

As the contract stipulated, I sent chapters to Microsoft Press on diskette and paper. (We all had email, of course, but email didn't support attachments at the time.) The edited chapters came back to me by mail decorated with proofreading marks and numerous sticky notes. I remember a page on which someone had drawn a thermometer indicating the increasing number of pages I was turning in with the caption "Temperature's Rising!"

Along the way, the focus of the book changed. Writing a book for "Programmers and Other Advanced Users" proved to be a flawed concept. I don't know who came up with the title *Programming Windows*.

The contract had a completion date of April, but I didn't finish until August and the book wasn't published until early 1988. The final page total was about 850. If these were normal book pages (that is, without program listings or diagrams) the word count would be about 400,000 rather than the 100,000 indicated in the contract.

The cover of the first edition of *Programming Windows* described it as "The Microsoft Guide to Programming for the MS-DOS Presentation Manager: Windows 2.0 and Windows/386." The reference to Presentation Manager reminds us of the days when Windows and the OS/2 Presentation Manager were supposed to peacefully coexist as similar environments for two different operating systems.

The first edition of *Programming Windows* went pretty much unnoticed by the programming community. When MS-DOS programmers gradually realized they needed to learn about the brave new environment of Windows, it was mostly the 2nd edition (published in 1990 and focusing on Windows 3) and the 3rd edition (1992, Windows 3.1) that helped out.

When the Windows API graduated from 16-bit to 32-bit, *Programming Windows* responded with the 4th edition (1996, Windows 95) and 5th edition (1998, Windows 98). Although the 5th edition is still in print, the email I receive from current readers indicates that the book is most popular in India and China.

From the 1st edition to the 5th, I used the C programming language. Sometime between the 3rd and 4th editions, my good friend Jeff Prosise said that he wanted to write *Programming Windows with MFC*, and that was fine by me. I didn't much care for the Microsoft Foundation Classes, which seemed to me a fairly light wrapper on the Windows API, and I wasn't that thrilled with C++ either.

As the years went by, *Programming Windows* acquired the reputation of being the book for programmers who needed to get close to the metal without any extraneous obstacles between their program code and the operating system.

But to me, the early editions of *Programming Windows* were nothing of the sort. In those days, getting close to the metal involved coding in assembly language, writing character output directly into video display memory, and resorting to MS-DOS only for file I/O. In contrast, programming for Windows involved a high-level language, completely unaccelerated graphics, and accessing hardware only through a heavy layer of APIs and device drivers.

This switch from MS-DOS to Windows represented a deliberate forfeit of speed and efficiency in return for other advantages. But what advantages? Many veteran programmers just couldn't see the point. Graphics? Pictures? Color? Fancy fonts? A mouse? That's not what computers are all about! The skeptics called it the WIMP (window-icon-menu-pointer) interface, which was not exactly a subtle implication about the people who chose to use such an environment or code for it.

If you wait long enough, a high-level language becomes a low-level language, and multiple layers of interface seemingly shrink down (at least in lingo) to a native API. Some C and C++ programmers of today reject a managed language like C# on grounds of efficiency, and Windows has even sparked some energetic controversy once again. Windows 8 is easily the most revolutionary updating to Windows since its very first release in 1985, but many old-time Windows users are wondering about the wisdom of bringing a touch-based interface tailored for smartphones and tablets to the mainstream desktop, and they grumble when they can't find familiar features.

I suppose that *Programming Windows* could only be persuaded to emerge from semi-retirement with an exciting and controversial new user interface on Windows, and an API and programming language suited to its modern aspirations.

More in the Future

I suspect that Windows 8 will dominate my programming life for a while, which means that I'm likely to be posting blog entries about various aspects of Windows 8 programming. You can access my blog and subscribe to the RSS feed at *www.charlespetzold.com*.

I always enjoy solving a thorny programming problem and posting a blog entry about it, so if you have a Windows 8 programming issue that you'd like me to take a look at and possibly figure out, write me at *cp@charlespetzold.com*.

Beginning with the January 2013 issue of *MSDN Magazine*, I will be writing a monthly column called "DirectX Factor," focusing specifically on using DirectX from Windows 8 and Windows Phone 8 applications. MSDN Magazine is available for free perusal at *http://msdn.microsoft.com/magazine*.

Behind the Scenes

This book exists only because Ben Ryan and Devon Musgrave at Microsoft Press developed an interesting way to release early content to the developer community and get advance sales of the final book simultaneously.

Part of the job duties of Devon and my technical reviewer Marc Young is to protect me from embarrassment by identifying blunders in my prose and code, and I thank them both for finding quite a few.

Thanks also to Andrew Whitechapel for giving me feedback on the C++ sample code; Brent Rector for an email with a crucial solution for an issue involving touch, as well as some background into *IBuffer*; Robert Levy for reflections about touch; Jeff Prosise for always seeming to have a dead-on answer when I'm puzzled; Larry Smith for finding numerous flaws in my prose; and Admiral for prodding me to make the book as useful as possible to C++ programmers.

The errors that remain in these chapters are my own fault, of course. Later in this Introduction is an email address for reporting errors to the publisher, but I'll also try to identify the most egregious issues on my website at www.charlespetzold.com/pw6.

Finally, I want to thank my wife Deirdre Sinnott for love and support and making the necessary adjustments to our lives that writing a book inevitably entails.

Charles Petzold
Roscoe, NY and New York City
December 31, 2012

Errata & Book Support

We've made every effort to ensure the accuracy of this book and its companion content. Any errors that have been reported since this book was published are listed on our Microsoft Press site at oreilly.com. Search for the book at *http://microsoftpress.oreilly.com*, and then click the "View/Submit Errata" link. If you find an error that is not already listed, you can report it to us through the same page.

If you need additional support, email Microsoft Press Book Support at *mspinput@microsoft.com*.

Please note that product support for Microsoft software is not offered through the addresses above.

We Want to Hear from You

At Microsoft Press, your satisfaction is our top priority, and your feedback our most valuable asset. Please tell us what you think of this book at

http://aka.ms/tellpress

The feedback form is very short, and we read every one of your comments and ideas. Thanks in advance for your input.

Stay in Touch

Let's keep the conversation going! We're on Twitter: *http://twitter.com/MicrosoftPress*

PART I

Elementals

CHAPTER 1

Markup and Code

E ver since the publication of Brian Kernighan and Dennis Ritchie's classic book *The C Programming Language* (Prentice Hall, 1978), it has been customary for programming tutorials to begin with a simple program that displays a short text string such as "hello, world." Let's create a few similar programs for the new world of Windows 8.

I'll assume you have Windows 8 installed as well as a recent version of Microsoft Visual Studio that supports the creation of Windows 8 applications.

Launch Visual Studio from the Windows 8 start screen, and let's get coding.

The First Project

On the opening screen in Visual Studio, the Get Started tab should already be selected. Over at the left you'll see a New Project option. Click that item, or select New Project from the File menu.

When the New Project dialog box opens, select Templates in the left panel, then Visual C#, and the option for creating a new Windows Store project. From the list of available templates in the central area, select Blank App. Toward the bottom of the dialog box, type a project name in the Name field: **Hello**, for example. Let the Solution Name be the same. Use the Browse button to select a directory location for this program, and click OK. (I'll generally use mouse terminology such as "click" when referring to Visual Studio, but I'll switch to touch terminology such as "tap" for the applications you'll be creating. A version of Visual Studio that is optimized for touch is probably at least a few years away.)

Visual Studio creates a solution named Hello and a project within that solution named Hello, as well as a bunch of files in the Hello project. These files are listed in the Solution Explorer on the far right of the Visual Studio screen. Every Visual Studio solution has at least one project, but a solution might contain additional application projects and library projects.

The list of files for this project includes one called MainPage.xaml, and if you click the little arrowhead next to that file, you'll see a file named MainPage.xaml.cs indented underneath MainPage.xaml:

You can view either of these two files by double-clicking the file name or by right-clicking the file name and choosing Open.

The MainPage.xaml and MainPage.xaml.cs files are linked in the Solution Explorer because they both contribute to the definition of a class named *MainPage*. For a simple program like Hello, this *MainPage* class defines all the visuals and user interface for the application.

Despite its funny file name, MainPage.xaml.cs definitely has a .cs extension, which stands for "C Sharp." Stripped of all its comments, the skeleton MainPage.xaml.cs file contains C# code that looks like this:

```
using System;
using System.Collections.Generic;
using System.IO;
using System.Linq;
using Windows.Foundation;
using Windows.Foundation.Collections;
using Windows.UI.Xaml;
using Windows.UI.Xaml.Controls;
using Windows.UI.Xaml.Controls.Primitives;
using Windows.UI.Xaml.Data;
using Windows.UI.Xaml.Input;
using Windows.UI.Xaml.Media;
using Windows.UI.Xaml.Navigation;

namespace Hello
{
    public sealed partial class MainPage : Page
    {
        public MainPage()
        {
```

```
            this.InitializeComponent();
        }
        protected override void OnNavigatedTo(NavigationEventArgs e)
        {
        }
    }
}
```

The file is dominated by *using* directives for all the namespaces that you are anticipated to need. You'll discover that most MainPage.xaml.cs files don't require all these namespaces and many others require some additional namespaces.

These namespaces fall into two general categories based on the first word in the name:

- **System.*** .NET for new Windows 8 applications

- **Windows.*** Windows Runtime (or WinRT)

As suggested by the list of *using* directives, namespaces that begin with *Windows.UI.Xaml* play a major role in the Windows Runtime.

Following the *using* directives, this MainPage.xaml.cs file defines a namespace named *Hello* (the same as the project name) and a class named *MainPage* that derives from *Page*, a class that is part of the Windows Runtime.

The documentation of the Windows 8 API is organized by namespace, so if you want to locate the documentation of the *Page* class, knowing the namespace where it's defined is useful. Let the mouse pointer rest on the name *Page* in the MainPage.xaml.cs source code, and you'll discover that *Page* is in the *Windows.UI.Xaml.Controls* namespace.

The constructor of the *MainPage* class calls an *InitializeComponent* method (which I'll discuss shortly), and the class also contains an override of a method named *OnNavigatedTo*. Windows 8 applications often have a page-navigation structure somewhat like a website, and hence they often consist of multiple classes that derive from *Page*. For navigational purposes, *Page* defines virtual methods named *OnNavigatingFrom*, *OnNavigatedFrom*, and *OnNavigatedTo*. The override of *OnNavigatedTo* is a convenient place to perform initialization when the page becomes active. But that's for later; most of the programs in the early chapters of this book will have only one page. I'll tend to refer to an application's "page" more than its "window." There is still a window underneath the application, but it doesn't play nearly as large a role as the page.

Notice the *partial* keyword on the *MainPage* class definition. This keyword usually means that the class definition is continued in another C# source code file. In reality (as you'll see), that's exactly the case.

Conceptually, however, the missing part of the *MainPage* class is not another C# code file but the MainPage.xaml file:

```
<Page
    x:Class="Hello.MainPage"
    xmlns="http://schemas.microsoft.com/winfx/2006/xaml/presentation"
    xmlns:x="http://schemas.microsoft.com/winfx/2006/xaml"
    xmlns:local="using:Hello"
    xmlns:d="http://schemas.microsoft.com/expression/blend/2008"
    xmlns:mc="http://schemas.openxmlformats.org/markup-compatibility/2006"
    mc:Ignorable="d">

    <Grid Background="{StaticResource ApplicationPageBackgroundThemeBrush}">

    </Grid>
</Page>
```

This file consists of markup conforming to the standard known as the eXtensible Application Markup Language, or XAML, pronounced "zammel." As the name implies, XAML is based on eXtensible Markup Language, or XML.

Generally, you'll use the XAML file for defining all the visual elements of the page, while the C# file handles jobs that can't be performed in markup, such as number crunching and responding to user input. The C# file is often referred to as the "code-behind" file for the corresponding XAML file.

The root element of this XAML file is *Page*, which you already know is a class in the Windows Runtime. But notice the *x:Class* attribute:

```
<Page
    x:Class="Hello.MainPage"
```

The *x:Class* attribute can appear only on the root element in a XAML file. This particular *x:Class* attribute translates as "a class named *MainPage* in the *Hello* namespace is defined as deriving from *Page*." It means the same thing as the class definition in the C# file!

Following that are a bunch of XML namespace declarations. As usual, these URIs don't actually reference interesting webpages but instead serve as unique identifiers maintained by particular companies or organizations. The first two are the most important:

```
xmlns="http://schemas.microsoft.com/winfx/2006/xaml/presentation"
xmlns:x="http://schemas.microsoft.com/winfx/2006/xaml"
```

The 2006 date harkens back to Microsoft's introduction of the Windows Presentation Foundation and the debut of XAML. WPF was part of the .NET Framework 3.0, which prior to its release was known as WinFX, hence the "winfx" in the URI. To a certain extent, XAML files are compatible among WPF, Silverlight, Windows Phone, and the Windows Runtime, but only if they use classes, properties, and features common to all the environments.

The first namespace declaration with no prefix refers to public classes, structures, and enumerations defined in the Windows Runtime, which includes all the controls and everything else that can appear in a XAML file, including the *Page* and *Grid* classes in this particular file. The word "presentation" in this URI refers to a visual user interface, and that distinguishes it from other types of applications that can use XAML. For example, if you were using XAML for the Windows Workflow Foundation (WF), you'd use a default namespace URI ending with the word "workflow."

The second namespace declaration associates an "x" prefix with elements and attributes that are intrinsic to XAML itself. Only nine of these are applicable in Windows Runtime applications, and obviously one of the most important is the *x:Class* attribute.

The third namespace declaration is interesting:

```
xmlns:local="using:Hello"
```

This associates an XML prefix of *local* with the *Hello* namespace of this particular application. You might create custom classes in your application, and you'd use the *local* prefix to reference them in XAML. If you need to reference classes in code libraries, you'll define additional XML namespace declarations that refer to the assembly name and namespace name of these libraries. You'll see how to do this in chapters ahead.

The remaining namespace declarations are for Microsoft Expression Blend. Expression Blend might insert special markup of its own that should be ignored by the Visual Studio compiler, so that's the reason for the *Ignorable* attribute, which requires yet another namespace declaration. For any program in this book, these last three lines of the *Page* root element can be deleted.

The *Page* element has a child element named *Grid*, which is another class defined in the *Windows.UI.Xaml.Controls* namespace. The *Grid* will become extremely familiar. It is sometimes referred to as a "container" because it can contain other visual objects, but it's more formally classified as a "panel" because it derives from the *Panel* class. Classes that derive from *Panel* play a very important role in layout in Windows 8 applications. In the MainPage.xaml file that Visual Studio creates for you, the *Grid* is assigned a background color (actually a *Brush* object) based on a predefined identifier using a syntax I'll discuss in Chapter 2, "XAML Syntax."

Generally, you'll divide a *Grid* into rows and columns to define individual cells (as I'll demonstrate in Chapter 5, "Control Interaction"), somewhat like a much improved version of an HTML table. A *Grid* without rows and columns is sometimes called a "single-cell *Grid*" and is still quite useful.

To display up to a paragraph of text in the Windows Runtime, you'll generally use a *TextBlock* (another class defined in the *Windows.UI.Xaml.Controls* namespace), so let's put a *TextBlock* in the single-cell *Grid* and assign a bunch of attributes. These attributes are actually properties defined by the *TextBlock* class:

Project: Hello | File: MainPage.xaml (excerpt)

```
<Grid Background="{StaticResource ApplicationPageBackgroundThemeBrush}">
    <TextBlock Text="Hello, Windows 8!"
               FontFamily="Times New Roman"
               FontSize="96"
               FontStyle="Italic"
               Foreground="Yellow"
               HorizontalAlignment="Center"
               VerticalAlignment="Center" />
</Grid>
```

Note In this book, whenever a block of code or markup is preceded by a heading like this one, you'll find the code among this book's downloadable companion content. Generally, I'll just show an excerpt of the total file but with enough context so that you know exactly where it is.

The order of these attributes doesn't matter, and of course the indentation doesn't matter, and all of them except the *Text* attribute can be skipped if you're in a hurry. As you type you'll notice that Visual Studio's IntelliSense feature suggests attribute names and possible values for you. Often you can just select the one you want. As you finish typing the *TextBlock*, Visual Studio's design view gives you a preview of the page's appearance.

You can also skip all the typing and simply drag a *TextBlock* from the Visual Studio Toolbox and then set the properties in a table, but I won't be doing that in this book. I'll instead describe the creation of these programs as if you and I actually type in the code and markup just like real programmers.

Press F5 to compile and run this program, or select Start Debugging from the Debug menu. Even for simple programs like this, it's best to run the program under the Visual Studio debugger. If all goes well, this is what you'll see:

The *HorizontalAlignment* and *VerticalAlignment* attributes on the *TextBlock* have caused the text to be centered, obviously without the need for you the programmer to explicitly determine the size of the video display and the size of the rendered text. You can alternatively set *HorizontalAlignment* to

Left or *Right*, and *VerticalAlignment* to *Top* or *Bottom* to position the *TextBlock* in one of nine places in the *Grid*. As you'll see in Chapter 4, "Presentation with Panels," the Windows Runtime supports precise pixel placement of visual objects, but usually you'll want to rely on the built-in layout features.

The *TextBlock* has *Width* and *Height* properties, but generally you don't need to bother setting those. In fact, if you set the *Width* and *Height* properties on this particular *TextBlock*, you might end up cropping part of the text or interfering with the centering of the text on the page. The *TextBlock* knows better than you how large it should be.

You might be running this program on a device that responds to orientation changes, such as a tablet. If so, you'll notice that the page content dynamically conforms to the change in orientation and aspect ratio, apparently without any interaction from the program. The *Grid*, the *TextBlock*, and the Windows 8 layout system are doing most of the work.

To terminate the Hello program, press Shift+F5 in Visual Studio, or select Stop Debugging from the Debug menu. You'll notice that the program hasn't merely been executed, but has actually been deployed to Windows 8 and is now executable from the start screen. If you've created the project yourself, the tile is not very pretty, but the program's tiles are all stored in the Assets directory of the project, so you can spruce them up if you want. (The projects in the downloadable companion content for this book have been given custom tiles.) You can run the program again outside of the Visual Studio debugger right from the Windows 8 start screen.

Another option is to run your programs in a simulator that lets you control resolution, orientation, and other characteristics. In the Visual Studio toolbar, you'll see a drop-down list with the current setting Local Machine. Simply change that to Simulator.

Graphical Greetings

Traditional "hello" programs display a greeting in text, but that's not the only way to do it. The HelloImage project accesses a bitmap from my website using a tiny piece of XAML:

Project: HelloImage | File: MainPage.xaml (excerpt)

```
<Grid Background="{StaticResource ApplicationPageBackgroundThemeBrush}">
    <Image Source="http://www.charlespetzold.com/pw6/PetzoldJersey.jpg" />
</Grid>
```

The *Image* element is defined in the *Windows.UI.Xaml.Controls* namespace, and it's the standard way to display bitmaps in a Windows Runtime program. By default, the bitmap is stretched to fit the space available for it while respecting the original aspect ratio:

If you make the page smaller—perhaps by changing the orientation or invoking a snap view—the image will change size to accommodate the new size of the page.

You can override the default display of this bitmap by using the *Stretch* property defined by *Image*. The default value is the enumeration member *Stretch.Uniform*. Try setting it to *Fill*:

```
<Grid Background="{StaticResource ApplicationPageBackgroundThemeBrush}">
    <Image Source="http://www.charlespetzold.com/pw6/PetzoldJersey.jpg"
           Stretch="Fill" />
</Grid>
```

Now the aspect ratio is ignored and the bitmap fills the container:

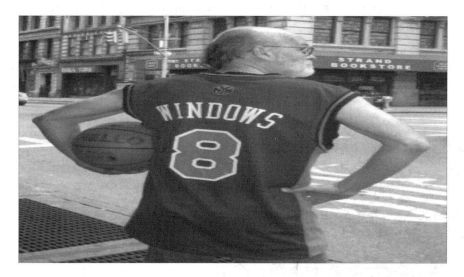

Set the *Stretch* property to *None* to display the image in its pixel dimensions (320 by 400):

You can control where it appears on the page by using the same *HorizontalAlignment* and *VerticalAlignment* properties you use with *TextBlock*.

The fourth option for the *Stretch* property is *UniformToFill*, which respects the aspect ratio but fills the container regardless. It achieves this feat by the only way possible: clipping the image. Which part of the image that gets clipped depends on the *HorizontalAlignment* and *VerticalAlignment* properties.

Accessing bitmaps over the Internet is dependent on a network connection and even then might require some time. A better guarantee of having an image immediately available is to bind the bitmap into the application itself.

You can create simple bitmaps right in Windows Paint. Let's run Paint and use the File Properties option to set a size of 480 by 320 (for example). Using a mouse, finger, or pen, you can create your own personalized greeting:

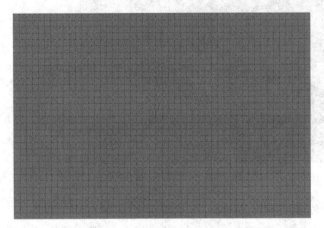

The Windows Runtime supports the popular BMP, JPEG, PNG, and GIF formats, as well as a couple less common formats. For images such as the preceding one, PNG is common, so save it with a name like Greeting.png.

Now create a new project: HelloLocalImage, for example. It's common to store bitmaps used by a project in a directory named Images. In the Solution Explorer, right-click the project name and choose Add and New Folder. (Or, if the project is selected in the Solution Explorer, pick New Folder from the Project menu.) Give the folder a name such as Images.

Now right-click the Images folder and choose Add and Existing Item. Navigate to the Greeting.png file you saved and click the Add button. Once the file is added to the project, you'll want to right-click the Greeting.png file name and select Properties. In the Properties panel, make sure the Build Action is set to Content. You want this image to become part of the content of the application.

The XAML file that references this image looks very much like one for accessing an image over the web:

Project: HelloLocalImage | File: MainPage.xaml (excerpt)

```
<Grid Background="{StaticResource ApplicationPageBackgroundThemeBrush}">
    <Image Source="Images/Greeting.png"
           Stretch="None" />
</Grid>
```

Notice that the *Source* property is set to the folder and file name. Here's how it looks:

Sometimes programmers prefer giving a name of Assets to the folder that stores application bitmaps. You'll notice that the standard project already contains an Assets folder containing program logo bitmaps. You can use that same folder for your other images instead of creating a separate folder.

Variations in Text

You might be tempted to refer to the *Grid*, *TextBlock*, and *Image* as "controls," perhaps based on the knowledge that these classes are in the *Windows.UI.Xaml.Controls* namespace. Strictly speaking, however, they are *not* controls. The Windows Runtime does define a class named *Control*, but these three classes do not descend from *Control*. Here's a tiny piece of the Windows Runtime class hierarchy showing the classes encountered so far:

Object
  DependencyObject
    UIElement
      FrameworkElement
        TextBlock
        Image
        Panel
          Grid
        Control
          UserControl
            Page

Page derives from *Control* but *TextBlock* and *Image* do not. *TextBlock* and *Image* instead derive from *UIElement* and *FrameworkElement*. For that reason, *TextBlock* and *Image* are more correctly referred to as "elements," the same word often used to describe items that appear in XML files.

The distinction between an element and a control is not always obvious, but the distinction is useful nonetheless. Visually, controls are built from elements, and the visual appearance of the control can be customizable through a template. A *Grid* is also an element, but it's more often referred to as a "panel," and that (as you'll see) is a very useful distinction.

Try this: In the original Hello program move the *Foreground* attribute and all the font-related attributes from the *TextBlock* element to the *Page*. The entire MainPage.xaml file now looks like this:

```
<Page
    x:Class="Hello.MainPage"
    xmlns="http://schemas.microsoft.com/winfx/2006/xaml/presentation"
    xmlns:x="http://schemas.microsoft.com/winfx/2006/xaml"
    xmlns:local="using:Hello"
    xmlns:d="http://schemas.microsoft.com/expression/blend/2008"
    xmlns:mc="http://schemas.openxmlformats.org/markup-compatibility/2006"
    mc:Ignorable="d"
    FontFamily="Times New Roman"
    FontSize="96"
    FontStyle="Italic"
    Foreground="Yellow">

    <Grid Background="{StaticResource ApplicationPageBackgroundThemeBrush}">
        <TextBlock Text="Hello, Windows 8!"
                   HorizontalAlignment="Center"
                   VerticalAlignment="Center" />
    </Grid>
</Page>
```

You'll discover that the result is exactly the same. When these attributes are set on the *Page* element, they apply to everything on that page.

Now try setting the *Foreground* property of the *TextBlock* to red:

```
<TextBlock Text="Hello, Windows 8!"
           Foreground="Red"
           HorizontalAlignment="Center"
           VerticalAlignment="Center" />
```

The local red setting overrides the yellow setting on the *Page*.

The *Page*, *Grid*, and *TextBlock* form what is called a "visual tree" of elements, except that in the XAML file the tree is upside-down. The *Page* is the trunk of the tree, and its descendants (*Grid* and *TextBlock*) form branches. You might imagine that the values of the font properties and *Foreground* property defined on the *Page* are propagated down through the visual tree from parent to child. This is true except for a little peculiarity: These properties don't exist in *Grid*. These properties are defined by *TextBlock* and separately defined by *Control*, which means that the properties manage to propagate from the *Page* to the *TextBlock* despite an intervening element that has very different DNA.

If you begin examining the documentation of these properties in the *TextBlock* or *Page* class, you'll discover that they seem to appear twice under somewhat different names. In the documentation of *TextBlock* you'll see a *FontSize* property of type *double*:

```
public double FontSize { set; get; }
```

You'll also see a property named *FontSizeProperty* of type *DependencyProperty*:

```
public static DependencyProperty FontSizeProperty { get; }
```

Notice that this *FontSizeProperty* property is get-only and static as well.

Many of the classes that you'll use in constructing the user interface of a Windows 8 application have conventional properties as well as corresponding properties called "dependency properties" of type *DependencyProperty*. Interestingly enough, the class hierarchy I just showed you has a class named *DependencyObject*. These two types are related: A class that derives from *DependencyObject* often declares static get-only properties of type *DependencyProperty*. Both *DependencyObject* and *DependencyProperty* are defined in the *Windows.UI.Xaml* namespace, suggesting how fundamental they are to the whole system.

Dependency properties are intended to solve some fundamental problems that come about in sophisticated user interfaces. In a Windows 8 application, properties can be set in a variety of ways. For example, you've already seen that properties can be set directly on an object or inherited through the visual tree. As you'll see in Chapter 2, "XAML Syntax," properties might also be set from a *Style* definition. In a future chapter you'll see properties set from animations. The *DependencyObject* and *DependencyProperty* classes are part of a system that helps maintain order in such an environment by establishing priorities for the different ways in which the property might be set. I don't want to go too deeply into the mechanism just yet; it's something you'll experience more intimately when you begin defining your own controls.

The *FontSize* property is sometimes said to be "backed by" the dependency property named *FontSizeProperty*. But sometimes a semantic shortcut is used and *FontSize* itself is referred to as a dependency property. Usually this is not confusing.

Many of the properties defined by *UIElement* and its descendent classes are dependency properties, but only a few of these properties are propagated through the visual tree. *Foreground* and all the font-related properties are, as well as a few others that I'll be sure to call your attention to as we encounter them. Dependency properties also have an intrinsic default value. If you remove all the *TextBlock* and *Page* attributes except *Text*, you'll get white text displayed with an 11-pixel system font in the upper-left corner of the page.

The *FontSize* property is in units of pixels and refers to the design height of a font. This design height includes space for descenders and diacritical marks. As you might know, font sizes are often specified in *points*, which in electronic typography are units of 1/72 inch. The equivalence between pixels and points requires knowing the resolution of the video display in dots-per-inch (DPI). Without that information, it's generally assumed that video displays have a resolution of 96 DPI, so a 96-pixel font is thus a 72-point font (one-inch high) and the default 11-pixel font is an 8¼-point font.

For high-resolution displays, Windows automatically adjusts sizes and coordinates. An application can obtain this information from the *DisplayProperties* class, which pretty much dominates the *Windows.Graphics.Display* namespace. For most purposes, however, assuming a resolution of 96 DPI is fine, and you'll use this same assumption for the printer. In accordance with this assumption, I tend to use pixel dimensions that represent simple fractions of inches: 48 (1/2"), 24 (1/4"), 12 (1/8"), and 6 (1/16").

You've seen that if you remove the *Foreground* attribute, you get white text on a dark background. The background is not exactly black, but the predefined *ApplicationPageBackgroundThemeBrush* identifier that the *Grid* references is close to it.

The Hello project also includes two other files that come in a pair: App.xaml and App.xaml.cs together define a class named *App* that derives from *Application*. Although an application can have multiple *Page* derivatives, it has only one *Application* derivative. This *App* class is responsible for settings or activities that affect the application as a whole.

Try this: In the root element of the App.xaml file, set the attribute *RequestedTheme* to *Light*.

```
<Application
    x:Class="Hello.App"
    xmlns="http://schemas.microsoft.com/winfx/2006/xaml/presentation"
    xmlns:x="http://schemas.microsoft.com/winfx/2006/xaml"
    xmlns:local="using:Hello"
    RequestedTheme="Light">
    ...
</Application>
```

The only options are *Light* and *Dark*. Now when you recompile and run the program, it has a light background, which means the color referenced by the *ApplicationPageBackgroundThemeBrush* identifier is different. If the *Foreground* property on the *Page* or *TextBlock* is not explicitly set, you'll also get black text, which means that the *Foreground* property has a different default value with this theme.

In many of the sample programs in the remainder of this book, I'll be using the light theme without mentioning it. I think the screen shots look better on the page, and they won't consume as much ink if you decide to print pages from the book. However, keep in mind that many small devices and an increasing number of larger devices have video displays built around organic light-emitting diode (OLED) technology and these displays consume less power if the screen isn't lit up like a billboard. Reduced power consumption is one reason why dark color schemes are becoming more popular.

Of course, you can completely specify your own colors by explicitly setting both the *Background* of the *Grid* and the *Foreground* of the *TextBlock*:

```
<Grid Background="Blue">
    <TextBlock Text="Hello, Windows 8!"
               Foreground="Yellow"
               ... />
</Grid>
```

For these properties, Visual Studio's IntelliSense provides 140 standard color names, plus *Transparent*. These are actually static properties of the *Colors* class. Alternatively, you can specify red-green-blue (RGB) values directly in hexadecimal with values ranging from 00 to FF prefaced by a pound sign:

```
Foreground="#FF8000"
```

That's maximum red, half green, and no blue. An optional fourth byte at the beginning is the alpha channel, with values ranging from 00 for transparent and FF for opaque. Here's a half-transparent red:

```
Foreground="#80FF0000"
```

When an alpha value is included at the beginning, these are sometimes referred to as ARGB colors. The *UIElement* class also defines an *Opacity* property that can be set to values between 0 (transparent) and 1 (opaque). In HelloImage, try setting the *Background* property of the *Grid* to a nonblack color (perhaps Blue) and set the *Opacity* property of the *Image* element to 0.5.

When you specify colors by using bytes, the values are in accordance with the familiar sRGB ("standard RGB") color space. This color space dates back to the era of cathode-ray tube displays where these bytes directly controlled the voltages illuminating the pixels. Very fortuitously, nonlinearities in pixel brightness and nonlinearities in the perception of brightness by the human eye roughly cancel each other out, so these byte values often seem perceptually linear, or nearly so.

An alternative is the scRGB color space, which uses values between 0 and 1 that are proportional to light intensity. Here's a value for medium gray:

```
Foreground="sc# 0.5 0.5 0.5"
```

Because of the logarithmic response of the human eye to light intensity, this gray will appear to be rather too light to be classified as medium.

If you need to display text characters that are not on your keyboard, you can specify them in Unicode by using standard XML character escaping. For example, if you want to display the text "This costs €55" and you're confined to an American keyboard, you can specify the Unicode Euro in decimal like this:

```
<TextBlock Text="This costs &#8364;55" ...
```

Or perhaps you prefer hexadecimal:

```
<TextBlock Text="This costs &#x20AC;55" ...
```

Or you can simply paste text into Visual Studio as I obviously did with a program later in this chapter.

As with standard XML, strings can contain special characters beginning with the ampersand:

- & is an ampersand
- ' is a single-quotation mark ("apostrophe")
- " is a double-quotation mark

- < is a left angle bracket ("less than")

- > is a right angle bracket ("greater than")

An alternative to setting the *Text* property of *TextBlock* requires separating the element into a start tag and end tag and specifying the text as content:

```
<TextBlock ... >
    Hello, Windows 8!
</TextBlock>
```

As I'll discuss in Chapter 2, setting text as content of the *TextBlock* is not exactly equivalent to setting the *Text* property. It's actually much more powerful. But even without taking advantage of additional features, specifying text as content is useful for displaying a larger quantity of text because you don't have to worry about extraneous white space as much as when you're dealing with quoted text. The WrappedText project displays a whole paragraph of text by specifying this text as content of the *TextBlock*:

Project: WrappedText | File: MainPage.xaml (excerpt)

```
<Grid Background="{StaticResource ApplicationPageBackgroundThemeBrush}">
    <TextBlock FontSize="48"
               TextWrapping="Wrap">
        For a long time I used to go to bed early. Sometimes, when I had put out
        my candle, my eyes would close so quickly that I had not even time to
        say "I'm going to sleep." And half an hour later the thought that it was
        time to go to sleep would awaken me; I would try to put away the book
        which, I imagined, was still in my hands, and to blow out the light; I
        had been thinking all the time, while I was asleep, of what I had just
        been reading, but my thoughts had run into a channel of their own,
        until I myself seemed actually to have become the subject of my book:
        a church, a quartet, the rivalry between François I and Charles V. This
        impression would persist for some moments after I was awake; it did not
        disturb my mind, but it lay like scales upon my eyes and prevented them
        from registering the fact that the candle was no longer burning. Then
        it would begin to seem unintelligible, as the thoughts of a former
        existence must be to a reincarnate spirit; the subject of my book would
        separate itself from me, leaving me free to choose whether I would form
        part of it or no; and at the same time my sight would return and I
        would be astonished to find myself in a state of darkness, pleasant and
        restful enough for the eyes, and even more, perhaps, for my mind, to
        which it appeared incomprehensible, without a cause, a matter dark
        indeed.
    </TextBlock>
</Grid>
```

When parsed, the end-of-line characters at the end of each line and the eight space characters at the beginning of each line are collapsed into a single space character.

Notice the *TextWrapping* property. The default is the *TextWrapping.NoWrap* enumeration member; *Wrap* is the only alternative. You can also set the *TextAlignment* property to members of the *TextAlignment* enumeration: *Left*, *Right*, *Center*, or *Justify*, which causes extra space to be inserted between words so that the text is even on both the left and right.

You can run this program in either portrait mode or landscape:

For a long time I used to go to bed early. Sometimes, when I had put out my candle, my eyes would close so quickly that I had not even time to say "I'm going to sleep." And half an hour later the thought that it was time to go to sleep would awaken me; I would try to put away the book which, I imagined, was still in my hands, and to blow out the light; I had been thinking all the time, while I was asleep, of what I had just been reading, but my thoughts had run into a channel of their own, until I myself seemed actually to have become the subject of my book: a church, a quartet, the rivalry between François I and Charles V. This impression would persist for some moments after I was awake; it did not disturb my mind, but it lay like scales upon my eyes and prevented them from registering the fact that the

If your display responds to orientation changes, the text is automatically reformatted. The Windows Runtime breaks lines at spaces or hyphens, but it does not break lines at nonbreaking spaces ('&#x00A0') or nonbreaking hyphens ('&#x2011'). Any soft hyphens ('&#x00AD') are ignored.

Not every element in XAML supports text content like *TextBlock*. You can't have text content in the *Page* or *Grid*, for example. XAML is not as free form as HTML because XAML syntax is based entirely on underlying classes and properties.

But the *Grid* can support multiple *TextBlock* children. The OverlappedStackedText project has two *TextBlock* elements in the *Grid* with different colors and font sizes:

Project: OverlappedStackedText | File: MainPage.xaml

```
<Grid Background="Yellow">
    <TextBlock Text="8"
               FontSize="864"
               FontWeight="Bold"
               Foreground="Red"
               HorizontalAlignment="Center"
               VerticalAlignment="Center" />

    <TextBlock Text="Windows"
               FontSize="192"
               FontStyle="Italic"
               Foreground="Blue"
               HorizontalAlignment="Center"
               VerticalAlignment="Center" />
</Grid>
```

Here's the result:

Notice that the second element is visually above the first. This visual stacking is often referred to as "Z order" because in a three-dimensional coordinate space, an imaginary Z axis comes out of the screen. In Chapter 4 you'll see a way to override this behavior.

Of course, overlapping is not a generalized solution to displaying multiple items of text! In Chapter 5 you'll see how to define rows and columns in the *Grid* for layout purposes, but another approach to organizing multiple elements in a single-cell *Grid* is to use various values of *HorizontalAlignment* and *VerticalAlignment* to prevent them from overlapping. The InternationalHelloWorld program displays "hello, world" in nine different languages. (Thank you, Google Translate.)

Project: InternationalHelloWorld | File: MainPage.xaml (excerpt)

```xaml
<Page
    x:Class="InternationalHelloWorld.MainPage"
    ...
    FontSize="40">

    <Grid Background="{StaticResource ApplicationPageBackgroundThemeBrush}">
        <!-- Chinese (simplified) -->
        <TextBlock Text="你好, 世界"
                   HorizontalAlignment="Left"
                   VerticalAlignment="Top" />

        <!-- Urdu -->
        <TextBlock Text="ہیلو دنیا،"
                   HorizontalAlignment="Center"
                   VerticalAlignment="Top" />
```

```
        <!-- Japanese -->
        <TextBlock Text="こんにちは、世界中のみなさん"
                   HorizontalAlignment="Right"
                   VerticalAlignment="Top" />

        <!-- Hebrew -->
        <TextBlock Text="שלום, עולם"
                   HorizontalAlignment="Left"
                   VerticalAlignment="Center" />

        <!-- Esperanto -->
        <TextBlock Text="Saluton, mondo"
                   HorizontalAlignment="Center"
                   VerticalAlignment="Center" />

        <!-- Arabic -->
        <TextBlock Text="مرحبا، العالم"
                   HorizontalAlignment="Right"
                   VerticalAlignment="Center" />

        <!-- Korean -->
        <TextBlock Text="안녕하세요, 전 세계"
                   HorizontalAlignment="Left"
                   VerticalAlignment="Bottom" />

        <!-- Russian -->
        <TextBlock Text="Здравствуй, мир"
                   HorizontalAlignment="Center"
                   VerticalAlignment="Bottom" />

        <!-- Hindi -->
        <TextBlock Text="नमस्ते दुनिया है,"
                   HorizontalAlignment="Right"
                   VerticalAlignment="Bottom" />
    </Grid>
</Page>
```

Notice the *FontSize* attribute set in the root element to apply to all nine *TextBlock* elements. Property inheritance is obviously one way to reduce repetition in XAML, and you'll see other approaches as well in the next chapter.

你好，世界　　　　　　　بيلو دنيا،　　　　こんにちは、世界中のみなさん

שלום, עולם　　　　　Saluton, mondo　　　　مرحبا، العالم

안녕하세요, 전 세계　　　Здравствуй, мир　　　नमस्ते दुनिया है,

Media As Well

So far you've seen greetings in text and bitmaps. The HelloAudio project plays an audio greeting from a file on my website. I made the recording using the Windows 8 Sound Recorder application, which automatically saves in WMA format. The XAML file looks like this:

Project: HelloAudio | **File:** MainPage.xaml (excerpt)

```
<Grid Background="{StaticResource ApplicationPageBackgroundThemeBrush}">
    <MediaElement Source="http://www.charlespetzold.com/pw6/AudioGreeting.wma" />
</Grid>
```

The *MediaElement* class derives from *FrameworkElement* and has no user interface, although it provides enough information for you to build your own.

You can also use *MediaElement* for playing movies. The HelloVideo program plays a video from my website:

Project: HelloVideo | **File:** MainPage.xaml (excerpt)

```
<Grid Background="{StaticResource ApplicationPageBackgroundThemeBrush}">
    <MediaElement Source="http://www.charlespetzold.com/pw6/VideoGreeting.wmv" />
</Grid>
```

The Code Alternatives

It's not necessary to instantiate elements or controls in XAML. You can alternatively create them entirely in code. Indeed, very much of what can be done in XAML can be done in code instead. Code is particularly useful for creating many objects of the same type because there's no such thing as a *for* loop in XAML.

Let's create a new project named HelloCode, but let's visit the MainPage.xaml file only long enough to give the *Grid* a name:

Project: HelloCode | **File:** MainPage.xaml (excerpt)

```
<Grid Name="contentGrid"
      Background="{StaticResource ApplicationPageBackgroundThemeBrush}">

</Grid>
```

Setting the *Name* attribute allows the *Grid* to be accessed from the code-behind file. Alternatively, you can use *x:Name*:

```
<Grid x:Name="contentGrid"
      Background="{StaticResource ApplicationPageBackgroundThemeBrush}">

</Grid>
```

For most cases, there's really no practical difference between *Name* and *x:Name*. As the "x" prefix indicates, the *x:Name* attribute is intrinsic to XAML itself, and you can use it to identify any object in the XAML file. The *Name* attribute is more restrictive: *Name* is defined by *FrameworkElement*, so you can use it only with classes that derive from *FrameworkElement*. For a class not derived from *FrameworkElement*, you'll need to use *x:Name* instead. Some programmers prefer to be consistent by using *x:Name* throughout. I tend to use *Name* whenever I can and *x:Name* otherwise. (However, when naming a custom control that is defined in the application assembly, sometimes *Name* doesn't work and *x:Name* is required.)

Whether you use *Name* or *x:Name*, the rules for the name you choose are the same as the rules for variable names. The name can't contain spaces or begin with a number, for example. All names within a particular XAML file must be unique.

In the MainPage.xaml.cs file you'll want two additional *using* directives:

Project: HelloCode | **File:** MainPage.xaml.cs (excerpt)

```
using Windows.UI;
using Windows.UI.Text;
```

The first is for the *Colors* class; the second is for a *FontStyle* enumeration. It's not strictly necessary that you insert these *using* directives manually. If you use the *Colors* class or *FontStyle* enumeration, Visual Studio will indicate with a red squiggly underline that it can't resolve the identifier, at which point you can right-click it and select Resolve from the shortcut menu. The new *using* directive will be added to the others in correct alphabetical order (as long as the existing *using* directives are alphabetized). When you're all finished with the code file, you can right-click anywhere in the file and select

Organize Usings and Remove Unused Usings to clean up the list. (I've done that with this MainPage.xaml.cs file.)

The constructor of the *MainPage* class is a handy place to create a *TextBlock*, assign properties, and then add it to the *Grid*:

Project: HelloCode | File: MainPage.xaml.cs (excerpt)

```
public MainPage()
{
    this.InitializeComponent();

    TextBlock txtblk = new TextBlock();
    txtblk.Text = "Hello, Windows 8!";
    txtblk.FontFamily = new FontFamily("Times New Roman");
    txtblk.FontSize = 96;
    txtblk.FontStyle = FontStyle.Italic;
    txtblk.Foreground = new SolidColorBrush(Colors.Yellow);
    txtblk.HorizontalAlignment = HorizontalAlignment.Center;
    txtblk.VerticalAlignment = VerticalAlignment.Center;

    contentGrid.Children.Add(txtblk);
}
```

Notice that the last line of code here references the *Grid* named *contentGrid* in the XAML file just as if it were a normal object, perhaps stored as a field. (As you'll see, it actually *is* a normal object and it *is* a field!) Although not evident in XAML, the *Grid* has a property named *Children* that it inherits from *Panel*. This *Children* property is of type *UIElementCollection*, which is a collection that implements the *IList<UIElement>* and *IEnumerable<UIElement>* interfaces. This is why the *Grid* can support multiple child elements.

Code often tends to be a little wordier than XAML partially because the XAML parser works behind the scenes to create additional objects and perform conversions. The code reveals that the *FontFamily* property requires that a *FontFamily* object be created and that *Foreground* is of type *Brush* and requires an instance of a *Brush* derivative, such as *SolidColorBrush*. *Colors* is a class that contains 141 static properties of type *Color*. You can alternatively create a *Color* value from ARGB bytes by using the static *Color.FromArgb* method.

The *FontStyle*, *HorizontalAlignment*, and *VerticalAlignment* properties are all enumeration types, where the enumeration is the same name as the property. Indeed, the *Text* and *FontSize* properties seem odd in that they are primitive types: a string and a double-precision floating-point number.

You can reduce the code bulk a little by using a style of property initialization introduced in C# 3.0:

```
TextBlock txtblk = new TextBlock
{
    Text = "Hello, Windows 8!",
    FontFamily = new FontFamily("Times New Roman"),
    FontSize = 96,
    FontStyle = FontStyle.Italic,
    Foreground = new SolidColorBrush(Colors.Yellow),
    HorizontalAlignment = HorizontalAlignment.Center,
    VerticalAlignment = VerticalAlignment.Center
};
```

I've tended to use this style a lot in this book. (However, I have not used another popular feature introduced in C# 3.0—implicit typing using the *var* keyword—because it tends to obscure rather than illuminate the code.) Either way, you can now compile and run the HelloCode project and the result should look the same as the XAML version. It looks the same because it basically *is* the same.

You can alternatively create the *TextBlock* and add it to the *Children* collection of the *Grid* in the *OnNavigatedTo* override. Or you can create the *TextBlock* in the constructor, save it as a field, and add it to the *Grid* in *OnNavigatedTo*.

Notice that I put the code after the *InitializeComponent* call in the *MainPage* constructor. You can create the *TextBlock* prior to *InitializeComponent*, but you must add it to the *Grid* after *InitializeComponent* because the *Grid* does not exist prior to that call. The *InitializeComponent* method basically parses the XAML at run time and instantiates all the XAML objects and puts them all together in a tree. *InitializeComponent* is obviously an important method, which is why you might be puzzled when you can't find it in the documentation.

Here's the story: When Visual Studio compiles the application, it generates some intermediate files. You can find these files with Windows Explorer by navigating to the HelloCode solution, the HelloCode project, and then the obj and Debug directories. Among the list of files are MainPage.g.cs and MainPage.g.i.cs. The "g" stands for "generated." Both these files define *MainPage* classes derived from *Page* with the *partial* keyword. The composite *MainPage* class thus consists of the MainPage.xaml.cs file under your control plus these two generated files, which you don't mess with. Although you don't edit these files, they are important to know about because they might pop up in Visual Studio if a run-time error occurs involving the XAML file.

The MainPage.g.i.cs file is the more interesting of the two. Here you'll find the definition of the *InitializeComponent* method, which calls a static method named *Application.LoadComponent* to load the MainPage.xaml file. Notice also that this partial class definition contains a private field named *contentGrid*, which is the name you've assigned to the *Grid* in the XAML file. The *InitializeComponent* method concludes by setting that field to the actual *Grid* object created by *Application.LoadComponent*.

The *contentGrid* field is thus accessible throughout the *MainPage* class, but the value will be *null* until *InitializeComponent* is called.

In summary, parsing the XAML is a two-stage process. At compile time the XAML is parsed to extract all the element names (among other tasks) and generate the intermediate C# files in the obj directory. These generated C# files are compiled along with the C# files under your control. At run time the XAML file is parsed again to instantiate all the elements, assemble them in a visual tree, and obtain references to them.

Where is the standard *Main* method that serves as an entry point to any C# program? That's in App.g.i.cs, one of two files generated by Visual Studio based on App.xaml.

Let me show you something else that will serve as just a little preview of dependency properties:

As I mentioned earlier, many properties that we've been dealing with—*FontFamily*, *FontSize*, *FontStyle*, *Foreground*, *Text*, *HorizontalAlignment*, and *VerticalAlignment*—have corresponding static dependency properties, named *FontFamilyProperty*, *FontSizeProperty*, and so forth. You might amuse yourself by changing a normal statement like this:

```
txtblk.FontStyle = FontStyle.Italic;
```

to an alternative that might look quite peculiar:

```
txtblk.SetValue(TextBlock.FontStyleProperty, FontStyle.Italic);
```

What you're doing here is calling a method named *SetValue* defined by *DependencyObject* and inherited by *TextBlock*. You're calling this method on the *TextBlock* object but passing to it the static *FontStyleProperty* object of type *DependencyProperty* defined by *TextBlock* and the value you want for that property. There is no real difference between these two ways of setting the *FontStyle* property. Within *TextBlock*, the *FontStyle* property is very likely defined something like this:

```
public FontStyle FontStyle
{
    set
    {
        SetValue(TextBlock.FontStyleProperty, value);
    }
    get
    {
        return (FontStyle)GetValue(TextBlock.FontStyleProperty);
    }
}
```

I say "very likely" because I'm not privy to the Windows Runtime source code, and that source code is likely written in C++ rather than C#, but if the *FontStyle* property is defined like all other properties backed by dependency properties, the *set* and *get* accessors simply call *SetValue* and *GetValue* with the *TextBlock.FontStyleProperty* dependency property. This is extremely standard code, and it's a pattern you'll come to be so familiar with that you'll generally define your own dependency properties without so much white space like this:

```
public FontStyle FontStyle
{
    set { SetValue(TextBlock.FontStyleProperty, value); }
    get { return (FontStyle)GetValue(TextBlock.FontStyleProperty); }
}
```

Earlier you saw how you can set the *Foreground* and font-related properties in XAML on the *Page* tag rather than the *TextBlock* and how these properties are inherited by the *TextBlock*. Of course you can do the same thing in code:

```
public MainPage()
{
    this.InitializeComponent();

    this.FontFamily = new FontFamily("Times New Roman");
    this.FontSize = 96;
    this.FontStyle = FontStyle.Italic;
    this.Foreground = new SolidColorBrush(Colors.Yellow);
```

```
TextBlock txtblk = new TextBlock();
txtblk.Text = "Hello, Windows 8!";
txtblk.HorizontalAlignment = HorizontalAlignment.Center;
txtblk.VerticalAlignment = VerticalAlignment.Center;

contentGrid.Children.Add(txtblk);
}
```

C# doesn't require the *this* prefix to access properties and methods of the class, but when you're editing the files in Visual Studio, typing the *this* prefix invokes IntelliSense to give you a list of available methods, properties, and events.

Images in Code

The HelloImage and HelloLocalImage projects earlier in this chapter used the *Image* element to display bitmaps. In XAML, you set the *Source* property to a URI indicating the location of a bitmap. Judging solely from the XAML file, you might have assumed that this *Source* property is defined as a string or perhaps the *Uri* type. It's actually more complex than that: The *Source* property is of type *ImageSource*, which encapsulates the actual image that the *Image* element is responsible for displaying. *ImageSource* doesn't define anything on its own and cannot be instantiated, but several important classes descend from *ImageSource*, as shown in this partial class hierarchy:

Object
   DependencyObject
     ImageSource
       BitmapSource
         BitmapImage
         WriteableBitmap

ImageSource is defined in the *Windows.UI.Xaml.Media* namespace, but the descendent classes are in *Windows.UI.Xaml.Media.Imaging*. A *BitmapSource* can't be instantiated either, but it defines public *PixelWidth* and *PixelHeight* properties as well as a *SetSource* method that lets you read in bitmap data from a file or network stream. *BitmapImage* inherits these members and also defines a *UriSource* property.

You can use *BitmapImage* for displaying a bitmap from code. Besides defining this *UriSource* property, *BitmapImage* also defines a constructor that accepts a *Uri* object. In the HelloImageCode project, the *Grid* has been given a name of "contentGrid" and a *using* directive for *Windows.UI.Xaml. Media.Imaging* has been added to the code-behind file. Here's the *MainPage* constructor:

Project: HelloImageCode | **File:** MainPage.xaml.cs (excerpt)

```
public MainPage()
{
    this.InitializeComponent();

    Uri uri = new Uri("http://www.charlespetzold.com/pw6/PetzoldJersey.jpg");
    BitmapImage bitmap = new BitmapImage(uri);
```

```
Image image = new Image();
image.Source = bitmap;
contentGrid.Children.Add(image);
}
```

Setting a *Name* of "contentGrid" on the *Grid* is not strictly necessary for accessing the *Grid* from code. The *Grid* is actually set to the *Content* property of the *Page*, so rather than accessing the *Grid* like so:

```
contentGrid.Children.Add(image);
```

you can do it like this:

```
Grid grid = this.Content as Grid;
grid.Children.Add(image);
```

In fact, the *Grid* isn't even necessary in such a simple program. You can effectively remove the *Grid* from the visual tree by setting the *Image* directly to the *Content* property of *MainPage*:

```
this.Content = image;
```

The *Content* property that *MainPage* inherits from *UserControl* is of type *UIElement*, so it can support only one child. Generally, the child of the *MainPage* is a *Panel* derivative that supports multiple children, but if you need only one child, you can use the *Content* property of the *MainPage* directly.

It's also possible to make a hybrid of the XAML and code approaches: to instantiate the *Image* element in XAML and create the *BitmapImage* in code, or to instantiate both the *Image* element and *BitmapImage* in XAML and then set the *UriSource* property of *BitmapImage* from code. I've used the first approach in the HelloLocalImageCode project, which has an Images directory with the Greeting. png file. The XAML file already contains the *Image* element, but it doesn't reference an actual bitmap:

Project: HelloLocalImageCode | File: MainPage.xaml (excerpt)

```
<Grid Background="{StaticResource ApplicationPageBackgroundThemeBrush}">
    <Image Name="image"
           Stretch="None" />
</Grid>
```

The code-behind file sets the *Source* property of the *Image* element in a single line:

Project: HelloLocalImageCode | File: MainPage.xaml.cs (excerpt)

```
public sealed partial class MainPage : Page
{
    public MainPage()
    {
        this.InitializeComponent();
        image.Source = new BitmapImage(new Uri("ms-appx:///Images/Greeting.png"));
    }
}
```

Look at that special URL for referencing the content bitmap file from code. In XAML, that special prefix is optional.

Are there general rules to determine when to use XAML and when to use code? Not really. I tend to use XAML whenever possible except when the repetition becomes ridiculous. My normal rule for code is "three or more: use a *for*," but I'll often allow somewhat more repetition in XAML before moving it into code. A lot depends on how concise and elegant you've managed to make the XAML and how much effort it would be to change something.

Not Even a Page

Insights into how a Windows Runtime program starts up can be obtained by examining the *OnLaunched* override in the standard App.xaml.cs file. You'll discover that it creates a *Frame* object, uses this *Frame* object to navigate to an instance of *MainPage* (which is how *MainPage* gets instantiated), and then sets this *Frame* object to a precreated *Window* object accessible through the *Window.Current* static property. Here's the simplified code:

```
var rootFrame = new Frame();
rootFrame.Navigate(typeof(MainPage));
Window.Current.Content = rootFrame;
Window.Current.Activate();
```

A Windows 8 application doesn't require a *Page* derivative, a *Frame*, or even any XAML files at all. Let's conclude this chapter by creating a new project named StrippedDownHello and begin by deleting the App.xaml, App.xaml.cs, MainPage.xaml, and MainPage.xaml.cs files, as well as the entire Common folder. Yes, delete them all! Now the project has no code files and no XAML files. It's left with just an app manifest, assembly information, and some PNG files.

Right-click the project name and select Add and New Item. Select either a new class or code file and name it App.cs. Here's what you'll want it to look like:

Project: StrippedDownHello | **File:** App.cs

```
using Windows.ApplicationModel.Activation;
using Windows.UI;
using Windows.UI.Xaml;
using Windows.UI.Xaml.Controls;
using Windows.UI.Xaml.Media;

namespace StrippedDownHello
{
    public class App : Application
    {
        static void Main(string[] args)
```

```
        {
            Application.Start((p) => new App());
        }

        protected override void OnLaunched(LaunchActivatedEventArgs args)
        {
            TextBlock txtblk = new TextBlock
            {
                Text = "Stripped-Down Windows 8",
                FontFamily = new FontFamily("Lucida sans Typewriter"),
                FontSize = 96,
                Foreground = new SolidColorBrush(Colors.Red),
                HorizontalAlignment = HorizontalAlignment.Center,
                VerticalAlignment = VerticalAlignment.Center
            };

            Window.Current.Content = txtblk;
            Window.Current.Activate();
        }
    }
}
```

That's all you need (and obviously much less if you want default properties on the *TextBlock*).
The static *Main* method is the entry point and that creates a new *App* object and starts it going, and
the *OnLaunched* override creates a *TextBlock* and makes it the content of the application's default
window.

I won't be pursuing this approach to creating Windows 8 applications in this book, but obviously
it works.

CHAPTER 2

XAML Syntax

A Windows 8 application is divided into code and markup because each has its own strength. Despite the limitations of markup in performing complex logic or computational tasks, it's good to get as much of a program into markup as possible. Markup is easier to edit with tools and shows a clearer sense of the visual layout of a page. Of course, everything in markup is a string, so markup sometimes becomes cumbersome in representing complex objects. Because markup doesn't have the loop processing common in programming languages, it can also be prone to repetition.

These issues have been addressed in the syntax of XAML in several ways, the most important of which are explored in this chapter. But let me begin this vital subject with a topic that will at first appear to be completely off topic: defining a gradient brush.

The Gradient Brush in Code

The *Background* property in *Grid* and the *Foreground* property of the *TextBlock* are both of type *Brush*. The programs shown so far have set these properties to a derivative of *Brush* called *SolidColorBrush*. As demonstrated in Chapter 1, "Markup and Code," you can create a *SolidColorBrush* in code and give it a *Color* value; in XAML this is done for you behind the scenes.

SolidColorBrush is only one of four available brushes, as shown in this class hierarchy:

> *Object*
>   *DependencyObject*
>   *Brush*
>   *SolidColorBrush*
>   *GradientBrush*
>   *LinearGradientBrush*
>   *TileBrush*
>   *ImageBrush*
>   *WebViewBrush*

Only *SolidColorBrush*, *LinearGradientBrush*, *ImageBrush*, and *WebViewBrush* are instantiable. Like many other graphics-related classes, most of these brush classes are defined in the *Windows.UI.Xaml .Media* namespace, although *WebViewBrush* is defined in *Windows.UI.Xaml.Controls*.

The *LinearGradientBrush* creates a gradient between two or more colors. For example, suppose you want to display some text with blue at the left gradually turning to red at the right. While we're at it, let's set a similar gradient on the *Background* property of the *Grid* but going the other way.

In the GradientBrushCode program, a *TextBlock* is instantiated in XAML, and both the *Grid* and the *TextBlock* have names:

Project: GradientBrushCode | **File:** MainPage.xaml (excerpt)

```
<Grid Name="contentGrid"
      Background="{StaticResource ApplicationPageBackgroundThemeBrush}">

    <TextBlock Name="txtblk"
               Text="Hello, Windows 8!"
               FontSize="96"
               FontWeight="Bold"
               HorizontalAlignment="Center"
               VerticalAlignment="Center" />
</Grid>
```

The constructor of the code-behind file creates two separate *LinearGradientBrush* objects to set to the *Background* property of the *Grid* and *Foreground* property of the *TextBlock*:

Project: GradientBrushCode | **File:** MainPage.xaml.cs (excerpt)

```
public MainPage()
{
    this.InitializeComponent();

    // Create the foreground brush for the TextBlock
    LinearGradientBrush foregroundBrush = new LinearGradientBrush();
    foregroundBrush.StartPoint = new Point(0, 0);
    foregroundBrush.EndPoint = new Point(1, 0);

    GradientStop gradientStop = new GradientStop();
    gradientStop.Offset = 0;
    gradientStop.Color = Colors.Blue;
    foregroundBrush.GradientStops.Add(gradientStop);

    gradientStop = new GradientStop();
    gradientStop.Offset = 1;
    gradientStop.Color = Colors.Red;
    foregroundBrush.GradientStops.Add(gradientStop);

    txtblk.Foreground = foregroundBrush;

    // Create the background brush for the Grid
    LinearGradientBrush backgroundBrush = new LinearGradientBrush
    {
        StartPoint = new Point(0, 0),
        EndPoint = new Point(1, 0)
    };
    backgroundBrush.GradientStops.Add(new GradientStop
    {
        Offset = 0,
        Color = Colors.Red
    });
```

```
backgroundBrush.GradientStops.Add(new GradientStop
{
    Offset = 1,
    Color = Colors.Blue
});

contentGrid.Background = backgroundBrush;
}
```

The two brushes are created with two different styles of property initialization, but otherwise they're basically the same. The *LinearGradientBrush* class defines two properties named *StartPoint* and *EndPoint* of type *Point*, which is a structure with *X* and *Y* properties representing a two-dimensional coordinate point. The *StartPoint* and *EndPoint* properties are relative to the object to which the brush is applied based on the standard windowing coordinate system: *X* values increase to the right and *Y* values increase going down. The relative point (0, 0) is the upper-left corner and (1, 0) is the upper-right corner, so the brush gradient extends along an imaginary line between these two points, and all lines parallel to that line. The *StartPoint* and *EndPoint* defaults are (0, 0) and (1, 1), which defines a gradient from the upper-left to the lower-right corners of the target object.

LinearGradientBrush also has a property named *GradientStops* that is a collection of *GradientStop* objects. Each *GradientStop* indicates an *Offset* relative to the gradient line and a *Color* at that offset. Generally the offsets range from 0 to 1, but for special purposes they can go beyond the range encompassed by the brush. *LinearGradientBrush* defines additional properties to indicate how the gradient is calculated and what happens beyond the smallest *Offset* and the largest *Offset*.

Here's the result:

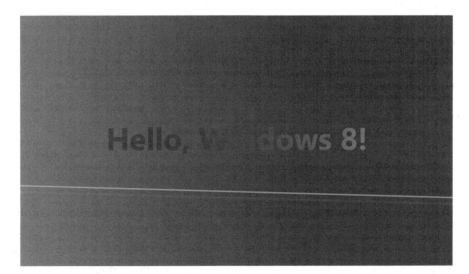

If you now consider defining these same brushes in XAML, all of a sudden the limitations of markup become all too evident. XAML lets you define a *SolidColorBrush* by just specifying the color, but how on earth do you set a *Foreground* or *Background* property to a text string defining two points and two or more offsets and colors?

Property-Element Syntax

Fortunately, there is a way. As you've seen, you normally indicate that you want a *SolidColorBrush* in XAML simply by specifying the color of the brush:

```
<TextBlock Text="Hello, Windows 8!"
           Foreground="Blue"
           FontSize="96" />
```

The *SolidColorBrush* is created for you behind the scenes.

However, it's possible to use a variation of this syntax that gives you the option of being more explicit about the nature of this brush. Remove that *Foreground* property, and separate the *TextBlock* element into start and end tags:

```
<TextBlock Text="Hello, Windows 8!"
           FontSize="96">

</TextBlock>
```

Within those tags, insert additional start and end tags consisting of the element name, a period, and a property name:

```
<TextBlock Text="Hello, Windows 8!"
           FontSize="96">
    <TextBlock.Foreground>

    </TextBlock.Foreground>
</TextBlock>
```

And within those tags put the object you want to set to that property:

```
<TextBlock Text="Hello, Windows 8!"
           FontSize="96">
    <TextBlock.Foreground>
        <SolidColorBrush Color="Blue" />
    </TextBlock.Foreground>
</TextBlock>
```

Now it's explicit that *Foreground* is being set to an instance of a *SolidColorBrush*.

This is called *property-element syntax*, and it's an important feature of XAML. At first it might seem to you (as it did to me) that this syntax is an extension or aberration of standard XML, but it's definitely not. Periods are perfectly valid characters in XML element names.

In reference to that last little snippet of XAML it is now possible to categorize three types of XAML syntax:

- The *TextBlock* and *SolidColorBrush* are both examples of "object elements" because they are XML elements that result in the creation of objects.

- The *Text*, *FontSize*, and *Color* settings are examples of "property attributes." They are XML attributes that specify the settings of properties.

- The *TextBlock.Foreground* tag is a "property element." It is a property expressed as an XML element.

XAML poses a restriction on property-element tags: Nothing else can go in the start tag. The object being set to the property must be content that goes between the start and end tags.

The following example uses a second set of property-element tags for the *Color* property of the *SolidColorBrush*:

```
<TextBlock Text="Hello, Windows 8!"
           FontSize="96">
    <TextBlock.Foreground>
        <SolidColorBrush>
            <SolidColorBrush.Color>
                Blue
            </SolidColorBrush.Color>
        </SolidColorBrush>
    </TextBlock.Foreground>
</TextBlock>
```

If you want, you can set the other two properties of the *TextBlock* similarly:

```
<TextBlock>
    <TextBlock.Text>
        Hello, Windows 8
    </TextBlock.Text>

    <TextBlock.FontSize>
        96
    </TextBlock.FontSize>

    <TextBlock.Foreground>
        <SolidColorBrush>
            <SolidColorBrush.Color>
                Blue
            </SolidColorBrush.Color>
        </SolidColorBrush>
    </TextBlock.Foreground>
</TextBlock>
```

But there's really no point. For these simple properties, the property attribute syntax is shorter and clearer. Where property-element syntax comes to the rescue is in expressing more complex objects like *LinearGradientBrush*. Let's begin again with the property-element tags:

```
<TextBlock Text="Hello, Windows 8!"
           FontSize="96">
    <TextBlock.Foreground>

    </TextBlock.Foreground>
</TextBlock>
```

Put a *LinearGradientBrush* in there, separated into start tags and end tags. Set the *StartPoint* and *EndPoint* properties in this start tag:

```
<TextBlock Text="Hello, Windows 8!"
           FontSize="96">
    <TextBlock.Foreground>
        <LinearGradientBrush StartPoint="0 0" EndPoint="1 0">

        </LinearGradientBrush>
    </TextBlock.Foreground>
</TextBlock>
```

Notice that the two properties of type *Point* are specified with two numbers separated by a space. You can separate the number pair with a comma if you choose.

The *LinearGradientBrush* has a *GradientStops* property that is a collection of *GradientStop* objects, so include the *GradientStops* property with another property element:

```
<TextBlock Text="Hello, Windows 8!"
           FontSize="96">
    <TextBlock.Foreground>
        <LinearGradientBrush StartPoint="0 0" EndPoint="1 0">
            <LinearGradientBrush.GradientStops>

            </LinearGradientBrush.GradientStops>
        </LinearGradientBrush>
    </TextBlock.Foreground>
</TextBlock>
```

The *GradientStops* property is of type *GradientStopCollection*, so let's add that in as well:

```
<TextBlock Text="Hello, Windows 8!"
           FontSize="96">
    <TextBlock.Foreground>
        <LinearGradientBrush StartPoint="0 0" EndPoint="1 0">
            <LinearGradientBrush.GradientStops>
                <GradientStopCollection>

                </GradientStopCollection>
            </LinearGradientBrush.GradientStops>
        </LinearGradientBrush>
    </TextBlock.Foreground>
</TextBlock>
```

Finally, add the two *GradientStop* objects to the collection:

```
<TextBlock Text="Hello, Windows 8!"
           FontSize="96">
    <TextBlock.Foreground>
        <LinearGradientBrush StartPoint="0 0" EndPoint="1 0">
            <LinearGradientBrush.GradientStops>
                <GradientStopCollection>
                    <GradientStop Offset="0" Color="Blue" />
                    <GradientStop Offset="1" Color="Red" />
                </GradientStopCollection>
            </LinearGradientBrush.GradientStops>
        </LinearGradientBrush>
    </TextBlock.Foreground>
</TextBlock>
```

And there we have it: a rather complex property setting expressed entirely in markup.

Content Properties

The syntax I've just shown you for instantiating and initializing the *LinearGradientBrush* is actually a bit more extravagant than what you actually need. You might be persuaded of this fact when you consider that all the XAML files we've seen so far have apparently been missing some properties and elements. Look at this little snippet of markup:

```
<Page ... >
    <Grid ... >
        <TextBlock ... />
        <TextBlock ... />
        <TextBlock ... />
    </Grid>
</Page>
```

We know from working with the classes in code that the *TextBlock* elements are added to the *Children* collection of the *Grid*, and the *Grid* is set to the *Content* property of the *Page*. But where are those *Children* and *Content* properties in the markup?

Well, you can include them if you want. Here are the *Page.Content* and *Grid.Children* property elements as they are allowed to appear in a XAML file:

```
<Page ... >
    <Page.Content>
        <Grid ... >
            <Grid.Children>
                <TextBlock ... />
                <TextBlock ... />
                <TextBlock ... />
            </Grid.Children>
        </Grid>
    </Page.Content>
</Page>
```

This markup is still missing the *UIElementCollection* object that is set to the *Children* property of the *Grid*. That cannot be explicitly included because only elements with parameterless public constructors can be instantiated in XAML files, and the *UIElementCollection* class is missing such a constructor.

The real question is this: Why aren't the *Page.Content* and *Grid.Children* property elements required in the XAML file?

Simple: All classes referenced in XAML are allowed to have one (and only one) property that is designated as a "content" property. For this content property, and only this property, property-element tags are not required.

The content property for a particular class is specified as a .NET attribute. Somewhere in the actual class definition of the *Panel* class (from which *Grid* derives) is an attribute named *ContentProperty*. If these classes were defined in C#, it would look like this:

```
[ContentProperty(Name="Children")]
public class Panel : FrameworkElement
{
    ...
}
```

What this means is simple. Whenever the XAML parser encounters some markup like this:

```
<Grid ... >
    <TextBlock ... />
    <TextBlock ... />
    <TextBlock ... />
</Grid>
```

then it checks the *ContentProperty* attribute of the *Grid* and discovers that these *TextBlock* elements should be added to the *Children* property.

Similarly, the definition of the *UserControl* class (from which *Page* derives) defines the *Content* property as its content property (which might sound appropriately redundant if you say it out loud):

```
[ContentProperty(Name="Content")]
public class UserControl : Control
{
    ...
}
```

You can define a *ContentProperty* attribute in your own classes. The *ContentPropertyAttribute* class required for this is in the *Windows.UI.Xaml.Markup* namespace.

Unfortunately, at the time I'm writing this book, the documentation for the Windows Runtime indicates only when a *ContentProperty* attribute has been set on a class—look in the Attributes section of the home page for the *Panel* class, for example—but not what that property actually is! Perhaps the documentation will be enhanced in the future, but until then, you'll just have to learn by example and retain by habit.

Fortunately, many content properties are defined to be the most convenient property of the class. For *LinearGradientBrush*, the content property is *GradientStops*. Although *GradientStops* is of type *GradientStopCollection*, XAML does not require collection objects to be explicitly included. Here's the excessively wordy form of the *LinearGradientBrush* syntax:

```
<TextBlock Text="Hello, Windows 8!"
           FontSize="96">
    <TextBlock.Foreground>
        <LinearGradientBrush StartPoint="0 0" EndPoint="1 0">
            <LinearGradientBrush.GradientStops>
                <GradientStopCollection>
                    <GradientStop Offset="0" Color="Blue" />
                    <GradientStop Offset="1" Color="Red" />
                </GradientStopCollection>
            </LinearGradientBrush.GradientStops>
        </LinearGradientBrush>
    </TextBlock.Foreground>
</TextBlock>
```

Neither the *LinearGradientBrush.GradientStops* property elements nor the *GradientStopCollection* tags are required, so it simplifies to this:

```
<TextBlock Text="Hello, Windows 8!"
           FontSize="96">
    <TextBlock.Foreground>
        <LinearGradientBrush StartPoint="0 0" EndPoint="1 0">
            <GradientStop Offset="0" Color="Blue" />
            <GradientStop Offset="1" Color="Red" />
        </LinearGradientBrush>
    </TextBlock.Foreground>
</TextBlock>
```

Now it's difficult to imagine how it can get any simpler and still be valid XML.

It is now possible to rewrite the GradientBrushCode program so that everything is done in XAML:

Project: GradientBrushMarkup | File: MainPage.xaml (excerpt)

```
<Grid>
    <Grid.Background>
        <LinearGradientBrush StartPoint="0 0" EndPoint="1 0">
            <GradientStop Offset="0" Color="Red" />
            <GradientStop Offset="1" Color="Blue" />
        </LinearGradientBrush>
    </Grid.Background>

    <TextBlock Name="txtblk"
               Text="Hello, Windows 8!"
               FontSize="96"
               FontWeight="Bold"
               HorizontalAlignment="Center"
               VerticalAlignment="Center">
        <TextBlock.Foreground>
            <LinearGradientBrush StartPoint="0 0" EndPoint="1 0">
                <GradientStop Offset="0" Color="Blue" />
```

```
            <GradientStop Offset="1" Color="Red" />
        </LinearGradientBrush>
    </TextBlock.Foreground>
    </TextBlock>
</Grid>
```

Even with the property-element syntax, it's more readable than the code version. What code illustrates most clearly is how something is built. Markup shows the completed construction.

Here's something to watch out for. Suppose you define a property element on a *Grid* with multiple children:

```
<Grid>
    <Grid.Background>
        <SolidColorBrush Color="Blue" />
    </Grid.Background>

    <TextBlock Text="one" />
    <TextBlock Text="two" />
    <TextBlock Text="three" />
</Grid>
```

You can alternatively put the property element at the bottom:

```
<Grid>
    <TextBlock Text="one" />
    <TextBlock Text="two" />
    <TextBlock Text="three" />

    <Grid.Background>
        <SolidColorBrush Color="Blue" />
    </Grid.Background>
</Grid>
```

But you can't have some content before the property element and some content after it:

```
<!-- This doesn't work! -->
<Grid>
    <TextBlock Text="one" />

    <Grid.Background>
        <SolidColorBrush Color="Blue" />
    </Grid.Background>

    <TextBlock Text="two" />
    <TextBlock Text="three" />
</Grid>
```

Why the prohibition? The problem becomes very apparent when you include the property-element tags for the *Children* property:

```
<!-- This doesn't work! -->
<Grid>
    <Grid.Children>
        <TextBlock Text="one" />
    </Grid.Children>
```

```
    <Grid.Background>
        <SolidColorBrush Color="Blue" />
    </Grid.Background>

    <Grid.Children>
        <TextBlock Text="two" />
        <TextBlock Text="three" />
    </Grid.Children>
</Grid>
```

Now it's obvious that the *Children* property is defined twice with two separate collections, and that's not legal.

The *TextBlock* Content Property

As you saw in the WrappedText program in Chapter 1, *TextBlock* allows you to specify text as content. However, the content property of *TextBlock* is not the *Text* property. It is instead a property named *Inlines* of type *InlineCollection*, a collection of *Inline* objects, or more precisely, instances of *Inline* derivatives. The *Inline* class and its derivatives can all be found in the *Windows.UI.Xaml.Documents* namespace. Here's the hierarchy:

Object
  DependencyObject
    TextElement
      Block
        Paragraph
      Inline
        InlineUIContainer
        LineBreak
        Run (defines *Text* property)
        Span (defines *Inlines* property)
          Bold
          Italic
          Underline

These classes allow you to specify varieties of formatted text in a single *TextBlock*. *TextElement* defines *Foreground* and all the font-related properties: *FontFamily*, *FontSize*, *FontStyle*, *FontWeight* (for setting bold), *FontStretch* (expanded and compressed for fonts that support it), and *CharacterSpacing*, and these are inherited by all the descendent classes.

The *Block* and *Paragraph* classes are mostly used in connection with a souped-up version of *TextBlock* called *RichTextBlock* that I'll discuss in Chapter 16, "Rich Text." The remainder of this discussion will focus entirely on classes that derive from *Inline*.

The *Run* element is the only class here that defines a *Text* property, and *Text* is also the content property of *Run*. Any text content in an *InlineCollection* is converted to a *Run*, except when that text is already content of a *Run*. You can also use *Run* objects explicitly to specify different font properties of the text strings.

Span defines an *Inlines* property just like *TextBlock*. This allows *Span* and its descendent classes to be nested. The three descendent classes of *Span* are shortcuts. For example, the *Bold* class is equivalent to *Span* with the *FontWeight* attribute set to *Bold*.

As an example, here's a *TextBlock* with a small *Inlines* collection using the shortcut classes with nesting:

```
<TextBlock>
    Text in <Bold>bold</Bold> and <Italic>italic</Italic> and
    <Bold><Italic>bold italic</Italic></Bold>
</TextBlock>
```

As this is parsed, all those pieces of loose text are converted to *Run* objects, so the *Inlines* collection of the *TextBlock* contains six items: instances of *Run*, *Bold*, *Run*, *Italic*, *Run*, and *Bold*. The *Inlines* collection of the first *Bold* item contains a single *Run* object as does the *Inlines* collection of the first *Italic* item. The *Inlines* collection of the second *Bold* item contains an *Italic* object, whose *Inlines* collection contains a *Run* object.

The use of *Bold* and *Italic* with a *TextBlock* demonstrates clearly how the syntax of XAML is based on the classes and properties that support these elements. It wouldn't be possible to nest an *Italic* tag in a *Bold* tag if *Bold* didn't have an *Inlines* collection.

Here's a somewhat more extensive *TextBlock* that shows off more formatting features:

Project: TextFormatting | File: MainPage.xaml (excerpt)

```
<Grid Background="{StaticResource ApplicationPageBackgroundThemeBrush}">
    <TextBlock Width="400"
               FontSize="24"
               TextWrapping="Wrap"
               HorizontalAlignment="Center"
               VerticalAlignment="Center">
        Here is text in a
        <Run FontFamily="Times New Roman">Times New Roman</Run> font,
        as well as text in a
        <Run FontSize="36">36-pixel</Run> height.
        <LineBreak />
        <LineBreak />
        Here is some <Bold>bold</Bold> and here is some
        <Italic>italic</Italic> and here is some
        <Underline>underline</Underline> and here is some
        <Bold><Italic><Underline>bold italic underline and
        <Span FontSize="36">bigger and
        <Span Foreground="Red">Red</Span> as well</Span>
        </Underline></Italic></Bold>.
    </TextBlock>
</Grid>
```

The *TextBlock* is given an explicit 400-pixel width so that it doesn't sprawl too wide. Individual *Run* elements can always be used to format pieces of text as shown in the first several lines in this paragraph, but if you want nested formatting—and particularly in connection with the shortcut classes—you'll want to switch to *Span* and its derivatives:

As you can see, the *LineBreak* element can arbitrarily break lines. In theory, the *InlineUIContainer* class allows you to embed any *UIElement* in the text (for example, *Image* elements), but it only works with *RichTextBlock* and not the regular *TextBlock*.

Sharing Brushes (and Other Resources)

Suppose you have multiple *TextBlock* elements on a page, and you want several of them to have the same brush. If this is a *SolidColorBrush*, the repetitive markup is not too bad. However, if it's a *LinearGradientBrush*, it gets messier. A *LinearGradientBrush* requires at least six tags, and all that repetitive markup becomes very painful, particularly if something needs to be changed.

The Windows Runtime has a feature called the "XAML resource" that lets you share objects among multiple elements. Sharing brushes is one common application of the XAML resource, but the most common is defining and sharing styles.

XAML resources are stored in a *ResourceDictionary*, a dictionary whose keys and values are both of type *object*. Very often, however, the keys are strings. Both *FrameworkElement* and *Application* define a property named *Resources* of type *ResourceDictionary*.

The SharedBrush project shows a typical way to share a *LinearGradientBrush* (and a couple other objects) among several elements on a page. Toward the top of the XAML file I've defined a *Resources* property element for the collection of resources for that page:

Project: SharedBrush | File: MainPage.xaml (excerpt)

```
<Page ... >

    <Page.Resources>
        <x:String x:Key="appName">Shared Brush App</x:String>

        <LinearGradientBrush x:Key="rainbowBrush">
            <GradientStop Offset="0" Color="Red" />
            <GradientStop Offset="0.17" Color="Orange" />
            <GradientStop Offset="0.33" Color="Yellow" />
            <GradientStop Offset="0.5" Color="Green" />
            <GradientStop Offset="0.67" Color="Blue" />
            <GradientStop Offset="0.83" Color="Indigo" />
            <GradientStop Offset="1" Color="Violet" />
        </LinearGradientBrush>

        <FontFamily x:Key="fontFamily">Times New Roman</FontFamily>

        <x:Double x:Key="fontSize">96</x:Double>
    </Page.Resources>
    ...
</Page>
```

Often the definition of resources near the top of a XAML file is referred to as a "resources section." This particular *Resources* dictionary is initialized with four items of four different types: *String*, *LinearGradientBrush*, *FontFamily*, and *Double*. Notice the "x" prefix on *String* and *Double*. These are .NET primitive types, of course, but they are not Windows Runtime types, and hence they are not in the default XAML namespace. Also available are *x:Boolean* and *x:Int32* types.

Notice as well that each of these objects has an *x:Key* attribute. The *x:Key* attribute is valid only in a *Resources* dictionary. As the name suggests, the *x:Key* attribute is the key for that item in the dictionary.

In the body of the XAML file, an element references the resource by using this key in some special markup called a XAML *markup extension*.

There are just a few XAML markup extensions, and you'll always recognize them by curly braces. The markup extension for referencing a resource consists of the keyword *StaticResource* and the key name. In fact, you've already seen the *StaticResource* markup extension numerous times: It provides the standard *Grid* with a background brush. The rest of this XAML file uses *StaticResource* to obtain items defined in the *Resources* dictionary:

Project: SharedBrush | File: MainPage.xaml (excerpt)

```
<Page ... >
    ...
    <Grid Background="{StaticResource ApplicationPageBackgroundThemeBrush}">
        <TextBlock Text="{StaticResource appName}"
                    FontSize="48"
```

```
                    HorizontalAlignment="Center"
                    VerticalAlignment="Center" />

        <TextBlock Text="Top Text"
                    Foreground="{StaticResource rainbowBrush}"
                    FontFamily="{StaticResource fontFamily}"
                    FontSize="{StaticResource fontSize}"
                    HorizontalAlignment="Center"
                    VerticalAlignment="Top" />

        <TextBlock Text="Left Text"
                    Foreground="{StaticResource rainbowBrush}"
                    FontFamily="{StaticResource fontFamily}"
                    FontSize="{StaticResource fontSize}"
                    HorizontalAlignment="Left"
                    VerticalAlignment="Center" />

        <TextBlock Text="Right Text"
                    Foreground="{StaticResource rainbowBrush}"
                    FontFamily="{StaticResource fontFamily}"
                    FontSize="{StaticResource fontSize}"
                    HorizontalAlignment="Right"
                    VerticalAlignment="Center" />

        <TextBlock Text="Bottom Text"
                    Foreground="{StaticResource rainbowBrush}"
                    FontFamily="{StaticResource fontFamily}"
                    FontSize="{StaticResource fontSize}"
                    HorizontalAlignment="Center"
                    VerticalAlignment="Bottom" />
    </Grid>
</Page>
```

Here's the result:

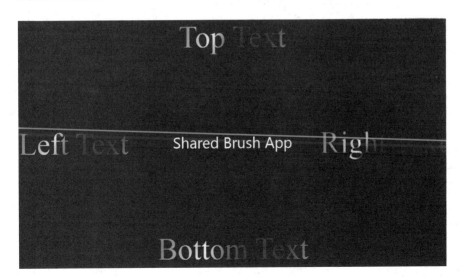

A few notes:

Referencing the same three resources in four *TextBlock* elements cries out for a more efficient approach, namely, a style, which I'll discuss later in this chapter.

Resources must be defined in a XAML file lexically preceding their use. This is why it's most common for the *Resources* dictionary to be near the top of a XAML file and most conveniently defined on the root element.

However, every *FrameworkElement* descendent can support a *Resources* dictionary, so you might include them further down the visual tree. The keys must be unique within any *Resources* dictionary, but you can use duplicate keys in other *Resources* dictionaries. When the XAML parser encounters a *StaticResource* markup extension, it begins searching up the visual tree for a *Resources* dictionary with a matching key and it uses the first one it encounters. You can effectively override the values of *Resources* keys with those in more local dictionaries.

If the XAML parser cannot find a matching key by searching up the visual tree, it checks the *Resources* dictionary in the *Application* object. The App.xaml file is an ideal place for defining resources that are used throughout the application. To use a bunch of resources across multiple applications, you can define them in a separate XAML file with a root element of *ResourceDictionary*. Include that file in a project, reference it in the App.xaml file, and you can then use items in that dictionary.

Indeed, an example is already provided for you in the standard Visual Studio projects for Windows 8 applications. The Common folder contains a file named StandardStyles.xaml that has a root element of *ResourceDictionary*:

```
<ResourceDictionary
    xmlns="http://schemas.microsoft.com/winfx/2006/xaml/presentation"
    xmlns:x="http://schemas.microsoft.com/winfx/2006/xaml">


    ...


</ResourceDictionary>
```

This file is referenced in the standard App.xaml file. In fact, referencing this resources collection is just about all that the standard App.xaml file does:

```
<Application
    x:Class="SharedBrush.App"
    xmlns="http://schemas.microsoft.com/winfx/2006/xaml/presentation"
    xmlns:x="http://schemas.microsoft.com/winfx/2006/xaml"
    xmlns:local="using:SharedBrush">

    <Application.Resources>
        <ResourceDictionary>
            <ResourceDictionary.MergedDictionaries>
                <ResourceDictionary Source="Common/StandardStyles.xaml"/>
            </ResourceDictionary.MergedDictionaries>
        </ResourceDictionary>
    </Application.Resources>
</Application>
```

You can include your own collections of resources by inserting additional *ResourceDictionary* tags in the *MergedDictionaries* collection. Or you can include your own resources directly in the *App* object's *Resources* dictionary.

You can also reference the *Resources* dictionary from code. Following the *InitializeComponent* call, you can retrieve an item from the dictionary with an indexer:

```
FontFamily fntfam = this.Resources["fontFamily"] as FontFamily;
```

Now try this: Comment out the "fontFamily" entry in the MainPage.xaml file, but add that item to the dictionary in the *MainPage* constructor *prior* to the *InitializeComponent* call.

```
this.Resources.Add("fontFamily", new FontFamily("Times New Roman"));
```

When the XAML file is parsed by *InitializeComponent*, this object will be available within that XAML file.

The *ResourceDictionary* class does not define a public method that searches up the visual tree for dictionaries in ancestor classes. If you need something like that to search for resources in code, you can easily write it yourself by "climbing the visual tree" using the *Parent* property defined by *FrameworkElement* or the *VisualTreeHelper* class defined in the *Windows.UI.Xaml.Media* namespace. The *Application* object for the application is available from the static *Application.Current* property.

The predefined resources (such as the *ApplicationPageBackgroundThemeBrush* referenced by the *Grid*) don't seem to be documented, but you can get a list of their values (in the Default, Light, and High Contrast themes) in the file:

C:\Program Files (x86)\Windows Kits\8.0\Include\winrt\xaml\design\themeresources.xaml

After *ApplicationPageBackgroundThemeBrush*, the next most important predefined resource identifier is *ApplicationForegroundThemeBrush*, which is black in the light theme, and white in the dark theme. If you need a color to properly contrast with the background (as I will shortly), this is it. For a convenient highlight color that contrasts with both background and foreground, create a *SolidColorBrush* based on the *Highlight* color available from the *UIElementColor* method of the *UISettings* class.

Resources Are Shared

Are resource objects truly shared among the elements that reference them? Or are separate instances created for each *StaticResource* reference?

Try inserting the following code after the *InitializeComponent* call in the SharedBrush.xaml.cs file:

```
TextBlock txtblk = (this.Content as Grid).Children[1] as TextBlock;
LinearGradientBrush brush = txtblk.Foreground as LinearGradientBrush;
brush.StartPoint = new Point(0, 1);
brush.EndPoint = new Point(0, 0);
```

This code references the *LinearGradientBrush* of the second *TextBlock* in the *Children* collection of the *Grid* and changes the *StartPoint* and *EndPoint* properties. Lo and behold, all the *TextBlock* elements referencing that *LinearGradientBrush* are affected:

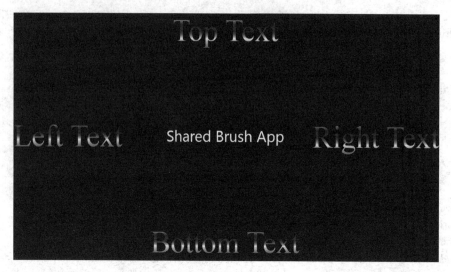

Conclusion: Resources are shared.

It's also easy to verify that even if a resource is not referenced by any element, it is still instantiated.

Exploring Vector Graphics

As you've seen, displaying text and bitmaps in a Windows 8 application involves creating objects of type *TextBlock* and *Image* and attaching them to a visual tree. There's no concept of "drawing" or "painting," at least not on the application level. Internal to the Windows Runtime, the *TextBlock* and *Image* elements are rendering themselves.

Similarly, if you wish to display some vector graphics—lines, curves, and filled areas—you don't do it by calling methods like *DrawLine* and *DrawBezier*. These methods do not exist in the Windows Runtime! Methods with names like those exist in DirectX, which you can use in a Windows 8 application, but when using the Windows Runtime you instead create elements of type *Line*, *Polyline*, *Polygon*, and *Path*. These classes derive from the *Shape* class (which itself derives from *FrameworkElement*) and can all be found in the *Windows.UI.Xaml.Shapes* namespace, which is sometimes referred to as the *Shapes* library.

The most powerful members of the *Shapes* library are *Polyline* and *Path*. *Polyline* renders a collection of connected straight lines, but its real purpose is to draw complex curves. All you need to do is keep the individual lines short and supply plenty of them. Don't hesitate to give *Polyline* thousands of lines. That's what it's there for.

Let's use *Polyline* to draw an Archimedean spiral. The XAML file for the Spiral program instantiates the *Polyline* object but doesn't include the points that define the figure:

Project: Spiral | File: MainPage.xaml (excerpt)

```
<Grid Background="{StaticResource ApplicationPageBackgroundThemeBrush}">
    <Polyline Name="polyline"
            Stroke="{StaticResource ApplicationForegroundThemeBrush}"
            StrokeThickness="3"
            HorizontalAlignment="Center"
            VerticalAlignment="Center" />
</Grid>
```

The *Stroke* property (inherited from *Shape*) is the brush used to draw the actual lines. Generally, this is a *SolidColorBrush*, but you'll see shortly that it doesn't have to be. I've used *StaticResource* with the predefined identifier that provides a white brush with a dark theme and a black brush with a light theme. *StrokeThickness* (also inherited from *Shape*) is the width of the lines in pixels, and you've seen *HorizontalAlignment* and *VerticalAlignment* before.

It might seem a little strange to specify *HorizontalAlignment* and *VerticalAlignment* for a chunk of vector graphics, so a little explanation might be in order.

Two-dimensional vector graphics involve the use of coordinate points in the form (*X*, *Y*) on a Cartesian coordinate system, where *X* is a position on the horizontal axis and *Y* is a position on the vertical axis. Vector graphics in the Windows Runtime use a coordinate convention commonly associated with windowing environments: Values of *X* increase to the right (as is normal), but values of *Y* increase going down (which is opposite the mathematical convention).

When only positive values of *X* and *Y* are used, the origin—the point (0, 0)—is the upper-left corner of the graphical figure.

Negative coordinates can be used to indicate points to the left of the origin or above the origin. However, when the Windows Runtime calculates the dimensions of a vector graphics object for layout purposes, these negative coordinates are ignored. For example, suppose you draw a polyline with points that have *X* coordinates ranging from –100 to 300 and *Y* coordinates ranging from –200 to 400. This implies that the polyline has a dimension of 400 pixels wide and 600 pixels high, and that is certainly true. But for purposes of layout and alignment, the polyline is treated as if it were 300 pixels wide and 400 pixels tall.

For a vector graphics figure to be treated in a predictable manner in the Windows Runtime layout system, all that's required is that you regard the point (0, 0) as the upper-left corner. For purposes of layout, the maximum positive *X* coordinate becomes the element's width and the maximum positive *Y* coordinate becomes the element's height.

For specifying a coordinate point, the *Windows.Foundation* namespace includes a *Point* structure that has two properties of type *double* named *X* and *Y*. In addition, the *Windows.UI.Xaml.Media* namespace includes a *PointCollection*, which is a collection of *Point* objects.

The only property that *Polyline* defines on its own is *Points* of type *PointCollection*. A collection of points can be assigned to the *Points* property in XAML, but for very many points calculated algorithmically, code is ideal. In the constructor of the *Spiral* class, a *for* loop goes from 0 to 3600 degrees, effectively spinning around a circle 10 times:

Project: Spiral | File: MainPage.xaml.cs (excerpt)

```
public MainPage()
{
    this.InitializeComponent();

    for (int angle = 0; angle < 3600; angle++)
    {
        double radians = Math.PI * angle / 180;
        double radius = angle / 10;
        double x = 360 + radius * Math.Sin(radians);
        double y = 360 + radius * Math.Cos(radians);
        polyline.Points.Add(new Point(x, y));
    }
}
```

The *radians* variable converts degrees to radians for the .NET trig functions, and *radius* is calculated to range from 0 through 360 depending on the *angle*, which means that the maximum radius will be 360 pixels. The values returned by the *Math.Sin* and *Math.Cos* static methods are multiplied by *radius*, which means these products will range between −360 and 360 pixels.

To shift this figure so that all pixels have positive values relative to an upper-left origin, 360 is added to both products. The spiral is thus centered at the point (360, 360) and extends no more than 360 pixels in all directions.

The loop concludes by instantiating a *Point* value and adding it to the *Points* collection of the *Polyline*. Here it is:

Without the *HorizontalAlignment* and *VerticalAlignment* settings, the figure would be aligned at the upper-left corner of the page. If the adjustment for the spiral's center is also removed from the calculation, the center would be in the upper-left corner of the page and three-quarters of the figure would not be visible. If you keep *HorizontalAlignment* and *VerticalAlignment* set to *Center* but remove the adjustment for the spiral's center, you'll see the figure positioned so that the lower-right quadrant is centered.

The spiral almost fills the screen, but that's only because the screen I'm using for these images has a height of 768 pixels. What if we wanted to ensure that the spiral filled the screen regardless of the screen's size?

One solution is to base the numbers going into the calculation of the spiral coordinates directly on the pixel size of the screen. You'll see how to do that in Chapter 3, "Basic Event Handling."

Another solution requires noticing that the *Shape* class defines a property named *Stretch* that you use in exactly the same way you use the *Stretch* property of *Image*. By default, the *Stretch* property for *Polyline* is the enumeration member *Stretch.None*, which means no stretching, but you can set it to *Uniform* so that the figure fills the container while maintaining its aspect ratio.

The StretchedSpiral project demonstrates this. The XAML file sets a larger stroke width as well:

Project: StretchedSpiral | File: MainPage.xaml (excerpt)

```
<Grid Background="{StaticResource ApplicationPageBackgroundThemeBrush}">
    <Polyline Name="polyline"
              Stroke="{StaticResource ApplicationForegroundThemeBrush}"
              StrokeThickness="6"
              Stretch="Uniform" />
</Grid>
```

The code-behind file calculates the coordinates of the spiral using arbitrary coordinates, which in this case I've chosen based on a radius of 1000:

Project: StretchedSpiral | File: MainPage.xaml.cs (excerpt)

```
public MainPage()
{
    this.InitializeComponent();

    for (int angle = 0; angle < 3600; angle++)
    {
        double radians = Math.PI * angle / 180;
        double radius = angle / 3.6;
        double x = 1000 + radius * Math.Sin(radians);
        double y = 1000 - radius * Math.Cos(radians);
        polyline.Points.Add(new Point(x, y));
    }
}
```

You might also notice that I changed a plus to a minus in the *y* calculation so that the spiral ends at the top rather than the bottom. The switch to the light theme demonstrates the convenience of using *ApplicationForegroundThemeBrush* for the *Stroke* color:

Try setting the *Stretch* property to *Fill* to see this circular spiral be distorted into an elliptical spiral.

You'll recall how *LinearGradientBrush* adapts itself to the size of whatever element it's applied to. The same is true when using that brush with vector graphics. Let's instead try an *ImageBrush*, which is a brush created from a bitmap.

The code-behind file for ImageBrushedSpiral is the same as StretchedSpiral. The XAML file widens the stroke considerably and instantiates an *ImageBrush*:

Project: ImageBrushedSpiral | File: MainPage.xaml (excerpt)

```
<Grid Background="{StaticResource ApplicationPageBackgroundThemeBrush}">
    <Polyline Name="polyline"
              StrokeThickness="25"
              Stretch="Uniform">
        <Polyline.Stroke>
            <ImageBrush ImageSource="http://www.charlespetzold.com/pw6/PetzoldJersey.jpg"
                        Stretch="UniformToFill"
                        AlignmentY="Top" />
        </Polyline.Stroke>
    </Polyline>
</Grid>
```

The *ImageSource* property of *ImageBrush* is of type *ImageSource*, just like the *Source* property of *Image*. In XAML you can just set it to a URL. *ImageBrush* has its own *Stretch* property, which by default is *Fill*. This means that the bitmap is stretched to fill the area without respecting the aspect ratio. For the image I'm using, that would make me look fat, so I switched to *UniformToFill*, which maintains the image's aspect ratio while filling the area. Doing so requires part of the image to be cropped. Use the *AlignmentX* and *AlignmentY* properties to indicate how the bitmap should be aligned with the graphical figure, and consequently, where the image should be cropped. For this bitmap, I prefer that the bottom be cropped rather than my head:

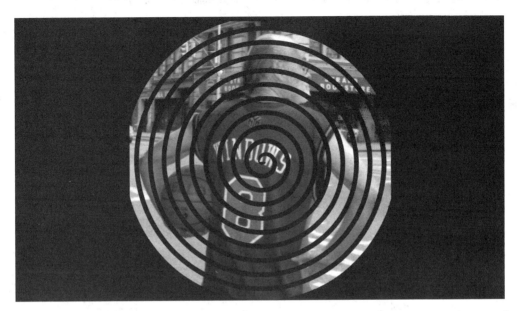

Notice that the alignment of the image seems to be based on the geometric line of the spiral rather than the line rendered with a width of 25 pixels. This causes areas at the top, left, and right sides to be shaved off. The problem can be fixed with the *Transform* property of *ImageBrush*, but that's a little too advanced for this chapter.

You may have noticed that *ImageBrush* derives from *TileBrush*. That heritage might suggest that you could repeat bitmap images horizontally and vertically to tile a surface, but doing so is not supported by the Windows Runtime.

Any curve that you can define with parametric formulas, you can render with *Polyline*. But if the complex curves you need are arcs (that is, curves on the circumference of an ellipse), cubic Bézier splines (the standard sort), or quadratic Bézier splines (which have only one control point), you don't need to use *Polyline*. These curves are all supported with the *Path* element.

Path defines just one property on its own called *Data*, of type *Geometry*, a class defined in *Windows.UI.Xaml.Media*. In the Windows Runtime, *Geometry* and related classes represent pure analytic geometry. The *Geometry* object defines lines and curves using coordinate points, and the *Path* renders those lines with a particular stroke brush and thickness.

The most powerful and flexible *Geometry* derivative is *PathGeometry*. The content property of *PathGeometry* is named *Figures*, which is a collection of *PathFigure* objects. Each *PathFigure* is a series of connected straight lines and curves. The content property of *PathFigure* is *Segments*, a collection of *PathSegment* objects. *PathSegment* is the parent class to *LineSegment*, *PolylineSegment*, *BezierSegment*, *PolyBezierSegment*, *QuadraticBezierSegment*, *PolyQuadraticBezierSegment*, and *ArcSegment*.

Let's display the word HELLO using *Path* and *PathGeometry*:

Project: HelloVectorGraphics | **File:** MainPage.xaml (excerpt)

```xml
<Grid Background="{StaticResource ApplicationPageBackgroundThemeBrush}">
    <Path Stroke="Red"
          StrokeThickness="12"
          StrokeLineJoin="Round"
          HorizontalAlignment="Center"
          VerticalAlignment="Center">
        <Path.Data>
            <PathGeometry>
                <!-- H -->
                <PathFigure StartPoint="0 0">
                    <LineSegment Point="0 100" />
                </PathFigure>
                <PathFigure StartPoint="0 50">
                    <LineSegment Point="50 50" />
                </PathFigure>
                <PathFigure StartPoint="50 0">
                    <LineSegment Point="50 100" />
                </PathFigure>

                <!-- E -->
                <PathFigure StartPoint="125 0">
                    <BezierSegment Point1="60 -10" Point2="60 60" Point3="125 50" />
                    <BezierSegment Point1="60 40" Point2="60 110" Point3="125 100" />
                </PathFigure>

                <!-- L -->
                <PathFigure StartPoint="150 0">
                    <LineSegment Point="150 100" />
                    <LineSegment Point="200 100" />
                </PathFigure>

                <!-- L -->
                <PathFigure StartPoint="225 0">
                    <LineSegment Point="225 100" />
                    <LineSegment Point="275 100" />
                </PathFigure>

                <!-- O -->
                <PathFigure StartPoint="300 50">
                    <ArcSegment Size="25 50" Point="300 49.9" IsLargeArc="True" />
                </PathFigure>
            </PathGeometry>
        </Path.Data>
    </Path>
</Grid>
```

Each letter is one or more *PathFigure* objects, which always specifies a starting point for a series of connected lines. The *PathSegment* derivatives continue the figure from that point. For example, to draw the "E," *BezierSegment* specifies two control points and an end point. The next *BezierSegment* then continues from the end of the previous segment. (In the *ArcSegment*, the end point for the arc can't be the same as the start point or nothing will be drawn. That why it's set to 1/10th pixel short. A better alternative is to split the *ArcSegment* into two, each drawing half the circle.)

The result suggests that a pair of Bézier splines was perhaps not the best way to render a capital E:

Try setting the *Stretch* property of *Path* to *Fill* for a "really big hello":

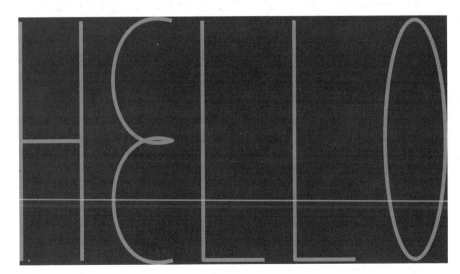

Of course you can assemble the *PathFigure* and *PathSegment* objects in code, but let me show you an easier way to do it in XAML. A Path Markup Syntax is available that consists of single letters, coordinate points, an occasional size, and a couple Boolean values that reduce the markup considerably. The HelloVectorGraphicsPath project creates the same figure as HelloVectorGraphics:

Project: HelloVectorGraphicsPath | **File:** MainPage.xaml (excerpt)

```
<Grid Background="{StaticResource ApplicationPageBackgroundThemeBrush}">
    <Path Stroke="Red"
          StrokeThickness="12"
          StrokeLineJoin="Round"
          HorizontalAlignment="Center"
          VerticalAlignment="Center"
          Data="M 0 0 L 0 100 M 0 50 L 50 50 M 50 0 L 50 100
                M 125 0 C 60 -10, 60 60, 125 50, 60 40, 60 110, 125 100
                M 150 0 L 150 100, 200 100
                M 225 0 L 225 100, 275 100
                M 300 50 A 25 50 0 1 0 300 49.9" />
</Grid>
```

The *Data* property is now one big string, but I've separated it into five lines corresponding to the five letters. The M code is a "move" followed by *x* and *y* coordinate points. This indicates the start of a figure. The L is a line (or, more precisely, a polyline) followed by one or more points; C is a cubic Bézier curve, followed by control points and an end point, but more than one can be included; and A is an arc. The arc is by far the most complex: The first two numbers indicate the horizontal and vertical radii of an ellipse, which is rotated a number of degrees given by the next argument. Following are two flags for the *IsLargeArc* property and sweep direction, followed by the end point. Not used here is the often useful Z, which closes a figure with a straight line back to the start point.

Defining a complex geometry in terms of Path Markup Syntax is one example of something that can be done only in XAML. Whatever class performs this conversion is not publicly exposed in the Windows Runtime. It is available only to the XAML parser. To convert a string of Path Markup Syntax to a *Geometry* in code would require some way to convert XAML to an object in code.

Fortunately, something like that is available. It's a static method named *XamlReader.Load* in the *Windows.UI.Xaml.Markup* namespace. Pass it a string of XAML and get out an instance of the root element with all the other parts of the tree instantiated and assembled. *XamlReader.Load* has some restrictions—the XAML it parses can't refer to event handlers in external code, for example—but it is a very powerful facility. In Chapter 8, "App Bars and Popups," I'll show you the source code for a tool called XamlCruncher that lets you interactively experiment with XAML.

Meanwhile, here's a *Path* with Path Markup Syntax created entirely in code:

Project: PathMarkupSyntaxCode | **File:** MainPage.xaml.cs

```
using Windows.UI;                    // for Colors
using Windows.UI.Xaml;
using Windows.UI.Xaml.Controls;
using Windows.UI.Xaml.Markup;        // for XamlReader
using Windows.UI.Xaml.Media;
using Windows.UI.Xaml.Shapes;        // for Path
```

```
namespace PathMarkupSyntaxCode
{
    public sealed partial class MainPage : Page
    {
        public MainPage()
        {
            this.InitializeComponent();

            Path path = new Path
            {
                Stroke = new SolidColorBrush(Colors.Red),
                StrokeThickness = 12,
                StrokeLineJoin = PenLineJoin.Round,
                HorizontalAlignment = HorizontalAlignment.Center,
                VerticalAlignment =  VerticalAlignment.Center,
                Data = PathMarkupToGeometry(
                    "M 0 0 L 0 100 M 0 50 L 50 50 M 50 0 L 50 100 " +
                    "M 125 0 C 60 -10, 60 60, 125 50, 60 40, 60 110, 125 100 " +
                    "M 150 0 L 150 100, 200 100 " +
                    "M 225 0 L 225 100, 275 100 " +
                    "M 300 50 A 25 50 0 1 0 300 49.9")
            };

            (this.Content as Grid).Children.Add(path);
        }

        Geometry PathMarkupToGeometry(string pathMarkup)
        {
            string xaml =
                "<Path " +
                "xmlns='http://schemas.microsoft.com/winfx/2006/xaml/presentation'>" +
                "<Path.Data>" + pathMarkup + "</Path.Data></Path>";

            Path path = XamlReader.Load(xaml) as Path;

            // Detach the PathGeometry from the Path
            Geometry geometry = path.Data;
            path.Data = null;
            return geometry;
        }
    }
}
```

Watch out when working with the *Path* class in code: The MainPage.xaml.cs file that Visual Studio generates does not include a *using* directive for *Windows.UI.Xaml.Shapes* where *Path* resides but does include a *using* directive for *System.IO*, which has a very different *Path* class for working with files and directories.

The magic method is down at the bottom. It assembles a tiny piece of legal XAML with *Path* as the root element and property-element syntax to enclose the string of Path Markup Syntax. Notice that the XAML must include the standard XML namespace declaration. If *XamlReader.Load* doesn't encounter any errors, it returns a *Path* with a *Data* property set to a *PathGeometry*. However, you can't use this *PathGeometry* for another *Path* unless you disconnect it from this *Path*, which requires setting the *Data* property of the returned *Path* to *null*.

Stretching with *Viewbox*

Both the *Image* class and the *Shape* class define a *Stretch* property that can stretch the bitmap or vector graphics to the size of its container. This property is not universal among the *FrameworkElement* derivatives. After all, why would you ever want to stretch a *TextBlock* in such a way?

Well, sometimes you need to do precisely that. Suppose you were displaying a bunch of objects with text titles. You want these items to look similar with each title restricted to a particular rectangular area. But the length of the text might be variable. Perhaps the user types in this text. If the text is very long, you might prefer that it be shrunk down a bit to fit the rectangle. While you could always perform a *FontSize* calculation in the code-behind file, it would be nice to have the *TextBlock* sized automatically to fit a particular space.

This a job for *Viewbox*, which has a *Child* property of type *UIElement* and which stretches that child to its own size. Like *Image* and *Shape*, *Viewbox* defines a *Stretch* property. The default setting is *Uniform* (the same default as *Image*), but the following program sets *Stretch* to *Fill* to ignore the aspect ratio of a *TextBlock* and make it fill the screen:

Project: TextStretch | File: MainPage.xaml (excerpt)

```
<Grid Background="{StaticResource ApplicationPageBackgroundThemeBrush}">
    <Viewbox Stretch="Fill">
        <TextBlock Text="Stretch Windows 8!" />
    </Viewbox>
</Grid>
```

TextBlock always calculates its height to encompass diacritics and descenders even if they don't exist in the text, which is why the text doesn't quite extend to the full height of the window:

Still, it definitely no longer has the correct aspect ratio.

Unlike *Image* and *Shape*, *Viewbox* defines a *StretchDirection* property that can take on values of *UpOnly*, *DownOnly*, or *Both* (the default). This instructs *Viewbox* to only increase the size of its child or only decrease the size if that's what you want.

Suppose you wanted to modify the HelloVectorGraphics program so that each letter is a different color. Instead of using one *Path* element you'd need to split it up into five *Path* elements. But if you then try to use the *Stretch* property of *Path* to stretch each letter to the size of the window, it wouldn't work because each letter has a different size.

Instead, put all five *Path* elements in a *Grid*, and put the *Grid* inside a *Viewbox*:

Project: VectorGraphicsStretch | File: MainPage.xaml (excerpt)

```
<Grid Background="{StaticResource ApplicationPageBackgroundThemeBrush}">
    <Viewbox Stretch="Fill">
        <Grid Margin="6 6 0 0">
            <!-- H -->
            <Path Stroke="Red"
                  StrokeThickness="12"
                  StrokeLineJoin="Round"
                  Data="M 0 0 L 0 100 M 0 50 L 50 50 M 50 0 L 50 100" />

            <!-- E -->
            <Path Stroke="#C00040"
                  StrokeThickness="12"
                  StrokeLineJoin="Round"
                  Data="M 125 0 C 60 -10, 60 60, 125 50, 60 40, 60 110, 125 100" />

            <!-- L -->
            <Path Stroke="#800080"
                  StrokeThickness="12"
                  StrokeLineJoin="Round"
                  Data="M 150 0 L 150 100, 200 100" />

            <!-- L -->
            <Path Stroke="#4000C0"
                  StrokeThickness="12"
                  StrokeLineJoin="Round"
                  Data="M 225 0 L 225 100, 275 100" />

            <!-- O -->
            <Path Stroke="Blue"
                  StrokeThickness="12"
                  StrokeLineJoin="Round"
                  Data="M 300 50 A 25 50 0 1 0 300 49.9" />
        </Grid>
    </Viewbox>
</Grid>
```

Now the whole ensemble of vector graphics is sized uniformly:

Notice also that the *Viewbox* increases the stroke width along with the size of the graphics, whereas setting *Stretch* on the *Path* element does not.

Styles

You've seen how brushes can be defined as resources and shared among elements. By far the most common use of resources is to define styles, which are instances of the *Style* class. A style is basically a collection of property definitions that can be shared among multiple elements. The use of styles not only reduces repetitive markup, but also allows easier global changes.

After this discussion, much of the StandardStyles.xaml file included in the Common folder of your Visual Studio projects will be comprehensible, except for large sections within *ControlTemplate* tags. That's coming up in Chapter 11, "The Three Templates."

The SharedBrushWithStyle project is much the same as SharedBrush except that it uses a *Style* to consolidate several properties. Here's the new *Resources* section with the *Style* near the bottom:

Project: SharedBrushWithStyle | File: MainPage.xaml (excerpt)

```
<Page.Resources>
    <x:String x:Key="appName">Shared Brush with Style</x:String>

    <LinearGradientBrush x:Key="rainbowBrush">
        <GradientStop Offset="0" Color="Red" />
        <GradientStop Offset="0.17" Color="Orange" />
        <GradientStop Offset="0.33" Color="Yellow" />
        <GradientStop Offset="0.5" Color="Green" />
        <GradientStop Offset="0.67" Color="Blue" />
```

```
            <GradientStop Offset="0.83" Color="Indigo" />
            <GradientStop Offset="1" Color="Violet" />
        </LinearGradientBrush>

        <Style x:Key="rainbowStyle" TargetType="TextBlock">
            <Setter Property="FontFamily" Value="Times New Roman" />
            <Setter Property="FontSize" Value="96" />
            <Setter Property="Foreground" Value="{StaticResource rainbowBrush}" />
        </Style>
</Page.Resources>
```

Like all resources, the start tag of the *Style* includes an *x:Key* attribute. *Style* also requires a *TargetType* attribute indicating either *FrameworkElement* or a class that derives from *FrameworkElement*. Styles can be applied only to *FrameworkElement* derivatives.

The body of the *Style* includes a bunch of *Setter* tags, each of which specifies *Property* and *Value* attributes. Notice that the last one has its *Value* attribute set to a *StaticResource* of the previously defined *LinearGradientBrush*. For this reference to work, this particular *Style* must be defined later in the XAML file than the brush, although it can be in a different *Resources* section deeper in the visual tree.

Like other resources, an element references a *Style* by using the *StaticResource* markup extension on its *Style* property:

Project: SharedBrushWithStyle | File: MainPage.xaml (excerpt)

```
<Grid Background="{StaticResource ApplicationPageBackgroundThemeBrush}">
    <TextBlock Text="{StaticResource appName}"
               FontSize="48"
               HorizontalAlignment="Center"
               VerticalAlignment="Center" />

    <TextBlock Text="Top Text"
               Style="{StaticResource rainbowStyle}"
               HorizontalAlignment="Center"
               VerticalAlignment="Top" />

    <TextBlock Text="Left Text"
               Style="{StaticResource rainbowStyle}"
               HorizontalAlignment="Left"
               VerticalAlignment="Center" />

    <TextBlock Text="Right Text"
               Style="{StaticResource rainbowStyle}"
               HorizontalAlignment="Right"
               VerticalAlignment="Center" />

    <TextBlock Text="Bottom Text"
               Style="{StaticResource rainbowStyle}"
               HorizontalAlignment="Center"
               VerticalAlignment="Bottom" />
</Grid>
```

Except for the application name, the visuals are the same as the SharedBrush program.

There is an alternative way for this particular *Style* to incorporate the *LinearGradientBrush*. Just as you can use property-element syntax on elements to define an object with complex markup, you can use property-element syntax with the *Value* property of the *Setter* class:

```
<Style x:Key="rainbowStyle" TargetType="TextBlock">
    <Setter Property="FontFamily" Value="Times New Roman" />
    <Setter Property="FontSize" Value="96" />
    <Setter Property="Foreground">
        <Setter.Value>
            <LinearGradientBrush>
                <GradientStop Offset="0" Color="Red" />
                <GradientStop Offset="0.17" Color="Orange" />
                <GradientStop Offset="0.33" Color="Yellow" />
                <GradientStop Offset="0.5" Color="Green" />
                <GradientStop Offset="0.67" Color="Blue" />
                <GradientStop Offset="0.83" Color="Indigo" />
                <GradientStop Offset="1" Color="Violet" />
            </LinearGradientBrush>
        </Setter.Value>
    </Setter>
</Style>
```

I know it looks a little odd at first, but defining brushes within styles is very common. Notice that the *LinearGradientBrush* now has no *x:Key* of its own. Only items defined at the root level in a *Resources* collection can have *x:Key* attributes.

You can define a *Style* in code, for example, like so:

```
Style style = new Style(typeof(TextBlock));
style.Setters.Add(new Setter(TextBlock.FontSizeProperty, 96));
style.Setters.Add(new Setter(TextBlock.FontFamilyProperty,
                      new FontFamily("Times New Roman")));
```

You could then add this to the *Resources* collection of a *Page* prior to the *InitializeComponent* call so that it would be available to *TextBlock* elements defined in the XAML file. Or you could assign this *Style* object directly to the *Style* property of a *TextBlock*. This isn't common, however, because code offers other solutions for defining the same properties on several different elements, namely, the *for* or *foreach* loop.

Take careful note of the first argument to the *Setter* constructor in the code example. It's defined as a *DependencyProperty*, and what you specify is a static property of type *DependencyProperty* defined by (or inherited by) the target class of the style. This is an excellent example of how dependency properties allow a property of a class to be specified independently of a particular instance of that class.

The code also makes clear that the properties targeted by a *Style* can *only* be dependency properties. I mentioned earlier that dependency properties impose a hierarchy on the way that properties can be set. For example, suppose you have the following markup in this program:

```
<TextBlock Text="Top Text"
           Style="{StaticResource rainbowStyle}"
           FontSize="24"
           HorizontalAlignment="Center"
           VerticalAlignment="Top" />
```

The *Style* defines a *FontSize* value, but the *FontSize* property is also set locally on the *TextBlock*. As you might hope and expect, the local setting takes precedence over the *Style* setting, and both take precedence over a *FontSize* value propagated through the visual tree.

Once a *Style* object is set to the *Style* property of an element, the *Style* can no longer be changed. You can later set a different *Style* object to the element, and you can change properties of objects referenced by the style (such as brushes), but you cannot set or remove *Setter* objects or change their *Value* properties.

Styles can inherit property settings from other styles by using a *Style* property called *BasedOn*, which is usually set to a *StaticResource* markup extension referencing a previously defined *Style* definition:

```
<Style x:Key="baseTextBlockStyle" TargetType="TextBlock">
    <Setter Property="FontFamily" Value="Times New Roman" />
    <Setter Property="FontSize" Value="24" />
</Style>

<Style x:Key="gradientStyle" TargetType="TextBlock"
       BasedOn="{StaticResource baseTextBlockStyle}">
    <Setter Property="FontSize" Value="96" />
    <Setter Property="Foreground">
        <Setter.Value>
            <LinearGradientBrush>
                <GradientStop Offset="0" Color="Red" />
                <GradientStop Offset="1" Color="Blue" />
            </LinearGradientBrush>
        </Setter.Value>
    </Setter>
</Style>
```

The *Style* with the key "gradientStyle" is based on the previous *Style* with the key "baseTextBlockStyle," which means that it inherits the *FontFamily* setting, overrides the *FontSize* setting, and defines a new *Foreground* setting.

Here's another example:

```
<Style x:Key="centeredStyle" TargetType="FrameworkElement">
    <Setter Property="HorizontalAlignment" Value="Center" />
    <Setter Property="VerticalAlignment" Value="Center" />
</Style>
```

```xaml
<Style x:Key="rainbowStyle" TargetType="TextBlock"
        BasedOn="{StaticResource centeredStyle}">
    <Setter Property="FontSize" Value="96" />
    <Setter Property="Foreground">
        <Setter.Value>
            <LinearGradientBrush>
                <GradientStop Offset="0" Color="Red" />
                <GradientStop Offset="1" Color="Blue" />
            </LinearGradientBrush>
        </Setter.Value>
    </Setter>
</Style>
```

In this case, the first *Style* has a *TargetType* of *FrameworkElement*, which means that it can include only properties defined by *FrameworkElement* or inherited by *FrameworkElement*. You can still use this style for a *TextBlock* because *TextBlock* derives from *FrameworkElement*. The second *Style* is based on "centeredStyle" but has a *TargetType* of *TextBlock*, which means it can also include property settings specific to *TextBlock*. The *TargetType* must be the same as the *BasedOn* type or derived from the *BasedOn* type.

Despite all I've said about keys being required for resources, a *Style* is actually the only exception to this rule. A *Style* without an *x:Key* is a very special case called an *implicit style*. The *Resources* section of the ImplicitStyle project has an example:

Project: ImplicitStyle | File: MainPage.xaml (excerpt)

```xaml
<Page.Resources>
    <x:String x:Key="appName">Implicit Style App</x:String>

    <Style TargetType="TextBlock">
        <Setter Property="FontFamily" Value="Times New Roman" />
        <Setter Property="FontSize" Value="96" />
        <Setter Property="Foreground">
            <Setter.Value>
                <LinearGradientBrush>
                    <GradientStop Offset="0" Color="Red" />
                    <GradientStop Offset="0.17" Color="Orange" />
                    <GradientStop Offset="0.33" Color="Yellow" />
                    <GradientStop Offset="0.5" Color="Green" />
                    <GradientStop Offset="0.67" Color="Blue" />
                    <GradientStop Offset="0.83" Color="Indigo" />
                    <GradientStop Offset="1" Color="Violet" />
                </LinearGradientBrush>
            </Setter.Value>
        </Setter>
    </Style>
</Page.Resources>
```

A key is actually created behind the scenes. It's an object of type *RuntimeType* (which is not a public type) indicating the *TextBlock* type.

The implicit style is very powerful. Any *TextBlock* further down the visual tree that does not have its *Style* property set instead gets the implicit style. If you have a page already full of *TextBlock* elements and you then decide that you want them all to be styled the same way, the implicit style makes it very easy. Notice that none of these *TextBlock* elements have their *Style* properties set:

Project: ImplicitStyle | **File:** MainPage.xaml (excerpt)

```
<Grid Background="{StaticResource ApplicationPageBackgroundThemeBrush}">

    <TextBlock Text="{StaticResource appName}"
               FontFamily="Portable User Interface"
               FontSize="48"
               Foreground="{StaticResource ApplicationForegroundThemeBrush}"
               HorizontalAlignment="Center"
               VerticalAlignment="Center" />

    <TextBlock Text="Top Text"
               HorizontalAlignment="Center"
               VerticalAlignment="Top" />

    <TextBlock Text="Left Text"
               HorizontalAlignment="Left"
               VerticalAlignment="Center" />

    <TextBlock Text="Right Text"
               HorizontalAlignment="Right"
               VerticalAlignment="Center" />

    <TextBlock Text="Bottom Text"
               HorizontalAlignment="Center"
               VerticalAlignment="Bottom" />
</Grid>
```

Although I obviously intended for the implicit style to apply to most of the *TextBlock* elements on the page, I didn't want it to apply to the first one, which appears in the center. If you want certain elements on the page *not* to have this implicit style, you must give those elements an explicit style, or provide local settings that override the properties included in the *Style* object, or set the *Style* property to *null*. (I'll show you how to do that in XAML shortly.) In this example, I've effectively overridden the implicit style in the first *TextBlock* by giving it the default *FontFamily* name, an explicit *FontSize*, and a *Foreground* based on a predefined resource.

You cannot derive a style from an implicit style. However, an implicit style can be based on a nonimplicit style. Simply provide *TargetType* and *BasedOn* attributes and leave out the *x:Key*.

The implicit style is very powerful, but remember: With great power comes...and you know the rest. In a large application, styles can be defined all over the place and visual trees can extend over multiple XAML files. It sometimes happens that a style is implicitly applied to an element, but it's very hard to determine where that style is actually defined!

At this point, you can begin using (or at least start looking at) the *TextBlock* styles defined in the StandardStyles.xaml file. These are called BasicTextStyle, BaselineTextStyle, HeaderTextStyle, SubheaderTextStyle, TitleTextStyle, ItemTextStyle, BodyTextStyle, CaptionTextStyle, PageHeaderTextStyle, PageSubheaderTextStyle, and SnappedPageHeaderTextStyle, and obviously they are for more extensive text layout than I've been doing here.

A Taste of Data Binding

Another way to share objects in a XAML file is through data bindings. Basically, a data binding establishes a connection between two properties of different objects. As you'll see in Chapter 6, "WinRT and MVVM," data bindings find their greatest application in linking visual elements on a page with data sources, and they form a crucial part of implementing the popular Model-View-ViewModel (MVVM) architectural pattern. In MVVM, the target of the binding is a visual element in the View, and the source of the binding is a property in a corresponding View Model. As you'll see in Chapter 11, bindings are crucial in defining templates to display data objects.

You can also use data bindings to link properties of two elements. Like *StaticResource*, *Binding* is generally expressed as a markup extension, which means that it appears between a pair of curly braces. However, *Binding* is more elaborate than *StaticResource* and can alternatively be expressed in property-element syntax.

Here's the *Resources* section from the SharedBrushWithBinding project:

Project: SharedBrushWithBinding | **File:** MainPage.xaml (excerpt)

```
<Page.Resources>
    <x:String x:Key="appName">Shared Brush with Binding</x:String>

    <Style TargetType="TextBlock">
        <Setter Property="FontFamily" Value="Times New Roman" />
        <Setter Property="FontSize" Value="96" />
    </Style>
</Page.Resources>
```

The implicit style for the *TextBlock* no longer has a *Foreground* property. The *LinearGradientBrush* is defined on the first of the four *TextBlock* elements that use that brush, and the subsequent *TextBlock* elements reference that same brush through a binding:

Project: SharedBrushWithBinding | **File:** MainPage.xaml (excerpt)

```
<Grid Background="{StaticResource ApplicationPageBackgroundThemeBrush}">
    <TextBlock Text="{StaticResource appName}"
               FontFamily="Portable User Interface"
               FontSize="48"
               HorizontalAlignment="Center"
               VerticalAlignment="Center" />

    <TextBlock Name="topTextBlock"
               Text="Top Text"
               HorizontalAlignment="Center"
               VerticalAlignment="Top">
        <TextBlock.Foreground>
            <LinearGradientBrush>
                <GradientStop Offset="0" Color="Red" />
                <GradientStop Offset="0.17" Color="Orange" />
                <GradientStop Offset="0.33" Color="Yellow" />
                <GradientStop Offset="0.5" Color="Green" />
                <GradientStop Offset="0.67" Color="Blue" />
                <GradientStop Offset="0.83" Color="Indigo" />
```

```
            <GradientStop Offset="1" Color="Violet" />
          </LinearGradientBrush>
        </TextBlock.Foreground>
      </TextBlock>

      <TextBlock Text="Left Text"
              HorizontalAlignment="Left"
              VerticalAlignment="Center"
              Foreground="{Binding ElementName=topTextBlock, Path=Foreground}" />

      <TextBlock Text="Right Text"
              HorizontalAlignment="Right"
              VerticalAlignment="Center"
              Foreground="{Binding ElementName=topTextBlock, Path=Foreground}" />

      <TextBlock Text="Bottom Text"
              HorizontalAlignment="Center"
              VerticalAlignment="Bottom">
        <TextBlock.Foreground>
          <Binding ElementName="topTextBlock" Path="Foreground" />
        </TextBlock.Foreground>
      </TextBlock>
  </Grid>
```

Data bindings are said to have a *source* and a *target*. The target is always the property on which the binding is set, and the source is the property the binding references. The *TextBlock* with the name "topTextBlock" is considered the source of these data bindings; the three *TextBlock* elements that share the *Foreground* property are targets. Two of these targets show the more standard way of expressing the *Binding* object as a XAML markup extension:

```
Foreground="{Binding ElementName=topTextBlock, Path=Foreground}"
```

XAML markup extensions always appear in curly braces. In the markup extension for *Binding*, a couple properties and values usually need to be set. These properties are separated by commas. The *ElementName* property indicates the name of the element on which the desired property has been set; the *Path* provides the name of the property.

When I'm typing a *Binding* markup extension, I always want to put quotation marks around the property values, but that's wrong. Quotation marks do not appear in a binding expression.

The final *TextBlock* shows the *Binding* expressed in less common property-element syntax:

```
<TextBlock.Foreground>
    <Binding ElementName="topTextBlock" Path="Foreground" />
</TextBlock.Foreground>
```

With this syntax, the quotation marks around the element name and path are required.

You can also create a *Binding* object in code and set it on a target property by using the *SetBinding* method defined by *FrameworkElement*. When doing this, you'll discover that the binding target must be a dependency property.

The *Path* property of the *Binding* class is called *Path* because it can actually be several property names separated by periods. For example, replace one of the *Text* settings in this project with the following:

```
Text="{Binding ElementName=topTextBlock, Path=FontFamily.Source}"
```

The first part of the *Path* indicates that we want something from the *FontFamily* property. That property is set to an object of type *FontFamily*, which has a property named *Source* indicating the font family name. The text displayed by this *TextBlock* is therefore "Times New Roman." (This does not work in a C++ program. Compound and indexed binding paths are not currently supported.)

Try this on any *TextBlock* in this project:

```
Text="{Binding RelativeSource={RelativeSource Self}, Path=FontSize}"
```

That's a *RelativeSource* markup extension inside a *Binding* markup extension, and you use it to reference a property of the same element on which the binding is set.

With *StaticResource*, *Binding*, and *RelativeSource*, you've now seen 60 percent of the XAML markup extensions supported by the Windows Runtime. The *TemplateBinding* markup extension won't turn up until Chapter 11.

The remaining markup extension is not used very often, but when you need it, it's indispensable. Suppose you've defined an implicit style for the *Grid* that includes a *Background* property, and it does exactly what you want except for one *Grid* where you want the *Background* property to be its default value of *null*. How do you specify *null* in markup? Like so:

```
Background="{x:Null}"
```

Or suppose you've defined an implicit style and there's one element where you don't want any part of the style to apply. Inhibit the implicit style like so:

```
Style="{x:Null}"
```

You have now seen nearly all the elements and attributes that appear with an "x" prefix in Windows Runtime XAML files. These are the data types *x:Boolean*, *x:Double*, *x:Int32*, *x:String*, as well as the *x:Class*, *x:Name*, and *x:Key* attributes and the *x:Null* markup extension. The only one I haven't mentioned is *x:Uid*, which must be set to application-wide unique strings that reference resources for internationalization purposes.

CHAPTER 3

Basic Event Handling

The previous chapters have demonstrated how you can instantiate and initialize elements and other objects in either XAML or code. The most common procedure is to use XAML to define the initial layout and appearance of elements on a page but then to change properties of these elements from code as the program is running.

As you've seen, assigning a *Name* or *x:Name* to an element in XAML causes a field to be defined in the page class that gives the code-behind file easy access to that element. This is one of the two major ways that code and XAML interact. The second is through events. An event is a general-purpose mechanism that allows one object to communicate something of interest to other objects. The event is said to be "fired" or "triggered" or "raised" by the first object and "handled" by the other. In the Windows Runtime, one important application of events is to signal the presence of user input from touch, the mouse, a pen, or the keyboard.

Following initialization, a Windows Runtime program generally sits dormant in memory waiting for something interesting to happen. Almost everything the program does thereafter is in response to an event, so the job of event handling is one that will occupy much of the rest of this book.

The *Tapped* Event

The *UIElement* class defines all the basic user-input events. These include

- eight events beginning with the word *Pointer* that consolidate input from touch, the mouse, and the pen;

- five events beginning with the word *Manipulation* that combine input from multiple fingers;

- two *Key* events for keyboard input; and

- higher level events named *Tapped*, *DoubleTapped*, *RightTapped*, and *Holding*.

No, the *RightTapped* event is *not* generated by a finger on your right hand; it's mostly used to register right-button clicks on the mouse, but you can simulate a right tap with touch by holding your finger down for a moment and then lifting, a gesture that also generates *Holding* events. It's the application's responsibility to determine how it wants to handle these.

An extensive exploration of touch, mouse, and pen events awaits us in Chapter 13, "Touch, Etc." The only other events that *UIElement* defines are also related to user input:

- *GotFocus* and *LostFocus* signal when an element is the target of keyboard input; and
- *DragEnter*, *DragOver*, *DragLeave*, and *Drop* relate to drag-and-drop.

For now, let's focus on *Tapped* as a simple representative event. An element that derives from *UIElement* fires a *Tapped* event to indicate that the user has briefly touched the element with a finger, or clicked it with the mouse, or dinged it with the pen. To qualify as a *Tapped* event, the finger (or mouse or pen) cannot move very much and must be released in a short period of time.

All the user-input events have a similar pattern. Expressed in C# syntax, *UIElement* defines the *Tapped* event like so:

```
public event TappedEventHandler Tapped;
```

The *TappedEventHandler* is defined in the *Windows.UI.Xaml.Input* namespace. It's a delegate type that defines the signature of the event handler:

```
public delegate void TappedEventHandler(object sender, TappedRoutedEventArgs e);
```

In the event handler, the first argument indicates the source of the event (which is always an instance of a class that derives from *UIElement*) and the second argument provides properties and methods specific to the *Tapped* event.

The XAML file for the TapTextBlock program defines a *TextBlock* with a *Name* attribute as well as a handler for the *Tapped* event:

Project: TapTextBlock | File: MainPage.xaml (excerpt)

```
<Grid Background="{StaticResource ApplicationPageBackgroundThemeBrush}">
    <TextBlock Name="txtblk"
               Text="Tap Text!"
               FontSize="96"
               HorizontalAlignment="Center"
               VerticalAlignment="Center"
               Tapped="txtblk_Tapped_1" />
</Grid>
```

As you type *TextBlock* attributes in XAML, IntelliSense suggests events as well as properties. These are distinguished with little icons: a wrench for properties and a lightning bolt for events. (You'll also see a few with pairs of curly braces. These are attached properties that I'll describe in Chapter 4, "Presentation with Panels.") If you allow it, IntelliSense also suggests a name for the event handler, and I let it choose this one. Based solely on the XAML syntax, you really can't tell which attributes are properties and which are events.

The actual event handler is implemented in the code-behind file. If you allow Visual Studio to select a handler name for you, you'll discover that Visual Studio also creates a skeleton event handler in the MainPage.xaml.cs file:

```
private void txtblk_Tapped_1(object sender, TappedRoutedEventArgs e)
{

}
```

This is the method that is called when the user taps the *TextBlock*. In future projects, I'll change the names of event handlers to make them more to my liking. I'll remove the *private* keyword (because that's the default), I'll change the name to eliminate underscores and preface it with the word *On* (for example *OnTextBlockTapped*), and I'll change the argument named *e* to *args*. You can rename the method in the code file and then click a little global-rename icon to rename the method in the XAML file as well.

For this sample program, I decided I want to respond to the tap by setting the *TextBlock* to a random color. In preparation for that job, I defined fields for a *Random* object and a *byte* array for the red, green, and blue bytes:

Project: TapTextBlock | **File:** MainPage.xaml.cs (excerpt)

```
public sealed partial class MainPage : Page
{
    Random rand = new Random();
    byte[] rgb = new byte[3];

    public MainPage()
    {
        this.InitializeComponent();
    }

    private void txtblk_Tapped_1(object sender, TappedRoutedEventArgs e)
    {
        rand.NextBytes(rgb);
        Color clr = Color.FromArgb(255, rgb[0], rgb[1], rgb[2]);
        txtblk.Foreground = new SolidColorBrush(clr);
    }
}
```

I've removed the *OnNavigatedTo* method because it's not being used here. In the *Tapped* event handler, the *NextBytes* method of the *Random* object obtains three random bytes, and these are used to construct a *Color* value with the static *Color.FromArgb* method. The handler finishes by setting the *Foreground* property of the *TextBlock* to a *SolidColorBrush* based on that *Color* value.

When you run this program, you can tap the *TextBlock* with a finger, mouse, or pen and it will change to a random color. If you tap on an area of the screen outside the *TextBlock*, nothing happens. If you're using a mouse or pen, you might notice that you don't need to tap the actual strokes that comprise the letters. You can tap between and inside those strokes, and the *TextBlock* will still respond. It's as if the *TextBlock* has an invisible background that encompasses the full height of the font including diacritical marks and descenders, and that's precisely the case.

If you look inside the MainPage.g.cs file generated by Visual Studio, you'll see a *Connect* method containing the code that attaches the event handler to the *Tapped* event of the *TextBlock*. You can do this yourself in code. Try eliminating the *Tapped* handler assigned in the MainPage.xaml file and instead attach an event handler in the constructor of the code-behind file:

```
public MainPage()
{
    this.InitializeComponent();
    txtblk.Tapped += txtblk_Tapped_1;
}
```

No real difference.

Several properties of *TextBlock* need to be set properly for the *Tapped* event to work. The *IsHitTestVisible* and *IsTapEnabled* properties must both be set to their default values of *true*. The *Visibility* property must be set to its default value of *Visibility.Visible*. If set to *Visibility.Collapsed*, the *TextBlock* will not be visible at all and will not respond to user input.

The first argument to the *txtblk_Tapped_1* event handler is the element that sent the event, in this case the *TextBlock*. The second argument provides information about this particular event, including the coordinate point at which the tap occurred, and whether the tap came from a finger, mouse, or pen. This information will be explored in more detail in Chapter 13.

Routed Event Handling

Because the first argument to the *Tapped* event handler is the element that generates the event, you don't need to give the *TextBlock* a name to access it from within the event handler. You can simply cast the *sender* argument to an object of type *TextBlock*. This technique is particularly useful for sharing an event handler among multiple elements, and I've done precisely that in the RoutedEvents0 project.

RoutedEvents0 is the first of several projects that demonstrate the concept of *routed event handling*, which is an important feature of the Windows Runtime. But this particular program doesn't show any features particular to routed events. Hence the suffix of zero. For this project I created the *Tapped* handler first with the proper signature and my preferred name:

Project: RoutedEvents0 | File: MainPage.xaml.cs (excerpt)

```
public sealed partial class MainPage : Page
{
    Random rand = new Random();
    byte[] rgb = new byte[3];

    public MainPage()
    {
        this.InitializeComponent();
    }

    void OnTextBlockTapped(object sender, TappedRoutedEventArgs args)
    {
        TextBlock txtblk = sender as TextBlock;
```

```
        rand.NextBytes(rgb);
        Color clr = Color.FromArgb(255, rgb[0], rgb[1], rgb[2]);
        txtblk.Foreground = new SolidColorBrush(clr);
    }
}
```

Notice that the first line of the event handler casts the *sender* argument to *TextBlock*.

Because this event handler already exists in the code-behind file, Visual Studio suggests that name when you type the name of the event in the XAML file. This was handy because I added nine *TextBlock* elements to the *Grid*:

Project: RoutedEvents0 | File: MainPage.xaml (excerpt)

```
<Page
    x:Class="RoutedEvents0.MainPage"
    ...
    FontSize="48">

    <Grid Background="{StaticResource ApplicationPageBackgroundThemeBrush}">
        <TextBlock Text="Left / Top"
                   HorizontalAlignment="Left"
                   VerticalAlignment="Top"
                   Tapped="OnTextBlockTapped" />

        ...

        <TextBlock Text="Right / Bottom"
                   HorizontalAlignment="Right"
                   VerticalAlignment="Bottom"
                   Tapped="OnTextBlockTapped" />
    </Grid>
</Page>
```

I'm sure you don't need to see them all to get the general idea. Notice that *FontSize* is set for the *Page* so that it is inherited by all the *TextBlock* elements. When you run the program, you can tap the individual elements and each one changes its color independently of the others:

If you tap anywhere between the elements, nothing happens.

You might consider it a nuisance to set the same event handler on nine different elements in the XAML file. If so, you'll probably appreciate the following variation to the program. The RoutedEvents1 program uses *routed input handling*, a term used to describe how input events such as *Tapped* are fired by the element on which the event occurs but the events are then routed up the visual tree. Rather than set a *Tapped* handler for the individual *TextBlock* elements, you can instead set it on the parent of one of these elements (for example, the *Grid*). Here's an excerpt from the XAML file for the RoutedEvents1 program:

Project: RoutedEvents1 | File: MainPage.xaml (excerpt)

```
<Grid Background="{StaticResource ApplicationPageBackgroundThemeBrush}"
    Tapped="OnGridTapped">

    <TextBlock Text="Left / Top"
            HorizontalAlignment="Left"
            VerticalAlignment="Top" />

    ...

    <TextBlock Text="Right / Bottom"
            HorizontalAlignment="Right"
            VerticalAlignment="Bottom" />
</Grid>
```

In the process of moving the *Tapped* handler from the individual *TextBlock* elements to the *Grid*, I've also renamed it to more accurately describe the source of the event.

The event handler must also be modified. The previous *Tapped* handler cast the *sender* argument to a *TextBlock*. It could perform this cast with confidence because the event handler was set only on elements of type *TextBlock*. However, when the event handler is set on the *Grid* as it is here, the *sender* argument to the event handler will be the *Grid*. How can we determine which *TextBlock* was tapped?

Easy: The *TappedRoutedEventArgs* class—an instance of which appears as the second argument to the event handler—has a property named *OriginalSource*, and that indicates the source of the event. In this example, *OriginalSource* can be either a *TextBlock* (if you tap the text) or the *Grid* (if you tap between the text), so the new event handler must perform a check before casting:

Project: RoutedEvents1 | File: MainPage.xaml.cs (excerpt)

```
void OnGridTapped(object sender, TappedRoutedEventArgs args)
{
    if (args.OriginalSource is TextBlock)
    {
        TextBlock txtblk = args.OriginalSource as TextBlock;
        rand.NextBytes(rgb);
        Color clr = Color.FromArgb(255, rgb[0], rgb[1], rgb[2]);
        txtblk.Foreground = new SolidColorBrush(clr);
    }
}
```

Slightly more efficient is performing the cast first and then checking if the result is non-null.

TappedRoutedEventArgs derives from *RoutedEventArgs*, which defines *OriginalSource* and no other properties. Obviously, the *OriginalSource* property is a central concept of routed event handling. The property allows elements to process events that originate with their children and other descendents in the visual tree and to know the source of these events. Routed event handling lets a parent know what its children are up to, and *OriginalSource* identifies the particular child involved.

Alternatively, you can set the *Tapped* handler on *MainPage* rather than the *Grid*. But with *MainPage* there's an easier way. I mentioned earlier that *UIElement* defines all the user-input events. These events are inherited by all derived classes, but the *Control* class adds its own event interface consisting of a whole collection of virtual methods corresponding to these events. For example, for the *Tapped* event defined by *UIElement*, the *Control* class defines a virtual method named *OnTapped*. These virtual methods always begin with the word *On* followed by the name of the event, so they are sometimes referred to as "*On* methods." *Page* derives from *Control* through *UserControl*, so these methods are inherited by the *Page* and *MainPage* classes.

Here's an excerpt from the XAML file for RoutedEvents2 demonstrating that the XAML file defines no event handlers:

Project: RoutedEvents2 | File: MainPage.xaml (excerpt)

```
<Page
    x:Class="RoutedEvents2.MainPage"
    xmlns="http://schemas.microsoft.com/winfx/2006/xaml/presentation"
    xmlns:x="http://schemas.microsoft.com/winfx/2006/xaml"
    xmlns:local="using:RoutedEvents2"
    xmlns:d="http://schemas.microsoft.com/expression/blend/2008"
    xmlns:mc="http://schemas.openxmlformats.org/markup-compatibility/2006"
    mc:Ignorable="d"
    FontSize="48">

    <Grid Background="{StaticResource ApplicationPageBackgroundThemeBrush}">
        <TextBlock Text="Left / Top"
                   HorizontalAlignment="Left"
                   VerticalAlignment="Top" />

        ...

        <TextBlock Text="Right / Bottom"
                   HorizontalAlignment="Right"
                   VerticalAlignment="Bottom" />
    </Grid>
</Page>
```

Instead, the code-behind file has an override of the *OnTapped* method:

Project: RoutedEvents2 | File: MainPage.xaml.cs (excerpt)

```
protected override void OnTapped(TappedRoutedEventArgs args)
{
    if (args.OriginalSource is TextBlock)
    {
        TextBlock txtblk = args.OriginalSource as TextBlock;
        rand.NextBytes(rgb);
        Color clr = Color.FromArgb(255, rgb[0], rgb[1], rgb[2]);
        txtblk.Foreground = new SolidColorBrush(clr);
    }
    base.OnTapped(args);
}
```

When you're typing in Visual Studio and you want to override a virtual method like *OnTapped*, simply type the keyword *override* and press the space bar, and Visual Studio will provide a list of all the virtual methods defined for that class. When you select one, Visual Studio creates a skeleton method with a call to the base method. A call to the base method isn't really required here, but including it is a good habit to develop when overriding virtual methods. Depending on the method you're overriding, you might want to call the base method first, last, in the middle, or not at all.

The *On* methods are basically the same as the event handlers, but they have no *sender* argument because it would be redundant: *sender* would be the same as *this*, the instance of the *Page* that is processing the event.

The next project is RoutedEvents3. I decided to give the *Grid* a random background color if that's the element being tapped. The XAML file looks the same, but the revised *OnTapped* method looks like this:

Project: RoutedEvents3 | File: MainPage.xaml.cs (excerpt)

```
protected override void OnTapped(TappedRoutedEventArgs args)
{
    rand.NextBytes(rgb);
    Color clr = Color.FromArgb(255, rgb[0], rgb[1], rgb[2]);
    SolidColorBrush brush = new SolidColorBrush(clr);

    if (args.OriginalSource is TextBlock)
        (args.OriginalSource as TextBlock).Foreground = brush;

    else if (args.OriginalSource is Grid)
        (args.OriginalSource as Grid).Background = brush;

    base.OnTapped(args);
}
```

Now when you tap a *TextBlock* element, it changes color, but when you tap anywhere else on the screen, the *Grid* changes color.

Now suppose for one reason or another, you decide you want to go back to the original scheme of explicitly defining an event handler separately for each *TextBlock* element to change the text colors, but you also want to retain the *OnTapped* override for changing the *Grid* background color. In the

RoutedEvents4 project, the XAML file has the *Tapped* events restored for *TextBlock* elements and the *Grid* has been given a name:

Project: RoutedEvents4 | File: MainPage.xaml (excerpt)

```
<Grid Name="contentGrid"
      Background="{StaticResource ApplicationPageBackgroundThemeBrush}">

    <TextBlock Text="Left / Top"
               HorizontalAlignment="Left"
               VerticalAlignment="Top"
               Tapped="OnTextBlockTapped" />

    ...

    <TextBlock Text="Right / Bottom"
               HorizontalAlignment="Right"
               VerticalAlignment="Bottom"
               Tapped="OnTextBlockTapped" />
</Grid>
```

One advantage is that the methods to set the *TextBlock* and *Grid* colors are now separate and distinct, so there's no need for *if-else* blocks. The *Tapped* handler for the *TextBlock* elements can cast the *sender* argument with impunity, and the *OnTapped* override can simply access the *Grid* by name:

Project: RoutedEvents4 | File: MainPage.xaml.cs (excerpt)

```
public sealed partial class MainPage : Page
{
    Random rand = new Random();
    byte[] rgb = new byte[3];

    public MainPage()
    {
        this.InitializeComponent();
    }

    void OnTextBlockTapped(object sender, TappedRoutedEventArgs args)
    {
        TextBlock txtblk = sender as TextBlock;
        txtblk.Foreground = GetRandomBrush();
    }

    protected override void OnTapped(TappedRoutedEventArgs args)
    {
        contentGrid.Background = GetRandomBrush();
        base.OnTapped(args);
    }

    Brush GetRandomBrush()
    {
        rand.NextBytes(rgb);
        Color clr = Color.FromArgb(255, rgb[0], rgb[1], rgb[2]);
        return new SolidColorBrush(clr);
    }
}
```

However, the code might not do exactly what you want. When you tap a *TextBlock*, not only does the *TextBlock* change color, but the event continues to go up the visual tree where it's processed by the *OnTapped* override, and the *Grid* changes color as well! If that's what you want, you're in luck. If not, then I'm sure you'll be interested to know that the *TappedRoutedEventArgs* has a property specifically to prevent this. If the *OnTextBlockTapped* handler sets the *Handled* property of the event arguments to *true*, the event is effectively inhibited from further processing higher in the visual tree.

This is demonstrated in the RoutedEvents5 project, which is the same as RoutedEvents4 except for a single statement in the *OnTextBlockTapped* method:

Project: RoutedEvents5 | File: MainPage.xaml.cs (excerpt)

```
void OnTextBlockTapped(object sender, TappedRoutedEventArgs args)
{
    TextBlock txtblk = sender as TextBlock;
    txtblk.Foreground = GetRandomBrush();
    args.Handled = true;
}
```

Overriding the *Handled* Setting

You've just seen that when an element handles an event such as *Tapped* and concludes its event processing by setting the *Handled* property of the event arguments to *true*, the routing of the event effectively stops. The event isn't visible to elements higher in the visual tree.

In some cases, this behavior might be undesirable. Suppose you're working with an element that sets the *Handled* property to *true* in its event handler, but you still want to see that event higher in the visual tree. One solution is to simply change the code, but that option might not be available. The element might be implemented in a dynamic-link library, and you might not have access to the source code.

In RoutedEvents6, the XAML file is the same as in RoutedEvents5: Each *TextBlock* has a handler set for its *Tapped* event. The *Tapped* handler sets the *Handled* property to *true*. The class also defines a separate *OnPageTapped* handler that sets the background color of the *Grid*:

Project: RoutedEvents6 | File: MainPage.xaml.cs (excerpt)

```
public sealed partial class MainPage : Page
{
    Random rand = new Random();
    byte[] rgb = new byte[3];

    public MainPage()
    {
        this.InitializeComponent();

        this.AddHandler(UIElement.TappedEvent,
                        new TappedEventHandler(OnPageTapped),
                        true);
    }
```

```
        void OnTextBlockTapped(object sender, TappedRoutedEventArgs args)
        {
            TextBlock txtblk = sender as TextBlock;
            txtblk.Foreground = GetRandomBrush();
            args.Handled = true;
        }

        void OnPageTapped(object sender, TappedRoutedEventArgs args)
        {
            contentGrid.Background = GetRandomBrush();
        }

        Brush GetRandomBrush()
        {
            rand.NextBytes(rgb);
            Color clr = Color.FromArgb(255, rgb[0], rgb[1], rgb[2]);
            return new SolidColorBrush(clr);
        }
    }
}
```

But look at the interesting way that the constructor sets a *Tapped* handler for the *Page*. Normally, it would attach the event handler like so:

```
this.Tapped += OnPageTapped;
```

In that case the *OnPageTapped* handler would not get a *Tapped* event originating with the *TextBlock* because the *TextBlock* handler sets *Handled* to *true*. Instead, it attaches the handler with a method named *AddHandler*:

```
this.AddHandler(UIElement.TappedEvent,
                new TappedEventHandler(OnPageTapped),
                true);
```

AddHandler is defined by *UIElement*, which also defines the static *UIElement.TappedEvent* property. This property is of type *RoutedEvent*.

Just as a property like *FontSize* is backed by a static property named *FontSizeProperty* of type *DependencyProperty*, a routed event such as *Tapped* is backed by a static property named *TappedEvent* of type *RoutedEvent*. *RoutedEvent* defines nothing public on its own; it mainly exists to allow an event to be referenced in code without requiring an instance of an element.

The *AddHandler* method attaches a handler to that event. The second argument of *AddHandler* is defined as just an *object*, so creating a delegate object is required to reference the event handler. And here's the magic: Set the last argument to *true* if you want this handler to also receive routed events that have been flagged as *Handled*.

The *AddHandler* method isn't used often, but when you need it, it is essential.

Input, Alignment, and Backgrounds

I have just one more, very short program in the RoutedEvents series to make a couple important points about input events.

The XAML file for RoutedEvents7 has just one *TextBlock* and no event handlers defined:

Project: RoutedEvents7 | File: MainPage.xaml (excerpt)

```
<Page ...
    FontSize="48">

    <Grid Background="{StaticResource ApplicationPageBackgroundThemeBrush}">
        <TextBlock Text="Hello, Windows 8!"
                    Foreground="Red" />
    </Grid>
</Page>
```

The absence of *HorizontalAlignment* and *VerticalAlignment* settings on the *TextBlock* cause it to appear in the upper-left corner of the *Grid*.

Like RoutedEvents3, the code-behind file contains separate processing for an event originating from the *TextBlock* and an event coming from the *Grid*:

Project: RoutedEvents7 | File: MainPage.xaml.cs (excerpt)

```
public sealed partial class MainPage : Page
{
    Random rand = new Random();
    byte[] rgb = new byte[3];

    public MainPage()
    {
        this.InitializeComponent();
    }

    protected override void OnTapped(TappedRoutedEventArgs args)
    {
        rand.NextBytes(rgb);
        Color clr = Color.FromArgb(255, rgb[0], rgb[1], rgb[2]);
        SolidColorBrush brush = new SolidColorBrush(clr);

        if (args.OriginalSource is TextBlock)
            (args.OriginalSource as TextBlock).Foreground = brush;

        else if (args.OriginalSource is Grid)
            (args.OriginalSource as Grid).Background = brush;

        base.OnTapped(args);
    }
}
```

Here it is:

As you tap the *TextBlock*, it changes to a random color like normal, but when you tap outside the *TextBlock*, the *Grid* doesn't change color like it did earlier. Instead, the *TextBlock* changes color! It's as if...yes, it's as if the *TextBlock* is now occupying the entire page and snagging all the *Tapped* events for itself.

And that's precisely the case. This *TextBlock* has default values of *HorizontalAlignment* and *VerticalAlignment*, but those default values are not *Left* and *Top* like the visuals might suggest. The default values are named *Stretch*, and that means that the *TextBlock* is stretched to the size of its parent, the *Grid*. It's hard to tell because the text still has a 48-pixel font, but the *TextBlock* has a transparent background that now fills the entire page.

In fact, throughout the Windows Runtime, all elements have default *HorizontalAlignment* and *VerticalAlignment* values of *Stretch*, and it's an important part of the Windows Runtime layout system. More details are coming in Chapter 4.

Let's put *HorizontalAlignment* and *VerticalAlignment* values in this *TextBlock*:

```
<Grid Background="{StaticResource ApplicationPageBackgroundThemeBrush}">
    <TextBlock Text="Hello, Windows 8!"
               HorizontalAlignment="Left"
               VerticalAlignment="Top"
               Foreground="Red" />
</Grid>
```

Now the *TextBlock* is only occupying a small area in the upper-left corner of the page, and when you tap outside the *TextBlock*, the *Grid* changes color.

Now change *HorizontalAlignment* to *TextAlignment*:

```
<Grid Background="{StaticResource ApplicationPageBackgroundThemeBrush}">
    <TextBlock Text="Hello, Windows 8!"
               TextAlignment="Left"
               VerticalAlignment="Top"
               Foreground="Red" />
</Grid>
```

The program looks the same. The text is still positioned at the upper-left corner. But now when you tap to the right of the *TextBlock*, the *TextBlock* changes color rather than the *Grid*. The *TextBlock* has its default *HorizontalAlignment* property of *Stretch*, so it is now occupying the entire width of the screen, but within the total width that the *TextBlock* occupies, the text is aligned to the left.

The lesson: *HorizontalAlignment* and *TextAlignment* are not equivalent, although they might seem to be if you judge solely from the visuals.

Now try another experiment by restoring the *HorizontalAlignment* setting and removing the *Background* property of the *Grid*:

```
<Grid>
    <TextBlock Text="Hello, Windows 8!"
               HorizontalAlignment="Left"
               VerticalAlignment="Top"
               Foreground="Red" />
</Grid>
```

With a light theme, the *Grid* has an off-white background. When the *Background* property is removed, the background of the page changes to black. But you'll also experience a change in the behavior of the program: The *TextBlock* still changes color when you tap it, but when you tap outside the *TextBlock*, the *Grid* doesn't change color at all.

The default value of the *Background* property defined by *Panel* (and inherited by *Grid*) is *null*, and with a *null* background, the *Grid* doesn't trap touch events. They just fall right through.

One way to fix this without altering the visual appearance is to give the *Grid* a *Background* property of *Transparent*:

```
<Grid Background="Transparent">
    <TextBlock Text="Hello, Windows 8!"
               HorizontalAlignment="Left"
               VerticalAlignment="Top"
               Foreground="Red" />
</Grid>
```

It looks the same as *null*, but now you'll get *Tapped* events with an *OriginalSource* of *Grid*.

The lessons here are important: Looks can be deceiving. An element with default settings of *HorizontalAlignment* and *VerticalAlignment* might look the same as one with settings of *Left* and *Top*, but it is actually occupying the entire area of its container and might block events from reaching underlying elements. A *Panel* derivative with a default *Background* property of *null* might look the same as one with a setting of *Transparent*, but it does not respond to touch events.

I can almost guarantee that sometime in the future, one of these two issues will cause a bug in one of your programs that will drive you crazy for the good part of a day, and that this will happen even after many years of working with the XAML layout system.

I speak from experience.

Size and Orientation Changes

Many, many years ago when Windows was very young, information about Windows programming was hard to find. It wasn't until the December 1986 issue of *Microsoft Systems Journal* (the predecessor to *MSDN Magazine*) that the very first magazine article about Windows programming appeared. The article described a program called WHATSIZE (all capital letters, of course), which did little more than display the current size of the program's window. But as the size of the window changed, the displayed values reflected that change.

Obviously, the original WHATSIZE program was written for the Windows APIs of that era, so it redrew the display in response to a WM_PAINT message. In the original Windows API, this message occurred whenever the contents of part of a program's window became "invalid" and needed redrawing. A program could define its window so that the entire window was invalidated whenever its size changed.

The Windows Runtime has no equivalent of the WM_PAINT message, and indeed, the entire graphics paradigm is quite different. Previous versions of Windows implemented a "direct mode" graphics system in which applications drew to the actual video memory. Of course, this occurred through a software layer (the Graphics Device Interface) and a device driver, but at some point in the actual drawing functions, code was writing into video display memory.

The Windows Runtime is quite different. In its public programming interface, it doesn't even have a concept of drawing or painting. Instead, a Windows 8 application creates elements—that is, objects instantiated from classes that derive from *FrameworkElement*—and adds them to the application's visual tree. These elements are responsible for rendering themselves. When a Windows 8 application wants to display text, it doesn't draw text but instead creates a *TextBlock*. When the application wants to display a bitmap, it creates an *Image* element. Instead of drawing lines and Bézier splines and ellipses, the program creates *Polyline* and *Path* elements.

The Windows Runtime implements a "retained mode" graphics system. Between your application and the video display is a composition layer on which all the rendered output is assembled before it is presented to the user. Perhaps the most important benefit of retained mode graphics is flicker-free animation, as you'll witness for yourself toward the end of this chapter and in much of the remainder of this book.

Although the graphics system in the Windows Runtime is very different from earlier versions of Windows, in another sense a Windows 8 application is similar to its earlier brethren. Once a program is loaded into memory and starts running, it spends most of its time generally sitting dormant in memory, waiting for something interesting to happen. These notifications take the form of events and callbacks. Often these events signal user input, but there might be other interesting activity as well. One such callback is the *OnNavigatedTo* method. In a simple single-page program, this method is called soon after the constructor returns.

Another event that might be of interest to a Windows 8 application—particularly one that does what the old WHATSIZE program did—is named *SizeChanged*. Here's the XAML file for the Windows 8 WhatSize program. Notice that the root element defines a handler for the *SizeChanged* event:

Project: WhatSize | File: MainPage.xaml (excerpt)

```
<Page
    x:Class="WhatSize.MainPage"
    ...
    FontSize="36"
    SizeChanged="OnPageSizeChanged">

    <Grid Background="{StaticResource ApplicationPageBackgroundThemeBrush}">
        <TextBlock HorizontalAlignment="Center"
                   VerticalAlignment="Top">
            &#x21A4; <Run x:Name="widthText" /> pixels &#x21A6;
        </TextBlock>

        <TextBlock HorizontalAlignment="Center"
                   VerticalAlignment="Center"
                   TextAlignment="Center">
            &#x21A5;
            <LineBreak />
            <Run x:Name="heightText" /> pixels
            <LineBreak />
            &#x21A7;
        </TextBlock>
    </Grid>
</Page>
```

The remainder of the XAML file defines two *TextBlock* elements containing some *Run* objects surrounded by arrow characters. (You'll see what they look like soon.) It might seem excessive to set three properties to *Center* in the second *TextBlock*, but they're all necessary. The first two center the *TextBlock* in the page; setting *TextAlignment* to *Center* results in the two arrows being centered relative to the text. The two *Run* elements are given *x:Name* attributes so that the *Text* properties can be set in code. This happens in the *SizeChanged* event handler:

Project: WhatSize | File: MainPage.xaml.cs (excerpt)

```
public sealed partial class MainPage : Page
{
    public MainPage()
    {
        this.InitializeComponent();
    }

    void OnPageSizeChanged(object sender, SizeChangedEventArgs args)
    {
        widthText.Text = args.NewSize.Width.ToString();
        heightText.Text = args.NewSize.Height.ToString();
    }
}
```

Very conveniently, the event arguments supply the new size in the form of a *Size* structure, and the handler simply converts the *Width* and *Height* properties to strings and sets them to the *Text* properties of the two *Run* elements:

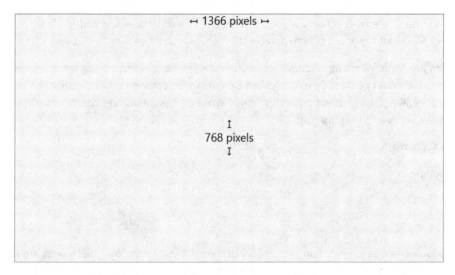

If you're running the program on a device that responds to orientation changes, you can try flipping the screen and observe how the numbers change. You can also sweep your finger from the left of the screen to invoke the snapped views and then divide the screen between this program and another to see how the width value changes.

You don't need to set the *SizeChanged* event handler in XAML. You can set it in code, perhaps during the *Page* constructor:

```
this.SizeChanged += OnPageSizeChanged;
```

SizeChanged is defined by *FrameworkElement* and inherited by all descendent classes. Despite the fact that *SizeChangedEventArgs* derives from *RoutedEventArgs*, this is not a routed event. You can tell it's not a routed event because the *OriginalSource* property of the event arguments is always *null*; there is no *SizeChangedEvent* property; and whatever element you set this event on, that's the element's size you get. But you can set *SizeChanged* handlers on any element. Generally, the order the events are fired proceeds down the visual tree: *MainPage* first (in this example), and then *Grid* and *TextBlock*.

If you need the rendered size of an element other than in the context of a *SizeChanged* handler, that information is available from the *ActualWidth* and *ActualHeight* properties defined by *FrameworkElement*. Indeed, the *SizeChanged* handler in WhatSize is actually a little shorter when accessing those properties:

```
void OnPageSizeChanged(object sender, SizeChangedEventArgs args)
{
    widthText.Text = this.ActualWidth.ToString();
    heightText.Text = this.ActualHeight.ToString();
}
```

What you probably do *not* want are the *Width* and *Height* properties. Those properties are also defined by *FrameworkElement*, but they have default values of "not a number" or NaN. A program can set *Width* and *Height* to explicit values (such as in the TextFormatting project in Chapter 2, "XAML Syntax"), but usually these properties remain at their default values and they are of no use in determining how large an element actually is. *FrameworkElement* also defines *MinWidth*, *MaxWidth*, *MinHeight*, and *MaxHeight* properties with default NaN values, but these aren't used very often.

If you access the *ActualWidth* and *ActualHeight* properties in the page's constructor, however, you'll find they have values of zero. Despite the fact that *InitializeComponent* has constructed the visual tree, that visual tree has not yet gone through a layout process. After the constructor finishes, the page gets several events in sequence:

- *OnNavigatedTo*
- *SizeChanged*
- *LayoutUpdated*
- *Loaded*

If the page later changes size, additional *SizeChanged* events and *LayoutUpdated* events are fired. *LayoutUpdated* can also be fired if elements are added to or removed from the visual tree or if an element is changed so as to affect layout.

If you need a place to perform initialization after initial layout when all the elements in the visual tree have nonzero sizes, the event you want is *Loaded*. It is very common for a *Page* derivative to attach a handler for the *Loaded* event. Generally, the *Loaded* event occurs only once during the lifetime of a *Page* object. I say "generally" because if the *Page* object is detached from its parent (a *Frame*) and reattached, the *Loaded* event will occur again. But this won't happen unless you deliberately make it happen. Also, the *Unloaded* event can let you know if the page has been detached from the visual tree.

Every *FrameworkElement* derivative has a *Loaded* event. As a visual tree is built, the *Loaded* events occur in a sequence going up the visual tree, ending with the *Page* derivative. When that *Page* object gets a *Loaded* event, it can assume that all its children have fired their own *Loaded* events and everything has been correctly sized.

Handling a *Loaded* event in a *Page* class is so common that some programmers perform *Loaded* processing right in the constructor using an anonymous handler:

```
public MainPage()
{
    this.InitializeComponent();

    Loaded += (sender, args) =>
        {
            ...
        };
}
```

Sometimes Windows 8 applications need to know when the orientation of the screen changes. In Chapter 1, "Markup and Code," I showed an InternationalHelloWorld program that looks fine in landscape mode but probably results in overlapping text if switched to portrait mode. To fix that, the ScalableInternationalHelloWorld program code-behind file changes the page's *FontSize* property to 24 in portrait mode:

Project: ScalableInternationalHelloWorld | File: MainPage.xaml.cs

```
public sealed partial class MainPage : Page
{
    public MainPage()
    {
        this.InitializeComponent();
        SetFont();
        DisplayProperties.OrientationChanged += OnDisplayPropertiesOrientationChanged;
    }

    void OnDisplayPropertiesOrientationChanged(object sender)
    {
        SetFont();
    }

    void SetFont()
    {
        bool isLandscape =
            DisplayProperties.CurrentOrientation == DisplayOrientations.Landscape ||
            DisplayProperties.CurrentOrientation == DisplayOrientations.LandscapeFlipped;

        this.FontSize = isLandscape ? 40 : 24;
    }
}
```

The *DisplayProperties* class and *DisplayOrientations* enumeration are defined in the *Windows .Graphics.Display* namespace. *DisplayProperties.OrientationChanged* is a static event, and when that event is fired, the static *DisplayProperties.CurrentOrientation* property provides the current orientation.

Somewhat more information, including snapped states, is provided by the *ViewStateChanged* event of the *AppicationView* class in the *Windows.UI.ViewManagement* namespace, but working with this event must await Chapter 12, "Pages and Navigation."

Bindings to *Run*?

In Chapter 2 I discussed data bindings. Data bindings can link properties of two elements so that when a source property changes, the target property also changes. Data bindings are particularly satisfying when they eliminate the need for event handlers.

Is it possible to rewrite WhatSize to use data bindings rather than a *SizeChanged* handler? It's worth a try.

In the WhatSize project, remove the *OnPageSizeChanged* handler from the MainPage.xaml.cs file (or just comment it out if you don't want to do *too* much damage to the file). In the root tag of the MainPage.xaml file, remove the *SizeChanged* attribute and give *MainPage* a name of "page." Then, set *Binding* markup extensions on the two *Run* objects referencing the *ActualWidth* and *ActualHeight* properties of the page:

```
<Page ...
    FontSize="36"
    Name="page">

    <Grid Background="{StaticResource ApplicationPageBackgroundThemeBrush}">
        <TextBlock HorizontalAlignment="Center"
                   VerticalAlignment="Top">
            &#x21A4;
            <Run Text="{Binding ElementName=page, Path=ActualWidth}" />
            pixels &#x21A6;
        </TextBlock>

        <TextBlock HorizontalAlignment="Center"
                   VerticalAlignment="Center"
                   TextAlignment="Center">
            &#x21A5;
            <LineBreak />
            <Run Text="{Binding ElementName=page, Path=ActualHeight}" /> pixels
            <LineBreak />
            &#x21A7;
        </TextBlock>
    </Grid>
</Page>
```

The program compiles fine, and it runs smoothly without any run-time exceptions. The only problem is: Where the numbers should appear is a discouraging 0.

This is likely to seem odd, particularly when you set the same bindings on the *Text* property of *TextBlock* instead of *Run*:

```
<Page ...
    FontSize="36"
    Name="page">

    <Grid Background="{StaticResource ApplicationPageBackgroundThemeBrush}">
        <TextBlock HorizontalAlignment="Center"
                   VerticalAlignment="Top"
                   Text="{Binding ElementName=page, Path=ActualWidth}" />

        <TextBlock HorizontalAlignment="Center"
                   VerticalAlignment="Center"
                   TextAlignment="Center"
                   Text="{Binding ElementName=page, Path=ActualHeight}" />
    </Grid>
</Page>
```

This works:

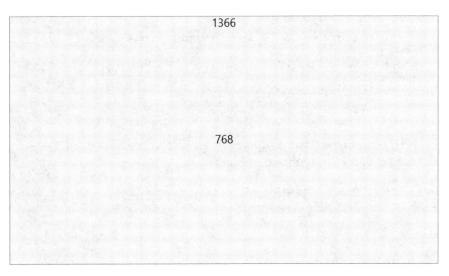

At least it appears to work at first. With the version of Windows 8 that I'm using to write this chapter, the numbers are not updated as you change the orientation or size of the page, and they really should be. In theory, a data binding is notified when a source property changes so that it can change the target property, but the application source code appears to have no event handlers and no moving parts. This is what is supposed to make data bindings so great.

Unfortunately, by giving up on the bindings to *Run* we've also lost the informative arrows. So, why do the data bindings work (or almost work) on the *Text* property of *TextBlock* but not at all on the *Text* property of *Run*?

It's very simple. The target of a data binding must be a dependency property. This fact is obvious when you define a data binding in code by using the *SetBinding* method. That's the difference: The *Text* property of *TextBlock* is backed by the *TextProperty* dependency property, but the *Text* property of *Run* is not. The *Run* version of *Text* is a plain old property that cannot serve as a target for a data binding. The XAML parser probably shouldn't allow a binding to be set on the *Text* property of *Run*, but it does.

In Chapter 4 I'll show you how to use a *StackPanel* to get the arrows back in a version of WhatSize that uses data bindings, and in Chapter 16, "Rich Text," I'll demonstrate a technique using *RichTextBlock*.

Timers and Animation

Sometimes a Windows 8 application needs to receive periodic events at a fixed interval. A clock application, for example, probably needs to update its display every second. The ideal class for this job is *DispatcherTimer*. Set a timer interval, set a handler for the *Tick* event, and go.

Here's the XAML file for a digital clock application. It's just a big *TextBlock*:

Project: DigitalClock | File: MainPage.xaml (excerpt)

```xaml
<Grid Background="{StaticResource ApplicationPageBackgroundThemeBrush}">
    <TextBlock Name="txtblk"
               FontFamily="Lucida Console"
               FontSize="120"
               HorizontalAlignment="Center"
               VerticalAlignment="Center" />
</Grid>
```

The code-behind file creates the *DispatcherTimer* with a 1-second interval and sets the *Text* property of the *TextBlock* in the event handler:

Project: DigitalClock | File: MainPage.xaml.cs (excerpt)

```csharp
public sealed partial class MainPage : Page
{
    public MainPage()
    {
        this.InitializeComponent();

        DispatcherTimer timer = new DispatcherTimer();
        timer.Interval = TimeSpan.FromSeconds(1);
        timer.Tick += OnTimerTick;
        timer.Start();
    }

    void OnTimerTick(object sender, object e)
    {
        txtblk.Text = DateTime.Now.ToString("h:mm:ss tt");
    }
}
```

And here it is:

Calls to the *Tick* handler occur in the same execution thread as the rest of the user interface, so if the program is busy doing something in that thread, the calls won't interrupt that work and might become somewhat irregular and even skip a few beats. In a multipage application, you might want to start the timer in the *OnNavigatedTo* override and stop it in *OnNavigatedFrom* to avoid the program wasting time doing work when the page is not visible.

This is a good illustration of the difference in how a desktop Windows application and a Windows 8 application update the video display. Both types of applications use a timer for implementing a clock, but rather than drawing and redrawing text every second by invalidating the contents of the window, the Windows 8 application changes the visual appearance of an existing element simply by changing one of its properties.

You can set the *DispatcherTimer* for an interval as low as you want, but you're not going to get calls to the *Tick* handler faster than the frame rate of the video display, which is probably 60 Hertz or about a 17-millisecond period. Of course, it doesn't make sense to update the video display faster than the frame rate. Updating the display precisely at the frame rate gives you as smooth an animation as possible. If you want to perform an animation in this way, don't use *DispatcherTimer*. A better choice is the static *CompositionTarget.Rendering* event, which is specifically designed to be called prior to a screen refresh.

Even better than *CompositionTarget.Rendering* are all the animation classes provided as part of the Windows Runtime. These classes let you define animations in XAML or code, they have lots of options, and some of them are performed in background threads.

But until I cover the animation classes in Chapter 9, "Animation"—and perhaps even after I do— the *CompositionTarget.Rendering* event is well suited for performing animations. These are sometimes called "manual" animations because the program itself has to carry out some calculations based on elapsed time.

Here's a little project called ExpandingText that changes the *FontSize* of a *TextBlock* in the *CompositionTarget.Rendering* event handler, making the text larger and smaller. The XAML file simply instantiates a *TextBlock*:

Project: ExpandingText | File: MainPage.xaml (excerpt)

```
<Grid Background="{StaticResource ApplicationPageBackgroundThemeBrush}">
    <TextBlock Name="txtblk"
               Text="Hello, Windows 8!"
               HorizontalAlignment="Center"
               VerticalAlignment="Center" />
</Grid>
```

In the code-behind file, the constructor starts a *CompositionTarget.Rendering* event simply by setting an event handler. The second argument to that handler is defined as type *object*, but it is actually of type *RenderingEventArgs*, which has a property named *RenderingTime* of type *TimeSpan*, giving you an elapsed time since the app was started:

Project: ExpandingText | **File:** MainPage.xaml.cs (excerpt)

```
public sealed partial class MainPage : Page
{
    public MainPage()
    {
        this.InitializeComponent();
        CompositionTarget.Rendering += OnCompositionTargetRendering;
    }

    void OnCompositionTargetRendering(object sender, object args)
    {
        RenderingEventArgs renderArgs = args as RenderingEventArgs;
        double t = (0.25 * renderArgs.RenderingTime.TotalSeconds) % 1;
        double scale = t < 0.5 ? 2 * t : 2 - 2 * t;
        txtblk.FontSize = 1 + scale * 143;
    }
}
```

I've attempted to generalize this code somewhat. The calculation of *t* causes it to repeatedly increase from 0 to 1 over the course of 4 seconds. During those same 4 seconds, the value of *scale* goes from 0 to 1 and back to 0, so *FontSize* ranges from 1 to 144 and back to 1. (The code ensures that the *FontSize* is never set to zero, which would raise an exception.) When you run this program, you might see a little jerkiness at first because fonts need to be rasterized at a bunch of different sizes. But after it settles into a rhythm, it's fairly smooth and there is definitely no flickering.

It's also possible to animate color, and I'll show you two different ways to do it. The second way is better than the first, but I want to make a point here, so here's the XAML file for the ManualBrushAnimation project:

Project: ManualBrushAnimation | **File:** MainPage.xaml (excerpt)

```
<Grid Name="contentGrid">
    <TextBlock Name="txtblk"
               Text="Hello, Windows 8!"
               FontFamily="Times New Roman"
               FontSize="96"
               FontWeight="Bold"
               HorizontalAlignment="Center"
               VerticalAlignment="Center" />
</Grid>
```

Neither the *Grid* nor the *TextBlock* have explicit brushes defined. Creating those brushes based on animated colors is the job of the *CompositionTarget.Rendering* event handler:

Project: ManualBrushAnimation | **File:** MainPage.xaml.cs (excerpt)

```
public sealed partial class MainPage : Page
{
    public MainPage()
    {
        this.InitializeComponent();
        CompositionTarget.Rendering += OnCompositionTargetRendering;
    }
```

```
void OnCompositionTargetRendering(object sender, object args)
{
    RenderingEventArgs renderingArgs = args as RenderingEventArgs;
    double t = (0.25 * renderingArgs.RenderingTime.TotalSeconds) % 1;
    t = t < 0.5 ? 2 * t : 2 - 2 * t;

    // Background
    byte gray = (byte)(255 * t);
    Color clr = Color.FromArgb(255, gray, gray, gray);
    contentGrid.Background = new SolidColorBrush(clr);

    // Foreground
    gray = (byte)(255 - gray);
    clr = Color.FromArgb(255, gray, gray, gray);
    txtblk.Foreground = new SolidColorBrush(clr);
}
}
```

As the background color of the *Grid* goes from black to white and back, the foreground color of the *TextBlock* goes from white to black and back, meeting halfway through.

The effect is nice, but notice that two *SolidColorBrush* objects are being created at the frame rate of the video display (which is probably about 60 times a second) and these objects are just as quickly discarded. This is not necessary. A much better approach is to create two *SolidColorBrush* objects initially in the XAML file:

Project: ManualColorAnimation | **File:** MainPage.xaml (excerpt)

```
<Grid>
    <Grid.Background>
        <SolidColorBrush x:Name="gridBrush" />
    </Grid.Background>

    <TextBlock Text="Hello, Windows 8!"
               FontFamily="Times New Roman"
               FontSize="96"
               FontWeight="Bold"
               HorizontalAlignment="Center"
               VerticalAlignment="Center">
        <TextBlock.Foreground>
            <SolidColorBrush x:Name="txtblkBrush" />
        </TextBlock.Foreground>
    </TextBlock>
</Grid>
```

These *SolidColorBrush* objects exist for the entire duration of the program, and they are given names for easy access from the *CompositionTarget.Rendering* handler:

Project: ManualColorAnimation | **File:** MainPage.xaml.cs (excerpt)

```
void OnCompositionTargetRendering(object sender, object args)
{
    RenderingEventArgs renderingArgs = args as RenderingEventArgs;
    double t = (0.25 * renderingArgs.RenderingTime.TotalSeconds) % 1;
    t = t < 0.5 ? 2 * t : 2 - 2 * t;
```

```
    // Background
    byte gray = (byte)(255 * t);
    gridBrush.Color = Color.FromArgb(255, gray, gray, gray);

    // Foreground
    gray = (byte)(255 - gray);
    txtblkBrush.Color = Color.FromArgb(255, gray, gray, gray);
}
```

At first this might not seem a whole lot different because two *Color* objects are being created and discarded at the video frame rate. But it's wrong to speak of *objects* here because *Color* is a structure rather than a class. It is more correct to speak of *Color* values. These *Color* values are stored on the stack rather than requiring a memory allocation from the heap.

It's best to avoid frequent allocations from the heap whenever possible, and particularly at the rate of 60 times per second. But what I like most about this example is the idea of *SolidColorBrush* objects remaining alive in the Windows Runtime composition system. This program is effectively reaching down into that composition layer and changing a property of the brush so that it renders differently.

This program also illustrates part of the wonders of dependency properties. Dependency properties are built to respond to changes in a very structured manner. As you'll discover, the built-in animation facilities of the Windows Runtime can target *only* dependency properties, and "manual" animations using *CompositionTarget.Rendering* have pretty much the same limitation. Fortunately, the *Foreground* property of *TextBlock* and the *Background* property of *Grid* are both dependency properties of type *Brush*, and the *Color* property of the *SolidColorBrush* is also a dependency property.

Indeed, whenever you encounter a dependency property, you might ask yourself, "How can I animate that?" For example, the *Offset* property in the *GradientStop* class is a dependency property, and you can animate it for some interesting effects.

Here's the XAML file for the RainbowEight project:

Project: RainbowEight | File: MainPage.xaml (excerpt)
```xml
<Grid Background="{StaticResource ApplicationPageBackgroundThemeBrush}">
    <TextBlock Name="txtblk"
               Text="8"
               FontFamily="CooperBlack"
               FontSize="1"
               HorizontalAlignment="Center">
        <TextBlock.Foreground>
            <LinearGradientBrush x:Name="gradientBrush">
                <GradientStop Offset="0.00" Color="Red" />
                <GradientStop Offset="0.14" Color="Orange" />
                <GradientStop Offset="0.28" Color="Yellow" />
                <GradientStop Offset="0.43" Color="Green" />
                <GradientStop Offset="0.57" Color="Blue" />
                <GradientStop Offset="0.71" Color="Indigo" />
                <GradientStop Offset="0.86" Color="Violet" />
                <GradientStop Offset="1.00" Color="Red" />
                <GradientStop Offset="1.14" Color="Orange" />
```

```
                    <GradientStop Offset="1.28" Color="Yellow" />
                    <GradientStop Offset="1.43" Color="Green" />
                    <GradientStop Offset="1.57" Color="Blue" />
                    <GradientStop Offset="1.71" Color="Indigo" />
                    <GradientStop Offset="1.86" Color="Violet" />
                    <GradientStop Offset="2.00" Color="Red" />
                </LinearGradientBrush>
            </TextBlock.Foreground>
        </TextBlock>
    </Grid>
```

A bunch of those *GradientStop* objects have *Offset* values above 1, so they're not going to be visible. Moreover, the *TextBlock* itself won't be very obvious because it has a *FontSize* of 1. However, during its *Loaded* event, the *Page* class obtains the *ActualHeight* of that tiny *TextBlock* and saves it in a field. It then starts a *CompositionTarget.Rendering* event going:

Project: RainbowEight | **File:** MainPage.xaml (excerpt)

```
public sealed partial class MainPage : Page
{
    double txtblkBaseSize;  // ie, for 1-pixel FontSize

    public MainPage()
    {
        this.InitializeComponent();
        Loaded += OnPageLoaded;
    }

    void OnPageLoaded(object sender, RoutedEventArgs args)
    {
        txtblkBaseSize = txtblk.ActualHeight;
        CompositionTarget.Rendering += OnCompositionTargetRendering;
    }

    void OnCompositionTargetRendering(object sender, object args)
    {
        // Set FontSize as large as it can be
        txtblk.FontSize = this.ActualHeight / txtblkBaseSize;

        // Calculate t from 0 to 1 repetitively
        RenderingEventArgs renderingArgs = args as RenderingEventArgs;
        double t = (0.25 * renderingArgs.RenderingTime.TotalSeconds) % 1;

        // Loop through GradientStop objects
        for (int index = 0; index < gradientBrush.GradientStops.Count; index++)
            gradientBrush.GradientStops[index].Offset = index / 7.0 - t;
    }
}
```

In the *CompositionTarget.Rendering* handler, the *FontSize* of the *TextBlock* is increased based on the *ActualHeight* property of the *Page*, rather like a manual version of *Viewbox*. It won't be the full height of the page because the *ActualHeight* of the *TextBlock* includes space for descenders and diacriticals, but it will be as large as is convenient to make it, and it will change when the display switches orientation.

Moreover, the *CompositionTarget.Rendering* handler goes on to change all the *Offset* properties of the *LinearGradientBrush* for an animated rainbow effect that I'm afraid can't quite be rendered on the static page of this book:

You might wonder: Isn't it inefficient to change the *FontSize* property of the *TextBlock* at the frame rate of the video display? Wouldn't it make more sense to set a *SizeChanged* handler for the *Page* and do it then?

Perhaps a little. But it is another feature of dependency properties that the object doesn't register a change unless the property really changes. If the property is being set to the value it already is, nothing happens, as you can verify by attaching a *SizeChanged* handler on the *TextBlock* itself.

CHAPTER 4

Presentation with Panels

A Windows Runtime program generally consists of one or more classes that derive from *Page*. Each page contains a visual tree of elements connected in a parent-child hierarchy. A *Page* object can have only one child set to its *Content* property, but in most cases this child is an instance of a class that derives from *Panel*. *Panel* defines a property named *Children* that is of type *UIElementCollection*—a collection of *UIElement* derivatives, including other panels.

These *Panel* derivatives form the core of the Windows Runtime dynamic layout system. As the size or orientation of a page changes, panels can reorganize their children to optimally fill the available space. Each type of panel arranges its children differently. The *Grid*, for example, arranges its children in rows and columns. The *StackPanel* stacks its children either horizontally or vertically. The *VariableSizedWrapGrid* also stacks its children horizontally or vertically but then uses additional rows or columns if necessary, much like the Windows 8 start screen. The *Canvas* allows its children to be positioned at specific pixel locations.

What makes a layout system complex is balancing the conflicting needs of parents and children. In part, a layout system needs to be "child-driven" in that each child should be allowed to determine how large it needs to be, and to obtain sufficient screen space for itself. But the layout system also needs to be "parent-driven." At any time, the page is fixed in size and cannot give its descendents in the visual tree more space than it has available.

Similar concepts are well known in the Web world. For example, a simple HTML page has a width that is parent-driven because it's constrained by the width of the video display or the browser window. However, the height of a page is child-driven because it depends on the content of the page. If that height exceeds the height of the browser window, scrollbars are required.

In contrast, the Windows 8 start screen is the other way around: The number of application tiles that can fit vertically is parent-driven because it's based on the height of the screen. The width of this tile display is child-driven. If tiles extend off the screen horizontally, they must be moved into view by scrolling.

The *Border* Element

Two of the most important properties connected with layout are *HorizontalAlignment* and *VerticalAlignment*. These properties are defined by *FrameworkElement* and set to members of enumerations with identical names: *HorizontalAlignment* and *VerticalAlignment*.

As you saw in Chapter 3, "Basic Event Handling," the default values of *HorizontalAlignment* and *VerticalAlignment* are not *Left* and *Top*. They are instead *HorizontalAlignment.Stretch* and *VerticalAlignment.Stretch*. These default *Stretch* settings imply parent-driven layout: Elements automatically stretch to become as large as their parents. This is not always visually apparent, but in the last chapter you saw how a *TextBlock* stretched to the size of its parent gets all the *Tapped* events anywhere within that parent.

When the *HorizontalAlignment* or *VerticalAlignment* properties are set to values other than *Stretch*, the element sets its own width or height based on its content. Layout becomes more child-driven.

The important role of *HorizontalAlignment* and *VerticalAlignment* also becomes apparent when you start adding more parents and children to the page. For example, suppose you want to display a *TextBlock* with a border around it. You might discover (perhaps with some dismay) that *TextBlock* has no properties that relate to a border. However, the *Windows.UI.Xaml.Controls* namespace contains a *Border* element with a property named *Child*. So, you put the *TextBlock* in a *Border* and put the *Border* in the *Grid*, like so:

Project: NaiveBorderedText | **File:** MainPage.xaml (excerpt)

```
<Page ... >

    <Grid Background="{StaticResource ApplicationPageBackgroundThemeBrush}">

        <Border BorderBrush="Red"
                BorderThickness="12"
                CornerRadius="24"
                Background="Yellow">

            <TextBlock Text="Hello Windows 8!"
                       FontSize="96"
                       Foreground="Blue"
                       HorizontalAlignment="Center"
                       VerticalAlignment="Center" />
        </Border>

    </Grid>
</Page>
```

The *BorderThickness* property defined by *Border* can be set to different values for the four sides. Just specify four different values in the order left, top, right, and bottom. If you specify only two values, the first applies to the left and right and the second applies to the top and bottom. The *CornerRadius* property defines the curvature of the corners. You can set it a uniform value or four different values in the order upper-left, upper-right, lower-right, and lower-left.

Notice the *HorizontalAlignment* and *VerticalAlignment* properties set on the *TextBlock*. The markup looks reasonable, but the result is probably not what you want:

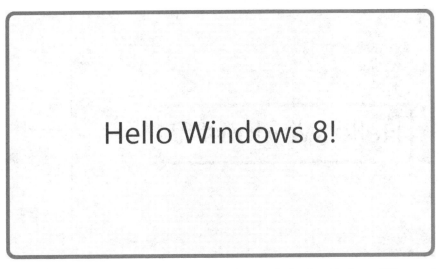

Because *Border* derives from *FrameworkElement*, it also has *HorizontalAlignment* and *VerticalAlignment* properties, and their default values are *Stretch*, which causes the size of the *Border* to be stretched to the size of its parent. To get the effect you probably want, you need to move the *HorizontalAlignment* and *VerticalAlignment* settings from the *TextBlock* to the *Border*:

Project: BetterBorderedText | **File:** MainPage.xaml (excerpt)

```
<Grid Background="{StaticResource ApplicationPageBackgroundThemeBrush}">

    <Border BorderBrush="Red"
            BorderThickness="12"
            CornerRadius="24"
            Background="Yellow"
            HorizontalAlignment="Center"
            VerticalAlignment="Center">

        <TextBlock Text="Hello Windows 8!"
                   FontSize="96"
                   Foreground="Blue"
                   Margin="24" />
    </Border>

</Grid>
```

I've also added a quarter-inch margin to the *TextBlock* by setting its *Margin* property. This causes the *Border* to be a quarter-inch larger than the size of the text on all four sides:

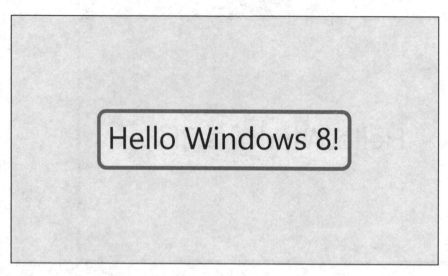

The *Margin* property is defined by *FrameworkElement*, so it is available on every element. The property is of type *Thickness* (the same as the type of the *BorderThickness* property)—a structure with four properties named *Left*, *Top*, *Right*, and *Bottom*. *Margin* is exceptionally useful for defining a little breathing room around elements so that they don't butt up against each other, and it appears a lot in real-life XAML. Like *BorderThickness*, *Margin* can potentially have four different values. In XAML, they appear in the order left, top, right, and bottom. Specify just two values and the first applies to the left and right, and the second to the top and bottom.

In addition, *Border* defines a *Padding* property, which is similar to *Margin* except that it applies to the inside of the element rather than the outside. Try removing the *Margin* property from *TextBlock* and instead set *Padding* on the *Border*:

```
<Border BorderBrush="Red"
        BorderThickness="12"
        CornerRadius="24"
        Background="Yellow"
        HorizontalAlignment="Center"
        VerticalAlignment="Center"
        Padding="24">

    <TextBlock Text="Hello Windows 8!"
               FontSize="96"
               Foreground="Blue" />
</Border>
```

The result is the same. In either case, any *HorizontalAlignment* or *VerticalAlignment* settings on the *TextBlock* are now irrelevant.

For layout purposes, *Margin* is considered to be part of the size of the element, but otherwise it is entirely out of the element's control. The element cannot control the background color of its margin, for example. That color depends on the element's parent. Nor does an element get user input from the margin area. If you tap in an element's margin area, the element's *parent* gets the *Tapped* event.

The *Padding* property is also of type *Thickness*, but only a few classes define a *Padding* property: *Control*, *Border*, *TextBlock*, *RichTextBlock*, and *RichTextBlockOverflow*. The *Padding* property defines an area *inside* the element. This area is considered to be part of the element for all purposes, including user input.

If you want a *TextBlock* to respond to taps not only on the text itself but also within a 100-pixel area surrounding the text, set the *Padding* property of the *TextBlock* to 100 rather than the *Margin* property.

Rectangle and Ellipse

As you saw in Chapter 2, "XAML Syntax," the *Windows.UI.Xaml.Shapes* namespace contains classes used to render vector graphics: lines, curves, and filled areas. The *Shape* class itself derives from *FrameworkElement* and defines various properties, including *Stroke* (for specifying the brush used to render straight lines and curves), *StrokeThickness*, and *Fill* (for specifying the brush used to render enclosed areas).

Six classes derive from *Shape*. *Line*, *Polyline*, and *Polygon* render straight lines based on coordinate points, and *Path* uses a series of classes in *Windows.UI.Xaml.Media* for rendering a series of straight lines, arcs, and Bézier curves.

The remaining two classes that derive from *Shape* are *Rectangle* and *Ellipse*. Despite the innocent names, these elements are real oddities in that they define figures without the use of coordinate points. Here, for example, is a tiny piece of XAML to render an ellipse:

Project: SimpleEllipse | **File:** MainPage.xaml (excerpt)

```
<Grid Background="{StaticResource ApplicationPageBackgroundThemeBrush}">
    <Ellipse Stroke="Red"
            StrokeThickness="24"
            Fill="Blue" />
</Grid>
```

Notice how the ellipse fills its container:

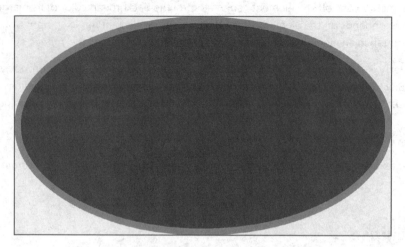

Like all other *FrameworkElement* derivatives, *Ellipse* has default *HorizontalAlignment* and *VerticalAlignment* settings of *Stretch*, but more than most other elements, *Ellipse* unashamedly flaunts the implications of these settings.

What happens if you set a nondefault *HorizontalAlignment* or *VerticalAlignment* on this *Ellipse* element? Try it! The ellipse shrinks down to nothing. It disappears. In fact, it's hard to imagine how it can legitimately have any other behavior. If you do not want the *Ellipse* or *Rectangle* element to fill its container, your only real alternative is to set explicit *Height* and *Width* values on it.

The *Shape* class also defines a *Stretch* property (not to be confused with the *Stretch* values of *HorizontalAlignment* and *VerticalAlignment*), which is similar to the *Stretch* property defined by *Image* and *Viewbox*. For example, in the SimpleEllipse program, if you set the *Stretch* property to *Uniform*, you'll get a special case of an ellipse that has equal horizontal and vertical radii. This is a circle, and its diameter is set to the minimum of the container's width and height. Setting the *Stretch* property to *UniformToFill* also gets you a circle, but now the diameter is the *maximum* of the container's width and height, so part of the circle is cropped:

You can control what part is cropped with the *HorizontalAlignment* and *VerticalAlignment* properties.

Rectangle is very similar to *Ellipse* and also shares several characteristics with *Border*, although the properties have different names:

Border	Rectangle
BorderBrush	Stroke
BorderThickness	StrokeThickness
Background	Fill
CornerRadius	RadiusX / RadiusY

The big difference between *Border* and *Rectangle* is that *Border* has a *Child* property and *Rectangle* does not.

The *StackPanel*

Panel and its derivative classes form the core of the Windows Runtime layout system. *Panel* defines just a few properties on its own, but one of them is *Children*, and that's crucial. A *Panel* derivative is the only type of element that supports multiple children.

This class hierarchy shows *Panel* and some of its derivatives:

Object
    DependencyObject
        UIElement
            FrameworkElement
                Panel
                    Canvas
                    Grid
                    StackPanel
                    VariableSizedWrapGrid

There are others, but they have restrictions that prevent them from being used except in controls of type *ItemsControl* (which I'll discuss in Chapter 11, "The Three Templates"). I'll save the *Grid* for Chapter 5, "Control Interaction," and I'll cover the other three here.

Of these standard panels, the *StackPanel* is certainly the easiest to use. Like the name suggests, it stacks its children, by default vertically. The children can be different heights, but each child gets only as much height as it needs. The SimpleVerticalStack program shows how it's done:

Project: SimpleVerticalStack | File: MainPage.xaml (excerpt)

```
<Grid Background="{StaticResource ApplicationPageBackgroundThemeBrush}">
    <StackPanel>
        <TextBlock Text="Right-Aligned Text"
                   FontSize="48"
                   HorizontalAlignment="Right" />
```

```
<Image Source="http://www.charlespetzold.com/pw6/PetzoldJersey.jpg"
        Stretch="None" />

<TextBlock Text="Figure 1. Petzold heading to the basketball court"
           FontSize="24"
           HorizontalAlignment="Center" />

<Ellipse Stroke="Red"
         StrokeThickness="12"
         Fill="Blue" />

<TextBlock Text="Left-Aligned Text"
           FontSize="36"
           HorizontalAlignment="Left" />
    </StackPanel>
</Grid>
```

In XAML the children of the *StackPanel* are simply listed in order, just as they appear on the screen:

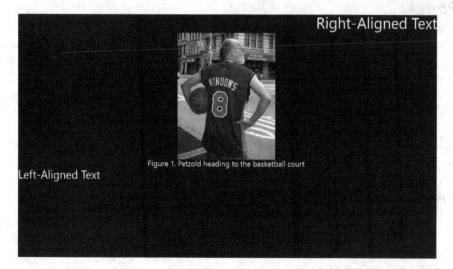

Notice that I made this *StackPanel* a child of the *Grid.* Panels can be nested, and they very often *are* nested. In this particular case I could have replaced the *Grid* with *StackPanel* and set that same *Background* property on it.

Each element in the *StackPanel* gets only as much height as it needs but can stretch to the panel's full width, as demonstrated by the first and last *TextBlock* aligned to the right and left. In a vertical *StackPanel*, any *VerticalAlignment* settings on the children are irrelevant and are basically ignored.

Notice that the *Stretch* property of the *Image* element is set to *None* to display the bitmap in its pixel dimensions. If left at its default value of *Uniform*, the *Image* is stretched to the width of the *StackPanel* (which is the same as the width of the *Page*) and its vertical dimension increases proportionally. This might cause all the elements below the *Image* to be pushed right off the bottom of the screen and into the bit bucket.

The XAML also includes an *Ellipse.* What happened to it? Like all the other children of the *StackPanel*, the *Ellipse* is given only as much vertical space as it needs, and it really doesn't need any, so it shrinks to nothing. If you want the *Ellipse* to be visible, give it at least a nonzero *Height*, for example, 48:

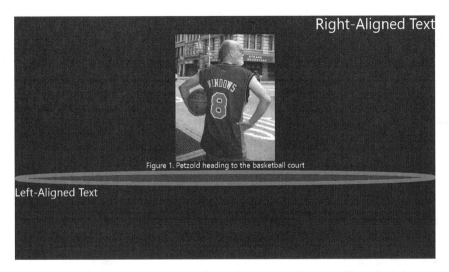

If you also set the *Stretch* property of the *Ellipse* to *Uniform*, you'll get a circle rather than a very wide ellipse.

This *StackPanel* occupies the entire page. How do I know this? When experimenting with panels, one very useful technique is to give each panel a unique *Background* so that you can see the footprint that the panel occupies on the screen. For example:

```
<StackPanel Background="Blue">
```

Like all other *FrameworkElement* derivatives, *StackPanel* also has *HorizontalAlignment* and *VerticalAlignment* properties. When set to nondefault values, these properties cause the *StackPanel* to tightly hug its children (so to speak), and the change can be dramatic. Here's what it looks like with the *StackPanel* getting a *Background* of *Blue* and *HorizontalAlignment* and *VerticalAlignment* values of *Center*:

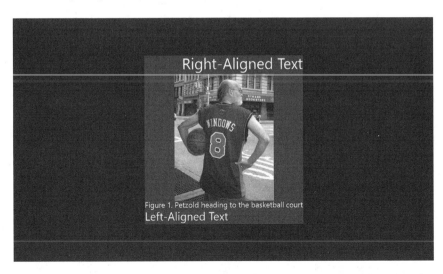

The width of the *StackPanel* is now governed by the width of its widest child, which is the totally honest caption under the photograph.

Horizontal Stacks

It is also possible to use *StackPanel* to stack elements horizontally by setting its *Orientation* property to *Horizontal*. The SimpleHorizontalStack program shows an example:

Project: SimpleHorizontalStack | **File:** MainPage.xaml (excerpt)

```xml
<Grid Background="{StaticResource ApplicationPageBackgroundThemeBrush}">

    <StackPanel Orientation="Horizontal"
                VerticalAlignment="Center"
                HorizontalAlignment="Center">

        <TextBlock Text="Rectangle: "
                VerticalAlignment="Center" />

        <Rectangle Stroke="Blue"
                Fill="Red"
                Width="72"
                Height="72"
                Margin="12 0"
                VerticalAlignment="Center" />

        <TextBlock Text="Ellipse: "
                VerticalAlignment="Center" />

        <Ellipse Stroke="Red"
                Fill="Blue"
                Width="72"
                Height="72"
                Margin="12 0"
                VerticalAlignment="Center" />

        <TextBlock Text="Petzold: "
                VerticalAlignment="Center" />

        <Image Source="http://www.charlespetzold.com/pw6/PetzoldJersey.jpg"
                Stretch="Uniform"
                Width="72"
                Margin="12 0"
                VerticalAlignment="Center" />

    </StackPanel>
</Grid>
```

Here it is:

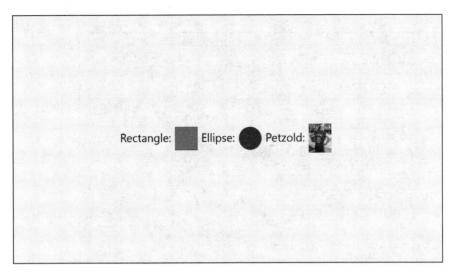

You might question the apparently excessive number of alignment settings. Try removing all the *VerticalAlignment* and *HorizontalAlignment* settings, and the result looks like this:

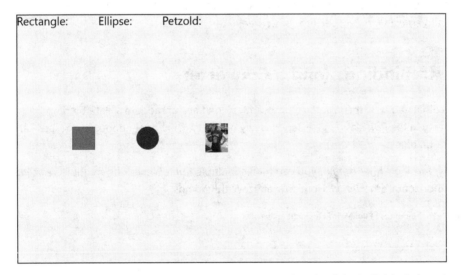

The *StackPanel* is now occupying the entire page, and each of the individual elements occupies the full height of the *StackPanel*. *TextBlock* aligns itself at the top, and the other elements are in the center. Setting the *HorizontalAlignment* and *VerticalAlignment* settings of the *Panel* to *Center* tightens up the space that the panel occupies and moves it to the center of the display, like this:

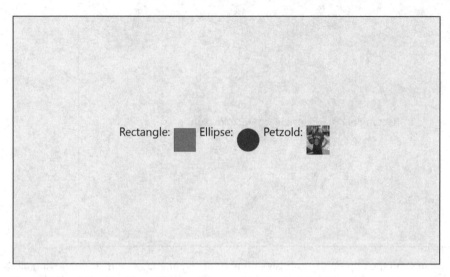

The height of the *StackPanel* is now governed by the height of its tallest element, but all the elements are stretched to that height. To center all the elements relative to each other, the easiest approach is to give them all *VerticalAlignment* settings of *Center*.

WhatSize with Bindings (and a Converter)

In Chapter 3 I discussed how the WhatSize program couldn't accommodate a data binding because the *Text* property in the *Run* class isn't a dependency property. Only dependency properties can be targets of data bindings.

Fortunately, for single lines of text, you can mimic multiple *Run* objects with multiple *TextBlock* elements in a horizontal *StackPanel*. Here's WhatSizeWithBindings:

Project: WhatSizeWithBindings | **File:** MainPage.xaml (excerpt)

```
<Page
    x:Class="WhatSizeWithBindings.MainPage"
    ...
    FontSize="36"
    Name="page">

    <Grid Background="{StaticResource ApplicationPageBackgroundThemeBrush}">
        <StackPanel Orientation="Horizontal"
                    HorizontalAlignment="Center"
                    VerticalAlignment="Top">
            <TextBlock Text="&#x21A4; " />
            <TextBlock Text="{Binding ElementName=page, Path=ActualWidth}" />
            <TextBlock Text=" pixels &#x21A6;" />
        </StackPanel>
```

```
        <StackPanel HorizontalAlignment="Center"
                    VerticalAlignment="Center">
            <TextBlock Text="&#x21A5;" TextAlignment="Center" />

            <StackPanel Orientation="Horizontal"
                        HorizontalAlignment="Center">
                <TextBlock Text="{Binding ElementName=page, Path=ActualHeight}" />
                <TextBlock Text=" pixels" />
            </StackPanel>

            <TextBlock Text="&#x21A7;" TextAlignment="Center" />
        </StackPanel>
    </Grid>
</Page>
```

Notice that the root element is now given a name of *page*, which is referenced in the two data bindings to obtain the *ActualWidth* and *ActualHeight* properties. The big advantage over the previous version is that there's no longer any need for an event handler in the code-behind file. And here it is:

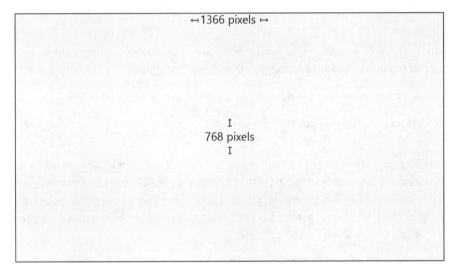

Although the values are initially correct, the bindings in the Windows 8 version that I'm using for this chapter unfortunately don't update the values with a different orientation or snap view.

These data bindings are automatically converting *double* values to *string* objects. But what if you wanted this conversion to work a little differently? Suppose you want to display a particular number of decimal places in the results? Or perhaps, more appropriate for this example, you want a comma separator to appear in the width so that it's 1,366?

It is possible to customize the data conversion that occurs in a binding by supplying a little piece of code to the *Binding* object. The *Binding* class has a property named *Converter* of type *IValueConverter*, an interface with two methods named *Convert* (to convert from a binding source to a binding target) and *ConvertBack* (for a conversion from the target back to the source in a two-way binding).

To create your own custom converter, you'll need to derive a class from *IValueConverter* and to fill in the two methods. Here's an example that shows these methods doing nothing:

```
public class NothingConverter : IValueConverter
{
    public object Convert(object value, Type targetType, object parameter, string language)
    {
        return value;
    }

    public object ConvertBack(object value, Type targetType, object parameter, string language)
    {
        return value;
    }
}
```

If you'll be using the binding only in a one-way mode, you can ignore the *ConvertBack* method. In the *Convert* method, the *value* argument is the value coming from the binding source. In the WhatSize example, this is a *double*. The *TargetType* is the type of the target—in the WhatSize example, a *string*.

If you're writing a binding converter specifically for WhatSize to convert floating-point numbers to strings with comma separators and no decimal points, the *Convert* method can be as simple as this:

```
public object Convert(object value, Type targetType, object parameter, string language)
{
    return ((double)value).ToString("N0");
}
```

But it's more common to generalize binding converters. For example, it might be useful for the converter to handle *value* arguments of any type that implements the *IFormattable* interface, which includes *double* as well as all the other numeric types and *DateTime*. The *IFormattable* interface defines a *ToString* method with two arguments: a formatting string and an object that implements *IFormatProvider*, which is generally a *CultureInfo* object.

Besides *value* and *targetType*, the *Convert* method also has *parameter* and *language* arguments. These come from two properties of the *Binding* class named *ConverterParameter* and *ConverterLanguage*, which are generally set right in the XAML file. This means that the formatting specification for *ToString* can be provided by the *parameter* argument to *Convert*, and a *CultureInfo* object could be created from the *language* argument. Here's one possibility:

Project: WhatSizeWithBindingConverter | File: FormattedStringConverter.cs

```
using System;
using System.Globalization;
using Windows.UI.Xaml.Data;

namespace WhatSizeWithBindingConverter
{
    public class FormattedStringConverter : IValueConverter
    {
        public object Convert(object value, Type targetType, object parameter, string language)
        {
```

```
        if (value is IFormattable &&
            parameter is string &&
            !String.IsNullOrEmpty(parameter as string) &&
            targetType == typeof(string))
        {
            if (String.IsNullOrEmpty(language))
                return (value as IFormattable).ToString(parameter as string, null);

            return (value as IFormattable).ToString(parameter as string,
                                                    new CultureInfo(language));
        }

        return value;
    }
    public object ConvertBack(object value, Type targetType, object parameter, string
        language)
    {
        return value;
    }
  }
}
```

The *Convert* method uses *ToString* only if several conditions are met. If the conditions are not met, the fallback is simply to return the incoming *value* argument.

In the XAML file, the binding converter is generally defined as a resource so that it can be shared among multiple bindings:

Project: WhatSizeWithBindingConverter | **File:** MainPage.xaml (excerpt)

```
<Page
    x:Class="WhatSizeWithBindingConverter.MainPage"
    ...
    FontSize="36"
    Name="page">

    <Page.Resources>
        <local:FormattedStringConverter x:Key="stringConverter" />
    </Page.Resources>

    <Grid Background="{StaticResource ApplicationPageBackgroundThemeBrush}">
        <StackPanel Orientation="Horizontal"
                    HorizontalAlignment="Center"
                    VerticalAlignment="Top">
            <TextBlock Text="&#x21A4; " />
            <TextBlock Text="{Binding ElementName=page,
                                      Path=ActualWidth,
                                      Converter={StaticResource stringConverter},
                                      ConverterParameter=N0}" />
            <TextBlock Text=" pixels &#x21A6;" />
        </StackPanel>

        <StackPanel HorizontalAlignment="Center"
                    VerticalAlignment="Center">
            <TextBlock Text="&#x21A5;" TextAlignment="Center" />

            <StackPanel Orientation="Horizontal"
                        HorizontalAlignment="Center">
```

```
            <TextBlock Text="{Binding ElementName=page,
                                       Path=ActualHeight,
                                       Converter={StaticResource stringConverter},
                                       ConverterParameter=N0}" />
            <TextBlock Text=" pixels" />
        </StackPanel>

        <TextBlock Text="&#x21A7;" TextAlignment="Center" />
    </StackPanel>
  </Grid>
</Page>
```

Take careful note of the *Binding* syntax. I've spread it out over four lines for purposes of clarity (and to stay within the margins of the book page), but notice that the *Binding* markup extension contains an embedded markup extension of *StaticResource* for referencing the binding converter resource. No quotation marks appear within either markup extension.

Now the width is formatted a little fancier:

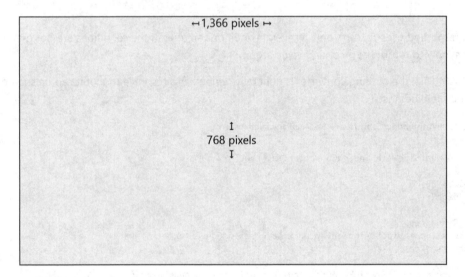

The *ScrollViewer* Solution

What happens if there are too many elements for *StackPanel* to display on the screen? In real life, that situation occurs quite often and it's why a *StackPanel* with more than just a few elements is almost always put inside a *ScrollViewer*.

The *ScrollViewer* has a property named *Content* that you can set to anything that might be too large to display in the space allowed for it—a single large *Image*, for example. *ScrollViewer* provides scrollbars for the mouse-users among us. Otherwise, you can just move the content around with your fingers. By default, *ScrollViewer* also adds a pinch interface so that you can use two fingers to make the content larger or smaller. This can be disabled if you want by setting the *ZoomMode* property to *Disabled*.

ScrollViewer defines a couple other crucial properties. Most often you'll be using *ScrollViewer* for vertical scrolling, such as with a vertical *StackPanel*. Consequently, the default value of the *VerticalScrollBarVisibility* property is the enumeration member *ScrollBarVisibility.Visible*. This setting doesn't mean that the scrollbar is actually visible all the time. For mouse users, the scrollbar appears only when the mouse is moved to the right side of the *ScrollViewer*, and then it fades from view if the mouse is moved away. A much thinner slider appears when you scroll using your finger.

Horizontal scrolling is different: The default value of *HorizontalScrollBarVisibility* property is *Disabled*, so you'll want to change that to enable horizontal scrolling. The other two options are *Hidden*, which allows scrolling with your fingers but not the mouse, and *Auto*, which is the same as *Visible* if the content requires scrolling and *Disabled* otherwise.

The XAML file for the StackPanelWithScrolling program contains a *StackPanel* in a *ScrollViewer*. Notice that the *FontSize* property is set in the root tag so that it can be inherited throughout the page:

Project: StackPanelWithScrolling | File: MainPage.xaml (excerpt)

```
<Page
    x:Class="StackPanelWithScrolling.MainPage"
    ...
    FontSize="26">

    <Grid Background="{StaticResource ApplicationPageBackgroundThemeBrush}">
        <ScrollViewer>
            <StackPanel Name="stackPanel" />
        </ScrollViewer>
    </Grid>
</Page>
```

Now all that's necessary in the code-behind file is to generate so many items for the *StackPanel* that they can't all be visible at once. Where do we get so many items? One convenient solution is to use .NET reflection to obtain all 141 static *Color* properties defined in the *Colors* class:

Project: StackPanelWithScrolling | File: MainPage.xaml.cs (excerpt)

```
public sealed partial class MainPage : Page
{
    public MainPage()
    {
        this.InitializeComponent();

        IEnumerable<PropertyInfo> properties =
                            typeof(Colors).GetTypeInfo().DeclaredProperties;

        foreach (PropertyInfo property in properties)
        {
            Color clr = (Color)property.GetValue(null);
            TextBlock txtblk = new TextBlock();
            txtblk.Text = String.Format("{0} \x2014 {1:X2}-{2:X2}-{3:X2}-{4:X2}",
                                property.Name, clr.A, clr.R, clr.G, clr.B);
            stackPanel.Children.Add(txtblk);
        }
    }
}
```

Windows 8 reflection works a little differently from .NET reflection. Generally, to get anything interesting from the *Type* object, you need to call a Windows 8 extension method *GetTypeInfo*. The returned *TypeInfo* object makes available additional information about the *Type*. In this program, the *DeclaredProperties* property of *TypeInfo* obtains all the properties of the *Colors* class in the form of *PropertyInfo* objects. Because all the properties in the *Colors* class are static, the value of these static properties can be obtained by calling *GetValue* on each *PropertyInfo* object with a *null* parameter. Each *TextBlock* gets the name of the color, an em-dash (Unicode 0x2014), and the hexadecimal color bytes. The display looks like this:

```
GreenYellow — FF-AD-FF-2F
Honeydew — FF-F0-FF-F0
HotPink — FF-FF-69-B4
IndianRed — FF-CD-5C-5C
Indigo — FF-4B-00-82
Ivory — FF-FF-FF-F0
Khaki — FF-F0-E6-8C
Lavender — FF-E6-E6-FA
LavenderBlush — FF-FF-F0-F5
LawnGreen — FF-7C-FC-00
LemonChiffon — FF-FF-FA-CD
LightBlue — FF-AD-D8-E6
LightCoral — FF-F0-80-80
LightCyan — FF-E0-FF-FF
LightGoldenrodYellow — FF-FA-FA-D2
LightGray — FF-D3-D3-D3
LightGreen — FF-90-EE-90
LightPink — FF-FF-B6-C1
LightSalmon — FF-FF-A0-7A
LightSeaGreen — FF-20-B2-AA
LightSkyBlue — FF-87-CE-FA
LightSlateGray — FF-77-88-99
LightSteelBlue — FF-B0-C4-DE
LightYellow — FF-FF-FF-E0
Lime — FF-00-FF-00
```

And, of course, you can scroll it with your finger or the mouse.

To simplify the use of reflection in the C++ version of this program, the program references a ReflectionHelper library in the solution that I wrote in C#. This library is also referenced in some subsequent projects in this chapter and other chapters. I'll discuss libraries later in this chapter.

As you play around with the program, you'll discover that the *ScrollViewer* incorporates a nice fluid response to your finger movements, including inertia and bounce. You'll want to use *ScrollViewer* for virtually all your scrolling needs. You'll discover that many controls that incorporate scrolling—such as the *ListBox* and *GridView* coming up in Chapter 11—have this same *ScrollViewer* built right in. I wouldn't be surprised if this same *ScrollViewer* is used in the Windows 8 start screen.

Wouldn't it be nice to see the actual colors as well as their names and values? That enhancement is coming up soon!

Several times already in this book I've shown you partial class hierarchies. If you've explored the Windows 8 documentation trying to find these class hierarchies, you've probably discovered that the documentation for each class shows only an ancestor class hierarchy but not derived classes. So, how exactly did I create the class hierarchies for this book?. They come from a program I wrote called DependencyObjectClassHierarchy, which uses a *ScrollViewer* and *StackPanel* to show all the classes that derive from *DependencyObject*.

```
        highlightBrush =
            new SolidColorBrush(new UISettings().UIElementColor(UIElementType.Highlight)));
```

The XAML file is similar to the previous one except I've specified a smaller font:

Project: DependencyObjectClassHierarchy | **File:** MainPage.xaml (excerpt)

```
<Page
    x:Class="DependencyObjectClassHierarchy.MainPage"
    ...
    FontSize="{StaticResource ControlContentThemeFontSize}">

    <Grid Background="{StaticResource ApplicationPageBackgroundThemeBrush}">
        <ScrollViewer>
            <StackPanel Name="stackPanel" />
        </ScrollViewer>
    </Grid>
</Page>
```

The program builds a tree of classes and their descendent classes. Each node is a particular class and a collection of its immediate descendent classes, so I added another code file to the project for a class that represents this node:

Project: DependencyObjectClassHierarchy | **File:** ClassAndSubclasses.cs

```
using System;
using System.Collections.Generic;

namespace DependencyObjectClassHierarchy
{
    class ClassAndSubclasses
    {
        public ClassAndSubclasses(Type parent)
        {
            this.Type = parent;
            this.Subclasses = new List<ClassAndSubclasses>();
        }

        public Type Type { protected set; get; }
        public List<ClassAndSubclasses> Subclasses { protected set; get; }
    }
}
```

Just as it's possible to use reflection to get all the properties defined by a class, you can use reflection to get all public classes defined in an assembly. These classes are available from the *ExportedTypes* property of the *Assembly* object. Conceptually, the entire Windows Runtime is associated with a single assembly, so to get a reference to that assembly you just need one type. You get the *Assembly* object from the *Assembly* property of the *TypeInfo* object for that type.

Project: DependencyObjectClassHierarchy | **File:** MainPage.xaml.cs (excerpt)

```
public sealed partial class MainPage : Page
{
    Type rootType = typeof(DependencyObject);
    TypeInfo rootTypeInfo = typeof(DependencyObject).GetTypeInfo();
```

```
List<Type> classes = new List<Type>();
Brush highlightBrush;

public MainPage()
{
    this.InitializeComponent();

    highlightBrush =
        new SolidColorBrush(new UISettings().UIElementColor(UIElementType.Highlight));

    // Accumulate all the classes that derive from DependencyObject
    AddToClassList(typeof(Windows.UI.Xaml.DependencyObject));

    // Sort them alphabetically by name
    classes.Sort((t1, t2) =>
        {
            return String.Compare(t1.GetTypeInfo().Name, t2.GetTypeInfo().Name);
        });

    // Put all these sorted classes into a tree structure
    ClassAndSubclasses rootClass = new ClassAndSubclasses(rootType);
    AddToTree(rootClass, classes);

    // Display the tree using TextBlock's added to StackPanel
    Display(rootClass, 0);
}

void AddToClassList(Type sampleType)
{
    Assembly assembly = sampleType.GetTypeInfo().Assembly;

    foreach (Type type in assembly.ExportedTypes)
    {
        TypeInfo typeInfo = type.GetTypeInfo();

        if (typeInfo.IsPublic && rootTypeInfo.IsAssignableFrom(typeInfo))
            classes.Add(type);
    }
}

void AddToTree(ClassAndSubclasses parentClass, List<Type> classes)
{
    foreach (Type type in classes)
    {
        Type baseType = type.GetTypeInfo().BaseType;

        if (baseType == parentClass.Type)
        {
            ClassAndSubclasses subClass = new ClassAndSubclasses(type);
            parentClass.Subclasses.Add(subClass);
            AddToTree(subClass, classes);
        }
    }
}
```

```
void Display(ClassAndSubclasses parentClass, int indent)
{
    TypeInfo typeInfo = parentClass.Type.GetTypeInfo();

    // Create TextBlock with type name
    TextBlock txtblk = new TextBlock();
    txtblk.Inlines.Add(new Run { Text = new string(' ', 8 * indent) });
    txtblk.Inlines.Add(new Run { Text = typeInfo.Name });

    // Indicate if the class is sealed
    if (typeInfo.IsSealed)
        txtblk.Inlines.Add(new Run
            {
                Text = " (sealed)",
                Foreground = highlightBrush
            });

    // Indicate if the class can't be instantiated
    IEnumerable<ConstructorInfo> constructorInfos = typeInfo.DeclaredConstructors;
    int publicConstructorCount = 0;

    foreach (ConstructorInfo constructorInfo in constructorInfos)
        if (constructorInfo.IsPublic)
            publicConstructorCount += 1;

    if (publicConstructorCount == 0)
        txtblk.Inlines.Add(new Run
        {
            Text = " (non-instantiable)",
            Foreground = highlightBrush
        });

    // Add to the StackPanel
    stackPanel.Children.Add(txtblk);

    // Call this method recursively for all subclasses
    foreach (ClassAndSubclasses subclass in parentClass.Subclasses)
        Display(subclass, indent + 1);
}
}
```

Notice how the *TextBlock* for each class is constructed by adding *Run* items to its *Inlines* collection. It's sometimes useful for a class hierarchy to display additional information, so the program also checks whether the class is marked as *sealed* and whether it can be instantiated. In the Windows Presentation Foundation and Silverlight, classes that can't be instantiated are generally defined as *abstract*. In the Windows Runtime, they have protected constructors instead.

Here's the section of the class hierarchy with *Panel* derivatives:

```
                        ProgressBar
                    ScrollBar (sealed)
                        Slider
                    RichEditBox
                SemanticZoom (sealed)
                    TextBox
                Thumb (sealed)
                ToggleSwitch (sealed)
                UserControl
                    Page
            Glyphs (sealed)
            Image (sealed)
            ItemsPresenter (sealed)
            MediaElement (sealed)
            Panel (non-instantiable)
                Canvas
                Grid
                    SwapChainBackgroundPanel
                StackPanel
                VariableSizedWrapGrid (sealed)
                VirtualizingPanel (non-instantiable)
                    CarouselPanel
                    OrientedVirtualizingPanel
                        VirtualizingStackPanel
                        WrapGrid (sealed)
            Popup (sealed)
            RichTextBlock (sealed)
            RichTextBlockOverflow (sealed)
            Shape (non-instantiable)
                Ellipse (sealed)
                Line (sealed)
                Path
                Polygon (sealed)
                Polyline (sealed)
                Rectangle (sealed)
            TextBlock (sealed)
            TickBar (sealed)
            Viewbox (sealed)
            WebView (sealed)
    VisualState (sealed)
    VisualStateGroup (sealed)
    VisualStateManager
    VisualTransition
```

Layout Weirdness or Normalcy?

Becoming acquainted with the mechanics of layout is an important part of being a crafty Windows Runtime developer, and the best way to make this acquaintance is to write your own *Panel* derivatives. That job awaits us in a Chapter 11, but you can also discover a lot by just experimenting.

Suppose you have a *StackPanel* and you decide that one of the items in this *StackPanel* should be a *ScrollViewer* with another *StackPanel*. To determine what happens in such a situation, you might experiment with the StackPanelWithScrolling project and change the XAML file like so:

```
<Grid Background="{StaticResource ApplicationPageBackgroundThemeBrush}">
    <StackPanel>
        <ScrollViewer>
            <StackPanel Name="stackPanel" />
        </ScrollViewer>
    </StackPanel>
</Grid>
```

When you try it out, you'll discover it doesn't work. You can't scroll. What happened?

The conflict here results from the different ways in which *StackPanel* and *ScrollViewer* calculate their desired heights. The *StackPanel* calculates a desired height based on the total height of all its children. In the vertical dimension (by default), *StackPanel* is entirely child-driven. To calculate a total height, it offers to each of its children an *infinite* height. (When you write your own *Panel* derivatives, you'll see that I'm not speaking metaphorically or abstractly. A *Double.PositiveInfinity* value actually comes into play!) The children respond by calculating a desired height based on their natural size. The *StackPanel* adds these heights to calculate its own desired height.

The height of the *ScrollViewer*, however, is parent-driven. Its height is only what its parent offers to it, and in our earlier example this was the height of the *Grid*, which was the height of the *Page*, which was the height of the window. The *ScrollViewer* is able to determine how to scroll its content because it knows the difference between the height of its child (often a *StackPanel*) and its own height.

Now put a vertically scrolling *ScrollViewer* as a child of a vertical *StackPanel*. To determine the desired size of this *ScrollViewer* child, the *StackPanel* offers it an infinite height. How tall does the *ScrollViewer* really want to be? The height of the *ScrollViewer* is now child-driven rather than parent-driven, and its desired height is the height of its child, which is the total height of the inner *StackPanel*, which is the total accumulated height of all the children in that *StackPanel*.

From the perspective of the *ScrollViewer*, its height is the same as the height of its content, which means that there's nothing to scroll.

In other words, when a vertically scrolling *ScrollViewer* is put in a vertical *StackPanel*, losing the ability to scroll is totally expected behavior!

Here's another seeming layout oddity that is actually quite normal: Try giving a *TextBlock* a very long chunk of text to display, and set the *TextWrapping* property to *Wrap*. In most cases, the text wraps as we might expect. Now put that *TextBlock* in a *StackPanel* with an *Orientation* property set to *Horizontal*. To determine how wide the *TextBlock* needs to be, the *StackPanel* offers it an infinite width, and in response to that infinite width, the *TextBlock* stops wrapping the text.

In the WhatSizeWithBindings and WhatSizeWithBindingConverter programs you saw how a horizontal *StackPanel* can effectively concatenate *TextBlock* elements, one of which has a binding on its *Text* property. But what if you wanted to use this same technique with a paragraph of wrapped text? What if you wanted part of the text of this paragraph to be a result of a binding? You can't do it with a horizontal *StackPanel* because the text will never wrap. You can't do it with a *Run* element of a *TextBlock* because the *Text* property of *Run* is not backed by a dependency property. The solution, of course, is to set that item from code. Another solution involves *RichTextBlock*, as you'll see in Chapter 16, "Rich Text."

A horizontal *StackPanel* can't impose text wrapping on child *TextBlock* elements, but a vertical *StackPanel* can. A vertical *StackPanel* has a finite width, so it's an ideal host for *TextBlock* elements that wrap text, as you'll see next.

Making an E-Book

A *TextBlock* item that goes into a vertical *StackPanel* can have its *TextWrapping* property set to *Wrap*, which means that it can actually be a whole paragraph rather than just a word or two. *Image* elements can also go into this same *StackPanel*, and the result can be a rudimentary illustrated e-book.

On the famous Project Gutenberg website, I found an illustrated version of Beatrix Potter's classic children's book *The Tale of Tom Kitten* (*http://www.gutenberg.org/ebooks/14837*), so I created a Visual Studio project named TheTaleOfTomKitten and I made a folder in that project called Images. From Project Gutenberg's HTML version of the book, it was easy to download all the illustrations in the form of JPEG files. These have names such as tomxx.jpg, where xx is the original page number of the book where that illustration appeared. From within the Visual Studio project, I then added all 28 of these JPEG files to the Images folder.

Most of the rest of the work involved the MainPage.xaml file. Each paragraph of the book became a *TextBlock*, and these I interspersed with *Image* elements referencing the JPEG files in the Images folder.

However, I felt it necessary to deviate somewhat from the ordering of the text and images in Project Gutenberg's HTML file. A PDF of the original edition of *The Tale of Tom Kitten* on the Internet Archive site (*http://archive.org/details/taleoftomkitten00pottuoft*) reveals how Miss Potter's illustrations are associated with the text of the book. There are two patterns:

1. Text appears on the verso (left-hand, even-numbered) page with an accompanying illustration on the recto (right-hand, odd-numbered) page.

2. Text appears on the recto page with an accompanying illustration on the verso page.

Adapting this paginated book to a continuous format required altering the order of the text and image in this second case so that the text appears *before* the accompanying illustration. That's why you'll see some page swaps in the XAML file.

Given the very many *TextBlock* and *Image* elements, styles seemed almost mandatory:

Project: TheTaleOfTomKitten | **File:** MainPage.xaml (excerpt)

```
<Page.Resources>
    <Style x:Key="commonTextStyle" TargetType="TextBlock">
        <Setter Property="FontFamily" Value="Century Schoolbook" />
        <Setter Property="FontSize" Value="36" />
        <Setter Property="Foreground" Value="Black" />
        <Setter Property="Margin" Value="0 12" />
    </Style>

    <Style x:Key="paragraphTextStyle" TargetType="TextBlock"
            BasedOn="{StaticResource commonTextStyle}">
        <Setter Property="TextWrapping" Value="Wrap" />
    </Style>

    <Style x:Key="frontMatterTextStyle" TargetType="TextBlock"
            BasedOn="{StaticResource commonTextStyle}">
        <Setter Property="TextAlignment" Value="Center" />
    </Style>

    <Style x:Key="imageStyle" TargetType="Image">
        <Setter Property="Stretch" Value="None" />
        <Setter Property="HorizontalAlignment" Value="Center" />
    </Style>
</Page.Resources>
```

Notice the *Margin* value that provides a little spacing between the paragraphs. Each *TextBlock* element references either *paragraphTextStyle* (for the actual paragraphs of the book) or *frontMatterTextStyle* (for all the titles and other information that appears in the front of the book). I could have made the style for the *Image* element an implicit style by simply removing the *x:Key* attribute and removing the *Style* attributes from the *Image* elements.

Many of the *TextBlock* elements that comprise the front matter have various local *FontSize* settings. Books generally are printed with black ink on white pages, so I hard-coded the *Foreground* of the *TextBlock* to black and set the *Background* of the *Grid* to white. To restrict the text to reasonable line lengths, the *StackPanel* is given a *MaxWidth* of 640 and centered within the *ScrollViewer*. Here's a little excerpt of the alternating *TextBlock* elements and *Image* elements:

Project: TheTaleOfTomKitten | **File:** MainPage.xaml (excerpt)

```xml
<Grid Background="White">
    <ScrollViewer>
        <StackPanel MaxWidth="640"
                    HorizontalAlignment="Center">
            ...
            <!-- pg. 38 -->
            <TextBlock Style="{StaticResource paragraphTextStyle}">
                  Mittens laughed so that she fell off the
                wall. Moppet and Tom descended after her; the pinafores
                and all the rest of Tom's clothes came off on the way down.
            </TextBlock>

            <TextBlock Style="{StaticResource paragraphTextStyle}">
                  "Come! Mr. Drake Puddle-Duck," said Moppet
                – "Come and help us to dress him! Come and button up Tom!"
            </TextBlock>

            <Image Source="Images/tom39.jpg" Style="{StaticResource imageStyle}" />

            <!-- pg. 41 -->
            <TextBlock Style="{StaticResource paragraphTextStyle}">
                  Mr. Drake Puddle-Duck advanced in a slow
                sideways manner, and picked up the various articles.
            </TextBlock>

            <Image Source="Images/tom40.jpg" Style="{StaticResource imageStyle}" />
            ...
        </StackPanel>
    </ScrollViewer>
</Grid>
```

The two   characters at the beginning of each paragraph are em-spaces. These provide a first-line indentation, which, unfortunately, is not provided by the *TextBlock* class. (This feature *is* provided by *RichTextBlock*, as you'll see in Chapter 16.)

You can read this book in either landscape or portrait mode:

Mrs. Tabitha dressed Moppet and Mittens in clean pinafores and tuckers; and then she took all sorts of elegant uncomfortable clothes out of a chest of drawers, in order to dress up her son Thomas.

Tom Kitten was very fat, and he had grown; several buttons burst off. His mother sewed them on again.

Fancier *StackPanel* Items

I mentioned earlier I'd be showing you a program that displays all 141 available Windows Runtime colors with the colors as well as their names and RGB values. My first example is called ColorList1, but let's begin with the screen shot of the completed program so that you can see the goal:

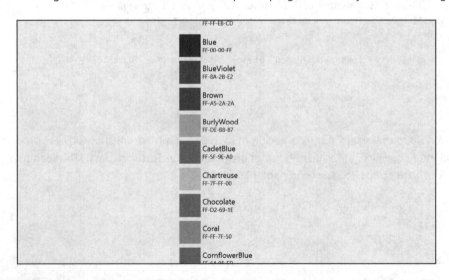

This program contains a total of 283 *StackPanel* elements. Each of the 141 colors gets a pair: A vertical *StackPanel* is parent to the two *TextBlock* elements, and a horizontal *StackPanel* is parent to a *Rectangle* and the vertical *StackPanel*. All the horizontal *StackPanel* elements are then children of the main vertical *StackPanel* in a *ScrollViewer*. The XAML file is responsible for centering that *StackPanel*:

Project: ColorList1 | File: MainPage.xaml (excerpt)

```
<Grid Background="{StaticResource ApplicationPageBackgroundThemeBrush}">
    <ScrollViewer>
        <StackPanel Name="stackPanel"
                    HorizontalAlignment="Center" />
    </ScrollViewer>
</Grid>
```

Although the *StackPanel* is aligned in the center of the *ScrollViewer* (and is as wide as its widest child), the *ScrollViewer* occupies the entire width of the page. Any visible sliders or scrollbars appear on the far right of the page. Alternatively, you can put the *HorizontalAlignment* setting on the *ScrollViewer*, in which case the contents will still be the center but the *ScrollViewer* will be only as wide as the *StackPanel*.

While enumerating through the static properties of the *Colors* class, the constructor in the code-behind file builds the nested *StackPanel* elements for each item:

Project: ColorList1 | File: MainPage.xaml.cs (excerpt)

```
public sealed partial class MainPage : Page
{
    public MainPage()
    {
        this.InitializeComponent();

        IEnumerable<PropertyInfo> properties = typeof(Colors).GetTypeInfo().DeclaredProperties;

        foreach (PropertyInfo property in properties)
        {
            Color clr = (Color)property.GetValue(null);

            StackPanel vertStackPanel = new StackPanel
            {
                VerticalAlignment = VerticalAlignment.Center
            };

            TextBlock txtblkName = new TextBlock
            {
                Text = property.Name,
                FontSize = 24
            };
            vertStackPanel.Children.Add(txtblkName);

            TextBlock txtblkRgb = new TextBlock
            {
                Text = String.Format("{0:X2}-{1:X2}-{2:X2}-{3:X2}",
                                clr.A, clr.R, clr.G, clr.B),
                FontSize = 18
            };
            vertStackPanel.Children.Add(txtblkRgb);
```

```
            StackPanel horzStackPanel = new StackPanel
            {
                Orientation = Orientation.Horizontal
            };

            Rectangle rectangle = new Rectangle
            {
                Width = 72,
                Height = 72,
                Fill = new SolidColorBrush(clr),
                Margin = new Thickness(6)
            };
            horzStackPanel.Children.Add(rectangle);
            horzStackPanel.Children.Add(vertStackPanel);
            stackPanel.Children.Add(horzStackPanel);
        }
    }
}
```

Now, there's nothing really wrong with this code, except that there are numerous ways to do it better, and by "better" I don't mean faster or more efficient but cleaner and more elegant and—most important—easier to maintain and modify.

Let's look at a better solution, but at the same time be aware that I won't be finished with this example until Chapter 11, where you'll see not only a better way of doing it, but the *best* way of doing it.

Deriving from *UserControl*

The key to making ColorList1 better is expressing those color items—the nested *StackPanel* and *TextBlock* and *Rectangle*—in XAML. Just offhand, this doesn't seem possible. We can't put this XAML in the MainPage.xaml file because we can't tell XAML to make 141 instances of the item unless we actually paste in 141 copies, and I suspect we're all agreed that would be the *worst* way to do it.

The ColorList2 program shows one common approach. After creating the ColorList2 project, I right-clicked the project name in the Solution Explorer and selected Add and New Item. In the Add New Item dialog box, I chose User Control and gave it a name of ColorItem.xaml. This process creates a pair of files: ColorItem.xaml accompanied by a code-behind file ColorItem.xaml.cs.

The ColorItem.xaml.cs file created by Visual Studio defines a *ColorItem* class in the *ColorList2* namespace that derives from *UserControl*:

```
namespace ColorList2
{
    public sealed partial class ColorItem : UserControl
    {
        public ColorItem()
        {
            this.InitializeComponent();
        }
    }
}
```

The ColorItem.xaml file created by Visual Studio says the same thing in XAML:

```
<UserControl
    x:Class="ColorList2.ColorItem"
    xmlns="http://schemas.microsoft.com/winfx/2006/xaml/presentation"
    xmlns:x="http://schemas.microsoft.com/winfx/2006/xaml"
    xmlns:local="using:ColorList2"
    xmlns:d="http://schemas.microsoft.com/expression/blend/2008"
    xmlns:mc="http://schemas.openxmlformats.org/markup-compatibility/2006"
    mc:Ignorable="d"
    d:DesignHeight="300"
    d:DesignWidth="400">

    <Grid>

    </Grid>
</UserControl>
```

You've actually already seen the *UserControl* class before because *Page* derives from *UserControl*. The "user" refers not to the end user of your application but to *you*, the programmer. Deriving from *UserControl* is the easiest way for you (the programmer) to make a custom control because you can define the visuals of the control in this XAML file. *UserControl* defines a property named *Content*, which is also the class's content property, so anything you add within the *UserControl* tags is set to this *Content* property.

Don't worry about the *d:DesignHeight* and *d:DesignWidth* properties in the ColorItem.xaml file. Those are for Microsoft Expression Blend. The actual size of this control depends on its contents.

The next step is to define the visuals of the color item in this ColorItem.xaml file:

Project: ColorList2 | **File:** ColorItem.xaml (excerpt)

```
<UserControl
    x:Class="ColorList2.ColorItem" ... >

    <Grid>
        <StackPanel Orientation="Horizontal">
            <Rectangle Name="rectangle"
                       Width="72"
                       Height="72"
                       Margin="6" />

            <StackPanel VerticalAlignment="Center">

                <TextBlock Name="txtblkName"
                           FontSize="24" />

                <TextBlock Name="txtblkRgb"
                           FontSize="18" />
            </StackPanel>
        </StackPanel>
    </Grid>
</UserControl>
```

It's the same element hierarchy as defined in code in ColorList1, but now it's actually readable. The *Rectangle* and the two *TextBlock* elements all have names, so they can be referenced in the code-behind file:

Project: ColorList2 | File: ColorItem.xaml.cs (excerpt)

```
public sealed partial class ColorItem : UserControl
{
    public ColorItem(string name, Color clr)
    {
        this.InitializeComponent();

        rectangle.Fill = new SolidColorBrush(clr);
        txtblkName.Text = name;
        txtblkRgb.Text = String.Format("{0:X2}-{1:X2}-{2:X2}-{3:X2}",
                                        clr.A, clr.R, clr.G, clr.B);
    }
}
```

I've redefined the constructor to accept a color name and a *Color* value as arguments. It uses those arguments to set the appropriate properties of the *Rectangle* and two *TextBlock* elements.

Let me warn you that defining a parameterized constructor in a *UserControl* derivative is *extremely* unorthodox. A much better approach is to define properties instead, but I don't want to do that right now because these properties should really be dependency properties, and that's too involved at the moment.

Without a parameterless constructor, this *ColorItem* class cannot be instantiated in XAML. But that's OK for this program because I'm not going to try instantiating it in XAML. The MainPage .xaml file for the ColorList2 project looks the same as the one for ColorList1. What's different is the simplicity of the code-behind file:

Project: ColorList2 | File: MainPage.xaml.cs (excerpt)

```
public sealed partial class MainPage : Page
{
    public MainPage()
    {
        this.InitializeComponent();

        IEnumerable<PropertyInfo> properties = typeof(Colors).GetTypeInfo().DeclaredProperties;

        foreach (PropertyInfo property in properties)
        {
            Color clr = (Color)property.GetValue(null);
            ColorItem clrItem = new ColorItem(property.Name, clr);
            stackPanel.Children.Add(clrItem);
        }
    }
}
```

Each *ColorItem* is instantiated with a name and *Color* and then added to the *StackPanel*.

Creating Windows Runtime Libraries

Let's create another version of this program, but this time the *ColorItem* class will be in a library that can be shared with other projects.

You can create a Visual Studio solution containing only a library project, but it's more common to add a library project to the solution of an existing application project. As you're developing the code in the library, you want to test it, and it really helps to have an application project in the same solution for that purpose. After developing a library in conjunction with an application, you can then share that library later if desired.

So let's create a new application project named ColorList3. In the Solution Explorer, add a library project to the solution by right-clicking the solution name and selecting Add and New Project. (Or pick Add New Project from the File menu.) In the Add New Project dialog box, at the left select Visual C# and the option for creating a new Windows 8 project. From the list of templates, select Class Library.

Generally, a library has a multilevel name separated by periods. This name also becomes the default namespace for that project. The library name usually begins with a company name (or its equivalent), so for this example I wanted to choose a library name of Petzold.Windows8.Controls. However, I had problems with a multileveled assembly name, so I left out the periods and used PetzoldWindow8Controls instead, and then later I changed the namespace to *Petzold.Windows8 .Controls*.

In a new library, Visual Studio automatically creates a file named Class1.cs, but you can delete that. Now right-click the library project name and select Add and New Item, and in the Add New Item dialog box, select User Control and give it a name of *ColorItem*. I decided to enhance the visuals of this *ColorItem* a little beyond the one you've already seen:

Solution: ColorList3 | **Project:** PetzoldWindows8Controls | **File:** ColorItem.xaml (excerpt)

```
<UserControl ... >
    <Grid>
        <Border BorderBrush="{StaticResource ApplicationForegroundThemeBrush}"
                BorderThickness="1"
                Width="336"
                Margin="6">
            <StackPanel Orientation="Horizontal">
                <Rectangle Name="rectangle"
                           Width="72"
                           Height="72"
                           Margin="6" />

                <StackPanel VerticalAlignment="Center">

                    <TextBlock Name="txtblkName"
                               FontSize="24" />

                    <TextBlock Name="txtblkRgb"
                               FontSize="18" />
                </StackPanel>
```

```
            </StackPanel>
        </Border>
    </Grid>
</UserControl>
```

Notice that I've given it a *Border* with an explicit *Width* property and a *Margin*. I chose this width empirically based on the longest color name (*LightGoldenrodYellow*). Notice also that the *BorderBrush* is set to a predefined identifier, which will be black with a light theme and white with a dark theme. Themes are set on applications rather than libraries—indeed, a library has no *App* class to set a theme—so this brush will be based on the theme of the application that uses *ColorItem*.

We still haven't touched the ColorList3 application project. Despite the fact that they're in the same solution, this application project will need a reference to the library, so right-click the References item under the ColorList3 project and select Add Reference. In the Reference Manager dialog box, at the left select Solution (indicating you want an assembly in the same solution), click PetzoldWindows8Controls, and click OK.

There is a distinct advantage to having both these projects in the same solution: Whenever you build ColorList3, Visual Studio will also rebuild the PetzoldWindows8Controls library if it's not up to date.

The MainPage.xaml file in ColorList3 is the same as in the previous two projects. The code-behind file needs a *using* directive for the namespace of the library, but otherwise it's the same as ColorList2:

Project: ColorList3 | File: MainPage.xaml.cs

```
using System.Collections.Generic;
using System.Reflection;
using Windows.UI;
using Windows.UI.Xaml.Controls;
using Petzold.Windows8.Controls;

namespace ColorList3
{
    public sealed partial class MainPage : Page
    {
        public MainPage()
        {
            this.InitializeComponent();

            IEnumerable<PropertyInfo> properties =
                        typeof(Colors).GetTypeInfo().DeclaredProperties;

            foreach (PropertyInfo property in properties)
            {
                Color clr = (Color)property.GetValue(null);
                ColorItem clrItem = new ColorItem(property.Name, clr);
                stackPanel.Children.Add(clrItem);
            }
        }
    }
}
```

Here's the result:

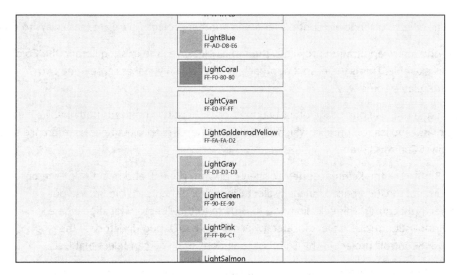

When creating the Petzold.Windows8.Controls library, I indicated that you should choose Class Library from the Add New Project dialog box. There is another option for creating a library labeled Windows Runtime Component. For this particular example, it doesn't matter which one you choose. In fact, you can right-click the library project name, select Properties, and in the Application screen change the Output type from Class Library to Windows Runtime Component. The ColorList3 program will run the same.

The big difference is this: The library you create by selecting Class Library can be accessed only from other C# and Visual Basic applications. A Windows Runtime Component can additionally be accessed from C++ and JavaScript. It is the Windows Runtime Component that allows language interoperability for Windows 8 applications.

Consequently, a Windows Runtime Component has some restrictions that a regular Class Library does not. Public classes must be sealed, for example. If you remove the *sealed* keyword from the definition of the *ColorItem* control, that class cannot be part of a Windows Runtime Component. The other major rules involve structures—you can't have any public members that are not fields—and the restriction of data types passing over the API to Windows Runtime types.

The C++ version of StackPanelWithScrolling includes a Windows Runtime Component named ReflectionHelper written in C# that simplifies the use of reflection by the C++ programs. Chapter 15, "Going Native," shows the opposite approach: a Windows Runtime Component written in C++ that gives C# programs access to DirectX classes.

The Wrap Alternative

Now let's use that PetzoldWindows8Controls library in another project. There are three ways to do it:

Method 1: Add a new application project to the same solution as the existing library: the ColorList3 solution, in this example. This is the easiest approach, and it certainly makes sense if the two applications are related some way.

Instead, I'm going to use one of the other two methods. These two methods both involve creating a new solution and application project, which I'll call ColorWrap. This project needs a reference to the PetzoldWindows8Controls library.

Method 2: Right-click the References item in the ColorWrap project, and select Add Reference. In the left column of the Reference Manager, select Browse, and then click the Browse button in the lower-right corner. This will allow you to browse to the directory location where the PetzoldWindows8Controls.dll file is located (which is the bin/Debug directory of the PetzoldWindows8Controls project in the ColorList3 solution), and you can select that DLL.

The disadvantage to this method is that you're assuming that the library is complete and finished and that you won't need to make any changes. You're referencing a DLL rather than the project with its source code. However, in my experience the *really* big disadvantage to this method is that it doesn't work quite right with the current release of Windows 8 when there are XAML files involved.

That leaves us with:

Method 3: In the ColorWrap solution, right-click the solution name and select Add and Existing Project. The existing project you want to add is the library. In the Add Existing Project dialog box, navigate to the PetzoldWindows8Controls.csproj file. This is the C# project file maintained by Visual Studio in the ColorList3 solution. Select that. The library project is not copied! Instead, only a reference is created to that library project. Regardless, Visual Studio can still determine if the library needs to be rebuilt, and it performs that rebuild if necessary.

Now the PetzoldWindows8Controls project is part of the ColorWrap solution, but the ColorWrap application project still needs a reference to the library. Right-click the References section under the ColorWrap project and select the library from the solution, just as you did in ColorList3.

It could be that you have two instances of Visual Studio running, perhaps with the ColorList3 and ColorWrap solutions loaded, both of which let you make changes to the PetzoldWindows8Controls library. That's generally OK as long as you save or compile after making changes. If the same file is open in both instances of Visual Studio and you make changes to that file, the other instance of Visual Studio will notify you of changes when that file is saved to disk.

With those preliminaries out of the way, let's focus on the ColorWrap program, which demonstrates how to display these colors with a *VariableSizedWrapGrid* panel. Despite the name of this panel, it *really* wants all the items to be the same size. That's why I added the explicit *Width* to the *Border* in *ColorItem*.

Like *StackPanel*, *VariableSizedWrapGrid* has an *Orientation* property and the default is *Vertical*. The first items in the *Children* collection are displayed in a column. The difference is that

VariableSizedWrapGrid will use multiple columns, just like the Windows 8 start screen. This means that the default *VariableSizedWrapGrid* must be horizontally scrolled, so *ScrollViewer* properties must be set accordingly. Here's the XAML file:

Project: ColorWrap | File: MainPage.xaml (excerpt)

```xaml
<Grid Background="{StaticResource ApplicationPageBackgroundThemeBrush}">
    <ScrollViewer HorizontalScrollBarVisibility="Visible"
                  VerticalScrollBarVisibility="Disabled">
        <VariableSizedWrapGrid Name="wrapPanel" />
    </ScrollViewer>
</Grid>
```

The code-behind file is similar to the previous program except that now it puts the items into *wrapPanel*:

Project: ColorWrap | File: MainPage.xaml.cs (excerpt)

```csharp
public sealed partial class MainPage : Page
{
    public MainPage()
    {
        this.InitializeComponent();

        IEnumerable<PropertyInfo> properties = typeof(Colors).GetTypeInfo().DeclaredProperties;

        foreach (PropertyInfo property in properties)
        {
            Color clr = (Color)property.GetValue(null);
            ColorItem clrItem = new ColorItem(property.Name, clr);
            wrapPanel.Children.Add(clrItem);
        }
    }
}
```

And here it is:

Scrolling is horizontal.

The *Canvas* and Attached Properties

The final *Panel* derivative I'll discuss in this chapter is the *Canvas*. In one sense, *Canvas* is the most "traditional" type of panel because it allows you to position elements at precise pixel locations.

But what property of the child element do you set to indicate the element's position relative to the *Canvas*? If you've scoured the properties defined by *UIElement* and *FrameworkElement* searching for something named *Location* or *Position* or *X* or *Y*, you haven't found it. Properties that let you specify coordinate positions exist for drawing vector graphics but not for other elements. Such a property doesn't make much sense in the Windows Runtime because it is not applicable when you're using a *Grid*, a *StackPanel*, or a *WrapPanel*. We've managed to make it this far without specifying pixel locations for positioning elements, and the only time one is needed is when the element is a child of a *Canvas*.

For that reason, *Canvas* itself defines the properties used to position elements relative to itself. These are a very special type of property known as *attached properties*, and they are a subset of dependency properties. Attached properties defined by one class (*Canvas*, in this example) are actually set on instances of other classes (children of the *Canvas*, in this case). The objects on which you set an attached property don't need to know what that property does or where it came from.

Let's see how this works. The TextOnCanvas project has a XAML file that contains a *Canvas* within the standard *Grid*. (You can alternatively replace the *Grid* with the *Canvas*.) The *Canvas* contains three *TextBlock* children:

Project: TextOnCanvas | File: MainPage.xaml (excerpt)

```
<Page
    x:Class="TextOnCanvas.MainPage"
    ...
    FontSize="48">

    <Grid Background="{StaticResource ApplicationPageBackgroundThemeBrush}">
        <Canvas>
            <TextBlock Text="Text on Canvas at (0, 0)"
                       Canvas.Left="0"
                       Canvas.Top="0" />

            <TextBlock Text="Text on Canvas at (200, 100)"
                       Canvas.Left="200"
                       Canvas.Top="100" />

            <TextBlock Text="Text on Canvas at (400, 200)"
                       Canvas.Left="400"
                       Canvas.Top="200" />
        </Canvas>
    </Grid>
</Page>
```

Here's the (rather unexciting) result:

Text on Canvas at (0, 0)

Text on Canvas at (200, 100)

Text on Canvas at (400, 200)

Look at that markup again, and take special note of the strange syntax:

```
<TextBlock Text="Text on Canvas at (200, 100)"
           Canvas.Left="200"
           Canvas.Top="100" />
```

Judging from their names, the *Canvas.Left* and *Canvas.Top* attributes appear to be defined by the *Canvas* class, and yet they are set on the children of the *Canvas* to indicate their positions. XAML attribute names identified with both class and property names like this are always attached properties.

The funny thing is, *Canvas* actually doesn't define any properties named *Left* and *Top*! It defines properties and methods with *similar* names but not those names exactly.

The nature of these attached properties might become a little clearer by examining how they are set in code. The XAML file for the TapAndShowPoint program contains only a named *Canvas* in the standard *Grid*:

Project: TapAndShowPoint | File: MainPage.xaml (excerpt)

```
<Grid Background="{StaticResource ApplicationPageBackgroundThemeBrush}">
    <Canvas Name="canvas" />
</Grid>
```

Everything else is the responsibility of the code-behind file. It overrides the *OnTapped* method to create a dot (an *Ellipse* element actually) and a *TextBlock*, both of which it adds to the *Canvas* at the point where the screen was tapped:

Project: TapAndShowPoint | File: MainPage.xaml.cs (excerpt)

```
public sealed partial class MainPage : Page
{
    public MainPage()
    {
```

```
        this.InitializeComponent();
    }

    protected override void OnTapped(TappedRoutedEventArgs args)
    {
        Point pt = args.GetPosition(this);

        // Create dot
        Ellipse ellipse = new Ellipse
        {
            Width = 3,
            Height = 3,
            Fill = this.Foreground
        };

        Canvas.SetLeft(ellipse, pt.X);
        Canvas.SetTop(ellipse, pt.Y);
        canvas.Children.Add(ellipse);

        // Create text
        TextBlock txtblk = new TextBlock
        {
            Text = String.Format("({0})", pt),
            FontSize = 24,
        };

        Canvas.SetLeft(txtblk, pt.X);
        Canvas.SetTop(txtblk, pt.Y);
        canvas.Children.Add(txtblk);

        args.Handled = true;
        base.OnTapped(args);
    }
}
```

As you tap the screen, the dots and text appear at the tap points:

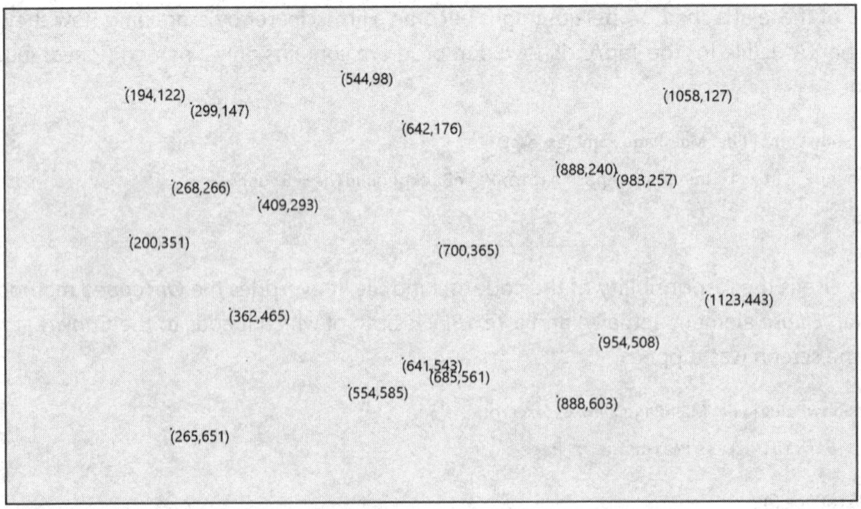

Here's how the position of the dot is specified in code as it's added to the *Children* collection of the *Canvas*:

```
Canvas.SetLeft(ellipse, pt.X);
Canvas.SetTop(ellipse, pt.Y);
canvas.Children.Add(ellipse);
```

The order doesn't matter: You could add the element to the *Canvas* first, and then set its position. The *Canvas.SetLeft* and *Canvas.SetTop* static methods play the same role here as the *Canvas.Left* and *Canvas.Top* attributes in XAML. They let you specify a coordinate point where a particular element is to be positioned. (However, there's a little flaw in the approach I've used to position the dots. This flaw becomes evident if you make the *Ellipse* a little larger. The program should really be putting the center of the dot at the tapped point, and instead the *Canvas.SetLeft* and *Canvas.SetTop* calls I've used position the upper-left corner of the *Ellipse* there. If you want the center of the *Ellipse* at the point *pt*, you'll want to subtract half its width from *pt.X* and half its height from *pt.Y*.)

I mentioned that *Canvas* doesn't define *Left* and *Top* properties specifically. Instead, *Canvas* defines static *SetLeft* and *SetTop* methods as well as static properties of type *DependencyProperty*. Here's how the two *DependencyProperty* objects might be defined if the *Canvas* class were written in C#:

```
public static DependencyProperty LeftProperty { get; }
public static DependencyProperty TopProperty { get; }
```

As you'll see in a later chapter, these are special types of dependency properties in that they can be set on elements other than *Canvas*.

Let me show you something interesting. The TapAndShowPoint program calls the static *Canvas.SetLeft* and *Canvas.SetTop* methods like this:

```
Canvas.SetLeft(ellipse, pt.X);
Canvas.SetTop(ellipse, pt.Y);
```

An alternative approach—just as legal, just as valid, and 100 percent equivalent—involves calling *SetValue* on the child element and referencing the static *DependencyProperty* objects defined by *Canvas*:

```
ellipse.SetValue(Canvas.LeftProperty, pt.X);
ellipse.SetValue(Canvas.TopProperty, pt.Y);
```

These statements are exactly equivalent to the *Canvas.SetLeft* and *Canvas.SetTop* calls, and it doesn't matter which form you use.

You've seen that *SetValue* method before. *SetValue* is defined by *DependencyObject* and inherited by very many classes in the Windows Runtime. A property like *FontSize* is actually defined in terms of the static dependency property that becomes an argument to this same *SetValue* method:

```
public double FontSize
{
    set { SetValue(FontSizeProperty, value); }
    get { return (double)GetValue(FontSizeProperty); }
}
```

In fact, although I have never seen the internal source code of the *Canvas* class, I can practically guarantee you that the *SetLeft* and *SetTop* static methods in *Canvas* are defined with code that's equivalent to this C# syntax:

```
public static void SetLeft(DependencyObject element, double value)
{
    element.SetValue(LeftProperty, value);
}
public static void SetTop(DependencyObject element, double value)
{
    element.SetValue(TopProperty, value);
}
```

These methods show very clearly how the dependency property is actually being set on the child element rather than the *Canvas*.

Canvas also defines *GetLeft* and *GetTop* methods, defined in code equivalent to this:

```
public static double GetLeft(DependencyObject element)
{
    return (double)element.GetValue(LeftProperty);
}
public static double GetTop(DependencyObject element)
{
    return (double)element.GetValue(TopProperty);
}
```

The *Canvas* class uses these methods internally to obtain the left and top settings on each of its children so that it can position them during the layout process.

The static *SetLeft*, *SetTop*, *GetLeft*, and *GetTop* methods suggest that the dependency property system involves a dictionary of sorts. The *SetValue* method allows an attached property like *Canvas .LeftProperty* to be stored in an element that has no knowledge of this property or its purpose. *Canvas* can later retrieve this property to determine where the child should appear relative to itself.

The Z-Index

Canvas has a third attached property that you can set in XAML with the attribute *Canvas.ZIndex*. The "Z" in *ZIndex* refers to a three-dimensional coordinate system, where the Z axis extends out of the screen toward the user.

When sibling elements overlap, they are normally displayed in the order they appear in the visual tree, which means that elements early in a panel's *Children* collection can be covered by elements later in the *Children* collection. For example, consider the following:

```
<Grid>
    <TextBlock Text="Blue Text" Foreground="Blue" FontSize="96" />
    <TextBlock Text="Red Text" Foreground="Red" FontSize="96" />
</Grid>
```

The red text obscures part of the blue text.

You can override that behavior with the *Canvas.ZIndex* attached property, and the weird thing is this: It works with all panels, and not just *Canvas*. To make the blue text appear on top of the red text, give it a higher z-index:

```
<Grid>
    <TextBlock Text="Blue Text" Foreground="Blue" FontSize="96" Canvas.ZIndex="1" />
    <TextBlock Text="Red Text" Foreground="Red" FontSize="96" Canvas.ZIndex="0" />
</Grid>
```

Canvas Weirdness

Much of what I've described about layout earlier in this chapter doesn't apply to the *Canvas*. Layout within a *Canvas* is always child-driven. The *Canvas* always offers its children an infinite size, which means that each child sets a natural size for itself and that's the only space the child occupies. *HorizontalAlignment* and *VerticalAlignment* settings have no effect on a child of a *Canvas*. Likewise, the *Stretch* property of *Image* has no effect when the *Image* is a child of a *Canvas*: *Image* always displays the bitmap in its pixel size. *Rectangle* and *Ellipse* shrink to nothing in a *Canvas* unless given an explicit width and height.

Although *HorizontalAlignment* and *VerticalAlignment* have no effect on a child of the *Canvas*, they do have an effect when set on the *Canvas* itself. With other panels, when you set the alignment properties to something other than *Stretch*, the panel becomes as small as possible while still encompassing its children. The *Canvas*, however, is different. Set *HorizontalAlignment* and *VerticalAlignment* to values other than *Stretch*, and the *Canvas* shrinks to nothing regardless of its children.

Even when the *Canvas* shrinks down to a zero size, the display of its children is not affected. Conceptually, the *Canvas* is more like a reference point than a container, and the size of the children of a *Canvas* are ignored in layout.

You can use this characteristic of the *Canvas* to your advantage. For example, suppose you try to display a *TextBlock* in a *Grid* that is obviously too small for it:

```
<Grid Width="200" Height="100">
    <TextBlock Text="Text in a Small Grid" FontSize="144" />
</Grid>
```

The *TextBlock* is clipped to the dimensions of the *Grid*. You could make the *Grid* larger of course, but you might be stuck with this *Grid* size, perhaps because of other child elements. Still, you want the *TextBlock* to be aligned with these other elements without being clipped to the *Grid*.

The extremely simple solution is to put a *Canvas* in the *Grid* and put the *TextBlock* in that *Canvas*:

```
<Grid Width="200" Height="100">
    <Canvas>
        <TextBlock Text="Text in a Small Grid" FontSize="144" />
    </Canvas>
</Grid>
```

Even though the *Canvas* is now clipped to the size of the *Grid*, the *TextBlock* is not. The *TextBlock* is still where you want it—aligned with the upper-left corner of the *Grid*—but it's now displayed without any clipping. The *TextBlock* essentially exists outside of normal layout.

It's a very simple technique that can be very useful when you need it.

CHAPTER 5

Control Interaction

Early on in this book I made a distinction between classes that derive from *FrameworkElement* and those that derive from *Control*. I've tended to refer to *FrameworkElement* derivatives (such as *TextBlock* and *Image*) as "elements" to preserve this distinction, but a deeper explication is now required.

The title of this chapter might suggest that elements are for presentation and controls are for interaction, but that's not necessarily so. It is the *UIElement* class that defines all the user-input events for touch, mouse, stylus, and keyboard, which means that elements as well as controls can interact with the user in very sophisticated ways.

Nor are elements deficient in layout, styling, or data binding capabilities. It's the *FrameworkElement* class that defines layout properties such as *Width*, *Height*, *HorizontalAlignment*, *VerticalAlignment*, and *Margin*, as well as the *Style* property and the *SetBinding* method.

The *Control* Difference

Visually and functionally, *FrameworkElement* derivatives are primitives—atoms, so to speak—while *Control* derivatives are assemblages of these primitives, or molecules in this analogy. A *Button* is actually constructed from a *Border* and a *TextBlock* (in many cases). A *Slider* consists of a couple of *Rectangle* elements with a *Thumb*, which itself is a *Control* probably built from a *Rectangle*. Anything that has visual content beyond text, a bitmap, or vector graphics is almost certainly a *Control* derivative.

Consequently, one of the most important properties defined by *Control* is called *Template*. As I'll demonstrate in Chapter 11, "The Three Templates," this property allows you to completely redefine the appearance of a control by defining a visual tree of your own invention. It makes sense to visually redefine a *Button* because (for example) you might want it to be round rather than rectangular because you want to put it on an application bar. It makes no sense to visually redefine a *TextBlock* or *Image* because there's nothing you can do with it beyond the text or bitmap itself. If you want to *add* something to a *TextBlock* or *Image*, you're defining a *Control* because you're constructing a visual tree that includes the element primitive.

Although you can derive a custom class from *FrameworkElement*, there is little you can do with the result. You can't give it any visuals. But when you derive from *Control*, you generally give your custom control a default visual appearance by defining a visual tree in XAML.

Control defines a bunch of properties that the *Control* class itself does not need. These are for use by classes that derive from *Control*, and consist of properties mostly associated with *TextBlock* (*CharacterSpacing*, *FontFamily*, *FontSize*, *FontStretch*, *FontStyle*, *FontWeight*, and *Foreground*) and *Border* (*Background*, *BorderBrush*, *BorderThickness*, and *Padding*). Not every *Control* derivative has text or a border, but if you need those properties when creating a new control or creating a new template for an existing control, they are conveniently provided. *Control* also provides two new properties named *HorizontalContentAlignment* and *VerticalContentAlignment* for purposes of defining control visuals.

A *Control* derivative often defines some new properties and events. Commonly, a *Control* derivative will process user-input events from the pointer, mouse, stylus, and keyboard and will convert that input into a higher-level event. For example, the *ButtonBase* class (from which all the buttons derive) defines a *Click* event. The *Slider* defines a *ValueChanged* event indicating when its *Value* property changes. The *TextBox* defines a *TextChanged* event indicating when its *Text* property changes.

It turns out that in real life, *Control* derivatives really *do* interact more with users, so the title of this chapter is accurate. For the convenience of working with user input, *Control* provides protected virtual methods corresponding to all the user-input events defined by *UIElement*. For example, *UIElement* defines the *Tapped* event, but *Control* defines the protected virtual method *OnTapped*. *Control* also defines an *IsEnabled* property so that controls can avoid user input if input is not currently applicable, and it defines an *IsEnabledChanged* event that is fired when the property changes. This is the only public event actually defined by *Control*.

The idea of a control having "input focus" is still applicable in Windows 8. When a control has the input focus, the user expects that particular control to get most keyboard events. (Of course, some keyboard events, such as the Windows key, transcend input focus.) For this purpose, *Control* defines a *Focus* method, as well as *OnGotFocus* and *OnLostFocus* virtual methods.

In connection with keyboard focus is the idea of being able to navigate among controls by using the keyboard Tab key. *Control* provides for this by defining *IsTabStop*, *TabIndex*, and *TabNavigation* properties.

Many *Control* derivatives are in the *Windows.UI.Xaml.Controls* namespace, but a few are in the *Windows.UI.Xaml.Controls.Primitives* namespace. The latter namespace is generally reserved for those controls that usually appear only as parts of other controls, but that's a suggestion rather than a restriction.

Most *Control* derivatives derive directly from *Control*, but four important classes derive from *Control* to define their own subcategories of controls. Here they are:

Object
  DependencyObject
    UIElement
      FrameworkElement
        Control
          ContentControl
          ItemsControl
          RangeBase
          UserControl

ContentControl—from which important classes like *Button*, *ScrollViewer*, and *AppBar* derive—seemingly does little more than define a property named *Content* of type *object*. For a *Button*, for example, this *Content* property is what you set to whatever you want to appear inside the *Button*. Most often this is text or a bitmap, but you can also use a panel that contains other content.

It is interesting that the *Content* property of *ContentControl* is of type *object* rather than *UIElement*. There's a good reason for that. You can actually put pretty much any type of object you want as the content of a *Button*, and you can supply a template (in the form of a visual tree) that tells the *Button* how to display this content. This feature is not so much used for *Button*, but it's used a great deal for items in *ItemsControl* derivatives. I'll show you how to define a content template in Chapter 11.

ItemsControl is the parent class to a bunch of controls that display collections of items. Here you'll find the familiar *ListBox* and *ComboBox* as well as the new Windows 8 controls *FlipView*, *GridView*, and *ListView*. Again, Chapter 11.

There are a couple ways to create custom controls. The really simple way is by defining a *Style* for the control, but more extensive visual changes require a template. In some cases you can derive from an existing control to add some features to it, or you can derive from *ContentControl* or *ItemsControl* if these controls provide features you need.

But one of the most common ways to create a custom control is by deriving from *UserControl*. This is not the approach you'll use if you want to market a custom control library, but it's great for controls that you use yourself within the context of an application.

The *Slider* for Ranges

In the *Control* class hierarchy shown above, the remaining important class is *RangeBase*, which has three derivatives: *ProgressBar*, *ScrollBar*, and *Slider*.

Which of these is not like the others? Obviously *ProgressBar*, which exists in this hierarchy mainly to inherit several properties from *RangeBase*: *Minimum*, *Maximum*, *SmallChange*, *LargeChange*, and *Value*. In every *RangeBase* control, the *Value* property takes on values of type *double* ranging from *Minimum* through *Maximum*. With the *ScrollBar* and *Slider*, the *Value* property changes when the user manipulates the control; with *ProgressBar*, the *Value* property is set programmatically to indicate the progress of a lengthy operation.

ProgressBar has an indeterminate mode to display a row of dots that skirt across the screen, but also available is *ProgressRing*, which displays a now familiar spinning circle of dots.

In the quarter-century evolution of Windows, the *ScrollBar* has slipped from its high perch in the control hierarchy and is commonly seen today only in a *ScrollViewer* control. Try to instantiate the Windows Runtime version of *ScrollBar*, and you won't even see it. If you want to use *ScrollBar*, you'll have to supply a template for it. Like *RangeBase*, *ScrollBar* is defined in the *Windows.UI.Xaml.Controls .Primitives* namespace, indicating that it's not something application programmers normally use.

For virtually all needs that involve choosing from a range of values, *ScrollBar* has been replaced with *Slider*, and with touch interfaces, *Slider* has become simpler than ever. In its default manifestation, *Slider* has no arrows. It simply jumps to the value corresponding to the point where you touch the *Slider* or drag your finger or mouse.

The *Value* property of the *Slider* can change either programmatically or through user manipulation. To obtain a notification when the *Value* property changes, attach an event handler for the *ValueChanged* event, such as shown in the SliderEvents project:

Project: SliderEvents | File: MainPage.xaml (excerpt)

```
<Grid Background="{StaticResource ApplicationPageBackgroundThemeBrush}">
    <StackPanel>
        <Slider ValueChanged="OnSliderValueChanged" />

        <TextBlock HorizontalAlignment="Center"
                   FontSize="48" />

        <Slider ValueChanged="OnSliderValueChanged" />

        <TextBlock HorizontalAlignment="Center"
                   FontSize="48" />
    </StackPanel>
</Grid>
```

Both *Slider* controls here share the same event handler. The idea behind this simple program is that the current *Value* of each *Slider* is displayed by the *TextBlock* below it. This might be considered somewhat challenging when you notice that nothing in this XAML file is assigned a name. However, the event handler makes a few assumptions. It assumes that the parent to the *Slider* is a *Panel*, and the next child in this *Panel* is a *TextBlock*:

Project: SliderEvents | File: MainPage.xaml.cs (excerpt)

```
void OnSliderValueChanged(object sender, RangeBaseValueChangedEventArgs args)
{
    Slider slider = sender as Slider;
    Panel parentPanel = slider.Parent as Panel;
    int childIndex = parentPanel.Children.IndexOf(slider);
    TextBlock txtblk = parentPanel.Children[childIndex + 1] as TextBlock;
    txtblk.Text = args.NewValue.ToString();
}
```

This little bit of "trickery" merely demonstrates that there's more than one way to access elements in the visual tree. In the final step, the *Text* property of the *TextBlock* is assigned the *NewValue* argument from the event arguments, converted to a string. Equally valid would be using the *Value* property of the *Slider*:

```
txtblk.Text = slider.Value.ToString();
```

Although *RangeBaseValueChangedEventArgs* derives from *RoutedEvent*, this is not a routed event. The event does not travel up the visual tree. The *sender* argument is always the *Slider*, and the *OriginalSource* property of the event arguments is always *null*.

When you run the program, you'll notice that the *TextBlock* elements initially display nothing. The *ValueChanged* event is not fired until *Value* actually changes from its default value of zero.

As you touch a *Slider* or click it with a mouse, the value jumps to that position. You can then sweep your finger or mouse pointer back and forth to change the value. As you manipulate the *Slider* controls, you'll see that they let you select values from 0 to 100, inclusive:

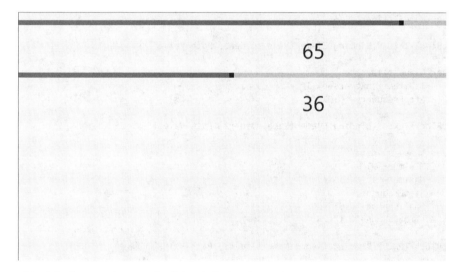

This default range is a result of the default values of the *Minimum* and *Maximum* properties, which are 0 and 100, respectively. Although the *Value* property is a *double*, it takes on integral values as a result of the default *StepFrequency* property, which is 1.

By default the *Slider* is oriented horizontally, but you can switch to vertical with the *Orientation* property. The thickness of the *Slider* cannot be changed except by redefining the visuals with a template. The total thickness of the control in layout includes a bit more space than the visuals imply. In layout, the default height of a horizontal *Slider* is 60 pixels; the default width of a vertical *Slider* is 45 pixels. In use, these dimensions are adequate for touch purposes.

If you press the Tab key while this program is running, you can change the keyboard input focus from one *Slider* to another and then use the keyboard arrow keys to make the value go up or down. Pressing Home and End shoots to the minimum and maximum values.

Some other variations are illustrated in the next project called SliderBindings, in which I've moved all the updating logic to the XAML file. Three *Slider* controls are instantiated in a *StackPanel* and alternated with *TextBlock* elements with bindings to the *Value* properties of each *Slider*. An implicit style for the *TextBlock* is defined to reduce repetitive markup:

Project: SliderBindings | File: MainPage.xaml (excerpt)

```xml
<Grid Background="{StaticResource ApplicationPageBackgroundThemeBrush}">
    <Grid.Resources>
        <Style TargetType="TextBlock">
            <Setter Property="FontSize" Value="48" />
            <Setter Property="HorizontalAlignment" Value="Center" />
        </Style>
    </Grid.Resources>

    <StackPanel>
        <Slider Name="slider1" />

        <TextBlock Text="{Binding ElementName=slider1, Path=Value}" />

        <Slider Name="slider2"
                IsDirectionReversed="True"
                StepFrequency="0.01" />

        <TextBlock Text="{Binding ElementName=slider2, Path=Value}" />

        <Slider Name="slider3"
                Minimum="-1"
                Maximum="1"
                StepFrequency="0.01"
                SmallChange="0.01"
                LargeChange="0.1" />

        <TextBlock Text="{Binding ElementName=slider3, Path=Value}" />
    </StackPanel>
</Grid>
```

Bindings obtain initial values and don't wait for the first *ValueChanged* event to be fired. The bindings then keep track of changing values resulting from user manipulation:

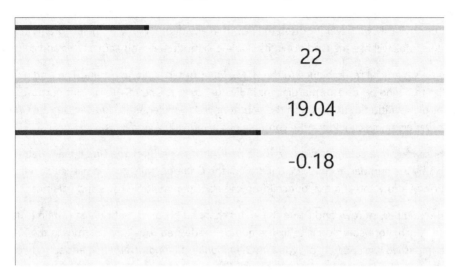

The markup for the second *Slider* sets the *StepFrequency* property to 0.01 and also sets *IsDirectionReversed* to *true* so that the minimum value of 0 occurs when the thumb is positioned to the far right. It's rather rare to set *IsDirectionReversed* to *true* for horizontal sliders but more common for vertical sliders. The default vertical slider has a minimum value when the slider is all the way down, and for some purposes that should be a maximum value.

For that second *Slider*, however, the keyboard arrow keys change the value in increments of 1 rather than the *StepFrequency* of 0.01. The keyboard interface is governed by the *SmallChange* property, which by default is 1.

The third *Slider* has a range from –1 to 1. When the *Slider* is first displayed, the thumb is set in the center at the default *Value* of 0. I've set both *StepFrequency* and *SmallChange* to 0.01, and *LargeChange* to 0.1, but I've found no way to trigger the *LargeChange* jump with either the mouse or keyboard.

The *Slider* class defines *TickFrequency* and *TickPlacement* properties to display tick marks adjacent to the *Slider*. If the *Background* and *Foreground* properties of the *Slider* are set, the *Slider* uses *Foreground* for the slider area associated with the minimum value and *Background* for the area associated with the maximum value, but it switches to default colors when the *Slider* is being manipulated or when the mouse hovers overhead.

As we begin creating more *Slider* controls, it becomes necessary to find a better way to lay them out on the page. It's time to get familiar with the *Grid*.

The *Grid*

The *Grid* probably seems like a familiar friend at this point because it's been in almost every program in this book, but obviously we haven't gotten to know it in any depth. Many of the programs in the remainder of this book will use the *Grid* not in its single-cell mode but with actual rows and columns.

The *Grid* has a superficial resemblance to the HTML *table*, but it's quite different. The *Grid* doesn't have any facility to define borders or margins for individual cells. It is strictly for layout purposes. Any sprucing up for presentation must occur on the parent or children elements: You can put the *Grid* in a *Border*, and *Border* elements can adorn the contents of the individual *Grid* cells.

The number of rows and columns in a *Grid* must be explicitly specified; the *Grid* cannot determine this information by the number of children. Children of the *Grid* generally go in a particular cell, which is an intersection of a row and column, but children can also span multiple rows and columns.

Although the numbers of rows and columns can be changed programmatically at run time, it's not often done. Much more common is to fix the number of desired rows and columns in the XAML file. This is accomplished with objects of type *RowDefinition* and *ColumnDefinition* added to two collections defined by *Grid* called *RowDefinitions* and *ColumnDefinitions*.

The size of each row and column can be defined in one of three ways:

- An explicit row height or column width in pixels
- *Auto*, meaning based on the size of the children
- Asterisk (or star), which allocates remaining space proportionally

In XAML, property-element syntax is used to fill the *RowDefinitions* and *ColumnDefinitions* collections, so a typical *Grid* looks like this:

```
<Grid>
    <Grid.RowDefinitions>
        <RowDefinition Height="Auto" />
        <RowDefinition Height="55" />
        <RowDefinition Height="*" />
    </Grid.RowDefinitions>

    <Grid.ColumnDefinitions>
        <ColumnDefinition Width="Auto" />
        <ColumnDefinition Width="10*" />
        <ColumnDefinition Width="20*" />
        <ColumnDefinition Width="Auto" />
    </Grid.ColumnDefinitions>

    <!-- Children go here -->

</Grid>
```

Notice that the *Grid* collection properties are named *RowDefinitions* and *ColumnDefinitions* (plural) but they contain objects of type *RowDefinition* and *ColumnDefinition* (singular). You can omit the *RowDefinitions* or *ColumnDefinitions* for a *Grid* that has only one row or one column.

This particular *Grid* has three rows and four columns, and it shows the various ways that the size of the rows and columns can be defined. A number by itself indicates a width (or height) in pixels. Explicit row heights and column widths are not generally used as much as the other two options.

The word *Auto* means to let the child decide. The calculated height of the row (or width of the column) is based on the maximum height (or width) of the children in that row (or column).

As in HTML, the asterisk (pronounced "star" in this context) directs the *Grid* to allocate the available space. In this *Grid*, the height of the third row is calculated by subtracting the height of the first and second rows from the total height of the *Grid*. For the columns, the second and third columns are allocated the remaining space calculated by subtracting the widths of the first and fourth columns from the total width of the *Grid*. The numbers before the asterisks indicate proportions, and here they mean that the third column gets twice the width of the second column.

The star values are applicable only when the size of the *Grid* is parent-driven! For example, suppose that this *Grid* is a child of a *StackPanel* with a vertical orientation. The *StackPanel* offers to the *Grid* an unconstrained infinite height. How can the *Grid* allocate that infinite height to its middle row? It cannot. The asterisk specification degenerates to *Auto*.

Similarly, if a *Grid* is a child of a *Canvas* and the *Grid* is not given an explicit *Height* and *Width*, all the star specifications degenerate to *Auto*. The same thing happens to a *Grid* that does not have default *Stretch* values of *HorizontalAlignment* and *VerticalAlignment*. In the *Grid* example shown earlier, the second column might actually become wider than the third if that's what the sizes of the children in those columns dictate.

However, if you have no *RowDefinition* objects with a star specification, the height of the *Grid* is child-driven. The *Grid* can go in a vertical *StackPanel* or *Canvas* or be given a non-default *VerticalAlignment* without weirdness happening.

The *Height* property of *RowDefinition* and the *Width* property of *ColumnDefinition* are both of type *GridLength*, a structure defined in *Windows.UI.Xaml* that lets you specify *Auto* or star sizes from code. *RowDefinition* also defines *MinHeight* and *MaxHeight* properties, and *ColumnDefinition* defines *MinWidth* and *MaxWidth*. These are all of type *double* and indicate minimum and maximum sizes in pixels. You can obtain the actual sizes with the *ActualHeight* property of *RowDefinition* and the *ActualWidth* property of *ColumnDefinition*.

Grid also defines four attached properties that you set on the children of a *Grid*: *Grid.Row* and *Grid.Column* have default values of 0, and *Grid.RowSpan* and *Grid.ColumnSpan* have default values of 1. This is how you indicate the cell in which a particular child resides and how many rows and columns it spans. A cell can contain more than one element.

You can nest a *Grid* within a *Grid* or put other panels in *Grid* cells, but the nesting of panels could degrade layout performance, so watch out if a deeply nested element is changing size based on an animation or if children are frequently being added to or removed from *Children* collections. You should probably try to avoid the layout of your page being recalculated at the video frame rate!

In Chapter 3, "Basic Event Handling," I presented a Windows 8 version of WHATSIZE, the first program to appear in a magazine article about Windows programming. The third article about Windows Programming to appear in a magazine was in the May 1987 issue of *Microsoft Systems Journal* and featured a program called COLORSCR ("color scroll"). Here it is as it looked in that article running under a beta version of Windows 2:

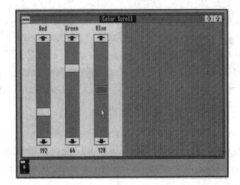

Manipulate the scrollbars to mix red, green, and blue values, and you'd see the result at the right. (In those days, most graphics displays didn't have full ranges of color, so dithering was used to approximate colors not renderable by the device.) The value of each scrollbar is also displayed beneath the scrollbar. The program performed a rather crude (and heavily arithmetic) attempt at dynamic layout, even changing the width of the scrollbars when the window size changed.

This seems like an ideal program to demonstrate a simple *Grid*. Considering the six instances of *TextBlock* and three instances of *Slider* required, the XAML file in the SimpleColorScroll project starts off with two implicit styles:

Project: SimpleColorScroll | File: MainPage.xaml (excerpt)

```
<Page.Resources>
    <Style TargetType="TextBlock">
        <Setter Property="Text" Value="00" />
        <Setter Property="FontSize" Value="24" />
        <Setter Property="HorizontalAlignment" Value="Center" />
        <Setter Property="Margin" Value="0 12" />
    </Style>

    <Style TargetType="Slider">
        <Setter Property="Orientation" Value="Vertical" />
        <Setter Property="IsDirectionReversed" Value="True" />
        <Setter Property="Maximum" Value="255" />
        <Setter Property="HorizontalAlignment" Value="Center" />
    </Style>
</Page.Resources>
```

I've decided to display the current value of each *Slider* in hexadecimal, so the *Style* for the *TextBlock* initializes the *Text* property to "00", which is the hexadecimal value corresponding to the minimum *Slider* position.

The *Grid* begins by defining three rows (for each *Slider* and two accompanying *TextBlock* labels) and four columns. Notice that the first three columns are all the same width but the fourth column is three times as wide:

Project: SimpleColorScroll | **File:** MainPage.xaml (excerpt)

```
<Grid Background="{StaticResource ApplicationPageBackgroundThemeBrush}">
    <Grid.ColumnDefinitions>
        <ColumnDefinition Width="*" />
        <ColumnDefinition Width="*" />
        <ColumnDefinition Width="*" />
        <ColumnDefinition Width="3*" />
    </Grid.ColumnDefinitions>

    <Grid.RowDefinitions>
        <RowDefinition Height="Auto" />
        <RowDefinition Height="*" />
        <RowDefinition Height="Auto" />
    </Grid.RowDefinitions>

    ...

</Grid>
```

The remainder of the XAML file instantiates 10 children of the *Grid*. Each one has both *Grid.Row* and *Grid.Column* attached properties set, although these aren't necessary for values of 0. When specifying attributes of *Grid* children, I tend to put these attached properties early but after at least one attribute (such as a *Name* or *Text*) that provides a quick visual identification of the element:

Project: SimpleColorScroll | **File:** MainPage.xaml (excerpt)

```
<Grid Background="{StaticResource ApplicationPageBackgroundThemeBrush}">

    ...

    <!-- Red -->
    <TextBlock Text="Red"
               Grid.Column="0"
               Grid.Row="0"
               Foreground="Red" />

    <Slider Name="redSlider"
            Grid.Column="0"
            Grid.Row="1"
            Foreground="Red"
            ValueChanged="OnSliderValueChanged" />

    <TextBlock Name="redValue"
               Grid.Column="0"
               Grid.Row="2"
               Foreground="Red" />
```

```
    <!-- Green -->
    <TextBlock Text="Green"
               Grid.Column="1"
               Grid.Row="0"
               Foreground="Green" />

    <Slider Name="greenSlider"
            Grid.Column="1"
            Grid.Row="1"
            Foreground="Green"
            ValueChanged="OnSliderValueChanged" />

    <TextBlock Name="greenValue"
               Grid.Column="1"
               Grid.Row="2"
               Foreground="Green" />

    <!-- Blue -->
    <TextBlock Text="Blue"
               Grid.Column="2"
               Grid.Row="0"
               Foreground="Blue" />

    <Slider Name="blueSlider"
            Grid.Column="2"
            Grid.Row="1"
            Foreground="Blue"
            ValueChanged="OnSliderValueChanged" />

    <TextBlock Name="blueValue"
               Grid.Column="2"
               Grid.Row="2"
               Foreground="Blue" />

    <!-- Result -->
    <Rectangle Grid.Column="3"
               Grid.Row="0"
               Grid.RowSpan="3">
        <Rectangle.Fill>
            <SolidColorBrush x:Name="brushResult"
                             Color="Black" />
        </Rectangle.Fill>
    </Rectangle>
</Grid>
```

Notice that all the *TextBlock* and *Slider* elements are given *Foreground* property assignments based on what color they represent.

The *Rectangle* at the bottom has the *Grid.RowSpan* attached property set to 3, indicating that it spans all three rows. The *SolidColorBrush* is set to *Black*, so that's consistent with the three initial *Slider* values. If you can't get everything initialized correctly in the XAML file, the constructor of the code-behind file (or the *Loaded* event) is usually the place to do it.

All three *Slider* controls have the same handler for the *ValueChanged* event. That's in the code-behind file:

Project: SimpleColorScroll | **File:** MainPage.xaml.cs (excerpt)

```
public sealed partial class MainPage : Page
{
    public MainPage()
    {
        this.InitializeComponent();
    }

    void OnSliderValueChanged(object sender, RangeBaseValueChangedEventArgs args)
    {
        byte r = (byte)redSlider.Value;
        byte g = (byte)greenSlider.Value;
        byte b = (byte)blueSlider.Value;

        redValue.Text = r.ToString("X2");
        greenValue.Text = g.ToString("X2");
        blueValue.Text = b.ToString("X2");

        brushResult.Color = Color.FromArgb(255, r, g, b);
    }
}
```

The event handler could obtain the actual *Slider* firing the event by casting the *sender* argument and obtain the new value from the *RangeBaseValueChangedEventArgs* object. But regardless of which *Slider* actually changes value, the event handler needs to create a whole new *Color* value, and that requires all three values. The only somewhat wasteful part of this code is setting all three text values when only one is changing, but fixing that would require accessing the *TextBlock* associated with the particular *Slider* firing the event.

Here's one of 16,777,216 possible results:

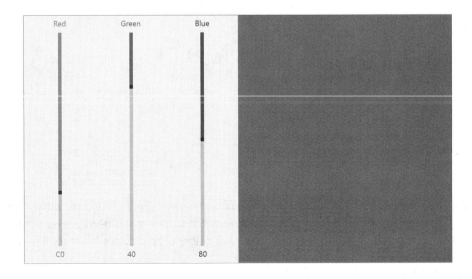

Orientation and Aspect Ratios

If you run SimpleColorScroll on a tablet and rotate it into portrait mode, the layout starts to look a little funny, and even if you run it in landscape mode, a snap view might cause some of the text labels to overlap. It might make sense to add some logic in the code-behind file that adjusts the layout based on the orientation or aspect ratio of the display.

Adjusting the layout with this particular program becomes much easier if the single *Grid* is split in two, one nested in the other. The inner *Grid* has three rows and three columns for the *TextBlock* elements and *Slider* controls. The outer *Grid* has just two children: the inner *Grid* and the *Rectangle*. In landscape mode, the outer *Grid* has two columns; in portrait mode, it has two rows.

The XAML file for the OrientableColorScroll project has the same *Style* definitions as SimpleColorScroll. The outer *Grid* is shown here:

Project: OrientableColorScroll | File: MainPage.xaml (excerpt)

```
<Grid Background="{StaticResource ApplicationPageBackgroundThemeBrush}"
      SizeChanged="OnGridSizeChanged">

    <Grid.ColumnDefinitions>
        <ColumnDefinition Width="*" />
        <ColumnDefinition x:Name="secondColDef" Width="*" />
    </Grid.ColumnDefinitions>

    <Grid.RowDefinitions>
        <RowDefinition Height="*" />
        <RowDefinition x:Name="secondRowDef" Height="0" />
    </Grid.RowDefinitions>

    <Grid Grid.Row="0"
          Grid.Column="0">

    ...

    </Grid>

    <!-- Result -->
    <Rectangle Name="rectangleResult"
               Grid.Column="1"
               Grid.Row="0">
        <Rectangle.Fill>
            <SolidColorBrush x:Name="brushResult"
                             Color="Black" />
        </Rectangle.Fill>
    </Rectangle>
</Grid>
```

The outer *Grid* has its *RowDefinitions* and *ColumnDefinitions* collections initialized for either contingency: two columns or two rows. In each collection, the second item has been given a name so that it can be accessed from code. The second row has a height of zero, so the initial configuration assumes a landscape mode.

The inner *Grid* (containing the *TextBlock* elements and *Slider* controls) is always in either the first column or first row:

```
<Grid Grid.Row="0"
      Grid.Column="0">

    ...

</Grid>
```

Setting *Grid.Row* and *Grid.Column* attributes on a *Grid* tag always looks a little peculiar to me. They refer not to the rows and columns of this *Grid* but to the rows and columns of the parent *Grid*. The default values of these attached properties are both zero, so these particular attribute settings aren't actually required.

The *Rectangle* is initially in the second column and first row:

```
<Rectangle Name="rectangleResult"
           Grid.Column="1"
           Grid.Row="0">
    ...
</Rectangle>
```

In this version of the program the *Rectangle* has a name, so these attached properties can be changed from the code-behind file. This is done in the *SizeChanged* event handler set on the outer *Grid*:

Project: OrientableColorScroll | File: MainPage.xaml.cs (excerpt)

```
void OnGridSizeChanged(object sender, SizeChangedEventArgs args)
{
    // Landscape mode
    if (args.NewSize.Width > args.NewSize.Height)
    {
        secondColDef.Width = new GridLength(1, GridUnitType.Star);
        secondRowDef.Height = new GridLength(0);

        Grid.SetColumn(rectangleResult, 1);
        Grid.SetRow(rectangleResult, 0);
    }
    // Portrait mode
    else
    {
        secondColDef.Width = new GridLength(0);
        secondRowDef.Height = new GridLength(1, GridUnitType.Star);

        Grid.SetColumn(rectangleResult, 0);
        Grid.SetRow(rectangleResult, 1);
    }
}
```

This code changes the second *RowDefinition* and *ColumnDefinition* in the outer *Grid*. These both apply to the *Rectangle*, which has its column and row attached properties changed so that it finds itself in the second column (for portrait mode) or second row (for landscape mode).

Here's the program running in a snap mode:

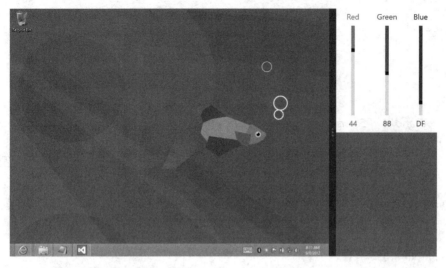

I'll have more to say about adjusting to snap modes in Chapter 12, "Pages and Navigation."

Slider and the Formatted String Converter

In both ColorScroll programs so far, the *TextBlock* labels at the bottom show the current values of the *Slider* in hexadecimal. It's not necessary to provide these values from the code-behind file. It could be done with a data binding from the *Slider* to the *TextBlock*. The only thing that's required is a binding converter that can convert a double into a two-digit hexadecimal string.

It's disturbing to discover that the *FormattedStringConverter* class I described in Chapter 4, "Presentation with Panels," in connection with the WhatSizeWithBindingConverter project will *not* work in this case. You're welcome to try it out, but you'll discover (if you don't already know) that a hexadecimal formatting specification of "X2" can be used only with integral types and the *Value* property of the *Slider* is a *double*.

However, in this case it might make more sense to write a very short ad hoc binding converter, particularly when you realize it can be used for two purposes, as I'll discuss next.

Tooltips and Conversions

As you manipulate the *Slider* controls in either ColorScroll program, you've probably noticed something peculiar: The *Slider* has a built-in tooltip that shows the current value in a little box. That's a nice feature except that this tooltip shows the value in decimal but the program insists on displaying the current value in hexadecimal.

If you think it's great for the *Slider* value to be displayed in *both* decimal and hexadecimal, skip to the next section. If you'd prefer that the two values be consistent—and that they both display the value in hexadecimal—you'll be pleased to know that the *Slider* defines a *ThumbToolTipValueConverter* property that lets you supply a class that performs the formatting you want. This class must implement the *IValueConverter* interface, which is the same interface you implement to write binding converters.

However, a converter class for the *ThumbToolTipValueConverter* property can't be as sophisticated as a converter class for a data binding because you don't have the option of supplying a parameter for the conversion. On the plus side, the converter class can be very simple and do only what is required for the particular case.

The ColorScrollWithValueConverter project defines a converter dedicated to converting a *double* to a two-character string indicating the value in hexadecimal. The name of this class is almost longer than the actual code:

Project: ColorScrollWithValueConverter | **File:** DoubleToStringHexByteConverter.cs

```
using System;
using Windows.UI.Xaml.Data;

namespace ColorScrollWithValueConverter
{
    public class DoubleToStringHexByteConverter : IValueConverter
    {
        public object Convert(object value, Type targetType, object parameter, string language)
        {
            return ((int)(double)value).ToString("X2");
        }
        public object ConvertBack(object value, Type targetType, object parameter, string lang)
        {
            return value;
        }
    }
}
```

This converter is suitable not only for formatting the tooltip value, but also for a binding converter used to display the value of the *Slider* in the *TextBlock*. The following variation of the ColorScroll program shows how it's done. (To keep things simple, this version doesn't adjust for aspect ratio.) The XAML file instantiates the converter in the *Resources* section:

Project: ColorScrollWithValueConverter | **File:** MainPage.xaml (excerpt)

```
<Page.Resources>
    <local:DoubleToStringHexByteConverter x:Key="hexConverter" />
    ...
</Page.Resources>
```

Here's the first set of *TextBlock* labels and *Slider*. The *hexConverter* resource is referenced both by a simple *StaticResource* markup extension by the *Slider*, and by the *Binding* on the *TextBlock*, which I've broken into three lines for easy readability:

Project: ColorScrollWithValueConverter | File: MainPage.xaml (excerpt)

```
<!-- Red -->
<TextBlock Text="Red"
           Grid.Column="0"
           Grid.Row="0"
           Foreground="Red" />

<Slider Name="redSlider"
        Grid.Column="0"
        Grid.Row="1"
        ThumbToolTipValueConverter="{StaticResource hexConverter}"
        Foreground="Red"
        ValueChanged="OnSliderValueChanged" />

<TextBlock Text="{Binding ElementName=redSlider,
                          Path=Value,
                          Converter={StaticResource hexConverter}}"
           Grid.Column="0"
           Grid.Row="2"
           Foreground="Red" />
```

Because the *ValueChanged* handler no longer needs to update the *TextBlock* labels, that code has been removed, but the handler still needs to calculate a new color:

Project: ColorScrollWithValueConverter | File: MainPage.xaml.cs (excerpt)

```
void OnSliderValueChanged(object sender, RangeBaseValueChangedEventArgs args)
{
    byte r = (byte)redSlider.Value;
    byte g = (byte)greenSlider.Value;
    byte b = (byte)blueSlider.Value;

    brushResult.Color = Color.FromArgb(255, r, g, b);
}
```

It's possible to remove the *ThumbToolTipValueConverter* from the individual *Slider* tags and move it to the *Slider* style:

```
<Style TargetType="Slider">
    <Setter Property="Orientation" Value="Vertical" />
    <Setter Property="IsDirectionReversed" Value="True" />
    <Setter Property="Maximum" Value="255" />
    <Setter Property="HorizontalAlignment" Value="Center" />
    <Setter Property="ThumbToolTipValueConverter" Value="{StaticResource hexConverter}" />
</Style>
```

Is it possible to go another step with the data bindings and eliminate the *ValueChanged* handler entirely? That would surely be feasible if it were possible to establish bindings on the individual properties of *Color*, like so:

```
<!-- Doesn't work! -->
<Rectangle Grid.Column="3"
           Grid.Row="0"
           Grid.RowSpan="3">
    <Rectangle.Fill>
        <SolidColorBrush>
            <SolidColorBrush.Color>
                <Color A="255"
                       R="{Binding ElementName=redSlider, Path=Value}"
                       G="{Binding ElementName=greenSlider, Path=Value}"
                       B="{Binding ElementName=blueSlider, Path=Value}" />
            </SolidColorBrush.Color>
        </SolidColorBrush>
    </Rectangle.Fill>
</Rectangle>
```

The big problem with this markup is that binding targets need to be backed by dependency properties, and the properties of *Color* are not. They can't be, because dependency properties can be implemented only in a class that derives from *DependencyObject* and *Color* isn't a class at all. It's a structure.

The *Color* property of *SolidColorBrush* is backed by a dependency property, and that could be the target of a data binding. However, in this program the *Color* property needs three values to be computed, and the Windows Runtime does not support data bindings with multiple sources.

The solution is to have a separate class devoted to the job of creating a *Color* object from red, green, and blue values, and I'll show you how to do it in Chapter 6, "WinRT and MVVM."

Sketching with Sliders

I'm not going to show you a screen shot of the next program. It's called SliderSketch, and it's a *Slider* version of a popular toy invented about 50 years ago. The user of SliderSketch must skillfully manipulate a horizontal *Slider* and a vertical *Slider* in tandem to control a conceptual stylus that progressively extends a continuous polyline. I'm not going to show you a screen shot because the program is very difficult to use, and I've never managed to get beyond the baby stage.

The XAML file defines a 2-by-2 *Grid*, but the screen is dominated by one cell containing a large *Border* and a *Polyline*. A vertical *Slider* is at the far left, and a horizontal *Slider* sits at the bottom. The cell in the lower-left corner is empty:

Project: SliderSketch | **File:** MainPage.xaml (excerpt)

```
<Grid Background="{StaticResource ApplicationPageBackgroundThemeBrush}">
    <Grid.RowDefinitions>
        <RowDefinition Height="*" />
        <RowDefinition Height="Auto" />
    </Grid.RowDefinitions>
```

```xml
    <Grid.ColumnDefinitions>
        <ColumnDefinition Width="Auto" />
        <ColumnDefinition Width="*" />
    </Grid.ColumnDefinitions>

    <Slider Name="ySlider"
            Grid.Row="0"
            Grid.Column="0"
            Orientation="Vertical"
            IsDirectionReversed="True"
            Margin="0 18"
            ValueChanged="OnSliderValueChanged" />

    <Slider Name="xSlider"
            Grid.Row="1"
            Grid.Column="1"
            Margin="18 0"
            ValueChanged="OnSliderValueChanged" />

    <Border Grid.Row="0"
            Grid.Column="1"
            BorderBrush="{StaticResource ApplicationForegroundThemeBrush}"
            BorderThickness="3 0 0 3"
            Background="#C0C0C0"
            Padding="24"
            SizeChanged="OnBorderSizeChanged">

        <Polyline Name="polyline"
                  Stroke="#404040"
                  StrokeThickness="3"
                  Points="0 0" />
    </Border>
</Grid>
```

It is very common for a *Grid* to define rows and columns at the edges using *Auto* and then make the whole interior as large as possible with a star specification. The content at the edges is effectively docked. Windows 8 has no *DockPanel*, but it's easy to mimic with *Grid*.

The *Margin* properties on the *Slider* controls were developed based on experimentation. For the program to work intuitively, the range of *Slider* values should be set equal to the number of pixels between the minimum and maximum positions, and the *Slider* thumbs should be approximately even with the pixel for that value. The calculation of the *Minimum* and *Maximum* values for each *Slider* occurs when the size of the display area changes:

Project: SliderSketch | File: MainPage.xaml.cs (excerpt)

```csharp
public sealed partial class MainPage : Page
{
    public MainPage()
    {
        this.InitializeComponent();
    }

    void OnBorderSizeChanged(object sender, SizeChangedEventArgs args)
```

```
    {
        Border border = sender as Border;
        xSlider.Maximum = args.NewSize.Width - border.Padding.Left
                                             - border.Padding.Right
                                             - polyline.StrokeThickness;

        ySlider.Maximum = args.NewSize.Height - border.Padding.Top
                                              - border.Padding.Bottom
                                              - polyline.StrokeThickness;
    }

    void OnSliderValueChanged(object sender, RangeBaseValueChangedEventArgs args)
    {
        polyline.Points.Add(new Point(xSlider.Value, ySlider.Value));
    }
}
```

After all that, it's really astonishing to see the actual "drawing" method down at the bottom: just a single line of code that adds a new *Point* to a *Polyline*.

But don't try turning your tablet upside down and shaking it to start anew. I haven't defined an erase function just yet.

The Varieties of Button Experience

The Windows Runtime supports several buttons that derive from the *ButtonBase* class:

Object
  DependencyObject
    UIElement
      FrameworkElement
        Control
          ContentControl
            ButtonBase
              Button
                HyperlinkButton
              RepeatButton
              ToggleButton
                CheckBox
                RadioButton

The ButtonVarieties program demonstrates the default appearances and functionality of all these buttons:

Project: ButtonVarieties | File: MainPage.xaml (excerpt)

```xaml
<Grid Background="{StaticResource ApplicationPageBackgroundThemeBrush}">
    <StackPanel>
        <Button Content="Just a plain old Button" />
        <HyperlinkButton Content="HyperlinkButton" />
```

```
        <RepeatButton Content="RepeatButton" />
        <ToggleButton Content="ToggleButton" />
        <CheckBox Content="CheckBox" />

        <RadioButton Content="RadioButton #1" />
        <RadioButton>RadioButton #2</RadioButton>
        <RadioButton>
            <RadioButton.Content>
                RadioButton #3
            </RadioButton.Content>
        </RadioButton>
        <RadioButton>
            <RadioButton.Content>
                <TextBlock Text="RadioButton #4" />
            </RadioButton.Content>
        </RadioButton>

        <ToggleSwitch />
    </StackPanel>
</Grid>
```

I've included four *RadioButton* instances, all with different approaches to setting the *Content* property, and they're all basically equivalent:

If you don't like the look of any of these, keep in mind that you can entirely redesign them with a *ControlTemplate* that I'll explore in Chapter 11.

Like all *FrameworkElement* derivatives, the default values of the *HorizontalAlignment* and *VerticalAlignment* properties are *Stretch*. However, by the time the button is loaded, the *HorizontalAlignment* property has been set to *Left*, the *VerticalAlignment* is *Center*, and a nonzero *Padding* has also been set. Although the *Margin* property is zero, the visuals contain a little built-in margin that surrounds the *Border*.

ButtonBase defines the *Click* event, which is fired when a finger, mouse, or stylus presses the control and then releases, but that behavior can be altered with the *ClickMode* property. Alternatively, a program can be notified that the button has been clicked through a command interface that I'll discuss in Chapter 6.

The classic button is *Button*. There's nothing really special about *HyperlinkButton* except that it looks different as a result of a different template. *RepeatButton* generates a series of *Click* events if held down for a moment; this is mostly intended for the repeat behavior of the *ScrollBar*.

Each click of the *ToggleButton* toggles it on and off. The screen shot shows the on state. *CheckBox* defines nothing public on its own; it simply inherits all the functionality of *ToggleButton* and achieves a different look with a template.

ToggleButton defines an *IsChecked* property to indicate the current state, as well as *Checked* and *Unchecked* events to signal when changing to the on or off state. In general, you'll want to install handlers for both these events, but you can share one handler for the job.

The *IsChecked* property of *ToggleButton* is not a *bool*. It is a *Nullable<bool>*, which means that it can have a value of *null*. This oddity is to accommodate toggle buttons that have a third "indeterminate" state. The classic example is a *CheckBox* labeled "Bold" in a word-processing program: If the selected text is bold, the box should be checked. If the selected text is not bold, it should be unchecked. If the selected text contains some bold and some nonbold, however, the *CheckBox* should show an indeterminate state. You'll need to set the *IsThreeState* property to *true* to enable this feature, and you'll want to install a handler for the *Indeterminate* event. *ToggleButton* does not have a unique appearance for the indeterminate state; *CheckBox* displays a little box rather than a checkmark.

With all that said, you might want to gravitate toward the *ToggleSwitch* control for your toggling needs because it's specifically designed for touch in Windows 8 applications. Although *ToggleSwitch* does not derive from *ButtonBase*, I've included one anyway at the bottom of the list. As you can see, it provides default labels of "Off" and "On", but you can change those. A header is also available, as you'll discover in Chapter 8, "App Bars and Popups."

The *RadioButton* is a special form of *ToggleButton* for selecting one item from a collection of mutually exclusive options. The name of the control comes from old car radios with buttons for preselected stations: Press a button, and the previously pressed button pops out. Similarly, when a *RadioButton* control is checked, it unchecks all other sibling *RadioButton* controls. The only thing you need to do is make them all children of the same panel. (Watch out: If you put a *RadioButton* in a *Border*, it is no longer a sibling with any other *RadioButton*. Use a template if you need a *Border* in the visuals of a *RadioButton*.) If you prefer to separate the *RadioButton* controls into multiple mutually exclusive groups within the same panel, a *GroupName* property is available for that purpose.

The *Control* class defines a *Foreground* property, many font-related properties, and several properties associated with *Border*, and setting these properties will change button appearance. For example, suppose you initialize a *Button* like so:

```
<Button Content="Not just a plain old Button anymore"
        Background="Yellow"
        BorderBrush="Red"
        BorderThickness="12"
        Foreground="Blue"
        FontSize="48"
        FontStyle="Italic" />
```

Now it looks like this:

However, certain visual characteristics are still governed by the template. For example, when you pass the mouse over this button or press it, the yellow background momentarily disappears and the button background changes to standard colors. Also, although you can change the *Border* color and thickness, you can't give it rounded corners.

ButtonBase derives from *ContentControl*, which defines a property named *Content*. Although the *Content* property is commonly set to text, it can be set to an *Image* or a panel. This is obviously very powerful. For example, here's how a *Button* can contain a bitmap and a caption for the bitmap:

```
<Button>
    <StackPanel>
        <Image Source="http://www.charlespetzold.com/pw6/PetzoldJersey.jpg"
               Width="100" />
        <TextBlock Text="Figure 1"
                   HorizontalAlignment="Center" />
    </StackPanel>
</Button>
```

In Chapter 11, I'll show you how the *Content* property can be set to virtually any object and how you can supply a template to display that object in a desirable way.

Let's make a simple telephone-like keypad. The keys are *Button* controls, and the telephone number that you type is displayed in a *TextBlock*.

In the following XAML file, the keypad is enclosed in a *Grid* that is given a *HorizontalAlignment* and *VerticalAlignment* of *Center* so that it sits in the center of the screen. Regardless of the size of this keypad and the contents of the buttons, it should have 12 buttons of exactly the same size. I handled the width and the height of these buttons in two different ways. A width of 288 (that is, 3 inches) is imposed on the keyboard *Grid* itself. I wanted a specific width because I realized that a user could type many numbers, and I didn't want the width of the keypad to expand to accommodate an extra-wide *TextBlock*. The *Height* of each *Button*, however, is specified in an implicit style:

Project: SimpleKeypad | File: MainPage.xaml (excerpt)

```
<Grid Background="{StaticResource ApplicationPageBackgroundThemeBrush}">

    <Grid HorizontalAlignment="Center"
          VerticalAlignment="Center"
          Width="288">

        <Grid.Resources>
            <Style TargetType="Button">
                <Setter Property="ClickMode" Value="Press" />
                <Setter Property="HorizontalAlignment" Value="Stretch" />
                <Setter Property="Height" Value="72" />
                <Setter Property="FontSize" Value="36" />
            </Style>
        </Grid.Resources>

        <Grid.RowDefinitions>
            <RowDefinition Height="Auto" />
            <RowDefinition Height="Auto" />
            <RowDefinition Height="Auto" />
            <RowDefinition Height="Auto" />
            <RowDefinition Height="Auto" />
        </Grid.RowDefinitions>

        <Grid.ColumnDefinitions>
            <ColumnDefinition Width="*" />
            <ColumnDefinition Width="*" />
            <ColumnDefinition Width="*" />
        </Grid.ColumnDefinitions>

        <Grid Grid.Row="0" Grid.Column="0" Grid.ColumnSpan="3">
            <Grid.ColumnDefinitions>
                <ColumnDefinition Width="*" />
                <ColumnDefinition Width="Auto" />
            </Grid.ColumnDefinitions>
```

```xaml
        <Border Grid.Column="0"
                HorizontalAlignment="Left">

            <TextBlock Name="resultText"
                       HorizontalAlignment="Right"
                       VerticalAlignment="Center"
                       FontSize="24" />
        </Border>

        <Button Name="deleteButton"
                Content="&#x21E6;"
                Grid.Column="1"
                IsEnabled="False"
                FontFamily="Segoe Symbol"
                HorizontalAlignment="Left"
                Padding="0"
                BorderThickness="0"
                Click="OnDeleteButtonClick" />
    </Grid>

    <Button Content="1"
            Grid.Row="1" Grid.Column="0"
            Click="OnCharButtonClick" />

    <Button Content="2"
            Grid.Row="1" Grid.Column="1"
            Click="OnCharButtonClick" />

    <Button Content="3"
            Grid.Row="1" Grid.Column="2"
            Click="OnCharButtonClick" />

    <Button Content="4"
            Grid.Row="2" Grid.Column="0"
            Click="OnCharButtonClick" />

    <Button Content="5"
            Grid.Row="2" Grid.Column="1"
            Click="OnCharButtonClick" />

    <Button Content="6"
            Grid.Row="2" Grid.Column="2"
            Click="OnCharButtonClick" />

    <Button Content="7"
            Grid.Row="3" Grid.Column="0"
            Click="OnCharButtonClick" />

    <Button Content="8"
            Grid.Row="3" Grid.Column="1"
            Click="OnCharButtonClick" />
```

```
<Button Content="9"
        Grid.Row="3" Grid.Column="2"
        Click="OnCharButtonClick" />

<Button Content="*"
        Grid.Row="4" Grid.Column="0"
        Click="OnCharButtonClick" />

<Button Content="0"
        Grid.Row="4" Grid.Column="1"
        Click="OnCharButtonClick" />

<Button Content="#"
        Grid.Row="4" Grid.Column="2"
        Click="OnCharButtonClick" />
    </Grid>
</Grid>
```

The hard part is the first row. This must accommodate a *TextBlock* to show the typed result as well as a delete button. I didn't want a very large delete button, so I made the whole first row of the *Grid* a separate *Grid* just for these two items. The attributes of the delete button override many of the properties set in the implicit style. Notice that the delete button is initially disabled. It should be enabled only when there are characters to delete.

The *TextBlock* was a little tricky. I wanted it to be left-justified during normal typing, but if the string got too long to be displayed, I wanted the *TextBlock* to be clipped at the left, not at the right. My solution was to enclose the *TextBlock* in a *Border*:

```
<Border Grid.Column="0"
        HorizontalAlignment="Left">

    <TextBlock Name="resultText"
            HorizontalAlignment="Right"
            VerticalAlignment="Center"
            FontSize="24" />
</Border>
```

The *Border* has a fixed limit to its width: It cannot get wider than the width of the overall *Grid* minus the width of the delete button. But within that area the *Border* is aligned to the left. It is sized to fit the *TextBlock*, so despite its *HorizontalAlignment* setting, the *TextBlock* is also positioned at the left. As more characters are typed, the *TextBlock* gets wider until it becomes wider than the *Border*. At that point, the *HorizontalAlignment* setting of *Right* comes into play and the left part of *TextBlock* is what gets clipped.

After that top row, everything else is smooth sailing. The implicit style helps keep the markup for each of the 12 numeric and symbol buttons as small as possible.

The code-behind file handles the *Click* event from the delete button and has a shared handler for the other 12 buttons:

Project: SimpleKeypad | File: MainPage.xaml.cs (excerpt)

```
public sealed partial class MainPage : Page
{
    string inputString = "";
    char[] specialChars = { '*', '#' };

    public MainPage()
    {
        this.InitializeComponent();
    }

    void OnCharButtonClick(object sender, RoutedEventArgs args)
    {
        Button btn = sender as Button;
        inputString += btn.Content as string;
        FormatText();
    }

    void OnDeleteButtonClick(object sender, RoutedEventArgs args)
    {
        inputString = inputString.Substring(0, inputString.Length - 1);
        FormatText();
    }

    void FormatText()
    {
        bool hasNonNumbers = inputString.IndexOfAny(specialChars) != -1;

        if (hasNonNumbers || inputString.Length < 4 || inputString.Length > 10)
            resultText.Text = inputString;

        else if (inputString.Length < 8)
            resultText.Text = String.Format("{0}-{1}", inputString.Substring(0, 3),
                                            inputString.Substring(3));

        else
            resultText.Text = String.Format("({0}) {1}-{2}", inputString.Substring(0, 3),
                                            inputString.Substring(3, 3),
                                            inputString.Substring(6));

        deleteButton.IsEnabled = inputString.Length > 0;
    }
}
```

The handler for the delete button removes a character from the *inputString* field, and the other handler adds a character. Each handler then calls *FormatText*, which attempts to format the string as a telephone number. At the end of the method, the delete button is enabled only if the input string contains characters.

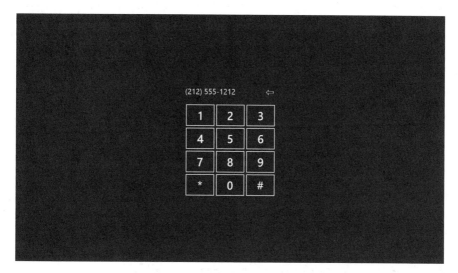

The *OnCharButtonClick* event handler uses the *Content* property of the button being pressed to determine which character to add to the string. Such an easy equivalence between the *Content* visuals of the button and the functionality of the button isn't always available. Sometimes sharing an event handler among multiple controls requires that the handler extract more information from the button being clicked. *FrameworkElement* defines a *Tag* property of type *object* specifically for this purpose. You can set *Tag* to an identifying string or object in the XAML file and check it in the event handler, as I'll demonstrate later in this chapter with *RadioButton*.

Defining Dependency Properties

Perhaps you're writing an application where you want all the *Button* controls to display text with a gradient brush. Of course, you can simply define the *Foreground* property of each *Button* to be a *LinearGradientBrush*, but the markup might start becoming a bit overwhelming. You could then try a *Style* with the *Foreground* property set to a *LinearGradientBrush*, but then each *Button* shares the same *LinearGradientBrush* with the same gradient colors, and perhaps you want more flexibility than that.

What you really want is a *Button* with two properties named *Color1* and *Color2* that you can set to the gradient colors. That sounds like a custom control. It's a class that derives from *Button* that creates a *LinearGradientBrush* in its constructor and defines *Color1* and *Color2* properties to control this gradient.

Can these *Color1* and *Color2* properties be just plain old .NET properties with *set* and *get* accessors? Yes, they can. However, defining the properties like that will limit them in some crucial ways. Such properties cannot be the targets of styles, bindings, or animations. Only dependency properties can do all that.

Dependency properties have a bit more overhead than regular properties, but learning how to define dependency properties in your own classes is an important skill. In a new project, begin by adding a new item to the project and select Class from the list. Give it a name of *GradientButton*, and in the file, make the class public and derived from *Button*:

```
public class GradientButton : Button
{

}
```

Now let's fill up that class. You will need to add some *using* directives along the way.

The two new properties are named *Color1* and *Color2* of type *Color*. These two properties require two dependency properties of type *DependencyProperty* named *Color1Property* and *Color2Property*. They must be public and static but settable only from within the class:

```
public static DependencyProperty Color1Property { private set; get; }
public static DependencyProperty Color2Property { private set; get; }
```

These *DependencyProperty* objects can be created in the static constructor. The *DependencyProperty* class defines a static method named *Register* for the job of creating *DependencyProperty* objects:

```
static GradientButton()
{
    Color1Property =
        DependencyProperty.Register("Color1",
            typeof(Color),
            typeof(GradientButton),
            new PropertyMetadata(Colors.White, OnColorChanged));

    Color2Property =
        DependencyProperty.Register("Color2",
            typeof(Color),
            typeof(GradientButton),
            new PropertyMetadata(Colors.Black, OnColorChanged));
}
```

A slightly different static method named *DependencyProperty.RegisterAttached* is used to create attached properties.

The first argument to *DependencyProperty.Register* is the text name of the property. This is used sometimes by the XAML parsers. The second argument is the type of the property. The third argument is the type of the class that is registering this dependency property.

The fourth argument is an object of type *PropertyMetadata*. The constructor comes in two versions. In one version, all you need to specify is a default value of the property. In the other, you also specify a method that is called when the property changes. This method will not be called if the property happens to be set to the same value it already has.

The default value you specify as the first argument to the *PropertyMetadata* constructor must match the type indicated in the second argument or a run-time exception will result. This is not as easy as it sounds. For example, it is very common for programmers to supply a default value of 0 for a property of type *double*. During compilation, the 0 is assumed to be an integer, so at run time a type mismatch is discovered and an exception is thrown. If you're defining a dependency property of type *double*, give it a default value of 0.0 so that the compiler knows the correct data type of this argument.

An alternative approach is to define *DependencyProperty* objects as private static fields and then return those objects from the public static properties:

```
static readonly DependencyProperty color1Property =
        DependencyProperty.Register("Color1",
                typeof(Color),
                typeof(GradientButton),
                new PropertyMetadata(Colors.White, OnColorChanged));

static readonly DependencyProperty color2Property =
        DependencyProperty.Register("Color2",
                typeof(Color),
                typeof(GradientButton),
                new PropertyMetadata(Colors.Black, OnColorChanged));

public static DependencyProperty Color1Property
{
    get { return color1Property; }
}

public static DependencyProperty Color2Property
{
    get { return color2Property; }
}
```

The explicit static constructor isn't required. It's also possible to do it WPF or Silverlight style, where you don't have public static properties at all but simply define the static fields as public. Note that the fields are now named *Color1Property* and *Color2Property*:

```
public static readonly DependencyProperty Color1Property =
        DependencyProperty.Register("Color1",
                typeof(Color),
                typeof(GradientButton),
                new PropertyMetadata(Colors.White, OnColorChanged));

public static readonly DependencyProperty Color2Property =
        DependencyProperty.Register("Color2",
                typeof(Color),
                typeof(GradientButton),
                new PropertyMetadata(Colors.Black, OnColorChanged));
```

This approach works with Windows 8, but I tend not to use it because all the public static *DependencyProperty* objects defined by the standard Windows Runtime controls are properties rather than fields.

Regardless of how you define the public static *DependencyProperty* objects, the *GradientButton* class also needs regular .NET property definitions of *Color1* and *Color2*. These properties are always of a very specific form:

```
public Color Color1
{
    set { SetValue(Color1Property, value); }
    get { return (Color)GetValue(Color1Property); }
}

public Color Color2
{
    set { SetValue(Color2Property, value); }
    get { return (Color)GetValue(Color2Property); }
}
```

The *set* accessor always calls *SetValue* (inherited from the *DependencyObject* class), referencing the dependency property object, and the *get* accessor always calls *GetValue* and casts the return value to the proper type for the property. You can make the *set* accessor *protected* or *private* if you don't want the property being set from outside the class.

In my *GradientButton* control, I want the *Foreground* property to be a *LinearGradientBrush* and I want the *Color1* and *Color2* properties to be the colors of the two *GradientStop* objects. Two *GradientStop* objects are thus defined as fields:

```
GradientStop gradientStop1, gradientStop2;
```

The regular instance constructor of the class creates those objects as well as the *LinearGradientBrush* to set it to the *Foreground* property:

```
public GradientButton()
{
    gradientStop1 = new GradientStop
    {
        Offset = 0,
        Color = this.Color1
    };

    gradientStop2 = new GradientStop
    {
        Offset = 1,
        Color = this.Color2
    };

    LinearGradientBrush brush = new LinearGradientBrush();
    brush.GradientStops.Add(gradientStop1);
    brush.GradientStops.Add(gradientStop2);

    this.Foreground = brush;
}
```

Notice how the property initializers for the two *GradientStop* objects access the *Color1* and *Color2* properties. This is how the colors in the *LinearGradientBrush* are set to the default colors defined by the two dependency properties.

You'll recall that in the definition of the two dependency properties, a method named *OnColorChanged* was specified as the method to be called whenever either the *Color1* or *Color2* property changes value. Because this property-changed method is referenced in a static constructor, the method itself must also be static:

```
static void OnColorChanged(DependencyObject obj, DependencyPropertyChangedEventArgs args)
{

}
```

Now this is kind of weird, because the whole point of defining this *GradientButton* class is to use it multiple times in an application, and now we're defining a static property that is called whenever the *Color1* or *Color2* property in an instance of this class changes. How do you know to what instance this method call applies?

Easy: It's the first argument. That first argument to this *OnColorChanged* method is always a *GradientButton* object, and you can safely cast it to a *GradientButton* and then access fields and properties in the particular *GradientButton* instance.

What I like to do in the static property-changed method is call an instance method of the same name, passing to it the second argument:

```
static void OnColorChanged(DependencyObject obj, DependencyPropertyChangedEventArgs args)
{
    (obj as GradientButton).OnColorChanged(args);
}
void OnColorChanged(DependencyPropertyChangedEventArgs args)
{

}
```

This second method then does all the work accessing instance fields and properties of the class.

The *DependencyPropertyChangedEventArgs* object contains some useful information. The *Property* property is of type *DependencyProperty* and indicates the property that's been changed. In this example, the *Property* property will be either *Color1Property* or *Color2Property*. *DependencyPropertyChangedEventArgs* also has properties named *OldValue* and *NewValue* of type *object*.

In *GradientButton*, the property-changed handler sets the *Color* property of the appropriate *GradientStop* object from *NewValue*:

```
void OnColorChanged(DependencyPropertyChangedEventArgs args)
{
    if (args.Property == Color1Property)
        gradientStop1.Color = (Color)args.NewValue;

    if (args.Property == Color2Property)
        gradientStop2.Color = (Color)args.NewValue;
}
```

And that's it for *GradientButton*. The only job left to do is arrange all these pieces of the *GradientButton* class in the class in an order that makes sense to you. I like to put all fields at the top, static constructor next, static properties next, and then the instance constructor, instance properties, and all methods. Here's the complete *GradientButton* class from the DependencyProperties project:

Project: DependencyProperties | **File:** GradientButton.cs

```
using Windows.UI;
using Windows.UI.Xaml;
using Windows.UI.Xaml.Controls;
using Windows.UI.Xaml.Media;

namespace DependencyProperties
{
    public class GradientButton : Button
    {
        GradientStop gradientStop1, gradientStop2;

        static GradientButton()
        {
            Color1Property =
                DependencyProperty.Register("Color1",
                    typeof(Color),
                    typeof(GradientButton),
                    new PropertyMetadata(Colors.White, OnColorChanged));

            Color2Property =
                DependencyProperty.Register("Color2",
                    typeof(Color),
                    typeof(GradientButton),
                    new PropertyMetadata(Colors.Black, OnColorChanged));
        }

        public static DependencyProperty Color1Property { private set; get; }

        public static DependencyProperty Color2Property { private set; get; }

        public GradientButton()
        {
            gradientStop1 = new GradientStop
            {
                Offset = 0,
                Color = this.Color1
            };

            gradientStop2 = new GradientStop
            {
                Offset = 1,
                Color = this.Color2
            };
```

```
            LinearGradientBrush brush = new LinearGradientBrush();
            brush.GradientStops.Add(gradientStop1);
            brush.GradientStops.Add(gradientStop2);

            this.Foreground = brush;
        }

        public Color Color1
        {
            set { SetValue(Color1Property, value); }
            get { return (Color)GetValue(Color1Property); }
        }

        public Color Color2
        {
            set { SetValue(Color2Property, value); }
            get { return (Color)GetValue(Color2Property); }
        }

        static void OnColorChanged(DependencyObject obj,
                            DependencyPropertyChangedEventArgs args)
        {
            (obj as GradientButton).OnColorChanged(args);
        }

        void OnColorChanged(DependencyPropertyChangedEventArgs args)
        {
            if (args.Property == Color1Property)
                gradientStop1.Color = (Color)args.NewValue;

            if (args.Property == Color2Property)
                gradientStop2.Color = (Color)args.NewValue;
        }
    }
}
```

There are some alternate ways of writing the property-changed handler. If you specify separate handlers for each property, you don't need to look at the *Property* property of the event arguments.

Another option: Rather than access the *NewValue* property, you can just get the value of the property from the class. For example:

```
gradientStop1.Color = this.Color1;
```

The *Color1* property has already been set to the new value by the time the property-changed handler is called.

Where are the actual values of the *Color1* and *Color2* properties stored? I suspect it's some kind of dictionary, perhaps optimized somewhat (one would hope) but otherwise inaccessible through the API. The state of these properties is managed by the operating system, and the only access to their values is through *SetValue* and *GetValue*.

The XAML file in this project defines a couple styles, one with *Setter* elements for *Color1* and *Color2*, and applies these styles to two instances of *GradientButton*. Any reference to *GradientButton* in this XAML file must be preceded by the *local* XML namespace that is associated with the *DependencyProperties* namespace in which *GradientButton* is defined. Notice the *local* prefix in both the *TargetType* of the *Style* and when the buttons are instantiated:

Project: DependencyProperties | **File:** MainPage.xaml (excerpt)

```
<Page ...
    xmlns:local="using:DependencyProperties"
    ... >

    <Page.Resources>
        <Style x:Key="baseButtonStyle" TargetType="local:GradientButton">
            <Setter Property="FontSize" Value="48" />
            <Setter Property="HorizontalAlignment" Value="Center" />
            <Setter Property="Margin" Value="0 12" />
        </Style>

        <Style x:Key="blueRedButtonStyle"
               TargetType="local:GradientButton"
               BasedOn="{StaticResource baseButtonStyle}">
            <Setter Property="Color1" Value="Blue" />
            <Setter Property="Color2" Value="Red" />
        </Style>
    </Page.Resources>

    <Grid Background="{StaticResource ApplicationPageBackgroundThemeBrush}">
        <StackPanel>
            <local:GradientButton Content="GradientButton #1"
                                  Style="{StaticResource baseButtonStyle}" />

            <local:GradientButton Content="GradientButton #2"
                                  Style="{StaticResource blueRedButtonStyle}" />

            <local:GradientButton Content="GradientButton #3"
                                  Style="{StaticResource baseButtonStyle}"
                                  Color1="Aqua"
                                  Color2="Lime" />
        </StackPanel>
    </Grid>
</Page>
```

The first one gets the default settings of *Color1* and *Color2*, the second one gets the settings defined in the *Style*, and the third gets local settings Here it is:

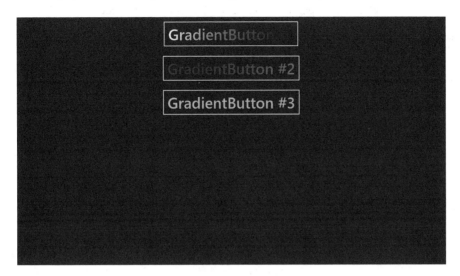

I want to show you an alternative way to create the *GradientButton* class that lets you define the *LinearGradientBrush* in XAML and eliminate the property-changed handlers. Interested?

In a separate project, to create the *GradientButton* class, rather than adding a new item and picking Class from the list, add a new item, pick User Control from the list, and give it a name of *GradientButton*. As usual you'll get a pair of files: GradientButton.xaml and GradientButton.xaml.cs. The *GradientButton* class derives from *UserControl*. Here's the class definition in the GradientButton.xaml.cs file:

```
public sealed partial class GradientButton : UserControl
{
    public GradientButton()
    {
        this.InitializeComponent();
    }
}
```

Change the base class from *UserControl* to *Button*:

```
public sealed partial class GradientButton : Button
{
    public GradientButton()
    {
        this.InitializeComponent();
    }
}
```

The body of this class will be very much like the first *GradientButton* class except the instance constructor doesn't do anything except call *InitializeComponent*. There are no property-changed handlers. Here's how it looks in the DependencyPropertiesWithBindings project:

Project: DependencyPropertiesWithBindings | **File:** GradientButton.xaml.cs

```
public sealed partial class GradientButton : Button
{
    static GradientButton()
    {
        Color1Property =
            DependencyProperty.Register("Color1",
                typeof(Color),
                typeof(GradientButton),
                new PropertyMetadata(Colors.White));

        Color2Property =
            DependencyProperty.Register("Color2",
                typeof(Color),
                typeof(GradientButton),
                new PropertyMetadata(Colors.Black));
    }

    public static DependencyProperty Color1Property { private set; get; }

    public static DependencyProperty Color2Property { private set; get; }

    public GradientButton()
    {
        this.InitializeComponent();
    }

    public Color Color1
    {
        set { SetValue(Color1Property, value); }
        get { return (Color)GetValue(Color1Property); }
    }

    public Color Color2
    {
        set { SetValue(Color2Property, value); }
        get { return (Color)GetValue(Color2Property); }
    }
}
```

When first created, the GradientButton.xaml file has a root element that indicates the class derives from *UserControl*:

```
<UserControl
    x:Class="DependencyPropertiesWithBindings.GradientButton" ... >
    ...
</UserControl>
```

Change that to *Button* as well:

```
<Button
    x:Class="DependencyPropertiesWithBindings.GradientButton" ... >
    ...
</Button>
```

Normally, when you put stuff between the root tags of a XAML file, you're implicitly setting the *Content* property. But in this case we don't want to set the *Content* property of the *Button*. We want to set the *Foreground* property of *GradientButton* to a *LinearGradientBrush*. This requires property-element tags of *Button.Foreground*. Here's the complete XAML file:

Project: DependencyPropertiesWithBindings | File: GradientButton.xaml

```
<Button
    x:Class="DependencyPropertiesWithBindings.GradientButton"
    xmlns="http://schemas.microsoft.com/winfx/2006/xaml/presentation"
    xmlns:x="http://schemas.microsoft.com/winfx/2006/xaml"
    Name="root">

    <Button.Foreground>
        <LinearGradientBrush>
            <GradientStop Offset="0"
                          Color="{Binding ElementName=root,
                                          Path=Color1}" />
            <GradientStop Offset="1"
                          Color="{Binding ElementName=root,
                                          Path=Color2}" />
        </LinearGradientBrush>
    </Button.Foreground>
</Button>
```

Notice the cool way that the *Color* properties of the *GradientStop* objects are set: The root element is given a name of "root" so that it can be the source of two data bindings referencing the custom dependency properties.

The MainPage.xaml file for this project is the same as the previous project, and the result is also the same.

RadioButton Tags

A group of *RadioButton* controls allows a user to choose between one of several mutually exclusive items. From the program's perspective, often it is convenient that each *RadioButton* in a particular group corresponds with a member of an enumeration and that the enumeration value be identifiable from the *RadioButton* object. This allows all the buttons in a group to share the same event handler.

The *Tag* property is ideal for this purpose. You can set *Tag* to anything you want to identify the control. For example, suppose you want to write a program that lets you experiment with the *StrokeStartLineCap*, *StrokeEndLineCap*, and *StrokeLineJoin* properties defined by the *Shape* class. When rendering thick lines, these properties govern the shape of the ends of the line and the shape where two lines join. The *StrokeStartLineCap* and *StrokeEndLineCap* properties are set to members of the *PenLineCap* enumeration type, and the *StrokeLineJoin* property is set to members of the *PenLineJoin* enumeration.

For example, one of the members of the *PenLineJoin* enumeration is *Bevel*. You might define a *RadioButton* to represent this option like so:

```
<RadioButton Content="Bevel join"
             Tag="Bevel"
             ... />
```

The problem is that "Bevel" is interpreted by the XAML parser as a string, so in the event handler in the code-behind file, you need to use *switch* and *case* to differentiate between the different strings or *Enum.TryParse* to convert the string into an actual *PenLineJoin.Bevel* value.

A better way of defining the *Tag* property involves breaking it out as a property element and explicitly indicating that it's being set to a value of type *PenLineJoin*:

```
<RadioButton Content="Bevel join"
             ... >
    <RadioButton.Tag>
        <PenLineJoin>Bevel</PenLineJoin>
    </RadioButton.Tag>
</RadioButton>
```

Of course, this is a bit wordy and cumbersome. Nevertheless, I've used this approach in the LineCapsAndJoins project. The XAML file defines three groups of *RadioButton* controls for the three *Shape* properties. Each group contains three or four controls corresponding to the appropriate enumeration members.

Project: LineCapsAndJoins | **File:** MainPage.xaml (excerpt)

```
<Grid Background="{StaticResource ApplicationPageBackgroundThemeBrush}">
    <Grid.RowDefinitions>
        <RowDefinition Height="*" />
        <RowDefinition Height="Auto" />
    </Grid.RowDefinitions>

    <Grid.ColumnDefinitions>
        <ColumnDefinition Width="Auto" />
        <ColumnDefinition Width="*" />
        <ColumnDefinition Width="Auto" />
    </Grid.ColumnDefinitions>

    <StackPanel Name="startLineCapPanel"
                Grid.Row="0" Grid.Column="0"
                Margin="24">

        <RadioButton Content="Flat start"
                     Checked="OnStartLineCapRadioButtonChecked">
            <RadioButton.Tag>
                <PenLineCap>Flat</PenLineCap>
            </RadioButton.Tag>
        </RadioButton>
```

```xml
    <RadioButton Content="Round start"
                 Checked="OnStartLineCapRadioButtonChecked">
        <RadioButton.Tag>
            <PenLineCap>Round</PenLineCap>
        </RadioButton.Tag>
    </RadioButton>

    <RadioButton Content="Square start"
                 Checked="OnStartLineCapRadioButtonChecked">
        <RadioButton.Tag>
            <PenLineCap>Square</PenLineCap>
        </RadioButton.Tag>
    </RadioButton>

    <RadioButton Content="Triangle start"
                 Checked="OnStartLineCapRadioButtonChecked">
        <RadioButton.Tag>
            <PenLineCap>Triangle</PenLineCap>
        </RadioButton.Tag>
    </RadioButton>
</StackPanel>

<StackPanel Name="endLineCapPanel"
            Grid.Row="0" Grid.Column="2"
            Margin="24">
    <RadioButton Content="Flat end"
                 Checked="OnEndLineCapRadioButtonChecked">
        <RadioButton.Tag>
            <PenLineCap>Flat</PenLineCap>
        </RadioButton.Tag>
    </RadioButton>

    <RadioButton Content="Round end"
                 Checked="OnEndLineCapRadioButtonChecked">
        <RadioButton.Tag>
            <PenLineCap>Round</PenLineCap>
        </RadioButton.Tag>
    </RadioButton>

    <RadioButton Content="Square end"
                 Checked="OnEndLineCapRadioButtonChecked">
        <RadioButton.Tag>
            <PenLineCap>Square</PenLineCap>
        </RadioButton.Tag>
    </RadioButton>

    <RadioButton Content="Triangle End"
                 Checked="OnEndLineCapRadioButtonChecked">
        <RadioButton.Tag>
            <PenLineCap>Triangle</PenLineCap>
        </RadioButton.Tag>
    </RadioButton>
</StackPanel>

<StackPanel Name="lineJoinPanel"
            Grid.Row="1" Grid.Column="1"
            HorizontalAlignment="Center"
            Margin="24">
```

```
                    <RadioButton Content="Bevel join"
                                 Checked="OnLineJoinRadioButtonChecked">
                        <RadioButton.Tag>
                            <PenLineJoin>Bevel</PenLineJoin>
                        </RadioButton.Tag>
                    </RadioButton>

                    <RadioButton Content="Miter join"
                                 Checked="OnLineJoinRadioButtonChecked">
                        <RadioButton.Tag>
                            <PenLineJoin>Miter</PenLineJoin>
                        </RadioButton.Tag>
                    </RadioButton>

                    <RadioButton Content="Round join"
                                 Checked="OnLineJoinRadioButtonChecked">
                        <RadioButton.Tag>
                            <PenLineJoin>Round</PenLineJoin>
                        </RadioButton.Tag>
                    </RadioButton>
                </StackPanel>

                <Polyline Name="polyline"
                          Grid.Row="0"
                          Grid.Column="1"
                          Points="0 0, 500 1000, 1000 0"
                          Stroke="{StaticResource ApplicationForegroundThemeBrush}"
                          StrokeThickness="100"
                          Stretch="Fill"
                          Margin="24" />
        </Grid>
```

Each of the three groups of *RadioButton* controls is in its own *StackPanel*, and all the controls within each *StackPanel* share the same handler for the *Checked* event.

The markup doesn't put any *RadioButton* in its checked state. This is the responsibility of the *Loaded* handler defined in the constructor in the code-behind file. (Oddly, when performing the initialization in the constructor rather than the *Loaded* handler, the line-join *RadioButton* gets initialized but not the other two.)

At the bottom of the markup is a thick *Polyline* waiting for its *StrokeStartLineCap*, *StrokeEndLineCap*, and *StrokeLineJoin* properties to be set. This happens in the three *Checked* event handlers also in the code-behind file:

Project: LineCapsAndJoins | File: MainPage.xaml.cs (excerpt)

```
public sealed partial class MainPage : Page
{
    public MainPage()
    {
        this.InitializeComponent();

        Loaded += (sender, args) =>
            {
```

```
            foreach (UIElement child in startLineCapPanel.Children)
                (child as RadioButton).IsChecked =
                    (PenLineCap)(child as RadioButton).Tag == polyline.StrokeStartLineCap;

            foreach (UIElement child in endLineCapPanel.Children)
                (child as RadioButton).IsChecked =
                    (PenLineCap)(child as RadioButton).Tag == polyline.StrokeEndLineCap;

            foreach (UIElement child in lineJoinPanel.Children)
                (child as RadioButton).IsChecked =
                    (PenLineJoin)(child as RadioButton).Tag == polyline.StrokeLineJoin;
        };
    }

    void OnStartLineCapRadioButtonChecked(object sender, RoutedEventArgs args)
    {
        polyline.StrokeStartLineCap = (PenLineCap)(sender as RadioButton).Tag;
    }

    void OnEndLineCapRadioButtonChecked(object sender, RoutedEventArgs args)
    {
        polyline.StrokeEndLineCap = (PenLineCap)(sender as RadioButton).Tag;
    }

    void OnLineJoinRadioButtonChecked(object sender, RoutedEventArgs args)
    {
        polyline.StrokeLineJoin = (PenLineJoin)(sender as RadioButton).Tag;
    }
}
```

The *Loaded* handler loops through all the *RadioButton* controls in each group, setting the *IsChecked* property to *true* if the *Tag* value matches the corresponding property of the *Polyline*. Any further *RadioButton* checking occurs under the user's control. The event handlers simply need to set a property of the *Polyline* based on the *Tag* property of the checked *RadioButton*. Here's the result:

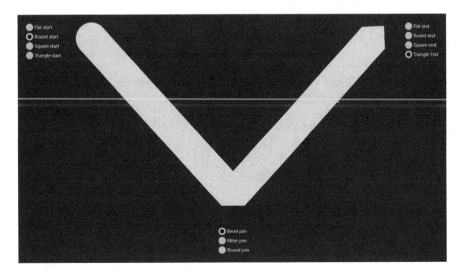

Although the markup is very explicit about setting the *Tag* property to a member of the *PenLineCap* or *PenLineJoin* enumeration, the XAML parser actually assigns the *Tag* an integer corresponding to the underlying enumeration value. This integer can easily be cast into the correct enumeration member, but it's definitely not the enumeration member itself.

Much of the awkward markup in LineCapsAndJoins can be eliminated by defining a couple simple custom controls. These custom controls don't need to have dependency properties; they can have just a very simple regular .NET property for a tag corresponding to a particular type.

The LineCapsAndJoinsWithCustomClass shows how this works. Here's a *RadioButton* derivative specifically for representing a *PenLineCap* value:

Project: LineCapsAndJoinsWithCustomClass | File: LineCapRadioButton.cs

```
using Windows.UI.Xaml.Controls;
using Windows.UI.Xaml.Media;

namespace LineCapsAndJoinsWithCustomClass
{
    public class LineCapRadioButton : RadioButton
    {
        public PenLineCap LineCapTag { set; get; }
    }
}
```

Similarly, here's one for *PenLineJoin* values:

Project: LineCapsAndJoinsWithCustomClass | File: LineJoinRadioButton.cs

```
using Windows.UI.Xaml.Controls;
using Windows.UI.Xaml.Media;

namespace LineCapsAndJoinsWithCustomClass
{
    public class LineJoinRadioButton : RadioButton
    {
        public PenLineJoin LineJoinTag { set; get; }
    }
}
```

Let me show you just a little piece of the XAML (the last group of three *RadioButton* controls) to demonstrate how the property-element syntax has been eliminated:

Project: LineCapsAndJoinsWithCustomClass | File: MainPage.xaml (excerpt)

```
<StackPanel Name="lineJoinPanel"
            Grid.Row="1" Grid.Column="1"
            HorizontalAlignment="Center"
            Margin="24">

    <local:LineJoinRadioButton Content="Bevel join"
                               LineJoinTag="Bevel"
                               Checked="OnLineJoinRadioButtonChecked" />
```

```
<local:LineJoinRadioButton Content="Miter join"
                           LineJoinTag="Miter"
                           Checked="OnLineJoinRadioButtonChecked" />

<local:LineJoinRadioButton Content="Round join"
                           LineJoinTag="Round"
                           Checked="OnLineJoinRadioButtonChecked" />
</StackPanel>
```

You'll notice that as you type this markup, IntelliSense correctly recognizes the *LineCapTag* and *LineJoinTag* properties to be an enumeration type and gives you an option of typing in one of the enumeration members. Nice!

This switch to custom *RadioButton* derivatives mostly affects the XAML file. The code-behind file is pretty much the same except for somewhat less casting:

Project: LineCapsAndJoinsWithCustomClass | File: MainPage.xaml.cs (excerpt)

```
public sealed partial class MainPage : Page
{
    public MainPage()
    {
        this.InitializeComponent();

        Loaded += (sender, args) =>
            {
                foreach (UIElement child in startLineCapPanel.Children)
                    (child as LineCapRadioButton).IsChecked =
                        (child as LineCapRadioButton).LineCapTag == polyline.StrokeStartLineCap;

                foreach (UIElement child in endLineCapPanel.Children)
                    (child as LineCapRadioButton).IsChecked =
                        (child as LineCapRadioButton).LineCapTag == polyline.StrokeEndLineCap;

                foreach (UIElement child in lineJoinPanel.Children)
                    (child as LineJoinRadioButton).IsChecked =
                        (child as LineJoinRadioButton).LineJoinTag == polyline.StrokeLineJoin;
            };
    }

    void OnStartLineCapRadioButtonChecked(object sender, RoutedEventArgs args)
    {
        polyline.StrokeStartLineCap = (sender as LineCapRadioButton).LineCapTag;
    }

    void OnEndLineCapRadioButtonChecked(object sender, RoutedEventArgs args)
    {
        polyline.StrokeEndLineCap = (sender as LineCapRadioButton).LineCapTag;
    }

    void OnLineJoinRadioButtonChecked(object sender, RoutedEventArgs args)
    {
        polyline.StrokeLineJoin = (sender as LineJoinRadioButton).LineJoinTag;
    }
}
```

Keyboard Input and *TextBox*

Keyboard input in Windows 8 applications is complicated somewhat by the on-screen touch keyboard that allows the user to enter text by tapping on the screen. Although the touch keyboard is important for tablets and other devices that don't have real keyboards attached, it can also be invoked as a supplement to a real keyboard.

It is vital that the touch keyboard not pop up and disappear in an annoying fashion. For this reason, many controls—including custom controls—do not automatically receive keyboard input. If they did, the system would need to invoke the touch keyboard whenever these controls received input focus. Consequently, if you create a custom control and install event handlers for the *KeyUp* and *KeyDown* events (or override the *OnKeyUp* and *OnKeyDown* methods), you'll discover that nothing comes through. You need to write code that gives the control input focus.

If you are interested in getting keyboard input from the physical keyboard only and you don't care about the touch keyboard—perhaps for a program intended only for yourself or for testing purposes—there is a fairly easy way to do it. In the constructor of your page, obtain your application's *CoreWindow* object:

```
CoreWindow coreWindow = Window.Current.CoreWindow;
```

This class is defined in the *Windows.UI.Core* namespace. You can then install event handlers on this object for *KeyDown* and *KeyUp* (which indicate keys on the keyboard) as well as *CharacterReceived* (which translates keys to text characters).

If you need to create a custom control that obtains keyboard input from both the physical keyboard and the touch keyboard, the process is rather more involved. You need to derive a class from *FrameworkElementAutomationPeer* that implements the *ITextProvider* and *IValueProvider* interfaces and return this class in an override of the *OnCreateAutomationPeer* method of your custom control.

Obviously this is a nontrivial task, but I'll provide full details in Chapter 16, "Rich Text."

Meanwhile, if your program needs text input, the best approach is to use one of the controls specifically provided for this purpose:

- *TextBox* features single-line or multiline input with a uniform font, much like the traditional Windows Notepad program.

- *RichEditBox* features formatted text, much like the traditional Windows WordPad program.

- *PasswordBox* allows a single line of masked input.

I'll be focusing on *TextBox* in this brief discussion, and I'll provide more examples in the chapters ahead. I'll save *RichTextBox* for Chapter 16.

TextBox defines a *Text* property that lets code set the text in the *TextBox* or obtain the current text. The *SelectedText* property is the text that's selected (if any), and the *SelectionStart* and *SelectionLength* properties indicate the offset and length of the selection. If *SelectionLength* is 0, *SelectionStart* is the position of the cursor. Setting the *IsReadOnly* property to *true* inhibits typed input but allows text to be selected and copied to the Clipboard. All cut, copy, and paste interaction occurs through context menus. The *TextBox* defines both *TextChanged* and *SelectionChanged* events.

By default, a *TextBox* allows only a single line of input. Two properties can change that behavior:

- Normally the *TextBox* ignores the Return key, but setting *AcceptsReturn* to *true* causes the *TextBox* to begin a new line when Return is pressed.

- The default setting of the *TextWrapping* property is *NoWrap*. Setting that to *Wrap* causes the *TextBox* to generate a new line when the user types beyond the end of the current line.

These properties can be set independently. Either will cause a *TextBox* to grow vertically as additional lines are added. *TextBox* has a built-in *ScrollViewer*. If you don't want the *TextBox* to grow indefinitely, set the *MaxLength* property.

There is not just one touch keyboard but several, and some are more suitable for entering numbers or email addresses or URIs. A *TextBox* specifies what type of keyboard it wants with the *InputScope* property.

The following TextBoxInputScopes program lets you experiment with different keyboard layouts, as well as different modes of multiline *TextBox* instances and (as a bonus) *PasswordBox*:

Project: TextBoxInputScopes | File: MainPage.xaml (excerpt)

```xml
<Page ... >
    <Page.Resources>
        <Style TargetType="TextBlock">
            <Setter Property="FontSize" Value="24" />
            <Setter Property="VerticalAlignment" Value="Center" />
            <Setter Property="Margin" Value="6" />
        </Style>

        <Style TargetType="TextBox">
            <Setter Property="Width" Value="320" />
            <Setter Property="VerticalAlignment" Value="Center" />
            <Setter Property="Margin" Value="0 6" />
        </Style>
    </Page.Resources>

    <Grid Background="{StaticResource ApplicationPageBackgroundThemeBrush}">
        <Grid HorizontalAlignment="Center">
            <Grid.RowDefinitions>
                <RowDefinition Height="Auto" />
                <RowDefinition Height="Auto" />
                <RowDefinition Height="Auto" />
                <RowDefinition Height="Auto" />
                <RowDefinition Height="Auto" />
                <RowDefinition Height="Auto" />
                <RowDefinition Height="Auto" />
                <RowDefinition Height="Auto" />
                <RowDefinition Height="Auto" />
                <RowDefinition Height="Auto" />
            </Grid.RowDefinitions>
        </Grid.RowDefinitions>
```

```xml
<Grid.ColumnDefinitions>
    <ColumnDefinition Width="Auto" />
    <ColumnDefinition Width="Auto" />
</Grid.ColumnDefinitions>

<!-- Multiline with Return, no wrapping -->
<TextBlock Text="Multiline (accepts Return, no wrap):"
        Grid.Row="0" Grid.Column="0" />

<TextBox AcceptsReturn="True"
        Grid.Row="0" Grid.Column="1" />

<!-- Multiline with no Return, wrapping -->
<TextBlock Text="Multiline (ignores Return, wraps):"
        Grid.Row="1" Grid.Column="0" />

<TextBox TextWrapping="Wrap"
        Grid.Row="1" Grid.Column="1" />

<!-- Multiline with Return and wrapping -->
<TextBlock Text="Multiline (accepts Return, wraps):"
        Grid.Row="2" Grid.Column="0" />

<TextBox AcceptsReturn="True"
        TextWrapping="Wrap"
        Grid.Row="2" Grid.Column="1" />

<!-- Default input scope -->
<TextBlock Text="Default input scope:"
        Grid.Row="3" Grid.Column="0" />

<TextBox Grid.Row="3" Grid.Column="1"
        InputScope="Default" />

<!-- Email address input scope -->
<TextBlock Text="Email address input scope:"
        Grid.Row="4" Grid.Column="0" />

<TextBox Grid.Row="4" Grid.Column="1"
        InputScope="EmailSmtpAddress" />

<!-- Number input scope -->
<TextBlock Text="Number input scope:"
        Grid.Row="5" Grid.Column="0" />

<TextBox Grid.Row="5" Grid.Column="1"
        InputScope="Number" />

<!-- Search input scope -->
<TextBlock Text="Search input scope:"
        Grid.Row="6" Grid.Column="0" />

<TextBox Grid.Row="6" Grid.Column="1"
        InputScope="Search" />
```

```
            <!-- Telephone number input scope -->
            <TextBlock Text="Telephone number input scope:"
                       Grid.Row="7" Grid.Column="0" />

            <TextBox Grid.Row="7" Grid.Column="1"
                     InputScope="TelephoneNumber" />

            <!-- URL input scope -->
            <TextBlock Text="URL input scope:"
                       Grid.Row="8" Grid.Column="0" />

            <TextBox Grid.Row="8" Grid.Column="1"
                     InputScope="Url" />

            <!-- PasswordBox -->
            <TextBlock Text="PasswordBox:"
                       Grid.Row="9" Grid.Column="0" />

            <PasswordBox Grid.Row="9" Grid.Column="1" />
        </Grid>
    </Grid>
</Page>
```

This is a program you'll want to experiment with before choosing a multiline mode or an *InputScope* value.

Touch and *Thumb*

In Chapter 13, "Touch, Etc.," I'll discuss touch input and how you can use it to manipulate objects on the screen. Meanwhile, a modest control called *Thumb* provides some rudimentary touch functionality. *Thumb* is defined in the *Windows.UI.Xaml.Controls.Primitives* namespace, and it is primarily intended as a building block for the *Slider* and *Scrollbar*. In Chapter 8, I'll use it in a custom grid-splitter control.

The *Thumb* control generates three events based on mouse, stylus, or touch movement relative to itself: *DragStarted*, *DragDelta*, and *DragCompleted*. The *DragStarted* event occurs when you put your finger on a *Thumb* control or move the mouse to its surface and click. Thereafter, *DragDelta* events indicate how the finger or mouse is moving. You can use these events to move the *Thumb* (and anything else), most conveniently on a *Canvas*. *DragCompleted* indicates a lift of a finger or the release of the mouse button.

In the AlphabetBlocks program, a series of buttons labeled with letters, numbers, and some punctuation surrounds the perimeter. Click one, and an alphabet block appears that you can drag with your finger or the mouse. I know that you'll want to send this alphabet block scurrying across the screen with a flick of your finger, but it won't respond in that way. The *Thumb* does not incorporate touch inertia. For inertia, you'll have to tap into the actual touch events beginning with the word *Manipulation*.

For the alphabet blocks themselves, a *UserControl* derivative named *Block* has a XAML file that defines a 144-pixel square image with a *Thumb*, some graphics, and a *TextBlock*:

Project: AlphabetBlocks | File: Block.xaml

```
<UserControl
    x:Class="AlphabetBlocks.Block"
    xmlns="http://schemas.microsoft.com/winfx/2006/xaml/presentation"
    xmlns:x="http://schemas.microsoft.com/winfx/2006/xaml"
    xmlns:local="using:AlphabetBlocks"
    Width="144"
    Height="144"
    Name="root">

    <Grid>
        <Thumb DragStarted="OnThumbDragStarted"
               DragDelta="OnThumbDragDelta"
               Margin="18 18 6 6" />

        <!-- Left -->
        <Polygon Points="0 6, 12 18, 12 138, 0 126"
                 Fill="#E0C080" />

        <!-- Top -->
        <Polygon Points="6 0, 18 12, 138 12, 126 0"
                 Fill="#F0D090" />

        <!-- Edge -->
        <Polygon Points="6 0, 18 12, 12 18, 0 6"
                 Fill="#E8C888" />

        <Border BorderBrush="{Binding ElementName=root, Path=Foreground}"
                BorderThickness="12"
                Background="#FFE0A0"
                CornerRadius="6"
                Margin="12 12 0 0"
                IsHitTestVisible="False" />

        <TextBlock FontFamily="Courier New"
                   FontSize="156"
                   FontWeight="Bold"
                   Text="{Binding ElementName=root, Path=Text}"
                   HorizontalAlignment="Center"
                   VerticalAlignment="Center"
                   Margin="12 18 0 0"
                   IsHitTestVisible="False" />
    </Grid>
</UserControl>
```

The *Polygon* shape is similar to *Polyline* except that it automatically closes the figure and then fills the figure with the brush referenced by the *Fill* property.

The *Thumb* has *DragStarted* and *DragDelta* event handlers installed. The two elements that sit on top of the *Thumb*—the *Border* and *TextBlock*—visually hide the *Thumb* but have their *IsHitTestVisible* properties set to *false* so that they don't block touch input from reaching the *Thumb*.

The *BorderBrush* property of the *Border* has a binding to the *Foreground* property of the root element. *Foreground*, you'll recall, is defined by the *Control* class and inherited by *UserControl* and propagated through the visual tree. The *Foreground* property of the *TextBlock* automatically gets this same brush. The *Text* property of the *TextBlock* element is bound to the *Text* property of the control. *UserControl* doesn't have a *Text* property, which strongly suggests that *Block* defines it.

The code-behind file confirms that supposition. Much of this class is devoted to defining a *Text* property backed by a dependency property:

Project: AlphabetBlocks | File: Block.xaml.cs

```
using Windows.UI.Xaml;
using Windows.UI.Xaml.Controls;
using Windows.UI.Xaml.Controls.Primitives;

namespace AlphabetBlocks
{
    public sealed partial class Block : UserControl
    {
        static int zindex;

        static Block()
        {
            TextProperty = DependencyProperty.Register("Text",
                typeof(string),
                typeof(Block),
                new PropertyMetadata("?"));
        }

        public static DependencyProperty TextProperty { private set; get; }

        public static int ZIndex
        {
            get { return ++zindex; }
        }

        public Block()
        {
            this.InitializeComponent();
        }

        public string Text
        {
            set { SetValue(TextProperty, value); }
            get { return (string)GetValue(TextProperty); }
        }

        void OnThumbDragStarted(object sender, DragStartedEventArgs args)
        {
            Canvas.SetZIndex(this, ZIndex);
        }

        void OnThumbDragDelta(object sender, DragDeltaEventArgs args)
        {
            Canvas.SetLeft(this, Canvas.GetLeft(this) + args.HorizontalChange);
            Canvas.SetTop(this, Canvas.GetTop(this) + args.VerticalChange);
        }
    }
}
```

This *Block* class also defines a static *ZIndex* property that requires an explanation. As you click buttons in this program and *Block* objects are created and added to a *Canvas*, each subsequent *Block* appears on top of the previous *Block* objects because of the way they're ordered in the collection. However, when you later put your finger on a *Block*, you want that object to pop to the top of the pile, which means that it should have a z-index higher than every other *Block*.

The static *ZIndex* property defined here helps achieve that. Notice that the value is incremented each time it's called. Whenever a *DragStarted* event occurs, which means that the user has touched one of these controls, the *Canvas.SetZIndex* method gives the *Block* a z-index higher than all the others. Of course, this process will break down eventually when the *ZIndex* property reaches its maximum value, but it's highly unlikely that will happen. (The Windows Runtime imposes an arbitrary maximum value of 1,000,000, so if you move one block per second without stopping, the program will go out on an exception during the 12th day.)

The *DragDelta* event of the *Thumb* reports how touch or the mouse has moved relative to itself in the form of *HorizontalChange* and *VerticalChange* properties. These are simply used to increment the *Canvas.Left* and *Canvas.Top* attached properties.

The MainPage.xaml file is very bare. The XAML is dominated by some text that displays the name of the program in the center of the page:

Project: AlphabetBlocks | File: MainPage.xaml (excerpt)

```
<Grid Background="{StaticResource ApplicationPageBackgroundThemeBrush}"
      SizeChanged="OnGridSizeChanged">

    <TextBlock Text="Alphabet Blocks"
               FontStyle="Italic"
               FontWeight="Bold"
               FontSize="96"
               TextWrapping="Wrap"
               HorizontalAlignment="Center"
               VerticalAlignment="Center"
               TextAlignment="Center"
               Opacity="0.1" />

    <Canvas Name="buttonCanvas" />
    <Canvas Name="blockcanvas" />
</Grid>
```

Notice the *SizeChanged* handler on the *Grid*. Whenever the size of the page changes, the handler is responsible for re-creating all the *Button* objects and distributing them equally around the perimeter of the page. That code dominates that code-behind file:

Project: AlphabetBlocks | File: MainPage.xaml.cs (excerpt)

```
public sealed partial class MainPage : Page
{
    const double BUTTON_SIZE = 60;
    const double BUTTON_FONT = 18;
    string blockChars = "ABCDEFGHIJKLMNOPQRSTUVWXYZ0123456789!?-+*/%=";
    Color[] colors = { Colors.Red, Colors.Green, Colors.Orange, Colors.Blue, Colors.Purple };
    Random rand = new Random();
```

```
public MainPage()
{
    this.InitializeComponent();
}

void OnGridSizeChanged(object sender, SizeChangedEventArgs args)
{
    buttonCanvas.Children.Clear();

    double widthFraction = args.NewSize.Width /
                    (args.NewSize.Width + args.NewSize.Height);
    int horzCount = (int)(widthFraction * blockChars.Length / 2);
    int vertCount = (int)(blockChars.Length / 2 - horzCount);
    int index = 0;

    double slotWidth = (args.NewSize.Width - BUTTON_SIZE) / horzCount;
    double slotHeight = (args.NewSize.Height - BUTTON_SIZE) / vertCount + 1;

    // Across top
    for (int i = 0; i < horzCount; i++)
    {
        Button button = MakeButton(index++);
        Canvas.SetLeft(button, i * slotWidth);
        Canvas.SetTop(button, 0);
        buttonCanvas.Children.Add(button);
    }

    // Down right side
    for (int i = 0; i < vertCount; i++)
    {
        Button button = MakeButton(index++);
        Canvas.SetLeft(button, this.ActualWidth - BUTTON_SIZE);
        Canvas.SetTop(button, i * slotHeight);
        buttonCanvas.Children.Add(button);
    }

    // Across bottom from right
    for (int i = 0; i < horzCount; i++)
    {
        Button button = MakeButton(index++);
        Canvas.SetLeft(button, this.ActualWidth - i * slotWidth - BUTTON_SIZE);
        Canvas.SetTop(button, this.ActualHeight - BUTTON_SIZE);
        buttonCanvas.Children.Add(button);
    }

    // Up left side
    for (int i = 0; i < vertCount; i++)
    {
        Button button = MakeButton(index++);
        Canvas.SetLeft(button, 0);
        Canvas.SetTop(button, this.ActualHeight - i * slotHeight - BUTTON_SIZE);
        buttonCanvas.Children.Add(button);
    }
}
```

```
Button MakeButton(int index)
{
    Button button = new Button
    {
        Content = blockChars[index].ToString(),
        Width = BUTTON_SIZE,
        Height = BUTTON_SIZE,
        FontSize = BUTTON_FONT,
        Tag = new SolidColorBrush(colors[index % colors.Length]),
    };
    button.Click += OnButtonClick;
    return button;
}

void OnButtonClick(object sender, RoutedEventArgs e)
{
    Button button = sender as Button;

    Block block = new Block
    {
        Text = button.Content as string,
        Foreground = button.Tag as Brush
    };
    Canvas.SetLeft(block, this.ActualWidth / 2 - 144 * rand.NextDouble());
    Canvas.SetTop(block, this.ActualHeight / 2 - 144 * rand.NextDouble());
    Canvas.SetZIndex(block, Block.ZIndex);
    blockcanvas.Children.Add(block);
}
}
```

A *Block* is created in the *Click* handler for the *Button* and given a random location somewhere close to the center of the screen. It's the responsibility of the user to then move the blocks to discover yet another way to say Hello to Windows 8:

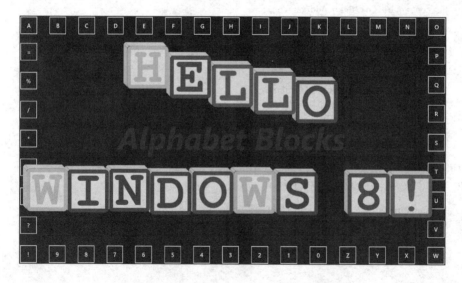

CHAPTER 6

WinRT and MVVM

In structuring software, one of the primary guiding rules is the separation of concerns. A large application is best developed, debugged, and maintained by being separated into specialized layers. In highly interactive graphical environments, one obvious separation is between presentation and content. The presentation layer is the part of the program that displays controls (and other graphics) and interacts with the user. Underlying this presentation layer is business logic and data providers.

To help programmers conceptualize and implement separations of concerns, architectural patterns are developed. In XAML-based programming environments, one pattern that has become extremely popular is Model-View-ViewModel, or MVVM. MVVM is particularly suited for implementing a presentation layer in XAML and linking to the underlying business logic through data bindings and commands.

Unfortunately, books such as this one tend to contain very small programs to illustrate particular features and concepts. Very small programs often become somewhat larger when they are made to fit an architectural pattern! MVVM is overkill for a small application and may very well obfuscate rather than clarify.

Nevertheless, data binding and commanding are an important part of the Windows Runtime, and you should see how they help implement an MVVM architecture.

MVVM (Brief and Simplified)

As the name suggests, an application using the Model-View-ViewModel pattern is split into three layers:

- The Model is the layer that deals with data and raw content. It is often involved with obtaining and maintaining data from files or web services.

- The View is the presentation layer of controls and graphics, generally implemented in XAML.

- The View Model sits between the Model and View. In the general case, it is responsible for making the data or content from the Model more conducive to the View.

It's not uncommon for the Model layer to be unnecessary and therefore absent, and that's the case for the programs shown in this chapter.

If all the interaction between these three layers occurs through procedural method calls, a calling hierarchy would be imposed:

View → View Model → Model

Calls in the other direction are not allowed except for events. The Model can define an event that the View Model handles, and the View Model can define an event that the View handles. Events allow the View Model (for example) to signal to the View that updated data is available. The View can then call into the View Model to obtain that updated data.

Most often, the View and View Model interact through data bindings and commands. Consequently, most or all of these method calls and event handling actually occur under the covers. These data bindings and commands serve to allow three types of interactions:

- The View can transfer user input to the View Model.

- The View Model can notify the View when updated data is available.

- The View can obtain and display updated data from the View Model.

One of the goals inherent in MVVM is to minimize the code-behind file—at least on the page or window level. MVVM mavens are happiest when all the connections between the View and View Model are accomplished through bindings in the XAML file.

Data Binding Notifications

In Chapter 5, "Control Interaction," you saw data bindings that looked like this:

```
<TextBlock Text="{Binding ElementName=slider, Path=Value}" />
```

This is a binding between two *FrameworkElement* derivatives. The target of this data binding is the *Text* property of the *TextBlock*. The binding source is the *Value* property of a *Slider* identified by the name *slider*. Both the target and source properties are backed by dependency properties. This is a requirement for the binding target but not (as you'll see) for the source.

Whenever the *Value* property of the *Slider* changes, the text displayed by the *TextBlock* changes accordingly. How does this work? When the binding source is a dependency property, the actual mechanism is internal to the Windows Runtime. Undoubtedly an event is involved. The *Binding* object installs a handler for an event that provides a notification when the *Value* property of the *Slider* changes, and the *Binding* object sets that changed value to the *Text* property of the *TextBlock*, converting from *double* to *string* in the process. This shouldn't be very mysterious, considering that *Slider* has a public *ValueChanged* event that is also fired when the *Value* property changes.

When implementing a View Model, the data bindings are a little different: The binding targets are still elements in the XAML file, but the binding sources are properties in the View Model class. This is the basic way that the View Model and the View (the XAML file) transfer data back and forth.

A binding source is not required to be backed by a dependency property. But in order for the binding to work properly, the binding source must implement some other kind of notification mechanism to signal to the *Binding* object when a property has changed. This notification does not happen automatically; it must be implemented through an event.

The standard way for a View Model to serve as a binding source is by implementing the *INotifyPropertyChanged* interface defined in the *System.ComponentModel* namespace. This interface has an exceptionally simple definition:

```
public interface INotifyPropertyChanged
{
    event PropertyChangedEventHandler PropertyChanged;
}
```

The *PropertyChangedEventHandler* delegate is associated with the *PropertyChangedEventArgs* class, which defines one property: *PropertyName* of type *string*. When a class implements *INotifyPropertyChanged*, it fires a *PropertyChanged* event whenever one of its properties changes.

Here's a simple example of a class that implements *INotifyPropertyChanged*. The single property named *TotalScore* fires the *PropertyChanged* event when the property changes:

```
public class SimpleViewModel : INotifyPropertyChanged
{
    double totalScore;

    public event PropertyChangedEventHandler PropertyChanged;

    public double TotalScore
    {
        set
        {
            if (totalScore != value)
            {
                totalScore = value;

                if (PropertyChanged != null)
                    PropertyChanged(this, new PropertyChangedEventArgs("TotalScore"));
            }
        }
        get
        {
            return totalScore;
        }
    }
}
```

The *TotalScore* property is backed by the *totalScore* field. Notice that the *TotalScore* property checks the value coming into the *set* accessor against the *totalScore* field and fires the *PropertyChanged* event only when the property actually changes. Do not skimp on this step just to make these *set* accessors a little shorter! The event is called *PropertyChanged* and not *PropertySetAndPerhapsChangedOrMaybeNot*.

Also notice that it's possible for a class to legally implement *INotifyPropertyChanged* and not actually fire any *PropertyChanged* events, but that would be considered *very* bad behavior.

When a class has more than a couple properties, it starts making sense to define a protected method named *OnPropertyChanged* and let that method do the actual event firing. It's also possible to automate part of this class, as you'll see shortly.

As you design a View and View Model, it helps to start thinking of controls as visual manifestations of data types. Through data bindings, the controls in the View are connected to properties of these types in the View Model. For example, a *Slider* is a *double*, a *TextBox* is a *string*, a *CheckBox* or *ToggleSwitch* is a *bool*, and a group of *RadioButton* controls is an enumeration.

A View Model for ColorScroll

The ColorScroll programs in Chapter 5 showed how to use data bindings to update a *TextBlock* from the value property of a *Slider*. However, defining a data binding to change the color based on the three *Slider* values proved much more elusive. Is it possible at all?

The solution is to have a separate class devoted to the job of creating a *Color* object from the values of *Red*, *Green*, and *Blue* properties. Any change to one of these three properties triggers a recalculation of the *Color* property. In the XAML file, bindings connect the *Slider* controls with the *Red*, *Green*, and *Blue* properties and the *SolidColorBrush* with the *Color* property. Even if we don't call this class a View Model, that's what it is.

Here's an *RgbViewModel* class that implements the *INotifyPropertyChanged* interface to fire *PropertyChanged* events whenever its *Red*, *Green*, *Blue*, or *Color* properties change:

Project: ColorScrollWithViewModel | **File:** RgbViewModel.cs

```
using System.ComponentModel;        // for INotifyPropertyChanged
using Windows.UI;                   // for Color

namespace ColorScrollWithViewModel
{
    public class RgbViewModel : INotifyPropertyChanged
    {
        double red, green, blue;
        Color color = Color.FromArgb(255, 0, 0, 0);

        public event PropertyChangedEventHandler PropertyChanged;

        public double Red
        {
            set
            {
                if (red != value)
                {
                    red = value;
                    OnPropertyChanged("Red");
                    Calculate();
                }
            }
```

```
        }
        get
        {
            return red;
        }
    }

    public double Green
    {
        set
        {
            if (green != value)
            {
                green = value;
                OnPropertyChanged("Green");
                Calculate();
            }
        }
        get
        {
            return green;
        }
    }

    public double Blue
    {
        set
        {
            if (blue != value)
            {
                blue = value;
                OnPropertyChanged("Blue");
                Calculate();
            }
        }
        get
        {
            return blue;
        }
    }

    public Color Color
    {
        protected set
        {
            if (color != value)
            {
                color = value;
                OnPropertyChanged("Color");
            }
        }
        get
        {
            return color;
        }
    }
```

```
    void Calculate()
    {
        this.Color = Color.FromArgb(255, (byte)this.Red, (byte)this.Green, (byte)this.Blue);
    }

    protected void OnPropertyChanged(string propertyName)
    {
        if (PropertyChanged != null)
            PropertyChanged(this, new PropertyChangedEventArgs(propertyName));
    }
  }
}
```

The *OnPropertyChanged* method at the bottom of the class has the job of actually firing the *PropertyChanged* event with the name of the property.

I've defined the *Red*, *Green*, and *Blue* properties as *double* to facilitate data bindings. These properties are basically input to the View Model, and they'll probably come from controls such as *Slider*, so the *double* type is the most generalized.

Each of the *Red*, *Green*, and *Blue* property *set* accessors fires a *PropertyChanged* event and then calls *Calculate*, which sets a new *Color* value, which causes another *PropertyChanged* event to be fired for the *Color* property. The *Color* property itself has a protected *set* accessor, indicating that this class isn't designed to calculate *Red*, *Green*, and *Blue* values from a new *Color* value. (I'll explore this issue shortly.)

The *RgbViewModel* class is part of the ColorScrollWithViewModel project. The MainPage.xaml file instantiates the *RgbViewModel* in its *Resources* section.

Project: ColorScrollWithViewModel | **File:** MainPage.xaml (excerpt)

```
<Page.Resources>
    <local:RgbViewModel x:Key="rgbViewModel" />
    ...
</Page.Resources>
```

Notice the namespace prefix of *local*.

Defining the View Model as a resource is one of two basic ways that a XAML file can get access to the object. As was demonstrated in Chapter 2, "XAML Syntax," a class included in a *Resources* section is instantiated only once and shared among all *StaticResource* references. That behavior is essential for an application such as this, in which all the bindings need to reference the same object.

Each of the *Slider* controls is similar. Only one is shown here:

Project: ColorScrollWithViewModel | **File:** MainPage.xaml (excerpt)

```
<!-- Red -->
<TextBlock Text="Red"
           Grid.Column="0"
           Grid.Row="0"
           Foreground="Red" />
```

```
<Slider Grid.Column="0"
        Grid.Row="1"
        Value="{Binding Source={StaticResource rgbViewModel},
                        Path=Red,
                        Mode=TwoWay}"
        Foreground="Red" />

<TextBlock Text="{Binding Source={StaticResource rgbViewModel},
                          Path=Red,
                          Converter={StaticResource hexConverter}}"
           Grid.Column="0"
           Grid.Row="2"
           Foreground="Red" />
```

Notice that the *Slider* element no longer has a *Name* attribute because no other element in the XAML file refers to this element, and neither does the code-behind file. There's no *ValueChanged* event handler because that's not needed either. The code-behind file contains nothing except a call to *InitializeComponent*.

Take careful note of the binding on the *Slider*:

```
<Slider ...
        Value="{Binding Source={StaticResource rgbViewModel},
                        Path=Red,
                        Mode=TwoWay}" ... />
```

This binding is a little long, so I've broken it into three lines. It does not specify an *ElementName* because it's not referencing another element in the XAML file. Instead, it's referencing an object instantiated as a XAML resource, so it must use *Source* with *StaticResource*. The syntax of this binding implies that the binding target is the *Value* property of the *Slider* and the binding source is the *Red* property of the *RgbViewModel* instance.

Does this seem backward? Shouldn't the *Slider* be providing a value to *RgbViewModel*?

Yes, but *RgbViewModel* must be a binding source rather than a target. It can't be a binding target because it has no dependency properties. Despite the syntax implying that *Value* is the binding target, in reality we want the *Slider* to provide a value to the *Red* property. For this reason, the *Mode* property of *Binding* must be set to *TwoWay*, which means

- an updated source value causes a change to the target property (the normal case for a data binding), and

- an updated target value causes a change to the source property (which is actually the essential transfer here).

The default *Mode* setting is *OneWay*. The only other option is *OneTime*, which means that the target is updated from the source property only when the binding is established. With *OneTime*, no updating occurs when the source property later changes. You can use *OneTime* if the source has no notification mechanism.

Also notice that the *TextBlock* showing the current value now has a binding to the *RgbViewModel* object:

```
<TextBlock Text="{Binding Source={StaticResource rgbViewModel},
                          Path=Red,
                          Converter={StaticResource hexConverter}}" ... />
```

This binding could instead refer directly to the *Slider* as in the previous project, but I thought it would be better that it also refer to the *RgbViewModel* instance. The default *OneWay* mode is fine here because data only needs to go from the source to the target.

The *OneWay* mode is also good for the binding on the *Color* property of the *SolidColorBrush*:

Project: ColorScrollWithViewModel | File: MainPage.xaml (excerpt)

```
<Rectangle Grid.Column="3"
           Grid.Row="0"
           Grid.RowSpan="3">
    <Rectangle.Fill>
        <SolidColorBrush Color="{Binding Source={StaticResource rgbViewModel},
                                         Path=Color}" />
    </Rectangle.Fill>
</Rectangle>
```

The *SolidColorBrush* no longer has an *x:Name* attribute because there's nothing in the code-behind file that refers to it.

Of course, the code in the *RgbViewModel* class is much longer than the *ValueChanged* event handler we've managed to remove from the code-behind file. I warned you at the outset that MVVM is overkill for small programs. Even in larger applications, often there's an initial price to pay for cleaner architecture, but the separation of presentation and business logic usually has long-term advantages.

In the *RgbViewModel* class I made the *set* accessor of *Color* protected so that it can be accessed only from within the class. Is this really necessary? Perhaps the *Color* property can be defined so that an external change to the property causes new values of the *Red*, *Green*, and *Blue* properties to be calculated:

```
public Color Color
{
    set
    {
        if (color != value)
        {
            color = value;
            OnPropertyChanged("Color");
            this.Red = color.R;
            this.Green = color.G;
            this.Blue = color.B;
        }
    }
    get
    {
        return color;
    }
}
```

At first this might seem like asking for trouble because it causes recursive property changes and recursive calls to *OnPropertyChanged*. But that doesn't happen because the *set* accessors do nothing if the property is not actually changing, so this should be safe.

But it's actually flawed. Suppose the *Color* property is currently the RGB value (0, 0, 0) and it's set to value (255, 128, 0). When the *Red* property is set to 255 in the code, a *PropertyChanged* event is fired, but now *Color* (and *color*) is set to (255, 0, 0), so the code here continues with *Green* and *Blue* being set to the new *color* values of 0.

Rather than guard against re-entry, try searching for a change in logic that does what you want. This version works OK, even though it causes a flurry of *PropertyChanged* events:

```
public Color Color
{
    set
    {
        if (color != value)
        {
            color = value;
            OnPropertyChanged("Color");
            this.Red = value.R;
            this.Green = value.G;
            this.Blue = value.B;
        }
    }
    get
    {
        return color;
    }
}
```

I'll make the *set* accessor of *Color* property public in the next version of the program.

Syntactic Shortcuts

You might have concluded from the *RgbViewModel* code that implementing *INotifyPropertyChanged* is a bit of a hassle, and that's true. To make it somewhat easier, Visual Studio creates a *BindableBase* class in the Common folder for projects of type Grid App and Split App. (Don't confuse this class with the *BindingBase* class from which *Binding* derives.)

However, Visual Studio does *not* create this *BindableBase* class in the Blank App project. But let's take a look at it and see if we can learn anything.

The *BindableBase* class is defined in a namespace that consists of the project name followed by a period and the word *Common*. Stripped of comments and attributes, here's what it looks like:

```
public abstract class BindableBase : INotifyPropertyChanged
{
    public event PropertyChangedEventHandler PropertyChanged;
```

```
    protected bool SetProperty<T>(ref T storage, T value,
                                  [CallerMemberName] String propertyName = null)
    {
        if (object.Equals(storage, value)) return false;

        storage = value;
        this.OnPropertyChanged(propertyName);
        return true;
    }

    protected void OnPropertyChanged([CallerMemberName] string propertyName = null)
    {
        var eventHandler = this.PropertyChanged;
        if (eventHandler != null)
        {
            eventHandler(this, new PropertyChangedEventArgs(propertyName));
        }
    }
}
```

A class that derives from *BindableBase* calls *SetProperty* in the *set* accessor of its property definitions. The signature for the *SetProperty* method looks a little hairy, but it's very easy to use. For a property named *Red* of type *double*, for example, you would have a backing field defined like this:

```
double red;
```

You call *SetProperty* in the *set* accessor like so:

```
SetProperty<double>(ref red, value, "Red");
```

Notice the use of *CallerMemberName* in *BindableBase*. This is an attribute added to .NET 4.5 that C# 5.0 can use to obtain information about code that's calling a particular property or method, which means that you can call *SetProperty* without that last argument. If you're calling *SetProperty* from the *set* accessor of the *Red* property, the name will be automatically provided:

```
SetProperty<double>(ref red, value);
```

The return value from *SetProperty* is *true* if the property is actually changing. You'll probably want to use the return in logic that does something with the new value. For the next project, called ColorScrollWithDataContext, I've created an alternate version of *RgbViewModel* that steals some code from *BindableBase*, and I've given *Color* a public *set* accessor:

Project: ColorScrollWithDataContext | File: RgbViewModel.cs

```
using System.ComponentModel;
using System.Runtime.CompilerServices;
using Windows.UI;

namespace ColorScrollWithDataContext
{
    public class RgbViewModel : INotifyPropertyChanged
    {
        double red, green, blue;
```

```csharp
Color color = Color.FromArgb(255, 0, 0, 0);

public event PropertyChangedEventHandler PropertyChanged;

public double Red
{
    set
    {
        if (SetProperty<double>(ref red, value, "Red"))
            Calculate();
    }
    get
    {
        return red;
    }
}

public double Green
{
    set
    {
        if (SetProperty<double>(ref green, value))
            Calculate();
    }
    get
    {
        return green;
    }
}

public double Blue
{
    set
    {
        if (SetProperty<double>(ref blue, value))
            Calculate();
    }
    get
    {
        return blue;
    }
}

public Color Color
{
    set
    {
        if (SetProperty<Color>(ref color, value))
        {
            this.Red = value.R;
            this.Green = value.G;
            this.Blue = value.B;
        }
    }
    get
    {
        return color;
```

```
        }
    }

    void Calculate()
    {
        this.Color = Color.FromArgb(255, (byte)this.Red, (byte)this.Green, (byte)this.Blue);
    }

    protected bool SetProperty<T>(ref T storage, T value,
                                 [CallerMemberName] string propertyName = null)
    {
        if (object.Equals(storage, value))
            return false;

        storage = value;
        OnPropertyChanged(propertyName);
        return true;
    }

    protected void OnPropertyChanged(string propertyName)
    {
        if (PropertyChanged != null)
            PropertyChanged(this, new PropertyChangedEventArgs(propertyName));
    }
    }
}
```

This form of the *INotifyPropertyChanged* implementation is somewhat cleaner and certainly sleeker. I'll use this version in the ColorScrollWithDataContext project in the next section.

The DataContext Property

So far you've seen three ways to specify a source object in a binding: *ElementName*, *RelativeSource*, and *Source*. *ElementName* is ideal for referencing a named element in XAML, and *RelativeSource* allows a binding to reference a property in the target object. (*RelativeSource* actually has a more important but also more esoteric use that you'll discover in Chapter 11, "The Three Templates.") The third option is the *Source* property, which is generally used with *StaticResource* for accessing an object in the *Resources* collection.

There's a fourth way to specify a binding source: If *ElementName*, *RelativeSource*, and *Source* are all *null*, the *Binding* object checks the *DataContext* property of the binding target.

The *DataContext* property is defined by *FrameworkElement*, and it has the wonderful (and essential) characteristic of propagating down through the visual tree. Not many properties propagate through the visual tree in this way. *Foreground* and all the font-related properties do so, but not many others. *DataContext* is one of the big exceptions to the rule. The constructor of a code-behind file can instantiate a View Model and set that instance to the *DataContext* of the page. Here's how it's done in the MainPage.xaml.cs file of the ColorScrollWithDataContext project:

Project: ColorScrollWithDataContext | File: MainPage.xaml.cs

```
public MainPage()
{
    this.InitializeComponent();
    this.DataContext = new RgbViewModel();

    // Initialize to highlight color
    (this.DataContext as RgbViewModel).Color =
            new UISettings().UIElementColor(UIElementType.Highlight);

}
```

Instantiating the View Model in code might be necessary or desirable for one reason or another. Perhaps the View Model has a constructor that requires an argument. That's something XAML can't do.

Notice that I've also taken the opportunity to test the settability of the *Color* property by initializing it to the system highlight color.

One big advantage to the *DataContext* approach is the simplification of the data bindings. Because they no longer require *Source* settings, they can look like this:

```
<Slider ... Value="{Binding Path=Red, Mode=TwoWay}" ... />
```

Moreover, if the *Path* item is the first item in the binding markup, the *Path=* part can be removed:

```
<Slider ... Value="{Binding Red, Mode=TwoWay}" ... />
```

Now that's a simple *Binding* syntax!

You can remove the *Path=* part of any binding specification regardless of the source, but only if *Path* is the first item. Whenever I use *Source* or *ElementName*, I prefer for that part of the *Binding* specification to appear first, so I'll drop *Path=* only when the *DataContext* comes into play.

Here's an excerpt from the XAML file showing the new bindings. They've become so short that I've stopped breaking them into multiple lines:

Project: ColorScrollWithDataContext | File: MainPage.xaml (excerpt)

```
<!-- Red -->
<TextBlock Text="Red"
           Grid.Column="0"
           Grid.Row="0"
           Foreground="Red" />

<Slider Grid.Column="0"
        Grid.Row="1"
        Value="{Binding Red, Mode=TwoWay}"
        Foreground="Red" />
```

```
<TextBlock Text="{Binding Red, Converter={StaticResource hexConverter}}"
           Grid.Column="0"
           Grid.Row="2"
           Foreground="Red" />
...
<!-- Result -->
<Rectangle Grid.Column="3"
           Grid.Row="0"
           Grid.RowSpan="3">
    <Rectangle.Fill>
        <SolidColorBrush Color="{Binding Color}" />
    </Rectangle.Fill>
</Rectangle>
```

It's possible to mix the two approaches. For example, you can instantiate the View Model in the *Resources* collection of the XAML file:

```
<Page.Resources>
    ...
    <local:RgbViewModel x:Key="rgbViewModel" />
    ...
</Page.Resources>
```

Then at the earliest convenient place in the visual tree, you can set a *DataContext* property:

```
<Grid ... DataContext="{StaticResource rgbViewModel}" ... >
```

Or:

```
<Grid ... DataContext="{Binding Source={StaticResource rgbViewModel}}" ... >
```

The second form is particularly useful if you want to set the *DataContext* to a property of the View Model. You'll see examples when I begin discussing collections in Chapter 11.

Bindings and *TextBox*

One of the big advantages to isolating underlying business logic is the ability to completely revamp the user interface without touching the View Model. For example, suppose you want a color-selection program that is similar to ColorScroll but where each color component is entered in a *TextBox*. Such a program might be a little clumsy to use, but it should be possible.

The ColorTextBoxes project has the same *RgbViewModel* class as the ColorScrollWithDataContext program. The code-behind file has the same constructor as that project as well:

Project: ColorTextBoxes | File: MainPage.xaml.cs (excerpt)

```
public MainPage()
{
    this.InitializeComponent();
    this.DataContext = new RgbViewModel();
```

```
    // Initialize to highlight color
    (this.DataContext as RgbViewModel).Color =
            new UISettings().UIElementColor(UIElementType.Highlight);


}
```

The XAML file instantiates three *TextBox* controls and defines data bindings between the *Red*, *Green*, and *Blue* properties of *RgbViewModel*:

Project: ColorTextBoxes | **File:** MainPage.xaml (excerpt)

```
<Page ... >

    <Page.Resources>
        <Style TargetType="TextBlock">
            <Setter Property="FontSize" Value="24" />
            <Setter Property="Margin" Value="24 0 0 0" />
            <Setter Property="VerticalAlignment" Value="Center" />
        </Style>

        <Style TargetType="TextBox">
            <Setter Property="Margin" Value="24 48 96 48" />
            <Setter Property="VerticalAlignment" Value="Center" />
        </Style>
    </Page.Resources>

    <Grid Background="{StaticResource ApplicationPageBackgroundThemeBrush}">
        <Grid.ColumnDefinitions>
            <ColumnDefinition Width="*" />
            <ColumnDefinition Width="*" />
        </Grid.ColumnDefinitions>

        <Grid Grid.Column="0">
            <Grid.RowDefinitions>
                <RowDefinition Height="Auto" />
                <RowDefinition Height="Auto" />
                <RowDefinition Height="Auto" />
            </Grid.RowDefinitions>

            <Grid.ColumnDefinitions>
                <ColumnDefinition Width="Auto" />
                <ColumnDefinition Width="*" />
            </Grid.ColumnDefinitions>

            <TextBlock Text="Red: "
                    Grid.Row="0"
                    Grid.Column="0" />

            <TextBox Text="{Binding Red, Mode=TwoWay}"
                    Grid.Row="0"
                    Grid.Column="1" />

            <TextBlock Text="Green: "
                    Grid.Row="1"
                    Grid.Column="0" />
```

```
            <TextBox Text="{Binding Green, Mode=TwoWay}"
                    Grid.Row="1"
                    Grid.Column="1" />

            <TextBlock Text="Blue: "
                    Grid.Row="2"
                    Grid.Column="0" />

            <TextBox Text="{Binding Blue, Mode=TwoWay}"
                    Grid.Row="2"
                    Grid.Column="1" />
        </Grid>

        <!-- Result -->
        <Rectangle Grid.Column="1">
            <Rectangle.Fill>
                <SolidColorBrush Color="{Binding Color}" />
            </Rectangle.Fill>
        </Rectangle>
    </Grid>
</Page>
```

When the program runs, the individual *TextBox* controls are initialized with color values, all the necessary data conversions being performed behind the scenes:

Now tap one of the *TextBox* controls, and try entering another number. Nothing happens. Now tap another *TextBox*, or press the Tab key to shift the input focus to the next *TextBox*. Aha! Now the number you entered in the first *TextBox* has finally been acknowledged and used to update the color.

As you experiment with this program, you'll find that the Windows Runtime is extremely lenient about accepting letters and symbols in these text strings without raising exceptions but that any new value you type registers only when the *TextBox* loses input focus.

This behavior is by design. Suppose a View Model bound to a *TextBox* is using a Model to update a database through a network connection. As the user types text into a *TextBox*—perhaps making mistakes and backspacing—do you really want each and every change going over the network? For that reason, user entry in the *TextBox* is considered to be completed and ready for processing only when the *TextBox* loses input focus.

Unfortunately, there's currently no option to change this behavior. Nor is there any way to include validation in these data bindings. If the *TextBox* binding behavior is unacceptable, and if you prefer not duplicating *TextBox* logic with a control of your own, the only real choice you have is abandoning bindings for this case and using the *TextChanged* event handler instead.

The ColorTextBoxesWithEvents project shows one possible approach. The project still uses the same *RgbViewModel* class. The XAML file is similar to the previous project except that the *TextBox* controls now have names and *TextChanged* handlers assigned:

Project: ColorTextBoxesWithEvents | **File:** MainPage.xaml (excerpt)

```
<TextBlock Text="Red: "
           Grid.Row="0"
           Grid.Column="0" />

<TextBox Name="redTextBox"
         Grid.Row="0"
         Grid.Column="1"
         Text="0"
         TextChanged="OnTextBoxTextChanged" />

<TextBlock Text="Green: "
           Grid.Row="1"
           Grid.Column="0" />

<TextBox Name="greenTextBox"
         Grid.Row="1"
         Grid.Column="1"
         Text="0"
         TextChanged="OnTextBoxTextChanged" />

<TextBlock Text="Blue: "
           Grid.Row="2"
           Grid.Column="0" />

<TextBox Name="blueTextBox"
         Grid.Row="2"
         Grid.Column="1"
         Text="0"
         TextChanged="OnTextBoxTextChanged" />
```

The *Rectangle*, however, still has the same data binding as in the earlier programs.

Because we're replacing two-way bindings, not only do we need event handlers on the *TextBox* controls, but we need to install a handler for the *PropertyChanged* event of *RgbViewModel*. Updating a *TextBox* when a View Model property changes is fairly easy, but I also decided I wanted to actually validate the text entered by the user:

Project: ColorTextBoxesWithEvents | File: MainPage.xaml.cs (excerpt)

```
public sealed partial class MainPage : Page
{
    RgbViewModel rgbViewModel;
    Brush textBoxTextBrush;
    Brush textBoxErrorBrush = new SolidColorBrush(Colors.Red);

    public MainPage()
    {
        this.InitializeComponent();

        // Get TextBox brush
        textBoxTextBrush = this.Resources["TextBoxForegroundThemeBrush"] as SolidColorBrush;

        // Create RgbViewModel and save as field
        rgbViewModel = new RgbViewModel();
        rgbViewModel.PropertyChanged += OnRgbViewModelPropertyChanged;
        this.DataContext = rgbViewModel;

        // Initialize to highlight color
        rgbViewModel.Color = new UISettings().UIElementColor(UIElementType.Highlight);
    }

    void OnRgbViewModelPropertyChanged(object sender, PropertyChangedEventArgs args)
    {
        switch (args.PropertyName)
        {
            case "Red":
                redTextBox.Text = rgbViewModel.Red.ToString("F0");
                break;

            case "Green":
                greenTextBox.Text = rgbViewModel.Green.ToString("F0");
                break;

            case "Blue":
                blueTextBox.Text = rgbViewModel.Blue.ToString("F0");
                break;
        }
    }

    void OnTextBoxTextChanged(object sender, TextChangedEventArgs args)
    {
        byte value;

        if (sender == redTextBox && Validate(redTextBox, out value))
            rgbViewModel.Red = value;

        if (sender == greenTextBox && Validate(greenTextBox, out value))
            rgbViewModel.Green = value;
```

```
            if (sender == blueTextBox && Validate(blueTextBox, out value))
                rgbViewModel.Blue = value;
    }

    bool Validate(TextBox txtbox, out byte value)
    {
        bool valid = byte.TryParse(txtbox.Text, out value);
        txtbox.Foreground = valid ? textBoxTextBrush : textBoxErrorBrush;
        return valid;
    }
}
```

The *Validate* method uses the standard *TryParse* method to convert the text into a *byte* value. If successful, the View Model is updated with the value. If not, the text is displayed in red, indicating a problem.

This works well except when the numbers being entered are preceded with leading blanks or zeros. For example, suppose you type **0** in the first *TextBox*. That's a valid *byte*, so the *Red* property in *RgbViewModel* is updated with this value, which triggers a *PropertyChanged* method, and the *TextBox* is assigned a *Text* value of "0". No problem. Now type a **5**. The *TextBox* contains "05". The *TryParse* method considers this to be a valid *byte* string, and the *Red* property is updated with the value 5. Now the *PropertyChanged* handler sets the *Text* property of the *TextBox* to the string "5", replacing "05". But the cursor location is not changed, so it's in front of the 5 instead of being after the 5.

Perhaps the best way to prevent this problem is to ignore *PropertyChanged* events from the View Model while setting a property in the View Model from the *TextChanged* handler. You can do this with a simple flag:

```
bool blockViewModelUpdates;

...

void OnRgbViewModelPropertyChanged(object sender, PropertyChangedEventArgs args)
{
    if (blockViewModelUpdates)
        return;
    ...
}

void OnTextBoxTextChanged(object sender, TextChangedEventArgs args)
{
    blockViewModelUpdates = true;
    ...
    blockViewModelUpdates = false;
}
```

You'll probably also want to clean up the displayed values when each *TextBox* loses input focus.

In some cases, data entry validation might more properly be under the jurisdiction of View Model rather than the View.

Buttons and MVVM

At first, the idea that you can use MVVM to eliminate most of a code-behind file seems valid only for controls that generate values. The concept starts to crumble when you consider buttons. A *Button* fires a *Click* event. That *Click* event must be handled in the code-behind file. If a View Model is actually implementing the logic for that button (which is likely), the *Click* handler must call a method in the View Model. That might be architecturally legal, but it's still rather cumbersome.

Fortunately, there's an alternative to the *Click* event that is ideal for MVVM. This is sometimes informally referred to as the "command interface." *ButtonBase* defines properties named *Command* (of type *ICommand*) and *CommandParameter* (of type object) that allow a *Button* to effectively make a call into a View Model through a data binding. *Command* and *CommandParameter* are both backed by dependency properties, which means they can be binding targets. *Command* is almost always the target of a data binding. *CommandParameter* is optional. It's useful for differentiating between buttons bound to the same *Command* object, and it's usually treated like a *Tag* property.

Perhaps you've written a calculator application where you've implemented the engine as a View Model that's set as the *DataContext*. The calculator button for the + (plus) command might be instantiated in XAML like so:

```
<Button Content="+"
        Command="{Binding CalculateCommand}"
        CommandParameter="add" />
```

What this means is that the View Model has a property named *CalculateCommand* of type *ICommand*, perhaps defined like this:

```
public ICommand CalculateCommand { protected set; get; }
```

The View Model must initialize the *CalculateCommand* property by setting it to an instance of a class that implements the *ICommand* interface, which is defined like so:

```
public interface ICommand
{
    void Execute(object param);
    bool CanExecute(object param)
    event EventHandler<object> CanExecuteChanged;
}
```

When this particular *Button* is clicked, the *Execute* method is called in the object referenced by *CalculateCommand* with an argument of *"add"*. This is how a *Button* basically makes a call right into the View Model (or rather, the class containing that *Execute* method).

The other two-thirds of the *ICommand* interface contain the phrase "can execute" and involve the validity of the particular command at a particular time. If this command is not currently valid—perhaps the calculator can't add right now because no number has been entered—the *Button* should be disabled.

Here's how it works: As the XAML is being parsed and loaded at run time, the *Command* property of the *Button* is assigned a binding to (in this example) the *CalculateCommand* object. The *Button* installs a handler for the *CanExecuteChanged* event and calls the *CanExecute* method in this object with an argument (in this example) of *"add"*. If *CanExecute* returns *false*, the *Button* disables itself. Thereafter, the *Button* calls *CanExecute* again whenever the *CanExecuteChanged* event is fired.

To include a command in your View Model, you must provide a class that implements the *ICommand* interface. However, it's very likely that this class needs to access properties in the View Model class, and vice versa.

So you might wonder: Can these two classes be one and the same?

In theory, yes they can, but only if you use the same *Execute* and *CanExecute* methods for all the buttons on the page, which means that each button must have a unique *CommandParameter* so that the methods can distinguish between them. But let me show you the standard way of implementing commands in a View Model.

The *DelegateCommand* Class

Let's rewrite the SimpleKeypad application from Chapter 5 so that it uses a View Model to accumulate the keystrokes and generate a formatted text string. Besides implementing the *INotifyPropertyChanged* interface, the View Model will also process commands from all the buttons in the keypad. There will be no more *Click* handlers.

Here's the problem: For the View Model to process button commands, it must have one or more properties of type *ICommand*, which means that we need one or more classes that implement the *ICommand* interface. To implement *ICommand*, these classes must contain *Execute* and *CanExecute* methods and the *CanExecuteChanged* event. Yet, the bodies of these methods undoubtedly need to interact with the other parts of the View Model.

The solution is to define all the *Execute* and *CanExecute* methods in the View Model class but with different and unique names. Then, a special class can be defined that implements *ICommand* but that actually calls the methods in the View Model.

This special class is often named *DelegateCommand*, and if you search around, you'll find several somewhat different implementations of this class, including one in Microsoft's Prism framework, which helps developers implement MVVM in Windows Presentation Foundation (WPF) and Silverlight. The version here is my variation.

DelegateCommand implements the *ICommand* interface, which means it has *Execute* and *CanExecute* methods and the *CanExecuteChanged* event, but it turns out that *DelegateCommand* also needs another method to fire the *CanExecuteChanged* event. Let's call this additional method

RaiseCanExecuteChanged. The first job is to define an interface that implements *ICommand* plus this additional method:

Project: KeypadWithViewModel | File: IDelegateCommand.cs

```
using System.Windows.Input;

namespace KeypadWithViewModel
{
    public interface IDelegateCommand : ICommand
    {
        void RaiseCanExecuteChanged();
    }
}
```

The *DelegateCommand* class implements the *IDelegateCommand* interface and makes use of a couple simple (but useful) generic delegates defined in the *System* namespace. These predefined delegates have the names *Action* and *Func* with anything from 1 to 16 arguments. The *Func* delegates return an object of a particular type; the *Action* delegates do not. The *Action<object>* delegate represents a method with a single *object* argument and a *void* return value; this is the signature of the *Execute* method. The *Func<object, bool>* delegate represents a method with an *object* argument that returns a *bool*; this is the signature of the *CanExecute* method. *DelegateCommand* defines two fields of these types for storing methods with these signatures:

Project: KeypadWithViewModel | File: DelegateCommand.cs

```
using System;

namespace KeypadWithViewModel
{
    public class DelegateCommand : IDelegateCommand
    {
        Action<object> execute;
        Func<object, bool> canExecute;

        // Event required by ICommand
        public event EventHandler CanExecuteChanged;

        // Two constructors
        public DelegateCommand(Action<object> execute, Func<object, bool> canExecute)
        {
            this.execute = execute;
            this.canExecute = canExecute;
        }
        public DelegateCommand(Action<object> execute)
        {
            this.execute = execute;
            this.canExecute = this.AlwaysCanExecute;
        }

        // Methods required by ICommand
        public void Execute(object param)
        {
            execute(param);
        }
```

```
        public bool CanExecute(object param)
        {
            return canExecute(param);
        }

        // Method required by IDelegateCommand
        public void RaiseCanExecuteChanged()
        {
            if (CanExecuteChanged != null)
                CanExecuteChanged(this, EventArgs.Empty);
        }

        // Default CanExecute method
        bool AlwaysCanExecute(object param)
        {
            return true;
        }
    }
}
```

This class implements *Execute* and *CanExecute* methods, but these methods merely call the methods saved as fields. These fields are set by the constructor of the class from constructor arguments.

For example, if the calculator View Model has a command to calculate, it can define the *CalculateCommand* property like so:

```
public IDelegateCommand CalculateCommand { protected set; get; }
```

The View Model also defines two methods named *ExecuteCalculate* and *CanExecuteCalculate*:

```
void ExecuteCalculate(object param)
{
    ...
}

bool CanExecuteCalculate(object param)
{
    ...
}
```

The constructor of the View Model class creates the *CalculateCommand* property by instantiating *DelegateCommand* with these two methods:

```
this.CalculateCommand = new DelegateCommand(ExecuteCalculate, CanExecuteCalculate);
```

Now that you see the general idea, let's look at the View Model for the keypad. For the text entered into and displayed by the keypad, this View Model defines two properties named *InputString* and the formatted version, *DisplayText*.

The View Model also defines two properties of type *IDelegateCommand* named *AddCharacterCommand* (for all the numeric and symbol keys) and *DeleteCharacterCommand*. These properties are created by instantiating *DelegateCommand* with the methods *ExecuteAddCharacter*,

ExecuteDeleteCharacter, and *CanExecuteDeleteCharacter*. There's no *CanExecuteAddCharacter* because the keys are always valid.

Project: KeypadWithViewModel | File: KeypadViewModel.cs

```csharp
using System;
using System.ComponentModel;
using System.Runtime.CompilerServices;

namespace KeypadWithViewModel
{
    public class KeypadViewModel : INotifyPropertyChanged
    {
        string inputString = "";
        string displayText = "";
        char[] specialChars = { '*', '#' };

        public event PropertyChangedEventHandler PropertyChanged;

        // Constructor
        public KeypadViewModel()
        {
            this.AddCharacterCommand = new DelegateCommand(ExecuteAddCharacter);
            this.DeleteCharacterCommand =
                new DelegateCommand(ExecuteDeleteCharacter, CanExecuteDeleteCharacter);
        }

        // Public properties
        public string InputString
        {
            protected set
            {
                bool previousCanExecuteDeleteChar = this.CanExecuteDeleteCharacter(null);

                if (this.SetProperty<string>(ref inputString, value))
                {
                    this.DisplayText = FormatText(inputString);

                    if (previousCanExecuteDeleteChar != this.CanExecuteDeleteCharacter(null))
                        this.DeleteCharacterCommand.RaiseCanExecuteChanged();
                }
            }

            get { return inputString; }
        }

        public string DisplayText
        {
            protected set { this.SetProperty<string>(ref displayText, value); }
            get { return displayText; }
        }
```

```csharp
// ICommand implementations
public IDelegateCommand AddCharacterCommand { protected set; get; }

public IDelegateCommand DeleteCharacterCommand { protected set; get; }

// Execute and CanExecute methods
void ExecuteAddCharacter(object param)
{
    this.InputString += param as string;
}

void ExecuteDeleteCharacter(object param)
{
    this.InputString = this.InputString.Substring(0, this.InputString.Length - 1);
}

bool CanExecuteDeleteCharacter(object param)
{
    return this.InputString.Length > 0;
}

// Private method called from InputString
string FormatText(string str)
{
    bool hasNonNumbers = str.IndexOfAny(specialChars) != -1;
    string formatted = str;

    if (hasNonNumbers || str.Length < 4 || str.Length > 10)
    {
    }
    else if (str.Length < 8)
    {
        formatted = String.Format("{0}-{1}", str.Substring(0, 3),
                                             str.Substring(3));
    }
    else
    {
        formatted = String.Format("({0}) {1}-{2}", str.Substring(0, 3),
                                                   str.Substring(3, 3),
                                                   str.Substring(6));
    }
    return formatted;
}

protected bool SetProperty<T>(ref T storage, T value,
                             [CallerMemberName] string propertyName = null)
{
    if (object.Equals(storage, value))
        return false;

    storage = value;
    OnPropertyChanged(propertyName);
    return true;
```

```
        }

        protected void OnPropertyChanged(string propertyName)
        {
            if (PropertyChanged != null)
                PropertyChanged(this, new PropertyChangedEventArgs(propertyName));
        }
    }
}
```

The *ExecuteAddCharacter* method expects that the parameter is the character entered by the user. This is how the single command is shared among multiple buttons.

The *CanExecuteDeleteCharacter* returns *true* only if there are characters to delete. The delete button should be disabled otherwise. But this method is called initially when the binding is first established and thereafter only if the *CanExecuteChanged* event is fired. The logic to fire this event is in the *set* accessor of *InputString*, which compares the *CanExecuteDeleteCharacter* return values before and after the input string is modified.

The XAML file instantiates the View Model as a resource and then defines a *DataContext* in the *Grid*. Notice the simplicity of the *Command* bindings on the thirteen *Button* controls and the use of *CommandParameter* on the numeric and symbol keys:

Project: KeypadWithViewModel | File: MainPage.xaml (excerpt)

```xml
<Page ... >

    <Page.Resources>
        <local:KeypadViewModel x:Key="viewModel" />
    </Page.Resources>

    <Grid Background="{StaticResource ApplicationPageBackgroundThemeBrush}"
          DataContext="{StaticResource viewModel}">

        <Grid HorizontalAlignment="Center"
              VerticalAlignment="Center"
              Width="288">

            <Grid.Resources>
                <Style TargetType="Button">
                    <Setter Property="ClickMode" Value="Press" />
                    <Setter Property="HorizontalAlignment" Value="Stretch" />
                    <Setter Property="Height" Value="72" />
                    <Setter Property="FontSize" Value="36" />
                </Style>
            </Grid.Resources>

            <Grid.RowDefinitions>
                <RowDefinition Height="Auto" />
                <RowDefinition Height="Auto" />
                <RowDefinition Height="Auto" />
                <RowDefinition Height="Auto" />
                <RowDefinition Height="Auto" />
            </Grid.RowDefinitions>
```

```
<Grid.ColumnDefinitions>
    <ColumnDefinition Width="*" />
    <ColumnDefinition Width="*" />
    <ColumnDefinition Width="*" />
</Grid.ColumnDefinitions>

<Grid Grid.Row="0" Grid.Column="0" Grid.ColumnSpan="3">
    <Grid.ColumnDefinitions>
        <ColumnDefinition Width="*" />
        <ColumnDefinition Width="Auto" />
    </Grid.ColumnDefinitions>

    <Border Grid.Column="0"
            HorizontalAlignment="Left">

        <TextBlock Text="{Binding DisplayText}"
                   HorizontalAlignment="Right"
                   VerticalAlignment="Center"
                   FontSize="24" />
    </Border>

    <Button Content="&#x21E6;"
            Command="{Binding DeleteCharacterCommand}"
            Grid.Column="1"
            FontFamily="Segoe Symbol"
            HorizontalAlignment="Left"
            Padding="0"
            BorderThickness="0" />
</Grid>

<Button Content="1"
        Command="{Binding AddCharacterCommand}"
        CommandParameter="1"
        Grid.Row="1" Grid.Column="0" />

...

<Button Content="#"
        Command="{Binding AddCharacterCommand}"
        CommandParameter="#"
        Grid.Row="4" Grid.Column="2" />
            </Grid>
        </Grid>
</Page>
```

The really boring part of this project is the code-behind file, which now contains nothing but a call to *InitializeComponent*.

Mission accomplished.

CHAPTER 7

Asynchronicity

These days programmers are discouraged from making frequent use of message boxes, but I'm sure we can all acknowledge how useful they can be to give the user some important information in a very direct manner, or to obtain a vital Yes, No, or Cancel.

The Windows Runtime supports a message box with the *MessageDialog* class, and it's actually quite versatile: Up to three buttons can be labeled with whatever text you'd like. However, there is no *Show* method in this class. The expected *Show* method has been replaced with *ShowAsync*.

That *Async* suffix is short for "asynchronous," and that's a very important sequence of five letters in the Windows Runtime. It's not just a change of name; it's a change in how you use the method and ultimately a change in philosophy in how we code for modern operating systems like Windows 8.

Threads and the User Interface

Like applications for earlier versions of Windows, a Windows 8 program is structured much like a state machine. Following initialization, the program usually sits dormant in memory waiting for events. Very often these events signal user interaction with the program, but sometimes they signal systemwide changes, such as a switch in the orientation of the display.

It's important that applications process events as quickly as possible and then return control back to the operating system to wait for more events. If an application doesn't process an event quickly, it could become unresponsive and annoy the user. For this reason, applications should relegate very lengthy jobs to secondary threads of execution. The thread devoted to the user interface should remain free and unencumbered of heavy processing.

But what if a particular method call in the Windows Runtime itself takes a long time to complete? Is the application programmer expected to anticipate that problem and put that call in a secondary thread?

No, that seems unreasonable. For that reason, when the Microsoft developers were designing the Windows Runtime, they attempted to identify any method call that could require more than 50 milliseconds to return control to the application. Approximately 10–15 percent of the Windows Runtime qualified. These methods were made asynchronous, meaning that the methods themselves spin off secondary threads to do the lengthy processing. They return control back to the application very quickly and later notify the application when they've completed.

You'll encounter asynchronous methods most often when working with file I/O or accessing the Internet. But they also turn up when invoking dialog boxes implemented in Windows 8, such as *MessageDialog* and a couple file pickers you'll see later in this chapter. All asynchronous methods in the Windows Runtime are identified with the *Async* suffix, and they all have similar definition patterns. Fortunately, working with asynchronous methods has become much less onerous as a result of powerful .NET libraries and enhancements to the C# programming language.

A skill in asynchronous programming is likely to become much more important in the years ahead. In consumer computers of the past, all threads of execution ran on the same processor. It was the job of the operating system to switch quickly among these threads, giving the appearance that they run simultaneously. In recent years, however, computers frequently have multiple processors, usually occupying the same chip in a multicore configuration. This type of hardware allows different threads to run on different processors.

Some types of heavy computational tasks—such as array processing—can take advantage of multiple processors by running a bunch of calculations in parallel. To support asynchronous and parallel processing, support was added to .NET called the Task-based Asynchronous Pattern, or TAP, which is centered around the *Task* class in the *System.Threading.Tasks* namespace. This part of .NET can be accessed by Windows Runtime applications coded in C# and Visual Basic, and it is much more powerful and versatile than the asynchronous support in the Windows Runtime itself.

Working with *MessageDialog*

To get a feel for the syntax of using asynchronous functions, let's look at *MessageDialog*. The *MessageDialog* constructor accepts a message string and (optionally) a title and by default displays a single button named "Close." This is suitable for delivering some essential information to the user. You also have the option of defining up to three custom buttons by using *UICommand* objects. Here's an example from a project called HowToAsync1:

```
MessageDialog msgdlg = new MessageDialog("Choose a color", "How To Async #1");
msgdlg.Commands.Add(new UICommand("Red", null, Colors.Red));
msgdlg.Commands.Add(new UICommand("Green", null, Colors.Green));
msgdlg.Commands.Add(new UICommand("Blue", null, Colors.Blue));
```

The first argument to the *UICommand* constructor is the text that appears on the button, and the third argument is an ID of type *object* that can be anything you like to identify the button. I've chosen to use the actual *Color* value indicated by the label. I'll discuss the second argument shortly.

The *UICommand* class implements the *IUICommand* interface. When the *MessageDialog* informs your program what button has been pressed, it does so with an object of type *IUICommand*.

The asynchronous processing occurs when you call the *ShowAsync* method. The method has no arguments and returns quickly back to the application. The message box itself is handled by a secondary thread of execution. Here's the call:

```
IAsyncOperation<IUICommand> asyncOp = msgdlg.ShowAsync();
```

What *ShowAsync* returns is an object that implements the generic *IAsyncOperation* interface. The generic argument is the *IUICommand* interface, which means that the *MessageDialog* returns an object of type *IUICommand*, except not right away. It can't return a value until the user presses one of the buttons and the *MessageDialog* is dismissed, and the *MessageDialog* hasn't even been displayed yet! For that reason, an object like *IAsyncOperation* is sometimes called a "future" or a "promise."

IAsyncOperation<T> derives from the *IAsyncInfo* interface, which defines methods named *Cancel* and *Close* and properties named *Id*, *Status*, and *ErrorCode*. The *IAsyncOperation<T>* interface additionally defines a property named *Completed*, which is a delegate of type *AsyncOperationCompletedHandler<T>*.

What you set to this *Completed* property is a callback method in your code. Although *Completed* is defined as a property, it functions like an event, in that it signals something of interest to your program. (The difference is that an event can have multiple handlers, but a property can have only one.) Here's how it's done:

```
asyncOp.Completed = OnMessageDialogShowAsyncCompleted;
```

If the method in your program that calls *ShowAsync* and sets the *Completed* handler contains any additional code, that code will be executed next. Only after the method calling *ShowAsync* returns control back to the operating system will the *MessageDialog* be displayed:

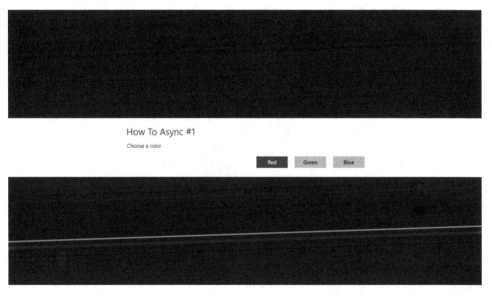

This *MessageDialog* is handled by a thread created specifically for this purpose. Although the user interface of your program is disabled while the *MessageDialog* is displayed, the user interface thread of your program is not blocked. It can continue to do work.

You'll notice the button labeled Red is colored differently from the others. This is the default button that is effectively triggered when the user presses Enter. You can change which button is the default using the *DefaultCommandIndex* property of *MessageDialog*. You can also select a button to be triggered when the user presses Esc by setting the *CancelCommandIndex* property.

When the user presses a button, the message box is dismissed and the *Completed* callback method in your program is called. The first argument to this method is the same object that *ShowAsync* returned, but I've given it a somewhat different name (*asyncInfo*) because now it actually has some information for us:

```
void OnMessageDialogShowAsyncCompleted(IAsyncOperation<IUICommand> asyncInfo,
                                       AsyncStatus asyncStatus)
{
    // Get the Color value
    IUICommand command = asyncInfo.GetResults();
    Color clr = (Color)command.Id;
    ...
}
```

This *IAsyncOperation* argument has a property named *Status* of type *AsyncStatus*, an enumeration with four members: *Started*, *Completed*, *Canceled*, or *Error*. This value is reproduced as the second argument to the *Completed* handler. If an error has occurred—which is not relevant for the *MessageDialog* class but certainly possible when dealing with file I/O or Internet access—the *ErrorCode* property of *IAsyncOperation* is an object of type *Exception*.

In the general case, you should check that the status is *Completed* before calling *GetResults*. The *GetResults* method returns an object of the same type as the generic argument to *IAsyncOperation*, in this case an object of type *IUICommand* indicating the pressed button. From this, you can get the *Id* property that comes from the third argument to the *UICommand* constructor. In this code it can be cast to a *Color* value.

And now, perhaps, the program can use this color to set the background brush on a *Grid*:

```
contentGrid.Background = new SolidColorBrush(clr);
```

Not so fast!

When your program calls *ShowAsync*, the *MessageDialog* class creates a secondary thread of execution to display the message box and buttons. When the user presses a button, the *Completed* handler in your code is called, but it runs in that secondary thread, and you cannot access user interface objects from this secondary thread!

For any particular window, there can be only one application thread that handles user input and displays controls and graphics that interact with this input. This "UI thread" (as it's called) is consequently very important and very special to Windows applications because all interaction with the user must occur through this thread. But only code that runs in that thread can access the elements and controls that constitute the user interface.

This prohibition can be generalized: *DependencyObject* is not thread safe. Any object based on a class that derives from *DependencyObject* can only be accessed by the thread that creates that object.

In this particular example, a *Color* value can be obtained by a secondary thread of execution because *Color* is a structure and hence does not derive from *DependencyObject*. However, any code that applies that *Color* value to the user interface must run in the UI thread.

Fortunately, there's a way to do it. To compensate for the fact that it is not thread safe, *DependencyObject* has a property named *Dispatcher* that returns an object of type *CoreDispatcher*. This *Dispatcher* property is an exception to the rule that prohibits you from accessing a *DependencyObject* from another thread. The *HasThreadAccess* property of *CoreDispatcher* lets you know if you can access this particular *DependencyObject* from the thread in which the code is running. If you can't (and even if you can), you can put a chunk of code on a queue for execution by the thread that created the object.

You queue up some code to run on the user interface thread by calling the *RunAsync* method defined by *CoreDispatcher*. This is another asynchronous method, and you pass to it a method that you want to run in the user interface thread:

```
void OnMessageDialogShowAsyncCompleted(IAsyncOperation<IUICommand> asyncInfo,
                                       AsyncStatus asyncStatus)
{
    ...
    this.Dispatcher.RunAsync(CoreDispatcherPriority.Normal, OnDispatcherRunAsyncCallback);
}

void OnDispatcherRunAsyncCallback()
{
    contentGrid.Background = new SolidColorBrush(clr);
}
```

Usually the *CoreDispatcher* object obtained from the *Dispatcher* property is not saved as a variable; the *RunAsync* method is just called on the *Dispatcher* property itself, as shown here. The callback you pass to the *RunAsync* method can safely access elements in the user interface. However, notice that there's no way to pass arbitrary information to this method, which means that *OnMessageDialogShowAsyncCompleted* must first save the *Color* value as a field.

It doesn't matter from which user interface element you obtain this *CoreDispatcher* object; all the user interface objects are created in the same UI thread, so they all work identically.

Although I haven't shown it in this code, the *RunAsync* method of *CoreDispatcher* returns an object of *IAsyncAction*:

```
IAsyncAction asyncAction = this.Dispatcher.RunAsync(CoreDispatcherPriority.Normal,
                                                    OnDispatcherRunAsyncCallback);
```

IAsyncAction is very similar to the *IAsyncOperation* object returned from the *ShowAsync* method of *MessageDialog*. Both of them implement the *IAsyncInfo* interface. The big difference is that *IAsyncOperation* is used for asynchronous methods that need to return something to the program (hence the generic argument), while *IAsyncAction* is used for asynchronous methods that do not return information.

Here's an interface hierarchy:

IAsyncInfo
> *IAsyncAction*
> *IAsyncActionWithProgress<TProgress>*
> *IAsyncOperation<TResult>*
> *IAsyncOperationWithProgress<TResult, TProgress>*

Some asynchronous methods are capable of reporting progress while performing the asynchronous job, and those have their own interfaces.

At any rate, you can set a *Completed* handler on the *IAsyncAction* object returned from the *RunAsync* method of *CoreDispatcher* and use that for accessing the user interface:

```
void OnMessageDialogShowAsyncCompleted(IAsyncOperation<IUICommand> asyncInfo,
                                       AsyncStatus asyncStatus)
{
    ...
    IAsyncAction asyncAction = this.Dispatcher.RunAsync(CoreDispatcherPriority.Normal,
                                                        OnDispatcherRunAsyncCallback);

    asyncAction.Completed = OnDispatcherRunAsyncCompleted;
}

void OnDispatcherRunAsyncCompleted(IAsyncAction asyncInfo, AsyncStatus asyncStatus)
{
    contentGrid.Background = new SolidColorBrush(clr);
}
```

This particular *Completed* handler runs in the user interface thread. But there's no real purpose for this additional method; you can't set the second argument of the *RunAsync* method to *null*, so you still need that method as well.

Here's the entire HowToAsync1 project. The XAML file has a button specifically for invoking the *MessageDialog*:

Project: HowToAsync1 | File: MainPage.xaml (excerpt)

```
<Grid Name="contentGrid"
      Background="{StaticResource ApplicationPageBackgroundThemeBrush}">

    <Button Content="Show me a MessageDialog!"
            HorizontalAlignment="Center"
            VerticalAlignment="Center"
            Click="OnButtonClick" />

</Grid>
```

Nothing in the code-behind file should be surprising at this point:

Project: HowToAsync1 | File: MainPage.xaml.cs (excerpt)

```
public sealed partial class MainPage : Page
{
    Color clr;

    public MainPage()
    {
        this.InitializeComponent();
    }

    void OnButtonClick(object sender, RoutedEventArgs args)
    {
        MessageDialog msgdlg = new MessageDialog("Choose a color", "How To Async #1");
        msgdlg.Commands.Add(new UICommand("Red", null, Colors.Red));
        msgdlg.Commands.Add(new UICommand("Green", null, Colors.Green));
        msgdlg.Commands.Add(new UICommand("Blue", null, Colors.Blue));

        // Show the MessageDialog with a Completed handler
        IAsyncOperation<IUICommand> asyncOp = msgdlg.ShowAsync();
        asyncOp.Completed = OnMessageDialogShowAsyncCompleted;
    }

    void OnMessageDialogShowAsyncCompleted(IAsyncOperation<IUICommand> asyncInfo,
                                           AsyncStatus asyncStatus)
    {
        // Get the Color value
        IUICommand command = asyncInfo.GetResults();
        clr = (Color)command.Id;

        // Use a Dispatcher to run in the UI thread
        IAsyncAction asyncAction = this.Dispatcher.RunAsync(CoreDispatcherPriority.Normal,
                                                OnDispatcherRunAsyncCallback);
    }

    void OnDispatcherRunAsyncCallback()
    {
        // Set the background brush
        contentGrid.Background = new SolidColorBrush(clr);
    }
}
```

The optional second argument to the *UICommand* constructor is a callback method of the delegate type *UICommandInvokedHandler*:

```
void OnMessageDialogCommand(IUICommand command)
{
    ...
}
```

This callback runs in the UI thread, and for that reason it represents perhaps an easier alternative to get the button pressed by the user.

Callbacks as Lambda Functions

To more gracefully handle callback methods is one reason why C# 3.0 added a support of anonymous methods, also known as lambda functions or lambda expressions. All the callback logic in HowToAsync1 can be moved to lambda functions in the *Click* handler, and the *Color* value doesn't need to be saved as a field. This is shown in the HowToAsync2 project:

Project: HowToAsync2 | File: MainPage.xaml.cs (excerpt)

```
void OnButtonClick(object sender, RoutedEventArgs args)
{
    MessageDialog msgdlg = new MessageDialog("Choose a color", "How To Async #2");
    msgdlg.Commands.Add(new UICommand("Red", null, Colors.Red));
    msgdlg.Commands.Add(new UICommand("Green", null, Colors.Green));
    msgdlg.Commands.Add(new UICommand("Blue", null, Colors.Blue));

    // Show the MessageDialog with a Completed handler
    IAsyncOperation<IUICommand> asyncOp = msgdlg.ShowAsync();
    asyncOp.Completed = (asyncInfo, asyncStatus) =>
        {
            // Get the Color value
            IUICommand command = asyncInfo.GetResults();
            Color clr = (Color)command.Id;

            // Use a Dispatcher to run in the UI thread
            IAsyncAction asyncAction = this.Dispatcher.RunAsync(CoreDispatcherPriority.Normal,
                                                                () =>
                {
                    // Set the background brush
                    contentGrid.Background = new SolidColorBrush(clr);
                });
        };
}
```

Although everything has been moved to the single *Click* handler, obviously this code does not run all at once. The *Completed* handler for the *MessageDialog* runs only after the box is dismissed, and the callback of the *CoreDispatcher* class runs only when the user interface thread is available for running some code.

This particular assemblage of two lambda functions isn't too bad, but it's easy for nested lambda functions to get rather more entangled. Once you start working with file I/O, for example, often several steps must be executed in sequence, many of which are asynchronous. The nested lambda functions start piling up and begin obscuring the actual structure of the code. Lambda functions are certainly convenient, but they are often not very readable. In some cases, lambda functions can even turn common procedural code inside out and make it difficult to execute a simple *return* statement or deal with an exception.

Another solution is desperately needed. Fortunately, it exists.

The Amazing *await* Operator

The C# 5.0 keyword *await* allows us to work with asynchronous operations as if they were relatively normal method calls without callback methods. Here's the code I've been using to obtain the *IAsyncOperation* object:

```
IAsyncOperation<IUICommand> asyncOp = msgdlg.ShowAsync();
```

The earlier programs used a callback method to obtain that *IUICommand* object indicating the pressed button. The *await* operator effectively extracts that *IUICommand* object directly from the *IAsyncOperation* object:

```
IUICommand command = await asyncOp;
```

Very often, these two statements are combined into one, as shown in the HowToAsync3 program, which is functionally equivalent to the first two programs:

Project: HowToAsync3 | File: MainPage.xaml.cs (excerpt)

```
async void OnButtonClick(object sender, RoutedEventArgs args)
{
    MessageDialog msgdlg = new MessageDialog("Choose a color", "How To Async #3");
    msgdlg.Commands.Add(new UICommand("Red", null, Colors.Red));
    msgdlg.Commands.Add(new UICommand("Green", null, Colors.Green));
    msgdlg.Commands.Add(new UICommand("Blue", null, Colors.Blue));

    // Show the MessageDialog
    IUICommand command = await msgdlg.ShowAsync();

    // Get the Color value
    Color clr = (Color)command.Id;

    // Set the background brush
    contentGrid.Background = new SolidColorBrush(clr);
}
```

Nice, wouldn't you say?

The *await* keyword is a full-fledged C# operator, and it's perfectly legal to embed it in more complex code. This single statement does the work of the last three statements shown above:

```
contentGrid.Background = new SolidColorBrush((Color)(await msgdlg.ShowAsync()).Id);
```

Let me emphasize again: HowToAsync3 is functionally identical to the two previous programs. Yet, the syntax is considerably cleaner, and it all results from the *await* operator. The *await* operator seems to bypass all the messy callback stuff and return the *IUICommand* directly. It looks like magic, but much of the messy implementation details are now hidden. The C# compiler recognizes the pattern of the *ShowAsync* method and generates the callback and the *GetResults* call.

What the *await* operator essentially does is break up the method in which it's used and turn it into a state machine. This *OnButtonClick* method begins executing normally until *ShowAsync* is called and the *await* appears. Despite its name, that *await* does *not* wait until the operation completes. Instead, the *Click* handler is exited at that point. Control returns to Windows. Other code on the program's user interface thread can then run, as can the *MessageDialog* itself. When the *MessageDialog* is dismissed and a result is ready and the UI thread is ready to run some code, execution of the *Click* handler continues with the assignment to the *IUICommand* object. The method then proceeds until the next *await* operator, if there is one.

However, there are no more *await* operators required in this particular *Click* handler: When the *IUICommand* object is assigned a value, the code is running in the user interface thread and a dispatcher is not required.

Prior to *await*, calling asynchronous operations in C# always seemed to me to violate the imperative structure of the language. The *await* operator brings back that imperative structure and turns asynchronous calls into what appears to be a series of sequential normal method calls. But despite the ease of *await*, you'll probably want to keep in mind that a method in which *await* appears is actually chopped into pieces behind the scenes with callbacks that you cannot see.

This can be a problem in some cases. Sometimes when Windows calls a method in your program, Windows expects that the method has completed when the method returns control back to the operating system. If that method has an *await* operator, that's not necessarily the case. The method with the *await* actually returns control back to Windows prior to the execution of the code following the *await* operator.

To let Windows know that a method using the *await* operator hasn't yet completed, a "deferral" object is involved. You'll see how this works later in this chapter when handling the *Suspending* event of the *Application* class.

There are some other restrictions on the *await* operator. If cannot appear in the *catch* or *finally* clause of an exception handler. However, it *can* appear in the *try* clause, and this is precisely how you'll trap errors that occur in the asynchronous method or determine if the asynchronous operation has been cancelled (as you'll see shortly).

The method in which the *await* operator appears must be flagged as *async* as this *Click* handler is:

```
async void OnButtonClick(object sender, RoutedEventArgs args)
{
    // ... code with await operators
}
```

But this *async* keyword doesn't do much of anything. In earlier versions of C#, *await* was not a keyword, so programmers could use the word for variable names or property names or whatever. Adding a new *await* keyword to C# 5.0 would break this code, but restricting *await* to methods flagged with *async* avoids that problem. The *async* modifier does not change the signature of the method—the method is still a valid *Click* handler. But you can't use *async* (and hence *await*) with methods that serve as entry points, specifically *Main* or class constructors.

If you need to call asynchronous methods during page initialization, call these methods in the handler for the *Loaded* event and flag that handler as *async*:

```
public MainPage()
{
    this.InitializeComponent();
    ...
    Loaded += OnLoaded;
}

async void OnLoaded(object sender, RoutedEventArgs arg)
{
    ...
}
```

Or, if you prefer defining the *Loaded* handler as an anonymous method:

```
public MainPage()
{
    this.InitializeComponent();
    ...
    Loaded += async (sender, args) =>
        {
            ...
        };
}
```

See the *async* before the argument list?

Cancelling an Asynchronous Operation

Not all asynchronous operations can be as cleanly structured as the *ShowAsync* call of *MessageDialog*. Three characteristics of asynchronous operations often make them more complex:

- **Cancellation**   Many asynchronous operations can be cancelled, either by a user deliberately stopping an operation that might be taking too long or in some other way.

- **Progress**   Some asynchronous operations report progress as they are performing a lengthy job. Often users appreciate seeing a progress report, either with a *ProgressBar* or text.

- **Errors**   An asynchronous operation might encounter a problem—for example, trying to open a file that no longer exists.

Let's tackle the cancellation issue first. Cancelling a message box—that is, removing it from the screen prior to the user pressing a button—is not very common, but it might make sense in certain scenarios.

The *IAsyncInfo* interface—which the four other standard Windows Runtime asynchronous interfaces implement—defines a method named *Cancel* that cancels the operation. As I mentioned earlier, the *IAsyncInfo* interface also includes a *Status* property that takes on a value of the

AsyncStatus enumeration, which has four members: *Started*, *Completed*, *Canceled*, and *Error*. For the last case, *IAsyncInfo* also defines an *ErrorCode* property of type *Exception*.

If you use a callback for the asynchronous operation, generally you need to check this status at the top of the callback method and make sure that the status is *Completed* rather than *Canceled* or *Error* before calling *GetResults*.

If you use *await*, put the *await* statement in a *try* block. If the asynchronous operation is cancelled, an exception is thrown of type *TaskCanceledException*. If an actual error occurs in the asynchronous operation, the exception indicates that error.

The HowToAsync3 program called the *ShowAsync* method of *MessageDialog* like this:

```
IUICommand command = await msgdlg.ShowAsync();
```

You can alternatively break this statement down to reveal the *IAsyncOperation* object:

```
IAsyncOperation<IUICommand> asyncOp = msgdlg.ShowAsync();
IUICommand command = await asyncOp;
```

No difference. This means that you can save the *asyncOp* object as a field so that some other method in the class can call the *Cancel* method on that object.

Let's simulate a cancellation of *MessageDialog* with a timer. The HowToCancelAsync program starts a five-second *DispatcherTimer* when the *MessageDialog* is displayed. If the *MessageDialog* is not dismissed in five seconds, the timer *Tick* callback calls *Cancel* on the *IAsyncOperation* object stored as a field:

Project: HowToCancelAsync | **File:** MainPage.xaml.cs (excerpt)

```
public sealed partial class MainPage : Page
{
    IAsyncOperation<IUICommand> asyncOp;

    public MainPage()
    {
        this.InitializeComponent();
    }

    async void OnButtonClick(object sender, RoutedEventArgs args)
    {
        MessageDialog msgdlg = new MessageDialog("Choose a color", "How To Cancel Async");
        msgdlg.Commands.Add(new UICommand("Red", null, Colors.Red));
        msgdlg.Commands.Add(new UICommand("Green", null, Colors.Green));
        msgdlg.Commands.Add(new UICommand("Blue", null, Colors.Blue));

        // Start a five-second timer
        DispatcherTimer timer = new DispatcherTimer();
        timer.Interval = TimeSpan.FromSeconds(5);
        timer.Tick += OnTimerTick;
        timer.Start();
```

```
    // Show the MessageDialog
    asyncOp = msgdlg.ShowAsync();
    IUICommand command = null;

    try
    {
        command = await asyncOp;
    }
    catch (Exception)
    {
        // The exception in this case will be TaskCanceledException
    }

    // Stop the timer
    timer.Stop();

    // If the operation was cancelled, exit the method
    if (command == null)
        return;

    // Get the Color value and set the background brush
    Color clr = (Color)command.Id;
    contentGrid.Background = new SolidColorBrush(clr);
}

void OnTimerTick(object sender, object args)
{
    // Cancel the asynchronous operation
    asyncOp.Cancel();
}
}
```

The logic is a little messier than the noncancellable version, of course, but it's no messier than other code involving *try* and *catch* blocks, and it still maintains an imperative structure. Once again, everything up to the *await* operator is executed first, and then the method continues in the *try* block when the *MessageDialog* is dismissed. Either an exception is raised or not, and the program can determine if an exception has occurred with a *null* value of the *command* variable assigned in the *try* block.

Approaches to File I/O

Programmers who work with .NET are familiar with the *System.IO* namespace for performing file I/O. You can leverage some of this knowledge in Windows 8, but you'll find the Windows 8 version of *System.IO* to be a bit emaciated. Instead, much of the Windows Runtime file I/O support can be found in several namespaces beginning with *Windows.Storage*. Be prepared for plenty of new file I/O classes and concepts. The whole file and stream interface has been revamped, and any method that accesses a disk is asynchronous.

A Windows 8 application can take one of three basic approaches to file I/O, which I describe in the next three sections in order of preference.

Application Local Storage

If an application needs to retain information that is of no value to any other application or to the user's examination, it is best to keep this information in application local storage (sometimes called isolated storage). This is an area on the hard drive that is private to the application, but the application doesn't need to worry where it's actually located. If the application is ever uninstalled from the machine, the storage is automatically freed.

Getting access to this storage requires the *ApplicationData* class in the *Windows.Storage* namespace. An *ApplicationData* object applicable to the current application can be obtained from the static *Current* property:

```
ApplicationData appData = ApplicationData.Current;
```

The *ApplicationData* class defines several properties you can use with this object:

The *LocalSettings* and *RoamingSettings* properties give you access to an *ApplicationDataContainer* that provides a dictionary for storing application settings. These application settings are restricted to the basic Windows Runtime types (numbers and strings).

The *LocalFolder*, *RoamingFolder*, and *TemporaryFolder* properties return objects of type *StorageFolder*, an important class also defined in the *Windows.Storage* namespace. The *StorageFolder* class represents a directory, in this case a directory for private use by the application. The *StorageFolder* class contains methods to create subfolders and to create or access files represented as objects of type *StorageFile*. A *StorageFile* object can then be opened and return a stream object for reading and writing.

File Pickers

The *Windows.Storage.Pickers* namespace is devoted to the *FileOpenPicker*, *FileSavePicker*, and *FolderPicker*. These are the standard dialog boxes that a Windows 8 program can use to open and save files in the standard data folders, such as the Documents Library, Music Library, and Pictures Library.

Like *MessageDialog*, *FileOpenPicker* and *FileSavePicker* have asynchronous methods to display the dialogs and return information of type *StorageFile*; the *FolderPicker* returns an object of type *StorageFolder*.

Because the user effectively gives the application permission to access the file system by invoking one of the pickers and then guides the pickers through the file system, the pickers have a great deal of flexibility. However, the application is required to indicate the specific file types that it's interested in. When using the *FileOpenPicker*, for example, the application is required to specify at least one file type (such as ".txt") in the *FileTypeFilter* property. These file types cannot include wildcards.

A *FileOpenPicker* will list only the file types specified by the application in the *FileTypeFilter* collection. Although *FileOpenPicker* can display many different types of files, it cannot list *all* possible files.

Bulk Access

An application can also access the user's file system directly using the *FileInformation* and *FolderInformation* classes defined in the *Windows.Storage.BulkAccess* namespace. The application is allowed to query folders for subfolders and files and to manipulate these folders and files in a fairly flexible manner.

However, because this process is not guided by the user, the application needs to declare its needs. An application that uses bulk access is required to have a package.appxmanifest file that indicates what areas of storage the application is allowed to examine. In Visual Studio you can edit the package. appxmanifest file from a dialog box. In the Capabilities section of this dialog, the Documents Library, Music Library, Pictures Library, or Videos Library option must be selected to get access to these areas. These capabilities define the limitations of the application. For the Documents Library, the Declarations section must include File Type Associations, and all the file types that the application wants must be explicitly listed; all file queries are limited to these file types.

I'll demonstrate the use of the bulk access classes with the Pictures Library in the PhotoScatter program in Chapter 14, "Bitmaps." The other two approaches to file I/O are demonstrated in this chapter.

File Pickers and File I/O

Let's become familiar with the *FileOpenPicker* and *FileSavePicker* classes by writing a simple program called PrimitivePad similar to the classic Windows Notepad. This program is basically a big *TextBox* with a couple commands. Normally these commands would be implemented on an application bar, but I'm going to save that topic for Chapter 8, "App Bars and Popups."

PrimitivePad has just two buttons for file I/O: Open and Save As. If it were a real application, it would also have New and Save buttons and it would prompt you to save a file if you pressed New or Open without saving your previous work. That logic is also coming up in the next chapter.

PrimitivePad has a third button for the word-wrapping mode, which is saved as a program setting. Here's the XAML file:

Project: PrimitivePad | File: MainPage.xaml (excerpt)

```
<Page ... >
    <Page.Resources>
        <Style x:Key="buttonStyle" TargetType="ButtonBase">
            <Setter Property="HorizontalAlignment" Value="Center" />
            <Setter Property="Margin" Value="0 12" />
        </Style>
    </Page.Resources>
```

```xml
<Grid Background="{StaticResource ApplicationPageBackgroundThemeBrush}">
    <Grid.RowDefinitions>
        <RowDefinition Height="Auto" />
        <RowDefinition Height="*" />
    </Grid.RowDefinitions>

    <Grid.ColumnDefinitions>
        <ColumnDefinition Width="*" />
        <ColumnDefinition Width="*" />
        <ColumnDefinition Width="*" />
    </Grid.ColumnDefinitions>

    <Button Content="Open..."
            Grid.Row="0"
            Grid.Column="0"
            Style="{StaticResource buttonStyle}"
            Click="OnFileOpenButtonClick" />

    <Button Content="Save As..."
            Grid.Row="0"
            Grid.Column="1"
            Style="{StaticResource buttonStyle}"
            Click="OnFileSaveAsButtonClick" />

    <ToggleButton Name="wrapButton"
                  Content="No Wrap"
                  Grid.Row="0"
                  Grid.Column="2"
                  Style="{StaticResource buttonStyle}"
                  Checked="OnWrapButtonChecked"
                  Unchecked="OnWrapButtonChecked" />

    <TextBox Name="txtbox"
             Grid.Row="1"
             Grid.Column="0"
             Grid.ColumnSpan="3"
             FontSize="24"
             AcceptsReturn="True" />
</Grid>
</Page>
```

The three buttons are displayed at the top, and in the big *TextBox* you can perhaps type some poetry:

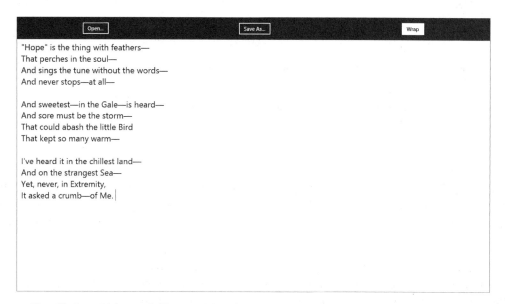

The *FileOpenPicker* and *FileSavePicker* classes invoke dialogs that take over the screen from your application and don't return control until they have been dismissed. If this is unacceptable to you, you'll want to explore the bulk access approach and navigate the directories on your own.

Both classes deliver an object of type *StorageFile* back to your application. (*FileOpenPicker* has an option for multiple selection that returns multiple *StorageFile* objects.) *StorageFile* is defined in the *Windows.Storage* namespace and represents an unopened file. Calling one of the *Open* methods on this *StorageFile* object gives you a stream object in the form of an interface such as *IInputStream* or *IRandomAccessStream* defined in the *Windows.Storage.Streams* namespace. You can then attach a *DataReader* or *DataWriter* object to this stream for reading or writing. Through extension methods defined in *System.IO*, it's also possible to create a .NET *Stream* object from the Windows Runtime stream objects and then use some familiar .NET objects, such as *StreamReader* or *StreamWriter*, for dealing with files. You might be able to salvage some existing code that uses .NET streams, and you'll also need these .NET stream objects for reading and writing XML files.

The only prerequisite for invoking *FileOpenPicker* is adding at least one string to the *FileTypeFilter* collection (for example, ".txt"). You then call the *PickSingleFileAsync* method. The standard file open picker is displayed, and the user selects an existing file and then presses Open or Cancel. If you use *await* with this method call, your program then gets back a *StorageFile* object indicating the file that the user selected. Here's the entire *Click* handler for the *Open* button:

Project: PrimitivePad | **File:** MainPage.xaml.cs (excerpt)

```
async void OnFileOpenButtonClick(object sender, RoutedEventArgs args)
{
    FileOpenPicker picker = new FileOpenPicker();
    picker.FileTypeFilter.Add(".txt");
    StorageFile storageFile = await picker.PickSingleFileAsync();
```

```
        // If user presses Cancel, result is null
        if (storageFile == null)
            return;

        using (IRandomAccessStream stream = await storageFile.OpenReadAsync())
        {
            using (DataReader dataReader = new DataReader(stream))
            {
                uint length = (uint)stream.Size;
                await dataReader.LoadAsync(length);
                txtbox.Text = dataReader.ReadString(length);
            }
        }
    }
}
```

PickSingleFileAsync actually returns an *IAsyncOperation<StorageFile>* object, but this is one of the few asynchronous calls in which the object represented by the generic argument can be *null*. This *null* value occurs when the user presses the Cancel button on the file open picker. For this case, nothing more needs to be done.

To open that *StorageFile* object for reading, you can call *OpenReadAsync* on it. That's another asynchronous operation, which of course makes sense because the call must access the disk. *OpenReadAsync* actually returns an object of type (hold your breath) *IAsyncOperation<IRandomAccessStreamWithContentType>*, but the *IRandomAccessStreamWithContentType* interface implements *IRandomAccessStream*, so I've used the shorter version. *IRandomAccessStream* implements *IDisposable*, so it's a good idea to put the stream object in a *using* block to be automatically disposed.

DataReader also implements *IDisposable*. This class provides access to many *Read* methods for the Windows Runtime primitive types, such as *ReadString*. These *Read* methods are not asynchronous because they don't involve disk accesses. The methods merely read bytes from an internal buffer (of type *IBuffer*) stored in memory and converts them to specific data types. The method call that actually accesses the disk file is *LoadAsync*, which loads a particular number of bytes from the file into this buffer and which must occur before any *Read* calls. For very large files, you might want to break down the file loading into smaller pieces. *DataReader* has an *UnconsumedBufferLength* property to help with this process.

Without the *await* operator, these three asynchronous methods would all require their own callbacks and a fourth callback would be required to run the code that sets the *Text* property of the *TextBox* in the user interface thread.

The file-saving logic is similar:

Project: PrimitivePad | File: MainPage.xaml.cs (excerpt)

```
async void OnFileSaveAsButtonClick(object sender, RoutedEventArgs args)
{
    FileSavePicker picker = new FileSavePicker();
    picker.DefaultFileExtension = ".txt";
    picker.FileTypeChoices.Add("Text", new List<string> { ".txt" });
```

```
        StorageFile storageFile = await picker.PickSaveFileAsync();

        // If user presses Cancel, result is null
        if (storageFile == null)
            return;

        using (IRandomAccessStream stream = await storageFile.OpenAsync(FileAccessMode.ReadWrite))
        {
            using (DataWriter dataWriter = new DataWriter(stream))
            {
                dataWriter.WriteString(txtbox.Text);
                await dataWriter.StoreAsync();
            }
        }
    }
}
```

The *StoreAsync* method of *DataWriter* returns a *DataWriteStoreOperation* object that implements *IAsyncOperation<uint>*. This *uint* indicates the number of bytes stored in the file. This value isn't used for anything here, and *StoreAsync* is the last statement of this method, so you might wonder if you need to use the *await* operator on this call. In general, you can call asynchronous methods that don't return values without the *await* operator, but keep in mind that the method making the call will continue execution while the asynchronous method runs, and that might be an issue if the method making the call implicitly expects the asynchronous method to complete before continuing execution. In this particular case, I'd be leery of omitting *await* because the *using* blocks implicitly close the *DataWriter* and *IRandomAccessStream* objects and you don't want that happening before *StoreAsync* completes.

The PrimitivePad program also gives you the option to set text wrapping on and off using a *ToggleButton*. The only part of the *MainPage* code-behind file you haven't seen yet is the portion of the program that is devoted to that feature:

Project: PrimitivePad | File: MainPage.xaml.cs (excerpt)

```
public sealed partial class MainPage : Page
{
    ApplicationDataContainer appData = ApplicationData.Current.LocalSettings;

    public MainPage()
    {
        this.InitializeComponent();

        Loaded += (sender, args) =>
            {
                if (appData.Values.ContainsKey("TextWrapping"))
                    txtbox.TextWrapping = (TextWrapping)appData.Values["TextWrapping"];

                wrapButton.IsChecked = txtbox.TextWrapping == TextWrapping.Wrap;
                wrapButton.Content = (bool)wrapButton.IsChecked ? "Wrap" : "No Wrap";

                txtbox.Focus(FocusState.Programmatic);
            };
    }
```

```
    ...
    void OnWrapButtonChecked(object sender, RoutedEventArgs args)
    {
        txtbox.TextWrapping = (bool)wrapButton.IsChecked ? TextWrapping.Wrap :
                                                            TextWrapping.NoWrap;
        wrapButton.Content = (bool)wrapButton.IsChecked ? "Wrap" : "No Wrap";
        appData.Values["TextWrapping"] = (int)txtbox.TextWrapping;
    }
}
```

A field obtains an *ApplicationDataContainer* object for this application. The *Values* property of this object is a dictionary that an application can use for saving program settings—at least those that can be expressed as primitive types. During the *Loaded* handler, if this dictionary contains a "TextWrapping" item, that item is used to set the property of the *TextBox*, and the *ToggleButton* is initialized accordingly.

Whenever the *ToggleButton* is checked or unchecked, the handler sets the *TextWrapping* property of the *TextBox* and saves the new value in the dictionary.

This is one way to save application settings. I'll show you another way later in this chapter involving the *Suspending* property of the *Application* class. If you ever need to locate these settings (and other local storage) on the hard drive, first use Visual Studio to check the Package Name of the application in the Packaging tab of the Package.appxmanifest file. (Or check the *Name* attribute of the Identity element in the actual file.) This is a GUID that uniquely identifies the application. The settings and local data can be found at the directory:

C:\Users\[user-name]\AppData\Local\Packages\[app-guid]

Handling Exceptions

If you work at it, you can crash the PrimitivePad program. For example, press the Open button in PrimitivePad, select a file in the picker, but before pressing the picker's Open button, use Windows Explorer (or something else) to delete the selected file. When PrimitivePad tries to open that nonexistent file, an exception is raised.

To catch errors such as these, the entire block of code after the check for a *null StorageFile* can be put in a *try* block. But watch out: You can't display a *MessageDialog* informing the user of the problem in the *catch* block because *await* isn't allowed in a *catch* block. A better way to handle exceptions looks more like this:

```
async void OnFileOpenButtonClick(object sender, RoutedEventArgs args)
{
    ...
    Exception exception = null;

    try
    {
        using (IRandomAccessStream stream = await storageFile.OpenReadAsync())
        {
```

```
        using (DataReader dataReader = new DataReader(stream))
        {
            uint length = (uint)stream.Size;
            await dataReader.LoadAsync(length);
            txtbox.Text = dataReader.ReadString(length);
        }
    }
}
catch (Exception exc)
{
    exception = exc;
}

if (exception != null)
{
    MessageDialog msgdlg = new MessageDialog(exception.Message,
                                             "File Read Error");
    await msgdlg.ShowAsync();
}
}
```

The final *if* statement determines if an exception has occurred by checking for a non-*null* value of the *exception* variable. At that point a *MessageDialog* can be used to display the error.

Consolidating Async Calls

Suppose you'd like to consolidate all the file-open and file-save logic into methods that are then called from the *Click* handlers of the buttons. This might be warranted if you're invoking these open and save pickers from more than one place in the program.

Let's imagine a method named *LoadFile* that displays the *FileOpenPicker*, reads the entire contents of a text file, and returns a string. The *OnFileOpenButtonClick* method can then be as simple as this:

```
void OnFileOpenButtonClick(object sender, RoutedEventArgs args)
{
    txtbox.Text = LoadFile();
}
```

Well, no, it actually can't be as simple as that. This *LoadFile* method cannot return a *string* because that *string* isn't available until multiple asynchronous operations have completed. Keep in mind that the *await* operator actually results in the creation of callback methods just as if you wrote them explicitly. Try writing a *LoadFile* method with explicit callback methods and then try to return a *string* from *LoadFile*. You can't do it.

You must be able to apply an *await* operator to *LoadFile* itself, which means you probably want to name it *LoadFileAsync*, which you'll call like this:

```
async void OnFileOpenButtonClick(object sender, RoutedEventArgs args)
{
    txtbox.Text = await LoadFileAsync();
}
```

But this should actually make you happy because it means that you can write *LoadFileAsync* without any exception handling and instead put the exception handling in the caller, in this case the *OnFileOpenButtonClick* handler.

But the real question is this: What should the return type of *LoadFileAsync* be? Judging from the asynchronous methods implemented in the Windows Runtime, you might guess *IAsyncOperation<string>*, but that's not so. The big problem is that the Windows Runtime does not define a public class that implements this interface.

Instead, as a C# programmer, you'll use classes in .NET that support asynchronous operations. The best return value of *LoadFileAsync* is *Task<string>*, and the method looks like this:

```
async Task<string> LoadFileAsync()
{
    FileOpenPicker picker = new FileOpenPicker();
    picker.FileTypeFilter.Add(".txt");
    StorageFile storageFile = await picker.PickSingleFileAsync();

    // If user presses Cancel, result is null
    if (storageFile == null)
        return null;

    using (IRandomAccessStream stream = await storageFile.OpenReadAsync())
    {
        using (DataReader dataReader = new DataReader(stream))
        {
            uint length = (uint)stream.Size;
            await dataReader.LoadAsync(length);
            return dataReader.ReadString(length);
        }
    }
}
```

Although this method is named *LoadFileAsync*, all the code that you supply to this method runs in the user interface thread. But it's considered an asynchronous method because parts of it run in secondary threads. Notice that the method returns *null* if the user presses Cancel on the picker. You can't assign a *null* to the *Text* property of *TextBox*, so the *Click* handler must accommodate that possibility:

```
async void OnFileOpenButtonClick(object sender, RoutedEventArgs args)
{
    string text = await LoadFileAsync();

    if (text != null)
        txtbox.Text = text;
}
```

What is *Task*? *Task* is a class defined in the *System.Threading.Tasks* namespace, and it is the core of the .NET support of asynchronous and parallel processing. It exists in both generic and nongeneric versions. You'll use the nongeneric version for a method that doesn't return anything, such as a method that consolidates all the save logic:

```
async void OnFileSaveAsButtonClick(object sender, RoutedEventArgs args)
{
    await SaveFileAsync(txtbox.Text);
}

async Task SaveFileAsync(string text)
{
    FileSavePicker picker = new FileSavePicker();
    picker.DefaultFileExtension = ".txt";
    picker.FileTypeChoices.Add("Text", new List<string> { ".txt" });
    StorageFile storageFile = await picker.PickSaveFileAsync();

    // If user presses Cancel, result is null
    if (storageFile == null)
        return;

    using (IRandomAccessStream stream = await storageFile.OpenAsync(FileAccessMode.ReadWrite))
    {
        using (DataWriter dataWriter = new DataWriter(stream))
        {
            dataWriter.WriteString(text);
            await dataWriter.StoreAsync();
        }
    }
}
```

Support of asynchronous processing in .NET and the Windows Runtime is similar enough that the types can be converted to each other. *Task* has an extension method named *AsAsyncAction* that returns an *IAsyncAction*, and *Task<T>* has an extension method *AsAsyncOperation<T>* that returns an *IAsyncOperation<T>*. Similarly, *IAsyncAction* has an *AsTask* method that returns a *Task*, and *IAsyncOperation<T>* has an *AsTask<T>* method that returns a *Task<T>*.

However, *Task* is much more powerful than the asynchronous support in the Windows Runtime, offering facilities to manage parallel processing and to await groups of tasks. *Task* really deserves a book of its own—this is not that book, but later in this chapter I'll show you how to use *Task* for your own lengthy processing jobs.

Streamlined File I/O

Although it's good for programmers to be familiar with file I/O using the *DataReader* and *DataWriter* classes, much of your file I/O jobs can probably be accomplished with some streamlined methods. These are available in the static *FileIO* and *PathIO* classes from the *Windows.Storage* namespace. Methods in these classes read or write whole files in single asynchronous calls.

For text files, the *FileIO.ReadLinesAsync* method can read a text file and return an *IList* of *string* objects (one per line) and *FileIO.ReadTextAsync* can return a file in a single *string* object. In

PrimitivePad, the block of two nested *using* statements in *OnFileOpenButtonClick* can be replaced with this:

```
txtbox.Text = await FileIO.ReadTextAsync(storageFile);
```

Similarly, the file save logic can be replaced with this single call:

```
await FileIO.WriteTextAsync(storageFile, txtbox.Text, UnicodeEncoding.Utf8);
```

For binary files, you can use *ReadBufferAsync* and *WriteBufferAsync*. These methods work with an object of type *IBuffer*. An *IBuffer* object is basically an array of bytes that exists in system memory. References to an *IBuffer* are tracked so that Windows can remove it from memory if it's no longer needed.

The *IBuffer* object can't be accessed directly from a C# program, but you can get at it indirectly. To create a binary file, you can create a *DataWriter* object, write into it, and then save the internal *IBuffer* object that the *DataWriter* created:

```
DataWriter dataWriter = new DataWriter();
// ... write to dataWriter
await FileIO.WriteBufferAsync(storageFile, dataWriter.DetachBuffer());
```

For reading a binary file, you first obtain an *IBuffer* object by reading the file and then create a *DataReader* from that:

```
IBuffer buffer = await FileIO.ReadBufferAsync(storageFile);
DataReader dataReader = DataReader.FromBuffer(buffer);
// ... read from dataReader
```

If you include the *System.Runtime.InteropServices.WindowsRuntime* namespace in your program, you can convert an *IBuffer* object to a .NET *Stream* object and then use this *Stream* to create other classes defined in the *System.IO* namespace: *BinaryReader*, *BinaryWriter*, *StreamReader*, and *StreamWriter*. Or you can convert an *IBuffer* to an array of bytes.

The *PathIO* class is similar to *FileIO* but instead of passing *StorageFile* objects to the static methods, you pass a string URI. This URI generally begins with "ms-appx:///" to access files stored as program content and "ms-appdata:///" to access files in application storage, as I'll demonstrate shortly.

The *HttpClient* class is the main class for uploading or downloading files over the Web, but if you don't need that flexibility, *RandomAccessStreamReference* comes in very handy:

```
Uri uri = new Uri("http://...");
RandomAccessStreamReference streamRef = RandomAccessStreamReference.CreateFromUri(uri);

using (IRandomAccessStream stream = await streamRef.OpenReadAsync())
{
    ...
}
```

You can then call *ReadAsync* on that *IRandomAccessStream* to read the contents of the file into an *IBuffer*, and then pass the *IBuffer* to the static *DataReader.FromBuffer* method.

Application Lifecycle Issues

The PrimitivePad program has a subtle flaw that needs to be addressed. As you know, if you run the regular Windows desktop Notepad program, type in some text, and then try to terminate the program—by pressing the Close button at the upper right corner, by pressing Alt+F4, by selecting Exit from the File menu, or by shutting down Windows—Notepad will display a "Do you want to save changes...?" message box. You can select Save, Don't Save, or Cancel.

We're all familiar with this convention, but it is no longer a good solution. Computing no longer exclusively involves sitting down at your desk, turning on the computer, doing some work, and then shutting the computer down. It's just as likely that you'll pull a tablet out of your handbag or off the coffee table, unlock the screen, spend some time with it, and then toss it back where it came from, perhaps putting it to sleep by pressing the on/off button or letting it go to sleep by itself.

Do you want your Windows applications to ask you to save data when the computer is going to sleep? No, you do not. By putting the computer to sleep (or even by turning your eyes away from the screen) you've signaled that continued interaction with the computer is precisely what you do *not* want.

But here's the problem: What if that tablet now sitting on the coffee table determines that the battery is getting too low to continue maintaining even the sleep state and it decides to turn itself off? In a practical sense, it can't warn you that this is happening.

Or perhaps you're using the computer and Windows needs to free up some memory. One way it can do this is by terminating applications that haven't been used in a while. Again, as a user, you probably don't want to be notified of this event.

For these reasons, a polite Windows 8 application saves information so that it can provide a continuous user experience regardless of whether it's terminated or not. If an application contains some unsaved data that the user might regret losing and that application is terminated, then the next time that application runs, it should display that data. (Obviously, for some applications this is more important than for others. For a calculator, for example, it probably doesn't matter all that much if the program discards the data. But for a spreadsheet it's a very big deal.)

This is easy, right? As a programmer all you need to know about is the event that is fired when the application is about to be terminated. You can use this event to save any unsaved data in local application storage and then restore that data the next time the program is run.

The only problem is: There's no such event.

However, there is an event that indicates when an application is being *suspended*. An application is always suspended before it's terminated (unless the termination is abnormal, such as crash), but a suspension doesn't necessarily result in termination. There's another event that indicates when the application is being resumed following a suspension.

An application is suspended when it's no longer running in the foreground—that is, when you bring up the Windows start screen or sweep your finger from the left edge to bring another program to the foreground. An application is also suspended when you press Alt+F4 to terminate it or when you put the computer to sleep. In all these cases, there's actually about a 10-second delay before the application is suspended; this delay is for Windows (and the application) to avoid doing work if the program is resumed shortly.

After a program is suspended, it might be resumed or it might be terminated. Much time might elapse after suspension before resumption or termination. Because there is no event to indicate when a program is being terminated, the application must use the suspension to save everything it needs to resume, even though that suspension might not end in a termination. (Now perhaps you can see why there's no specific event for program termination: If the program is already suspended, Windows would need to resume the application just to fire the termination event!)

The *Application* class defines two events for this purpose: *Suspending* and *Resuming*. The *Suspending* event is much more important than *Resuming*. An application uses this event to save unsaved data in local application storage. The program *does* not need to restore this data during the *Resuming* event. Windows restores the application itself. All the program needs to do is load the data the next time it's run.

However, an application can choose to do other chores during the *Suspending* event and undo those during the *Resuming* event. For example, the program can try to minimize its footprint in memory by letting go of large resources that it can re-create. Or it might use the *Resuming* event to refresh itself with updated data coming from a Web source.

When a program is running under the Visual Studio debugger, it does not get suspended and resumed the same way as when it's running by itself. An application running by itself is suspended when the program is no longer running in the foreground, but an application running under the Visual Studio debugger is not.

Another difference: A program is *not* suspended prior to termination if the termination is abnormal. Abnormal termination can occur by an unhandled exception or—keep this in mind when you're experimenting—when you use the Stop Debugging command of Visual Studio.

However, if you terminate an application running under the Visual Studio debugger with Alt+F4, the program gets a *Suspending* event and the program is terminated, but that process is delayed about 10 seconds, during which time Visual Studio still believes that the program is running!

To compensate for these issues, Visual Studio has commands on the Debug Location toolbar to manually Suspend, Resume, or Suspend And Shutdown an application. These commands are essential for developing suspension and resumption code while running the program under the debugger.

Because it's hard to examine normal *Suspending* and *Resuming* events while a program is running under Visual Studio, I've written a little program that logs these events to a file that it stores in local application storage. This program is intended to be run outside the Visual Studio debugger.

The XAML file of the SuspendResumeLog program contains a read-only *TextBox*:

Project: SuspendResumeLog | File: MainPage.xaml (excerpt)

```
<Grid Background="{StaticResource ApplicationPageBackgroundThemeBrush}">
    <TextBox Name="txtbox"
             AcceptsReturn="True"
             IsReadOnly="True" />
</Grid>
```

The code-behind file handles three events: the *Loaded* event of *MainPage* (which is executed once when the program is launched), and the *Suspending* and *Resuming* events of the current *Application* object. All these events are logged to a file named logfile.txt that is saved in local application storage:

Project: SuspendResumeLog | File: MainPage.xaml.cs (excerpt)

```
public sealed partial class MainPage : Page
{
    StorageFile logfile;

    public MainPage()
    {
        this.InitializeComponent();

        Loaded += OnLoaded;
        Application.Current.Suspending += OnAppSuspending;
        Application.Current.Resuming += OnAppResuming;
    }

    async void OnLoaded(object sender, RoutedEventArgs args)
    {
        // Create or obtain the log file
        StorageFolder localFolder = ApplicationData.Current.LocalFolder;
        logfile = await localFolder.CreateFileAsync("logfile.txt",
                                        CreationCollisionOption.OpenIfExists);

        // Load the file and display it
        txtbox.Text = await FileIO.ReadTextAsync(logfile);

        // Log the launch
        txtbox.Text += String.Format("Launching at {0}\r\n", DateTime.Now.ToString());
        await FileIO.WriteTextAsync(logfile, txtbox.Text);
    }

    async void OnAppSuspending(object sender, SuspendingEventArgs args)
    {
        SuspendingDeferral deferral = args.SuspendingOperation.GetDeferral();
```

```
            // Log the suspension
            txtbox.Text += String.Format("Suspending at {0}\r\n", DateTime.Now.ToString());
            await FileIO.WriteTextAsync(logfile, txtbox.Text);

            deferral.Complete();
        }

        async void OnAppResuming(object sender, object args)
        {
            // Log the resumption
            txtbox.Text += String.Format("Resuming at {0}\r\n", DateTime.Now.ToString());
            await FileIO.WriteTextAsync(logfile, txtbox.Text);
        }
    }
```

During the *Loaded* event, the program obtains the *StorageFolder* associated with local storage for this application and creates a file named logfile.txt. Using the handy *CreationCollisionOption* .*OpenIfExists* argument, this *CreateFileAsync* call is the same as a *GetFileAsync* if the file already exists, which it will the second and subsequent times this program is run.

The *OpenIfExists* enumeration member is somewhat misnamed. It should really be *GetIfExists* because the file is not opened for reading and writing in the normal sense. However, the file is created with a zero-byte length, and a reference to that file is obtained. The *FileIO.ReadTextAsync* and *FileIO* .*WriteTextAsync* calls actually open the file, read or write to it, and close the file.

Notice the use of the *SuspendingDeferral* object in the *Suspending* event handler. Without that, Windows would think that the *Suspending* handler had completed when it calls the *WriteTextAsync* call because that's when the handler is exited for the first time.

Normally, when a program maintains unsaved data in local storage, the program only needs to load the data during the *Loaded* event (or some other initialization event) and save it during the *Suspending* event. The SuspendResumeLog program also saves the file during the *Loaded* event and *Resuming* event. Although the program is most designed to run outside the Visual Studio debugger, I added this code in case the program is running under the Visual Studio debugger and terminates with Stop Debugging. Without those saves, that data would be lost because the *Suspending* handler is not fired for this type of termination.

When testing a program's ability to save and restore data running in the Visual Studio debugger, it might be best to get into the habit of terminating the program by using the Suspend And Shutdown command rather than Stop Debugging.

You can replace the *FileIO.ReadTextAsync* call with this:

```
txtbox.Text = await PathIO.ReadTextAsync("ms-appdata:///local/logfile.txt");
```

And you can replace the *FileIO.WriteTextAsync* calls with this:

```
await PathIO.WriteTextAsync("ms-appdata:///local/logfile.txt", txtbox.Text);
```

The *ms-appdata* prefix indicates application isolated storage. What appears to be a directory named *local* actually differentiates this area from *roaming* or *temp*. Even if you use these file URIs for reading and writing, you still need to create the *StorageFile* object by using a method of *StorageFolder*.

Normally, code that updates log files appends text to an existing file. There are methods in *FileIO* and *PathIO* for appending text, but I decided not to do that in the SuspendResumeLog program because the same text would need to be appended to both the *TextBox* and the log file, or the *TextBox* would need to be reloaded from the appended log file.

The QuickNotes project is similar to SuspendResumeLog in that it consists of a *TextBox* and saves the contents in local application storage. However, QuickNotes lets you type text in the *TextBox*, and of course it's automatically saved for the next time you bring up the program. Here's the XAML file:

Project: QuickNotes | File: MainPage.xaml (excerpt)

```
<Grid Background="{StaticResource ApplicationPageBackgroundThemeBrush}">
    <TextBox Name="txtbox"
             AcceptsReturn="True"
             TextWrapping="Wrap" />
</Grid>
```

The code-behind file uses *FileIO.ReadTextAsync* to read the file (because it already has a *StorageFile* object handy) but *PathIO.WriteTextAsync* for writing the file:

Project: QuickNotes | File: MainPage.xaml.cs (excerpt)

```
public sealed partial class MainPage : Page
{
    public MainPage()
    {
        this.InitializeComponent();
        Loaded += OnLoaded;
        Application.Current.Suspending += OnAppSuspending;
    }

    async void OnLoaded(object sender, RoutedEventArgs args)
    {
        StorageFolder localFolder = ApplicationData.Current.LocalFolder;
        StorageFile storageFile = await localFolder.CreateFileAsync("QuickNotes.txt",
                                            CreationCollisionOption.OpenIfExists);
        txtbox.Text = await FileIO.ReadTextAsync(storageFile);
        txtbox.SelectionStart = txtbox.Text.Length;
        txtbox.Focus(FocusState.Programmatic);
    }

    async void OnAppSuspending(object sender, SuspendingEventArgs args)
    {
        SuspendingDeferral deferral = args.SuspendingOperation.GetDeferral();
        await PathIO.WriteTextAsync("ms-appdata:///local/QuickNotes.txt", txtbox.Text);
        deferral.Complete();
    }
}
```

Your Own Asynchronous Methods

Earlier I demonstrated how to write a method with the word *Async* at the end that calls one or more other asynchronous methods. The code that you supply for such a method runs in the user interface thread, even though the asynchronous methods that are called within that method run in secondary threads.

Sometimes an application needs to perform a lengthy computational job that has the potential of grinding the UI thread to a halt. If you can chop the job into tiny pieces, you might be able to use a *DispatcherTimer* or a *CompositionTarget.Rendering* event to do it. The event handlers run in the UI thread, but the job is spread out in such a way that the user interface remains responsive.

Or you can do the job in a secondary thread. One approach is to make use of the *ThreadPool* class in the *Windows.System.Threading* namespace, but the *Task* class is much more versatile, so that's the approach I'll be demonstrating here.

The simplest *Task.Run* method has an argument of type *Action* (a method with no arguments and no return value) and runs that argument in a thread obtained from the thread pool. Generally, you'll use a lambda function for this argument.

For example, suppose you have a method (perhaps with a couple arguments) that requires a long time to run:

```
void BigJob(object arg1, object arg2)
{
    // ... heavy processing job
}
```

You don't want to run this method directly from the user interface thread, but you can *await* this method by putting it in the body of a lambda function that you pass to *Task.Run*:

```
await Task.Run(() => BigJob("abc", 555));
```

Because *Task.Run* runs *BigJob* in a secondary thread, *BigJob* cannot contain any code that accesses user interface objects. (Or rather, if it *does* need to contain code that accesses user interface objects, it must do so using the *RunAsync* method of *CoreDispatcher*. If *BigJob* needs to *await* that *RunAsync* call, *BigJob* must be declared as *async* and return a *Task* object.)

Here's another method that requires lots of processing time but returns a value:

```
double CalculateMagicNumber(string str, double x)
{
    double magicNumber = 0;

    // ... big job

    return magicNumber;
}
```

Again, you don't want to call this method on the user interface thread, but you can do so safely with *Task.Run*:

```
double magicNum = await Task.Run(() =>
    {
        return CalculateMagicNumber("abc", 5);
    });
```

Because the method in the body of the lambda function passed to *Task.Run* returns a *double* (the return value from *CalculateMagicNumber*), the return value of *Task.Run* is *Task<double>*. Notice the *await* operator that returns the *double* value that *CalculateMagicNumber* calculated.

Or you can define a *CalculateMagicNumberAsync* method like so:

```
Task<double> CalculateMagicNumberAsync(string str, double x)
{
    return Task.Run(() =>
        {
            return CalculateMagicNumber(str, x);
        });
}
```

You can then call this method from the user interface thread:

```
double magicNum = await CalculateMagicNumberAsync("xyz", 333);
```

Or you can consolidate the entire big job in a single method:

```
Task<double> CalculateMagicNumberAsync(string str, double x)
{
    return Task.Run(() =>
        {
            double magicNumber = 0;

            // ... big job in non-UI thread

            return magicNumber;
        });
}
```

If the calculation requires some calls to other asynchronous methods, those methods should be preceded with *await* and the lambda function should be declared with *async*:

```
Task<double> CalculateMagicNumberAsync(string str, double x)
{
    return Task.Run(async () =>
        {
            double magicNumber = 0;

            // ... big job with await's

            return magicNumber;
        });
}
```

This last form—with everything in this one method—is the easiest if you want to incorporate cancellation and progress reports.

It is very likely that the asynchronous method that you're defining contains some kind of loop:

```
Task<double> CalculateMagicNumberAsync(string str, double x)
{
    return Task.Run(async () =>
    {
        double magicNumber = 0;

        for (int i = 0; i < 100; i++)
        {
            // ... big job with await's
        }
        return magicNumber;
    });
}
```

This loop is a good place to perform both cancellation and progress, but some judgment and prudence are required. You don't want to check for cancellation or report progress thousands of times per second, or every five seconds. Every second or several times a second is about right. For a loop that executes thousands or millions of times, you might want to include some logic that checks for cancellation or reports progress only if the loop variable is equally divisible by 100, for example.

To incorporate cancellation into this method, you add a method parameter of type *CancellationToken* and at a convenient point, call the *ThrowIfCancellationRequested* method on that argument:

```
Task<double> CalculateMagicNumberAsync(string str, double x,
                            CancellationToken cancellationToken)
{
    return Task.Run(async () =>
    {
        double magicNumber = 0;

        for (int i = 0; i < 100; i++)
        {
            cancellationToken.ThrowIfCancellationRequested();

            // ... big job with await's
        }
        return magicNumber;
    }, cancellationToken);
}
```

Notice that the *cancellationToken* parameter is also passed as a second argument to *Task.Run*. This allows the task to be cancelled before it's even started.

Now, when calling the *CalculateMagicNumberAsync* method, you must pass a *CancellationToken* as the last argument. To obtain this object, you'll need to define an object of type *CancellationTokenSource* as a field:

```
CancellationTokenSource cts;
```

This object must be defined as a field because it needs to be accessed from a method that triggers the cancellation, very likely based on the user's initiative:

```
void OnCancelButtonClick(object sender, RoutedEventArgs args)
{
    cts.Cancel();
}
```

Prior to calling *CalculateMagicNumberAsync*, a new *CancellationTokenSource* must be created and its *Token* property passed to the method in a *try* block:

```
cts = new CancellationTokenSource();
double magicNum = 0;

try
{
    magicNum = await CalculateMagicNumberAsync("xyz", 333, cts.Token);
}
catch (OperationCanceledException)
{
    // ... cancellation logic
}
catch (Exception exc)
{
    // ... other exceptions logic
}
```

When the *Cancel* method of *CancellationTokenSource* is called, the next time the asynchronous method calls the *ThrowIfCancellationRequested* method of the *CancellationToken* object, an exception is raised of type *OperationCanceledException*, and this is caught by the code calling the asynchronous method. Other exceptions that might be raised (most likely as a result of file I/O or web access calls) are trapped in the second *catch* block.

If you want the asynchronous method to report progress, you add another parameter to the method for that purpose. This parameter is of type *IProgress<T>*, where *T* is the type you prefer for marking the progress. Generally *T* will be a *double*, but whether the progress ranges from 0 to 1 or 0 to 100 is up to you. If the latter, *T* can be an *int*. I've even seen an example where *T* is a *bool*, with *true* indicating the job is complete!

At a convenient place—perhaps at the same point you check for cancellation—you can report progress:

```
Task<double> CalculateMagicNumberAsync(string str, double x,
                            CancellationToken cancellationToken,
                            IProgress<double> progress)
{
```

```
    return Task.Run(async () =>
    {
        double magicNumber = 0;

        for (int i = 0; i < 100; i++)
        {
            cancellationToken.ThrowIfCancellationRequested();
            progress.Report((double)i);

            // ... big job with await's
        }
        return magicNumber;
    }, cancellationToken);
}
```

This code just casts the loop variable to a *double* so it ranges from 0 to 100 and represents a percentage (which makes it convenient for setting the *Value* property of a *ProgressBar*). In some cases you might want to explicitly report a zero progress at the beginning of the method and a maximum progress at the end.

You'll also want a method that has the progress type you've selected as a parameter and which displays that progress:

```
void ProgressCallback(double progress)
{
    progressBar.Value = progress;
}
```

This callback is called in the user interface thread.

When calling *CalculateMagicNumberAsync* (which, as you'll recall, is inside a *try* block), you create an object of type *Progress* with the callback method you've defined and pass that as the last argument:

```
magicNum = await CalculateMagicNumberAsync("xyz", 333, cts.Token,
                            new Progress<double>(ProgressCallback));
```

The progress callback doesn't need to be a separate function. It can be a simple lambda expression:

```
magicNum = await CalculateMagicNumberAsync("xyz", 333, cts.Token,
                    new Progress<double>((percent) => progressBar.Value = percent));
```

Let's look at a real example.

For the author of a programming tutorial, one of the hard parts of demonstrating asynchronous operations is coming up with a reasonably simple example that requires an appreciable amount of time to execute. One finds oneself deliberately writing inefficient code just so that there's time to see the *ProgressBar* move and to hit the Cancel button before the job is done!

The WordFreq project reads a text file—such as a plain-text e-book from the famous Project Gutenberg website—and calculates word frequencies, letting you determine, for example, how many times the word "whale" appears in Herman Melville's *Moby-Dick*. In fact, WordFreq is hard-coded for *Moby-Dick*, but of course the word-counting code in the *GetWordFrequenciesAsync* method is generalized.

GetWordFrequenciesAsync has a .NET Stream argument because I wanted to use the .NET *StreamReader* within the method to read the file line by line. It also includes *CancellationToken* and *IProgress* arguments.

But the return value is a bit hairy. The method uses a .NET *Dictionary* object to accumulate the counts of each unique word in the file. Hence, the *Dictionary* key is of type *string* and the value is of type *int*. At the end of the method, the LINQ *OrderByDescending* function sorts the dictionary by value—that is, the highest frequency words at the beginning. The result is a collection of objects of type:

```
KeyValuePair<string, int>
```

The actual collection returned by *OrderByDescending* is an object of the generic type *IOrderedEnumerable*:

```
IOrderedEnumerable<KeyValuePair<string, int>>
```

This means that the return value of the *GetWordFrequenciesAsync* method is:

```
Task<IOrderedEnumerable<KeyValuePair<string, int>>>
```

And here it is:

Project: WordFreq | File: MainPage.xaml.cs (excerpt)

```
Task<IOrderedEnumerable<KeyValuePair<string, int>>> GetWordFrequenciesAsync(Stream stream,
                                              CancellationToken cancellationToken,
                                              IProgress<double> progress)
{
    return Task.Run(async () =>
        {
            Dictionary<string, int> dictionary = new Dictionary<string, int>();

            using (StreamReader streamReader = new StreamReader(stream))
            {
                // Read the first line
                string line = await streamReader.ReadLineAsync();

                while (line != null)
                {
                    cancellationToken.ThrowIfCancellationRequested();
                    progress.Report(100.0 * stream.Position / stream.Length);

                    string[] words = line.Split(' ', ',', '.', ';', ':');

                    foreach (string word in words)
                    {
                        string charWord = word.ToLower();

                        while (charWord.Length > 0 && !Char.IsLetter(charWord[0]))
                            charWord = charWord.Substring(1);
```

```
                while (charWord.Length > 0 &&
                            !Char.IsLetter(charWord[charWord.Length - 1]))
                    charWord = charWord.Substring(0, charWord.Length - 1);

                if (charWord.Length == 0)
                    continue;

                if (dictionary.ContainsKey(charWord))
                    dictionary[charWord] += 1;
                else
                    dictionary.Add(charWord, 1);
            }
            line = await streamReader.ReadLineAsync();
        }
    }

    // Return the dictionary sorted by Value (the word count)
    return dictionary.OrderByDescending(i => i.Value);
    }, cancellationToken);
}
```

Notice that the body of the method passed to *Task.Run* has occurrences of the *await* operator with calls to the *ReadLineAsync* method of *StreamReader*. Consequently, the lambda function passed to *Task.Run* is flagged with *async*. For every line in the file, the *CancellationToken* is checked and progress is reported as a percentage based on the amount of the *Stream* object that's been read. The Project Gutenberg e-book of *Moby-Dick* contains over 22,000 lines, so these two calls are rather too frequent, but reducing their number probably involves keeping track of line counts.

This method has no exception handling. If the *StreamReader* constructor or *ReadLineAsync* call raises an exception, that must be handled by the code calling this method.

The XAML file for the program has two buttons for Start and Cancel (the latter initially disabled), a *ProgressBar* for reporting progress, a *TextBlock* for reporting errors, and a *StackPanel* in a *ScrollViewer* for the list of words and word counts:

Project: WordFreq | File: MainPage.xaml (excerpt)
```xml
<Grid Background="{StaticResource ApplicationPageBackgroundThemeBrush}">
    <Grid HorizontalAlignment="Center">
        <Grid.RowDefinitions>
            <RowDefinition Height="Auto" />
            <RowDefinition Height="Auto" />
            <RowDefinition Height="Auto" />
            <RowDefinition Height="*" />
        </Grid.RowDefinitions>

        <Grid.ColumnDefinitions>
            <ColumnDefinition Width="*" />
            <ColumnDefinition Width="*" />
        </Grid.ColumnDefinitions>
```

```xml
<Button Name="startButton"
        Content="Start"
        Grid.Row="0" Grid.Column="0"
        HorizontalAlignment="Center"
        Margin="24 12"
        Click="OnStartButtonClick" />

<Button Name="cancelButton"
        Content="Cancel"
        Grid.Row="0" Grid.Column="1"
        IsEnabled="false"
        HorizontalAlignment="Center"
        Margin="24 12"
        Click="OnCancelButtonClick" />

<ProgressBar Name="progressBar"
             Grid.Row="1" Grid.Column="0" Grid.ColumnSpan="2"
             Margin="24" />

<TextBlock Name="errorText"
           Grid.Row="2" Grid.Column="0" Grid.ColumnSpan="2"
           FontSize="24"
           TextWrapping="Wrap" />

<ScrollViewer Grid.Row="3" Grid.Column="0" Grid.ColumnSpan="2">
    <StackPanel Name="stackPanel" />
</ScrollViewer>
        </Grid>
</Grid>
```

The code-behind file contains the *GetWordFrequenciesAsync* method as well as a couple of short methods for cancellation and progress:

Project: WordFreq | **File:** MainPage.xaml.cs (excerpt)

```csharp
public sealed partial class MainPage : Page
{
    // Project Gutenberg ebook of Herman Melville's "Moby-Dick"
    Uri uri = new Uri("http://www.gutenberg.org/ebooks/2701.txt.utf-8");
    CancellationTokenSource cts;

    public MainPage()
    {
        this.InitializeComponent();
    }

    async void OnStartButtonClick(object sender, RoutedEventArgs args)
    {
        ...
    }

    void OnCancelButtonClick(object sender, RoutedEventArgs args)
    {
        cts.Cancel();
    }
```

```
void ProgressCallback(double progress)
{
    progressBar.Value = progress;
}

Task<IOrderedEnumerable<KeyValuePair<string, int>>> GetWordFrequenciesAsync(Stream stream,
                                        CancellationToken cancellationToken,
                                        IProgress<double> progress)

{
    ...
}
}
```

The only code you haven't seen yet is the *Click* handler for the *Start* button. The handler is designed to be called multiple times while the program is running, but it's not re-entrant—that is, it's not designed to be started a second time until it's exited the first time. Much of the logic in the method involves initializing the *StackPanel*, initializing the *ProgressBar*, and enabling and disabling the buttons. Notice all the file accesses as well as the call to *GetWordFrequenciesAsync* are in a *try* block:

Project: WordFreq | File: MainPage.xaml.cs (excerpt)

```
async void OnStartButtonClick(object sender, RoutedEventArgs args)
{
    stackPanel.Children.Clear();
    progressBar.Value = 0;
    errorText.Text = "";
    startButton.IsEnabled = false;
    IOrderedEnumerable<KeyValuePair<string, int>> wordList = null;

    try
    {
        RandomAccessStreamReference streamRef = RandomAccessStreamReference.CreateFromUri(uri);

        using (IRandomAccessStream raStream = await streamRef.OpenReadAsync())
        {
            using (Stream stream = raStream.AsStream())
            {
                cancelButton.IsEnabled = true;
                cts = new CancellationTokenSource();

                wordList = await GetWordFrequenciesAsync(stream, cts.Token,
                                        new Progress<double>(ProgressCallback));

                cancelButton.IsEnabled = false;
            }
        }
    }
    catch (OperationCanceledException)
    {
        progressBar.Value = 0;
        cancelButton.IsEnabled = false;
        startButton.IsEnabled = true;
        return;
    }
```

```
    catch (Exception exc)
    {
        progressBar.Value = 0;
        cancelButton.IsEnabled = false;
        startButton.IsEnabled = true;
        errorText.Text = "Error: " + exc.Message;
        return;
    }

    // Transfer the list of words and counts to the StackPanel
    foreach (KeyValuePair<string, int> word in wordList)
    {
        if (word.Value > 1)
        {
            TextBlock txtblk = new TextBlock
            {
                FontSize = 24,
                Text = word.Key + " \x2014 " + word.Value.ToString()
            };
            stackPanel.Children.Add(txtblk);
        }
        await Task.Yield();
    }

    startButton.IsEnabled = true;
}
```

But another issue has arisen: After the asynchronous method has returned, the program must transfer the items into the *StackPanel*. This job is handled by the *foreach* block at the end of the method. This loop involves extreme interaction with user interface objects—creating a *TextBlock* and adding it to the *StackPanel*—and it simply can't be handled in another thread. Even limiting the list to those words that show up at least twice in *Moby-Dick* (as I've done) involves almost 10,000 items. Such a loop has the potential of freezing the user interface, preventing it from responding to user input, and even preventing the prompt appearance of the items on the screen.

The solution—not entirely successful—involves this statement:

```
await Task.Yield();
```

This call with *await* effectively allows other code on the user interface thread to run and then returns when that code has completed. The other code that executes includes code implemented in the *StackPanel* class that lays out the *TextBlock* children and user input that might want to scroll the *StackPanel* within the *ScrollViewer*.

Without that call to *Task.Yield*, the list of words doesn't appear on the screen for about five seconds after the *ProgressBar* has signaled maximum progress. To be sure, the repeated calls to *Task.Yield* slow down the loop considerably. It will take longer to complete (as you can see for yourself when running the program by the delay before the Start button is enabled), but you'll see results almost immediately. You should also be able to scroll the list before it has completed, and you'll discover that the *Moby-Dick* file contains 963 occurrences of the word "whale":

```
be — 1030
him — 1046
so — 1046
whale — 963
you — 930
one — 892
or — 795
had — 777
have — 771
there — 771
now — 768
were — 681
they — 661
which — 648
their — 619
then — 619
are — 616
some — 615
me — 612
when — 599
an — 594
my — 587
```

A better solution for this program is not to use a *StackPanel* at all. As you'll discover in Chapter 11, "The Three Templates," there are controls specifically for displaying lists of items. These controls can use a *VirtualizingStackPanel*, which doesn't create actual elements until they are scrolled into view.

Although Windows 8, .NET, and C# have made working with asynchronous methods easier than ever, attention to detail and testing are still required. For example, on the machine I'm using for this book, the *GetWordFrequenciesAsync* method requires three to four seconds to finish. However, if I remove the check for cancellation and progress reporting, the method requires less than one second. I don't know about you, but I find it questionable whether cancellation and progress are suitable for a one-second asynchronous method.

These things are not easy, and they're not easy because in one sense we're trying to do the impossible: We're trying to give our computers lots of work to do but make it seem as if they're doing nothing at all. Windows 8 applications should appear as if they can engage in heavy lifting without breaking a sweat, and that's still a challenge for programmers.

CHAPTER 8

App Bars and Popups

By assembling the elements, controls, and panels discussed in Chapter 4, "Presentation with Panels," and Chapter 5, "Control Interaction," it is possible to construct an entire user interface on the surface of a page. But for many programs, it's preferable that most commands and program options remain hidden until the user specifically needs to use them.

Windows applications of the past generally used menus and dialog boxes to consolidate commands and options. While the top level of a menu always remains visible, the actual commands are usually on drop-down submenus. Some menu commands have the effect of invoking a dialog box for presenting a group of related program options.

Windows 8 instead places emphasis on application content rather than chrome. In many cases, program options formerly on an application menu will be moved to an application bar, which is normally hidden from view but invoked when the user sweeps a finger on the top or bottom edge of the screen, or moves the mouse pointer to that location. The application bar is a *ContentControl* derivative named *AppBar*, and I'll show you how to use it in this chapter.

In addition, a Windows 8 program can display a list of commands in a simple object of type *PopupMenu* (often used as a context menu) or a more extensive collection of controls that you present to the user through an element named *Popup*. I'll show you how to use both types of popups in this chapter.

This chapter concludes with the most extensive application so far in this book—a program called XamlCruncher that lets you interactively experiment with XAML.

Implementing Context Menus

A context menu is a menu that is invoked with a right click of a mouse or a press-hold-and-release finger gesture. The menu pops up at the point where the screen was touched and generally disappears when one of the commands is selected. Very often, the context menu is associated with a particular control or a particular area of a single control; this is what justifies the "context" part of the name.

The *TextBox* control includes a context menu. To see it, run any program in this book that uses a *TextBox*. Type some text into it, select some, and then right-click the control or perform the press-hold-and-release gesture. A menu appears that potentially contains up to five commands, depending on the selection and the state of the clipboard:

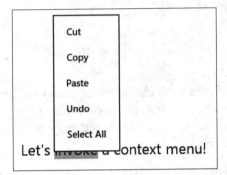

To make your own custom context menu you create an object of type *PopupMenu*. This class is defined in the *Windows.UI.Popups* namespace along with *MessageDialog* (which you encountered in Chapter 7, "Asynchronicity") and *UICommand*, which is what you use to specify commands in both *MessageDialog* and *PopupMenu*.

PopupMenu derives from *Object*, so it's very unlikely that you'll instantiate it in a visual tree in a XAML file. Instead, you'll probably want to construct a *PopupMenu* object entirely in code at the time it's invoked, most likely in response to a *RightTapped* event.

Here's a XAML file containing a *TextBlock* centered on the page with a handler assigned for the *RightTapped* event:

Project: SimpleContextMenu | File: MainPage.xaml (excerpt)

```
<Grid Background="{StaticResource ApplicationPageBackgroundThemeBrush}">
    <TextBlock Name="textBlock"
               FontSize="24"
               HorizontalAlignment="Center"
               VerticalAlignment="Center"
               TextAlignment="Center"
               RightTapped="OnTextBlockRightTapped">
        Simple Context Menu
        <LineBreak />
        <LineBreak />
        (right-click or press-and-hold-and-release to invoke)
    </TextBlock>
</Grid>
```

Just as with *MessageDialog*, you indicate the commands you want to appear on the menu with instances of *UICommand*. Call *ShowAsync* to display it:

Project: SimpleContextMenu | File: MainPage.xaml.cs (excerpt)

```
public sealed partial class MainPage : Page
{
    public MainPage()
    {
        this.InitializeComponent();
    }

    async void OnTextBlockRightTapped(object sender, RightTappedRoutedEventArgs args)
    {
        PopupMenu popupMenu = new PopupMenu();
        popupMenu.Commands.Add(new UICommand("Larger Font", OnFontSizeChanged, 1.2));
        popupMenu.Commands.Add(new UICommand("Smaller Font", OnFontSizeChanged, 1 / 1.2));
        popupMenu.Commands.Add(new UICommandSeparator());
        popupMenu.Commands.Add(new UICommand("Red", OnColorChanged, Colors.Red));
        popupMenu.Commands.Add(new UICommand("Green", OnColorChanged, Colors.Green));
        popupMenu.Commands.Add(new UICommand("Blue", OnColorChanged, Colors.Blue));

        await popupMenu.ShowAsync(args.GetPosition(this));
    }

    void OnFontSizeChanged(IUICommand command)
    {
        textBlock.FontSize *= (double)command.Id;
    }

    void OnColorChanged(IUICommand command)
    {
        textBlock.Foreground = new SolidColorBrush((Color)command.Id);
    }
}
```

Notice the *UICommandSeparator* object to create a horizontal line in the menu.

Just as with *MessageDialog*, the *ShowAsync* call returns an object of type *IAsyncOperation<IUICommand>*, from which you can obtain the command selected by the user. I have chosen instead to specify two custom handlers for the commands in the *UICommand* constructors, and I've used the third argument of that constructor to specify a value that helps the handler process the command with as little fuss as possible.

The *ShowAsync* method requires a *Point* value to indicate where the menu is to be displayed. This point should be relative to the application's window, which usually means that it can be relative to the page. The menu is generally horizontally centered at this point and positioned vertically *above* the point. This makes sense for a touch interface: You don't want the menu obscured by the user's hand!

Here's how it appears when I right-click at the top of the 'S' in "Simple":

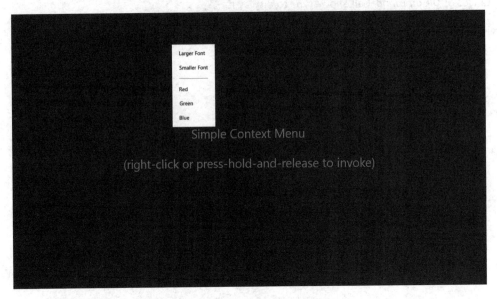

Of course, if you click outside the *TextBlock*, nothing will happen.

If the point you specify is too close to the left, top, or right edge of the window, the location will be automatically shifted so that the menu is not cropped. The menu is always displayed with black text on a white background regardless of the *RequestedTheme* value.

The menu has a keyboard interface, but not much of one: You can use the arrow keys to move a selection among the items, and then press Enter to choose one. The menu disappears when you select a command, if you tap or click anywhere outside the menu, or if you press any other key on the keyboard. If you choose to process the *IUICommand* object returned from *ShowAsync*, that object will be *null* if the menu was dismissed without a command being selected.

You have now seen virtually everything you can do with *PopupMenu*. The only other option is an alternative method to invoke the menu called *ShowForSelectionAsync*. This method requires a *Rect* value and an optional member of the *Placement* enumeration, which has members *Default*, *Above*, *Below*, *Left*, and *Right*. This is only a *preferred* location: The actual location will be chosen so that the entire menu appears within the program's window.

You can't display any commands in a *PopupMenu* in a shaded disabled state. If a particular command isn't currently applicable, don't include it!

Nor can you display any commands with check marks to indicate a selected item. If you want to display anything beyond simple commands, you need to graduate from *PopupMenu* to *Popup*.

The *Popup* Dialog

The *Popup* class (which derives from *FrameworkElement*) is the closest thing the Windows Runtime has to the traditional dialog box. *Popup* has a *Child* property of type *UIElement* that you'll likely set to a *Panel* containing a bunch of controls or to a *Border* with a *Panel* child.

The SimpleContextDialog project is functionally equivalent to the previous project, and the XAML file is very similar:

Project: SimpleContextDialog | **File:** MainPage.xaml (excerpt)

```
<Grid Background="{StaticResource ApplicationPageBackgroundThemeBrush}">
    <TextBlock Name="textBlock"
               FontSize="24"
               HorizontalAlignment="Center"
               VerticalAlignment="Center"
               TextAlignment="Center"
               RightTapped="OnTextBlockRightTapped">
        Simple Context Dialog
        <LineBreak />
        <LineBreak />
        (right-click or press-hold-and-release to invoke)
    </TextBlock>
</Grid>
```

The handler for the *RightTapped* event on the *TextBlock* assembles two *Button* controls and three *RadioButton* controls in a *StackPanel* that is made a child of a *Border* that is then set to the *Child* property of a *Popup*. That's the long part. Much shorter are the *Click* handler for the *Button* controls and the *Checked* handler for the *RadioButton* controls:

Project: SimpleContextDialog | **File:** MainPage.xaml.cs (excerpt)

```
public sealed partial class MainPage : Page
{
    public MainPage()
    {
        this.InitializeComponent();
    }

    void OnTextBlockRightTapped(object sender, RightTappedRoutedEventArgs args)
    {
        StackPanel stackPanel = new StackPanel();

        // Create two Button controls and add to StackPanel
        Button btn1 = new Button
        {
            Content = "Larger font",
            Tag = 1.2,
            HorizontalAlignment = HorizontalAlignment.Center,
            Margin = new Thickness(12)
        };
```

```
btn1.Click += OnButtonClick;
stackPanel.Children.Add(btn1);

Button btn2 = new Button
{
    Content = "Smaller font",
    Tag = 1 / 1.2,
    HorizontalAlignment = HorizontalAlignment.Center,
    Margin = new Thickness(12)
};
btn2.Click += OnButtonClick;
stackPanel.Children.Add(btn2);

// Create three RadioButton controls and add to StackPanel
string[] names = { "Red", "Green", "Blue" };
Color[] colors = { Colors.Red, Colors.Green, Colors.Blue };

for (int i = 0; i < names.Length; i++)
{
    RadioButton radioButton = new RadioButton
    {
        Content = names[i],
        Foreground = new SolidColorBrush(colors[i]),
        IsChecked = (textBlock.Foreground as SolidColorBrush).Color == colors[i],
        Margin = new Thickness(12)
    };
    radioButton.Checked += OnRadioButtonChecked;
    stackPanel.Children.Add(radioButton);
}

// Create a Border for the StackPanel
Border border = new Border
{
    Child = stackPanel,
    Background =
        this.Resources["ApplicationPageBackgroundThemeBrush"] as SolidColorBrush,
    BorderBrush = this.Resources["ApplicationForegroundThemeBrush"] as SolidColorBrush,
    BorderThickness = new Thickness(1),
    Padding = new Thickness(24),
};

// Create the Popup object
Popup popup = new Popup
{
    Child = border,
    IsLightDismissEnabled = true
};

// Adjust location based on content size
border.Loaded += (loadedSender, loadedArgs) =>
    {
        Point point = args.GetPosition(this);
        point.X -= border.ActualWidth / 2;
        point.Y -= border.ActualHeight;
```

```
            // Leave at least a quarter inch margin
            popup.HorizontalOffset =
                Math.Min(this.ActualWidth - border.ActualWidth - 24,
                    Math.Max(24, point.X));

            popup.VerticalOffset =
                Math.Min(this.ActualHeight - border.ActualHeight - 24,
                    Math.Max(24, point.Y));

            // Set keyboard focus to first element
            btn1.Focus(FocusState.Programmatic);
        };

    // Open the popup
    popup.IsOpen = true;
}

void OnButtonClick(object sender, RoutedEventArgs args)
{
    textBlock.FontSize *= (double)(sender as Button).Tag;
}

void OnRadioButtonChecked(object sender, RoutedEventArgs args)
{
    textBlock.Foreground = (sender as RadioButton).Foreground;
}
}
```

To position the *Popup*, it is necessary to set the *HorizontalOffset* and *VerticalOffset* properties to values relative to the program's window. However, these properties cannot be set intelligently without knowing the size of the content that the *Popup* is hosting, and that's generally not available until the *Popup* is displayed. For that reason, this code sets a *Loaded* handler on the *Border*, which is the content element of the *Popup*. The *Popup* is then positioned centered above the right-tap point (much like *PopupMenu*), but I've also allowed at least a 24-pixel margin between the *Popup* and the program's window.

The *RightTapped* handler concludes by setting the *IsOpen* property of the *Popup* to *true*. This causes the *Popup* to be displayed on the screen. Normally the user can still interact with the rest of the program's page. But notice that the *IsLightDismissEnabled* property of the *Popup* is set to *true*. This allows the *Popup* to be dismissed with a click or a tap outside the *Popup* or with a press of the Esc key. Without this property set, multiple copies of this dialog can be displayed and the program would need to remove the *Popup* from the screen by setting the *IsOpen* property of *false*, probably in response to an event of one of the child controls. *Popup* also defines *Opened* and *Closed* properties if you need that information for initialization or cleanup.

Here's a click on the upper end of the right parenthesis with the font already having been increased in size:

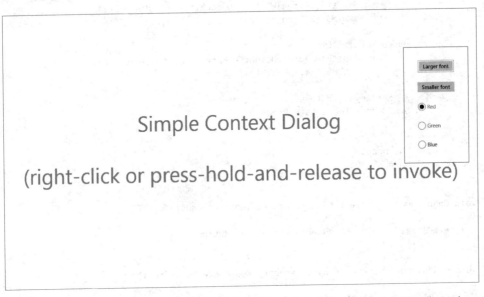

You can use the Tab key to navigate among the items. By default these dialogs have the same color theme as the application, so using a *Border* as I've done helps to set off the dialog visually on the page.

This dialog box has no OK or Cancel button. Instead, I've implemented this dialog so that clicking the buttons changes the underlying display immediately and the *Popup* is dismissed by clicking or pressing anywhere outside it. In more complex dialogs, you might want a button to restore defaults.

Of course, defining the entire content of the *Popup* in code is a nuisance. It's more common to define a *UserControl* specifically for the dialog and then make an instance of that the child of the *Popup*. However, you then need to provide some way for this *UserControl* to convey the user selections back to the program, and the best way to do that is with bindings between the dialog and the application, either directly or through a view model. You'll see examples of both approaches later in this chapter.

Application Bars

The Windows 8 application bar is intended to implement program commands and options in a manner similar to a traditional menu or toolbar. The application bar is a class named *AppBar*, and it is invoked when the user sweeps a finger on the top or bottom of the screen. Application bars can appear at the top of the page, the bottom, or both. The application bar often disappears when a command has been selected, but that's not required.

The *Page* class defines two properties named *TopAppBar* and *BottomAppBar* that you generally set to *AppBar* tags in XAML. *AppBar* derives from *ContentControl*, and you'll usually set the *Content* property to a panel that contains the controls that appear on the application bar. *AppBar* does not have a fixed height: The height is based on the controls it hosts.

Certainly the best way to become familiar with the use of application bars in real programs is to explore some of the standard applications that are part of Windows 8. Mostly you'll see application bars that consist of a row of circular *Button* controls, but the application bars in the Windows 8 version of Internet Explorer demonstrate that an application bar can contain a variety of controls. In Internet Explorer, the bottom application bar contains a *TextBox* into which you can type a URL; the top application bar displays a collection of visited web pages.

Here's a program with a rather unconventional pair of application bars:

Project: UnconventionalAppBar | **File:** MainPage.xaml (excerpt)

```xml
<Page ... >
    <Grid Background="LightGray">
        <TextBlock Name="textBlock"
                   Text="Unconventional App Bar"
                   HorizontalAlignment="Center"
                   VerticalAlignment="Center"
                   FontSize="{Binding ElementName=slider, Path=Value}" />
    </Grid>

    <Page.TopAppBar>
        <AppBar Name="topAppBar">
            <Slider Name="slider"
                    Minimum="8"
                    Maximum="196"
                    Value="24" />
        </AppBar>
    </Page.TopAppBar>

    <Page.BottomAppBar>
        <AppBar Name="bottomAppBar">
            <StackPanel Orientation="Horizontal"
                        HorizontalAlignment="Right">

                <Button Content="Red"
                        Foreground="Red"
                        Margin="24 12"
                        Click="OnAppBarButtonClick" />

                <Button Content="Green"
                        Foreground="Green"
                        Margin="24 12"
                        Click="OnAppBarButtonClick" />

                <Button Content="Blue"
                        Foreground="Blue"
                        Margin="24 12"
                        Click="OnAppBarButtonClick" />
            </StackPanel>
        </AppBar>
    </Page.BottomAppBar>
</Page>
```

Again, a *TextBlock* sits in the center of the screen, but this one has its *FontSize* bound to a *Slider* that is the only content of an *AppBar* that appears at the top. The second *AppBar* is set to the *BottomAppBar* property and contains a horizontal *StackPanel* with three *Button* controls. The Button controls share a *Click* handler in the code-behind file:

Project: UnconventionalAppBar | **File:** MainPage.xaml.cs (excerpt)

```
void OnAppBarButtonClick(object sender, RoutedEventArgs args)
{
    textBlock.Foreground = (sender as Button).Foreground;
}
```

It is generally much easier working with an application bar than a *Popup* or *PopupMenu* because the *AppBar* is part of the visual tree of the page, which eases the setting of bindings and event handlers. The only difference between controls on an *AppBar* and controls on the page is that the application bars are usually not visible until the user sweeps a finger on the top or bottom of the screen. At that point, the user can interact with the controls:

An application bar and controls are colored according to the *RequestedTheme* of the application, which is set to *Light* in this program. I gave the main *Grid* a *LightGray* background to contrast with those colors. Most programs that use application bars seem to have *Dark* themes.

An application bar is automatically dismissed and goes back into hiding when you click or press anywhere outside the application bar, or if you press Esc. If you prefer that the application bar is not dismissed in this way, set the *IsSticky* property of *AppBar* to *true*. In that case, to get rid of the application bar, the user needs to perform another finger sweep or you'll need to set the *IsOpen* property of one or both *AppBar* objects to *false* in the code-behind file.

There are some cases where a program might want to dismiss the application bar from code. For example, in this particular program, to change the text color, a user needs to bring up the application bar with a finger sweep, press a button, and then dismiss the application bar with another finger sweep or by pressing outside the bar. You might choose to dismiss the application bars from code when a button is pressed:

```
void OnAppBarButtonClick(object sender, RoutedEventArgs args)
{
    textBlock.Foreground = (sender as Button).Foreground;
    topAppBar.IsOpen = false;
    bottomAppBar.IsOpen = false;
}
```

This is very common, and you know you'll need to do it when you get tired of dismissing an application bar after you've clicked a button on it. However, sometimes the user might find it convenient to set several options in a row without re-invoking the application bar. This is a judgment call.

Some applications might want to require the user to interact with an application bar the first time the program is run. In that case, initializing the *IsOpen* property to *true* is fine. Like *Popup*, *AppBar* has *Opened* and *Closed* events for initialization and cleanup.

The Application Bar Button Style

Many Windows 8 applications have only a bottom application bar containing a row of circular *Button* controls. The buttons are usually identified both with a symbol in a circle and a short text command.

The basis of this circular button is a *Style* defined in StandardStyles.xaml with the key name AppBarButtonStyle. StandardStyles.xaml is the file located in the Common folder of every C#, Visual Basic, or C++ Windows 8 project created by Visual Studio. The file is included in the *Resources* section of the App.xaml file and hence is available to any Windows 8 application.

The AppBarButtonStyle *Style* definition contains a long *ControlTemplate* that defines the visuals of this circular button. You might want to take a closer look at this *ControlTemplate* after assimilating Chapter 11, "The Three Templates." Meanwhile, you can just use this *Style* without knowing exactly how the template works.

The AppBarButtonStyle contains a *Setter* object that sets the *FontFamily* to Segoe UI Symbol, and the symbol that appears in the button is a character from this font.

As the name indicates, Segoe UI Symbol is a symbol font. However, it is not like an old-fashioned symbol font where a bunch of symbols replace the common letters and numbers. The normal characters still exist in this font, and you can use this font for normal purposes. But the Unicode standard allows fonts such as this to include custom characters by defining the range of codes from 0xE000 through 0xF8FF as a "private use area," which means that these character codes are font-specific. The Segoe UI Symbol doesn't fill up this whole area with custom symbols, but the range of 0xE100 through 0xE1F4 is a collection of glyphs that symbolize a bunch of common computer chores and hence are suitable for application bar buttons.

For example, if you want to display a button with a little house and the word "Home," you can put such a button on an application bar like so:

```
<Page.BottomAppBar>
    <AppBar>
        <StackPanel Orientation="Horizontal">
            <Button Style="{StaticResource AppBarButtonStyle}"
                    Content="&#xE10F;"
                    AutomationProperties.Name="Home"
                    Click="OnButtonClick" />
            ...
        </StackPanel>
    </AppBar>
</Page.BottomAppBar>
```

You've seen the *Content* and *Click* attributes before. The *AutomationProperties* class is a collection of attached properties, of which *Name* is one. These properties normally allow user interface elements to be identified for purposes of testing, and for accessibility by assistive technologies such as screen readers. The *ControlTemplate* defined within AppBarButtonStyle references the *AutomationProperties.Name* property to display a text string under the button. Here's how this particular button appears with a dark theme:

The StandardStyles.xaml file also defines individual styles based on AppBarButtonStyle for many (but not all) of the Segoe UI Symbol character codes from 0xE100 through 0xE1E9. For example, here's a *Style* definition for HomeAppBarButtonStyle:

```
<Style x:Key="HomeAppBarButtonStyle" TargetType="ButtonBase"
                        BasedOn="{StaticResource AppBarButtonStyle}">
    <Setter Property="AutomationProperties.AutomationId" Value="HomeAppBarButton"/>
    <Setter Property="AutomationProperties.Name" Value="Home"/>
    <Setter Property="Content" Value="&#xE10F;"/>
</Style>
```

Obviously these styles can be very handy because someone has already matched up the symbols, names, and suggested functionality. However, in the standard StandardStyles.xaml files, these styles are all commented out and you need to remove the comments in order to use them. Here's how you would reference this *Style* in a XAML file:

```
<Button Style="{StaticResource HomeAppBarButtonStyle}"
        Click="OnButtonClick" />
```

But feel free to specify your own text if you want:

```
<Button Style="{StaticResource HomeAppBarButtonStyle}"
        AutomationProperties.Name="Head on Home"
        Click="OnButtonClick" />
```

Wouldn't it be nice to get a complete list of the application bar button styles defined in StandardStyles.xaml with the symbols and text labels? That's provided by the LookAtAppBarButtonStyles program. The XAML file contains a *ScrollViewer* and *StackPanel* ready for filling, and an application bar with a couple standard *RadioButton* controls:

Project: LookAtAppBarButtonStyles | **File:** MainPage.xaml (excerpt)

```xml
<Page ... >
    <Grid Background="{StaticResource ApplicationPageBackgroundThemeBrush}">
        <ScrollViewer FontSize="20">
            <StackPanel Name="stackPanel" />
        </ScrollViewer>
    </Grid>

    <Page.BottomAppBar>
        <AppBar>
            <StackPanel Orientation="Horizontal">
                <RadioButton Name="symbolSortRadio"
                             Content="Sort by symbol"
                             Checked="OnRadioButtonChecked" />

                <RadioButton Name="textSortRadio"
                             Content="Sort by text"
                             Checked="OnRadioButtonChecked" />

            </StackPanel>
        </AppBar>
    </Page.BottomAppBar>
</Page>
```

In the handler for the *Loaded* event, the code-behind file gets access to the *ResourceDictionary* provided by StandardStyles.xaml by referencing the *MergedDictionaries* property of the *Resources* collection associated with the current *Application* instance. The code locates the *Style* with the key name "AppBarButtonStyle" and then saves all *Style* instances with a *BasedOn* property equal to that *Style* in a collection of type *Item*, an internal class:

Project: LookAtAppBarButtonStyles | **File:** MainPage.xaml.cs (excerpt)

```csharp
public sealed partial class MainPage : Page
{
    class Item
    {
        public string Key;
        public char Symbol;
        public string Text;
    }

    List<Item> appbarStyles = new List<Item>();
    FontFamily segoeSymbolFont = new FontFamily("Segoe UI Symbol");

    public MainPage()
    {
        this.InitializeComponent();
        Loaded += OnLoaded;
    }
```

```
    void OnLoaded(object sender, RoutedEventArgs args)
    {
        // Basically gets StandardStyles.xaml
        ResourceDictionary dictionary = Application.Current.Resources.MergedDictionaries[0];
        Style baseStyle = dictionary["AppBarButtonStyle"] as Style;

        // Find all styles based on AppBarButtonStyle
        foreach (object key in dictionary.Keys)
        {
            Style style = dictionary[key] as Style;

            if (style != null && style.BasedOn == baseStyle)
            {
                Item item = new Item
                {
                    Key = key as string
                };

                foreach (Setter setter in style.Setters)
                {
                    if (setter.Property.Equals(AutomationProperties.NameProperty))
                        item.Text = setter.Value as string;

                    if (setter.Property.Equals(ButtonBase.ContentProperty))
                        item.Symbol = (setter.Value as string)[0];
                }

                appbarStyles.Add(item);
            }
        }

        // Display items by checking RadioButton
        symbolSortRadio.IsChecked = true;
    }
    ...
}
```

The *Loaded* event concludes by checking one of the two *RadioButton* controls in the application bar. This causes a call to the *Checked* handler for the *RadioButton*, which sorts the collection of styles in one of two different ways:

Project: LookAtAppBarButtonStyles | File: MainPage.xaml.cs (excerpt)

```
void OnRadioButtonChecked(object sender, RoutedEventArgs args)
{
    if (sender == symbolSortRadio)
    {
        // Sort by symbol
        appbarStyles.Sort((item1, item2) =>
        {
            return item1.Symbol.CompareTo(item2.Symbol);
        });
    }
    else
```

```
    {
        // Sort by text
        appbarStyles.Sort((item1, item2) =>
        {
            return item1.Text.CompareTo(item2.Text);
        });
    }

    // Close app bar and display the items
    this.BottomAppBar.IsOpen = false;
    DisplayList();
}
```

Processing of the *Checked* handler concludes with a call to *DisplayList* that creates lines of text for each item. (Notice that the *FontFamily* for the first *TextBlock* in each line uses the Segoe UI Symbol font.) Each of these items is added to the *StackPanel* in the *ScrollViewer*.

Project: LookAtAppBarButtonStyles | **File:** MainPage.xaml.cs (excerpt)

```
void DisplayList()
{
    // Clear the StackPanel
    stackPanel.Children.Clear();

    // Loop through the styles
    foreach (Item item in appbarStyles)
    {
        // A StackPanel for each item
        StackPanel itemPanel = new StackPanel
        {
            Orientation = Orientation.Horizontal,
            Margin = new Thickness(0, 6, 0, 6)
        };

        // The symbol itself
        TextBlock textBlock = new TextBlock
        {
            Text = item.Symbol.ToString(),
            FontFamily = segoeSymbolFont,
            Margin = new Thickness(24, 0, 24, 0)
        };
        itemPanel.Children.Add(textBlock);

        // The Unicode identifier
        textBlock = new TextBlock
        {
            Text = "0x" + ((int)item.Symbol).ToString("X4"),
            Width = 96
        };
        itemPanel.Children.Add(textBlock);

        // The text for the button
        textBlock = new TextBlock
        {
            Text = "\"" + item.Text + "\"",
            Width = 240,
        };
```

```
itemPanel.Children.Add(textBlock);

// The key name
textBlock = new TextBlock
{
    Text = item.Key
};
itemPanel.Children.Add(textBlock);

stackPanel.Children.Add(itemPanel);
    }
}
```

Here's an excerpt of part of the list:

▦	0xE144	"Keyboard"	KeyboardAppBarButtonStyle
▣	0xE145	"Dock Left"	DockLeftAppBarButtonStyle
▢	0xE146	"Dock Right"	DockRightAppBarButtonStyle
▭	0xE147	"Dock Bottom"	DockBottomAppBarButtonStyle
✕	0xE148	"Remote"	RemoteAppBarButtonStyle
↻	0xE149	"Sync"	SyncAppBarButtonStyle
⌒	0xE14A	"Rotate"	RotateAppBarButtonStyle
⇅	0xE14B	"Shuffle"	ShuffleAppBarButtonStyle
☰	0xE14C	"List"	ListAppBarButtonStyle
▮	0xE14D	"Shop"	ShopAppBarButtonStyle
▦	0xE14E	"Select All"	SelectAllAppBarButtonStyle
⮡	0xE14F	"Orientation"	OrientationAppBarButtonStyle
←ı	0xE150	"Import"	ImportAppBarButtonStyle
←∷	0xE151	"Import All"	ImportAllAppBarButtonStyle
▢	0xE155	"Browse Photos"	BrowsePhotosAppBarButtonStyle
[▲]	0xE156	"Webcam"	WebcamAppBarButtonStyle
▣	0xE158	"Pictures"	PicturesAppBarButtonStyle
⊟	0xE159	"Save Local"	SaveLocalAppBarButtonStyle
▯	0xE15A	"Caption"	CaptionAppBarButtonStyle
■	0xE15B	"Stop"	StopAppBarButtonStyle

Don't feel restricted to the items in this list. You can use any character in the Segoe UI Symbol font for application bar buttons, or you can specify a different font.

Inside the Segoe UI Symbol Font

Besides the characters in the private-use area, the Segoe UI Symbol font also supports character codes from 0x2600 through 0x26FF that the Unicode standard classifies as "miscellaneous symbols." Some of these characters might also be suitable for application bar buttons.

The Segoe UI Symbol font also goes beyond the range of 16-bit codes and contains glyphs for character codes 0x1F300 through 0x1F5FF that map to emoji characters. These are icon characters that originated in Japan but that have also found their way into the Microsoft Windows Phone and the Apple iPhone.

The Segoe UI Symbol font also supports common emoticon characters in the range 0x1F600 through 0x1F64F, including nine cat emoticons and a trio of see-no-evil, hear-no-evil, speak-no-evil monkeys.

Also supported is the range from 0x1F680 through 0x1F6C5 containing transportation and map symbols.

To help you (and me) select additional symbols for application bars, I've written a program named SegoeSymbols that displays all the characters from 0 through 0x1FFFF in the Segoe UI Symbol font.

As you might know, Unicode started out as a 16-bit character encoding with codes ranging from 0x0000 through 0xFFFF. When it became evident that 65,536 code points were not sufficient, Unicode began incorporating character codes in the range 0x10000 through 0x10FFFF, increasing the number of characters to over 1.1 million. This expansion of Unicode also included a system to represent these additional characters using a pair of 16-bit values.

The use of a single 32-bit code to represent Unicode characters is known as 32-bit Unicode Transformation Format, or UTF-32. But that's a bit of misnomer because with UTF-32 there is no transformation: A one-to-one mapping exists from the 32-bit numeric codes to character glyphs.

UTF-32 is extremely rare. Indeed, most people don't even think of Unicode as a 32-bit character encoding because the 32-bit part of Unicode is really tacked on to the 16-bit encoding.

Accordingly, most modern programming languages and operating systems instead support UTF-16. The *Char* structure in the Windows Runtime is basically a 16-bit integer, and that's the basis for the *char* data type in C#. To represent the additional characters in the range 0x10000 through 0x10FFFF, UTF-16 uses two 16-bit characters in sequence. These are known as *surrogates*, and a special range of 16-bit codes in Unicode has been set aside for their use. The leading surrogate is in the range 0xD800 through 0xDBFF, and the trailing surrogate is in the range 0xDC00 through 0xDFFF. That's 1,024 possible leading surrogates, and 1,024 possible trailing surrogates, which is sufficient for the 1,048,576 codes in the range 0x10000 through 0x10FFFF. (You'll see the actual algorithm shortly.)

Text in languages that use the Latin alphabet is mostly restricted to ASCII character codes in the range 0x0020 and 0x007E, so most webpages and other files save lots of space by using a system called UTF-8 for storing text. UTF-8 encodes these 7-bit characters directly but uses one to three additional bytes for other Unicode characters.

Because I wrote SegoeSymbols mostly to let me examine the symbols that might be useful in application bars, the program only goes up to character codes of 0x1FFFF. The XAML file has a simple title, a *Grid* awaiting rows and columns to display a block of 256 characters, and a *Slider*:

Project: SegoeSymbols | File: MainPage.xaml (excerpt)

```
<Page ... >

    <Page.Resources>
        <local:DoubleToStringHexByteConverter x:Key="hexByteConverter" />
    </Page.Resources>
```

```
<Grid Background="{StaticResource ApplicationPageBackgroundThemeBrush}">
    <Grid.RowDefinitions>
        <RowDefinition Height="Auto" />
        <RowDefinition Height="*" />
        <RowDefinition Height="Auto" />
    </Grid.RowDefinitions>

    <TextBlock Name="titleText"
               Grid.Row="0"
               Text="Segoe UI Symbol"
               HorizontalAlignment="Center"
               Style="{StaticResource HeaderTextStyle}" />

    <Grid Name="characterGrid"
          Grid.Row="1"
          HorizontalAlignment="Center"
          VerticalAlignment="Center" />

    <Slider Grid.Row="2"
            Orientation="Horizontal"
            Margin="24 0"
            Minimum="0"
            Maximum="511"
            SmallChange="1"
            LargeChange="16"
            ThumbToolTipValueConverter="{StaticResource hexByteConverter}"
            ValueChanged="OnSliderValueChanged" />
</Grid>
</Page>
```

Notice that the *Slider* has a *Maximum* value of 511, which is the maximum character code I want to display (0x1FFFF) divided by 256. The *DoubleToStringHexByteConverter* class referenced in the *Resources* section is similar to one you've seen before, but it displays a couple underlines as well to be consistent with the screen visuals:

Project: SegoeSymbols | File: DoubleToStringHexByteConverter.cs (excerpt)

```
public class DoubleToStringHexByteConverter : IValueConverter
{
    public object Convert(object value, Type targetType, object parameter, string language)
    {
        return ((int)(double)value).ToString("X2") + "__";
    }
    public object ConvertBack(object value, Type targetType, object parameter, string language)
    {
        return value;
    }
}
```

Each *Slider* value corresponds to a display of 256 characters in a 16 × 16 array. The code to build the *Grid* that displays these 256 characters is rather messy because I decided that there should be lines between all the rows and columns of characters and that these lines should have their own rows and columns in the *Grid*.

Project: SegoeSymbols | File: MainPage.xaml.cs (excerpt)

```csharp
public sealed partial class MainPage : Page
{
    const int CellSize = 36;
    const int LineLength = (CellSize + 1) * 16 + 18;
    FontFamily symbolFont = new FontFamily("Segoe UI Symbol");

    TextBlock[] txtblkColumnHeads = new TextBlock[16];
    TextBlock[,] txtblkCharacters = new TextBlock[16, 16];

    public MainPage()
    {
        this.InitializeComponent();

        for (int row = 0; row < 34; row++)
        {
            RowDefinition rowdef = new RowDefinition();

            if (row == 0 || row % 2 == 1)
                rowdef.Height = GridLength.Auto;
            else
                rowdef.Height = new GridLength(CellSize, GridUnitType.Pixel);

            characterGrid.RowDefinitions.Add(rowdef);

            if (row != 0 && row % 2 == 0)
            {
                TextBlock txtblk = new TextBlock
                {
                    Text = (row / 2 - 1).ToString("X1"),
                    VerticalAlignment = VerticalAlignment.Center
                };
                Grid.SetRow(txtblk, row);
                Grid.SetColumn(txtblk, 0);
                characterGrid.Children.Add(txtblk);
            }

            if (row % 2 == 1)
            {
                Rectangle rectangle = new Rectangle
                {
                    Stroke = this.Foreground,
                    StrokeThickness = row == 1 || row == 33 ? 1.5 : 0.5,
                    Height = 1
                };
                Grid.SetRow(rectangle, row);
                Grid.SetColumn(rectangle, 0);
                Grid.SetColumnSpan(rectangle, 34);
                characterGrid.Children.Add(rectangle);
            }
        }

        for (int col = 0; col < 34; col++)
        {
            ColumnDefinition coldef = new ColumnDefinition();
```

```
            if (col == 0 || col % 2 == 1)
                coldef.Width = GridLength.Auto;
            else
                coldef.Width = new GridLength(CellSize);

            characterGrid.ColumnDefinitions.Add(coldef);

            if (col != 0 && col % 2 == 0)
            {
                TextBlock txtblk = new TextBlock
                {
                    Text = "00" + (col / 2 - 1).ToString("X1") + "_",
                    HorizontalAlignment = HorizontalAlignment.Center
                };
                Grid.SetRow(txtblk, 0);
                Grid.SetColumn(txtblk, col);
                characterGrid.Children.Add(txtblk);
                txtblkColumnHeads[col / 2 - 1] = txtblk;
            }

            if (col % 2 == 1)
            {
                Rectangle rectangle = new Rectangle
                {
                    Stroke = this.Foreground,
                    StrokeThickness = col == 1 || col == 33 ? 1.5 : 0.5,
                    Width = 1
                };
                Grid.SetRow(rectangle, 0);
                Grid.SetColumn(rectangle, col);
                Grid.SetRowSpan(rectangle, 34);
                characterGrid.Children.Add(rectangle);
            }
        }

    for (int col = 0; col < 16; col++)
        for (int row = 0; row < 16; row++)
        {
            TextBlock txtblk = new TextBlock
            {
                Text = ((char)(16 * col + row)).ToString(),
                FontFamily = symbolFont,
                FontSize = 24,
                HorizontalAlignment = HorizontalAlignment.Center,
                VerticalAlignment = VerticalAlignment.Center
            };
            Grid.SetRow(txtblk, 2 * row + 2);
            Grid.SetColumn(txtblk, 2 * col + 2);
            characterGrid.Children.Add(txtblk);
            txtblkCharacters[col, row] = txtblk;
        }
    }
    ...
}
```

The *ValueChanged* handler for the *Slider* has the relatively easier job of inserting the correct text into the existing *TextBlock* elements, but there's also that irksome matter of dealing with character codes above 0xFFFF:

Project: SegoeSymbols | File: MainPage.xaml.cs (excerpt)

```
void OnSliderValueChanged(object sender, RangeBaseValueChangedEventArgs args)
{
    int baseCode = 256 * (int)args.NewValue;

    for (int col = 0; col < 16; col++)
    {
        txtblkColumnHeads[col].Text = (baseCode / 16 + col).ToString("X3") + "_";

        for (int row = 0; row < 16; row++)
        {
            int code = baseCode + 16 * col + row;
            string strChar = null;

            if (code <= 0x0FFFF)
            {
                strChar = ((char)code).ToString();
            }
            else
            {
                code -= 0x10000;
                int lead = 0xD800 + code / 1024;
                int trail = 0xDC00 + code % 1024;
                strChar = ((char)lead).ToString() + (char)trail;
            }
            txtblkCharacters[col, row].Text = strChar;
        }
    }
}
```

Four statements toward the end of the handler demonstrate the mathematics that separate a Unicode character code between 0x10000 and 0x10FFFF into two 10-bit values to construct leading and trailing surrogates, which together in a string define a single character.

If you're the type of person who prefers not witnessing how sausage is made, you can replace those four lines with

```
strChar = Char.ConvertFromUtf32(code);
```

For a *code* value of 0xFFFF and below, *Char.ConvertFromUtf32* returns a string consisting of one character; for codes above 0xFFFF, the string has two characters. Passing the method a surrogate code (0xD800 through 0xDFFF) raises an exception.

The areas that are of most interest in constructing application bar buttons begin at 0x2600 (the miscellaneous symbols area), 0xE100 (the private use area used by the Seqoe UI Symbol font), and 0x1F300 (emoji, emoticons, and transportation and map symbols). Here's the first screen of the emoji characters:

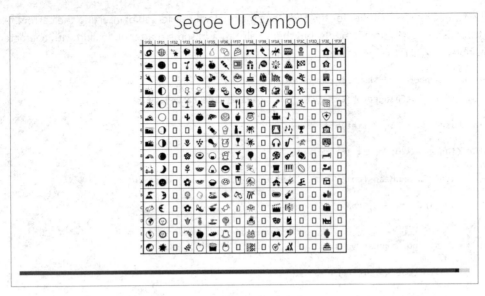

You can specify a character beyond 0xFFFF in XAML like so:

```
<TextBlock FontFamily="Segoe UI Symbol"
           FontSize="24"
           Text="&#x1F3B7;" />
```

That's the saxophone symbol. Visual Studio sometimes complains, but the program compiles and runs just fine.

Here's a row of application bar buttons obviously for a very musical application:

```
<Button Style="{StaticResource AppBarButtonStyle}"
        Content="&#x1F3B7;"
        AutomationProperties.Name="Saxophone"
        Click="OnMusicButtonClick" />

<Button Style="{StaticResource AppBarButtonStyle}"
        Content="&#x1F3B8;"
        AutomationProperties.Name="Guitar"
        Click="OnMusicButtonClick" />

<Button Style="{StaticResource AppBarButtonStyle}"
        Content="&#x1F3B9;"
        AutomationProperties.Name="Piano"
        Click="OnMusicButtonClick" />

<Button Style="{StaticResource AppBarButtonStyle}"
        Content="&#x1F3BA;"
        AutomationProperties.Name="Trumpet"
        Click="OnMusicButtonClick" />

<Button Style="{StaticResource AppBarButtonStyle}"
        Content="&#x1F3BB;"
        AutomationProperties.Name="Violin"
        Click="OnMusicButtonClick" />
```

And here it is:

App Bar *CheckBox* and *RadioButton*

Circular buttons that function like *CheckBox* or *RadioButton* can be seen on the application bars of several standard Windows 8 applications. In the Calendar application, the Day, Week, and Month buttons work like a trio of *RadioButton* controls, and the Show Traffic button in the Maps application works like a *CheckBox*.

The AppBarButtonStyle has a *TargetType* of *ButtonBase*, which means that you can use it to style a *CheckBox* or a *RadioButton*. However, in the version of StandardStyles.xaml that I'm seeing, the *ControlTemplate* for AppBarButtonStyle has a reference to *BackgroundCheckedGlyph*, which is not defined in the template. If you get an error when using these styles with *CheckBox* or *RadioButton*, comment out the *ObjectAnimationUsingKeyFrames* object that references *BackgroundCheckedGlyph*.

This is what I've done for the TextFormattingAppBar, which has a *TextBlock* sitting in the center of the page with an application bar with three *CheckBox* controls and three *RadioButton* controls, all with styles based on AppBarButtonStyle:

Project: TextFormattingAppBar | **File:** MainPage.xaml (excerpt)

```
<Page ... >
    <Grid Background="LightGray">
        <TextBlock Name="textBlock"
                   FontFamily="Times New Roman"
                   FontSize="96"
                   HorizontalAlignment="Center"
                   VerticalAlignment="Center">
            <Run>Text Formatting AppBar</Run>
        </TextBlock>
    </Grid>

    <Page.BottomAppBar>
        <AppBar>
            <StackPanel Orientation="Horizontal">
                <CheckBox Style="{StaticResource BoldAppBarButtonStyle}"
                          Checked="OnBoldAppBarCheckBoxChecked"
                          Unchecked="OnBoldAppBarCheckBoxChecked" />

                <CheckBox Style="{StaticResource ItalicAppBarButtonStyle}"
                          Checked="OnItalicAppBarCheckBoxChecked"
                          Unchecked="OnItalicAppBarCheckBoxChecked" />

                <CheckBox Style="{StaticResource UnderlineAppBarButtonStyle}"
                          Checked="OnUnderlineAppBarCheckBoxChecked"
                          Unchecked="OnUnderlineAppBarCheckBoxChecked" />
```

```
                    <Polyline Points="0 12, 0 48"
                              Stroke="{StaticResource ApplicationForegroundThemeBrush}"
                              VerticalAlignment="Top" />

                    <RadioButton Name="redRadioButton"
                                 Style="{StaticResource FontColorAppBarButtonStyle}"
                                 Foreground="Red"
                                 AutomationProperties.Name="Red"
                                 Checked="OnFontColorAppBarRadioButtonChecked" />

                    <RadioButton Style="{StaticResource FontColorAppBarButtonStyle}"
                                 Foreground="Green"
                                 AutomationProperties.Name="Green"
                                 Checked="OnFontColorAppBarRadioButtonChecked" />

                    <RadioButton Style="{StaticResource FontColorAppBarButtonStyle}"
                                 Foreground="Blue"
                                 AutomationProperties.Name="Blue"
                                 Checked="OnFontColorAppBarRadioButtonChecked" />

                </StackPanel>
            </AppBar>
        </Page.BottomAppBar>
</Page>
```

When such a button is selected, it's displayed in reverse colors, but it doesn't quite work as nicely for the *RadioButton* indicating color:

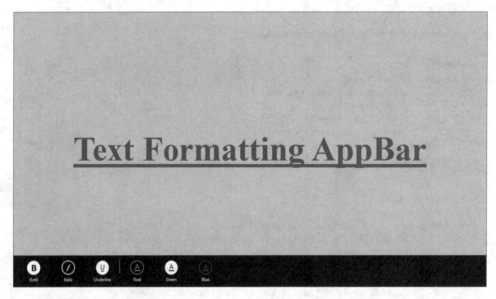

If you have another idea about how to color a selected *CheckBox* or *RadioButton*, you can always make changes to AppBarButtonStyle.

The code-behind file is much as you might expect, except that implementing the underline option is exceptionally kludgy:

Project: TextFormattingAppBar | **File:** MainPage.xaml (excerpt)

```
public sealed partial class MainPage : Page
{
    public MainPage()
    {
        this.InitializeComponent();
    }

    void OnBoldAppBarCheckBoxChecked(object sender, RoutedEventArgs args)
    {
        CheckBox chkbox = sender as CheckBox;
        textBlock.FontWeight = (bool)chkbox.IsChecked ? FontWeights.Bold : FontWeights.Normal;
    }

    void OnItalicAppBarCheckBoxChecked(object sender, RoutedEventArgs args)
    {
        CheckBox chkbox = sender as CheckBox;
        textBlock.FontStyle = (bool)chkbox.IsChecked ? FontStyle.Italic : FontStyle.Normal;
    }

    void OnUnderlineAppBarCheckBoxChecked(object sender, RoutedEventArgs args)
    {
        CheckBox chkbox = sender as CheckBox;
        Inline inline = textBlock.Inlines[0];

        if ((bool)chkbox.IsChecked && !(inline is Underline))
        {
            Underline underline = new Underline();
            textBlock.Inlines[0] = underline;
            underline.Inlines.Add(inline);
        }
        else if (!(bool)chkbox.IsChecked && inline is Underline)
        {
            Underline underline = inline as Underline;
            Run run = underline.Inlines[0] as Run;
            underline.Inlines.Clear();
            textBlock.Inlines[0] = run;
        }
    }

    void OnFontColorAppBarRadioButtonChecked(object sender, RoutedEventArgs args)
    {
        textBlock.Foreground = (sender as RadioButton).Foreground;
    }
}
```

Styling a *CheckBox* or *RadioButton* is not the only way to implement this type of functionality. Another approach to mimic a *CheckBox* is illustrated in the Weather application. When tapped, the *Button* labeled "Change to Celsius" changes to "Change to Fahrenheit."

A button on an application bar can also invoke a *PopupMenu* or *Popup*. For example, press the button with the wrench icon in Windows 8 Internet Explorer. A little popup appears with at least two additional commands: "Find on page" and "View on the desktop." Or try the Map Style button in Maps to see two mutually exclusive options "Road View" and "Aerial View" with a check mark indicating the current selection. Or press the Camera Options command in the Camera application. You get a popup with combo boxes, a toggle switch, and a link for "More," which displays a larger popup dialog.

Using *PopupMenu* and *Popup* with an application bar is very similar to invoking them with a right-click: You just need to position them intelligently, as I'll demonstrate shortly.

If you sweep your finger on the right side of the screen while an application is running, you'll bring up the standard list of charms: Search, Share, Start, Devices, and Settings. I'll demonstrate in Chapter 17, "Share and Print," how your application can hook into these charms. In particular, the Settings button often invokes a list of options that can include About and Help as well as Settings. However, some applications include an Options item on the application bar, and the application bar can also contain a Settings item. Indeed, StandardStyles.xaml includes a SettingsAppBarButtonStyle that displays a gear icon and the word "Settings." How you divide program functionality among these items is up to you, but generally you'll use an application bar Options button for items accessed more frequently than the Settings and you'll use the Settings button on the application bar for items accessed more frequently than those on the Settings charm.

An App Bar for a Note Pad

The PrimitivePad program in Chapter 7 had three buttons at the top of its page labeled "Open," "Save As," and a *ToggleButton* with "Wrap" alternating with "No Wrap." Let's convert these to application bar buttons, as well as implementing the text-wrapping option as a *Popup* and adding buttons to increase and decrease the font size. But I won't attempt to make the file I/O logic more sophisticated.

Here's the MainPage.xaml file for AppBarPad:

Project: AppBarPad | File: MainPage.xaml (excerpt)

```
<Page ... >
    <Grid Background="{StaticResource ApplicationPageBackgroundThemeBrush}">
        <TextBox Name="txtbox"
                 IsEnabled="False"
                 FontSize="24"
                 AcceptsReturn="True" />
    </Grid>

    <Page.BottomAppBar>
        <AppBar>
            <Grid>
                <StackPanel Orientation="Horizontal"
                            HorizontalAlignment="Left">

                    <Button Style="{StaticResource FontIncreaseAppBarButtonStyle}"
                            Click="OnFontIncreaseAppBarButtonClick" />

                    <Button Style="{StaticResource FontDecreaseAppBarButtonStyle}"
                            Click="OnFontDecreaseAppBarButtonClick" />
```

```
                        <Button Style="{StaticResource SettingsAppBarButtonStyle}"
                                AutomationProperties.Name="Wrap Option"
                                Click="OnWrapOptionAppBarButtonClick" />
                    </StackPanel>

                    <StackPanel Orientation="Horizontal"
                                HorizontalAlignment="Right">

                        <Button Style="{StaticResource OpenFileAppBarButtonStyle}"
                                Click="OnOpenAppBarButtonClick" />

                        <Button Style="{StaticResource SaveAppBarButtonStyle}"
                                AutomationProperties.Name="Save As"
                                Click="OnSaveAsAppBarButtonClick" />
                    </StackPanel>
                </Grid>
            </AppBar>
        </Page.BottomAppBar>
</Page>
```

Generally, an application bar has some buttons on the left and some on the right. When holding a tablet, these are more convenient than buttons in the middle. You can use XAML in a couple ways to divide the buttons between left and right. Perhaps the easiest approach is to put two horizontal *StackPanel* elements in a single-cell *Grid* and align them on the right and left.

It's recommended that a New (or Add) button be on the far right, and although this program does not have a New button, the other file-related buttons should also appear on the right side because they are related to New. I supplied a name of "Save As" to replace "Save" for the Button styled with the *SaveAppBarButtonStyle*.

The program options are on the left: buttons to increase and decrease the font size, and another (using a generic *SettingsAppBarButtonStyle*) for the word-wrap setting. When you sweep your finger on the top or bottom of the screen, here's what you'll see:

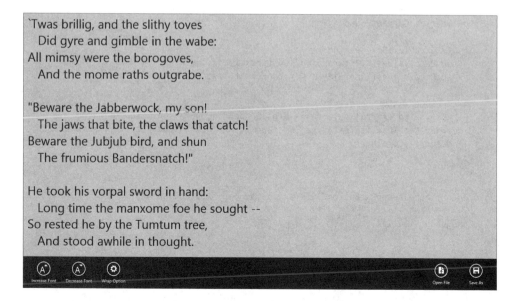

The program saves user settings (and the content of the *TextBox*) in response to the *Suspending* event defined by *Application*. These settings are loaded in the *Loaded* handler. For convenience, I've defined both of these as anonymous methods in the *MainPage* constructor. Also shown here are the simple handlers for the font size increase and decrease buttons:

Project: AppBarPad | **File:** MainPage.xaml.cs (excerpt)

```
public sealed partial class MainPage : Page
{
    public MainPage()
    {
        this.InitializeComponent();

        // Get local settings object
        ApplicationDataContainer appData = ApplicationData.Current.LocalSettings;

        Loaded += async (sender, args) =>
            {
                // Load TextBox settings
                if (appData.Values.ContainsKey("TextWrapping"))
                    txtbox.TextWrapping = (TextWrapping)appData.Values["TextWrapping"];

                if (appData.Values.ContainsKey("FontSize"))
                    txtbox.FontSize = (double)appData.Values["FontSize"];

                // Load TextBox content
                StorageFolder localFolder = ApplicationData.Current.LocalFolder;
                StorageFile storageFile = await localFolder.CreateFileAsync("AppBarPad.txt",
                                                    CreationCollisionOption.OpenIfExists);
                txtbox.Text = await FileIO.ReadTextAsync(storageFile);

                // Enable the TextBox and give it input focus
                txtbox.IsEnabled = true;
                txtbox.Focus(FocusState.Programmatic);
            };

        Application.Current.Suspending += async (sender, args) =>
        {
            // Save TextBox settings
            appData.Values["TextWrapping"] = (int)txtbox.TextWrapping;
            appData.Values["FontSize"] = txtbox.FontSize;

            // Save TextBox content
            SuspendingDeferral deferral = args.SuspendingOperation.GetDeferral();
            await PathIO.WriteTextAsync("ms-appdata:///local/AppBarPad.txt", txtbox.Text);
            deferral.Complete();
        };
    }

    void OnFontIncreaseAppBarButtonClick(object sender, RoutedEventArgs args)
    {
        ChangeFontSize(1.1);
    }
```

```
    void OnFontDecreaseAppBarButtonClick(object sender, RoutedEventArgs args)
    {
        ChangeFontSize(1/1.1);
    }

    void ChangeFontSize(double multiplier)
    {
        txtbox.FontSize *= multiplier;
    }
    ...
}
```

When the *Button* labeled "Wrap Options" is clicked, the program displays a little dialog with "Wrap" and "No wrap" items. I've defined the layout of this little dialog as a *UserControl* called *WrapOptionsDialog*. The XAML file represents the two options with *RadioButton* controls:

Project: AppBarPad | File: WrapOptionsDialog.xaml (excerpt)

```
<UserControl ... >

    <Grid Background="{StaticResource ApplicationPageBackgroundThemeBrush}">
        <StackPanel Name="stackPanel"
                    Margin="24">
            <RadioButton Content="Wrap"
                         Checked="OnRadioButtonChecked">
                <RadioButton.Tag>
                    <TextWrapping>Wrap</TextWrapping>
                </RadioButton.Tag>
            </RadioButton>

            <RadioButton Content="No wrap"
                         Checked="OnRadioButtonChecked">
                <RadioButton.Tag>
                    <TextWrapping>NoWrap</TextWrapping>
                </RadioButton.Tag>
            </RadioButton>
        </StackPanel>
    </Grid>
</UserControl>
```

You'll notice that this *Grid* has the standard background brush. It needs to have some kind of brush or the background will be transparent. I've retained a dark theme in this program, so this dialog will have a white foreground and black background and hence contrast with the *TextBox*.

The code-behind file for the dialog defines a dependency property named *TextWrapping* of type *TextWrapping*. The property-changed handler checks a *RadioButton* when this property is set, and the property is set when a user selects a *RadioButton*:

Project: AppBarPad | File: WrapOptionsDialog.xaml.cs (excerpt)

```
public sealed partial class WrapOptionsDialog : UserControl
{
    static WrapOptionsDialog()
    {
        TextWrappingProperty = DependencyProperty.Register("TextWrapping",
            typeof(TextWrapping),
```

```
                typeof(WrapOptionsDialog),
                new PropertyMetadata(TextWrapping.NoWrap, OnTextWrappingChanged));
    }

    public static DependencyProperty TextWrappingProperty { private set; get; }

    public WrapOptionsDialog()
    {
        this.InitializeComponent();
    }

    public TextWrapping TextWrapping
    {
        set { SetValue(TextWrappingProperty, value); }
        get { return (TextWrapping)GetValue(TextWrappingProperty); }
    }

    static void OnTextWrappingChanged(DependencyObject obj,
                                DependencyPropertyChangedEventArgs args)
    {
        (obj as WrapOptionsDialog).OnTextWrappingChanged(args);
    }

    void OnTextWrappingChanged(DependencyPropertyChangedEventArgs args)
    {
        foreach (UIElement child in stackPanel.Children)
        {
            RadioButton radioButton = child as RadioButton;
            radioButton.IsChecked =
                (TextWrapping)radioButton.Tag == (TextWrapping)args.NewValue;
        }
    }

    void OnRadioButtonChecked(object sender, RoutedEventArgs args)
    {
        this.TextWrapping = (TextWrapping)(sender as RadioButton).Tag;
    }
}
```

The event handler for the "Wrap Options" application bar button is in the *MainPage* code-behind
file. The event handler instantiates a *WrapOptionsDialog* object and initializes its *TextWrapping* property from the *TextWrapping* property of the *TextBox*. It then defines a binding in code between the
two *TextWrapping* properties. This allows the user to see the result of changing this property directly
in the *TextBox*. The *WrapOptionsDialog* object is then made a child of a new *Popup* object:

Project: AppBarPad | File: MainPage.xaml.cs (excerpt)

```
void OnWrapOptionsAppBarButtonClick(object sender, RoutedEventArgs args)
{
    // Create dialog
    WrapOptionsDialog wrapOptionsDialog = new WrapOptionsDialog
    {
        TextWrapping = txtbox.TextWrapping
    };
```

```
    // Bind dialog to TextBox
    Binding binding = new Binding
    {
        Source = wrapOptionsDialog,
        Path = new PropertyPath("TextWrapping"),
        Mode = BindingMode.TwoWay
    };
    txtbox.SetBinding(TextBox.TextWrappingProperty, binding);

    // Create popup
    Popup popup = new Popup
    {
        Child = wrapOptionsDialog,
        IsLightDismissEnabled = true
    };

    // Adjust location based on content size
    wrapOptionsDialog.Loaded += (dialogSender, dialogArgs) =>
    {
        // Get Button location relative to screen
        Button btn = sender as Button;
        Point pt = btn.TransformToVisual(null).TransformPoint(new Point(btn.ActualWidth / 2,
                                                                        btn.ActualHeight / 2));

        popup.HorizontalOffset = pt.X - wrapOptionsDialog.ActualWidth / 2;
        popup.VerticalOffset = this.ActualHeight - wrapOptionsDialog.ActualHeight
                                                 - this.BottomAppBar.ActualHeight - 48;
    };

    // Open the popup
    popup.IsOpen = true;
}
```

Generally, popups such as this are positioned just above the application bar, which means that you need to know the height of the popup, the height of the page, and the height of the application bar to get it right. I also wanted to position the *Popup* horizontally so that it's aligned with the button that invoked it. This requires making use of the *TransformToVisual* method (which I'll discuss in Chapter 10, "Transforms") to obtain the coordinates of the center of the button relative to the screen. You can perform calculations such as these during either the *Loaded* or the *SizeChanged* event on the child of the *Popup*.

The *Click* handler concludes by setting the *IsOpen* property of the *Popup* to *true*, and here it is:

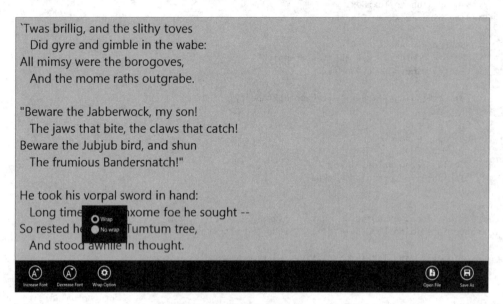

The *Popup* is automatically dismissed when the user taps anywhere outside the *Popup*, and then the user needs to tap once more to dismiss the application bar. Because both *AppBar* and *Popup* have *Opened* and *Closed* events for performing initialization or cleanup, it's possible to install a handler for the *Closed* event of *Popup* and use that to set the *IsOpen* property of the *AppBar* to *false* (for example).

The file I/O logic uses the simple static *FileIO* methods but without exception handling:

Project: AppBarPad | File: MainPage.xaml.cs (excerpt)

```csharp
public sealed partial class MainPage : Page
{
    ...
    async void OnOpenAppBarButtonClick(object sender, RoutedEventArgs args)
    {
        FileOpenPicker picker = new FileOpenPicker();
        picker.FileTypeFilter.Add(".txt");
        StorageFile storageFile = await picker.PickSingleFileAsync();

        // If user presses Cancel, result is null
        if (storageFile == null)
            return;

        txtbox.Text = await FileIO.ReadTextAsync(storageFile);
    }

    async void OnSaveAsAppBarButtonClick(object sender, RoutedEventArgs args)
    {
        FileSavePicker picker = new FileSavePicker();
        picker.DefaultFileExtension = ".txt";
        picker.FileTypeChoices.Add("Text", new List<string> { ".txt" });
        StorageFile storageFile = await picker.PickSaveFileAsync();
```

```
        // If user presses Cancel, result is null
        if (storageFile == null)
            return;

        await FileIO.WriteTextAsync(storageFile, txtbox.Text);
    }
}
```

Introducing XamlCruncher

Even after becoming familiar with various features of the Windows Runtime, putting it all together to create an application can still be a challenge. But with the ability to create application bars and dialog boxes, it is now possible to build something that looks like a real application.

XamlCruncher lets you type XAML into a *TextBox* and see the result. The magic method that XamlCruncher uses is *XamlReader.Load*, which you had a brief glimpse of in the PathMarkupSyntaxCode project in Chapter 2, "XAML Syntax." The XAML processed by *XamlReader .Load* cannot reference event handlers or external assemblies, but a tool such as XamlCruncher is very useful for interactively experimenting with XAML and learning about it. I won't pretend that this program is commercial grade, but it's a real program with real Windows 8 features.

Here's a view of the program with some XAML in the editor on the left and the resultant objects in a display area on the right:

The editor doesn't include any amenities. It won't even automatically generate a closing tag when you type a start tag; it doesn't use different colors for elements, attributes, and strings; and it doesn't have anything close to IntelliSense. However, the configuration of the page is changeable: You can put the edit window on the top, right, or bottom.

The application bar has Add, Open, Save, and Save As buttons as well as a Refresh button and a button for application settings:

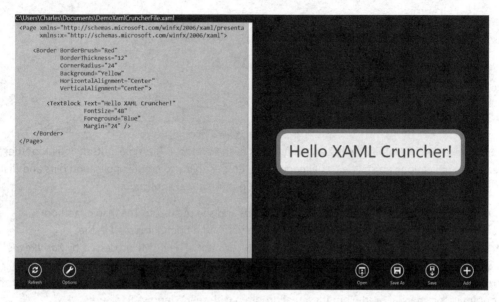

You can select whether XamlCruncher reparses the XAML with each keystroke or only with a press of the Refresh button. That option and others are available from the dialog invoked when you press the Settings button:

I've turned on the Ruler and Grid Lines options to show you the result in the display area on the right. All these settings are saved for the next time the program is run.

Most of the page is a custom *UserControl* derivative called *SplitContainer*. In the center is a *Thumb* control that lets you select the proportion of space in the left and right panels (or top and bottom panels). In the screen shots, this *Thumb* is a lighter gray vertical bar in the center of the screen. The XAML file for *SplitContainer* consists of a *Grid* defined for both horizontal and vertical configurations:

Project: XamlCruncher | File: SplitContainer.xaml

```xml
<UserControl
    x:Class="XamlCruncher.SplitContainer"
    xmlns="http://schemas.microsoft.com/winfx/2006/xaml/presentation"
    xmlns:x="http://schemas.microsoft.com/winfx/2006/xaml"
    xmlns:local="using:XamlCruncher">

    <Grid>
        <!-- Default Orientation is Horizontal -->
        <Grid.ColumnDefinitions>
            <ColumnDefinition x:Name="coldef1" Width="*" MinWidth="100" />
            <ColumnDefinition Width="Auto" />
            <ColumnDefinition x:Name="coldef2" Width="*" MinWidth="100" />
        </Grid.ColumnDefinitions>

        <!-- Alternative Orientation is Vertical -->
        <Grid.RowDefinitions>
            <RowDefinition x:Name="rowdef1" Height="*" />
            <RowDefinition Height="Auto" />
            <RowDefinition x:Name="rowdef2" Height="0" />
        </Grid.RowDefinitions>

        <Grid Name="grid1"
            Grid.Row="0"
            Grid.Column="0" />

        <Thumb Name="thumb"
            Grid.Row="0"
            Grid.Column="1"
            Width="12"
            DragStarted="OnThumbDragStarted"
            DragDelta="OnThumbDragDelta" />

        <Grid Name="grid2"
            Grid.Row="0"
            Grid.Column="2" />
    </Grid>
</UserControl>
```

In Chapter 5 you've seen similar markup in the OrientableColorScroll program, which altered a *Grid* when the aspect ratio of the page changed between landscape and portrait.

The code-behind file defines five properties backed by dependency properties. Normally the *Child1* and *Child2* properties are set to the elements to appear in the left and right of the control, but where they actually appear is governed by the *Orientation* and *SwapChildren* properties:

Project: XamlCruncher | **File:** SplitContainer.xaml.cs (excerpt)

```
public sealed partial class SplitContainer : UserControl
{
    // Static constructor and properties
    static SplitContainer()
    {
        Child1Property =
            DependencyProperty.Register("Child1",
                typeof(UIElement), typeof(SplitContainer),
                new PropertyMetadata(null, OnChildChanged));

        Child2Property =
            DependencyProperty.Register("Child2",
                typeof(UIElement), typeof(SplitContainer),
                new PropertyMetadata(null, OnChildChanged));

        OrientationProperty =
            DependencyProperty.Register("Orientation",
                typeof(Orientation), typeof(SplitContainer),
                new PropertyMetadata(Orientation.Horizontal, OnOrientationChanged));

        SwapChildrenProperty =
            DependencyProperty.Register("SwapChildren",
                typeof(bool), typeof(SplitContainer),
                new PropertyMetadata(false, OnSwapChildrenChanged));

        MinimumSizeProperty =
            DependencyProperty.Register("MinimumSize",
                typeof(double), typeof(SplitContainer),
                new PropertyMetadata(100.0, OnMinSizeChanged));
    }

    public static DependencyProperty Child1Property { private set; get; }
    public static DependencyProperty Child2Property { private set; get; }
    public static DependencyProperty OrientationProperty { private set; get; }
    public static DependencyProperty SwapChildrenProperty { private set; get; }
    public static DependencyProperty MinimumSizeProperty { private set; get; }

    // Instance constructor and properties
    public SplitContainer()
    {
        this.InitializeComponent();
    }

    public UIElement Child1
    {
        set { SetValue(Child1Property, value); }
        get { return (UIElement)GetValue(Child1Property); }
    }
```

```
    public UIElement Child2
    {
        set { SetValue(Child2Property, value); }
        get { return (UIElement)GetValue(Child2Property); }
    }

    public Orientation Orientation
    {
        set { SetValue(OrientationProperty, value); }
        get { return (Orientation)GetValue(OrientationProperty); }
    }

    public bool SwapChildren
    {
        set { SetValue(SwapChildrenProperty, value); }
        get { return (bool)GetValue(SwapChildrenProperty); }
    }

    public double MinimumSize
    {
        set { SetValue(MinimumSizeProperty, value); }
        get { return (double)GetValue(MinimumSizeProperty); }
    }
    ...
}
```

The *Orientation* property is of type *Orientation*, the same enumeration used for *StackPanel* and *VariableSizedWrapGrid*. It's always nice to use existing types for dependency properties rather than inventing your own. Notice that the *MinimumSize* is of type *double* and hence is initialized as 100.0 rather than 100 to prevent a type mismatch at run time.

The property-changed handlers show two different approaches that programmers use in calling the instance property-changed handler from the static handler. I've already shown you the approach where the static handler simply calls the instance handler with the same *DependencyPropertyChangedEventArgs* object. Sometimes—as with the handlers for the *Orientation*, *SwapChildren*, and *MinimumSize* properties—it's more convenient for the static handler to call the instance handler with the old value and new value cast to the proper type:

Project: XamlCruncher | File: SplitContainer.xaml.cs (excerpt)

```
public sealed partial class SplitContainer : UserControl
{
    ...
    // Property-changed handlers
    static void OnChildChanged(DependencyObject obj,
                          DependencyPropertyChangedEventArgs args)
    {
        (obj as SplitContainer).OnChildChanged(args);
    }
```

```csharp
void OnChildChanged(DependencyPropertyChangedEventArgs args)
{
    Grid targetGrid = (args.Property == Child1Property ^ this.SwapChildren) ? grid1 : grid2;
    targetGrid.Children.Clear();

    if (args.NewValue != null)
        targetGrid.Children.Add(args.NewValue as UIElement);
}

static void OnOrientationChanged(DependencyObject obj,
                                 DependencyPropertyChangedEventArgs args)
{
    (obj as SplitContainer).OnOrientationChanged((Orientation)args.OldValue,
                                                 (Orientation)args.NewValue);
}

void OnOrientationChanged(Orientation oldOrientation, Orientation newOrientation)
{
    // Shouldn't be necessary, but...
    if (newOrientation == oldOrientation)
        return;

    if (newOrientation == Orientation.Horizontal)
    {
        coldef1.Width = rowdef1.Height;
        coldef2.Width = rowdef2.Height;

        coldef1.MinWidth = this.MinimumSize;
        coldef2.MinWidth = this.MinimumSize;

        rowdef1.Height = new GridLength(1, GridUnitType.Star);
        rowdef2.Height = new GridLength(0);

        rowdef1.MinHeight = 0;
        rowdef2.MinHeight = 0;

        thumb.Width = 12;
        thumb.Height = Double.NaN;

        Grid.SetRow(thumb, 0);
        Grid.SetColumn(thumb, 1);

        Grid.SetRow(grid2, 0);
        Grid.SetColumn(grid2, 2);
    }
    else
    {
        rowdef1.Height = coldef1.Width;
        rowdef2.Height = coldef2.Width;

        rowdef1.MinHeight = this.MinimumSize;
        rowdef2.MinHeight = this.MinimumSize;

        coldef1.Width = new GridLength(1, GridUnitType.Star);
        coldef2.Width = new GridLength(0);
```

```
            coldef1.MinWidth = 0;
            coldef2.MinWidth = 0;

            thumb.Height = 12;
            thumb.Width = Double.NaN;

            Grid.SetRow(thumb, 1);
            Grid.SetColumn(thumb, 0);

            Grid.SetRow(grid2, 2);
            Grid.SetColumn(grid2, 0);
        }
    }

    static void OnSwapChildrenChanged(DependencyObject obj,
                                DependencyPropertyChangedEventArgs args)
    {
        (obj as SplitContainer).OnSwapChildrenChanged((bool)args.OldValue,
                                                (bool)args.NewValue);
    }

    void OnSwapChildrenChanged(bool oldOrientation, bool newOrientation)
    {
        grid1.Children.Clear();
        grid2.Children.Clear();

        grid1.Children.Add(newOrientation ? this.Child2 : this.Child1);
        grid2.Children.Add(newOrientation ? this.Child1 : this.Child2);
    }

    static void OnMinSizeChanged(DependencyObject obj,
                            DependencyPropertyChangedEventArgs args)
    {
        (obj as SplitContainer).OnMinSizeChanged((double)args.OldValue,
                                            (double)args.NewValue);
    }

    void OnMinSizeChanged(double oldValue, double newValue)
    {
        if (this.Orientation == Orientation.Horizontal)
        {
            coldef1.MinWidth = newValue;
            coldef2.MinWidth = newValue;
        }
        else
        {
            rowdef1.MinHeight = newValue;
            rowdef2.MinHeight = newValue;
        }
    }
    ...
}
```

My original version of the property-changed handler for *Orientation* assumed that the *Orientation* property was actually changing, as should be the case whenever a property-changed handler is called. However, I discovered that sometimes the property-changed handler was called when the property was set to its existing value.

All that's left for *SplitContainer* is examining the event handlers for the *Thumb*. The idea here is that the two columns (or rows) of the *Grid* are allocated size based on the star specification so that the relative size of the columns (or rows) remains the same when the size or aspect ratio of the *Grid* changes. However, to keep the *Thumb* dragging logic reasonably simple, it helps if the numeric proportions associated with the star specifications are actual pixel dimensions. These are initialized in the *OnThumbDragStarted* method and changed in *OnDragThumbDelta*:

Project: XamlCruncher | File: SplitContainer.xaml.cs (excerpt)

```
public sealed partial class SplitContainer : UserControl
{
    ...
    // Thumb event handlers
    void OnThumbDragStarted(object sender, DragStartedEventArgs args)
    {
        if (this.Orientation == Orientation.Horizontal)
        {
            coldef1.Width = new GridLength(coldef1.ActualWidth, GridUnitType.Star);
            coldef2.Width = new GridLength(coldef2.ActualWidth, GridUnitType.Star);
        }
        else
        {
            rowdef1.Height = new GridLength(rowdef1.ActualHeight, GridUnitType.Star);
            rowdef2.Height = new GridLength(rowdef2.ActualHeight, GridUnitType.Star);
        }
    }

    void OnThumbDragDelta(object sender, DragDeltaEventArgs args)
    {
        if (this.Orientation == Orientation.Horizontal)
        {
            double newWidth1 = Math.Max(0, coldef1.Width.Value + args.HorizontalChange);
            double newWidth2 = Math.Max(0, coldef2.Width.Value - args.HorizontalChange);

            coldef1.Width = new GridLength(newWidth1, GridUnitType.Star);
            coldef2.Width = new GridLength(newWidth2, GridUnitType.Star);
        }
        else
        {
            double newHeight1 = Math.Max(0, rowdef1.Height.Value + args.VerticalChange);
            double newHeight2 = Math.Max(0, rowdef2.Height.Value - args.VerticalChange);

            rowdef1.Height = new GridLength(newHeight1, GridUnitType.Star);
            rowdef2.Height = new GridLength(newHeight2, GridUnitType.Star);
        }
    }
}
```

The last of the earlier screen shots of XamlCruncher showed a ruler and grid lines in the display area. The ruler is in units of inches, based on 96 pixels to the inch, so the grid lines are 24 pixels apart.

The ruler and grid lines are useful if you're interactively designing some vector graphics or other precise layout.

The ruler and grid lines are independently optional. The *UserControl* derivative that displays them is called *RulerContainer*. As you'll see when the XamlCruncher page is constructed, an instance of *RulerContainer* is set to the *Child2* property of the *SplitContainer* object. Here's the XAML file for *RulerContainer*:

Project: XamlCruncher | **File:** RulerContainer.xaml (excerpt)

```
<UserControl ... >
    <Grid SizeChanged="OnGridSizeChanged">
        <Canvas Name="rulerCanvas" />
        <Grid Name="innerGrid">
            <Grid Name="gridLinesGrid" />
            <Border Name="border" />
        </Grid>
    </Grid>
</UserControl>
```

This *RulerContainer* control has a *Child* property, and the child of this control is set to the *Child* property of the *Border*. Visually behind this *Border* is the grid of horizontal and vertical lines, which are children of the *Grid* labeled "gridLinesGrid." If the ruler is also present, the *Grid* labeled "innerGrid" is given a nonzero *Margin* on the left and top to accommodate this ruler. The tick marks and numbers that comprise the ruler are children of the *Canvas* named "rulerCanvas."

Here's all the overhead for the dependency property definitions in the code-behind file:

Project: XamlCruncher | **File:** RulerContainer.xaml.cs (excerpt)

```
public sealed partial class RulerContainer : UserControl
{
    ...
    static RulerContainer()
    {
        ChildProperty =
            DependencyProperty.Register("Child",
                typeof(UIElement), typeof(RulerContainer),
                new PropertyMetadata(null, OnChildChanged));

        ShowRulerProperty =
            DependencyProperty.Register("ShowRuler",
                typeof(bool), typeof(RulerContainer),
                new PropertyMetadata(false, OnShowRulerChanged));

        ShowGridLinesProperty =
            DependencyProperty.Register("ShowGridLines",
                typeof(bool), typeof(RulerContainer),
                new PropertyMetadata(false, OnShowGridLinesChanged));
    }

    public static DependencyProperty ChildProperty { private set; get; }
    public static DependencyProperty ShowRulerProperty { private set; get; }
    public static DependencyProperty ShowGridLinesProperty { private set; get; }
```

```csharp
    public RulerContainer()
    {
        this.InitializeComponent();
    }

    public UIElement Child
    {
        set { SetValue(ChildProperty, value); }
        get { return (UIElement)GetValue(ChildProperty); }
    }

    public bool ShowRuler
    {
        set { SetValue(ShowRulerProperty, value); }
        get { return (bool)GetValue(ShowRulerProperty); }
    }

    public bool ShowGridLines
    {
        set { SetValue(ShowGridLinesProperty, value); }
        get { return (bool)GetValue(ShowGridLinesProperty); }
    }

    // Property changed handlers
    static void OnChildChanged(DependencyObject obj,
                              DependencyPropertyChangedEventArgs args)
    {
        (obj as RulerContainer).border.Child = (UIElement)args.NewValue;
    }

    static void OnShowRulerChanged(DependencyObject obj,
                                 DependencyPropertyChangedEventArgs args)
    {
        (obj as RulerContainer).RedrawRuler();
    }

    static void OnShowGridLinesChanged(DependencyObject obj,
                                     DependencyPropertyChangedEventArgs args)
    {
        (obj as RulerContainer).RedrawGridLines();
    }

    void OnGridSizeChanged(object sender, SizeChangedEventArgs args)
    {
        RedrawRuler();
        RedrawGridLines();
    }

    ...

}
```

Also shown here are the property-changed handlers (which are simple enough to use in the static versions) as well as the *SizeChanged* handler for the *Grid*. Two redraw methods handle all the drawing, which involves creating *Line* elements and *TextBlock* elements and organizing them in the two panels:

Project: XamlCruncher | File: RulerContainer.xaml.cs (excerpt)

```
public sealed partial class RulerContainer : UserControl
{
    const double RULER_WIDTH = 12;
    ...
    void RedrawGridLines()
    {
        gridLinesGrid.Children.Clear();

        if (!this.ShowGridLines)
            return;

        // Vertical grid lines every 1/4"
        for (double x = 24; x < gridLinesGrid.ActualWidth; x += 24)
        {
            Line line = new Line
            {
                X1 = x,
                Y1 = 0,
                X2 = x,
                Y2 = gridLinesGrid.ActualHeight,
                Stroke = this.Foreground,
                StrokeThickness = x % 96 == 0 ? 1 : 0.5
            };
            gridLinesGrid.Children.Add(line);
        }

        // Horizontal grid lines every 1/4"
        for (double y = 24; y < gridLinesGrid.ActualHeight; y += 24)
        {
            Line line = new Line
            {
                X1 = 0,
                Y1 = y,
                X2 = gridLinesGrid.ActualWidth,
                Y2 = y,
                Stroke = this.Foreground,
                StrokeThickness = y % 96 == 0 ? 1 : 0.5
            };
            gridLinesGrid.Children.Add(line);
        }
    }

    void RedrawRuler()
    {
        rulerCanvas.Children.Clear();

        if (!this.ShowRuler)
        {
            innerGrid.Margin = new Thickness();
            return;
        }

        innerGrid.Margin = new Thickness(RULER_WIDTH, RULER_WIDTH, 0, 0);
```

```
// Ruler across the top
for (double x = 0; x < gridLinesGrid.ActualWidth - RULER_WIDTH; x += 12)
{
    // Numbers every inch
    if (x > 0 && x % 96 == 0)
    {
        TextBlock txtblk = new TextBlock
        {
            Text = (x / 96).ToString("F0"),
            FontSize = RULER_WIDTH - 2
        };

        txtblk.Measure(new Size());
        Canvas.SetLeft(txtblk, RULER_WIDTH + x - txtblk.ActualWidth / 2);
        Canvas.SetTop(txtblk, 0);
        rulerCanvas.Children.Add(txtblk);
    }
    // Tick marks every 1/8"
    else
    {
        Line line = new Line
        {
            X1 = RULER_WIDTH + x,
            Y1 = x % 48 == 0 ? 2 : 4,
            X2 = RULER_WIDTH + x,
            Y2 = x % 48 == 0 ? RULER_WIDTH - 2 : RULER_WIDTH - 4,
            Stroke = this.Foreground,
            StrokeThickness = 1
        };
        rulerCanvas.Children.Add(line);
    }
}

// Heavy line underneath the tick marks
Line topLine = new Line
{
    X1 = RULER_WIDTH - 1,
    Y1 = RULER_WIDTH - 1,
    X2 = rulerCanvas.ActualWidth,
    Y2 = RULER_WIDTH - 1,
    Stroke = this.Foreground,
    StrokeThickness = 2
};
rulerCanvas.Children.Add(topLine);

// Ruler down the left side
for (double y = 0; y < gridLinesGrid.ActualHeight - RULER_WIDTH; y += 12)
{
    // Numbers every inch
    if (y > 0 && y % 96 == 0)
    {
        TextBlock txtblk = new TextBlock
        {
            Text = (y / 96).ToString("F0"),
            FontSize = RULER_WIDTH - 2,
        };
```

```
            txtblk.Measure(new Size());
            Canvas.SetLeft(txtblk, 2);
            Canvas.SetTop(txtblk, RULER_WIDTH + y - txtblk.ActualHeight / 2);
            rulerCanvas.Children.Add(txtblk);
        }
        // Tick marks every 1/8"
        else
        {
            Line line = new Line
            {
                X1 = y % 48 == 0 ? 2 : 4,
                Y1 = RULER_WIDTH + y,
                X2 = y % 48 == 0 ? RULER_WIDTH - 2 : RULER_WIDTH - 4,
                Y2 = RULER_WIDTH + y,
                Stroke = this.Foreground,
                StrokeThickness = 1
            };
            rulerCanvas.Children.Add(line);
        }
    }

    Line leftLine = new Line
    {
        X1 = RULER_WIDTH - 1,
        Y1 = RULER_WIDTH - 1,
        X2 = RULER_WIDTH - 1,
        Y2 = rulerCanvas.ActualHeight,
        Stroke = this.Foreground,
        StrokeThickness = 2
    };
    rulerCanvas.Children.Add(leftLine);
    }
}
```

These two methods make extensive use of the *Line* element, which renders a single straight line between the points (*X1, Y1*) and (*X2, Y2*).

This *RedrawRuler* code also illustrates a technique for obtaining the rendered size of a *TextBlock*: When you create a new *TextBlock*, the *ActualWidth* and *ActualHeight* properties are both zero. These properties are normally not calculated until the *TextBlock* becomes part of a visual tree and is subjected to layout. However, you can force the *TextBlock* to calculate a size for itself by calling its *Measure* method. This method is defined by *UIElement* and is an important component of the layout system.

The argument to the *Measure* method is a *Size* value indicating the size available for the element, but you can set the size to zero for this purpose:

```
txtblk.Measure(new Size());
```

If you need to find the size of a *TextBlock* that wraps text, you must supply a nonzero first argument to the *Size* constructor so that *TextBlock* knows the width in which to wrap the text.

Following the *Measure* call, the *ActualWidth* and *ActualHeight* properties of *TextBlock* are valid and usable for positioning the *TextBlock* in a *Canvas*. Calling the *Canvas.SetLeft* and *Canvas.SetTop* properties is necessary only when positioning the *TextBlock* elements in the *Canvas*. In either a single-cell *Grid* or *Canvas*, the *Line* elements are positioned based on their coordinates.

As you'll see, an instance of *RulerContainer* is set to the *Child2* property of the *SplitContainer* that dominates the XamlCruncher page. The *Child1* property appears to be a *TextBox*, but it's actually an instance of another custom control named *TabbableTextBox*, which derives from *TextBox*.

The standard *TextBox* does not respond to the Tab key, and when you're typing XAML into an editor, you really want tabs. That's the primary feature of *TabbableTextBox*, shown here in its entirety:

Project: XamlCruncher | **File:** TabbableTextBox.cs

```
using Windows.System;
using Windows.UI.Xaml;
using Windows.UI.Xaml.Controls;
using Windows.UI.Xaml.Input;

namespace XamlCruncher
{
    public class TabbableTextBox : TextBox
    {
        static TabbableTextBox()
        {
            TabSpacesProperty =
                DependencyProperty.Register("TabSpaces",
                    typeof(int), typeof(TabbableTextBox),
                    new PropertyMetadata(4));
        }

        public static DependencyProperty TabSpacesProperty { private set; get; }

        public int TabSpaces
        {
            set { SetValue(TabSpacesProperty, value); }
            get { return (int)GetValue(TabSpacesProperty); }
        }

        public bool IsModified { set; get; }

        protected override void OnKeyDown(KeyRoutedEventArgs args)
        {
            this.IsModified = true;

            if (args.Key == VirtualKey.Tab)
            {
                int line, col;
                GetPositionFromIndex(this.SelectionStart, out line, out col);
                int insertCount = this.TabSpaces - col % this.TabSpaces;
                this.SelectedText = new string(' ', insertCount);
                this.SelectionStart += insertCount;
                this.SelectionLength = 0;
                args.Handled = true;
                return;
```

```
        }
        base.OnKeyDown(args);
    }

    public void GetPositionFromIndex(int index, out int line, out int col)
    {
        if (index > Text.Length)
        {
            line = col = -1;
            return;
        }

        line = col = 0;
        int i = 0;

        while (i < index)
        {
            if (Text[i] == '\n')
            {
                line++;
                col = 0;
            }
            else if (Text[i] == '\r')
            {
                index++;
            }
            else
            {
                col++;
            };
            i++;
        }
    }
    }
    }
}
```

The class intercepts the *OnKeyDown* method to determine if the Tab key is being pressed. If that's the case, it inserts blanks into the *Text* object so that the cursor moves to a text column that is an integral multiple of the *TabSpaces* property. This calculation requires knowing the character position of the cursor on the current line. To obtain this information, it uses the *GetPositionFromIndex* method also defined in this class. (Although the lines in the *Text* property of the *TextBox* are delimited by a carriage return and line feed, the *SelectionStart* index is calculated based on just one end-of-line character.) This method is public and is also used by XamlCruncher to display the current position of the cursor and the current selection (if any).

Another property—not backed by a dependency property—is also defined by *TabbableTextBox*. This is *IsModified*, which is set to *true* whenever a *KeyDown* event occurs.

Like many programs that deal with documents, XamlCruncher keeps track if the text file has changed since the last save. If the user initiates an operation to create a new file or open an existing file, and the current document is in a modified state, the program asks if the user wants to save that document.

Often this logic occurs entirely external to the *TextBox* control. The program sets an *IsModified* flag to *false* when a new file is loaded or the file is saved and to *true* on receipt of a *TextChanged* event. However, the *TextChanged* event is fired when the *Text* property of the *TextBox* is set programmatically, so even if the *TextBox* is being set to a newly loaded file, the *TextChanged* event is fired and the *IsModified* flag would be set by the *TextChanged* handler. You might think that setting the *IsModified* flag in that case might be avoided by setting a flag when the *Text* property is set programmatically. However, the *TextChanged* handler is not called until the method setting the *Text* property has returned control to the operating system, which makes the logic rather messy. Implementing the *IsModified* flag in the *TextBox* derivative helps.

Application Settings and View Models

Many applications maintain user settings and preferences between invocations of the program. As you've seen, the Windows Runtime provides an isolated area of application data storage for storing settings or entire files.

In this program, I've consolidated user settings in a class named *AppSettings*. This class implements *INotifyPropertyChanged* to let it be used for data binding. It's basically a View Model, or perhaps (in a larger application) part of a View Model.

One program option that should be saved is the orientation of the edit and display areas. As you'll recall, the *SplitContainer* has two properties named *Orientation* and *SwapChildren*. For storing user settings, I wanted something more specific to this application. The *TextBox* (or rather, the *TabbableTextBox*) can be on the left, top, right, or bottom, and this enumeration encapsulates those options:

Project: XamlCruncher | File: EditOrientation.cs

```
namespace XamlCruncher
{
    public enum EditOrientation
    {
        Left, Top, Right, Bottom
    }
}
```

Here's *AppSettings* showing all the properties that comprise program settings. The constructor loads the settings, and a *Save* method saves them. All the property values are backed by fields initialized with the program's default settings. Notice that the *EditOrientation* property is based on the *EditOrientation* enumeration:

Project: XamlCruncher | File: AppSettings.cs

```
public class AppSettings : INotifyPropertyChanged
{
    // Application settings initial values
    EditOrientation editOrientation = EditOrientation.Left;
    Orientation orientation = Orientation.Horizontal;
    bool swapEditAndDisplay = false;
```

```csharp
bool autoParsing = false;
bool showRuler = false;
bool showGridLines = false;
double fontSize = 18;
int tabSpaces = 4;

public event PropertyChangedEventHandler PropertyChanged;

public AppSettings()
{
    ApplicationDataContainer appData = ApplicationData.Current.LocalSettings;

    if (appData.Values.ContainsKey("EditOrientation"))
        this.EditOrientation = (EditOrientation)(int)appData.Values["EditOrientation"];

    if (appData.Values.ContainsKey("AutoParsing"))
        this.AutoParsing = (bool)appData.Values["AutoParsing"];

    if (appData.Values.ContainsKey("ShowRuler"))
        this.ShowRuler = (bool)appData.Values["ShowRuler"];

    if (appData.Values.ContainsKey("ShowGridLines"))
        this.ShowGridLines = (bool)appData.Values["ShowGridLines"];

    if (appData.Values.ContainsKey("FontSize"))
        this.FontSize = (double)appData.Values["FontSize"];

    if (appData.Values.ContainsKey("TabSpaces"))
        this.TabSpaces = (int)appData.Values["TabSpaces"];
}

public EditOrientation EditOrientation
{
    set
    {
        if (SetProperty<EditOrientation>(ref editOrientation, value))
        {
            switch (editOrientation)
            {
                case EditOrientation.Left:
                    this.Orientation = Orientation.Horizontal;
                    this.SwapEditAndDisplay = false;
                    break;

                case EditOrientation.Top:
                    this.Orientation = Orientation.Vertical;
                    this.SwapEditAndDisplay = false;
                    break;

                case EditOrientation.Right:
                    this.Orientation = Orientation.Horizontal;
                    this.SwapEditAndDisplay = true;
                    break;
```

```csharp
                    case EditOrientation.Bottom:
                        this.Orientation = Orientation.Vertical;
                        this.SwapEditAndDisplay = true;
                        break;
                }
            }
        }
        get { return editOrientation; }
    }

    public Orientation Orientation
    {
        protected set { SetProperty<Orientation>(ref orientation, value); }
        get { return orientation; }
    }

    public bool SwapEditAndDisplay
    {
        protected set { SetProperty<bool>(ref swapEditAndDisplay, value); }
        get { return swapEditAndDisplay; }
    }

    public bool AutoParsing
    {
        set { SetProperty<bool>(ref autoParsing, value); }
        get { return autoParsing; }
    }

    public bool ShowRuler
    {
        set { SetProperty<bool>(ref showRuler, value); }
        get { return showRuler; }
    }

    public bool ShowGridLines
    {
        set { SetProperty<bool>(ref showGridLines, value); }
        get { return showGridLines; }
    }

    public double FontSize
    {
        set { SetProperty<double>(ref fontSize, value); }
        get { return fontSize; }
    }

    public int TabSpaces
    {
        set { SetProperty<int>(ref tabSpaces, value); }
        get { return tabSpaces; }
    }

    public void Save()
    {
        ApplicationDataContainer appData = ApplicationData.Current.LocalSettings;
        appData.Values.Clear();
```

```
            appData.Values.Add("EditOrientation", (int)this.EditOrientation);
            appData.Values.Add("AutoParsing", this.AutoParsing);
            appData.Values.Add("ShowRuler", this.ShowRuler);
            appData.Values.Add("ShowGridLines", this.ShowGridLines);
            appData.Values.Add("FontSize", this.FontSize);
            appData.Values.Add("TabSpaces", this.TabSpaces);
    }

    protected bool SetProperty<T>(ref T storage, T value,
                                 [CallerMemberName] string propertyName = null)
    {
        if (object.Equals(storage, value))
            return false;

        storage = value;
        OnPropertyChanged(propertyName);
        return true;
    }

    protected void OnPropertyChanged(string propertyName)
    {
        if (PropertyChanged != null)
            PropertyChanged(this, new PropertyChangedEventArgs(propertyName));
    }
}
```

Besides *EditOrientation*, *AppSettings* defines two additional properties that more directly correspond to properties of the *SplitContainer*: *Orientation* and *SwapEditAndDisplay*. The *set* accessors are protected, and the properties are set only from the *set* accessor of *EditOrientation*. These two properties are not saved with the other application settings, but they are easily derived from application settings and make the bindings easier.

The XamlCruncher Page

Sufficient pieces have now been created to let us begin assembling this application. Here's MainPage.xaml:

Project: XamlCruncher | **File:** MainPage.xaml (excerpt)

```
<Page ... >

    <Grid Background="{StaticResource ApplicationPageBackgroundThemeBrush}">
        <Grid.RowDefinitions>
            <RowDefinition Height="Auto" />
            <RowDefinition Height="*" />
            <RowDefinition Height="Auto" />
        </Grid.RowDefinitions>

        <Grid.ColumnDefinitions>
            <ColumnDefinition Width="*" />
            <ColumnDefinition Width="Auto" />
        </Grid.ColumnDefinitions>
```

```xml
<TextBlock Name="filenameText"
           Grid.Row="0"
           Grid.Column="0"
           Grid.ColumnSpan="2"
           FontSize="18"
           TextTrimming="WordEllipsis" />

<local:SplitContainer x:Name="splitContainer"
                       Orientation="{Binding Orientation}"
                       SwapChildren="{Binding SwapEditAndDisplay}"
                       MinimumSize="200"
                       Grid.Row="1"
                       Grid.Column="0"
                       Grid.ColumnSpan="2">
    <local:SplitContainer.Child1>
        <local:TabbableTextBox x:Name="editBox"
                               AcceptsReturn="True"
                               FontSize="{Binding FontSize}"
                               TabSpaces="{Binding TabSpaces}"
                               TextChanged="OnEditBoxTextChanged"
                               SelectionChanged="OnEditBoxSelectionChanged"/>
    </local:SplitContainer.Child1>

    <local:SplitContainer.Child2>
        <local:RulerContainer x:Name="resultContainer"
                              ShowRuler="{Binding ShowRuler}"
                              ShowGridLines="{Binding ShowGridLines}" />
    </local:SplitContainer.Child2>
</local:SplitContainer>

<TextBlock Name="statusText"
           Text="OK"
           Grid.Row="2"
           Grid.Column="0"
           FontSize="18"
           TextWrapping="Wrap" />

<TextBlock Name="lineColText"
           Grid.Row="2"
           Grid.Column="1"
           FontSize="18" />
</Grid>

<Page.BottomAppBar>
    <AppBar>
        <Grid>
            <StackPanel Orientation="Horizontal" HorizontalAlignment="Left">
                <Button Style="{StaticResource RefreshAppBarButtonStyle}"
                        Click="OnRefreshAppBarButtonClick" />

                <Button Style="{StaticResource SettingsAppBarButtonStyle}"
                        Click="OnSettingsAppBarButtonClick" />
            </StackPanel>
```

```
            <StackPanel Orientation="Horizontal" HorizontalAlignment="Right">
                <Button Style="{StaticResource OpenAppBarButtonStyle}"
                        Click="OnOpenAppBarButtonClick" />

                <Button Style="{StaticResource SaveLocalAppBarButtonStyle}"
                        AutomationProperties.Name="Save As"
                        Click="OnSaveAsAppBarButtonClick" />

                <Button Style="{StaticResource SaveAppBarButtonStyle}"
                        Click="OnSaveAppBarButtonClick" />

                <Button Style="{StaticResource AddAppBarButtonStyle}"
                        Click="OnAddAppBarButtonClick" />
            </StackPanel>
        </Grid>
    </AppBar>
</Page.BottomAppBar>
</Page>
```

The main *Grid* has three rows:

- for the name of the loaded file (the *TextBlock* named "filenameText"),
- the *SplitContainer*,
- and the status bar at the bottom.

The status bar consists of two *TextBlock* elements named "statusText" (to indicate possible XAML parsing errors) and "lineColText" (for the line and column of the *TabbableTextBox*). The *Grid* is further divided into two columns for the two components of that status bar.

Most of the page is occupied by the *SplitContainer*, and you'll see that it contains bindings to the *Orientation* and *SwapEditAndDisplay* properties of *AppSettings*. The *SplitContainer* contains a *TabbableTextBox* (with bindings to the *FontSize* and *TabSpaces* properties of *AppSettings*) and a *RulerContainer* (with bindings to *ShowRuler* and *ShowGridLines*). All these bindings strongly suggest that the *DataContext* of *MainPage* is set to an instance of *AppSettings*.

The bottom of the XAML file has the *Button* definitions for the application bar.

As you might expect, the code-behind file is the longest file in the project, but I'm going to discuss it in various modular sections so that it won't be too overwhelming. Here are the constructor, *Loaded* handler, and a few simple methods:

Project: XamlCruncher | File: MainPage.xaml.cs (excerpt)

```
public sealed partial class MainPage : Page
{
    ...
    AppSettings appSettings;
    StorageFile loadedStorageFile;

    public MainPage()
    {
        this.InitializeComponent();

        ...
```

```csharp
        // Why aren't these set in the generated C# files?
        editBox = splitContainer.Child1 as TabbableTextBox;
        resultContainer = splitContainer.Child2 as RulerContainer;

        // Set a fixed-pitch font for the TextBox
        Language language =
            new Language(Windows.Globalization.Language.CurrentInputLanguageTag);
        LanguageFontGroup languageFontGroup = new LanguageFontGroup(language.LanguageTag);
        LanguageFont languageFont = languageFontGroup.FixedWidthTextFont;
        editBox.FontFamily = new FontFamily(languageFont.FontFamily);

        Loaded += OnLoaded;
        Application.Current.Suspending += OnApplicationSuspending;
    }

    async void OnLoaded(object sender, RoutedEventArgs args)
    {
        // Load AppSettings and set to DataContext
        appSettings = new AppSettings();
        this.DataContext = appSettings;

        // Load any file that may have been saved
        StorageFolder localFolder = ApplicationData.Current.LocalFolder;
        StorageFile storageFile = await localFolder.CreateFileAsync("XamlCruncher.xaml",
                                            CreationCollisionOption.OpenIfExists);
        editBox.Text = await FileIO.ReadTextAsync(storageFile);

        if (editBox.Text.Length == 0)
            await SetDefaultXamlFile();

        // Other initialization
        ParseText();
        editBox.Focus(FocusState.Programmatic);
        DisplayLineAndColumn();
        ...
    }

    async void OnApplicationSuspending(object sender, SuspendingEventArgs args)
    {
        // Save application settings
        appSettings.Save();

        // Save text content
        SuspendingDeferral deferral = args.SuspendingOperation.GetDeferral();
        await PathIO.WriteTextAsync("ms-appdata:///local/XamlCruncher.xaml", editBox.Text);
        deferral.Complete();
    }

    async Task SetDefaultXamlFile()
    {
        editBox.Text =
            "<Page xmlns=\"http://schemas.microsoft.com/winfx/2006/xaml/presentation\"\r\n" +
            "      xmlns:x=\"http://schemas.microsoft.com/winfx/2006/xaml\">\r\n\r\n" +
            "    <TextBlock Text=\"Hello, Windows 8!\"\r\n" +
            "               FontSize=\"48\" />\r\n\r\n" +
            "</Page>";
```

```
        editBox.IsModified = false;
        loadedStorageFile = null;
        filenameText.Text = "";
    }
    ...
    void OnEditBoxSelectionChanged(object sender, RoutedEventArgs args)
    {
        DisplayLineAndColumn();
    }

    void DisplayLineAndColumn()
    {
        int line, col;
        editBox.GetPositionFromIndex(editBox.SelectionStart, out line, out col);
        lineColText.Text = String.Format("Line {0} Col {1}", line + 1, col + 1);

        if (editBox.SelectionLength > 0)
        {
            editBox.GetPositionFromIndex(editBox.SelectionStart + editBox.SelectionLength - 1,
                                         out line, out col);
            lineColText.Text += String.Format(" - Line {0} Col {1}", line + 1, col + 1);
        }
    }
    ...
}
```

The constructor begins by fixing a little bug involving the *editBox* and *resultContainer* fields. The XAML parser definitely creates these fields during compilation, but they are not set by the *InitializeComponent* call at run time.

The remainder of the constructor sets a fixed-pitch font in the *TabbableTextBox* based on the predefined fonts available from the *LanguageFontGroup* class. This is apparently the only way to get actual font family names from the Windows Runtime. (In Chapter 15, "Going Native," I demonstrate how to use DirectWrite to obtain the collection of fonts installed on the system.)

The remaining initialization occurs in the *Loaded* event handler. The *DataContext* of the page is set to the *AppSettings* instance, as you probably anticipated from the data bindings in the MainPage.xaml file.

The *OnLoaded* method continues by loading a previously saved file or (if it doesn't exist) setting a default piece of XAML in the *TabbableTextBox* and calling *ParseText* to parse it. (You'll see how this works soon.) The *TabbableTextBox* is assigned keyboard input focus, and *OnLoaded* concludes by displaying the initial line and column, which is then updated whenever the *TextBox* selection changes.

You might wonder why *SetDefaultXamlFile* is defined as *async* and returns *Task* when it does not actually contain any asynchronous code. You'll see later that this method is used as an argument to another method in the file I/O logic, and that's the sole reason I had to define it oddly. The compiler generates a warning message because it doesn't contain any *await* logic.

Parsing the XAML

The major job of XamlCruncher is to pass a piece of XAML to *XamlReader.Load* and get out an object. A property of the *AppSettings* class named *AutoParsing* allows this to happen with every keystroke, or the program waits until you press the Refresh button on the application bar.

If *XamlReader.Load* encounters an error, it raises an exception, and the program then displays that error in red in the status bar at the bottom of the page and also colors the text in the *TabbableTextBox* red.

Project: XamlCruncher | **File:** MainPage.xaml.cs (excerpt)

```
public sealed partial class MainPage : Page
{
    Brush textBlockBrush, textBoxBrush, errorBrush;
    ...
    public MainPage()
    {
        ...
        // Set brushes
        textBlockBrush = Resources["ApplicationForegroundThemeBrush"] as SolidColorBrush;
        textBoxBrush = Resources["TextBoxForegroundThemeBrush"] as SolidColorBrush;
        errorBrush = new SolidColorBrush(Colors.Red);
        ...
    }
    ...

    void OnRefreshAppBarButtonClick(object sender, RoutedEventArgs args)
    {
        ParseText();
        this.BottomAppBar.IsOpen = false;
    }
    ...
    void OnEditBoxTextChanged(object sender, RoutedEventArgs e)
    {
        if (appSettings.AutoParsing)
            ParseText();
    }

    void ParseText()
    {
        object result = null;

        try
        {
            result = XamlReader.Load(editBox.Text);
        }
        catch (Exception exc)
        {
            SetErrorText(exc.Message);
            return;
        }

        if (result == null)
```

```
        {
            SetErrorText("Null result");
        }
        else if (!(result is UIElement))
        {
            SetErrorText("Result is " + result.GetType().Name);
        }
        else
        {
            resultContainer.Child = result as UIElement;
            SetOkText();
            return;
        }
    }

    void SetErrorText(string text)
    {
        SetStatusText(text, errorBrush, errorBrush);
    }

    void SetOkText()
    {
        SetStatusText("OK", textBlockBrush, textBoxBrush);
    }

    void SetStatusText(string text, Brush statusBrush, Brush editBrush)
    {
        statusText.Text = text;
        statusText.Foreground = statusBrush;
        editBox.Foreground = editBrush;
    }
}
```

It could be that a chunk of XAML successfully passes *XamlReader.Load* with no errors but then raises an exception later on. This can happen particularly when XAML animations are involved because the animation doesn't start up until the visual tree is loaded.

The only real solution is to install a handler for the *UnhandledException* event defined by the *Application* object, and that's done in the conclusion of the *Loaded* handler:

Project: XamlCruncher | File: MainPage.xaml.cs (excerpt)

```
async void OnLoaded(object sender, RoutedEventArgs args)
{
    ...
    Application.Current.UnhandledException += (excSender, excArgs) =>
        {
            SetErrorText(excArgs.Message);
            excArgs.Handled = true;
        };
}
```

The problem with something like this is that you want to make sure that the program isn't going to have some other kind of unhandled exception that isn't a result of some errant code.

Also, when Visual Studio is running a program in its debugger, it wants to snag the unhandled exceptions so that it can report them to you. Use the Exceptions dialog from the Debug menu to indicate which exceptions you want Visual Studio to intercept and which should be left to the program.

XAML Files In and Out

Whenever I approach the code involved in loading and saving documents, I always think it's going to be easier than it turns out to be. Here's the basic problem: Whenever a New or Open command occurs, you need to check if the current document has been modified without being saved. If that's the case, a message box should be displayed asking whether the user wants to save the file. The options are Save, Don't Save, and Cancel.

The easy answer is Cancel. The program doesn't need to do anything further. If the user selects the Don't Save option, the current document can be abandoned and the New or Open command can proceed.

If the user answers Save, the existing document needs to be saved under its file name. But that file name might not exist if the document wasn't loaded from a disk file or previously saved. At that point, the Save As dialog box needs to be displayed. But the user can select Cancel from that dialog box as well, and the New or Open operation ends. Otherwise, the existing file is first saved.

Let's first look at the methods involved in saving documents. The application button has Save and Save As buttons, but the Save button needs to invoke the Save As dialog box if it doesn't have a file name for the document:

Project: XamlCruncher | File: MainPage.xaml.cs (excerpt)

```
async void OnSaveAsAppBarButtonClick(object sender, RoutedEventArgs args)
{
    StorageFile storageFile = await GetFileFromSavePicker();

    if (storageFile == null)
        return;

    await SaveXamlToFile(storageFile);
}

async void OnSaveAppBarButtonClick(object sender, RoutedEventArgs args)
{
    Button button = sender as Button;
    button.IsEnabled = false;

    if (loadedStorageFile != null)
    {
        await SaveXamlToFile(loadedStorageFile);
    }
    else
    {
        StorageFile storageFile = await GetFileFromSavePicker();

        if (storageFile != null)
```

```
            {
                await SaveXamlToFile(storageFile);
            }
        }
        button.IsEnabled = true;
}

async Task<StorageFile> GetFileFromSavePicker()
{
    FileSavePicker picker = new FileSavePicker();
    picker.DefaultFileExtension = ".xaml";
    picker.FileTypeChoices.Add("XAML", new List<string> { ".xaml" });
    picker.SuggestedSaveFile = loadedStorageFile;
    return await picker.PickSaveFileAsync();
}

async Task SaveXamlToFile(StorageFile storageFile)
{
    loadedStorageFile = storageFile;
    string exception = null;

    try
    {
        await FileIO.WriteTextAsync(storageFile, editBox.Text);
    }
    catch (Exception exc)
    {
        exception = exc.Message;
    }

    if (exception != null)
    {
        string message = String.Format("Could not save file {0}: {1}",
                                    storageFile.Name, exception);
        MessageDialog msgdlg = new MessageDialog(message, "XAML Cruncher");
        await msgdlg.ShowAsync();
    }
    else
    {
        editBox.IsModified = false;
        filenameText.Text = storageFile.Path;
    }
}
```

For the Save button, the handler disables the button and then enables it when it's completed. I'm worried that the button might be re-pressed during the time the file is being saved and there might even be a reentrancy problem if the handler tries to save it again when the first save hasn't completed.

In the final method, the *FileIO.WriteTextAsync* call is in a *try* block. If an exception occurs while saving the file, the program wants to use *MessageDialog* to inform the user. But asynchronous methods such as *ShowAsync* can't be called in a *catch* block, so the exception is simply saved for checking afterward.

For both Add and Open, XamlCruncher needs to check if the file has been modified. If so, a message box must be displayed to inform the user and request further direction. This occurs in a method I've called *CheckIfOkToTrashFile*. Because this method is applicable for both the Add and Open buttons, I gave this method an argument named *commandAction* of type *Func<Task>*, a delegate meaning a method with no arguments that returns a *Task*. The *Click* handler for the Open button passes the *LoadFileFromOpenPicker* method as this argument, and the handler for the Add button uses the aforementioned *SetDefaultXamlFile*.

Project: XamlCruncher | **File:** MainPage.xaml.cs (excerpt)

```
async void OnAddAppBarButtonClick(object sender, RoutedEventArgs args)
{
    Button button = sender as Button;
    button.IsEnabled = false;
    await CheckIfOkToTrashFile(SetDefaultXamlFile);
    button.IsEnabled = true;
    this.BottomAppBar.IsOpen = false;
}

async void OnOpenAppBarButtonClick(object sender, RoutedEventArgs args)
{
    Button button = sender as Button;
    button.IsEnabled = false;
    await CheckIfOkToTrashFile(LoadFileFromOpenPicker);
    button.IsEnabled = true;
    this.BottomAppBar.IsOpen = false;
}

async Task CheckIfOkToTrashFile(Func<Task> commandAction)
{
    if (!editBox.IsModified)
    {
        await commandAction();
        return;
    }

    string message =
        String.Format("Do you want to save changes to {0}?",
            loadedStorageFile == null ? "(untitled)" : loadedStorageFile.Name);

    MessageDialog msgdlg = new MessageDialog(message, "XAML Cruncher");
    msgdlg.Commands.Add(new UICommand("Save", null, "save"));
    msgdlg.Commands.Add(new UICommand("Don't Save", null, "dont"));
    msgdlg.Commands.Add(new UICommand("Cancel", null, "cancel"));
    msgdlg.DefaultCommandIndex = 0;
    msgdlg.CancelCommandIndex = 2;
    IUICommand command = await msgdlg.ShowAsync();

    if ((string)command.Id == "cancel")
        return;
```

```csharp
    if ((string)command.Id == "dont")
    {
        await commandAction();
        return;
    }

    if (loadedStorageFile == null)
    {
        StorageFile storageFile = await GetFileFromSavePicker();

        if (storageFile == null)
            return;

        loadedStorageFile = storageFile;
    }

    await SaveXamlToFile(loadedStorageFile);
    await commandAction();
}

async Task LoadFileFromOpenPicker()
{
    FileOpenPicker picker = new FileOpenPicker();
    picker.FileTypeFilter.Add(".xaml");
    StorageFile storageFile = await picker.PickSingleFileAsync();

    if (storageFile != null)
    {
        string exception = null;

        try
        {
            editBox.Text = await FileIO.ReadTextAsync(storageFile);
        }
        catch (Exception exc)
        {
            exception = exc.Message;
        }

        if (exception != null)
        {
            string message = String.Format("Could not load file {0}: {1}",
                                    storageFile.Name, exception);
            MessageDialog msgdlg = new MessageDialog(message, "XAML Cruncher");
            await msgdlg.ShowAsync();
        }
        else
        {
            editBox.IsModified = false;
            loadedStorageFile = storageFile;
            filenameText.Text = loadedStorageFile.Path;
        }
    }
}
```

The Settings Dialog

When the user clicks the Settings button, the handler instantiates a *UserControl* derivative named *SettingsDialog* and makes it the child of a *Popup*. Among these options is the orientation of the display. You'll recall I defined an *EditOrientation* enumeration for the four possibilities. Accordingly, the project also contains an *EditOrientationRadioButton* for storing one of the four values as a custom tag:

Project: XamlCruncher | **File:** EditOrientationRadioButton.cs

```
using Windows.UI.Xaml.Controls;

namespace XamlCruncher
{
    public class EditOrientationRadioButton : RadioButton
    {
        public EditOrientation EditOrientationTag { set; get; }
    }
}
```

The SettingsDialog.xaml file arranges all the controls in a *StackPanel*:

Project: XamlCruncher | **File:** SettingsDialog.xaml (excerpt)

```
<UserControl ... >

    <UserControl.Resources>
        <Style x:Key="DialogCaptionTextStyle"
               TargetType="TextBlock"
               BasedOn="{StaticResource CaptionTextStyle}">
            <Setter Property="FontSize" Value="14.67" />
            <Setter Property="FontWeight" Value="SemiLight" />
            <Setter Property="Margin" Value="7 0 0 0" />
        </Style>
    </UserControl.Resources>

    <Border Background="{StaticResource ApplicationPageBackgroundThemeBrush}"
            BorderBrush="{StaticResource ApplicationForegroundThemeBrush}"
            BorderThickness="1">
        <StackPanel Margin="24">
            <TextBlock Text="XamlCruncher settings"
                       Style="{StaticResource SubheaderTextStyle}"
                       Margin="0 0 0 12" />

            <!-- Auto parsing -->
            <ToggleSwitch Header="Automatic parsing"
                          IsOn="{Binding AutoParsing, Mode=TwoWay}" />

            <!-- Orientation -->
            <TextBlock Text="Orientation"
                       Style="{StaticResource DialogCaptionTextStyle}" />

            <Grid Name="orientationRadioButtonGrid"
                  Margin="7 0 0 0">
                <Grid.RowDefinitions>
                    <RowDefinition Height="Auto" />
                    <RowDefinition Height="Auto" />
```

```
        </Grid.RowDefinitions>

        <Grid.ColumnDefinitions>
            <ColumnDefinition Width="Auto" />
            <ColumnDefinition Width="Auto" />
        </Grid.ColumnDefinitions>

        <Grid.Resources>
            <Style TargetType="Border">
                <Setter Property="BorderBrush"
                        Value="{StaticResource ApplicationForegroundThemeBrush}" />
                <Setter Property="BorderThickness" Value="1" />
                <Setter Property="Padding" Value="3" />
            </Style>

            <Style TargetType="TextBlock">
                <Setter Property="TextAlignment" Value="Center" />
            </Style>

            <Style TargetType="local:EditOrientationRadioButton">
                <Setter Property="Margin" Value="0 6 12 6" />
            </Style>
        </Grid.Resources>

        <local:EditOrientationRadioButton Grid.Row="0" Grid.Column="0"
                                    EditOrientationTag="Left"
                Checked="OnOrientationRadioButtonChecked">
            <StackPanel Orientation="Horizontal">
                <Border>
                    <TextBlock Text="edit" />
                </Border>
                <Border>
                    <TextBlock Text="display" />
                </Border>
            </StackPanel>
        </local:EditOrientationRadioButton>

        <local:EditOrientationRadioButton Grid.Row="0" Grid.Column="1"
                                    EditOrientationTag="Bottom"
                Checked="OnOrientationRadioButtonChecked">
            <StackPanel>
                <Border>
                    <TextBlock Text="display" />
                </Border>
                <Border>
                    <TextBlock Text="edit" />
                </Border>
            </StackPanel>
        </local:EditOrientationRadioButton>

        <local:EditOrientationRadioButton Grid.Row="1" Grid.Column="0"
                                    EditOrientationTag="Top"
                Checked="OnOrientationRadioButtonChecked">
            <StackPanel>
                <Border>
                    <TextBlock Text="edit" />
                </Border>
```

```
                    <Border>
                        <TextBlock Text="display" />
                    </Border>
                </StackPanel>
            </local:EditOrientationRadioButton>

            <local:EditOrientationRadioButton Grid.Row="1" Grid.Column="1"
                                              EditOrientationTag="Right"
                            Checked="OnOrientationRadioButtonChecked">
                <StackPanel Orientation="Horizontal">
                    <Border>
                        <TextBlock Text="display" />
                    </Border>
                    <Border>
                        <TextBlock Text="edit" />
                    </Border>
                </StackPanel>
            </local:EditOrientationRadioButton>
        </Grid>

        <!-- Ruler -->
        <ToggleSwitch Header="Ruler"
                      OnContent="Show"
                      OffContent="Hide"
                      IsOn="{Binding ShowRuler, Mode=TwoWay}" />

        <!-- Grid lines -->
        <ToggleSwitch Header="Grid lines"
                      OnContent="Show"
                      OffContent="Hide"
                      IsOn="{Binding ShowGridLines, Mode=TwoWay}" />

        <!-- Font size -->
        <TextBlock Text="Font size"
                   Style="{StaticResource DialogCaptionTextStyle}" />

        <Slider Value="{Binding FontSize, Mode=TwoWay}"
                Minimum="10"
                Maximum="48"
                Margin="7 0 0 0" />

        <!-- Tab spaces -->
        <TextBlock Text="Tab spaces"
                   Style="{StaticResource DialogCaptionTextStyle}" />

        <Slider Value="{Binding TabSpaces, Mode=TwoWay}"
                Minimum="1"
                Maximum="12"
                Margin="7 0 0 0" />
    </StackPanel>
  </Border>
</UserControl>
```

All the two-way bindings strongly suggest that the *DataContext* is set to an instance of *AppSettings*, just like *MainPage*. It's actually the *same* instance of *AppSettings*, which means that any changes in this dialog are automatically applied to the program.

This means that you can't make a bunch of changes in the dialog and hit Cancel. There is no Cancel button. To compensate, it might make sense for a dialog to have a Defaults button that restores everything to its factory-new condition.

A significant chunk of the XAML file is devoted to the four *EditOrientationRadioButton* controls. The content of each of these is a *StackPanel* with two bordered *TextBlock* elements, to create a little graphic that resembles the four layout options you saw in the earlier screen shot (that is, the third screen shot in the "Introducing XamlCruncher" section).

The dialog contains three instances of *ToggleSwitch*. By default, the *OnContent* and *OffContent* properties are set to the text string "On" and "Off," but I thought "Show" and "Hide" were better for the ruler and grid displays.

ToggleSwitch also has a *Header* property that displays text above the switch. In the screen shot I just referred to, the labels "Automatic parsing," "Ruler," and "Grid lines" are all displayed by the *ToggleSwitch*. I thought the labels looked good, so I made an effort to duplicate the font and placement with the *Style* labeled as "DialogCaptionTextStyle."

A *Slider* is used to set the font size, which might seem reasonable, but I also use a *Slider* to set the number of tab spaces, which I'll admit doesn't seem reasonable at all. Even though the *AppSettings* class defines the *TabSpaces* property as an integer, the binding with the *Value* property of the *Slider* works regardless, and the *Slider* proves to be a convenient way to change the property.

The only chore left for the code-behind file is to manage the *RadioButton* controls:

Project: XamlCruncher | File: SettingsDialog.xaml.cs

```
using Windows.UI.Xaml;
using Windows.UI.Xaml.Controls;

namespace XamlCruncher
{
    public sealed partial class SettingsDialog : UserControl
    {
        public SettingsDialog()
        {
            this.InitializeComponent();
            Loaded += OnLoaded;
        }

        // Initialize RadioButton for edit orientation
        void OnLoaded(object sender, RoutedEventArgs args)
        {
            AppSettings appSettings = DataContext as AppSettings;
```

```
                if (appSettings != null)
                {
                    foreach (UIElement child in orientationRadioButtonGrid.Children)
                    {
                        EditOrientationRadioButton radioButton =
                            child as EditOrientationRadioButton;
                        radioButton.IsChecked =
                            appSettings.EditOrientation == radioButton.EditOrientationTag;
                    }
                }
            }

            // Set EditOrientation based on checked RadioButton
            void OnOrientationRadioButtonChecked(object sender, RoutedEventArgs args)
            {
                AppSettings appSettings = DataContext as AppSettings;
                EditOrientationRadioButton radioButton = sender as EditOrientationRadioButton;

                if (appSettings != null)
                    appSettings.EditOrientation = radioButton.EditOrientationTag;
            }
        }
    }
```

The display of the dialog is very similar to the AppBarPad program:

Project: XamlCruncher | File: MainPage.xaml.cs (excerpt)

```
public sealed partial class MainPage : Page
{
    ...
    void OnSettingsAppBarButtonClick(object sender, RoutedEventArgs args)
    {
        SettingsDialog settingsDialog = new SettingsDialog();
        settingsDialog.DataContext = appSettings;

        Popup popup = new Popup
        {
            Child = settingsDialog,
            IsLightDismissEnabled = true
        };

        settingsDialog.Loaded += (dialogSender, dialogArgs) =>
            {
                popup.VerticalOffset = this.ActualHeight - settingsDialog.ActualHeight
                                        - this.BottomAppBar.ActualHeight - 24;

                popup.HorizontalOffset = 24;
            };
```

```
        popup.Closed += (popupSender, popupArgs) =>
            {
                this.BottomAppBar.IsOpen = false;
            };
        popup.IsOpen = true;
    }
    ...
}
```

The *Closed* event handler for the *Popup* closes the application bar. The new settings are saved in the handler for the *Suspending* event that you've already seen.

Beyond the Windows Runtime

Earlier I mentioned some limitations to the XAML that you can enter in XamlCruncher. Elements cannot have their events set because events require event handlers and event handlers must be implemented in code. Nor can the XAML contain references to external classes or assemblies.

However, the parsed XAML runs in the XamlCruncher process, which means that it does have access to any classes that XamlCruncher has access to, including the custom classes I created for the program. Here's a piece of XAML that includes a namespace declaration for *local*. This enables it to use the *SplitContainer* and nests two instances of it:

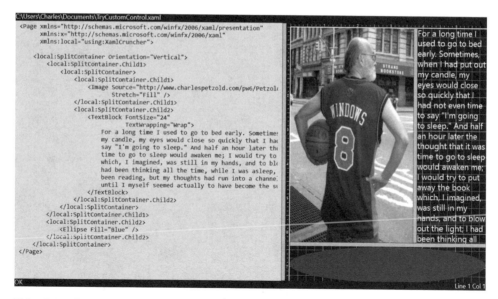

This piece of XAML is among the downloadable code for this chapter, as is the XAML used for the earlier screen shots.

This is interesting because it means that XamlCruncher really can go beyond the Windows Runtime and let you experiment with custom classes.

CHAPTER 9

Animation

The topic of animation might at first seem as if it doesn't quite belong in the "Elementals" section of this book. Perhaps the subject is more suited for advanced programmers working on games or physics simulations. Animation just doesn't seem appropriate in sedate and dignified business applications (except perhaps on casual Fridays).

But animation has more of a central role in Windows 8 applications than you might think. You'll discover part of that role in Chapter 11, "The Three Templates," which shows how to use XAML to create *ControlTemplate* objects that entirely redefine the appearances of controls. Although the most important part of a *ControlTemplate* is a visual tree, the template must also indicate how the appearance of the control changes under certain conditions. For example, a *Button* might be highlighted when it's pressed and "grayed out" when it's disabled. All these changes in appearance within the *ControlTemplate* are defined as animations—even if the change is instantaneous and doesn't really seem much like an animation.

Animations also come into play to define transitions between different application views or the movement of items during changes to a collection. Try moving a tile on the Start screen from one location to another and you'll see neighboring tiles shift in response. These are animations, and this is an important part of the fluid nature of Windows 8 aesthetics.

The *Windows.UI.Xaml.Media.Animation* Namespace

In Chapter 3, "Basic Event Handling," I demonstrated how to animate objects by using the *CompositionTarget.Rendering* event, a technique I referred to as a "manual" animation. Although a manual animation can be powerful, it has some limitations. The callback method always runs in the user interface thread, which means that the animation can interfere with program responsiveness to user input.

Also, the animations I demonstrated with *CompositionTarget.Rendering* were all linear—that is, they increased or decreased a value linearly over a period of time. Animations are often more pleasant when they have a little variation, usually by speeding up at the beginning and slowing down toward the end, perhaps with a little "bounce" for extra realism. You can certainly perform animations of this sort using *CompositionTarget.Rendering*, but the mathematics can be challenging.

In contrast, in this chapter I'll be demonstrating instead the built-in Windows Runtime animation facility that consists of 71 classes, 4 enumerations, and 2 structures in the *Windows.UI.Xaml.Media .Animation* namespace. These animations often run on background threads and support several features for sophisticated effects. Very often, you can define animations entirely in XAML and then trigger them from code or (in one particular but common case) directly from XAML.

Of course, the very idea of mastering an animation facility with 71 classes can be intimidating. Fortunately, these classes fall into just a few general categories, and by the end of this chapter, the namespace should be entirely comprehensible.

Animation involves change, and what these animations change is a property of an object. This property is often referred to as the "target" of the animation. The Windows Runtime animations require this target property to be backed by a dependency property and therefore defined in a class that derives from *DependencyObject*.

Some graphical environments have animations that are *frame-based*, meaning that the pacing of the animation is based on the frame rate of the video display. Different video frame rates on different hardware platforms might result in animations of different speeds. The Windows Runtime animations are instead *time-based*, meaning that they are based on actual durations of clock time: seconds and milliseconds.

What happens if the thread running an animation needs to do some work and the animation misses a few ticks? A frame-based animation generally continues where it left off. A Windows Runtime time-based animation adjusts itself based on clock time and catches up to where it should be.

Animation Basics

Let's begin with the animation of the *FontSize* property of a *TextBlock*, much like the ExpandingText program in Chapter 3. The SimpleAnimation project has a two-row *Grid* with a *TextBlock* and a *Button* to start the animation going. Very often, animations are defined in the *Resources* section of the root element of the XAML file. A simple animation like this one consists of a *Storyboard* and a *DoubleAnimation*:

Project: SimpleAnimation | File: MainPage.xaml (excerpt)

```
<Page ... >

    <Page.Resources>
        <Storyboard x:Key="storyboard">
            <DoubleAnimation Storyboard.TargetName="txtblk"
                             Storyboard.TargetProperty="FontSize"
                             EnableDependentAnimation="True"
                             From="1" To="144" Duration="0:0:3" />
        </Storyboard>
    </Page.Resources>

    <Grid Background="{StaticResource ApplicationPageBackgroundThemeBrush}">
        <Grid.RowDefinitions>
            <RowDefinition Height="*" />
```

```
                    <RowDefinition Height="*" />
                </Grid.RowDefinitions>

                <TextBlock Name="txtblk"
                           Text="Animated Text"
                           Grid.Row="0"
                           FontSize="48"
                           HorizontalAlignment="Center"
                           VerticalAlignment="Center" />

                <Button Content="Trigger!"
                        Grid.Row="1"
                        HorizontalAlignment="Center"
                        VerticalAlignment="Center"
                        Click="OnButtonClick" />
        </Grid>
</Page>
```

The name of the *DoubleAnimation* class doesn't mean that it performs two animations! This is an animation that targets properties of type *Double*. As you'll see, the Windows Runtime also supports animations that target properties of type *Point*, *Color*, and *Object*. (An animation that targets properties of type *Object* might seem as if it's the only animation you'd need, but in reality it's limited to setting discrete property values rather than smoothly animating them.)

The Windows Runtime requires that an animation object such as *DoubleAnimation* be a child of a *Storyboard*. A *Storyboard* can have multiple children performing parallel animations, and the job of the *Storyboard* is to provide a framework for synchronizing the children.

Storyboard also defines two attached properties named *TargetName* and *TargetProperty*. You set these properties in the animation object to indicate the name of the object you're targeting, and the property of that object you wish to animate:

```
<Storyboard x:Key="storyboard">
    <DoubleAnimation Storyboard.TargetName="txtblk"
                     Storyboard.TargetProperty="FontSize"
                     ... />
</Storyboard>
```

By default, animations are performed in a secondary thread so that the user interface thread remains free to respond to user input. However, an animation that targets the *FontSize* property of a *TextBlock* must run in the user interface thread because a change in the font size triggers a layout change. The Windows Runtime is reluctant to run animations in the user-interface thread, even to the extent of implementing a default behavior to disallow them! To let the Windows Runtime know your intention—yes, you want the animation to run even if it happens in the user interface thread—you must set the *EnableDependentAnimation* property to *true*:

```
<Storyboard x:Key="storyboard">
    <DoubleAnimation Storyboard.TargetName="txtblk"
                     Storyboard.TargetProperty="FontSize"
                     EnableDependentAnimation="True"
                     ... />
</Storyboard>
```

In this context, the word "dependent" means "dependent on the user interface thread."

The remainder of this particular animation indicates that we want to animate the value of the *FontSize* property from 1 to 144 over the course of three seconds:

```
<Storyboard x:Key="storyboard">
    <DoubleAnimation Storyboard.TargetName="txtblk"
                     Storyboard.TargetProperty="FontSize"
                     EnableDependentAnimation="True"
                     From="1" To="144" Duration="0:0:3" />
</Storyboard>
```

The duration of the animation is specified in hours, minutes, and seconds. All three values and two colons are required. If you specify just one number, it will be interpreted as an integral number of hours; two numbers separated by a colon are interpreted as hours and minutes. The seconds can include fractional seconds. If you need an animation that runs more than a day, you can precede the hours with a number of days and a period.

When you first run this program, the *TextBlock* is displayed with a 48-pixel height, as specified in the *TextBlock* element in the XAML file:

The *Storyboard* doesn't run by itself. It needs to be triggered, usually by something happening in the user interface. In this program, the *Click* handler for the *Button* obtains a reference to the *Storyboard* by accessing the *Resources* collection, and then it calls *Begin*:

Project: SimpleAnimation | File: MainPage.xaml.cs

```
using Windows.UI.Xaml;
using Windows.UI.Xaml.Controls;
using Windows.UI.Xaml.Media.Animation;
```

```
namespace SimpleAnimation
{
    public sealed partial class MainPage : Page
    {
        public MainPage()
        {
            this.InitializeComponent();
        }

        void OnButtonClick(object sender, RoutedEventArgs args)
        {
            (this.Resources["storyboard"] as Storyboard).Begin();
        }
    }
}
```

Notice the *using* directive for *Windows.UI.Xaml.Media.Animation*. This is not provided for you automatically by the Visual Studio template.

When the storyboard is started, the *TextBlock* immediately jumps to a *FontSize* of 1 (the *From* value in *DoubleAnimation*), and then the *FontSize* increases to 144 over the course of three seconds. The increase is linear: At the one-second mark, the FontSize is 48-2/3 pixels, and at two seconds, it's 96-1/3. At the end of three seconds, the animation stops and the *TextBlock* remains at the 144-pixel size:

You can click the button again, and the animation starts over again. In fact, you can click the button repeatedly while the animation is running, and each time it starts over again at the 1-pixel size.

Animation Variation Appreciation

When the animation in the SimpleAnimation program completes, the *FontSize* remains at the value specified by the *To* property of *DoubleAnimation*. This is a result of the value of the *FillBehavior* property of *DoubleAnimation*, which by default is the enumeration member *HoldEnd*. You can alternatively set it to *Stop*:

```
<Storyboard x:Key="storyboard">
    <DoubleAnimation Storyboard.TargetName="txtblk"
                     Storyboard.TargetProperty="FontSize"
                     EnableDependentAnimation="True"
                     FillBehavior="Stop"
                     From="1" To="144" Duration="0:0:3" />
</Storyboard>
```

Now at the end of the animation, the animation is released from the target property and *FontSize* reverts to its pre-animation value of 48.

Another variation is to leave out the *From* or *To* value. For example,

```
<Storyboard x:Key="storyboard">
    <DoubleAnimation Storyboard.TargetName="txtblk"
                     Storyboard.TargetProperty="FontSize"
                     EnableDependentAnimation="True"
                     From="1" Duration="0:0:3" />
</Storyboard>
```

Now the animation begins at 1 but goes up only to the pre-animation value of 48. The increase in size proceeds at a slower rate because the duration is still three seconds.

This animation causes *FontSize* to go from its current value up to 144 over three seconds:

```
<Storyboard x:Key="storyboard">
    <DoubleAnimation Storyboard.TargetName="txtblk"
                     Storyboard.TargetProperty="FontSize"
                     EnableDependentAnimation="True"
                     To="144" Duration="0:0:3" />
</Storyboard>
```

I say the *FontSize* goes from "its current value" because that value isn't necessarily the pre-animation value of 48. Click the button, and while the *TextBlock* is still increasing in size, click the button again. Each successive click effectively terminates the existing animation and starts a new animation from the current *FontSize*. Each new click slows down the rate of increase because the length of the animation is still three seconds.

You might assume that the *DoubleAnimation* class defines the *To* and *From* properties as type *double*. That's *almost* true. They are actually of type nullable *double*, and *null* is the default value. This is how *DoubleAnimation* can determine whether these properties are set.

The other option is *By*:

```
<Storyboard x:Key="storyboard">
    <DoubleAnimation Storyboard.TargetName="txtblk"
                     Storyboard.TargetProperty="FontSize"
                     EnableDependentAnimation="True"
                     By="100" Duration="0:0:3" />
</Storyboard>
```

Now each click of the button triggers an animation that increases the *FontSize* by another 100 pixels over the course of three seconds. The text just gets larger and larger and larger.

Try going back to the original settings and add an attribute that sets *AutoReverse* to *true*:

```
<Storyboard x:Key="storyboard">
    <DoubleAnimation Storyboard.TargetName="txtblk"
                     Storyboard.TargetProperty="FontSize"
                     EnableDependentAnimation="True"
                     From="1" To="144" Duration="0:0:3"
                     AutoReverse="True" />
</Storyboard>
```

When this animation is triggered, the *FontSize* jumps down to 1, goes up to 144 over the course of three seconds, and then goes back down to 1 over another three seconds, at which time the animation is completed. The entire animation is six seconds in length. Set *FillBehavior* to *Stop*, and the *FontSize* will jump back to its pre-animation value of 48 at the end of those six seconds.

You can also set a *RepeatBehavior* attribute with or without *AutoReverse*. The following combination indicates that you want to perform three entire cycles of increasing and decreasing the *FontSize*:

```
<Storyboard x:Key="storyboard">
    <DoubleAnimation Storyboard.TargetName="txtblk"
                     Storyboard.TargetProperty="FontSize"
                     EnableDependentAnimation="True"
                     From="1" To="144" Duration="0:0:3"
                     AutoReverse="True"
                     RepeatBehavior="3x" />
</Storyboard>
```

The entire animation lasts for 18 seconds.

You can also set *RepeatBehavior* to a duration:

```
<Storyboard x:Key="storyboard">
    <DoubleAnimation Storyboard.TargetName="txtblk"
                     Storyboard.TargetProperty="FontSize"
                     EnableDependentAnimation="True"
                     From="1" To="144" Duration="0:0:3"
                     AutoReverse="True"
                     RepeatBehavior="0:0:7.5" />
</Storyboard>
```

The total animation lasts 7.5 seconds. The *FontSize* increases from 1 to 144 over the course of three seconds, decreases from 144 to 1 in another three seconds, and then starts to increase again but stops. The final *FontSize* value is 73.5.

You can also set *RepeatBehavior* to *Forever*:

```
<Storyboard x:Key="storyboard">
    <DoubleAnimation Storyboard.TargetName="txtblk"
                     Storyboard.TargetProperty="FontSize"
                     EnableDependentAnimation="True"
                     From="1" To="144" Duration="0:0:3"
                     AutoReverse="True"
                     RepeatBehavior="Forever" />
</Storyboard>
```

And it does exactly that (or at least until you get bored and terminate the program).

You can delay the start of an animation with the *BeginTime* property:

```
<Storyboard x:Key="storyboard">
    <DoubleAnimation Storyboard.TargetName="txtblk"
                     Storyboard.TargetProperty="FontSize"
                     EnableDependentAnimation="True"
                     BeginTime="0:0:1.5"
                     From="1" To="144" Duration="0:0:3" />
</Storyboard>
```

When you click the button, nothing will seem to happen for a second and a half, and then the *TextBlock* will jump to a 1-pixel size and start to expand. The animation concludes 4.5 seconds after the button click.

Even with all these variations, all the animations so far have been linear. The *FontSize* always increases or decreases linearly by a certain number of pixels per second. One easy way to create a nonlinear animation is by setting the *EasingFunction* property defined by *DoubleAnimation*. Break out the property as a property element, and specify one of the 11 classes that derive from *EasingFunctionBase*. Here's *ElasticEase*:

```
<Storyboard x:Key="storyboard">
    <DoubleAnimation Storyboard.TargetName="txtblk"
                     Storyboard.TargetProperty="FontSize"
                     EnableDependentAnimation="True"
                     From="1" To="144" Duration="0:0:3">
        <DoubleAnimation.EasingFunction>
            <ElasticEase />
        </DoubleAnimation.EasingFunction>
    </DoubleAnimation>
</Storyboard>
```

You really need to try this out to see the effect. As the *TextBlock* gets larger, it actually goes *beyond* the 144-pixel size and then decreases to below 144 and back and forth a couple times, finally settling at the *To* value. (That behavior rather stretches the meaning of the word "ease"!)

EasingFunctionBase defines an *EasingMode* property that is inherited by all 11 derived classes. The default setting is the enumeration member *EasingMode.EaseOut*, which means that the animation begins linearly and the special effect is applied at the end of the animation. You can specify *EaseIn* to apply the effect to the beginning of the animation or *EaseInOut* to the beginning and the end.

Some *EasingFunctionBase* derivatives define their own properties for a little variation. *ElasticEase* defines an *Oscillations* property (an integer with a default value of 3 that indicates how many times the values swings back and forth) and a *Springiness* property, a *double* also with a default setting of 3. The lower the *Springiness* value, the more extreme the effect. Try this:

```
<Storyboard x:Key="storyboard">
    <DoubleAnimation Storyboard.TargetName="txtblk"
                     Storyboard.TargetProperty="FontSize"
                     EnableDependentAnimation="True"
                     From="1" To="144" Duration="0:0:3">
        <DoubleAnimation.EasingFunction>
            <ElasticEase Oscillations="10"
                         Springiness="0" />
        </DoubleAnimation.EasingFunction>
    </DoubleAnimation>
</Storyboard>
```

A program to explore the easing functions is coming up soon.

I mentioned earlier that an animation object such as *DoubleAnimation* must be a child of a *Storyboard*. Interestingly, *Storyboard* and *DoubleAnimation* are siblings in the class hierarchy:

Object
  DependencyObject
    Timeline
      Storyboard
      DoubleAnimation
      ...

Storyboard defines a *Children* property of type *TimelineCollection*, the attached properties *TargetName* and *TargetProperty*, as well as methods to pause and resume the animation. *DoubleAnimation* defines *From*, *To*, *By*, *EnableDependentAnimation*, and *EasingFunction*.

All the other properties you've seen so far—*AutoReverse*, *BeginTime*, *Duration*, *FillBehavior*, and *RepeatBehavior*—are defined by *Timeline*, which means that you can set these properties on *Storyboard* to define behavior for all the children of the *Storyboard*.

Timeline also defines a property named *SpeedRatio*:

```
<Storyboard x:Key="storyboard">
    <DoubleAnimation Storyboard.TargetName="txtblk"
                     Storyboard.TargetProperty="FontSize"
                     EnableDependentAnimation="True"
                     SpeedRatio="10"
                     From="1" To="144" Duration="0:0:3" />
</Storyboard>
```

This *SpeedRatio* setting causes the animation to go 10 times faster! Setting *SpeedRatio* on the *DoubleAnimation* is certainly allowed, but it's much more common to set it on a *Storyboard* so that it applies to all the animation children within that *Storyboard*. You can use *SpeedRatio* for fine-tuning the speed of an animation without changing all the individual *Duration* times or for debugging complex collections of animations. For example, set the *SpeedRatio* to 0.1 to slow down the animation so that you can better see what it's doing.

Timeline also defines a *Completed* event, which you can set on either a *Storyboard* or a *DoubleAnimation* to be notified when an animation has completed.

It's also possible to define an animation entirely in code. The XAML file for the SimpleAnimationCode project has a *Grid* with nine *Button* elements sharing the same *Click* event handler. No *Storyboard* or *DoubleAnimation* appears in the XAML file:

Project: SimpleAnimationCode | **File:** MainPage.xaml (excerpt)

```
<Page ... >
    <Page.Resources>
        <Style TargetType="Button">
            <Setter Property="Content" Value="Trigger!" />
            <Setter Property="FontSize" Value="48" />
            <Setter Property="HorizontalAlignment" Value="Center" />
            <Setter Property="VerticalAlignment" Value="Center" />
            <Setter Property="Margin" Value="12" />
        </Style>
    </Page.Resources>

    <Grid Background="{StaticResource ApplicationPageBackgroundThemeBrush}">
        <Grid HorizontalAlignment="Center"
              VerticalAlignment="Center">
            <Grid.RowDefinitions>
                <RowDefinition Height="Auto" />
                <RowDefinition Height="Auto" />
                <RowDefinition Height="Auto" />
            </Grid.RowDefinitions>

            <Grid.ColumnDefinitions>
                <ColumnDefinition Width="Auto" />
                <ColumnDefinition Width="Auto" />
                <ColumnDefinition Width="Auto" />
            </Grid.ColumnDefinitions>

            <Button Grid.Row="0" Grid.Column="0" Click="OnButtonClick" />
            <Button Grid.Row="0" Grid.Column="1" Click="OnButtonClick" />
            <Button Grid.Row="0" Grid.Column="2" Click="OnButtonClick" />
            <Button Grid.Row="1" Grid.Column="0" Click="OnButtonClick" />
            <Button Grid.Row="1" Grid.Column="1" Click="OnButtonClick" />
            <Button Grid.Row="1" Grid.Column="2" Click="OnButtonClick" />
            <Button Grid.Row="2" Grid.Column="0" Click="OnButtonClick" />
            <Button Grid.Row="2" Grid.Column="1" Click="OnButtonClick" />
            <Button Grid.Row="2" Grid.Column="2" Click="OnButtonClick" />
        </Grid>
    </Grid>
</Page>
```

In the code-behind file, you can create the *Storyboard* and *DoubleAnimation* once and reuse the objects whenever you need to trigger the animation, or you can create them anew as needed. The first approach only works when the animation target is always the same object. This program potentially needs nine independent animations for the nine buttons, so it's easiest just creating them on demand. Everything is in the *Click* handler:

Project: SimpleAnimationCode | **File:** MainPage.xaml.cs (excerpt)

```
void OnButtonClick(object sender, RoutedEventArgs args)
{
    DoubleAnimation anima = new DoubleAnimation
    {
        EnableDependentAnimation = true,
        To = 96,
        Duration = new Duration(new TimeSpan(0, 0, 1)),
        AutoReverse = true,
        RepeatBehavior = new RepeatBehavior(3)
    };
    Storyboard.SetTarget(anima, sender as Button);
    Storyboard.SetTargetProperty(anima, "FontSize");

    Storyboard storyboard = new Storyboard();
    storyboard.Children.Add(anima);
    storyboard.Begin();
}
```

In the earlier XAML definition of *DoubleAnimation*, the attached properties *Storyboard.TargetName* and *Storyboard.TargetProperty* indicate the object and property to animate. In code, it's a little different: You continue to use the static method *Storyboard.SetTargetProperty* to set the property name, but you use *Storyboard.SetTarget*—not *Storyboard.SetTargetName*—to set the target object rather than the XAML name of the target object. If the target object is a *TextBlock* in XAML with the name "txtblk," the *SetTarget* call would look like this:

```
Storyboard.SetTarget(anima, txtblk);
```

It's the object variable name, not the text name. In this code example I've set the target object to the *Button* generating the *Click* event.

Also notice how the *Duration* property is set. Using a *TimeSpan* is the most common approach, but *Duration* also has two static properties: *Automatic* (which means one second in this context) and *Forever* (which is not recommended because it makes the animation infinitely slow). The default value is *Automatic*, which is handy if you forget to specify it.

Because the change in each *FontSize* affects the size of each *Button*, the *Grid* needs to recalculate the width and height of its cells. It's fun to get all the animations going at once to watch how the *Grid* changes size:

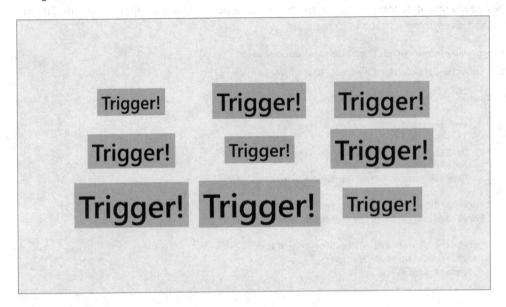

Other Double Animations

A *DoubleAnimation* can animate any property of type *double* that's backed by a dependency property, for example, *Width* or *Height* (or both):

Project: EllipseBlobAnimation | File: MainPage.xaml (excerpt)

```
<Page ... >

    <Page.Resources>
        <Storyboard x:Key="storyboard"
                    RepeatBehavior="Forever"
                    AutoReverse="True">
            <DoubleAnimation Storyboard.TargetName="ellipse"
                    Storyboard.TargetProperty="Width"
                    EnableDependentAnimation="True"
                    From="100" To="600" Duration="0:0:1" />

            <DoubleAnimation Storyboard.TargetName="ellipse"
                    Storyboard.TargetProperty="Height"
                    EnableDependentAnimation="True"
                    From="600" To="100" Duration="0:0:1" />

        </Storyboard>
    </Page.Resources>
```

```
<Grid Background="{StaticResource ApplicationPageBackgroundThemeBrush}">
    <Ellipse Name="ellipse">
        <Ellipse.Fill>
            <LinearGradientBrush>
                <GradientStop Offset="0" Color="Pink" />
                <GradientStop Offset="1" Color="LightBlue" />
            </LinearGradientBrush>
        </Ellipse.Fill>
    </Ellipse>
</Grid>
</Page>
```

The two animations run in parallel. The first animates the *Width* of the *Ellipse* from 100 to 600, and the second animates the *Height* of the *Ellipse* from 600 to 100. The two dimensions only briefly meet up in the middle to make a circle. The settings of *AutoReverse* and *RepeatBehavior* can be set on either the *Storyboard* (as I've done) or on the individual animations.

The animation is triggered when the page is loaded, and it runs "forever":

Project: EllipseBlobAnimation | File: MainPage.xaml.cs (excerpt)

```
public sealed partial class MainPage : Page
{
    public MainPage()
    {
        this.InitializeComponent();

        Loaded += (sender, args) =>
            {
                (this.Resources["storyboard"] as Storyboard).Begin();
            };
    }
}
```

Because the *LinearGradientBrush* that colors the *Ellipse* has a default gradient from the upper-left corner of a bounding rectangle to the lower-right corner, the gradient actually shifts a bit during the animation:

Width and *Height* aren't the only properties of *Ellipse* that can be animated. The *StrokeThickness* property defined by *Shape* is also a *double* and is backed by a dependency property. Here's an *Ellipse* with a dotted line around its circumference, and the animation targets the *thickness* of that dotted line:

Project AnimateStrokeThickness | File: MainPage.xaml (excerpt)

```
<Page ... >
    <Page.Resources>
        <Storyboard x:Key="storyboard">
            <DoubleAnimation Storyboard.TargetName="ellipse"
                             Storyboard.TargetProperty="StrokeThickness"
                             EnableDependentAnimation="True"
                             From="1" To="100" Duration="0:0:4"
                             AutoReverse="True"
                             RepeatBehavior="Forever" />
        </Storyboard>
    </Page.Resources>

    <Grid Background="{StaticResource ApplicationPageBackgroundThemeBrush}">
        <Ellipse Name="ellipse"
                 Stroke="Red"
                 StrokeDashCap="Round"
                 StrokeDashArray="0 2" />
    </Grid>
</Page>
```

The animation is triggered during the *Loaded* event with the same code as the previous program.

The "0 2" value of the *StrokeDashArray* indicates that the dashed line consists of a dash that is zero units long followed by a gap two units long, where these units indicate multiples of the *StrokeThickness*. This dash has rounded ends benefit of the *StrokeDashCap* property, and the rounded ends add to the length of the dash, so the dash actually becomes a dot with a diameter equal to the *StrokeThickness*. The centers of these dots are separated by a gap equal to twice the *StrokeThickness*, so the dots themselves are separated by the *StrokeThickness*.

In this animation, the number of dots actually decreases and then increases as the *StrokeThickness* is increased and decreased by the animation. The dots seem to disappear and reappear at the far right of the *Ellipse*:

Can you find another property of *Ellipse* of type *double*? How about *StrokeDashOffset*, which indicates where the dashes and gaps of a dotted line begin in a dashed line? Here's some XAML that uses a *Path* with Bézier curves to draw an infinity sign with dotted lines. The animation targets *Stroke-DashOffset* to make the dots seem to travel around the figure:

Project: AnimateDashOffset | **File:** MainPage.xaml (excerpt)

```
<Page ... >
    <Page.Resources>
        <Storyboard x:Key="storyboard">
            <DoubleAnimation Storyboard.TargetName="path"
                        Storyboard.TargetProperty="StrokeDashOffset"
                        EnableDependentAnimation="True"
                        From="0" To="1.5" Duration="0:0:1"
                        RepeatBehavior="Forever" />
        </Storyboard>
    </Page.Resources>
```

```
<Grid Background="{StaticResource ApplicationPageBackgroundThemeBrush}">
    <Viewbox>
        <Path Name="path"
            Margin="12"
            Stroke="{StaticResource ApplicationForegroundThemeBrush}"
            StrokeThickness="24"
            StrokeDashArray="0 1.5"
            StrokeDashCap="Round"
            Data="M 100    0
                  C  45    0,    0   45, 0 100
                  S  45  200,  100  200
                  S 200  150,  250  100
                  S 345    0,  400    0
                  S 500   45,  500  100
                  S 455  200,  400  200
                  S 300  150,  250  100
                  S 155    0,  100    0" />
    </Viewbox>
</Grid>
</Page>
```

Unfortunately, I can't show the dots traveling around the infinity sign on the printed page:

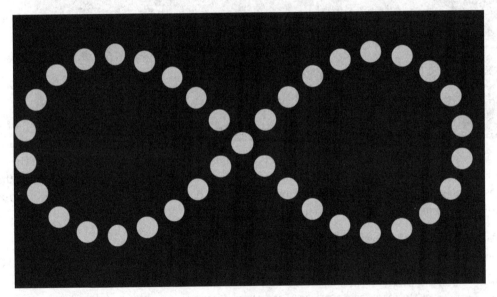

The *Path* definition in this program incorporates a well-known Bézier approximation to a quarter circle. For a circle centered at the point (0, 0), the lower-right quarter-circle arc begins at (100, 0) and ends at (0, 100). This can be approximated very well with a Bézier curve that also begins at (100, 0) and ends at (0, 100) with two control points (100, 55) and (55, 100). You can draw an entire circle using four of these "Bezier 55" arcs.

Thus, the quarter-circle arc that begins this infinity sign at the upper-left corner starts at (100, 0) and ends at (0, 100), but the center is (100, 100) rather than (0, 0), so the first control point is 55 units to the left of (100, 0), and the second is 55 units above (0, 100), or (45, 0), and (0, 45). The next Bézier should continue the figure around the lower-left corner starting at (0, 100)—the end of the previous Bézier—and ending at (100, 200) with control points (0, 155) and (45, 200). But the remainder of the path markup geometry continues not with figures indicated by C, which stands for "Cubic Bézier," but with S, which stands for "Smooth Bézier." It is well known that two connected Bézier curves have a smooth connection if their common point and two adjacent control points are collinear (that is, lie on the same line). The S figure in path markup syntax causes the first control point to be automatically derived so that it is collinear with the start point and previous control point and the same distance from the start point as the previous collinear point. Thus, based on the point (0, 45) and (0, 100) in the first Bézier curve, the first S figure derives the first control point to be (0, 155).

When drawing a dashed line whose end connects back with its beginning, it is very likely that there will be a discontinuity at the start point where only a partial dash will be displayed. The *StrokeThickness* of 24 was derived experimentally and need not necessarily be a whole number. For the Windows Phone version of this program, I settled upon a *StrokeThickness* of 23.98.

When exploring the rest of the *Shapes* library for properties of type *double* to animate, you'll also discover the *X1*, *Y1*, *X2*, and *Y2* properties of *Line*. Later in this chapter I'll demonstrate how to animate properties of type *Point* that show up in many of the *PathSegment* derivatives.

The *Opacity* property is a very common animation target, and it's used to fade elements in and out. You can set *Opacity* to a value ranging from 0 (transparent) to 1 (opaque). Here's an *Opacity* animation based on John Tenniel's illustrations of the Cheshire Cat for the original edition of Lewis Carroll's *Alice's Adventures in Wonderland* (1865):

Project: CheshireCat | File: MainPage.xaml (excerpt)

```xml
<Page ... >

    <Page.Resources>
        <Storyboard x:Key="storyboard">
            <DoubleAnimation Storyboard.TargetName="image2"
                             Storyboard.TargetProperty="Opacity"
                             From="0" To="1" Duration="0:0:2"
                             AutoReverse="True"
                             RepeatBehavior="Forever" />
        </Storyboard>
    </Page.Resources>

    <!-- Images from Project Gutenberg Book #114
         http://www.gutenberg.org/ebooks/114
         John Tenniel's illustrations for Lewis Carroll's "Alice in Wonderland" -->

    <Grid Background="{StaticResource ApplicationPageBackgroundThemeBrush}">
        <Viewbox>
            <Grid>
                <Image Source="Images/alice23a.gif"
                       Width="640" />

                <TextBlock FontFamily="Century Schoolbook"
                           FontSize="24"
                           Foreground="Black"
                           TextWrapping="Wrap"
```

```
                    TextAlignment="Justify"
                    Width="320"
                    Margin="0 0 24 60"
                    HorizontalAlignment="Right"
                    VerticalAlignment="Bottom">
              "All right," said the Cat; and this
            time it vanished quite slowly, beginning with the end
            of the tail, and ending with the grin, which
            remained some time after the rest of it had gone.
            <LineBreak />
            <LineBreak />
              "Well! I've often seen a cat without a
            grin," thought Alice; "but a grin without a cat! It's
            the most curious thing I ever saw in all my life!"
                </TextBlock>

                <Image Name="image2"
                       Source="Images/alice24a.gif"
                       Stretch="None"
                       VerticalAlignment="Top">
                    <Image.Clip>
                        <RectangleGeometry Rect="320 70 320 240" />
                    </Image.Clip>
                </Image>
            </Grid>
        </Viewbox>
    </Grid>
</Page>
```

As the comment in the XAML file indicates, I obtained the images from Project Gutenberg. In the original edition of *Alice's Adventures in Wonderland*, the two images were both the width of the page, but the first image also extended to the full height of the page to show Alice standing by the tree. The images on the Project Gutenberg site, however, don't have the same width. The first image (alice23a.gif) is 342 × 480 pixels and the second (alice24a.gif) is 640 × 435. When I forced them to have the same rendered width, they seemed to line up very well considering that they're definitely two different drawings. Still, I decided to use a rectangular clipping area to restrict the second image to only the disappearing cat. The text that I added is not the same as that which appeared in this spot in the original edition.

"All right," said the Cat; and this time it vanished quite slowly, beginning with the end of the tail, and ending with the grin, which remained some time after the rest of it had gone.

"Well! I've often seen a cat without a grin," thought Alice; "but a grin without a cat! It's the most curious thing I ever saw in all my life!"

The utility of *DoubleAnimation* increases enormously when you begin animating the classes that derive from *Transform*. This is a subject for the next chapter (Chapter 10, "Transforms"). You might remember the RainbowEight program from Chapter 3 that animated the *Offset* property of 15 *GradientStop* objects in tandem. You can do a similar program using 15 *DoubleAnimation* objects, but in the next chapter I'll show you how to do it with one *DoubleAnimation* animating a *TranslateTransform* set on the *LinearGradientBrush*.

Animating Attached Properties

One of the simple uses of transforms that I'll explore in the next chapter involves moving an object around the screen. But you don't need transforms for that. You can put the object in a *Canvas* and animate the *Canvas.Left* and *Canvas.Top* attached properties. Animating attached properties requires a special syntax for *Storyboard.TargetProperty*, as shown here:

Project: AttachedPropertyAnimation | File: MainPage.xaml (excerpt)

```
<Page ... >

    <Page.Resources>
        <Storyboard x:Key="storyboard">
            <DoubleAnimation Storyboard.TargetName="ellipse"
                        Storyboard.TargetProperty="(Canvas.Left)"
                        From="0" Duration="0:0:2.51"
                        AutoReverse="True"
                        RepeatBehavior="Forever" />
```

```
                <DoubleAnimation Storyboard.TargetName="ellipse"
                                 Storyboard.TargetProperty="(Canvas.Top)"
                                 From="0" Duration="0:0:1.01"
                                 AutoReverse="True"
                                 RepeatBehavior="Forever" />
        </Storyboard>
    </Page.Resources>

    <Grid Background="{StaticResource ApplicationPageBackgroundThemeBrush}">
        <Canvas SizeChanged="OnCanvasSizeChanged"
                Margin="0 0 48 48">
            <Ellipse Name="ellipse"
                     Width="48"
                     Height="48"
                     Fill="Red" />
        </Canvas>
    </Grid>
</Page>
```

The *Canvas.Left* and *Canvas.Top* attached properties are simply enclosed in parentheses. The target is an *Ellipse* colored red and hence easily recognizable as a ball.

Notice the absence of an *EnableDependentAnimation* setting. This indicates that these animations do not occur in the user interface thread. If you're unsure whether to use *EnableDependentAnimation*, try leaving it out. If the animation works, it's OK!

This *Storyboard* has two *DoubleAnimation* children that run in synchronization. Notice that each of these *DoubleAnimation* definitions has *AutoReverse* set to *True* and *RepeatBehavior* set to *Forever* and *Duration* values set to 1.01 seconds and 2.51 seconds, respectively. I chose prime numbers here (101 and 251) to avoid repetitive patterns. The two animations include *From* values but no *To* values. That happens in the code-behind file:

Project: AttachedPropertyAnimation | File: MainPage.xaml.cs (excerpt)

```
public sealed partial class MainPage : Page
{
    public MainPage()
    {
        this.InitializeComponent();

        Loaded += (sender, args) =>
            {
                (this.Resources["storyboard"] as Storyboard).Begin();
            };
    }

    void OnCanvasSizeChanged(object sender, SizeChangedEventArgs args)
    {
        Storyboard storyboard = this.Resources["storyboard"] as Storyboard;

        // Canvas.Left animation
        DoubleAnimation anima = storyboard.Children[0] as DoubleAnimation;
        anima.To = args.NewSize.Width;
```

```
        // Canvas.Top animation
        anima = storyboard.Children[1] as DoubleAnimation;
        anima.To = args.NewSize.Height;
    }
}
```

The storyboard is started in the *Loaded* event handler. Whenever the size of the *Canvas* changes (which happens when the size of the window changes), new *To* values are calculated based on the height and width of the *Canvas*, which has a *Margin* setting in the XAML file to compensate for the size of the *Ellipse*. You might assume that you wouldn't be allowed to change values of an ongoing animation, but it seems to work fine. The effect is a ball that appears to bounce between the edges of the screen:

Both *DoubleAnimation* definitions include the same *AutoReverse* and *RepeatBehavior* settings. As I mentioned earlier, these properties are defined by *Timeline*, which is also the parent class to *Storyboard*. Might these two settings be moved to the *Storyboard* tag? Try it:

```
<Storyboard x:Key="storyboard"
            AutoReverse="True"
            RepeatBehavior="Forever">
    <DoubleAnimation Storyboard.TargetName="ellipse"
                     Storyboard.TargetProperty="(Canvas.Left)"
                     From="0" Duration="0:0:2.51" />

    <DoubleAnimation Storyboard.TargetName="ellipse"
                     Storyboard.TargetProperty="(Canvas.Top)"
                     From="0" Duration="0:0:1.01" />
</Storyboard>
```

This is perfectly legal, but it doesn't work the same as the previous markup. The duration of a *Storyboard* is the duration of the longest animation child of that *Storyboard*, which in this case is 2.51 seconds. The animation begins by moving the ball both horizontally and vertically. But at the end of 1.01 seconds, the ball hits an edge. In landscape mode, this is the bottom edge. The animation of the *Canvas.Top* property has completed, but the animation of *Canvas.Left* continues to move the ball horizontally for another 1.5 seconds. At that point the ball is in the lower-right corner of the screen. Both animations have now completed, so the *Storyboard* reverses the animation we've just seen until the ball is in the upper-left corner again. Then that same pattern repeats forever.

Only if all the animations in a *Storyboard* are the same length can the *AutoReverse* and *RepeatBehavior* properties be moved to the *Storyboard*.

The Easing Functions

Suppose a *DoubleAnimation* has a *From* value of 100, a *To* value of 500, and a *Duration* of five seconds. By default the *DoubleAnimation* is linear, which means that the target property takes on values from 100 through 500 based on a linear relationship with elapsed time:

Time	Value
0 sec	100
1	180
2	260
3	340
4	420
5	500

Or, perhaps more clearly:

$$\text{Value} = \text{From} + \frac{Time}{Duration} \times (\text{To} - \text{From})$$

The purpose of the easing functions is to make this more interesting.

I was originally planning to begin this discussion by demonstrating how to derive from *EasingFunctionBase* to create a custom easing function, but for reasons that I'm sure are very good reasons, you cannot derive from *EasingFunctionBase*. If you were able to, you could create your own easing function by simply overriding the *Ease* method and implementing a transfer function. The *Ease* method has a *double* argument that ranges from 0 to 1. The method returns a *double* value. When the argument is 0, the method returns 0. When the argument is 1, the method returns 1. In between, anything goes. In this way, the easing function effectively bends time so that the relationship between elapsed time and the animation value becomes nonlinear.

When an easing function is in effect, the elapsed time is normalized to a value between 0 and 1 by dividing by the *Duration* (just as in the formula above). The *Ease* function is called, and the return value is used to calculate a value:

$$Value = From + Ease\left(\frac{Time}{Duration}\right) \times (To - From)$$

For example, the *ExponentialEase* function with the default *EasingMode* setting of *EaseOut* has this transfer function:

$$t' = \frac{1-e^{-Nt}}{1-e^{-N}}$$

where *t* is the argument to the *Ease* function, *t'* is the result, and *N* is the setting of the *Exponent* property. If *N* equals 2 (the default value), the animation shown in the table above is instead like this:

Time	t	t'	Value
0 sec	0.0	0.000	100
1	0.2	0.381	252
2	0.4	0.637	355
3	0.6	0.808	423
4	0.8	0.923	469
5	1.0	1.000	500

It's faster at the beginning and then seems to slow down.

The AnimationEaseGrapher program provides a visual representation of the easing functions and lets you experiment with them:

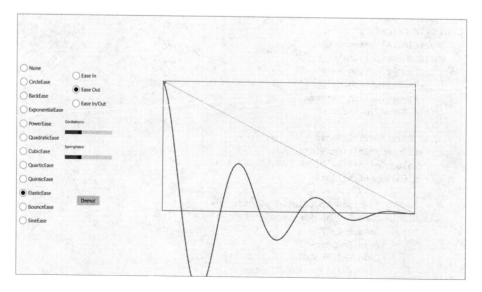

The graph is the transfer function with the horizontal access representing *t* from 0 to 1, and the vertical access representing *t'* with 0 at the top and 1 at the bottom. The dotted line from upper left to lower right is a linear transfer function, and the blue line is the selected transfer function. The points of that *Polyline* are assigned from the code-behind file by repeatedly calling the *Ease* method of the selected easing class. When you press the *Demo* button, the little red ball in the upper-left corner is animated horizontally with a regular linear animation and animated vertically with the se-lected ease function, and—amazingly enough—it follows the graph.

Here's the program's XAML file with the animation for the red ball defined at the top. The easing function for this animation is assigned from the code-behind file. The *To* and *From* values are adjusted based on the 6-pixel radius of the ball (which appears way down at the bottom):

Project: AnimationEaseGrapher | File: MainPage.xaml (excerpt)

```xml
<Page ... >
    <Page.Resources>
        <Storyboard x:Key="storyboard"
                    FillBehavior="Stop">
            <DoubleAnimation Storyboard.TargetName="redBall"
                            Storyboard.TargetProperty="(Canvas.Left)"
                            From="-6" To="994" Duration="0:0:3" />

            <DoubleAnimation x:Name="anima2"
                            Storyboard.TargetName="redBall"
                            Storyboard.TargetProperty="(Canvas.Top)"
                            From="-6" To="494" Duration="0:0:3" />
        </Storyboard>
    </Page.Resources>

    <Grid Background="{StaticResource ApplicationPageBackgroundThemeBrush}">
        <Grid.ColumnDefinitions>
            <ColumnDefinition Width="Auto" />
            <ColumnDefinition Width="*" />
        </Grid.ColumnDefinitions>

        <!-- Control panel -->
        <Grid Grid.Column="0"
              VerticalAlignment="Center">
            <Grid.RowDefinitions>
                <RowDefinition Height="*" />
                <RowDefinition Height="*" />
                <RowDefinition Height="*" />
            </Grid.RowDefinitions>

            <Grid.ColumnDefinitions>
                <ColumnDefinition Width="Auto" />
                <ColumnDefinition Width="Auto" />
            </Grid.ColumnDefinitions>

            <!-- Easing function (populated by code) -->
            <StackPanel Name="easingFunctionStackPanel"
                        Grid.Row="0"
                        Grid.RowSpan="3"
                        Grid.Column="0"
                        VerticalAlignment="Center">
```

```xml
            <RadioButton Content="None"
                         Margin="6"
                         Checked="OnEasingFunctionRadioButtonChecked" />
        </StackPanel>

        <!-- Easing mode -->
        <StackPanel Name="easingModeStackPanel"
                    Grid.Row="0"
                    Grid.Column="1"
                    HorizontalAlignment="Center"
                    VerticalAlignment="Center">
            <RadioButton Content="Ease In"
                         Margin="6"
                         Checked="OnEasingModeRadioButtonChecked">
                <RadioButton.Tag>
                    <EasingMode>EaseIn</EasingMode>
                </RadioButton.Tag>
            </RadioButton>

            <RadioButton Content="Ease Out"
                         Margin="6"
                         Checked="OnEasingModeRadioButtonChecked">
                <RadioButton.Tag>
                    <EasingMode>EaseOut</EasingMode>
                </RadioButton.Tag>
            </RadioButton>

            <RadioButton Content="Ease In/Out"
                         Margin="6"
                         Checked="OnEasingModeRadioButtonChecked">
                <RadioButton.Tag>
                    <EasingMode>EaseInOut</EasingMode>
                </RadioButton.Tag>
            </RadioButton>
        </StackPanel>

        <!-- Easing properties (populated by code) -->
        <StackPanel Name="propertiesStackPanel"
                    Grid.Row="1"
                    Grid.Column="1"
                    HorizontalAlignment="Center"
                    VerticalAlignment="Center" />

        <!-- Demo button -->
        <Button Grid.Row="2"
                Grid.Column="1"
                Content="Demo!"
                HorizontalAlignment="Center"
                VerticalAlignment="Center"
                Click="OnDemoButtonClick" />
    </Grid>

    <!-- Graph using arbitrary coordinates and scaled to window -->
    <Viewbox Grid.Column="1">
        <Grid Width="1000"
              Height="500"
              Margin="0 250 0 250">
```

```
            <!-- Rectangle outline -->
            <Polygon Points="0 0, 1000 0, 1000 500, 0 500"
                     Stroke="{StaticResource ApplicationForegroundThemeBrush}"
                     StrokeThickness="3" />

            <Canvas>
                <!-- Linear transfer -->
                <Polyline Points="0 0, 1000 500"
                          Stroke="{StaticResource ApplicationForegroundThemeBrush}"
                          StrokeThickness="1"
                          StrokeDashArray="3 3" />

                <!-- Points set by code based on easing function -->
                <Polyline Name="polyline"
                          Stroke="Blue"
                          StrokeThickness="3" />

                <!-- Animated ball -->
                <Ellipse Name="redBall"
                         Width="12"
                         Height="12"
                         Fill="Red" />
            </Canvas>
        </Grid>
      </Viewbox>
    </Grid>
</Page>
```

The code-behind file uses reflection to obtain all the classes that derive from *EasingFunction-Base* and creates a *RadioButton* element for each one. When one is selected, reflection also comes to the rescue to obtain a parameterless constructor for the class. This allows the class to be instantiated. Additional reflection lets the program obtain all the public properties the particular *EasingFunctionBase* derivative has defined on its own. Fortunately, all these public properties are restricted to *int* or *double* types, so a *Slider* control is created for each.

Project: AnimationEaseGrapher | File: MainPage.xaml.cs (excerpt)

```
public sealed partial class MainPage : Page
{
    EasingFunctionBase easingFunction;

    public MainPage()
    {
        this.InitializeComponent();
        Loaded += OnMainPageLoaded;
    }

    void OnMainPageLoaded(object sender, RoutedEventArgs args)
    {
        Type baseType = typeof(EasingFunctionBase);
        TypeInfo baseTypeInfo = baseType.GetTypeInfo();
        Assembly assembly = baseTypeInfo.Assembly;

        // Enumerate through all Windows Runtime types
        foreach (Type type in assembly.ExportedTypes)
```

```
        {
            TypeInfo typeInfo = type.GetTypeInfo();

            // Create RadioButton for each easing function
            if (typeInfo.IsPublic &&
                baseTypeInfo.IsAssignableFrom(typeInfo) &&
                type != baseType)
            {
                RadioButton radioButton = new RadioButton
                {
                    Content = type.Name,
                    Tag = type,
                    Margin = new Thickness(6),

                };
                radioButton.Checked += OnEasingFunctionRadioButtonChecked;
                easingFunctionStackPanel.Children.Add(radioButton);
            }
        }

        // Check the first RadioButton in the StackPanel (the one labeled "None")
        (easingFunctionStackPanel.Children[0] as RadioButton).IsChecked = true;
    }

    void OnEasingFunctionRadioButtonChecked(object sender, RoutedEventArgs args)
    {
        RadioButton radioButton = sender as RadioButton;
        Type type = radioButton.Tag as Type;
        easingFunction = null;
        propertiesStackPanel.Children.Clear();

        // type is only null for "None" button
        if (type != null)
        {
            TypeInfo typeInfo = type.GetTypeInfo();

            // Find a parameterless constructor and instantiate the easing function
            foreach (ConstructorInfo constructorInfo in typeInfo.DeclaredConstructors)
            {
                if (constructorInfo.IsPublic && constructorInfo.GetParameters().Length == 0)
                {
                    easingFunction = constructorInfo.Invoke(null) as EasingFunctionBase;
                    break;
                }
            }

            // Enumerate the easing function properties
            foreach (PropertyInfo property in typeInfo.DeclaredProperties)
            {
                // We can only deal with properties of type int and double
                if (property.PropertyType != typeof(int) &&
                    property.PropertyType != typeof(double))
                {
                    continue;
                }
```

```csharp
            // Create a TextBlock for the property name
            TextBlock txtblk = new TextBlock
            {
                Text = property.Name + ":"
            };
            propertiesStackPanel.Children.Add(txtblk);

            // Create a Slider for the property value
            Slider slider = new Slider
            {
                Width = 144,
                Minimum = 0,
                Maximum = 10,
                Tag = property
            };

            if (property.PropertyType == typeof(int))
            {
                slider.StepFrequency = 1;
                slider.Value = (int)property.GetValue(easingFunction);
            }
            else
            {
                slider.StepFrequency = 0.1;
                slider.Value = (double)property.GetValue(easingFunction);
            }

            // Define the Slider event handler right here
            slider.ValueChanged += (sliderSender, sliderArgs) =>
                {
                    Slider sliderChanging = sliderSender as Slider;
                    PropertyInfo propertyInfo = sliderChanging.Tag as PropertyInfo;

                    if (property.PropertyType == typeof(int))
                        property.SetValue(easingFunction, (int)sliderArgs.NewValue);
                    else
                        property.SetValue(easingFunction, (double)sliderArgs.NewValue);

                    DrawNewGraph();
                };
            propertiesStackPanel.Children.Add(slider);
        }
    }

    // Initialize EasingMode radio buttons
    foreach (UIElement child in easingModeStackPanel.Children)
    {
        RadioButton easingModeRadioButton = child as RadioButton;
        easingModeRadioButton.IsEnabled = easingFunction != null;

        easingModeRadioButton.IsChecked =
            easingFunction != null &&
            easingFunction.EasingMode == (EasingMode)easingModeRadioButton.Tag;
    }
```

```
            DrawNewGraph();
    }

    void OnEasingModeRadioButtonChecked(object sender, RoutedEventArgs args)
    {
        RadioButton radioButton = sender as RadioButton;
        easingFunction.EasingMode = (EasingMode)radioButton.Tag;
        DrawNewGraph();
    }

    void OnDemoButtonClick(object sender, RoutedEventArgs args)
    {
        // Set the selected easing function and start the animation
        Storyboard storyboard = this.Resources["storyboard"] as Storyboard;
        (storyboard.Children[1] as DoubleAnimation).EasingFunction = easingFunction;
        storyboard.Begin();
    }

    void DrawNewGraph()
    {
        polyline.Points.Clear();

        if (easingFunction == null)
        {
            polyline.Points.Add(new Point(0, 0));
            polyline.Points.Add(new Point(1000, 500));
            return;
        }

        for (decimal t = 0; t <= 1; t += 0.01m)
        {
            double x = (double)(1000 * t);
            double y = 500 * easingFunction.Ease((double)t);
            polyline.Points.Add(new Point(x, y));
        }
    }
}
}
```

There is some redundancy in these easing functions: The *QuadraticEase*, *CubicEase*, *QuarticEase*, and *QuinticEase* are all special cases of the *PowerEase* class, and they can be duplicated with *PowerEase* by setting the *Power* property to 2, 3, 4, and 5, respectively.

The above screen shot (a few pages ago) with *ElasticEase* shows that this particular *Ease* function returns values outside the range of 0 and 1. The same is true with *BackEase*. Because the transfer function possibly returns values less than 0 or greater than 1, the animation could take on values outside the range of its *From* and *To* settings.

For many properties, this is no problem. But for some properties an exception could be raised. *Opacity*, for example, can't be set to values less than 0 or greater than 1. *Width* and *Height* can't be set to negative values, and *FontSize* must be greater than 0. Applying an animation to these properties that results in an illegal value will raise a run-time exception.

Although the easing functions usually cause animations to slow down and speed up in various ways, it's possible to use the easing functions in somewhat unorthodox ways. For example, *SineEase* has this transfer function when *EasingMode* is set to the default value of *EaseOut*:

$$t' = \sin\left(\frac{\pi}{2}\,t\right)$$

It's the first quarter of a sine curve, starting fast and slowing down. For *EaseIn*, it's the first quarter of a cosine curve but flipped around to go from 0 to 1:

$$t' = 1 - \cos\left(\frac{\pi}{2}\,t\right)$$

It starts slow and speeds up.

SineEase with an *EasingMode* setting of *EaseInOut* is the first half of a cosine curve, adjusted to go from 0 to 1:

$$t' = \frac{1 - \cos(\pi t)}{2}$$

It starts slow, speeds up, and then slows down again. If you were to use the *EaseInOut* variation of *SineEase* with a *DoubleAnimation* applied to the *Canvas.Left* property of an *Ellipse* and you set *AutoReverse* equal to *True* and *RepeatBehavior* to *Forever*, you would get motion that resembles a pendulum: slow right before and after the motion reverses, but faster in the middle.

If you apply a similar animation to *Canvas.Top* but offset by half a cycle, you can move an object around in a circle, as the following program demonstrates:

Project: CircleAnimation | File: MainPage.xaml (excerpt)

```
<Page ... >
    <Page.Resources>
        <Storyboard x:Key="storyboard" SpeedRatio="3">
            <DoubleAnimation Storyboard.TargetName="ball"
                             Storyboard.TargetProperty="(Canvas.Left)"
                             From="-350" To="350" Duration="0:0:2"
                             AutoReverse="True"
                             RepeatBehavior="Forever">
                <DoubleAnimation.EasingFunction>
                    <SineEase EasingMode="EaseInOut" />
                </DoubleAnimation.EasingFunction>
            </DoubleAnimation>

            <DoubleAnimation Storyboard.TargetName="ball"
                             Storyboard.TargetProperty="(Canvas.Top)"
                             BeginTime="0:0:1"
                             From="-350" To="350" Duration="0:0:2"
                             AutoReverse="True"
                             RepeatBehavior="Forever">
                <DoubleAnimation.EasingFunction>
                    <SineEase EasingMode="EaseInOut" />
```

```
            </DoubleAnimation.EasingFunction>
        </DoubleAnimation>
    </Storyboard>
</Page.Resources>

<Grid Background="{StaticResource ApplicationPageBackgroundThemeBrush}">
    <Canvas HorizontalAlignment="Center"
            VerticalAlignment="Center"
            Margin="0 0 48 48">
        <Ellipse Name="ball"
                 Width="48"
                 Height="48"
                 Fill="Red" />
    </Canvas>
</Grid>
</Page>
```

The *Canvas* is aligned in the center but offset by the size of the ellipse, which means that the point (0, 0) relative to the *Canvas* is 24 pixels to the left and 24 pixels above the center of the window. The *Ellipse* has default zero values of *Canvas.Left* and *Canvas.Top* and sits in the center. The animations move that *Ellipse* 350 pixels to the left and right and up and down.

Notice that the second animation has a *BeginTime* of one second, so for the first second after the program is loaded, the first animation moves the ellipse horizontally from −350 pixels to 0, and then the second animation kicks in and begins moving the ball vertically from −350 to 0 as it is moving horizontally from 0 to 350. Although the easing functions are intended to slow down and speed up animations, the *Ellipse* has a constant angular velocity as it travels around in a circle.

I'll show you a more direct way of implementing revolution by using a *RotateTransform* in the next chapter.

All-XAML Animations

Several of the programs shown so far in this chapter have triggered the *Storyboard* in the handler for the page's *Loaded* event. This is handy when you need to start an animation when a program or page is loaded or for "demo" animations that simply run forever.

Triggering an animation in the *Loaded* event can actually be done entirely in XAML using a legacy property named *Triggers* inherited from the Windows Presentation Foundation. In the long journey from WPF to the Windows Runtime, the *Triggers* property has lost virtually all its earlier functionality, but it can still trigger a storyboard:

```
<Page.Triggers>
    <EventTrigger>
        <BeginStoryboard>
            <Storyboard ... >
                ...
            </Storyboard>
        </BeginStoryboard>
    </EventTrigger>
</Page.Triggers>
```

The *Triggers* property element usually appears on the root element of a XAML file, traditionally toward the bottom of the file, but you can actually define the *Triggers* property element on any ancestor element of the animation target.

Notice *EventTrigger* and *BeginStoryboard*. This is the only context in which you'll see those tags. *EventTrigger* has a *RoutedEvent* property, but if you try setting it to anything (including the reasonable "Loaded" or "Page.Loaded"), you'll generate a run-time error. *BeginStoryboard* can have multiple *Storyboard* children.

Here's a program that's similar to the ManualColorAnimation of Chapter 3. The background of the *Grid* and the *Foreground* of a *TextBlock* are animated from black to white in different directions. The two *ColorAnimation* objects target the *Color* properties of two *SolidColorBrush* objects:

Project: ForeverColorAnimation | **File:** MainPage.xaml (excerpt)

```
<Page ... >
    <Grid>
        <Grid.Background>
            <SolidColorBrush x:Name="gridBrush" />
        </Grid.Background>

        <TextBlock Text="Color Animation"
                   FontFamily="Times New Roman"
                   FontSize="96"
                   FontWeight="Bold"
                   HorizontalAlignment="Center"
                   VerticalAlignment="Center">
            <TextBlock.Foreground>
                <SolidColorBrush x:Name="txtblkBrush" />
            </TextBlock.Foreground>
        </TextBlock>
    </Grid>

    <Page.Triggers>
        <EventTrigger>
            <BeginStoryboard>
                <Storyboard RepeatBehavior="Forever"
                            AutoReverse="True">
                    <ColorAnimation Storyboard.TargetName="gridBrush"
                                    Storyboard.TargetProperty="Color"
                                    From="Black" To="White" Duration="0:0:2" />

                    <ColorAnimation Storyboard.TargetName="txtblkBrush"
                                    Storyboard.TargetProperty="Color"
                                    From="White" To="Black" Duration="0:0:2" />
                </Storyboard>
            </BeginStoryboard>
        </EventTrigger>
    </Page.Triggers>
</Page>
```

ColorAnimation is perhaps the second most common animation class after *DoubleAnimation*. It's pretty much limited to targeting the *Color* property of *SolidColorBrush* and *GradientStop*, but these brushes show up frequently, so it's more versatile than it might seem. Notice the *RepeatBehavior* and *AutoReverse* settings in the *Storyboard*.

The code-behind file contains nothing but an *InitializeComponent* call in the page's constructor. What this means is that you can copy this XAML file into the editor in the XamlCruncher program presented in Chapter 8, "App Bars and Popups," remove the *x:Class* attribute, and run the animation without help from any code. XamlCruncher (or another XAML-editing program) is a fine way to experiment with animations.

It's also possible to animate properties of type *Point*. Properties of type *Point* aren't very common, but *EllipseGeometry* has a *Center* property of type *Point*. If you create a circle or ellipse using *Path* and *EllipseGeometry* rather than the *Ellipse* class, you can move it around the screen by animating the *Center* property. Unlike animating *Canvas.Left* and *Canvas.Top*, this *Path* doesn't need to be in a *Canvas*, and the position of the figure is specified relative to its center rather than the upper-left corner.

However, you can't animate the *X* and *Y* properties of a *Point* value separately. *Point* is a structure rather than a class, which means it doesn't derive from *DependencyObject*, which means that the *X* and *Y* properties aren't backed by dependency properties.

Properties of type *Point* also show up in some *PathSegment* derivatives: *ArcSegment*, *BezierSegment*, *LineSegment*, and *QuadraticBezierSegment* all have properties of type *Point*. Animating these *Point* properties allows you to dynamically alter graphical figures. Here's a program that uses the Bézier approximation to a circle I discussed earlier but then animates all 13 points so that the circle deforms into a square. Just to demonstrate that the *Triggers* property element doesn't need to be defined on the root element of the XAML file, I've defined it right on the *Path*:

Project: SquaringTheCircle | **File:** MainPage.xaml (excerpt)

```
<Page ... >
    <Grid Background="{StaticResource ApplicationPageBackgroundThemeBrush}">
        <Canvas HorizontalAlignment="Center"
                VerticalAlignment="Center">
            <Path Fill="{StaticResource ApplicationPressedForegroundThemeBrush}"
                  Stroke="{StaticResource ApplicationForegroundThemeBrush}"
                  StrokeThickness="3" >
                <Path.Data>
                    <PathGeometry>
                        <PathFigure x:Name="bezier1" IsClosed="True">
                            <BezierSegment x:Name="bezier2" />
                            <BezierSegment x:Name="bezier3" />
                            <BezierSegment x:Name="bezier4" />
                            <BezierSegment x:Name="bezier5" />
                        </PathFigure>
                    </PathGeometry>
                </Path.Data>
```

```
<Path.Triggers>
    <EventTrigger>
        <BeginStoryboard>
            <Storyboard RepeatBehavior="Forever">
                <PointAnimation Storyboard.TargetName="bezier1"
                                Storyboard.TargetProperty="StartPoint"
                                EnableDependentAnimation="True"
                                From="0 200" To="0 250"
                                AutoReverse="True" />

                <PointAnimation Storyboard.TargetName="bezier2"
                                Storyboard.TargetProperty="Point1"
                                EnableDependentAnimation="True"
                                From="110 200" To="125 125"
                                AutoReverse="True" />

                <PointAnimation Storyboard.TargetName="bezier2"
                                Storyboard.TargetProperty="Point2"
                                EnableDependentAnimation="True"
                                From="200 110" To="125 125"
                                AutoReverse="True" />

                <PointAnimation Storyboard.TargetName="bezier2"
                                Storyboard.TargetProperty="Point3"
                                EnableDependentAnimation="True"
                                From="200 0" To="250 0"
                                AutoReverse="True" />

                <PointAnimation Storyboard.TargetName="bezier3"
                                Storyboard.TargetProperty="Point1"
                                EnableDependentAnimation="True"
                                From="200 -110" To="125 -125"
                                AutoReverse="True" />

                <PointAnimation Storyboard.TargetName="bezier3"
                                Storyboard.TargetProperty="Point2"
                                EnableDependentAnimation="True"
                                From="110 -200" To="125 -125"
                                AutoReverse="True" />

                <PointAnimation Storyboard.TargetName="bezier3"
                                Storyboard.TargetProperty="Point3"
                                EnableDependentAnimation="True"
                                From="0 -200" To="0 -250"
                                AutoReverse="True" />

                <PointAnimation Storyboard.TargetName="bezier4"
                                Storyboard.TargetProperty="Point1"
                                EnableDependentAnimation="True"
                                From="-110 -200" To="-125 -125"
                                AutoReverse="True" />

                <PointAnimation Storyboard.TargetName="bezier4"
                                Storyboard.TargetProperty="Point2"
                                EnableDependentAnimation="True"
                                From="-200 -110" To="-125 -125"
                                AutoReverse="True" />
```

```xml
                        <PointAnimation Storyboard.TargetName="bezier4"
                                        Storyboard.TargetProperty="Point3"
                                        EnableDependentAnimation="True"
                                        From="-200 0" To="-250 0"
                                        AutoReverse="True" />

                        <PointAnimation Storyboard.TargetName="bezier5"
                                        Storyboard.TargetProperty="Point1"
                                        EnableDependentAnimation="True"
                                        From="-200 110" To="-125 125"
                                        AutoReverse="True" />

                        <PointAnimation Storyboard.TargetName="bezier5"
                                        Storyboard.TargetProperty="Point2"
                                        EnableDependentAnimation="True"
                                        From="-110 200" To="-125 125"
                                        AutoReverse="True" />

                        <PointAnimation Storyboard.TargetName="bezier5"
                                        Storyboard.TargetProperty="Point3"
                                        EnableDependentAnimation="True"
                                        From="0 200" To="0 250"
                                        AutoReverse="True" />
                    </Storyboard>
                </BeginStoryboard>
            </EventTrigger>
        </Path.Triggers>
    </Path>
</Canvas>
    </Grid>
</Page>
```

Here's the figure somewhere between a square and a circle:

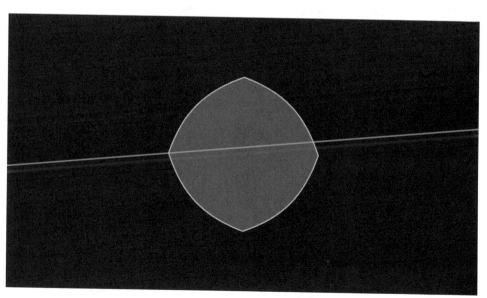

Animating Custom Classes

Yes, you can animate properties of custom classes. But the animatable properties must be backed by dependency properties.

Here's a class named *PieSlice* that derives from *Path* to render a pie slice such as used in pie charts. The custom properties are *Center*, *Radius*, *StartAngle* (in degrees, measured clockwise from 12:00), and *SweepAngle* (in degrees, measured clockwise from *StartAngle*):

Project: AnimatedPieSlice | File: PieSlice.cs

```
using System;
using Windows.Foundation;
using Windows.UI.Xaml;
using Windows.UI.Xaml.Media;
using Windows.UI.Xaml.Shapes;

namespace AnimatedPieSlice
{
    public class PieSlice : Path
    {
        PathFigure pathFigure;
        LineSegment lineSegment;
        ArcSegment arcSegment;

        static PieSlice()
        {
            CenterProperty = DependencyProperty.Register("Center",
                typeof(Point), typeof(PieSlice),
                new PropertyMetadata(new Point(100, 100), OnPropertyChanged));

            RadiusProperty = DependencyProperty.Register("Radius",
                typeof(double), typeof(PieSlice),
                new PropertyMetadata(100.0, OnPropertyChanged));

            StartAngleProperty = DependencyProperty.Register("StartAngle",
                typeof(double), typeof(PieSlice),
                new PropertyMetadata(0.0, OnPropertyChanged));

            SweepAngleProperty = DependencyProperty.Register("SweepAngle",
                typeof(double), typeof(PieSlice),
                new PropertyMetadata(90.0, OnPropertyChanged));
        }

        public PieSlice()
        {
            pathFigure = new PathFigure { IsClosed = true };
            lineSegment = new LineSegment();
            arcSegment = new ArcSegment { SweepDirection = SweepDirection.Clockwise };
            pathFigure.Segments.Add(lineSegment);
            pathFigure.Segments.Add(arcSegment);

            PathGeometry pathGeometry = new PathGeometry();
            pathGeometry.Figures.Add(pathFigure);

            this.Data = pathGeometry;
            UpdateValues();
        }
```

```
    public static DependencyProperty CenterProperty { private set; get; }

    public static DependencyProperty RadiusProperty { private set; get; }

    public static DependencyProperty StartAngleProperty { private set; get; }

    public static DependencyProperty SweepAngleProperty { private set; get; }

    public Point Center
    {
        set { SetValue(CenterProperty, value); }
        get { return (Point)GetValue(CenterProperty); }
    }

    public double Radius
    {
        set { SetValue(RadiusProperty, value); }
        get { return (double)GetValue(RadiusProperty); }
    }

    public double StartAngle
    {
        set { SetValue(StartAngleProperty, value); }
        get { return (double)GetValue(StartAngleProperty); }
    }

    public double SweepAngle
    {
        set { SetValue(SweepAngleProperty, value); }
        get { return (double)GetValue(SweepAngleProperty); }
    }

    static void OnPropertyChanged(DependencyObject obj,
                                DependencyPropertyChangedEventArgs args)
    {
        (obj as PieSlice).UpdateValues();
    }

    void UpdateValues()
    {
        pathFigure.StartPoint = this.Center;

        double x = this.Center.X + this.Radius * Math.Sin(Math.PI * this.StartAngle / 180);
        double y = this.Center.Y - this.Radius * Math.Cos(Math.PI * this.StartAngle / 180);
        lineSegment.Point = new Point(x, y);

        x = this.Center.X + this.Radius * Math.Sin(Math.PI * (this.StartAngle +
                                                    this.SweepAngle) / 180);

        y = this.Center.Y - this.Radius * Math.Cos(Math.PI * (this.StartAngle +
                                                    this.SweepAngle) / 180);
        arcSegment.Point = new Point(x, y);
        arcSegment.IsLargeArc = this.SweepAngle >= 180;

        arcSegment.Size = new Size(this.Radius, this.Radius);
    }
}
```

Just about everything in this class is overhead for the dependency properties except the *UpdateValues* method, and that method is critical. *UpdateValues* is called whenever any of the four properties changes. Any of those four properties can be the target of an animation, which means that *UpdateValues* might be called 60 times per second for an indefinite period of time.

In methods called so frequently you should be careful about creating objects that require memory allocations on the heap. Creating new *double* and *Point* values is fine because those are stored on the stack. But a not very good way to implement this method would be to create new *PathFigure, LineSegment*, and *ArcSegment* objects during every call because that generates a lot of activity allocating memory that must later be freed. Try re-using or caching objects rather than re-creating them.

The *PieSlice* class is part of the AnimatedPieSlice project, which includes a MainPage.xaml that instantiates, initializes, and animates it:

Project: AnimatedPieSlice | File: MainPage.xaml (excerpt)

```
<Page ... >
    <Grid Background="{StaticResource ApplicationPageBackgroundThemeBrush}">
        <local:PieSlice x:Name="pieSlice"
                        Center="400 400"
                        Radius="200"
                        Stroke="Red"
                        StrokeThickness="3"
                        Fill="Yellow" />
    </Grid>

    <Page.Triggers>
        <EventTrigger>
            <BeginStoryboard>
                <Storyboard>
                    <DoubleAnimation Storyboard.TargetName="pieSlice"
                                     Storyboard.TargetProperty="SweepAngle"
                                     EnableDependentAnimation="True"
                                     From="1" To="359" Duration="0:0:3"
                                     AutoReverse="True"
                                     RepeatBehavior="Forever" />
                </Storyboard>
            </BeginStoryboard>
        </EventTrigger>
    </Page.Triggers>
</Page>
```

The result is a pie slice that ranges from 1 degree to 359 degrees, back and forth forever:

Key Frame Animations

All the programs you've seen so far have animated properties from one value to another, usually specified as the *From* and *To* properties of *DoubleAnimation*, *ColorAnimation*, and *PointAnimation* classes, and the only variations have involved nonlinear ways to get from *From* to *To* and then reversing animations to go from *To* to *From*.

What if you need to animate a property from one value to another value and then to a third value, and maybe even beyond? A solution that might occur to you is to define several animations in the storyboard targeting the same property and to use *BeginTime* to delay some of those animations so that they don't overlap. But that's illegal. You can't have more than one animation in a storyboard targeting a particular property.

The correct solution is a *key frame* animation, so called because you define the progress of the animation through a series of key frames. Each key frame indicates what the value of the property should be at a particular elapsed time and how to get from the previous key frame value to the new value in that key frame.

Here's a simple example of a key frame animation that targets the *Center* property of an *EllipseGeometry* to move the circle around the screen:

Project: SimpleKeyFrameAnimation | **File:** MainPage.xaml (excerpt)

```
<Page ... >
    <Grid Background="{StaticResource ApplicationPageBackgroundThemeBrush}">
        <Path Fill="Blue">
            <Path.Data>
                <EllipseGeometry x:Name="ellipse"
                                 RadiusX="24"
                                 RadiusY="24" />
```

```
            </Path.Data>
        </Path>
    </Grid>

    <Page.Triggers>
        <EventTrigger>
            <BeginStoryboard>
                <Storyboard>
                    <PointAnimationUsingKeyFrames Storyboard.TargetName="ellipse"
                                            Storyboard.TargetProperty="Center"
                                            EnableDependentAnimation="True"
                                            RepeatBehavior="Forever">
                        <DiscretePointKeyFrame KeyTime="0:0:0" Value="100 100" />
                        <LinearPointKeyFrame KeyTime="0:0:2" Value="700 700" />
                        <LinearPointKeyFrame KeyTime="0:0:2.1" Value="700 100" />
                        <LinearPointKeyFrame KeyTime="0:0:4.1" Value="100 700" />
                        <LinearPointKeyFrame KeyTime="0:0:4.2" Value="100 100" />
                    </PointAnimationUsingKeyFrames>
                </Storyboard>
            </BeginStoryboard>
        </EventTrigger>
    </Page.Triggers>
</Page>
```

Rather than a *PointAnimation*, the *Storyboard* contains a *PointAnimationUsingKeyFrames*. Rather than specifying *From*, *To*, and *Duration* properties in the *PointAnimation*, the *PointAnimationUsingKeyFrames* contains children of type *DiscretePointKeyFrame* and *LinearPointKeyFrame*.

Each key frame in a collection specifies what you want the value of the target property to be at that particular time from the beginning of the animation. Very often a collection of key frames will begin with a *Discrete* item with a *KeyTime* of zero, basically initializing the property to that value:

```
<DiscretePointKeyFrame KeyTime="0:0:0" Value="100 100" />
```

The next key frame in the collection is

```
<LinearPointKeyFrame KeyTime="0:0:2" Value="700 700" />
```

What this means is that the target property is linearly increased from the previous point (100, 100) to the point (700, 700) over the course of two seconds. At an elapsed time of two seconds, the value is (700, 700).

The next key frame specifies a much faster animation:

```
<LinearPointKeyFrame KeyTime="0:0:2.1" Value="700 100" />
```

From an elapsed time of two seconds to 2.1 seconds, the point changes from (700, 700) to (700, 100). The animation then slows up again for the next two seconds:

```
<LinearPointKeyFrame KeyTime="0:0:4.1" Value="100 700" />
```

The last key frame is:

```
<LinearPointKeyFrame KeyTime="0:0:4.2" Value="100 100" />
```

At an elapsed time of 4.2 seconds, the value of the target property is (100, 100) and the animation is finished. At this point, it can reverse (if *AutoReverse* is *true*) or start over again (if an appropriate value of *RepeatBehavior* is set).

It's possible for programmers to "overthink" key frames, so here are two extraordinarily simple rules that might prevent confusion:

- A key frame always indicates the desired value of the property at that elapsed time.

- The duration of an animation is the highest key time in the collection.

To store the collection of key frames, the *PointAnimationUsingKeyFrames* class defines a property named *KeyFrames* of type *PointKeyFrameCollection*, which is a collection of *PointKeyFrame* objects. *PointKeyFrame* defines the *KeyTime* and *Value* properties. Four classes derive from *PointKeyFrame*, and you've already seen two of them:

- *DiscretePointKeyFrame* jumps to a particular value.

- *LinearPointKeyFrame* performs a linear animation.

- *SplinePointKeyFrame* can speed up or slow down.

- *EasingPointKeyFrame* animates with an easing function.

Similarly, the Windows Runtime includes a *DoubleAnimationUsingKeyFrames* class, which has children of type *DoubleKeyFrame*, from which similar *Discrete*, *Linear*, *Spline*, and *Easing* classes derive, and *ColorAnimationUsingKeyFrames* with children of type *ColorKeyFrame*, also with *Discrete*, *Linear*, *Spline*, and *Easing* derivatives.

The following project uses *ColorAnimationUsingKeyFrames* to color the background of the grid with colors that animate through the rainbow:

Project: RainbowAnimation | **File:** MainPage.xaml (excerpt)

```
<Page ... >
    <Grid>
        <Grid.Background>
            <SolidColorBrush x:Name="brush" />
        </Grid.Background>
    </Grid>

    <Page.Triggers>
        <EventTrigger>
            <BeginStoryboard>
                <Storyboard RepeatBehavior="Forever">
                    <ColorAnimationUsingKeyFrames Storyboard.TargetName="brush"
                                        Storyboard.TargetProperty="Color">
                        <DiscreteColorKeyFrame KeyTime="0:0:0" Value="#FF0000" />
                        <LinearColorKeyFrame KeyTime="0:0:1" Value="#FFFF00" />
                        <LinearColorKeyFrame KeyTime="0:0:2" Value="#00FF00" />
                        <LinearColorKeyFrame KeyTime="0:0:3" Value="#00FFFF" />
                        <LinearColorKeyFrame KeyTime="0:0:4" Value="#0000FF" />
```

```
                    <LinearColorKeyFrame KeyTime="0:0:5" Value="#FF00FF" />
                    <LinearColorKeyFrame KeyTime="0:0:6" Value="#FF0000" />
                </ColorAnimationUsingKeyFrames>
            </Storyboard>
        </BeginStoryboard>
    </EventTrigger>
  </Page.Triggers>
</Page>
```

The animation is 6 seconds in length, and it ends up at the same value it started with, which means there won't be any discontinuities when it starts over again from the beginning.

Here's a pair of *PointAnimationUsingKeyFrames* objects that animate the *StartPoint* and *EndPoint* properties of a *LinearGradientBrush* object to make the gradient go around in circles:

Project: GradientBrushPointAnimation | File: MainPage.xaml (excerpt)

```
<Page ... >
    <Grid>
        <Grid.Background>
            <LinearGradientBrush x:Name="gradientBrush">
                <GradientStop Offset="0" Color="Red" />
                <GradientStop Offset="1" Color="Blue" />
            </LinearGradientBrush>
        </Grid.Background>
    </Grid>

    <Page.Triggers>
        <EventTrigger>
            <BeginStoryboard>
                <Storyboard RepeatBehavior="Forever">
                    <PointAnimationUsingKeyFrames Storyboard.TargetName="gradientBrush"
                                                  Storyboard.TargetProperty="StartPoint"
                                                  EnableDependentAnimation="True">
                        <LinearPointKeyFrame KeyTime="0:0:0" Value="0 0" />
                        <LinearPointKeyFrame KeyTime="0:0:1" Value="1 0" />
                        <LinearPointKeyFrame KeyTime="0:0:2" Value="1 1" />
                        <LinearPointKeyFrame KeyTime="0:0:3" Value="0 1" />
                        <LinearPointKeyFrame KeyTime="0:0:4" Value="0 0" />
                    </PointAnimationUsingKeyFrames>

                    <PointAnimationUsingKeyFrames Storyboard.TargetName="gradientBrush"
                                                  Storyboard.TargetProperty="EndPoint"
                                                  EnableDependentAnimation="True">
                        <LinearPointKeyFrame KeyTime="0:0:0" Value="1 1" />
                        <LinearPointKeyFrame KeyTime="0:0:1" Value="0 1" />
                        <LinearPointKeyFrame KeyTime="0:0:2" Value="0 0" />
                        <LinearPointKeyFrame KeyTime="0:0:3" Value="1 0" />
                        <LinearPointKeyFrame KeyTime="0:0:4" Value="1 1" />
                    </PointAnimationUsingKeyFrames>
                </Storyboard>
            </BeginStoryboard>
        </EventTrigger>
    </Page.Triggers>
</Page>
```

The *SplineDoubleKeyFrame*, *SplineColorKeyFrame*, and *SplinePointKeyFrame* objects are not used as much as they once were because much of their functionality has been superseded by *EasingDoubleKeyFrame*, *EasingColorKeyFrame*, and *EasingPointKeyFrame*. With the *Spline* variations of the key frame, you use a *KeySpline* object to define two control points of a Bézier spline that begins at the point (0, 0) and ends at (1, 1). This spline performs the same role as an easing function in that it bends time and causes an animation to speed up and slow down. I'll have an example in the next chapter.

The *Object* Animation

The Windows Runtime animation system is also capable of animating properties of type *Object*, which implicitly seems to encompass everything, but there's a catch: There is no *ObjectAnimation* class with *From* and *To* properties. There is only an *ObjectAnimationUsingKeyFrames* class, and the only class that derives from *ObjectKeyFrame* is *DiscreteObjectKeyFrame*.

In other words, you can indeed define an animation to target a property of any type (as long as that property is backed by a dependency property), but you can use the animation only to set that property to discrete values.

In practice, object animations are used mostly for targeting properties of enumeration types or *Brush* types, which allows setting the property to a predefined brush resource. These are mostly used in control templates, as you'll see in Chapter 11.

But here's an example that moves an *Ellipse* around a screen while animating its *Visibility* property with the enumeration members *Visible* and *Collapsed* and its *Fill* property with predefined brushes. Because these animations cause the *Ellipse* to flicker on and off, and with different discrete colors, the project is called FastNotFluid:

Project: FastNotFluid | **File:** MainPage.xaml (excerpt)

```
<Page ... >

    <Grid Background="Gray">
        <Canvas SizeChanged="OnCanvasSizeChanged"
                Margin="0 0 96 96">
            <Ellipse Name="ellipse"
                    Width="96"
                    Height="96" />
        </Canvas>
    </Grid>

    <Page.Triggers>
        <EventTrigger>
            <BeginStoryboard>
                <Storyboard>
                    <DoubleAnimation x:Name="horzAnima"
                                Storyboard.TargetName="ellipse"
                                Storyboard.TargetProperty="(Canvas.Left)"
                                From="0" Duration="0:0:2.51"
                                AutoReverse="True"
                                RepeatBehavior="Forever" />
```

```xml
            <DoubleAnimation x:Name="vertAnima"
                             Storyboard.TargetName="ellipse"
                             Storyboard.TargetProperty="(Canvas.Top)"
                             From="0" Duration="0:0:1.01"
                             AutoReverse="True"
                             RepeatBehavior="Forever" />

            <ObjectAnimationUsingKeyFrames
                             Storyboard.TargetName="ellipse"
                             Storyboard.TargetProperty="Visibility"
                             RepeatBehavior="Forever">
                <DiscreteObjectKeyFrame KeyTime="0:0:0" Value="Visible" />
                <DiscreteObjectKeyFrame KeyTime="0:0:0.2" Value="Collapsed" />
                <DiscreteObjectKeyFrame KeyTime="0:0:0.25" Value="Visible" />
                <DiscreteObjectKeyFrame KeyTime="0:0:0.3" Value="Collapsed" />
                <DiscreteObjectKeyFrame KeyTime="0:0:0.45" Value="Visible" />
            </ObjectAnimationUsingKeyFrames>

            <ObjectAnimationUsingKeyFrames
                             Storyboard.TargetName="ellipse"
                             Storyboard.TargetProperty="Fill"
                             RepeatBehavior="Forever">
                <DiscreteObjectKeyFrame KeyTime="0:0:0"
                    Value="{StaticResource ApplicationPageBackgroundThemeBrush}" />
                <DiscreteObjectKeyFrame KeyTime="0:0:0.2"
                    Value="{StaticResource ApplicationForegroundThemeBrush}" />
                <DiscreteObjectKeyFrame KeyTime="0:0:0.4"
                    Value="{StaticResource ApplicationPressedForegroundThemeBrush}" />
                <DiscreteObjectKeyFrame KeyTime="0:0:0.6"
                    Value="{StaticResource ApplicationPageBackgroundThemeBrush}" />
            </ObjectAnimationUsingKeyFrames>
          </Storyboard>
        </BeginStoryboard>
      </EventTrigger>
    </Page.Triggers>
</Page>
```

It is interesting that the *Value* property of the *DiscreteObjectKeyFrame* can be set directly to the name of an enumeration member or set to a *StaticResource* without causing confusion about the type.

Another advantage of defining the *Storyboard* and animations in a *Triggers* section is accessing the individual animations by name in the code-behind file:

Project: FastNotFluid | **File:** MainPage.xaml.cs (excerpt)

```csharp
void OnCanvasSizeChanged(object sender, SizeChangedEventArgs args)
{
    horzAnima.To = args.NewSize.Width;
    vertAnima.To = args.NewSize.Height;
}
```

Predefined Animations and Transitions

I said at the outset that the *Windows.UI.Xaml.Media.Animation* contained 71 classes, but if you've been keeping count, you probably haven't reached that number yet.

Besides the classes I've mentioned so far, the namespace also includes 14 predefined animations that derive from *Timeline* with names that end with *ThemeAnimation*. These animations already have all their properties and target properties set and need only a target object that you set with a *TargetName* property. So that you can experiment with these predefined animations, I've created a program where 12 of these animations (excluding *SplitOpenThemeAnimation* and *SplitCloseThemeAnimation*, which don't quite fit in the scheme of this program) are associated with their own *Storyboard* objects where the *TargetName* is set to an element with the name of "button":

Project: PreconfiguredAnimations | MainPage.xaml (excerpt)

```
<Page ... >
    <Page.Resources>
        <Style TargetType="Button">
            <Setter Property="Margin" Value="0 6" />
        </Style>

        <Storyboard x:Key="fadeIn">
            <FadeInThemeAnimation TargetName="button" />
        </Storyboard>

        <Storyboard x:Key="fadeOut">
            <FadeOutThemeAnimation TargetName="button" />
        </Storyboard>

        <Storyboard x:Key="popIn">
            <PopInThemeAnimation TargetName="button" />
        </Storyboard>

        <Storyboard x:Key="popOut">
            <PopOutThemeAnimation TargetName="button" />
        </Storyboard>

        <Storyboard x:Key="reposition">
            <RepositionThemeAnimation TargetName="button" />
        </Storyboard>

        <Storyboard x:Key="pointerUp">
            <PointerUpThemeAnimation TargetName="button" />
        </Storyboard>

        <Storyboard x:Key="pointerDown">
            <PointerDownThemeAnimation TargetName="button" />
        </Storyboard>

        <Storyboard x:Key="swipeBack">
            <SwipeBackThemeAnimation TargetName="button" />
        </Storyboard>
```

```
        <Storyboard x:Key="swipeHint">
            <SwipeHintThemeAnimation TargetName="button" />
        </Storyboard>

        <Storyboard x:Key="dragItem">
            <DragItemThemeAnimation TargetName="button" />
        </Storyboard>

        <Storyboard x:Key="dropTargetItem">
            <DropTargetItemThemeAnimation TargetName="button" />
        </Storyboard>

        <Storyboard x:Key="dragOver">
            <DragOverThemeAnimation TargetName="button" />
        </Storyboard>
    </Page.Resources>

    <Grid Background="{StaticResource ApplicationPageBackgroundThemeBrush}">
        <Grid.ColumnDefinitions>
            <ColumnDefinition Width="Auto" />
            <ColumnDefinition Width="*" />
        </Grid.ColumnDefinitions>

        <StackPanel Name="animationTriggersStackPanel"
                    Grid.Column="0"
                    VerticalAlignment="Center">

            <Button Content="Fade In"
                    Tag="fadeIn"
                    Click="OnButtonClick" />

            <Button Content="Fade Out"
                    Tag="fadeOut"
                    Click="OnButtonClick" />

            <Button Content="Pop In"
                    Tag="popIn"
                    Click="OnButtonClick" />

            <Button Content="Pop Out"
                    Tag="popOut"
                    Click="OnButtonClick" />

            <Button Content="Reposition"
                    Tag="reposition"
                    Click="OnButtonClick" />

            <Button Content="Pointer Up"
                    Tag="pointerUp"
                    Click="OnButtonClick" />

            <Button Content="Pointer Down"
                    Tag="pointerDown"
                    Click="OnButtonClick" />
```

```
            <Button Content="Swipe Back"
                    Tag="swipeBack"
                    Click="OnButtonClick" />

            <Button Content="Swipe Hint"
                    Tag="swipeHint"
                    Click="OnButtonClick" />

            <Button Content="Drag Item"
                    Tag="dragItem"
                    Click="OnButtonClick" />

            <Button Content="Drop Target Item"
                    Tag="dropTargetItem"
                    Click="OnButtonClick" />

            <Button Content="Drag Over"
                    Tag="dragOver"
                    Click="OnButtonClick" />
        </StackPanel>

        <!-- Animation target -->
        <Button Name="button"
                Grid.Column="1"
                Content="Big Button"
                FontSize="48"
                HorizontalAlignment="Center"
                VerticalAlignment="Center" />
    </Grid>
</Page>
```

Besides the *Button* named "button", the XAML file also defines a *Button* for each of the preconfigured animations. The code-behind file uses the *Tag* property to trigger the corresponding *Storyboard*:

Project: PreconfiguredAnimations | **File:** MainPage.xaml.cs (excerpt)

```
void OnButtonClick(object sender, RoutedEventArgs args)
{
    Button btn = sender as Button;
    string key = btn.Tag as string;
    Storyboard storyboard = this.Resources[key] as Storyboard;
    storyboard.Begin();
}
```

Watch out! Some of these animations cause the target *Button* to disappear, and others are rather subtle, but you'll get an idea of some of the effects that you might want to add to your own application.

Another set of predefined animations is the eight classes that derive from *Transition*. These are rather more complex sets of animations that you set to one of the following properties of type *TransitionCollection*:

- *Transitions* property defined by *UIElement*

- *ContentTransitions* property defined by *ContentControl*

- *ChildrenTransitions* property defined by *Panel*

- *ItemContainerTransitions* property defined by *ItemsControl*

For example, try replacing the *StackPanel* tag in the PreconfiguredAnimations program with the following:

```
<StackPanel Name="animationTriggersStackPanel"
            Grid.Column="0"
            VerticalAlignment="Center">
    <StackPanel.ChildrenTransitions>
        <TransitionCollection>
            <EntranceThemeTransition />
        </TransitionCollection>
    </StackPanel.ChildrenTransitions>
```

Now, as the page is loaded, the buttons seem to appear a little offset from their actual positions and then shift into place.

I'll have more to say about these transitions in Chapter 11 and Chapter 12, "Pages and Navigation."

Transforms

In Chapter 9, "Animation," you saw how to use animations to move objects around the screen, change their size or color or opacity, and even move the dots in a dotted line. But certain types of animations were missing. What if you want to use an animation to *rotate* a button when the button is clicked? And I don't necessarily mean to make the button spin around crazy, but maybe just jiggle a little as if the button is saying, "I simply can't restrain my enthusiasm to be carrying out the command you desire."

What you need for this job (and others like it) are *transforms*. Back in the old days, transforms were called *graphics transforms* or even—perhaps to scare away the uninitiated—*matrix transforms*. But in recent years transforms have been liberated from the greedy clutches of the graphics mavens and made available to all programmers.

This is not to imply that transforms no longer have anything to do with mathematics. (Yes, there will be math.) But it's possible to use transforms in the Windows Runtime without getting involved in the mathematics that enable their capabilities.

A Brief Overview

A transform is basically a mathematical formula that is applied to a point (x, y) to create a new point (x', y'). If you apply the same formula to all the points of a visual object, you can effectively move the object, or make it a different size, or rotate it, or even distort the object in various ways.

Transforms are supported in the Windows Runtime with three properties defined by *UIElement*: *RenderTransform*, *RenderTransformOrigin*, and *Projection*. Because these properties are defined by *UIElement*, transforms are not limited to vector graphics as they were in the old days. You can apply transforms to any element, including *Image*, *TextBlock*, and *Button*. If you apply a transform to a *Panel* derivative such as a *Grid*, it also applies to all the children of that panel.

To apply a transform to an element, use property-element syntax to set the *RenderTransform* property to an instance of a class that derives from *Transform*, for example, *RotateTransform*:

Project: SimpleRotate | File: MainPage.xaml (excerpt)

```
<Grid Background="{StaticResource ApplicationPageBackgroundThemeBrush}">
    <Image Source="http://www.charlespetzold.com/pw6/PetzoldJersey.jpg"
           Stretch="None"
           HorizontalAlignment="Right"
           VerticalAlignment="Bottom">
        <Image.RenderTransform>
            <RotateTransform Angle="135" />
        </Image.RenderTransform>
    </Image>
</Grid>
```

The *Angle* property of the *RotateTransform* indicates a clockwise rotation of 135 degrees:

But the result only appears reasonable because I knew that the *Image* would be rotated relative to its upper-left corner, so I deliberately positioned the *Image* element in the lower-right corner of the page. Rotation in two dimensions always occurs around a particular point—like a pin that attaches a photograph to a cork board—and setting that point correctly turns out to be one of the trickier aspects of working with transforms.

You can set the *RenderTransform* property to any one of the seven classes that derive from *Transform*, arranged here roughly in order of increasing mathematical complexity:

Object
  DependencyObject
    GeneralTransform
      Transform
        TranslateTransform
        ScaleTransform
        RotateTransform
        SkewTransform
        CompositeTransform
        MatrixTransform
        TransformGroup

These classes define traditional two-dimensional affine transforms. The word "affine" suggests that the transformed object has certain affinities with the nontransformed object: A straight line is always transformed to another straight line. The line possibly assumes a different location, size, or orientation, but it is still a straight line. Lines that are parallel prior to an affine transform continue to be parallel after the transform. An affine transform never causes anything to shoot off into infinity. Indeed, the mathematical definition of affine is "preserving finiteness."

The Windows Runtime also supports a certain type of non-affine transform commonly used in three-dimensional perspective. You can use the Windows Runtime to achieve three-dimensional effects by setting the *Projection* property defined by *UIElement* to an instance of one of the two classes that derive from *Projection*:

Object
  DependencyObject
    Projection
      PlaneProjection
      Matrix3DProjection

Rotation in three dimensions is always around an axis. Rotation around the *Y* (vertical) axis is demonstrated in the SimpleProjection project:

Project: SimpleProjection | File: MainPage.xaml (excerpt)

```
<Grid Background="{StaticResource ApplicationPageBackgroundThemeBrush}">
    <Image Source="http://www.charlespetzold.com/pw6/PetzoldJersey.jpg"
           HorizontalAlignment="Center"
           VerticalAlignment="Center">
        <Image.Projection>
            <PlaneProjection RotationY="-60" />
        </Image.Projection>
    </Image>
</Grid>
```

This creates a rather different sort of rotation, seeming to add a third dimension to the two dimensions of the screen:

Obviously, parallel lines are not preserved in this type of transform. That's what makes it appear as if it exists in 3D space.

The *Projection* transforms are sometimes called *pseudo-3D* transforms and are intended to provide a little "3Dishness" to the Windows Runtime. You can define an animation to make an element seem to swing into view like a door or flip around like a playing card. But the element itself stays flat. This is why one of the *Projection* classes refers to a "plane." You're basically taking a flat element and moving it in 3D space.

Math-oriented programmers might be able to persuade *Matrix3DProjection* to display actual 3D objects in the Windows Runtime. But the Windows Runtime is missing some crucial features of 3D, such as surface shading based on light sources, or clipping when one object is partially hidden behind another. If you need to bring real 3D graphics into your Windows 8 application, you'll want to use Direct3D, which is only accessible from C++ and (it grieves me to say) beyond the scope of this book.

Rotation (Manual and Animated)

It's common for tutorials such as this to begin the subject of transforms with the mathematically simple ones: *TranslateTransform* to move objects and *ScaleTransform* to make them larger or smaller. But these aren't very impressive because you've already seen animations that move an object around the screen or change its size. That's why I'm starting with something you can't do in other ways.

I just demonstrated that you can set the *Angle* property of *RotateTransform* directly in XAML, but it's much more fun to change the *Angle* property dynamically with a data binding or an animation, and the result can also be more revealing of what's actually going on. Here's a XAML file with the

Angle property of a *RotateTransform* bound to the *Value* property of a *Slider* with a range from 0 through 360:

Project: RotateTheText | **File:** MainPage.xaml (excerpt)

```xaml
<Grid Background="{StaticResource ApplicationPageBackgroundThemeBrush}">
    <Border BorderBrush="{StaticResource ApplicationForegroundThemeBrush}"
            BorderThickness="1"
            HorizontalAlignment="Center"
            VerticalAlignment="Center">
        <Grid>
            <Grid.RowDefinitions>
                <RowDefinition Height="Auto" />
                <RowDefinition Height="Auto" />
            </Grid.RowDefinitions>

            <Slider Name="slider"
                    Grid.Row="0"
                    Minimum="0"
                    Maximum="360" />

            <TextBlock Text="Rotate Text with Slider"
                    Grid.Row="1"
                    FontSize="48">
                <TextBlock.RenderTransform>
                    <RotateTransform Angle="{Binding ElementName=slider, Path=Value}" />
                </TextBlock.RenderTransform>
            </TextBlock>
        </Grid>
    </Border>
</Grid>
```

The *Slider* and *TextBlock* occupy two rows of a *Grid* that's inside a *Border*. Here's how it looks when the screen first comes up:

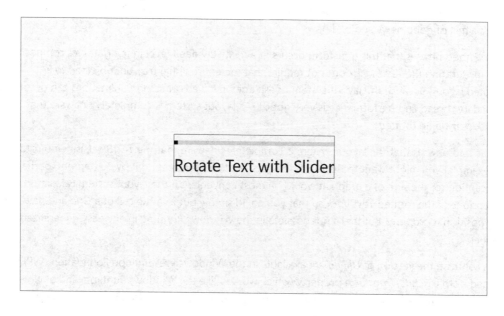

The *TextBlock* width determines the *Grid* width, which then determines the *Slider* width and the *Border* width.

As you use the mouse or your fingers to change the *Slider* value, the *TextBlock* rotates in a clockwise direction. Here it is at 120 degrees:

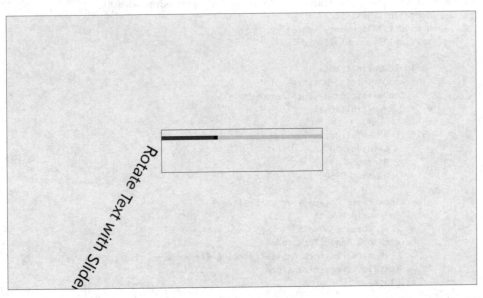

It's obvious that the size of the *Grid* and the *Border* continue to be based on the unrotated *TextBlock*, and the rotated *TextBlock* has broken free of the boundaries of its ancestors in the visual tree.

The property of *UIElement* to which you set the *RotateTransform* is named *RenderTransform*, and you'll want to mull over that property name a little bit. That word *render* means that the transform affects only how the element is *rendered* and *not* how the element appears to the layout system. That's a mix of good news and bad news.

The good news is that this transform occurs at a relatively deep level in the graphics composition system. Rotating the *TextBlock* does not require that the entire visual tree be subjected to an updated layout. Because the layout system doesn't get involved, transform animations can occur in a secondary thread and performance is very good. The layout system is completely unaware that the *TextBlock* is being rotated.

The bad news is that the layout system is completely unaware that the *TextBlock* is being rotated. For example, you might want to display a sideways *TextBlock* by rotating it by 90 degrees, perhaps as a caption for the side of a graph. It would be most convenient if the layout system calculated the dimensions of the rotated *TextBlock* so that you could simply put it in the cell of a *Grid* and have the *Grid* position it properly. But that's not possible in the Windows Runtime in any easy generalized manner.

In contrast, the version of *UIElement* available in the Windows Presentation Foundation (WPF) defined both a *RenderTransform* property (which worked like the Windows Runtime) and a *LayoutTransform* property, which allowed specifying a transform recognized by the layout system.

That *LayoutTransform* property was lost in the transition from WPF to Silverlight and the Windows Runtime, and mimicking it requires a bit of work.

Let's go back to the running RotateTheText program. Manipulate the *Slider* so that the *TextBlock* partially lies on top of the *Slider*:

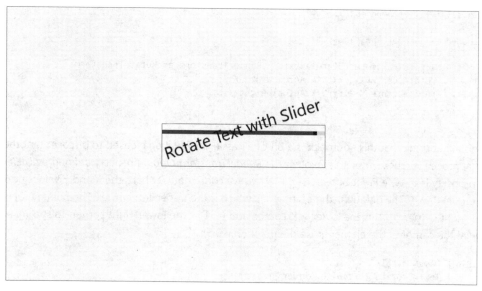

Now remove all fingers from the screen (or release the mouse button), and try touching or clicking the *Slider* in a spot where the *TextBlock* overlaps. The *Slider* doesn't respond because the *TextBlock* is blocking the mouse or touch input. The lesson learned is this: Although the layout system doesn't know that the *TextBlock* has moved, hit-testing logic continues to be aware exactly where it is. (On the other hand, while you're in the actual process of manipulating the *Slider*, the *TextBlock* doesn't interfere because the *Slider* has *captured* this input, which is a concept I'll discuss in Chapter 13, "Touch, Etc.")

You'll also notice that the rotation of the *TextBlock* is relative to its upper-left corner, which conceptually is the origin of the *TextBlock*: the point (0, 0). In many graphics systems, it is common for graphics transforms to be relative to the origin of the canvas on which the graphics object is positioned. In the Windows Runtime, all transforms are relative to the element to which they're applied.

Very often you'll prefer that rotation be relative to some point other than the upper-left corner. This point is sometimes referred to as "the center of rotation," and you can specify it in three different ways:

The first way is the one that is most illuminating of the underlying mathematics of the transform, but I'll save it for later.

The second way involves the *RotateTransform* class itself. The class defines *CenterX* and *CenterY* properties that are 0 by default. If you want this particular *TextBlock* to rotate relative to its center, set *CenterX* to half the width of the *TextBlock* and *CenterY* to half its height. This information can be obtained during the *Loaded* handler, so you can add something like the following to the constructor of the code-behind file. Fortunately, I gave the *TextBlock* a name even though that name isn't used in the XAML file:

```
public MainPage()
{
    this.InitializeComponent();

    Loaded += (sender, args) =>
        {
            RotateTransform rotate = txtblk.RenderTransform as RotateTransform;
            rotate.CenterX = txtblk.ActualWidth / 2;
            rotate.CenterY = txtblk.ActualHeight / 2;
        };
}
```

You might think that this approach is a bit of a hassle, so you'll be pleased to discover that the third approach is much simpler. It involves the *RenderTransformOrigin* property defined by *UIElement*. This property is of type *Point* but you set it to *relative* coordinates, where the *X* and *Y* values normally range from 0 to 1. The default is the point (0, 0), which is the upper-left corner. The point (1, 0) is the upper-right corner, (0, 1) is the lower-left corner, and (1, 1) is the lower-right corner. To specify an origin at the center of the element, use the point (0.5, 0.5):

```
<TextBlock Name="txtblk"
           Text="Rotate Text with Slider"
           Grid.Row="1"
           FontSize="48"
           RenderTransformOrigin="0.5 0.5">
    <TextBlock.RenderTransform>
        <RotateTransform Angle="{Binding ElementName=slider, Path=Value}" />
    </TextBlock.RenderTransform>
</TextBlock>
```

Notice that *CenterX* and *CenterY* are properties of *RotateTransform*, but the *RenderTransformOrigin* property is defined by *UIElement* and common to all elements. If you set *RenderTransformOrigin* in addition to *CenterX* and *CenterY*, the effects are compounded. In this example, the compounded effect of both examples would cause rotation to be around the lower-right corner of the *TextBlock*.

You can specify a center of rotation that is outside the element. Here's a XAML file that positions a *TextBlock* in the top center of the page and then starts up a "forever" animation to rotate it:

Project: RotateAroundCenter | File: MainPage.xaml (excerpt)

```
<Page ... >
    <Grid Background="{StaticResource ApplicationPageBackgroundThemeBrush}">
        <TextBlock Name="txtblk"
                   Text="Rotated Text"
                   FontSize="48"
                   HorizontalAlignment="Center"
                   VerticalAlignment="Top">
```

```
        <TextBlock.RenderTransform>
            <RotateTransform x:Name="rotate" />
        </TextBlock.RenderTransform>
    </TextBlock>
</Grid>

<Page.Triggers>
    <EventTrigger>
        <BeginStoryboard>
            <Storyboard RepeatBehavior="Forever">
                <DoubleAnimation Storyboard.TargetName="rotate"
                                 Storyboard.TargetProperty="Angle"
                                 From="0" To="360" Duration="0:0:2" />
            </Storyboard>
        </BeginStoryboard>
    </EventTrigger>
</Page.Triggers>
</Page>
```

Without any additional code, this program would rotate the *TextBlock* around its upper-left corner, and it would sweep right off the screen at certain times during the animation. But the constructor of the code-behind file defines two event handlers to set the *CenterX* and *CenterY* properties of the *RotateTransform*:

Project: RotateAroundCenter | **File:** MainPage.xaml.cs (excerpt)

```
public sealed partial class MainPage : Page
{
    public MainPage()
    {
        this.InitializeComponent();

        Loaded += (sender, args) =>
            {
                rotate.CenterX = txtblk.ActualWidth / 2;
            };

        SizeChanged += (sender, args) =>
            {
                rotate.CenterY = args.NewSize.Height / 2;
            };
    }
}
```

The center of rotation is set to a point aligned with the horizontal center of the *TextBlock* but a distance below the *TextBlock* equal to half the height of the page. The result is that the *TextBlock* rotates in a circle around the page center:

Visual Feedback

An animated transform can be effective for alerting the user to something on the screen that requires attention or for confirming that an operation has been initiated. In the JiggleButtonDemo program, I added a new *UserControl* item that I named *JiggleButton*, but then I changed the base class in the XAML and C# files from *UserControl* to *Button*. Here's the complete JiggleButton.xaml file:

Project: JiggleButtonDemo | JiggleButton.xaml

```
<Button
    x:Class="JiggleButtonDemo.JiggleButton"
    xmlns="http://schemas.microsoft.com/winfx/2006/xaml/presentation"
    xmlns:x="http://schemas.microsoft.com/winfx/2006/xaml"
    RenderTransformOrigin="0.5 0.5"
    Click="OnJiggleButtonClick">

    <Button.Resources>
        <Storyboard x:Key="jiggleAnimation">
            <DoubleAnimation Storyboard.TargetName="rotate"
                             Storyboard.TargetProperty="Angle"
                             From="0" To="10" Duration="0:0:0.33"
                             AutoReverse="True">
                <DoubleAnimation.EasingFunction>
                    <ElasticEase EasingMode="EaseIn" />
                </DoubleAnimation.EasingFunction>
            </DoubleAnimation>
        </Storyboard>
    </Button.Resources>
```

```
<Button.RenderTransform>
    <RotateTransform x:Name="rotate" />
</Button.RenderTransform>
</Button>
```

The content of the *Button* isn't defined in this XAML file but three *Button* properties are set: *RenderTransformOrigin* (in the root tag), *Resources*, and *RenderTransform*. Normally, if you wanted to jiggle an element with a rotation, you'd need to use key frames because you first want to rotate from 0 to 10 degrees (for example), then from 10 degrees to –10 degrees several times, and then back to 0 degrees. But *ElasticEase* with an *EasingMode* of *EaseIn* is a great alternative. The *DoubleAnimation* is defined to rotate the button 10 degrees and then back to zero, but the *ElasticEase* function incorporates wide negative swing, so the animation actually ranges from –10 to 10 degrees.

The code-behind file for the *JiggleButton* simply triggers the animation in a *Click* event handler:

Project: JiggleButtonDemo | JiggleButton.xaml.cs

```
using Windows.UI.Xaml;
using Windows.UI.Xaml.Controls;
using Windows.UI.Xaml.Media.Animation;

namespace JiggleButtonDemo
{
    public sealed partial class JiggleButton : Button
    {
        public JiggleButton()
        {
            this.InitializeComponent();
        }

        void OnJiggleButtonClick(object sender, RoutedEventArgs args)
        {
            (this.Resources["jiggleAnimation"] as Storyboard).Begin();
        }
    }
}
```

The MainPage.xaml file instantiates a *JiggleButton* so that you can play with it:

Project: JiggleButtonDemo | File: MainPage.xaml (excerpt)

```
<Grid Background="{StaticResource ApplicationPageBackgroundThemeBrush}">
    <local:JiggleButton Content="JiggleButton Demo"
                        FontSize="24"
                        HorizontalAlignment="Center"
                        VerticalAlignment="Center" />
</Grid>
```

Keep in mind that *JiggleButton* derives from *Button*, so you can use it just like any other *Button*, except that you shouldn't set the *RenderTransform* or *RenderTransformOrigin* properties on it because doing so would interfere with the jiggle animation.

Translation

TranslateTransform defines two properties *X* and *Y* that cause an element to be rendered offset to its original position. One simple application of the *TranslateTransform* is to display text with an "embossed" or "engraved" appearance, or with a drop shadow like this:

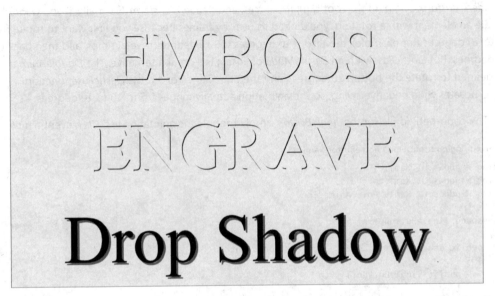

Because light normally comes from above—and perhaps also because we're accustomed to the convention that 3D-ish objects on the computer screen are illuminated with a light source from the upper left—the text on the top appears as if it has shadows at the right and bottom, and hence the letters are projecting outward from the screen. The engraved effect is opposite that: The shadows are on the left and top, and so the letters appear to be carved out.

The page that displays those three text strings actually consists of six *TextBlock* elements. In the first two pairs, a *TextBlock* colored with the default foreground brush is covered by another *TextBlock* colored with the default background brush but offset by 2 pixels in the horizontal and vertical directions:

Project: TextEffects | File: MainPage.xaml (excerpt)

```
<Page ... >
    <Page.Resources>
        <Style TargetType="TextBlock">
            <Setter Property="FontFamily" Value="Times New Roman" />
            <Setter Property="FontSize" Value="192" />
            <Setter Property="HorizontalAlignment" Value="Center" />
            <Setter Property="VerticalAlignment" Value="Center" />
        </Style>
    </Page.Resources>
```

```xaml
<Grid Background="{StaticResource ApplicationPageBackgroundThemeBrush}">
    <Grid.RowDefinitions>
        <RowDefinition Height="*" />
        <RowDefinition Height="*" />
        <RowDefinition Height="*" />
    </Grid.RowDefinitions>

    <TextBlock Text="EMBOSS"
            Grid.Row="0" />

    <TextBlock Text="EMBOSS"
            Grid.Row="0"
            Foreground="{StaticResource ApplicationPageBackgroundThemeBrush}">
        <TextBlock.RenderTransform>
            <TranslateTransform X="-2" Y="-2" />
        </TextBlock.RenderTransform>
    </TextBlock>

    <TextBlock Text="ENGRAVE"
            Grid.Row="1" />

    <TextBlock Text="ENGRAVE"
            Grid.Row="1"
            Foreground="{StaticResource ApplicationPageBackgroundThemeBrush}">
        <TextBlock.RenderTransform>
            <TranslateTransform X="2" Y="2" />
        </TextBlock.RenderTransform>
    </TextBlock>

    <TextBlock Text="Drop Shadow"
            Grid.Row="2"
            Foreground="Gray">
        <TextBlock.RenderTransform>
            <TranslateTransform X="6" Y="6" />
        </TextBlock.RenderTransform>
    </TextBlock>

    <TextBlock Text="Drop Shadow"
            Grid.Row="2" />
</Grid>
</Page>
```

Notice that the embossing effect requires negative offsets (so that the *TextBlock* on top is shifted to the left and up) whereas the engraving effect has positive offsets. You can use these same effects just slightly less successfully with a dark theme, but you'll have to switch the signs of the *X* and *Y* values.

A drop-shadow effect is similar except that the text on top is colored normally and a gray shadow is offset underneath.

I don't recommend using the following technique on a regular basis, but you can give your on-screen text a little bit of depth—that's *visual* depth and not *intellectual* depth, alas—using a bunch of *TextBlock* elements offset from each other by one pixel:

The generation of these elements is handled entirely in the code-behind file:

Project: DepthText | File: MainPage.xaml.cs (excerpt)

```
public sealed partial class MainPage : Page
{
    const int COUNT = 48;    // ~1/2 inch

    public MainPage()
    {
        this.InitializeComponent();

        Grid grid = this.Content as Grid;
        Brush foreground = this.Resources["ApplicationForegroundThemeBrush"] as Brush;
        Brush grayBrush = new SolidColorBrush(Colors.Gray);

        for (int i = 0; i < COUNT; i++)
        {
            bool firstOrLast = i == 0 || i == COUNT - 1;

            TextBlock txtblk = new TextBlock
            {
                Text = "DEPTH",
                FontSize = 192,
                FontWeight = FontWeights.Bold,
                HorizontalAlignment = HorizontalAlignment.Center,
```

```
            VerticalAlignment = VerticalAlignment.Center,
            RenderTransform = new TranslateTransform
            {
                X = COUNT - i - 1,
                Y = i - COUNT + 1,
            },
            Foreground = firstOrLast ? foreground : grayBrush
        };
        grid.Children.Add(txtblk);
    }
  }
}
```

A *TranslateTransform* is a great way to move something a little bit from the position determined by the layout system. You'll see a couple examples of *TranslateTransform* used in this way in the StandardStyles.xaml file.

In Chapter 9 I showed an example of animating *Canvas.Left* and *Canvas.Top* attached properties to move an object around the screen. You can do the same type of animation by defining a *TranslateTransform* on the element you wish to move and using the animation to target the *X* and *Y* properties. One advantage is that the element being animated need not be a child of a *Canvas*, but there doesn't seem to be a performance difference. Both types of animations are performed in secondary threads.

Transform Groups

I mentioned earlier that there are three ways to set a center of rotation but I was going to save the first way for a later discussion. Now is the time. It's a little more complicated because it involves a transform that is constructed from other transforms.

One of the classes that derives from *Transform* is *TransformGroup*, which has a property named *Children* of type *TransformCollection*, which you can use to construct a composite transform from multiple *Transform* derivatives.

You might define a *RotateTransform* like this:

```
<RotateTransform Angle="A" CenterX="CX" CenterY="CY" />
```

where *A*, *CX*, and *CY* are actual numbers or perhaps data bindings. That transform is equivalent to the following *TransformGroup*:

```
<TransformGroup>
    <TranslateTransform X="-CX" Y="-CY" />
    <RotateTransform Angle="A" />
    <TranslateTransform X="CX" Y="CY" />
</TransformGroup>
```

The two *TranslateTransform* tags seem to cancel each other out, but they surround a *RotateTransform*. Let me demonstrate in two ways that this transform group is equivalent to the first *RotateTransform* by itself.

The following ImageRotate program references a bitmap on my website that I know is 320 pixels wide and 400 pixels tall. To rotate that bitmap around its center the *RotateTransform* would normally have *CenterX* and *CenterY* set to half those values (160 and 200), but I've instead used a pair of *TranslateTransform* objects:

Project: ImageRotate | File: MainPage.xaml (excerpt)

```
<Page ... >
    <Grid Background="{StaticResource ApplicationPageBackgroundThemeBrush}">
        <Image Source="http://www.charlespetzold.com/pw6/PetzoldJersey.jpg"
               Stretch="None"
               HorizontalAlignment="Center"
               VerticalAlignment="Center">
            <Image.RenderTransform>
                <TransformGroup>
                    <TranslateTransform X="-160" Y="-200" />
                    <RotateTransform x:Name="rotate" />
                    <TranslateTransform X="160" Y="200" />
                </TransformGroup>
            </Image.RenderTransform>
        </Image>
    </Grid>

    <Page.Triggers>
        <EventTrigger>
            <BeginStoryboard>
                <Storyboard RepeatBehavior="Forever">
                    <DoubleAnimation Storyboard.TargetName="rotate"
                                     Storyboard.TargetProperty="Angle"
                                     From="0" To="360" Duration="0:0:3">
                        <DoubleAnimation.EasingFunction>
                            <ElasticEase EasingMode="EaseInOut" />
                        </DoubleAnimation.EasingFunction>
                    </DoubleAnimation>
                </Storyboard>
            </BeginStoryboard>
        </EventTrigger>
    </Page.Triggers>
</Page>
```

The *ElasticEase* animation with a mode of *EaseInOut* causes the image to rock back and forth crazily before and after it actually spins around, but you can see that the rotation is clearly around the image's center:

The following screenshot shows the process in the individual steps: The lightest *TextBlock* is positioned in the center of the page. The next darkest *TextBlock* shows the effect of a *TranslateTransform* that shifts the *TextBlock* left by half its width and up by half its height. The next darkest *TextBlock* is rotated relative to its origin—the upper-left corner of the original *TextBlock*. The final black *TextBlock* is then shifted by half its width and height. The final result is the original *TextBlock* rotated around its center:

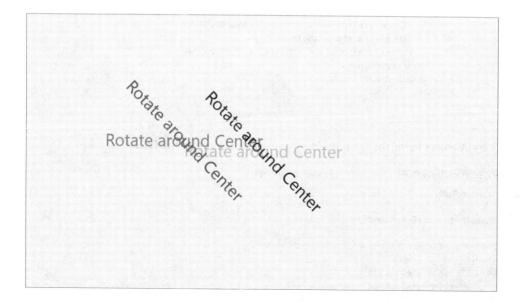

Here's the XAML file that created that image:

Project: RotationCenterDemo | **File:** MainPage.xaml (excerpt)

```xml
<Page ... >
    <Page.Resources>
        <Style TargetType="TextBlock">
            <Setter Property="Text" Value="Rotate around Center" />
            <Setter Property="FontSize" Value="48" />
            <Setter Property="HorizontalAlignment" Value="Center" />
            <Setter Property="VerticalAlignment" Value="Center" />
        </Style>
    </Page.Resources>

    <Grid Background="{StaticResource ApplicationPageBackgroundThemeBrush}">
        <TextBlock Name="txtblk"
                   Foreground="#D0D0D0" />

        <TextBlock Foreground="#A0A0A0">
            <TextBlock.RenderTransform>
                <TranslateTransform x:Name="translateBack1" />
            </TextBlock.RenderTransform>
        </TextBlock>

        <TextBlock Foreground="#707070">
            <TextBlock.RenderTransform>
                <TransformGroup>
                    <TranslateTransform x:Name="translateBack2" />
                    <RotateTransform Angle="45" />
                </TransformGroup>
            </TextBlock.RenderTransform>
        </TextBlock>

        <TextBlock Foreground="{StaticResource ApplicationForegroundThemeBrush}">
            <TextBlock.RenderTransform>
                <TransformGroup>
                    <TranslateTransform x:Name="translateBack3" />
                    <RotateTransform Angle="45" />
                    <TranslateTransform x:Name="translate" />
                </TransformGroup>
            </TextBlock.RenderTransform>
        </TextBlock>
    </Grid>
</Page>
```

The X and Y values for all the *TranslateTransform* tags are set from the *Loaded* handler:

Project: RotationCenterDemo | **File:** MainPage.xaml.cs (excerpt)

```csharp
public MainPage()
{
    this.InitializeComponent();

    Loaded += (sender, args) =>
        {
            translateBack1.X =
            translateBack2.X =
            translateBack3.X = -(translate.X = txtblk.ActualWidth / 2);
```

```
                translateBack1.Y =
                translateBack2.Y =
                translateBack3.Y = -(translate.Y = txtblk.ActualHeight / 2);
        };
}
```

Transforms can be combined for some very interesting effects that might initially seem beyond the scope of the nonmathematical, nongraphics programmer. Here's a XAML file that uses a *Polygon* element to define a simple propeller shape, and then applies three transforms to it, a *RotateTransform*, a *TranslateTransform*, and another *RotateTransform*:

Project: Propeller | File: MainPage.xaml (excerpt)

```
<Page ... >
    <Grid Background="{StaticResource ApplicationPageBackgroundThemeBrush}">
        <Polygon Points="40   0,  60  0, 53 47,
                        100   40, 100 60, 53 53,
                         60 100,  40 100, 47 53,
                          0  60,   0  40, 47 47"
                Stroke="{StaticResource ApplicationForegroundThemeBrush}"
                Fill="SteelBlue"
                HorizontalAlignment="Center"
                VerticalAlignment="Center"
                RenderTransformOrigin="0.5 0.5">
            <Polygon.RenderTransform>
                <TransformGroup>
                    <RotateTransform x:Name="rotate1" />
                    <TranslateTransform X="300" />
                    <RotateTransform x:Name="rotate2" />
                </TransformGroup>
            </Polygon.RenderTransform>
        </Polygon>
    </Grid>

    <Page.Triggers>
        <EventTrigger>
            <BeginStoryboard>
                <Storyboard>
                    <DoubleAnimation Storyboard.TargetName="rotate1"
                                    Storyboard.TargetProperty="Angle"
                                    From="0" To="360" Duration="0:0:0.5"
                                    RepeatBehavior="Forever" />

                    <DoubleAnimation Storyboard.TargetName="rotate2"
                                    Storyboard.TargetProperty="Angle"
                                    From="0" To="360" Duration="0:0:6"
                                    RepeatBehavior="Forever" />
                </Storyboard>
            </BeginStoryboard>
        </EventTrigger>
    </Page.Triggers>
</Page>
```

The *Storyboard* contains two *DoubleAnimation* objects. The first *DoubleAnimation* targets the first *RotateTransform* object to rotate the propeller itself around its center at the speed of 2 cycles per second. The *TranslateTransform* moves this rotating propeller 300 pixels to the right of the center of the page, and the second *DoubleAnimation* targets the second *RotateTransform* to rotate the propeller again. But this rotation is relative to the original center of the propeller, which means that the propeller circles the center of the page with a radius of 300 pixels at the rate of 10 revolutions per minute.

Now it's perhaps clear how *RenderTransformOrigin* works: *RenderTransformOrigin* is equivalent to performing a *TranslateTransform* with negative *X* and *Y* values prior to the transform specified as the *RenderTransform* property, and performing another *TranslateTransform* with positive *X* and *Y* values after the *RenderTransform*.

The Scale Transform

The *ScaleTransform* class defines properties named *ScaleX* and *ScaleY* that increase or decrease the size of an element independently in the horizontal and vertical directions. If you want to preserve the correct aspect ratio of a target, you'll need to use the same values for *ScaleX* and *ScaleY*. If it's an animation, you need two animation objects.

The *ScaleTransform* does not affect the *ActualWidth* and *ActualHeight* properties of an element.

You've seen how to use a *Viewbox* to stretch a *TextBlock* in ways that violate its typographically correct aspect ratio. Here's how to do it with a *ScaleTransform*:

Project: OppositelyScaledText | File: MainPage.xaml (excerpt)

```xml
<Page ... >
    <Grid Background="{StaticResource ApplicationPageBackgroundThemeBrush}">
        <TextBlock Text="Scaled Text"
                   FontSize="144"
                   HorizontalAlignment="Center"
                   VerticalAlignment="Center"
                   RenderTransformOrigin="0.5 0.5">
            <TextBlock.RenderTransform>
                <ScaleTransform x:Name="scale" />
            </TextBlock.RenderTransform>
        </TextBlock>
    </Grid>

    <Page.Triggers>
        <EventTrigger>
            <BeginStoryboard>
                <Storyboard>
                    <DoubleAnimation Storyboard.TargetName="scale"
                                     Storyboard.TargetProperty="ScaleX"
                                     BeginTime="0:0:2"
                                     From="1" To="0.01" Duration="0:0:2"
                                     AutoReverse="True"
                                     RepeatBehavior="Forever" />

                    <DoubleAnimation Storyboard.TargetName="scale"
                                     Storyboard.TargetProperty="ScaleY"
                                     From="10" To="0.1" Duration="0:0:2"
                                     AutoReverse="True"
                                     RepeatBehavior="Forever" />
                </Storyboard>
            </BeginStoryboard>
        </EventTrigger>
    </Page.Triggers>
</Page>
```

This is actually not quite the way I wanted to write this program. I originally gave the *TextBlock* a *FontSize* of 1 and then animated *ScaleX* from 1 to 144 and *ScaleY* from 144 to 1, both reversed and repeated forever. That should probably have worked, but it resulted in the 1-pixel-high font being increased in size by a factor of 144 rather than becoming a 144-pixel-high font. To get the program to work in a way I wanted, I gave the *TextBlock* a 144-pixel size and started the animations offset from each other. The *TextBlock* alternately stretches out horizontally and vertically:

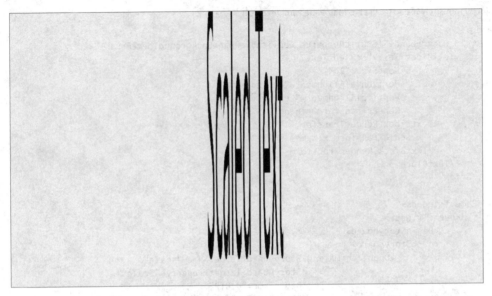

Scaling is like rotation in that it is always in reference to a center point. The *ScaleTransform* class defines *CenterX* and *CenterY* properties just like *RotateTransform*, or you can set *RenderTransformOrigin* as I've done in the *OppositelyScaledText* program. The scaling center is the point that remains in the same location when the scaling occurs.

Scaling and rotation centers play a big role in manipulating on-screen objects (such as photographs) with your fingers. As you stretch, pinch, and rotate a photograph, the scaling and rotation centers change as your fingers move relative to each other. I'll discuss the technique for calculating these rotation centers in Chapter 13.

Negative scaling factors flip an element around the horizontal or vertical axis. This technique is particularly useful for creating reflection effects. Unfortunately, the Windows Runtime is missing an important contributor to this effect: a *UIElement* property named *OpacityMask* of type *Brush* that allows defining a graduated opacity based on the alpha channel of the colors of a gradient brush. In the Windows Runtime, you'll have to mimic a graduated fade-out by covering up the element with another element that has a gradient brush incorporating transparency and the background color.

This is demonstrated in the ReflectedFadeOutImage project. The upper half of a *Grid* is shared by two items: an *Image* and another *Grid*. That second *Grid* contains the same *Image* covered by a

Rectangle with a *LinearGradientBrush* that fades from the background color at top to transparent at the bottom:

Project: ReflectedFadeOutImage | **File:** MainPage.xaml (excerpt)

```xaml
<Page ... >
    <Grid Background="{StaticResource ApplicationPageBackgroundThemeBrush}">
        <Grid.RowDefinitions>
            <RowDefinition Height="*" />
            <RowDefinition Height="*" />
        </Grid.RowDefinitions>

        <Image Source="http://www.charlespetzold.com/pw6/PetzoldJersey.jpg"
               HorizontalAlignment="Center" />

        <Grid RenderTransformOrigin="0 1"
              HorizontalAlignment="Center">
            <Grid.RenderTransform>
                <ScaleTransform ScaleY="-1" />
            </Grid.RenderTransform>
            <Image Source="http://www.charlespetzold.com/pw6/PetzoldJersey.jpg" />
            <Rectangle>
                <Rectangle.Fill>
                    <LinearGradientBrush StartPoint="0 0" EndPoint="0 1" >
                        <GradientStop Offset="0"
                            Color="{Binding
                                Source={StaticResource ApplicationPageBackgroundThemeBrush},
                                Path=Color}" />
                        <GradientStop Offset="1" Color="Transparent" />
                    </LinearGradientBrush>
                </Rectangle.Fill>
            </Rectangle>
        </Grid>
    </Grid>
</Page>
```

That inner *Grid* is also reflected around its bottom edge. The *RenderTransformOrigin* assigns a transform center at the lower left, and the *ScaleTransform* sets *ScaleY* to –1, which flips the element around the horizontal axis:

In Chapter 14, "Bitmaps," I'll demonstrate another way to achieve this effect accessing the pixels of a bitmap and setting the transparency appropriately.

Building an Analog Clock

An analog clock is round. This simple fact implies that drawing the clock would probably be mathematically easiest if you use arbitrary coordinates—that is, coordinates not in units of pixels but in units you choose for convenience—with the origin in the center. Putting the origin in the center also means you probably won't need to mess around with *CenterX* or *CenterY* settings for the *RotateTransform* objects that position the hands of the clock because the origin is also the center of rotation.

The traditional analog clock in a graphical environment adapts itself to whatever size it's given. It is tempting to use a *Viewbox* for this job, but with an analog clock that could be a problem. The layout system (and *Viewbox*) perceives the size of a vector graphics object to be the maximum *X* and *Y* values of its coordinate points. Negative coordinates are ignored, including those in three-quarters of an analog clock with an origin in the center.

The layout system (and *Viewbox*) will not correctly determine the size of graphics objects with negative coordinates, and a little "help" is required. Fortunately, transforms cascade from parent to child. You can set a transform on a *Grid*, and it will apply to everything in that *Grid*. The contents of the *Grid* can then have their own transforms.

That's what I've done in the AnalogClock program. All the graphics are in a *Grid* that is fixed in size with a 200-pixel *Width* and *Height* implying a 100-pixel radius:

```
<Grid Width="200" Height="200">

    ... clock graphics go here

</Grid>
```

Within that *Grid* are five *Path* elements that render the tick marks around the circumference of the clock, as well as the hour, minute, and second hands. These are all based on a coordinate system with *X* and *Y* values ranging from –100 to 100. If you could see that *Grid* (outlined here in red) and the clock, it would look like this:

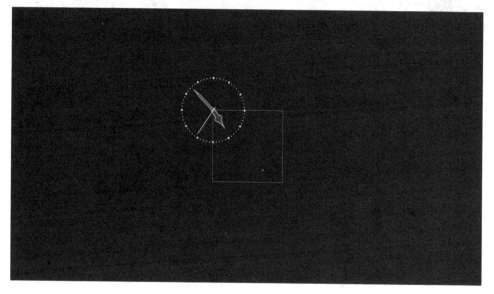

The *Grid* is positioned in the center of the page thanks to its default alignment, but the center of the clock is positioned at the upper-left corner of the *Grid* because that's where the point (0, 0) is.

Now let's put that *Grid* in a *Viewbox*, like so:

```
<Viewbox>
    <Grid Width="200" Height="200">

        ... clock graphics go here

    </Grid>
</Viewbox>
```

The *Viewbox* can correctly handle elements that have an origin at the upper-left corner but not graphics with negative coordinates:

Fortunately, the fix is fairly easy. All that's necessary is to shift the *Grid* and the clock. This transform occurs before the *Viewbox* gets ahold of the element, so it's merely by 100 pixels:

```
<Viewbox>
    <Grid Width="200" Height="200">
        <Grid.RenderTransform>
            <TranslateTransform X="100" Y="100" />
        </Grid.RenderTransform>

        ... clock graphics go here

    </Grid>
</Viewbox>
```

And here it is:

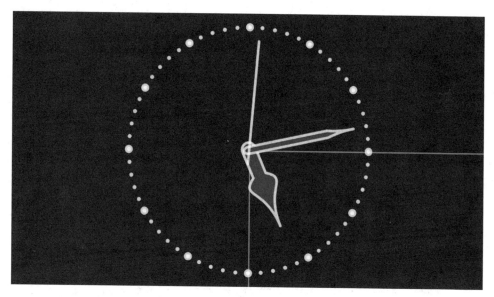

Now all that's needed is to get rid of that red border.

The clock consists of five *Path* elements. Each of the three hands is defined by path markup syntax consisting of straight lines and Bézier curves. Here's the hour hand pointing to the 12:00 position. Because the hand is initially mostly on the top half of this clock, most of the hand has negative *Y* coordinates with only a few positive *Y* coordinates as it loops around the center.

```
<Path Data="M 0 -60 C 0 -30, 20 -30, 5 -20 L 5 0
                     C 5 7.5, -5 7.5, -5 0 L -5 -20
                     C -20 -30, 0 -30, 0 -60">
    <Path.RenderTransform>
        <RotateTransform x:Name="rotateHour" />
    </Path.RenderTransform>
</Path>
```

The tick marks are actually dotted lines. Here's the *Path* element for the small tick marks:

```
<Path Fill="{x:Null}"
      StrokeThickness="3"
      StrokeDashArray="0 3.14159">
    <Path.Data>
        <EllipseGeometry RadiusX="90" RadiusY="90" />
    </Path.Data>
</Path>
```

This creates a circle with a radius of 90, so the circumference is 2π90, which means that the 60 tick marks are separated by 3π, which not coincidentally is the product of the *StrokeThickness* and number in the *StrokeDashArray* indicating the distance between the dots in units of the *StrokeThickness*.

Since you enjoyed that one, here's the *Path* for the large tick marks:

```
<Path Fill="{x:Null}"
      StrokeThickness="6"
      StrokeDashArray="0 7.854">
    <Path.Data>
        <EllipseGeometry RadiusX="90" RadiusY="90" />
    </Path.Data>
</Path>
```

Again, the circumference is 2π90, but there are only 12 tick marks, so they are separated by 15π, which is close enough to the product of 6 and 7.854. Here's everything put together:

Project: AnalogClock | File: MainPage.xaml (excerpt)

```
<Page ... >

    <Page.Resources>
        <Style TargetType="Path">
            <Setter Property="Stroke"
                    Value="{StaticResource ApplicationForegroundThemeBrush}" />
            <Setter Property="StrokeThickness" Value="2" />
            <Setter Property="StrokeStartLineCap" Value="Round" />
            <Setter Property="StrokeEndLineCap" Value="Round" />
            <Setter Property="StrokeLineJoin" Value="Round" />
            <Setter Property="StrokeDashCap" Value="Round" />
            <Setter Property="Fill" Value="Blue" />
        </Style>
    </Page.Resources>

    <Grid Background="{StaticResource ApplicationPageBackgroundThemeBrush}">

        <Viewbox>
            <!-- Grid containing all graphics based on (0, 0) origin, 100-pixel radius -->
            <Grid Width="200" Height="200">

                <!-- Transform for entire clock -->
                <Grid.RenderTransform>
                    <TranslateTransform X="100" Y="100" />
                </Grid.RenderTransform>

                <!-- Small tick marks -->
                <Path Fill="{x:Null}"
                      StrokeThickness="3"
                      StrokeDashArray="0 3.14159">
                    <Path.Data>
                        <EllipseGeometry RadiusX="90" RadiusY="90" />
                    </Path.Data>
                </Path>

                <!-- Large tick marks -->
                <Path Fill="{x:Null}"
                      StrokeThickness="6"
                      StrokeDashArray="0 7.854">
                    <Path.Data>
                        <EllipseGeometry RadiusX="90" RadiusY="90" />
                    </Path.Data>
                </Path>
```

```
<!-- Hour hand pointing straight up -->
<Path Data="M 0 -60 C 0 -30, 20 -30, 5 -20 L 5 0
                      C 5 7.5, -5 7.5, -5 0 L -5 -20
                      C -20 -30, 0 -30, 0 -60">
    <Path.RenderTransform>
        <RotateTransform x:Name="rotateHour" />
    </Path.RenderTransform>
</Path>

<!-- Minute hand pointing straight up -->
<Path Data="M 0 -80 C 0 -75, 0 -70, 2.5 -60 L 2.5 0
                      C 2.5 5, -2.5 5, -2.5 0 L -2.55 -60
                      C 0 -70, 0 -75, 0 -80">
    <Path.RenderTransform>
        <RotateTransform x:Name="rotateMinute" />
    </Path.RenderTransform>
</Path>

<!-- Second hand pointing straight up -->
<Path Data="M 0 10 L 0 -80">
    <Path.RenderTransform>
        <RotateTransform x:Name="rotateSecond" />
    </Path.RenderTransform>
</Path>
        </Grid>
    </Viewbox>
    </Grid>
</Page>
```

The code-behind file is responsible for calculating angles measured clockwise from 12:00 for the three *RotateTransform* objects:

Project: AnalogClock | File: MainPage.xaml.cs (excerpt)

```
public sealed partial class MainPage : Page
{
    public MainPage()
    {
        this.InitializeComponent();
        CompositionTarget.Rendering += OnCompositionTargetRendering;
    }

    void OnCompositionTargetRendering(object sender, object args)
    {
        DateTime dt = DateTime.Now;
        rotateSecond.Angle = 6 * (dt.Second + dt.Millisecond / 1000.0);
        rotateMinute.Angle = 6 * dt.Minute + rotateSecond.Angle / 60;
        rotateHour.Angle = 30 * (dt.Hour % 12) + rotateMinute.Angle / 12;
    }
}
```

This clock has a "sweep" second hand that seems to move continuously. If you prefer a "tick" second hand that jumps by seconds, you can simply remove the milliseconds from the calculation. But a better solution is using a *DispatcherTimer* with an interval of 1 second rather than *CompositionTarget.Rendering*, which always goes at the video refresh rate.

Skew

I discussed earlier that all the classes that derive from *Transform* are restricted to defining two-dimensional affine transforms, and one of the characteristics of an affine transform is the preservation of parallel lines. However, an affine transform does not necessarily preserve angles between lines. For example, an affine transform is capable of transforming a square to a parallelogram:

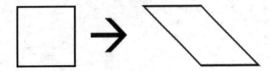

In the Windows Runtime, this type of transform is known as a *skew*, but in other graphics environments it might be called a *shear*. The figure is progressively shifted positively or negatively in the horizontal or vertical direction. In a sense, the skew is the most extreme of the affine transforms, but it still preserves a great deal of the original geometry. A skew transform applied to a circle or ellipse never results in anything other than an ellipse:

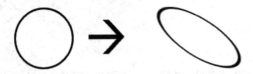

Similarly, a skewed Bézier curve remains a Bézier curve.

The *SkewTransform* has *AngleX* and *AngleY* properties that you set to an angle in degrees. The examples shown were created with a *SkewTransform* with *AngleX* set to 45 degrees, which skews the bottom to the right. Set the angle negative to skew the bottom to the left. For text, negative *AngleX* values create an oblique effect (similar to italic but without any typographical changes to the characters). Here's *AngleX* set to –30 degrees:

Nonzero settings of *AngleY* cause skew in the vertical direction. Positive values of *AngleY* cause the right side of figures to skew down:

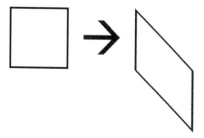

Negative values cause the right sides to skew up. By default, the upper-left corner of the figure stays in the same location with the skew, but you can change that with *CenterX* and *CenterY* properties or with *RenderTransformOrigin*.

The following program demonstrates what happens when you combine *AngleX* and *AngleY* skewing:

Project: SkewPlusSkew | File: MainPage.xaml (excerpt)

```
<Page ... >
    <Grid Background="{StaticResource ApplicationPageBackgroundThemeBrush}">
        <TextBlock Text="SKEW"
                   FontSize="288"
                   FontWeight="Bold"
                   HorizontalAlignment="Center"
                   VerticalAlignment="Center"
                   RenderTransformOrigin="0.5 0.5">
            <TextBlock.RenderTransform>
                <SkewTransform x:Name="skew" />
            </TextBlock.RenderTransform>
        </TextBlock>
    </Grid>

    <Page.Triggers>
        <EventTrigger>
            <BeginStoryboard>
                <Storyboard SpeedRatio="0.5" RepeatBehavior="Forever">
                    <DoubleAnimationUsingKeyFrames Storyboard.TargetName="skew"
                                                   Storyboard.TargetProperty="AngleX">

                        <!-- Back and forth for 4 seconds -->
                        <DiscreteDoubleKeyFrame KeyTime="0:0:0" Value="0" />
                        <LinearDoubleKeyFrame KeyTime="0:0:1" Value="90" />
                        <LinearDoubleKeyFrame KeyTime="0:0:2" Value="0" />
                        <LinearDoubleKeyFrame KeyTime="0:0:3" Value="-90" />
                        <LinearDoubleKeyFrame KeyTime="0:0:4" Value="0" />
```

```
            <!-- Do nothing for 4 seconds -->
            <DiscreteDoubleKeyFrame KeyTime="0:0:8" Value="0" />

            <!-- Back and forth for 4 seconds -->
            <LinearDoubleKeyFrame KeyTime="0:0:9" Value="90" />
            <LinearDoubleKeyFrame KeyTime="0:0:10" Value="0" />
            <LinearDoubleKeyFrame KeyTime="0:0:11" Value="-90" />
            <LinearDoubleKeyFrame KeyTime="0:0:12" Value="0" />
        </DoubleAnimationUsingKeyFrames>

        <DoubleAnimationUsingKeyFrames Storyboard.TargetName="skew"
                                 Storyboard.TargetProperty="AngleY">

            <!-- Do nothing for 4 seconds -->
            <DiscreteDoubleKeyFrame KeyTime="0:0:0" Value="0" />
            <DiscreteDoubleKeyFrame KeyTime="0:0:4" Value="0" />

            <!-- Back and forth for 4 seconds -->
            <LinearDoubleKeyFrame KeyTime="0:0:5" Value="-90" />
            <LinearDoubleKeyFrame KeyTime="0:0:6" Value="0" />
            <LinearDoubleKeyFrame KeyTime="0:0:7" Value="90" />
            <LinearDoubleKeyFrame KeyTime="0:0:8" Value="0" />

            <!-- Back and forth for 4 seconds -->
            <LinearDoubleKeyFrame KeyTime="0:0:9" Value="-90" />
            <LinearDoubleKeyFrame KeyTime="0:0:10" Value="0" />
            <LinearDoubleKeyFrame KeyTime="0:0:11" Value="90" />
            <LinearDoubleKeyFrame KeyTime="0:0:12" Value="0" />
        </DoubleAnimationUsingKeyFrames>
    </Storyboard>
   </BeginStoryboard>
  </EventTrigger>
 </Page.Triggers>
</Page>
```

I've set the *SpeedRatio* on the Storyboard to 0.5 so that you can better relish the effects, but I'll use the key frame times to discuss what's going on. During the first four seconds, the first animation animates the *AngleX* property to 90 degrees, back to zero, to –90 degrees, and back to zero. During the next four seconds the second animation animates the *AngleY* property between –90 and 90. During the final four seconds, the two animations go together.

You may or may not be surprised that combining *AngleX* and *AngleY* in this way results in rotation:

However, as a result of the mathematics, the figure gets larger as well.

Skew is often used to give a little 3D-like depth to elements, but it works best in combination with an unskewed element, as I'll demonstrate later in this chapter.

Making an Entrance

Sometimes you want an animated transform to occur on an element when a page is first loaded. For example, an element might slide in from the side and then come to rest, or expand in size, or spin in from above.

It's generally easiest to begin by positioning the element in its final location with no transforms. You can then define the transforms and animations so that the element ends up in that spot. Often you can simply leave out the *To* value of a *DoubleAnimation* on a transform because the *To* value is the same as the pre-animation default value.

This is demonstrated in the SkewSlideInText project. As you can see, the *TextBlock* has some transforms defined, but with default values the element simply sits in the center of the display. That's the final location and orientation of the *TextBlock*, and the animations conclude at that spot.

Project: SkewSlideInText | File: MainPage.xaml (excerpt)

```
<Page ... >
    <Grid Background="{StaticResource ApplicationPageBackgroundThemeBrush}">
        <TextBlock Text="Hello!"
                   FontSize="192"
                   HorizontalAlignment="Center"
                   VerticalAlignment="Center"
```

```
                    RenderTransformOrigin="0.5 1">
          <TextBlock.RenderTransform>
              <TransformGroup>
                  <SkewTransform x:Name="skew" />
                  <TranslateTransform x:Name="translate" />
              </TransformGroup>
          </TextBlock.RenderTransform>
      </TextBlock>
  </Grid>

  <Page.Triggers>
      <EventTrigger>
          <BeginStoryboard>
              <Storyboard>
                  <DoubleAnimation Storyboard.TargetName="translate"
                                   Storyboard.TargetProperty="X"
                                   From="-1000" Duration="0:0:1" />

                  <DoubleAnimationUsingKeyFrames
                                   Storyboard.TargetName="skew"
                                   Storyboard.TargetProperty="AngleX">
                      <DiscreteDoubleKeyFrame KeyTime="0:0:0" Value="15" />
                      <LinearDoubleKeyFrame KeyTime="0:0:1" Value="30" />
                      <EasingDoubleKeyFrame KeyTime="0:0:1.5" Value="0">
                          <EasingDoubleKeyFrame.EasingFunction>
                              <ElasticEase />
                          </EasingDoubleKeyFrame.EasingFunction>
                      </EasingDoubleKeyFrame>
                  </DoubleAnimationUsingKeyFrames>
              </Storyboard>
          </BeginStoryboard>
      </EventTrigger>
  </Page.Triggers>
</Page>
```

The *DoubleAnimation* applied to the *TranslateTransform* has a *From* value that starts the *TextBlock* 1000 pixels to the left of its final location. The absence of a *To* value means that the animation ends at the pre-animation value, which is 0.

As that's happening, a *DoubleAnimationUsingKeyFrames* makes the skew progress from an *AngleX* value of 15 degrees to 30 degrees, as if the *TextBlock* is being pulled into the center of the screen. The final key frame then animates the *AngleX* back to its pre-animation value of 0, shaking it back and forth in the process.

Transform Mathematics

I stated at the outset of this chapter that a transform is a formula that converts a point (x, y) into (x', y') and performs that conversion for all the points of an element. It's now time to look at that math.

Suppose a *TranslateTransform* has its *X* and *Y* properties set to *TX* and *TY*. The transform formulas add these translation factors to *x* and *y*:

$$x' = x + TX$$

$$y' = y + TY$$

If the *ScaleX* and *ScaleY* properties of a *ScaleTransform* are set to *SX* and *SY*, the transform formulas are also fairly obvious:

$$x' = SX \cdot x$$

$$y' = SY \cdot y$$

Now that we have the basics down, let's start combining transforms, such as in a *TransformGroup*. If the *ScaleTransform* occurs first, followed by the *TranslateTransform*, the formulas are:

$$x' = SX \cdot x + TX$$

$$y' = SY \cdot y + TY$$

But if the translate transform is applied first, followed by the scale transform, it's a little different:

$$x' = SX \cdot (x + TX)$$

$$y' = SY \cdot (y + TY)$$

The translation factors are now effectively multiplied by the scaling factors.

The *ScaleTransform* defines *ScaleX* and *ScaleY* properties but also *CenterX* and *CenterY*. I discussed earlier how the center point is used to construct two translations. The first translation is negative, which is then followed by the scale or rotation, followed by positive translation. Suppose *CenterX* and *CenterY* are set to the values *CX* and *CY*. The composite scaling formulas are:

$$x' = SX \cdot (x - CX) + CX$$

$$y' = SX \cdot (y - CY) + CY$$

You can easily confirm that the point (*CX*, *CY*) is transformed to the point (*CX*, *CY*), which is the characteristic of the center of scaling: the point that the transform leaves unchanged.

In all the cases so far, *x'* has depended solely on constants multiplied by and added to *x*, and *y'* has depended only on constants multiplied by and added to *y*. With rotation, it gets a bit messier because *x'* depends on both *x* and *y*, and *y'* also depends on both *x* and *y*. If the *Angle* property of a *RotateTransform* is set to *A*, the transform formulas are:

$$x' = \cos(A) \cdot x - \sin(A) \cdot y$$

$$y' = \sin(A) \cdot x + \cos(A) \cdot y$$

These formulas are pretty easy to confirm for simple cases. If A is zero, the formulas are just:

$$x' = x$$

$$y' = y$$

If A is 90 degrees, the sine is 1, and the cosine is 0, so

$$x' = -y$$

$$y' = x$$

For example, the point (1, 0) is transformed to (0, 1), and (0, 1) is transformed to (–1, 0). When A is 180 degrees, the sine is 0 and the cosine is –1, so

$$x' = -x$$

$$y' = -y$$

It's a reflection around the origin, and you can get the same effect with a *ScaleTransform* with *ScaleX* and *ScaleY* both set to –1. When A is 270 degrees,

$$x' = y$$

$$y' = -x$$

Here's the first diagram of a skew transform shown earlier:

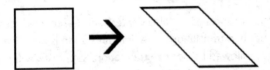

The transform formulas for this particular skew (*AngleX* set to 45 degrees) are

$$x' = x + y$$

$$y' = y$$

When y equals 0 (at the top of the figure), x' simply equals x and y' equals y. But as you move down the figure, y gets larger, so x' becomes increasing greater than x. The generalized formulas for *SkewTransform* when *AngleX* is set to *AX* and *AngleY* is set to *AY* are

$$x' = x + \sin(AX) \cdot y$$

$$y' = \sin(AY) \cdot x + y$$

When you begin exploring combinations of rotation with other transforms, this type of notation starts to become rather clumsy. Fortunately, matrix algebra comes to the rescue. When individual transforms are expressed as matrices, transforms can be combined through the well-established process of matrix multiplication.

Let's represent a point (x, y) as a 2×1 matrix:

$$\begin{vmatrix} x & y \end{vmatrix}$$

And let's represent the transform as a 2×2 matrix:

$$\begin{vmatrix} M11 & M12 \\ M21 & M22 \end{vmatrix}$$

Applying the transform can then be represented with a matrix multiplication. The result is the transformed point:

$$\begin{vmatrix} x & y \end{vmatrix} \times \begin{vmatrix} M11 & M12 \\ M21 & M22 \end{vmatrix} = \begin{vmatrix} x' & y' \end{vmatrix}$$

The rules of matrix multiplication imply the following formulas:

$$x' = M11 \cdot x + M21 \cdot y$$

$$y' = M12 \cdot x + M22 \cdot y$$

This process works for scaling if *M11* is the *ScaleX* value and *M22* is the *ScaleY* value, and *M21* and *M12* are zero. It also works for rotation and skewing, which both involve factors that are multiplied by *x* and *y*.

But it does not work for translation. The translation formulas look like this:

$$x' = x + TX$$

$$y' = y + TY$$

These translation factors are added in by themselves, not multiplied by *x* or *y*. How can we represent a generalized transform by a matrix if it doesn't allow for translation, which is arguably the simplest type of transform of them all?

The interesting solution is to introduce a third dimension. In addition to the *X* and *Y* axes on the plane of the computer screen, a conceptual *Z* axis extends out from the screen. Let's assume that we're still drawing on a two-dimensional plane, but that plane exists in 3D space with a constant *Z* coordinate equal to 1.

This means that the point (x, y) is actually the point $(x, y, 1)$ and we can represent it as a 3×1 matrix:

$$\begin{vmatrix} x & y & 1 \end{vmatrix}$$

The matrix transform is now a 3×3 matrix, and the multiplication looks like this:

$$\begin{vmatrix} x & y & 1 \end{vmatrix} \times \begin{vmatrix} M11 & M12 & M13 \\ M21 & M22 & M23 \\ M31 & M32 & M33 \end{vmatrix} = \begin{vmatrix} x' & y' & z' \end{vmatrix}$$

The formulas implied by the matrix multiplication are:

$$x' = M11 \cdot x + M21 \cdot y + M31$$

$$y' = M12 \cdot x + M22 \cdot y + M32$$

$$z' = M13 \cdot x + M23 \cdot y + M33$$

This is a partial success because the transform formulas now include translation factors of *M31* and *M32*. These two numbers aren't multiplied by *x* or *y*.

But it's not a total success because *z'* is generally not equal to 1, which means that we've shifted off the plane where *z* always equals 1. One way to get back to that plane is simply to set all those errant *z'* values to 1. But shouldn't points that are transformed a long distance away from the plane where *z* equals 1 be distinguished from those that end up close to it?

One clever way to get the *z* values to 1 without simply ignoring them is to take the 3×1 matrix result and divide all three coordinates by *z'*:

$$\left(\frac{x'}{z'}, \frac{y'}{z'}, \frac{z'}{z'} \right) = \left(\frac{x'}{z'}, \frac{y'}{z'}, 1 \right)$$

This approach to representing two-dimensional transforms with three-dimensional coordinates is called *homogenous coordinates*, and it was developed by August Möbius in the 1820s as a way to represent infinity, which results when *z'* is zero. But for us, infinite coordinates are a problem. If we want to avoid infinite coordinates, *z'* cannot be allowed to be zero. Indeed, we can avoid dividing by *z'* entirely if we ensure that *z'* is always equal to 1.

It's possible to do that by setting M13 and M23 in the matrix to 0 and M33 to 1. Now the transform is represented by formulas that remain entirely in the same plane:

$$\begin{vmatrix} x & y & 1 \end{vmatrix} \times \begin{vmatrix} M11 & M12 & 0 \\ M21 & M22 & 0 \\ M31 & M32 & 1 \end{vmatrix} = \begin{vmatrix} x' & y' & 1 \end{vmatrix}$$

This is the standard matrix representation of the two-dimensional affine transform. (Allowing other values in the third column results in a non-affine transform. Because such a matrix is capable of transforming parallel lines to nonparallel lines, it is sometimes also called a *taper* transform.)

With the notation I was using earlier, the *ScaleTransform* where *ScaleX* is set to *SX* and *ScaleY* is set to *SY* is

$$\begin{vmatrix} x & y & 1 \end{vmatrix} \times \begin{vmatrix} SX & 0 & 0 \\ 0 & SY & 0 \\ 0 & 0 & 1 \end{vmatrix} = \begin{vmatrix} x' & y' & 1 \end{vmatrix}$$

A *TranslateTransform* with *TX* and *TY* factors is

$$\begin{vmatrix} x & y & 1 \end{vmatrix} \times \begin{vmatrix} 1 & 0 & 0 \\ 0 & 1 & 0 \\ TX & TY & 1 \end{vmatrix} = \begin{vmatrix} x' & y' & 1 \end{vmatrix}$$

A *ScaleTransform* with center (*CX*, *CY*) is effectively a multiplication of three 3×3 transforms:

$$\begin{vmatrix} x & y & 1 \end{vmatrix} \times \begin{vmatrix} 1 & 0 & 0 \\ 0 & 1 & 0 \\ -CX & -CY & 1 \end{vmatrix} \times \begin{vmatrix} SX & 0 & 0 \\ 0 & SY & 0 \\ 0 & 0 & 1 \end{vmatrix} \times \begin{vmatrix} 1 & 0 & 0 \\ 0 & 1 & 0 \\ CX & CY & 1 \end{vmatrix} = \begin{vmatrix} x' & y' & 1 \end{vmatrix}$$

Similarly, a *RotateTransform* with angle *A* and center (*CX*, *CY*) also informs three transforms:

$$\begin{vmatrix} x & y & 1 \end{vmatrix} \times \begin{vmatrix} 1 & 0 & 0 \\ 0 & 1 & 0 \\ -CX & -CY & 1 \end{vmatrix} \times \begin{vmatrix} \cos(A) & \sin(A) & 0 \\ -\sin(A) & \cos(A) & 0 \\ 0 & 0 & 1 \end{vmatrix} \times \begin{vmatrix} 1 & 0 & 0 \\ 0 & 1 & 0 \\ CX & CY & 1 \end{vmatrix} = \begin{vmatrix} x' & y' & 1 \end{vmatrix}$$

And here's the *SkewTransform* with angles *AX* and *AY* and a center:

$$\begin{vmatrix} x & y & 1 \end{vmatrix} \times \begin{vmatrix} 1 & 0 & 0 \\ 0 & 1 & 0 \\ -CX & -CY & 1 \end{vmatrix} \times \begin{vmatrix} 1 & \sin(AY) & 0 \\ \sin(AX) & 1 & 0 \\ 0 & 0 & 1 \end{vmatrix} \times \begin{vmatrix} 1 & 0 & 0 \\ 0 & 1 & 0 \\ CX & CY & 1 \end{vmatrix} = \begin{vmatrix} x' & y' & 1 \end{vmatrix}$$

A well-known property of matrix multiplication is that it is not commutative. The order of multiplication makes a difference. This has already been demonstrated with translation and scaling. If the translation comes first, the translation factors themselves are also scaled by the scaling factors.

However, certain types of transforms can be safely multiplied in any order:

- Multiple *TranslateTransform* objects. The total translation is the sum of the individual translation factors.

- Multiple *ScaleTransform* objects with the same scaling center. The total scaling is the product of the individual scaling factors.

- Multiple *RotateTransforms* with the same rotation center. The total rotation is the sum of the angles of the individual rotations.

In addition, if a *ScaleTransform* has equal *ScaleX* and *ScaleY* properties, it can be multiplied by a *RotateTransform* or a *SkewTransform* in either order.

The Windows Runtime defines a *Matrix* structure that has six properties that correspond to the cells of the matrix like this:

$$\begin{vmatrix} M11 & M12 & 0 \\ M21 & M22 & 0 \\ OffsetX & OffsetY & 1 \end{vmatrix}$$

The last row of this matrix is fixed. You cannot use this *Matrix* structure to define a taper transform or anything "crazier" than what you've already seen. *OffsetX* and *OffsetY* are the translation properties. The default values for *M11* and *M22* are 1, and the default values for the other four properties are zero. That's the identity matrix with a diagonal of 1s:

$$\begin{vmatrix} 1 & 0 & 0 \\ 0 & 1 & 0 \\ 0 & 0 & 1 \end{vmatrix}$$

The *Matrix* structure has a static *Identity* property that returns this value and an *IsIdentity* property that returns *true* if the *Matrix* value is the identity matrix.

Along with the "easy" *Transform* derivatives like *ScaleTransform* and *RotateTransform*, there is also the low-level alternative *MatrixTransform*, which has a property of type *Matrix*. If you know the matrix transform you want, you can specify it directly in six numbers in the order *M11, M12, M21, M22, OffsetX, OffsetY*. Here's one way to set this transform:

```
<TextBlock ... >
    <TextBlock.RenderTransform>
        <MatrixTransform Matrix="10 0 0 5 0 100" />
    </TextBlock.RenderTransform>
</TextBlock>
```

This transform scales in the horizontal direction by a factor of 10 (*M11*) and in the vertical direction by a factor of 5 (*M22*), and then it shifts the *TextBlock* down by 100 pixels (*OffsetY*). But you can also set the transform directly to the *RenderTransform* property:

```
<TextBlock ...
            RenderTransform="10 0 0 5 0 100"
            ... />
```

The preview design view in Microsoft Visual Studio doesn't particularly care for this syntax, but it's no problem for the compiler or Windows 8.

Using this implicit form of *MatrixTransform* is handy for several common rotation transforms that are shown in the following program. Each *TextBlock* displays the transform applied to it:

Project: CommonMatrixTransforms | **File:** MainPage.xaml (excerpt)

```xml
<Page ... >
    <Page.Resources>
        <Style TargetType="TextBlock">
            <Setter Property="FontSize" Value="24" />
            <Setter Property="RenderTransformOrigin" Value="0 0.5" />
        </Style>
    </Page.Resources>

    <Grid Background="{StaticResource ApplicationPageBackgroundThemeBrush}">

        <!-- Move origin to center -->
        <Canvas HorizontalAlignment="Center"
                VerticalAlignment="Center">

            <TextBlock Text="  RenderTransform='1 0 0 1 0 0'"
                    RenderTransform="1 0 0 1 0 0" />

            <TextBlock Text="  RenderTransform='.7 .7 -.7 .7 0 0'"
                    RenderTransform=".7 .7 -.7 .7 0 0" />

            <TextBlock Text="  RenderTransform='0 1 -1 0 0 0'"
                    RenderTransform="0 1 -1 0 0 0" />

            <TextBlock Text="  RenderTransform='-.7 .7 -.7 -.7 0 0"
                    RenderTransform="-.7 .7 -.7 -.7 0 0" />

            <TextBlock Text="  RenderTransform='-1 0 0 -1 0 0'"
                    RenderTransform="-1 0 0 -1 0 0" />

            <TextBlock Text="  RenderTransform='-.7 -.7 .7 -.7 0 0'"
                    RenderTransform="-.7 -.7 .7 -.7 0 0" />

            <TextBlock Text="  RenderTransform='0 -1 1 0 0 0'"
                    RenderTransform="0 -1 1 0 0 0" />

            <TextBlock Text="  RenderTransform='.7 -.7 .7 .7 0 0"
                    RenderTransform=".7 -.7 .7 .7 0 0" />
        </Canvas>
    </Grid>
</Page>
```

The frequent references to .7 should more accurately be .707, the sine and cosine of 45 degrees and (not coincidentally) half the square root of 2. These eight transforms result in each *TextBlock* being rotated an additional 45 degrees from the previous one:

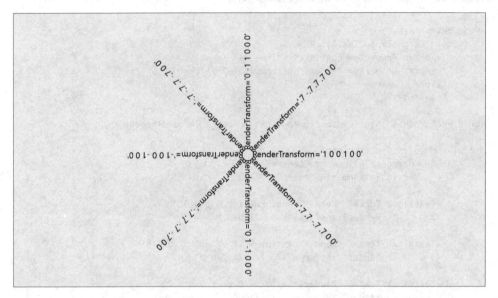

If you're working in code, the *Matrix* structure has a *Transform* method that applies the transform to a *Point* value and returns the transformed *Point*.

However, the *Matrix* structure is missing many amenities. It's missing a multiplication operator that would allow you to easily perform your own matrix multiplications in code. You could write the multiplication code yourself, or you can use *TransformGroup*, which internally performs matrix multiplications and makes the result available in a read-only *Value* property of type *Matrix*. If you need to perform matrix multiplications, you can create a *TransformGroup* in code, add a couple initialized *Transform* derivatives to it, and access the *Value* property.

I'll have an important example in Chapter 13. Matrix transform calculations become essential in computing scaling and rotation centers when using touch to manipulate on-screen objects.

The Composite Transform

When combining transforms of various types, the order makes a difference. In practical use, however, it turns out that you usually want various transforms to be applied in a fairly standard order.

For example, suppose you want to rotate, scale, and translate an element. *ScaleTransform* usually comes first because generally you want to specify the scaling in terms of the unrotated element. The *TranslateTransform* comes last because generally you don't want scaling or rotation to affect the translation factors. That means the *RotateTransform* is in the middle. The order is: scale, rotate, translate.

If that's the order you want, you can use *CompositeTransform*. *CompositeTransform* has a bunch of properties defined to perform transforms in the order:

- Scale
- Skew
- Rotate
- Translate

The properties are

- *CenterX* and *CenterY* for the center of scaling, skewing, and rotation
- *ScaleX* and *ScaleY*
- *SkewX* and *SkewY*
- *Rotation*
- *TranslateX* and *TranslateY*

Here's a little program that uses a *CompositeTransform* as a convenient way to combine scaling and skewing:

Project: TiltedShadow | **File:** MainPage.xaml (excerpt)

```
<Page ... >
    <Page.Resources>
        <Style TargetType="TextBlock">
            <Setter Property="Text" Value="quirky" />
            <Setter Property="FontFamily" Value="Times New Roman" />
            <Setter Property="FontSize" Value="192" />
            <Setter Property="HorizontalAlignment" Value="Center" />
            <Setter Property="VerticalAlignment" Value="Center" />
        </Style>
    </Page.Resources>
```

```
<Grid Background="{StaticResource ApplicationPageBackgroundThemeBrush}">
    <!-- Shadow TextBlock -->
    <TextBlock Foreground="Gray"
               RenderTransformOrigin="0 1">
        <TextBlock.RenderTransform>
            <CompositeTransform ScaleY="1.5" SkewX="-60" />
        </TextBlock.RenderTransform>
    </TextBlock>

    <!-- TextBlock with all styled properties -->
    <TextBlock />
</Grid>
</Page>
```

The XAML instantiates two *TextBlock* elements with mostly the same properties specified in the *Style*, including the *Text* property, and as far as the layout system is concerned, they both occupy the same space. The bottom one is gray, however, and has scale and skew transforms applied:

Notice that the *RenderTransformOrigin* is set to the point (0, 1), which means that the transform is relative to the lower-left corner. However, that point could be specified as (1, 1) or anything in between, and it would work the same. All that's required is that the two *TextBlock* elements share the same bottom edge. A *ScaleY* of 1.5 is applied to increase the height of the shadow by 50 percent. The *SkewX* value of –60 degrees should shift the bottom to the left, but because the bottom is the center of scaling and skewing, the top is skewed to the right.

Look closely and you'll notice that the bottoms of the descenders don't quite meet up. That's because the *TextBlock* actually extends a little below the bottom of the descenders. Change the *RenderTransformOrigin* to (0, 0.96) for a somewhat better match.

What if you wanted a similar effect with text with no descenders? Here's an example:

The problem is that you need to come up with a *RenderTransformOrigin* with a *Y* value equal to the relative height of the text above the baseline. That's dependent on the font. For this particular screenshot, I experimented until I came up with (0, 0.78), but that's appropriate only for the Times New Roman font. To do something like this in a generalized way, you'd need access to font metrics, which are available to a Windows 8 application only through DirectX. I'll show you how to do that in Chapter 15, "Going Native."

Geometry Transforms

The *Geometry* class defines a *Transform* property, which naturally raises the question: What is the difference between applying a transform to a *Path* element and applying a transform to a *Geometry* object that is set to the *Data* property of a *Path*?

The big difference is that a *Transform* applied to the *RenderTransform* property of a *Path* increases the width of the strokes, whereas a *Transform* applied to the *Geometry* does not.

Here's a *Path* element based on a *RectangleGeometry* with a height and width of 10 but with a transform applied to the geometry to increase it by a factor of 20:

```
<Path Stroke="Black"
      StrokeThickness="1"
      StrokeDashArray="1 1">
   <Path.Data>
      <RectangleGeometry Rect="0 0 10 10"
                         Transform="20 0 0 20 0 0" />
   </Path.Data>
</Path>
```

The result is as if the *Rect* value in the *RectangleGeometry* had a height and width of 200:

This XAML has the same initial *RectangleGeometry* but the transform is applied to the *Path*:

```
<Path Stroke="Black"
      StrokeThickness="1"
      StrokeDashArray="1 1"
      RenderTransform="20 0 0 20 0 0">
    <Path.Data>
        <RectangleGeometry Rect="0 0 10 10" />
    </Path.Data>
</Path>
```

The result is quite different:

To the layout system, however, these elements appear to be identical. Both *Path* elements are perceived to have a width and height of 10.

Brush Transforms

The *Brush* class defines two transform-related properties: *Transform* and *RelativeTransform*, which are distinguished by letting you specify translation factors based on the pixel size of the brush or relative to its size. *RelativeTransform* is often easier to use unless you've given the brushed element a specific pixel size.

Here's a program that replicates the RainbowEight program from Chapter 3, "Basic Event Handling," but using an animated brush transform. I've substituted a *Path* rendition of the 8 rather than using a *TextBlock* because I couldn't get the brush to repeat with the *SpreadMethod* property of *Repeat* for a *TextBlock*.

Project: RainbowEightTransform | File: MainPage.xaml (excerpt)

```xml
<Page ... >
    <Grid Background="{StaticResource ApplicationPageBackgroundThemeBrush}">
        <Viewbox>
            <Path StrokeThickness="50"
                  Margin="0 25 0 0">
                <Path.Data>
                    <PathGeometry>
                        <PathFigure StartPoint="110 0">
                            <ArcSegment Size="90 90" Point="110 180"
                                        SweepDirection="Clockwise" />
                            <ArcSegment Size="110 110" Point="110 400"
                                        SweepDirection="Counterclockwise" />
                            <ArcSegment Size="110 110" Point="110 180"
                                        SweepDirection="Counterclockwise" />
                            <ArcSegment Size="90 90" Point="110 0"
                                        SweepDirection="Clockwise" />
                        </PathFigure>
                    </PathGeometry>
                </Path.Data>
                <Path.Stroke>
                    <LinearGradientBrush StartPoint="0 0" EndPoint="1 1"
                                         SpreadMethod="Repeat">
                        <LinearGradientBrush.RelativeTransform>
                            <TranslateTransform x:Name="translate" />
                        </LinearGradientBrush.RelativeTransform>

                        <GradientStop Offset="0.00" Color="Red" />
                        <GradientStop Offset="0.14" Color="Orange" />
                        <GradientStop Offset="0.28" Color="Yellow" />
                        <GradientStop Offset="0.43" Color="Green" />
                        <GradientStop Offset="0.57" Color="Blue" />
                        <GradientStop Offset="0.71" Color="Indigo" />
                        <GradientStop Offset="0.86" Color="Violet" />
                        <GradientStop Offset="1.00" Color="Red" />
                    </LinearGradientBrush>
                </Path.Stroke>
            </Path>
        </Viewbox>
    </Grid>

    <Page.Triggers>
        <EventTrigger>
            <BeginStoryboard>
                <Storyboard>
                    <DoubleAnimation Storyboard.TargetName="translate"
                                     Storyboard.TargetProperty="Y"
                                     EnableDependentAnimation="True"
                                     From="0" To="-1.36" Duration="0:0:10"
                                     RepeatBehavior="Forever" />
```

```
            </Storyboard>
        </BeginStoryboard>
    </EventTrigger>
</Page.Triggers>
</Page>
```

Here's the image:

There's a "magic number" in the markup. It's the *To* value of the *DoubleAnimation*. That's the value that is applied to the *Y* property of the *TranslateTransform*, and it was chosen so that the translated brush with that value is identical to the untranslated brush. The magic number, you can see, is –1.36, and I'm sure you want to know where it came from.

If the *LinearGradientBrush* went from top to bottom—with a *StartPoint* of (0, 0) and an *EndPoint* of (0, 1)—this *To* value would simply be –1. If the gradient went from left to right—with a *StartPoint* of (0, 0) and an *EndPoint* of (1, 0)—the *X* property of the *TranslateTransform* would be the animation target, and again a *To* value of 1 or –1 would be used.

But when the gradient goes from one corner to the opposite—with the default *StartPoint* of (0, 0) and *EndPoint* of (1, 1)—then that's not quite right. When covering a *Path* element with a brush, the Windows Runtime computes a bounding rectangle that includes the geometric size of the element plus the stroke width. The brush is then stretched to this bounding rectangle:

The gradient line runs along the diagonal, which means that lines of constant color are at right angles to this gradient line.

When the brush has a *SpreadMethod* of *Repeat*, the brush conceptually repeats beyond the specified offsets. This *SpreadMethod* setting is useful when applying a *TranslateTransform* to the brush because the brush seems to repeat regardless how it's shifted.

If you shift this brush up by the height of the element (that is, a Y value of –1 in the *TranslateTransform*), the bottom edge of the untransformed brush becomes the top edge of the transformed brush, but you can see the result in the following image, and it's not the same as the previous image:

To get a smooth animation, you need to shift it up some more. But by how much?

Let's extend this figure to show part of the repeating brush, and let's label the width of the element with 'w', the height with 'h', the diagonal with 'd', and the increase in height with 'Δh'.

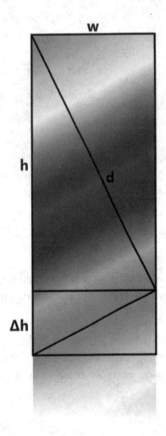

You can figure out Δh in a variety of ways, but perhaps the most straightforward is based on similar triangles:

$$\frac{d}{h} = \frac{h + \Delta h}{d}$$

from which it's easy to derive

$$\Delta h = \frac{w^2}{h}$$

or, the number we really want:

$$\frac{h + \Delta h}{h} = 1 + \left(\frac{w}{h}\right)^2$$

Try plugging in the numbers from the *Path* shown earlier. You'll need to add the *StrokeThickness* to the widths and heights of the geometry. With a width of 270 and a height of 450, Δh is 162. Add that to *h* and divide by *h*, and that's the magic number of 1.36.

Would you like to hear about an easier approach? Simply use two *DoubleAnimation* objects in the *Storyboard*, where one targets the *Y* property and the other targets *X*. Set the *To* value of both to –1 and the brush shifts both up and left with every cycle.

Dude, Where's My Element?

Earlier I mentioned that a computed *Matrix* value is available from *TransformGroup*, but it's not available from other sources where you might expect it. For example, *GeneralTransform*—from which *Transform* and all the other transform classes derive—might be expected to have a *Matrix* property, but it does not.

However, the *GeneralTransform* class has a *TransformPoint* method and a *TransformBounds* method, which applies the transform to a *Rect* value, and these actually come in handy in some circumstances.

Suppose an element is a child of a panel. The panel is responsible for positioning the element relative to itself, but the element could also have a *RenderTransform* applied with translation, scale, rotation, or skewing. For purposes of hit-testing, the location and orientation of that element are known internal to the system. But can your own program find where the element is actually located?

Yes! The essential (but obscure) method is defined by *UIElement* and called *TransformToVisual*. Generally, you'll call this method on an element with an argument that is the element's parent or some other ancestor:

```
GeneralTransform xform = element.TransformToVisual(parent);
```

The *GeneralTransform* object returned from the method maps from *element* coordinates to *parent* coordinates. But you can't actually see what this transform is! It won't give you a *Matrix* value. All you can do with it is call *TransformPoint* or *TransformBounds* or use the *Inverse* property. But this is often all you need.

Here's a XAML file that animates properties of a *CompositeTransform* to make a *TextBlock* go crazy all over the screen:

Project: WheresMyElement | File: MainPage.xaml (excerpt)

```
<Page ... >
    <Grid Name="contentGrid"
          Background="{StaticResource ApplicationPageBackgroundThemeBrush}">
        <TextBlock Name="txtblk"
                   Text="Tap to Find"
                   FontSize="96"
                   HorizontalAlignment="Center"
                   VerticalAlignment="Center"
                   RenderTransformOrigin="0.5 0.5">
```

```
            <TextBlock.RenderTransform>
                <CompositeTransform x:Name="transform" />
            </TextBlock.RenderTransform>
        </TextBlock>

        <Polygon Name="polygon" Stroke="Blue" />
        <Path Name="path" Stroke="Red" />
    </Grid>

    <Page.Triggers>
        <EventTrigger>
            <BeginStoryboard>
                <Storyboard x:Name="storyboard">
                    <DoubleAnimation Storyboard.TargetName="transform"
                                Storyboard.TargetProperty="TranslateX"
                                From="-300" To="300" Duration="0:0:2.11"
                                AutoReverse="True" RepeatBehavior="Forever" />
                    <DoubleAnimation Storyboard.TargetName="transform"
                                Storyboard.TargetProperty="TranslateY"
                                From="-300" To="300" Duration="0:0:2.23"
                                AutoReverse="True" RepeatBehavior="Forever" />
                    <DoubleAnimation Storyboard.TargetName="transform"
                                Storyboard.TargetProperty="Rotation"
                                From="0" To="360" Duration="0:0:2.51"
                                AutoReverse="True" RepeatBehavior="Forever" />
                    <DoubleAnimation Storyboard.TargetName="transform"
                                Storyboard.TargetProperty="ScaleX"
                                From="1" To="2" Duration="0:0:2.77"
                                AutoReverse="True" RepeatBehavior="Forever" />
                    <DoubleAnimation Storyboard.TargetName="transform"
                                Storyboard.TargetProperty="ScaleY"
                                From="1" To="2" Duration="0:0:3.07"
                                AutoReverse="True" RepeatBehavior="Forever" />
                    <DoubleAnimation Storyboard.TargetName="transform"
                                Storyboard.TargetProperty="SkewX"
                                From="-30" To="30" Duration="0:0:3.31"
                                AutoReverse="True" RepeatBehavior="Forever" />
                    <DoubleAnimation Storyboard.TargetName="transform"
                                Storyboard.TargetProperty="SkewY"
                                From="-30" To="30" Duration="0:0:3.53"
                                AutoReverse="True" RepeatBehavior="Forever" />
                </Storyboard>
            </BeginStoryboard>
        </EventTrigger>
    </Page.Triggers>
</Page>
```

Notice that the *Grid* also contains a blue *Polygon* and a red *Path*, but with no actual coordinate points.

The code-behind file uses the *Tapped* event to take a "snapshot" of the *TextBlock* by calling *TransformToVisual* and pausing the *Storyboard* (resumed on the next tap). *TransformToVisual* returns a *GeneralTransform* object that describes the relationship between the *TextBlock* and the *Grid*. The program uses this to transform the four corners of the *TextBlock* to *Grid* coordinates for the *Polygon*, which effectively draws a rectangle around the *TextBlock*:

Project: WheresMyElement | **File:** MainPage.xaml.cs (excerpt)

```
public sealed partial class MainPage : Page
{
    bool storyboardPaused;

    public MainPage()
    {
        this.InitializeComponent();
    }

    protected override void OnTapped(TappedRoutedEventArgs args)
    {
        if (storyboardPaused)
        {
            storyboard.Resume();
            storyboardPaused = false;
            return;
        }

        GeneralTransform xform = txtblk.TransformToVisual(contentGrid);

        // Draw blue polygon around element
        polygon.Points.Clear();
        polygon.Points.Add(xform.TransformPoint(new Point(0, 0)));
        polygon.Points.Add(xform.TransformPoint(new Point(txtblk.ActualWidth, 0)));
        polygon.Points.Add(xform.TransformPoint(new Point(txtblk.ActualWidth,
                                                txtblk.ActualHeight)));
        polygon.Points.Add(xform.TransformPoint(new Point(0, txtblk.ActualHeight)));

        // Draw red bounding box
        path.Data = new RectangleGeometry
        {
            Rect = xform.TransformBounds(new Rect(new Point(0, 0), txtblk.DesiredSize))
        };

        storyboard.Pause();
        storyboardPaused = true;
        base.OnTapped(args);
    }
}
```

The call to *TransformBounds* obtains something a little different: a rectangle describing a boundary box with sides parallel to the horizontal and vertical large enough to encompass the element. This is drawn in red:

That boundary rectangle is easily calculable from the maximum and minimum *X* and *Y* coordinates of the transformed four corners, but it's nice to have it conveniently available.

Projection Transforms

Earlier in this chapter I discussed why a two-dimensional graphics transform is mathematically described by a 3×3 matrix and requires a flirtation with the third dimension. By a similar analogy, a three-dimensional graphics transform is expressed by a 4×4 matrix, and the Windows Runtime has one.

The *Windows.UI.Xaml.Media.Media3D* namespace contains exactly two items: a *Matrix3D* structure available for all programmers, and a *Matrix3DHelper* class that's mostly of value to C++ programmers because they can't access any of the methods defined by *Matrix3D*. The properties of *Matrix3D* are analogous to those in the regular *Matrix* structure except that every cell of the matrix is available:

$$
\begin{vmatrix}
M11 & M12 & M13 & M14 \\
M21 & M22 & M23 & M24 \\
M31 & M32 & M33 & M34 \\
OffsetX & OffsetY & OffsetZ & M44
\end{vmatrix}
$$

However, few programmers ever really get close to this matrix. Most of them are content to use the *PlaneProjection* class that I briefly demonstrated at the beginning of this chapter.

PlaneProjection is intended mostly to let you rotate two-dimensional elements in three-dimensional space. Rotation in 3D space is always around an axis, and *PlaneProjection* lets you rotate an element around a horizontal axis (using the *RotationX* property), the vertical axis (with *RotationY*), or the *Z* axis that conceptually pokes out of the screen. Rotation around the *Z* axis is simply two-dimensional rotation, so that's not nearly as exciting as the other two.

You can anticipate the direction of rotation using the right-hand rule: Point the thumb of your right hand in the direction of the positive axis. That's right for the *X* axis, down for the *Y* axis, and out of the screen for *Z*. The curve of your fingers indicates the direction of rotation for positive angles. *PlaneProjection* applies the rotations in the order *X*, *Y*, and *Z*, but generally you'll be using only one of them.

With a little discreet use of *PlaneProjection*, you can have elements swing into view or even conceptually flip over to reveal something on the "other side" (as I'll demonstrate shortly).

And then there's the not-so-discreet uses. The ThreeDeeSpinningText program lets you independently animate the *RotationX*, *RotationY*, and *RotationZ* properties to spin a *TextBlock* around in 3D space. Here's the XAML file with a group of Begin/Stop and Play/Pause buttons at the bottom:

Project: ThreeDeeSpinningText | File: MainPage.xaml (excerpt)

```
<Page ... >
    <Page.Resources>
        <Storyboard x:Key="xAxisAnimation" RepeatBehavior="Forever">
            <DoubleAnimation Storyboard.TargetName="projection"
                             Storyboard.TargetProperty="RotationX"
                             From="0" To="360" Duration="0:0:1.9" />
        </Storyboard>

        <Storyboard x:Key="yAxisAnimation" RepeatBehavior="Forever">
            <DoubleAnimation Storyboard.TargetName="projection"
                             Storyboard.TargetProperty="RotationY"
                             From="0" To="360" Duration="0:0:3.1" />
        </Storyboard>

        <Storyboard x:Key="zAxisAnimation" RepeatBehavior="Forever">
            <DoubleAnimation Storyboard.TargetName="projection"
                             Storyboard.TargetProperty="RotationZ"
                             From="0" To="360" Duration="0:0:4.3" />
        </Storyboard>
    </Page.Resources>

    <Grid Background="{StaticResource ApplicationPageBackgroundThemeBrush}">
        <Grid.RowDefinitions>
            <RowDefinition Height="*" />
            <RowDefinition Height="Auto" />
        </Grid.RowDefinitions>

        <TextBlock Text="3D-ish"
                   FontSize="384"
                   HorizontalAlignment="Center"
                   VerticalAlignment="Center">
            <TextBlock.Projection>
```

```xml
                <PlaneProjection x:Name="projection" />
            </TextBlock.Projection>
        </TextBlock>

        <!-- Control Panel -->
        <Grid Grid.Row="1" HorizontalAlignment="Center">
            <Grid.RowDefinitions>
                <RowDefinition Height="Auto" />
                <RowDefinition Height="Auto" />
                <RowDefinition Height="Auto" />
            </Grid.RowDefinitions>

            <Grid.ColumnDefinitions>
                <ColumnDefinition Width="Auto" />
                <ColumnDefinition Width="Auto" />
                <ColumnDefinition Width="Auto" />
            </Grid.ColumnDefinitions>

            <Grid.Resources>
                <Style TargetType="TextBlock">
                    <Setter Property="FontSize"
                            Value="{StaticResource ControlContentThemeFontSize}" />
                    <Setter Property="VerticalAlignment" Value="Center" />
                </Style>

                <Style TargetType="Button">
                    <Setter Property="Width" Value="120" />
                    <Setter Property="Margin" Value="12" />
                </Style>
            </Grid.Resources>

            <TextBlock Text="X Axis: " Grid.Row="0" Grid.Column="0"
                       Tag="xAxisAnimation" />
            <Button Content="Begin" Grid.Row="0" Grid.Column="1"
                    Click="OnBeginStopButton" />
            <Button Content="Pause" Grid.Row="0" Grid.Column="2"
                    IsEnabled="False"
                    Click="OnPauseResumeButton" />

            <TextBlock Text="Y Axis: " Grid.Row="1" Grid.Column="0"
                       Tag="yAxisAnimation" />
            <Button Content="Begin" Grid.Row="1" Grid.Column="1"
                    Click="OnBeginStopButton" />
            <Button Content="Pause" Grid.Row="1" Grid.Column="2"
                    IsEnabled="False"
                    Click="OnPauseResumeButton" />

            <TextBlock Text="Z Axis: " Grid.Row="2" Grid.Column="0"
                       Tag="zAxisAnimation" />
            <Button Content="Begin" Grid.Row="2" Grid.Column="1"
                    Click="OnBeginStopButton" />
            <Button Content="Pause" Grid.Row="2" Grid.Column="2"
                    IsEnabled="False"
                    Click="OnPauseResumeButton" />

        </Grid>
    </Grid>
</Page>
```

The durations of the individual *DoubleAnimation* objects all have somewhat different times to avoid repetitive patterns when they're all going at once. The buttons in the code-behind file use the *Begin*, *Stop*, *Pause*, and *Resume* methods of *Storyboard* to control the activity:

Project: ThreeDeeSpinningText | File: MainPage.xaml.cs (excerpt)

```csharp
public sealed partial class MainPage : Page
{
    public MainPage()
    {
        this.InitializeComponent();
    }

    void OnBeginStopButton(object sender, RoutedEventArgs args)
    {
        Button btn = sender as Button;
        string key = GetSibling(btn, -1).Tag as string;
        Storyboard storyboard = this.Resources[key] as Storyboard;
        Button pauseResumeButton = GetSibling(btn, 1) as Button;
        pauseResumeButton.Content = "Pause";

        if (btn.Content as string == "Begin")
        {
            storyboard.Begin();
            btn.Content = "Stop";
            pauseResumeButton.IsEnabled = true;
        }
        else
        {
            storyboard.Stop();
            btn.Content = "Begin";
            pauseResumeButton.IsEnabled = false;
        }
    }

    void OnPauseResumeButton(object sender, RoutedEventArgs args)
    {
        Button btn = sender as Button;
        string key = GetSibling(btn, -2).Tag as string;
        Storyboard storyboard = this.Resources[key] as Storyboard;

        if (btn.Content as string == "Pause")
        {
            storyboard.Pause();
            btn.Content = "Resume";
        }
        else
        {
            storyboard.Resume();
            btn.Content = "Pause";
        }
    }

    FrameworkElement GetSibling(FrameworkElement element, int relativeIndex)
    {
        Panel parent = element.Parent as Panel;
        int index = parent.Children.IndexOf(element);
```

```
            return parent.Children[index + relativeIndex] as FrameworkElement;
        }
}
```

And here's a sample image:

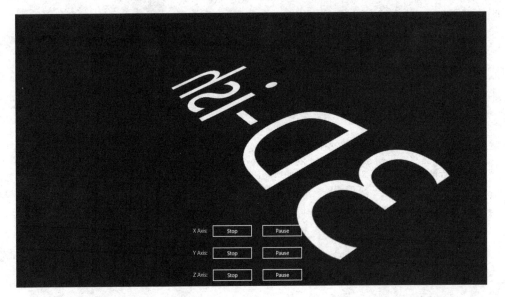

The *PlaneProjection* class has a bunch of additional properties. The *CenterOfRotationX* and *CenterOfRotationY* properties are both in coordinates relative to the element. The default values are 0.5, which is the center of the element and usually what you want. The *CenterOfRotationZ* property is in pixels with a default value of 0, corresponding to the surface of the screen. For purposes of internal calculations, it is assumed that the "camera" (or you, the user) is viewing the screen from a distance of 1000 pixels, or about 10 inches.

PlaneProjection also defines three *LocalOffset* properties for the *X*, *Y*, and *Z* dimensions and three *GlobalOffset* properties. These are translation factors in pixels. The *LocalOffset* values are applied before the rotation, and the *GlobalOffset* values are applied after the rotation. Most often, you'll be setting the *GlobalOffset* properties.

Here's a little example of a "flip panel," a technique that was once quite difficult and involved real 3D programming. The idea is that you have a little collection of controls on a panel and a way to flip that panel over to use a different (but related) set of controls. In this example, I've represented the front and "back" of this panel with two *Grid* panels with different background colors containing a *TextBlock* each:

Project: TapToFlip | File: MainPage.xaml (excerpt)

```
<Grid Background="{StaticResource ApplicationPageBackgroundThemeBrush}">
    <Grid HorizontalAlignment="Center"
        VerticalAlignment="Center"
        Tapped="OnGridTapped">

        <Grid Name="grid1"
```

```
            Background="Cyan"
            Canvas.ZIndex="1">
        <TextBlock Text="Hello"
                   HorizontalAlignment="Center"
                   FontSize="192" />
    </Grid>

    <Grid Name="grid2"
          Background="Yellow"
          Canvas.ZIndex="0">
        <TextBlock Text="Windows 8"
                   FontSize="192" />
    </Grid>

    <Grid.Projection>
        <PlaneProjection x:Name="projection" />
    </Grid.Projection>
    </Grid>
</Grid>
```

Notice the *Canvas.ZIndex* settings. These ensure that the *grid1* is visually on top of *grid2* even though it comes earlier in the children collection of their mutual parent.

The *Resources* section contains two *Storyboard* definitions, one to flip and the other to flip back:

Project: TapToFlip | **File:** MainPage.xaml (excerpt)

```
<Page.Resources>
    <Storyboard x:Key="flipStoryboard">
        <DoubleAnimationUsingKeyFrames
                       Storyboard.TargetName="projection"
                       Storyboard.TargetProperty="RotationY">
            <DiscreteDoubleKeyFrame KeyTime="0:0:0" Value="0" />
            <LinearDoubleKeyFrame KeyTime="0:0:0.99" Value="90" />
            <DiscreteDoubleKeyFrame KeyTime="0:0:1.01" Value="-90" />
            <LinearDoubleKeyFrame KeyTime="0:0:2" Value="0" />
        </DoubleAnimationUsingKeyFrames>

        <DoubleAnimation Storyboard.TargetName="projection"
                       Storyboard.TargetProperty="GlobalOffsetZ"
                       From="0" To="-1000" Duration="0:0:1"
                       AutoReverse="True" />

        <ObjectAnimationUsingKeyFrames
                       Storyboard.TargetName="grid1"
                       Storyboard.TargetProperty="(Canvas.ZIndex)">
            <DiscreteObjectKeyFrame KeyTime="0:0:0" Value="1" />
            <DiscreteObjectKeyFrame KeyTime="0:0:1" Value="0" />
        </ObjectAnimationUsingKeyFrames>

        <ObjectAnimationUsingKeyFrames
                       Storyboard.TargetName="grid2"
                       Storyboard.TargetProperty="(Canvas.ZIndex)">
            <DiscreteObjectKeyFrame KeyTime="0:0:0" Value="0" />
            <DiscreteObjectKeyFrame KeyTime="0:0:1" Value="1" />
        </ObjectAnimationUsingKeyFrames>
    </Storyboard>
```

```
<Storyboard x:Key="flipBackStoryboard">
    <DoubleAnimationUsingKeyFrames
                    Storyboard.TargetName="projection"
                    Storyboard.TargetProperty="RotationY">
        <DiscreteDoubleKeyFrame KeyTime="0:0:0" Value="0" />
        <LinearDoubleKeyFrame KeyTime="0:0:0.99" Value="-90" />
        <DiscreteDoubleKeyFrame KeyTime="0:0:1.01" Value="90" />
        <LinearDoubleKeyFrame KeyTime="0:0:2" Value="0" />
    </DoubleAnimationUsingKeyFrames>

    <DoubleAnimation Storyboard.TargetName="projection"
                    Storyboard.TargetProperty="GlobalOffsetZ"
                    From="0" To="-1000" Duration="0:0:1"
                    AutoReverse="True" />

    <ObjectAnimationUsingKeyFrames
                    Storyboard.TargetName="grid1"
                    Storyboard.TargetProperty="(Canvas.ZIndex)">
        <DiscreteObjectKeyFrame KeyTime="0:0:0" Value="0" />
        <DiscreteObjectKeyFrame KeyTime="0:0:1" Value="1" />
    </ObjectAnimationUsingKeyFrames>

    <ObjectAnimationUsingKeyFrames
                    Storyboard.TargetName="grid2"
                    Storyboard.TargetProperty="(Canvas.ZIndex)">
        <DiscreteObjectKeyFrame KeyTime="0:0:0" Value="1" />
        <DiscreteObjectKeyFrame KeyTime="0:0:1" Value="0" />
    </ObjectAnimationUsingKeyFrames>
    </Storyboard>
</Page.Resources>
```

These two storyboards are very similar. Each of them contains a *DoubleAnimationUsingKeyFrames* to target the *RotationY* property of the *PlaneProjection* object. The property is rotated from 0 to either 90 or –90 degrees (at which point it's at right angles to the user), and then it's switched 180 degrees so that the animation can continue in the same direction back to 0.

At the same time, the *GlobalOffsetZ* property is animated from 0 to –1000 and back to 0. This makes it seem as if the panel is dropping behind the screen in preparation for performing the flip (perhaps so that the flipping panel won't smack the user in the nose).

Halfway through each *Storyboard*, the *Canvas.ZIndex* indices are swapped. The *Canvas.ZIndex* property is another appropriate target of an *ObjectAnimationUsingKeyFrames*.

The animations are triggered by a tap, which is handled in the code-behind file:

Project: TapToFlip | File: MainPage.xaml.cs (excerpt)

```
public sealed partial class MainPage : Page
{
    Storyboard flipStoryboard, flipBackStoryboard;
    bool flipped = false;

    public MainPage()
    {
```

```
        this.InitializeComponent();
        flipStoryboard = this.Resources["flipStoryboard"] as Storyboard;
        flipBackStoryboard = this.Resources["flipBackStoryboard"] as Storyboard;
    }

    void OnGridTapped(object sender, TappedRoutedEventArgs args)
    {
        if (flipStoryboard.GetCurrentState() == ClockState.Active ||
            flipBackStoryboard.GetCurrentState() == ClockState.Active)
        {
            return;
        }

        Storyboard storyboard = flipped ? flipBackStoryboard : flipStoryboard;
        storyboard.Begin();
        flipped ^= true;
    }
}
```

Much of the logic here is to prevent one *Storyboard* from starting when the previous one hasn't yet finished. With the way these storyboards are defined, that would cause discontinuities. (Try removing the *return* statement from *OnGridTapped* to see the unsatisfactory result.) I would prefer that a tap while an animation is in progress simply reverses the operation, but that would require somewhat more complex logic.

Deriving a *Matrix3D*

Let's get into some hairy math, OK?

As you discovered earlier, two-dimensional graphics requires a 3×3 transform matrix to accommodate translation as well as scaling, rotation, and skew. Conceptually, a point (x, y) is treated as if it exists in 3D space with the coordinates $(x, y, 1)$.

The application of the generalized two-dimensional affine transform looks like this:

$$\begin{vmatrix} x & y & 1 \end{vmatrix} \times \begin{vmatrix} M11 & M12 & 0 \\ M21 & M22 & 0 \\ OffsetX & OffsetY & 1 \end{vmatrix} = \begin{vmatrix} x' & y' & 1 \end{vmatrix}$$

Those are the actual fields of the *Matrix* structure provided for this purpose. The fixed third column restricts it to affine transforms. The transform formulas implied by the matrix multiplication are

$$x' = M11 \cdot x + M21 \cdot y + OffsetX$$
$$y' = M12 \cdot x + M22 \cdot y + OffsetY$$

Because this is an affine transform, a square is always transformed into a parallelogram. This parallelogram is defined by three corners, and the fourth corner is determined by the other three.

Is it possible to derive the affine transform that maps a unit square into an arbitrary parallelogram? What we want is a mapping like this:

$$(0,0) \rightarrow (x_0, y_0)$$
$$(0,1) \rightarrow (x_1, y_1)$$
$$(1,0) \rightarrow (x_2, y_2)$$

If you begin substituting these points into the transform formulas, it is easy to derive the following cells of the required matrix:

$$M11 = x_2 - x_0$$
$$M12 = y_2 - y_0$$
$$M21 = x_1 - x_0$$
$$M22 = y_1 - y_0$$
$$OffsetX = x_0$$
$$OffsetY = y_0$$

In 3D graphics programming, a 4×4 transform matrix is required and a point (x, y, z) is treated as if it exists in 4D space with coordinates $(x, y, z, 1)$. Because there are no remaining letters after x, y, and z, that fourth dimension is usually referred to with the letter w. Application of a transform looks like this:

$$\begin{vmatrix} x & y & z & 1 \end{vmatrix} \times \begin{vmatrix} M11 & M12 & M13 & M14 \\ M21 & M22 & M23 & M24 \\ M31 & M32 & M33 & M34 \\ OffsetX & OffsetY & OffsetZ & M44 \end{vmatrix} = \begin{vmatrix} x' & y' & z' & w' \end{vmatrix}$$

Those are the actual fields of the *Matrix3D* structure.

That resultant 4×1 matrix is then converted back to a point in three-dimensional space by dividing all the coordinates by w':

$$\begin{vmatrix} x' & y' & z' & w' \end{vmatrix} \rightarrow \left(\frac{x'}{w'}, \frac{y'}{w'}, \frac{z'}{w'} \right)$$

In conventional 2D graphics, a potential division by zero is generally undesired. But in 3D graphics, division by a value that might equal zero is essential because this is how perspective is achieved. You want parallel lines to meet at infinity because that's how the world looks in real life.

The only purpose of this *Matrix3D* structure in the Windows Runtime is to set to the *ProjectionMatrix* property of a *Matrix3DProjection* object, which you can then set to the *Projection* property of an element as an alternative to *PlaneProjection*. In XAML, it might look like this:

```
<Image ... >
    <Image.Projection>
        <Matrix3DProjection>
            <Matrix3DProjection.ProjectionMatrix>
                1 0 0 0, 0 1 0 0, 0 0 1 0, 0 0 0 1
            </Matrix3DProjection.ProjectionMatrix>
        </Matrix3DProjection>
    </Image.Projection>
</Image>
```

You can't actually instantiate a *Matrix3D* value in XAML, so instead you need to specify the 16 numbers that make up the matrix, starting with the first row. This example shows the identity matrix, with its characteristic diagonal of 1s.

This full-blown 4×4 matrix isn't entirely used in this context because the element that it's applied to is flat and has a *Z* coordinate of zero, so the application of the matrix really looks like this:

$$\begin{vmatrix} x & y & 0 & 1 \end{vmatrix} \times \begin{vmatrix} M11 & M12 & M13 & M14 \\ M21 & M22 & M23 & M24 \\ M31 & M32 & M33 & M34 \\ OffsetX & OffsetY & OffsetZ & M44 \end{vmatrix} = \begin{vmatrix} x' & y' & z' & w' \end{vmatrix}$$

This means that the cells that make up the entire third row—the values of *M31*, *M32*, *M33*, and *M34*—are irrelevant. They are multiplied by 0 and hence do not enter the calculation.

Moreover, the 3D point derived from this process is collapsed on the *Z* axis to obtain a 2D point for mapping to the video display:

$$\left(\frac{x'}{w'}, \frac{y'}{w'}, \frac{z'}{w'} \right) \rightarrow \left(\frac{x'}{w'}, \frac{y'}{w'} \right)$$

This is a process that happens in standard 3D graphics as well, but there's usually much more work involved because the *Z* values also indicate what's visible to the camera and what's obscured.

Moreover, in standard 3D graphics, only a range of *Z* values is retained. A "near plane" and "far plane" are defined in terms of *Z*, and only coordinates between these two planes are visible. The rest are simply thrown away because they are conceptually too near or too far from the camera. In the Windows Runtime, only coordinates with *Z* values between the values of 0 and 1 are retained. To avoid losing part of a transformed element, *M13* and *M23* should be set to zero. *OffsetZ* can be set to any value between 0 and 1, but it's convenient to set it to zero as well.

When applying a *Matrix3DProjection* to a two-dimensional element, the transform formulas are therefore

$$x' = M11 \cdot x + M21 \cdot y + OffsetX$$

$$y' = M12 \cdot x + M22 \cdot y + OffsetY$$

$$w' = M14 \cdot x + M24 \cdot y + M44$$

If *M14* and *M24* are zero and *M44* is 1, this is simply a two-dimensional affine transform. Nonzero values of *M14* and *M24* are the non-affine parts of these formulas. *M44* can be something other than 1, but if it's not zero, you can always find an equivalent transform where *M44* equals 1. Just multiply all the fields by 1/*M44*.

With a non-affine transform, a square is not necessarily transformed to a parallelogram. However, a non-affine matrix transform still has limitations. It can't transform a square to any arbitrary quadrilateral. The transformed lines cannot cross each other and the four angles must be convex.

Let's attempt to derive a non-affine transform that maps the four corners of a square to four arbitrary points:

$$(0,0) \rightarrow (x_0, y_0)$$

$$(0,1) \rightarrow (x_1, y_1)$$

$$(1,0) \rightarrow (x_2, y_2)$$

$$(1,1) \rightarrow (x_3, y_3)$$

This exercise will be easier if we break this down into two transforms:

$$(0,0) \rightarrow (0,0) \rightarrow (x_0, y_0)$$

$$(0,1) \rightarrow (0,1) \rightarrow (x_1, y_1)$$

$$(1,0) \rightarrow (1,0) \rightarrow (x_2, y_2)$$

$$(1,1) \rightarrow (a,b) \rightarrow (x_3, y_3)$$

The first transform is obviously a non-affine transform that I'll call **B**. The second is something that we'll force to be an affine transform called **A** (for affine). The way we'll force it to be an affine transform is by deriving values of *a* and *b*. The composite transform is **B×A**.

I've already shown you the derivation of the affine transform, and I don't even need to change notation when switching from the 3×3 matrix to the 4×4 matrix. But we also want this affine transform to map the point (a, b) to the arbitrary point (x_3, y_3). By applying the derived affine transform to (a, b) and solving for a and b, we get this:

$$a = \frac{M22 \cdot x_3 - M21 \cdot y_3 + M21 \cdot OffsetY - M22 \cdot OffsetX}{M11 \cdot M22 - M12 \cdot M21}$$

$$b = \frac{M11 \cdot y_3 - M12 \cdot x_3 + M12 \cdot OffsetX - M11 \cdot OffsetY}{M11 \cdot M22 - M12 \cdot M21}$$

Now let's take a shot at the non-affine transform, which needs to yield the following mappings:

$$(0,0) \rightarrow (0,0)$$

$$(0,1) \rightarrow (0,1)$$

$$(1,0) \rightarrow (1,0)$$

$$(1,1) \rightarrow (a,b)$$

Here are the transform formulas from earlier:

$$x' = M11 \cdot x + M21 \cdot y + OffsetX$$

$$y' = M12 \cdot x + M22 \cdot y + OffsetY$$

$$w' = M14 \cdot x + M24 \cdot y + M44$$

Keep in mind that x' and y' must be divided by w' to get the transformed point.

If (0, 0) maps to (0, 0), then *OffsetX* and *OffsetY* are zero and *M44* is nonzero. Let's go out on a limb and set *M44* to 1.

If (0, 1) maps to (0, 1), then *M21* must be zero (to calculate a zero value of x') and y' divided by w' must equal 1, which means *M24* equals *M22* minus 1.

If (1, 0) maps to (1, 0), then *M12* is zero (for the zero value of y') and x' divided by w' must equal 1, or *M14* equals *M11* minus 1.

If (1, 1) maps to (a, b), then a bit of algebra derives

$$M11 = \frac{a}{a + b - 1}$$

$$M22 = \frac{b}{a + b - 1}$$

And a and b have already been derived.

Now let's code it up. I want to display the actual matrix that's derived from this process. That's the purpose of a *UserControl* derivative named *DisplayMatrix3D*. The XAML file consists of little more than a 4×4 *Grid* of *TextBlock* elements:

Project: NonAffineStretch | File: DisplayMatrix3D.xaml (excerpt)

```xaml
<UserControl ... >
    <UserControl.Resources>
        <Style TargetType="TextBlock">
            <Setter Property="TextAlignment" Value="Right" />
            <Setter Property="Margin" Value="6 0" />
        </Style>
    </UserControl.Resources>

    <Border BorderBrush="{StaticResource ApplicationForegroundThemeBrush}"
            BorderThickness="1 0">
        <Grid>
            <Grid.RowDefinitions>
                <RowDefinition Height="Auto" />
                <RowDefinition Height="Auto" />
                <RowDefinition Height="Auto" />
                <RowDefinition Height="Auto" />
            </Grid.RowDefinitions>

            <Grid.ColumnDefinitions>
                <ColumnDefinition Width="Auto" />
                <ColumnDefinition Width="Auto" />
                <ColumnDefinition Width="Auto" />
                <ColumnDefinition Width="Auto" />
            </Grid.ColumnDefinitions>

            <TextBlock Name="m11" Grid.Row="0" Grid.Column="0" />
            <TextBlock Name="m12" Grid.Row="0" Grid.Column="1" />
            <TextBlock Name="m13" Grid.Row="0" Grid.Column="2" />
            <TextBlock Name="m14" Grid.Row="0" Grid.Column="3" />

            <TextBlock Name="m21" Grid.Row="1" Grid.Column="0" />
            <TextBlock Name="m22" Grid.Row="1" Grid.Column="1" />
            <TextBlock Name="m23" Grid.Row="1" Grid.Column="2" />
            <TextBlock Name="m24" Grid.Row="1" Grid.Column="3" />

            <TextBlock Name="m31" Grid.Row="2" Grid.Column="0" />
            <TextBlock Name="m32" Grid.Row="2" Grid.Column="1" />
            <TextBlock Name="m33" Grid.Row="2" Grid.Column="2" />
            <TextBlock Name="m34" Grid.Row="2" Grid.Column="3" />

            <TextBlock Name="m41" Grid.Row="3" Grid.Column="0" />
            <TextBlock Name="m42" Grid.Row="3" Grid.Column="1" />
            <TextBlock Name="m43" Grid.Row="3" Grid.Column="2" />
            <TextBlock Name="m44" Grid.Row="3" Grid.Column="3" />
        </Grid>
    </Border>
</UserControl>
```

The code-behind file defines a dependency property of type *Matrix3D*, so it receives a notification whenever the property is changed. Watch out: The notification will not occur if a *property* of the existing *Matrix3D* structure is changed. The entire structure must be replaced.

Project: NonAffineStretch | File: DisplayMatrix3D.xaml.cs (excerpt)

```
public sealed partial class DisplayMatrix3D : UserControl
{
    static DependencyProperty matrix3DProperty =
        DependencyProperty.Register("Matrix3D",
            typeof(Matrix3D), typeof(DisplayMatrix3D),
            new PropertyMetadata(Matrix3D.Identity, OnPropertyChanged));

    public DisplayMatrix3D()
    {
        this.InitializeComponent();
    }

    public static DependencyProperty Matrix3DProperty
    {
        get { return matrix3DProperty; }
    }

    public Matrix3D Matrix3D
    {
        set { SetValue(Matrix3DProperty, value); }
        get { return (Matrix3D)GetValue(Matrix3DProperty); }
    }

    static void OnPropertyChanged(DependencyObject obj,
                                  DependencyPropertyChangedEventArgs args)
    {
        (obj as DisplayMatrix3D).OnPropertyChanged(args);
    }

    void OnPropertyChanged(DependencyPropertyChangedEventArgs args)
    {
        m11.Text = this.Matrix3D.M11.ToString("F3");
        m12.Text = this.Matrix3D.M12.ToString("F3");
        m13.Text = this.Matrix3D.M13.ToString("F3");
        m14.Text = this.Matrix3D.M14.ToString("F6");

        m21.Text = this.Matrix3D.M21.ToString("F3");
        m22.Text = this.Matrix3D.M22.ToString("F3");
        m23.Text = this.Matrix3D.M23.ToString("F3");
        m24.Text = this.Matrix3D.M24.ToString("F6");

        m31.Text = this.Matrix3D.M31.ToString("F3");
        m32.Text = this.Matrix3D.M32.ToString("F3");
        m33.Text = this.Matrix3D.M33.ToString("F3");
        m34.Text = this.Matrix3D.M34.ToString("F6");

        m41.Text = this.Matrix3D.OffsetX.ToString("F0");
        m42.Text = this.Matrix3D.OffsetY.ToString("F0");
        m43.Text = this.Matrix3D.OffsetZ.ToString("F0");
        m44.Text = this.Matrix3D.M44.ToString("F0");
    }
}
```

The formatting specifications were chosen based on a bit of experience with the common ranges of these cells.

The XAML file for *MainPage* includes an instance of the *DisplayMatrix3D* control, but it also references an image from my website and adorns it with four *Thumb* controls. These *Thumb* controls allow us to drag any corner to an arbitrary location. The prefixes "ul", "ur", "ll", and "lr" stand for "upper-left," "upper-right," "lower-left," and "lower-right."

Project: NonAffineStretch | File: MainPage.xaml (excerpt)

```
<Page ... >
    <Page.Resources>
        <Style TargetType="Thumb">
            <Setter Property="Width" Value="48" />
            <Setter Property="Height" Value="48" />
            <Setter Property="HorizontalAlignment" Value="Left" />
            <Setter Property="VerticalAlignment" Value="Top" />
        </Style>
    </Page.Resources>

    <Grid Background="{StaticResource ApplicationPageBackgroundThemeBrush}">
        <Image Source="http://www.charlespetzold.com/pw6/PetzoldJersey.jpg"
               Stretch="None"
               HorizontalAlignment="Left"
               VerticalAlignment="Top">
            <Image.Projection>
                <Matrix3DProjection x:Name="matrixProjection" />
            </Image.Projection>
        </Image>

        <Thumb DragDelta="OnThumbDragDelta">
            <Thumb.RenderTransform>
                <TransformGroup>
                    <TranslateTransform X="-24" Y="-24" />
                    <TranslateTransform x:Name="ulTranslate" X="100" Y="100" />
                </TransformGroup>
            </Thumb.RenderTransform>
        </Thumb>

        <Thumb DragDelta="OnThumbDragDelta">
            <Thumb.RenderTransform>
                <TransformGroup>
                    <TranslateTransform X="-24" Y="-24" />
                    <TranslateTransform x:Name="urTranslate" X="420" Y="100" />
                </TransformGroup>
            </Thumb.RenderTransform>
        </Thumb>

        <Thumb DragDelta="OnThumbDragDelta">
            <Thumb.RenderTransform>
                <TransformGroup>
                    <TranslateTransform X="-24" Y="-24" />
                    <TranslateTransform x:Name="llTranslate" X="100" Y="500" />
                </TransformGroup>
            </Thumb.RenderTransform>
        </Thumb>
```

```
    <Thumb DragDelta="OnThumbDragDelta">
        <Thumb.RenderTransform>
            <TransformGroup>
                <TranslateTransform X="-24" Y="-24" />
                <TranslateTransform x:Name="lrTranslate" X="420" Y="500" />
            </TransformGroup>
        </Thumb.RenderTransform>
    </Thumb>

    <local:DisplayMatrix3D HorizontalAlignment="Right"
                           VerticalAlignment="Bottom"
                           FontSize="24"
                           Matrix3D="{Binding ElementName=matrixProjection,
                                      Path=ProjectionMatrix}" />
    </Grid>
</Page>
```

The code-behind file implements the math I just showed you, except that another matrix is needed for mapping from the actual size and location of the image to a unit square. That's the matrix called *S* in the *CalculateNewTransform* code:

Project: NonAffineStretch | File: MainPage.xaml.cs (excerpt)

```
public sealed partial class MainPage : Page
{
    // Location and Size of Image with no transform
    Rect imageRect = new Rect(0, 0, 320, 400);

    public MainPage()
    {
        this.InitializeComponent();

        Loaded += (sender, args) =>
            {
                CalculateNewTransform();
            };
    }

    void OnThumbDragDelta(object sender, DragDeltaEventArgs args)
    {
        Thumb thumb = sender as Thumb;
        TransformGroup xformGroup = thumb.RenderTransform as TransformGroup;
        TranslateTransform translate = xformGroup.Children[1] as TranslateTransform;
        translate.X += args.HorizontalChange;
        translate.Y += args.VerticalChange;
        CalculateNewTransform();
    }

    void CalculateNewTransform()
    {
        Matrix3D matrix = CalculateNewTransform(imageRect,
                          new Point(ulTranslate.X, ulTranslate.Y),
                          new Point(urTranslate.X, urTranslate.Y),
                          new Point(llTranslate.X, llTranslate.Y),
                          new Point(lrTranslate.X, lrTranslate.Y));
```

```
        matrixProjection.ProjectionMatrix = matrix;
    }


    // The returned transform maps the points (0, 0),
    //   (0, 1), (1, 0), and (1, 1) to the points
    //   ptUL, ptUR, ptLL, and ptLR normalized based on rect.
    static Matrix3D CalculateNewTransform(Rect rect, Point ptUL, Point ptUR,
                                                      Point ptLL, Point ptLR)
    {
        // Scale and translate normalization transform
        Matrix3D S = new Matrix3D()
        {
            M11 = 1 / rect.Width,
            M22 = 1 / rect.Height,
            OffsetX = -rect.Left / rect.Width,
            OffsetY = -rect.Top / rect.Height,
            M44 = 1
        };

        // Affine transform: Maps
        //      (0, 0) --> ptUL
        //      (1, 0) --> ptUR
        //      (0, 1) --> ptLL
        //      (1, 1) --> (x2 + x1 + x0, y2 + y1 + y0)
        Matrix3D A = new Matrix3D()
        {
            OffsetX = ptUL.X,
            OffsetY = ptUL.Y,
            M11 = (ptUR.X - ptUL.X),
            M12 = (ptUR.Y - ptUL.Y),
            M21 = (ptLL.X - ptUL.X),
            M22 = (ptLL.Y - ptUL.Y),
            M44 = 1
        };

        // Non-affine transform
        Matrix3D B = new Matrix3D();
        double den = A.M11 * A.M22 - A.M12 * A.M21;
        double a = (A.M22 * ptLR.X - A.M21 * ptLR.Y +
                        A.M21 * A.OffsetY - A.M22 * A.OffsetX) / den;
        double b = (A.M11 * ptLR.Y - A.M12 * ptLR.X +
                        A.M12 * A.OffsetX - A.M11 * A.OffsetY) / den;

        B.M11 = a / (a + b - 1);
        B.M22 = b / (a + b - 1);
        B.M14 = B.M11 - 1;
        B.M24 = B.M22 - 1;
        B.M44 = 1;

        // Product of three transforms
        return S * B * A;
    }
}
```

Unlike the two-dimensional *Matrix* structure, the *Matrix3D* structure implements the multiplication operator, which makes array manipulation much easier.

It is certainly possible to drag one of the thumbs to a position where the image disappears because at least one of the angles is concave or the lines cross each other. But under those restrictions you can indeed stretch the image to a non-affine shape:

0.595	-0.261	0.000	-0.000369
-0.364	0.215	0.000	-0.001584
0.000	0.000	0.000	0.000000
188	173	0	1

Obviously, it's a little bit of work to persuade the Windows Runtime to apply a taper transform of a desired form, but the work is compensated by the pleasures of distorting photographs to make people look funny.

CHAPTER 11

The Three Templates

The word "template" generally refers to a kind of pattern or mold used for creating identical or similar objects. In the Windows Runtime, a template is a chunk of XAML that Windows uses to create a visual tree of elements. This might not seem so astonishing. You've seen Windows turning XAML into visual trees since the first pages of this book. But templates almost always contain data bindings, so a single template can result in many visual trees of somewhat different appearances based on the binding sources. For this reason, templates are very often defined as resources so that they can be shared and used multiple times.

The title of this chapter refers to three templates. These correspond to the three classes that derive from *FrameworkTemplate*:

```
Object
    DependencyObject
        FrameworkTemplate (non-instantiable)
            DataTemplate
            ControlTemplate
            ItemsPanelTemplate
```

You cannot define a template in code. You must use XAML. And don't expect to get any deeper knowledge of these classes by consulting the Windows Runtime documentation. *DataTemplate* defines just one public method, *ControlTemplate* defines just one public property, and *ItemsPanelTemplate* defines nothing on its own. Virtually everything connected with the actual mechanics of the template classes is internal to the Windows Runtime.

You use *DataTemplate* to give a visual appearance to data objects that don't necessarily have intrinsic visuals. I will first demonstrate *DataTemplate* in connection with controls that derive from *ContentControl*, and it will initially seem to have limited applicability. But *DataTemplate* is essential for displaying individual items in collections, which involves controls that derive from *ItemsControl*.

You use *ControlTemplate* to redefine the appearance of standard controls; this is a very powerful tool for customizing the visuals of an application.

ItemsPanelTemplate is much simpler than the other two and plays a role only in classes that derive from *ItemsControl*.

As might be expected from so versatile a tool, the templates defined as part of a *DataTemplate* or *ControlTemplate* can be complex. Many programmers cherish the help that Expression Blend brings in designing their templates. As usual, however, I will demonstrate here how to create templates "by hand." Even if you end up using Expression Blend, you'll be in better shape for understanding the XAML that Expression Blend generates.

By the end of this chapter, everything in the StandardStyles.xaml file that Visual Studio generates as part of standard projects should be entirely comprehensible.

Data in a Button

Several common elements and controls in the Windows Runtime can have visual children. The most obvious is *Panel*, which can support multiple children through its *Children* property of type *UIElementCollection*. The *Border* can have one child; its *Child* property is of type *UIElement*. When you create a custom control from *UserControl*, you set a visual tree to its *Content* property, which is also of type *UIElement*.

Button has a *Content* property as well, but this *Content* property is of type *Object*. Why is that?

The easy answer is: Because *Button* derives from *ContentControl*, and *ContentControl* defines a *Content* property of type *Object*:

```
Object
    DependencyObject
        UIElement
            FrameworkElement
                Control
                    ContentControl
                        ButtonBase
                            Button
```

But that's really not a good answer.

Most of the time, you do not set the *Content* property of *Button* to any old object. Most of the time you set the *Content* property to text, and you probably (and correctly) presume that a *TextBlock* is being created behind the scenes to display that text.

For fancier buttons, you can set the *Content* property to anything that derives from *UIElement*. For example, here's a button with a panel containing a bitmap and formatted text:

```
<Button HorizontalAlignment="Center">
    <StackPanel>
        <Image Source="http://www.charlespetzold.com/pw6/PetzoldJersey.jpg"
               Width="100" />
        <TextBlock>
            <Italic>Tap</Italic> to shoot the basket
        </TextBlock>
    </StackPanel>
</Button>
```

And here it is:

But if the *Content* property of *Button* is truly of type *Object*, we should be able to set it to something that does not derive from *UIElement*. What do you suppose happens in that case? Try it out by setting the content of a button to a *LinearGradientBrush*, for example:

```
<Button HorizontalAlignment="Center">
    <LinearGradientBrush>
        <GradientStop Offset="0" Color="Red" />
        <GradientStop Offset="1" Color="Blue" />
    </LinearGradientBrush>
</Button>
```

That's perfectly legal, even though it's not quite clear what you're trying to do. Brushes are commonly set to various properties of elements (such as the *Background* or *Foreground* properties of *Button*) to color them in various ways. But a brush doesn't have any visual representation of its own. For that reason what you'll see displayed in the button is the *ToString* representation of the brush. *ToString* might return something meaningful for some classes but the default implementation simply returns the fully qualified class name:

This is not very satisfying.

This problem is fixable! *ContentControl* defines (and *Button* inherits) not only a *Content* property but also a property named *ContentTemplate*. You set the *ContentTemplate* property to an object of type *DataTemplate*, in which you define a visual tree. This visual tree usually contains bindings that reference the object set to the *Content* property.

Let's first add property-element tags for the *ContentTemplate* property of *Button* and set to that a *DataTemplate*:

```
<Button HorizontalAlignment="Center">
    <LinearGradientBrush>
        <GradientStop Offset="0" Color="Red" />
        <GradientStop Offset="1" Color="Blue" />
    </LinearGradientBrush>
```

```
        <Button.ContentTemplate>
            <DataTemplate>

            </DataTemplate>
        </Button.ContentTemplate>
</Button>
```

Within those *DataTemplate* tags we can define a visual tree of elements that make use of the button content in some way. Let's try an *Ellipse*:

```
<Button HorizontalAlignment="Center">
    <LinearGradientBrush>
        <GradientStop Offset="0" Color="Red" />
        <GradientStop Offset="1" Color="Blue" />
    </LinearGradientBrush>

    <Button.ContentTemplate>
        <DataTemplate>
            <Ellipse Width="120"
                     Height="144"
                     Fill="{Binding}" />
        </DataTemplate>
    </Button.ContentTemplate>
</Button>
```

Notice the *Binding* markup extension on the *Fill* property of the *Ellipse*. This is obviously a very simple binding. It doesn't need a *Source* because the *DataContext* of this template has been set to the content of the button. The binding doesn't have a *Path* because we want the *Fill* property set directly to the content of the button. The template makes the button content visible:

Visually, it's the same as setting an *Ellipse* as content of the button and defining the *LinearGradientBrush* directly on the *Fill* property, like so:

```
<Button HorizontalAlignment="Center">
    <Ellipse Width="120"
             Height="144">
        <Ellipse.Fill>
            <LinearGradientBrush>
                <GradientStop Offset="0" Color="Red" />
```

```
                <GradientStop Offset="1" Color="Blue" />
            </LinearGradientBrush>
        </Ellipse.Fill>
    </Ellipse>
</Button>
```

However, the template could be part of a style that is shared among multiple buttons, so the template approach is definitely more flexible and versatile.

The data bindings in a *DataTemplate* need not be as simple as the one I just showed you. Here's a more extensive template that references the *Color* property of the second *GradientStop* object in the button's content and uses that to set the color of a *SolidColorBrush* that strokes the circumference of the ellipse:

```
<Button HorizontalAlignment="Center">
    <LinearGradientBrush>
        <GradientStop Offset="0" Color="Red" />
        <GradientStop Offset="1" Color="Blue" />
    </LinearGradientBrush>

    <Button.ContentTemplate>
        <DataTemplate>
            <Ellipse Width="120"
                     Height="144"
                     Fill="{Binding}"
                     StrokeThickness="6">
                <Ellipse.Stroke>
                    <SolidColorBrush Color="{Binding Path=GradientStops[1].Color}" />
                </Ellipse.Stroke>
            </Ellipse>
        </DataTemplate>
    </Button.ContentTemplate>
</Button>
```

The *Binding* on the *Color* property of the *SolidColorBrush* uses a *Path* to reference the *GradientStops* property of the *LinearGradientBrush*, an index to obtain a particular *GradientStop* object, and then *Color* to get a property of that object:

```
<SolidColorBrush Color="{Binding Path=GradientStops[1].Color}" />
```

A *Binding* in a *DataTemplate* usually doesn't have an *ElementName* or *Source* setting because that source is provided as the data context. Because *Path* is the first (and only) item in the *Binding*, the "Path=" part can be removed:

```
<SolidColorBrush Color="{Binding GradientStops[1].Color}" />
```

This is how you'll almost always see bindings in data templates, and here's what results:

Of course, the template is relying on the content being a *LinearGradientBrush*. If it's not, the bindings won't work.

You can define a *DataTemplate* in the *Resources* section of a page (or other XAML file):

```
<Page.Resources>
    <DataTemplate x:Key="ellipseTemplate">
        <Ellipse Width="120"
                 Height="144"
                 Fill="{Binding}"
                 StrokeThickness="6">
            <Ellipse.Stroke>
                <SolidColorBrush Color="{Binding GradientStops[1].Color}" />
            </Ellipse.Stroke>
        </Ellipse>
    </DataTemplate>
</Page.Resources>
```

Referencing this template in a button requires only the standard *StaticResource* markup extension:

```
<Button HorizontalAlignment="Center"
        ContentTemplate="{StaticResource ellipseTemplate}">
    <LinearGradientBrush>
        <GradientStop Offset="0" Color="Red" />
        <GradientStop Offset="1" Color="Blue" />
    </LinearGradientBrush>
</Button>
```

The template can be shared among multiple buttons (or other *ContentControl* derivatives). Normally, visual trees cannot be shared because visual elements can't have more than one parent. But the template works quite differently. When a template is shared, it is used to generate a unique visual tree for each control that references it. If 100 buttons have their *ContentTemplate* properties set to this template, 100 *Ellipse* elements will be created.

Very often, a template is defined within a *Style* so that other properties can be applied to the control at the same time. The SharedStyleWithDataTemplate project defines an implicit style in the *Resources* section of the page:

Project: SharedStyleWithDataTemplate | **File:** MainPage.xaml (excerpt)

```xml
<Page ... >
    <Page.Resources>
        <Style TargetType="Button">
            <Setter Property="HorizontalAlignment" Value="Center" />
            <Setter Property="VerticalAlignment" Value="Center" />
            <Setter Property="ContentTemplate">
                <Setter.Value>
                    <DataTemplate>
                        <Ellipse Width="144"
                                 Height="192"
                                 Fill="{Binding}" />
                    </DataTemplate>
                </Setter.Value>
            </Setter>
        </Style>
    </Page.Resources>

    <Grid Background="{StaticResource ApplicationPageBackgroundThemeBrush}">
        <Grid.ColumnDefinitions>
            <ColumnDefinition Width="*" />
            <ColumnDefinition Width="*" />
            <ColumnDefinition Width="*" />
        </Grid.ColumnDefinitions>

        <Button Grid.Column="0">
            <SolidColorBrush Color="Green" />
        </Button>

        <Button Grid.Column="1">
            <LinearGradientBrush>
                <GradientStop Offset="0" Color="Blue" />
                <GradientStop Offset="1" Color="Red" />
            </LinearGradientBrush>
        </Button>

        <Button Grid.Column="2">
            <ImageBrush ImageSource="http://www.charlespetzold.com/pw6/PetzoldJersey.jpg" />
        </Button>
    </Grid>
</Page>
```

The implicit style sets the properties of each *Button* automatically, including the *ContentTemplate* property. All that's left for the individual buttons is to define a *Brush* derivative as content:

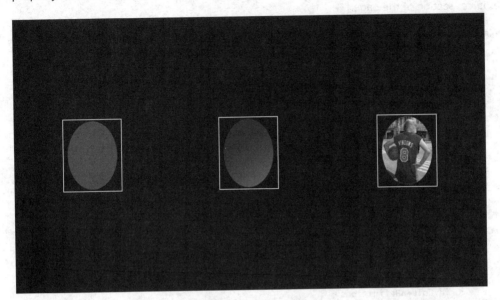

A template references objects through normal data bindings, so if the source object implements a notification mechanism—most likely *INotifyPropertyChanged*—then the visuals are dynamically updated. For example, suppose you create a *Clock* class that uses a *CompositionTarget.Rendering* event to obtain the current time and use that to set several properties, each of which fires a *PropertyChanged* event:

Project: ClockButton | File: Clock.cs

```
using System;
using System.ComponentModel;
using System.Runtime.CompilerServices;
using Windows.UI.Xaml.Media;

namespace ClockButton
{
    public class Clock : INotifyPropertyChanged
    {
        bool isEnabled;
        int hour, minute, second;
        int hourAngle, minuteAngle, secondAngle;

        public event PropertyChangedEventHandler PropertyChanged;

        public bool IsEnabled
        {
            set
            {
                if (SetProperty<bool>(ref isEnabled, value, "IsEnabled"))
                {
                    if (isEnabled)
                        CompositionTarget.Rendering += OnCompositionTargetRendering;
```

```
                else
                    CompositionTarget.Rendering -= OnCompositionTargetRendering;
            }
        }
        get
        {
            return isEnabled;
        }
    }

    public int Hour
    {
        set { SetProperty<int>(ref hour, value); }
        get { return hour; }
    }

    public int Minute
    {
        set { SetProperty<int>(ref minute, value); }
        get { return minute; }
    }

    public int Second
    {
        set { SetProperty<int>(ref second, value); }
        get { return second; }
    }

    public int HourAngle
    {
        set { SetProperty<int>(ref hourAngle, value); }
        get { return hourAngle; }
    }

    public int MinuteAngle
    {
        set { SetProperty<int>(ref minuteAngle, value); }
        get { return minuteAngle; }
    }
    public int SecondAngle
    {
        set { SetProperty<int>(ref secondAngle, value); }
        get { return secondAngle; }
    }

    void OnCompositionTargetRendering(object sender, object args)
    {
        DateTime dateTime = DateTime.Now;
        this.Hour = dateTime.Hour;
        this.Minute = dateTime.Minute;
        this.Second = dateTime.Second;

        this.HourAngle = 30 * dateTime.Hour + dateTime.Minute / 2;
        this.MinuteAngle = 6 * dateTime.Minute + dateTime.Second / 10;
        this.SecondAngle = 6 * dateTime.Second + dateTime.Millisecond / 166;
    }
```

```
        protected bool SetProperty<T>(ref T storage, T value,
                            [CallerMemberName] string propertyName = null)
        {
            if (object.Equals(storage, value))
                return false;

            storage = value;
            OnPropertyChanged(propertyName);
            return true;
        }

        protected virtual void OnPropertyChanged(string propertyName)
        {
            if (PropertyChanged != null)
                PropertyChanged(this, new PropertyChangedEventArgs(propertyName));
        }
    }
}
```

You can then set an instance of this class to the content of a *Button* and use a *DataTemplate* to
define how this object is rendered:

Project: ClockButton | MainPage.xaml (excerpt)

```
<Grid Background="{StaticResource ApplicationPageBackgroundThemeBrush}">
    <Button HorizontalAlignment="Center"
            VerticalAlignment="Center">

        <local:Clock IsEnabled="True" />

        <Button.ContentTemplate>
            <DataTemplate>
                <Grid Width="144" Height="144">
                    <Grid.Resources>
                        <Style TargetType="Polyline">
                            <Setter Property="Stroke"
                                    Value="{StaticResource ApplicationForegroundThemeBrush}" />
                        </Style>
                    </Grid.Resources>

                    <Polyline Points="72 80, 72 24"
                            StrokeThickness="6">
                        <Polyline.RenderTransform>
                            <RotateTransform Angle="{Binding HourAngle}"
                                            CenterX="72"
                                            CenterY="72" />
                        </Polyline.RenderTransform>
                    </Polyline>

                    <Polyline Points="72 88, 72 12"
                            StrokeThickness="3">
                        <Polyline.RenderTransform>
                            <RotateTransform Angle="{Binding MinuteAngle}"
                                            CenterX="72"
                                            CenterY="72" />
                        </Polyline.RenderTransform>
                    </Polyline>
```

```
                    <Polyline Points="72 88, 72 6"
                              StrokeThickness="1">
                        <Polyline.RenderTransform>
                            <RotateTransform Angle="{Binding SecondAngle}"
                                             CenterX="72"
                                             CenterY="72" />
                        </Polyline.RenderTransform>
                    </Polyline>
                </Grid>
            </DataTemplate>
        </Button.ContentTemplate>
    </Button>
</Grid>
```

Notice that I've defined an implicit *Style* for *Polyline* within the visual tree of the *DataTemplate*. This applies to all the *Polyline* elements within that visual tree. These *Polyline* elements have their *RenderTransform* properties set to a *RotateTransform*, the *Angle* of which is bound to various properties of the *Clock* class. Together, these three *Polyline* elements constitute a primitive clock that tells time along with functioning as part of a completely functional *Button*:

Keep in mind that the *DataTemplate* set to the *ContentTemplate* property of the *Button* defines only the appearance of the button content and not the button's chrome. The button still has a rectangular border, for example, and (in the dark theme) it still assumes a somewhat grayer appearance when the mouse passes over and it displays a white background when it's clicked. Changing those aspects of the button's appearance requires working with a *ControlTemplate* object set to the button's *Template* property, as you'll see later in this chapter.

Making Decisions

XAML is not a real programming language because it doesn't have loops and *if* statements. XAML isn't capable of making decisions, so it cannot contain blocks of markup that are conditionally executed.

But we can always try.

Let's expand upon the *Clock* class in the previous project to make it differentiate between morning and afternoon. To do this we'll derive a new class from *Clock* with a new property named *Hour12* that ranges from 1 through 12. Let's also give this new class a couple Boolean properties named *IsAm* and *IsPm* in the hopes that we might use these properties for displaying something a little different depending on their values.

The ConditionalClockButton project contains a link to the Clock.cs file from the *ClockButton* project and defines a *TwelveHourClock* class that derives from *Clock*:

Project: ConditionalClockButton | File: TwelveHourClock.cs

```
namespace ConditionalClockButton
{
    public class TwelveHourClock : ClockButton.Clock
    {
        // Initialize for Hour value of 0
        int hour12 = 1;
        bool isAm = true;
        bool isPm = false;

        public int Hour12
        {
            set { SetProperty<int>(ref hour12, value); }
            get { return hour12; }
        }

        public bool IsAm
        {
            set { SetProperty<bool>(ref isAm, value); }
            get { return isAm; }
        }

        public bool IsPm
        {
            set { SetProperty<bool>(ref isPm, value); }
            get { return isPm; }
        }

        protected override void OnPropertyChanged(string propertyName)
        {
            if (propertyName == "Hour")
            {
                this.Hour12 = (this.Hour - 1) % 12 + 1;
                this.IsAm = this.Hour < 12;
```

```
                this.IsPm = !this.IsAm;
            }

        base.OnPropertyChanged(propertyName);
        }
    }
}
```

Fortunately, I defined the *OnPropertyChanged* method in *Clock* as virtual, so this new class can override that method and check if the *propertyName* argument equals "Hour." If so, all three new properties are set, and those properties also call *SetProperty* and hence *OnPropertyChanged* to fire their own *PropertyChanged* events.

Suppose you want a *Button* that says, "It's after 9 in the morning" or "It's after 3 in the afternoon." This *TwelveHourClock* class has all the information you need, and you might begin defining the button like so:

```
<Button>

    <local:TwelveHourClock />

    <Button.ContentTemplate>
        <DataTemplate>
            <StackPanel Orientation="Horizontal">
                <TextBlock Text="It's after&#x00A0;" />
                <TextBlock Text="{Binding Hour12}" />
                <TextBlock Text=" o'clock" />
                <TextBlock Text=" in the morning!" />
                <TextBlock Text=" in the afternoon!" />
            </StackPanel>
        </DataTemplate>
    </Button.ContentTemplate>
</Button>
```

However, one of those two last *TextBlock* elements needs to be suppressed. The first of that pair should be displayed only when the *IsAm* property is *true*, and the second should be displayed only when *IsPm* is *true*. As you'll recall, elements have a *Visibility* property that can be set to members of the *Visibility* enumeration, either *Visible* or *Collapsed*. If there were some way to convert the Boolean properties of *TwelveHourClock* to members of the *Visibility* enumeration, we'd be in great shape.

I introduced binding converters in Chapter 4, "Presentation with Panels," and it turns out that one of the most popular binding converters is often named *BooleanToVisibilityConverter*. Indeed, if you create a project of type Grid App or Split App in Visual Studio, you get one of these converters for free in the Common folder, but writing one isn't hard:

Project: ConditionalClockButton | **File:** BooleanToVisibilityConverter.cs

```
using System;
using Windows.UI.Xaml;
using Windows.UI.Xaml.Data;
```

```
namespace ConditionalClockButton
{
    public sealed class BooleanToVisibilityConverter : IValueConverter
    {
        public object Convert(object value, Type targetType, object parameter, string language)
        {
            return (bool)value ? Visibility.Visible : Visibility.Collapsed;
        }

        public object ConvertBack(object value, Type targetType, object parameter, string lang)
        {
            return (Visibility)value == Visibility.Visible;
        }
    }
}
```

The version that Visual Studio generates is just a bit more elaborate than this: It checks that the *value* arguments are actually of the types to which they are cast. But if you're restricting the use of a converter to some specific markup, you can relax the type checking. A restricted use is certainly the case in this program, in which the converter is instantiated not in the *Resources* section of the *Page* but in a *Resources* section within the template:

Project: ConditionalClockButton | File: MainPage.xaml (excerpt)

```
<Grid Background="{StaticResource ApplicationPageBackgroundThemeBrush}">
    <Button HorizontalAlignment="Center"
            VerticalAlignment="Center"
            FontSize="24">

        <local:TwelveHourClock IsEnabled="True" />

        <Button.ContentTemplate>
            <DataTemplate>
                <StackPanel Orientation="Horizontal">
                    <StackPanel.Resources>
                        <local:BooleanToVisibilityConverter x:Key="booleanToVisibility" />
                    </StackPanel.Resources>

                    <TextBlock Text="It's after&#x00A0;" />
                    <TextBlock Text="{Binding Hour12}" />
                    <TextBlock Text=" o'clock" />
                    <TextBlock Text=" in the morning!"
                               Visibility="{Binding IsAm,
                                   Converter={StaticResource booleanToVisibility}}" />

                    <TextBlock Text=" in the afternoon!"
                               Visibility="{Binding IsPm,
                                   Converter={StaticResource booleanToVisibility}}" />

                </StackPanel>
            </DataTemplate>
        </Button.ContentTemplate>
    </Button>
</Grid>
```

The *Visibility* properties of the last two *TextBlock* items are now bound to the *IsAm* and *IsPm* properties of *TwelveHourClock*, and the *BooleanToVisibilityConverter* determines which one is visible:

Collection Controls and the *Real* Use of *DataTemplate*

I've been demonstrating the use of *DataTemplate* with a representative class that derives from *ContentControl*, but there aren't very many of those classes, and to be honest, the use of *DataTemplate* with these classes is not very common.

The real use of *DataTemplate* is with controls that derive from *ItemsControl*, which are controls that store a collection of objects, usually of the same type:

Object
    DependencyObject
        UIElement
            FrameworkElement
                Control
                    ItemsControl
                        Selector (non-instantiable)
                            ComboBox
                            FlipView
                            ListBox
                            ListViewBase (non-instantiable)
                                GridView
                                ListView

Certainly the most famous of these is *ListBox*, which has existed in Windows (in one form or another) from the very beginning. The archetypal *ListBox* presents a vertical list of items through which a user can scroll and select using the keyboard or mouse. (The modern *ListBox* is more flexible and allows touch manipulation.) The *ComboBox* came a little later in Windows and got its name because it combined a text-editing field with a drop-down list of items. *FlipView* is new in Windows 8.

The *GridView* and *ListView* are rather more sophisticated than the others and I'll leave those for Chapter 12, "Pages and Navigation."

When working with these various controls, it's easy to neglect *ItemsControl* itself, from which everything else derives. *ItemsControl* simply displays a collection of items for presentation purposes; there's no concept of selection. The *Selector* class adds selection logic, and all the other classes derive from that. I'll generally refer to this entire group of controls as *items controls*. All of them display a collection of items.

You can get objects into an items control in one of four ways: individually in XAML, individually in code, in bulk in code, or in bulk in XAML, usually with a data binding. The objects that you put into an items control usually do *not* derive from *UIElement*. Very often these items are business objects or view models.

For a brief list of items, you can specify them right in the XAML file:

```
<Grid Background="{StaticResource ApplicationPageBackgroundThemeBrush}">
    <ItemsControl FontSize="24">
        <x:String>One potato</x:String>
        <x:String>Two potato</x:String>
        <x:String>Three potato</x:String>
        <x:String>Four</x:String>
        <x:String>Five potato</x:String>
        <x:String>Six potato</x:String>
        <x:String>Seven potato</x:String>
        <x:String>More</x:String>
    </ItemsControl>
</Grid>
```

The content property of *ItemsControl* is *Items*, which is an object of type *ItemCollection*, a class that implements *IList*, *IEnumerable*, and *IObservableVector*. (I'll have more to say about these interfaces shortly.)

In this example the items being added to the *ItemsControl* are objects of type *String*, so they just display as text:

```
One potato
Two potato
Three potato
Four
Five potato
Six potato
Seven potato
More
```

This particular use of *ItemsControl* is not much better than a *StackPanel* except that you can fill it with items of type *String* rather than using *TextBlock*. Behind the scenes, of course, a *TextBlock* is generated for each item.

Unlike the controls that derive from *ItemsControl*, *ItemsControl* itself does not have a built-in facility for scrolling. It you have a bunch of items that might require scrolling, you'll want to put the *ItemsControl* inside a *ScrollViewer*, like so:

```
<Grid Background="{StaticResource ApplicationPageBackgroundThemeBrush}">
    <ScrollViewer>
        <ItemsControl FontSize="24">
            <Color>AliceBlue</Color>
            <Color>AntiqueWhite</Color>
            <Color>Aqua</Color>

            ...
            <Color>WhiteSmoke</Color>
            <Color>Yellow</Color>
            <Color>YellowGreen</Color>
        </ItemsControl>
    </ScrollViewer>
</Grid>
```

This list scrolls, but it's not exactly informative because each *Color* item is displayed with its *ToString* representation:

```
Windows.Foundation.IReference`1<Windows.UI.Color>
Windows.Foundation.IReference`1<Windows.UI.Color>
Windows.Foundation.IReference`1<Windows.UI.Color>
Windows.Foundation.IReference`1<Windows.UI.Color>
Windows.Foundation.IReference`1<Windows.UI.Color>
Windows.Foundation.IReference`1<Windows.UI.Color>
Windows.Foundation.IReference`1<Windows.UI.Color>
Windows.Foundation.IReference`1<Windows.UI.Color>
Windows.Foundation.IReference`1<Windows.UI.Color>
Windows.Foundation.IReference`1<Windows.UI.Color>
Windows.Foundation.IReference`1<Windows.UI.Color>
Windows.Foundation.IReference`1<Windows.UI.Color>
Windows.Foundation.IReference`1<Windows.UI.Color>
Windows.Foundation.IReference`1<Windows.UI.Color>
Windows.Foundation.IReference`1<Windows.UI.Color>
Windows.Foundation.IReference`1<Windows.UI.Color>
Windows.Foundation.IReference`1<Windows.UI.Color>
Windows.Foundation.IReference`1<Windows.UI.Color>
Windows.Foundation.IReference`1<Windows.UI.Color>
Windows.Foundation.IReference`1<Windows.UI.Color>
Windows.Foundation.IReference`1<Windows.UI.Color>
Windows.Foundation.IReference`1<Windows.UI.Color>
Windows.Foundation.IReference`1<Windows.UI.Color>
Windows.Foundation.IReference`1<Windows.UI.Color>
Windows.Foundation.IReference`1<Windows.UI.Color>
```

Whenever you see a list of type names in an items control, don't fret! You should actually be quite happy to see a binding working because it means that you can display these items better. All you need do is set the *ItemTemplate* property of *ItemsControl* to a *DataTemplate* with bindings for rendering these items:

```
<Grid Background="{StaticResource ApplicationPageBackgroundThemeBrush}">
    <ScrollViewer>
        <ItemsControl>
            <ItemsControl.ItemTemplate>
                <DataTemplate>
                    <Rectangle Width="144"
                               Height="72"
                               Margin="12">
                        <Rectangle.Fill>
                            <SolidColorBrush Color="{Binding}" />
                        </Rectangle.Fill>
                    </Rectangle>
                </DataTemplate>
            </ItemsControl.ItemTemplate>

            <Color>AliceBlue</Color>
            <Color>AntiqueWhite</Color>
            <Color>Aqua</Color>
            ...
            <Color>WhiteSmoke</Color>
            <Color>Yellow</Color>
            <Color>YellowGreen</Color>
        </ItemsControl>
    </ScrollViewer>
</Grid>
```

The *ItemTemplate* property of *ItemsControl* is analogous to the *ContentTemplate* property of *ContentControl*. Both properties are of type *DataTemplate*. With the *ItemTemplate* property, however, the template is used to generate a visual tree for each item. Here's how it looks now:

As the *ItemsControl* is being constructed, the *DataTemplate* is used to generate 141 *Rectangle* elements and 141 *SolidColorBrush* objects, one for each item in the control.

Of course, you probably don't want a whole list of 141 *Color* items in the XAML file. You'll probably want to generate them in code. In the ColorItems project, the XAML file contains no items but it does have a more elaborate template that also displays the components of the color:

Project: ColorItems | **File:** MainPage.xaml (excerpt)

```xml
<Grid Background="{StaticResource ApplicationPageBackgroundThemeBrush}">
    <ScrollViewer>
        <ItemsControl Name="itemsControl"
                      FontSize="24">
            <ItemsControl.ItemTemplate>
                <DataTemplate>
                    <Grid Width="240"
                          Margin="0 12">
                        <Grid.ColumnDefinitions>
                            <ColumnDefinition Width="144" />
                            <ColumnDefinition Width="Auto" />
                        </Grid.ColumnDefinitions>

                        <Grid.RowDefinitions>
                            <RowDefinition Height="Auto" />
                            <RowDefinition Height="Auto" />
                            <RowDefinition Height="Auto" />
                            <RowDefinition Height="Auto" />
                        </Grid.RowDefinitions>
```

```xml
            <Rectangle Grid.Column="0"
                       Grid.Row="0"
                       Grid.RowSpan="4"
                       Margin="12 0">
                <Rectangle.Fill>
                    <SolidColorBrush Color="{Binding}" />
                </Rectangle.Fill>
            </Rectangle>

            <StackPanel Grid.Column="1"
                        Grid.Row="0"
                        Orientation="Horizontal">
                <TextBlock Text="A =&#x00A0;" />
                <TextBlock Text="{Binding A}" />
            </StackPanel>

            <StackPanel Grid.Column="1"
                        Grid.Row="1"
                        Orientation="Horizontal">
                <TextBlock Text="R =&#x00A0;" />
                <TextBlock Text="{Binding R}" />
            </StackPanel>

            <StackPanel Grid.Column="1"
                        Grid.Row="2"
                        Orientation="Horizontal">
                <TextBlock Text="G =&#x00A0;" />
                <TextBlock Text="{Binding G}" />
            </StackPanel>

            <StackPanel Grid.Column="1"
                        Grid.Row="3"
                        Orientation="Horizontal">
                <TextBlock Text="B =&#x00A0;" />
                <TextBlock Text="{Binding B}" />
            </StackPanel>
        </Grid>
    </DataTemplate>
</ItemsControl.ItemTemplate>
        </ItemsControl>
    </ScrollViewer>
</Grid>
```

The items themselves are generated in code. As you probably expect by now, the code-behind file uses reflection to obtain all the *Color* properties defined by the static *Colors* class. Each *Color* value is added to the *ItemsControl* using the *Add* method defined by *ItemCollection*. This represents the second method of putting items in an items control:

Project: ColorItems | File: MainPage.xaml (excerpt)

```csharp
public MainPage()
{
    this.InitializeComponent();
```

```
    IEnumerable<PropertyInfo> properties = typeof(Colors).GetTypeInfo().DeclaredProperties;

    foreach (PropertyInfo property in properties)
    {
        Color clr = (Color)property.GetValue(null);
        itemsControl.Items.Add(clr);
    }
}
```

And now we get the color display with the decimal values of the components of each color:

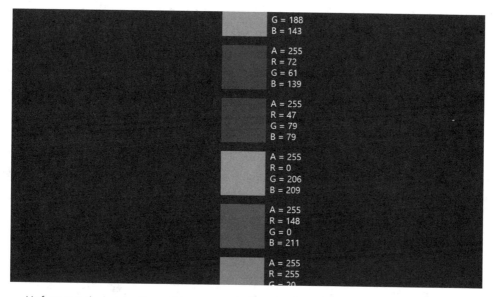

Unfortunately, we can't use this same technique to display the name of each color because that's not part of the *Color* structure. If we want to display the name along with the color, we'll need to fill the *ItemsControl* with instances of a class that provides this name.

Let's create this class. In a library project I've called Petzold.ProgrammingWindows6.Chapter11, I've defined a class called *NamedColor*:

Project: Petzold.ProgrammingWindows6.Chapter11 | File: NamedColor.cs (excerpt)

```
public class NamedColor
{
    static NamedColor()
    {
        List<NamedColor> colorList = new List<NamedColor>();
        IEnumerable<PropertyInfo> properties = typeof(Colors).GetTypeInfo().DeclaredProperties;

        foreach (PropertyInfo property in properties)
        {
            NamedColor namedColor = new NamedColor
            {
                Name = property.Name,
                Color = (Color)property.GetValue(null)
            };
```

```
            colorList.Add(namedColor);
        }

        All = colorList;
    }

    public static IEnumerable<NamedColor> All { private set; get; }

    public string Name { private set; get; }

    public Color Color { private set; get; }
}
```

The *NamedColor* class has two public properties: a *Name* property of type *string*, and a *Color* property of type *Color*. It also defines a static property named *All* of type *IEnumerable<NamedColor>*. This property is set from the static constructor to consist of a collection of all *NamedColor* objects obtained using reflection of the static *Colors* class.

I have not defined this class as implementing *INotifyPropertyChanged* because the properties of any *NamedColor* object do not change after the object is initialized.

For displaying hexadecimal color values, the Petzold.ProgrammingWindows6.Chapter11 library also contains a *ByteToHexStringConverter*:

Project: Petzold.ProgrammingWindows6.Chapter11 | File: ByteToHexStringConverter.cs

```
using System;
using Windows.UI.Xaml.Data;

namespace Petzold.ProgrammingWindows6.Chapter11
{
    public class ByteToHexStringConverter : IValueConverter
    {
        public object Convert(object value, Type targetType, object parameter, string language)
        {
            return ((byte)value).ToString("X2");
        }
        public object ConvertBack(object value, Type targetType, object parameter, string lang)
        {
            return value;
        }
    }
}
```

As with many of the projects in the rest of this chapter, the ColorItemsSource solution contains a link to this library project: With the ColorItemsSource solution in Visual Studio, I right-clicked the solution name in the Solution Explorer and chose Add and Existing Project. Then I navigated to the Petzold.ProgrammingWindows6.Chapter11.csproj file. I then defined a reference to this project: I right-clicked the References under the ColorItemsSource project and in the Reference Manager dialog box I selected Projects (under Solution) at the left and the library at the right. The MainPage.xaml file contains an XML namespace declaration for the library:

```
xmlns:ch11="using:Petzold.ProgrammingWindows6.Chapter11"
```

The MainPage.xaml.cs file contains a *using* directive for this namespace:

```
using Petzold.ProgrammingWindows6.Chapter11;
```

This project is called ColorItemsSource for a reason: I've already shown you how to fill up an *ItemCollection* object accessible from the *Items* property of *ItemsControl* from either XAML or code. An alternative is the *ItemsSource* property. This property is defined as type *object* but you'll undoubtedly set *ItemsSource* to something that implements the *IEnumerable* interface. The object you set to *ItemsSource* becomes the collection for the *ItemsControl*, at which point the *Items* property becomes read-only.

You can set the *ItemsSource* property from either code or XAML. Let me show you the code approach first. Here's the XAML file, the bulk of which is a *DataTemplate* defining the visual tree for each *NamedColor* item in the collection.

Project: ColorItemsSource | **File:** MainPage.xaml (excerpt)

```
<Page ...
    xmlns:ch11="using:Petzold.ProgrammingWindows6.Chapter11"
    ... >
    <Page.Resources>
        <ch11:ByteToHexStringConverter x:Key="byteToHexString" />
    </Page.Resources>

    <Grid Background="{StaticResource ApplicationPageBackgroundThemeBrush}">
        <ScrollViewer>
            <ItemsControl Name="itemsControl">

                <ItemsControl.ItemTemplate>
                    <DataTemplate>
                        <Border BorderBrush="{StaticResource ApplicationForegroundThemeBrush}"
                                BorderThickness="1"
                                Width="336"
                                Margin="6">
                            <Grid>
                                <Grid.ColumnDefinitions>
                                    <ColumnDefinition Width="Auto" />
                                    <ColumnDefinition Width="*"/>
                                </Grid.ColumnDefinitions>

                                <Rectangle Grid.Column="0"
                                           Height="72"
                                           Width="72"
                                           Margin="6">
                                    <Rectangle.Fill>
                                        <SolidColorBrush Color="{Binding Color}" />
                                    </Rectangle.Fill>
                                </Rectangle>
```

```
                    <StackPanel Grid.Column="1"
                                VerticalAlignment="Center">
                        <TextBlock FontSize="24"
                                   Text="{Binding Name}" />

                        <ContentControl FontSize="18">
                            <StackPanel Orientation="Horizontal">
                                <TextBlock Text="{Binding Color.A,
                                    Converter={StaticResource byteToHexString}}" />
                                <TextBlock Text="-" />
                                <TextBlock Text="{Binding Color.R,
                                    Converter={StaticResource byteToHexString}}" />
                                <TextBlock Text="-" />
                                <TextBlock Text="{Binding Color.G,
                                    Converter={StaticResource byteToHexString}}" />
                                <TextBlock Text="-" />
                                <TextBlock Text="{Binding Color.B,
                                    Converter={StaticResource byteToHexString}}" />
                            </StackPanel>
                        </ContentControl>
                    </StackPanel>
                </Grid>
            </Border>
        </DataTemplate>
    </ItemsControl.ItemTemplate>
</ItemsControl>
</ScrollViewer>
</Grid>
</Page>
```

Notice the seven *TextBlock* elements displaying the *Color* components. These are all within a horizontal *StackPanel*, which is then in a *ContentControl*. The sole reason for this *ContentControl* is to provide a *FontSize* that is inherited by the seven *TextBlock* elements. An implicit *Style* would also have worked fine.

The bindings on the *SolidColorBrush* and *TextBlock* elements obviously imply that an object of type *NamedColor* is being displayed, but no objects of *NamedColor* are instantiated in the XAML file. Instead, the *ItemsSource* property of the *ItemsControl* is set in the constructor of the code-behind file:

Project: ColorItemsSource | **File:** MainPage.xaml.cs (excerpt)

```
public MainPage()
{
    this.InitializeComponent();

    itemsControl.ItemsSource = NamedColor.All;
}
```

When *ItemsSource* is set, the *ItemsControl* generates visual trees for all the items in collection:

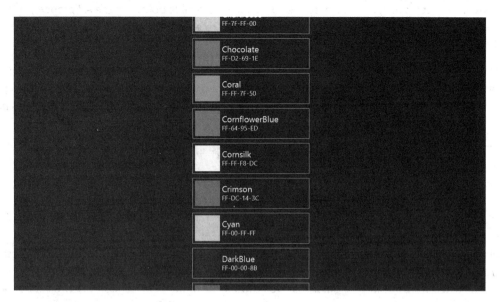

It is also possible to implement a XAML-only solution by binding the *ItemsSource* property to the collection. The ColorItemsSourceWithBinding project is very similar to the ColorItemsSource project in that it also uses the Petzold.ProgrammingWindows6.Chapter11 library, and it defines the same *DataTemplate* in the XAML file. But a *NamedColor* object is instantiated as a resource, and a binding to the *All* property is defined in the *ItemsSource* property of the *ItemsControl*:

Project: ColorItemsSourceWithBinding | File: MainPage.xaml (excerpt)

```
<Page ...
    xmlns:ch11="using:Petzold.ProgrammingWindows6.Chapter11"
    ... >
    <Page.Resources>
        <ch11:NamedColor x:Key="namedColor" />
        <ch11:ByteToHexStringConverter x:Key="byteToHexString" />
    </Page.Resources>

    <Grid Background="{StaticResource ApplicationPageBackgroundThemeBrush}">
        <ScrollViewer>
            <ItemsControl ItemsSource="{Binding Source={StaticResource namedColor},
                                        Path=All}">
                <ItemsControl.ItemTemplate>
                    <DataTemplate>
                    ...
                    </DataTemplate>
                </ItemsControl.ItemTemplate>
            </ItemsControl>
        </ScrollViewer>
    </Grid>
</Page>
```

If the resource itself were a collection object, *ItemsSource* could be set to a *StaticResource* markup extension of that resource, but because the collection is accessible only from the *All* property of *NamedColor*, a *Binding* markup extension is necessary to reference the *NamedColor* object and the *All* property.

You'll recall that Chapter 4 has a couple programs that display lists of colors in various ways and that I indicated that we'd need to wait for Chapter 11 to see the best way of doing it. This is it. A class defines the type of the items you wish to display, and a *DataTemplate* on an *ItemsControl* defines how you want these items rendered.

This is the coming together of collections and bindings and templates, and it represents an essential aspect of Windows Runtime programming.

Collections and Interfaces

Normally, in constructing a class such as *NamedColor* I would have defined the instance constructor as *protected* or *private* because it doesn't make much sense for an individual *NamedColor* object to be instantiated from outside the class. That would work fine in the ColorItemsSource project but not in ColorItemsSourceWithBinding. In this second program, *NamedColor* needs a public parameterless constructor because the class must be instantiated in XAML as a resource. That particular instance of *NamedColor* isn't otherwise used: It just provides a way to access the static *All* property in the binding. In most programs, you'll probably have a view model class that is instantiated once (the so-called singleton pattern) and that provides instance properties of particular collections. (I'll define such a class in the next chapter.)

In *NamedColor*, I had some choice in defining the type of the *All* property. I could have defined it as what it actually is: a *List<NamedColor>*. Or I could have gone to the other extreme and defined it as *object*. That's not a problem. When the *ItemsSource* property of an items control is set, the control itself checks whether the object set to *ItemsSource* implements *IEnumerable*. That's all it needs to access the actual items in the collection. That's why I defined the property as *IEnumerable<NamedColor>*. Regardless of how I later change the internals of *NamedColor* class, I know that property should always implement *IEnumerable* because it must provide a suitable collection source for an items control.

When you begin looking at the documentation of collections and interfaces, it's apt to be a bit confusing. Programmers working with .NET recognize the *IEnumerable<T>* interface defined in the *System.Collections.Generic* namespace. Yet in some contexts this interface is referred to as *IIterable<T>*, which is defined in the *Windows.Foundations.Collections* namespace. It's the same interface, but C# and Visual Basic programmers refer to it as *IEnumerable*, while C++ programmers use *IIterable*.

C# and Visual Basic programmers are also accustomed to working with two basic types of collections: *List<T>*, which is an ordered collection of objects of type *T*, and *Dictionary<TKey, TValue>*, which is an ordered collection of unique non-*null* keys and corresponding values. C++

programmers, however, know these two basic types of collections under the names *vector* and *map*, respectively. For that reason, the *Windows.Foundations.Collections* namespace includes the interfaces *IVector<T>* and *IMap<K, V>*, but C# and Visual Basic programmers see these interfaces as *IList<T>* and *IDictionary<TKey, TValue>*, both defined in *System.Collections.Generic*.

If you just remember "a vector is a list; a map is a dictionary," you'll certainly be less confused.

You've already acquired a familiarity with the *INotifyPropertyChanged* interface defined in *System.ComponentModel*. (C++ programmers use an interface of the same name but defined in *Windows.UI.Xaml.Data*.) If an item in a collection that is set to *ItemsSource* implements the *INotifyPropertyChanged* interface, any change to the properties of those items will be reflected in the visual elements bound to those properties. In other words, the bindings in the *DataTemplate* can respond to property changes. You've seen this with the ClockButton project for a single item of type *Clock*. It also works with items in collections, as you'll see in the next chapter.

When working with collections and items controls, there is another important interface named *INotifyCollectionChanged* defined in *System.Collections.Specialized*. This interface defines a *CollectionChanged* event that is fired when changes to the collection itself occur—that is, when items are added to the collection or removed from the collection, or items are reordered. If the collection set to the *ItemsSource* property of an items control implements *INotifyCollectionChanged*, these changes will be perceived by the items control and items will be dynamically added to the display or removed from the display.

For C# programmers, the *ObservableCollection<T>* class implements *INotifyCollectionChanged*, and this is the class to use for this purpose in Windows Runtime programming.

Tapping and Selecting

In the ColorItemsSource and ColorItemsSourceWithBinding projects, the visuals of each item are defined by a *DataTemplate*, but that doesn't prohibit you from getting input events from the individual items. In either ColorItemsSource or ColorItemsSourceWithBinding, give the *Border* that begins the *DataTemplate* a non-*null* background and define a handler for the *Tapped* event:

```
<Border BorderBrush="{StaticResource ApplicationForegroundThemeBrush}"
        BorderThickness="1"
        Width="336"
        Margin="6"
        Background="{StaticResource ApplicationPageBackgroundThemeBrush}"
        Tapped="OnItemTapped">
```

This gives each of the 144 *Border* elements the same *Tapped* handler. In that handler, the *sender* argument is the *Border*; the *OriginalSource* property of the event arguments is either that *Border* or another element in the template. Regardless, the *DataContext* of that element is the particular

NamedColor object associated with that item, which means that you can extract the *Color* value and use that to color the background:

```
void OnItemTapped(object sender, TappedRoutedEventArgs args)
{
    object dataContext = (args.OriginalSource as FrameworkElement).DataContext;
    Color clr = (dataContext as NamedColor).Color;
    (this.Content as Grid).Background = new SolidColorBrush(clr);
}
```

Here's the result when the Brown item has been tapped:

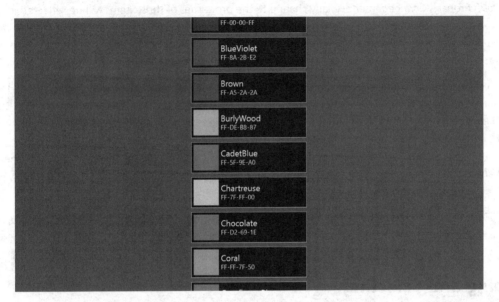

Considering that you can easily implement a tap or click interface in an *ItemsControl*, you might wonder why you need controls that derive from *Selector*, most notably *ListBox*.

One simple answer is that tapping is not selecting. When an item in a *ListBox* is selected, it has a different visual appearance. In addition, the selection can be moved from item to item by using the keyboard arrow keys. If these aren't features you need, obviously *ItemsControl* might be a satisfactory solution.

To indicate the currently selected item, *Selector* defines three different (but obviously related) properties:

- *SelectedIndex* is the index of the selected item within the collection, or –1 if no item is currently selected.

- *SelectedItem* is the selected item itself, or *null* if no item is selected.

- *SelectedValue* is generally the value of a property of the selected item, as indicated by *SelectedValuePath*. (More on this shortly.)

If *SelectedIndex* is not –1, *SelectedItem* is the same object obtained from indexing the *Items* property with *SelectedIndex*. All these properties can be set programmatically or in XAML. When a *ListBox* is first filled with items, its *SelectedIndex* will be –1 and its *SelectedItem* will be *null* until these properties are explicitly changed or until the user selects an item with a finger or mouse.

Selector defines a *SelectionChanged* event that is fired when the selection changes. The handler then obtains the selected item by using one of these properties.

SelectedItem is backed by a dependency property, which means that it can be the target of a data binding, but it's more commonly used as a binding source. The SimpleListBox project uses *NamedColor.All* as a binding source for the *Items* property, but it does not define a template. Instead, it uses a somewhat different technique for displaying items:

Project: SimpleListBox | File: MainPage.xaml (excerpt)

```xaml
<Page ... >
    <Page.Resources>
        <ch11:NamedColor x:Key="namedColor" />
    </Page.Resources>

    <Grid>
        <ListBox Name="lstbox"
                 ItemsSource="{Binding Source={StaticResource namedColor},
                                       Path=All}"
                 DisplayMemberPath="Name"
                 Width="288"
                 HorizontalAlignment="Center" />

        <Grid.Background>
            <SolidColorBrush Color="{Binding ElementName=lstbox,
                                             Path=SelectedItem.Color}" />
        </Grid.Background>
    </Grid>
</Page>
```

The *ListBox* incorporates its own *ScrollViewer*, but it tends to grab as much screen space as possible regardless of the settings of *HorizontalAlignment* and *VerticalAlignment*. You'll want to give *ListBox* a specific *Width*, as I've done here. As you'll discover shortly, there are very good reasons why a *ListBox* can't determine its own width based on the maximum width of its items.

Rather than defining a *DataTemplate* for displaying the *NamedColor* items, I've set the *DisplayMemberPath* to "Name," which refers to the *Name* property of the items in the *ListBox*. These items are of type *NamedColor*, and fortunately, *NamedColor* includes a *Name* property. This is the property that *ListBox* uses to display the items. Initially, the *SolidColorBrush* set to the *Grid* will reference a default *Color* value because there is no selected item, but once you select an item, that color will form the background of the window:

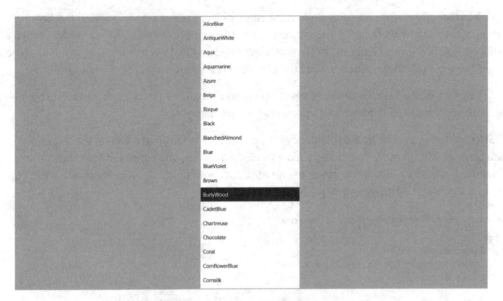

This program has a dark theme. The light background of the *ListBox* items and the selection highlight represent default behavior for the *ListBox*. You'll see how to change this highlighting later in this chapter. If you experiment with this program, you'll discover that you can move the selection by using the keyboard arrow keys, Page Up and Page Down, and Home and End.

There's an alternative way to defining the binding to the selected item. Similar to *DisplayMemberPath* that you use to indicate the property of the item you want displayed is *SelectedValuePath*, which is the name of the property to expose as the *SelectedValue*:

```
<Grid>
    <ListBox Name="lstbox"
             ItemsSource="{Binding Source={StaticResource namedColor},
                                   Path=All}"
             DisplayMemberPath="Name"
             SelectedValuePath="Color"
             Width="288"
             HorizontalAlignment="Center" />

    <Grid.Background>
        <SolidColorBrush Color="{Binding ElementName=lstbox,
                                         Path=SelectedValue}" />
    </Grid.Background>
</Grid>
```

The *SelectedValuePath* property of the *ListBox* indicates that the *Color* property of the *ListBox* items should be exposed as the *SelectedValue* property, so the binding on the *SolidColorBrush* is simplified.

It's easy to confuse *SelectedItem* and *SelectedValue*. They are the same if no *SelectedValuePath* property has been set. Otherwise, *SelectedItem* is an object in the collection, and *SelectedValue* is a property of that object.

It is more common for *ListBox* to have its *ItemTemplate* property set to a *DataTemplate*, as this one does. I've simplified the item template to not show the hexadecimal representation of the color, but otherwise it's the same as the ones you've seen already:

Project: ListBoxWithItemTemplate | **File:** MainPage.xaml (excerpt)

```xml
<Page ... >
    <Page.Resources>
        <ch11:NamedColor x:Key="namedColor" />
    </Page.Resources>

    <Grid>
        <ListBox Name="lstbox"
                ItemsSource="{Binding Source={StaticResource namedColor},
                                    Path=All}"
                Width="388">
            <ListBox.ItemTemplate>
                <DataTemplate>
                    <Border
                        BorderBrush="{Binding RelativeSource={RelativeSource TemplatedParent},
                                        Path=Foreground}"
                            BorderThickness="1"
                            Width="336"
                            Margin="6"
                            Loaded="OnItemLoaded">
                        <Grid>
                            <Grid.ColumnDefinitions>
                                <ColumnDefinition Width="Auto" />
                                <ColumnDefinition Width="*"/>
                            </Grid.ColumnDefinitions>

                            <Rectangle Grid.Column="0"
                                        Height="72"
                                        Width="72"
                                        Margin="6">
                                <Rectangle.Fill>
                                    <SolidColorBrush Color="{Binding Color}" />
                                </Rectangle.Fill>
                            </Rectangle>

                            <TextBlock Grid.Column="1"
                                        FontSize="24"
                                        Text="{Binding Name}"
                                        VerticalAlignment="Center" />
                        </Grid>
                    </Border>
                </DataTemplate>
            </ListBox.ItemTemplate>
        </ListBox>

        <Grid.Background>
            <SolidColorBrush Color="{Binding ElementName=lstbox,
                                        Path=SelectedItem.Color}" />
```

```
        </Grid.Background>
    </Grid>
</Page>
```

Very early in the item template, you might notice a big difference in how the *Border* is colored. In the programs using *ItemsControl*, the *Border* could be colored with a reference to the theme foreground brush:

```
BorderBrush="{StaticResource ApplicationForegroundThemeBrush}"
```

With a dark theme (which I've been using throughout the chapter), that's white.

However, we have discovered that the *ListBox* items get a white background by default, which means that white brush would disappear against the background. We really want to set it to the *Foreground* property of the ancestor element being templated, and the option of doing that is provided for with a special binding syntax:

```
BorderBrush="{Binding RelativeSource={RelativeSource TemplatedParent},
                      Path=Foreground}"
```

The only two options for *RelativeSource* are *Self* and *TemplatedParent*, and you can't use *Self* here because *Border* doesn't have a *Foreground* property.

What is the *TemplatedParent* exactly? In this context, it's a *ContentPresenter*, which is a class that you rarely see unless you're writing another type of template (a control template) that I'll discuss later in this chapter. The *TextBlock* doesn't need any binding to obtain the correct color because it simply inherits the *Foreground* property, and both elements are properly flipped in color when the item is selected:

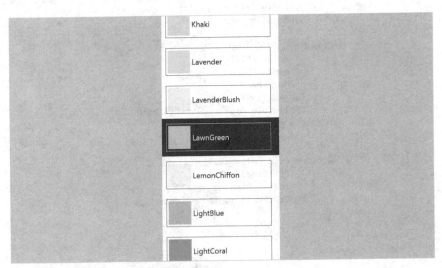

ListBox supports multiple selection if you need it. Set the *SelectionMode* property to *Multiple* or *Extended*, and use the *SelectedItems* property for obtaining the selected items.

Panels and Virtualizing Panels

I've done something in ListBoxWithItemTemplate that I haven't often done in this book: I've left in a bit of debugging code. The sole purpose of this is to give you a firsthand glimpse of something very important going on internally within *ListBox*.

The *Border* element that surrounds each item defines a handler for the *Loaded* event:

```
<Border BorderBrush="{Binding RelativeSource={RelativeSource TemplatedParent},
                              Path=Foreground}"
        BorderThickness="1"
        Width="336"
        Margin="6"
        Loaded="OnItemLoaded">
```

In the *Loaded* handler, a call to *System.Diagnostics.Debug.WriteLine* displays the *Name* property of the *NamedColor* object set to the loaded element's *DataContext* property:

```
void OnItemLoaded(object sender, RoutedEventArgs args)
{
    System.Diagnostics.Debug.WriteLine("Item Loaded: " +
        ((sender as FrameworkElement).DataContext as NamedColor).Name);
}
```

Run this program under the Visual Studio debugger, and watch the Output window. When the program first loads, you'll see only several of these colors and definitely not all 141 of them. On my tablet, the 768-pixel-tall screen allows for the display of 6 full items (from *AliceBlue* through *Beige*) and a half of the next item. The list in the Visual Studio Output window shows that visual trees for 11 items have been loaded, from *AliceBlue* to *BlueViolet*.

Now start scrolling the list. You might see a few more items in the Output window—I see *Brown*, *BurlyWood*, and *CadetBlue*—but then the list stops. What exactly is going on?

The *ListBox* is being efficient. It's building visual trees only for those items initially displayed (plus a couple more), and it's re-using these visual trees when some items are scrolled out of view and others are scrolled into view. And why not? All it needs to do is change the bindings.

This virtualization is essential when you start binding your *ListBox* control with collections of hundreds or thousands of items. But it also means that *ListBox* can't determine the width it needs to display all its items.

Watch out: There might be something peculiar about the items in your collection that have issues with this virtualization. I'll discuss such a case in Chapter 16, "Rich Text," that involves visual trees that contain links to each other. In that case, you can basically turn off this virtualization feature. An items control always uses a *Panel* of some sort to display the items, and you can specify which *Panel* derivative it uses or supply your own. *ItemsControl* defines (and *ListBox* inherits) a property named *ItemsPanel* that you can set to an object of type *ItemsPanelTemplate*. This is the second of the three templates referred to in the title of this chapter, but it's certainly the simplest of the three. *ItemsPanelTemplate* only needs one item: a *Panel* derivative. This is the panel that the items control uses for hosting the child items. In a regular *ItemsControl*, it's a *StackPanel*. In a *ListBox*, it's a *VirtualizingStackPanel*.

In ListBoxWithItemTemplate, you can set the *ItemsPanel* property of the *ListBox* to the default value with the following markup:

```
<ListBox Name="lstbox"
         ItemsSource="{Binding Source={StaticResource namedColor},
                               Path=All}"
         Width="380">
    <ListBox.ItemTemplate>
    ...
    </ListBox.ItemTemplate>

    <ListBox.ItemsPanel>
        <ItemsPanelTemplate>
            <VirtualizingStackPanel />
        </ItemsPanelTemplate>
    </ListBox.ItemsPanel>
</ListBox>
```

Now try changing that to a regular *StackPanel*:

```
<ListBox.ItemsPanel>
    <ItemsPanelTemplate>
        <StackPanel />
    </ItemsPanelTemplate>
</ListBox.ItemsPanel>
```

Now all the items are created when the *ListBox* is first loaded, as a glance at the Output window in Visual Studio will verify.

However, you can also do this:

```
<ListBox.ItemsPanel>
    <ItemsPanelTemplate>
        <VirtualizingStackPanel Orientation="Horizontal" />
    </ItemsPanelTemplate>
</ListBox.ItemsPanel>
```

And that will turn your vertical *ListBox* into a horizontal *ListBox*.

Well, not quite. You'll also need to make some adjustments to the *ListBox* size and the internal *ScrollViewer* properties, as I've done in the HorizontalListBox project:

Project: HorizontalListBox | **File:** MainPage.xaml (excerpt)

```
<Page ... >
    <Page.Resources>
        <ch11:NamedColor x:Key="namedColor" />
    </Page.Resources>

    <Grid>
        <ListBox Name="lstbox"
```

```
                ItemsSource="{Binding Source={StaticResource namedColor},
                                      Path=All}"
              Height="120"
              ScrollViewer.HorizontalScrollMode="Enabled"
              ScrollViewer.HorizontalScrollBarVisibility="Auto"
              ScrollViewer.VerticalScrollMode="Disabled"
              ScrollViewer.VerticalScrollBarVisibility="Disabled">
            <ListBox.ItemTemplate>
                <DataTemplate>
                    <Border
                        BorderBrush="{Binding RelativeSource={RelativeSource TemplatedParent},
                                              Path=Foreground}"
                        BorderThickness="1"
                        Width="336"
                        Margin="6"
                        Loaded="OnItemLoaded">
                        <Grid>
                            <Grid.ColumnDefinitions>
                                <ColumnDefinition Width="Auto" />
                                <ColumnDefinition Width="*"/>
                            </Grid.ColumnDefinitions>

                            <Rectangle Grid.Column="0"
                                       Height="72"
                                       Width="72"
                                       Margin="6">
                                <Rectangle.Fill>
                                    <SolidColorBrush Color="{Binding Color}" />
                                </Rectangle.Fill>
                            </Rectangle>

                            <TextBlock Grid.Column="1"
                                       FontSize="24"
                                       Text="{Binding Name}"
                                       VerticalAlignment="Center" />
                        </Grid>
                    </Border>
                </DataTemplate>
            </ListBox.ItemTemplate>

            <ListBox.ItemsPanel>
                <ItemsPanelTemplate>
                    <VirtualizingStackPanel Orientation="Horizontal" />
                </ItemsPanelTemplate>
            </ListBox.ItemsPanel>
        </ListBox>

        <Grid.Background>
            <SolidColorBrush Color="{Binding ElementName=lstbox,
                                             Path=SelectedItem.Color}" />
        </Grid.Background>
    </Grid>
</Page>
```

ScrollViewer defines several properties that govern the control's appearance and functionality, but sometimes the *ScrollViewer* itself is inaccessible, as it is when it's inside a *ListBox*. For situations like that, *ScrollViewer* has conveniently defined several attached properties that you can set right in the *ListBox* tag.

The only differences between this program and the previous *ListBox* are the use of a horizontal *VirtualizingStackPanel* and some changes in the *ListBox* tag to alter the dimensions of the control and provide for horizontal scrolling. The result is a fully functional horizontal *ListBox*:

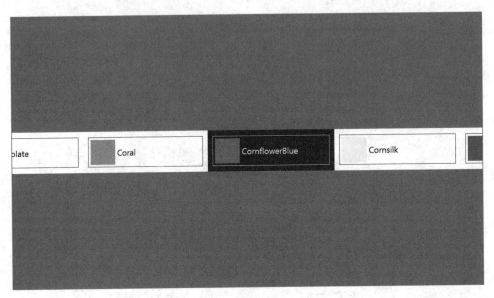

Oddly enough, I have not had success using a *WrapGrid* or a *VariableSizedWrapGrid* panel with *ListBox*. Attempting to do so raises an exception with the message "The Panel you are using for the Control is not allowed as an ItemsPanel for the Control." But I will provide something similar to these wrap panels in the next section.

Custom Panels

Perhaps the primary reason to write a custom *Panel* derivative is to use as an *ItemsPanelTemplate* of an items control. Each type of custom *Panel* can lay out children in a different manner.

Writing a *Panel* derivative that lays out its children in an unusual way—in a circle, perhaps—is easiest if all the items can fit on the screen and no scrolling is required. If scrolling is required, the layout of the items needs to be conducive to the abilities of *ScrollViewer*. Or, *ScrollViewer* itself needs to be replaced with some custom scrolling mechanism.

Panel derivatives can define dependency properties and attached properties. Both *Grid* and *Canvas* define attached properties, for example. However, generally a *Panel* derivative that has attached properties cannot be used as the *ItemsPanelTemplate* because there's usually no sensible way to set these attached properties from the *DataTemplate*.

A *Panel* derivative always overrides two virtual protected methods: *MeasureOverride* and *ArrangeOverride*. These correspond to the two passes of layout. During the *MeasureOverride* method, the *Panel* derivative calls the *Measure* method on all its children and calculates a desired size for itself. During the *ArrangeOverride* method, the *Panel* derivative calls *Arrange* on all its children, which sizes and positions each child relative to itself.

The two method names *MeasureOverride* and *ArrangeOverride* might seem somewhat peculiar. These method names originated in the Windows Presentation Foundation and involve the difference between the WPF versions of the *UIElement* and *FrameworkElement* classes. *UIElement* implements a comparatively simpler layout system involving the methods *Measure* and *Arrange*. To the WPF *UIElement*, however, *FrameworkElement* added the properties *HorizontalAlignment*, *VerticalAlignment*, and *Margin*, which make layout considerably more complicated. Hence, *FrameworkElement* also defines *MeasureOverride* and *ArrangeOverride* to supersede the *Measure* and *Arrange* methods, although *Measure* and *Arrange* still continue to play a role in layout.

In summary, a *Panel* overrides *MeasureOverride* and *ArrangeOverride* and within these methods calls *Measure* and *Arrange* on all its children. Internally, these *Measure* and *Arrange* methods in the child call the child's *MeasureOverride* and *ArrangeOverride* methods. The child then uses the opportunity to call *Measure* and *Arrange* on all its children, and the process continues down the tree.

You can override *MeasureOverride* and *ArrangeOverride* in any *FrameworkElement* derivative, but programs written for the Windows Runtime generally do not do so except in *Panel* derivatives.

A *Panel* derivative does *not* need to bother itself with any of the following properties set on itself or its children:

- *Width*, *MinWidth*, and *MaxWidth*

- *Height*, *MinHeight*, and *MaxHeight*

- *HorizontalAlignment* and *VerticalAlignment*

- *Margin*

- *Visibility*

- *Opacity* (does not affect layout)

- *RenderTransform* (does not affect layout)

All these properties are handled automatically.

In a *Panel* derivative, the *MeasureOverride* method looks like this:

```
protected override Size MeasureOverride(Size availableSize)
{
    ...

    return desiredSize;
}
```

The *availableSize* argument is of type *Size*, which (as you know) has two properties of type *double* named *Width* and *Height*. This *availableSize* argument is sometimes very simple: If this panel is the content of a *Page*, for example, the *availableSize* indicates the size of the page, which is usually the size of the application's window. If this panel is in a cell of a *Grid* and that *Grid* cell has specific pixel dimensions, the *availableSize* is the size of that cell.

However, there are also common cases where the available size *Width* or *Height* or both might be infinite. Within the *MeasureOverride* method, you can test *Width* and *Height* for infinity using the static *Double.IsPositiveInfinity* method.

An infinite *Width* or *Height* property of *availableSize* means that the parent of the panel is offering the panel as much horizontal or vertical space as it needs. If the panel is a child of a vertical *StackPanel*, the *Height* property will be infinite; if the panel is a child of a horizontal *StackPanel*, the *Width* property will be infinite. If the panel is a child of a *Canvas*, both *Width* and *Height* will be infinite. If the panel is in a *Grid* cell where the cell width and height are both *Auto*, the *Width* and *Height* properties of *availableSize* will be infinite.

The *MeasureOverride* method must properly deal with these cases. The *desiredSize* returned from the method must *not* have infinite *Width* or *Height* properties. In other words, *MeasureOverride* cannot simply return *availableSize*. That will not work.

The *MeasureOverride* method must call *Measure* on each of its children; otherwise, the children will not be visible. On return from each *Measure* call, the child's *DesiredSize* property will be valid, and the panel can use the desired sizes of all its children to compute its own desired size.

When *MeasureOverride* calls *Measure* on a child, it provides an available size for the child. One or both properties of this available size can be infinite. For example, a vertical *StackPanel* calls *Measure* on all its children with an available *Width* that equals its own available *Width* and an available *Height* of infinity:

```
protected override Size MeasureOverride(Size availableSize)
{
    double maxWidth = 0;
    double totalHeight = 0;

    foreach (UIElement child in this.Children)
    {
        child.Measure(new Size(availableSize.Width, Double.PositiveInfinity));
        maxWidth = Math.Max(maxWidth, child.DesiredSize.Width);
        totalHeight += child.DesiredSize.Height;
    }
    return new Size(maxWidth, totalHeight);
}
```

This *MeasureOverride* for a vertical stack then accumulates a maximum width and a total height of all its children. That becomes its desired size.

The *ArrangeOverride* method has an argument that indicates the size computed for this panel. For a vertical stack panel, the method again loops through all its children and stacks them, giving to each its own width and the child's desired height:

```
protected override Size ArrangeOverride(Size finalSize)
{
    double y = 0;

    foreach (UIElement child in this.Children)
    {
        child.Arrange(new Rect(0, y, finalSize.Width, child.DesiredSize.Height));
        y += child.DesiredSize.Height;
    }
    return base.ArrangeOverride(finalSize);
}
```

One *Panel* derivative that I find useful when programming with WPF is called the *UniformGrid*. It's similar to a regular *Grid* but every cell has the same size. The children are simply distributed one to a cell so that no attached properties are required. Although the size of the children can vary, the *UniformGrid* treats the children as if they all have the same size. This size is based on the maximum child size or the space available for the *UniformGrid*.

My version of *UniformGrid* defines two properties named *Rows* and *Columns* of type *int*, but the default values are –1, indicating no preset values. If neither of these two properties is set, *UniformGrid* attempts to determine an optimum number of rows and columns; otherwise, if one of the two properties is set, the other is calculated based on the number of children. It is not recommended that both properties be set: If the product of *Rows* and *Columns* is less than the number of children, some of the children might not appear in the panel.

In most uses of *UniformGrid*, *Rows* and *Columns* are left at their default –1 values or one or the other of these properties is set to 1. If *Rows* or *Columns* is set to 1, *UniformGrid* behaves like a *Grid* with a single column or single row, or like a *StackPanel* where every child has the same size.

If the *Width* and *Height* properties of *availableSize* are both finite values, *UniformGrid* attempts to fit all the children into that space. Otherwise, it uses the maximum child size to lay out its children. The only situation *UniformGrid* can't handle is when *Rows* and *Columns* are both left at –1 and available *Width* and *Height* are both infinite. In that case, an exception is raised.

Like *StackPanel*, *UniformGrid* also defines an *Orientation* property. Here are the property definitions and the property-changed handler they all share:

Project: Petzold.ProgrammingWindows6.Chapter11 | File: UniformGrid.cs (excerpt)

```
public class UniformGrid : Panel
{
    // Set by MeasureOverride, used in ArrangeOverride
    protected int rows, cols;

    static UniformGrid()
```

```
    {
        RowsProperty = DependencyProperty.Register("Rows",
            typeof(int),
            typeof(UniformGrid),
            new PropertyMetadata(-1, OnPropertyChanged));

        ColumnsProperty = DependencyProperty.Register("Columns",
            typeof(int),
            typeof(UniformGrid),
            new PropertyMetadata(-1, OnPropertyChanged));

        OrientationProperty = DependencyProperty.Register("Orientation",
            typeof(Orientation),
            typeof(UniformGrid),
            new PropertyMetadata(Orientation.Vertical, OnPropertyChanged));
    }

    public static DependencyProperty RowsProperty { private set; get; }

    public static DependencyProperty ColumnsProperty { private set; get; }

    public static DependencyProperty OrientationProperty { private set; get; }

    public int Rows
    {
        set { SetValue(RowsProperty, value); }
        get { return (int)GetValue(RowsProperty); }
    }

    public int Columns
    {
        set { SetValue(ColumnsProperty, value); }
        get { return (int)GetValue(ColumnsProperty); }
    }

    public Orientation Orientation
    {
        set { SetValue(OrientationProperty, value); }
        get { return (Orientation)GetValue(OrientationProperty); }
    }
    ...

    static void OnPropertyChanged(DependencyObject obj, DependencyPropertyChangedEventArgs args)
    {
        if (args.Property == UniformGrid.OrientationProperty)
        {
            (obj as UniformGrid).InvalidateArrange();
        }
        else
        {
            (obj as UniformGrid).InvalidateMeasure();
        }
    }
}
```

In the property-changed handler, the *InvalidateMeasure* and *InvalidateArrange* calls signal the layout system that a new layout is required. A call to *InvalidateMeasure* triggers both measure and arrange passes; a call to *InvalidateArrange* triggers only an arrange pass, skipping the measure pass. In that case, everything remains the same size, but children might be moved to different locations.

Of course, these are not the only ways that layout is invalidated. Any change in the number of children in the panel triggers a new layout, for example.

The *MeasureOverride* method begins by performing a couple validity checks and then calculating the *rows* and *cols* fields by using the *Rows* and *Columns* properties and the number of children:

Project: Petzold.ProgrammingWindows6.Chapter11 | File: UniformGrid.cs (excerpt)

```
protected override Size MeasureOverride(Size availableSize)
{
    // Only bother if children actually exist
    if (this.Children.Count == 0)
        return new Size();

    // Throw exceptions if the properties aren't OK
    if (this.Rows != -1 && this.Rows < 1)
        throw new ArgumentOutOfRangeException("UniformGrid Rows must be greater than zero");

    if (this.Columns != -1 && this.Columns < 1)
        throw new ArgumentOutOfRangeException("UniformGrid Columns must be greater than zero");

    // Determine the actual number of rows and columns
    // ---------------------------------------
    // This option is discouraged
    if (this.Rows != -1 && this.Columns != -1)
    {
        rows = this.Rows;
        cols = this.Columns;
    }
    // These two options often appear with values of 1
    else if (this.Rows != -1)
    {
        rows = this.Rows;
        cols = (int)Math.Ceiling((double)this.Children.Count / rows);
    }
    else if (this.Columns != -1)
    {
        cols = this.Columns;
        rows = (int)Math.Ceiling((double)this.Children.Count / cols);
    }
    // No values yet if both Rows and Columns are both -1, but
    //      check for infinite availableSize
    else if (Double.IsInfinity(availableSize.Width) &&
             Double.IsInfinity(availableSize.Height))
    {
        throw new NotSupportedException("Completely unconstrained UniformGrid " +
                                "requires Rows or Columns property to be set");
    }
    ...
}
```

Processing of *MeasureOverride* continues with a calculation of the maximum child size. This is the code that enumerates through the *Children* collection and performs the crucial calls to the *Measure* method of each child. Without this *Measure* call, the child has zero size. Following the *Measure* call, the *DesiredSize* property of the child is valid:

Project: Petzold.ProgrammingWindows6.Chapter11 | File: UniformGrid.cs (excerpt)

```
protected override Size MeasureOverride(Size availableSize)
{
    ...

    // Determine the maximum size of all children
    // -------------------------------------------
    Size maximumSize = new Size();
    Size infiniteSize = new Size(Double.PositiveInfinity,
                                 Double.PositiveInfinity);

    // Find the maximum size of all children
    foreach (UIElement child in this.Children)
    {
        child.Measure(infiniteSize);
        Size childSize = child.DesiredSize;
        maximumSize.Width = Math.Max(maximumSize.Width, childSize.Width);
        maximumSize.Height = Math.Max(maximumSize.Height, childSize.Height);
    }

    ...
}
```

This is a calculation that occurs in many *Panel* derivatives. However, the *Measure* method isn't always called with infinite height and widths. In this particular case, *UniformGrid* wants to determine the "natural size" of each element, and this is the way to do it.

I mentioned earlier that the *Panel* derivative does not need to take account of any *Margin* property set on itself or its children. The available size that's passed as an argument to *MeasureOverride* excludes any *Margin* property set on the element. However, when the panel calls *Measure* on its children, that size implicitly includes the child's *Margin*. The *Measure* method in the child then decreases that available size by the child's *Margin* setting. (Of course, if the size is infinite, as it is in this case, the result is the same.) That size without the *Margin* is then passed to the child's *MeasureOverride* method, and the child calculates a size for itself that it returns from *MeasureOverride*. The child's *Measure* method continues by adding the child's *Margin* to the size returned from *MeasureOverride* and set's the child's *DesiredSize* property to that increased size.

This is how *Margin* is accounted for in layout despite *MeasureOverride* not bothering with it.

Now that the maximum child size has been calculated, a desired size for the *Panel* can be calculated. But there is still potentially a rather lengthy calculation: If both *Rows* and *Columns* have been left at their default values, the *Panel* itself needs to calculate an optimum number of rows and columns based on available size and the maximum child size:

Project: Petzold.ProgrammingWindows6.Chapter11 | **File:** UniformGrid.cs (excerpt)

```
protected override Size MeasureOverride(Size availableSize)
{
    ...

    // Find rows and cols if Rows and Colunms are both -1
    if (this.Rows == -1 && this.Columns == -1)
    {
        if (Double.IsInfinity(availableSize.Width))
        {
            rows = (int)Math.Max(1, availableSize.Height / maximumSize.Height);
            cols = (int)Math.Ceiling((double)this.Children.Count / rows);
        }
        else if (Double.IsInfinity(availableSize.Height))
        {
            cols = (int)Math.Max(1, availableSize.Width / maximumSize.Width);
            rows = (int)Math.Ceiling((double)this.Children.Count / cols);
        }
        // Neither dimension is infinite -- the hard one
        else
        {
            double aspectRatio = maximumSize.Width / maximumSize.Height;
            double bestHeight = 0;
            double bestWidth = 0;

            for (int tryRows = 1; tryRows < this.Children.Count; tryRows++)
            {
                int tryCols = (int)Math.Ceiling((double)this.Children.Count / tryRows);
                double childHeight = availableSize.Height / tryRows;
                double childWidth = availableSize.Width / tryCols;

                // Adjust for aspect ratio
                if (childWidth > aspectRatio * childHeight)
                    childWidth = aspectRatio * childHeight;
                else
                    childHeight = childWidth / aspectRatio;

                // Check if it's larger than other trials
                if (childHeight > bestHeight)
                {
                    bestHeight = childHeight;
                    bestWidth = childWidth;
                    rows = tryRows;
                    cols = tryCols;
                }
            }
        }
    }
    // Return desired size
    Size desiredSize = new Size(Math.Min(cols * maximumSize.Width, availableSize.Width),
                               Math.Min(rows * maximumSize.Height, availableSize.Height));

    return desiredSize;
}
```

Normally, the panel's desired size is based entirely on the size of its children and any overhead that may be required. That size might well be larger than *availableSize*. That's how *ScrollViewer* knows how to scroll a child element. With a non-infinite *availableSize* on the *UniformGrid*, however, I want to restrict the panel to just that size.

The *ArrangeOverride* method is often much simpler than *MeasureOverride*. The *finalSize* argument is the finite size allocated for the panel. The only requirement for *ArrangeOverride* is that the *Arrange* method be called on each child, passing to it a *Rect* object indicating the location of the child relative to the panel, and the size of the child. Very often this size is the child's *DesiredSize* property, but in this case I want the total size of the panel to be allocated equally for the rows and columns:

Project: Petzold.ProgrammingWindows6.Chapter11 | File: UniformGrid.cs (excerpt)

```
protected override Size ArrangeOverride(Size finalSize)
{
    int index = 0;
    double cellWidth = finalSize.Width / cols;
    double cellHeight = finalSize.Height / rows;

    if (this.Orientation == Orientation.Vertical)
    {
        for (int row = 0; row < rows; row++)
        {
            double y = row * cellHeight;

            for (int col = 0; col < cols; col++)
            {
                double x = col * cellWidth;

                if (index < this.Children.Count)
                    this.Children[index].Arrange(new Rect(x, y, cellWidth, cellHeight));

                index++;
            }
        }
    }
    else
    {
        for (int col = 0; col < cols; col++)
        {
            double x = col * cellWidth;

            for (int row = 0; row < rows; row++)
            {
                double y = row * cellHeight;

                if (index < this.Children.Count)
                    this.Children[index].Arrange(new Rect(x, y, cellWidth, cellHeight));

                index++;
            }
        }
    }

    return base.ArrangeOverride(finalSize);
}
```

This is the only place in *UniformGrid* where *Orientation* plays a role and governs whether the children should be positioned left to right first, or from top to bottom first. The *ArrangeOverride* method almost always returns *finalSize*, which is what the base method returns.

Let's try this out for a situation where *availableSize* has finite *Width* and *Height* properties. This is the case for an *ItemsControl* that is not in a *ScrollViewer*, such as this one:

Project: AllColorsItemsControl | **File:** MainPage.xaml (excerpt)

```xaml
<Page ... >
    <Page.Resources>
        <ch11:NamedColor x:Key="namedColor" />
        <ch11:ColorToContrastColorConverter x:Key="colorConverter" />
    </Page.Resources>

    <Grid Background="{StaticResource ApplicationPageBackgroundThemeBrush}">
        <ItemsControl ItemsSource="{Binding Source={StaticResource namedColor},
                                    Path=All}">
            <ItemsControl.ItemTemplate>
                <DataTemplate>
                    <Border
                        BorderBrush="{Binding RelativeSource={RelativeSource TemplatedParent},
                                         Path=Foreground}"
                            BorderThickness="2"
                            Margin="2">
                        <Border.Background>
                            <SolidColorBrush Color="{Binding Color}" />
                        </Border.Background>

                        <Viewbox>
                            <TextBlock Text="{Binding Name}"
                                       HorizontalAlignment="Center"
                                       VerticalAlignment="Center">
                                <TextBlock.Foreground>
                                    <SolidColorBrush Color="{Binding Color,
                                               Converter={StaticResource colorConverter}}" />
                                </TextBlock.Foreground>
                            </TextBlock>
                        </Viewbox>
                    </Border>
                </DataTemplate>
            </ItemsControl.ItemTemplate>

            <ItemsControl.ItemsPanel>
                <ItemsPanelTemplate>
                    <ch11:UniformGrid />
                </ItemsPanelTemplate>
            </ItemsControl.ItemsPanel>
        </ItemsControl>
    </Grid>
</Page>
```

Notice the *UniformGrid* toward the bottom used as the control's *ItemsPanel*.

I've made the item template a little simpler than previous examples. It now consists of a *Border* with its *Background* property constructed from a binding to the *Color* property of *NamedColor*, and a *TextBlock* child displaying the name of the color. Notice that the *TextBlock* is inside a *Viewbox*, so the text size should adapt itself to the available size for the child. Also notice that I've bound the *Foreground* of the *TextBlock* to the *Color* property but passed through a converter named *ColorToContrastColorConverter*. This converter calculates a gray shade corresponding to the input color and then selects *Colors.Black* or *Colors.White* to contrast:

Project: Petzold.ProgrammingWindows6.Chapter11 | File: ColorToContrastColorConverter.cs

```
public class ColorToContrastColorConverter : IValueConverter
{
    public object Convert(object value, Type targetType, object parameter, string language)
    {
        Color clr = (Color)value;
        double grayShade = 0.30 * clr.R + 0.59 * clr.G + 0.11 * clr.B;
        return grayShade > 128 ? Colors.Black : Colors.White;
    }
    public object ConvertBack(object value, Type targetType, object parameter, string language)
    {
        return value;
    }
}
```

This works well for every color except *Transparent*:

AliceBlue	AntiqueWhite	Aqua	Aquamarine	Azure	Beige	Bisque
Black	BlanchedAlmond	Blue	BlueViolet	Brown	BurlyWood	CadetBlue
Chartreuse	Chocolate	Coral	CornflowerBlue	Cornsilk	Crimson	Cyan
DarkBlue	DarkCyan	DarkGoldenrod	DarkGray	DarkGreen	DarkKhaki	DarkMagenta
DarkOliveGreen	DarkOrange	DarkOrchid	DarkRed	DarkSalmon	DarkSeaGreen	DarkSlateBlue
DarkSlateGray	DarkTurquoise	DarkViolet	DeepPink	DeepSkyBlue	DimGray	DodgerBlue
Firebrick	FloralWhite	ForestGreen	Fuchsia	Gainsboro	GhostWhite	Gold
Goldenrod	Gray	Green	GreenYellow	Honeydew	HotPink	IndianRed
Indigo	Ivory	Khaki	Lavender	LavenderBlush	LawnGreen	LemonChiffon
LightBlue	LightCoral	LightCyan	LightGoldenrodYellow	LightGray	LightGreen	LightPink
LightSalmon	LightSeaGreen	LightSkyBlue	LightSlateGray	LightSteelBlue	LightYellow	Lime
LimeGreen	Linen	Magenta	Maroon	MediumAquamarine	MediumBlue	MediumOrchid
MediumPurple	MediumSeaGreen	MediumSlateBlue	MediumSpringGreen	MediumTurquoise	MediumVioletRed	MidnightBlue
MintCream	MistyRose	Moccasin	NavajoWhite	Navy	OldLace	Olive
OliveDrab	Orange	OrangeRed	Orchid	PaleGoldenrod	PaleGreen	PaleTurquoise
PaleVioletRed	PapayaWhip	PeachPuff	Peru	Pink	Plum	PowderBlue
Purple	Red	RosyBrown	RoyalBlue	SaddleBrown	Salmon	SandyBrown
SeaGreen	SeaShell	Sienna	Silver	SkyBlue	SlateBlue	SlateGray
Snow	SpringGreen	SteelBlue	Tan	Teal	Thistle	Tomato
	Turquoise	Violet	Wheat	White	WhiteSmoke	Yellow
YellowGreen						

All 141 colors fit within the window, which was the objective here. The cells and text become smaller when the program is in a snap view:

AliceBlue	AntiqueWhite	Aqua	Aquamarine	Azure	Beige
Bisque	Black	BlanchedAlmond	Blue	BlueViolet	Brown
BurlyWood	CadetBlue	Chartreuse	Chocolate	Coral	CornflowerBlue
Cornsilk	Crimson	Cyan	DarkBlue	DarkCyan	DarkGoldenrod
DarkGray	DarkGreen	DarkKhaki	DarkMagenta	DarkOliveGreen	DarkOrange
DarkOrchid	DarkRed	DarkSalmon	DarkSeaGreen	DarkSlateBlue	DarkSlateGray
DarkTurquoise	DarkViolet	DeepPink	DeepSkyBlue	DimGray	DodgerBlue
Firebrick	FloralWhite	ForestGreen	Fuchsia	Gainsboro	GhostWhite
Gold	Goldenrod	Gray	Green	GreenYellow	Honeydew
HotPink	IndianRed	Indigo	Ivory	Khaki	Lavender
LavenderBlush	LawnGreen	LemonChiffon	LightBlue	LightCoral	LightCyan
LightGoldenrodYellow	LightGray	LightGreen	LightPink	LightSalmon	LightSeaGreen
LightSkyBlue	LightSlateGray	LightSteelBlue	LightYellow	Lime	LimeGreen
Linen	Magenta	Maroon	MediumAquamarine	MediumBlue	MediumOrchid
MediumPurple	MediumSeaGreen	MediumSlateBlue	MediumSpringGreen	MediumTurquoise	MediumVioletRed
MidnightBlue	MintCream	MistyRose	Moccasin	NavajoWhite	Navy
OldLace	Olive	OliveDrab	Orange	OrangeRed	Orchid
PaleGoldenrod	PaleGreen	PaleTurquoise	PaleVioletRed	PapayaWhip	PeachPuff
Peru	Pink	Plum	PowderBlue	Purple	Red
RosyBrown	RoyalBlue	SaddleBrown	Salmon	SandyBrown	SeaGreen
SeaShell	Sienna	Silver	SkyBlue	SlateBlue	SlateGray
Snow	SpringGreen	SteelBlue	Tan	Teal	Thistle
Tomato		Turquoise	Violet	Wheat	White
WhiteSmoke	Yellow	YellowGreen			

However, if the cells become too small, the visuals break down a bit.

Now let's try *UniformGrid* in a *ListBox*. I've retained the simplified data template, but I've given the *Border* and *TextBlock* specific sizes:

Project: ListBoxWithUniformGrid | **File:** MainPage.xaml (excerpt)

```xml
<Page ... >
    <Page.Resources>
        <ch11:NamedColor x:Key="namedColor" />
        <ch11:ColorToContrastColorConverter x:Key="colorConverter" />
    </Page.Resources>

    <Grid Background="{StaticResource ApplicationPageBackgroundThemeBrush}">
        <ListBox ItemsSource="{Binding Source={StaticResource namedColor},
                               Path=All}">
            <ListBox.ItemTemplate>
                <DataTemplate>
                    <Border
                        BorderBrush="{Binding RelativeSource={RelativeSource TemplatedParent},
                                      Path=Foreground}"
                            Width="288"
                            Height="72"
                            BorderThickness="3"
                            Margin="3">
                        <Border.Background>
                            <SolidColorBrush Color="{Binding Color}" />
                        </Border.Background>

                        <TextBlock Text="{Binding Name}"
                                   FontSize="24"
                                   HorizontalAlignment="Center"
```

```
                                    VerticalAlignment="Center">
                        <TextBlock.Foreground>
                            <SolidColorBrush Color="{Binding Color,
                                    Converter={StaticResource colorConverter}}" />
                        </TextBlock.Foreground>
                    </TextBlock>
                </Border>
            </DataTemplate>
        </ListBox.ItemTemplate>

        <ListBox.ItemsPanel>
            <ItemsPanelTemplate>
                <ch11:UniformGrid />
            </ItemsPanelTemplate>
        </ListBox.ItemsPanel>
    </ListBox>
    </Grid>
</Page>
```

In this case, the *availableSize* argument to the *MeasureOverride* method in *UniformGrid* has an infinite *Height* property for vertical scrolling. *UniformGrid* calculates a number of columns based on the available width and maximum child width. The number of rows is calculated from that. *UniformGrid* has a desired size that is based on its total height, and the panel becomes vertically scrollable:

It's fairly easy to switch to horizontal scrolling. Simply set the *ScrollViewer* attached properties as you saw earlier in the HorizontalListBox project and then set the *Orientation* property of the *UniformGrid* to *Horizontal*:

```
<ListBox ItemsSource="{Binding Source={StaticResource namedColor},
                        Path=All}"
        ScrollViewer.HorizontalScrollMode="Enabled"
        ScrollViewer.HorizontalScrollBarVisibility="Auto"
```

```
            ScrollViewer.VerticalScrollMode="Disabled"
            ScrollViewer.VerticalScrollBarVisibility="Disabled">
        <ListBox.ItemTemplate>
            <DataTemplate>
                ...
            </DataTemplate>
        </ListBox.ItemTemplate>

        <ListBox.ItemsPanel>
            <ItemsPanelTemplate>
                <ch11:UniformGrid Orientation="Horizontal" />
            </ItemsPanelTemplate>
        </ListBox.ItemsPanel>
    </ListBox>
```

The *Horizontal* setting of *Orientation* isn't strictly required but causes the children to be ordered differently, first from top to bottom and then from left to right:

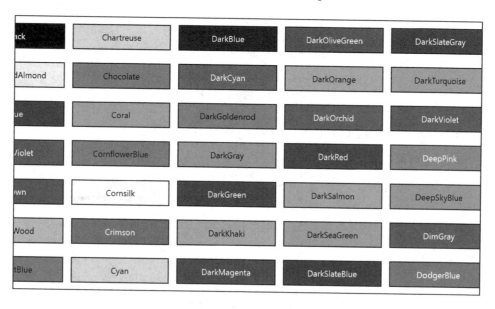

The Item Template Bar Chart

One of the great "parlor tricks" with an items control involves creating a bar chart with a minimum of fuss. All you really need is a data item containing a numeric property suitable for binding, a *Rectangle* in an *ItemTemplate*, and a *UniformGrid* or *StackPanel* to hold the items.

The RgbBarChart project demonstrates this technique. This *ItemsSource* for the *ItemsControl* is, of course, the collection of *NamedColor* objects. The *DataTemplate* is a vertical *StackPanel* containing three *Rectangle* elements, the *Height* properties of each bound to the *R*, *G*, and *B* properties of the *Color* property of the items. Normally, this would create a stack of three *Rectangle* elements that start at the top of the *StackPanel*, and I wanted a more traditional looking stacked bar chart oriented at the bottom, so I used a *RenderTransform* to flip the bars upside down:

Project: RgbBarChart | **File:** MainPage.xaml (excerpt)

```xml
<Page ... >
    <Page.Resources>
        <ch11:NamedColor x:Key="namedColor" />
    </Page.Resources>

    <Grid Background="{StaticResource ApplicationPageBackgroundThemeBrush}">
        <ItemsControl ItemsSource="{Binding Source={StaticResource namedColor},
                                    Path=All}">
            <ItemsControl.ItemTemplate>
                <DataTemplate>
                    <StackPanel Name="stackPanel"
                                Height="765"
                                RenderTransformOrigin="0.5 0.5"
                                Margin="1 0">
                        <StackPanel.RenderTransform>
                            <ScaleTransform ScaleY="-1" />
                        </StackPanel.RenderTransform>

                        <Rectangle Fill="Red"
                                   Height="{Binding Color.R}" />
                        <Rectangle Fill="Green"
                                   Height="{Binding Color.G}" />
                        <Rectangle Fill="Blue"
                                   Height="{Binding Color.B}" />

                        <ToolTipService.ToolTip>
                            <ToolTip x:Name="tooltip"
                                     PlacementTarget="{Binding ElementName=stackPanel}">

                                <!-- Set DataContext to StackPanel containing items-->
                                <Grid DataContext="{Binding ElementName=tooltip,
                                                    Path=PlacementTarget}">

                                    <!-- Set DataContext to NamedColor -->
                                    <StackPanel DataContext="{Binding DataContext}">
                                        <TextBlock Text="{Binding Name}"
                                                   HorizontalAlignment="Center" />
                                        <StackPanel DataContext="{Binding Color}"
                                                    Orientation="Horizontal"
                                                    HorizontalAlignment="Center">
                                            <TextBlock Text="R=" />
                                            <TextBlock Text="{Binding R}" />
                                            <TextBlock Text=" G=" />
                                            <TextBlock Text="{Binding G}" />
                                            <TextBlock Text=" B=" />
                                            <TextBlock Text="{Binding B}" />
                                        </StackPanel>
                                    </StackPanel>
                                </Grid>
                            </ToolTip>
                        </ToolTipService.ToolTip>
```

```
                </StackPanel>
            </DataTemplate>
        </ItemsControl.ItemTemplate>

        <ItemsControl.ItemsPanel>
            <ItemsPanelTemplate>
                <ch11:UniformGrid Rows="1" />
            </ItemsPanelTemplate>
        </ItemsControl.ItemsPanel>
    </ItemsControl>
  </Grid>
</Page>
```

Of course, bars by themselves can be pretty vague, and one good way to identify them is with tooltips invoked when the mouse hovers. That turned out to be rather messier. You can attach a tooltip to an element by setting a *ToolTipService.ToolTip* attached property as a child of the element and defining a *ToolTip* control as a child of that. *ToolTip* derives from *ContentControl*. However, this *ToolTip* element is not actually part of the visual tree because it "floats" outside the tree. It doesn't inherit properties through the visual tree, including the all-important *DataContext* property. I had to get at that through the *PlacementTarget* property of *ToolTip*.

Here's the bar chart showing the relative red, green, and blue components of all 141 colors, and a tooltip for one of them showing the color name and RGB values:

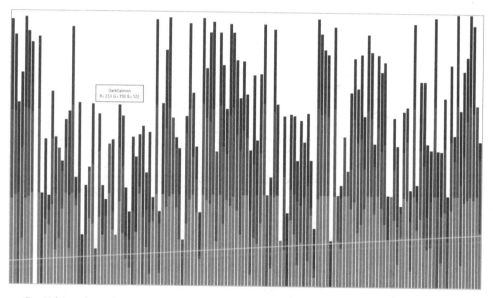

For White, the color components total to 765, just a touch under the 768-pixel height of the screen. Of course, these bars can be shortened for smaller screens (or larger values) using a *RenderTransform*.

The *FlipView* Control

One of my favorite controls introduced in the Windows Runtime is *FlipView*, which (like *ListBox*) derives from *ItemsControl* by way of *Selector*. *FlipView* displays only one item at a time, and that item is the selected item, so it shouldn't replace *ListBox* for most applications. But it has a nice touch interface, and it's good to keep it in mind for some special purposes.

Like many of the other projects in this chapter, the FlipViewColors project uses the Petzold.ProgrammingWindows.Chapter11 library. The *Resources* section of MainPage.xaml contains the usual reference to the *NamedColor* class but also defines a *DataTemplate* and *ItemsPanelTemplate* and then references both of those in a *Style* definition that also includes the *ItemsSource* binding. A *Border* and *TextBlock* have *SolidColorBrush* definitions with bindings to two *FlipView* controls:

Project: FlipViewColors | File: MainPage.xaml (excerpt)

```
<Page ... >
    <Page.Resources>
        <ch11:NamedColor x:Key="namedColor" />
        <ch11:ColorToContrastColorConverter x:Key="colorConverter" />

        <DataTemplate x:Key="colorTemplate">
            <Border BorderBrush="{Binding RelativeSource={RelativeSource TemplatedParent},
                                          Path=Foreground}"
                    Width="288"
                    Height="72"
                    BorderThickness="3"
                    Margin="3">
                <Border.Background>
                    <SolidColorBrush Color="{Binding Color}" />
                </Border.Background>

                <TextBlock Text="{Binding Name}"
                           FontSize="24"
                           HorizontalAlignment="Center"
                           VerticalAlignment="Center">
                    <TextBlock.Foreground>
                        <SolidColorBrush Color="{Binding Color,
                                          Converter={StaticResource colorConverter}}" />
                    </TextBlock.Foreground>
                </TextBlock>
            </Border>
        </DataTemplate>

        <ItemsPanelTemplate x:Key="panelTemplate">
            <VirtualizingStackPanel />
        </ItemsPanelTemplate>

        <Style TargetType="FlipView">
            <Setter Property="Width" Value="300" />
            <Setter Property="Height" Value="100" />
            <Setter Property="ItemsSource" Value="{Binding Source={StaticResource namedColor},
                                          Path=All}" />
            <Setter Property="ItemTemplate" Value="{StaticResource colorTemplate}" />
            <Setter Property="ItemsPanel" Value="{StaticResource panelTemplate}" />
```

```
                <Setter Property="SelectedValuePath" Value="Color" />
            </Style>
        </Page.Resources>

        <Grid Background="{StaticResource ApplicationPageBackgroundThemeBrush}">
            <Grid.RowDefinitions>
                <RowDefinition Height="Auto" />
                <RowDefinition Height="*" />
            </Grid.RowDefinitions>

            <Grid.ColumnDefinitions>
                <ColumnDefinition Width="*" />
                <ColumnDefinition Width="*" />
            </Grid.ColumnDefinitions>

            <Border Grid.Row="0"
                    Grid.Column="0"
                    Grid.ColumnSpan="2"
                    BorderThickness="12"
                    CornerRadius="48"
                    Margin="48"
                    Padding="48"
                    HorizontalAlignment="Center">
                <Border.Background>
                    <SolidColorBrush Color="{Binding ElementName=flipView1,
                                              Path=SelectedValue}" />
                </Border.Background>

                <Border.BorderBrush>
                    <SolidColorBrush Color="{Binding ElementName=flipView2,
                                              Path=SelectedValue}" />
                </Border.BorderBrush>

                <TextBlock FontFamily="Times New Roman"
                        FontSize="96">
                    The <Italic>FlipView</Italic> Control
                    <TextBlock.Foreground>
                        <SolidColorBrush Color="{Binding ElementName=flipView2,
                                                  Path=SelectedValue}" />
                    </TextBlock.Foreground>
                </TextBlock>
            </Border>

            <FlipView Name="flipView1"
                    Grid.Row="1"
                    Grid.Column="0" />

            <FlipView Name="flipView2"
                    Grid.Row="1"
                    Grid.Column="1" />
        </Grid>
    </Page>
```

By default, the *ItemsPanelTemplate* for *FlipView* is a *VirtualizingStackPanel* like *ListBox* but with a horizontal orientation. I've replaced that with a vertical *VirtualizingStackPanel*. Like *ListBox*, *FlipView* controls tend to sprawl out over the available space, so it's good to set explicit *Height* and *Width* properties. The idea here is that you "dial" the controls to two different colors. The first color controls the background of the *Border*; the second controls the border itself and the text:

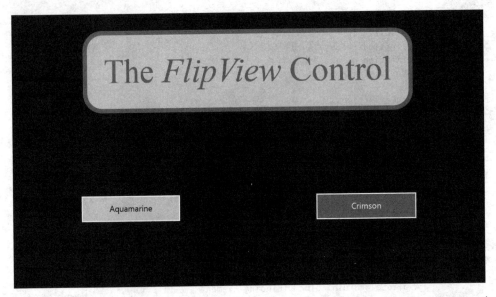

Chapter 16 demonstrates how to use a *FlipView* control as a simple e-book reader. I got the idea because the standard printer dialog uses a *FlipView* for previewing pages, as is demonstrated in Chapter 17, "Share and Print." In that chapter I also use a *FlipView* for a control that allows date selection.

The Basic Control Template

You've seen how you can set a *DataTemplate* to the *ContentTemplate* property of a *ContentControl* derivative, or to the *ItemTemplate* of an *ItemsControl* derivative to format the display of data objects.

You've also seen how you can define an *ItemsPanelTemplate* to set to the *ItemsPanel* of an *ItemsControl* derivative to provide a panel for hosting the items.

The third type of template is of type *ControlTemplate*. The *Control* class defines a *Template* property of type *ControlTemplate* that allows you to entirely redefine the visuals of the control itself—not the content of the control but the part of the control commonly referred to as "chrome."

The existence of the *Template* property is probably the most important difference between a *Control* derivative and a mere *FrameworkElement* derivative. Controls have chrome, and the appearance of this chrome is entirely under your control.

Whenever you think you need a custom control, you should probably ask yourself whether it's truly a new control or simply an existing control with a different appearance. Sometimes you get lucky and discover that you can adapt an existing control simply by using a *Style*. Other times, however, you'll need a *ControlTemplate*.

Like a *Style*, the *ControlTemplate* is often defined as a resource so that it can be shared. Like a *Style* as well, the *ControlTemplate* has a *TargetType*, which is the type of the control for which the template is designed. The *Template* property defined by *Control* is backed by a dependency property, which means that the *Template* property can be set in a *Style*. This is very common, and here's what it might look like in a *Resources* section:

```
<Style x:Key="buttonStyle" TargetType="Button">
    <Setter Property="Margin" Value="12" />
    <Setter Property="Template">
        <Setter.Value>
            <ControlTemplate TargetType="Button">
                ...
            </ControlTemplate>
        </Setter.Value>
    </Setter>
</Style>
```

Generally, you'll want to use *Setter* objects to set some properties of the control together with defining the template. These *Setter* tags define new default properties for the control, but they can be overridden by local property settings for the control that uses this style.

For purposes of clarity in the next several pages, I'll be defining a *ControlTemplate* right on the control itself. To demonstrate the basics of control templates, I'm going to redefine the appearance of a *Button*, but it won't be all that different from the existing *Button*.

Here's a standard *Button* as it might appear in a visual tree. It has content, an event handler, and some common properties:

```
<Button Content="Click me!"
        Click="OnButtonClick"
        HorizontalAlignment="Center"
        VerticalAlignment="Center" />
```

Let's define a new *ControlTemplate* on this *Button* by breaking out the *Template* property as a property element:

```
<Button Content="Click me!"
        Click="OnButtonClick"
        HorizontalAlignment="Center"
        VerticalAlignment="Center">
    <Button.Template>
        <ControlTemplate TargetType="Button">

        </ControlTemplate>
    </Button.Template>
</Button>
```

Notice the *TargetType* on the *ControlTemplate*. Sometimes you can leave this out and the template will still work except that it will stop working if the template references a property that is defined by the target control and not defined by *Control*.

A *Button* with an empty *ControlTemplate* can still be instantiated, but it no longer has any visual appearance. Because it has no visuals, there is no way for a user to see it, let alone click it. Just to make sure that we haven't caused too much damage, let's put a temporary *TextBlock* between those *ControlTemplate* tags:

```
<Button Content="Click me!"
        Click="OnButtonClick"
        HorizontalAlignment="Center"
        VerticalAlignment="Center">
    <Button.Template>
        <ControlTemplate TargetType="Button">
            <TextBlock Text="temporary" />
        </ControlTemplate>
    </Button.Template>
</Button>
```

Now the *Button* again has a visual appearance that consists solely of this text, and it is also functional. That *Click* event definitely fires when you tap or click the *TextBlock*. The visuals, however, are static. There is no longer any special appearance to indicate that the mouse pointer is hovering over the *Button* or that the *Button* is in the process of being clicked. Along with the standard visuals, those special appearances are defined within the template.

You can put a *Border* around the *TextBlock*:

```
<Button Content="Click me!"
        Click="OnButtonClick"
        HorizontalAlignment="Center"
        VerticalAlignment="Center">
    <Button.Template>
        <ControlTemplate TargetType="Button">
            <Border BorderBrush="Red"
                    BorderThickness="3">
                <TextBlock Text="temporary" />
            </Border>
        </ControlTemplate>
    </Button.Template>
</Button>
```

And here's what it looks like:

But do you really want to hard-code a red brush in the template? If you're defining a template for a single *Button* as I'm doing here, that's fine. But in the general case, you'll be defining templates as shared resources, and sometimes you might want this *Border* to be red, and other times you might want it to be something else.

Control itself defines *BorderBrush* and *BorderThickness* properties, and *Button* inherits those properties, so it would make more sense to define those properties on the *Button* itself:

```
<Button Content="Click me!"
        Click="OnButtonClick"
        HorizontalAlignment="Center"
        VerticalAlignment="Center"
        BorderBrush="Red"
        BorderThickness="3">
    <Button.Template>
        <ControlTemplate TargetType="Button">
            <Border>
                <TextBlock Text="temporary" />
            </Border>
        </ControlTemplate>
    </Button.Template>
</Button>
```

But now the *Border* has disappeared entirely from the *Button* visuals! The *Border* in the template doesn't magically pick up the properties set on the *Button*. The *Border* in the template needs some kind of binding to reference the properties defined in the *Button*.

This is a very special kind of binding called a *TemplateBinding*, and it has its own markup extension:

```
<Button Content="Click me!"
        Click="OnButtonClick"
        HorizontalAlignment="Center"
        VerticalAlignment="Center"
        BorderBrush="Red"
        BorderThickness="3">
    <Button.Template>
        <ControlTemplate TargetType="Button">
            <Border BorderBrush="{TemplateBinding BorderBrush}"
                    BorderThickness="{TemplateBinding BorderThickness}">
                <TextBlock Text="temporary" />
            </Border>
        </ControlTemplate>
    </Button.Template>
</Button>
```

What the *TemplateBinding* does is bind properties of an element in the visual tree of a *ControlTemplate* to properties of the control on which the *ControlTemplate* is applied. The *Button* visuals now contain a red *Border* as before.

The *TemplateBinding* syntax is exceptionally simple: It always targets a dependency property of an element in the visual tree of a *ControlTemplate*. It always references a property of the control to which the template is applied. Nothing else can go in the *TemplateBinding* markup. The *TemplateBinding* only appears on visual trees in a *ControlTemplate*.

TemplateBinding is actually a shortcut for a *RelativeSource* binding. The following bindings work as well, but they're obviously syntactically messier:

```
<Button Content="Click me!"
        Click="OnButtonClick"
        HorizontalAlignment="Center"
        VerticalAlignment="Center"
        BorderBrush="Red"
        BorderThickness="3">
    <Button.Template>
        <ControlTemplate TargetType="Button">
            <Border BorderBrush="{Binding RelativeSource={RelativeSource TemplatedParent},
                                          Path=BorderBrush}"
                    BorderThickness="{Binding RelativeSource={RelativeSource TemplatedParent},
                                              Path=BorderThickness}">
                <TextBlock Text="temporary" />
            </Border>
        </ControlTemplate>
    </Button.Template>
</Button>
```

You'll use this verbose syntax if you ever need to establish a two-way binding in a *ControlTemplate*. *TemplateBinding* is one-way only and does not allow a *Mode* setting.

Now suppose you want this red border to be the default in your new button but you want to allow individual buttons to override this default. In that case, you can define this *ControlTemplate* as part of a *Style*. Keep in mind that normally this *Style* would be defined as a resource and shared by multiple buttons, but I'm attaching it directly to the button for this exercise:

```xml
<Button Content="Click me!"
        Click="OnButtonClick"
        HorizontalAlignment="Center"
        VerticalAlignment="Center">
    <Button.Style>
        <Style TargetType="Button">
            <Setter Property="BorderBrush" Value="Red" />
            <Setter Property="BorderThickness" Value="3" />
            <Setter Property="Template">
                <Setter.Value>
                    <ControlTemplate TargetType="Button">
                        <Border BorderBrush="{TemplateBinding BorderBrush}"
                                BorderThickness="{TemplateBinding BorderThickness}">
                            <TextBlock Text="temporary" />
                        </Border>
                    </ControlTemplate>
                </Setter.Value>
            </Setter>
        </Style>
    </Button.Style>
</Button>
```

Now you can set *BorderBrush* and *BorderThickness* properties on the *Button* itself and these will override those set in the *Style*. Let's add default *Background* and *Foreground* properties to this *Style*, as well as a *FontSize* to make the text a little larger:

```xml
<Button Content="Click me!"
        Click="OnButtonClick"
        HorizontalAlignment="Center"
        VerticalAlignment="Center">
    <Button.Style>
        <Style TargetType="Button">
            <Setter Property="Background" Value="White" />
            <Setter Property="Foreground" Value="Blue" />
            <Setter Property="BorderBrush" Value="Red" />
            <Setter Property="BorderThickness" Value="3" />
            <Setter Property="FontSize" Value="24" />
            <Setter Property="Template">
                <Setter.Value>
                    <ControlTemplate TargetType="Button">
                        <Border Background="{TemplateBinding Background}"
                                BorderBrush="{TemplateBinding BorderBrush}"
                                BorderThickness="{TemplateBinding BorderThickness}">
                            <TextBlock Text="temporary" />
                        </Border>
                    </ControlTemplate>
                </Setter.Value>
            </Setter>
        </Style>
    </Button.Style>
</Button>
```

Notice the *TemplateBinding* on the *Background* property of the *Border*. However, the *TextBlock* doesn't need a *TemplateBinding* for the *Foreground* or *FontSize* properties because those properties are inherited through the visual tree. The *TextBlock* now shows up with blue text a little larger than before:

So far, each *TemplateBinding* has bound a property of an element in the visual tree with a property of the same name in the control. This one-to-one equivalence isn't required. Within the template, you could easily swap the bindings of *Background* and *BorderBrush* because both are of type *Brush*.

```
<ControlTemplate TargetType="Button">
    <Border Background="{TemplateBinding BorderBrush}"
            BorderBrush="{TemplateBinding Background}"
            BorderThickness="{TemplateBinding BorderThickness}">
        <TextBlock Text="temporary" />
    </Border>
</ControlTemplate>
```

There's nothing wrong with this except for the bafflement that it might cause.

Perhaps you want this new *Button* to have rounded corners on the *Border*. There's no property in *Control* or *Button* that corresponds to that, so unless we want to define a class derived from *Button* that includes a *CornerRadius* property, we'll have to hard-code it. Here's only the *ControlTemplate* part of the markup:

```
<ControlTemplate TargetType="Button">
    <Border Background="{TemplateBinding Background}"
            BorderBrush="{TemplateBinding BorderBrush}"
            BorderThickness="{TemplateBinding BorderThickness}"
            CornerRadius="12">
        <TextBlock Text="temporary" />
    </Border>
</ControlTemplate>
```

Here's what we're up to so far:

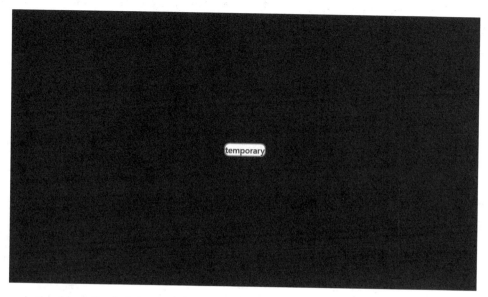

Let's address the little issue of the *TextBlock* with the temporary text. Based on what you've seen so far, you might be tempted to replace that temporary text with a *TemplateBinding* to the *Content* property of the *Button*:

```
<TextBlock Text="{TemplateBinding Content}" />
```

This works in this example, but it is very wrong. I began this chapter by discussing how the *Content* property of a *ContentControl* derivative such as *Button* is of type *object*, and *TextBlock* only works for text. It doesn't even work when the content is set to a bitmap.

Fortunately, there is a special class designed expressly to display content inside a *ContentControl* derivative. That class is *ContentPresenter*, and like *ContentControl* it has a *Content* property of type *object*:

```
<ControlTemplate TargetType="Button">
    <Border Background="{TemplateBinding Background}"
            BorderBrush="{TemplateBinding BorderBrush}"
            BorderThickness="{TemplateBinding BorderThickness}"
            CornerRadius="12">
        <ContentPresenter Content="{TemplateBinding Content}" />
    </Border>
</ControlTemplate>
```

You'll find a *ContentPresenter* in most every template for *ContentControl* derivatives. *ContentPresenter* derives from *FrameworkElement*, but it also generates its own visual tree to render the content. In this specific example, *ContentPresenter* creates a *TextBlock* to display its *Content* property.

ContentPresenter is also entrusted with the job of building a visual tree to display any kind of content based on the *ContentTemplate* property of the control. Indeed, *ContentPresenter* has its own *ContentTemplate* property that you can bind to the *ContentTemplate* property of the control:

```
<ControlTemplate TargetType="Button">
    <Border Background="{TemplateBinding Background}"
            BorderBrush="{TemplateBinding BorderBrush}"
            BorderThickness="{TemplateBinding BorderThickness}"
            CornerRadius="12">
        <ContentPresenter Content="{TemplateBinding Content}"
                          ContentTemplate="{TemplateBinding ContentTemplate}" />

    </Border>
</ControlTemplate>
```

These two template bindings on *ContentPresenter* are so standard and so essential that they're not actually required! *ContentPresenter* will automatically pick up the values of these properties from the control in which it's being used. If you want to leave them out, you can do so. I personally feel more comfortable seeing them in there.

You might recall that *Control* defines a property named *Padding* that is intended to provide a little space between the control's chrome and the control's content. Try setting the *Padding* property in this *Button*:

```
<Button Content="Click me!"
        Click="OnButtonClick"
        HorizontalAlignment="Center"
        VerticalAlignment="Center"
        Padding="24">
    ...
</Button>
```

Nothing happens. You need to add something to the *ControlTemplate* to explicitly leave a little space between the *Border* and the *ContentPresenter*. This can be a *TemplateBinding* on the *Padding* property of the *Border*, but the more common approach is to set a *TemplateBinding* on the *Margin* property of the *ContentPresenter*:

```
<ControlTemplate TargetType="Button">
    <Border Background="{TemplateBinding Background}"
            BorderBrush="{TemplateBinding BorderBrush}"
            BorderThickness="{TemplateBinding BorderThickness}"
            CornerRadius="12">
        <ContentPresenter Content="{TemplateBinding Content}"
                          ContentTemplate="{TemplateBinding ContentTemplate}"
                          Margin="{TemplateBinding Padding}" />

    </Border>
</ControlTemplate>
```

Now try setting the *HorizontalAlignment* and *VerticalAlignment* properties of the *Button* to *Stretch*. The *Button* properly expands to fill the page:

This is good because it means that these properties are being handled automatically. However, the content is at the upper-left corner of the button. *Control* defines two properties named *HorizontalContentAlignment* and *VerticalContentAlignment* that govern how content should be positioned within the button, but if you try setting these properties, you'll find that they don't work.

This means you'll have to add something to the template to get them to work. The standard way is for these properties to be bound to the *HorizontalAlignment* and *VerticalAlignment* properties of the *ContentPresenter*:

```
<ControlTemplate TargetType="Button">
    <Border Background="{TemplateBinding Background}"
            BorderBrush="{TemplateBinding BorderBrush}"
            BorderThickness="{TemplateBinding BorderThickness}"
            CornerRadius="12">
        <ContentPresenter Content="{TemplateBinding Content}"
                          ContentTemplate="{TemplateBinding ContentTemplate}"
                          Margin="{TemplateBinding Padding}"
                          HorizontalAlignment="{TemplateBinding HorizontalContentAlignment}"
                          VerticalAlignment="{TemplateBinding VerticalContentAlignment}" />
    </Border>
</ControlTemplate>
```

These properties position the *ContentPresenter* within its parent, which in this case is the *Border*. I'm going to add one more *TemplateBinding* on the *ContentPresenter* and then declare it ready for the next step:

```xml
<Button Content="Click me!"
        Click="OnButtonClick"
        HorizontalAlignment="Center"
        VerticalAlignment="Center"
        Padding="24">
    <Button.ContentTransitions>
        <TransitionCollection>
            <EntranceThemeTransition />
        </TransitionCollection>
    </Button.ContentTransitions>
    <Button.Style>
        <Style TargetType="Button">
            <Setter Property="Background" Value="White" />
            <Setter Property="Foreground" Value="Blue" />
            <Setter Property="BorderBrush" Value="Red" />
            <Setter Property="BorderThickness" Value="3" />
            <Setter Property="FontSize" Value="24" />
            <Setter Property="Template">
                <Setter.Value>
                    <ControlTemplate TargetType="Button">
                        <Border Background="{TemplateBinding Background}"
                                BorderBrush="{TemplateBinding BorderBrush}"
                                BorderThickness="{TemplateBinding BorderThickness}"
                                CornerRadius="12">
                            <ContentPresenter Content="{TemplateBinding Content}"
                                              ContentTemplate="{TemplateBinding ContentTemplate}"
                                              Margin="{TemplateBinding Padding}"
                                              HorizontalAlignment=
                                                  "{TemplateBinding HorizontalContentAlignment}"
                                              VerticalAlignment=
                                                  "{TemplateBinding VerticalContentAlignment}"
                                              ContentTransitions=
                                                  "{TemplateBinding ContentTransitions}" />
                        </Border>
                    </ControlTemplate>
                </Setter.Value>
            </Setter>
        </Style>
    </Button.Style>
</Button>
```

The *ContentTransitions* property of *ContentPresenter* is now bound to the *ContentTransitions* property of the *Button*, and I've added an *EntranceThemeTransition* to the *Button* to test it out. Now when the *Button* loads, the text slides in from the right.

The Visual State Manager

If you've been playing along defining new *Button* visuals, you might have noted that this *Button* has always remained fully functional in firing *Click* events when it's been clicked or tapped. However, it has been deficient in providing visual feedback to the user. Normal buttons assume somewhat different appearances when they are disabled, or have keyboard input focus, or are in the process of being clicked, or when the mouse passes over.

These different appearances are known as *visual states*, and you build them right into the template by using classes that are part of the Visual State Manager.

The *Button* has seven visual states divided into two groups:

- **CommonStates**   *Normal*, *PointerOver*, *Pressed*, and *Disabled*

- **FocusStates**   *Focused*, *Unfocused*, *PointerFocused*

Within each group, the states are mutually exclusive. For example, there is no visual state that applies to a disabled button that is also pressed.

The underlying code for the control is responsible for putting the control into these states with calls to *VisualStateManager.GoToState*. These states are always referred to with text names.

Often these visual states are implemented with additional elements in the visual tree of the template; these elements are normally invisible. This invisibility can result from the use of a color that matches a background color, a *Visibility* property of *Collapsed*, or an *Opacity* of 0. An animation then targets this property to make the element visible. Often these animations have a duration of zero, which means they occur instantaneously, but you can stretch out your animations if you wish.

Be forewarned that accounting for these visual states is certainly the most complex part of defining a template. If you will be using a control only in a particular application, you might want to cut a few corners. For example, if you know that a control will never be disabled, you don't need to provide a visual state for that.

In the *ControlTemplate* I've been building I'm going to handle the *Pressed*, *Disabled*, and *Focused* states and then declare it complete.

In the standard *Button*, keyboard input focus is indicated by a dotted line that surrounds the button's border. I'm going to instead make it a dotted line that surrounds the content of the button, which means it goes inside the *Border* along with the *ContentPresenter*, which means that both this dotted line and *ContentPresenter* need to go in a single-cell *Grid*. Here's the dotted line implemented with a *Rectangle* that has the name "focusRectangle":

```
<ControlTemplate TargetType="Button">
    <Border Background="{TemplateBinding Background}"
            BorderBrush="{TemplateBinding BorderBrush}"
            BorderThickness="{TemplateBinding BorderThickness}"
            CornerRadius="12">
        <Grid>
```

```
    <ContentPresenter Content="{TemplateBinding Content}"
                      ContentTemplate="{TemplateBinding ContentTemplate}"
                      Margin="{TemplateBinding Padding}"
                      HorizontalAlignment="{TemplateBinding HorizontalContentAlignment}"
                      VerticalAlignment="{TemplateBinding VerticalContentAlignment}"
                      ContentTransitions="{TemplateBinding ContentTransitions}" />

    <Rectangle Name="focusRectangle"
               Stroke="{TemplateBinding Foreground}"
               StrokeThickness="1"
               StrokeDashArray="2 2"
               Margin="4"
               RadiusX="12"
               RadiusY="12" />
    </Grid>
  </Border>
</ControlTemplate>
```

And here's what it looks like now:

Of course, you don't want that *Rectangle* to appear all the time. One way to make it invisible is to give it an *Opacity* of 0:

```
<Rectangle Name="focusRectangle"
           Stroke="{TemplateBinding Foreground}"
           Opacity="0"
           StrokeThickness="1"
           StrokeDashArray="2 2"
           Margin="4"
           RadiusX="12"
           RadiusY="12" />
```

Then, customarily within the root element in the visual tree that makes up the *ControlTemplate*—in this example, right after the start tag for *Border*—you want a *VisualStateManager.VisualStateGroups* section. Within that are *VisualStateGroup* tags for each group, and within those, *VisualState* tags for each state in that group. All are identified with *x:Name* attributes:

```
<VisualStateManager.VisualStateGroups>
    <VisualStateGroup x:Name="CommonStates">
        <VisualState x:Name="Normal">
        ...
        </VisualState>

        <VisualState x:Name="PointerOver">
        ...
        </VisualState>

        <VisualState x:Name="Pressed">
        ...
        </VisualState>

        <VisualState x:Name="Disabled">
        ...
        </VisualState>
    </VisualStateGroup>

    <VisualStateGroup x:Name="FocusedStates">
        <VisualState x:Name="Unfocused">
        ...
        </VisualState>

        <VisualState x:Name="Focused">
        ...
        </VisualState>

        <VisualState x:Name="PointerFocused">
        ...
        </VisualState>
    </VisualStateGroup>
</VisualStateManager.VisualStateGroups>
```

If the visual part of your basic template is designed for the *Normal* and *Unfocused* states, you can make those empty tags. And if you don't wish to handle various states, you can make those tags empty as well:

```
<VisualStateManager.VisualStateGroups>
    <VisualStateGroup x:Name="CommonStates">
        <VisualState x:Name="Normal" />
        <VisualState x:Name="PointerOver" />

        <VisualState x:Name="Pressed">
        ...
        </VisualState>

        <VisualState x:Name="Disabled">
        ...
        </VisualState>
    </VisualStateGroup>
```

```
<VisualStateGroup x:Name="FocusedStates">
    <VisualState x:Name="Unfocused" />

    <VisualState x:Name="Focused">
    ...
    </VisualState>

    <VisualState x:Name="PointerFocused" />
</VisualStateGroup>
</VisualStateManager.VisualStateGroups>
```

But don't delete them. Within a particular group you should have tags for all the states. Leave one out and any transition back to that state won't occur.

For the states you want to handle, put a *Storyboard* between the *VisualState* tags that contains animations that target the elements you've supplied for this purpose. For example:

```
<VisualStateGroup x:Name="FocusedStates">
    <VisualState x:Name="Unfocused" />

    <VisualState x:Name="Focused">
        <Storyboard>
            <DoubleAnimation Storyboard.TargetName="focusRectangle"
                             Storyboard.TargetProperty="Opacity"
                             To="1" Duration="0" />
        </Storyboard>
    </VisualState>

    <VisualState x:Name="PointerFocused" />
</VisualStateGroup>
```

Notice the absence of a *From* property. You want to indicate only what the value should end up at—not what it starts at.

With this in place, when the underlying control receives input focus, its *OnGotFocus* method is called. The control responds by calling *VisualStateManager.GoToState* with "Focused." This triggers the *Storyboard*, which sets the target *Opacity* property to 1. When the underlying control loses input focus, it calls *VisualStateManager.GoToState* with "Unfocused," which undoes that animation.

For the disabled state, I want the entire control grayed out, and a good way to do that is to cover the entire control with a semi-transparent black rectangle with a *Visibility* of *Collapsed*. So, let's put the *Border* in another *Grid* and add a named *Rectangle* to that *Grid* that sits visually on top of the *Border*. In doing this, I've also moved the Visual State Manager markup to the outermost *Grid*:

```
<ControlTemplate TargetType="Button">
    <Grid>
        <VisualStateManager.VisualStateGroups>
            ...
        </VisualStateManager.VisualStateGroups>

        <Border Name="border" ... >
            <Grid>
                <ContentPresenter Name="contentPresenter" ... />
                <Rectangle Name="focusRectangle" ...  />
```

```
            </Grid>
        </Border>

        <Rectangle Name="disabledRect"
                   Visibility="Collapsed"
                   Fill="Black"
                   Opacity="0.5" />
    </Grid>
</ControlTemplate>
```

I've also given the *Border* and *ContentPresenter* names so that I can reference those in animations. For the *Disabled* state, I've defined an animation to make the *disabledRect* visible, and for the *Pressed* state, I've defined two animations to set the background and foreground colors of the control.

These can be seen in the CustomButtonTemplate project, which has the final style and template. Primarily to avoid extremely long line lengths on the printed page, I have defined the *ControlTemplate* as a separate object in the *Resources* dictionary and referenced that from the *Style*:

Project: CustomButtonTemplate | **File:** MainPage.xaml (excerpt)

```
<Page ... >
    <Page.Resources>
        <ControlTemplate x:Key="buttonTemplate" TargetType="Button">
            <Grid>
                <VisualStateManager.VisualStateGroups>
                    <VisualStateGroup x:Name="CommonStates">
                        <VisualState x:Name="Normal" />
                        <VisualState x:Name="PointerOver" />

                        <VisualState x:Name="Pressed">
                            <Storyboard>
                                <ObjectAnimationUsingKeyFrames
                                            Storyboard.TargetName="border"
                                            Storyboard.TargetProperty="Background">
                                    <DiscreteObjectKeyFrame KeyTime="0"
                                                    Value="LightGray" />
                                </ObjectAnimationUsingKeyFrames>

                                <ObjectAnimationUsingKeyFrames
                                            Storyboard.TargetName="contentPresenter"
                                            Storyboard.TargetProperty="Foreground">
                                    <DiscreteObjectKeyFrame KeyTime="0"
                                                    Value="Black" />
                                </ObjectAnimationUsingKeyFrames>
                            </Storyboard>
                        </VisualState>

                        <VisualState x:Name="Disabled">
                            <Storyboard>
                                <ObjectAnimationUsingKeyFrames
                                            Storyboard.TargetName="disabledRect"
                                            Storyboard.TargetProperty="Visibility">
                                    <DiscreteObjectKeyFrame KeyTime="0"
                                                    Value="Visible" />
                                </ObjectAnimationUsingKeyFrames>
                            </Storyboard>
                        </VisualState>
```

```xml
            </VisualState>
        </VisualStateGroup>

        <VisualStateGroup x:Name="FocusedStates">
            <VisualState x:Name="Unfocused" />

            <VisualState x:Name="Focused">
                <Storyboard>
                    <DoubleAnimation Storyboard.TargetName="focusRectangle"
                                     Storyboard.TargetProperty="Opacity"
                                     To="1" Duration="0" />
                </Storyboard>
            </VisualState>

            <VisualState x:Name="PointerFocused" />
        </VisualStateGroup>
    </VisualStateManager.VisualStateGroups>

    <Border Name="border"
            Background="{TemplateBinding Background}"
            BorderBrush="{TemplateBinding BorderBrush}"
            BorderThickness="{TemplateBinding BorderThickness}"
            CornerRadius="12">

        <Grid>
            <ContentPresenter Name="contentPresenter"
                              Content="{TemplateBinding Content}"
                              ContentTemplate="{TemplateBinding ContentTemplate}"
                              Margin="{TemplateBinding Padding}"
                    HorizontalAlignment="{TemplateBinding HorizontalContentAlignment}"
                      VerticalAlignment="{TemplateBinding VerticalContentAlignment}"
                      ContentTransitions="{TemplateBinding ContentTransitions}" />

            <Rectangle Name="focusRectangle"
                       Stroke="{TemplateBinding Foreground}"
                       Opacity="0"
                       StrokeThickness="1"
                       StrokeDashArray="2 2"
                       Margin="4"
                       RadiusX="12"
                       RadiusY="12" />
        </Grid>
    </Border>

    <Rectangle Name="disabledRect"
               Visibility="Collapsed"
               Fill="Black"
               Opacity="0.5" />

    </Grid>
</ControlTemplate>

<Style x:Key="buttonStyle" TargetType="Button">
    <Setter Property="Background" Value="White" />
    <Setter Property="Foreground" Value="Blue" />
    <Setter Property="BorderBrush" Value="Red" />
```

```
                <Setter Property="BorderThickness" Value="3" />
                <Setter Property="FontSize" Value="24" />
                <Setter Property="Padding" Value="12" />
                <Setter Property="Template" Value="{StaticResource buttonTemplate}" />
            </Style>
        </Page.Resources>

        <Grid Background="{StaticResource ApplicationPageBackgroundThemeBrush}">
            <Grid.ColumnDefinitions>
                <ColumnDefinition Width="*" />
                <ColumnDefinition Width="*" />
                <ColumnDefinition Width="*" />
            </Grid.ColumnDefinitions>

            <Button Content="Disable center button"
                    Grid.Column="0"
                    Style="{StaticResource buttonStyle}"
                    Click="OnButton1Click"
                    HorizontalAlignment="Center"
                    VerticalAlignment="Center" />

            <Button Name="centerButton"
                    Content="Center button"
                    Grid.Column="1"
                    Style="{StaticResource buttonStyle}"
                    FontSize="48"
                    Background="DarkGray"
                    Foreground="Red"
                    HorizontalAlignment="Center"
                    VerticalAlignment="Center" />

            <Button Content="Enable center button"
                    Grid.Column="2"
                    Style="{StaticResource buttonStyle}"
                    Click="OnButton3Click"
                    HorizontalAlignment="Center"
                    VerticalAlignment="Center" />
        </Grid>
</Page>
```

The XAML file concludes with three buttons, with the center one getting some local property values that override those in the *Style*. The outer two buttons disable and enable the center button:

Project: CustomButtonTemplate | File: MainPage.xaml.cs (excerpt)

```
void OnButton1Click(object sender, RoutedEventArgs args)
{
    centerButton.IsEnabled = false;
}

void OnButton3Click(object sender, RoutedEventArgs args)
{
    centerButton.IsEnabled = true;
}
```

In this screen shot, the center button has indeed been disabled and the third button has keyboard input focus:

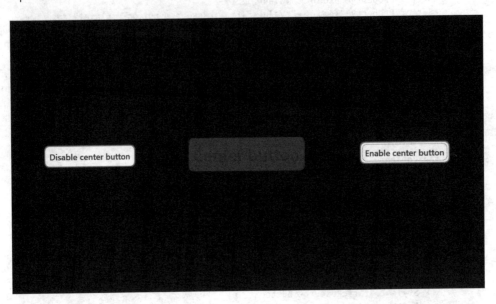

Using generic.xaml

Look in the following directory of the machine on which you've installed Visual Studio:

C:\Program Files (x86)\Windows Kits\8.0\Include\winrt\xaml\design

You should see two files there. The shorter one, themeresources.xaml, contains mostly *SolidColorBrush* definitions for the standard colors available to Windows Runtime applications, including the famous *ApplicationPageBackgroundThemeBrush* and *ApplicationForegroundThemeBrush* colors. Entire sets of these colors are in three sections: Default (meaning the dark theme), Light, and HighContrast. A user can select a high-contrast display from the Ease of Access section in the PC Settings program accessible from the Settings charm.

The larger file, generic.xaml, contains the same definitions as themeresources.xaml, plus all the default *Style* and *ControlTemplate* definitions for all the standard controls.

If you want to become good at designing custom templates for controls, studying the default templates in generic.xaml is essential. Within these templates is also (apparently) the only documentation of the visual states associated with each control, as well as the named parts that I'll discuss in the next section.

To find the default *Style* for a particular control, do a search of TargetType=" followed by the control name.

Often the templates reference the brushes defined earlier in generic.xaml, and there are special brushes for various visual states. For example, visual state animations in the default *Button* template reference brushes with names such as *ButtonPressedBackgroundThemeBrush* and *ButtonPressedForegroundThemeBrush*. The actual colors of these brushes are different based on the Light or Dark theme the application has selected or the HighContrast theme that the user might have selected.

These *Style* definitions for all the standard controls have no key names. They are basically implicit styles that are applied to the control when the control is instantiated. Anything the application provides is in addition to this implicit style.

One good way to develop a new template for a control is simply to copy the entire existing *Style* definition from generic.xaml into your own XAML file and then begin making changes.

Template Parts

As I guided you through the process of constructing a template for a *Button*, you were possibly wondering how this concept works with more sophisticated controls. Consider the *Slider*, for example. The *Slider* has moving parts. How does the underlying control reference these parts of the template?

The underlying code for a control such as *Slider* assumes that certain elements that comprise the template have specific names. During initialization, the control code gets references to these elements in an override of the *OnApplyTemplate* method by calling the *GetTemplateChild* method with these names. The control code can save these element objects as fields, install event handlers on them, and alter their properties as the user manipulates the control.

Unfortunately, these named parts are not yet indicated in any documentation I've seen for the Windows Runtime. You'll have to study the default templates in generic.xaml to figure out what they are. In many cases, you don't have to know about each and every one. It is considered proper for controls to not raise exceptions if certain pieces of the template are missing.

To be minimally functional, a *Slider* template must contain a template for both horizontal and vertical orientations. These separate templates are generally of type *Grid*. Give these names of "HorizontalTemplate" and "VerticalTemplate".

Within each *Grid* must be a *Rectangle* that encompasses the full extent of the *Slider* named "HorizontalTrackRect" or "VerticalTrackRect", a *Thumb* named "HorizontalThumb" or "VerticalThumb", and a second *Rectangle* that appears to the left of the *Thumb* named "HorizontalDecreaseRect" or "VerticalDecreaseRect". When the user manipulates the *Thumb* or clicks or taps anywhere within the *Slider*, the underlying control changes the size of this second rectangle to reflect the value of the *Slider*.

Let's look at a nearly minimally functional *Slider* template that contains several explicit property settings and ignores the *TickBar* elements that provide optional tick marks. This is a project I call BareBonesSlider:

Project: BareBonesSlider | File: MainPage.xaml (excerpt)

```xml
<Page ... >
    <Page.Resources>
        <ControlTemplate x:Key="sliderTemplate"
                         TargetType="Slider">
            <Grid>
                <Grid Name="HorizontalTemplate"
                      Background="Transparent"
                      Height="48">
                    <Grid.ColumnDefinitions>
                        <ColumnDefinition Width="Auto" />
                        <ColumnDefinition Width="Auto" />
                        <ColumnDefinition Width="*" />
                    </Grid.ColumnDefinitions>

                    <Rectangle Name="HorizontalTrackRect"
                               Grid.Column="0"
                               Grid.ColumnSpan="3"
                               Fill="Blue"
                               Margin="0 12" />

                    <Thumb Name="HorizontalThumb"
                           Grid.Column="1"
                           DataContext="{TemplateBinding Value}"
                           Width="24" />

                    <Rectangle Name="HorizontalDecreaseRect"
                               Grid.Column="0"
                               Fill="Red"
                               Margin="0 12" />
                </Grid>

                <Grid Name="VerticalTemplate"
                      Visibility="Collapsed"
                      Background="Transparent"
                      Width="48">
                    <Grid.RowDefinitions>
                        <RowDefinition Height="*" />
                        <RowDefinition Height="Auto" />
                        <RowDefinition Height="Auto" />
                    </Grid.RowDefinitions>

                    <Rectangle Name="VerticalTrackRect"
                               Grid.Row="0"
                               Grid.RowSpan="3"
                               Fill="Blue"
                               Margin="12 0" />
```

```
            <Thumb Name="VerticalThumb"
                   Grid.Row="1"
                   DataContext="{TemplateBinding Value}"
                   Height="24" />

            <Rectangle Name="VerticalDecreaseRect"
                       Grid.Row="2"
                       Fill="Red"
                       Margin="12 0" />
        </Grid>
      </Grid>
    </ControlTemplate>
  </Page.Resources>

  <Grid Background="{StaticResource ApplicationPageBackgroundThemeBrush}">
    <Grid.RowDefinitions>
      <RowDefinition Height="Auto" />
      <RowDefinition Height="*" />
    </Grid.RowDefinitions>

    <Slider Grid.Row="0"
            Template="{StaticResource sliderTemplate}"
            Margin="48" />

    <Slider Grid.Row="1"
            Template="{StaticResource sliderTemplate}"
            Orientation="Vertical"
            Margin="48" />
  </Grid>
</Page>
```

At the bottom of the XAML file are two *Slider* controls, one horizontal and one vertical, that reference these templates.

I'll describe the template for the horizontal *Slider*; the vertical is structured similarly.

The total width of the *Grid* named "HorizontalTemplate" is the width of the *Slider* control in layout. The *Grid* has three columns. The *Rectangle* named "HorizontalTrackRect" spans all three columns so that *Rectangle* will always be the width of the *Slider* itself. The *Rectangle* named "HorizontalDecreaseRect" occupies the first column in the *Grid*, which has a width of *Auto*, which has the effect of reducing that *Rectangle* to a zero width. The *Thumb* occupies the center column in the *Grid*, which also has a width of *Auto*, which means that this center column is the size of the *Thumb*.

The underlying code allows the *Thumb* to move horizontally only and not past the limits of the *Slider*. As the user manipulates the *Thumb* or presses or taps anywhere else on the *Slider*, the underlying code sets the *Width* property of the "HorizontalDecreaseRect" element accordingly. For the minimum value of the *Slider*, this *Width* property is set to zero; for the maximum value, it's set to the width of the "HorizontalTrackRect" element minus the width of the *Thumb*. I've given sizes and margins to these components so that the *Thumb* is a little larger than the rectangles:

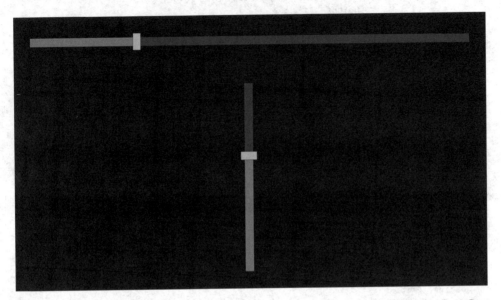

You'll notice that the template contains a single *TemplateBinding* that binds the *DataContext* of the *Thumb* to the *Value* property of the *Slider*. This is required to get the *Slider* popup tooltip to display the correct value.

As you manipulate the *Thumb* in BareBonesSlider, you'll discover that it becomes a nearly transparent black as it is being pressed. *Thumb* derives from Control and hence can be given its own template. This is done in the default *Slider* template in a *Resources* section attached to the outermost *Grid* of the template.

With just a little alteration of the BareBonesSlider program, you can do something fancy. Here's something I call a SpringLoadedSlider:

Project: SpringLoadedSlider | File: MainPage.xaml (excerpt)

```
<Page ... >
    <Page.Resources>
        <ControlTemplate x:Key="sliderTemplate"
                         TargetType="Slider">
            <Grid>
                <Grid.Resources>
                    <Style TargetType="Path">
                        <Setter Property="StrokeThickness" Value="6" />
                        <Setter Property="StrokeLineJoin" Value="Round" />
                        <Setter Property="Stretch" Value="Fill" />
                    </Style>
                </Grid.Resources>
```

```xml
<Grid Name="HorizontalTemplate"
      Background="Transparent"
      Height="48">

    <Grid.ColumnDefinitions>
        <ColumnDefinition Width="Auto" />
        <ColumnDefinition Width="Auto" />
        <ColumnDefinition Width="*" />
    </Grid.ColumnDefinitions>

    <Rectangle Name="HorizontalTrackRect"
               Grid.Column="0"
               Grid.ColumnSpan="3"
               Fill="Transparent" />

    <Thumb Name="HorizontalThumb"
           Grid.Column="1"
           DataContext="{TemplateBinding Value}"
           Width="12" />

    <Rectangle Name="HorizontalDecreaseRect"
               Grid.Column="0"
               Fill="Transparent" />

    <Path Stroke="Red"
          Grid.Column="0"
          Width="{Binding ElementName=HorizontalDecreaseRect,
                          Path=Width}"
          Data="M 0 0 L 100 100, 200 0, 300 100, 400 0,
                400 100, 300 0, 200 100, 100 0, 0 100 Z" />

    <Path Stroke="Blue"
          Grid.Column="2"
          Data="M 0 0 L 100 100, 200 0, 300 100, 400 0,
                400 100, 300 0, 200 100, 100 0, 0 100 Z" />
</Grid>

<Grid Name="VerticalTemplate"
      Visibility="Collapsed"
      Background="Transparent"
      Width="48">
    <Grid.RowDefinitions>
        <RowDefinition Height="*" />
        <RowDefinition Height="Auto" />
        <RowDefinition Height="Auto" />
    </Grid.RowDefinitions>

    <Rectangle Name="VerticalTrackRect"
               Grid.Row="0"
               Grid.RowSpan="3"
               Fill="Transparent" />
```

```
<Thumb Name="VerticalThumb"
       Grid.Row="1"
       DataContext="{TemplateBinding Value}"
       Height="12" />

<Rectangle Name="VerticalDecreaseRect"
           Grid.Row="2"
           Fill="Transparent" />

<Path Stroke="Red"
      Grid.Row="2"
      Height="{Binding ElementName=VerticalDecreaseRect,
                        Path=Height}"
      Data="M 0 0 L 100 100, 0 200, 100 300, 0 400,
            100 400, 0 300, 100 200, 0 100, 100 0 Z" />

<Path Stroke="Blue"
      Grid.Row="0"
      Data="M 0 0 L 100 100, 0 200, 100 300, 0 400,
            100 400, 0 300, 100 200, 0 100, 100 0 Z" />

        </Grid>
      </Grid>
    </ControlTemplate>
  </Page.Resources>

  <Grid Background="{StaticResource ApplicationPageBackgroundThemeBrush}">
    <Grid.RowDefinitions>
      <RowDefinition Height="Auto" />
      <RowDefinition Height="*" />
    </Grid.RowDefinitions>

    <Slider Grid.Row="0"
            Template="{StaticResource sliderTemplate}"
            Margin="48" />

    <Slider Grid.Row="1"
            Template="{StaticResource sliderTemplate}"
            Orientation="Vertical"
            Margin="48" />

  </Grid>
</Page>
```

The two templates are structured the same, except that the *Rectangle* elements have all been given *Fill* colors of *Transparent*. In addition, two *Path* elements have been added to each template. The first *Path* sits in the first column (for a horizontal *Slider*) and is colored red. The *Width* of this *Path* is bound to the *Width* of the element named "HorizontalDecreaseRect". The second *Path* is blue and occupies the third column. Each has the same geometry—a crisscrossing lattice—with a *Stretch* mode of *Fill*, meaning that it will fill the space allowed for it.

This gives the appearance of springs on either side of the *Thumb*:

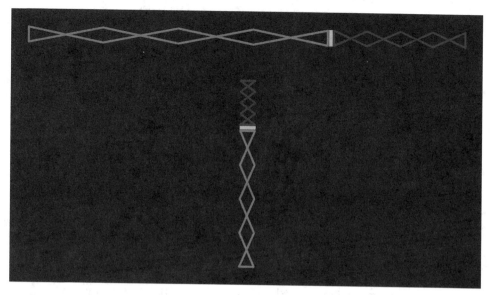

The default template for the *ProgressBar* is rather elaborate because it needs to encompass both determinate and indeterminate appearances. However, if you restrict yourself to just the determinate *ProgressBar*, it becomes very simple: The underlying code changes the width of an element named "ProgressBarIndicator" between 0 and the width of an element named "DeterminateRoot". In the default template, "DeterminateRoot" is a *Border* that contains a left-aligned *Rectangle* named "ProgressBarIndicator".

In SpeedometerProgressBar, neither "DeterminateRoot" nor "ProgressBarIndicator" are visible, but the *Width* of "DeterminateRoot" is hard-coded as 180. This means that the *Width* of "ProgressBarIndicator" will range from 0 to 180. A binding from the *Width* property of "ProgressBarIndicator" targets the *Angle* property of a *RotateTransform*, which rotates an arrow indicator from 0 through 180 degrees:

Project: SpeedometerProgressBar | **File:** MainPage.xaml (excerpt)

```
<Page ... >
    <Page.Resources>
        <ControlTemplate x:Key="progressTemplate"
                         TargetType="ProgressBar">
            <Grid>
                <Grid.Resources>
                    <Style TargetType="Line">
                        <Setter Property="Stroke" Value="Black" />
                        <Setter Property="StrokeThickness" Value="1" />
                        <Setter Property="X1" Value="-85" />
                        <Setter Property="X2" Value="-95" />
                    </Style>
```

```xml
                    <Style TargetType="TextBlock">
                        <Setter Property="FontSize" Value="11" />
                        <Setter Property="Foreground" Value="Black" />
                    </Style>
                </Grid.Resources>

                <Border Width="270" Height="120"
                        BorderBrush="{TemplateBinding BorderBrush}"
                        BorderThickness="{TemplateBinding BorderThickness}"
                        Background="White">

                    <!-- Canvas for positioning graphics-->
                    <Canvas Width="0" Height="0"
                            RenderTransform="1 0 0 1 0 50" >

                        <!-- The required parts of the ProgressBar template -->
                        <Border Name="DeterminateRoot"
                                Width="180">
                            <Rectangle Name="ProgressBarIndicator"
                                       HorizontalAlignment="Left" />
                        </Border>

                        <Line RenderTransform=" 1.00 0.00 -0.00 1.00 0 0" />
                        <Line RenderTransform=" 0.95 0.31 -0.31 0.95 0 0" />
                        <Line RenderTransform=" 0.81 0.59 -0.59 0.81 0 0" />
                        <Line RenderTransform=" 0.59 0.81 -0.81 0.59 0 0" />
                        <Line RenderTransform=" 0.31 0.95 -0.95 0.31 0 0" />
                        <Line RenderTransform=" 0.00 1.00 -1.00 0.00 0 0" />
                        <Line RenderTransform="-0.31 0.95  0.95 0.31 0 0" />
                        <Line RenderTransform="-0.59 0.81  0.81 0.59 0 0" />
                        <Line RenderTransform="-0.81 0.59  0.59 0.81 0 0" />
                        <Line RenderTransform="-0.95 0.31  0.31 0.95 0 0" />
                        <Line RenderTransform="-1.00 0.00  0.00 1.00 0 0" />

                        <TextBlock Text="0%" Canvas.Left="-115" Canvas.Top="-6" />
                        <TextBlock Text="20%" Canvas.Left="-104" Canvas.Top="-65" />
                        <TextBlock Text="40%" Canvas.Left="-42" Canvas.Top="-105" />
                        <TextBlock Text="60%" Canvas.Left="25" Canvas.Top="-105" />
                        <TextBlock Text="80%" Canvas.Left="82" Canvas.Top="-65" />
                        <TextBlock Text="100%" Canvas.Left="100" Canvas.Top="-6" />

                        <!-- Arrow to point to percentage -->
                        <Polygon Points="5 5 5 -5 -75 0"
                                 Stroke="Black"
                                 Fill="Red">
                            <Polygon.RenderTransform>
                                <RotateTransform
                                        Angle="{Binding ElementName=ProgressBarIndicator,
                                                        Path=Width}" />
                            </Polygon.RenderTransform>
                        </Polygon>
                    </Canvas>
                </Border>
            </Grid>
        </ControlTemplate>
    </Page.Resources>
```

```
<Grid Background="{StaticResource ApplicationPageBackgroundThemeBrush}">
    <Grid.RowDefinitions>
        <RowDefinition Height="Auto" />
        <RowDefinition Height="*" />
    </Grid.RowDefinitions>

    <ProgressBar Grid.Row="0"
                 Template="{StaticResource progressTemplate}"
                 Margin="48"
                 Value="{Binding ElementName=slider, Path=Value}" />

    <Slider Name="slider"
            Grid.Row="1"
            Margin="48"
            VerticalAlignment="Center" />
    </Grid>
</Page>
```

The bottom of the XAML file instantiates a *ProgressBar* with this template and binds it to a *Slider* for testing purposes:

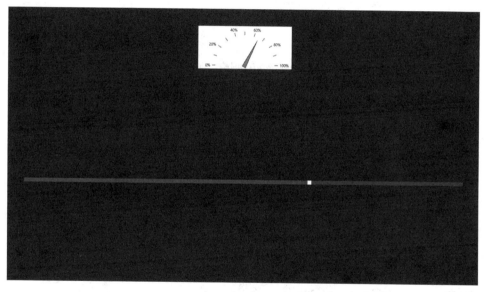

The SpringLoadedSlider and SpeedometerProgressBar are based on XAML files I originally created for WPF for an article in the January 2007 issue of *MSDN Magazine*. Although I needed to alter the templates somewhat to account for the differences between WPF and the Windows Runtime, for the most part they are quite similar. Although we don't have complete portability between all XAML-based environments, it is certainly the case that work done six years ago can be readily adapted to newer platforms.

Custom Controls

When you create a custom control in a Windows Runtime library, you probably want to make that control available to a variety of applications and perhaps even market it to other programmers. In this case, you should supply a default *Style* for that control, including a default *ControlTemplate*.

A library that contains custom control classes should also contain a file named generic.xaml in a folder named Themes. Like the generic.xaml file you've already seen, this generic.xaml file has a root element of *ResourceDictionary* and contains a *Style* definition with a *TargetType* indicating the custom control name and no dictionary key. This *Style* should incorporate a default *ControlTemplate*.

Visual Studio will generate a skeleton generic.xaml file for you. In the Petzold.ProgrammingWindows6.Chapter11 library I've been using for this chapter, I invoked the Add New Item dialog box and selected Templated Control, giving it a name of *NewToggle*. Visual Studio generated a NewToggle.cs file with a bunch of *using* directives and the following class definition:

```
namespace Petzold.ProgrammingWindows6.Chapter11
{
    public sealed class NewToggle : Control
    {
        public NewToggle()
        {
            this.DefaultStyleKey = typeof(NewToggle);
        }
    }
}
```

This is not a partial class definition! There is no corresponding NewToggle.xaml file, and the constructor does not contain a call to *InitializeComponent*. The *DefaultStyleKey* property indicates the type to use when searching for implicit styles.

Visual Studio also generated a Themes folder and a generic.xaml file containing this implicit style:

```
<ResourceDictionary
    xmlns="http://schemas.microsoft.com/winfx/2006/xaml/presentation"
    xmlns:x="http://schemas.microsoft.com/winfx/2006/xaml"
    xmlns:local="using:Petzold.ProgrammingWindows6.Chapter11">

    <Style TargetType="local:NewToggle">
        <Setter Property="Template">
            <Setter.Value>
                <ControlTemplate TargetType="local:NewToggle">
                    <Border
                        Background="{TemplateBinding Background}"
                        BorderBrush="{TemplateBinding BorderBrush}"
                        BorderThickness="{TemplateBinding BorderThickness}">
                    </Border>
                </ControlTemplate>
            </Setter.Value>
        </Setter>
    </Style>
</ResourceDictionary>
```

If your library has multiple custom controls, this same file will contain default *Style* definitions for all of them. This file has a specific name and location for a reason: It will forever be associated with the custom control defined in this library and doesn't need to be referenced in any other way.

The *NewToggle* control is intended to implement toggle button functionality by showing two different pieces of content at the same time, one associated with the unchecked state and the other with the checked state. Tap one of those pieces of content to change the check state. How the visuals change to reflect that change is the responsibility of the template.

I made *NewToggle* derive from *ContentControl* so that it inherits the *Content* and *ContentTemplate* properties. The class defines two new dependency properties, *CheckedContent* and *IsChecked*:

Project: Petzold.ProgrammingWindows6.Chapter11 | **File:** NewToggle.cs

```
public class NewToggle : ContentControl
{
    public event EventHandler CheckedChanged;
    Button uncheckButton, checkButton;

    static NewToggle()
    {
        CheckedContentProperty = DependencyProperty.Register("CheckedContent",
            typeof(object),
            typeof(NewToggle),
            new PropertyMetadata(null));

        IsCheckedProperty = DependencyProperty.Register("IsChecked",
            typeof(bool),
            typeof(NewToggle),
            new PropertyMetadata(false, OnCheckedChanged));
    }

    public NewToggle()
    {
        this.DefaultStyleKey = typeof(NewToggle);
    }

    public static DependencyProperty CheckedContentProperty { private set; get; }

    public static DependencyProperty IsCheckedProperty { private set; get; }

    public object CheckedContent
    {
        set { SetValue(CheckedContentProperty, value); }
        get { return GetValue(CheckedContentProperty); }
    }

    public bool IsChecked
    {
        set { SetValue(IsCheckedProperty, value); }
        get { return (bool)GetValue(IsCheckedProperty); }
    }

    protected override void OnApplyTemplate()
    {
```

```
        if (uncheckButton != null)
            uncheckButton.Click -= OnButtonClick;

        if (checkButton != null)
            checkButton.Click -= OnButtonClick;

        uncheckButton = GetTemplateChild("UncheckButton") as Button;
        checkButton = GetTemplateChild("CheckButton") as Button;

        if (uncheckButton != null)
            uncheckButton.Click += OnButtonClick;

        if (checkButton != null)
            checkButton.Click += OnButtonClick;

        base.OnApplyTemplate();
    }

    void OnButtonClick(object sender, RoutedEventArgs args)
    {
        this.IsChecked = sender == checkButton;
    }

    static void OnCheckedChanged(DependencyObject obj,
                        DependencyPropertyChangedEventArgs args)
    {
        (obj as NewToggle).OnCheckedChanged(EventArgs.Empty);
    }

    protected virtual void OnCheckedChanged(EventArgs args)
    {
        VisualStateManager.GoToState(this,
                            this.IsChecked ? "Checked" : "Unchecked",
                            true);

        if (CheckedChanged != null)
            CheckedChanged(this, args);
    }
}
```

The *OnApplyTemplate* override assumes that the template has two *Button* controls with the names "UncheckButton" and "CheckButton." If so, these are saved as fields and *Click* handlers are attached. If one of these buttons is then clicked, the *IsChecked* property is changed, the *CheckedChanged* event is fired, and the static *VisualStateManager.GoToState* is called with states of "Checked" or "Unchecked."

The template in generic.xaml contains the two buttons with these names as well as *Storyboard* objects defined for the two states:

Project: Petzold.ProgrammingWindows11.Chapter11 | File: generic.xaml (excerpt)

```
<Style TargetType="local:NewToggle">
    <Setter Property="BorderBrush" Value="{StaticResource ApplicationForegroundThemeBrush}" />
    <Setter Property="BorderThickness" Value="1" />
    <Setter Property="Template">
        <Setter.Value>
            <ControlTemplate TargetType="local:NewToggle">
```

```
<Border Background="{TemplateBinding Background}"
        BorderBrush="{TemplateBinding BorderBrush}"
        BorderThickness="{TemplateBinding BorderThickness}">

    <VisualStateManager.VisualStateGroups>
        <VisualStateGroup x:Name="CheckStates">
            <VisualState x:Name="Unchecked" />

            <VisualState x:Name="Checked">
                <Storyboard>
                    <ObjectAnimationUsingKeyFrames
                            Storyboard.TargetName="UncheckButton"
                            Storyboard.TargetProperty="BorderThickness">
                        <DiscreteObjectKeyFrame KeyTime="0"
                                                Value="0" />
                    </ObjectAnimationUsingKeyFrames>

                    <ObjectAnimationUsingKeyFrames
                            Storyboard.TargetName="CheckButton"
                            Storyboard.TargetProperty="BorderThickness">
                        <DiscreteObjectKeyFrame KeyTime="0"
                                                Value="8" />
                    </ObjectAnimationUsingKeyFrames>
                </Storyboard>
            </VisualState>
        </VisualStateGroup>
    </VisualStateManager.VisualStateGroups>

    <local:UniformGrid Rows="1">
        <Button Name="UncheckButton"
                Content="{TemplateBinding Content}"
                ContentTemplate="{TemplateBinding ContentTemplate}"
                FontSize="{TemplateBinding FontSize}"
                BorderBrush="Red"
                BorderThickness="8"
                HorizontalAlignment="Stretch" />

        <Button Name="CheckButton"
                Content="{TemplateBinding CheckedContent}"
                ContentTemplate="{TemplateBinding ContentTemplate}"
                FontSize="{TemplateBinding FontSize}"
                BorderBrush="Green"
                BorderThickness="0"
                HorizontalAlignment="Stretch" />
    </local:UniformGrid>
</Border>
                </ControlTemplate>
            </Setter.Value>
        </Setter>
    </Style>
```

Keep in mind that in more extensive templates, the two buttons can themselves be templated. Here they contain template bindings to the *Content* and *CheckedContent* properties and share the same *ContentTemplate* of the control. The item that's checked is highlighted with a thick border, red for the left button and green for the right button.

This *NewToggle* control is demonstrated by the NewToggleDemo project:

Project: NewToggleDemo | File: MainPage.xaml (excerpt)

```xaml
<Page ... >
    <Page.Resources>
        <Style TargetType="ch11:NewToggle">
            <Setter Property="HorizontalAlignment" Value="Center" />
            <Setter Property="VerticalAlignment" Value="Center" />
        </Style>
    </Page.Resources>

    <Grid Background="{StaticResource ApplicationPageBackgroundThemeBrush}">
        <Grid.ColumnDefinitions>
            <ColumnDefinition Width="*" />
            <ColumnDefinition Width="*" />
        </Grid.ColumnDefinitions>

        <ch11:NewToggle Content="Don't do it!"
                        CheckedContent="Let's go for it!"
                        Grid.Column="0"
                        FontSize="24" />

        <ch11:NewToggle Grid.Column="1">
            <ch11:NewToggle.Content>
                <Image Source="Images/MunchScream.jpg" />
            </ch11:NewToggle.Content>

            <ch11:NewToggle.CheckedContent>
                <Image Source="Images/BotticelliVenus.jpg" />
            </ch11:NewToggle.CheckedContent>
        </ch11:NewToggle>
    </Grid>
</Page>
```

The first *NewToggle* has content that consists of two text strings. It's in an unchecked state. The second *NewToggle* uses two famous images for the two states and is currently checked:

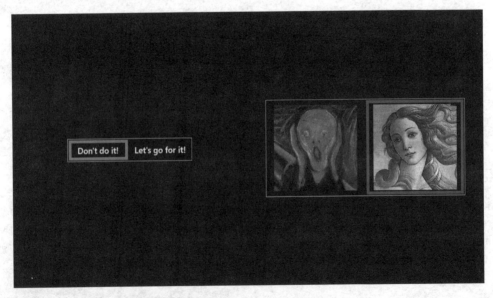

In Chapter 13, "Touch, Etc.," I have another example of a custom control called *XYSlider*.

If you're using a custom control in a single application, you can define the control right in the application project, and the default template can indeed go in a XAML file that contributes to a partial class definition for the control.

Templates and Item Containers

Templating an *ItemsControl* derivative such as *ListBox* is very similar to templating any other type of control except that the template contains an element named *ItemsPresenter*. This is basically a placeholder that represents the list of items. It requires no template bindings. As you can see by looking at the default template for *ListBox*, the bulk of the template is a *ScrollViewer*. You can replace *ScrollViewer* in a *ListBox* if you find that you can code something better or more appropriate for your application.

As you tap or click an item in a *ListBox*, or as you use the keyboard arrow keys to navigate through the list, the selected item is highlighted. Where does that highlight come from? Who is responsible?

The class actually performing the highlighting belongs to a category of *ContentControl* derivatives I haven't discussed yet. These are controls that derive from *SelectorItem*:

```
Object
    DependencyObject
        UIElement
            FrameworkElement
                Control
                    ContentControl
                        SelectorItem (non-instantiable)
                            ComboBoxItem
                            FlipViewItem
                            GridViewItem
                            ListBoxItem
                            ListViewItem
```

These five classes map to the five instantiable classes that derive from *Selector*, as shown earlier in this chapter, and they are used to host the individual items in those items controls. *ItemsControl* has no class for its items because the items can't be selected.

You haven't seen these classes yet because normally you don't instantiate them on your own. Instead, the *Selector* control itself is responsible for generating the items. Because these classes derive from *ContentControl* they have their own default templates (defined in generic.xaml), and these templates involve a *ContentPresenter*.

Suppose you want to provide a different type of selection highlighting. How is this done? How do you apply a style to a *ListBoxItem* class that you don't even see?

ItemsControl defines an *ItemContainerStyle* property that you can set to a *Style* object. When working with a *ListBox*, for example, you would provide a *Style* with a *TargetType* of *ListBoxItem*. That *Style* can include a setting for the *Template* property.

If you look at the default *ListBoxItem* style in generic.xaml, you'll see a visual state group named *SelectionStates* that has six mutually exclusive states: *Unselected*, *Selected*, *SelectedUnfocused*, *SelectedDisabled*, *SelectedPointerOver*, and *SelectedPressed*.

If you'd like all the selected states to be the same, you can define the template to reflect a selected state, and then you can define a *Storyboard* for the *Unselected* state. This is the approach I took in the CustomListBoxItemStyle project. This is similar to the ListBoxWithItemTemplate project except that it also includes a *Style* set to the *ItemContainerStyle* property.

Project: CustomListBoxItemStyle | File: MainPage.xaml (excerpt)

```
<Page ... >
    <Page.Resources>
        <ch11:NamedColor x:Key="namedColor" />
    </Page.Resources>

    <Grid>
        <ListBox Name="lstbox"
                 ItemsSource="{Binding Source={StaticResource namedColor},
                                       Path=All}"
                 Width="380">
            <ListBox.ItemTemplate>
                <DataTemplate>
                    ...
                </DataTemplate>
            </ListBox.ItemTemplate>

            <ListBox.ItemContainerStyle>
                <Style TargetType="ListBoxItem">
                    <Setter Property="Background" Value="Transparent" />
                    <Setter Property="TabNavigation" Value="Local" />
                    <Setter Property="Padding" Value="8,10" />
                    <Setter Property="HorizontalContentAlignment" Value="Left" />
                    <Setter Property="Template">
                        <Setter.Value>
                            <ControlTemplate TargetType="ListBoxItem">
                                <Border Background="{TemplateBinding Background}"
                                        BorderBrush="{TemplateBinding BorderBrush}"
                                        BorderThickness="{TemplateBinding BorderThickness}">

                                    <VisualStateManager.VisualStateGroups>
                                        <VisualStateGroup x:Name="SelectionStates">
                                            <VisualState x:Name="Unselected">
                                                <Storyboard>
                                                    <ObjectAnimationUsingKeyFrames
                                                        Storyboard.TargetName="ContentPresenter"
                                                        Storyboard.TargetProperty="FontStyle">
```

```xml
                                        <DiscreteObjectKeyFrame KeyTime="0"
                                                    Value="Normal" />
                                </ObjectAnimationUsingKeyFrames>

                                <ObjectAnimationUsingKeyFrames
                                        Storyboard.TargetName="ContentPresenter"
                                        Storyboard.TargetProperty="FontWeight">
                                    <DiscreteObjectKeyFrame KeyTime="0"
                                                    Value="Normal" />
                                </ObjectAnimationUsingKeyFrames>
                            </Storyboard>
                        </VisualState>

                        <VisualState x:Name="Selected" />
                        <VisualState x:Name="SelectedUnfocused" />
                        <VisualState x:Name="SelectedDisabled" />
                        <VisualState x:Name="SelectedPointerOver" />
                        <VisualState x:Name="SelectedPressed" />
                    </VisualStateGroup>
                </VisualStateManager.VisualStateGroups>

                <Grid Background="Transparent">
                    <ContentPresenter x:Name="ContentPresenter"
                                    FontStyle="Italic"
                                    FontWeight="Bold"
                                    Content="{TemplateBinding Content}"
                        ContentTransitions=
                            "{TemplateBinding ContentTransitions}"
                        ContentTemplate=
                            "{TemplateBinding ContentTemplate}"
                        HorizontalAlignment=
                            "{TemplateBinding HorizontalContentAlignment}"
                        VerticalAlignment=
                            "{TemplateBinding VerticalContentAlignment}"
                        Margin="{TemplateBinding Padding}" />
                </Grid>
            </Border>
        </ControlTemplate>
    </Setter.Value>
    </Setter>
    </Style>
    </ListBox.ItemContainerStyle>
    </ListBox>

    <Grid.Background>
        <SolidColorBrush Color="{Binding ElementName=lstbox,
                                Path=SelectedItem.Color}" />
    </Grid.Background>
    </Grid>
</Page>
```

The *Style* set to the *ItemContainerStyle* of the *ListBox* can be defined as a resource of course. I decided that I wanted a selected item to have text in bold italic, and that's how the *FontStyle* and *FontWeight* properties of the *ContentPresenter* are defined. When the item is unselected (which is actually the normal case), the *FontStyle* and *FontWeight* are animated to normal. Here's how it looks:

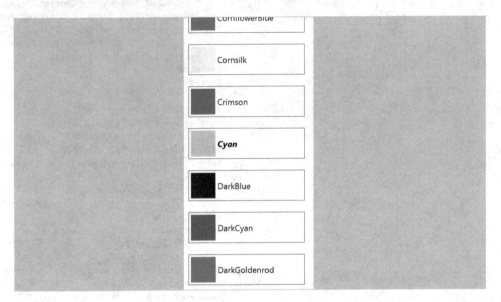

That's a rather odd way to highlight an item, but for some applications an unusual highlighting might be exactly what is desired.

The real purpose of templates is not to make controls more unusual (although that is certainly fun) but to make them more usable—to adapt the visuals of the control to its functionality.

In the next chapter I'll continue the discussion of items controls with the *ListViewBase* derivatives (*ListView* and *GridView*) and explore the use of these controls with view models.

CHAPTER 12

Pages and Navigation

M ost Windows 8 applications are built around instances of the *Page* class. This is certainly not a requirement, but it offers some conveniences such as the easy integration of application bars. Up until this chapter, I've been focusing on programs that have only one instance of a *Page* derivative called *MainPage*, but now is the time to explore programs that allow Web-like navigation among multiple *Page* derivatives.

Visual Studio has two project templates for applications with multiple pages called Grid App and Split App. These templates are built around the powerful *ListView* and *GridView* controls and use these controls with view models. These templates are also layout-aware, meaning that they respond to changes in screen orientation and snap modes, so an exploration into window resizing issues offers a convenient place to begin this chapter.

Responding to window size changes is not new to Windows programmers. Most traditional Windows desktop programs have a sizing border that allows the user a great deal of control over the size and aspect ratio of the application's window. Windows programmers have been taught for 25 years to try to write their programs to adapt to whatever size the user selects. Of course, this is not always feasible: What's a spreadsheet program to do if the user shrinks the window down so far that no cells are visible? Some programs—for example, the Windows Calculator—simply set a fixed window size adequate to display all the program's content. For traditional desktop applications, this is suitable only when the window is guaranteed to be smaller than the screen.

Windows 8 applications mostly run in full screen mode and actually have a greater assurance of getting a minimum screen size. However, Windows 8 applications are also susceptible to changes in orientation and snap modes, and many applications should be aware of these changes.

Screen Resolution Issues

A computer screen has a particular horizontal and vertical size in pixels and also a physical size that is usually specified as a diagonal measurement in inches. Using the Pythagorean Theorem, you can combine these sizes and calculate a resolution in pixels per inch, also known as dots per inch (DPI).

For example, a 1024 × 768 pixel screen has a diagonal of 1280 pixels. If the screen measures 12 inches diagonally, that's a resolution of 106 DPI. A 23-inch desktop monitor with a standard high-definition size of 1920 × 1080 pixels has about 2203 pixels on the diagonal for a resolution of 96 DPI. A 27-inch monitor with 2560 × 1440 pixels has a resolution of about 109 DPI.

Early on in this book, I said that it's proper to assume that the screen has a resolution of 96 pixels per inch. As you can see, this is a good assumption for these three example monitors, although you might encounter monitors where this rule is stretched somewhat: For much of this book I've been using a Samsung tablet that has a pixel size of 1366 × 768, with a 11.6-inch diagonal of about 1567 pixels, for a resolution of 135 DPI. When I draw a 96-pixel square on this screen, I want it to be a square inch, it's closer to 7/10th inch square.

The 96 DPI assumption most commonly breaks down for small screens with lots of pixels. For example, consider a 10.6-inch screen that crams in 1920 × 1080 pixels. Such a screen has a resolution of 208 DPI, so what the programmer thinks is an inch actually shows up as less than half an inch. Text gets tinier and although it might still be readable because of the high pixel density, it probably offers an insufficiently large touch target.

For this reason, Windows 8 attempts to compensate for high-resolution screens in a manner that is fairly transparent to applications: If a screen has a pixel size of 2560 × 1440 or above and a physical size—for example, 12 inches—that results in a resolution of 240 DPI or greater, Windows adjusts all pixel coordinates and dimensions used or encountered by the application by 180 percent. The 2560 × 1440 screen appears to the application to have a size of 1422 × 800 pixels.

If a screen doesn't have quite that high a pixel density but it does have a pixel size of 1920 × 1080 or greater and a physical size small enough to result in a resolution of 174 DPI or greater, Windows 8 adjusts all pixel dimensions by 140 percent, so a 1920 × 1080 display seems to have a size of 1371 × 771 pixels.

Keep in mind that these automatic adjustments occur only for physically small screens with many pixels. A physically large screen that has an actual resolution of under 174 DPI will not be adjusted, and hence the application will see the full size.

The Windows Runtime refers to the assumed resolution of the video display as a *logical DPI*. Normally, the logical DPI is 96, but for displays of high pixel density, logical DPI can be either 134.4 (that is, 96 DPI scaled by 140 percent) or 172.8 (96 DPI scaled by 180 percent).

Let's see how this works. The WhatRes program is similar to the WhatSize program first introduced in Chapter 3, "Basic Event Handling," but in addition to displaying the size of the window (which is also the size of the page), it obtains information about the resolution of the screen.

The XAML file in WhatRes simply instantiates a *TextBlock*:

Project: WhatRes | File: MainPage.xaml (excerpt)

```
<Grid Background="{StaticResource ApplicationPageBackgroundThemeBrush}">
    <TextBlock Name="textBlock"
               HorizontalAlignment="Center"
               VerticalAlignment="Center"
               FontSize="24" />
</Grid>
```

The code-behind file sets handlers for the *SizeChanged* event of the page and also the static *LogicalDpiChanged* event from the *DisplayProperties* class defined in the *Windows.Graphics.Display* namespace.

```
public sealed partial class MainPage : Page
{
    public MainPage()
    {
        this.InitializeComponent();

        this.SizeChanged += OnMainPageSizeChanged;
        DisplayProperties.LogicalDpiChanged += OnLogicalDpiChanged;

        Loaded += (sender, args) =>
        {
            UpdateDisplay();
        };
    }

    void OnMainPageSizeChanged(object sender, SizeChangedEventArgs args)
    {
        UpdateDisplay();
    }

    void OnLogicalDpiChanged(object sender)
    {
        UpdateDisplay();
    }

    void UpdateDisplay()
    {
        double logicalDpi = DisplayProperties.LogicalDpi;
        int pixelWidth = (int)Math.Round(logicalDpi * this.ActualWidth / 96);
        int pixelHeight = (int)Math.Round(logicalDpi * this.ActualHeight / 96);

        textBlock.Text =
            String.Format("Window size = {0} x {1}\r\n" +
                          "ResolutionScale = {2}\r\n" +
                          "Logical DPI = {3}\r\n" +
                          "Pixel size = {4} x {5}",
                          this.ActualWidth, this.ActualHeight,
                          DisplayProperties.ResolutionScale,
                          DisplayProperties.LogicalDpi,
                          pixelWidth, pixelHeight);
    }
}
```

In real life, the *DisplayProperties.LogicalDpiChanged* event will not be fired very often because video displays don't change pixel size or physical size while a program is running. However, the event could be fired if a second monitor is attached to a Windows 8 computer, the two monitors have different logical DPI settings, and the program is moved from one display to another.

The WhatRes program obtains the window size by using the *ActualWidth* and *ActualHeight* properties of the page, but then it calculates an actual pixel size based on the *DisplayProperties .LogicalDpi* setting.

Here's how the program looks on the 1366 × 768 tablet I've been using for most of this book:

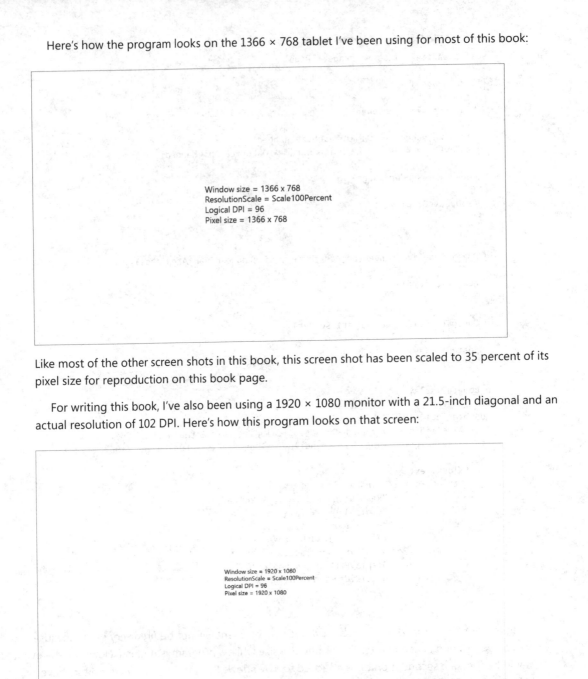

Window size = 1366 x 768
ResolutionScale = Scale100Percent
Logical DPI = 96
Pixel size = 1366 x 768

Like most of the other screen shots in this book, this screen shot has been scaled to 35 percent of its pixel size for reproduction on this book page.

For writing this book, I've also been using a 1920 × 1080 monitor with a 21.5-inch diagonal and an actual resolution of 102 DPI. Here's how this program looks on that screen:

Window size = 1920 x 1080
ResolutionScale = Scale100Percent
Logical DPI = 96
Pixel size = 1920 x 1080

This screen shot has a greater pixel dimension than the previous screen shot, so I had to size it to 25 percent to occupy the same area on this page of the book. In real life, the text is about the same size whether the program is running on the tablet or the big screen, but the text is smaller relative to the big screen, indicating the application has a bigger area in which to play.

WhatRes is a good program to run on the Windows 8 simulator that you can select from the standard toolbar in Visual Studio. The simulator allows you to run the application in some common display sizes. For example, here's WhatRes running on a simulated 1920 × 1080 display with a 10.6-inch diagonal:

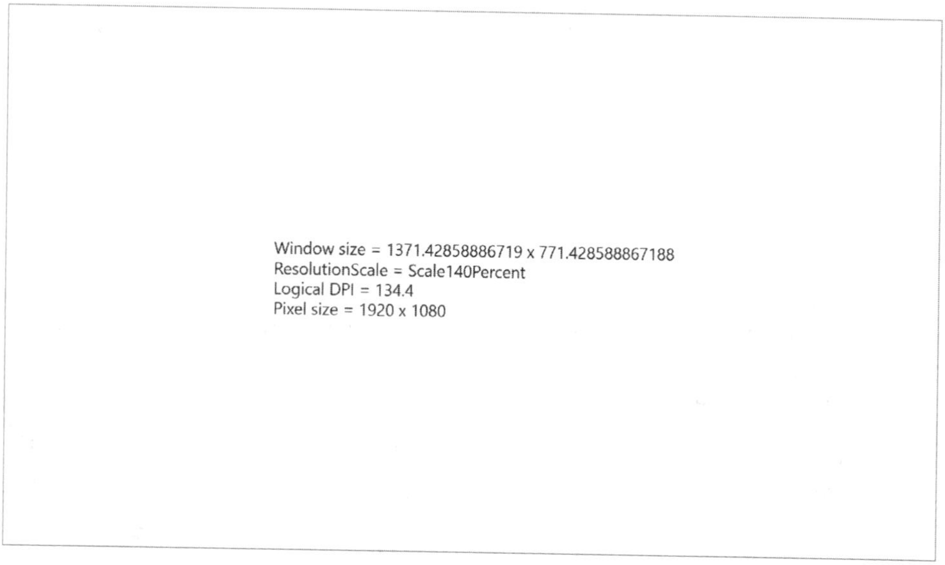

Window size = 1371.42858886719 x 771.428588867188
ResolutionScale = Scale140Percent
Logical DPI = 134.4
Pixel size = 1920 x 1080

Like the previous screen shot, this screen shot has been scaled to 25 percent to fit on this page. To the Windows 8 application, the window appears to have a dimension of 1371 × 771, and all the text and graphics it displays will be based on that size. The calculated pixel size matches the pixel dimensions of the display. As you can see, the 18-point text appears to occupy about the same relative area of the screen as the 1366 × 768 display.

Here's the same program running on a simulated 2560 × 1440 pixel 10.6-inch screen:

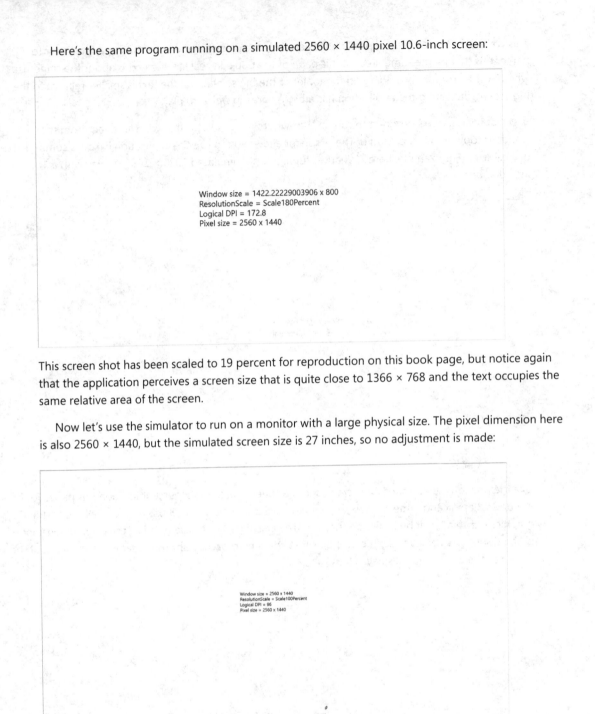

Window size = 1422.22229003906 x 800
ResolutionScale = Scale180Percent
Logical DPI = 172.8
Pixel size = 2560 x 1440

This screen shot has been scaled to 19 percent for reproduction on this book page, but notice again that the application perceives a screen size that is quite close to 1366 × 768 and the text occupies the same relative area of the screen.

Now let's use the simulator to run on a monitor with a large physical size. The pixel dimension here is also 2560 × 1440, but the simulated screen size is 27 inches, so no adjustment is made:

Window size = 2560 x 1440
ResolutionScale = Scale100Percent
Logical DPI = 96
Pixel size = 2560 x 1440

Like the previous screen shot, I had to reduce the size to 19 percent, which makes the text appear very tiny. However, this text has quite a reasonable size on a 27-inch monitor, and what the tiny text here really indicates is how the application has a much roomier playground in which to stretch out.

Scaling Issues

As a Windows programmer, you're accustomed to dealing with coordinates and sizes in units of pixels. As you've seen, when your program runs on a physically small screen with a high pixel density, Windows scales these coordinates and sizes by 140 percent or 180 percent, depending on the display size and resolution.

So, instead of saying that we draw or size controls in *pixels*, we might more correctly say that we deal in *device-independent units* (DIUs), or simply *units*. Some people refer to these units as *device-independent pixels*, but that seems like too much of an oxymoron to my ears.

In the following table, the first column shows the units you use in a program for drawing and sizing, and the other columns show how these translate to the actual pixels of the video display:

	Resolution Scale		
DIUs	100%	140%	180%
5	5	7	9
10	10	14	18
15	15	21	27
20	20	28	36

You can continue the chart yourself.

What this chart shows is that if you stick with sizes and coordinates that are multiples of five units, these units convert to an integral number of pixels. This integral conversion can sometimes help in preserving the fidelity of the graphics.

When Windows makes these adjustments, it scales text and vector graphics without loss of resolution. For example, if you specify a *FontSize* of 20 and your program runs on a display with 180 percent resolution scale, you don't get a 20-pixel-tall font scaled up by 180 percent with resultant jaggies or blurring. You get a smooth authentic 36-pixel *FontSize* font.

But bitmaps are different. Bitmaps have particular pixel sizes, and if you display a 200-pixel-square bitmap at its actual pixel size, there is no choice for Windows except to scale this image by 140 percent or 180 percent to make it larger and hence fuzzier.

To avoid this problem, you can create bitmaps in three different sizes (for example, 200-pixel-square, 280-pixel-square, and 360-pixel-square) for use by your application. It's even possible to store these images as program assets and have Windows automatically select the correct one!

The AutoImageSelection project demonstrates how this is done. I started with a rather high-resolution bitmap and cropped it to 2304 pixels square size. Working from that, I then resized the image three times: to 640 pixels square, to 896 pixels square, and to 1152 pixels square. These correspond to the three resolution scales: 896 pixels is 140 percent of 640, and 1152 pixels is 180 percent of 640. I also used Windows Paint to embed some text in each image indicating the actual pixel size. I had to use three different text sizes to make the text approximately the same size in all three images.

I then added these three images to the AutoImageSelection project twice in two different folders with two different naming conventions, as shown here in the Visual Studio Solution Explorer:

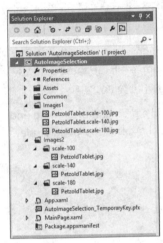

In the Images1 folder, the three bitmaps have been given different names. Notice that periods separate the "scale-100", "scale-140", and "scale-180" parts of the name from the "PetzoldTablet" name and the "jpg" extension.

In the Images2 directory, the three bitmaps have identical names, but they reside in three different subfolders indicating the scaling.

In both cases, the scale-100 bitmap is 640 pixels square, the scale-140 bitmap is 896 pixels square, and the scale-180 bitmap is 1152 pixels square.

The MainPage.xaml file contains two *Image* elements that reference a bitmap in the Images1 and Images2 directories. In both cases, the part of the filename or file path indicating the scaling is absent from these paths:

Project: AutoImageSelection | File: MainPage.xaml (excerpt)

```
<Grid Background="{StaticResource ApplicationPageBackgroundThemeBrush}">
    <Grid.ColumnDefinitions>
        <ColumnDefinition Width="*" />
        <ColumnDefinition Width="*" />
    </Grid.ColumnDefinitions>
```

```
<Image Source="Images1/PetzoldTablet.jpg"
       Grid.Column="0"
       Width="640"
       Height="640"
       HorizontalAlignment="Center"
       VerticalAlignment="Center" />

<Image Source="Images2/PetzoldTablet.jpg"
       Grid.Column="1"
       Width="640"
       Height="640"
       HorizontalAlignment="Center"
       VerticalAlignment="Center" />
</Grid>
```

Notice that the two *Image* elements are given explicit *Width* and *Height* settings corresponding to the pixel size of the 100 percent bitmap. This is crucial! Don't count on a *Stretch* mode of *None* to force the *Image* element to perform the scaling correctly.

Let's run this program on three different 10.6-inch diagonal (simulated) monitors. (When you're doing this with the Windows 8 simulator, don't switch resolutions while the program is running. Instead, terminate the program, switch resolutions, and then run the program again.) Here's the 1366 × 768 display:

As usual, this 1366 × 768 screen shot is scaled to 35 percent for the page.

Here's the program running on a 1920 × 1080 monitor with a 10.6-inch diagonal:

This screen shot is sized to 25 percent to fit on the page. Even though a Windows 8 program perceives this display to have a 1371 × 771 pixel size, the 896-pixel-square bitmap has been chosen and effectively displayed in its native size: Each pixel of the bitmap corresponds to a pixel of the display.

And here's the program running on a 2560 × 1440 monitor with a 10.6-inch diagonal:

The screen shot has been sized to 19 percent, but on a real display there will be a one-to-one correspondence between the bitmap pixels and the screen pixels.

When run on screens of the same physical size, the bitmaps should also have the same physical size, as shown in these examples, but the rendition of the bitmap should be better for screens of higher density, as is also the case. On displays of a larger physical size, the images will be much smaller relative to the size of the screen but roughly the same physical size.

Snap Views

A Windows 8 machine requires a display of at least 1024 × 768 pixels to run Windows Store applications. This display size has an aspect ratio of 4:3, consistent with movies before the advent of widescreen in the early 1950s and consistent with classical television and computer displays prior to widescreen.

On a tablet, the screen can switch between landscape and portrait modes, so a display size of 768 × 1024 will also be encountered by applications running on this machine. But on a display of this size, these are the only two dimensions that a Windows Store application needs to handle.

The next step up is a display of 1366 × 768, which has an aspect ratio of approximately 16:9, consistent with high-definition television. Such a display has a portrait mode of 768 × 1366.

In addition, 1366 × 768 is the smallest display size that supports snap modes. Snap modes allow two programs to share the screen, but they are available only in the landscape orientation.

The *Windows.UI.ViewManagement* namespace contains an *ApplicationView* class with a static property named *Value* that is of type *ApplicationViewState*, an enumeration that indicates the current snap mode of an application. There is no event corresponding with this information. If your program needs to be notified when the view changes, check the value during a *SizeChanged* handler.

The WhatSnap program is similar to WhatRes except that it includes a display of the *ApplicationView.Value* property:

Project: WhatSnap | **File:** MainPage.xaml.cs (excerpt)

```
void UpdateDisplay()
{
    double logicalDpi = DisplayProperties.LogicalDpi;
    int pixelWidth = (int)Math.Round(logicalDpi * this.ActualWidth / 96);
    int pixelHeight = (int)Math.Round(logicalDpi * this.ActualHeight / 96);

    textBlock.Text =
        String.Format("ApplicationViewState = {0}\r\n" +
                    "Window size = {1} x {2}\r\n" +
                    "ResolutionScale = {3}\r\n" +
                    "Logical DPI = {4}\r\n" +
                    "Pixel size = {5} x {6}",
                    ApplicationView.Value,
                    this.ActualWidth, this.ActualHeight,
                    DisplayProperties.ResolutionScale,
                    DisplayProperties.LogicalDpi,
                    pixelWidth, pixelHeight);
}
```

In addition, the *TextBlock* is in a *Viewbox* so that it can still be viewed if the screen gets too narrow:

Project: WhatSnap | File: MainPage.xaml (excerpt)

```
<Grid Background="{StaticResource ApplicationPageBackgroundThemeBrush}">
    <Viewbox HorizontalAlignment="Center"
             VerticalAlignment="Center"
             StretchDirection="DownOnly"
             Margin="24">

        <TextBlock Name="textBlock"
                   FontSize="24" />
    </Viewbox>
</Grid>
```

The *ApplicationViewState* enumeration has four members. In portrait mode, the only applicable member is *FullScreenPortrait*:

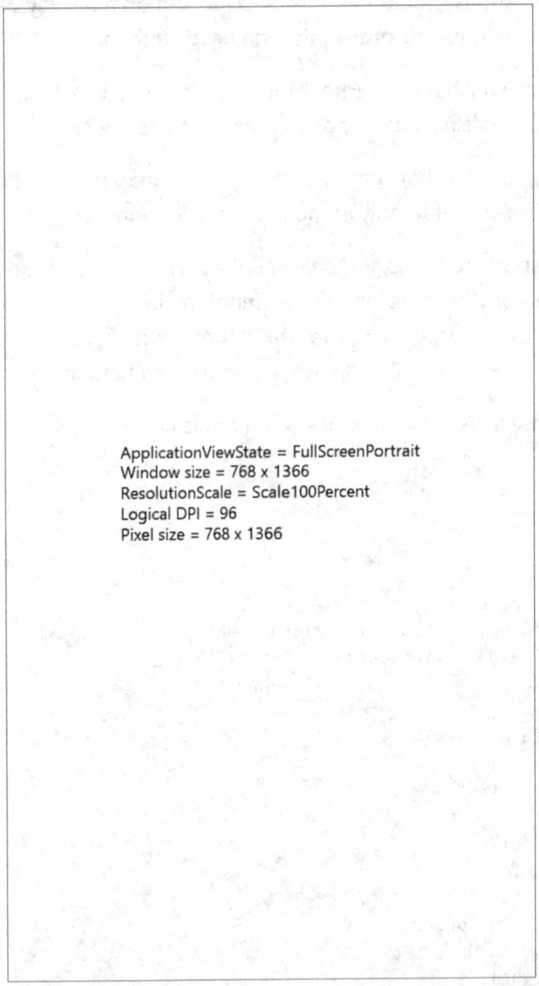

```
ApplicationViewState = FullScreenPortrait
Window size = 768 x 1366
ResolutionScale = Scale100Percent
Logical DPI = 96
Pixel size = 768 x 1366
```

Snap modes play a role in landscape only. If the application occupies the full screen, the *ApplicationViewState* has a value of *FullScreenLandscape*:

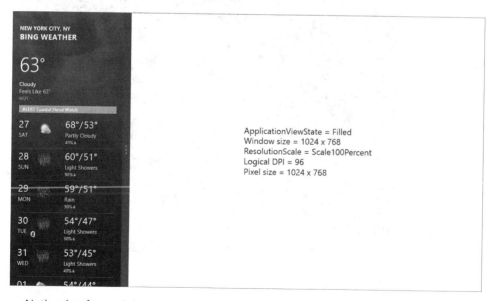

ApplicationViewState = FullScreenLandscape
Window size = 1366 x 768
ResolutionScale = Scale100Percent
Logical DPI = 96
Pixel size = 1366 x 768

If you sweep your finger on the left edge of the screen just a bit and then go back, you can get a columnar display of other applications. If you drag your finger farther, you can bring another program into a partial view. At this point, the *ApplicationViewState* becomes *Filled*:

ApplicationViewState = Filled
Window size = 1024 x 768
ResolutionScale = Scale100Percent
Logical DPI = 96
Pixel size = 1024 x 768

Notice that for a minimum size screen that supports snap modes—1366 × 768—the *Filled* size is 1024 × 768, which is the minimum size screen that runs Windows Store applications.

Drag that bar farther to the right, and *ApplicationViewState* becomes *Snapped*:

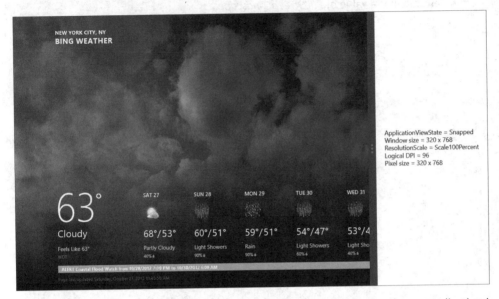

Those are the only four possibilities. You get the same *Snapped* value if your application is on the left rather than the right:

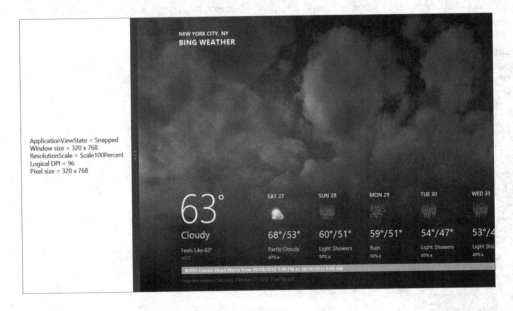

Continue dragging that bar to the right, and your program goes into the *Filled* mode again:

The *Snapped* view is always 320 units wide. The *Filled* view is always the total screen width minus 320 units for the other application minus 22 units for the drag bar.

For example, if you run this program on a 2560 × 1440 pixel 10.6-inch diagonal display, the screen has a total width of 1422 units, which separates into 1080 units for the *Filled* mode, 320 units for the *Snapped* mode, and 22 units for the divider.

If you run the program on a 2560 × 1440 pixel 27-inch diagonal display, device-independent units are the same as pixels. The screen has a total width of 2560 units, which separates into 2218 units for the *Filled* mode, 320 units for the *Snapped* mode, and 22 units for the divider.

In the *Filled* mode, a program can determine the full size of the screen in device-independent units by adding 320 and 22 to the width. By further incorporating the *LogicalDpi* setting, the program can determine the full size of the screen in pixels.

Because there are a very limited number of display modes—and particularly because the *Snapped* mode always has a width of 320 units—it is expected that applications will be tailored to do something intelligent for each mode. As you can see, the Bing Weather application reorients its display of daily weather forecasts for the *Snapped* mode. However, it's unlikely you'll need to do something different for the *Filled* mode.

Changing the orientation of a *StackPanel* is one simple way to deal with the *Snapped* mode. Juggling rows and columns of a *Grid* is another, as I demonstrated in the OrientableColorScroll program in Chapter 5, "Control Interaction." Later in this chapter, you'll see that it's possible to switch between a *GridView* and a *ListView* for displaying collections of items.

But obviously there is no solution that will be adequate for every application. This is really an issue that needs to be addressed individually.

The *ApplicationView* class has a static *TryUnsnap* method that attempts to unsnap a foreground application, but using this method is discouraged and it's hard to think of a reason to do so.

Orientation Changes

At the same time that you're adapting your application to *Filled* and *Snapped* modes, you can also adapt your application to landscape and portrait modes. Even if you believe that your application will run only on a desktop and never a tablet, you should be aware that some desktop monitors are capable of flipping into portrait mode and these monitors are much appreciated by people who tend to do a lot of writing.

You've seen earlier in this chapter that the *ApplicationView.Value* property indicates portrait mode with the *ApplicationViewState.FullScreenPortrait* enumeration member, but if you need more information—and if you'd prefer an event that tells you when orientation changes—then you'll want to use the *DisplayProperties* class in the *Windows.Graphics.Display* namespace. This is the same class that provides the logical DPI scaling information.

The *Windows.Graphics.Display* namespace defines a *DisplayOrientations* enumeration with five members, shown here with their values in parentheses:

- *None* (0)   Used only for *DisplayProperties.AutoRotationPreferences*

- *Landscape* (1)   90 degrees clockwise rotation from *PortraitFlipped*

- *Portrait* (2)   90 degrees clockwise rotation from *Landscape*

- *LandscapeFlipped* (4)   90 degrees clockwise rotation from *Portrait*

- *PortraitFlipped* (8)   90 degrees clockwise rotation from *LandscapeFlipped*

The "90 degrees clockwise rotation" mentioned here refers to the user turning the tablet (or computer screen) 90 degrees clockwise. As you've seen, Windows 8 automatically responds by rotating the contents of the screen in the opposite direction so that it maintains the same orientation.

The static *DisplayProperties.NativeOrientation* property indicates the orientation of the screen that is "native" or "most natural." This can be either *Landscape* or *Portrait*, generally governed on the location of buttons or logos on the device. The static *DisplayProperties.CurrentOrientation* can be any of the non-zero values.

The *DisplayProperties.OrientationChanged* event is fired when *CurrentOrientation* changes (as a result of the user turning the screen) or *NativeOrientation* changes, which happens more rarely when an application is moved to another monitor. This *OrientationChanged* event is *not* fired when an application starts up regardless of the initial orientation, so it's a good idea to duplicate *OrientationChanged* event handling during program initialization.

The XAML file in the NativeUp program displays an arrow pointing up:

Project: NativeUp | File: MainPage.xaml (excerpt)

```
<Grid Background="{StaticResource ApplicationPageBackgroundThemeBrush}">
    <StackPanel HorizontalAlignment="Center"
                VerticalAlignment="Center"
                RenderTransformOrigin="0.5 0.5">
        <Path Data="M 100 0 L 200 100, 150 100, 150 500, 50 500, 50 100, 0 100 Z"
              Stroke="Yellow"
              StrokeThickness="12"
              Fill="Red"
              RenderTransformOrigin="0.5 0.5"
              HorizontalAlignment="Center" />

        <TextBlock Text="Native Up"
                   FontSize="96" />

        <StackPanel.RenderTransform>
            <RotateTransform x:Name="rotate" />
        </StackPanel.RenderTransform>
    </StackPanel>
</Grid>
```

Normally, if you run such a program on a tablet and turn it around in your hands, Windows 8 would change the orientation of the display so that the arrow always points up, or nearly up given the 90 degree increments of rotation.

However, the code-behind file in this particular program uses the *OrientationChanged* event to counteract that rotation. The result is that the arrow always points toward the top of the computer as if the program were not subject to orientation changes:

Project: NativeUp | File: MainPage.xaml.cs (excerpt)

```
public sealed partial class MainPage : Page
{
    public MainPage()
    {
        this.InitializeComponent();

        SetRotation();
        DisplayProperties.OrientationChanged += OnOrientationChanged;
    }

    void OnOrientationChanged(object sender)
    {
        SetRotation();
    }

    void SetRotation()
    {
        rotate.Angle = 90 * (Log2(DisplayProperties.CurrentOrientation) -
                             Log2(DisplayProperties.NativeOrientation));
    }

    int Log2(DisplayOrientations orientation)
```

```
    {
        int value = (int)orientation;
        int log = 0;

        while (value > 0 && (value & 1) == 0)
        {
            value >>= 1;
            log += 1;
        }
        return log;
    }
}
```

For example, suppose you start the program in its native orientation. The arrow points up. Then you turn the tablet 90 degrees clockwise. Windows reorients the program 90 degrees counterclockwise, but the *OrientationChanged* handler turns the text and arrow 90 degrees clockwise. You can still see that there's an orientation change occurring because the screen contracts slightly, but the arrow's orientation relative to the screen doesn't change.

The program relies on the values of the *DisplayOrientations* enumeration members being 1, 2, 4, and 8 in order of clockwise rotation. The base-2 logarithms of these values are 0, 1, 2, and 3, so each increase by 1 is equivalent to a 90 degree clockwise change.

It is possible for an application to request a particular desired orientation. There are two ways to do this. You can open the Package.appmanifest file in Visual Studio, select the Application UI tab, and check one or more of the four orientations:

Whatever you select becomes the initial value of the static *DisplayProperties* *.AutoRotationPreferences* property, but during program initialization you can set that property to one or more *DisplayOrientations* enumeration members combined with the C# bitwise OR operator (|).

The key word here is *preferences*. Windows 8 is free to ignore what you request. For example, if you request that your application run only in portrait mode but the program happens to be running on a desktop computer with a landscape screen, the program will run in landscape mode. Even if the application is running on a tablet but the tablet is in a docking station in landscape mode, it's only going to run in landscape.

In other words, Windows 8 overrides the program's preferences if the preferences don't make sense in the current environment. This is reasonable: Regardless of what the program wants, the user shouldn't be required to look at the screen sideways.

I recommend that you avoid specifying orientation preferences and instead code your program to accommodate all orientations. The only possible exceptions to this rule involve games that rely upon bitmap graphics that must be oriented in a particular way, or programs that make use of the orientation sensors such as those in Chapter 18, "Sensors and GPS."

But keep in mind that restricting your program to a particular orientation might cause user confusion. For example, suppose you request that your program run only in landscape mode but it's running on a tablet that the user is holding in portrait mode. Normally, the user swipes a finger on the left or right of the screen to invoke the application switcher or charms bar. If the program is running in landscape mode, but the tablet is held in portrait mode, the user must swipe the top or bottom of the screen to invoke the application switcher or charms bar, and these two features will be displayed sideways because they have the same orientation as the current application.

Simple Page Navigation

Until this point, virtually all the applications in this book have been built around a single instance of a class called *MainPage* that derives from *Page*. As a result, it hasn't even been noticeable that this instance of *MainPage* is set to the *Content* property of an object of type *Frame*, and this *Frame* object is set to the *Content* property of an instance of the *Window* class.

You can see this hierarchy come together in the *OnLaunched* method in the standard *App* class. The actual code (which you'll see later in this chapter) checks for errors and ensures that initialization occurs only once, but basically it does this in the simple case:

```
Frame rootFrame = new Frame();
Window.Current.Content = rootFrame;
rootFrame.Navigate(typeof(MainPage), args.Arguments);
Window.Current.Activate();
```

Frame derives from *ContentControl*, but the *Content* property isn't set directly. Instead, the *Navigate* method accepts a *Type* argument that references a *Page* derivative. The *Navigate* method instantiates this type (in this case *MainPage*) and this instance becomes the *Content* property of the *Frame* object and the main focus of user interaction.

Within your programs, you'll use this same *Navigate* method to move from one page to another. *Navigate* comes in two versions: The version in the *OnLaunched* method passes some data to the *Page* object, but the other version does not. (You'll see how this works later in this chapter.)

Very conveniently, the *Page* class defines a *Frame* property, so within a *Page* derivative you can call *Navigate* like so:

```
this.Frame.Navigate(pageType);
```

Within a multipage application, *Navigate* is often called numerous times with various *Page* type arguments. Internally, the *Frame* class maintains a stack of visited pages. The *Frame* class also defines *GoBack* and *GoForward* methods, as well as *CanGoBack* and *CanGoForward* properties of type *bool*.

The SimplePageNavigation project contains two classes that derive from *Page* rather than just one. I've continued to use the Blank App template for this project, so the *MainPage* class is created by Visual Studio as usual. To add another *Page* derivative to a project, I selected Add New Item from the Project menu and then Blank Page (not Basic Page) from the Add New Item dialog. I gave my new page class a name of *SecondPage*.

The SimplePageNavigation project demonstrates how pages can navigate to each other in a variety of ways. MainPage.xaml instantiates a *TextBlock* to identify the page, a *TextBox* to enter some text, and three buttons with the text "Go to Second Page," "Go Forward," and "Go Back":

Project: SimplePageNavigation | File: MainPage.xaml (excerpt)

```xml
<Page ... >
    <Grid Background="{StaticResource ApplicationPageBackgroundThemeBrush}">
        <StackPanel>
            <TextBlock Text="Main Page"
                       FontSize="48"
                       HorizontalAlignment="Center"
                       Margin="48" />

            <TextBox Name="txtbox"
                     Width="320"
                     HorizontalAlignment="Center"
                     Margin="48" />

            <Button Content="Go to Second Page"
                    HorizontalAlignment="Center"
                    Margin="48"
                    Click="OnGotoButtonClick" />

            <Button Name="forwardButton"
                    Content="Go Forward"
                    HorizontalAlignment="Center"
                    Margin="48"
                    Click="OnForwardButtonClick" />

            <Button Name="backButton"
                    Content="Go Back"
                    HorizontalAlignment="Center"
                    Margin="48"
                    Click="OnBackButtonClick" />
        </StackPanel>
    </Grid>
</Page>
```

The code-behind file uses the *OnNavigatedTo* override to enable the forward and back buttons depending on the *CanGoForward* and *CanGoBack* properties defined by *Frame*. The three *Click* handlers call *Navigate* (referencing the *SecondPage* object), *GoForward*, and *GoBack*:

Project: SimplePageNavigation | File: MainPage.xaml.cs (excerpt)

```csharp
public sealed partial class MainPage : Page
{
    public MainPage()
    {
        this.InitializeComponent();
    }
```

```
protected override void OnNavigatedTo(NavigationEventArgs args)
{
    forwardButton.IsEnabled = this.Frame.CanGoForward;
    backButton.IsEnabled = this.Frame.CanGoBack;
}

void OnGotoButtonClick(object sender, RoutedEventArgs args)
{
    this.Frame.Navigate(typeof(SecondPage));
}

void OnForwardButtonClick(object sender, RoutedEventArgs args)
{
    this.Frame.GoForward();
}

void OnBackButtonClick(object sender, RoutedEventArgs args)
{
    this.Frame.GoBack();
}
}
```

The *SecondPage* class is exactly the same except that it uses the *OnGotoButtonClick* method to navigate to *MainPage*:

Project: SimplePageNavigation | **File:** SecondPage.xaml.cs (excerpt)

```
void OnGotoButtonClick(object sender, RoutedEventArgs args)
{
    this.Frame.Navigate(typeof(MainPage));
}
```

Here's how the program appears when you first run it:

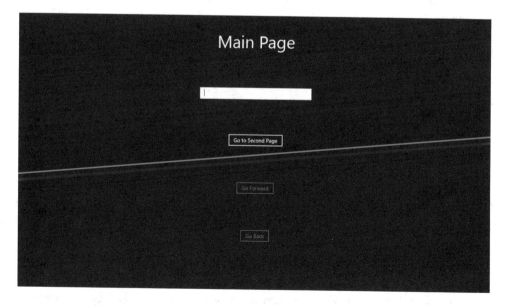

Neither the forward nor the back button is enabled. When you click the "Go to Second Page" button, the program navigates to that page:

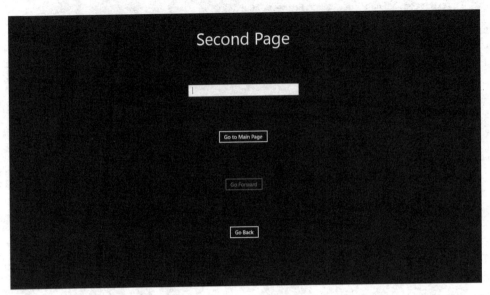

Now the "Go Back" button is enabled, and it will take you back to *MainPage*. The "Go to Second Page" will do that as well, but with a difference: When you press "Go Back" to go back to *MainPage*, the "Go Forward" button will be enabled but "Go Back" will not be. When you press "Go to Second Page," "Go Back" will be enabled but "Go Forward" won't be.

Before we begin exploring this in detail, I want to show you another way to enable the "Go Forward" and "Go Back" buttons. The *CanGoBack* and *CanGoForward* properties of *Frame* can be *Binding* sources, like so:

```
<Page ... Name="page">
    ...
            <Button Name="forwardButton"
                    IsEnabled="{Binding ElementName=page, Path=Frame.CanGoForward}"
                    ... />

            <Button Name="backButton"
                    IsEnabled="{Binding ElementName=page, Path=Frame.CanGoBack}"
                    ... />
    ...
</Page>
```

That would eliminate the need for the *OnNavigatedTo* method in this program, but any program that implements page navigation will probably make other uses of that method as well as its companion, *OnNavigatedFrom*.

You'll discover an important characteristic of navigation if you experiment with SimplePageNavigation by pressing the various buttons to navigate, go forward, and go back, all the while typing a few characters into each *TextBox* that you encounter along the way. You will discover that whenever you move from one page to another—whether by means of calls to the *Navigate*, *GoForward*, or *GoBack* methods—the *TextBox* is initially blank. What this means is that a new instance of *MainPage* or *SecondPage* is being created on each *Button* click. Whatever you've typed into that *TextBox* has been lost because the *Page* instance containing that *TextBox* has been abandoned.

This is likely surprising. You probably expect a new instance to be created when you press the "Go to Main Page" or "Go to Second Page" button, but you probably also expect that pressing "Go Forward" or "Go Back" navigates to a previous instance of the page. But this is not the case. New instances are created regardless.

The *Page* class defines three virtual methods that assist the page in handling navigation. These are named *OnNavigatingFrom*, *OnNavigatedFrom*—notice the tense difference in those two method names!—and *OnNavigatedTo*. If you were to log calls to those three methods, as well as the constructor of these *Page* classes and firings of the *Loaded* and *Unloaded* events, you would discover the following sequence during the transition from one page to another:

From Page	To Page
OnNavigatingFrom	
	Constructor
OnNavigatedFrom	
	OnNavigatedTo
	Loaded
Unloaded	

This sequence occurs regardless of whether the transition is a result of *Navigate*, *GoForward*, or *GoBack*.

Up until this chapter, we've been treating *MainPage* as if it lasts for the duration of the application, as it does if it's the only *Page* derivative around. However, once you begin dealing with multipage applications, you need to think about *Page* derivatives being created and discarded. It's a good idea to architect your *Page* derivatives so that they attach event handlers and obtain resources during *OnNavigatedTo* or *Loaded* and detach those handlers and release those resources during *OnNavigatedFrom* or *Unloaded*.

If you want a new instance of your *Page* derivatives created whenever that page is navigated to, you're obviously in good shape because this is what happens by default. If you prefer something a little different, there are two alternatives, one of which is very easy and the other not quite so easy.

The easy alternative is setting the *NavigationCacheMode* property of the *Page* to something other than the default *Disabled* enumeration member. For example:

```
public MainPage()
{
    this.InitializeComponent();
    this.NavigationCacheMode = NavigationCacheMode.Enabled;
}
```

The other option is *Required*, but for this program *Enabled* and *Required* both work the same. When you set *Enabled* or *Required* on a *Page* object, only one instance of each *Page* derivative is created and cached, and that instance is reused every time the page is visited, regardless of whether that occurs with *Navigate*, *GoForward*, or *GoBack*. The sequence of method calls and events that occur is the same as the table shown earlier the first time a particular page type is navigated to; subsequently, it's the same sequence but without the constructor. You can set the *NavigationCacheMode* property differently for different *Page* classes.

This option might be ideal for a "hub" architecture where one *MainPage* can navigate to several different secondary pages that can then go back to *MainPage*. The difference between *Enabled* and *Required* is that *Enabled* might cause instantiated pages to be discarded if the number of cached pages exceeds the *CacheSize* property of *Frame*, which is 10 by default but can be changed.

In the general case, however, you probably want a new instance to be created for a *Navigate* call but existing instances to be used for *GoForward* and *GoBack*. This option is not provided with a simple property setting, but I'll show you how to do it shortly.

The Back Stack

Back in the dark ages, Web browsers had Back buttons but not Forward buttons. The browser implemented the Back button in a very simple manner by storing visited pages in a familiar data structure known as the *stack*. In the context of the browser, this was called the *back stack*: Whenever the browser navigated to a new page, it pushed the previous page on the stack. Whenever the user pressed the Back button, the browser popped a page off the stack and navigated to that. When the stack became empty, the Back button was disabled.

Implementing a Forward button complicates this process somewhat. Rather than a stack to store visited pages, the browser requires an ordered list. (This list is still often referred to as the back stack, however.) This list includes the current page. Whenever the browser navigates to a new page, it adds that new page to the end of the list. However, when the user presses the Back button, the page being navigated from is *not* removed from the list. That page must remain in the list because the user might then press the Forward button.

For example, perhaps the user begins at a page that I'll call Page Zero and from there navigates to Page One, then to Page Two, Page Three, Page Four, and Page Five. The back stack looks like this, with the most recent new page at the top and the arrow pointing to the current page:

        Page Five   ←
        Page Four
        Page Three
        Page Two

Page One
Page Zero

Now suppose the user presses the Back button four times. The current page is now Page One:

Page Five
Page Four
Page Three
Page Two
Page One   ←
Page Zero

Then the user presses the Forward button, and the current page is now Page Two:

Page Five
Page Four
Page Three
Page Two   ←
Page One
Page Zero

Obviously, using the Back and Forward buttons, the user can navigate anywhere among these six pages. When the current page reaches the bottom, the Back button is disabled. When the current page reaches the top, the Forward button is disabled.

But now suppose that from Page Two the user instead navigates to Page Six. An entire section of the list must be discarded. This discarded part of the list has previously been saved for presses of the Forward button but those pages are no longer navigable following navigation to a new page:

Page Six   ←
Page Two
Page One
Page Zero

The Forward button is now disabled. The Forward button will be re-enabled only when the user presses the Back button.

The *Frame* class internally maintains this back stack of visited pages. However, the back stack is not accessible by an application. You can't even obtain the size of the back stack.

But you can obtain the position of the current page within the back stack from the get-only *BackStackDepth* property. When an application begins running and navigates to the initial page, *BackStackDepth* reports a value of zero. In the four examples shown earlier, *BackStackDepth* equals 5, 1, 2, and 3, respectively.

This *BackStackDepth* is important information, for it allows a particular page class to uniquely identify a particular instance of itself. Let's see how.

Navigation Events and Page Restoration

In the normal case, when a program calls *GoBack* or *GoForward* to return to a particular page, you want the user to see the same content on the previously visited page. You've already seen that you can't get this automatically: When *NavigationCacheMode* is set to its default value of *Disabled*, the *GoBack* and *GoForward* calls always result in a new instance of the particular *Page* class to be created. When set to *Enabled* or *Required*, existing instances of the *Page* class are re-used but they're re-used for *Navigate* as well.

As I mentioned earlier, the *Page* class defines three virtual methods that involve navigation. The *OnNavigatingFrom* call kicks off a navigation sequence. This method is not often used. The event arguments are of type *NavigatingCancelEventArgs* that allows the navigation to be cancelled.

During navigation from one page to another—whether a result of a call to *Navigate*, *GoBack*, or *GoForward*—the *OnNavigatedFrom* in the first page is followed shortly by a call to *OnNavigatedTo* in the second page. These two methods both have event arguments of type *NavigationEventArgs*. These event arguments are used in other contexts (such as the *WebView* class), so some of the properties are irrelevant when used with these two overrides. Here are the important ones for the navigation events:

- The *Parameter* property of type *object*. This is set from the optional second argument of the *Navigate* method, and it is used to pass data from one page to another. I'll have more to say about this process shortly.

- The *Content* and *SourcePageType* properties always refer to the page being navigated to. The *Content* object is the actual instance of the *Page* derivative, and *SourcePageType* is the type of that instance—in other words, the first argument to the *Navigate* call used to create that page. This information is only of real value in an *OnNavigatedFrom* override. In an *OnNavigatedTo* override, the *Content* property is equal to *this* and *SourcePageType* is equal to a call to *GetType*.

- The *NavigationMode* property is a member of the *NavigationMode* enumeration, with members *New*, *Refresh*, *Back*, and *Forward*. The value is *New* or *Refresh* for a navigation initiated by the *Navigate* method. The value is *Refresh* if the page is navigating to itself. The value is *Back* or *Forward* for a navigation initiated by the *GoBack* or *GoForward* methods, respectively.

The *NavigationMode* property is the key to implementing an architecture where new page content is created for *Navigate* calls (that is, when *NavigationMode* is *New*) but not when the page has been previously visited and navigation occurs though *Back* or *Forward*.

The first step is for the *Page* derivative to define a field that allows it to save and restore its state:

```
Dictionary<string, object> pageState;
```

You use this dictionary in much the same way you use *ApplicationData.LocalSettings* dictionary that I first demonstrated in connection with the PrimitivePad program in Chapter 7, "Asynchronicity." However, instead, of saving application settings during the *Application.Suspending* event and restoring them when the application runs again, you save page state into the dictionary during the *OnNavigatedFrom* override and restore it in *OnNavigatedTo*.

What is page state? It's generally input by the user and anything that results from that input: the state of check boxes, radio buttons, sliders, and particularly text input. In the sample application I've been using, the only really important page state is the content of the *TextBox*. You can save that during *OnNavigatedFrom* with a made-up key name like so:

```
pageState.Add("TextBoxText", txtbox.Text);
```

You restore it during *OnNavigatedTo*:

```
txtbox.Text = pageState["TextBoxText"] as string;
```

There are conceivably other properties of the *TextBox* you might want to save and restore—for example, *SelectionStart* and *SelectionLength*—but let's keep it simple for now.

This process of saving and restoring page state in this dictionary is totally useless if the *Page* class is being instantiated for every navigation event because a new instance of *pageState* is created as part of the new page! What you need in addition is to save instances of this dictionary in another dictionary that's defined as static so that it's shared among all the instances of that page:

```
static Dictionary<int, Dictionary<string, object>> pages;
```

The values in this dictionary are the instances of the *Dictionary* I've called *pageState*. The keys to this dictionary are values of *BackStackDepth*, thus allowing different *pageState* dictionaries to be associated with fixed locations of the page instance within the back stack.

If you have multiple page derivatives using this same technique, you'll want to define both dictionaries in a *Page* derivative that you'll use as a base class for other pages. The static *pages* dictionary can then be shared by all the pages in the application.

Let's see how this works in the context of a simple application. The VisitedPageSave program defines a class named *SaveStatePage*. I used the simple Class template to create this class; there is no XAML file associated with it. The class derives from *Page*, and the two dictionaries are defined as *protected* so that they can be accessed from derived classes:

Project: VisitedPageSave | File: SaveStatePage.cs (excerpt)
```
public class SaveStatePage : Page
{
    protected Dictionary<string, object> pageState;

    static protected Dictionary<int, Dictionary<string, object>> pages =
                        new Dictionary<int, Dictionary<string, object>>();
    ...
}
```

The static dictionary is instantiated in its definition (or it could be instantiated in the static constructor), and the instance dictionary is not. As you'll see, it will be instantiated in the *OnNavigatedTo* override when the *NavigationMode* is *New*.

I created a *SecondPage* class just as in SimplePageNavigation, but in both the XAML files and code-behind files for *MainPage* and *SecondPage* I changed the base class from *Page* to *SaveStatePage*. Otherwise, the MainPage.xaml and SecondPage.xaml files are the same as in SimplePageNavigation. The two code-behind files are basically identical to each other. Here's MainPage.xaml.cs showing the same implementations of the button *Click* handlers you've seen before:

Project: VisitedPageSave | File: MainPage.xaml.cs (excerpt)

```
public sealed partial class MainPage : SaveStatePage
{
    public MainPage()
    {
        this.InitializeComponent();
    }

    ...

    void OnGotoButtonClick(object sender, RoutedEventArgs args)
    {
        this.Frame.Navigate(typeof(SecondPage));
    }

    void OnForwardButtonClick(object sender, RoutedEventArgs args)
    {
        this.Frame.GoForward();
    }

    void OnBackButtonClick(object sender, RoutedEventArgs args)
    {
        this.Frame.GoBack();
    }
}
```

The *NavigationCacheMode* is left at its default setting of *Disabled* so that a new page object is instantiated during all navigation events.

In the *OnNavigatedTo* override, the integer key for the static dictionary is the *BackStackDepth* property. If the *NavigationMode* is not *New*, the method simply uses that key to obtain the *pageState* dictionary corresponding to this location in the back stack, and then it uses that dictionary to initialize the page, in this example the *TextBox*:

Project: VisitedPageSave | File: MainPage.xaml.cs (excerpt)

```
protected override void OnNavigatedTo(NavigationEventArgs args)
{
    // Enable buttons
    forwardButton.IsEnabled = this.Frame.CanGoForward;
    backButton.IsEnabled = this.Frame.CanGoBack;

    // Construct a dictionary key
    int pageKey = this.Frame.BackStackDepth;

    if (args.NavigationMode != NavigationMode.New)
    {
```

```
            // Get the page state dictionary for this page
            pageState = pages[pageKey];

            // Get the page state from the dictionary
            txtbox.Text = pageState["TextBoxText"] as string;
        }

        base.OnNavigatedTo(args);
    }
}
```

If the *NavigationMode* is *New*, however, we know that this page was reached with a call to *Navigate* and should be regarded as a fresh uninitialized page. This additional logic occurs in the implementation of *OnNavigatedTo* in *SaveStatePage*, which you'll note is called at the end of the *OnNavigatedTo* overrides in *MainPage* and *SecondPage*. This code creates a new *pageState* dictionary and adds that to the static *pages* dictionary:

Project: VisitedPageSave | **File:** SaveStatePage.cs (excerpt)

```
public class SaveStatePage : Page
{
    ...
    protected override void OnNavigatedTo(NavigationEventArgs args)
    {
        if (args.NavigationMode == NavigationMode.New)
        {
            // Construct a dictionary key
            int pageKey = this.Frame.BackStackDepth;

            // Remove page key and higher page keys
            for (int key = pageKey; pages.Remove(key); key++) ;

            // Create a new page state dictionary and save it
            pageState = new Dictionary<string, object>();
            pages.Add(pageKey, pageState);
        }

        base.OnNavigatedTo(args);
    }
}
```

However, the static *pages* dictionary must also be cleared of any possible entries with equal or higher *BackStackDepth* keys. These entries result from *GoBack* calls not balanced by *GoForward* calls. The *for* statement that removes these entries is more comprehensible when you realize that the *Remove* method of *Dictionary* returns *false* if the key does not exist:

```
for (int key = pageKey; pages.Remove(key); key++) ;
```

In both *MainPage* and *SecondPage*, the *OnNavigatedFrom* override is much simpler and just saves the page state in the existing *pageState* dictionary:

Project: VisitedPageSave | File: MainPage.xaml.cs (excerpt)

```
protected override void OnNavigatedFrom(NavigationEventArgs args)
{
    pageState.Clear();

    // Save the page state in the dictionary
    pageState.Add("TextBoxText", txtbox.Text);

    base.OnNavigatedFrom(args);
}
```

Also keep in mind that the *pageState* dictionary can store many more items—as many as you need to re-create the state of the entire page.

Perhaps the easiest way to check whether this program is working correctly is to simply type 1, 2, 3, and so forth into the *TextBox* in consecutive pages. You'll see those restored entries when you press the "Go Forward" and "Go Back" buttons.

If you suspend and then resume the application from Visual Studio, you'll see that everything is restored correctly. However, the application is not saving anything when it's suspended, so if the application is terminated following suspension, the next time it is launched it will appear in a new and pristine state. This is probably not what you desire, but it's not hard to fix.

Saving and Restoring Application State

If an application such as VisitedPageSave is terminated and then relaunched, you probably want the program to appear as if it had never been terminated. You probably want all the previously created pages to be restored with their previous content, plus you want the application displaying the same page that the user last visited.

In other words, not only do you need to save (and later restore) the state of each page, but you need to save (and later restore) the state of the back stack. Restoring the state of each page is actually *useless* without restoring the back stack because without that back stack there's no record of what pages must be restored!

I mentioned earlier that the back stack is entirely internal to the *Frame* object. Fortunately, *Frame* provides two methods that let you save and restore the back stack state without knowing its internal structure: The *GetNavigationState* returns a string that you can save in application settings; the next time your program runs you can retrieve that string and pass it as an argument to *SetNavigationState*.

What is this string? Well, you can look at it if you want. You'll find that it contains the class names of the pages in the back stack with some numbers. What these numbers are is undocumented and might change in the future, so you should really only use this string for passing from *GetNavigationState* to *SetNavigationState*.

GetNavigationState actually does a little more than just return a string that encodes the state of the back stack. Calling this method causes the current page to get an *OnNavigatedFrom* call with a *NavigationMode* of *Forward*. This allows the current page to save its page state, but it also means that you just can't call *GetNavigationState* any time you want. It should be called only when the application is being suspended. An excellent place to do this is in the *OnSuspending* event handler in App .xaml.cs.

Here's what I've done in a program called ApplicationStateSave:

Project: ApplicationStateSave | File: App.xaml.cs (excerpt)

```
private void OnSuspending(object sender, SuspendingEventArgs e)
{
    var deferral = e.SuspendingOperation.GetDeferral();
    //TODO: Save application state and stop any background activity

    // Code added for ApplicationStateSave project
    ApplicationDataContainer appData = ApplicationData.Current.LocalSettings;
    appData.Values["NavigationState"] = (Window.Current.Content as Frame).GetNavigationState();
    // End of code added for ApplicationStateSave project

    deferral.Complete();
}
```

I've left the version of *OnSuspending* that Visual Studio generated intact and merely added two lines of code surrounded by comments. This code obtains the *GetNavigationState* string from the *Frame* and saves it in application settings with a name of "NavigationState."

Some earlier programs in this book save application settings from *MainPage*. Why not do the same thing here? Recall that *Page* derivatives in a multipage environment should attach any event handlers they need during *OnNavigatedTo* or *Loaded* and detach them during *OnNavigatedFrom* or *Unloaded*, which means that every *Page* derivative in your application would need to set a *Suspending* handler to perform this job. But this is not really a job for the *Page* derivative. This job involves saving a navigation state that defines the navigational relationship among multiple pages, so it should really be the responsibility of the application itself.

That's one reason why the code goes in the *App* class. The other reason is that restoring the navigation state also needs to go in the *App* class as well, and actually in a particular place in the *App* class because it's effectively overriding default logic encoded there.

To restore the back stack, you call *SetNavigationState* with the saved string originally obtained from *GetNavigationState*. Calling *SetNavigationState* causes navigation to the previously current page. The *OnNavigatedTo* method of that page is called with a *NavigationMode* of *Back*, allowing the page to reload its own page settings without believing that it's a new page.

It is essential that *SetNavigationState* be called at a particular place in the *OnLaunched* method in App.xaml.cs. Here it is in the ApplicationStateSave project. I've left all the generated code and comments in *OnLaunched* intact:

Project: ApplicationStateSave | File: App.xaml.cs (excerpt)

```
protected override void OnLaunched(LaunchActivatedEventArgs args)
{
    Frame rootFrame = Window.Current.Content as Frame;

    // Do not repeat app initialization when the Window already has content,
    // just ensure that the window is active
    if (rootFrame == null)
    {
        // Create a Frame to act as the navigation context and navigate to the first page
        rootFrame = new Frame();

        if (args.PreviousExecutionState == ApplicationExecutionState.Terminated)
        {
            //TODO: Load state from previously suspended application

            // Code added for ApplicationStateSave project
            ApplicationDataContainer appData = ApplicationData.Current.LocalSettings;

            if (appData.Values.ContainsKey("NavigationState"))
                rootFrame.SetNavigationState(appData.Values["NavigationState"] as string);
            // End of code added for ApplicationStateSave project
        }

        // Place the frame in the current Window
        Window.Current.Content = rootFrame;
    }

    if (rootFrame.Content == null)
    {
        // When the navigation stack isn't restored navigate to the first page,
        // configuring the new page by passing required information as a navigation
        // parameter
        if (!rootFrame.Navigate(typeof(MainPage), args.Arguments))
        {
            throw new Exception("Failed to create initial page");
        }
    }
    // Ensure the current window is active
    Window.Current.Activate();

    ...
}
```

Again, I've used comments to identify the code I've added for this project. (Notice the ellipsis down at the bottom. I'll discuss the additional code I've added to App.xaml.cs in the next section.)

Toward the bottom of the *OnLaunched* method is a call to the *Navigate* method with the *MainPage* class. You do *not* want this call to occur if you are restoring the back state because this *Navigate* call will navigate away from the previously current page and possibly cause part of the back stack to be removed in the *OnNavigatedTo* method of *MainPage*. For this reason, the back stack must be restored prior to this call, which ensures that the *Content* property of the *Frame* object is set to the previously current page and the navigation to *MainPage* is skipped.

The code you've seen so far saves and restores the back stack. The second part of this job involves saving and restoring all the page states. In the previous project, I defined a class named *SaveStatePage* that maintained two dictionaries—one instance and one static—for saving page state. Both *MainPage* and *SecondPage* derived from this class.

I've retained that architecture for this program. Indeed, *MainPage* and *SecondPage* are identical to the classes in the previous project. But *SaveStatePage* has been enhanced to save all the settings for all the pages in application local storage, and to retrieve them.

If a particular back stack references four instances of *MainPage* and three instances of *SecondPage*, there is a total of seven settings with the key name "TextBoxText." These must all be distinguished from each other. Fortunately, the *ApplicationDataContainer* used for storing application settings has a "container" feature, somewhat similar to folders or subdirectories. This feature seems ideal for isolating the settings for each page. The container is identified by a name, and the name I chose for each *Page* instance indicates the location of that instance within the back stack, which is the same as the integer key of the *pages* dictionary converted to a string.

Here's both the static constructor and the *Suspending* handler in this enhanced version of *SaveStatePage*. The handler for the *Suspending* event is attached by the static constructor so that it's only executed once to save the settings for all the pages, of course without knowing anything about those settings:

Project: ApplicationStateSave | **File:** SaveStatePage.cs (excerpt)

```
public class SaveStatePage : Page
{
    protected Dictionary<string, object> pageState;

    static protected Dictionary<int, Dictionary<string, object>> pages =
                        new Dictionary<int, Dictionary<string, object>>();

    static SaveStatePage()
    {
        // Set handler for Suspending event
        Application.Current.Suspending += OnApplicationSuspending;

        ApplicationDataContainer appData = ApplicationData.Current.LocalSettings;

        // Loop through containers, one for each page in the back stack
        foreach (ApplicationDataContainer container in appData.Containers.Values)
        {
            // Create a page state dictionary for that page
            Dictionary<string, object> pageState = new Dictionary<string, object>();

            // Fill it up with saved values
            foreach (string key in container.Values.Keys)
            {
                pageState.Add(key, container.Values[key]);
```

```
        }

        // Save in static dictionary
        int pageKey = Int32.Parse(container.Name);
        pages[pageKey] = pageState;
    }
}

static void OnApplicationSuspending(object sender, SuspendingEventArgs args)
{
    ApplicationDataContainer appData = ApplicationData.Current.LocalSettings;

    foreach (int pageKey in pages.Keys)
    {
        // Create container based on location within back state
        string containerName = pageKey.ToString();

        // Get container with that name and clear it
        ApplicationDataContainer container =
            appData.CreateContainer(containerName,
                                    ApplicationDataCreateDisposition.Always);
        container.Values.Clear();

        // Save settings for each page in that container
        foreach (string key in pages[pageKey].Keys)
            container.Values.Add(key, pages[pageKey][key]);
    }
}
...
}
```

By the time the static constructor concludes, the *pages* dictionary contains one entry for each page on the back stack. None of these individual pages has yet been instantiated. As each *SaveStatePage* derivative is instantiated, however, it obtains its own *pageState* dictionary during the *OnNavigatedTo* override, either by retrieving it from the *pages* dictionary or by creating a new one.

Navigational Accelerators and Mouse Buttons

Do you use a mouse that has five buttons rather than the usual three? Neither do I, but some people do, and some of those people are accustomed to using the extra two buttons to navigate forward and back in Internet Explorer. Other Internet Explorer users have become accustomed to using the left and right arrow keys in conjunction with Alt to navigate back and forward. Some keyboards have special keys to perform these operations.

You might want to implement these same shortcuts to allow users to navigate among the pages of your application. To do this, you need two events that you haven't seen yet: *PointerPressed* and *AcceleratorKeyActivated*.

The *AcceleratorKeyActivated* event isn't available in the *Page* or *Frame* classes or even the *Window* class that underlies *Frame*. But it is available from *CoreWindow*, which is the object that supports input events for *Window*, and you can obtain the *CoreWindow* object from the current *Window* object.

The handler for *AcceleratorKeyActivated* gets first dibs on keystrokes, and if this handler identifies a particular key as a command accelerator, it can inhibit further visibility of that key by the application by setting the *Handled* property of the event arguments to *true*.

As you'll learn in Chapter 13, "Touch, Etc.," the *PointerPressed* event is fired for a mouse button press or a finger or pen touching the screen. This event is defined by *UIElement* and inherited by *Frame* and *Page*, but for purposes of getting button clicks for page navigation, you can define a handler for this event on the *CoreWindow* as well.

Because these keyboard and mouse accelerators function at a higher level than the page, it is convenient to put them in the *App* class.

Earlier I showed you an *OnLaunched* method in the *App* class of the ApplicationStateSave project. That method had an ellipsis at the bottom indicating that the method contains a bit more code. Here it is:

Project: ApplicationStateSave | **File:** App.xaml.cs (excerpt)

```
protected override void OnLaunched(LaunchActivatedEventArgs args)
{
    ...
    // Code added for ApplicationStateSave project
    Window.Current.CoreWindow.Dispatcher.AcceleratorKeyActivated += OnAcceleratorKeyActivated;
    Window.Current.CoreWindow.PointerPressed += OnPointerPressed;
    // End of code added for ApplicationStateSave project
}
```

The *PointerPressed* event handler is the simpler of the two, so let's look at that first. The states of all five mouse buttons are available from the *Properties* property of the *CurrentPoint* property of the event arguments. The two extra buttons commonly used for navigation are identified as *XButton1* and *XButton2*. We're only interested in cases where all the regular buttons are unpressed and only one of these extra buttons is pressed—that is, their states aren't equal to each other:

Project: ApplicationStateSave | **File:** App.xaml.cs (excerpt)

```
void OnPointerPressed(CoreWindow sender, PointerEventArgs args)
{
    PointerPointProperties props = args.CurrentPoint.Properties;

    if (!props.IsLeftButtonPressed &&
        !props.IsMiddleButtonPressed &&
        !props.IsRightButtonPressed &&
        props.IsXButton1Pressed != props.IsXButton2Pressed)
    {
        if (props.IsXButton1Pressed)
            GoBack();
        else
            GoForward();

        args.Handled = true;
    }
}

void GoBack()
```

```
    {
        Frame frame = Window.Current.Content as Frame;

        if (frame != null && frame.CanGoBack)
            frame.GoBack();
    }

    void GoForward()
    {
        Frame frame = Window.Current.Content as Frame;

        if (frame != null && frame.CanGoForward)
            frame.GoForward();
    }
```

If the event results in a call to the *GoBack* or *GoForward* method, the event handler sets the *Handled* property of the event arguments to *true*.

For the keyboard accelerators, the event handler is able to use members of the *VirtualKey* enumeration for the Left and Right arrow keys, but *VirtualKey* doesn't have members for the special browser keys. In the Win32 API, these are identified as VK_BROWSER_BACK and VK_BROWSER_FORWARD and have values of 166 and 167, respectively:

Project: ApplicationStateSave | File: App.xaml.cs (excerpt)

```
void OnAcceleratorKeyActivated(CoreDispatcher sender, AcceleratorKeyEventArgs args)
{
    if ((args.EventType == CoreAcceleratorKeyEventType.SystemKeyDown ||
         args.EventType == CoreAcceleratorKeyEventType.KeyDown) &&
        (args.VirtualKey == VirtualKey.Left ||
         args.VirtualKey == VirtualKey.Right ||
         (int)args.VirtualKey == 166 ||
         (int)args.VirtualKey == 167))
    {
        CoreWindow window = Window.Current.CoreWindow;
        CoreVirtualKeyStates down = CoreVirtualKeyStates.Down;

        // Ignore key combinations where Shift or Ctrl is down
        if ((window.GetKeyState(VirtualKey.Shift) & down) == down ||
            (window.GetKeyState(VirtualKey.Control) & down) == down)
        {
            return;
        }

        // Get alt key state
        bool alt = (window.GetKeyState(VirtualKey.Menu) & down) == down;

        // Go back for Alt-Left key or browser left key
        if (args.VirtualKey == VirtualKey.Left && alt ||
            (int)args.VirtualKey == 166 && !alt)
        {
            GoBack();
            args.Handled = true;
        }
```

```
        // Go forward for Alt-Right key or browser right key
        if (args.VirtualKey == VirtualKey.Right && alt ||
            (int)args.VirtualKey == 167 && !alt)
        {
            GoForward();
            args.Handled = true;
        }
    }
}
}
```

The Left and Right arrow keys function as accelerators only when the Alt key (also known as the Menu key) is down but neither Shift nor Ctrl is down, and the special browser keys are accepted only when no modifier key is down.

The *GetKeyState* method is a little clumsy to use because it can return one of three members of the *CoreVirtualKeyStates* enumeration: *None* (equal to 0), *Down* (equal to 1), or *Locked* (equal to 2). Internally, all the keys are treated as toggles, and the enumeration members are flags. A key that is up begins with a key state of 0. When the key is pressed, it has a state of 3, and when it is released, it has a state of 2. Press it down again for a state of 1, and release it to 0 again.

Passing and Returning Data

Very often pages need to share data. It's common for pages to share a view model, for example. A good place to maintain data shared among pages is the *App* class. Don't hesitate about adding methods and properties to this class. For example, you can add a public property named *ViewModel* that has a public *get* accessor but a private *set* accessor so that the property can be initialized in the *App* constructor.

On the other hand, under the philosophy that data should be visible only to classes that need to know this data, don't put *everything* in the *App* class. There are very structured ways for one page to pass data to another page during navigation and for the second page to return data to the first page.

The DataPassingAndReturning project has two simple pages that demonstrate these techniques. The first page is called *MainPage* as usual, and the second page is called *DialogPage* because it functions much like a dialog box. *MainPage* can navigate only to *DialogPage*, and *DialogPage* can only go back to *MainPage*.

Because the navigation between these two pages is limited, the pages don't need to save page state. To keep the program even simpler, it doesn't save navigation state or page state during suspension and it doesn't implement keyboard or mouse shortcuts. Despite the simplicity of the program, it illustrates basic data-passing techniques.

The XAML file for *DialogPage* has three *RadioButton* controls for Red, Green, and Blue, and a regular *Button* labeled "Finished":

Project: DataPassingAndReturning | File: DialogPage.xaml (excerpt)

```xaml
<Grid Background="{StaticResource ApplicationPageBackgroundThemeBrush}">
    <StackPanel>
        <TextBlock Text="Color Dialog"
                   FontSize="48"
                   HorizontalAlignment="Center"
                   Margin="48" />

        <StackPanel Name="radioStack"
                   HorizontalAlignment="Center"
                   Margin="48">
            <RadioButton Content="Red" Margin="12">
                <RadioButton.Tag>
                    <Color>Red</Color>
                </RadioButton.Tag>
            </RadioButton>

            <RadioButton Content="Green" Margin="12">
                <RadioButton.Tag>
                    <Color>Green</Color>
                </RadioButton.Tag>
            </RadioButton>

            <RadioButton Content="Blue" Margin="12">
                <RadioButton.Tag>
                    <Color>Blue</Color>
                </RadioButton.Tag>
            </RadioButton>
        </StackPanel>

        <Button Content="Finished"
                HorizontalAlignment="Center"
                Margin="48"
                Click="OnReturnButtonClick" />
    </StackPanel>
</Grid>
```

Notice that each *RadioButton* has its *Tag* property set to a *Color* value corresponding to that button. The code-behind file for *DialogPage* is responsible for obtaining the selected *Color* from these buttons and returning that back to *MainPage*.

Interestingly, MainPage.xaml is very similar to DialogPage.xaml, except that the *Grid* has a name, the middle *RadioButton* is checked, and the *Button* is labeled "Get Color":

Project: DataPassingAndReturning | File: MainPage.xaml (excerpt)

```xaml
<Grid Name="contentGrid"
      Background="{StaticResource ApplicationPageBackgroundThemeBrush}">
    <StackPanel>
        <TextBlock Text="Main Page"
                   FontSize="48"
```

```
                HorizontalAlignment="Center"
                Margin="48" />

        <StackPanel Name="radioStack"
                HorizontalAlignment="Center"
                Margin="48">
            <RadioButton Content="Red" Margin="12">
                <RadioButton.Tag>
                    <Color>Red</Color>
                </RadioButton.Tag>
            </RadioButton>

            <RadioButton Content="Green" Margin="12"
                    IsChecked="True">
                <RadioButton.Tag>
                    <Color>Green</Color>
                </RadioButton.Tag>
            </RadioButton>

            <RadioButton Content="Blue" Margin="12">
                <RadioButton.Tag>
                    <Color>Blue</Color>
                </RadioButton.Tag>
            </RadioButton>
        </StackPanel>

        <Button Content="Get Color"
                HorizontalAlignment="Center"
                Margin="48"
                Click="OnGotoButtonClick" />
    </StackPanel>
</Grid>
```

The idea here is that you use the *RadioButton* controls in MainPage to select an initial value for the *RadioButton* controls in *DialogPage*, which means that *MainPage* needs to pass data to *DialogPage*.

The data that *MainPage* and *DialogPage* are passing between each other is only a *Color* value, but for real applications it could be much, much more. Let's reflect that possibility by defining classes specifically for the purpose of passing data between pages. Here's the class for the data that *MainPage* passes to *DialogPage*:

Project: DataPassingAndReturning | File: PassData.cs

```
using Windows.UI;

namespace DataPassingAndReturning
{
    public class PassData
    {
        public Color InitializeColor { set; get; }
    }
}
```

For this simple example, the data returned from *DialogPage* to *MainPage* is quite similar:

Project: DataPassingAndReturning | File: ReturnData.cs

```
using Windows.UI;

namespace DataPassingAndReturning
{
    public class ReturnData
    {
        public Color ReturnColor { set; get; }
    }
}
```

I could have used the same class in this example, of course, but in the general case you'll be using different classes for these two tasks.

Watch out! I'm going to be jumping back and forth between the *MainPage* and *DialogPage* code-behind files in accordance with the flow of logic and data.

The easy transfer of data is from *MainPage* to *DialogPage*. When you click the "Get Color" button in *MainPage*, the code-behind file creates an object of type *PassData* and then scans through the collection of *RadioButton* controls to see which one is checked. That's the *Color* value assigned to the *InitializeColor* property of *PassData*. That *PassData* object then becomes the second argument to *Navigate*:

Project: DataPassingAndReturning | File: MainPage.xaml.cs (excerpt)

```
void OnGotoButtonClick(object sender, RoutedEventArgs args)
{
    // Create PassData object
    PassData passData = new PassData();

    // Set the InitializeColor property from the RadioButton controls
    foreach (UIElement child in radioStack.Children)
        if ((child as RadioButton).IsChecked.Value)
            passData.InitializeColor = (Color)(child as RadioButton).Tag;

    // Pass that object to Navigate
    this.Frame.Navigate(typeof(DialogPage), passData);
}
```

When the *OnNavigatedTo* override in *DialogPage* is called, the *Parameter* property of the event arguments is the object passed as the second argument to *Navigate*. *DialogPage* uses that to initialize its own set of *RadioButton* controls:

Project: DataPassingAndReturning | File: DialogPage.xaml.cs (excerpt)

```
protected override void OnNavigatedTo(NavigationEventArgs args)
{
    // Get the object passed as the second argument to Navigate
    PassData passData = args.Parameter as PassData;

    // Use that to initialize the RadioButton controls
    foreach (UIElement child in radioStack.Children)
        if ((Color)(child as RadioButton).Tag == passData.InitializeColor)
            (child as RadioButton).IsChecked = true;
```

```
    base.OnNavigatedTo(args);
}
```

Now you can click the three *RadioButton* controls to select a *Color* value. When satisfied with the selection press the Finished button. The handler simply calls *GoBack* to return to *MainPage*.

Project: DataPassingAndReturning | File: DialogPage.xaml.cs (excerpt)

```
void OnReturnButtonClick(object sender, RoutedEventArgs args)
{
    this.Frame.GoBack();
}
```

It would be nice if *GoBack* had an optional parameter that you could set to return data to the target page. But it does not. There is no mechanism for doing this, and another technique is required.

One possibility is this: After *DialogPage* calls *GoBack*, the *OnNavigatedFrom* override in *DialogPage* is called. The *Content* property of the event arguments is the instance of *MainPage* about to be navigated to. This means that *MainPage* could define a public property or method expressly for obtaining information from *DialogPage*, and *DialogPage* could set that property or call that method during its *OnNavigatedFrom* override.

Architecturally, though, it's a little cheesy because *DialogPage* must be familiar with the page types that are navigating to it. In general, this is not a good solution.

A much better solution is for *DialogPage* to define a *Completed* event with the type of the data it needs to return:

Project: DataPassingAndReturning | File: DialogPage.xaml.cs (excerpt)

```
public sealed partial class DialogPage : Page
{
    public event EventHandler<ReturnData> Completed;
    ...
}
```

MainPage needs to set a handler for that event. The only place *MainPage* can do this is within the *OnNavigatedFrom* method because the event arguments include a *Content* property that is the instance of *DialogPage* that is being navigated to:

Project: DataPassingAndReturning | File: MainPage.xaml.cs (excerpt)

```
protected override void OnNavigatedFrom(NavigationEventArgs args)
{
    if (args.SourcePageType.Equals(typeof(DialogPage)))
        (args.Content as DialogPage).Completed += OnDialogPageCompleted;

    base.OnNavigatedFrom(args);
}
```

MainPage knows about *DialogPage* because it's navigating to *DialogPage*. But it could be navigating to other pages as well, so it checks the *SourcePageType* property of the event arguments to make sure that it knows what type of page this particular *OnNavigatedFrom* event indicates.

With this scheme, *DialogPage* doesn't need to know about *MainPage*, and that's how it should be. Hiding a consumer of information from the provider of information is one of the primary purposes of events within the context of object-oriented programming.

DialogPage could fire the *Completed* event in the *Click* handler for the *Button*, but I've chosen to implement that logic in *OnNavigatedFrom*.

Project: DataPassingAndReturning | File: DialogPage.xaml.cs (excerpt)

```
protected override void OnNavigatedFrom(NavigationEventArgs args)
{
    if (Completed != null)
    {
        // Create ReturnData object
        ReturnData returnData = new ReturnData();

        // Set the ReturnColor property from the RadioButton controls
        foreach (UIElement child in radioStack.Children)
            if ((child as RadioButton).IsChecked.Value)
                returnData.ReturnColor = (Color)(child as RadioButton).Tag;

        // Fire the Completed event
        Completed(this, returnData);
    }

    base.OnNavigatedFrom(args);
}
```

If there is indeed a handler for the *Completed* event, *DialogPage* instantiates a *ReturnData* object and then sets the *ReturnColor* property from the collection of *RadioButton* controls.

In the *Completed* handler, *MainPage* uses the data from *DialogPage* to set the *Background* property of its *Grid* and check a *RadioButton*:

Project: DataPassingAndReturning | File: MainPage.xaml.cs (excerpt)

```
void OnDialogPageCompleted(object sender, ReturnData args)
{
    // Set background from returned color
    contentGrid.Background = new SolidColorBrush(args.ReturnColor);

    // Set RadioButton for returned color
    foreach (UIElement child in radioStack.Children)
        if ((Color)(child as RadioButton).Tag == args.ReturnColor)
            (child as RadioButton).IsChecked = true;

    (sender as DialogPage).Completed -= OnDialogPageCompleted;
}
```

The handler concludes by detaching itself from the sender.

But there's a flaw in the code as I've presented it: By default, the instance of *MainPage* that sets a handler for the *Completed* event in *DialogPage* is not the instance of *MainPage* that *DialogPage* returns back to! To fix that little problem requires setting *NavigationCacheMode* to something other than *Disabled*.

```
public sealed partial class MainPage : Page
{
    public MainPage()
    {
        this.InitializeComponent();
        this.NavigationCacheMode = NavigationCacheMode.Enabled;
    }
    ...
}
```

You only need to do this in *MainPage*, and guaranteeing a single instance makes perfect sense for a page that is architecturally the hub of the application. The instance of *MainPage* that invokes *DialogPage* should be the same instance that gets data back from it.

Visual Studio Standard Templates

A confession: I've been coding page-navigation logic in various Windows environments for several years now, and it never occurred to me to implement shortcuts with accelerator keys or mouse buttons. The code I showed you earlier is adapted from a class generated by Visual Studio named *LayoutAwarePage* that derives from *Page* and implements several helpful features.

LayoutAwarePage and other assorted classes are automatically added to your Visual Studio projects when you invoke the Add New Item dialog box and add an item called Basic Page rather than Blank Page. These files are also part of the Grid App and Split App templates. The page class created by selecting Basic Page derives from *LayoutAwarePage* rather than just *Page*. *LayoutAwarePage* defines virtual methods named *SaveState* and *LoadState* that allow the page instance to save and load its state and that do much of the work for you in conjunction with another generated class named *SuspensionManager*.

LayoutAwarePage also works in conjunction with *SuspensionManager* to save application state (including the back stack) when a program is being suspended and reload that state when it's relaunched.

LayoutAwarePage is named as it is because it uses the *SizeChanged* method to check the *ApplicationView.Value* property and call *VisualStateManager.GoToState* with strings corresponding to the members of the *ApplicationViewState* enumeration: "FullScreenLandscape", "FullScreenPortrait", "Filled", and "Snapped". These states allow XAML files to implement view changes themselves through Visual State Manager markup.

It's up to you whether you want to use these classes or implement these features (or similar features) on your own. Whether you use them or not, it doesn't hurt to study these classes and see what you can learn from them.

When creating new projects in Visual Studio, I've been using Blank App, but there are two alternatives: Grid App and Split App. These templates make use of *LayoutAwarePage* and *SuspensionManager*, as well as a sample view model in the *DataModel* folder. These templates demonstrate a recommended approach to laying out data on the screen. Perhaps most important, the Grid App and Split App templates demonstrate rudimentary use of the two remaining *ItemsControl* derivatives: *GridView* and *ListView*.

Both *GridView* and *ListView* derive from *ItemsControl* by way of *Selector* and *ListViewBase*. Neither *GridView* nor *ListView* defines any public properties or methods on its own, but they share many properties and methods from *ListViewBase*. Also, if you check generic.xaml, you'll discover that the templates for *GridView*, *ListView*, *GridViewItem*, and *ListViewItem* are different. In particular, by default *GridView* uses a *WrapGrid* for displaying its items, and *ListView* uses a *VirtualizingStackPanel*.

GridView and *ListView* are also suitable for grouping items. You define how the items are grouped, and the appearance of a header that delimits the groups. You'll see examples of this in the Grid App and Split App templates.

The Windows 8 start screen itself is a *GridView* or something very similar to a *GridView*. As you probably know, you can swipe items on the start screen to select them. This type of selection is supported by *ListViewBase* (and hence by *GridView* and *ListView*), but it is disabled in the Visual Studio templates.

The Windows 8 start screen allows you to move items around. This feature is also supported by *ListViewBase* (but interestingly, not while items are grouped). The Windows 8 start screen also supports semantic zoom: If you use your fingers to pinch the start screen, it collapses to give you a broader view of the groups, and then you can select whole groups. You can do this in your own application by using the *SemanticZoom* class.

For now, let's take a closer look at the Grid App template. (You can study Split App on your own.) The project contains three *LayoutAwarePage* derivatives.

Grid App initializes itself by displaying a *GroupedItemsPage*.

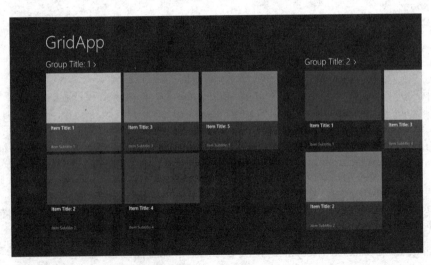

In a real application, those gray boxes would probably be pictures or other graphics.

The page has a title and a *GridView* control with horizontal scrolling. The individual items are defined by a *DataTemplate* resource named "Standard250x250ItemTemplate" defined in StandardStyles.xaml. The appearance of the headers ("Group Title: 1 >" and so forth) is defined in the GroupedItemsPage.xaml file by the *HeaderTemplate* property of the *GroupStyle* property of *GridView*.

The page has the same appearance in the *Filled* view, but in the *Snapped* view it switches to a vertically scrollable *ListView*:

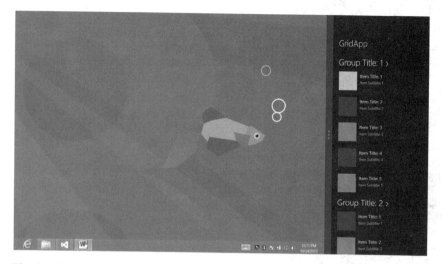

The *ItemTemplate* property is now the *DataTemplate* resource "Standard80ItemTemplate." Notice that the page title is also formatted differently. It's a "SnappedPageHeaderTextStyle" rather than the normal "PageHeaderTextStyle," both defined in StandardStyles.xaml.

The switch between the *GridView* and *ListView* when the program is in a *Snapped* mode occurs in the GroupedItemsPage.xaml file based on the calls to the *VisualStateManager* in *LayoutAwarePage*. The GroupedItemsPage.xaml file contains a Visual State Manager section that responds to the *Snapped* state as well as the *FullScreenPortrait* state.

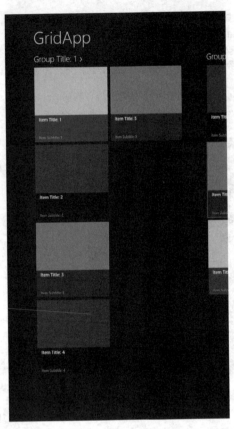

This is a *GridView* just as in the wider landscape views, but you might notice a little less margin around the sides. Defining changes like these in XAML is one of the advantages of using the Visual State Manager to signal different views.

If you click one of the header titles, you'll navigate to a *GroupDetailPage*:

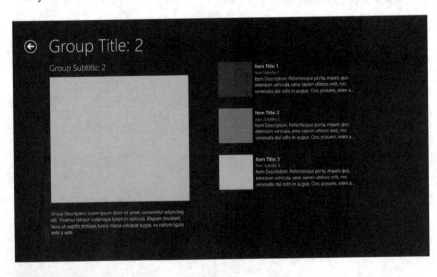

Notice that the Back button is implemented as a circled arrow in the upper-left corner. The *Button* has its *Style* set to the "BackButtonStyle" resources defined in StandardStyles.xaml. This is again a *GridView*, except that the header is very large and appears at the left. The individual items are now displayed with an *ItemTemplate* based on the "Standard500x130ItemTemplate" resources from StandardStyles.xaml.

Again, the page switches to a *ListView* in the *Snapped* state:

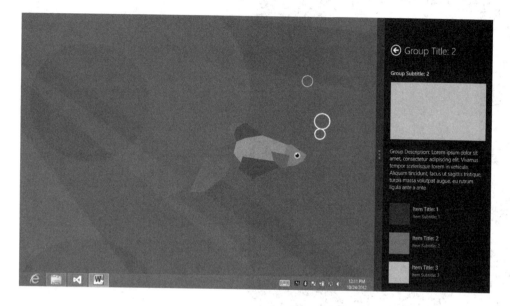

Notice that the *Button* has changed appearance as well. StandardStyles.xaml has a SnappedBackButtonStyle as well as a PortraitBackButtonStyle. Here's the portrait view:

From either this *GroupedItemsPage* or the *GroupDetailPage* you can navigate to a page for the individual item:

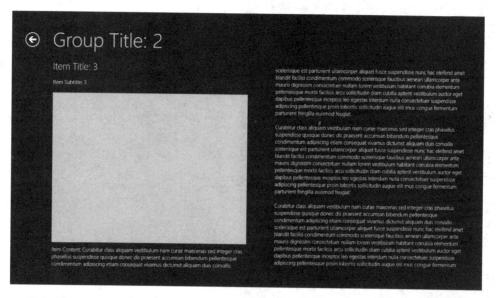

At first it appears to be a single item; however, you can horizontally scroll to see other items in the same group. The bulk of the page is actually a *FlipView*. Each item in this *FlipView* is a *ScrollViewer* containing a collection of *RichTextBlock* elements. I'll discuss *RichTextBlock* in Chapter 16, "Rich Text." In the Grid App template, the *RichTextBlock* elements are generated by a *RichTextColumns* class that you'll find in the Common folder.

The item view also has a different appearance in the *Snapped* state:

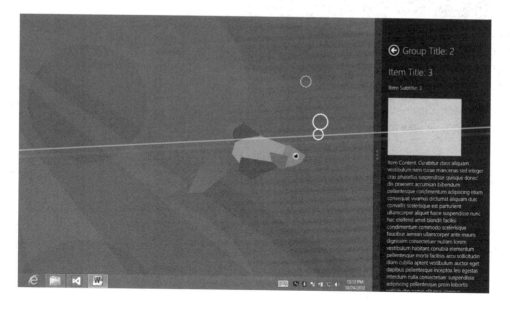

The *Portrait* view is also different:

Although I'll continue to use the Blank App and Blank Page templates in the projects in this book, I'll implement some of the features from the more sophisticated templates in a simplified and (I hope) more comprehensible manner.

View Models and Collections

As you saw in Chapter 11, "The Three Templates," the *Colors* class provides a convenient source of objects to display in an *ItemsControl* and *ListBox*. However, when graduating to the *GridView* and *ListView* controls, it's good to move to example data that is a little more sophisticated and a little more real.

For that purpose, the *http://www.charlespetzold.com/Students* directory of my website contains a file named students.xml that contains information on 69 students of a high school. The directory also contains lovely photographs of these students that originated in high school yearbooks from El Paso, Texas, for the years 1912 through 1914. The yearbooks are in the public domain, and they were digitized by the El Paso Public Library and made available to the public at *http://www.elpasotexas.gov/ library/ourlibraries/main_library/yearbooks/yearbooks.asp.*

The ElPasoHighSchool project is a library that accesses this XML file and constructs a view model to make the information available to applications. The following *Student* class represents a single student. Notice that the class implements *INotifyPropertyChanged* to make it suitable for data bindings:

Project: ElPasoHighSchool | File: Student.cs

```
using System.ComponentModel;
using System.Runtime.CompilerServices;

namespace ElPasoHighSchool
{
    public class Student : INotifyPropertyChanged
    {
        string fullName, firstName, middleName, lastName, sex, photoFilename;
        double gradePointAverage;

        public event PropertyChangedEventHandler PropertyChanged;

        public string FullName
        {
            set { SetProperty<string>(ref fullName, value); }
            get { return fullName; }
        }

        public string FirstName
        {
            set { SetProperty<string>(ref firstName, value); }
            get { return firstName; }
        }

        public string MiddleName
        {
            set { SetProperty<string>(ref middleName, value); }
            get { return middleName; }
        }

        public string LastName
        {
            set { SetProperty<string>(ref lastName, value); }
            get { return lastName; }
        }

        public string Sex
        {
            set { SetProperty<string>(ref sex, value); }
            get { return sex; }
        }
    }
```

```
        public string PhotoFilename
        {
            set { SetProperty<string>(ref photoFilename, value); }
            get { return photoFilename; }
        }

        public double GradePointAverage
        {
            set { SetProperty<double>(ref gradePointAverage, value); }
            get { return gradePointAverage; }
        }

        protected bool SetProperty<T>(ref T storage, T value,
                          [CallerMemberName] string propertyName = null)
        {
            if (object.Equals(storage, value))
                return false;

            storage = value;
            OnPropertyChanged(propertyName);
            return true;
        }

        protected void OnPropertyChanged(string propertyName)
        {
            if (PropertyChanged != null)
                PropertyChanged(this, new PropertyChangedEventArgs(propertyName));
        }
    }
}
```

The *StudentBody* class shown next also implements *INotifyPropertyChanged*. The class contains the name of the school and an *ObservableCollection* of type *Student* to store all the *Student* objects:

Project: ElPasoHighSchool | File: StudentBody.cs

```
using System.Collections.ObjectModel;
using System.ComponentModel;
using System.Runtime.CompilerServices;

namespace ElPasoHighSchool
{
    public class StudentBody : INotifyPropertyChanged
    {
        string school;
        ObservableCollection<Student> students = new ObservableCollection<Student>();

        public event PropertyChangedEventHandler PropertyChanged;

        public string School
        {
            set { SetProperty<string>(ref school, value); }
            get { return school; }
        }

        public ObservableCollection<Student> Students
        {
```

```
            set { SetProperty<ObservableCollection<Student>>(ref students, value); }
            get { return students; }
        }

        protected bool SetProperty<T>(ref T storage, T value,
                          [CallerMemberName] string propertyName = null)
        {
            if (object.Equals(storage, value))
                return false;

            storage = value;
            OnPropertyChanged(propertyName);
            return true;
        }

        protected void OnPropertyChanged(string propertyName)
        {
            if (PropertyChanged != null)
                PropertyChanged(this, new PropertyChangedEventArgs(propertyName));
        }
    }
}
```

ObservableCollection implements the *INotifyCollectionChanged* interface, which defines a *CollectionChanged* event. *ObservableCollection* fires this event whenever an item is added to or removed from the collection or existing items are reordered. When you set an object to the *ItemsSource* property of an items control, the control checks whether the object implements *INotifyCollectionChanged*. If so, it attaches a handler for the *CollectionChanged* event and modifies its display when items are added, removed, or reordered.

The student.xml file on my website looks like this:

File: http://www.charlespetzold.com/Students/students.xml (excerpt)

```
<?xml version="1.0" encoding="utf-8" ?>
<StudentBody xmlns:xsd="http://www.w3.org/2001/XMLSchema"
             xmlns:xsi="http://www.w3.org/2001/XMLSchema-instance">
  <School>El Paso High School</School>-<Students>
    <Student>
      <FullName>Adkins Bowden</FullName>
      <FirstName>Adkins</FirstName>
      <MiddleName/>
      <LastName>Bowden</LastName>
      <Sex>Male</Sex>
      <PhotoFilename>
        http://www.charlespetzold.com/Students/AdkinsBowden.png
      </PhotoFilename>
      <GradePointAverage>2.71</GradePointAverage>
    </Student>
    <Student>
      <FullName>Alfred Black</FullName>
      <FirstName>Alfred</FirstName>
      <MiddleName/>
      <LastName>Black</LastName>
      <Sex>Male</Sex>
      <PhotoFilename>
        http://www.charlespetzold.com/Students/AlfredBlack.png
```

```
        </PhotoFilename>
        <GradePointAverage>2.87</GradePointAverage>
      </Student>
      <Student>
        <FullName>Alice Bishop</FullName>
        <FirstName>Alice</FirstName>
        <MiddleName/>
        <LastName>Bishop</LastName>
        <Sex>Female</Sex>
        <PhotoFilename>
          http://www.charlespetzold.com/Students/AliceBishop.png
        </PhotoFilename>
        <GradePointAverage>3.68</GradePointAverage>
      </Student>
      ...
      <Student>
        <FullName>William Sheley Warnock</FullName>
        <FirstName>William</FirstName>
        <MiddleName>Sheley</MiddleName>
        <LastName>Warnock</LastName>
        <Sex>Male</Sex>
        <PhotoFilename>
          http://www.charlespetzold.com/Students/WilliamSheleyWarnock.png
        </PhotoFilename>
        <GradePointAverage>1.82</GradePointAverage>
      </Student>
    </Students>
</StudentBody>
```

The *Student* and *StudentBody* element tags conveniently correspond to the *Student* and *StudentBody* classes you've just seen. I created this XML file by using .NET serialization with the *XmlSerializer* class, and it can be deserialized in the same way. This is the purpose of the *StudentBodyPresenter* class, which again implements *INotifyPropertyChanged* but has just one property of type *StudentBody*:

Project: ElPasoHighSchool | File: StudentBodyPresenter.cs (excerpt)

```
public class StudentBodyPresenter : INotifyPropertyChanged
{
    StudentBody studentBody;
    Random rand = new Random();
    Window currentWindow = Window.Current;

    public event PropertyChangedEventHandler PropertyChanged;

    public StudentBodyPresenter()
    {
        // Download XML file
        HttpClient httpClient = new HttpClient();
        Task<string> task =
            httpClient.GetStringAsync("http://www.charlespetzold.com/Students/students.xml");
        task.ContinueWith(GetStringCompleted);
    }

    async void GetStringCompleted(Task<string> task)
    {
```

```
            if (task.Exception == null && !task.IsCanceled)
            {
                string xml = task.Result;

                // Deserialize XML
                StringReader reader = new StringReader(xml);
                XmlSerializer serializer = new XmlSerializer(typeof(StudentBody));

                await currentWindow.Dispatcher.RunAsync(CoreDispatcherPriority.Normal, () =>
                    {
                        this.StudentBody = serializer.Deserialize(reader) as StudentBody;

                        // Set a timer for random changes
                        DispatcherTimer timer = new DispatcherTimer
                        {
                            Interval = TimeSpan.FromMilliseconds(100)
                        };
                        timer.Tick += OnTimerTick;
                        timer.Start();
                    });
            }
        }

        public StudentBody StudentBody
        {
            set { SetProperty<StudentBody>(ref studentBody, value); }
            get { return studentBody; }
        }

        // Mimic changing grade point averages
        void OnTimerTick(object sender, object args)
        {
            int index = rand.Next(studentBody.Students.Count);
            Student student = this.StudentBody.Students[index];
            double factor = 1 + (rand.NextDouble() - 0.5) / 5;
            student.GradePointAverage =
                Math.Max(0.0,
                    Math.Min(5.0, (int)(100 * factor * student.GradePointAverage) / 100.0));
        }

        protected bool SetProperty<T>(ref T storage, T value,
                        [CallerMemberName] string propertyName = null)
        {
            if (object.Equals(storage, value))
                return false;

            storage = value;
            OnPropertyChanged(propertyName);
            return true;
        }

        protected void OnPropertyChanged(string propertyName)
        {
            if (PropertyChanged != null)
                PropertyChanged(this, new PropertyChangedEventArgs(propertyName));
        }
    }
```

This class caused me some problems. I wanted to initiate the loading and deserializing of the XML file from the class's constructor, but constructors cannot be declared as *async*, so I needed an explicit continuation handler instead. However, the continuation handler does not run in the user-interface thread. This is a problem because this method needs to set the *StudentBody* property, which causes a *PropertyChanged* event to be fired and possibly an updating of a binding on a user-interface object. The class needs to set the *StudentBody* property in the user-interface thread using a *CoreDispatcher*, but where does this *CoreDispatcher* object come from? The class has no access to objects created in the user-interface thread, which are the usual sources of *CoreDispatcher*.

Fortunately, the *Window* object has a *Dispatcher* property, and it's easy to get the current window through the *Window.Current* static property. The *StudentBodyPresenter* class also sets a *DispatcherTimer* for simulating real-time changes in the students' grade point averages to give the *PropertyChanged* event a little workout.

Let's create a new solution and project named DisplayHighSchoolStudents. To this solution add the existing ElPasoHighSchool project. In the References section of the DisplayHighSchoolStudents project, set a reference to the ElPasoHighSchool project, and in the MainPage.xaml file, create a new XML namespace prefix:

```
xmlns:elpaso="using:ElPasoHighSchool"
```

You can then instantiate the *StudentBodyPresenter* class in the *Resources* section of MainPage.xaml:

```
<Page.Resources>
    <elpaso:StudentBodyPresenter x:Key="presenter" />
</Page.Resources>
```

And now you can begin experimenting with accessing items from this view model.

For example, the markup

```
<Grid Background="{StaticResource ApplicationPageBackgroundThemeBrush}">
    <TextBlock Text="{Binding Source={StaticResource presenter}}"
            FontSize="24" />
</Grid>
```

causes the *TextBlock* to display the fully qualified class name "ElPasoHighSchool.StudentBodyPresenter". The markup

```
<TextBlock Text="{Binding Source={StaticResource presenter},
                        Path=StudentBody}"
        FontSize="24" />
```

displays the fully qualified class name "ElPasoHighSchool.StudentBody".

Try going another property deeper, like so:

```
<TextBlock Text="{Binding Source={StaticResource presenter},
                         Path=StudentBody.School}"
           FontSize="24" />
```

Now you get some real data: the value of the *School* property or "El Paso High School".

The other property in *StudentBody* is *Students*. Try that in the markup:

```
<TextBlock Text="{Binding Source={StaticResource presenter},
                         Path=StudentBody.Students}"
           FontSize="24" />
```

The displayed text is another fully qualified class name, this one quite lengthy: "System.Collections .ObjectModel.ObservableCollection`1[ElPasoHighSchool.Student]".

However, you can index the *Students* property in the markup:

```
<TextBlock Text="{Binding Source={StaticResource presenter},
                         Path=StudentBody.Students[23]}"
           FontSize="24" />
```

The result is another fully qualified class name, "ElPasoHighSchool.Student", but now we're at the point where we can see actual properties of that class.

One property of the *Student* class is *FullName*, so try this:

```
<TextBlock Text="{Binding Source={StaticResource presenter},
                         Path=StudentBody.Students[23].FullName}"
           FontSize="24" />
```

The result is the student's name: "Elizabeth Barnes".

Try replacing that *TextBlock* with an *Image* element, and reference the *PhotoFilename* property of *Student*:

```
<Grid Background="{StaticResource ApplicationPageBackgroundThemeBrush}">
    <Image Source="{Binding Source={StaticResource presenter},
                          Path=StudentBody.Students[23].PhotoFilename}" />
</Grid>
```

And there she is:

Now let's try replacing that *Image* element with a *GridView* with the *ItemsSource* property set to the *Students* property of *StudentBody*:

```
<Grid Background="{StaticResource ApplicationPageBackgroundThemeBrush}">
    <GridView ItemsSource="{Binding Source={StaticResource presenter},
                         Path=StudentBody.Students}" />

</Grid>
```

The result is a display of *Student* objects:

ElPasoHighSchool.Student ElPasoHighSchool.Student ElPasoHighSchool.Student ElPasoHighSchool.Student ElPasoHighSchool.Student
ElPasoHighSchool.Student ElPasoHighSchool.Student ElPasoHighSchool.Student ElPasoHighSchool.Student ElPasoHighSchool.Student
ElPasoHighSchool.Student ElPasoHighSchool.Student ElPasoHighSchool.Student ElPasoHighSchool.Student ElPasoHighSchool.Student
ElPasoHighSchool.Student ElPasoHighSchool.Student ElPasoHighSchool.Student ElPasoHighSchool.Student ElPasoHighSchool.Student
ElPasoHighSchool.Student ElPasoHighSchool.Student ElPasoHighSchool.Student ElPasoHighSchool.Student ElPasoHighSchool.Student
ElPasoHighSchool.Student ElPasoHighSchool.Student ElPasoHighSchool.Student ElPasoHighSchool.Student ElPasoHighSchool.Student
ElPasoHighSchool.Student ElPasoHighSchool.Student ElPasoHighSchool.Student ElPasoHighSchool.Student ElPasoHighSchool.Student
ElPasoHighSchool.Student ElPasoHighSchool.Student ElPasoHighSchool.Student ElPasoHighSchool.Student ElPasoHighSchool.Student
ElPasoHighSchool.Student ElPasoHighSchool.Student ElPasoHighSchool.Student ElPasoHighSchool.Student ElPasoHighSchool.Student
ElPasoHighSchool.Student ElPasoHighSchool.Student ElPasoHighSchool.Student ElPasoHighSchool.Student
ElPasoHighSchool.Student ElPasoHighSchool.Student ElPasoHighSchool.Student ElPasoHighSchool.Student
ElPasoHighSchool.Student ElPasoHighSchool.Student ElPasoHighSchool.Student ElPasoHighSchool.Student
ElPasoHighSchool.Student ElPasoHighSchool.Student ElPasoHighSchool.Student ElPasoHighSchool.Student
ElPasoHighSchool.Student ElPasoHighSchool.Student ElPasoHighSchool.Student ElPasoHighSchool.Student
ElPasoHighSchool.Student ElPasoHighSchool.Student ElPasoHighSchool.Student ElPasoHighSchool.Student

Although the *Student* objects are shown only as fully qualified class names, you can still detect some workings of the *GridView*. The display bounces a bit if you try to scroll it, and you can select individual items:

Let's simplify the *Binding* by moving part of it to the *Grid* as a *DataContext* property:

```
<Grid Background="{StaticResource ApplicationPageBackgroundThemeBrush}"
      DataContext="{Binding Source={StaticResource presenter},
                            Path=StudentBody}">
    <Grid.RowDefinitions>
        <RowDefinition Height="Auto" />
        <RowDefinition Height="*" />
    </Grid.RowDefinitions>

    <TextBlock Text="{Binding School}"
               Grid.Row="0"
               Style="{StaticResource PageHeaderTextStyle}" />

    <GridView ItemsSource="{Binding Students}"
              Grid.Row="1" />
</Grid>
```

Anything within that *Grid* can now access properties of the *StudentBody* class with very simple bindings. A *TextBlock* in the *Grid* references the *School* property.

Now all that's necessary is to add a *DataTemplate* to the *GridView* for the *Student* items:

```
<Grid Background="{StaticResource ApplicationPageBackgroundThemeBrush}"
      DataContext="{Binding Source={StaticResource presenter},
                            Path=StudentBody}">
    <Grid.RowDefinitions>
        <RowDefinition Height="Auto" />
        <RowDefinition Height="*" />
    </Grid.RowDefinitions>
```

```
<TextBlock Text="{Binding School}"
           Grid.Row="0"
           Style="{StaticResource PageHeaderTextStyle}" />

<GridView ItemsSource="{Binding Students}"
          Grid.Row="1">
    <GridView.ItemTemplate>
        <DataTemplate>
            <Border BorderBrush="{StaticResource ApplicationForegroundThemeBrush}"
                    BorderThickness="1">
                <Grid Height="120">
                    <Grid.ColumnDefinitions>
                        <ColumnDefinition Width="80" />
                        <ColumnDefinition Width="200" />
                    </Grid.ColumnDefinitions>

                    <Image Source="{Binding PhotoFilename}"
                           Grid.Column="0" />

                    <TextBlock Text="{Binding FullName}"
                               Grid.Column="1"
                               VerticalAlignment="Center"
                               Margin="5 0" />
                </Grid>
            </Border>
        </DataTemplate>
    </GridView.ItemTemplate>
</GridView>
</Grid>
```

And here they are, horizontally scrollable, of course:

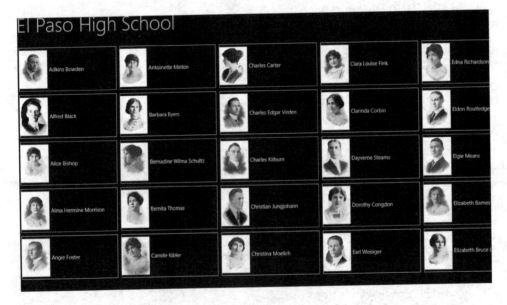

ListViewBase differentiates between clicking an item as if it were a button and selecting an item. Much of the selection support is inherited from *Selector* and is similar to *ListBox*. By default, when you tap an item, that item is selected. The item is displayed with a colored background and a checkmark, and the control fires a *SelectionChanged* event.

By default, item clicking is disabled, but you can enable this feature by setting a property and an event handler:

```
<GridView ItemsSource="{Binding Students}"
          Grid.Row="1"
          IsItemClickEnabled="True"
          ItemClick="OnGridViewItemClick">
```

Now when you tap an item, the item is *not* selected and instead an *ItemClick* event is fired. The event arguments to the *ItemClick* handler include the item, in this case an object of type *Student*.

However, the user can still select and unselect items by swiping them or right-clicking them. You can turn off selection entirely by setting the *SelectionMode* to *None*:

```
<GridView ItemsSource="{Binding Students}"
          Grid.Row="1"
          SelectionMode="None"
          IsItemClickEnabled="True"
          ItemClick="OnGridViewItemClick">
```

You can also set *SelectionMode* to *Multiple*, but obviously you don't want to implement selection at all if the program can't do anything with selected items.

Even when *SelectionMode* is set to *None*, you can still swipe items. The swiped item moves, but nothing is selected. You probably want to keep swiping in effect if you're going to implement dragging and reordering with the *AllowDrop* and *CanRecorderItems* properties:

```
<GridView ItemsSource="{Binding Students}"
          Grid.Row="1"
          SelectionMode="None"
          AllowDrop="True"
          CanReorderItems="True"
          IsItemClickEnabled="True"
          ItemClick="OnGridViewItemClick">
```

However, if you're not going to allow selection or reordering, it's probably best to disable swiping entirely:

```
<GridView ItemsSource="{Binding Students}"
          Grid.Row="1"
          SelectionMode="None"
          IsSwipeEnabled="False"
          IsItemClickEnabled="True"
          ItemClick="OnGridViewItemClick" />
```

In the complete DisplayHighSchoolStudents project, I have attempted to emulate the general layout of the Visual Studio standard Grid App while still using Blank App. The code-behind file for *MainPage* uses the *SizeChanged* handler to set a visual state based on the current view:

Project: DisplayHighSchoolStudents | **File:** MainPage.xaml.cs (excerpt)

```
public sealed partial class MainPage : Page
{
    public MainPage()
    {
        this.InitializeComponent();
        SizeChanged += OnPageSizeChanged;
    }

    void OnPageSizeChanged(object sender, SizeChangedEventArgs args)
    {
        VisualStateManager.GoToState(this, ApplicationView.Value.ToString(), true);
    }
    ...
}
```

The XAML file has a *GridView* for all view states except *Snapped*, and a *ListView* for *Snapped*. The two controls share a *DataTemplate* for displaying the items. This is defined in the *Resources* section of the XAML file along with the view model:

Project: DisplayHighSchoolStudents | **File:** MainPage.xaml (excerpt)

```
<Page ... >
    <Page.Resources>
        <elpaso:StudentBodyPresenter x:Key="presenter" />

        <DataTemplate x:Key="studentTemplate">
            <Border Height="120"
                    Width="280">
                <Grid>
                    <Grid.RowDefinitions>
                        <RowDefinition Height="*" />
                        <RowDefinition Height="*" />
                    </Grid.RowDefinitions>

                    <Grid.ColumnDefinitions>
                        <ColumnDefinition Width="Auto" />
                        <ColumnDefinition Width="*" />
                    </Grid.ColumnDefinitions>

                    <Image Grid.Row="0" Grid.Column="0" Grid.RowSpan="2"
                           Source="{Binding PhotoFilename}"
                           Height="120"
                           Margin="5" />

                    <TextBlock Text="{Binding FullName}"
                               Grid.Row="0" Grid.Column="1"
                               VerticalAlignment="Center"
                               Margin="5 0" />

                    <StackPanel Grid.Row="1" Grid.Column="1"
```

```
                              Orientation="Horizontal"
                              VerticalAlignment="Center"
                              Margin="5 0">
                      <TextBlock Text="GPA =&#x00A0;" />
                      <TextBlock Text="{Binding GradePointAverage}" />
                  </StackPanel>
              </Grid>
          </Border>
      </DataTemplate>
  </Page.Resources>
  ...
</Page>
```

Because this *DataTemplate* is shared between the *GridView* and *ListView*, and because the *ListView* is used in *Snapped* mode, and because *Snapped* mode always implies a 320-unit width, a template defined for *Snapped* needs to be narrower than 320 units. Of course, it's always possible to use different item templates for the two controls as the Grid App template does.

The page is divided into two rows, with the top row dedicated to an invisible Back button and page title:

Project: DisplayHighSchoolStudents | **File:** MainPage.xaml (excerpt)

```
<Page ... >
  ...
  <Grid Background="{StaticResource ApplicationPageBackgroundThemeBrush}"
        DataContext="{Binding Source={StaticResource presenter},
                              Path=StudentBody}">
      <Grid.RowDefinitions>
          <RowDefinition Height="140" />
          <RowDefinition Height="*" />
      </Grid.RowDefinitions>

      <Grid Grid.Row="0">
          <Grid.ColumnDefinitions>
              <ColumnDefinition Width="Auto" />
              <ColumnDefinition Width="*" />
          </Grid.ColumnDefinitions>

          <Button Name="backButton"
                  Grid.Column="0"
                  Style="{StaticResource BackButtonStyle}"
                  IsEnabled="False" />

          <TextBlock Name="pageTitle"
                     Text="{Binding School}"
                     Grid.Column="1"
                     Style="{StaticResource PageHeaderTextStyle}" />
      </Grid>
      ...
  </Grid>
</Page>
```

Notice that the *Button* is disabled because this is the main page. The standard style for this button hides the button entirely when it's disabled. The *TextBlock* is also based on a standard style, and it has a binding to the *School* property.

The second row of the *Grid* contains both the *GridView* and *ListView*, but the *ListView* has its *Visibility* property set to *Collapsed*:

Project: DisplayHighSchoolStudents | **File:** MainPage.xaml (excerpt)

```
<Page ... >
    ...
    <Grid Background="{StaticResource ApplicationPageBackgroundThemeBrush}"
          DataContext="{Binding Source={StaticResource presenter},
                                Path=StudentBody}">
        <Grid.RowDefinitions>
            <RowDefinition Height="140" />
            <RowDefinition Height="*" />
        </Grid.RowDefinitions>
        ...
        <GridView Name="gridView"
                  Grid.Row="1"
                  ItemsSource="{Binding Students}"
                  Padding="116 0 40 46"
                  SelectionMode="None"
                  IsSwipeEnabled="False"
                  IsItemClickEnabled="True"
                  ItemClick="OnGridViewItemClick"
                  ItemTemplate="{StaticResource studentTemplate}" />

        <ListView Name="listView"
                  Grid.Row="1"
                  ItemsSource="{Binding Students}"
                  Visibility="Collapsed"
                  SelectionMode="None"
                  IsSwipeEnabled="False"
                  IsItemClickEnabled="True"
                  ItemClick="OnGridViewItemClick"
                  ItemTemplate="{StaticResource studentTemplate}" />
        ...
    </Grid>
</Page>
```

Obviously, the *GridView* and *ListView* share a bunch of properties. These could be defined in a *Style* with a *TargetType* of *ListViewBase*. Selection has been disabled, but both controls have an *ItemClick* event set to a handler in the code-behind file.

Finally, *MainPage* has a section for Visual State Manager markup. The primary purpose is to hide the *GridView* and show the *ListView* when the application is in the *Snapped* state:

Project: DisplayHighSchoolStudents | **File:** MainPage.xaml (excerpt)

```
<Page ... >
    ...
    <Grid Background="{StaticResource ApplicationPageBackgroundThemeBrush}"
          DataContext="{Binding Source={StaticResource presenter},
                                Path=StudentBody}">
```

```
...
    <VisualStateManager.VisualStateGroups>
        <VisualStateGroup x:Name="ApplicationViewStates">

            <VisualState x:Name="FullScreenLandscape" />

            <VisualState x:Name="Filled" />

            <VisualState x:Name="FullScreenPortrait">
                <Storyboard>
                    <ObjectAnimationUsingKeyFrames Storyboard.TargetName="backButton"
                                                   Storyboard.TargetProperty="Style">
                        <DiscreteObjectKeyFrame KeyTime="0"
                                Value="{StaticResource PortraitBackButtonStyle}" />
                    </ObjectAnimationUsingKeyFrames>

                    <ObjectAnimationUsingKeyFrames Storyboard.TargetName="gridView"
                                                   Storyboard.TargetProperty="Padding">
                        <DiscreteObjectKeyFrame KeyTime="0" Value="96 0 10 56" />
                    </ObjectAnimationUsingKeyFrames>
                </Storyboard>
            </VisualState>

            <VisualState x:Name="Snapped">
                <Storyboard>
                    <ObjectAnimationUsingKeyFrames Storyboard.TargetName="gridView"
                                                   Storyboard.TargetProperty="Visibility">
                        <DiscreteObjectKeyFrame KeyTime="0" Value="Collapsed" />
                    </ObjectAnimationUsingKeyFrames>

                    <ObjectAnimationUsingKeyFrames Storyboard.TargetName="listView"
                                                   Storyboard.TargetProperty="Visibility">
                        <DiscreteObjectKeyFrame KeyTime="0" Value="Visible" />
                    </ObjectAnimationUsingKeyFrames>

                    <ObjectAnimationUsingKeyFrames Storyboard.TargetName="backButton"
                                                   Storyboard.TargetProperty="Style">
                        <DiscreteObjectKeyFrame KeyTime="0"
                                Value="{StaticResource SnappedBackButtonStyle}" />
                    </ObjectAnimationUsingKeyFrames>

                    <ObjectAnimationUsingKeyFrames Storyboard.TargetName="pageTitle"
                                                   Storyboard.TargetProperty="Style">
                        <DiscreteObjectKeyFrame KeyTime="0"
                                Value="{StaticResource SnappedPageHeaderTextStyle}" />
                    </ObjectAnimationUsingKeyFrames>
                </Storyboard>
            </VisualState>
        </VisualStateGroup>
    </VisualStateManager.VisualStateGroups>
</Grid>
</Page>
```

In addition to swapping the visibility of the *GridView* and *ListView*, this Visual State Manager section also changes button and title styles and the *GridView* padding.

Here's the program running normally:

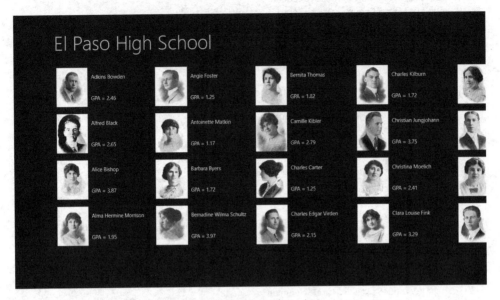

It won't take long to see the grade point averages changing.

In *Snapped* mode, the program switches to a *ListView* with a smaller title:

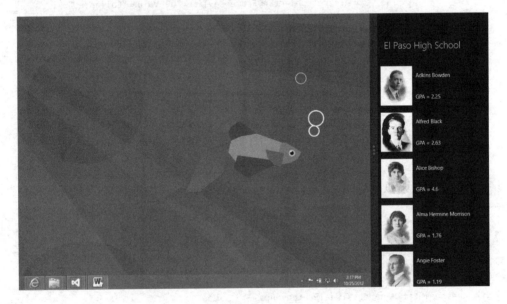

In portrait mode, the extra space at the sides closes up a bit:

Whenever an item is clicked, the *GridView* or *ListView* fires an *ItemClick* event. This initiates navigation to a *Page* derivative of type *StudentPage*, passing to it the *ClickedItem* property of the event arguments, which is an object of type *Student*:

Project: DisplayHighSchoolStudents | **File:** MainPage.xaml.cs (excerpt)

```
public sealed partial class MainPage : Page
{
    ...
    void OnGridViewItemClick(object sender, ItemClickEventArgs args)
    {
        this.Frame.Navigate(typeof(StudentPage), args.ClickedItem);
    }
}
```

In the *OnNavigatedTo* override in *StudentPage*, this *Student* object is set to the *DataContext* of the page:

Project: DisplayHighSchoolStudents | **File:** StudentPage.xaml.cs (excerpt)

```
public sealed partial class StudentPage : Page
{
    public StudentPage()
    {
        this.InitializeComponent();
        SizeChanged += OnPageSizeChanged;
    }

    void OnPageSizeChanged(object sender, SizeChangedEventArgs args)
    {
        VisualStateManager.GoToState(this, ApplicationView.Value.ToString(), true);
    }

    protected override void OnNavigatedTo(NavigationEventArgs args)
    {
        this.DataContext = args.Parameter;
        base.OnNavigatedTo(args);
    }

    void OnBackButtonClick(object sender, RoutedEventArgs args)
    {
        this.Frame.GoBack();
    }
}
```

Also notice the call to *VisualStateManager.GoToState* as well as a *Click* handler to go back to *Main-Page*.

The StudentPage.xaml file simply displays a couple properties of the *Student* class:

Project: DisplayHighSchoolStudents | **File:** StudentPage.xaml (excerpt)

```
<Page ...
    Name="page"
    FontSize="24">

    <Grid Background="{StaticResource ApplicationPageBackgroundThemeBrush}">
        <Grid.RowDefinitions>
            <RowDefinition Height="140" />
            <RowDefinition Height="*" />
        </Grid.RowDefinitions>

        <Grid Grid.Row="0">
            <Grid.ColumnDefinitions>
                <ColumnDefinition Width="Auto" />
                <ColumnDefinition Width="*" />
            </Grid.ColumnDefinitions>

            <Button Name="backButton"
                    Grid.Column="0"
                    Style="{StaticResource BackButtonStyle}"
                    IsEnabled="{Binding ElementName=page, Path=Frame.CanGoBack}"
```

```
                                  Click="OnBackButtonClick" />

        <TextBlock Name="pageTitle"
                   Text="{Binding FullName}"
                   Grid.Column="1"
                   Style="{StaticResource PageHeaderTextStyle}" />
    </Grid>

    <StackPanel Grid.Row="1"
                HorizontalAlignment="Center">
        <Image Source="{Binding PhotoFilename}"
               Width="240" />

        <TextBlock Text="{Binding Sex}"
                   HorizontalAlignment="Center"
                   Margin="10" />

        <StackPanel Orientation="Horizontal"
                    HorizontalAlignment="Center"
                    Margin="10">
            <TextBlock Text="GPA =&#x00A0;" />
            <TextBlock Text="{Binding GradePointAverage}" />
        </StackPanel>
    </StackPanel>

    <VisualStateManager.VisualStateGroups>
        <VisualStateGroup x:Name="ApplicationViewStates">

            <VisualState x:Name="FullScreenLandscape" />

            <VisualState x:Name="Filled" />

            <VisualState x:Name="FullScreenPortrait">
                <Storyboard>
                    <ObjectAnimationUsingKeyFrames Storyboard.TargetName="backButton"
                                                   Storyboard.TargetProperty="Style">
                        <DiscreteObjectKeyFrame KeyTime="0"
                                Value="{StaticResource PortraitBackButtonStyle}" />
                    </ObjectAnimationUsingKeyFrames>
                </Storyboard>
            </VisualState>

            <VisualState x:Name="Snapped">
                <Storyboard>
                    <ObjectAnimationUsingKeyFrames Storyboard.TargetName="backButton"
                                                   Storyboard.TargetProperty="Style">
                        <DiscreteObjectKeyFrame KeyTime="0"
                                Value="{StaticResource SnappedBackButtonStyle}" />
                    </ObjectAnimationUsingKeyFrames>

                    <ObjectAnimationUsingKeyFrames Storyboard.TargetName="pageTitle"
                                                   Storyboard.TargetProperty="Style">
                        <DiscreteObjectKeyFrame KeyTime="0"
                                Value="{StaticResource SnappedPageHeaderTextStyle}" />
                    </ObjectAnimationUsingKeyFrames>
                </Storyboard>
            </VisualState>
```

```
            </VisualStateGroup>
        </VisualStateManager.VisualStateGroups>
    </Grid>
</Page>
```

The Visual State Manager isn't as elaborate as before because there's no longer a *GridView* and *ListView* to switch between. The only real issues involve styles. Here it is in portrait mode:

Grouping the Items

To group items in a *GridView* or *ListView*, your view model needs a property of type *ObservableCollection* corresponding to the groups. The items within that collection are instances of a class that includes a title to identify the group and its own *ObservableCollection* for the items themselves. You'll use this view model in conjunction with a proxy collection class called *CollectionViewSource*.

My *StudentBodyPresenter* view model doesn't have such a property, but it's easy to create a new class for this purpose.

The GroupBySex project demonstrates how to group the students by male and female. This project supplements the view model implemented in the ElPasoHighSchool project with a couple extra classes. The first is called *StudentGroup* and has two just properties. The *Title* property serves as a title for the group, and the *Students* property is a collection of *Student* objects:

Project: GroupBySex | File: StudentGroup.cs

```
public class StudentGroup : INotifyPropertyChanged
{
    string title;
    ObservableCollection<Student> students = new ObservableCollection<Student>();

    public event PropertyChangedEventHandler PropertyChanged;

    public StudentGroup()
    {
        this.Students = new ObservableCollection<Student>();
    }

    public string Title
    {
        set { SetProperty<string>(ref title, value); }
        get { return title; }
    }

    public ObservableCollection<Student> Students
    {
        set { SetProperty<ObservableCollection<Student>>(ref students, value); }
        get { return students; }
    }

    protected bool SetProperty<T>(ref T storage, T value,
                        [CallerMemberName] string propertyName = null)
    {
        if (object.Equals(storage, value))
            return false;

        storage = value;
        OnPropertyChanged(propertyName);
        return true;
    }

    protected void OnPropertyChanged(string propertyName)
    {
        if (PropertyChanged != null)
            PropertyChanged(this, new PropertyChangedEventArgs(propertyName));
    }
}
```

The *StudentGroups* class (notice the plural) has only one getable property named *Groups*, which is a collection of *StudentGroup* objects. It also has a set-only *Source* property of type *StudentBodyPresenter* that constructs the *StudentGroups* and *StudentGroup* classes. I made *Source* a property so that it can be set in XAML.

```csharp
public class StudentGroups : INotifyPropertyChanged
{
    StudentBodyPresenter presenter;
    ObservableCollection<StudentGroup> groups = new ObservableCollection<StudentGroup>();

    public event PropertyChangedEventHandler PropertyChanged;

    public StudentBodyPresenter Source
    {
        set
        {
            if (value != null)
            {
                presenter = value;
                presenter.PropertyChanged += OnHighSchoolPropertyChanged;
            }
        }
    }

    void OnHighSchoolPropertyChanged(object sender, PropertyChangedEventArgs args)
    {
        if (args.PropertyName == "StudentBody" && presenter.StudentBody != null)
        {
            this.Groups = new ObservableCollection<StudentGroup>();
            this.Groups.Add(new StudentGroup { Title = "Male" });
            this.Groups.Add(new StudentGroup { Title = "Female" });

            foreach (Student student in presenter.StudentBody.Students)
                if (student.Sex == "Male")
                    this.Groups[0].Students.Add(student);
                else
                    this.Groups[1].Students.Add(student);
        }
    }

    public ObservableCollection<StudentGroup> Groups
    {
        set { SetProperty<ObservableCollection<StudentGroup>>(ref groups, value); }
        get { return groups; }
    }

    protected bool SetProperty<T>(ref T storage, T value,
                        [CallerMemberName] string propertyName = null)
    {
        if (object.Equals(storage, value))
            return false;

        storage = value;
        OnPropertyChanged(propertyName);
        return true;
    }

    protected void OnPropertyChanged(string propertyName)
    {
        if (PropertyChanged != null)
            PropertyChanged(this, new PropertyChangedEventArgs(propertyName));
    }
}
```

When the *Source* property is set to an instance of *StudentBodyPresenter*, the *set* accessor attaches a handler for the *PropertyChanged* event and waits for the *StudentBody* property to be set and available. At that time, it can create two instances of the *StudentGroup* class and fill those with the male and female students.

For purposes of clarity I've kept the MainPage.xaml file to nearly the bare necessities: It has only a *GridView*, and it doesn't change the layout for different views. There is virtually no formatting aside from the *DataTemplate* used to display each item, and I've excluded that template from this listing because it's the same as in the previous program.

The *Resources* section contains three classes that contribute to the collection used by the *GridView*. The *StudentBodyPresenter* class is first, as in the previous project. Next, *StudentGroups* is instantiated with its *Source* property set to the *StudentBodyPresenter* instance. Finally, a *CollectionViewSource* (the proxy collection) has its *Source* property bound to the *Groups* property of *StudentGroups*. This *StudentGroups* object is a collection of *StudentGroup* objects. The *CollectionViewSource* needs to know that this source represents a collection of groups, and it also needs the property of the *StudentGroups* class that contains the actual items, in this case *Students*:

Project: GroupBySex | File: MainPage.xaml (excerpt)

```xaml
<Page ... >
    <Page.Resources>
        <elpaso:StudentBodyPresenter x:Key="presenter" />

        <local:StudentGroups x:Key="studentGroups"
                        Source="{StaticResource presenter}" />

        <CollectionViewSource x:Key="collectionView"
                        Source="{Binding Source={StaticResource studentGroups},
                                    Path=Groups}"
                        IsSourceGrouped="True"
                        ItemsPath="Students" />

        <DataTemplate x:Key="studentTemplate">
        ...
        </DataTemplate>
    </Page.Resources>

    <Grid Background="{StaticResource ApplicationPageBackgroundThemeBrush}">
        <GridView ItemsSource="{Binding Source={StaticResource collectionView}}"
                ItemTemplate="{StaticResource studentTemplate}">

            <!-- The Panel for the groups themselves -->
            <GridView.ItemsPanel>
                <ItemsPanelTemplate>
                    <WrapGrid />
                </ItemsPanelTemplate>
            </GridView.ItemsPanel>

            <GridView.GroupStyle>
                <GroupStyle>
                    <!-- The content of the header -->
                    <GroupStyle.HeaderTemplate>
                        <DataTemplate>
```

```
                    <TextBlock Text="{Binding Title}"
                                Style="{StaticResource GroupHeaderTextStyle}" />
                </DataTemplate>
            </GroupStyle.HeaderTemplate>

            <!-- The panel for the items within each group -->
            <GroupStyle.Panel>
                <ItemsPanelTemplate>
                    <VariableSizedWrapGrid Orientation="Vertical" />
                </ItemsPanelTemplate>
            </GroupStyle.Panel>
        </GroupStyle>
    </GridView.GroupStyle>
</GridView>
        </Grid>
</Page>
```

The *ItemsSource* of the *GridView* is bound to that *CollectionViewSource*, but a few other properties also set here: Two panels and a *DataTemplate* for the header. The first of these two panels—the *WrapGrid* set to the *ItemsPanel* property—is the same as in the default template for *GridView* so that markup isn't required. However, it helps to show explicitly that there are two types of panel at work here, one for the groups and another for the items within each group.

Here's the result scrolled so that you can see the end of the boys and the start of the girls:

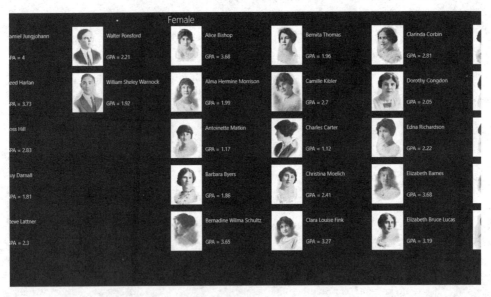

Although I've been instantiating view models in the XAML file, in the general case you probably want to share a view model among multiple pages. A good place to instantiate a single instance of the view model is in the *App* class, and from there you can make it available to the rest of the application as a public property.

Specialties

CHAPTER 13

Touch, Etc.

One of the most forward-looking aspects of the Windows Runtime is the consolidation of touch, mouse, and pen input. No longer is it necessary to add touch to an existing mouse-oriented application, or add some mouse support to a touch application. From the very beginning, the programmer treats all these forms of input in a fairly interchangeable manner. In accordance with the Windows Runtime programming interface, I will be using the word *pointer* to refer to input from touch, mouse, and the pen (also known as the stylus) when it's not necessary to distinguish the actual input device.

The best way to handle pointer input is through the existing Windows Runtime controls. As you've seen, standard controls such as *Button*, *Slider*, *ScrollViewer*, and *Thumb* all respond to pointer input and use that to deliver higher-level input to your application.

In some cases, however, the programmer needs to obtain actual pointer input, and for that purpose *UIElement* defines three different families of events:

- Eight low-level events beginning with the word *Pointer*

- Five higher-level events beginning with the word *Manipulation*

- *Tapped*, *RightTapped*, *DoubleTapped*, and *Holding* events

The *Control* class supplements these events with virtual protected methods beginning with the word *On* and followed by the event name.

To receive pointer input, a *FrameworkElement* derivative must have its *IsHitTestVisible* property set to *true* and its *Visibility* property set to *Visible*. A *Control* derivative must have its *IsEnabled* property set to *true*. The element must have some kind of graphical representation on the screen; a *Panel* derivative can have a *Transparent* background but not a *null* background.

All these events are associated with the element that is underneath your finger or mouse or pen at the time of the event. The only exception is when a pointer has been "captured" by an element, as you'll see later in this chapter.

If you need to track individual fingers, you'll want to use the *Pointer* events. Each event is accompanied by an ID number that uniquely identifies either an individual finger or pen touching the screen, or the mouse or pen. In this chapter I'll demonstrate how to use *Pointer* events for a finger-paint program and a piano keyboard (unfortunately without sound). Both these programs obviously need to handle simultaneous input from multiple fingers.

In a sense, the *Pointer* events are the only events you need. For example, if you wish to implement a feature that allows the user to stretch a photograph with two fingers, you can track *Pointer* events for those two fingers and measure how far they're moving apart. But calculations of this sort are provided for you in the *Manipulation* events. The *Manipulation* events consolidate multiple fingers into a single action, and they're ideal for moving, stretching, pinching, and rotating visual objects.

For some applications you might be puzzled whether to use *Pointer* or *Manipulation* events. The *Manipulation* events should probably be your first choice. Particularly if you think to yourself "I hope the user's not going to start using a second finger because I'll just have to ignore it," you probably want to use the *Manipulation* events. Then, if the user does use two or more fingers when only one finger is necessary, the multiple fingers will be averaged.

However, you'll also discover that the *Manipulation* events have an intrinsic lag. A finger touching the screen needs to move a bit before that finger is interpreted as contributing to a manipulation. *Manipulation* events are not fired if a finger taps or holds. Sometimes this lag will be enough to persuade you to use the *Pointer* events instead. The *XYSlider* custom control shown in this chapter is a case in point. The version shown in this chapter is written with *Manipulation* events because it wouldn't know what to do with extra fingers. But the lag time is a definite problem, so I have another version in Chapter 14, "Bitmaps," that uses *Pointer* events.

Pointer events are generated on a window level by the *CoreWindow* object, and you can derive *Manipulation* events on your own using the *GestureRecognizer*, but I'll be ignoring those facilities in this chapter and sticking with the events defined by *UIElement* and the virtual methods defined by *Control*. I also won't get into information about hardware input devices available from classes in the *Windows.Devices.Input* namespace.

Input from the pen has some special considerations involving the selection, erasing, and storage of pen strokes, as well as handwriting recognition. Those topics will be saved for Chapter 19, "Pen (Also Known as Stylus)." The Microsoft Surface tablet introduced in October 2012 does not support pen input.

A *Pointer* Roadmap

Of the eight *Pointer* events, five are very common. If you touch a finger to an enabled and visible *UIElement* derivative, move it, and lift it, these five *Pointer* events are generated in the following order:

- *PointerEntered*

- *PointerPressed*

- *PointerMoved* (multiple occurrences in the general case)

- *PointerReleased*

- *PointerExited*

A finger generates *Pointer* events only when the finger is touching the screen or when it has just been removed. There is no such thing as "hover" with touch.

The mouse is a little different. The mouse generates *PointerMoved* events even without the mouse button pressed. Suppose you move the mouse pointer to a particular element, press the button, move the mouse some more, release the button, and then move the mouse off the element. The element generates the following series of events:

- *PointerEntered*

- *PointerMoved* (multiple)

- *PointerPressed*

- *PointerMoved* (multiple)

- *PointerReleased*

- *PointerMoved* (multiple)

- *PointerExited*

Multiple *PointerPressed* and *PointerReleased* events can also be generated if the user presses and releases various mouse buttons.

Now let's try a pen. The element begins reacting to the pen before it actually touches the screen, so you'll first see a *PointerEntered* event followed by *PointerMoved*. As the pen touches the screen, a *PointerPressed* event is generated. Move the pen, and lift it. The element continues to fire *PointerMoved* events after *PointerReleased*, but it culminates with a *PointerExited* when the pen is moved farther away from the screen. It's the same sequence of events as the mouse.

When the user spins the mouse wheel, the following event is generated:

- *PointerWheelChanged*

The remaining two events are rarer:

- *PointerCaptureLost*

- *PointerCanceled*

I'll discuss pointer capture later in this chapter, at which time the *PointerCaptureLost* event becomes much more important.

I have never seen a *PointerCanceled* event even when I've unplugged the mouse from the computer, but the event exists to report an error of that sort.

All these events are accompanied by an instance of *PointerRoutedEventArgs*, defined in the *Windows.UI.Xaml.Input* namespace. (Watch out: There's also a *PointerEventArgs* class in the *Windows.UI.Core* namespace, but that's used for the processing of pointer input on the window level.) As the name of this class indicates, these *Pointer* events are all routed events that travel up the visual tree.

PointerRoutedEventArgs defines two properties common for routed events:

- *OriginalSource* indicates the element that raised the event.

- *Handled* lets you stop further routing of the event up the visual tree.

Lots of other information is available from the *PointerRoutedEventArgs* object. The following description covers only the highlights. The class also defines these members:

- *Pointer* property of type *Pointer*

- *KeyModifiers* property indicating the status of the Shift, Control, Menu (otherwise known as Alt), and Windows keys

- *GetCurrentPoint* method that returns a *PointerPoint* object

Watch out: Already we're dealing with classes named *Pointer* (defined in the *Windows.UI.Xaml.Input* namespace) and *PointerPoint* (defined in *Windows.UI.Input*).

The *Pointer* class has just four properties:

- *PointerId* property is an unsigned integer identifying the mouse, or an individual finger or pen.

- *PointerDeviceType* is an enumeration value *Touch*, *Mouse*, or *Pen*.

- *IsInRange* is a *bool* that indicates whether the device is in range of the screen.

- *IsInContact* is a *bool* indicating whether the finger or pen is touching the screen, or whether the mouse button is down.

The *PointerId* property is extremely important. This is what you use to track the movement of individual fingers. Almost always, a program that handles *Pointer* events will define a dictionary in which this *PointerId* property serves as a key.

The *GetCurrentPoint* method of *PointerRoutedEventArgs* sounds as if it returns the current coordinate location of the pointer, and it does, except that it also provides a whole lot more. Because it's convenient to get the location relative to a particular element, *GetCurrentPoint* accepts an argument of type *UIElement*. The *PointerPoint* object returned from this method duplicates some information from *Pointer* (the *PointerId* and *IsInContact* properties) and provides some other information:

- *Position* of type *Point*, the (x, y) location of the pointer at the time of the event

- *Timestamp* of type *ulong*

- *Properties* of type *PointerPointProperties* (defined in *Windows.UI.Input*)

The *Position* property is always relative to the upper-left corner of the element you pass to the *GetCurrentPoint* method.

PointerRoutedEventArgs also defines a method named *GetIntermediatePoints* that is similar to *GetCurrentPoint* except that it returns a collection of *PointerPoint* objects. Very often this collection has just one item—the same *PointerPoint* returned from *GetCurrentPoint*—but for the *PointerMoved* event there could be more than one, particularly if the event handler isn't very fast. I've particularly noticed *GetIntermediatePoints* returning multiple *PointerPoint* objects on the Microsoft Surface.

The *PointerPointProperties* class defines 22 properties that provide detailed information about the event, including which mouse buttons are pressed, whether the button on the pen barrel is pressed, how the pen is tilted, the contact rectangle of the finger with the screen (if that's available), the pressure of a finger or pen against the screen (if that's available), and *MouseWheelDelta*.

You can use as little or as much of this information as you need. Obviously, some of it will not be applicable to every pointer device and will therefore have default values.

A First Dab at Finger Painting

Perhaps the archetypal multitouch application is one that lets you paint with your fingers on the screen. You can write such a program handling just three *Pointer* events and examining just two properties from the event arguments, but I'm afraid the result has a flaw not quite compensated for by its simplicity.

The MainPage.xaml file of FingerPaint1 simply provides a name for the standard *Grid*:

Project: FingerPaint1 | File: MainPage.xaml (excerpt)

```
<Page ... >
    <Grid Name="contentGrid"
        Background="{StaticResource ApplicationPageBackgroundThemeBrush}" />
</Page>
```

The very first thing that the code-behind file does is define a *Dictionary* with a key of type *uint*. I mentioned earlier that virtually every program that handles *Pointer* events has a *Dictionary* of this sort. The type of the items you store in the *Dictionary* is dependent on the application; sometimes an application will define a class or structure specifically for this purpose. In a rudimentary finger-painting application, each finger touching the screen will be drawing a unique *Polyline*, so the *Dictionary* can store that *Polyline* instance:

Project: FingerPaint1 | File: MainPage.xaml.cs (excerpt)

```
public sealed partial class MainPage : Page
{
    Dictionary<uint, Polyline> pointerDictionary = new Dictionary<uint, Polyline>();
    Random rand = new Random();
    byte[] rgb = new byte[3];

    public MainPage()
    {
        this.InitializeComponent();
    }

    protected override void OnPointerPressed(PointerRoutedEventArgs args)
    {
        // Get information from event arguments
        uint id = args.Pointer.PointerId;
        Point point = args.GetCurrentPoint(this).Position;
```

```
        // Create random color
        rand.NextBytes(rgb);
        Color color = Color.FromArgb(255, rgb[0], rgb[1], rgb[2]);

        // Create Polyline
        Polyline polyline = new Polyline
        {
            Stroke = new SolidColorBrush(color),
            StrokeThickness = 24,
        };
        polyline.Points.Add(point);

        // Add to Grid
        contentGrid.Children.Add(polyline);

        // Add to dictionary
        pointerDictionary.Add(id, polyline);
        base.OnPointerPressed(args);
    }

    protected override void OnPointerMoved(PointerRoutedEventArgs args)
    {
        // Get information from event arguments
        uint id = args.Pointer.PointerId;
        Point point = args.GetCurrentPoint(this).Position;

        // If ID is in dictionary, add the point to the Polyline
        if (pointerDictionary.ContainsKey(id))
            pointerDictionary[id].Points.Add(point);

        base.OnPointerMoved(args);
    }

    protected override void OnPointerReleased(PointerRoutedEventArgs args)
    {
        // Get information from event arguments
        uint id = args.Pointer.PointerId;

        // If ID is in dictionary, remove it
        if (pointerDictionary.ContainsKey(id))
            pointerDictionary.Remove(id);

        base.OnPointerReleased(args);
    }
}
```

In the *OnPointerPressed* override, the program creates a *Polyline* and gives it a random color. The first point is the location of the pointer. The *Polyline* is added to the *Grid* and also to the dictionary.

When subsequent *OnPointerMoved* calls occur, the *PointerId* property identifies the finger, so the particular *Polyline* associated with that finger can be accessed from the dictionary and the new *Point* value can be added to the *Polyline*. Because it's the same instance as the *Polyline* in the *Grid*, the on-screen object will seem to grow in length as the finger moves.

The *OnPointerReleased* processing simply removes the entry from the dictionary. That particular *Polyline* is completed.

When you run the program, of course the first thing you'll want to do is sweep your whole hand across the screen like the glaciers that created the Finger Lakes in upstate New York.

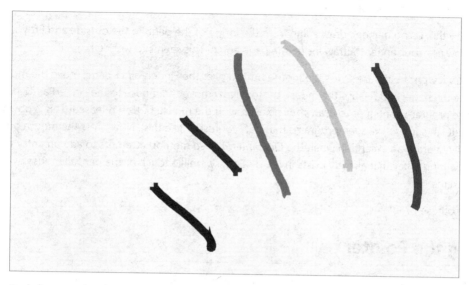

Each finger paints its own polyline as a single series of connected points of a particular color, and you'll discover that you can use the mouse and pen as well.

I mentioned that this code has a flaw. The *OnPointerMoved* and *OnPointerReleased* overrides are very careful to check that the particular ID exists as a key in the dictionary before using it to access the dictionary. This is very important for mouse and pen processing because these devices generate *PointerMoved* events prior to *OnPointerPressed*.

But try this: Put the program in a snap mode, and with your finger, draw a line that goes outside the page and then back in.

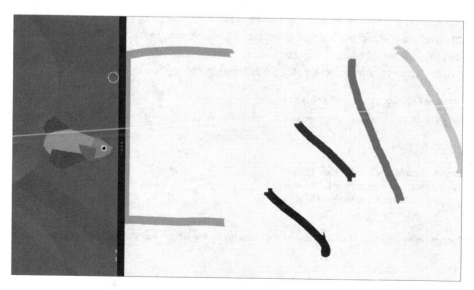

Look at that straight line down the left side. That line is drawn when the finger reenters the page, and it indicates that the program doesn't get *PointerMoved* events during the time the finger strays outside. Try it with the mouse. Same thing.

Now try this: Using a finger, draw a line from the inside of the page to the outside and lift your finger. Now use your finger to draw inside the page again. This seems to work OK.

Now try it with the mouse. Press the mouse button over the FingerPaint1 page, move the mouse to outside the page, and release the mouse button. Now move the mouse to the FingerPaint1 page again. The program continues to draw the line even with the mouse button released! This is obviously wrong (but I'm sure you've seen programs that get "confused" like this). Now press the mouse button, and you'll generate an exception when the *OnPointerPressed* method attempts to add an entry to the dictionary using a key that already exists in the dictionary. Unlike touch or the pen, all mouse events have the same ID.

Let's fix these problems.

Capturing the Pointer

To allow me (and you) to get a better sense of the sequence of *Pointer* events, I wrote a program called PointerLog that logs all the *Pointer* events on the screen. The core of the program is a *UserControl* called *LoggerControl*. The *Grid* in the LoggerControl.xaml file has been given a name but is otherwise initially empty:

Project: PointerLog | File: LoggerControl.xaml (excerpt)

```
<UserControl ... >

    <Grid Name="contentGrid" Background="Transparent" />

</UserControl>
```

The code-behind file has overrides of all eight *Pointer* methods, all of which call a method named *Log* with the event name and event arguments. Like all *Pointer* programs, a *Dictionary* is defined, but the values in this one are not simple objects. Instead, I defined a nested class named *PointerInfo* right at the top of the *LoggerControl* class for storing per-finger information in this dictionary.

Project: PointerLog | File: LoggerControl.xaml.cs (excerpt)

```
public sealed partial class LoggerControl : UserControl
{
    class PointerInfo
    {
        public StackPanel stackPanel;
        public string repeatEvent;
        public TextBlock repeatTextBlock;
    };

    Dictionary<uint, PointerInfo> pointerDictionary = new Dictionary<uint, PointerInfo>();
```

```csharp
public LoggerControl()
{
    this.InitializeComponent();
}

public bool CaptureOnPress { set; get; }

protected override void OnPointerEntered(PointerRoutedEventArgs args)
{
    Log("Entered", args);
    base.OnPointerEntered(args);
}

protected override void OnPointerPressed(PointerRoutedEventArgs args)
{
    if (this.CaptureOnPress)
        CapturePointer(args.Pointer);

    Log("Pressed", args);
    base.OnPointerPressed(args);
}

protected override void OnPointerMoved(PointerRoutedEventArgs args)
{
    Log("Moved", args);
    base.OnPointerMoved(args);
}

protected override void OnPointerReleased(PointerRoutedEventArgs args)
{
    Log("Released", args);
    base.OnPointerReleased(args);
}

protected override void OnPointerExited(PointerRoutedEventArgs args)
{
    Log("Exited", args);
    base.OnPointerExited(args);
}

protected override void OnPointerCaptureLost(PointerRoutedEventArgs args)
{
    Log("CaptureLost", args);
    base.OnPointerCaptureLost(args);
}

protected override void OnPointerCanceled(PointerRoutedEventArgs args)
{
    Log("Canceled", args);
    base.OnPointerCanceled(args);
}

protected override void OnPointerWheelChanged(PointerRoutedEventArgs args)
{
    Log("WheelChanged", args);
    base.OnPointerWheelChanged(args);
}
```

```
void Log(string eventName, PointerRoutedEventArgs args)
{
    uint id = args.Pointer.PointerId;
    PointerInfo pointerInfo;

    if (pointerDictionary.ContainsKey(id))
    {
        pointerInfo = pointerDictionary[id];
    }
    else
    {
        // New ID, so new StackPanel and header
        TextBlock header = new TextBlock
        {
            Text = args.Pointer.PointerId + " - " + args.Pointer.PointerDeviceType,
            FontWeight = FontWeights.Bold
        };
        StackPanel stackPanel = new StackPanel();
        stackPanel.Children.Add(header);

        // New PointerInfo for dictionary
        pointerInfo = new PointerInfo
        {
            stackPanel = stackPanel
        };
        pointerDictionary.Add(id, pointerInfo);

        // New column in the Grid for the StackPanel
        ColumnDefinition coldef = new ColumnDefinition
        {
            Width = new GridLength(1, GridUnitType.Star)
        };
        contentGrid.ColumnDefinitions.Add(coldef);
        Grid.SetColumn(stackPanel, contentGrid.ColumnDefinitions.Count - 1);
        contentGrid.Children.Add(stackPanel);
    }

    // Don't repeat PointerMoved and PointerWheelChanged events
    TextBlock txtblk = null;

    if (eventName == pointerInfo.repeatEvent)
    {
        txtblk = pointerInfo.repeatTextBlock;
    }
    else
    {
        txtblk = new TextBlock();
        pointerInfo.stackPanel.Children.Add(txtblk);
    }

    txtblk.Text = eventName + " ";

    if (eventName == "WheelChanged")
    {
        txtblk.Text += args.GetCurrentPoint(this).Properties.MouseWheelDelta;
```

```
        }
        else
        {
            txtblk.Text += args.GetCurrentPoint(this).Position;
        }

        txtblk.Text += args.Pointer.IsInContact ? " C" : "";
        txtblk.Text += args.Pointer.IsInRange ? " R" : "";

        if (eventName == "Moved" || eventName == "WheelChanged")
        {
            pointerInfo.repeatEvent = eventName;
            pointerInfo.repeatTextBlock = txtblk;
        }
        else
        {
            pointerInfo.repeatEvent = null;
            pointerInfo.repeatTextBlock = null;
        }
    }

    public void Clear()
    {
        contentGrid.ColumnDefinitions.Clear();
        contentGrid.Children.Clear();
        pointerDictionary.Clear();
    }
}
```

The *Log* method seems rather complicated, but every time it encounters a new *PointerId* value in the event arguments, it adds a new column to the *Grid*, puts a *TextBlock* at the top indicating the ID and device type, and adds an entry to the dictionary. All subsequent events with that ID go in that column, except that consecutive *PointerMoved* and *PointerWheelChanged* events don't get extra entries. There's no scrolling facility and eventually there will be too many columns, but a public *Clear* method restores everything to a pristine condition.

The *LoggerControl* only gets *Pointer* events for that control. To ease the examination of what happens when fingers move between controls, I made *LoggerControl* part of a larger page with the program name at the top and three buttons at the bottom:

Project: PointerLog | File: MainPage.xaml (excerpt)

```
<Grid Background="{StaticResource ApplicationPageBackgroundThemeBrush}">
    <Grid.RowDefinitions>
        <RowDefinition Height="Auto" />
        <RowDefinition Height="*" />
        <RowDefinition Height="Auto" />
    </Grid.RowDefinitions>

    <TextBlock Text="Pointer Event Log"
               Grid.Row="0"
               Style="{StaticResource HeaderTextStyle}"
```

```xaml
                        HorizontalAlignment="Center"
                        Margin="12" />

    <local:LoggerControl x:Name="logger"
                         Grid.Row="1"
                         FontSize="{StaticResource ControlContentThemeFontSize}" />


    <Grid Grid.Row="2">
        <Grid.ColumnDefinitions>
            <ColumnDefinition Width="*" />
            <ColumnDefinition Width="*" />
            <ColumnDefinition Width="*" />
        </Grid.ColumnDefinitions>

        <Button Content="Clear"
                Grid.Column="0"
                HorizontalAlignment="Center"
                Click="OnClearButtonClick" />

        <ToggleButton Name="captureButton"
                      Content="Capture on Press"
                      Grid.Column="1"
                      HorizontalAlignment="Center"
                      Checked="OnCaptureToggleButtonChecked"
                      Unchecked="OnCaptureToggleButtonChecked" />

        <Button Content="Release Captures in 5 seconds"
                Grid.Column="2"
                IsEnabled="{Binding ElementName=captureButton, Path=IsChecked}"
                HorizontalAlignment="Center"
                Click="OnReleaseCapturesButtonClick" />
    </Grid>
</Grid>
```

Notice the final *Button* is enabled only when the *ToggleButton* is toggled on.

The code-behind file just handles the buttons (which I'll discuss shortly):

Project: PointerLog | File: MainPage.xaml.cs (excerpt)

```csharp
public sealed partial class MainPage : Page
{
    DispatcherTimer timer;

    public MainPage()
    {
        this.InitializeComponent();
        timer = new DispatcherTimer { Interval = TimeSpan.FromSeconds(5) };
        timer.Tick += OnTimerTick;
    }

    void OnClearButtonClick(object sender, RoutedEventArgs args)
    {
        logger.Clear();
    }

    void OnCaptureToggleButtonChecked(object sender, RoutedEventArgs args)
```

```
    {
        ToggleButton toggle = sender as ToggleButton;
        logger.CaptureOnPress = toggle.IsChecked.Value;
    }

    void OnReleaseCapturesButtonClick(object sender, RoutedEventArgs args)
    {
        timer.Start();
    }

    void OnTimerTick(object sender, object args)
    {
        logger.ReleasePointerCaptures();
        timer.Stop();
    }
}
```

You can see from the screen that each new finger press gets a unique ID and generates only five events. Each new series of pen events also gets its own ID (using the same numbering sequence as touch) with a few more events. The mouse always has an ID of 1:

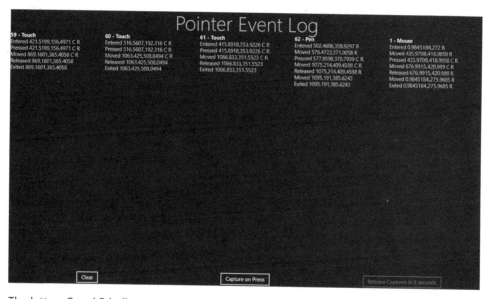

The letters C and R indicate *true* values of the *IsInContact* and *IsInRange* properties of the *Pointer* object. As you can see, for the pen and mouse you can use the *IsInRange* property to distinguish between *PointerMoved* events that occur when the pen is touching the screen or when the mouse button is pressed.

By default, an element gets *Pointer* input only when the pointer is within the boundaries of the element. This can sometimes result in a loss of information. To demonstrate this, I deliberately designed the program so that *LoggerControl* does not extend to the full height of the screen. Above it is an area for the program title, and below is the button area. These areas are the domain of *MainPage*. This configuration allows you to experiment with input that moves from one element to another.

For example, touch the PointerLog screen somewhere in the middle, move your finger around, and then move the finger to the top title area or the bottom button area. Lift it off the screen. The program does not receive that *PointerReleased* event, and it has no idea that the pointer has been released. It will never get another event with that particular ID number, but it's living in a state of ignorance. The entry in the dictionary is never removed.

Similarly, touch the screen in the top or bottom area and move your finger to the central area. The program registers *PointerEntered* and *PointerMoved* events but not a *PointerPressed* event.

Often while tracking a particular pointer, you want to continue getting input even if it drifts outside the element. Not getting that pointer input accounts for the flaws in the FingerPaint1 program.

You can get what you want with a process called "capturing the pointer," which you do with a call to the *CapturePointer* method defined by *UIElement*. The method has an argument of type *Pointer* and returns a *bool* indicating if the pointer capture has been successful. When will it not be successful? If you call *CapturePointer* during an event prior to *PointerPressed* or during *PointerReleased* or later.

For this reason—and for the sake of program politeness—it really only makes sense to call *CapturePointer* during a *PointerPressed* event. By pressing a finger (or pen or mouse button) on a particular element, the user is generally indicating a desire to interact with that element even if the finger sometimes drifts outside the element.

If you toggle on the "Capture on Press" button at the bottom of the PointerLog screen, the program calls

```
CapturePointer(args.Pointer);
```

during the *OnPointerPressed* override.

Now if you press in the central area of the PointerLog program, move your finger to the top or bottom, and then release, the program logs the *PointerReleased* event as well as a final *PointerCaptureLost* event following *PointerExited*.

A program can get a list of all the captured pointers with a call to *PointerCaptures* and release a particular capture with a *ReleasePointerCapture* call or release all pointer captures with *ReleasePointerCaptures*.

In a real-life application it is tempting to simply ignore the *PointerCaptureLost* event, but it's not a good idea. If Windows needs to communicate something urgent to the user, it's possible that pointer capture will be snatched from a program involuntarily. I have not actually seen this happen under Windows 8, but historically it occurs upon the display of a system modal dialog box—a dialog box that considers itself so important that it gets all user input until it's dismissed.

To demonstrate what happens in such a case, I've defined the third button to set a *DispatcherTimer* for five seconds and then conclude by calling *ReleasePointerCaptures* for the *LoggerControl*. When that happens, a pointer that has been captured fires a *PointerCaptureLost* event. The element continues to receive other *Pointer* events if the pointer is still over the element but not if it drifts outside the element.

What an application should do when it receives an unexpected *PointerCaptureLost* depends on the application. For a finger-paint program you might want to move *PointerReleased* logic into *PointerCaptureLost*, for example, and treat both expected and unexpected losses of capture as the same.

Or, it might make sense to entirely discard that particular drawing event.

In fact, you might want to build this feature into your program. Suppose you decide that the user should be able to press the Esc key to jettison a drawing event that's in progress. You could then implement Esc-key processing with a simple call to *ReleasePointerCaptures*.

The FingerPaint2 program does precisely that. The XAML file is the same as FingerPaint1, and so is the code-behind file with the following exceptions:

Project: FingerPaint2 | File: MainPage.xaml.cs (excerpt)

```
public sealed partial class MainPage : Page
{
    ...
    public MainPage()
    {
        this.InitializeComponent();
        this.IsTabStop = true;
    }

    protected override void OnPointerPressed(PointerRoutedEventArgs args)
    {
        ...
        // Capture the Pointer
        CapturePointer(args.Pointer);

        // Set input focus
        Focus(FocusState.Programmatic);

        base.OnPointerPressed(args);
    }
    ...
    protected override void OnPointerCaptureLost(PointerRoutedEventArgs args)
    {
        // Get information from event arguments
        uint id = args.Pointer.PointerId;

        // If ID is in dictionary, abandon the drawing operation
        if (pointerDictionary.ContainsKey(id))
        {
            contentGrid.Children.Remove(pointerDictionary[id]);
            pointerDictionary.Remove(id);
        }

        base.OnPointerCaptureLost(args);
    }
```

```
protected override void OnKeyDown(KeyRoutedEventArgs args)
{
    if (args.Key == VirtualKey.Escape)
        ReleasePointerCaptures();

    base.OnKeyDown(args);
}
}
```

In the constructor, the *IsTabStop* property must be set to *true* for the element to receive keyboard input. Only one element can receive keyboard input at any time. This is called the element with keyboard "focus," and some controls indicate they have keyboard focus with a special appearance, such as a dotted line. Often an element can give itself keyboard focus by calling the *Focus* method when the element is tapped or (in this case) during the *OnPointerPressed* event. That override concludes its processing by calling the *Focus* method as well as *CapturePointer*.

The *OnPointerCaptureLost* method removes the *Polyline* in progress from the *Grid* and removes the ID from the dictionary. However, the *PointerCaptureLost* event can occur normally after a finger has been released from the screen, so this ID will still be in the dictionary only if the page didn't get a call to *OnPointerReleased*.

The *OnKeyDown* method gets keystrokes and calls *ReleasePointerCaptures* for Esc. This call has no effect if no pointers are captured.

Try the problematic actions identified with the FingerPaint1, and you'll find that they're gone in this version. Moreover, now you can be drawing on the screen and press Esc, and what you're currently drawing will disappear and the finger will have no further effect until it's released and pressed again. (Let's hope that's what you want.)

Editing with a Popup Menu

Let's add an editing feature to this program. If you click an existing *Polyline* with the right mouse button—or you do something equivalent with a finger or pen—a little menu pops up with the options "Change color" and "Delete."

In the previous two FingerPaint programs, the *Polyline* was created, initialized, and added to the content *Grid* and touch dictionary like so:

```
// Create Polyline
Polyline polyline = new Polyline
{
    Stroke = new SolidColorBrush(color),
    StrokeThickness = 24,
};
polyline.Points.Add(point);

// Add to Grid
contentGrid.Children.Add(polyline);

// Add to dictionary
pointerDictionary.Add(id, polyline);
```

For FingerPaint3 let's add some additional code that sets two event handlers on this *Polyline*. The goal here is to use the handler for the *RightTapped* event of the *Polyline* to display a popup menu:

Project: FingerPaint3 | File: MainPage.xaml.cs (excerpt)

```
protected override void OnPointerPressed(PointerRoutedEventArgs args)
{
    ...
    // Create Polyline
    Polyline polyline = new Polyline
    {
        Stroke = new SolidColorBrush(color),
        StrokeThickness = 24,
    };
    polyline.PointerPressed += OnPolylinePointerPressed;
    polyline.RightTapped += OnPolylineRightTapped;
    polyline.Points.Add(point);
    ...
}
```

Although we're interested only in the *RightTapped* event for the *Polyline*, I've also set a handler for the *PointerPressed* event. That handler is not very interesting, but it's very important:

Project: FingerPaint3 | File: MainPage.xaml.cs (excerpt)

```
void OnPolylinePointerPressed(object sender, PointerRoutedEventArgs args)
{
    args.Handled = true;
}
```

You'll definitely want to try this program without this particular handler, and here's why: When a *PointerPressed* event is fired, that event is associated with the topmost element that is enabled for user input. If you're clicking or right-clicking a *Polyline* rather than the surface of *MainPage*, the *PointerPressed* event is fired for that *Polyline*.

However, *PointerPressed* is a routed event, and you'll recall from Chapter 3, "Basic Event Handling," that routed events travel up the visual tree, which means that if the *Polyline* isn't interested in this event, it will go to *MainPage*, which will assume that you want to begin drawing a new figure. To prevent that from happening in this program, the *Polyline* handles the *PointerPressed* event by setting the *Handled* property on the event arguments to *true*. This prevents the event from reaching *MainPage*.

The popup menu logic occurs in the *RightTapped* event:

Project: FingerPaint3 | File: MainPage.xaml.cs (excerpt)

```
async void OnPolylineRightTapped(object sender, RightTappedRoutedEventArgs args)
{
    Polyline polyline = sender as Polyline;
    PopupMenu popupMenu = new PopupMenu();
    popupMenu.Commands.Add(new UICommand("Change color", OnMenuChangeColor, polyline));
    popupMenu.Commands.Add(new UICommand("Delete", OnMenuDelete, polyline));
    await popupMenu.ShowAsync(args.GetPosition(this));
}
```

As I demonstrated in Chapter 8, "App Bars and Popups," it's fairly easy to use *PopupMenu*. After creating the object, you can add up to six items to the menu. Each item consists of a text label, a callback, and an optional object to help the callback identify the event. The *ShowAsync* method displays the menu at a particular location.

The handlers can obtain that last argument passed to the *UICommand* constructor by casting the *Id* property of the callback method's *IUICommand* argument:

Project: FingerPaint3 | **File:** MainPage.xaml.cs (excerpt)

```
void OnMenuChangeColor(IUICommand command)
{
    Polyline polyline = command.Id as Polyline;
    rand.NextBytes(rgb);
    Color color = Color.FromArgb(255, rgb[0], rgb[1], rgb[2]);
    (polyline.Stroke as SolidColorBrush).Color = color;
}

void OnMenuDelete(IUICommand command)
{
    Polyline polyline = command.Id as Polyline;
    contentGrid.Children.Remove(polyline);
}
```

I'm sure you already know how to use the mouse to right-click a *Polyline*. With touch, you'll need to hold your finger steady on a *Polyline* for a moment, and then release. You'll see a square form when you've held long enough. Similarly with a pen, hold it until you see a circle form, and then release. The menu appears:

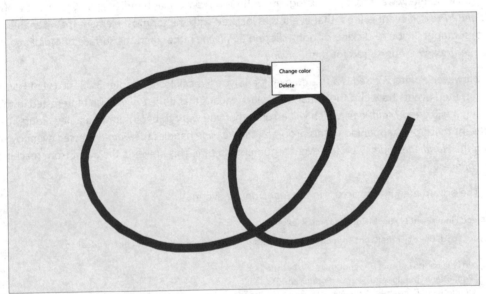

The square and circle you see when you hold your finger or the pen to the screen are actually associated with the *Holding* event. If you set the *IsHoldingEnabled* property on the *Polyline* to *false*, they won't appear and the user might be a little uncertain how long to press. The *RightTapped* event isn't fired until the user lifts the finger or pen from the screen.

The *OnMenuDelete* method in FingerPaint3 actually has a subtle bug. If one finger is drawing a line while another finger invokes the menu for that line, *OnMenuDelete* removes the *Polyline* from the screen but not the dictionary entry with that *Polyline*. Nothing bad will happen, but the dictionary might accumulate some abandoned entries. Logic to fix this would have to search through the dictionary for the deleted *Polyline* and then remove the key for that entry.

As I demonstrated with routed events in Chapter 3, whenever you're dealing with events generated by different elements, you can structure your event handling in various ways. For example, an *OnPointerPressed* override in *MainPage* can incorporate the logic that I put in *OnPolylinePointerPressed*, and you can perform all the *RightTapped* handling in an *OnRightTapped* override. All you need do is check the *OriginalSource* property on the event arguments to determine whether the input is coming from the *Polyline* or *MainPage*.

The program now has a little drawback. You can't draw a new line if you want to begin that line on a point occupied by an existing line. Any *PointerPressed* event received by the *Polyline* is flagged as *Handled* and essentially discarded.

What if you wanted to give the user both options? If the user presses an existing *Polyline* and starts moving, a new figure is started. If the user presses and holds, that's a menu.

Probably the easiest approach is abandoning the use of the *RightTapped* event and handling everything through the *Pointer* logic. When *OnPointerPressed* occurs on an existing *Polyline*, set a *DispatcherTimer* for one second, but cancel that timer (and start a drawing operation) if *OnPointerMoved* occurs, indicating that the finger has moved a distance greater than some preset criteria. If the timer fires, display the menu.

Pressure Sensitivity

The lines drawn by the various FingerPaint programs are of a uniform stroke thickness—24 pixels to be precise—but some touch devices can differentiate heavier touches from lighter touches, and a really good FingerPaint program would respond by varying the stroke thickness.

There are two properties that might influence line thickness in a finger-painting program, and both are defined by the *PointerPointProperties* object returned from the *Properties* property of the *PointerPoint* class (which in turn is obtained by a call to the *GetCurrentPoint* method of the *PointerRoutedEventArgs* event arguments).

The first property is *ContactRect*, a *Rect* value that is intended to report the rectangular bounding box of the contact area of a finger (or pen point) on the screen. This property will probably only apply to rather esoteric touch devices. On the tablet I've been using for most of this book, this *Rect* always has a *Width* and *Height* of zero regardless of the pointer device. On the first versions of the Microsoft Surface tablet, the *Width* and *Height* values are low-value integers, such as 1, 2, and 3, that don't seem as if they can be used for much. (But I might be wrong.)

The second property is *Pressure*, which is a *float* value that can take on values between 0 and 1. On the tablet I've been using for most of this book, this *Pressure* value is the default value of 0.5 for fingers and the mouse, but it is variable for the pen, and so I had the opportunity to try it out. (On the first versions of the Microsoft Surface tablet, the *Pressure* value is always 0.5.)

For purposes of simplicity, the FingerPaint4 program does not include Esc-key processing or the editing feature, but it does implement pointer capturing. The big difference is that the *Polyline* approach to drawing must be abandoned because a *Polyline* has only a single *StrokeThickness* property. In this new program each stroke must instead be composed of very short individual lines, each a unique *StrokeThickness* that is calculated from the *Pressure* value, but all the same color. This implies that the dictionary needs to contain values of type *Color* (or better yet, a *Brush*) and the previous *Point*. This is now two items, so let's define a custom structure for that purpose that I called *PointerInfo*:

Project: FingerPaint4 | File: MainPage.xaml.cs (excerpt)

```csharp
public sealed partial class MainPage : Page
{
    struct PointerInfo
    {
        public Brush Brush;
        public Point PreviousPoint;
    }

    Dictionary<uint, PointerInfo> pointerDictionary = new Dictionary<uint, PointerInfo>();
    Random rand = new Random();
    byte[] rgb = new byte[3];

    public MainPage()
    {
        this.InitializeComponent();
    }

    protected override void OnPointerPressed(PointerRoutedEventArgs args)
    {
        // Get information from event arguments
        uint id = args.Pointer.PointerId;
        Point point = args.GetCurrentPoint(this).Position;

        // Create random color
        rand.NextBytes(rgb);
        Color color = Color.FromArgb(255, rgb[0], rgb[1], rgb[2]);

        // Create PointerInfo
        PointerInfo pointerInfo = new PointerInfo
        {
            PreviousPoint = point,
            Brush = new SolidColorBrush(color)
        };
```

```
        // Add to dictionary
        pointerDictionary.Add(id, pointerInfo);

        // Capture the Pointer
        CapturePointer(args.Pointer);

        base.OnPointerPressed(args);
    }

    ...

    protected override void OnPointerReleased(PointerRoutedEventArgs args)
    {
        // Get information from event arguments
        uint id = args.Pointer.PointerId;

        // If ID is in dictionary, remove it
        if (pointerDictionary.ContainsKey(id))
            pointerDictionary.Remove(id);

        base.OnPointerReleased(args);
    }

    protected override void OnPointerCaptureLost(PointerRoutedEventArgs args)
    {
        // Get information from event arguments
        uint id = args.Pointer.PointerId;

        // If ID is still in dictionary, remove it
        if (pointerDictionary.ContainsKey(id))
            pointerDictionary.Remove(id);

        base.OnPointerCaptureLost(args);
    }
}
```

The earlier *PointerPressed* handlers created a *Polyline*, gave it an initial point, and added it to the *Grid* and *Dictionary*. In this program, only a *PointerInfo* value is created and added to the dictionary. Much more work occurs in the *PointerMoved* handler, particularly because I've also decided to use *GetIntermediatePoints* rather than *GetCurrentPoint*, resulting (at least theoretically) in smoother strokes on the Microsoft Surface. But one oddity I discovered is that these points are in the collection in reverse order!

This code loops through the points. For each new point and the previous point, a *Line* element is constructed and added to the *Grid*. The last point then replaces the previous point in the *PointerInfo* value:

Project: FingerPaint4 | File: MainPage.xaml.cs (excerpt)

```
protected override void OnPointerMoved(PointerRoutedEventArgs args)
{
    // Get ID from event arguments
    uint id = args.Pointer.PointerId;

    // If ID is in dictionary, start a loop
    if (pointerDictionary.ContainsKey(id))
    {
        PointerInfo pointerInfo = pointerDictionary[id];
        IList<PointerPoint> pointerpoints = args.GetIntermediatePoints(this);

        for (int i = pointerpoints.Count - 1; i >= 0; i--)
        {
            PointerPoint pointerPoint = pointerpoints[i];

            // For each point, create a new Line element and add to Grid
            Point point = pointerPoint.Position;
            float pressure = pointerPoint.Properties.Pressure;

            Line line = new Line
            {
                X1 = pointerInfo.PreviousPoint.X,
                Y1 = pointerInfo.PreviousPoint.Y,
                X2 = point.X,
                Y2 = point.Y,
                Stroke = pointerInfo.Brush,
                StrokeThickness = pressure * 24,
                StrokeStartLineCap = PenLineCap.Round,
                StrokeEndLineCap = PenLineCap.Round
            };
            contentGrid.Children.Add(line);

            // Update PointerInfo
            pointerInfo.PreviousPoint = point;
        }
        // Store PointerInfo back in dictionary
        pointerDictionary[id] = pointerInfo;
    }
    base.OnPointerMoved(args);
}
```

Notice that the *StrokeThickness* is set to 24 times the *Pressure* value. This results in a maximum stroke thickness of 24 and a stroke thickness of 12 for non-pressure-sensitive devices. Notice also that the *StrokeStartLineCap* and *StrokeEndLineCap* properties are set to *Round*. Try commenting out these property settings and see what happens when a stroke has sharp turns: Little gaps appear because two short lines are at an angle to each other. The line caps cover those gaps.

Here's a little, umm, artwork I did entirely with the pen:

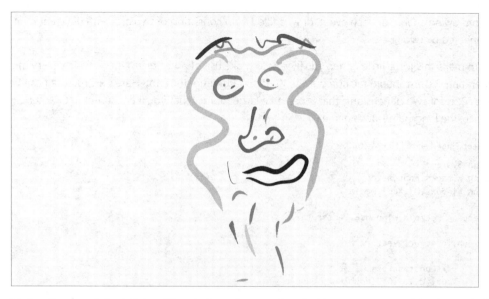

Notice the graceful subtlety of the strokes when rendered with a pressure-sensitive input device.

It is my experience that *PointerMoved* events can be fired as quickly as 100 times per second, which is faster than the frame rate of the video display but not quite fast enough for extremely energetic fingers.

Smoothing the Tapers

Have you ever noticed that solving one problem often reveals another problem? To my mind, allowing for pressure sensitivity is an important feature in a finger-painting program. Yet, if you draw something very fast with a pressure-sensitive pen in FingerPaint4, you might notice that lines don't seem to taper correctly. Instead, they increase or decrease in size with discrete jumps:

Well, of course. Each of those pieces in the lower-right portion of that squiggle is a separate *Line* element with its own *StrokeThickness*. I drew the squiggle with such speed that the pressure varied considerably between each event, which made the thickness jump in visible discontinuities.

If you consider that a particular *Line* element can have only one constant *StrokeThickness*, it might seem difficult to fix this problem. But the solution is actually quite easy (at least conceptually): Rather than drawing a *Line* for each event, draw a filled *Path* consisting of two arcs with different radii connected by two lines.

To make this job a little easier, you'll want to make use of a *Vector* structure, which every modern operating system should include but the Windows Runtime does not. Here's a structure I call *Vector2* (the "2" is for two dimensions) that is part of a larger library that you'll encounter in Chapter 14. Hence, the long namespace name:

Project: FingerPaint5 | File: Vector2.cs

```
using System;
using Windows.Foundation;
using Windows.UI.Xaml.Media;

namespace Petzold.Windows8.VectorDrawing
{
    public struct Vector2
    {
        // Constructors
        public Vector2(double x, double y)
            : this()
        {
            X = x;
            Y = y;
        }

        public Vector2(Point p)
            : this()
        {
            X = p.X;
            Y = p.Y;
        }

        public Vector2(double angle)
            : this()
        {
            X = Math.Cos(Math.PI * angle / 180);
            Y = Math.Sin(Math.PI * angle / 180);
        }

        // Properties
        public double X { private set; get; }
        public double Y { private set; get; }

        public double LengthSquared
        {
            get { return X * X + Y * Y; }
        }

        public double Length
        {
            get { return Math.Sqrt(LengthSquared); }
        }

        public Vector2 Normalized
```

```csharp
{
    get
    {
        double length = this.Length;

        if (length != 0)
        {
            return new Vector2(this.X / length,
                               this.Y / length);
        }
        return new Vector2();
    }
}

// Methods
public Vector2 Rotate(double angle)
{
    RotateTransform xform = new RotateTransform { Angle = angle };
    Point pt = xform.TransformPoint(new Point(X, Y));
    return new Vector2(pt.X, pt.Y);
}

// Static methods
public static double AngleBetween(Vector2 v1, Vector2 v2)
{
    return 180 * (Math.Atan2(v2.Y, v2.X) - Math.Atan2(v1.Y, v1.X)) / Math.PI;
}

// Operators
public static Vector2 operator +(Vector2 v1, Vector2 v2)
{
    return new Vector2(v1.X + v2.X, v1.Y + v2.Y);
}

public static Point operator +(Vector2 v, Point p)
{
    return new Point(v.X + p.X, v.Y + p.Y);
}

public static Point operator +(Point p, Vector2 v)
{
    return new Point(v.X + p.X, v.Y + p.Y);
}

public static Vector2 operator -(Vector2 v1, Vector2 v2)
{
    return new Vector2(v1.X - v2.X, v1.Y - v2.Y);
}

public static Point operator -(Point p, Vector2 v)
{
    return new Point(p.X - v.X, p.Y - v.Y);
}

public static Vector2 operator *(Vector2 v, double d)
{
    return new Vector2(d * v.X, d * v.Y);
}
}
```

```csharp
        public static Vector2 operator *(double d, Vector2 v)
        {
            return new Vector2(d * v.X, d * v.Y);
        }

        public static Vector2 operator /(Vector2 v, double d)
        {
            return new Vector2(v.X / d, v.Y / d);
        }

        public static Vector2 operator -(Vector2 v)
        {
            return new Vector2(-v.X, -v.Y);
        }

        public static explicit operator Point(Vector2 v)
        {
            return new Point(v.X, v.Y);
        }

        // Overrides
        public override string ToString()
        {
            return String.Format("({0} {1})", X, Y);
        }
    }
}
```

FingerPaint5 saves the previous radius (based on the pressure setting) along with the previous point. In this diagram, I've represented two consecutive finger locations as circles with independent radii. The smaller circle has a center $c0$ and radius $r0$, and the larger circle has a center $c1$ and radius $r1$:

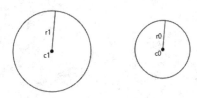

The goal here is to derive a *Path* that encompasses those two circles and the area between them. To do this, we must connect the two circles with lines that are tangent to both circles, and that's a little tricky (mathematically speaking). Let's first connect the centers of the two circles with a line labeled d:

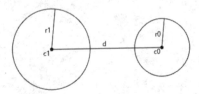

A *Vector2* value lets us obtain the length of that line and a normalized vector representing its direction:

```
Vector2 vCenters = new Vector2(c0) - new Vector2(c1);
double d = vCenters.Length;
vCenters = vCenters.Normalized;
```

Now let's define another length named *e* based on *d* and the radii of the two circles. The point *F* is *e* distance from *c0* and in the same direction as the vector between the two centers:

```
double e = d * r0 / (r1 - r0);
Point F = c0 + e * vCenters;
```

Here it is:

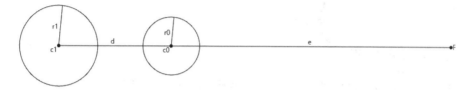

I called that point *F* because I think of it as a "focal point." I contend that there exist lines from *F* that are tangent to both circles, meaning a right angle is formed with that line and a radius line:

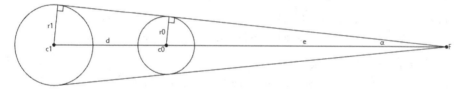

I know this because of the way that *e* was defined. The ratio of *e* to *r0* is the same as the ratio of *d* plus *e* to *r1*. That angle α (toward the right of the figure) is simply calculated like so:

```
double alpha = 180 * Math.Asin(r0 / e) / Math.PI;
```

If the argument to the *Math.Asin* method is greater than 1, the method returns NaN (not a number). This can happen only if *r0* plus *d* is less than *r1*—that is, if the smaller circle is entirely enclosed in the larger circle. That makes this problem easy to anticipate.

The lengths of those triangle legs from *F* to the tangent points can be calculated with the Pythagorean theorem:

```
double leg0 = Math.Sqrt(e * e - r0 * r0);
double leg1 = Math.Sqrt((e + d) * (e + d) - r1 * r1);
```

The *Vector2* structure has a convenient *Rotate* method that allows us to rotate the *vCenters* vector by α and $-\alpha$ degrees:

```
Vector2 vRight = -vCenters.Rotate(alpha);
Vector2 vLeft = -vCenters.Rotate(-alpha);
```

The "right" and "left" parts of the variable names are from the perspective of *F*. In the diagram, the *vRight* vector corresponds to the tangent line on the top of the circles, and *vLeft* to the bottom. The vectors and the lengths allow us to calculate the actual tangent points:

```
Point t0R = F + leg0 * vRight;
Point t0L = F + leg0 * vLeft;
Point t1R = F + leg1 * vRight;
Point t1L = F + leg1 * vLeft;
```

These points can then be used to construct a *PathGeometry* that consists of two *ArcSegment* objects and two *LineSegment* objects, shown here as a heavy outline:

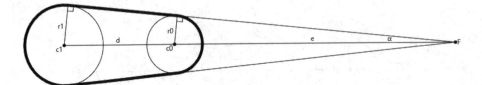

Notice that the *ArcSegment* on the smaller circle is always less than 180 degrees and the *ArcSegment* on the larger circle is always greater than 180 degrees. These characteristics affect the *IsLargeArc* property of *ArcSegment*. Also keep in mind that one of the two *LineSegment* objects can be created implicitly by specifying that the figure should be closed.

Here's the actual algorithm defined in FingerPaint5. Notice that it also must implement the relatively simpler case where the two radii are the same, or where one circle is enclosed in the other:

Project: FingerPaint5 | File: MainPage.xaml.cs (excerpt)

```
Geometry CreateTaperedLineGeometry(Point c0, double r0, Point c1, double r1)
{
    // Swap the centers and radii so that c0 is
    //       the center of the smaller circle.
    if (r1 < r0)
    {
        Point point = c0;
        c0 = c1;
        c1 = point;

        double radius = r0;
        r0 = r1;
        r1 = radius;
    }

    // Get vector from c1 to c0
    Vector2 vCenters = new Vector2(c0) - new Vector2(c1);

    // Get length and normalized version
    double d = vCenters.Length;
    vCenters = vCenters.Normalized;

    // Determine if one circle is enclosed in the other
    bool enclosed = r0 + d < r1;
```

```csharp
// Define tangent points derived in both algorithms
Point t0R = new Point();
Point t0L = new Point();
Point t1R = new Point();
Point t1L = new Point();

// Case for two circles of same size
if (r0 == r1 || enclosed)
{
    // Rotate centers vector 90 degrees
    Vector2 vLeft = new Vector2(-vCenters.Y, vCenters.X);

    // Rotate -90 degrees
    Vector2 vRight = -vLeft;

    // Find tangent points
    t0R = c0 + r0 * vRight;
    t0L = c0 + r0 * vLeft;
    t1R = c1 + r1 * vRight;
    t1L = c1 + r1 * vLeft;
}
// A bit more difficult for two circles of unequal size
else
{
    // Create focal point F extending from c0
    double e = d * r0 / (r1 - r0);
    Point F = c0 + e * vCenters;

    // Find angle and length of right-triangle legs
    double alpha = 180 * Math.Asin(r0 / e) / Math.PI;
    double leg0 = Math.Sqrt(e * e - r0 * r0);
    double leg1 = Math.Sqrt((e + d) * (e + d) - r1 * r1);

    // Vectors of tangent lines
    Vector2 vRight = -vCenters.Rotate(alpha);
    Vector2 vLeft = -vCenters.Rotate(-alpha);

    // Find tangent points
    t0R = F + leg0 * vRight;
    t0L = F + leg0 * vLeft;
    t1R = F + leg1 * vRight;
    t1L = F + leg1 * vLeft;
}

// Create PathGeometry with implied closing line
PathGeometry pathGeometry = new PathGeometry();
PathFigure pathFigure = new PathFigure
{
    StartPoint = t0R,
    IsClosed = true,
    IsFilled = true
};
pathGeometry.Figures.Add(pathFigure);

// Arc around smaller circle
ArcSegment arc0Segment = new ArcSegment
```

```
    {
        Point = t0L,
        Size = new Size(r0, r0),
        SweepDirection = SweepDirection.Clockwise,
        IsLargeArc = false
    };
    pathFigure.Segments.Add(arc0Segment);

    // Line connecting smaller circle to larger circle
    LineSegment lineSegment = new LineSegment
    {
        Point = t1L
    };
    pathFigure.Segments.Add(lineSegment);

    // Arc around larger circle
    ArcSegment arc1Segment = new ArcSegment
    {
        Point = t1R,
        Size = new Size(r1, r1),
        SweepDirection = SweepDirection.Clockwise,
        IsLargeArc = true
    };
    pathFigure.Segments.Add(arc1Segment);

    return pathGeometry;
}
```

The remainder of FingerPaint5 should be entirely comprehensible at this point. The
OnPointerReleased and *OnPointerCaptureLost* overrides are the same as FingerPaint4. The internal
PointerInfo class now includes a *PreviousRadius* field:

Project: FingerPaint5 | File: MainPage.xaml.cs (excerpt)

```
public sealed partial class MainPage : Page
{
    struct PointerInfo
    {
        public Brush Brush;
        public Point PreviousPoint;
        public double PreviousRadius;
    }

    Dictionary<uint, PointerInfo> pointerDictionary = new Dictionary<uint, PointerInfo>();
    Random rand = new Random();
    byte[] rgb = new byte[3];

    public MainPage()
    {
        this.InitializeComponent();
    }

    protected override void OnPointerPressed(PointerRoutedEventArgs args)
    {
        // Get information from event arguments
        uint id = args.Pointer.PointerId;
        PointerPoint pointerPoint = args.GetCurrentPoint(this);
```

```
        // Create random color
        rand.NextBytes(rgb);
        Color color = Color.FromArgb(255, rgb[0], rgb[1], rgb[2]);

        // Create PointerInfo
        PointerInfo pointerInfo = new PointerInfo
        {
            PreviousPoint = pointerPoint.Position,
            PreviousRadius = 24 * pointerPoint.Properties.Pressure,
            Brush = new SolidColorBrush(color)
        };

        // Add to dictionary
        pointerDictionary.Add(id, pointerInfo);

        // Capture the Pointer
        CapturePointer(args.Pointer);
        base.OnPointerPressed(args);
    }

    protected override void OnPointerMoved(PointerRoutedEventArgs args)
    {
        // Get ID from event arguments
        uint id = args.Pointer.PointerId;

        // If ID is in dictionary, start a loop
        if (pointerDictionary.ContainsKey(id))
        {
            PointerInfo pointerInfo = pointerDictionary[id];
            IList<PointerPoint> pointerpoints = args.GetIntermediatePoints(this);

            for (int i = pointerpoints.Count - 1; i >= 0; i--)
            {
                PointerPoint pointerPoint = pointerpoints[i];

                // For each point, create a Path element and add to Grid
                Point point = pointerPoint.Position;
                float pressure = pointerPoint.Properties.Pressure;
                double radius = 24 * pressure;

                Geometry geometry =
                    CreateTaperedLineGeometry(pointerInfo.PreviousPoint,
                                              pointerInfo.PreviousRadius,
                                              point,
                                              radius);
                Path path = new Path
                {
                    Data = geometry,
                    Fill = pointerInfo.Brush
                };
                contentGrid.Children.Add(path);

                // Update PointerInfo
                pointerInfo.PreviousPoint = point;
                pointerInfo.PreviousRadius = radius;
            }
```

```
            // Store PointerInfo back in dictionary
            pointerDictionary[id] = pointerInfo;
        }
        base.OnPointerMoved(args);
    }

    protected override void OnPointerReleased(PointerRoutedEventArgs args)
    {
        ...
    }

    protected override void OnPointerCaptureLost(PointerRoutedEventArgs args)
    {
        ...
    }

    Geometry CreateTaperedLineGeometry(Point c0, double r0, Point c1, double r1)
    {
        ...
    }
}
```

And now when you draw even very quickly on a pressure-sensitive device, the lines taper smoothly instead of as discrete steps:

How Do I Save My Drawings?

None of the finger-painting programs has any facility to save the drawings, but how would you implement such a thing?

Each program draws by adding *Polyline* or *Line* or *Path* elements to a *Grid*. One way to save your drawing would be to access those objects and save all the points and other information in a file, perhaps in an XML format. You could then add a feature to load them back in and create new *Polyline* or *Line* or *Path* elements from this information.

But you might be more inclined to save a *bitmap* of your drawing. (Traditionally, "draw" programs work with vectors while "paint" programs work with bitmaps.) Indeed, it makes sense for a FingerPaint program to perform *all* its painting on a bitmap.

This is possible, but it's not as easy as you might think. The easiest approach is to use *WriteableBitmap,* but you'd have to implement your own line-drawing logic to render lines on that bitmap. I'll show you how in Chapter 14. It's also possible using DirectX with some C++ coding. That's coming in Chapter 15, "Going Native."

Real and Surreal Finger Painting

In recent years, paint programs have attempted to mimic real-life drawing materials, such as pencil, chalk, and water colors. Of course, doing something like this requires combining visual sensitivity and programming skill with some degree of randomness.

You can, of course, go in the opposite direction and render something on the screen that you'll never encounter in the real world. The Whirligig program is very similar in structure to the FingerPaint series, but it renders spiraled lines that look like this:

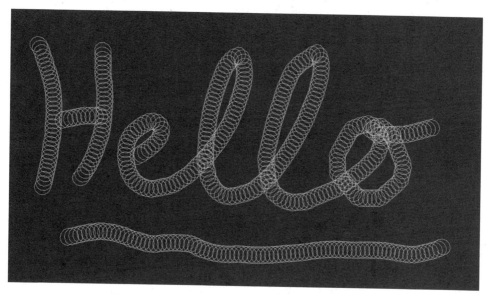

The Whirligig program implements pointer capture but not Esc-key termination, so the *OnPointerReleased* and *OnPointerCaptureLost* overrides are the same as in the past couple projects. For each finger stroke, the program renders a single *Polyline* much like the early versions of the program, except that *Polyline* is only one pixel in thickness and it turns around in circles:

Project: Whirligig | File: MainPage.xaml.cs (excerpt)

```
public sealed partial class MainPage : Page
{
    const double Radius = 24;          // 1/4 inch
    const double AngleIncrement = 0.5; // radians per pixel

    class TouchInfo
    {
        public Point LastPoint;
        public Polyline Polyline;
        public double Angle;
    }

    Dictionary<uint, TouchInfo> pointerDictionary = new Dictionary<uint, TouchInfo>();

    public MainPage()
```

```csharp
{
    this.InitializeComponent();
}

protected override void OnPointerPressed(PointerRoutedEventArgs args)
{
    // Get information from event arguments
    uint id = args.Pointer.PointerId;
    Point point = args.GetCurrentPoint(this).Position;

    // Create Polyline
    Polyline polyline = new Polyline
    {
        Stroke = this.Resources["ApplicationForegroundThemeBrush"] as Brush,
        StrokeThickness = 1,
    };

    // Add to Grid
    contentGrid.Children.Add(polyline);

    // Create TouchInfo
    TouchInfo touchInfo = new TouchInfo
    {
        LastPoint = point,
        Polyline = polyline
    };

    // Add to dictionary
    pointerDictionary.Add(id, touchInfo);

    // Capture the Pointer
    CapturePointer(args.Pointer);
    base.OnPointerPressed(args);
}

protected override void OnPointerMoved(PointerRoutedEventArgs args)
{
    // Get information from event arguments
    uint id = args.Pointer.PointerId;
    Point point = args.GetCurrentPoint(this).Position;

    // If ID is not in dictionary, don't do anything
    if (!pointerDictionary.ContainsKey(id))
        return;

    // Get TouchInfo objects
    Polyline polyline = pointerDictionary[id].Polyline;
    Point lastPoint = pointerDictionary[id].LastPoint;
    double angle = pointerDictionary[id].Angle;

    // Distance from last point to this point
    double distance = Math.Sqrt(Math.Pow(point.X - lastPoint.X, 2) +
                                Math.Pow(point.Y - lastPoint.Y, 2));

    int divisions = (int)distance;

    for (int i = 0; i < divisions; i++)
```

```
    {
        // Sub-divide the distance between the last point and the new
        double x = (i * point.X + (divisions - i) * lastPoint.X) / divisions;
        double y = (i * point.Y + (divisions - i) * lastPoint.Y) / divisions;
        Point pt = new Point(x, y);

        // Increase the angle
        angle += distance * AngleIncrement / divisions;

        // Rotate the point
        pt.X += Radius * Math.Cos(angle);
        pt.Y += Radius * Math.Sin(angle);

        // Add to Polyline
        polyline.Points.Add(pt);
    }

    // Save new information
    pointerDictionary[id].LastPoint = point;
    pointerDictionary[id].Angle = angle;

    base.OnPointerMoved(args);
}
...
}
```

Along with the *Polyline* itself, the *TouchInfo* class saves a *LastPoint* value and an *Angle* value. For each *PointerMoved* event, the program subdivides the distance from the current point to the previous point into pixel-sized lengths. For each of these pixel-sized lengths, it appends approximately 30 degrees of the circular pattern. (The 30 degrees is a result of the *AngleIncrement* constant.) Instead of rendering the actual point, it rotates the point by the accumulated angle and adds it to the *Polyline*.

A Touch Piano

Not all touch applications fall into the same pattern. For example, consider an on-screen piano keyboard. Obviously, you want to be able to play chords with your fingers, so this is a job for the *Pointer* events rather than the *Manipulation* events.

But what you also *really* want to do with an on-screen piano keyboard is run your fingers up and down the keys making glissandi. If you couldn't do that with an on-screen keyboard, you would undoubtedly consider it broken. What that implies, however, is that you're probably not exclusively concerned with *PointerPressed* and *PointerReleased*. Yes, you can press down on one key and release on another, but in between you could be playing many other keys just by sweeping your finger.

There are basically two ways to construct this piano keyboard. You can use one control for the whole keyboard, or you can use many controls (and by "many" I really mean one control for each key).

A single control must draw all the keys and also evaluate *PointerMoved* events by comparing pointer positions with the boundaries of these keys. You'll be tracking each finger to determine when a *PointerMoved* event indicates a key coming within a key boundary and when it leaves a key boundary. This is classic "hit testing"—you're examining pointer positions to determine if they lie within a boundary.

However, if each key is a separate control, that key doesn't need to perform hit testing. If it's getting a *Pointer* event, the *Pointer* is within the boundaries of that control (unless the control has captured the pointer, but pointer capturing makes no sense in this application).

What *Pointer* events are necessary to implement a piano key? Don't start by thinking about presses and releases. Think about glissandi. If we're talking about a keyboard that reacts solely to touch, the only two *Pointer* events that are necessary are *PointerEntered* and *PointerExited*.

However, you probably want the keyboard to respond reasonably to the mouse and pen as well. A piano key will get *PointerEntered* and *PointerExited* events for a mouse when the mouse button is not pressed, and that's a problem. The *PointerEntered* handler will need to examine the *IsInContact* property to correctly handle the mouse and pen. That property is always *true* for touch but only *true* for a mouse if the button is down or for the pen if it's in contact with the screen.

Moreover, when considering a single element, the mouse and pen generate *PointerEntered* events before *PointerPressed* and *PointerExited* after *PointerReleased*, so *PointerPressed* and *PointerReleased* must be handled as well.

Let's construct a two-octave piano keyboard from the bottom up, starting with the keys. The following *Key* class is a *Control* derivative without a default template, so it has no default visible appearance. But it does define an *IsPressed* dependency property, and a property-changed handler for *IsPressed* that toggles between two visual states called Normal and Pressed.

Project: SilentPiano | File: Key.cs (excerpt)

```
namespace SilentPiano
{
    public class Key : Control
    {
        static readonly DependencyProperty isPressedProperty =
                DependencyProperty.Register("IsPressed",
                        typeof(bool), typeof(Key),
                        new PropertyMetadata(false, OnIsPressedChanged));

        List<uint> pointerList = new List<uint>();

        public static DependencyProperty IsPressedProperty
        {
            get { return isPressedProperty; }
        }

        public bool IsPressed
        {
            set { SetValue(IsPressedProperty, value); }
            get { return (bool)GetValue(IsPressedProperty); }
        }
```

```
protected override void OnPointerEntered(PointerRoutedEventArgs args)
{
    if (args.Pointer.IsInContact)
        AddToList(args.Pointer.PointerId);
    base.OnPointerEntered(args);
}

protected override void OnPointerPressed(PointerRoutedEventArgs args)
{
    AddToList(args.Pointer.PointerId);
    base.OnPointerPressed(args);
}

protected override void OnPointerReleased(PointerRoutedEventArgs args)
{
    RemoveFromList(args.Pointer.PointerId);
    base.OnPointerReleased(args);
}

protected override void OnPointerExited(PointerRoutedEventArgs args)
{
    RemoveFromList(args.Pointer.PointerId);
    base.OnPointerExited(args);
}

void AddToList(uint id)
{
    if (!pointerList.Contains(id))
        pointerList.Add(id);

    CheckList();
}

void RemoveFromList(uint id)
{
    if (pointerList.Contains(id))
        pointerList.Remove(id);

    CheckList();
}

void CheckList()
{
    this.IsPressed = pointerList.Count > 0;
}

static void OnIsPressedChanged(DependencyObject obj,
                               DependencyPropertyChangedEventArgs args)
{
    VisualStateManager.GoToState(obj as Key,
                (bool)args.NewValue ? "Pressed" : "Normal", false);
}
```

Because you can use two fingers to play the same key, this control still needs to track individual fingers. But it doesn't need a *Dictionary* to retain information for each ID. It can simply use a *List*. IDs are put into this *List* in the *OnPointerEntered* override (but only if *IsInContact* is *true*) and in *OnPointerPressed*, and removed in *OnPointerReleased* and *OnPointerExited*, and that triggers the change in visual state. The *IsPressed* property is *true* if the *List* contains at least one entry. The *PointerPressed* and *PointerReleased* event handlers are only for the benefit of the mouse and pen.

Two templates—one for white keys and one for black keys—are defined in the Octave.xaml file. The two templates differ only by the size of a *Polygon* that defines the key shape and the default color. (The shape is a rectangle for both keys. Originally, I wanted to make the various white keys different shapes as they are on a real piano, but the uniform approach was a lot easier and required far fewer templates.) Both templates switch the color to red during a Pressed state:

Project: SilentPiano | **File:** Octave.xaml (excerpt)

```
<UserControl ... >
    <UserControl.Resources>
        <ControlTemplate x:Key="whiteKey" TargetType="local:Key">
            <Grid Width="80">
                <Polygon Points="2 0, 78 0, 78 320, 02 320">
                    <Polygon.Fill>
                        <SolidColorBrush x:Name="brush" Color="White" />
                    </Polygon.Fill>
                </Polygon>

                <VisualStateManager.VisualStateGroups>
                    <VisualStateGroup x:Name="CommonStates">
                        <VisualState x:Name="Normal"/>
                        <VisualState x:Name="Pressed">
                            <Storyboard>
                                <ColorAnimationUsingKeyFrames Storyboard.TargetName="brush"
                                                     Storyboard.TargetProperty="Color">
                                    <DiscreteColorKeyFrame KeyTime="0" Value="Red" />
                                </ColorAnimationUsingKeyFrames>
                            </Storyboard>
                        </VisualState>
                    </VisualStateGroup>
                </VisualStateManager.VisualStateGroups>
            </Grid>
        </ControlTemplate>

        <ControlTemplate x:Key="blackKey" TargetType="local:Key">
            <Grid>
                <Polygon Points="0 0, 40 0, 40 220, 0 220">
                    <Polygon.Fill>
                        <SolidColorBrush x:Name="brush" Color="Black" />
                    </Polygon.Fill>
                </Polygon>
```

```
            <VisualStateManager.VisualStateGroups>
                <VisualStateGroup x:Name="CommonStates">
                    <VisualState x:Name="Normal"/>
                    <VisualState x:Name="Pressed">
                        <Storyboard>
                            <ColorAnimationUsingKeyFrames Storyboard.TargetName="brush"
                                             Storyboard.TargetProperty="Color">
                                <DiscreteColorKeyFrame KeyTime="0" Value="Red" />
                            </ColorAnimationUsingKeyFrames>
                        </Storyboard>
                    </VisualState>
                </VisualStateGroup>
            </VisualStateManager.VisualStateGroups>
        </Grid>
    </ControlTemplate>
</UserControl.Resources>

<Grid>
    <StackPanel Orientation="Horizontal">
        <local:Key Template="{StaticResource whiteKey}" />
        <local:Key Template="{StaticResource whiteKey}" />
        <local:Key Template="{StaticResource whiteKey}" />
        <local:Key Template="{StaticResource whiteKey}" />
        <local:Key Template="{StaticResource whiteKey}" />
        <local:Key Template="{StaticResource whiteKey}" />
        <local:Key Template="{StaticResource whiteKey}" />
        <local:Key x:Name="lastKey"
                   Template="{StaticResource whiteKey}"
                   Visibility="Collapsed" />
    </StackPanel>
    <Canvas>
        <local:Key Template="{StaticResource blackKey}"
                   Canvas.Left="60" Canvas.Top="0" />
        <local:Key Template="{StaticResource blackKey}"
                   Canvas.Left="140" Canvas.Top="0" />
        <local:Key Template="{StaticResource blackKey}"
                   Canvas.Left="300" Canvas.Top="0" />
        <local:Key Template="{StaticResource blackKey}"
                   Canvas.Left="380" Canvas.Top="0" />
        <local:Key Template="{StaticResource blackKey}"
                   Canvas.Left="460" Canvas.Top="0" />
    </Canvas>
</Grid>
</UserControl>
```

Eight white keys are arranged horizontally in a *StackPanel*, but the five black keys are in a *Canvas*. This configuration allows the white keys to define the size of the control but lets the black keys sit on top of the white keys and cover parts of them.

The eight white keys go from C to C. Very often small keyboards start with C and end with C as well, but you don't want a pair of adjacent C keys where two octaves meet up. That's the reason why the last key has a *Visibility* of *Collapsed*. That *Visibility* property is set to *Visible* or *Collapsed* by the code-behind file based on the setting of the *LastKeyVisible* dependency property:

Project: SilentPiano | File: Octave.xaml.cs (excerpt)

```
public sealed partial class Octave : UserControl
{
    static readonly DependencyProperty lastKeyVisibleProperty =
            DependencyProperty.Register("LastKeyVisible",
                    typeof(bool), typeof(Octave),
                    new PropertyMetadata(false, OnLastKeyVisibleChanged));

    public Octave()
    {
        this.InitializeComponent();
    }

    public static DependencyProperty LastKeyVisibleProperty
    {
        get { return lastKeyVisibleProperty; }
    }

    public bool LastKeyVisible
    {
        set { SetValue(LastKeyVisibleProperty, value); }
        get { return (bool)GetValue(LastKeyVisibleProperty); }
    }

    static void OnLastKeyVisibleChanged(DependencyObject obj,
                                    DependencyPropertyChangedEventArgs args)
    {
        (obj as Octave).lastKey.Visibility =
            (bool)args.NewValue ? Visibility.Visible : Visibility.Collapsed;
    }
}
```

All that's left is to instantiate two *Octave* objects in the MainPage.xaml file, the second one with *LastKeyVisible* set to *true*:

Project: SilentPiano | File: MainPage.xaml (excerpt)

```
<Page ... >
    <Grid Background="Gray">
        <StackPanel Orientation="Horizontal"
                    HorizontalAlignment="Center"
                    VerticalAlignment="Center">
            <local:Octave />
            <local:Octave LastKeyVisible="True" />
        </StackPanel>
    </Grid>
</Page>
```

And here I am playing my favorite chord (consonant with a major programming language):

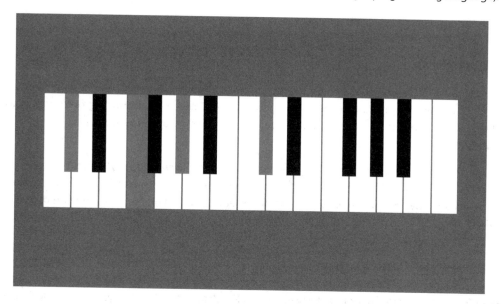

Manipulation, Fingers, and Elements

The great advantage of the *Pointer* events is that you can track individual fingers. The great advantage of the *Manipulation* events is that you can't track individual fingers.

The *Manipulation* events combine multiple fingers—and by "multiple" we're really often talking about "two"—into higher-level gestures such as pinch and rotate. These gestures correspond to common graphics transforms: translation, scaling (although limited to equal scaling in the horizontal and vertical directions), and rotation. Capture is intrinsic to manipulation. As a bonus, inertia is also available.

Keep in mind that multiple fingers are combined into a single series of *Manipulation* events not for the entire window, but for each element handling these events. What this means is that you can use a finger or a pair of fingers to manipulate one element, while using another couple fingers to manipulate a second element.

UIElement defines five *Manipulation* events that an element generally receives in the following order (and take heed that the first two have extremely similar names):

- *ManipulationStarting*
- *ManipulationStarted*
- *ManipulationDelta* (many)
- *ManipulationInertiaStarting*

- *ManipulationDelta* (more)

- *ManipulationCompleted*

The *Control* class defines virtual methods corresponding to these five events named *OnManipulationStarting*, and so forth.

Although the mouse or pen can generate *Manipulation* events, these occur only when a mouse button is pressed or when the pen is touching the screen. A *ManipulationStarting* event occurs when a finger first touches an element, or the mouse button is pressed over an element, or the pen is touched to an element.

The *ManipulationStarted* event generally occurs soon after *ManipulationStarting* (but, as I'll discuss shortly, the key word here is "generally"). What follows is usually a bunch of *ManipulationDelta* events as the fingers move on the screen. When all fingers leave an element, *ManipulationInertiaStarting* is fired. The element continues to generate *ManipulationDelta* events representing inertia, but *ManipulationCompleted* indicates that the sequence is over.

Although the *ManipulationStarting* event occurs when a finger first touches an element (or a mouse click or pen press occurs), this event is not necessarily followed by a *ManipulationStarted* event and *ManipulationStarted* might be delayed a little. The problem is that the system must distinguish between a tap or a hold and an actual manipulation. *ManipulationStarted* is fired when the finger (or mouse or pen) moves a little bit.

For example, if you touch an element with a sweeping motion, *ManipulationStarting* is followed very quickly by *ManipulationStarted* and multiple *ManipulationDelta* events. But put a finger down in one place and hold it, and the *ManipulationStarted* event can be delayed quite some time.

If the user taps, or right-taps, or double-taps the screen, a *ManipulationStarted* event won't occur at all. However, it's possible for a *Holding* event to be fired after *ManipulationStarting* and for the user to then move the finger and generate *ManipulationStarted* and the rest of the events. Another *Holding* event is then fired with a *HoldingState* property indicating *Canceled*.

By default, however, an element doesn't generate any *Manipulation* events whatsoever! The *Manipulation* events must first be enabled on a per-element basis. To allow a program to specify exactly what types of manipulation it wants, *UIElement* defines a *ManipulationMode* property of the enumeration type *ManipulationModes*. (The property name is singular; the enumeration name is plural.) The default setting of *ManipulationMode* is *ManipulationModes.System*, which for an application is equivalent to *ManipulationModes.None*. To enable an element for manipulation you'll need to set it to at least one other *ManipulationModes* member. The enumeration members are defined as bit flags, so you can combine them with the bitwise OR operator (|).

Although some applications need to handle all five *Manipulation* events, it's possible to write code that only examines *ManipulationDelta*.

This is the case with the ManipulationTracker program. The program displays a bunch of *CheckBox* controls for the members of the *ManipulationModes* enumeration and three *Rectangle* elements that you can manipulate. To ease some of the code and markup, a custom *CheckBox* derivative is used to store and display the *ManipulationModes* members:

Project: ManipulationTracker | **File:** ManipulationModeCheckBox.cs

```
using Windows.UI.Xaml.Controls;
using Windows.UI.Xaml.Input;

namespace ManipulationTracker
{
    public class ManipulationModeCheckBox : CheckBox
    {
        public ManipulationModes ManipulationModes { set; get; }
    }
}
```

Ten instances of this custom *CheckBox* are arranged in a *StackPanel* in MainPage.xaml, each identified both with the name of the enumeration member (with spaces inserted in the name to be more readable) and the integer value:

Project: ManipulationTracker | **File:** MainPage.xaml (excerpt)

```
<Page ... >
    <Page.Resources>
        <Style TargetType="local:ManipulationModeCheckBox">
            <Setter Property="Margin" Value="12 6 24 6" />
        </Style>

        <Style TargetType="Rectangle">
            <Setter Property="Width" Value="144" />
            <Setter Property="Height" Value="144" />
            <Setter Property="HorizontalAlignment" Value="Left" />
            <Setter Property="VerticalAlignment" Value="Top" />
            <Setter Property="RenderTransformOrigin" Value="0.5 0.5" />
        </Style>
    </Page.Resources>

    <Grid Background="{StaticResource ApplicationPageBackgroundThemeBrush}">
        <Grid.ColumnDefinitions>
            <ColumnDefinition Width="Auto" />
            <ColumnDefinition Width="*" />
        </Grid.ColumnDefinitions>

        <StackPanel Name="checkBoxPanel"
                    Grid.Column="0">
            <local:ManipulationModeCheckBox Checked="OnManipulationModeCheckBoxChecked"
                                            Unchecked="OnManipulationModeCheckBoxChecked"
                                            Content="Translate X (1)"
                                            ManipulationModes="TranslateX" />

            <local:ManipulationModeCheckBox Checked="OnManipulationModeCheckBoxChecked"
                                            Unchecked="OnManipulationModeCheckBoxChecked"
                                            Content="Translate Y (2)"
                                            ManipulationModes="TranslateY" />
```

```xml
        <local:ManipulationModeCheckBox Checked="OnManipulationModeCheckBoxChecked"
                                        Unchecked="OnManipulationModeCheckBoxChecked"
                                        Content="Translate Rails X (4)"
                                        ManipulationModes="TranslateRailsX" />

        <local:ManipulationModeCheckBox Checked="OnManipulationModeCheckBoxChecked"
                                        Unchecked="OnManipulationModeCheckBoxChecked"
                                        Content="Translate Rails Y (8)"
                                        ManipulationModes="TranslateRailsY" />

        <local:ManipulationModeCheckBox Checked="OnManipulationModeCheckBoxChecked"
                                        Unchecked="OnManipulationModeCheckBoxChecked"
                                        Content="Rotate (16)"
                                        ManipulationModes="Rotate" />

        <local:ManipulationModeCheckBox Checked="OnManipulationModeCheckBoxChecked"
                                        Unchecked="OnManipulationModeCheckBoxChecked"
                                        Content="Scale (32)"
                                        ManipulationModes="Scale" />

        <local:ManipulationModeCheckBox Checked="OnManipulationModeCheckBoxChecked"
                                        Unchecked="OnManipulationModeCheckBoxChecked"
                                        Content="Translate Inertia (64)"
                                        ManipulationModes="TranslateInertia" />

        <local:ManipulationModeCheckBox Checked="OnManipulationModeCheckBoxChecked"
                                        Unchecked="OnManipulationModeCheckBoxChecked"
                                        Content="Rotate Inertia (128)"
                                        ManipulationModes="RotateInertia" />

        <local:ManipulationModeCheckBox Checked="OnManipulationModeCheckBoxChecked"
                                        Unchecked="OnManipulationModeCheckBoxChecked"
                                        Content="Scale Inertia (256)"
                                        ManipulationModes="ScaleInertia" />

        <local:ManipulationModeCheckBox Checked="OnManipulationModeCheckBoxChecked"
                                        Unchecked="OnManipulationModeCheckBoxChecked"
                                        Content="All (0xFFFF)"
                                        ManipulationModes="All" />

    </StackPanel>

    <Grid Name="rectanglePanel"
          Grid.Column="1">
        <Rectangle Fill="Red">
            <Rectangle.RenderTransform>
                <CompositeTransform />
            </Rectangle.RenderTransform>
        </Rectangle>

        <Rectangle Fill="Green">
            <Rectangle.RenderTransform>
                <CompositeTransform />
            </Rectangle.RenderTransform>
        </Rectangle>
```

```
            <Rectangle Fill="Blue">
                <Rectangle.RenderTransform>
                    <CompositeTransform />
                </Rectangle.RenderTransform>
            </Rectangle>
        </Grid>
    </Grid>
</Page>
```

In the larger cell of the *Grid* are three *Rectangle* elements, with the three colors of the state flag of Computerstan: red, green, and blue.

In the code-behind file, any checking or unchecking of the custom *CheckBox* controls causes a calculation of a new *ManipulationModes* value by combining enumeration members associated with the checked check boxes with the bitwise OR operator. This composite *ManipulationModes* value is then set to the *ManipulationMode* property of the three *Rectangle* elements:

Project: ManipulationTracker | **File:** MainPage.xaml.cs (excerpt)

```
public sealed partial class MainPage : Page
{
    public MainPage()
    {
        this.InitializeComponent();
    }

    void OnManipulationModeCheckBoxChecked(object sender, RoutedEventArgs args)
    {
        // Get composite ManipulationModes value of checked CheckBoxes
        ManipulationModes manipulationModes = ManipulationModes.None;

        foreach (UIElement child in checkBoxPanel.Children)
        {
            ManipulationModeCheckBox checkBox = child as ManipulationModeCheckBox;

            if ((bool)checkBox.IsChecked)
                manipulationModes |= checkBox.ManipulationModes;
        }

        // Set ManipulationMode property of each Rectangle
        foreach (UIElement child in rectanglePanel.Children)
            child.ManipulationMode = manipulationModes;
    }

    protected override void OnManipulationDelta(ManipulationDeltaRoutedEventArgs args)
    {
        // OriginalSource is always Rectangle because nothing else has its
        //      ManipulationMode set to anything other than ManipulationModes.None
        Rectangle rectangle = args.OriginalSource as Rectangle;
        CompositeTransform transform = rectangle.RenderTransform as CompositeTransform;
```

```
        transform.TranslateX += args.Delta.Translation.X;
        transform.TranslateY += args.Delta.Translation.Y;

        transform.ScaleX *= args.Delta.Scale;
        transform.ScaleY *= args.Delta.Scale;

        transform.Rotation += args.Delta.Rotation;

        base.OnManipulationDelta(args);
    }
}
```

The final part of the program is the *OnManipulationDelta* override, which is a virtual method defined by the *Control* class that provides easier access to the *ManipulationDelta* event defined by *UIElement*. *ManipulationDelta* is the primary *Manipulation* event and indicates in what kinds of manipulation the user's fingers are engaged.

Notice that the *OnManipulationDelta* override casts the *OriginalSource* property of the event arguments to *Rectangle* without even checking if the cast is successful. In theory, the *OriginalSource* property can be *MainPage* or any child of *MainPage*. However, only the *Rectangle* elements are enabled for manipulation, so only the *Rectangle* elements can generate *ManipulationDelta* events.

The override obtains the *CompositeTransform* set to the *RenderTransform* property of that particular *Rectangle* and adjusts five properties of the transform based on the *Delta* property of the event arguments. This *Delta* property is of type *ManipulationDelta*, a structure with four properties. (Watch out! This structure has the same name as the event that delivers it!) The values indicate change since the last *ManipulationDelta* event.

Three of the four *ManipulationDelta* properties are accessed by this code. The fourth is *Expansion*, and it's similar to *Scale* except expressed in pixels rather than a multiplicative scaling factor. The *Translation* property of the *ManipulationDelta* structure indicates the average distance the fingers have moved since the last *ManipulationDelta* event, so these are just added to the *TranslateX* and *TranslateY* properties of the *CompositeTransform*. If there is no movement, these values are zero.

Similarly (but handled rather differently), the *Scale* property of the *ManipulationDelta* structure indicates the increase in the distance between the fingers since the last event. The *ScaleX* and *ScaleY* properties of the *CompositeTransform* are multiplied by this factor. (Because the *Manipulation* events don't provide separate scaling factors for horizontal and vertical scaling, all manipulation scaling is necessarily isotropic—equal in both directions.) If there is no scaling (or scaling has not been enabled), the *Scale* value is 1. The *Rotate* property of *ManipulationDelta* is a change in the rotation angle caused by turning the fingers relative to each other, and this is added to the *Rotation* property of *CompositeTransform*.

Check a few check boxes, and you can indeed move the rectangles with the mouse or pen or use multiple fingers to move, scale, and rotate the rectangles pretty much as you might expect, even manipulating two or three at once:

For a program using *Manipulation* events, the rules are very simple: Always set the *ManipulationMode* property to a non-default value on the element or elements that you want to generate *Manipulation* events. Each element you do this to generates its own independent stream of *Manipulation* events. You can set a handler for the *ManipulationDelta* event of the element itself, or you can handle that event by an ancestor in the visual tree.

I said that this manipulation works pretty much as you might expect, but it's not entirely correct. You'll notice that neither the code nor XAML has any reference to centers of scaling or rotation, except that *RenderTransformOrigin* is set to the relative point (0.5, 0.5). Hence all scaling and rotation are relative to the center of each particular rectangle.

This is not correct behavior. For example, suppose you put one finger near a corner of a rectangle and hold it steady. You use a second finger to grab the opposite edge and pull it or rotate it. The scaling and rotation that results should be relative to the first finger. In other words, the part of the rectangle under that first finger should remain in place while the rest of the rectangle is scaled or rotated around it.

It turns out that fixing this problem takes rather more complex logic, so I'm going to ignore it until later in this chapter.

Meanwhile, you can play with some of the other types of manipulation. There are three types of inertia—for translation, scaling, and rotation—and you can indeed flick or spin a rectangle right off the screen. There are ways to control the extent of inertia that I'll discuss later.

You can set an equivalent *ManipulationMode* property shown in the preceding screen shot like this in code:

```
rectangle.ManipulationMode = ManipulationModes.TranslateX |
                             ManipulationModes.TranslateY |
                             ManipulationModes.Scale |
                             ManipulationModes.Rotate;
```

But not in XAML. Setting the *ManipulationMode* property in XAML is limited to just a single enumeration member, and in a real-life application, that would probably be *All*.

If you want to restrict manipulation to horizontal movement only, you can specify the *ManipulationModes* member *TranslateX* but not *TranslateY*:

```
rectangle.ManipulationMode = ManipulationModes.TranslateX;
```

Similarly, to restrict movement to the vertical, specify *TranslateY* but not *TranslateX*.

Two of the members of the *ManipulationModes* enumeration are called *TranslateRailsX* and *TranslateRailsY*. These only work as they are intended if you also specify both *TranslateX* and *TranslateY*. For example,

```
rectangle.ManipulationMode = ManipulationModes.TranslateX |
                             ManipulationModes.TranslateY |
                             ManipulationModes.TranslateRailsX;
```

This configuration still allows you to freely move the element in the horizontal and vertical directions. *However*, if the manipulation *begins* with movement in the horizontal direction, the element gets stuck in the rails (so to speak) and all further movement is restricted to the horizontal until you lift off your finger and start over again.

Similarly, this configuration restricts movement to the vertical if the manipulation begins with vertical movement:

```
rectangle.ManipulationMode = ManipulationModes.TranslateX |
                             ManipulationModes.TranslateY |
                             ManipulationModes.TranslateRailsY;
```

You can also specify both:

```
rectangle.ManipulationMode = ManipulationModes.TranslateX |
                             ManipulationModes.TranslateY |
                             ManipulationModes.TranslateRailsX |
                             ManipulationModes.TranslateRailsY;
```

Begin dragging the element diagonally, and you can move it any which way. But begin with horizontal or vertical movement, and the element gets stuck in the rails.

As you saw earlier in the code listing, the ManipulationTracker program uses the *Delta* property of the *ManipulationDeltaRoutedEventArgs* argument to make changes to a *CompositeTransform*:

```
transform.TranslateX += args.Delta.Translation.X;
```

```
transform.TranslateY += args.Delta.Translation.Y;

transform.ScaleX *= args.Delta.Scale;
transform.ScaleY *= args.Delta.Scale;

transform.Rotation += args.Delta.Rotation;
```

If you've examined the properties of *ManipulationDeltaRoutedEventArgs*, you'll have discovered that besides the *Delta* property there is a *Cumulative* property, also of type *ManipulationDelta*. The *Delta* property indicates change since the last *ManipulationDelta* event, but *Cumulative* indicates change since *ManipulationStarted*.

You might suspect that this *Cumulative* property is easier to work with than the *Delta* property because you can just transfer the values to the corresponding properties of the *CompositeTransform*, like this:

```
transform.TranslateX = args.Cumulative.Translation.X;
transform.TranslateY = args.Cumulative.Translation.Y;

transform.ScaleX = args.Cumulative.Scale;
transform.ScaleY = args.Cumulative.Scale;

transform.Rotation = args.Cumulative.Rotation;
```

With this code, the first time you manipulate an element, it seems to work just fine. But lift your fingers off and try another manipulation on the same element. The element jumps back to its original position in the upper-left corner of the screen!

The *Cumulative* property is not cumulative from the beginning of the program but only from a particular *ManipulationStarted* event.

Working with Inertia

The *Manipulation* events support inertia for translation, scaling, and rotation, but if you don't want inertia, simply don't specify those *ManipulationModes*.

If at any time you want to stop the manipulation or the inertia, the event arguments accompanying the *ManipulationStarted* and *ManipulationDelta* events have a *Complete* method, which causes a firing of the *ManipulationCompleted* event.

If you'd like to handle inertia on your own, you can do that as well. The event arguments accompanying the *ManipulationDelta* and *ManipulationInertiaStarting* events have a *Velocities* property that indicates the linear, scaling, and rotational velocities. For linear movement, the *Velocities* property is in pixels per millisecond, which I suspect aren't exactly intuitive units. As I experimented with giving on-screen objects a good flick with my finger, I came close to 10 pixels per millisecond but could never get it higher than that. That's 10,000 pixels per second, which is equivalent to about 100 inches per second, or about 8 feet per second, or not quite 6 miles per hour.

Default deceleration is provided, but if you'd like to set your own you need to handle the *ManipulationInertiaStarting* event. The *ManipulationInertiaStartingRoutedEventArgs* class defines these three properties:

- *TranslationBehavior* of type *InertiaTranslationBehavior*
- *ExpansionBehavior* of type *InertiaExpansionBehavior*
- *RotationBehavior* of type *InertiaRotationBehavior*

The *InertiaTranslationBehavior* class (for example) lets you set linear deceleration in two ways: with a *DesiredDisplacement* property in units of pixels (which is how much farther you want the object to travel) or a *DesiredDeceleration* property in units of pixels per millisecond squared. Both properties have default values of NaN (not a number).

The *DesiredDeceleration* values are generally very small, but perhaps a physics review is in order here.

From basic physics, we know that with a constant acceleration applied to an object at rest, the distance the object travels in time *t* is

$$x = \frac{1}{2}at^2$$

For example, an object in free fall near the surface of the Earth without air resistance experiences a constant acceleration of 32 feet per second per second, or 32 feet per second squared. Set *a* to 32, and you can calculate that the object falls 16 feet at the end of 1 second, a total of 64 feet at the end of 2 seconds, and a total of 144 feet at the end of 3 seconds.

The velocity *v* is calculated as the first derivative of the distance with respect to time:

$$v = \frac{dx}{dt} = at$$

Again, for an object in free fall, the velocity is 32 feet per second at the end of 1 second, 64 feet per second at the end of 2 seconds, and 96 feet per second at the end of 3 seconds. Every second the velocity increases by 32 feet per second.

Deceleration is the same process in reverse. From that second formula we know that

$$a = \frac{v}{t}$$

If an object is traveling at velocity *v*, a constant deceleration *a* will bring it to rest in *t* seconds. If an on-screen object is traveling at the rate of 5 pixels per millisecond, you can use this formula to calculate a deceleration necessary to stop it in a fixed number of seconds, for example, 5 seconds or 5000 milliseconds:

$$a = \frac{5}{5000} = 0.001 \; pixels \, / \, msec^2$$

The FlickAndBounce project makes a similar calculation, except that the deceleration time is set via a *Slider* and can range from 1 second to 60 seconds. The XAML file includes that *Slider* and also an *Ellipse* with a *ManipulationMode* setting and three *Manipulation* events. Although *ManipulationMode* is set to *All* (because there's not much of an alternative in XAML), the program uses translation only and moves the *Ellipse* by setting *Canvas.Left* and *Canvas.Top* attached properties rather than a transform:

Project: FlickAndBounce | File: MainPage.xaml (excerpt)

```
<Page ... >
    <Grid Name="contentGrid"
          Background="{StaticResource ApplicationPageBackgroundThemeBrush}">
        <Canvas>
            <Ellipse Name="ellipse"
                     Fill="Red"
                     Width="144"
                     Height="144"
                     ManipulationMode="All"
                     ManipulationStarted="OnEllipseManipulationStarted"
                     ManipulationDelta="OnEllipseManipulationDelta"
                     ManipulationInertiaStarting="OnEllipseManipulationInertiaStarting" />
        </Canvas>

        <Slider x:Name="slider"
                Value="5" Minimum="1" Maximum="60"
                VerticalAlignment="Bottom"
                Margin="24 0" />
    </Grid>
</Page>
```

Of course, any deceleration would be wasted if the object just skittered off past the edge of the screen. For that reason, the *ManipulationDelta* handler detects when the *Ellipse* has moved past the edges of the screen. It moves the *Ellipse* back into view as if it's bounced off the edge and reverses further movement using the *xDirection* and *YDirection* fields.

Notice that this logic uses the *IsInertial* property for the bounce logic. It doesn't stop you from dragging the *Ellipse* past the edges of the screen:

Project: FlickAndBounce | File: MainPage.xaml.cs (excerpt)

```
public sealed partial class MainPage : Page
{
    int xDirection;
    int yDirection;

    public MainPage()
    {
        this.InitializeComponent();
    }

    void OnEllipseManipulationStarted(object sender, ManipulationStartedRoutedEventArgs args)
    {
```

```
        // Initialize directions
        xDirection = 1;
        yDirection = 1;
    }

    void OnEllipseManipulationDelta(object sender, ManipulationDeltaRoutedEventArgs args)
    {
        // Find new position of ellipse regardless of edges
        double x = Canvas.GetLeft(ellipse) + xDirection * args.Delta.Translation.X;
        double y = Canvas.GetTop(ellipse) + yDirection * args.Delta.Translation.Y;

        if (args.IsInertial)
        {
            // Bounce it off the edges
            Size playground = new Size(contentGrid.ActualWidth - ellipse.Width,
                                    contentGrid.ActualHeight - ellipse.Height);

            while (x < 0 || y < 0 || x > playground.Width || y > playground.Height)
            {
                if (x < 0)
                {
                    x = -x;
                    xDirection *= -1;
                }
                if (x > playground.Width)
                {
                    x = 2 * playground.Width - x;
                    xDirection *= -1;
                }
                if (y < 0)
                {
                    y = -y;
                    yDirection *= -1;
                }
                if (y > playground.Height)
                {
                    y = 2 * playground.Height - y;
                    yDirection *= -1;
                }
            }
        }

        Canvas.SetLeft(ellipse, x);
        Canvas.SetTop(ellipse, y);
    }

    void OnEllipseManipulationInertiaStarting(object sender,
                                        ManipulationInertiaStartingRoutedEventArgs args)
    {
        double maxVelocity = Math.Max(Math.Abs(args.Velocities.Linear.X),
                                    Math.Abs(args.Velocities.Linear.Y));

        args.TranslationBehavior.DesiredDeceleration = maxVelocity / (1000 * slider.Value);
    }
}
```

In the *ManipulationInertiaStarting* handler down at the bottom, the maximum of the absolute values of the horizontal and vertical velocities is used to calculate a deceleration based on a *Slider* value in seconds.

An *XYSlider* Control

An *XYSlider* control is similar to a *Slider* except that it allows you to select a point in a two-dimensional surface by changing the location of a crosshair (or something similar). At first, it seems like the *Pointer* events would be fine for this control, until you realize that the control really doesn't want to deal with multiple fingers. If it used the *Manipulation* events instead, it could avoid all that.

That was my original thought, anyway. But let's try it.

I derived *XYSlider* from *ContentControl* so that it could display whatever you wanted as a background simply by setting the *Content* property. Sitting on top of that is a crosshair that you move around with a finger, mouse, or pen. The control has one property, *Value* of type *Point*, and a *ValueChanged* event. The *X* and *Y* coordinates of the *Point* property are normalized to the range 0 to 1 relative to the content, which relieves the control of defining *Minimum* and *Maximum* values like *RangeBase* or an *IsDirectionReversed* property like *Slider*. (Actually, it would need a pair of *IsDirectionReversed* properties for the *X* and *Y* axes.)

The control definition itself is templateless, but it wants two parts in the template: the customary *ContentPresenter* normally found in a *ContentControl* template, and something that visually resembles a cross-hair. This cross-hair is moved around by code using *Canvas.Left* and *Canvas.Top* attached properties, strongly suggesting that the template needs to define this cross-hair in a *Canvas*.

Project: XYSliderDemo | File: XYSlider.cs

```
namespace XYSliderDemo
{
    public class XYSlider : ContentControl
    {
        ContentPresenter contentPresenter;
        FrameworkElement crossHairPart;

        static readonly DependencyProperty valueProperty =
                DependencyProperty.Register("Value",
                        typeof(Point), typeof(XYSlider),
                        new PropertyMetadata(new Point(0.5, 0.5), OnValueChanged));

        public event EventHandler<Point> ValueChanged;

        public XYSlider()
        {
            this.DefaultStyleKey = typeof(XYSlider);
        }

        public static DependencyProperty ValueProperty
        {
            get { return valueProperty; }
```

```
        }

        public Point Value
        {
            set { SetValue(ValueProperty, value); }
            get { return (Point)GetValue(ValueProperty); }
        }

        protected override void OnApplyTemplate()
        {
            // Detach event handlers
            if (contentPresenter != null)
            {
                contentPresenter.ManipulationStarted -= OnContentPresenterManipulationStarted;
                contentPresenter.ManipulationDelta -= OnContentPresenterManipulationDelta;
                contentPresenter.SizeChanged -= OnContentPresenterSizeChanged;
            }

            // Get new parts
            crossHairPart = GetTemplateChild("CrossHairPart") as FrameworkElement;
            contentPresenter = GetTemplateChild("ContentPresenterPart") as ContentPresenter;

            // Attach event handlers
            if (contentPresenter != null)
            {
                contentPresenter.ManipulationMode = ManipulationModes.TranslateX |
                                                    ManipulationModes.TranslateY;
                contentPresenter.ManipulationStarted += OnContentPresenterManipulationStarted;
                contentPresenter.ManipulationDelta += OnContentPresenterManipulationDelta;
                contentPresenter.SizeChanged += OnContentPresenterSizeChanged;
            }

            // Make cross-hair transparent to touch
            if (crossHairPart != null)
            {
                crossHairPart.IsHitTestVisible = false;
            }

            base.OnApplyTemplate();
        }

        void OnContentPresenterManipulationStarted(object sender,
                                            ManipulationStartedRoutedEventArgs args)
        {
            RecalculateValue(args.Position);
        }

        void OnContentPresenterManipulationDelta(object sender,
                                            ManipulationDeltaRoutedEventArgs args)
        {
            RecalculateValue(args.Position);
        }

        void OnContentPresenterSizeChanged(object sender, SizeChangedEventArgs args)
```

```
        {
            SetCrossHair();
        }

        void RecalculateValue(Point absolutePoint)
        {
            double x = Math.Max(0,Math.Min(1, absolutePoint.X / contentPresenter.ActualWidth));
            double y = Math.Max(0,Math.Min(1, absolutePoint.Y / contentPresenter.ActualHeight));
            this.Value = new Point(x, y);
        }

        void SetCrossHair()
        {
            if (contentPresenter != null && crossHairPart != null)
            {
                Canvas.SetLeft(crossHairPart, this.Value.X * contentPresenter.ActualWidth);
                Canvas.SetTop(crossHairPart, this.Value.Y * contentPresenter.ActualHeight);
            }
        }

        static void OnValueChanged(DependencyObject obj,
                                   DependencyPropertyChangedEventArgs args)
        {
            (obj as XYSlider).SetCrossHair();
            (obj as XYSlider).OnValueChanged((Point)args.NewValue);
        }

        protected void OnValueChanged(Point value)
        {
            if (ValueChanged != null)
                ValueChanged(this, value);
        }
    }
}
```

When the *Value* property is set programmatically, the class must set the cross-hair to the correct position by multiplying the width and height of the *ContentPresenter* by the relative coordinates. This happens in the *SetCrossHair* method. The *ManipulationStarted* and *ManipulationDelta* event handlers are set on the *ContentPresenter* object. Both call the *RecalculateValue* method to convert the absolute coordinates of the pointer to relative coordinates for the *Value* property.

The *ManipulationStarted* and *ManipulationDelta* handlers both reference a property of the event arguments named *Position*, which I haven't mentioned yet. For a mouse or pen, this *Position* property is simply the location of the mouse pointer or pen tip relative to the control generating these *Manipulation* events—the *ContentPresenter* in this case. For touch, the *Position* property is the average location of all the fingers involved in the manipulation. It provides a convenient way to deal with multiple fingers when you really want the position of only one finger.

The MainPage.xaml file instantiates an *XYSlider* and references a flattened map of the Earth that I obtained from a NASA website. But most of the XAML file is dedicated to defining a template for the *XYSlider* and particularly the cross-hair. Notice that I put the *ContentPresenter* and the *Canvas* in a *Grid* and assigned some properties to the *Grid* normally assigned to the *ContentPresenter*. This means that the upper-left corners of the *ContentPresenter* and *Canvas* are aligned, which makes it easier to convert between *ContentPresenter* coordinates and relative coordinates:

Project: XYSliderDemo | File: MainPage.xaml (excerpt)

```
<Page ... >
    <Page.Resources>
        <ControlTemplate x:Key="xySliderTemplate" TargetType="local:XYSlider">
            <Border BorderBrush="{TemplateBinding BorderBrush}"
                    BorderThickness="{TemplateBinding BorderThickness}"
                    Background="{TemplateBinding Background}">

                <Grid Margin="{TemplateBinding Padding}"
                      HorizontalAlignment="{TemplateBinding HorizontalContentAlignment}"
                      VerticalAlignment="{TemplateBinding VerticalContentAlignment}">

                    <ContentPresenter Name="ContentPresenterPart"
                                      Content="{TemplateBinding Content}"
                                      ContentTemplate="{TemplateBinding ContentTemplate}" />
                    <Canvas>
                        <Path Name="CrossHairPart"
                              Stroke="{TemplateBinding Foreground}"
                              StrokeThickness="3"
                              Fill="Transparent">
                            <Path.Data>
                                <GeometryGroup FillRule="Nonzero">
                                    <EllipseGeometry RadiusX="48" RadiusY="48" />
                                    <EllipseGeometry RadiusX="6" RadiusY="6" />
                                    <LineGeometry StartPoint="-48 0" EndPoint="-6 0" />
                                    <LineGeometry StartPoint="48 0" EndPoint="6 0" />
                                    <LineGeometry StartPoint="0 -48" EndPoint="0 -6" />
                                    <LineGeometry StartPoint="0 48" EndPoint="0 6" />
                                </GeometryGroup>
                            </Path.Data>
                        </Path>
                    </Canvas>
                </Grid>
            </Border>
        </ControlTemplate>

        <Style TargetType="local:XYSlider">
            <Setter Property="Template" Value="{StaticResource xySliderTemplate}" />
        </Style>
    </Page.Resources>

    <Grid Background="{StaticResource ApplicationPageBackgroundThemeBrush}">
        <Grid.RowDefinitions>
            <RowDefinition Height="*" />
            <RowDefinition Height="Auto" />
        </Grid.RowDefinitions>
```

```
<local:XYSlider x:Name="xySlider"
                Grid.Row="0"
                Margin="48"
                ValueChanged="OnXYSliderValueChanged">
    <!-- Image courtesy of NASN/JPL-Caltech (http://maps.jpl.nasa.gov) -->
    <Image Source="Images/ear0xuu2.jpg" />
</local:XYSlider>

<TextBlock Name="label"
           Grid.Row="1"
           Style="{StaticResource SubheaderTextStyle}"
           HorizontalAlignment="Center" />
    </Grid>
</Page>
```

The code-behind file has a handler for the *ValueChanged* event of *XYSlider* and uses that to display the corresponding longitude and latitude. Just to check that the code works the other way, it also uses the *Geolocator* class to obtain the current geographical location of the computer on which the program is running:

Project: XYSliderDemo | File: MainPage.xaml.cs (excerpt)

```
public sealed partial class MainPage : Page
{
    bool manualChange = false;

    public MainPage()
    {
        this.InitializeComponent();

        // Initialize position of cross-hair in XYSlider
        Loaded += async (sender, args) =>
            {
                Geolocator geolocator = new Geolocator();

                // Might not have permission!
                try
                {
                    Geoposition position = await geolocator.GetGeopositionAsync();

                    if (!manualChange)
                    {
                        double x = (position.Coordinate.Longitude + 180) / 360;
                        double y = (90 - position.Coordinate.Latitude) / 180;
                        xySlider.Value = new Point(x, y);
                    }
                }
                catch
                {
                }
            };
    }

    void OnXYSliderValueChanged(object sender, Point point)
    {
        double longitude = 360 * point.X - 180;
        double latitude = 90 - 180 * point.Y;
```

```
        label.Text = String.Format("Longitude: {0:F0} Latitude: {1:F0}",
                                    longitude, latitude);
        manualChange = true;
    }
}
```

Using the *Geolocator* class requires that you edit the Package.appxmanifest class to request Location capabilities. In Visual Studio, select the Package.appxmanifest file, select the Capabilities tab, and click Location. At run time, Windows 8 will then ask the user if it's OK for the program to know the computer's location. If the user denies permission, the *GetGeopositionAsync* call raises an exception.

Here's how it looks:

Longitude: -75 Latitude: 42

In an earlier version of this control that I wrote for Windows Phone 7, I used a templated *Thumb* for the cross-hair. I wasn't happy with that version because it required the user to drag the *Thumb* from its current location to a new location. For this new version, I wanted the cross-hair to snap to a new position with a simple touch.

But I'm not sure this version entirely succeeds either. As I mentioned earlier (and as you'll experience), simply touching a location does not snap the cross-hair to that point because some movement is required before the *ManipulationStarted* event is fired.

At first I thought I could make it respond faster by substituting a *PointerPressed* event for the *ManipulationStarted* event. However, apparently the simple act of calling *GetCurrentPoint* on the *PointerRoutedEventArgs* object inhibits *Manipulation* events.

Perhaps this is a case where the *Pointer* events are really best, and if there are multiple fingers attempting to move the crosshair they should just be averaged together. I wouldn't be surprised if there's a better version of *XYSlider* in the next chapter, when it's used for a color-selection control in a bitmap-based finger-painting program.

Centered Scaling and Rotation

When I first introduced the scaling and rotation features of the *Manipulation* events, I mentioned that applying these transforms with reference to a center point was a little tricky. Yet, in many cases it's important. The satisfaction of a touch interface depends a lot on how close the connection feels between a user's fingers and on-screen objects.

There is a technique to determine the scaling and rotation center involving the *Position* property that I used in the last section. This property is the average of the positions of all the fingers relative to the element being manipulated. It is not the center of scaling and rotation, but it can be used to derive that center.

The CenteredTransforms project has a XAML file that references a bitmap on my website:

Project: CenteredTransforms | **File:** MainPage.xaml (excerpt)

```
<Page ... >
    <Grid Background="{StaticResource ApplicationPageBackgroundThemeBrush}">
        <Image Name="image"
               Source="http://www.charlespetzold.com/pw6/PetzoldJersey.jpg"
               Stretch="None"
               HorizontalAlignment="Left"
               VerticalAlignment="Top">
            <Image.RenderTransform>
                <TransformGroup x:Name="xformGroup">
                    <MatrixTransform x:Name="matrixXform" />
                    <CompositeTransform x:Name="compositeXform" />
                </TransformGroup>
            </Image.RenderTransform>
        </Image>
    </Grid>
</Page>
```

Notice that the *RenderTransform* property is now set to a *TransformGroup* containing both a *MatrixTransform* and a *CompositeTransform*.

The code-behind file enables all forms of *Manipulation* except those involving rails:

Project: CenteredTransforms | **File:** MainPage.xaml.cs (excerpt)

```
public sealed partial class MainPage : Page
{
    public MainPage()
    {
        this.InitializeComponent();
        image.ManipulationMode = ManipulationModes.All &
                            ~ManipulationModes.TranslateRailsX &
                            ~ManipulationModes.TranslateRailsY;
    }

    protected override void OnManipulationDelta(ManipulationDeltaRoutedEventArgs args)
    {
        // Make this the entire transform to date
        matrixXform.Matrix = xformGroup.Value;
```

```
    // Use that to transform the Position property
    Point center = matrixXform.TransformPoint(args.Position);

    // That becomes the center of the new incremental transform
    compositeXform.CenterX = center.X;
    compositeXform.CenterY = center.Y;

    // Set the other properties
    compositeXform.TranslateX = args.Delta.Translation.X;
    compositeXform.TranslateY = args.Delta.Translation.Y;
    compositeXform.ScaleX = args.Delta.Scale;
    compositeXform.ScaleY = args.Delta.Scale;
    compositeXform.Rotation = args.Delta.Rotation;

    base.OnManipulationDelta(args);
}
}
```

The *OnManipulationDelta* override juggles around the three transform objects defined in the XAML file. At any time, the *Value* property of the *TransformGroup* (which is a *Matrix* value) represents the entire transform, which is the product of the transforms represented by the *MatrixTransform* and *CompositeTransform* objects. The *ManipulationDelta* handler first sets the *Matrix* value from the *TransformGroup* to the *MatrixTransform*, which means that the *MatrixTransform* is now the entire transform up to this point. This transform is also applied to the *Position* property, and that becomes the *CenterX* and *CenterY* properties for the *CompositeTransform*. The new values from the *ManipulationDelta* structure can then be set directly to the other properties of the *CompositeTransform*.

Does it work? You'll definitely want to try it out because you can't tell from this screen shot:

Try holding one finger still on a corner and pulling the opposite corner away or rotate it, and you'll see that the image follows your fingers—given the restriction of the isotropic scaling, of course.

To make this technique a little easier to use, I wrote a tiny class called *ManipulationManager* that performs this calculation in its own private collection of transforms created in the constructor and saved in fields:

Project: ManipulationManagerDemo | File: ManipulationManager.cs

```
using Windows.Foundation;
using Windows.UI.Input;
using Windows.UI.Xaml.Media;

namespace ManipulationManagerDemo
{
    public class ManipulationManager
    {
        TransformGroup xformGroup;
        MatrixTransform matrixXform;
        CompositeTransform compositeXform;

        public ManipulationManager()
        {
            xformGroup = new TransformGroup();
            matrixXform = new MatrixTransform();
            xformGroup.Children.Add(matrixXform);
            compositeXform = new CompositeTransform();
            xformGroup.Children.Add(compositeXform);
            this.Matrix = Matrix.Identity;
        }

        public Matrix Matrix { private set; get; }

        public void AccumulateDelta(Point position, ManipulationDelta delta)
        {
            matrixXform.Matrix = xformGroup.Value;
            Point center = matrixXform.TransformPoint(position);
            compositeXform.CenterX = center.X;
            compositeXform.CenterY = center.Y;
            compositeXform.TranslateX = delta.Translation.X;
            compositeXform.TranslateY = delta.Translation.Y;
            compositeXform.ScaleX = delta.Scale;
            compositeXform.ScaleY = delta.Scale;
            compositeXform.Rotation = delta.Rotation;
            this.Matrix = xformGroup.Value;
        }
    }
}
```

The public *AccumulateDelta* method accepts a *ManipulationDelta* value directly and calculates a new *Matrix* property. This allows elements that must be manipulated in this way to have only a single transform:

Project: ManipulationManagerDemo | File: MainPage.xaml (excerpt)

```
<Page ... >
    <Grid Background="{StaticResource ApplicationPageBackgroundThemeBrush}">
        <Image Name="image"
               Source="http://www.charlespetzold.com/pw6/PetzoldJersey.jpg"
```

```
                    Stretch="None"
                    HorizontalAlignment="Left"
                    VerticalAlignment="Top">
                <Image.RenderTransform>
                    <MatrixTransform x:Name="matrixXform" />
                </Image.RenderTransform>
            </Image>
        </Grid>
</Page>
```

The code-behind file creates an instance of *ManipulationManager* and uses that to calculate a new transform for the *Image*:

Project: ManipulationManagerDemo | File: MainPage.xaml.cs (excerpt)

```
public sealed partial class MainPage : Page
{
    ManipulationManager manipulationManager = new ManipulationManager();

    public MainPage()
    {
        this.InitializeComponent();

        image.ManipulationMode = ManipulationModes.All &
                        ~ManipulationModes.TranslateRailsX &
                        ~ManipulationModes.TranslateRailsY;
    }

    protected override void OnManipulationDelta(ManipulationDeltaRoutedEventArgs args)
    {
        manipulationManager.AccumulateDelta(args.Position, args.Delta);
        matrixXform.Matrix = manipulationManager.Matrix;
        base.OnManipulationDelta(args);
    }
}
```

If you had multiple manipulable objects on the screen, you'd need an instance of *ManipulationManager* for each one. In the next chapter I'll use a variation of *ManipulationManager* in a PhotoScatter project that displays the images in your Pictures directory and lets you pore through them with your fingers.

Single-Finger Rotation

Although the *ManipulationStarting* event doesn't necessarily signal that a manipulation will actually occur, it offers a few ways for a program to initialize the manipulation, all involving properties of *ManipulationStartingRoutedEventArgs*:

- The *Mode* property is of the familiar enumeration type *ManipulationModes*, and here it lets you set the types of manipulation you want to handle. But keep in mind that you'll get a *ManipulationStarting* event only if the element has its *ManipulationMode* property set to something other than *ManipulationModes.None* or *ManipulationModes.System*.

- The *Container* property is read-only in all the other *Manipulation* events but writeable in the *ManipulationStarting* event. By default, the *Container* property is the same as the *OriginalSource* property, but in later events it's the element that the *Position* property is relative to. If you want the *Position* property to be relative to an element other than *OriginalSource*, set the *Container* property to that element.

- The *Pivot* property enables single-finger rotation, and that's what I'll show you here.

Suppose a photograph is sitting on a table. (I'm referring here to a *real* photograph sitting on a *real* table.) You touch your finger to a corner and pull it toward you. Does the photograph stay in the same orientation? Not necessarily. If you're touching it fairly lightly, friction between the table and photograph causes the photograph to rotate a bit and the rest of it drags behind the corner that you're pulling.

You get a similar effect with single-finger rotation, but you need to use the technique I just showed you for rotating objects around a center. Indeed, this XAML file is basically the same as the CenteredTransforms project:

Project: SingleFingerRotate | File: MainPage.xaml (excerpt)

```
<Page ... >
    <Grid Background="{StaticResource ApplicationPageBackgroundThemeBrush}">
        <Image Name="image"
               Source="http://www.charlespetzold.com/pw6/PetzoldJersey.jpg"
               Stretch="None"
               HorizontalAlignment="Left"
               VerticalAlignment="Top"
               RenderTransformOrigin="0 0">
            <Image.RenderTransform>
                <TransformGroup x:Name="xformGroup">
                    <MatrixTransform x:Name="matrixXform" />
                    <CompositeTransform x:Name="compositeXform" />
                </TransformGroup>
            </Image.RenderTransform>
        </Image>
    </Grid>
</Page>
```

The code-behind file is nearly identical as well with the exception of the *OnManipulationStarting* override:

Project: SingleFingerRotate | File: MainPage.xaml.cs (excerpt)

```
public sealed partial class MainPage : Page
{
    public MainPage()
    {
        this.InitializeComponent();

        image.ManipulationMode = ManipulationModes.All &
                            ~ManipulationModes.TranslateRailsX &
                            ~ManipulationModes.TranslateRailsY;
    }
```

```
protected override void OnManipulationStarting(ManipulationStartingRoutedEventArgs args)
{
    args.Pivot = new ManipulationPivot(new Point(image.ActualWidth / 2,
                                                 image.ActualHeight / 2),
                                       50);
    base.OnManipulationStarting(args);
}

protected override void OnManipulationDelta(ManipulationDeltaRoutedEventArgs args)
{
    // Make this the entire transform to date
    matrixXform.Matrix = xformGroup.Value;

    // Use that to transform the Position property
    Point center = matrixXform.TransformPoint(args.Position);

    // That becomes the center of the new incremental transform
    compositeXform.CenterX = center.X;
    compositeXform.CenterY = center.Y;

    // Set the other properties
    compositeXform.TranslateX = args.Delta.Translation.X;
    compositeXform.TranslateY = args.Delta.Translation.Y;
    compositeXform.ScaleX = args.Delta.Scale;
    compositeXform.ScaleY = args.Delta.Scale;
    compositeXform.Rotation = args.Delta.Rotation;

    base.OnManipulationDelta(args);
}
}
```

The key here is setting the *Pivot* property of the *ManipulationStartingRoutedEventArgs* object to a *ManipulationPivot* object. This object provides two things:

- A center of rotation, almost always the center of the object being manipulated

- A protection radius around the center, here set to 50 pixels

Without that second item your finger can get very close to the center of the element, whereupon just a little movement can give it a big spin.

This is one of those programs you really have to try out for yourself to get a feel for how single-finger rotation adds some realism to the dragging operation.

Remember the SliderSketch program from Chapter 5, "Control Interaction"? Remember how you asked, "Shouldn't these be dials rather than sliders?"? The DialSketch program that concludes this chapter uses a *Dial* control that incorporates single-finger rotation.

To make the *Dial* class a little easier to define, I decided it should derive from *RangeBase* just like *Slider*. This gives the control *Minimum*, *Maximum*, and *Value* properties all of type *double*, as well as a *ValueChanged* event. The *double* values in this control, however, are rotation angles, and the only enabled manipulation mode is rotation:

Project: DialSketch | File: Dial.cs

```
using System;
using Windows.Foundation;
using Windows.UI.Xaml.Controls.Primitives;
using Windows.UI.Xaml.Input;

namespace DialSketch
{
    public class Dial : RangeBase
    {
        public Dial()
        {
            ManipulationMode = ManipulationModes.Rotate;
        }

        protected override void OnManipulationStarting(ManipulationStartingRoutedEventArgs args)
        {
            args.Pivot = new ManipulationPivot(new Point(this.ActualWidth / 2,
                                                         this.ActualHeight / 2),
                                               48);
            base.OnManipulationStarting(args);
        }

        protected override void OnManipulationDelta(ManipulationDeltaRoutedEventArgs args)
        {
            this.Value = Math.Max(this.Minimum,
                        Math.Min(this.Maximum, this.Value + args.Delta.Rotation));

            base.OnManipulationDelta(args);
        }
    }
}
```

That's it! Of course, it doesn't have a template yet, nor does it access any transforms. It just sets a new *Value* property (which causes *RangeBase* to fire a *ValueChanged* event), and it expects everything else to be implemented elsewhere.

Two of these *Dial* controls are instantiated in the XAML file for DialSketch. The *Resources* section is devoted to supplying a *Style* for these two controls, including a *ControlTemplate*. The *Dial* control require visuals that let the user know it's rotating, so the template uses a dashed line with very short dashes to simulate tick marks.

Notice the *Minimum* and *Maximum* values set on the *Dial*. These imply that the *Dial* can be rotated 10 full times between its minimum and maximum positions. To draw a line from one edge of the DialSketch canvas to the opposite edge, you need to turn the dial 10 times:

Project: DialSketch | File: MainPage.xaml (excerpt)

```xml
<Page ... >
    <Page.Resources>
        <Style TargetType="local:Dial">
            <Setter Property="Minimum" Value="-1800" />
            <Setter Property="Maximum" Value="1800" />
            <Setter Property="RenderTransformOrigin" Value="0.5 0.5" />
            <Setter Property="Width" Value="144" />
            <Setter Property="Height" Value="144" />
            <Setter Property="Margin" Value="24" />
            <Setter Property="Template">
                <Setter.Value>
                    <ControlTemplate>
                        <Grid>
                            <Ellipse Fill="DarkRed" />
                            <Ellipse Stroke="Black"
                                     StrokeThickness="12"
                                     StrokeDashArray="0.1 1"
                                     Margin="3" />
                            <Ellipse Fill="Black"
                                     Width="6"
                                     Height="6" />
                        </Grid>
                    </ControlTemplate>
                </Setter.Value>
            </Setter>
        </Style>
    </Page.Resources>

    <Grid Background="{StaticResource ApplicationPageBackgroundThemeBrush}">
        <Grid.RowDefinitions>
            <RowDefinition Height="*" />
            <RowDefinition Height="Auto" />
        </Grid.RowDefinitions>

        <Grid.ColumnDefinitions>
            <ColumnDefinition Width="Auto" />
            <ColumnDefinition Width="*" />
            <ColumnDefinition Width="Auto" />
        </Grid.ColumnDefinitions>

        <Border Grid.Row="0"
                Grid.Column="0"
                Grid.ColumnSpan='3'
                BorderBrush="{StaticResource ApplicationForegroundThemeBrush}"
                BorderThickness="3 0 0 3"
                Background="#C0C0C0"
                Padding="24">
```

```
<Grid Name="drawingGrid">
    <Polyline Name="polyline"
              Stroke="#404040"
              StrokeThickness="3" />
</Grid>
</Border>

<local:Dial x:Name="horzDial"
            Grid.Row="1"
            Grid.Column="0"
            Maximum="1800"
            ValueChanged="OnDialValueChanged">
    <local:Dial.RenderTransform>
        <RotateTransform />
    </local:Dial.RenderTransform>
</local:Dial>

<Button Content="Clear"
        Grid.Row="1"
        Grid.Column="1"
        HorizontalAlignment="Center"
        VerticalAlignment="Center"
        Click="OnClearButtonClick" />

<local:Dial x:Name="vertDial"
            Grid.Row="1"
            Grid.Column="2"
            Maximum="1800"
            ValueChanged="OnDialValueChanged">
    <local:Dial.RenderTransform>
        <RotateTransform />
    </local:Dial.RenderTransform>
</local:Dial>
    </Grid>
</Page>
```

You'll notice that the *Maximum* settings are repeated on the individual *Dial* controls. In the version of Windows 8 that I'm using, the settings in the *Style* didn't seem to "take." Also notice that each *Dial* control has a *RotateTransform* attached to it.

The code-behind file initializes the *Polyline* to a point in the center. For each *ValueChanged* event from a *Dial*, the *RotateTranform* on the control is set and a new *Point* is added to the *Polyline*:

Project: DialSketch | File: MainPage.xaml.cs (excerpt)

```
public sealed partial class MainPage : Page
{
    public MainPage()
    {
        this.InitializeComponent();

        Loaded += (sender, args) =>
            {
                polyline.Points.Add(new Point(drawingGrid.ActualWidth / 2,
                                              drawingGrid.ActualHeight / 2));
            };
    }
```

```
void OnDialValueChanged(object sender, RangeBaseValueChangedEventArgs args)
{
    Dial dial = sender as Dial;
    RotateTransform rotate = dial.RenderTransform as RotateTransform;
    rotate.Angle = args.NewValue;

    double xFraction = (horzDial.Value - horzDial.Minimum) /
                            (horzDial.Maximum - horzDial.Minimum);

    double yFraction = (vertDial.Value - vertDial.Minimum) /
                            (vertDial.Maximum - vertDial.Minimum);

    double x = xFraction * drawingGrid.ActualWidth;
    double y = yFraction * drawingGrid.ActualHeight;
    polyline.Points.Add(new Point(x, y));
}

void OnClearButtonClick(object sender, RoutedEventArgs args)
{
    polyline.Points.Clear();
}
}
```

Of course, the program is still impossible to use, but it says "Hi" the best it can:

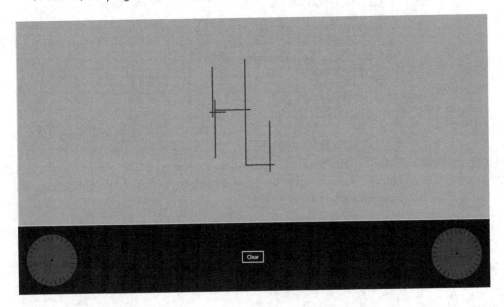

CHAPTER 14

Bitmaps

We've been working with bitmap images since the early pages of this book: displaying them, using them for brushes, stretching them, skewing them, and rotating them. But this chapter is all about reaching into the inner soul of bitmaps and manipulating their pixel bits. Almost every program in this chapter makes use of the *WriteableBitmap* class, which derives from *ImageSource* and therefore can be used as a source for *Image* and *ImageBrush*:

> *Object*
> > *DependencyObject*
> > > *ImageSource*
> > > > *BitmapSource*
> > > > > *BitmapImage*
> > > > > *WriteableBitmap*

From *BitmapSource*, *WriteableBitmap* inherits a *SetSource* method that you can use to load a bitmap file through an object that implements *IRandomAccessStream*.

What makes *WriteableBitmap* different is that it defines a *PixelBuffer* property that gives you access to the pixel bits. You can manipulate the pixels of an existing image or create an entire image from scratch. This chapter also discusses reading and writing various formats of image files (such as PNG and JPEG) based on arrays of pixel bits.

If you're familiar with the Silverlight version of *WriteableBitmap*, you might be disappointed to learn that the Windows Runtime version does not implement the *Render* method that allows you to render any *UIElement* on the surface of the image. This greatly limits *WriteableBitmap* for several common purposes.

For example, in Chapter 13, "Touch, Etc.," you saw a number of finger-painting programs that rendered pointer input with *Line*, *Polyline*, and *Path* elements. You probably noticed that I provided no way for you to save a painting to a file. One very reasonable way to save a painting is to render these *Line*, *Polyline*, and *Path* elements on a bitmap and then save this bitmap as a file. But the absence of a *Render* method in *WriteableBitmap* greatly inhibits this process.

In this chapter I'll show you how to draw lines on a bitmap algorithmically. This allows me to present a FingerPaint program (without any number on the project name) that lets you store your artwork as a bitmap. In Chapter 15, "Going Native," I'll show you how to use *SurfaceImageSource*, which also derives from *ImageSource* and can be drawn upon using DirectX drawing operations from C++ code.

It is not my policy to discuss third-party libraries in books about APIs, but if you need to draw complex graphics on bitmaps, you might find *WriteableBitmapEx* to be useful. This is available at *http://writeablebitmapex.codeplex.com*.

Pixel Bits

A bitmap image has an integral number of rows and columns. For any instance of a class that derives from *BitmapSource*, these dimensions are available from the *PixelHeight* and *PixelWidth* properties.

Conceptually, pixel bits are stored in a two-dimensional array with the two dimensions equal to *PixelHeight* and *PixelWidth*. In reality, the array has just one dimension, but the big issue is the nature of the individual pixels themselves. This is sometimes referred to as the bitmap's "color format" and could range from 1 bit per pixel (in a bitmap capable of only black and white) to 1 byte per pixel (in a gray-shade bitmap or a bitmap with a 256-color palette) to 3 or 4 bytes per pixel (for full-color with or without transparency) or even higher for more color resolution.

However, when working with *WriteableBitmap*, a uniform color format has been established. In every *WriteableBitmap*, each pixel consists of four bytes. The total number of bytes in the bitmap's pixel array is therefore

*PixelHeight * PixelWidth * 4*

The image begins with the topmost row, and each row goes from left to right. There is no row padding. For each pixel, the bytes are in this order:

Blue, Green, Red, Alpha

The bytes range from 0 to 255 just as in a *Color* value. The *WriteableBitmap* color values are assumed to be in accordance with sRGB ("standard RGB") and hence compatible with the Windows Runtime *Color* value (except for *Colors.Transparent*, as I'll discuss later).

The pixels in a *WriteableBitmap* are in a *premultiplied-alpha* format. I'll discuss what that means shortly.

The order Blue, Green, Red, Alpha might seem backward from how we usually refer to these color bytes (and their order in the *Color.FromArgb* method), but it makes more sense if you consider that a *WriteableBitmap* pixel is really a 32-bit unsigned integer with the Alpha value stored in the high byte and the Blue value in the low byte. That integer is stored in the bitmap in the little-endian order (lowest byte first) common in operating systems built around Intel microprocessors.

Let's construct a custom image by creating a *WriteableBitmap* and filling it with pixels. Just to make the math easy, this *WriteableBitmap* will have 256 rows and 256 columns. The upper-left corner will be black, the upper-right corner will be blue, the lower-left corner will be red, and the lower-right corner will be magenta, the combination of blue and red. This is a form of gradient, but it's not like any gradient available in the Windows Runtime.

Here's the XAML file with an *Image* element ready to receive an *ImageSource* derivative:

Project: CustomGradient | File: MainPage.xaml (excerpt)

```
<Grid Background="{StaticResource ApplicationPageBackgroundThemeBrush}">
    <Image Name="image" />
</Grid>
```

You cannot instantiate a *WriteableBitmap* in XAML because it doesn't have a parameterless constructor. The code-behind file creates and builds the *WriteableBitmap* in a handler for the *Loaded* event. Here's the complete file so that you can see the *using* directives as well. *WriteableBitmap* itself is defined in the *Windows.UI.Xaml.Media.Imaging* namespace:

Project: CustomGradient | File: MainPage.xaml.cs

```
using System.IO;
using System.Runtime.InteropServices.WindowsRuntime;
using Windows.UI.Xaml;
using Windows.UI.Xaml.Controls;
using Windows.UI.Xaml.Media.Imaging;

namespace CustomGradient
{
    public sealed partial class MainPage : Page
    {
        public MainPage()
        {
            this.InitializeComponent();
            Loaded += OnMainPageLoaded;
        }

        async void OnMainPageLoaded(object sender, RoutedEventArgs args)
        {
            WriteableBitmap bitmap = new WriteableBitmap(256, 256);
            byte[] pixels = new byte[4 * bitmap.PixelWidth * bitmap.PixelHeight];

            for (int y = 0; y < bitmap.PixelHeight; y++)
                for (int x = 0; x < bitmap.PixelWidth; x++)
                {
                    int index = 4 * (y * bitmap.PixelWidth + x);
                    pixels[index + 0] = (byte)x;      // Blue
                    pixels[index + 1] = 0;            // Green
                    pixels[index + 2] = (byte)y;      // Red
                    pixels[index + 3] = 255;          // Alpha
                }

            using (Stream pixelStream = bitmap.PixelBuffer.AsStream())
            {
                await pixelStream.WriteAsync(pixels, 0, pixels.Length);
            }
            bitmap.Invalidate();
            image.Source = bitmap;
        }
    }
}
```

The *WriteableBitmap* constructor requires a pixel width and height. The program then allocates a *byte* array for the pixels based on those dimensions:

```
byte[] pixels = new byte[4 * bitmap.PixelWidth * bitmap.PixelHeight];
```

The array size for a *WriteableBitmap* is always calculated like this.

The loops for the rows and columns touch every pixel in the bitmap. An index into the *pixels* array to reference a particular pixel is calculated like this:

```
int index = 4 * (y * bitmap.PixelWidth + x);
```

Each pixel can then be set in the order blue, green, red, alpha.

In this particular example, the two loops are addressing the pixels in the order in which they're stored in the array, so *index* really doesn't have to be recalculated for every pixel. It could be initialized at zero and then incremented like so:

```
int index = 0;
for (int y = 0; y < bitmap.PixelHeight; y++)
    for (int x = 0; x < bitmap.PixelWidth; x++)
    {
        pixels[index++] = (byte)x;      // Blue
        pixels[index++] = 0;            // Green
        pixels[index++] = (byte)y;      // Red
        pixels[index++] = 255;          // Alpha
    }
```

This is almost assuredly somewhat faster than the approach I've used, but in general it's less versatile. You could also define one loop for *index* and then calculate *x* and *y* from that. What's important (in most cases) is to access every pixel.

After the *byte* array has been filled, the pixels must be transferred into the *WriteableBitmap*. This process seems puzzling on first inspection. The *PixelBuffer* property defined by *WriteableBitmap* is of type *IBuffer*, which defines only two properties: *Capacity* and *Length*. As I discussed in Chapter 7, "Asynchronicity," an *IBuffer* object is usually an area of storage maintained within the operating system that is reference counted so that it can be deleted when no longer needed. You need to transfer bytes into this buffer.

Fortunately, an extension method named *AsStream* is defined to treat this *IBuffer* as a .NET *Stream* object:

```
Stream pixelStream = bitmap.PixelBuffer.AsStream();
```

To use this extension method, you must include a *using* directive for the *System.Runtime .InteropServices.WindowsRuntime* namespace. Without that *using* directive, IntelliSense won't reveal the method's existence.

You can then use the normal *Write* method defined by *Stream* to write the byte array to the *Stream* object, or you can use *WriteAsync* as I've done. Because this bitmap is not very large, and because the call merely transfers an array of bytes across the API, *Write* should be fast enough to justify doing the job in the user-interface thread. You can dispose of the *Stream* "manually" or let it be disposed of automatically, or you can put the *Stream* logic in a *using* statement as I've done:

```
using (Stream pixelStream = bitmap.PixelBuffer.AsStream())
{
    await pixelStream.WriteAsync(pixels, 0, pixels.Length);
}
```

Whenever you change the pixels of a *WriteableBitmap*, it's a good idea to get into the habit of calling *Invalidate* on the bitmap:

```
bitmap.Invalidate();
```

This call requests that the bitmap be redrawn. The call isn't strictly required in this particular context, but it's important in others.

Finally, do not forget to display the final bitmap! This program simply sets it to the *Source* property of the *Image* element in the XAML file:

```
image.Source = bitmap;
```

And here's the result:

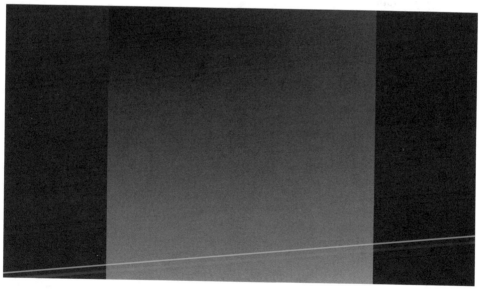

If you retain the *Stream* object and pixel array as a field for further manipulation of the bitmap— perhaps the image changes over time—you'll need to precede the *WriteAsync* call with a *Seek* call to set the current position back to the beginning:

```
pixelStream.Seek(0, SeekOrigin.Begin);
```

But notice also that you have the option of writing only part of the *byte* array to the bitmap. For example, suppose you've only modified pixels corresponding to the pixel coordinate (*x1, y1*) up to but not including (*x2, y2*). First find the byte indices corresponding to those two coordinates:

```
int index1 = 4 * (y1 * bitmap.PixelWidth + x1);
int index2 = 4 * (y2 * bitmap.PixelWidth + x2);
```

Then indicate that you want to update pixels at *index1* up to *index2*:

```
pixelStream.Seek(index1, SeekOrigin.Begin);
pixelStream.Write(pixels, index1, index2 - index1);
bitmap.Invalidate();
```

Let's try another custom gradient. This next program I call CircularGradient and the gradient is based on the angle a particular pixel makes with the center of the bitmap. (The math is easier than you might think.)

The XAML file defines an *Ellipse* with a thick outline and an *ImageBrush* for the *Stroke* property. An animation rotates the *Ellipse* around its center:

Project: CircularGradient | File: MainPage.xaml (excerpt)

```xml
<Page ... >
    <Grid Background="{StaticResource ApplicationPageBackgroundThemeBrush}">
        <Ellipse Width="576"
                 Height="576"
                 StrokeThickness="48"
                 RenderTransformOrigin="0.5 0.5">
            <Ellipse.Stroke>
                <ImageBrush x:Name="imageBrush" />
            </Ellipse.Stroke>

            <Ellipse.RenderTransform>
                <RotateTransform x:Name="rotate" />
            </Ellipse.RenderTransform>
        </Ellipse>
    </Grid>

    <Page.Triggers>
        <EventTrigger>
            <BeginStoryboard>
                <Storyboard>
                    <DoubleAnimation Storyboard.TargetName="rotate"
                                     Storyboard.TargetProperty="Angle"
                                     From="0" To="360" Duration="0:0:3"
                                     RepeatBehavior="Forever" />
                </Storyboard>
            </BeginStoryboard>
        </EventTrigger>
    </Page.Triggers>
</Page>
```

The *Loaded* handler in the code-behind file is similar to the previous program. As the two loops march through the rows and columns of the bitmap, each pixel has a position (*x, y*) relative to the upper-left corner. The pixel in the center has the coordinate (*bitmap.PixelWidth* / 2, *bitmap.PixelHeight* / 2). By subtracting that center from an individual pixel and dividing by the bitmap width and height, the pixel coordinate is converted to values between –1/2 and 1/2, which can then be passed to the *Math.Atan2* method to get exactly the angle we need:

Project: CircularGradient | File: MainPage.xaml.cs (excerpt)

```
public sealed partial class MainPage : Page
{
    public MainPage()
    {
        this.InitializeComponent();
        Loaded += OnMainPageLoaded;
    }

    async void OnMainPageLoaded(object sender, RoutedEventArgs args)
    {
        WriteableBitmap bitmap = new WriteableBitmap(256, 256);
        byte[] pixels = new byte[4 * bitmap.PixelWidth * bitmap.PixelHeight];
        int index = 0;
        int centerX = bitmap.PixelWidth / 2;
        int centerY = bitmap.PixelHeight / 2;

        for (int y = 0; y < bitmap.PixelHeight; y++)
            for (int x = 0; x < bitmap.PixelWidth; x++)
            {
                double angle =
                    Math.Atan2(((double)y - centerY) / bitmap.PixelHeight,
                               ((double)x - centerX) / bitmap.PixelWidth);
                double fraction = angle / (2 * Math.PI);
                pixels[index++] = (byte)(fraction * 255);        // Blue
                pixels[index++] = 0;                             // Green
                pixels[index++] = (byte)(255 * (1 - fraction));  // Red
                pixels[index++] = 255;                           // Alpha
            }

        using (Stream pixelStream = bitmap.PixelBuffer.AsStream())
        {
            await pixelStream.WriteAsync(pixels, 0, pixels.Length);
        }
        bitmap.Invalidate();
        imageBrush.ImageSource = bitmap;
    }
}
```

That angle is then converted to a fraction between 0 and 1 for calculating the gradient. Here's what the bitmap looks like in its entirety used for an *ImageBrush* set to the *Fill* property of a *Rectangle*:

However, it looks much more interesting when it's restricted to a circle and made to rotate. It seems as if the gradient itself is rotating:

As you've seen, brushes in the Windows Runtime are generally stretched to the element they're coloring. An *ImageBrush* does that as well, so in one sense the size of the underlying bitmap doesn't matter. But of course it does matter. A bitmap that is too small might not have the desired detail, and one that is too large is just a waste of pixels.

Transparency and Premultiplied Alphas

When a bitmap is rendered on a surface such as the video display, the pixels of the bitmap are generally not simply transferred to the video display surface. If the bitmap supports transparency, a pixel must be combined with the color of the existing surface at that point based on the Alpha setting of that pixel. It the Alpha value is 255 (opaque), the bitmap pixel can be simply copied to the surface. If the Alpha value is 0 (transparent), it doesn't need to be copied at all. If the Alpha value is 128, the result is the average of the bitmap pixel and the surface color prior to the rendering.

The following formulas show this calculation for a single pixel. In reality the values A, R, G, and B range from 0 to 255, but the following simplified formulas assume they've been normalized to values 0 through 1. The subscripts indicate the "result" of rendering a partially transparent "bitmap" pixel on an existing "surface":

$$R_{result} = \left(1 - A_{bitmap}\right) \cdot R_{surface} + A_{bitmap} \cdot R_{bitmap}$$

$$G_{result} = \left(1 - A_{bitmap}\right) \cdot G_{surface} + A_{bitmap} \cdot G_{bitmap}$$

$$B_{result} = \left(1 - A_{bitmap}\right) \cdot B_{surface} + A_{bitmap} \cdot B_{bitmap}$$

Notice that second multiplication in each line. That's a multiplication that involves only the bitmap pixel itself and not the surface. This implies that the entire process of rendering a bitmap on a surface can be speeded up if the R, G, and B values of the pixel have already been multiplied by the A value:

$$R_{result} = \left(1 - A_{bitmap}\right) \cdot R_{surface} + R_{bitmap}$$

$$G_{result} = \left(1 - A_{bitmap}\right) \cdot G_{surface} + G_{bitmap}$$

$$B_{result} = \left(1 - A_{bitmap}\right) \cdot B_{surface} + B_{bitmap}$$

This convention is called "premultiplied alpha."

For example, suppose a non-premultiplied alpha bitmap contains a pixel with the ARGB value (192, 40, 60, 255). That alpha value of 192 indicates 75 percent opacity (192 divided by 255). The equivalent pixel with a premultiplied alpha is (192, 30, 45, 192). The red, green, and blue values have been multiplied by 75 percent.

When rendering a *WriteableBitmap*, the operating system assumes that the pixel data has premultiplied alphas. For any pixel, none of the R, G, and B values should be greater than the A value. Nothing will "blow up" if that's not the case, but you won't get the colors and level of transparency you want.

Let's look at some examples. Back in Chapter 10, "Transforms," I showed you how to flip over an image and make it fade out so that it looked like a reflection. However, because the Windows

Runtime doesn't support an opacity mask, I had to fade out the reflected image by covering it with a partially transparent rectangle.

In the ReflectedAlphaImage project I take a different approach. The XAML file has two *Image* elements occupying the same top cell of a two-row *Grid*. The second *Image* element has a *RenderTransformOrigin* and *ScaleTransform* to flip it around its bottom edge, but no bitmap has been specified:

Project: ReflectedAlphaImage | File: MainPage.xaml (excerpt)

```
<Grid Background="{StaticResource ApplicationPageBackgroundThemeBrush}">
    <Grid.RowDefinitions>
        <RowDefinition Height="*" />
        <RowDefinition Height="*" />
    </Grid.RowDefinitions>

    <Image Source="http://www.charlespetzold.com/pw6/PetzoldJersey.jpg"
           HorizontalAlignment="Center" />

    <Image Name="reflectedImage"
           RenderTransformOrigin="0 1"
           HorizontalAlignment="Center">
        <Image.RenderTransform>
            <ScaleTransform ScaleY="-1" />
        </Image.RenderTransform>
    </Image>
</Grid>
```

The same bitmap referenced by the first *Image* element must be loaded independently in the code-behind file. (You might wonder if it's possible to obtain a *WriteableBitmap* based on the object that's set to the *Source* property of the first *Image* object. But that's an object of type *BitmapSource*, and you can't create a *WriteableBitmap* from a *BitmapSource*.) If it's not necessary to modify that downloaded bitmap, the code in the constructor might look something like this:

```
Loaded += async (sender, args) =>
    {
        Uri uri = new Uri("http://www.charlespetzold.com/pw6/PetzoldJersey.jpg");
        RandomAccessStreamReference streamRef = RandomAccessStreamReference.CreateFromUri(uri);
        IRandomAccessStreamWithContentType fileStream = await streamRef.OpenReadAsync();
        WriteableBitmap bitmap = new WriteableBitmap(1, 1);
        bitmap.SetSource(fileStream);
        reflectedImage.Source = bitmap;
    };
```

It's necessary to put this code in the *Loaded* handler because some asynchronous processing is involved. Notice that a *WriteableBitmap* can be created with essentially an "unknown" size if the data is coming from the *SetSource* method. When the *WriteableBitmap* reads that JPEG stream, it can figure out what the actual pixel dimensions are.

However, when that *fileStream* object is passed to the *SetSource* method of *WriteableBitmap* and when that *WriteableBitmap* is set to the *Source* property of the *Image* element, the bitmap has not yet been downloaded. That downloading occurs asynchronously within *WriteableBitmap*. This means that you can't yet start modifying the pixels because the pixels have not yet arrived! It would be nice if *WriteableBitmap* defined an event like *BitmapImage* does that indicates when *SetSource* completes loading the bitmap file, but that's not the case. Nor does the *ImageOpened* event of the *Image* element provide this information for a *WriteableBitmap*.

So, we're left with the job of loading in the bitmap file ourselves and then making the modifications to it. Some of the code I'm going to show you can be simplified with other classes covered later in this chapter, but let's look at how it's done without those classes. Here's the process:

Project: ReflectedAlphaImage | File: MainPage.xaml.cs (excerpt)

```
public sealed partial class MainPage : Page
{
    public MainPage()
    {
        this.InitializeComponent();
        Loaded += OnMainPageLoaded;
    }

    async void OnMainPageLoaded(object sender, RoutedEventArgs args)
    {
        Uri uri = new Uri("http://www.charlespetzold.com/pw6/PetzoldJersey.jpg");
        RandomAccessStreamReference streamRef = RandomAccessStreamReference.CreateFromUri(uri);

        // Create a buffer for reading the stream
        Windows.Storage.Streams.Buffer buffer = null;

        // Read the entire file
        using (IRandomAccessStreamWithContentType fileStream = await streamRef.OpenReadAsync())
        {
            buffer = new Windows.Storage.Streams.Buffer((uint)fileStream.Size);
            await fileStream.ReadAsync(buffer, (uint)fileStream.Size, InputStreamOptions.None);
        }

        // Create WriteableBitmap with unknown size
        WriteableBitmap bitmap = new WriteableBitmap(1, 1);

        // Create a memory stream for transferring the data
        using (InMemoryRandomAccessStream memoryStream = new InMemoryRandomAccessStream())
        {
            await memoryStream.WriteAsync(buffer);
            memoryStream.Seek(0);

            // Use the memory stream as the Bitmap source
            bitmap.SetSource(memoryStream);
        }
```

```
// Now get the pixels from the bitmap
byte[] pixels = new byte[4 * bitmap.PixelWidth * bitmap.PixelHeight];
int index = 0;

using (Stream pixelStream = bitmap.PixelBuffer.AsStream())
{
    await pixelStream.ReadAsync(pixels, 0, pixels.Length);

    // Apply opacity to the pixels
    for (int y = 0; y < bitmap.PixelHeight; y++)
    {
        double opacity = (double)y / bitmap.PixelHeight;

        for (int x = 0; x < bitmap.PixelWidth; x++)
            for (int i = 0; i < 4; i++)
            {
                pixels[index] = (byte)(opacity * pixels[index]);
                index++;
            }
    }

    // Put the pixels back in the bitmap
    pixelStream.Seek(0, SeekOrigin.Begin);
    await pixelStream.WriteAsync(pixels, 0, pixels.Length);
}
bitmap.Invalidate();
reflectedImage.Source = bitmap;
    }
}
```

The *Buffer* class needs a fully qualified name that includes the *Windows.Storage.Streams* namespace because the *System* namespace also includes a class named *Buffer*.

One objective here is to pass an object of type *IRandomAccessStream* to the *SetSource* method of the *WriteableBitmap*. However, immediately after this is done, we want to start working with the pixels of the resultant bitmap. This can't happen unless the file has been fully read.

That's the rationale for creating a *Buffer* object for reading the *fileStream* object, and then using that same *Buffer* object to write the contents to an *InMemoryRandomAccessStream*. As its name suggests, the *InMemoryRandomAccessStream* class implements the *IRandomAccessStream* interface so that it can be passed to the *SetSource* method of *WriteableBitmap*. (But notice that the stream position must first be set back to zero.)

It's important to realize that we're working with two very different chunks of data here. The *fileStream* references the PNG file, which in this case is 82,824 bytes of compressed image data. The *InMemoryRandomAccessStream* is that same chunk of data. Once that stream has been passed to the *SetSource* method of *WriteableBitmap*, it is decoded into rows and columns of pixels. The *pixels* array is 512,000 bytes in size, and the *pixelStream* object references those decompressed pixels. The *pixelStream* object is first used to read the pixels into the *pixels* array and then to write them back out into the bitmap.

Between those two calls is the actual application of the gradient opacity. If the pixels of a *WriteableBitmap* were not assumed by the Windows Runtime to have a premultiplied alpha format, only the Alpha byte would need to be modified. The premulitiplied format requires the color bytes to be multiplied as well. Here's the result:

If you want to see what happens if you adjust only the Alpha byte, substitute the following code for the inner loop:

```
for (int i = 0; i < 4; i++)
{
    if (i == 3)
        pixels[index] = (byte)(opacity * pixels[index]);
    index++;
}
```

You get the transparency you want, but only if the background is white. If the background is black, there's no transparency at all! Look at the formulas and it all becomes clear.

Suppose you wanted to alter the CircularGradient project so that the gradient is from a solid color to complete transparency. Here's the altered code to set the four bytes:

```
pixels[index++] = (byte)(fraction * 255);   // Blue
pixels[index++] = 0;                         // Green
pixels[index++] = 0;                         // Red
pixels[index++] = (byte)(fraction * 255);   // Alpha
```

The Blue component and the Alpha component get the same setting. With a non-premultiplied Alpha format, the Blue component would always be 255. Here's the result:

A Radial Gradient Brush

One of the many mysteriously missing pieces of the Windows Runtime is *RadialGradientBrush*, which is generally used to color a circle with a gradient from a point within that circle to the perimeter. One common use of *RadialGradientBrush* is to turn a circle into a three-dimensionalish "ball" that looks as if some light is reflecting off an area near the upper-left corner.

I began writing my *RadialGradientBrushSimulator* class with an idea about animating the *GradientOrigin* property of this class in a XAML file. For that reason, I made *RadialGradientBrushSimulator* a *FrameworkElement* derivative even though it doesn't display anything on its own. By making it derive from *FrameworkElement* I could more easily instantiate the class in XAML. And because I was thinking about animations and bindings, I defined all the properties as dependency properties. Here's the part of the class containing little more than the dependency property overhead:

Project: RadialGradientBrushDemo | **File:** RadialGradientBrushSimulator.cs (excerpt)

```
public class RadialGradientBrushSimulator : FrameworkElement
{
    ...
    static readonly DependencyProperty gradientOriginProperty =
            DependencyProperty.Register("GradientOrigin",
                    typeof(Point),
                    typeof(RadialGradientBrushSimulator),
                    new PropertyMetadata(new Point(0.5, 0.5), OnPropertyChanged));
```

```
    static readonly DependencyProperty innerColorProperty =
        DependencyProperty.Register("InnerColor",
            typeof(Color),
            typeof(RadialGradientBrushSimulator),
            new PropertyMetadata(Colors.White, OnPropertyChanged));

    static readonly DependencyProperty outerColorProperty =
        DependencyProperty.Register("OuterColor",
            typeof(Color),
            typeof(RadialGradientBrushSimulator),
            new PropertyMetadata(Colors.Black, OnPropertyChanged));

    static readonly DependencyProperty clipToEllipseProperty =
        DependencyProperty.Register("ClipToEllipse",
            typeof(bool),
            typeof(RadialGradientBrushSimulator),
            new PropertyMetadata(false, OnPropertyChanged));

    public static DependencyProperty imageSourceProperty =
        DependencyProperty.Register("ImageSource",
            typeof(ImageSource),
            typeof(RadialGradientBrushSimulator),
            new PropertyMetadata(null));

    public RadialGradientBrushSimulator()
    {
        SizeChanged += OnSizeChanged;
    }

    public static DependencyProperty GradientOriginProperty
    {
        get { return gradientOriginProperty; }
    }

    public static DependencyProperty InnerColorProperty
    {
        get { return innerColorProperty; }
    }

    public static DependencyProperty OuterColorProperty
    {
        get { return outerColorProperty; }
    }

    public static DependencyProperty ClipToEllipseProperty
    {
        get { return clipToEllipseProperty; }
    }

    public static DependencyProperty ImageSourceProperty
    {
        get { return imageSourceProperty; }
    }

    public Point GradientOrigin
    {
        set { SetValue(GradientOriginProperty, value); }
```

```
        get { return (Point)GetValue(GradientOriginProperty); }
    }

    public Color InnerColor
    {
        set { SetValue(InnerColorProperty, value); }
        get { return (Color)GetValue(InnerColorProperty); }
    }
    public Color OuterColor
    {
        set { SetValue(OuterColorProperty, value); }
        get { return (Color)GetValue(OuterColorProperty); }
    }
    public bool ClipToEllipse
    {
        set { SetValue(ClipToEllipseProperty, value); }
        get { return (bool)GetValue(ClipToEllipseProperty); }
    }

    public ImageSource ImageSource
    {
        private set { SetValue(ImageSourceProperty, value); }
        get { return (ImageSource)GetValue(ImageSourceProperty); }
    }

    void OnSizeChanged(object sender, SizeChangedEventArgs args)
    {
        this.RefreshBitmap();
    }

    static void OnPropertyChanged(DependencyObject obj, DependencyPropertyChangedEventArgs args)
    {
        (obj as RadialGradientBrushSimulator).RefreshBitmap();
    }
    ...
}
```

In the *RefreshBitmap* method shown later, the class uses the *GradientOrigin*, *InnerColor*, *OuterColor*, and *ClipToEllipse* properties (as well as the *ActualWidth* and *ActualHeight* of the element) to create a *WriteableBitmap* that the class exposes through the *ImageSource* property, allowing another element in the XAML file to reference that through a binding to the *ImageSource* property of an *ImageBrush*.

It was then that I discovered that the algorithm to make an image of a radial gradient brush was not exactly trivial. Conceptually, you're dealing with an ellipse, although you can use the bitmap to color a rectangle or anything else. The color at the boundary of the ellipse is the *OuterColor* property. The *GradientOrigin* property of type *Point* is in relative coordinates. For example, a value of (0.5, 0.5) would set the *GradientOrigin* to the center of the ellipse. The color at the *GradientOrigin* is the property *InnerColor*.

For any point (x, y) within the bitmap, the algorithm needs to find an interpolation factor to calculate a color between *InnerColor* and *OuterColor*. This interpolation factor is based on a straight line from the *GradientOrigin* through the point (x, y) to the circumference of the ellipse. Where the point (x, y) divides that line determines the value of the interpolation factor.

For best performance I wanted to avoid trigonometry. Instead, my strategy involved finding the intersection of the circumference of the ellipse with the line from the *GradientOrigin* to (*x, y*). This involved solving a quadratic equation for every point in the bitmap.

Here's the *RefreshBitmap* method:

Project: RadialGradientBrushDemo | **File:** RadialGradientBrushSimulator.cs (excerpt)

```
public class RadialGradientBrushSimulator : FrameworkElement
{
    WriteableBitmap bitmap;
    byte[] pixels;
    Stream pixelStream;
    ...
    void RefreshBitmap()
    {
        if (this.ActualWidth == 0 || this.ActualHeight == 0)
        {
            this.ImageSource = null;
            bitmap = null;
            pixels = null;
            pixelStream = null;
            return;
        }

        if (bitmap == null || (int)this.ActualWidth != bitmap.PixelWidth ||
                              (int)this.ActualHeight != bitmap.PixelHeight)
        {
            bitmap = new WriteableBitmap((int)this.ActualWidth, (int)this.ActualHeight);
            this.ImageSource = bitmap;
            pixels = new byte[4 * bitmap.PixelWidth * bitmap.PixelHeight];
            pixelStream = bitmap.PixelBuffer.AsStream();
        }
        else
        {
            for (int i = 0; i < pixels.Length; i++)
                pixels[i] = 0;
        }

        double xOrigin = 2 * this.GradientOrigin.X - 1;
        double yOrigin = 2 * this.GradientOrigin.Y - 1;

        byte aOutsideCircle = 0;
        byte rOutsideCircle = 0;
        byte gOutsideCircle = 0;
        byte bOutsideCircle = 0;

        if (!this.ClipToEllipse)
        {
            double opacity = this.OuterColor.A / 255.0;
            aOutsideCircle = this.OuterColor.A;
            rOutsideCircle = (byte)(opacity * this.OuterColor.R);
            gOutsideCircle = (byte)(opacity * this.OuterColor.G);
            gOutsideCircle = (byte)(opacity * this.OuterColor.B);
        }

        int index = 0;
```

```
for (int yPixel = 0; yPixel < bitmap.PixelHeight; yPixel++)
{
    // Calculate y relative to unit circle
    double y = 2.0 * yPixel / bitmap.PixelHeight - 1;

    for (int xPixel = 0; xPixel < bitmap.PixelWidth; xPixel++)
    {
        // Calculate x relative to unit circle
        double x = 2.0 * xPixel / bitmap.PixelWidth - 1;

        // Check if point is within circle
        if (x * x + y * y <= 1)
        {
            // relative length from gradient origin to point
            double length1 = 0;

            // relative length from point to unit circle
            //   (length1 + length2 = 1)
            double length2 = 0;

            if (x == xOrigin && y == yOrigin)
            {
                length2 = 1;
            }
            else
            {
                // Remember: xCircle^2 + yCircle^2 = 1
                double xCircle = 0, yCircle = 0;

                if (x == xOrigin)
                {
                    xCircle = x;
                    yCircle = (y < yOrigin ? -1 : 1) * Math.Sqrt(1 - x * x);
                }
                else if (y == yOrigin)
                {
                    xCircle = (x < xOrigin ? -1 : 1) * Math.Sqrt(1 - y * y);
                    yCircle = y;
                }
                else
                {
                    // Express line from origin to point as y = mx + k
                    double m = (yOrigin - y) / (xOrigin - x);
                    double k = y - m * x;

                    // Now substitute (mx + k) for y into x^2 + y^2 = 1
                    // x^2 + (mx + k)^2 = 1
                    // x^2 + (mx)^2 + 2mxk + k^2 - 1 = 0
                    // (1 + m^2)x^2 + (2mk)x + (k^2 - 1) = 0 is quadratic equation
                    double a = 1 + m * m;
                    double b = 2 * m * k;
                    double c = k * k - 1;

                    // Now solve for x
                    double sqrtTerm = Math.Sqrt(b * b - 4 * a * c);
                    double x1 = (-b + sqrtTerm) / (2 * a);
```

```
                    double x2 = (-b - sqrtTerm) / (2 * a);

                    if (x < xOrigin)
                        xCircle = Math.Min(x1, x2);
                    else
                        xCircle = Math.Max(x1, x2);

                    yCircle = m * xCircle + k;
                }

                // Length from origin to point
                length1 = Math.Sqrt(Math.Pow(x - xOrigin, 2) +
                    Math.Pow(y - yOrigin, 2));

                // Length from point to circle
                length2 = Math.Sqrt(Math.Pow(x - xCircle, 2) +
                    Math.Pow(y - yCircle, 2));

                // Normalize those lengths
                double total = length1 + length2;
                length1 /= total;
                length2 /= total;
            }

            // Interpolate color
            double alpha = length2 * this.InnerColor.A + length1 * this.OuterColor.A;
            double red= alpha * (length2 * this.InnerColor.R +
                                 length1 * this.OuterColor.R) / 255;
            double green = alpha * (length2 * this.InnerColor.G +
                                 length1 * this.OuterColor.G) / 255;
            double blue = alpha * (length2 * this.InnerColor.B +
                                 length1 * this.OuterColor.B) / 255;

            // Store in array
            pixels[index++] = (byte)blue;
            pixels[index++] = (byte)green;
            pixels[index++] = (byte)red;
            pixels[index++] = (byte)alpha;
        }
        else
        {
            pixels[index++] = bOutsideCircle;
            pixels[index++] = gOutsideCircle;
            pixels[index++] = rOutsideCircle;
            pixels[index++] = aOutsideCircle;
        }
    }
}
pixelStream.Seek(0, SeekOrigin.Begin);
pixelStream.Write(pixels, 0, pixels.Length);
bitmap.Invalidate();
    }
}
```

With an eye toward making this animatable, the array of pixels and the *Stream* object used to transfer the pixels into the bitmap are both saved as fields. No allocations from the heap are required in the

RefreshBitmap method unless the *WriteableBitmap* needs to be re-created because the size of the element has changed.

As it turned out, however, animation performance was very poor, even with rather small dimensions. But if you avoid animating the gradient itself, you can surely animate an object colored with this bitmap. The MainPage.xaml file instantiates both a *RadialGradientBrushSimulator* and an *Ellipse* with a binding to the simulator, as well as a couple animations:

Project: RadialGradientBrushDemo | File: MainPage.xaml (excerpt)

```
<Page ... >
    <Grid Background="{StaticResource ApplicationPageBackgroundThemeBrush}">
        <Canvas SizeChanged="OnCanvasSizeChanged"
                Margin="0 0 96 96">

            <Grid Name="ballContainer"
                  Width="96"
                  Height="96">

                <Ellipse Name="ellipse">
                    <Ellipse.Fill>
                        <ImageBrush ImageSource="{Binding ElementName=brushSimulator,
                                                          Path=ImageSource}" />

                    </Ellipse.Fill>
                </Ellipse>

                <local:RadialGradientBrushSimulator x:Name="brushSimulator"
                                                    InnerColor="White"
                                                    OuterColor="Red"
                                                    GradientOrigin="0.3 0.3" />

            </Grid>
        </Canvas>
    </Grid>

    <Page.Triggers>
        <EventTrigger>
            <BeginStoryboard>
                <Storyboard>
                    <DoubleAnimation x:Name="leftAnima"
                                     Storyboard.TargetName="ballContainer"
                                     Storyboard.TargetProperty="(Canvas.Left)"
                                     From="0" Duration="0:0:2.51"
                                     AutoReverse="True"
                                     RepeatBehavior="Forever" />

                    <DoubleAnimation x:Name="rightAnima"
                                     Storyboard.TargetName="ballContainer"
                                     Storyboard.TargetProperty="(Canvas.Top)"
                                     From="0" Duration="0:0:1.01"
                                     AutoReverse="True"
                                     RepeatBehavior="Forever" />

                </Storyboard>
            </BeginStoryboard>
        </EventTrigger>
    </Page.Triggers>
</Page>
```

Notice how I've put the *Ellipse* and the *RadialGradientBrushSimulator* in the same 96-pixel-square *Grid* so that both elements have the same size and the simulator generates a bitmap of exactly the same size as the *Ellipse* it's used to color. The code-behind file simply adjusts the *To* values on the animations based on the size of the *Canvas*:

Project: RadialGradientBrushDemo | **File:** MainPage.xaml.cs (excerpt)

```
void OnCanvasSizeChanged(object sender, SizeChangedEventArgs args)
{
    // Canvas.Left animation
    leftAnima.To = args.NewSize.Width;

    // Canvas.Top animation
    rightAnima.To = args.NewSize.Height;
}
```

The simulated light reflection makes the *Ellipse* come one step closer to looking like something that might be found in the real world:

Loading and Saving Image Files

As you've seen, you can give the *SetSource* method of *WriteableBitmap* a stream referencing a PNG file, and it will graciously decode that compressed file and convert it into an array of rows and columns. You can get closer to this process with classes in the *Windows.Graphics.Imaging* namespace. You can load a bitmap file as an array of pixel bits, and you can also go the other way: You can save an array of pixel bits from a *WriteableBitmap* that's been created in your program to a file in one of several popular image formats.

Bitmap file formats are generally differentiated by the type of compression they use (including none at all) and of course unique data structures, headers, and techniques for storing the compressed data. Code that knows how to read a specific file format and convert it into an array of pixels is known as a *decoder*. Decoders allow you to load image files into an application. The *BitmapDecoder* class in the *Windows.Graphics.Imaging* namespace supports the formats in the following table.

File Format	MIME Types	Filename Extensions
Windows Bitmap	image/bmp	.bmp .dib .rle
Windows Icon	image/ico image/x-icon	.ico .icon
GIF files	image/gif	.gif
JPEG	image/jpeg image/jpe image/jpg	.jpeg .jpe .jpg .jfif .exif
PNG	image/png	.png
TIFF	image/tiff image/tif	.tiff .tif
WMPhoto	image/vnd.ms-photo	.wdp .jxr

The *BitmapDecoder* class will determine what type of file it's been asked to load and will raise an exception if it can't figure it out.

Code that creates a file of a particular format from an array of pixel bits is called an *encoder*, and in the Windows Runtime it's the *BitmapEncoder* class. Using an encoder is a little different from using a decoder. A decoder can determine what type of file it's being requested to load, but an encoder can't read your mind and determine the file format for a save. It must be told. The *BitmapEncoder* class supports the same formats as the *BitmapDecoder* except for the Windows Icon file.

Sometimes encoders and decoders are referred to collectively as *codecs*, which conveniently stands for either "coder/decoder" or "compressor/decompressor."

The seven file formats shown in the preceding table are identified by global unique IDs (objects of type *Guid*) defined as static properties in the *BitmapEncoder* and *BitmapDecoder* classes, but you really don't need to hard-code these IDs in your program or, indeed, include much specific information at all.

The ImageFileIO program demonstrates how to use the *FileOpenPicker* and a *BitmapDecoder* to load a bitmap file into an application and how to use the *FileSavePicker* and a *BitmapEncoder* to select a file format and save a bitmap file from an application. In between, it has a couple application bar buttons to rotate the image by 90 degrees. Because this program uses the file pickers for obtaining *StorageFile* objects, it does not require any special permission for accessing the user's files.

The XAML file defines an *Image* element, a *TextBlock* for displaying some information about the loaded bitmap, and an *AppBar*:

Project: ImageFileIO | File: MainPage.xaml (excerpt)

```xml
<Page ... >
    <Grid Background="Gray">
        <Grid.RowDefinitions>
            <RowDefinition Height="Auto" />
            <RowDefinition Height="*" />
        </Grid.RowDefinitions>

        <TextBlock Name="txtblk"
                   Grid.Row="0"
                   HorizontalAlignment="Center"
                   FontSize="18" />

        <Image Name="image"
               Grid.Row="1" />
    </Grid>


    <Page.BottomAppBar>
        <AppBar IsOpen="True">
            <Grid>
                <StackPanel Orientation="Horizontal"
                            HorizontalAlignment="Left">

                    <Button Name="rotateLeftButton"
                            IsEnabled="False"
                            Style="{StaticResource AppBarButtonStyle}"
                            Content="&#x21B6;"
                            AutomationProperties.Name="Rotate Left"
                            Click="OnRotateLeftAppBarButtonClick" />

                    <Button Name="rotateRightButton"
                            IsEnabled="False"
                            Style="{StaticResource AppBarButtonStyle}"
                            Content="&#x21B7;"
                            AutomationProperties.Name="Rotate Right"
                            Click="OnRotateRightAppBarButtonClick" />
                </StackPanel>

                <StackPanel Orientation="Horizontal"
                            HorizontalAlignment="Right">

                    <Button Style="{StaticResource OpenFileAppBarButtonStyle}"
                            Click="OnOpenAppBarButtonClick" />

                    <Button Name="saveAsButton"
                            IsEnabled="False"
                            Style="{StaticResource SaveLocalAppBarButtonStyle}"
                            AutomationProperties.Name="Save As"
                            Click="OnSaveAsAppBarButtonClick" />
                </StackPanel>
```

```
        </Grid>
      </AppBar>
    </Page.BottomAppBar>
</Page>
```

Notice that the *AppBar* has its *IsOpen* property initialized to *true*. The program can't do anything until a file is loaded. All the other buttons on the *AppBar* are disabled.

To keep the program relatively simple, it doesn't retain a lot of information. Any bitmap the program loads from the disk is retained only as the *Source* property of the *Image* element. The only fields defined in the code-behind file serve solely to store bitmap resolution information, and that's not crucial:

Project: ImageFileIO | File: MainPage.xaml.cs (excerpt)

```
public sealed partial class MainPage : Page
{
    double dpiX, dpiY;

    public MainPage()
    {
        this.InitializeComponent();
    }
    ...
}
```

When the user clicks the Open button on the *AppBar*, the program creates a *FileOpenPicker* initialized to display the files in the Pictures folder:

Project: ImageFileIO | File: MainPage.xaml.cs (excerpt)

```
public sealed partial class MainPage : Page
{
    ...
    async void OnOpenAppBarButtonClick(object sender, RoutedEventArgs args)
    {
        // Create FileOpenPicker
        FileOpenPicker picker = new FileOpenPicker();
        picker.SuggestedStartLocation = PickerLocationId.PicturesLibrary;

        // Initialize with filename extensions
        IReadOnlyList<BitmapCodecInformation> codecInfos =
                            BitmapDecoder.GetDecoderInformationEnumerator();

        foreach (BitmapCodecInformation codecInfo in codecInfos)
            foreach (string extension in codecInfo.FileExtensions)
                picker.FileTypeFilter.Add(extension);

        // Get the selected file
        StorageFile storageFile = await picker.PickSingleFileAsync();
```

```
            if (storageFile == null)
                return;
            ...
        }
        ...
    }
```

The static *BitmapDecoder.GetDecoderInformationEnumerator* is of enormous assistance here. It returns a collection of seven *BitmapCodecInformation* objects corresponding to the seven file formats in the table shown a few pages ago. Each of these contains a collection of MIME types and a collection of filename extensions. (This is what I used to obtain the information shown in that table.) Those filename extensions can go right into the *FileOpenPicker* object, and the *FileOpenPicker* then displays all the files with those extensions.

If the *PickSingleFileAsync* call returns a non-null *StorageFile* object, the next step is to create a *BitmapDecoder* from that file:

Project: ImageFileIO | File: MainPage.xaml.cs (excerpt)

```
public sealed partial class MainPage : Page
{
    ...
    async void OnOpenAppBarButtonClick(object sender, RoutedEventArgs args)
    {
        ...
        // Open the stream and create a decoder
        BitmapDecoder decoder = null;

        using (IRandomAccessStreamWithContentType stream = await storageFile.OpenReadAsync())
        {
            string exception = null;

            try
            {
                decoder = await BitmapDecoder.CreateAsync(stream);
            }
            catch (Exception exc)
            {
                exception = exc.Message;
            }

            if (exception != null)
            {
                MessageDialog msgdlg =
                    new MessageDialog("That particular image file could not be loaded. " +
                                      "The system reports an error of: " + exception);
                await msgdlg.ShowAsync();
                return;
            }
            ...
        }
        ...
    }
}
```

BitmapDecoder.CreateAsync method could raise an exception if it is given a non-image file or something else it can't handle.

As you might know, a GIF file can contain multiple images that in sequence play a rudimentary animation. These individual images are known as *frames*, and they are supported by the Windows Runtime. After you create a *BitmapDecoder* object, the next step is generally to start extracting frames. However, if you don't want to bother with multiframe GIF files—and I don't blame you if you don't!—you can simply extract the first frame and call it a day. This is what I've done in the next section of the code:

Project: ImageFileIO | File: MainPage.xaml.cs (excerpt)

```
public sealed partial class MainPage : Page
{
    ...
    async void OnOpenAppBarButtonClick(object sender, RoutedEventArgs args)
    {
        ...
        // Get the first frame
        BitmapFrame bitmapFrame = await decoder.GetFrameAsync(0);

        // Set information title
        txtblk.Text = String.Format("{0}: {1} x {2} {3} {4} x {5} DPI",
                                    storageFile.Name,
                                    bitmapFrame.PixelWidth, bitmapFrame.PixelHeight,
                                    bitmapFrame.BitmapPixelFormat,
                                    bitmapFrame.DpiX, bitmapFrame.DpiY);

        // Save the resolution
        dpiX = bitmapFrame.DpiX;
        dpiY = bitmapFrame.DpiY;

        // Get the pixels
        PixelDataProvider dataProvider =
            await bitmapFrame.GetPixelDataAsync(BitmapPixelFormat.Bgra8,
                                    BitmapAlphaMode.Premultiplied,
                                    new BitmapTransform(),
                                    ExifOrientationMode.RespectExifOrientation,
                                    ColorManagementMode.ColorManageToSRgb);

        byte[] pixels = dataProvider.DetachPixelData();
        ...
    }
    ...
    }
    ...
}
```

The method displays information about the first frame in the *TextBlock* at the top of the page and saves the resolution settings as fields.

The *BitmapPixelFormat* and *BitmapAlphaMode* properties of the *BitmapFrame* contain important information about the format of the pixels. *BitmapPixelFormat* is an enumeration with the members *Rgba16* (red, green, blue, and alpha 16-bit values), *Rgba8* (red, green, blue, and alpha 8-bit values), or *Bgra8* (blue, green, red, and alpha 8-bit values), the last of which is compatible with the format associated with *WriteableBitmap*. Pixel data from the file is always converted into one of these formats. The *BitmapAlphaMode* property can indicate *Ignore*, *Straight*, or *Premultiplied*.

You can obtain a byte array of pixels in the pixel format of the frame simply by calling the *GetPixelDataAsync* method with no arguments. However, if you want to use the bitmap data to create a *WriteableBitmap*, you should call the longer version of *GetPixelDataAsync* as shown here to specify the format compatible with *WriteableBitmap*.

After *GetPixelDataAsync* obtains an array of bytes in the same format supported by *WriteableBitmap*, the code to create and display the bitmap is similar to what you've seen before:

Project: ImageFileIO | File: MainPage.xaml.cs (excerpt)

```
public sealed partial class MainPage : Page
{
    ...
    async void OnOpenAppBarButtonClick(object sender, RoutedEventArgs args)
    {
        ...
            // Create WriteableBitmap and set the pixels
            WriteableBitmap bitmap = new WriteableBitmap((int)bitmapFrame.PixelWidth,
                                                         (int)bitmapFrame.PixelHeight);

            using (Stream pixelStream = bitmap.PixelBuffer.AsStream())
            {
                await pixelStream.WriteAsync(pixels, 0, pixels.Length);
            }

            // Invalidate the WriteableBitmap and set as Image source
            bitmap.Invalidate();
            image.Source = bitmap;
        }

        // Enable the other buttons
        saveAsButton.IsEnabled = true;
        rotateLeftButton.IsEnabled = true;
        rotateRightButton.IsEnabled = true;
    }
    ...
}
```

That concludes the processing of the Open button. In summary, the *FileOpenPicker* returns a *StorageFile* object, this is opened and a stream is passed to *BitmapDecoder.CreateAsync*. The *BitmapDecoder* object exposes the images as *BitmapFrame* objects, and the *GetPixelDataAsync* method obtains an array of bytes that can be used to create a *WriteableBitmap*.

Here's the program displaying a bitmap I used in Chapter 13, "Touch, Etc.":

The Save As button on the application bar executes the *OnSaveAsAppBarButtonClick* method, which begins by creating a *FileSavePicker* object. The *BitmapEncoder* *.GetEncoderInformationEnumerator* provides information about the file formats supported by the *BitmapEncoder* class, but this information is used in a somewhat different way than with the *FileOpenPicker*.

The *FileSavePicker* wants a list of file types accompanied by one or more filename extensions for each type. The *FriendlyName* property of the *BitmapCodecInformation* object is unfortunately a string like "JPEG Encoder," so I use the *Split* method of *String* to extract just the first word (for example "JPEG"), and I combine that with the accumulated filename extensions. The code also constructs a dictionary of the supported MIME types and the *Guid* objects associated with those types:

Project: ImageFileIO | File: MainPage.xaml.cs (excerpt)

```
public sealed partial class MainPage : Page
{
    ...
    async void OnSaveAsAppBarButtonClick(object sender, RoutedEventArgs args)
    {
        FileSavePicker picker = new FileSavePicker();
        picker.SuggestedStartLocation = PickerLocationId.PicturesLibrary;

        // Get the encoder information
        Dictionary<string, Guid> imageTypes = new Dictionary<string, Guid>();
        IReadOnlyList<BitmapCodecInformation> codecInfos =
                            BitmapEncoder.GetEncoderInformationEnumerator();

        foreach (BitmapCodecInformation codecInfo in codecInfos)
        {
            List<string> extensions = new List<string>();
```

```
        foreach (string extension in codecInfo.FileExtensions)
            extensions.Add(extension);

        string filetype = codecInfo.FriendlyName.Split(' ')[0];
        picker.FileTypeChoices.Add(filetype, extensions);

        foreach (string mimeType in codecInfo.MimeTypes)
            imageTypes.Add(mimeType, codecInfo.CodecId);
    }

    // Get a selected StorageFile
    StorageFile storageFile = await picker.PickSaveFileAsync();

    if (storageFile == null)
        return;
    ...
    }
    ...
}
```

When the *FileSavePicker* displays itself, the user can select one of the file types from the popup box:

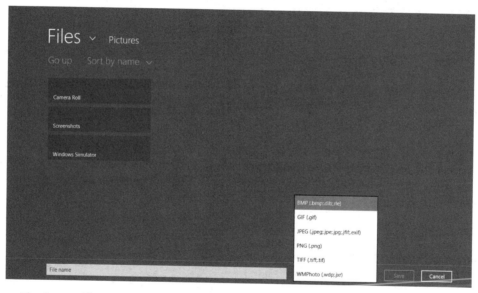

The *StorageFile* object returned from the *FileSavePicker* has a *ContentType* field, which is a MIME type string that identifies the file type that the user chose from that popup. The program can use this with its own dictionary to obtain the *Guid* object associated with that type:

Project: ImageFileIO | **File:** MainPage.xaml.cs (excerpt)

```
public sealed partial class MainPage : Page
{
    ...
    async void OnSaveAsAppBarButtonClick(object sender, RoutedEventArgs args)
    {
```

```
...
// Open the StorageFile
using (IRandomAccessStream fileStream =
                     await storageFile.OpenAsync(FileAccessMode.ReadWrite))
{
    // Create an encoder
    Guid codecId = imageTypes[storageFile.ContentType];
    BitmapEncoder encoder = await BitmapEncoder.CreateAsync(codecId, fileStream);

    // Get the pixels from the existing WriteableBitmap
    WriteableBitmap bitmap = image.Source as WriteableBitmap;
    byte[] pixels = new byte[4 * bitmap.PixelWidth * bitmap.PixelHeight];

    using (Stream pixelStream = bitmap.PixelBuffer.AsStream())
    {
        await pixelStream.ReadAsync(pixels, 0, pixels.Length);
    }

    // Write those pixels to the first frame
    encoder.SetPixelData(BitmapPixelFormat.Bgra8, BitmapAlphaMode.Premultiplied,
                    (uint)bitmap.PixelWidth, (uint)bitmap.PixelHeight,
                    dpiX, dpiY, pixels);

    await encoder.FlushAsync();
}
}
...
}
```

With the help of that *Guid*, the static *BitmapEncoder.CreateAsync* method returns a *BitmapEncoder* object. That object has a *SetPixelData* method that can be used to transfer a byte array into the first frame of the new image file. The Save As operation is complete.

The remainder of the program supports rotating the images by 90 degrees. This feature is actually available in the *BitmapEncoder* class. The class defines a *Transform* property that you can use to scale, flip, crop, or rotate the image in 90-degree increments as it's being saved. However, if you want to see the transformed image, you'll have to perform the logic yourself.

Here are the three methods involved in rotating the image by 90 degrees:

Project: ImageFileIO | File: MainPage.xaml.cs (excerpt)

```
public sealed partial class MainPage : Page
{
    ...
    void OnRotateLeftAppBarButtonClick(object sender, RoutedEventArgs args)
    {
        Rotate((BitmapSource bitmap, int x, int y) =>
            {
                return 4 * (bitmap.PixelWidth * x + (bitmap.PixelWidth - y - 1));
            });
    }
```

```
void OnRotateRightAppBarButtonClick(object sender, RoutedEventArgs args)
{
    Rotate((BitmapSource bitmap, int x, int y) =>
        {
            return 4 * (bitmap.PixelWidth * (bitmap.PixelHeight - x - 1) + y);
        });
}

async void Rotate(Func<BitmapSource, int, int, int> calculateSourceIndex)
{
    // Get the source bitmap pixels
    WriteableBitmap srcBitmap = image.Source as WriteableBitmap;
    byte[] srcPixels = new byte[4 * srcBitmap.PixelWidth * srcBitmap.PixelHeight];

    using (Stream pixelStream = srcBitmap.PixelBuffer.AsStream())
    {
        await pixelStream.ReadAsync(srcPixels, 0, srcPixels.Length);
    }

    // Create a destination bitmap and pixels array
    WriteableBitmap dstBitmap =
            new WriteableBitmap(srcBitmap.PixelHeight, srcBitmap.PixelWidth);
    byte[] dstPixels = new byte[4 * dstBitmap.PixelWidth * dstBitmap.PixelHeight];

    // Transfer the pixels
    int dstIndex = 0;
    for (int y = 0; y < dstBitmap.PixelHeight; y++)
        for (int x = 0; x < dstBitmap.PixelWidth; x++)
        {
            int srcIndex = calculateSourceIndex(srcBitmap, x, y);

            for (int i = 0; i < 4; i++)
                dstPixels[dstIndex++] = srcPixels[srcIndex++];
        }

    // Move the pixels into the destination bitmap
    using (Stream pixelStream = dstBitmap.PixelBuffer.AsStream())
    {
        await pixelStream.WriteAsync(dstPixels, 0, dstPixels.Length);
    }
    dstBitmap.Invalidate();

    // Swap the DPIs
    double dpi = dpiX;
    dpiX = dpiY;
    dpiY = dpi;

    // Display the new bitmap
    image.Source = dstBitmap;
}
}
```

The bulk of both jobs is handled by the same *Rotate* method, except that this method has an argument that is a function to calculate a source index based on *x* and *y* pixel locations of the destination bitmap. If you try this out on large files, you'll find that they require a couple seconds to rotate, strongly suggesting that routines like this should not be executed in the user-interface thread.

The rotation could be performed asynchronously by passing that block of nested *for* loops to *Task .Run* and awaiting the return. However, the asynchronous code cannot access the *WriteableBitmap* itself. You'll need to obtain the width and height of the bitmap before executing the asynchronous code and to redefine the *calculateSourceIndex* to accept a bitmap width and height rather than the bitmap. It would also be prudent to disable the application bar buttons during this time to prevent any interference with the job before it's completed.

Posterize and Monochromize

Most image-processing programs have an option to "posterize" a bitmap. The color resolution is reduced to a limited palette, and this causes the image to resemble a poster rather than a photograph. Another common option is to convert an image to monochrome. These two jobs represent perhaps the simplest image-processing operations.

The Posterizer program has Open File and Save As buttons like ImageFileIO, but the page also contains a "control panel"—a bunch of *RadioButton* controls that let you select a number of bits of color resolution (independently for the three color channels) and a *CheckBox* to convert the image to monochrome.

Suppose the user loads in a bitmap and clicks the *CheckBox* to convert it to monochrome and the program dutifully combines the Red, Green, and Blue values of each pixel into a gray shade. Then the user unchecks the *CheckBox*. Let's hope your program has saved the original image! This is why the Posterizer program maintains two entire pixel arrays, one with the original pixels (named *srcPixels* for "source pixels") and the other with modified pixels (named *dstPixels* for "destination pixels").

The XAML file contains the control panel, an *Image* element and an application bar:

Project: Posterizer | File: MainPage.xaml (excerpt)

```
<Page ... >
    <Page.Resources>
        <Style TargetType="TextBlock">
            <Setter Property="FontSize" Value="18" />
            <Setter Property="TextAlignment" Value="Center" />
        </Style>
    </Page.Resources>

    <Grid Background="{StaticResource ApplicationPageBackgroundThemeBrush}">
        <Grid.ColumnDefinitions>
            <ColumnDefinition Width="Auto" />
            <ColumnDefinition Width="*" />
        </Grid.ColumnDefinitions>
```

```xml
<Grid Name="controlPanelGrid"
      Grid.Column="0"
      Margin="12 0"
      HorizontalAlignment="Center"
      VerticalAlignment="Center">
    <Grid.ColumnDefinitions>
        <ColumnDefinition Width="*" />
        <ColumnDefinition Width="*" />
        <ColumnDefinition Width="*" />
        <ColumnDefinition Width="*" />
    </Grid.ColumnDefinitions>

    <Grid.RowDefinitions>
        <RowDefinition Height="Auto" />
        <RowDefinition Height="Auto" />
        <RowDefinition Height="Auto" />
        <RowDefinition Height="Auto" />
        <RowDefinition Height="Auto" />
        <RowDefinition Height="Auto" />
        <RowDefinition Height="Auto" />
        <RowDefinition Height="Auto" />
        <RowDefinition Height="Auto" />
        <RowDefinition Height="Auto" />
    </Grid.RowDefinitions>

    <TextBlock Text="Red" Grid.Row="0" Grid.Column="0" />
    <TextBlock Text="Green" Grid.Row="0" Grid.Column="1" />
    <TextBlock Text="Blue" Grid.Row="0" Grid.Column="2" />
    <TextBlock Text="All" Grid.Row="0" Grid.Column="3" />

    <CheckBox Name="monochromeCheckBox"
              Content="Monochrome"
              Grid.Row="9"
              Grid.Column="0"
              Grid.ColumnSpan="4"
              Margin="0 12"
              HorizontalAlignment="Center"
              Checked="OnCheckBoxChecked"
              Unchecked="OnCheckBoxChecked" />
</Grid>

<Image Name="image"
       Grid.Column="1" />
</Grid>

<Page.BottomAppBar>
    <AppBar>
        <Grid>
            <StackPanel Orientation="Horizontal"
                        HorizontalAlignment="Right">
                <Button Style="{StaticResource OpenFileAppBarButtonStyle}"
                        Click="OnOpenAppBarButtonClick" />
```

```
                    <Button Name="saveAsButton"
                            IsEnabled="False"
                            Style="{StaticResource SaveLocalAppBarButtonStyle}"
                            AutomationProperties.Name="Save As"
                            Click="OnSaveAsAppBarButtonClick" />
                </StackPanel>
            </Grid>
        </AppBar>
    </Page.BottomAppBar>
</Page>
```

However, the XAML file is missing the actual *RadioButton* controls. I decided I wanted to independently control the three color channels but have a fourth column to change all three color channels in one shot. The buttons are created in the *Loaded* handler with the convenient *Tag* property used to identify them:

Project: Posterizer | **File:** MainPage.xaml.cs (excerpt)

```
public sealed partial class MainPage : Page
{
    ...
    public MainPage()
    {
        this.InitializeComponent();
        Loaded += OnLoaded;
    }

    void OnLoaded(object sender, RoutedEventArgs args)
    {
        // Create the RadioButton controls
        // NOTE: 'a' here means "All" not "Alpha"!
        string[] prefix = { "r", "g", "b", "a" };

        for (int col = 0; col < 4; col++)
            for (int row = 1; row < 9; row++)
            {
                RadioButton radio = new RadioButton
                {
                    Content = row.ToString(),
                    Margin = new Thickness(12, 6, 12, 6),
                    GroupName = prefix[col],
                    Tag = prefix[col] + row,
                    IsChecked = row == 8
                };
                radio.Checked += OnRadioButtonChecked;

                Grid.SetColumn(radio, col);
                Grid.SetRow(radio, row);
                controlPanelGrid.Children.Add(radio);
            }
    }
    ...
}
```

The file I/O is very similar to the ImageFileIO project, except that when an image is loaded, a second array of pixels is created and a method named *UpdateBitmap* (which I'll describe shortly) is responsible for updating the *WriteableBitmap* with this second array of pixels. When a file is saved, the *dstPixels* array is used:

Project: Posterizer | File: MainPage.xaml.cs (excerpt)

```
public sealed partial class MainPage : Page
{
    WriteableBitmap bitmap;
    Stream pixelStream;
    byte[] srcPixels;
    byte[] dstPixels;
    ...
    async void OnOpenAppBarButtonClick(object sender, RoutedEventArgs args)
    {
        // Create FileOpenPicker
        FileOpenPicker picker = new FileOpenPicker();
        picker.SuggestedStartLocation = PickerLocationId.PicturesLibrary;

        // Initialize with filename extensions
        IReadOnlyList<BitmapCodecInformation> codecInfos =
                            BitmapDecoder.GetDecoderInformationEnumerator();

        foreach (BitmapCodecInformation codecInfo in codecInfos)
            foreach (string extension in codecInfo.FileExtensions)
                picker.FileTypeFilter.Add(extension);

        // Get the selected file
        StorageFile storageFile = await picker.PickSingleFileAsync();

        if (storageFile == null)
            return;

        // Open the stream and create a decoder
        BitmapDecoder decoder = null;

        using (IRandomAccessStreamWithContentType stream = await storageFile.OpenReadAsync())
        {
            string exception = null;

            try
            {
                decoder = await BitmapDecoder.CreateAsync(stream);
            }
            catch (Exception exc)
            {
                exception = exc.Message;
            }

            if (exception != null)
            {
                MessageDialog msgdlg =
                    new MessageDialog("That particular image file could not be loaded. " +
                                "The system reports on error of: " + exception);
```

```
                await msgdlg.ShowAsync();
                return;
        }

        // Get the first frame
        BitmapFrame bitmapFrame = await decoder.GetFrameAsync(0);

        // Get the source pixels
        PixelDataProvider dataProvider =
            await bitmapFrame.GetPixelDataAsync(BitmapPixelFormat.Bgra8,
                                        BitmapAlphaMode.Premultiplied,
                                        new BitmapTransform(),
                                        ExifOrientationMode.RespectExifOrientation,
                                        ColorManagementMode.ColorManageToSRgb);

        srcPixels = dataProvider.DetachPixelData();
        dstPixels = new byte[srcPixels.Length];

        // Create WriteableBitmap and set as Image source
        bitmap = new WriteableBitmap((int)bitmapFrame.PixelWidth,
                                    (int)bitmapFrame.PixelHeight);
        pixelStream = bitmap.PixelBuffer.AsStream();
        image.Source = bitmap;

        // Update bitmap from masked pixels
        UpdateBitmap();
    }

    // Enable the Save As button
    saveAsButton.IsEnabled = true;
}

async void OnSaveAsAppBarButtonClick(object sender, RoutedEventArgs args)
{
    FileSavePicker picker = new FileSavePicker();
    picker.SuggestedStartLocation = PickerLocationId.PicturesLibrary;

    // Get the encoder information
    Dictionary<string, Guid> imageTypes = new Dictionary<string, Guid>();
    IReadOnlyList<BitmapCodecInformation> codecInfos =
                        BitmapEncoder.GetEncoderInformationEnumerator();

    foreach (BitmapCodecInformation codecInfo in codecInfos)
    {
        List<string> extensions = new List<string>();

        foreach (string extension in codecInfo.FileExtensions)
            extensions.Add(extension);

        string filetype = codecInfo.FriendlyName.Split(' ')[0];
        picker.FileTypeChoices.Add(filetype, extensions);

        foreach (string mimeType in codecInfo.MimeTypes)
            imageTypes.Add(mimeType, codecInfo.CodecId);
    }
```

```
            // Get a selected StorageFile
            StorageFile storageFile = await picker.PickSaveFileAsync();

            if (storageFile == null)
                return;

            // Open the StorageFile
            using (IRandomAccessStream fileStream =
                            await storageFile.OpenAsync(FileAccessMode.ReadWrite))
            {
                // Create an encoder
                Guid codecId = imageTypes[storageFile.ContentType];
                BitmapEncoder encoder = await BitmapEncoder.CreateAsync(codecId, fileStream);

                // Write the destination pixels to the first frame
                encoder.SetPixelData(BitmapPixelFormat.Bgra8, BitmapAlphaMode.Premultiplied,
                                (uint)bitmap.PixelWidth, (uint)bitmap.PixelHeight,
                                96, 96, dstPixels);

                await encoder.FlushAsync();
            }
        }
        ...
}
```

The *RadioButton* event handler turned out to be rather tricky because of that fourth column of buttons. I wanted a click on a *RadioButton* in the fourth column to also check the other three buttons in that row, but what I certainly didn't want was multiple calls to *UpdateBitmap*. For this reason, an array of three byte masks is maintained as a field, and these are set in the *RadioButton* event handler. *UpdateBitmap* is called only if at least one of these mask values is changed:

Project: Posterizer | **File:** MainPage.xaml.cs (excerpt)

```
public sealed partial class MainPage : Page
{
    ...
    // Byte masks for blue, green, red
    byte[] masks = { 0xFF, 0xFF, 0xFF };
    ...
    void OnRadioButtonChecked(object sender, RoutedEventArgs args)
    {
        // Decode the RadioButton Tag property
        RadioButton radio = sender as RadioButton;
        string tag = radio.Tag as string;
        int maskIndex = -1;
        int bits = Int32.Parse(tag[1].ToString()); // 1 to 8
        byte mask = (byte)(0xFF << 8 - bits);
        bool needsUpdate;
```

```
        // Find the index of the masks array
        switch (tag[0])
        {
            case 'r': maskIndex = 2; break;
            case 'g': maskIndex = 1; break;
            case 'b': maskIndex = 0; break;
        }

        // For "All", check all the other buttons in the row
        if (tag[0] == 'a')
        {
            needsUpdate = masks[0] != mask && masks[1] != mask && masks[2] != mask;

            if (needsUpdate)
                masks[0] = masks[1] = masks[2] = mask;

            foreach (UIElement child in (radio.Parent as Panel).Children)
            {
                if (child != radio &&
                    Grid.GetRow(child as FrameworkElement) == Grid.GetRow(radio))
                {
                    (child as RadioButton).IsChecked = true;
                }
            }
        }
        else
        {
            needsUpdate = masks[maskIndex] != mask;

            if (needsUpdate)
                masks[maskIndex] = mask;
        }

        if (needsUpdate)
            UpdateBitmap();
    }

    void OnCheckBoxChecked(object sender, RoutedEventArgs args)
    {
        UpdateBitmap();
    }
    ...
}
```

All that's left is *UpdateBitmap* itself. The three mask values are applied to the blue, green, and red components, and then these components are combined to create a gray shade if the Monochrome button is checked. The weights for the gray shade are the standard conversion factors for the NTSC and PAL color television standards:

Project: Posterizer | **File:** MainPage.xaml.cs (excerpt)

```
void UpdateBitmap()
{
    if (bitmap == null)
        return;
```

```
    for (int index = 0; index < srcPixels.Length; index += 4)
    {
        // Mask source pixels
        byte B = (byte)(masks[0] & srcPixels[index + 0]);
        byte G = (byte)(masks[1] & srcPixels[index + 1]);
        byte R = (byte)(masks[2] & srcPixels[index + 2]);
        byte A = srcPixels[index + 3];

        // Possibly convert to gray shade
        if (monochromeCheckBox.IsChecked.Value)
            B = G = R = (byte)(0.30 * R + 0.59 * G + 0.11 * B);

        // Save destination pixels
        dstPixels[index + 0] = B;
        dstPixels[index + 1] = G;
        dstPixels[index + 2] = R;
        dstPixels[index + 3] = A;
    }

    // Update bitmap
    pixelStream.Seek(0, SeekOrigin.Begin);
    pixelStream.Write(dstPixels, 0, dstPixels.Length);
    bitmap.Invalidate();
}
```

If this were anything other than a sample program, I would put this processing in a second thread. But only the loops that alter the pixel bits should be in that thread. Any modification to the *Writeable-Bitmap* itself must be in the user-interface thread.

Here it is reducing the pixel resolution of an image to two bits, which means the entire image is displayed with just 64 colors:

Saving Finger Paint Artwork

The series of FingerPaint programs I discussed in the previous chapter all had a big drawback: You couldn't save your artwork. I suggested that one approach to saving the image is to enumerate the *Line* or *Polyline* or *Path* elements in the *Grid* and create some kind of text file (probably in an XML format) that would allow you to re-create all the elements when the file is reloaded.

Or you can draw on a bitmap and save that. The big problem here, however, is that the Windows Runtime version of *WriteableBitmap* doesn't support the rendering of elements such as *Line* and *Path*. You basically have to implement your own line- and arc-drawing algorithms. For a set of line-drawing coordinates and other parameters, these algorithms must figure out what pixels in the bitmap should be set to render these graphical objects.

Let's suppose you want to draw a line between two points:

A geometric line has zero width, but a rendered line must have a non-zero width, and in a finger-painting program, the width might be considerable (for example, 24 pixels). We really want to render this line by drawing a rectangle that extends on each side of the geometric line by half the total line width, 12 pixels on each side in this example:

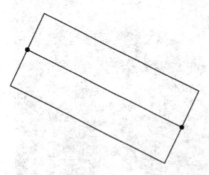

The four corners of that rectangle can be derived fairly easily by rotating the normalized vector between the two geometric points by 90 and –90 degrees and multiplying by half the total line thickness.

But if you're drawing one of these rectangles for each *PointerMoved* event, they're not going to join correctly for a curved line. Little gaps will appear. To avoid those gaps, you want to draw rounded caps on this rectangle:

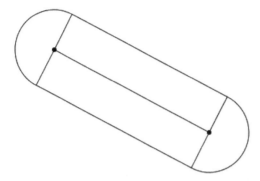

The radius of each of these arcs is half the total line thickness.

The overall shape consists of two arcs connected with two lines. (A similar shape is involved if the line increases or decreases in width between the two points, as I showed in the previous chapter.) But we don't want to draw that outline as I've done here. We need to fill the interior, which means coloring every pixel that appears within the overall shape.

From high school you are probably familiar with the equation for a line in the slope-intercept form:

$$y = mx + b$$

where *m* is the slope ("rise over run") and *b* is the value of *y* where the line intercepts the *Y* axis.

In traditional computer graphics, however, areas are filled based on horizontal scan lines, also known as raster lines. (The terms come from television technology.) The line equation should represent *x* as a function of *y*:

$$x = ay + b$$

For a line from *pt1* to *pt2*, you can calculate *a* and *b* like so:

$$a = \frac{pt2.X - pt1.X}{pt2.Y - pt1.Y}$$

$$b = pt1.X - a \cdot pt1.Y$$

For any *y* (that is, for any scan line), if *y* is between *pt1.Y* and *pt2.Y*, that value of *y* corresponds to a point on the line. The *x* coordinate of that point can be calculated from the equation of the line.

Look at the most recent diagram, and imagine horizontal scan lines intercepting the figure. For any *y* we can determine if the scan line crosses one or both of the outer two lines. If so, we can calculate *x* values for those two points. All the pixels between those *x* values must then be colored. This can be repeated for each *y*.

The process gets a little messier if the scan line passes through the rounded caps, but not much messier. A circle of radius *r* centered on the origin consists of all points (*x*, *y*) that satisfy the equation:

$$x^2 + y^2 = r^2$$

For a circle centered on the point (x_c, y_c), the equation is:

$$\left(x - x_c\right)^2 + \left(y - y_c\right)^2 = r^2$$

Or, expressed as a function of *y*,

$$x = x_c \pm \sqrt{r^2 - \left(y - y_c\right)^2}$$

For any *y*, if the expression in the square root is negative, then *y* is outside the circle entirely—somewhere above or below the circle. Otherwise, there are (in general) two values of *x* for every *y*. The only exception is when the square root is zero, which happens when *y* is exactly *r* units from y_c, which are the top and bottom points of the circle.

When dealing with an arc that goes only partway around the circle, it gets a little more complex. Any point on an arc forms an angle from the center of the circle. That angle can be calculated with the *Math.Atan2* method. If we know the start point and end point of the arc, *Math.Atan2* can calculate the angles corresponding to those two points. You can also use *Math.Atan2* to calculate the angle of any arbitrary point on the circle. If that point on the circle is between the start point and end point, the point is on the arc.

In general, for any *y* we can examine the two lines and two arcs and determine all points (*x*, *y*) that coincide with these four figures. At most, there will be only two such points: one where the scan line enters the figure and one where it exits. For that scan line, all pixels between these two points can be filled.

The FingerPaint solution contains a library project named *Petzold.Windows8.VectorDrawing* that contains several structures to implement line drawing on bitmaps. (I made them structures rather than classes because they will be instantiated and discarded very frequently.)

You've already seen the *Vector2* structure included in this library. All the other structures implement this little interface:

Project: Petzold.Windows8.VectorDrawing | File: IGeometrySegment.cs

```
using System.Collections.Generic;

namespace Petzold.Windows8.VectorDrawing
{
    public interface IGeometrySegment
    {
        void GetAllX(double y, IList<double> xCollection);
```

```
        }
    }
```

For any *y*, the *GetAllX* method adds items to a collection of *x* values. In actual practice, using the structures in the library that implement this interface, often this collection is returned empty. Sometimes it contains one item, and sometimes two.

Here's the *LineSegment* structure:

Project: Petzold.Windows8.VectorDrawing | File: LineSegment.cs

```
using System.Collections.Generic;
using Windows.Foundation;

namespace Petzold.Windows8.VectorDrawing
{
    public struct LineSegment : IGeometrySegment
    {
        readonly Point point1, point2;
        readonly double a, b;          // as in x = ay + b

        public LineSegment(Point point1, Point point2) : this()
        {
            this.point1 = point1;
            this.point2 = point2;

            a = (point2.X - point1.X) / (point2.Y - point1.Y);
            b = point1.X - a * point1.Y;
        }

        public void GetAllX(double y, IList<double> xCollection)
        {
            if ((point2.Y > point1.Y && y >= point1.Y && y < point2.Y) ||
                (point2.Y < point1.Y && y <= point1.Y && y > point2.Y))
            {
                xCollection.Add(a * y + b);
            }
        }
    }
}
```

Notice that the *if* statement in *GetAllX* checks if *y* is between *point1.Y* and *point2.Y*. It allows *y* values that equal *point1.Y* but not those that equal *point2.Y*. In other words, it defines the line to be all points from *point1* (inclusive) up to but not including *point2*. It helps to exercise some strict rules and caution in this regard. Otherwise, when dealing with connected lines and arcs, we'll get duplicate *x* values in the collection, and that makes the job harder.

No special consideration is given to horizontal lines, which are lines where *point1.Y* equals *point2.Y* and *a* equals infinity. In that case, the *if* statement is never satisfied and the line is ignored. A scan line never crosses a horizontal boundary line.

The *ArcSegment* structure is a generalized arc on the circumference of a circle:

Project: Petzold.Windows8.VectorDrawing | File: ArcSegment.cs

```
using System;
using System.Collections.Generic;
using Windows.Foundation;

namespace Petzold.Windows8.VectorDrawing
{
    public struct ArcSegment : IGeometrySegment
    {
        readonly Point center, point1, point2;
        readonly double radius;
        readonly double angle1, angle2;

        public ArcSegment(Point center, double radius,
                          Point point1, Point point2) :
            this()
        {
            this.center = center;
            this.radius = radius;
            this.point1 = point1;
            this.point2 = point2;
            this.angle1 = Math.Atan2(point1.Y - center.Y, point1.X - center.X);
            this.angle2 = Math.Atan2(point2.Y - center.Y, point2.X - center.X);
        }

        public void GetAllX(double y, IList<double> xCollection)
        {
            double sqrtArg = radius * radius - Math.Pow(y - center.Y, 2);

            if (sqrtArg >= 0)
            {
                double sqrt = Math.Sqrt(sqrtArg);
                TryY(y, center.X + sqrt, xCollection);
                TryY(y, center.X - sqrt, xCollection);
            }
        }

        void TryY(double y, double x, IList<double> xCollection)
        {
            double angle = Math.Atan2(y - center.Y, x - center.X);

            if ((angle1 < angle2 && (angle1 <= angle && angle < angle2)) ||
                (angle1 > angle2 && (angle1 <= angle || angle < angle2)))
            {
                xCollection.Add((float)x);
            }
        }
    }
}
```

The rather complex (but symmetrical) *if* clause in *TryY* accounts for the wrapping of angle values from π to $-\pi$ and back again. The comparison of *angle* with *angle1* and *angle2* implies that a scan line is considered to intersect the arc when *angle* equals *angle1* but not when *angle* equals *angle2*.

The *GetAllX* method in *LineSegment* puts either zero or one *x* value in the collection. The *GetAllX* method in *ArcSegment* can put zero, one, or two *x* values in the collection. The *RoundCappedLine* structure combines two *LineSegment* instances and two *ArcSegment* instances for the case of a line with uniform thickness:

Project: Petzold.Windows8.VectorDrawing | **File:** RoundCappedLine.cs

```
using System.Collections.Generic;
using Windows.Foundation;

namespace Petzold.Windows8.VectorDrawing
{
    public struct RoundCappedLine : IGeometrySegment
    {
        LineSegment lineSegment1;
        ArcSegment arcSegment1;
        LineSegment lineSegment2;
        ArcSegment arcSegment2;

        public RoundCappedLine(Point point1, Point point2, double radius) : this()
        {
            Vector2 vector = new Vector2(point2 - new Vector2(point1));
            Vector2 normVect = vector;
            normVect = normVect.Normalized;

            Point pt1a = point1 + radius * new Vector2(normVect.Y, -normVect.X);
            Point pt2a = pt1a + vector;
            Point pt1b = point1 + radius * new Vector2(-normVect.Y, normVect.X);
            Point pt2b = pt1b + vector;

            lineSegment1 = new LineSegment(pt1a, pt2a);
            arcSegment1 = new ArcSegment(point2, radius, pt2a, pt2b);
            lineSegment2 = new LineSegment(pt2b, pt1b);
            arcSegment2 = new ArcSegment(point1, radius, pt1b, pt1a);
        }

        public void GetAllX(double y, IList<double> xCollection)
        {
            arcSegment1.GetAllX(y, xCollection);
            lineSegment1.GetAllX(y, xCollection);
            arcSegment2.GetAllX(y, xCollection);
            lineSegment2.GetAllX(y, xCollection);
        }
    }
}
```

This structure implements *GetAllX* by calling the *GetAllX* methods in the two *LineSegment* instances and two *ArcSegment* instances. It is the responsibility of the code calling *GetAllX* in this structure to ensure that the collection has previously been cleared. The method returns a collection with zero, one, or two *x* values. The case of zero or one *x* value can be ignored for filling purposes. For two *x* values, the pixels between those two values can be filled.

The *RoundCappedPath* structure is similar except that it allows a line to have a different thickness at the beginning and at the end on a pressure-sensitive touch screen:

Project: Petzold.Windows8.VectorDrawing | File: RoundCappedPath.cs

```csharp
using System;
using System.Collections.Generic;
using Windows.Foundation;

namespace Petzold.Windows8.VectorDrawing
{
    public struct RoundCappedPath : IGeometrySegment
    {
        LineSegment lineSegment1;
        ArcSegment arcSegment1;
        LineSegment lineSegment2;
        ArcSegment arcSegment2;

        public RoundCappedPath(Point point1, Point point2, double radius1, double radius2)
            : this()
        {
            Point c0 = point1;
            Point c1 = point2;
            double r0 = radius1;
            double r1 = radius2;

            // Get vector from c1 to c0
            Vector2 vCenters = new Vector2(c0) - new Vector2(c1);

            // Get length and normalized version
            double d = vCenters.Length;
            vCenters = vCenters.Normalized;

            // Create focal point F extending from c0
            double e = d * r0 / (r1 - r0);
            Point F = c0 + e * vCenters;

            // Find angle and length of right-triangle legs
            double alpha = 180 * Math.Asin(r0 / e) / Math.PI;
            double leg0 = Math.Sqrt(e * e - r0 * r0);
            double leg1 = Math.Sqrt((e + d) * (e + d) - r1 * r1);

            // Vectors of tangent lines
            Vector2 vRight = -vCenters.Rotate(alpha);
            Vector2 vLeft = -vCenters.Rotate(-alpha);

            // Find tangent points
            Point t0R = F + leg0 * vRight;
            Point t0L = F + leg0 * vLeft;
            Point t1R = F + leg1 * vRight;
            Point t1L = F + leg1 * vLeft;

            lineSegment1 = new LineSegment(t1R, t0R);
            arcSegment1 = new ArcSegment(c0, r0, t0R, t0L);
            lineSegment2 = new LineSegment(t0L, t1L);
            arcSegment2 = new ArcSegment(c1, r1, t1L, t1R);
        }
```

```
        public void GetAllX(double y, IList<double> xCollection)
        {
            arcSegment1.GetAllX(y, xCollection);
            lineSegment1.GetAllX(y, xCollection);
            arcSegment2.GetAllX(y, xCollection);
            lineSegment2.GetAllX(y, xCollection);
        }
    }
}
```

I adapted some of this logic from the FingerPaint5 program in the previous chapter.

Using these structures in an actual program is not as easy as instantiating *Line* or *Polyline* or *Path*! Here is the *RenderOnBitmap* method from FingerPaint. This method makes use of a *WriteableBitmap* named *bitmap*, with a pixel array named *pixels*, and a *Stream* object named *pixelStream*. The method begins by determining whether it should use *RoundCappedLine* or *RoundCappedPath*:

Project: FingerPaint | **File:** MainPage.Pointer.cs (excerpt)

```
public sealed partial class MainPage : Page
{
    ...
    bool RenderOnBitmap(Point point1, double radius1, Point point2, double radius2, Color color)
    {
        bool bitmapNeedsUpdate = false;

        // Define a line between the two points with rounded caps
        IGeometrySegment geoseg = null;

        // Adjust the points for any bitmap scaling
        Point center1 = ScaleToBitmap(point1);
        Point center2 = ScaleToBitmap(point2);

        // Find the distance between them
        double distance = Math.Sqrt(Math.Pow(center2.X - center1.X, 2) +
                                    Math.Pow(center2.Y - center1.Y, 2));

        // Choose the proper way to render the segment
        if (radius1 == radius2)
            geoseg = new RoundCappedLine(center1, center2, radius1);

        else if (radius1 < radius2 && radius1 + distance < radius2)
            geoseg = new RoundCappedLine(center1, center2, radius2);

        else if (radius2 < radius1 && radius2 + distance < radius1)
            geoseg = new RoundCappedLine(center1, center2, radius1);

        else if (radius1 < radius2)
            geoseg = new RoundCappedPath(center1, center2, radius1, radius2);

        else
            geoseg = new RoundCappedPath(center2, center1, radius2, radius1);
```

```csharp
            // Find the minimum and maximum vertical coordinates
            int yMin = (int)Math.Min(center1.Y - radius1, center2.Y - radius2);
            int yMax = (int)Math.Max(center1.Y + radius1, center2.Y + radius1);

            yMin = Math.Max(0, Math.Min(bitmap.PixelHeight, yMin));
            yMax = Math.Max(0, Math.Min(bitmap.PixelHeight, yMax));

            // Loop through all the y coordinates that contain part of the segment
            for (int y = yMin; y < yMax; y++)
            {
                // Get the range of x coordinates in the segment
                xCollection.Clear();
                geoseg.GetAllX(y, xCollection);

                if (xCollection.Count == 2)
                {
                    // Find the minimum and maximum horizontal coordinates
                    int xMin = (int)(Math.Min(xCollection[0], xCollection[1]) + 0.5f);
                    int xMax = (int)(Math.Max(xCollection[0], xCollection[1]) + 0.5f);

                    xMin = Math.Max(0, Math.Min(bitmap.PixelWidth, xMin));
                    xMax = Math.Max(0, Math.Min(bitmap.PixelWidth, xMax));

                    // Loop through the X values
                    for (int x = xMin; x < xMax; x++)
                    {
                        {
                            // Set the pixel
                            int index = 4 * (y * bitmap.PixelWidth + x);
                            pixels[index + 0] = color.B;
                            pixels[index + 1] = color.G;
                            pixels[index + 2] = color.R;
                            pixels[index + 3] = 255;

                            bitmapNeedsUpdate = true;
                        }
                    }
                }
            }
        }
        // Update bitmap
        if (bitmapNeedsUpdate)
        {
            // Find the starting index and number of pixels
            int start = 4 * yMin * bitmap.PixelWidth;
            int count = 4 * (yMax - yMin) * bitmap.PixelWidth;

            pixelStream.Seek(start, SeekOrigin.Begin);
            pixelStream.Write(pixels, start, count);
            bitmap.Invalidate();
        }

        return bitmapNeedsUpdate;
    }
```

```
        Point ScaleToBitmap(Point pt)
        {
            return new Point((pt.X - imageOffset.X) / imageScale,
                             (pt.Y - imageOffset.Y) / imageScale);
        }
    }
```

Notice that the *RenderOnBitmap* concludes by restricting the updating to only the scan lines affected by this particular drawing operation. The *ScaleToBitmap* method adjusts points for bitmaps that are larger or smaller than the program's current page size.

To organize the source code files in the FingerPaint project in functional chunks, I've divided the code-behind logic for *MainPage* into three files: the normal MainPage.xaml.cs; MainPage.Pointer.cs, which contains all the *Pointer* event handling (including the *RenderOnBitmap* method I just showed you); and MainPage.File.cs, which contains the file I/O. The remainder of MainPage.Pointer.cs should look very familiar. Aside from the call to *RenderOnBitmap*, it's mostly the same as FingerPaint5:

Project: FingerPaint | File: MainPage.Pointer.cs (excerpt)

```
public sealed partial class MainPage : Page
{
    struct PointerInfo
    {
        public Brush Brush;
        public Point PreviousPoint;
        public double PreviousRadius;
    }

    Dictionary<uint, PointerInfo> pointerDictionary = new Dictionary<uint, PointerInfo>();
    List<double> xCollection = new List<double>();

    protected override void OnPointerPressed(PointerRoutedEventArgs args)
    {
        // Get information from event arguments
        uint id = args.Pointer.PointerId;
        PointerPoint pointerPoint = args.GetCurrentPoint(this);

        // Create PointerInfo
        PointerInfo pointerInfo = new PointerInfo
        {
            PreviousPoint = pointerPoint.Position,
            PreviousRadius = appSettings.Thickness * pointerPoint.Properties.Pressure,
            Brush = new SolidColorBrush(appSettings.Color)
        };

        // Add to dictionary
        pointerDictionary.Add(id, pointerInfo);

        // Capture the Pointer
        CapturePointer(args.Pointer);

        base.OnPointerPressed(args);
    }
```

```csharp
protected override void OnPointerMoved(PointerRoutedEventArgs args)
{
    // Get ID from event arguments
    uint id = args.Pointer.PointerId;

    // If ID is in dictionary, start a loop
    if (pointerDictionary.ContainsKey(id))
    {
        PointerInfo pointerInfo = pointerDictionary[id];

        foreach (PointerPoint pointerPoint in args.GetIntermediatePoints(this).Reverse())
        {
            // For each point, get new position and pressure
            Point point = pointerPoint.Position;
            double radius = appSettings.Thickness * pointerPoint.Properties.Pressure;

            // Render and flag that it's modified
            appSettings.IsImageModified =
                RenderOnBitmap(pointerInfo.PreviousPoint, pointerInfo.PreviousRadius,
                               point, radius,
                               appSettings.Color);

            // Update PointerInfo
            pointerInfo.PreviousPoint = point;
            pointerInfo.PreviousRadius = radius;
        }

        // Store PointerInfo back in dictionary
        pointerDictionary[id] = pointerInfo;
    }
    base.OnPointerMoved(args);
}

protected override void OnPointerReleased(PointerRoutedEventArgs args)
{
    // Get information from event arguments
    uint id = args.Pointer.PointerId;

    // If ID is in dictionary, remove it
    if (pointerDictionary.ContainsKey(id))
        pointerDictionary.Remove(id);

    base.OnPointerReleased(args);
}

protected override void OnPointerCaptureLost(PointerRoutedEventArgs args)
{
    // Get information from event arguments
    uint id = args.Pointer.PointerId;

    // If ID is still in dictionary, remove it
    if (pointerDictionary.ContainsKey(id))
        pointerDictionary.Remove(id);

    base.OnPointerCaptureLost(args);
}
...
}
```

Both *OnPointerPressed* and *OnPointerMoved* reference a field named *appSettings* of type *AppSettings*. This object saves settings in application local storage when the program is suspended, and it loads them back in when the program starts up. The overall structure of this class should look familiar by this point:

Project: FingerPaint | **File:** AppSettings.cs

```
using System.ComponentModel;
using System.Runtime.CompilerServices;
using Windows.Storage;
using Windows.UI;

namespace FingerPaint
{
    public class AppSettings : INotifyPropertyChanged
    {
        // Application settings initial values
        string loadedFilePath = null;
        string loadedFilename = null;
        bool isImageModified = false;
        Color color = Colors.Blue;
        double thickness = 16;

        public event PropertyChangedEventHandler PropertyChanged;

        public AppSettings()
        {
            ApplicationDataContainer appData = ApplicationData.Current.LocalSettings;

            if (appData.Values.ContainsKey("LoadedFilePath"))
                this.LoadedFilePath = (string)appData.Values["LoadedFilePath"];

            if (appData.Values.ContainsKey("LoadedFilename"))
                this.LoadedFilename = (string)appData.Values["LoadedFilename"];

            if (appData.Values.ContainsKey("IsImageModified"))
                this.IsImageModified = (bool)appData.Values["IsImageModified"];

            if (appData.Values.ContainsKey("Color.Red") &&
                appData.Values.ContainsKey("Color.Green") &&
                appData.Values.ContainsKey("Color.Blue"))
            {
                this.Color = Color.FromArgb(255,
                                    (byte)appData.Values["Color.Red"],
                                    (byte)appData.Values["Color.Green"],
                                    (byte)appData.Values["Color.Blue"]);
            }

            if (appData.Values.ContainsKey("Thickness"))
                this.Thickness = (double)appData.Values["Thickness"];

        }

        public string LoadedFilePath
        {
            set { SetProperty<string>(ref loadedFilePath, value); }
            get { return loadedFilePath; }
```

```
        }

        public string LoadedFilename
        {
            set { SetProperty<string>(ref loadedFilename, value); }
            get { return loadedFilename; }
        }

        public bool IsImageModified
        {
            set { SetProperty<bool>(ref isImageModified, value); }
            get { return isImageModified; }
        }

        public Color Color
        {
            set { SetProperty<Color>(ref color, value); }
            get { return color; }
        }

        public double Thickness
        {
            set { SetProperty<double>(ref thickness, value); }
            get { return thickness; }
        }

        public void Save()
        {
            ApplicationDataContainer appData = ApplicationData.Current.LocalSettings;
            appData.Values.Clear();
            appData.Values.Add("LoadedFilePath", this.LoadedFilePath);
            appData.Values.Add("LoadedFilename", this.LoadedFilename);
            appData.Values.Add("IsImageModified", this.IsImageModified);
            appData.Values.Add("Color.Red", this.Color.R);
            appData.Values.Add("Color.Green", this.Color.G);
            appData.Values.Add("Color.Blue", this.Color.B);
            appData.Values.Add("Thickness", this.Thickness);
        }

        protected bool SetProperty<T>(ref T storage, T value,
                                      [CallerMemberName] string propertyName = null)
        {
            if (object.Equals(storage, value))
                return false;

            storage = value;
            OnPropertyChanged(propertyName);
            return true;
        }

        protected void OnPropertyChanged(string propertyName)
        {
            if (PropertyChanged != null)
                PropertyChanged(this, new PropertyChangedEventArgs(propertyName));
        }
    }
}
```

One way you can use FingerPaint is to load in existing files, draw on them, and then save them. If that's what you're doing, the filename and full file path are part of user settings. If instead you've started with a blank canvas, the *LoadedFilename* and *LoadedFilePath* properties will both be *null*. Regardless, the *IsImageModified* property is *true* if the image has been modified without being saved to a named file.

In accordance with the concept of chromeless applications, the MainPage.xaml file simply instantiates an *Image* element and implements an application bar:

Project: FingerPaint | File: MainPage.xaml (excerpt)

```
<Page ... >
    <Grid Background="{StaticResource ApplicationPageBackgroundThemeBrush}">

        <Image Name="image" />

        <!-- Disable file I/O buttons in the Snapped state -->
        <VisualStateManager.VisualStateGroups>
            <VisualStateGroup x:Name="ApplicationViewStates">
                <VisualState x:Name="FullScreenLandscape" />
                <VisualState x:Name="Filled" />
                <VisualState x:Name="FullScreenPortrait" />

                <VisualState x:Name="Snapped">
                    <Storyboard>
                        <ObjectAnimationUsingKeyFrames Storyboard.TargetName="fileButtons"
                                                       Storyboard.TargetProperty="Visibility">
                            <DiscreteObjectKeyFrame KeyTime="0" Value="Collapsed" />
                        </ObjectAnimationUsingKeyFrames>
                    </Storyboard>
                </VisualState>
            </VisualStateGroup>
        </VisualStateManager.VisualStateGroups>
    </Grid>

    <Page.BottomAppBar>
        <AppBar>
            <Grid>
                <StackPanel Orientation="Horizontal"
                            HorizontalAlignment="Left">

                    <Button Style="{StaticResource AppBarButtonStyle}"
                            AutomationProperties.Name="Color"
                            Content="&#x1F308;"
                            Click="OnColorAppBarButtonClick" />

                    <Button Style="{StaticResource EditAppBarButtonStyle}"
                            AutomationProperties.Name="Thickness"
                            Click="OnThicknessAppBarButtonClick" />
                </StackPanel>

                <StackPanel Name="fileButtons"
                            Orientation="Horizontal"
                            HorizontalAlignment="Right">
```

```
                <Button Style="{StaticResource OpenFileAppBarButtonStyle}"
                        Click="OnOpenAppBarButtonClick" />

                <Button Style="{StaticResource SaveLocalAppBarButtonStyle}"
                        AutomationProperties.Name="Save As"
                        Click="OnSaveAsAppBarButtonClick" />

                <Button Style="{StaticResource SaveAppBarButtonStyle}"
                        Click="OnSaveAppBarButtonClick" />

                <Button Style="{StaticResource AddAppBarButtonStyle}"
                        Click="OnAddAppBarButtonClick" />
            </StackPanel>
        </Grid>
    </AppBar>
  </Page.BottomAppBar>
</Page>
```

Notice the Visual State Manager markup that makes all the file I/O buttons on the application bar disappear when the application is in the Snapped state. This is actually rather more important than just avoiding overlapping buttons: The file pickers don't work in the Snapped state.

When putting this program together, I encountered a little issue involving file I/O and restarting an application after it's been terminated. Suppose the user invokes the *FileOpenPicker* to select an existing file from the Pictures library. The program gets a *StorageFile* object back from *FileOpenPicker*, uses that to open the file, and retains the *StorageFile* object as a field. Then, when the user presses the Save button on the application bar, the program can simply use that existing *StorageFile* object to save the file.

However, suppose the program is suspended, terminated, and later restarted. That *StorageFile* object cannot be saved in local application storage! The program must abandon it and instead compensate by saving the full file path of the file (as I've done in the *AppSettings* class). When the program starts up again, and the user presses the Save button, the application doesn't have a *StorageFile* object for that file. Instead it must create one using the static *StorageFile. GetFileFromPathAsync* method. But using this method means that the program is accessing the file system without using a *StorageFile* object obtained from a file picker.

For this reason, the FingerPaint program needs permission to access the Pictures library. In Visual Studio, I displayed the properties of Package.appxmanifest and selected the Capabilities tab and checked Pictures Library. I didn't want the program to need this special permission, but the only alternative was forcing the user to save a previously loaded file by using *FileSavePicker*.

Here's the MainPage.File.cs file. You'll recognize some of the bitmap loading and saving logic from previous programs in this chapter, as well as some logic from the XamlCruncher application in Chapter 8, "App Bars and Popups," for asking the user to save a picture that's been modified:

Project: FingerPaint | File: MainPage.File.cs (excerpt)

```
public sealed partial class MainPage : Page
{
    WriteableBitmap bitmap;
    Stream pixelStream;
```

```csharp
byte[] pixels;

async Task CreateNewBitmapAndPixelArray()
{
    bitmap = new WriteableBitmap((int)this.ActualWidth, (int)this.ActualHeight);
    pixels = new byte[4 * bitmap.PixelWidth * bitmap.PixelHeight];

    // Set whole bitmap to white
    for (int index = 0; index < pixels.Length; index++)
        pixels[index] = 0xFF;

    await InitializeBitmap();

    appSettings.LoadedFilePath = null;
    appSettings.LoadedFilename = null;
    appSettings.IsImageModified = false;
}

async Task LoadBitmapFromFile(StorageFile storageFile)
{
    using (IRandomAccessStreamWithContentType stream = await storageFile.OpenReadAsync())
    {
        BitmapDecoder decoder = await BitmapDecoder.CreateAsync(stream);
        BitmapFrame bitmapframe = await decoder.GetFrameAsync(0);
        PixelDataProvider dataProvider =
            await bitmapframe.GetPixelDataAsync(BitmapPixelFormat.Bgra8,
                                                BitmapAlphaMode.Premultiplied,
                                                new BitmapTransform(),
                                                ExifOrientationMode.RespectExifOrientation,
                                                ColorManagementMode.ColorManageToSRgb);
        pixels = dataProvider.DetachPixelData();
        bitmap = new WriteableBitmap((int)bitmapframe.PixelWidth,
                                     (int)bitmapframe.PixelHeight);
        await InitializeBitmap();
    }
}

async Task InitializeBitmap()
{
    pixelStream = bitmap.PixelBuffer.AsStream();
    await pixelStream.WriteAsync(pixels, 0, pixels.Length);
    bitmap.Invalidate();
    image.Source = bitmap;
    CalculateImageScaleAndOffset();
}

async void OnAddAppBarButtonClick(object sender, RoutedEventArgs args)
{
    Button button = sender as Button;
    button.IsEnabled = false;

    await CheckIfOkToTrashFile(CreateNewBitmapAndPixelArray);

    button.IsEnabled = true;
    this.BottomAppBar.IsOpen = false;
}
```

```
async void OnOpenAppBarButtonClick(object sender, RoutedEventArgs args)
{
    Button button = sender as Button;
    button.IsEnabled = false;

    await CheckIfOkToTrashFile(LoadFileFromOpenPicker);

    button.IsEnabled = true;
    this.BottomAppBar.IsOpen = false;
}

async Task CheckIfOkToTrashFile(Func<Task> commandAction)
{
    if (!appSettings.IsImageModified)
    {
        await commandAction();
        return;
    }

    string message =
        String.Format("Do you want to save changes to {0}?",
                        appSettings.LoadedFilePath ?? "(untitled)");

    MessageDialog msgdlg = new MessageDialog(message, "Finger Paint");
    msgdlg.Commands.Add(new UICommand("Save", null, "save"));
    msgdlg.Commands.Add(new UICommand("Don't Save", null, "dont"));
    msgdlg.Commands.Add(new UICommand("Cancel", null, "cancel"));
    msgdlg.DefaultCommandIndex = 0;
    msgdlg.CancelCommandIndex = 2;
    IUICommand command = await msgdlg.ShowAsync();

    if ((string)command.Id == "cancel")
        return;

    if ((string)command.Id == "dont")
    {
        await commandAction();
        return;
    }

    if (appSettings.LoadedFilePath == null)
    {
        StorageFile storageFile = await GetFileFromSavePicker();

        if (storageFile == null)
            return;

        appSettings.LoadedFilePath = storageFile.Path;
        appSettings.LoadedFilename = storageFile.Name;
    }

    string exception = null;

    try
    {
        await SaveBitmapToFile(appSettings.LoadedFilePath);
    }
```

```
            catch (Exception exc)
            {
                exception = exc.Message;
            }

            if (exception != null)
            {
                msgdlg = new MessageDialog("The image file could not be saved. " +
                                    "The system reports an error of: " + exception,
                                    "Finger Paint");
                await msgdlg.ShowAsync();
                return;
            }
        }

        await commandAction();
    }

    async Task LoadFileFromOpenPicker()
    {
        // Create FileOpenPicker
        FileOpenPicker picker = new FileOpenPicker();
        picker.SuggestedStartLocation = PickerLocationId.PicturesLibrary;

        // Initialize with filename extensions
        IReadOnlyList<BitmapCodecInformation> codecInfos =
                            BitmapDecoder.GetDecoderInformationEnumerator();

        foreach (BitmapCodecInformation codecInfo in codecInfos)
            foreach (string extension in codecInfo.FileExtensions)
                picker.FileTypeFilter.Add(extension);

        // Get the selected file
        StorageFile storageFile = await picker.PickSingleFileAsync();

        if (storageFile == null)
            return;

        string exception = null;

        try
        {
            await LoadBitmapFromFile(storageFile);
        }
        catch (Exception exc)
        {
            exception = exc.Message;
        }

        if (exception != null)
        {
            MessageDialog msgdlg =
                new MessageDialog("The image file could not be loaded. " +
                            "The system reports an error of: " + exception,
                            "Finger Paint");
            await msgdlg.ShowAsync();
            return;
        }
    }
```

```
        appSettings.LoadedFilePath = storageFile.Path;
        appSettings.LoadedFilename = storageFile.Name;
        appSettings.IsImageModified = false;
}

async void OnSaveAppBarButtonClick(object sender, RoutedEventArgs args)
{
    Button button = sender as Button;
    button.IsEnabled = false;

    if (appSettings.LoadedFilePath != null)
    {
        await SaveWithErrorNotification(appSettings.LoadedFilePath);
    }
    else
    {
        StorageFile storageFile = await GetFileFromSavePicker();

        if (storageFile == null)
            return;

        await SaveWithErrorNotification(storageFile);
    }

    button.IsEnabled = true;
}

async void OnSaveAsAppBarButtonClick(object sender, RoutedEventArgs args)
{
    StorageFile storageFile = await GetFileFromSavePicker();

    if (storageFile == null)
        return;

    await SaveWithErrorNotification(storageFile);
}

async Task<StorageFile> GetFileFromSavePicker()
{
    FileSavePicker picker = new FileSavePicker();
    picker.SuggestedStartLocation = PickerLocationId.PicturesLibrary;
    picker.SuggestedFileName = appSettings.LoadedFilename ?? "MyFingerPainting";

    // Get the encoder information
    Dictionary<string, Guid> imageTypes = new Dictionary<string, Guid>();
    IReadOnlyList<BitmapCodecInformation> codecInfos =
                        BitmapEncoder.GetEncoderInformationEnumerator();

    foreach (BitmapCodecInformation codecInfo in codecInfos)
    {
        List<string> extensions = new List<string>();

        foreach (string extension in codecInfo.FileExtensions)
            extensions.Add(extension);

        string filetype = codecInfo.FriendlyName.Split(' ')[0];
```

```csharp
            picker.FileTypeChoices.Add(filetype, extensions);

            foreach (string mimeType in codecInfo.MimeTypes)
                imageTypes.Add(mimeType, codecInfo.CodecId);
        }

        // Get a selected StorageFile
        return await picker.PickSaveFileAsync();
    }

    async Task<bool> SaveWithErrorNotification(string filename)
    {
        StorageFile storageFile = await StorageFile.GetFileFromPathAsync(filename);
        return await SaveWithErrorNotification(storageFile);
    }

    async Task<bool> SaveWithErrorNotification(StorageFile storageFile)
    {
        string exception = null;

        try
        {
            await SaveBitmapToFile(storageFile);
        }
        catch (Exception exc)
        {
            exception = exc.Message;
        }

        if (exception != null)
        {
            MessageDialog msgdlg =
                new MessageDialog("The image file could not be saved. " +
                                  "The system reports an error of: " + exception,
                                  "Finger Paint");
            await msgdlg.ShowAsync();
            return false;
        }

        appSettings.LoadedFilePath = storageFile.Path;
        appSettings.IsImageModified = false;
        return true;
    }

    async Task SaveBitmapToFile(string filename)
    {
        StorageFile storageFile = await StorageFile.GetFileFromPathAsync(filename);
        await SaveBitmapToFile(storageFile);
    }

    async Task SaveBitmapToFile(StorageFile storageFile)
    {
        using (IRandomAccessStream fileStream =
                        await storageFile.OpenAsync(FileAccessMode.ReadWrite))
        {
            BitmapEncoder encoder =
                await BitmapEncoder.CreateAsync(BitmapEncoder.PngEncoderId, fileStream);
```

```
encoder.SetPixelData(BitmapPixelFormat.Bgra8, BitmapAlphaMode.Premultiplied,
                     (uint)bitmap.PixelWidth, (uint)bitmap.PixelHeight,
                     96, 96, pixels);
        await encoder.FlushAsync();
    }
  }
}
```

The MainPage.xaml.cs file shown next has several responsibilities. The code in this file saves application settings during program suspension and restores them when the program starts up. It also saves the current picture and reloads it. This logic makes use of methods in the MainPage.File.cs file, but of course it must ignore any exceptions that might occur.

This file is also responsible for handling the *SizeChanged* event, both for setting the visual state used in the XAML file and for setting the *imageScale* and *imageOffset* fields. Depending on the original size of the bitmap, the screen orientation, and the snapped state, the bitmap currently serving as the finger-painting canvas might be larger or smaller than the page. It's always displayed as large as possible without aspect ratio distortion, but touch coordinates must be converted to bitmap coordinates for drawing on it.

Project: FingerPaint | File: MainPage.xaml.cs (excerpt)

```
public sealed partial class MainPage : Page
{
    AppSettings appSettings = new AppSettings();
    double imageScale = 1;
    Point imageOffset = new Point();

    public MainPage()
    {
        this.InitializeComponent();

        SizeChanged += OnMainPageSizeChanged;
        Loaded += OnMainPageLoaded;
        Application.Current.Suspending += OnApplicationSuspending;
    }

    void OnMainPageSizeChanged(object sender, SizeChangedEventArgs args)
    {
        VisualStateManager.GoToState(this, ApplicationView.Value.ToString(), true);

        if (bitmap != null)
        {
            CalculateImageScaleAndOffset();
        }
    }

    void CalculateImageScaleAndOffset()
    {
        imageScale = Math.Min(this.ActualWidth / bitmap.PixelWidth,
                              this.ActualHeight / bitmap.PixelHeight);
        imageOffset = new Point((this.ActualWidth - imageScale * bitmap.PixelWidth) / 2,
                                (this.ActualHeight - imageScale * bitmap.PixelHeight) / 2);
    }
```

```
async void OnMainPageLoaded(object sender, RoutedEventArgs args)
{
    try
    {
        StorageFolder localFolder = ApplicationData.Current.LocalFolder;
        StorageFile storageFile = await localFolder.GetFileAsync("FingerPaint.png");
        await LoadBitmapFromFile(storageFile);
    }
    catch
    {
        // Ignore any errors
    }

    if (bitmap == null)
        await CreateNewBitmapAndPixelArray();
}

async void OnApplicationSuspending(object sender, SuspendingEventArgs args)
{
    // Save application settings
    appSettings.Save();

    // Save current bitmap
    SuspendingDeferral deferral = args.SuspendingOperation.GetDeferral();

    try
    {
        StorageFolder localFolder = ApplicationData.Current.LocalFolder;
        StorageFile storageFile = await localFolder.CreateFileAsync("FingerPaint.png",
                                            CreationCollisionOption.ReplaceExisting);
        await SaveBitmapToFile(storageFile);
    }
    catch
    {
        // Ignore any errors
    }

    deferral.Complete();
}
...
}
```

The MainPage.xaml.cs file is also responsible for handling the Color and Thickness application bar buttons by displaying *Popup* objects with *UserControl* derivatives named *ColorSettingDialog* and *ThicknessSettingDialog*.

Project: FingerPaint | **File:** MainPage.xaml.cs (excerpt)

```
public sealed partial class MainPage : Page
{
    ...
    void OnColorAppBarButtonClick(object sender, RoutedEventArgs args)
    {
        DisplayDialog(sender, new ColorSettingDialog());
    }
```

```
void OnThicknessAppBarButtonClick(object sender, RoutedEventArgs args)
{
    DisplayDialog(sender, new ThicknessSettingDialog());
}

void DisplayDialog(object sender, FrameworkElement dialog)
{
    dialog.DataContext = appSettings;

    Popup popup = new Popup
    {
        Child = dialog,
        IsLightDismissEnabled = true
    };

    dialog.SizeChanged += (dialogSender, dialogArgs) =>
    {
        // Get Button location relative to screen
        Button btn = sender as Button;
        Point pt = btn.TransformToVisual(null).TransformPoint(
                                        new Point(btn.ActualWidth / 2,
                                            btn.ActualHeight / 2));

        popup.HorizontalOffset = Math.Max(24, pt.X - dialog.ActualWidth / 2);

        if (popup.HorizontalOffset + dialog.ActualWidth > this.ActualWidth)
            popup.HorizontalOffset = this.ActualWidth - dialog.ActualWidth;

        popup.HorizontalOffset = Math.Max(0, popup.HorizontalOffset);

        popup.VerticalOffset = this.ActualHeight - dialog.ActualHeight
                                    - this.BottomAppBar.ActualHeight - 24;
    };

    popup.Closed += (popupSender, popupArgs) =>
    {
        this.BottomAppBar.IsOpen = false;
    };

    popup.IsOpen = true;
}
}
```

The *ThicknessSettingDialog* is definitely the simpler of the two. It simply contains a *ListBox* with a bunch of possible line-thickness values. I wanted powers of 2—such as 2, 4, 8, 16, 32—but I also wanted values between those as well, so basically the values increase by the cube root of 2 with rounding and elimination of redundancy:

Project: FingerPaint | **File:** ThicknessSettingDialog.xaml (excerpt)

```
<Grid>
    <Border Background="White"
            BorderBrush="Black"
            BorderThickness="3"
            Padding="32">
```

```xml
<ListBox SelectedItem="{Binding Thickness, Mode=TwoWay}"
        Width="150">
    <x:Double>2</x:Double>
    <x:Double>3</x:Double>
    <x:Double>4</x:Double>
    <x:Double>5</x:Double>
    <x:Double>6</x:Double>
    <x:Double>8</x:Double>
    <x:Double>10</x:Double>
    <x:Double>13</x:Double>
    <x:Double>16</x:Double>
    <x:Double>20</x:Double>
    <x:Double>25</x:Double>
    <x:Double>32</x:Double>
    <x:Double>40</x:Double>

    <ListBox.Foreground>
        <SolidColorBrush Color="{Binding Color}" />
    </ListBox.Foreground>

    <ListBox.ItemTemplate>
        <DataTemplate>
            <Grid Height="{Binding}"
                  Width="120">
                <Canvas VerticalAlignment="Center"
                        HorizontalAlignment="Center">
                <Polyline Points="-36 0 36 0"
                        Stroke="{Binding RelativeSource={RelativeSource TemplatedParent},
                                    Path=Foreground}"
                        StrokeThickness="{Binding}"
                        StrokeStartLineCap="Round"
                        StrokeEndLineCap="Round" />
                </Canvas>
            </Grid>
        </DataTemplate>
    </ListBox.ItemTemplate>

    <ListBox.ItemContainerStyle>
        <Style TargetType="ListBoxItem">
            <Setter Property="Background" Value="Transparent" />
            <Setter Property="Template">
                <Setter.Value>
                    <ControlTemplate TargetType="ListBoxItem">
                        <Grid>
                            <VisualStateManager.VisualStateGroups>
                                <VisualStateGroup x:Name="SelectionStates">
                                    <VisualState x:Name="Unselected">
                                        <Storyboard>
                                            <ObjectAnimationUsingKeyFrames
                                                Storyboard.TargetName="border"
                                                Storyboard.TargetProperty="BorderBrush">
                                                <DiscreteObjectKeyFrame
                                                        KeyTime="0"
                                                        Value="Transparent" />
                                            </ObjectAnimationUsingKeyFrames>
                                        </Storyboard>
                                    </VisualState>
```

```
                                <VisualState x:Name="Selected" />
                                <VisualState x:Name="SelectedUnfocused" />
                                <VisualState x:Name="SelectedDisabled" />
                                <VisualState x:Name="SelectedPointerOver" />
                                <VisualState x:Name="SelectedPressed" />
                            </VisualStateGroup>
                        </VisualStateManager.VisualStateGroups>

                        <Border Name="border"
                                BorderBrush="Black"
                                BorderThickness="1"
                                Background="Transparent"
                                Padding="12">

                            <ContentPresenter Content="{TemplateBinding Content}" />

                        </Border>
                    </Grid>
                </ControlTemplate>
            </Setter.Value>
        </Setter>
    </Style>
</ListBox.ItemContainerStyle>
        </ListBox>
    </Border>
</Grid>
```

Of course, all the "magic" occurs in the templates. (There is nothing in the code-behind file except a call to *InitializeComponent*.) The *ItemTemplate* uses the value in the *ListBox* as a thickness for an actual line, and the *ItemContainerStyle* causes a rectangle to be drawn around the selected value:

When *MainPage* displays this dialog, the *DataContext* is set to the *AppSettings* instance, so the value of the *Thickness* property in that class is updated through the data binding. That value is used in all subsequent drawing operations until the next change.

HSL Color Selection

You've probably seen a few too many color selectors in the book built from sliders that let you pick Red, Green, and Blue values. That's an easy way to pick color because it's the way that color is defined in video displays and in the Windows Runtime.

However, it's not really an intuitive way to select colors. People seem to prefer a system built around values named Hue, Saturation, and Lightness. Hue is basically a color of the rainbow, named by Isaac Newton as red, orange, yellow, green, blue, indigo, and violet. Using more "computerish" colors, Hue ranges continuously from red, through yellow, green, cyan, blue, magenta, and back to red. Notice the three additive primaries (red, green, and blue) and the three subtractive primaries (yellow, cyan, and magenta), which are combinations of the pair of additive primaries surrounding them.

The Hue is combined with a Saturation value. When the Saturation is a maximum value, the color is most vivid. At a minimum saturation, the color is gray. Then Lightness comes into play. Increasing the Lightness washes out the color and eventually turns it white at the maximum value. Decreasing the Lightness from its medium value turns the color black.

Hue-Saturation-Lightness (or HSL) color selection is used in Windows Paint and Microsoft Word, where a two-dimensional grid (similar to the *XYSlider* in Chapter 13) is used for the combination of Hue and Saturation and a regular slider is used for Lightness.

To mimic this type of color selection, I created an *HSL* structure for representing an HSL color value. This structure incorporates conversion routines between RGB and HSL:

Project: FingerPaint | File: HSL.cs

```csharp
public struct HSL
{
    public HSL(byte hue, byte saturation, byte lightness) :
        this(360 * hue / 255.0, saturation / 255.0, lightness / 255.0)
    {
    }

    // Hue from 0 to 360, saturation and lightness from 0 to 1
    public HSL(double hue, double saturation, double lightness) : this()
    {
        this.Hue = hue;
        this.Saturation = saturation;
        this.Lightness = lightness;

        double chroma = saturation * (1 - Math.Abs(2 * lightness - 1));
        double h = hue / 60;
```

```
        double x = chroma * (1 - Math.Abs(h % 2 - 1));
        double r = 0, g = 0, b = 0;

        if (h < 1)
        {
            r = chroma;
            g = x;
        }
        else if (h < 2)
        {
            r = x;
            g = chroma;
        }
        else if (h < 3)
        {
            g = chroma;
            b = x;
        }
        else if (h < 4)
        {
            g = x;
            b = chroma;
        }
        else if (h < 5)
        {
            r = x;
            b = chroma;
        }
        else
        {
            r = chroma;
            b = x;
        }

        double m = lightness - chroma / 2;
        this.Color = Color.FromArgb(255, (byte)(255 * (r + m)),
                                        (byte)(255 * (g + m)),
                                        (byte)(255 * (b + m)));

    }

    public HSL(Color color)
        : this()
    {
        this.Color = color;

        double r = color.R / 255.0;
        double g = color.G / 255.0;
        double b = color.B / 255.0;
        double max = Math.Max(r, Math.Max(g, b));
        double min = Math.Min(r, Math.Min(g, b));

        double chroma = max - min;
        this.Lightness = (max + min) / 2;

        if (chroma != 0)
        {
            if (r == max)
```

```
                   this.Hue = 60 * (g - b) / chroma;

               else if (g == max)
                   this.Hue = 120 + 60 * (b - r) / chroma;

               else
                   this.Hue = 240 + 60 * (r - g) / chroma;

               this.Hue = (this.Hue + 360) % 360;

               if (this.Lightness < 0.5)
                   this.Saturation = chroma / (2 * this.Lightness);
               else
                   this.Saturation = chroma / (2 - 2 * this.Lightness);
           }
       }

       public double Hue { private set; get; }

       public double Saturation { private set; get; }

       public double Lightness { private set; get; }

       public Color Color { private set; get; }
   }
```

Notice the two different constructors, one using *byte* arguments and the other using *double* arguments. For a particular call to an HSL constructor, the C# compiler needs to choose which constructor to use, and it will choose the first one only if all the arguments are *byte* values. There's no such ambiguity with the third constructor, which converts a *Color* value to HSL.

I presented an *XYSlider* control in the previous chapter but indicated that it would be more usable if it used *Pointer* events rather than *Manipulation* events. Here's the revised version. Because it's working with *Pointer* events, it needs to keep track of multiple fingers, but it simply averages the positions of those fingers to create a composite position. Otherwise, the control is basically the same:

Project: FingerPaint | File: XYSlider.cs (excerpt)

```
public class XYSlider : ContentControl
{
    ContentPresenter contentPresenter;
    FrameworkElement crossHairPart;
    Dictionary<uint, Point> pointerDictionary = new Dictionary<uint, Point>();

    static readonly DependencyProperty valueProperty =
            DependencyProperty.Register("Value",
                    typeof(Point), typeof(XYSlider),
                    new PropertyMetadata(new Point(), OnValueChanged));

    public event EventHandler<Point> ValueChanged;

    public XYSlider()
    {
        this.DefaultStyleKey = typeof(XYSlider);
```

```
            }

            public static DependencyProperty ValueProperty
            {
                get { return valueProperty; }
            }

            public Point Value
            {
                set { SetValue(ValueProperty, value); }
                get { return (Point)GetValue(ValueProperty); }
            }

            protected override void OnApplyTemplate()
            {
                // Detach event handlers
                if (contentPresenter != null)
                {
                    contentPresenter.PointerPressed -= OnContentPresenterPointerPressed;
                    contentPresenter.PointerMoved -= OnContentPresenterPointerMoved;
                    contentPresenter.PointerReleased -= OnContentPresenterPointerReleased;
                    contentPresenter.PointerCaptureLost -= OnContentPresenterPointerReleased;
                    contentPresenter.SizeChanged -= OnContentPresenterSizeChanged;
                }

                // Get new parts
                crossHairPart = GetTemplateChild("CrossHairPart") as FrameworkElement;
                contentPresenter = GetTemplateChild("ContentPresenterPart") as ContentPresenter;

                // Attach event handlers
                if (contentPresenter != null)
                {
                    contentPresenter.PointerPressed += OnContentPresenterPointerPressed;
                    contentPresenter.PointerMoved += OnContentPresenterPointerMoved;
                    contentPresenter.PointerReleased += OnContentPresenterPointerReleased;
                    contentPresenter.PointerCaptureLost += OnContentPresenterPointerReleased;
                    contentPresenter.SizeChanged += OnContentPresenterSizeChanged;
                }

                // Make cross-hair transparent to touch
                if (crossHairPart != null)
                {
                    crossHairPart.IsHitTestVisible = false;
                }

                base.OnApplyTemplate();
            }

            void OnContentPresenterPointerPressed(object sender, PointerRoutedEventArgs args)
            {
                uint id = args.Pointer.PointerId;
                Point point = args.GetCurrentPoint(contentPresenter).Position;
                pointerDictionary.Add(id, point);
                contentPresenter.CapturePointer(args.Pointer);

                RecalculateValue();
                args.Handled = true;
```

```
}

void OnContentPresenterPointerMoved(object sender, PointerRoutedEventArgs args)
{
    uint id = args.Pointer.PointerId;
    Point point = args.GetCurrentPoint(contentPresenter).Position;

    if (pointerDictionary.ContainsKey(id))
    {
        pointerDictionary[id] = point;
        RecalculateValue();
        args.Handled = true;
    }
}

void OnContentPresenterPointerReleased(object sender, PointerRoutedEventArgs args)
{
    uint id = args.Pointer.PointerId;

    if (pointerDictionary.ContainsKey(id))
    {
        pointerDictionary.Remove(id);
        RecalculateValue();
        args.Handled = true;
    }
}

void OnContentPresenterSizeChanged(object sender, SizeChangedEventArgs args)
{
    SetCrossHair();
}

void RecalculateValue()
{
    if (pointerDictionary.Values.Count > 0)
    {
        Point accumPoint = new Point();

        // Average all the current touch points
        foreach (Point point in pointerDictionary.Values)
        {
            accumPoint.X += point.X;
            accumPoint.Y += point.Y;
        }
        accumPoint.X /= pointerDictionary.Values.Count;
        accumPoint.Y /= pointerDictionary.Values.Count;

        RecalculateValue(accumPoint);
    }
}

void RecalculateValue(Point absolutePoint)
{
    double x = Math.Max(0, Math.Min(1, absolutePoint.X / contentPresenter.ActualWidth));
    double y = Math.Max(0, Math.Min(1, absolutePoint.Y / contentPresenter.ActualHeight));
    this.Value = new Point(x, y);
}
```

```
void SetCrossHair()
{
    if (contentPresenter != null && crossHairPart != null)
    {
        Canvas.SetLeft(crossHairPart, this.Value.X * contentPresenter.ActualWidth);
        Canvas.SetTop(crossHairPart, this.Value.Y * contentPresenter.ActualHeight);
    }
}

static void OnValueChanged(DependencyObject obj, DependencyPropertyChangedEventArgs args)
{
    (obj as XYSlider).SetCrossHair();
    (obj as XYSlider).OnValueChanged((Point)args.NewValue);
}

protected void OnValueChanged(Point value)
{
    if (ValueChanged != null)
        ValueChanged(this, value);
}
}
```

The next step is to build an *HslColorSelector* control. This is derived from *UserControl* and instantiates an *XYSlider*, *Slider*, and *TextBlock* in the XAML file. The *Resources* section defines *ControlTemplate* objects for the *XYSlider* and *Slider*. The *XYSlider* template is considerably simplified from what I showed for the corresponding control in Chapter 13 because I knew exactly the visuals I wanted and didn't add anything else.

Project: FingerPaint | File: HslColorSelector.xaml (excerpt)

```
<UserControl ... >
    <UserControl.Resources>
        <ControlTemplate x:Key="xySliderTemplate" TargetType="local:XYSlider">
            <Border>
                <Grid>
                    <ContentPresenter Name="ContentPresenterPart"
                                      Content="{TemplateBinding Content}" />
                    <Canvas>
                        <Path Name="CrossHairPart"
                              Fill="{TemplateBinding Foreground}"
                              Data="M 0 6 L -3 24 3 24 Z
                                    M 0 -6 L -3 -24 3 -24 Z
                                    M 6 0 L 24 -3 24 3 Z
                                    M -6 0 L -24 -2 -24 3 Z" />
                    </Canvas>
                </Grid>
            </Border>
        </ControlTemplate>

        <ControlTemplate x:Key="sliderTemplate" TargetType="Slider">
            <Grid>
                <Grid Name="HorizontalTemplate"
                      Background="Transparent"
                      Height="48">
                    <Grid.ColumnDefinitions>
                        <ColumnDefinition Width="*" />
```

```xml
                    <ColumnDefinition Width="Auto" />
                    <ColumnDefinition Width="Auto" />
                </Grid.ColumnDefinitions>

                <Rectangle Name="HorizontalTrackRect"
                        Grid.Column="0"
                        Grid.ColumnSpan="3"
                        Fill="{TemplateBinding Background}"
                        Height="12"
                        VerticalAlignment="Top" />

                <Thumb Name="HorizontalThumb"
                        Grid.Column="1"
                        DataContext="{TemplateBinding Value}">
                    <Thumb.Template>
                        <ControlTemplate TargetType="Thumb">
                            <Path Fill="{TemplateBinding Foreground}"
                                Data="M 0 24 L -3 48 3 48 Z" />
                        </ControlTemplate>
                    </Thumb.Template>
                </Thumb>

                <Rectangle Name="HorizontalDecreaseRect"
                        Grid.Column="2"
                        Fill="Transparent" />
        </Grid>

        <Grid Name="VerticalTemplate"
            Background="Transparent"
            Width="48">
            <Grid.RowDefinitions>
                <RowDefinition Height="*" />
                <RowDefinition Height="Auto" />
                <RowDefinition Height="Auto" />
            </Grid.RowDefinitions>

            <Rectangle Name="VerticalTrackRect"
                    Grid.Row="0"
                    Grid.RowSpan="3"
                    Fill="{TemplateBinding Background}"
                    Width="12"
                    HorizontalAlignment="Left" />

            <Thumb Name="VerticalThumb"
                    Grid.Row="1"
                    DataContext="{TemplateBinding Value}">
                <Thumb.Template>
                    <ControlTemplate TargetType="Thumb">
                        <Path Fill="{TemplateBinding Foreground}"
                            Data="M 24 0 L 48 -3 48 3 Z" />
                    </ControlTemplate>
                </Thumb.Template>
            </Thumb>

            <Rectangle Name="VerticalDecreaseRect"
                    Grid.Row="2"
                    Fill="Transparent" />
```

```
                </Grid>
            </Grid>
        </ControlTemplate>
    </UserControl.Resources>

    <Grid>
        <Grid.RowDefinitions>
            <RowDefinition Height="Auto" />
            <RowDefinition Height="Auto" />
            <RowDefinition Height="Auto" />
        </Grid.RowDefinitions>

        <local:XYSlider x:Name="xySlider"
                        Grid.Row="0"
                        Template="{StaticResource xySliderTemplate}"
                        ValueChanged="OnXYSliderValueChanged">
            <Image Name="hsImage"
                   Stretch="None" />
        </local:XYSlider>

        <Slider Name="slider"
                Grid.Row="1"
                Orientation="Horizontal"
                Template="{StaticResource sliderTemplate}"
                Width="256"
                Margin="0 12"
                ValueChanged="OnSliderValueChanged">
            <Slider.Background>
                <LinearGradientBrush StartPoint="0 0" EndPoint="1 0">
                    <GradientStop Offset="0" Color="Black" />
                    <GradientStop x:Name="sliderGradientStop" Offset="0.5" />
                    <GradientStop Offset="1" Color="White" />
                </LinearGradientBrush>
            </Slider.Background>
        </Slider>

        <TextBlock Name="txtblk"
                   Grid.Row="2"
                   HorizontalAlignment="Center"
                   TextAlignment="Center"
                   FontSize="24" />
    </Grid>
</UserControl>
```

Notice that the *ControlTemplate* for the *Slider* basically colors the control with its *Background* property. This *Background* property is defined on the *Slider* itself toward the bottom of the XAML file. It's a *LinearGradientBrush* that ranges from black to white with a color in the center settable from the code-behind file. That color is based on the combination of Hue and Saturation the user selects from the *XYSlider*.

The code-behind file defines a *DependencyProperty* named *Color* of type *Color*. Obviously, as a public property to be used in bindings, this *Color* property makes much more sense than a public property of type *HSL*. The *Loaded* handler is responsible for creating a bitmap for the main Hue-Saturation grid. It uses the *HSL* structure to convert from HSL (with an average Lightness value) to obtain RGB values for the bitmap pixels.

Project: FingerPaint | **File:** HslColorSelector.xaml.cs (excerpt)

```
public partial class HslColorSelector : UserControl
{
    bool doNotSetSliders = false;

    static readonly DependencyProperty colorProperty =
        DependencyProperty.Register("Color",
            typeof(Color),
            typeof(HslColorSelector),
            new PropertyMetadata(new Color(), OnColorChanged));

    public event EventHandler<Color> ColorChanged;

    public HslColorSelector()
    {
        this.InitializeComponent();
        Loaded += OnLoaded;
    }

    async void OnLoaded(object sender, RoutedEventArgs args)
    {
        // Build bitmap for hue/saturation grid
        WriteableBitmap bitmap = new WriteableBitmap(256, 256);
        byte[] pixels = new byte[4 * 256 * 256];
        int index = 0;

        for (int y = 0; y < 256; y++)
            for (int x = 0; x < 256; x++)
            {
                HSL hsl = new HSL((byte)x, (byte)(255 - y), (byte)128);
                Color clr = hsl.Color;

                pixels[index++] = clr.B;
                pixels[index++] = clr.G;
                pixels[index++] = clr.R;
                pixels[index++] = clr.A;
            }

        using (Stream pixelStream = bitmap.PixelBuffer.AsStream())
        {
            await pixelStream.WriteAsync(pixels, 0, pixels.Length);
        }
        bitmap.Invalidate();
        hsImage.Source = bitmap;
    }
```

```csharp
public static DependencyProperty ColorProperty
{
    get { return colorProperty; }
}

public Color Color
{
    set { SetValue(ColorProperty, value); }
    get { return (Color)GetValue(ColorProperty); }
}

// Event handlers for sliders
void OnXYSliderValueChanged(object sender, Point point)
{
    HSL hsl = new HSL(360 * point.X, 1 - point.Y, 0.5);
    sliderGradientStop.Color = hsl.Color;
    SetColorFromSliders();
}

void OnSliderValueChanged(object sender, RangeBaseValueChangedEventArgs args)
{
    SetColorFromSliders();
}

void SetColorFromSliders()
{
    Point point = xySlider.Value;
    double value = slider.Value;
    HSL hsl = new HSL(360 * point.X, 1 - point.Y, value / 100);

    doNotSetSliders = true;
    this.Color = hsl.Color;
    doNotSetSliders = false;
}

// Color property-changed handlers
static void OnColorChanged(DependencyObject obj, DependencyPropertyChangedEventArgs args)
{
    (obj as HslColorSelector).OnColorChanged((Color)args.NewValue);
}

protected void OnColorChanged(Color color)
{
    HSL hsl = new HSL(color);

    if (!doNotSetSliders)
    {
        xySlider.Value = new Point(hsl.Hue / 360, 1 - hsl.Saturation);
        slider.Value = 100 * hsl.Lightness;
    }
```

```
txtblk.Text = String.Format("RGB = ({0}, {1}, {2})",
                    this.Color.R, this.Color.G, this.Color.B);

    if (ColorChanged != null)
        ColorChanged(this, color);
    }
}
```

When a new *Color* property is set from outside the file, the *OnColorChanged* handler responds by setting the *XYSlider* and *Slider* values as well as using the *TextBlock* to display the RGB color value. When the user manipulates the *XYSlider* and *Slider* values, a new *Color* property is set and *OnColorChanged* is called. Normally, recursive calls to property-changed handlers are OK, but not in this case because a round-trip conversion—RGB to HSL to RGB—doesn't result in exactly the same value. That's the reason for the Boolean *doNotSetSliders* field when the *Color* property is changed from user input.

Finally, a *ColorSettingDialog* incorporates the *HslColorSelector*:

Project: FingerPaint | File: ColorSettingDialog.xaml (excerpt)

```
<Grid>
    <Border Background="White"
            BorderBrush="Black"
            BorderThickness="3"
            Padding="32">
        <StackPanel>
            <Path Data="M 0 50 C 80 0 160 100 256 0"
                StrokeStartLineCap="Round"
                StrokeEndLineCap="Round"
                StrokeThickness="{Binding Thickness}"
                Margin="0 12">
                <Path.Stroke>
                    <SolidColorBrush Color="{Binding Color}" />
                </Path.Stroke>
            </Path>

            <local:HslColorSelector x:Name="hslColorSelector"
                                    Foreground="Black"
                                    Color="{Binding Path=Color, Mode=TwoWay}" />
        </StackPanel>
    </Border>
</Grid>
```

For a preview, the control displays a squiggle based on the current thickness and color:

When you use Finger Paint on anything other than a very high resolution display, you'll probably notice that the drawing is a little grainier than the earlier FingerPaint programs from Chapter 13. There's a very good reason for this: When you render graphical objects with *Line*, *Polyline*, and *Path*, you get antialiasing. The boundary lines are a combination of the fill color and the background color, and perceptually the lines are smoother. But there is no antialiasing implemented in the Petzold.Windows8.VectorDrawing library. Either a pixel is colored, or it is not.

Reverse Painting

I once saw a little movie of someone painting over a large colorful mural with white paint and a roller, except that the movie was run in reverse so that it seemed as if the mural was being magically created by painting with the roller over a white surface.

A similar technique is illustrated in the ReversePaint program. The XAML file accesses a bitmap on my website and defines another *Image* element that lies on top:

Project: ReversePaint | File: MainPage.xaml (excerpt)

```
<Grid Background="{StaticResource ApplicationPageBackgroundThemeBrush}">
    <Image Source="http://www.charlespetzold.com/pw6/PetzoldJersey.jpg" />
    <Image Name="whiteImage" />
</Grid>
```

The bitmap for the second *Image* element is created in the *Loaded* handler to be the same size as the downloaded bitmap and all white. Like FingerPaint, there's a *CalculateImageScaleAndOffset* method that calculates factors for scaling pointer input to the bitmap. To streamline the presentation of the code, I've removed a lot of comments from the pointer event handlers, but you've seen the logic before. The *OnPointerMoved* method calls a simplified form of *RenderOnBitmap* with two points, a fixed line thickness, and a *Color* value representing transparency:

Project: ReversePaint | File: MainPage.xaml.cs (excerpt)

```
public sealed partial class MainPage : Page
{
    Dictionary<uint, Point> pointerDictionary = new Dictionary<uint, Point>();
    List<double> xCollection = new List<double>();

    WriteableBitmap bitmap;
    byte[] pixels;
    Stream pixelStream;

    Point imageOffset = new Point();
    double imageScale = 1;

    public MainPage()
    {
        this.InitializeComponent();

        SizeChanged += OnMainPageSizeChanged;
        Loaded += OnMainPageLoaded;
    }

    void OnMainPageSizeChanged(object sender, SizeChangedEventArgs args)
    {
        if (bitmap != null)
            CalculateImageScaleAndOffset();
    }

    async void OnMainPageLoaded(object sender, RoutedEventArgs args)
    {
        bitmap = new WriteableBitmap(320, 400);
        pixels = new byte[4 * bitmap.PixelWidth * bitmap.PixelHeight];

        // Initialize pixels to white
        for (int index = 0; index < pixels.Length; index++)
            pixels[index] = 0xFF;

        pixelStream = bitmap.PixelBuffer.AsStream();
        await pixelStream.WriteAsync(pixels, 0, pixels.Length);
        bitmap.Invalidate();

        // Set to Image element
        whiteImage.Source = bitmap;
        CalculateImageScaleAndOffset();
    }

    void CalculateImageScaleAndOffset()
    {
        imageScale = Math.Min(this.ActualWidth / bitmap.PixelWidth,
                              this.ActualHeight / bitmap.PixelHeight);
```

```
        imageOffset = new Point((this.ActualWidth - imageScale * bitmap.PixelWidth) / 2,
                                 (this.ActualHeight - imageScale * bitmap.PixelHeight) / 2);
}

protected override void OnPointerPressed(PointerRoutedEventArgs args)
{
    uint id = args.Pointer.PointerId;
    Point point = args.GetCurrentPoint(this).Position;
    pointerDictionary.Add(id, point);
    CapturePointer(args.Pointer);
    base.OnPointerPressed(args);
}

protected override void OnPointerMoved(PointerRoutedEventArgs args)
{
    uint id = args.Pointer.PointerId;
    Point point = args.GetCurrentPoint(this).Position;

    if (pointerDictionary.ContainsKey(id))
    {
        Point previousPoint = pointerDictionary[id];

        // Render the line
        RenderOnBitmap(previousPoint, point, 12, new Color());

        pointerDictionary[id] = point;
    }
        base.OnPointerMoved(args);
}

protected override void OnPointerReleased(PointerRoutedEventArgs args)
{
    uint id = args.Pointer.PointerId;

    if (pointerDictionary.ContainsKey(id))
        pointerDictionary.Remove(id);

    base.OnPointerReleased(args);
}

protected override void OnPointerCaptureLost(PointerRoutedEventArgs args)
{
    uint id = args.Pointer.PointerId;

    if (pointerDictionary.ContainsKey(id))
        pointerDictionary.Remove(id);

    base.OnPointerCaptureLost(args);
}

void RenderOnBitmap(Point point1, Point point2, double radius, Color color)
{
    bool bitmapNeedsUpdate = false;
```

```
// Adjust the points for any bitmap scaling
Point center1 = ScaleToBitmap(point1);
Point center2 = ScaleToBitmap(point2);

// Create object to render the line
RoundCappedLine line = new RoundCappedLine(center1, center2, radius);

// Find the minimum and maximum vertical coordinates
int yMin = (int)Math.Min(center1.Y - radius, center2.Y - radius);
int yMax = (int)Math.Max(center1.Y + radius, center2.Y + radius);

yMin = Math.Max(0, Math.Min(bitmap.PixelHeight, yMin));
yMax = Math.Max(0, Math.Min(bitmap.PixelHeight, yMax));

// Loop through all the y coordinates that contain part of the segment
for (int y = yMin; y < yMax; y++)
{
    // Get the range of x coordinates in the segment
    xCollection.Clear();
    line.GetAllX(y, xCollection);

    if (xCollection.Count == 2)
    {
        // Find the minimum and maximum horizontal coordinates
        int xMin = (int)(Math.Min(xCollection[0], xCollection[1]) + 0.5f);
        int xMax = (int)(Math.Max(xCollection[0], xCollection[1]) + 0.5f);

        xMin = Math.Max(0, Math.Min(bitmap.PixelWidth, xMin));
        xMax = Math.Max(0, Math.Min(bitmap.PixelWidth, xMax));

        // Loop through the X values
        for (int x = xMin; x < xMax; x++)
        {
            {
                // Set the pixel
                int index = 4 * (y * bitmap.PixelWidth + x);
                pixels[index + 0] = color.B;
                pixels[index + 1] = color.G;
                pixels[index + 2] = color.R;
                pixels[index + 3] = color.A;
                bitmapNeedsUpdate = true;
            }
        }
    }
}
// Update bitmap
if (bitmapNeedsUpdate)
{
    // Find the starting index and number of pixels
    int start = 4 * yMin * bitmap.PixelWidth;
    int count = 4 * (yMax - yMin) * bitmap.PixelWidth;

    pixelStream.Seek(start, SeekOrigin.Begin);
```

```
        pixelStream.Write(pixels, start, count);
        bitmap.Invalidate();
    }
}

Point ScaleToBitmap(Point pt)
{
    return new Point((pt.X - imageOffset.X) / imageScale,
                     (pt.Y - imageOffset.Y) / imageScale);
}
}
```

The *RenderOnBitmap* method is simpler than the one in FingerPaint because it's only dealing with a constant thickness and uses *RoundCappedLine* uniformly. Here's the result after "painting" the white bitmap with a few strokes of transparent pixels:

Notice that the *PointerMoved* method calls *RenderOnBitmap* like this:

```
RenderOnBitmap(previousPoint, point, 12, new Color());
```

The *Color* constructor creates a *Color* value with the *A*, *R*, *G*, and *B* properties all set to zero, a color sometimes known as "transparent black." For putting colors in a *WriteableBitmap*, this *Color* constructor is much better than the static *Colors.Transparent* property. *Colors.Transparent* returns a *Color* value with an *A* property equal to zero but *R*, *G*, *B* set to 255. This color is sometimes referred to as "transparent white," but it's not a premultiplied-alpha transparent color! For *WriteableBitmap* you need premultiplied-alpha colors, and that means that none of the *R*, *G*, and *B* properties should be greater than *A*.

Accessing the Pictures Library

It's possible for an application to access the Pictures library directly and to enumerate all the subfolders and files in those folders. The program can display those files on the screen most efficiently as thumbnails but can then access the actual bitmaps.

This is demonstrated in the PhotoScatter program. This program constructs a *ListBox* at the left of the page showing the directory structure of the Pictures library. Select a folder and the program displays the contents of that folder as thumbnails. You can use your fingers to move, scale, and rotate the images, at which time the real file is loaded so that it can be enlarged with more resolution.

Here's what the program looks like. You might recognize some of the 200-odd images currently stored in my Screenshots folder:

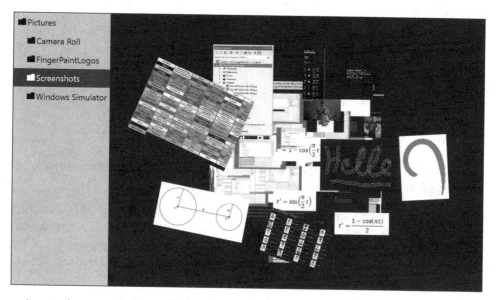

I wanted each of the items displayed here to be independently manipulable and to handle its own manipulation. To do that, I created a general-purpose *ContentControl* derivative named *ManipulableContentControl*. That control uses a somewhat fancier version of the *ManipulationManager* class I presented in Chapter 13:

Project: PhotoScatter | File: ManipulationManager.cs

```
public class ManipulationManager
{
    TransformGroup xformGroup;
    MatrixTransform matrixXform;
    CompositeTransform compositeXform;

    public ManipulationManager() : this(new CompositeTransform())
    {
    }
```

```
public ManipulationManager(CompositeTransform initialTransform)
{
    xformGroup = new TransformGroup();
    matrixXform = new MatrixTransform();
    xformGroup.Children.Add(matrixXform);
    compositeXform = initialTransform;
    xformGroup.Children.Add(compositeXform);
    this.Matrix = xformGroup.Value;
}

public Matrix Matrix { private set; get; }

public void AccumulateDelta(Point position, ManipulationDelta delta)
{
    matrixXform.Matrix = xformGroup.Value;
    Point center = matrixXform.TransformPoint(position);
    compositeXform.CenterX = center.X;
    compositeXform.CenterY = center.Y;
    compositeXform.TranslateX = delta.Translation.X;
    compositeXform.TranslateY = delta.Translation.Y;
    compositeXform.ScaleX = delta.Scale;
    compositeXform.ScaleY = delta.Scale;
    compositeXform.Rotation = delta.Rotation;
    this.Matrix = xformGroup.Value;
}
}
```

The only additional feature is a constructor that lets the orientation of the item be initialized with a *CompositeTransform* object that is then used within the class.

To create the *ManipulableContentControl* class, I created a new item in Visual Studio of type *User Control*. In both the XAML file and the code-behind file I then changed *UserControl* to *ContentControl*. In a *UserControl* derivative, normally the XAML file defines the content of the control. In this XAML file the content is left undefined but the *RenderTransform* is set to a *MatrixTransform* that is set from the code-behind file based on a *ManipulationManager* instance.

Project: PhotoScatter | File: ManipulableContentControl.xaml

```
<ContentControl
    x:Class="PhotoScatter.ManipulableContentControl"
    xmlns="http://schemas.microsoft.com/winfx/2006/xaml/presentation"
    xmlns:x="http://schemas.microsoft.com/winfx/2006/xaml"
    xmlns:local="using:PhotoScatter">

    <ContentControl.RenderTransform>
        <MatrixTransform x:Name="matrixXform" />
    </ContentControl.RenderTransform>
</ContentControl>
```

Here's the code-behind file. Notice the constructor, which takes a *CompositeTransform* that it uses to create a *ManipulationManager* object:

Project: PhotoScatter | File: ManipulableContentControl.xaml.cs (excerpt)

```
public sealed partial class ManipulableContentControl : ContentControl
{
    static int zIndex;
    ManipulationManager manipulationManager;

    public ManipulableContentControl(CompositeTransform initialTransform)
    {
        this.InitializeComponent();

        // Create the ManipulationManager and set MatrixTransform from it
        manipulationManager = new ManipulationManager(initialTransform);
        matrixXform.Matrix = manipulationManager.Matrix;

        this.ManipulationMode = ManipulationModes.All &
                            ~ManipulationModes.TranslateRailsX &
                            ~ManipulationModes.TranslateRailsY;
    }

    protected override void OnManipulationStarting(ManipulationStartingRoutedEventArgs args)
    {
        Canvas.SetZIndex(this, zIndex += 1);
        base.OnManipulationStarting(args);
    }

    protected override void OnManipulationDelta(ManipulationDeltaRoutedEventArgs args)
    {
        manipulationManager.AccumulateDelta(args.Position, args.Delta);
        matrixXform.Matrix = manipulationManager.Matrix;
        base.OnManipulationDelta(args);
    }
}
```

Notice also that the class maintains a static *zIndex* property that is incremented and used to bring the touched item to the top of the pile as soon as the manipulation begins.

Normally, a directory structure is displayed using a control named *TreeView* or something similar that provides visual indentation and an interface to expand and close up nodes of the tree. The Windows Runtime doesn't have a *TreeView* (yet), so I decided to use a plain old *ListBox* instead. There is no expanding and closing of nodes, but there is indentation.

The items in the *ListBox* are of type *FolderItem*:

Project: PhotoScatter | File: FolderItem.cs

```
public class FolderItem
{
    public StorageFolder StorageFolder { set; get; }

    public int Level { set; get; }
```

```
    public string Indent
    {
        get { return new string('\x00A0', this.Level * 4); }
    }

    public Grid DisplayGrid { set; get; }
}
```

Each *FolderItem* object represents a folder. The name of that folder is obtained from the *StorageFolder* object, the nesting level is set by code to the *Level* property, and the *Indent* property uses that value to construct a string of four blanks for each level.

FolderItem also defines a *DisplayGrid* property of type *Grid*. This *Grid* object is set the first time the user selects that particular folder, and it is filled with a bunch of *ManipulableContentControl* objects corresponding to the images in that folder. Retaining this *Grid* and everything in it avoids having the program re-enumerate the contents of each folder if the user skips around among them. (However, the program doesn't install a file watcher, so if items are later added to a folder, the program doesn't know about them.)

The *ItemTemplate* for the *ListBox* is defined in MainPage.xaml and references properties in *FolderItem*:

Project: PhotoScatter | File: MainPage.xaml (excerpt)

```
<Grid Background="{StaticResource ApplicationPageBackgroundThemeBrush}">
    <Grid.ColumnDefinitions>
        <ColumnDefinition Width="Auto" />
        <ColumnDefinition Width="*" />
    </Grid.ColumnDefinitions>

    <ListBox Name="folderListBox"
             Grid.Column="0"
             SelectionChanged="OnFolderListBoxSelectionChanged">
        <ListBox.ItemTemplate>
            <DataTemplate>
                <ContentControl FontSize="24">
                    <StackPanel Orientation="Horizontal">
                        <TextBlock Text="{Binding Indent}" />
                        <TextBlock Text="&#xE188;"
                                   FontFamily="Segoe UI Symbol" />
                        <TextBlock Text="{Binding StorageFolder.Name}" />
                    </StackPanel>
                </ContentControl>
            </DataTemplate>
        </ListBox.ItemTemplate>
    </ListBox>

    <Border Name="displayBorder"
            Grid.Column="1" />
</Grid>
```

Notice the 0xE188 codepoint in the Segoe UI Symbol font for displaying a little folder icon. That's preceded with the *Indent* string and followed by the *Name* property of the *StorageFolder* object in *FolderItem*.

The PhotoScatter program requires permission to access the Pictures library in the Capabilities section of Package.appxmanifest because during the *Loaded* event it obtains the complete directory tree by recursive calls to the *GetFoldersAsync* method of *StorageFolder*, in the process creating the *FolderItem* objects for the *ListBox*.

Project: PhotoScatter | File: MainPage.xaml.cs (excerpt)

```
public sealed partial class MainPage : Page
{
    ...

    public MainPage()
    {
        this.InitializeComponent();
        Loaded += OnMainPageLoaded;
    }

    void OnMainPageLoaded(object sender, RoutedEventArgs args)
    {
        StorageFolder storageFolder = KnownFolders.PicturesLibrary;
        BuildFolderListBox(storageFolder, 0);
        folderListBox.SelectedIndex = 0;
    }

    async void BuildFolderListBox(StorageFolder parentStorageFolder, int level)
    {
        FolderItem folderItem = new FolderItem
        {
            StorageFolder = parentStorageFolder,
            Level = level
        };
        folderListBox.Items.Add(folderItem);

        IReadOnlyList<StorageFolder> storageFolders =
                        await parentStorageFolder.GetFoldersAsync();

        foreach (StorageFolder storageFolder in storageFolders)
            BuildFolderListBox(storageFolder, level + 1);
    }
    ...
}
```

The *Loaded* handler concludes by setting the *SelectedIndex* of the *ListBox* to 0, which selects the first item, which is the Pictures folder itself. This triggers a call to the *SelectionChanged* handler, which uses the *GetFilesAsync* method of *StorageFolder* to obtain all the files in that folder. But for each *StorageFile*, the method calls *GetThumbnailAsync* to obtain the file's thumbnail image. (Loading thumbnails is much preferable to loading the actual images, which could take quite some time and consume a lot of memory.) A call to a method in *MainPage* named *LoadBitmapAsync* (which I'll describe shortly) creates an *Image* element and a *ManipulableContentControl* for displaying that thumbnail:

```csharp
public sealed partial class MainPage : Page
{
    Random rand = new Random();
    ...
    async void OnFolderListBoxSelectionChanged(object sender, SelectionChangedEventArgs args)
    {
        FolderItem folderItem = (sender as ListBox).SelectedItem as FolderItem;

        if (folderItem == null)
        {
            displayBorder.Child = null;
            return;
        }

        if (folderItem.DisplayGrid != null)
        {
            displayBorder.Child = folderItem.DisplayGrid;
            return;
        }

        Grid displayGrid = new Grid();
        folderItem.DisplayGrid = displayGrid;
        displayBorder.Child = displayGrid;

        StorageFolder storageFolder = folderItem.StorageFolder;
        IReadOnlyList<StorageFile> storageFiles = await storageFolder.GetFilesAsync();

        foreach (StorageFile storageFile in storageFiles)
        {
            StorageItemThumbnail thumbnail =
                    await storageFile.GetThumbnailAsync(ThumbnailMode.SingleItem);
            BitmapSource bitmap = await LoadBitmapAsync(thumbnail);

            if (bitmap == null)
                continue;

            // Create new Image element to display the thumbnail
            Image image = new Image
                {
                    Source = bitmap,
                    Stretch = Stretch.None,
                    Tag = ImageType.Thumbnail
                };

            // Create an initial CompositeTransform for the item
            CompositeTransform xform = new CompositeTransform();
            xform.TranslateX = (displayBorder.ActualWidth - bitmap.PixelWidth) / 2;
            xform.TranslateY = (displayBorder.ActualHeight - bitmap.PixelHeight) / 2;
            xform.TranslateX += 256 * (0.5 - rand.NextDouble());
            xform.TranslateY += 256 * (0.5 - rand.NextDouble());
```

```
                    // Create the ManipulableContentControl for the Image
                    ManipulableContentControl manipulableControl = new ManipulableContentControl(xform)
                    {
                        Content = image,
                        Tag = storageFile
                    };
                    manipulableControl.ManipulationStarted += OnManipulableControlManipulationStarted;

                    // Put it in the Grid
                    displayGrid.Children.Add(manipulableControl);
                }
        }
    ...
}
```

Because of the *await* operators on *GetThumbnailAsync* and *LoadBitmapAsync*, these *BitmapSource* objects, *Image* elements, and *ManipulableContentControl* instances are created sequentially, and each is displayed as it's created, which provides an entertaining show as the images are progressively stacked in a big, slightly random pile. The other option is to let them all go at the same time, but in most cases that would result in creating many more threads than processors to handle them.

The *SelectionChanged* handler for the *ListBox* is executed only once for each folder. The *Tag* property of the *ManipulableContentControl* is set to the *StorageFile* object associated with each item. This is later used to load the actual bitmap (if necessary). Also notice that the *Tag* property of each *Image* element is set to *ImageType.Thumbnail*. That's a member of the following enumeration:

Project: PhotoScatter | File: ImageType.cs (excerpt)

```
public enum ImageType
{
    Thumbnail,
    Full,
    Transitioning
}
```

That *Tag* property will change as the user begins manipulating a particular item. Although the *ManipulableContentControl* handles the *Manipulation* events necessary to allow the item to be moved, scaled, and rotated, a handler for the *ManipulationStarted* event is also attached by that *SelectionChanged* handler. This handler is responsible for replacing the thumbnail with the actual bitmap:

Project: PhotoScatter | File: MainPage.xaml.cs (excerpt)

```
public sealed partial class MainPage : Page
{
    ...
    async void OnManipulableControlManipulationStarted(object sender,
                                                ManipulationStartedRoutedEventArgs args)
    {
        ManipulableContentControl manipulableControl = sender as ManipulableContentControl;
        Image image = manipulableControl.Content as Image;
```

```
        if ((ImageType)image.Tag == ImageType.Thumbnail)
        {
            // Set tag to transitioning
            image.Tag = ImageType.Transitioning;

            // Load the actual bitmap file
            StorageFile storageFile = manipulableControl.Tag as StorageFile;
            BitmapSource newBitmap = await LoadBitmapAsync(storageFile);

            // This is the case for a file that BitmapDecoder can't handle
            if (newBitmap != null)
            {
                // Get the thumbnail from the Image element
                BitmapSource oldBitmap = image.Source as BitmapSource;

                // Find a ScaleTransform between old and new
                double scale = 1;

                if (oldBitmap.PixelWidth > oldBitmap.PixelHeight)
                    scale = (double)oldBitmap.PixelWidth / newBitmap.PixelWidth;
                else
                    scale = (double)oldBitmap.PixelHeight / newBitmap.PixelHeight;

                // Set properties on the Image element
                image.Source = newBitmap;
                image.RenderTransform = new ScaleTransform
                {
                    ScaleX = scale,
                    ScaleY = scale,
                };
            }
            image.Tag = ImageType.Full;
        }
    }
    ...
}
```

The replacement of the thumbnail by the bitmap is perhaps the trickiest part of the program. Because the *ManipulationStarted* handler contains asynchronous calls, it could be processing overlapping events from several items if the user is manipulating more than one simultaneously. The main logic takes place only if the *Tag* property of the *Image* is *ImageType.Thumbnail*. The *Tag* is then set to *ImageType.Transitioning* (not strictly necessary but it was helpful for debugging), and a call to *LoadBitmapAsync* obtains that image. When it finally replaces the thumbnail, the *Tag* property of the *Image* element is set to *ImageType.Full*.

I wanted the process to be as visually seamless as I could manage, and hence the routine calculates scaling factors that convert the size of the actual bitmap to the size of the thumbnail. The size and orientation of the item doesn't change, but the resolution improves.

Here, finally, are three overloads of *LoadBitmapAsync*, each of which returns a *BitmapSource*. Somewhat different approaches are used to obtain *IRandomAccessStream* objects for the image and its thumbnail, and then a common routine loads the file with code you've already seen.

```
public sealed partial class MainPage : Page
{
    ...
    async Task<BitmapSource> LoadBitmapAsync(StorageFile storageFile)
    {
        BitmapSource bitmapSource = null;

        // Open the StorageFile for reading
        using (IRandomAccessStreamWithContentType stream = await storageFile.OpenReadAsync())
        {
            bitmapSource = await LoadBitmapAsync(stream);
        }

        return bitmapSource;
    }

    async Task<BitmapSource> LoadBitmapAsync(StorageItemThumbnail thumbnail)
    {
        return await LoadBitmapAsync(thumbnail as IRandomAccessStream);
    }

    async Task<BitmapSource> LoadBitmapAsync(IRandomAccessStream stream)
    {
        WriteableBitmap bitmap = null;

        // Create a BitmapDecoder from the stream
        BitmapDecoder decoder = null;

        try
        {
            decoder = await BitmapDecoder.CreateAsync(stream);
        }
        catch
        {
            // Just skip ones that aren't valid
            return null;
        }

        // Get the first frame
        BitmapFrame bitmapFrame = await decoder.GetFrameAsync(0);

        // Get the pixels
        PixelDataProvider dataProvider =
                await bitmapFrame.GetPixelDataAsync(BitmapPixelFormat.Bgra8,
                                                    BitmapAlphaMode.Premultiplied,
                                                    new BitmapTransform(),
                                                    ExifOrientationMode.RespectExifOrientation,
                                                    ColorManagementMode.ColorManageToSRgb);

        byte[] pixels = dataProvider.DetachPixelData();

        // Create WriteableBitmap and set the pixels
        bitmap = new WriteableBitmap((int)bitmapFrame.PixelWidth,
                                     (int)bitmapFrame.PixelHeight);
```

```
            using (Stream pixelStream = bitmap.PixelBuffer.AsStream())
            {
                pixelStream.Write(pixels, 0, pixels.Length);
            }

            bitmap.Invalidate();
            return bitmap;
        }
    }
```

Capturing Camera Photos

You've seen how Windows Runtime applications can create *WriteableBitmap* objects from scratch or load existing bitmaps from files. There are other ways that programs can obtain bitmaps. In Chapter 17, "Share and Print," for example, you'll see how programs can obtain bitmaps from other applications, either directly or through the clipboard.

Your application can also get a bitmap from the computer's built-in camera. There are two approaches, and if you're willing to yield control to Windows 8 so that the operating system can display its normal camera interface, this process is exceptionally easy.

To enable your application to use the computer's camera, you must indicate that in the Package .appxmanifest file. In Visual Studio, open that file, select the Capabilities tab, and click Webcam.

I've done that for the EasyCameraCapture program. Here's the MainPage.xaml file:

Project: EasyCameraCapture | File: MainPage.xaml (excerpt)

```xml
<Grid Background="{StaticResource ApplicationPageBackgroundThemeBrush}">
    <Image Name="image" />

    <Button Content="Capture Photo!"
            FontSize="48"
            HorizontalAlignment="Left"
            VerticalAlignment="Top"
            Click="OnButtonClick" />
</Grid>
```

The *Click* handler for the *Button* instantiates the *CameraCaptureUI* class defined in the *Windows.Media.Capture* namespace and calls *CaptureFileAsync*:

Project: EasyCameraCapture | File: MainPage.xaml.cs (excerpt)

```csharp
async void OnButtonClick(object sender, RoutedEventArgs args)
{
    CameraCaptureUI cameraCap = new CameraCaptureUI();
    StorageFile storageFile = await cameraCap.CaptureFileAsync(CameraCaptureUIMode.Photo);

    if (storageFile != null)
    {
        IRandomAccessStreamWithContentType stream = await storageFile.OpenReadAsync();
```

```
    BitmapImage bitmap = new BitmapImage();
    await bitmap.SetSourceAsync(stream);
    image.Source = bitmap;
    }
}
```

Prior to calling *CaptureFileAsync* a program can set various properties of *CameraCaptureUI* to select a file format, select a pixel size, enable cropping, and so forth.

When your application calls *CaptureFileAsync*, Windows 8 switches to a screen that looks very much like the normal Windows 8 Camera application. The only substantial differences are that the Video Mode button is disabled (but that can be enabled by passing *CameraCaptureUIMode .PhotoOrVideo* to the *CaptureFileAsync* method) and a circled left arrow appears in the upper-left corner.

To return to the EasyCameraCapture application, you can press that circled left arrow, in which case the returned *StorageFile* is *null*. Or you can capture a picture by tapping or clicking the screen and then pressing a circled check mark at the bottom.

On return to the program, the *StorageFile* object references a file stored in the *TempState* directory of the application's local storage. The code in EasyCameraCapture simply displays the file:

Your application might want to invoke a *FileSavePicker* to let the user save the image, or you can save it automatically somewhere in the Pictures library. Perhaps your application does something unique with captured images and a special directory in the Pictures library would be convenient. (The standard Windows 8 Camera application stores photos in the Camera Roll directory of Pictures.) For doing this, you'll need to set your application capabilities to allow access to the Pictures library, just as the regular Windows 8 Camera application does.

You can drop to a lower level of interface to the camera and basically write your own complete camera application, including a video preview, selection of camera (if more than one), triggering the photo capture, and so forth.

The HarderCameraCapture project shows the basics. The XAML file contains something you haven't seen before—a *CaptureElement* for previewing the video—as well as an old friend:

Project: HarderCameraCapture | File: MainPage.xaml (excerpt)

```xaml
<Grid Background="{StaticResource ApplicationPageBackgroundThemeBrush}">
    <CaptureElement Name="captureElement" />
    <Image Name="image" />
</Grid>
```

The code-behind file uses the *Loaded* handler to perform initialization. The static *DeviceInformation.FindAllAsync* method allows obtaining a collection of video capture devices. The *DeviceInformation* object contains a string ID and an *EnclosureLocation* property that lets the program determine where on the computer each camera is located. This code attempts to find the camera on the front, but if it can't, it settles for the first (or possibly only) camera in the collection:

Project: HarderCameraCapture | File: MainPage.xaml.cs (excerpt)

```csharp
public sealed partial class MainPage : Page
{
    MediaCapture mediaCapture = new MediaCapture();
    ...

    public MainPage()
    {
        this.InitializeComponent();
        Loaded += OnMainPageLoaded;
    }

    async void OnMainPageLoaded(object sender, RoutedEventArgs args)
    {
        DeviceInformationCollection devInfos =
            await DeviceInformation.FindAllAsync(DeviceClass.VideoCapture);

        if (devInfos.Count == 0)
        {
            await new MessageDialog("No video capture devices found").ShowAsync();
            return;
        }

        string id = null;

        // Try to find the front webcam
        foreach (DeviceInformation devInfo in devInfos)
        {
            if (devInfo.EnclosureLocation != null &&
                    devInfo.EnclosureLocation.Panel == Windows.Devices.Enumeration.Panel.Front)
                id = devInfo.Id;
        }
```

```
        // If not available, just pick the first one
        if (id == null)
            id = devInfos[0].Id;

        // Create initialization settings
        MediaCaptureInitializationSettings settings = new MediaCaptureInitializationSettings();
        settings.VideoDeviceId = id;
        settings.StreamingCaptureMode = StreamingCaptureMode.Video;

        // Initialize the MediaCapture device
        await mediaCapture.InitializeAsync(settings);

        // Associate with the CaptureElement
        captureElement.Source = mediaCapture;

        // Start the preview
        await mediaCapture.StartPreviewAsync();
    }
    ...
}
```

Once a device ID has been obtained, the *Loaded* handler continues by creating a *MediaCaptureInitializationSettings* object and uses this to initialize a *MediaCapture* object defined as a field. This *MediaCapture* object is made the source of the *CaptureElement* instantiated in the XAML file.

At the conclusion of the *Loaded* handler, the preview is working. If a camera was found located on the front of the computer, you should be staring at a live video feed of yourself.

I've also implemented a *Tapped* handler for snapping a photo. The *MediaCapture* class has both *CapturePhotoToStorageFileAsync* and *CapturePhotoToStreamAsync* methods. I've chosen to use the stream approach and capture the photo to a memory stream. At that point a *BitmapDecoder* can obtain the pixel bits. The program borrows the HSL structure from the FingerPaint program to increase the saturation of all the pixels and then creates a *WriteableBitmap* from that:

Project: HarderCameraCapture | **File:** MainPage.xaml.cs (excerpt)

```
public sealed partial class MainPage : Page
{
    ...
    bool ignoreTaps = false;
    ...
    async protected override void OnTapped(TappedRoutedEventArgs args)
    {
        if (ignoreTaps)
            return;

        // Capture photo to memory stream
        ImageEncodingProperties imageEncodingProps = ImageEncodingProperties.CreateJpeg();
        InMemoryRandomAccessStream memoryStream = new InMemoryRandomAccessStream();
        await mediaCapture.CapturePhotoToStreamAsync(imageEncodingProps, memoryStream);
```

```
        // Use BitmapDecoder to get pixels array
        BitmapDecoder decoder = await BitmapDecoder.CreateAsync(memoryStream);
        PixelDataProvider pixelProvider = await decoder.GetPixelDataAsync();
        byte[] pixels = pixelProvider.DetachPixelData();

        // Saturate the colors
        for (int index = 0; index < pixels.Length; index += 4)
        {
            Color color = Color.FromArgb(pixels[index + 3],
                                         pixels[index + 2],
                                         pixels[index + 1],
                                         pixels[index + 0]);

            HSL hsl = new HSL(color);
            hsl = new HSL(hsl.Hue, 1.0, hsl.Lightness);
            color = hsl.Color;

            pixels[index + 0] = color.B;
            pixels[index + 1] = color.G;
            pixels[index + 2] = color.R;
            pixels[index + 3] = color.A;
        }

        // Create a WriteableBitmap and initialize it
        WriteableBitmap bitmap = new WriteableBitmap((int)decoder.PixelWidth,
                                                     (int)decoder.PixelHeight);
        Stream pixelStream = bitmap.PixelBuffer.AsStream();
        await pixelStream.WriteAsync(pixels, 0, pixels.Length);
        bitmap.Invalidate();

        // Display the bitmap
        image.Source = bitmap;

        // Set a timer for the image
        DispatcherTimer timer = new DispatcherTimer
        {
            Interval = TimeSpan.FromSeconds(2.5)
        };
        timer.Tick += OnTimerTick;
        timer.Start();
        ignoreTaps = true;

        base.OnTapped(args);
    }

    void OnTimerTick(object sender, object args)
    {
        // Disable the timer
        DispatcherTimer timer = sender as DispatcherTimer;
        timer.Stop();
        timer.Tick -= OnTimerTick;
```

```
        // Get rid of the bitmap
        image.Source = null;
        ignoreTaps = false;
    }
}
```

I don't want the picture to stick around forever, so the program sets a *DispatcherTimer* for 2.5 seconds. During this time, further taps are ignored, but after that period the photo is simply removed from the screen and we're back to the live video feed.

Of course, highly saturated colors can be somewhat frightening:

CHAPTER 15

Going Native

In the world of Windows 8 programming, it is a sad truth that all languages are not created equal. In theory, any programming language can access any class or function available to Windows Store applications, but that's only because the entire API is built on top of the Component Object Model (COM). In the real world of sane programming, the ease of accessing certain areas of the Windows 8 API depends on what programming language you're using.

For example, only programmers working with the managed languages of C# and Visual Basic have direct access to the .NET APIs for Windows 8 applications—those namespaces beginning with the word *System*. C++ programmers are expected to use C++ runtime libraries and classes in the *Platform* namespace for equivalent functionality.

On the other hand, Windows 8 applications can access a subset of the Win32 and COM API, but these functions and classes are only conveniently available to C++ programmers. To get at these same APIs, C# programmers need to jump through hoops.

This is a chapter showing how to jump through those hoops. I'll discuss two basic techniques. The first is called Platform Invoke (also known as PInvoke or P/Invoke), which has existed from the very beginning of .NET programming for accessing Win32 functions or functions in other dynamic-link libraries (DLLs). P/Invoke is particularly suited for accessing a "flat" API—that is, one in which functions are independent (or perhaps reference handles provided by other functions) rather than being consolidated into classes.

The second technique involves writing a "wrapper" DLL in C++ and then accessing that DLL from a C# program. This technique is more suited for object-oriented APIs and, in particular, the big chunk of high-performance graphics and audio classes collectively known as DirectX.

In a Windows 8 application, a DLL written in one language and accessed by another must be in a special format known as a Windows Runtime Component. Visual Studio lets you create a Windows Runtime Component, but there are a bunch of rules and restrictions on what these libraries may do.

Keep in mind that you can't use either of these techniques to give your program access to functions that aren't allowed in Windows Store applications. You can't use these techniques to access arbitrary Win32 functions. You're restricted to those in the subset allowed for Windows 8 applications. Nor can you call functions in DLLs that make calls to Win32 functions not in this subset.

An Introduction to P/Invoke

Suppose you're browsing through the subset of Win32 functions allowed for new Windows 8 applications and you encounter one that you'd like to use. Here's the way it appears in the documentation:

```
void WINAPI GetNativeSystemInfo(__out LPSYSTEM_INFO lpSystemInfo);
```

If you're completely unfamiliar with the Win32 API, this is likely to look like gibberish. The uppercase identifiers are generally defined using C #*define* or *typedef* statements in the various Windows header files. You'll find these header files in subdirectories of the *C:/Program Files (x86)/Windows Kits/8.0* directory on the machine on which you've installed Visual Studio. The most basic are Windows.h, WinDef.h, WinBase.h, and winnt.h. The WINAPI identifier is the same as __stdcall, which is the standard calling convention for C programs calling Win32 functions. LPSYSTEM_INFO is a long pointer—"long" meaning wider than a 16-bit pointer such as existed back when Windows was a wee child—to a SYSTEM_INFO structure. The SYSTEM_INFO structure is defined like this:

```
typedef struct _SYSTEM_INFO {
  union {
    DWORD   dwOemId;
    struct {
      WORD wProcessorArchitecture;
      WORD wReserved;
    };
  };
  DWORD       dwPageSize;
  LPVOID      lpMinimumApplicationAddress;
  LPVOID      lpMaximumApplicationAddress;
  DWORD_PTR dwActiveProcessorMask;
  DWORD       dwNumberOfProcessors;
  DWORD       dwProcessorType;
  DWORD       dwAllocationGranularity;
  WORD        wProcessorLevel;
  WORD        wProcessorRevision;
} SYSTEM_INFO;
```

The prefacing of field names with lowercase abbreviations of the data types is a form of simple Hungarian notation, so called because it was invented by Hungarian-born Charles Simonyi. Hungarian notation was popularized by the Windows API and some ancient books on Windows programming, but it is no longer widely used in application programming.

In Windows parlance, a WORD is a 16-bit unsigned value, which C# programmers know as a *ushort*. The DWORD is a double-WORD, or a 32-bit unsigned value or a *uint*. Watch out for references to *long*, which is not a 64-bit C# *long* but instead a C++ *long*, which is the same size as an *int*, or 32 bits.

LPVOID translates as a "long pointer to void" or, in standard C, void *, and DWORD_PTR is either an unsigned 32-bit or 64-bit integer, depending on whether Windows is running on a 32-bit or 64-bit processor. These are equivalent to the C# *IntPtr*.

The reason you need to know how these Windows API data types correspond to C# data types is because to use this structure from a C# program you need to redefine it in C#. Fortunately, the documentation of SYSTEM_INFO indicates that the *dwOemId* field is obsolete, which means that you can ignore the *union* and simply create a straight C# structure with public fields, perhaps giving the structure a more C#-ish name in the process:

```
struct SystemInfo
{
    public ushort wProcessorArchitecture;
    public ushort wReserved;
    public uint dwPageSize;
    public IntPtr lpMinimumApplicationAddress;
    public IntPtr lpMaximumApplicationAddress;
    public IntPtr dwActiveProcessorMask;
    public uint dwNumberOfProcessors;
    public uint dwProcessorType;
    public uint dwAllocationGranularity;
    public ushort wProcessorLevel;
    public ushort wProcessorRevision;
}
```

In C# the fields must be defined as *public* if you want to access them from outside the structure. If you want, you can also rename all the fields (for example, *ProcessorArchitecture* and *PageSize*).

You can also specify different data types of the same size—for example, *short* rather than *ushort* and *int* rather than *uint*—if you know that the actual values won't overrun the signed types. To the Windows API, all you're doing is supplying a block of memory. The total structure occupies 36 bytes of memory in 32-bit Windows and 48 bytes in 64-bit Windows.

Very often in P/Invoke code you'll see such a structure preceded by the following attribute:

```
[StructLayout(LayoutKind.Sequential)]
struct SystemInfo
{
    ...
}
```

The *StructLayoutAttribute* class and the *LayoutKind* enumeration are defined in the *System .Runtime.InteropServices* namespace, which has lots of other classes related to P/Invoke. This attribute indicates explicitly that these fields should be treated as contiguous and aligned on byte boundaries.

Now that you have a structure to be passed to the *GetNativeSystemInfo* function, you must declare the function itself. In doing so, you make use of the *DllImportAttribute*, also defined in *System .Runtime.InteropServices*. At the very least you must indicate the dynamic-link library in which this function can be found. The documentation indicates that *GetNativeSystemInfo* is defined in kernel32.dll. Here's the function declaration:

```
[DllImport("kernel32.dll")]
static extern void GetNativeSystemInfo(out SystemInfo systemInfo);
```

This declaration must appear inside a C# class definition at the same level as the other methods. The function must be declared as *static*, which is common in regular C# classes, but also as *extern*, which is not common but means that the actual implementation of this function is external to the class. If you want the function to be visible outside the class, give it a *public* keyword as well.

With the exception of *extern*, the function declaration otherwise appears to be a C# method. The method returns *void*, and the single argument is a reference to a *SystemInfo* object. Many Windows API calls require or return information in structures passed as arguments using pointers, and you'll define those arguments by using either *out* or *ref*. These are functionally identical, but with *ref* the C# compiler checks to see that you've initialized the value type before calling the function.

In some other method of the class, you can define a value of type *SystemInfo* and call the function as if it's a normal static method:

```
SystemInfo systemInfo;
GetNativeSystemInfo(out systemInfo);
```

Let's see how this works in the context of a complete program. The XAML file for SystemInfoPInvoke uses a *Grid* to format the information available from *GetNativeSystemInfo* in a table:

Project: SystemInfoPInvoke | File: MainPage.xaml (excerpt)

```
<Page ...
    FontSize="24">

    <Page.Resources>
        <Style x:Key="rightJustifiedText" TargetType="TextBlock">
            <Setter Property="TextAlignment" Value="Right" />
            <Setter Property="Margin" Value="12 0 0 0" />
        </Style>
    </Page.Resources>

    <Grid Background="{StaticResource ApplicationPageBackgroundThemeBrush}">
        <Grid HorizontalAlignment="Center"
            VerticalAlignment="Center">
            <Grid.RowDefinitions>
                <RowDefinition Height="Auto" />
                <RowDefinition Height="Auto" />
                <RowDefinition Height="Auto" />
                <RowDefinition Height="Auto" />
                <RowDefinition Height="Auto" />
                <RowDefinition Height="Auto" />
                <RowDefinition Height="Auto" />
                <RowDefinition Height="Auto" />
                <RowDefinition Height="Auto" />
            </Grid.RowDefinitions>
```

```xml
        <Grid.ColumnDefinitions>
            <ColumnDefinition Width="Auto" />
            <ColumnDefinition Width="Auto" />
        </Grid.ColumnDefinitions>

        <TextBlock Text="Processor Architecture: " Grid.Row="0" Grid.Column="0" />
        <TextBlock Name="processorArchitecture" Grid.Row="0" Grid.Column="1"
                Style="{StaticResource rightJustifiedText}" />

        <TextBlock Text="Page Size: " Grid.Row="1" Grid.Column="0" />
        <TextBlock Name="pageSize" Grid.Row="1" Grid.Column="1"
                Style="{StaticResource rightJustifiedText}" />

        <TextBlock Text="Minimum Application Addresss: " Grid.Row="2" Grid.Column="0" />
        <TextBlock Name="minAppAddr" Grid.Row="2" Grid.Column="1"
                Style="{StaticResource rightJustifiedText}" />

        <TextBlock Text="Maximum Application Addresss: " Grid.Row="3" Grid.Column="0" />
        <TextBlock Name="maxAppAddr" Grid.Row="3" Grid.Column="1"
                Style="{StaticResource rightJustifiedText}" />

        <TextBlock Text="Active Processor Mask: " Grid.Row="4" Grid.Column="0" />
        <TextBlock Name="activeProcessorMask" Grid.Row="4" Grid.Column="1"
                Style="{StaticResource rightJustifiedText}" />

        <TextBlock Text="Number of Processors: " Grid.Row="5" Grid.Column="0" />
        <TextBlock Name="numberProcessors" Grid.Row="5" Grid.Column="1"
                Style="{StaticResource rightJustifiedText}" />

        <TextBlock Text="Allocation Granularity: " Grid.Row="6" Grid.Column="0" />
        <TextBlock Name="allocationGranularity" Grid.Row="6" Grid.Column="1"
                Style="{StaticResource rightJustifiedText}" />

        <TextBlock Text="Processor Level: " Grid.Row="7" Grid.Column="0" />
        <TextBlock Name="processorLevel" Grid.Row="7" Grid.Column="1"
                Style="{StaticResource rightJustifiedText}" />

        <TextBlock Text="Processor Revision: " Grid.Row="8" Grid.Column="0" />
        <TextBlock Name="processorRevision" Grid.Row="8" Grid.Column="1"
                Style="{StaticResource rightJustifiedText}" />
    </Grid>
  </Grid>
</Page>
```

In the code-behind file, both the structure and the external function declaration are defined within the *MainPage* class. The external function must be declared within a class definition, but the structure need not be, and it can be in a different file entirely, just like any normal C# structure. Here's the complete code-behind file:

Project: SystemInfoPInvoke | File: MainPage.xaml.cs

```csharp
using System;
using System.Runtime.InteropServices;
using Windows.UI.Xaml.Controls;
```

```
namespace SystemInfoPInvoke
{
    public sealed partial class MainPage : Page
    {
        [StructLayout(LayoutKind.Sequential)]
        struct SystemInfo
        {
            public ushort wProcessorArchitecture;
            public byte wReserved;
            public uint dwPageSize;
            public IntPtr lpMinimumApplicationAddress;
            public IntPtr lpMaximumApplicationAddress;
            public IntPtr dwActiveProcessorMask;
            public uint dwNumberOfProcessors;
            public uint dwProcessorType;
            public uint dwAllocationGranularity;
            public ushort wProcessorLevel;
            public ushort wProcessorRevision;
        }

        [DllImport("kernel32.dll")]
        static extern void GetNativeSystemInfo(out SystemInfo systemInfo);

        enum ProcessorType
        {
            x86 = 0,
            ARM = 5,
            ia64 = 6,
            x64 = 9,
            Unknown = 65535
        };

        public MainPage()
        {
            this.InitializeComponent();

            SystemInfo systemInfo = new SystemInfo();
            GetNativeSystemInfo(out systemInfo);

            processorArchitecture.Text =
                        ((ProcessorType)systemInfo.wProcessorArchitecture).ToString();
            pageSize.Text = systemInfo.dwPageSize.ToString();
            minAppAddr.Text = ((ulong)systemInfo.lpMinimumApplicationAddress).ToString("X");
            maxAppAddr.Text = ((ulong)systemInfo.lpMaximumApplicationAddress).ToString("X");
            activeProcessorMask.Text = ((ulong)systemInfo.dwActiveProcessorMask).ToString("X");
            numberProcessors.Text = systemInfo.dwNumberOfProcessors.ToString("X");
            allocationGranularity.Text = systemInfo.dwAllocationGranularity.ToString();
            processorLevel.Text = systemInfo.wProcessorLevel.ToString();
            processorRevision.Text = systemInfo.wProcessorRevision.ToString("X");
        }
    }
}
```

The documentation indicates that the *wProcessorArchitecture* field can take on values of 0 (for x86 architectures), 6 (for Intel Itanium), 9 (for x64), and 0xFFFF for "unknown." The value for ARM processors (such as the first release of the Microsoft Surface) isn't indicated in the documentation I'm seeing, but all the possible values are constants beginning with PROCESSOR_ARCHITECTURE defined in winnt.h, and PROCESSOR_ARCHITECTURE_ARM is defined as 5.

To ease the formatting of the *wProcessorArchitecture* value, I defined a little *enum* called *ProcessorType* and cast the *wProcessorArchitecture* value to that enumeration. For the *IntPtr* fields, I cast to *ulong* and then displayed them as hexadecimal. Here's the screen running on the tablet I'm using to write this book:

```
Processor Architecture:              x64
Page Size:                          4096
Minimum Application Addresss:      10000
Maximum Application Addresss:  FFFFFFFFFFFEFFFF
Active Processor Mask:                 F
Number of Processors:                  4
Allocation Granularity:            65536
Processor Level:                       6
Processor Revision:                 2A07
```

That tablet has a 64-bit processor. Running on the Microsoft Surface, the program looks like this:

```
Processor Architecture:              ARM
Page Size:                          4096
Minimum Application Addresss:      10000
Maximum Application Addresss:  7FFEFFFF
Active Processor Mask:                 F
Number of Processors:                  4
Allocation Granularity:            65536
Processor Level:                    3081
Processor Revision:                  209
```

Some Help

When you use P/Invoke to define structures and declare functions, you are taking on the responsibility for getting it right. You must supply the correct filename of the DLL in which the function is located, for example. (While I began developing the first project in this chapter I typed "kernel32.lib" rather than "kernel32.dll" and couldn't figure out why it wasn't working.) If you're accessing something other than a system DLL, you must make sure the DLL is referenced by the application. You must also spell the function name correctly and declare all the arguments correctly. There's no IntelliSense for P/Invoke!

These structures and function declarations can often be complex. To help out, there is a wiki website *www.pinvoke.net*, to which many people have contributed structure definitions and function declarations that you can just copy and paste into your own code. You're even allowed to contribute some of your own!

Time Zone Information

Suppose you'd like to write a Windows Store application that displays a bunch of clocks set for various locations around the world, perhaps similar to the ClockRack program I wrote for *PC Magazine* back in the year 2000. Perhaps the Windows 8 version would look something like this:

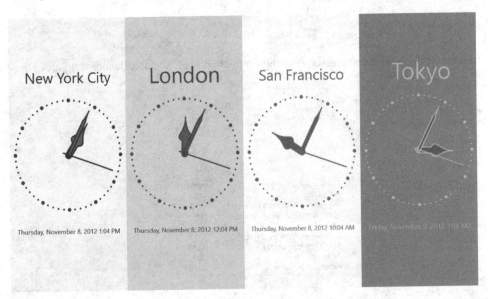

Such a program would let you add new clocks, set their locations and time zones, give them unique colors, and retain this information in application settings.

It would be great to take advantage of the built-in support of Windows for computing the time in various time zones and particularly for handling the problem of daylight saving time (known in some places as "summer time").

You might be very enthusiastic upon finding the *TimeZoneInfo* class in the *System* namespace and noting that the static *GetSystemTimeZones* method returns a collection of *TimeZoneInfo* objects for all the time zones around the world. However, when you try to use this method, you'll discover that it's not available for Windows 8 applications. The only *TimeZoneInfo* object you can obtain in a Windows 8 application is one that's appropriate for the current system time zone setting or the trivial one for Universal Coordinated Time (UTC), also known (more commonly but less accurately) as Greenwich Mean Time.

However, a Windows 8 application does have access to several Win32 functions that provide much of the information you'll need. The Win32 *EnumDynamicTimeZoneInformation* function enumerates all the time zones around the world in the form of DYNAMIC_TIME_ZONE_INFORMATION structures:

```
typedef struct _TIME_DYNAMIC_ZONE_INFORMATION {
    LONG        Bias;
    WCHAR       StandardName[32];
    SYSTEMTIME  StandardDate;
    LONG        StandardBias;
    WCHAR       DaylightName[32];
    SYSTEMTIME  DaylightDate;
    LONG        DaylightBias;
    WCHAR       TimeZoneKeyName[128];
    BOOLEAN     DynamicDaylightTimeDisabled;
} DYNAMIC_TIME_ZONE_INFORMATION, *PDYNAMIC_TIME_ZONE_INFORMATION;
```

This is an extended version of the TIME_ZONE_INFORMATION structure:

```
typedef struct _TIME_ZONE_INFORMATION {
    LONG        Bias;
    WCHAR       StandardName[32];
    SYSTEMTIME  StandardDate;
    LONG        StandardBias;
    WCHAR       DaylightName[32];
    SYSTEMTIME  DaylightDate;
    LONG        DaylightBias;
} TIME_ZONE_INFORMATION, *PTIME_ZONE_INFORMATION;
```

WCHAR is a wide 16-bit Unicode character, and arrays of these characters are essentially zero-terminated strings. The *StandardName* is a string like "Eastern Standard Time", and *DaylightName* is a string like "Eastern Daylight Time". The *TimeZoneKeyName* in the DYNAMIC_TIME_ZONE_INFORMATION structure is a key used in the Windows registry. In Windows 8, these registry entries can be found at HKEY_LOCAL_MACHINE/SOFTWARE/Microsoft/Windows NT/CurrentVersion/Time Zones, and the registry key matches *StandardName*.

The *Bias* field is a number of minutes to subtract from Universal Coordinated Time to get local time. For the eastern US time zone, that's 300 minutes. The *StandardBias* is always zero, while *DaylightBias* is the number of minutes to subtract from standard time to convert to summer time, usually −60.

The *DaylightDate* and *StandardDate* fields indicate when the switch to daylight saving time and back to standard occurs, and they are of type SYSTEMTIME:

```
typedef struct _SYSTEMTIME {
  WORD wYear;
  WORD wMonth;
  WORD wDayOfWeek;
  WORD wDay;
  WORD wHour;
  WORD wMinute;
  WORD wSecond;
  WORD wMilliseconds;
} SYSTEMTIME, *PSYSTEMTIME;
```

The SYSTEMTIME structure is mostly used with the Win32 *GetLocalTime* and *GetSystemTime* functions to obtain current local time and UTC, respectively. The SYSTEMTIME values in the TIME_ZONE_INFORMATION structure are specially coded for the purpose of indicating a transition date: The *wHour* and *wMinute* fields indicate the time of the transition, the *wMonth* field indicates the month of the transition (for example, 3 for March), the *wDayOfWeek* field indicates the day of the week of the transition (for example, 1 for Sunday), and the *wDay* field indicates the particular occurrence of that day of the week within the specified month (for example, 2 for the second Sunday of the month or 5 for the last Sunday).

Windows makes a distinction between locales that switch between standard time and daylight saving time on days indicated like that and those locales that dynamically change the date every year. These latter are referred to as using Dynamic DST, but the information by year is not directly available.

A function named *GetTimeZoneInformationForYear* accepts a year argument and a pointer to a DYNAMIC_TIME_ZONE_INFORMATION structure and returns a pointer to a TIME_ZONE_INFORMATION structure with the information appropriate for that year. The *SystemTimeToTzSpecificLocalTime* accepts a pointer to this TIME_ZONE_INFORMATION structure and a pointer to a SYSTEMTIME structure probably obtained from the *GetSystemTime* function and returns a SYSTEMTIME structure indicating local time for that time zone. Thus, it is not necessary for programs to perform their own time conversions.

A program such as ClockRack needs a facility for the user to choose a time zone for a particular locale. Most preferable would be something consistent with the facility that Windows 8 provides for users to select a time zone.

Take a look at what Windows 8 provides for users: Invoke the Windows 8 charms, select Settings, and tap the Change PC Settings label at the bottom. This invokes a program with the title PC Settings and a list. Select General, and you'll see a combo box at the top with the time zones. Each time zone is identified by an offset from UTC, sometimes the name of the time zone, and often some sample cities. For example, for Romance Standard Time, the combo box displays

(UTC+01:00) Brussels, Copenhagen, Madrid, Paris

In the Windows registry section for time zones, you'll find these labels identified with a name of "Display," but this information is not provided by the Win32 functions. You'd need to access the registry to obtain it, and there are no Win32 functions available to Windows 8 applications to access the registry.

Of course, nothing prevents you from writing a little desktop .NET program to access the full *TimeZoneInfo* class and format the resultant strings so that they define a *Dictionary* object that you can then include in a Windows 8 program. That's what I've done here. The code in the .NET program I used to generate this list is shown in the comment above the *Dictionary* definition:

Project: ClockRack | File: TimeZoneManager.Display.cs (excerpt)

```csharp
namespace ClockRack
{
    public partial class TimeZoneManager
    {
        // Generated from tiny .NET program:
        // foreach (TimeZoneInfo info in TimeZoneInfo.GetSystemTimeZones())
        //    Console.WriteLine("{{ \"{0}\", \"{1}\" }},", info.StandardName, info.DisplayName);
        static Dictionary<string, string> displayStrings = new Dictionary<string, string>
        {
            { "Dateline Standard Time", "(UTC-12:00) International Date Line West" },
            { "UTC-11", "(UTC-11:00) Coordinated Universal Time-11" },
            { "Hawaiian Standard Time", "(UTC-10:00) Hawaii" },
            { "Alaskan Standard Time", "(UTC-09:00) Alaska" },
            { "Pacific Standard Time (Mexico)", "(UTC-08:00) Baja California" },

            ...

            { "Kamchatka Standard Time", "(UTC+12:00) Petropavlovsk-Kamchatsky - Old" },
            { "Tonga Standard Time", "(UTC+13:00) Nuku'alofa" },
            { "Samoa Standard Time", "(UTC+13:00) Samoa" }
        };
    }
}
```

This dictionary is part of a class in the ClockRack project I called *TimeZoneManager*. This is the class I've used to consolidate all the P/Invoke logic. No code outside of the *TimeZoneManager* accesses any Win32 function or structure.

The *TimeZoneManager* class is designed to be instantiated only once and to be used for the duration of the application. The class makes time zone data available to the rest of the program as a collection of the following values:

Project: ClockRack | File: TimeZoneDisplayInfo.cs

```csharp
namespace ClockRack
{
    public struct TimeZoneDisplayInfo
    {
        public int Bias { set; get; }
        public string TimeZoneKey { set; get; }
        public string Display { set; get; }
    }
}
```

The *Bias* property is only used for sorting. The *TimeZoneKey* is the same string as the *TimeZoneKeyName* in the DYNAMIC_TIME_ZONE_INFORMATION structure, and the *Display* property is obtained from the *displayStrings* dictionary.

The portion of the *TimeZoneManager* class in the main TimeZoneManager.cs file begins by defining the necessary Win32 structures and declaring three Win32 functions the class requires:

Project: ClockRack | File: TimeZoneManager.cs (excerpt)

```csharp
public partial class TimeZoneManager
{
    [StructLayout(LayoutKind.Sequential)]
    struct SYSTEMTIME
    {
        public ushort wYear;
        public ushort wMonth;
        public ushort wDayOfWeek;
        public ushort wDay;
        public ushort wHour;
        public ushort wMinute;
        public ushort wSecond;
        public ushort wMilliseconds;
    }

    [StructLayout(LayoutKind.Sequential, CharSet = CharSet.Unicode)]
    struct TIME_ZONE_INFORMATION
    {
        public int Bias;
        [MarshalAs(UnmanagedType.ByValTStr, SizeConst = 32)]
        public string StandardName;
        public SYSTEMTIME StandardDate;
        public int StandardBias;
        [MarshalAs(UnmanagedType.ByValTStr, SizeConst = 32)]
        public string DaylightName;
        public SYSTEMTIME DaylightDate;
        public int DaylightBias;
    }

    [StructLayout(LayoutKind.Sequential, CharSet = CharSet.Unicode)]
    struct DYNAMIC_TIME_ZONE_INFORMATION
    {
        public int Bias;
        [MarshalAs(UnmanagedType.ByValTStr, SizeConst = 32)]
        public string StandardName;
        public SYSTEMTIME StandardDate;
        public int StandardBias;
        [MarshalAs(UnmanagedType.ByValTStr, SizeConst = 32)]
        public string DaylightName;
        public SYSTEMTIME DaylightDate;
        public int DaylightBias;
        [MarshalAs(UnmanagedType.ByValTStr, SizeConst = 128)]
        public string TimeZoneKeyName;
        public byte DynamicDaylightTimeDisabled;
    }

    [DllImport("Advapi32.dll")]
```

```
            static extern uint EnumDynamicTimeZoneInformation(uint index,
                                      ref DYNAMIC_TIME_ZONE_INFORMATION dynamicTzi);

            [DllImport("kernel32.dll")]
            static extern byte GetTimeZoneInformationForYear(ushort year,
                                      ref DYNAMIC_TIME_ZONE_INFORMATION dtzi,
                                      out TIME_ZONE_INFORMATION tzi);

            [DllImport("kernel32.dll")]
            static extern byte SystemTimeToTzSpecificLocalTime(ref TIME_ZONE_INFORMATION tzi,
                                      ref SYSTEMTIME utc, out SYSTEMTIME local);
            ...
        }
```

You'll recall that several of the fields in the DYNAMIC_TIME_ZONE_INFORMATION and TIME_ZONE_INFORMATION structures are defined as arrays of WCHAR. This wouldn't work in C# because a C# array is always a pointer to memory allocated from the heap. Instead, the *MarshalAs* attribute allows indicating that these fields should be treated as C# strings of a particular maximum length.

The constructor of the *TimeZoneManager* class repeatedly calls *EnumDynamicTimeZoneInformation* until it returns a nonzero value, indicating that it's at the end of the list. The number of items might change slightly with different versions of Windows, but I'm seeing a total of 101. Each item is stored in a private dictionary, and each item is also turned into a *TimeZoneDisplayInfo* value and added to the publicly available collection named *DisplayInformation*:

Project: ClockRack | File: TimeZoneManager.cs (excerpt)

```
public partial class TimeZoneManager
{
    ...
    // Internal dictionary for looking up DYNAMIC_TIME_ZONE_INFORMATION values from keys
    Dictionary<string, DYNAMIC_TIME_ZONE_INFORMATION> dynamicTzis =
                            new Dictionary<string, DYNAMIC_TIME_ZONE_INFORMATION>();

    public TimeZoneManager()
    {
        uint index = 0;
        DYNAMIC_TIME_ZONE_INFORMATION tzi = new DYNAMIC_TIME_ZONE_INFORMATION();
        List<TimeZoneDisplayInfo> displayInformation = new List<TimeZoneDisplayInfo>();

        // Enumerate through time zones
        while (0 == EnumDynamicTimeZoneInformation(index, ref tzi))
        {
            dynamicTzis.Add(tzi.TimeZoneKeyName, tzi);

            // Create TimeZoneDisplayInfo for public property
            TimeZoneDisplayInfo displayInfo = new TimeZoneDisplayInfo
            {
                Bias = tzi.Bias,
                TimeZoneKey = tzi.TimeZoneKeyName
            };

            // Look up the display string
            if (displayStrings.ContainsKey(tzi.TimeZoneKeyName))
            {
```

```
            displayInfo.Display = displayStrings[tzi.TimeZoneKeyName];
        }
        else if (displayStrings.ContainsKey(tzi.StandardName))
        {
            displayInfo.Display = displayStrings[tzi.StandardName];
        }
        // Or calculate one
        else
        {
            if (tzi.Bias == 0)
                displayInfo.Display = "(UTC) ";
            else
                displayInfo.Display = String.Format("(UTC{0}{1:D2}:{2:D2}) ",
                                                tzi.Bias > 0 ? '-' : '+',
                                                Math.Abs(tzi.Bias) / 60,
                                                Math.Abs(tzi.Bias) % 60);
            displayInfo.Display += tzi.TimeZoneKeyName;
        }

        // Add to collection
        displayInformation.Add(displayInfo);

        // Prepare for next iteration
        index += 1;
        tzi = new DYNAMIC_TIME_ZONE_INFORMATION();
    }

    // Sort the display information items
    displayInformation.Sort((TimeZoneDisplayInfo info1, TimeZoneDisplayInfo info2) =>
        {
            return info2.Bias.CompareTo(info1.Bias);
        });

    // Set to the publicly available property
    this.DisplayInformation = displayInformation;
    }

    // Public interface
    public IList<TimeZoneDisplayInfo> DisplayInformation { protected set; get; }
    ...
}
```

As you'll see shortly, this *DisplayInformation* property is used as an *ItemsSource* for a *ComboBox*.

The only remaining method in *TimeZoneManager* converts a UTC time into local time based on a time zone key value. This is the same string as the *TimeZoneKeyName* field of the DYNAMIC_TIME_ZONE_INFORMATION structure and the *TimeZoneKey* property of the *TimeZoneDisplayInfo* structure:

Project: ClockRack | File: TimeZoneManager.cs (excerpt)

```
public partial class TimeZoneManager
{
    ...
    public DateTime GetLocalTime(string timeZoneKey, DateTime utc)
    {
        // Convert to Win32 SYSTEMTIME
        SYSTEMTIME utcSysTime = new SYSTEMTIME
        {
```

```
            wYear = (ushort)utc.Year,
            wMonth = (ushort)utc.Month,
            wDay = (ushort)utc.Day,
            wHour = (ushort)utc.Hour,
            wMinute = (ushort)utc.Minute,
            wSecond = (ushort)utc.Second,
            wMilliseconds = (ushort)utc.Millisecond
        };

        // Convert to local time
        DYNAMIC_TIME_ZONE_INFORMATION dtzi = dynamicTzis[timeZoneKey];
        TIME_ZONE_INFORMATION tzi = new TIME_ZONE_INFORMATION();
        GetTimeZoneInformationForYear((ushort)utc.Year, ref dtzi, out tzi);

        SYSTEMTIME localSysTime = new SYSTEMTIME();
        SystemTimeToTzSpecificLocalTime(ref tzi, ref utcSysTime, out localSysTime);

        // Convert SYSTEMTIME to DateTime
        return new DateTime(localSysTime.wYear, localSysTime.wMonth, localSysTime.wDay,
                            localSysTime.wHour, localSysTime.wMinute,
                            localSysTime.wSecond, localSysTime.wMilliseconds);
    }
}
```

The method converts a .NET *DateTime* to a Win32 SYSTEMTIME, obtains a DYNAMIC_TIME_ZONE_ INFORMATION from the private dictionary, and then calls *GetTimeZoneInformationForYear*, which returns information in the form of a TIME_ZONE_INFORMATION structure, which is then passed to the *SystemTimeToTzSpecificLocalTime* function. The resultant SYSTEMTIME is converted back to a .NET *DateTime*.

I'm not entirely happy with this method, and let me tell you why. The ClockRack program displays multiple clocks and uses a *CompositionTarget.Rendering* method to obtain an updated *DateTime.UtcNow* value, which it uses for all the clocks. (I figured this was probably more efficient than for this *GetLocalTime* method to call the Win32 *GetSystemTime* function to obtain a SYSTEMTIME value for UTC for each clock.) What I'm not happy about is repeatedly calling the *GetTimeZoneInformationForYear* method. This function really only needs to be called once for each time zone, and then the TIME_ZONE_INFORMATION can be reused in subsequent calls. However, if the program is running from December 31 to January 1, it needs to be called again for the New Year. I decided not to clutter up the class with logic of this sort.

The year passed to *GetTimeZoneInformationForYear* should be a local year, not a UTC year, and that's something else I'm not quite doing correctly. These two years are potentially only different during a 24-hour period surrounding the UTC New Year, and it really shouldn't matter in a program like this because the transition between standard time and daylight saving time occurs much later in the year.

However, if a particular locale in the southern hemisphere decided to observe daylight saving time in one calendar year but not the next, or vice versa, that locale would experience a local time change at midnight on December 31st, and the time would not be calculated incorrectly in the hours around New Year in the transition between those two years.

But let's move on.

You'll recognize much of the actual clock (a *UserControl* derivative called *TimeZoneClock*) from the AnalogClock program from Chapter 10, "Transforms," but I've converted it to use a view model through data bindings. I've also reduced all the coordinates and sizes by a factor of 10. Because there might be many clocks displayed in a very tiny space (such as a snapped view), the clocks must be able to vary widely in size. The approach I've used here—involving a *Viewbox* and a custom panel—worked best when the clocks had a defined size that was smaller than they would ever be.

Another difference is that the analog clock face is now surrounded by two *TextBlock* elements. The top one displays a location, and the bottom one displays the current date and time. Without that text time at the bottom, you might be a little confused about whether the time was before noon or after.

Each of the two *TextBlock* elements has a fixed height from the *RowDefinition* settings on the *Grid*, but they are also each in a *Viewbox*—if the text gets too long, it is compressed to fit. Overall, the entire clock is in a single-cell *Grid* with a *Background* property set to a binding. This *Grid* will occupy the full area available for it. Within that *Grid* is a *Viewbox*, which will adjust the size of its contents. Those contents are another *Grid* with a fixed size of 30 by 20, but the actual size is governed by the *Viewbox* based on available space:

Project: ClockRack | File: TimeZoneClock.xaml (excerpt)

```
<UserControl ...
    Name="ctrl">

    <UserControl.Resources>
        <Style TargetType="TextBlock">
            <Setter Property="Margin" Value="12 0" />
            <Setter Property="TextAlignment" Value="Center" />
        </Style>

        <Style TargetType="Path">
            <Setter Property="StrokeThickness" Value="0.2" />
            <Setter Property="StrokeStartLineCap" Value="Round" />
            <Setter Property="StrokeEndLineCap" Value="Round" />
            <Setter Property="StrokeLineJoin" Value="Round" />
            <Setter Property="StrokeDashCap" Value="Round" />
            <Setter Property="Fill" Value="Gray" />
        </Style>
    </UserControl.Resources>

    <UserControl.Foreground>
        <SolidColorBrush Color="{Binding Foreground}" />
    </UserControl.Foreground>

    <Grid>
        <Grid.Background>
            <SolidColorBrush Color="{Binding Background}" />
        </Grid.Background>

        <Viewbox>
            <Grid Width="20"
                  Height="30"
                  HorizontalAlignment="Center"
                  VerticalAlignment="Center">
```

```
<Grid.RowDefinitions>
    <RowDefinition Height="5" />
    <RowDefinition Height="20" />
    <RowDefinition Height="5" />
</Grid.RowDefinitions>

<Viewbox Grid.Row="0">
    <TextBlock Text="{Binding Location}" />
</Viewbox>

<Grid Grid.Row="1">

    <!-- Transform for entire clock -->
    <Grid.RenderTransform>
        <TranslateTransform X="10" Y="10" />
    </Grid.RenderTransform>

    <!-- Small tick marks -->
    <Path Fill="{x:Null}"
          Stroke="{Binding ElementName=ctrl, Path=Foreground}"
          StrokeThickness="0.3"
          StrokeDashArray="0 3.14159">
        <Path.Data>
            <EllipseGeometry RadiusX="90" RadiusY="90" />
        </Path.Data>
    </Path>

    <!-- Large tick marks -->
    <Path Fill="{x:Null}"
          Stroke="{Binding ElementName=ctrl, Path=Foreground}"
          StrokeThickness="0.6"
          StrokeDashArray="0 7.854">
        <Path.Data>
            <EllipseGeometry RadiusX="90" RadiusY="90" />
        </Path.Data>
    </Path>

    <!-- Hour hand pointing straight up -->
    <Path Data="M 0 -6 C 0 -3, 2 -3, 0.5 -2 L 0.5 0
                    C 0.5 0.75, --/5 0.75, -0.5 0 L -0.5 -2
                    C -2 -3, 0 -3, 0 -6"
          Stroke="{Binding ElementName=ctrl, Path=Foreground}">
        <Path.RenderTransform>
            <RotateTransform Angle="{Binding HourAngle}" />
        </Path.RenderTransform>
    </Path>

    <!-- Minute hand pointing straight up -->
    <Path Data="M 0 -8 C 0 -7.5, 0 -7, 0.25 -6 L 0.25 0
                    C 0.25 0.5, -0.25 0.5, -0.25 0 L -0.255 -6
                    C 0 -7, 0 -7.5, 0 -8.0"
          Stroke="{Binding ElementName=ctrl, Path=Foreground}">
        <Path.RenderTransform>
            <RotateTransform Angle="{Binding MinuteAngle}" />
        </Path.RenderTransform>
    </Path>
```

```
        <!-- Second hand pointing straight up -->
        <Path Data="M 0 1 L 0 -8"
                Stroke="{Binding ElementName=ctrl, Path=Foreground}">
            <Path.RenderTransform>
                <RotateTransform Angle="{Binding SecondAngle}" />
            </Path.RenderTransform>
        </Path>
    </Grid>

    <Viewbox Grid.Row="2">
        <TextBlock Text="{Binding FormattedDateTime}" />
    </Viewbox>
            </Grid>
        </Viewbox>
    </Grid>
</UserControl>
```

Both *TextBlock* elements and all the *RotateTransform* elements have bindings to properties in a view model. Toward the top of the TimeZoneClock.xaml file you'll see that this view model also includes properties of type *Color* named *Foreground* and *Background*. The code-behind file has nothing but a call to *InitializeComponent*.

To keep this program relatively simple, I decided to limit the colors for the background and foreground of each clock to those 140 colors that have names and hence correspond to members of the static *Colors* class. The view model for the *TimeZoneClock* class defines *Foreground* and *Background* properties of type *Color* as you might expect, but it also defines *ForegroundName* and *BackgroundName* properties, and whenever one of these properties is changed, the other changes as well with a little reflection logic:

Project: ClockRack | File: TimeZoneClockViewModel.cs (excerpt)
```
public class TimeZoneClockViewModel : INotifyPropertyChanged
{
    string location = "New York City", timeZoneKey = "Eastern Standard Time";
    Color background = Colors.Yellow, foreground = Colors.Blue;
    string backgroundName = "Yellow", foregroundName = "Blue";
    DateTime dateTime;
    string formattedDateTime;
    double hourAngle, minuteAngle, secondAngle;
    TypeInfo colorsTypeInfo = typeof(Colors).GetTypeInfo();

    public event PropertyChangedEventHandler PropertyChanged;

    public string Location
    {
        set { SetProperty<string>(ref location, value); }
        get { return location; }
    }

    public string TimeZoneKey
    {
        set { SetProperty<string>(ref timeZoneKey, value); }
        get { return timeZoneKey; }
    }
```

```csharp
    public string BackgroundName
    {
        set
        {
            if (SetProperty<string>(ref backgroundName, value))
                this.Background = NameToColor(value);
        }
        get { return backgroundName; }
    }

    public Color Background
    {
        set
        {
            if (SetProperty<Color>(ref background, value))
                this.BackgroundName = ColorToName(value);
        }
        get { return background; }
    }

    public string ForegroundName
    {
        set
        {
            if (SetProperty<string>(ref foregroundName, value))
                this.Foreground = NameToColor(value);
        }
        get { return foregroundName; }
    }

    public Color Foreground
    {
        set
        {
            if (SetProperty<Color>(ref foreground, value))
                this.ForegroundName = ColorToName(value);
        }
        get { return foreground; }
    }

    public DateTime DateTime
    {
        set
        {
            if (SetProperty<DateTime>(ref dateTime, value))
            {
                this.FormattedDateTime = String.Format("{0:D} {1:t}", value, value);
                this.SecondAngle = 6 * (dateTime.Second + dateTime.Millisecond / 1000.0);
                this.MinuteAngle = 6 * dateTime.Minute + this.SecondAngle / 60;
                this.HourAngle = 30 * (dateTime.Hour % 12) + this.MinuteAngle / 12;
            }
        }
        get { return dateTime; }
    }

    public string FormattedDateTime
    {
```

```csharp
        set { SetProperty<string>(ref formattedDateTime, value); }
        get { return formattedDateTime; }
    }

    public double HourAngle
    {
        set { SetProperty<double>(ref hourAngle, value); }
        get { return hourAngle; }
    }

    public double MinuteAngle
    {
        set { SetProperty<double>(ref minuteAngle, value); }
        get { return minuteAngle; }
    }

    public double SecondAngle
    {
        set { SetProperty<double>(ref secondAngle, value); }
        get { return secondAngle; }
    }

    Color NameToColor(string name)
    {
        return (Color)colorsTypeInfo.GetDeclaredProperty(name).GetValue(null);
    }

    string ColorToName(Color color)
    {
        foreach (PropertyInfo property in colorsTypeInfo.DeclaredProperties)
            if (color.Equals((Color)property.GetValue(null)))
                return property.Name;

        return "";
    }

    protected bool SetProperty<T>(ref T storage, T value,
                                  [CallerMemberName] string propertyName = null)
    {
        if (object.Equals(storage, value))
            return false;

        storage = value;
        OnPropertyChanged(propertyName);
        return true;
    }

    protected void OnPropertyChanged(string propertyName)
    {
        if (PropertyChanged != null)
            PropertyChanged(this, new PropertyChangedEventArgs(propertyName));
    }
}
```

This view model also includes a *DateTime* property, and whenever that changes, the *HourAngle*, *MinuteAngle*, and *SecondAngle* properties also change, driving the three *RotateTransform* objects in TimeZoneClock.xaml.

To display multiple clocks, I wanted a type of panel that would allow all the clocks to be displayed within the confines of the page but that allocated optimum space for each child. The *UniformGrid* panel I developed in Chapter 11, "The Three Templates," seemed close to what I wanted but not exactly. For example, suppose there are seven clocks and the *UniformGrid* determines that they should be displayed in two rows of five clocks each. *UniformGrid* would put five clocks in the first row and two clocks in the second. It would be more aesthetically pleasing for the panel to distribute the clocks among the two rows more equally—four clocks in one row and three clocks in the other.

The ClockRack program includes a reference to the Petzold.ProgrammingWindows6.Chapter11 library from Chapter 11 but derives from *UniformGrid* a panel named *DistributedUniformGrid*. The logic in this new class allocates approximately an equal number of items to each row. Within each row, the items are equally spaced:

Project: ClockRack | File: DistributedUniformGrid.cs

```
using System;
using Windows.Foundation;
using Windows.UI.Xaml.Controls;
using Petzold.ProgrammingWindows6.Chapter11;

namespace ClockRack
{
    public class DistributedUniformGrid : UniformGrid
    {
        protected override Size ArrangeOverride(Size finalSize)
        {
            int index = 0;
            double cellWidth = finalSize.Width / cols;
            double cellHeight = finalSize.Height / rows;
            int displayed = 0;

            if (this.Orientation == Orientation.Vertical)
            {
                for (int row = 0; row < rows; row++)
                {
                    double y = row * cellHeight;
                    int accumDisplay = (int)Math.Ceiling((row + 1.0) *
                        this.Children.Count / rows);
                    int display = accumDisplay - displayed;
                    cellWidth = Math.Round(finalSize.Width / display);
                    double x = 0;

                    for (int col = 0; col < display; col++)
                    {
                        if (index < this.Children.Count)
                            this.Children[index].Arrange(new Rect(x, y, cellWidth, cellHeight));

                        x += cellWidth;
                        index++;
                    }
                }
```

```
                    displayed += display;
                }
            }
            else
            {
                for (int col = 0; col < cols; col++)
                {
                    double x = col * cellWidth;
                    int accumDisplay =
                            (int)Math.Ceiling((col + 1.0) * this.Children.Count / cols);
                    int display = accumDisplay - displayed;
                    cellHeight = Math.Round(finalSize.Height / display);
                    double y = 0;

                    for (int row = 0; row < display; row++)
                    {
                        if (index < this.Children.Count)
                            this.Children[index].Arrange(new Rect(x, y, cellWidth, cellHeight));

                        y += cellHeight;
                        index++;
                    }
                    displayed += display;
                }
            }
            return finalSize;
        }
    }
}
```

The MainPage.xaml file consists of little more than a *DistributedUniformGrid* to hold the clock controls:

Project: ClockRack | File: MainPage.xaml (excerpt)

```
<Page ... >
    <Grid Background="{StaticResource ApplicationPageBackgroundThemeBrush}">
        <Grid Name="contentGrid"
              Background="Transparent">

            <DistributedUniformGrid Name="uniformGrid"
                                    Orientation="Vertical" />
        </Grid>
    </Grid>
</Page>
```

The constructor of the *MainPage* class is responsible for populating the *DistributedUniformGrid* from application settings. The program uses the *ApplicationData* class in the *Windows.Storage* namespace for storing four text items per clock: the location name (selected by the user), the time zone key identifying the time zone for the clock, a foreground color name, and a background color name. For the first clock, these are stored using keys "0Location", "0TimeZoneKey", "0Foreground", and "0Background"; the second clock has keys that begin with the number 1, and so forth. As each set of settings is retrieved, a *TimeZoneClock* and *TimeZoneClockViewModel* are created and initialized:

Project: ClockRack | File: MainPage.xaml.cs (excerpt)

```csharp
public sealed partial class MainPage : Page
{
    ...
    IPropertySet appSettings = ApplicationData.Current.LocalSettings.Values;

    public MainPage()
    {
        this.InitializeComponent();

        // Load application settings for clocks
        int index = 0;

        while (appSettings.ContainsKey(index.ToString() + "Location"))
        {
            string preface = index.ToString();

            TimeZoneClock clock = new TimeZoneClock
            {
                DataContext = new TimeZoneClockViewModel
                {
                    Location = appSettings[preface + "Location"] as string,
                    TimeZoneKey = appSettings[preface + "TimeZoneKey"] as string,
                    ForegroundName = appSettings[preface + "Foreground"] as string,
                    BackgroundName = appSettings[preface + "Background"] as string
                },
            };
            uniformGrid.Children.Add(clock);
            index += 1;
        }

        // If there are no settings, make a default Clock
        if (uniformGrid.Children.Count == 0)
        {
            TimeZoneClock clock = new TimeZoneClock
            {
                DataContext = new TimeZoneClockViewModel()
            };
            uniformGrid.Children.Add(clock);
        }

        // Set the Suspending handler
        Application.Current.Suspending += OnApplicationSuspending;

        // Start the Rendering event
        CompositionTarget.Rendering += OnCompositionTargetRendering;
    }
```

```
void OnApplicationSuspending(object sender, SuspendingEventArgs args)
{
    appSettings.Clear();

    for (int index = 0; index < uniformGrid.Children.Count; index++)
    {
        TimeZoneClock timeZoneClock = uniformGrid.Children[index] as TimeZoneClock;
        TimeZoneClockViewModel viewModel =
                timeZoneClock.DataContext as TimeZoneClockViewModel;
        string preface = index.ToString();

        appSettings[preface + "Location"] = viewModel.Location;
        appSettings[preface + "TimeZoneKey"] = viewModel.TimeZoneKey;
        appSettings[preface + "Foreground"] = viewModel.ForegroundName;
        appSettings[preface + "Background"] = viewModel.BackgroundName;
    }
}
...
}
```

As usual, these settings are saved during the *Suspending* event.

The constructor concludes by starting up a *CompositionTarget.Rendering* event. This is responsible for using the *TimeZoneManager* instance to obtain a local time based on the current UTC time with the time zone key for each clock:

Project: ClockRack | File: MainPage.xaml.cs (excerpt)

```
public sealed partial class MainPage : Page
{
    TimeZoneManager timeZoneManager = new TimeZoneManager();
    ...
    void OnCompositionTargetRendering(object sender, object args)
    {
        // Get the time once
        DateTime utc = DateTime.UtcNow;

        foreach (UIElement child in uniformGrid.Children)
        {
            TimeZoneClockViewModel viewModel =
                    (child as FrameworkElement).DataContext as TimeZoneClockViewModel;
            string timeZoneKey = viewModel.TimeZoneKey;

            // Set the local time from the TimeZoneManager
            viewModel.DateTime = timeZoneManager.GetLocalTime(timeZoneKey, utc);
        }
    }
    ...
}
```

A right tap displays a *PopupMenu* with three items: Add, Edit, and Delete. The Edit and Delete items pertain to the particular clock being tapped, so the *OnRightTapped* override begins by finding that tapped clock. That object is passed to the handlers for these three items. Even for Add, the tapped clock is needed because the logic inserts the new clock after that tapped clock. The Delete item appears on the menu only if there's more than one clock:

Project: ClockRack | File: MainPage.xaml.cs (excerpt)

```
async protected override void OnRightTapped(RightTappedRoutedEventArgs args)
{
    // Check if the parent of the click element is a TimeZoneClock
    FrameworkElement element = args.OriginalSource as FrameworkElement;

    while (element != null)
    {
        if (element is TimeZoneClock)
            break;

        element = element.Parent as FrameworkElement;
    }

    if (element == null)
        return;

    // Create a PopupMenu
    PopupMenu popupMenu = new PopupMenu();
    popupMenu.Commands.Add(new UICommand("Add...", OnAddMenuItem, element));
    popupMenu.Commands.Add(new UICommand("Edit...", OnEditMenuItem, element));

    if (uniformGrid.Children.Count > 1)
        popupMenu.Commands.Add(new UICommand("Delete", OnDeleteMenuItem, element));

    args.Handled = true;
    base.OnRightTapped(args);

    // Display the menu
    await popupMenu.ShowAsync(args.GetPosition(this));
}
```

For the Add menu item, a new *TimeZoneClock* (with a corresponding *TimeZoneClockViewModel*) must be created and inserted into the collection. This new clock is always inserted after the clock that was tapped:

Project: ClockRack | File: MainPage.xaml.cs (excerpt)

```
void OnAddMenuItem(IUICommand command)
{
    // Create new TimeZoneClock
    TimeZoneClock timeZoneClock = new TimeZoneClock
    {
        DataContext = new TimeZoneClockViewModel()
    };

    // Insert after the tapped clock
    TimeZoneClock clickedClock = command.Id as TimeZoneClock;
    int index = uniformGrid.Children.IndexOf(clickedClock);
    uniformGrid.Children.Insert(index + 1, timeZoneClock);
}
```

The Delete item is also fairly easy, but the program insists on getting a confirmation of the deletion using a *MessageDialog*:

Project: ClockRack | File: MainPage.xaml.cs (excerpt)

```
async void OnDeleteMenuItem(IUICommand command)
{
    TimeZoneClock timeZoneClock = command.Id as TimeZoneClock;
    TimeZoneClockViewModel viewModel = timeZoneClock.DataContext as TimeZoneClockViewModel;

    MessageDialog msgdlg = new MessageDialog("Delete clock from collection?",
                                             viewModel.Location);
    msgdlg.Commands.Add(new UICommand("OK"));
    msgdlg.Commands.Add(new UICommand("Cancel"));
    msgdlg.DefaultCommandIndex = 0;
    msgdlg.CancelCommandIndex = 1;

    IUICommand msgDlgCommand = await msgdlg.ShowAsync();

    if (msgDlgCommand.Label == "OK")
        uniformGrid.Children.Remove(command.Id as TimeZoneClock);
}
```

Of course, the Edit option is more involved, and unless you're entirely satisfied with a clock for New York City with a blue foreground on a yellow background, you're going to be invoking the Edit menu right after you add a new clock. The Edit option instantiates a *SettingsDialog* (which you'll see shortly) as a child of a *Popup* object. Because *SettingsDialog* needs to access the *TimeZoneManager* instance, the *TimeZoneManager* object is supplied to the *SettingsDialog* constructor. The bulk of this method is responsible for positioning the *Popup* so that it is visually associated with the tapped clock but doesn't hang off the edge of the screen:

Project: ClockRack | File: MainPage.xaml.cs (excerpt)

```
void OnEditMenuItem(IUICommand command)
{
    TimeZoneClock timeZoneClock = command.Id as TimeZoneClock;
    SettingsDialog settingsDialog = new SettingsDialog(timeZoneManager);
    settingsDialog.DataContext = timeZoneClock.DataContext;

    // Create Popup with SettingsDialog child
    Popup popup = new Popup
    {
        Child = settingsDialog,
        IsLightDismissEnabled = true
    };

    settingsDialog.SizeChanged += (sender, args) =>
        {
            // Get clock center
            Point position = new Point(timeZoneClock.ActualWidth / 2,
                                       timeZoneClock.ActualHeight / 2);

            // Convert to Page coordinates
            position = timeZoneClock.TransformToVisual(this).TransformPoint(position);

            // Position popup so lower-left or lower-right corner
```

```
//       aligns with center of edited clock
if (position.X > this.ActualWidth / 2)
    position.X -= settingsDialog.ActualWidth;
position.Y -= settingsDialog.ActualHeight;

// Adjust for size of page
if (position.X + settingsDialog.ActualWidth > this.ActualWidth)
    position.X = this.ActualWidth - settingsDialog.ActualWidth;

if (position.X < 0)
    position.X = 0;

if (position.Y < 0)
    position.Y = 0;

// Set the Popup position
popup.HorizontalOffset = position.X;
popup.VerticalOffset = position.Y;
        };

    popup.IsOpen = true;
}
```

Here's what the *SettingsDialog* looks like. The first field is an *EditBox* that simply allows you to type in a label; the other three fields use a *ComboBox* to display the currently selected item. The *ComboBox* opens up to display a list of items when the control receives input focus:

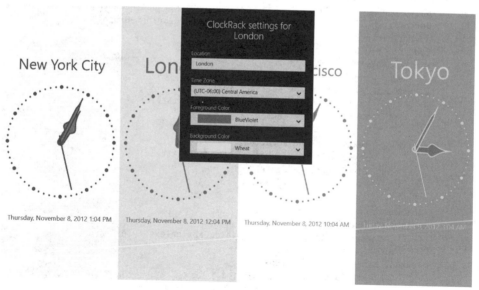

The *DataContext* of the *SettingsDialog* object is set to the *DataContext* of the *TimeZoneClock* being edited. That *DataContext* property is an object of *TimeZoneClockViewModel*, and the XAML file has bindings to the *Location*, *TimeZoneKey*, *ForegroundName*, and *BackgroundName* properties of that class. Notice that the *TextBox* bound to the *Location* property has its *TextChanged* event set; this allows the code-behind file to update the *Location* property in *TimeZoneClockViewModel* "manually," which then updates the display at the top of the popup.

```xaml
<UserControl ... >
    <UserControl.Resources>
        <Style x:Key="DialogCaptionTextStyle"
                TargetType="TextBlock"
                BasedOn="{StaticResource CaptionTextStyle}">
            <Setter Property="FontSize" Value="14.67" />
            <Setter Property="FontWeight" Value="SemiLight" />
            <Setter Property="Margin" Value="0 16 0 8" />
        </Style>

        <DataTemplate x:Key="colorItemTemplate">
            <!-- Item is SettingsDialog.ColorItem -->
            <StackPanel Orientation="Horizontal">
                <Rectangle Width="96" Height="24" Margin="12 6">
                    <Rectangle.Fill>
                        <SolidColorBrush Color="{Binding Color}" />
                    </Rectangle.Fill>
                </Rectangle>

                <TextBlock Text="{Binding Name}"
                           VerticalAlignment="Center" />

            </StackPanel>
        </DataTemplate>
    </UserControl.Resources>

    <!-- DataContext is TimeZoneClockViewModel -->
    <Border Background="{StaticResource ApplicationPageBackgroundThemeBrush}"
            BorderBrush="{StaticResource ApplicationForegroundThemeBrush}"
            BorderThickness="1"
            Padding="7 0 0 0"
            Width="384">
        <StackPanel Margin="24">
            <TextBlock Text="ClockRack settings for"
                       Style="{StaticResource SubheaderTextStyle}"
                       TextAlignment="Center" />

            <TextBlock Text="{Binding Location}"
                       Style="{StaticResource SubheaderTextStyle}"
                       TextAlignment="Center"
                       Margin="0 0 0 12" />

            <!-- Location -->
            <TextBlock Text="Location"
                       Style="{StaticResource DialogCaptionTextStyle}" />

            <TextBox Name="locationTextBox"
                     Text="{Binding Location}"
                     TextChanged="OnLocationTextBoxTextChanged" />

            <!-- Time Zone -->
            <TextBlock Text="Time Zone"
                       Style="{StaticResource DialogCaptionTextStyle}" />

            <ComboBox Name="timeZoneComboBox"
                      SelectedValuePath="TimeZoneKey"
```

```
                         SelectedValue="{Binding TimeZoneKey, Mode=TwoWay}">
            <ComboBox.ItemTemplate>
                <!-- Data is TimeZoneDisplayInfo -->
                <DataTemplate>
                    <TextBlock Text="{Binding Display}" />
                </DataTemplate>
            </ComboBox.ItemTemplate>
        </ComboBox>

        <!-- Foreground and Background Colors -->
        <TextBlock Text="Foreground Color"
                   Style="{StaticResource DialogCaptionTextStyle}" />

        <ComboBox Name="foregroundComboBox"
                  ItemTemplate="{StaticResource colorItemTemplate}"
                  SelectedValuePath="Name"
                  SelectedValue="{Binding ForegroundName, Mode=TwoWay}" />

        <TextBlock Text="Background Color"
                   Style="{StaticResource DialogCaptionTextStyle}" />

        <ComboBox Name="backgroundComboBox"
                  ItemTemplate="{StaticResource colorItemTemplate}"
                  SelectedValuePath="Name"
                  SelectedValue="{Binding BackgroundName, Mode=TwoWay}" />
      </StackPanel>
   </Border>
</UserControl>
```

The code-behind file (shown next) supplies collections for the three *ComboBox* controls. The *ComboBox* for the time zone is filled from the *DisplayInformation* property of the *TimeZoneManager*, and the markup for that first *ComboBox* references the *TimeZoneKey* and *Display* properties.

Because I was already using the Petzold.ProgrammingWindows6.Chapter11 library for *UniformGrid*, I decided to use the *NamedColor* class to get a collection of *NamedColor* objects. As you can see in the XAML file, the *ItemTemplate* used for those two *ComboBox* controls references the *Color* and *Name* properties of *NamedColor*, and each *ComboBox* indicates that the *SelectedValuePath* is the *Name* property.

Project: ClockRack | File: SettingsDialog.xaml.cs (excerpt)

```
public sealed partial class SettingsDialog : UserControl
{
    public SettingsDialog(TimeZoneManager timeZoneManager)
    {
        this.InitializeComponent();

        // Set ItemsSource for time zone ComboBox
        timeZoneComboBox.ItemsSource = timeZoneManager.DisplayInformation;

        // Set ItemsSource for foreground and background ComboBoxes
        foregroundComboBox.ItemsSource = NamedColor.All;
        backgroundComboBox.ItemsSource = NamedColor.All;
    }
```

```
    void OnLocationTextBoxTextChanged(object sender, TextChangedEventArgs args)
    {
        (this.DataContext as TimeZoneClockViewModel).Location = (sender as TextBox).Text;
    }
}
```

That concludes the code for ClockRack.

A Windows Runtime Component Wrapper for DirectX

While P/Invoke is fine for accessing various functions in the flat Win32 API, getting at DirectX is a different matter. DirectX is a bit awkward for P/Invoke and is best accessed from C++ code. If you want to use DirectX from a C# program, you can write a Windows Runtime Component in C++ containing all the DirectX code and then access that library from the C# program. For some small areas of DirectX, you might do this on your own, or you can pursue a more extensive solution such as the open-source SharpDX library available at *http://code.google.com/p/sharpdx*.

However, you might ponder if you are deceiving yourself in some way by accessing DirectX from a C# program through a wrapper library. One reason to use DirectX is for performance, and often that involves not only the performance of the DirectX library itself (which is independent of the language using it) but the performance of your application code. Your application code will generally run faster if it's coded in C++ rather than C# (even though you might code faster and with fewer errors using C#). Consequently, you might want to make the choice to code some or all of your DirectX application in C++.

The DirectXWrapper library I'll be presenting here is *extremely* sparse. I've deliberately limited it to three specific jobs: obtaining a list of fonts installed on the system, obtaining font metrics for a particular font, and drawing lines on a *SurfaceImageSource* object. This *SurfaceImageSource* is actually a bitmap except you don't have to implement your own line-drawing algorithms as I did in Chapter 14, "Bitmaps."

To create this library in Visual Studio, I made a new solution and project named DirectXWrapper. In the left column of the New Project dialog box, I specified that it was a C++ Windows Store project. The template I chose in the central area of the dialog box was Windows Runtime Component. This is a type of Windows 8 library that can be coded in one language (C++ in this case) and accessed from any other Windows Store application, including those written in C#, Visual Basic, and JavaScript. Because of this flexibility, Windows Runtime Components have very stringent limitations. They can't do something that's foreign to one of these languages.

The most significant of the limitations of a Windows Runtime Component are these:

- Public classes must be sealed or non-instantiable.

- Parameters and return values of public methods must be Windows Runtime types.

- Public C++ classes and structures must be defined as *ref* (meaning reference counted).

- Public members of structures are restricted to fields.

Other limitations are described in the Windows 8 documentation. (Do a search for "Creating Windows Runtime Components.")

This DirectXWrapper project needs to reference some C++ libraries not included by default. In the Solution Explorer, I right-clicked the project name and selected Properties. A dialog appears entitled DirectXWrapper Property Pages. At the top of the dialog is a Platform combo box. In this I selected All Platforms. At the left of the dialog I selected Configuration Properties, Linker, and Input. At the top of the resultant list of items is a field titled Additional Dependencies. Click that field and select Edit. You'll see an Additional Dependencies dialog box. To the list I added three DirectX libraries:

- d2d1.lib

- d3d11.lib

- dwrite.lib

The first two of these are for 2D and 3D graphics and are required for drawing on a *SurfaceImageSource*. The third is the library for DirectWrite.

The DirectXWrapper library also requires accessing some header files associated with these libraries. In the pch.h ("precompiled headers") file, I included the required header files:

Project: DirectXWrapper | File: pch.h

```
#pragma once

#include <wrl.h>
#include <d2d1_1.h>
#include <d3d11_1.h>
#include <dwrite.h>
#include <windows.ui.xaml.media.dxinterop.h>
```

The wrl.h header file stands for "Windows Runtime Library" and contains definitions useful for working with COM in Windows 8 applications. The windows.ui.xaml.media.dxinterop.h header file has a declaration for the *ISurfaceImageSourceNative* interface required for using the *SurfaceImageSource* class.

DirectWrite and Fonts

DirectWrite is the subset of DirectX dedicated to the high-performance display of text. Even if you don't need that performance, DirectWrite provides a couple facilities missing from the Windows Runtime, specifically obtaining a list of installed fonts and obtaining font metrics.

For accessing DirectWrite, I decided that I would define classes in my DirectXWrapper library in a one-to-one correspondence with DirectWrite interfaces. These interfaces all begin with *IDWrite*: The *I* is for "interface" and *DWrite* is for "DirectWrite." My corresponding classes simply begin with *Write*.

This is bound to be a little confusing at first, but here's the correspondence in the order I'll be discussing them:

DirectWrite Interface	DirectXWrapper Class
IDWriteFactory	WriteFactory
IDWriteFontCollection	WriteFontCollection
IDWriteFontFamily	WriteFontFamily
IDWriteFont	WriteFont
IDWriteLocalizedString	WriteLocalizedStrings

In many cases, method names in the DirectWrite interfaces (for example, the *GetMetrics* method in *IDWriteFont*) have simply been duplicated: My *WriteFont* class also has a *GetMetrics* method. I have not attempted to duplicate *all* the methods in these interfaces.

A program that wishes to use DirectWrite begins by calling the *DWriteCreateFactory* function to obtain an object of type *IDWriteFactory*. Among many other methods, this *IDWriteFactory* interface defines *GetSystemFontCollection* for obtaining the fonts currently installed on the system.

I wrapped *IDWriteFactory* in my own class named *WriteFactory*. Here's the C++ header file:

Project: DirectXWrapper | File: WriteFactory.h

```
#pragma once

#include "WriteFontCollection.h"

namespace DirectXWrapper
{
    public ref class WriteFactory sealed
    {
    private:
        Microsoft::WRL::ComPtr<IDWriteFactory> pFactory;

    public:
        WriteFactory();
        WriteFontCollection^ GetSystemFontCollection();
        WriteFontCollection^ GetSystemFontCollection(bool checkForUpdates);
    };
}
```

The class is defined with *ref* and *sealed*, which is required for public C++ classes in a Windows Runtime Component. The *ref* indicates that the class must be instantiated with *ref new* rather than just *new*, and the constructor returns a reference-counted handle rather than a pointer.

The *IDWriteFactory* object obtained from *DWriteCreateFactory* is stored as a private field as a *ComPtr*, which is defined in the *Microsoft.Wrl* namespace (or *Microsoft::WRL* namespace using C++ syntax). *ComPtr* is short for "Common Object Model pointer"—it turns a pointer to a COM object such as *IDWriteFactory* into a "smart pointer" that is reference counted and that properly releases its own resources. This is the recommended way to maintain pointers to COM objects in your Windows 8 DirectX code.

Three public methods are also defined in the header file: a constructor and two versions of a *GetSystemFontCollection* method. These methods return a *WriteFontCollection* object. This is *not* a DirectWrite type. It can't be because public methods in a Windows Runtime Component can return Windows Runtime types only. Instead, it is another class in the DirectXWrapper library. The hat (^) means that *WriteFontCollection* is a handle rather than a pointer, which means that it's also defined with the *ref* keyword and instantiated in C++ with *ref new* rather than just *new*.

The mention of the *WriteFontCollection* class in this header file requires the inclusion of the WriteFontCollection.h header file at the top.

The implementation of the *WriteFactory* class is in the WriteFactory.cpp file:

Project: DirectXWrapper | File: WriteFactory.cpp

```
#include "pch.h"
#include "WriteFactory.h"

using namespace DirectXWrapper;
using namespace Platform;
using namespace Microsoft::WRL;

WriteFactory::WriteFactory()
{
    HRESULT hr = DWriteCreateFactory(DWRITE_FACTORY_TYPE_SHARED,
                                __uuidof(IDWriteFactory),
                                &pFactory);

    if (!SUCCEEDED(hr))
        throw ref new COMException(hr);
}

WriteFontCollection^ WriteFactory::GetSystemFontCollection()
{
    return GetSystemFontCollection(false);
}

WriteFontCollection^ WriteFactory::GetSystemFontCollection(bool checkForUpdates)
{
    ComPtr<IDWriteFontCollection> pFontCollection;

    HRESULT hr = pFactory->GetSystemFontCollection(&pFontCollection, checkForUpdates);

    if (!SUCCEEDED(hr))
        throw ref new COMException(hr);

    return ref new WriteFontCollection(pFontCollection);
}
```

The constructor calls the *DWriteCreateFactory* function to obtain the *IDWriteFactory* object. The *__uuidof* operator obtains a GUID identifying this object. Very often DirectX functions and methods return values of type HRESULT. This is simply a number indicating success or failure, but it's important not to ignore them. The standard approach in a Windows 8 program is to raise an exception of type *COMException* if an error has occurred. Notice the *ref new* used to instantiate that *COMException* class; that's a Windows Runtime type.

The *GetSystemFontCollection* method in my *WriteFactory* class uses the *IDWriteFactory* object to call the *GetSystemFontCollection* method of that interface to obtain a pointer to a DirectWrite *IDWriteFontCollection* interface. This is passed to the *WriteFontCollection* constructor. Again, notice the *ref new*.

Here's the *WriteFontCollection* header file:

Project: DirectXWrapper | File: WriteFontCollection.h

```
#pragma once

#include "WriteFontFamily.h"

namespace DirectXWrapper
{
    public ref class WriteFontCollection sealed
    {
    private:
        Microsoft::WRL::ComPtr<IDWriteFontCollection> pFontCollection;

    internal:
        WriteFontCollection(Microsoft::WRL::ComPtr<IDWriteFontCollection> pFontCollection);

    public:
        bool FindFamilyName(Platform::String^ familyName, int * index);
        int GetFontFamilyCount();
        WriteFontFamily^ GetFontFamily(int index);
    };
}
```

The constructor is defined as *internal* to the library. It can't be *private* because then it couldn't be accessed from outside the class (and obviously the *WriteFontFactory* class needs to call it). But it can't be *public* because the constructor argument is not a Windows Runtime type. Also notice the use of the *String* class defined in the *Platform* namespace. This *String* class *is* a Windows Runtime type, and it is equivalent to the C# *String* class defined in the *System* namespace.

Here's the implementation of *WriteFontCollection*:

Project: DirectXWrapper | File: WriteFontCollection.cpp

```
#include "pch.h"
#include "WriteFontCollection.h"
#include "WriteFontFamily.h"

using namespace DirectXWrapper;
using namespace Platform;
using namespace Microsoft::WRL;

WriteFontCollection::WriteFontCollection(ComPtr<IDWriteFontCollection> pFontCollection)
{
    this->pFontCollection = pFontCollection;
}

bool WriteFontCollection::FindFamilyName(String^ familyName, int * index)
{
    uint32 familyIndex;
```

```
        BOOL exists;
        HRESULT hr = this->pFontCollection->FindFamilyName(familyName->Data(),&familyIndex,&exists);

        if (!SUCCEEDED(hr))
            throw ref new COMException(hr);

        *index = familyIndex;

        return exists != 0;
    }

    int WriteFontCollection::GetFontFamilyCount()
    {
        return pFontCollection->GetFontFamilyCount();
    }

    WriteFontFamily^ WriteFontCollection::GetFontFamily(int index)
    {
        ComPtr<IDWriteFontFamily> pfontFamily;

        HRESULT hr = pFontCollection->GetFontFamily(index, &pfontFamily);

        if (!SUCCEEDED(hr))
            throw ref new COMException(hr);

        return ref new WriteFontFamily(pfontFamily);
    }
```

Obtaining a particular font family from this collection is a two-step process. First, *FindFamilyName* must be called with a particular name (such as "Times New Roman") to obtain an index within the collection. That index is then passed to *GetFontFamily* to obtain an *IDWriteFontFamily* object (when using DirectWrite) or a *WriteFontFamily* object (when using the DirectXWrapper library).

Alternatively, all the fonts in the collection can be enumerated by passing indices to *GetFontFamily* up to the value returned from *GetFontFamilyCount*.

Here's the *WriteFontFamily* header file:

Project: DirectXWrapper | File: WriteFontFamily.h

```
#pragma once

#include "WriteLocalizedStrings.h"
#include "WriteFont.h"

namespace DirectXWrapper
{
    public ref class WriteFontFamily sealed
    {
    private:
        Microsoft::WRL::ComPtr<IDWriteFontFamily> pFontFamily;

    internal:
        WriteFontFamily(Microsoft::WRL::ComPtr<IDWriteFontFamily> pFontFamily);
```

```
public:
    WriteLocalizedStrings^ GetFamilyNames();
    WriteFont^ GetFirstMatchingFont(Windows::UI::Text::FontWeight fontWeight,
                                    Windows::UI::Text::FontStretch fontStretch,
                                    Windows::UI::Text::FontStyle fontStyle);
};
}
```

Look at those arguments to *GetFirstMatchingFont*: Those are Windows Runtime types because they're defined in the *Windows.UI.Text* namespace. *FontWeight* is a structure, which is the type of the static properties in the *FontWeights* class, and *FontStretch* and *FontStyle* are both enumerations. In the *GetFirstMatchingFont* method implemented by the *IDWriteFontFamily* interface, the arguments are of type DWRITE_FONT_WEIGHT, DWRITE_FONT_STRETCH, and DWRITE_FONT_STYLE, all of which are enumerations. Interestingly, the *FontStretch* and *FontStyle* values can be converted directly: The two enumerations have the same values, strongly indicating that DirectWrite forms the foundation of Windows Runtime text output.

Project: DirectXWrapper | File: WriteFontFamily.cpp

```cpp
#include "pch.h"
#include "WriteFontFamily.h"

using namespace DirectXWrapper;
using namespace Platform;
using namespace Microsoft::WRL;
using namespace Windows::UI::Text;

WriteFontFamily::WriteFontFamily(ComPtr<IDWriteFontFamily> pFontFamily)
{
    this->pFontFamily = pFontFamily;
}

WriteLocalizedStrings^ WriteFontFamily::GetFamilyNames()
{
    ComPtr<IDWriteLocalizedStrings> pFamilyNames;

    HRESULT hr = pFontFamily->GetFamilyNames(&pFamilyNames);

    if (!SUCCEEDED(hr))
        throw ref new COMException(hr);

    return ref new WriteLocalizedStrings(pFamilyNames);
}

WriteFont^ WriteFontFamily::GetFirstMatchingFont(FontWeight fontWeight,
                                                 FontStretch fontStretch,
                                                 FontStyle fontStyle)
{
    // Convert font weight from Windows Runtime to DirectX
    DWRITE_FONT_WEIGHT writeFontWeight = DWRITE_FONT_WEIGHT_NORMAL;
```

```
        if (fontWeight.Equals(FontWeights::Black))
            writeFontWeight = DWRITE_FONT_WEIGHT_BLACK;

        else if (fontWeight.Equals(FontWeights::Bold))
            writeFontWeight = DWRITE_FONT_WEIGHT_BOLD;

        else if (fontWeight.Equals(FontWeights::ExtraBlack))
            writeFontWeight = DWRITE_FONT_WEIGHT_EXTRA_BLACK;

        else if (fontWeight.Equals(FontWeights::ExtraBold))
            writeFontWeight = DWRITE_FONT_WEIGHT_EXTRA_BOLD;

        else if (fontWeight.Equals(FontWeights::ExtraLight))
            writeFontWeight = DWRITE_FONT_WEIGHT_EXTRA_LIGHT;

        else if (fontWeight.Equals(FontWeights::Light))
            writeFontWeight = DWRITE_FONT_WEIGHT_LIGHT;

        else if (fontWeight.Equals(FontWeights::Medium))
            writeFontWeight = DWRITE_FONT_WEIGHT_MEDIUM;

        else if (fontWeight.Equals(FontWeights::Normal))
            writeFontWeight = DWRITE_FONT_WEIGHT_NORMAL;

        else if (fontWeight.Equals(FontWeights::SemiBold))
            writeFontWeight = DWRITE_FONT_WEIGHT_SEMI_BOLD;

        else if (fontWeight.Equals(FontWeights::SemiLight))
            writeFontWeight = DWRITE_FONT_WEIGHT_SEMI_LIGHT;

        else if (fontWeight.Equals(FontWeights::Thin))
            writeFontWeight = DWRITE_FONT_WEIGHT_THIN;

    // Convert font stretch from Windows Runtime to DirectX
    DWRITE_FONT_STRETCH writeFontStretch = (DWRITE_FONT_STRETCH)fontStretch;

    // Convert font style from Windows Runtime to DirectX
    DWRITE_FONT_STYLE writeFontStyle = (DWRITE_FONT_STYLE)fontStyle;

    ComPtr<IDWriteFont> pWriteFont = nullptr;
    HRESULT hr = pFontFamily->GetFirstMatchingFont(writeFontWeight,
                                                   writeFontStretch,
                                                   writeFontStyle,
                                                   &pWriteFont);
    if (!SUCCEEDED(hr))
        throw ref new COMException(hr);

    return ref new WriteFont(pWriteFont);
}
```

A font family usually has a name such as "Times New Roman," but in DirectWrite a font family can have several names that are specific to different locales and languages. The *GetFamilyNames* method returns not one name but a collection of names stored in an *IDWriteLocalizedStrings*. These strings are identified by standard locale names—for example, "en-us" for United States English:

Project: DirectXWrapper | File: WriteLocalizedStrings.h

```
#pragma once

namespace DirectXWrapper
{
    public ref class WriteLocalizedStrings sealed
    {
    private:
        Microsoft::WRL::ComPtr<IDWriteLocalizedStrings> pLocalizedStrings;

    internal:
        WriteLocalizedStrings(Microsoft::WRL::ComPtr<IDWriteLocalizedStrings>
                                                        pLocalizedStrings);
    public:
        int GetCount();
        Platform::String^ GetLocaleName(int index);
        Platform::String^ GetString(int index);
        bool FindLocaleName(Platform::String^ localeName, int * index);
    };
}
```

Here's the implementation:

Project: DirectXWrapper | File: WriteLocalizedStrings.cpp

```
#include "pch.h"
#include "WriteLocalizedStrings.h"

using namespace DirectXWrapper;
using namespace Platform;
using namespace Microsoft::WRL;

WriteLocalizedStrings::WriteLocalizedStrings(ComPtr<IDWriteLocalizedStrings> pLocalizedStrings)
{
    this->pLocalizedStrings = pLocalizedStrings;
}

int WriteLocalizedStrings::GetCount()
{
    return this->pLocalizedStrings->GetCount();
}

String^ WriteLocalizedStrings::GetLocaleName(int index)
{
    UINT32 length = 0;
    HRESULT hr = this->pLocalizedStrings->GetLocaleNameLength(index, &length);

    if (!SUCCEEDED(hr))
        throw ref new COMException(hr);
```

```cpp
    wchar_t* str = new (std::nothrow) wchar_t[length + 1];

    if (str == nullptr)
        throw ref new COMException(E_OUTOFMEMORY);

    hr = this->pLocalizedStrings->GetLocaleName(index, str, length + 1);

    if (!SUCCEEDED(hr))
        throw ref new COMException(hr);

    String^ string = ref new String(str);
    delete[] str;
    return string;
}

String^ WriteLocalizedStrings::GetString(int index)
{
    UINT32 length = 0;
    HRESULT hr = this->pLocalizedStrings->GetStringLength(index, &length);

    if (!SUCCEEDED(hr))
        throw ref new COMException(hr);

    wchar_t* str = new (std::nothrow) wchar_t[length + 1];

    if (str == nullptr)
        throw ref new COMException(E_OUTOFMEMORY);

    hr = this->pLocalizedStrings->GetString(index, str, length + 1);

    if (!SUCCEEDED(hr))
        throw ref new COMException(hr);

    String^ string = ref new String(str);
    delete[] str;
    return string;
}

bool WriteLocalizedStrings::FindLocaleName(String^ localeName, int * index)
{
    uint32 localeIndex = 0;
    BOOL exists = false;
    HRESULT hr = this->pLocalizedStrings->FindLocaleName(localeName->Data(),
                                                &localeIndex, &exists);
    if (!SUCCEEDED(hr))
        throw ref new COMException(hr);

    *index = localeIndex;

    return exists != 0;
}
```

Much of the "messiness" in this code involves allocating C++ strings (which are really arrays of characters) for calling the DirectWrite methods, and then converting to Windows Runtime *String* objects for returning from the DirectXWrapper implementation.

Here's the *WriteFont* header file:

Project: DirectXWrapper | File: WriteFont.h

```
#pragma once

#include "WriteFontMetrics.h"

namespace DirectXWrapper
{
    public ref class WriteFont sealed
    {
    private:
        Microsoft::WRL::ComPtr<IDWriteFont> pWriteFont;

    internal:
        WriteFont(Microsoft::WRL::ComPtr<IDWriteFont> pWriteFont);

    public:
        bool HasCharacter(UINT32 unicodeValue);
        bool IsSymbolFont();
        WriteFontMetrics GetMetrics();
    };
}
```

And the implementation:

Project: DirectXWrapper | File: WriteFont.cpp

```
#include "pch.h"
#include "WriteFont.h"

using namespace DirectXWrapper;
using namespace Platform;
using namespace Microsoft::WRL;

WriteFont::WriteFont(ComPtr<IDWriteFont> pWriteFont)
{
    this->pWriteFont = pWriteFont;
}

WriteFontMetrics WriteFont::GetMetrics()
{
    DWRITE_FONT_METRICS fontMetrics;
    this->pWriteFont->GetMetrics(&fontMetrics);

    WriteFontMetrics writeFontMetrics =
    {
        fontMetrics.designUnitsPerEm,
        fontMetrics.ascent,
        fontMetrics.descent,
        fontMetrics.lineGap,
        fontMetrics.capHeight,
```

```
                    fontMetrics.xHeight,
                    fontMetrics.underlinePosition,
                    fontMetrics.underlineThickness,
                    fontMetrics.strikethroughPosition,
                    fontMetrics.strikethroughThickness
        };

        return writeFontMetrics;
    }

    bool WriteFont::HasCharacter(UINT32 unicodeValue)
    {
        BOOL exists = 0;
        HRESULT hr = this->pWriteFont->HasCharacter(unicodeValue, &exists);

        if (!SUCCEEDED(hr))
            throw ref new COMException(hr);

        return exists != 0;
    }

    bool WriteFont::IsSymbolFont()
    {
        return this->pWriteFont->IsSymbolFont() != 0;
    }
```

The DirectWrite version of the *GetMetrics* method fills in a structure of type DWRITE_FONT_METRICS. Of course, a Windows Runtime Component can't return that directly, so I defined my own version of this structure:

Project: DirectXWrapper | File: WriteFontMetrics.h

```
#pragma once

namespace DirectXWrapper
{
    public value struct WriteFontMetrics
    {
        UINT16 DesignUnitsPerEm;
        UINT16 Ascent;
        UINT16 Descent;
        INT16  LineGap;
        UINT16 CapHeight;
        UINT16 XHeight;
        INT16  UnderlinePosition;
        UINT16 UnderlineThickness;
        INT16  StrikethroughPosition;
        UINT16 StrikethroughThickness;
    };
}
```

You have now seen all the DirectWrite code implemented in the DirectXWrapper library. Obviously, there is much more to DirectWrite than what I've attempted to make available to a C# program, but I now have what I need for two basic jobs.

Let's enumerate the installed fonts. The EnumerateFonts project is a normal Windows 8 C# project, except that in the Solution Explorer I right-clicked the solution name and selected Add and Existing Project. The project I added was DirectXWrapper. As usual when referencing a library project, I also right-clicked the References section in EnumerateFonts, selected Add Reference, and in the Add Reference dialog box selected Projects at the left and DirectXWrapper.

The XAML file in EnumerateFonts contains a *ListBox*:

Project: EnumerateFonts | File: MainPage.xaml (excerpt)

```xaml
<Grid Background="{StaticResource ApplicationPageBackgroundThemeBrush}">
    <ListBox Name="lstbox">
        <ListBox.ItemTemplate>
            <DataTemplate>
                <TextBlock Text="{Binding}"
                           FontFamily="{Binding}"
                           FontSize="24" />
            </DataTemplate>
        </ListBox.ItemTemplate>
    </ListBox>
</Grid>
```

The *ItemTemplate* obviously anticipates that the *ListBox* will be filled with font family names. Each name is displayed with a font based on that family. That *ListBox* is filled from the constructor of the code-behind file:

Project: EnumerateFonts | File: MainPage.xaml.cs

```csharp
using Windows.UI.Xaml.Controls;
using DirectXWrapper;

namespace EnumerateFonts
{
    public sealed partial class MainPage : Page
    {
        public MainPage()
        {
            this.InitializeComponent();

            WriteFactory writeFactory = new WriteFactory();
            WriteFontCollection writeFontCollection =
                        writeFactory.GetSystemFontCollection();

            int count = writeFontCollection.GetFontFamilyCount();
            string[] fonts = new string[count];

            for (int i = 0; i < count; i++)
            {
                WriteFontFamily writeFontFamily =
                            writeFontCollection.GetFontFamily(i);

                WriteLocalizedStrings writeLocalizedStrings =
                            writeFontFamily.GetFamilyNames();
                int index;

                if (writeLocalizedStrings.FindLocaleName("en-us", out index))
```

```
            {
                fonts[i] = writeLocalizedStrings.GetString(index);
            }
            else
            {
                fonts[i] = writeLocalizedStrings.GetString(0);
            }
        }
        lstbox.ItemsSource = fonts;
    }
  }
}
```

As you can see, the classes and methods in DirectXWrapper are accessed and used as if they were normal Windows Runtime classes. The program attempts to find a font with the locale named "en-us"; if that's not available, it just gets the first one in the collection. In reality, many Windows 8 fonts have only one name, but some designed for languages of the Far East have alternative names in Chinese, Korean, or Japanese.

Here's the beginning of a list such as you might see on your own system:

SimSun-ExtB

KodchiangUPC

Kokila

Shonar Bangla

Mangal

BrowalliaUPC

Sakkal Majalla

LilyUPC

Palatino Linotype

MoolBoran

Franklin Gothic

Cordia New

Arial

AngsanaUPC

JasmineUPC

Configurations and Platforms

The Visual Studio standard toolbar includes two drop-down combo boxes identified by the tooltips "Solution Configurations" and "Solution Platforms."

The Solution Configurations box has three options:

- Debug

- Release

■ Configuration Manager...

The first two items allow you to compile your program in two different ways, Normally, you'll want to use the Debug configuration during program development. But when most of the debugging has been completed, you'll want to switch over to the Release configuration for better code optimization and performance.

In all the projects in this book prior to EnumerateFonts, the Solution Platforms box displays five options:

■ Any CPU

■ ARM

■ x64

■ x86

■ Configuration Manager...

In all the projects in this book prior to EnumerateFonts, that Solution Platforms box has probably displayed the default for C# projects, which is Any CPU.

This is as it should be. When you compile a C# program in Visual Studio, your source code is compiled into Intermediate Language, or IL. When the program runs, this IL is compiled into native code appropriate for the processor on which the program is running. This is one of the big advantages of using a managed language like C#: The distributable executable consists of Intermediate Language that is independent of the processor that later runs the program. This is true even if your program uses P/Invoke to access Win32 functions.

With a C# project, you have the ability to use the Solution Platforms combo box to change the platform to ARM, x64, or x86. The compiler still generates Intermediate Language but the executable will run only on specific processors. If you specify ARM, the program will run on machines with ARM processors only. If you specify x64, the program will run on 64-bit Intel processors only. If you specify x86, the program will run on both 32-bit and 64-bit Intel processors.

In general, unless you have a reason for doing so, you do *not* want to restrict your C# program to specific processors. You want the Solution Platforms box to read Any CPU. (If you want your program to do something a little different on Intel and ARM processors, you can use the *GetNativeSystemInfo* function described earlier in this chapter.)

However, once you begin introducing C++ code into your application, everything changes. Visual Studio does *not* compile C++ code to Intermediate Language; it's compiled to native machine code for a specific processor. That executable will run only on a processor of that sort—with the exception that code compiled for a 32-bit Intel processor will also run on 64-bit Intel processors.

Moreover, if you have a multiproject application that consists of some C# code and some C++ code (such as the EnumerateFonts solution), the platforms of the multiple projects must be the same and they must match the platform on which you're running the application. It might seem reasonable that an "Any CPU" C# project can reference an "x64" C++ project, but that is not the case.

To see the platforms of the individual projects, you can invoke the Configuration Manager dialog box by selecting Configuration Manager from either combo box. For the C# projects in the solution, the platform options are

- Any CPU

- ARM

- x64

- x86

For C++ projects, the platform options are

- ARM

- Win32

- x64

The C++ Win32 platform option is equivalent to the C# x86 platform.

The only possible combinations of platform options that work are these:

- C# ARM and C++ ARM running on an ARM processor

- C# x64 and C++ x64 running on an Intel 64-bit processor

- C# x86 and C++ Win32 running on an Intel 32-bit or 64-bit processor

If you select ARM, x64, x86, or Win32 from the Solution Platforms combo box, you'll get one of these three combinations.

In any program in this book, try selecting ARM from the Solution Platforms combo box and then pressing F5. The program will build just fine but it won't deploy because you're not running Visual Studio on an ARM-based machine. I know this for a fact because Visual Studio does not run on ARM processors.

If you have an ARM-based machine running Windows 8—such as the initial release of the Microsoft Surface machines—you probably want to test your programs on it. However, you can't run Visual Studio on the Surface, so you have to get the application on that machine in another way.

For debugging and testing purposes, the easy way is remote deployment, which works over a WiFi network and is described in a blog entry by Tim Heuer: *http://timheuer.com/blog/archive/2012/10/26/ remote-debugging-windows-store-apps-on-surface-arm-devices.aspx*. Once you have everything set up and your Surface is running the Remote Debugger and it's not asleep or displaying the lock screen, make the following two selections:

- Select the platform of the remote machine from the Solution Platforms combo box.

- Select Remote Machine from the drop-down to the left of the Solution Configurations combo box.

It's helpful to make these two selections in this order because the target machine is associated with the platform. If you select Remote Machine first and then the platform, Visual Studio will switch back to Local Machine.

If your solution consists solely of C# code, the Solution Platforms combo box should be Any CPU regardless what machine you're deploying to. If your solution has some C++ code and you're deploying to an ARM-based machine such as Microsoft Surface, select ARM from the Solution Platforms combo box.

For distribution purposes—whether you're uploading an application to the Windows Store or you're putting together a program for deployment to other machines—another approach is involved. This requires creating application packages in Visual Studio by selecting Create App Packages from the Store menu.

During this process, you'll encounter a dialog box with the heading "Select and Configure Packages" with a table of architectures. If your project has only C# code, you can select an architecture of "Neutral," which is equivalent to Any CPU. However, if your project has C++ code, you can't select that. You must select one or more of the other options: x64, x86, and ARM. You'll probably want to select all three for deployment on any type of machine.

If you're not uploading a package to the Windows Store but want to install it on another machine, Visual Studio creates directories for the various architectures that you've selected. Each of these directories contains a Windows PowerShell script—a file with the extension ps1—that you can run to deploy the application. One approach is to copy the directory to a USB thumb drive (or have Visual Studio create it there), bring the thumb drive to the other machine (such as a Microsoft Surface), and run the script to install the application on that machine.

Interpreting Font Metrics

Font metrics is the term that refers to the sizes of characters and character strings in a particular font. For most cases, you don't need font metric information when working with text in a Windows 8 program. The *TextBlock* element determines a size for the particular text and font it's being asked to display, and usually that's adequate. However, if you're going to be doing sophisticated text layout, font metrics are a necessity, and occasionally they are required for some unusual tasks.

I'm going to restrict this discussion to vertical measurements—heights rather than widths. These vertical measurements vary by font, font style (italics), font weight (bold), and font size, but they are independent of any particular character or string.

The LookAtFontMetrics program provides a visual demonstration of the correlation between the size of a text string as calculated by the *TextBlock* element and the font metrics provided by

DirectWrite. The project has the same references to the DirectXWrapper project as EnumerateFonts. The XAML file has a similar *ListBox* but also includes a *TextBlock* in a *Border* with some semidefined *Line* elements:

Project: LookAtFontMetrics | File: MainPage.xaml (excerpt)

```xml
<Grid Background="{StaticResource ApplicationPageBackgroundThemeBrush}">
    <Grid.ColumnDefinitions>
        <ColumnDefinition Width="Auto" />
        <ColumnDefinition Width="*" />
    </Grid.ColumnDefinitions>

    <ListBox Name="lstbox"
             Grid.Column="0"
             Width="300"
             SelectionChanged="OnListBoxSelectionChanged">
        <ListBox.ItemTemplate>
            <DataTemplate>
                <TextBlock Text="{Binding}"
                           FontFamily="{Binding}"
                           FontSize="24" />
            </DataTemplate>
        </ListBox.ItemTemplate>
    </ListBox>

    <Grid Grid.Column="1"
          HorizontalAlignment="Center"
          VerticalAlignment="Center">
        <Border BorderBrush="{StaticResource ApplicationForegroundThemeBrush}"
                BorderThickness="1">
            <Grid>
                <Grid.Resources>
                    <Style TargetType="Line">
                        <Setter Property="Stroke" Value="Red" />
                        <Setter Property="StrokeThickness" Value="2" />
                        <Setter Property="X1" Value="0" />
                    </Style>
                </Grid.Resources>

                <TextBlock Name="txtblk"
                           Text="Texting"
                           FontSize="192"
                           SizeChanged="OnTextBlockSizeChanged" />

                <Line x:Name="ascenderLine" Y1="0" Y2="0" />
                <Line x:Name="capsHeightLine" />
                <Line x:Name="xHeightLine" />
                <Line x:Name="baselineLine" Stroke="Blue" />
                <Line x:Name="descenderLine" />
                <Line x:Name="lineGapLine" />
            </Grid>
        </Border>
    </Grid>
</Grid>
```

The constructor of this program is pretty much the same as the previous program in that it fills up the *ListBox* with the available fonts. The program also handles a *SelectionChanged* event from the *ListBox* by setting the *FontFamily* property of the *TextBlock* and obtaining a *WriteFontMetrics* value from DirectXWrapper. The program then uses these font metrics to set the *Y1* and *Y2* properties of the various *Line* elements:

Project: LookAtFontMetrics | File: MainPage.xaml.cs (excerpt)

```
public sealed partial class MainPage : Page
{
    WriteFactory writeFactory;
    WriteFontCollection writeFontCollection;

    public MainPage()
    {
        this.InitializeComponent();

        writeFactory = new WriteFactory();
        writeFontCollection = writeFactory.GetSystemFontCollection();
        int count = writeFontCollection.GetFontFamilyCount();
        string[] fonts = new string[count];

        for (int i = 0; i < count; i++)
        {
            WriteFontFamily writeFontFamily = writeFontCollection.GetFontFamily(i);
            WriteLocalizedStrings writeLocalizedStrings = writeFontFamily.GetFamilyNames();
            int nameCount = writeLocalizedStrings.GetCount();
            int index;

            if (writeLocalizedStrings.FindLocaleName("en-us", out index))
            {
                fonts[i] = writeLocalizedStrings.GetString(index);
            }
        }

        lstbox.ItemsSource = fonts;

        Loaded += (sender, args) =>
            {
                lstbox.SelectedIndex = 0;
            };
    }

    void OnListBoxSelectionChanged(object sender, SelectionChangedEventArgs args)
    {
        string fontFamily = (sender as ListBox).SelectedItem as string;

        if (fontFamily == null)
            return;

        txtblk.FontFamily = new FontFamily(fontFamily);
```

```
            int index;
            if (writeFontCollection.FindFamilyName(fontFamily, out index))
            {
                WriteFontFamily writeFontFamily = writeFontCollection.GetFontFamily(index);
                WriteFont writeFont = writeFontFamily.GetFirstMatchingFont(FontWeights.Normal,
                                                                           FontStretch.Normal,
                                                                           FontStyle.Normal);
                WriteFontMetrics fontMetrics = writeFont.GetMetrics();
                double fontSize = txtblk.FontSize;
                double ascent = fontSize * fontMetrics.Ascent / fontMetrics.DesignUnitsPerEm;
                double capsHeight = fontSize * fontMetrics.CapHeight / fontMetrics.DesignUnitsPerEm;
                double xHeight = fontSize * fontMetrics.XHeight / fontMetrics.DesignUnitsPerEm;
                double descent = fontSize * fontMetrics.Descent / fontMetrics.DesignUnitsPerEm;
                double lineGap = fontSize * fontMetrics.LineGap / fontMetrics.DesignUnitsPerEm;

                baselineLine.Y1 = baselineLine.Y2 = ascent;
                capsHeightLine.Y1 = capsHeightLine.Y2 = ascent - capsHeight;
                xHeightLine.Y1 = xHeightLine.Y2 = ascent - xHeight;
                descenderLine.Y1 = descenderLine.Y2 = ascent + descent;
                lineGapLine.Y1 = lineGapLine.Y2 = ascent + descent + lineGap;
            }
        }

        void OnTextBlockSizeChanged(object sender, SizeChangedEventArgs args)
        {
            double width = txtblk.ActualWidth;
            ascenderLine.X2 = width;
            capsHeightLine.X2 = width;
            xHeightLine.X2 = width;
            baselineLine.X2 = width;
            descenderLine.X2 = width;
            lineGapLine.X2 = width;
        }
    }
}
```

The DWRITE_FONT_METRICS in DirectWrite has a field named *designUnitsPerEm* that for most fonts is a nice round number such as 256, 1024, 2048, or 4096 and only occasionally a peculiar value like 1000. As the name implies, this is the height of the grid the typographer used to define the characters of the font. All the other heights in the structure are relative to this design height. This is how all the fields of the structure can be integers. To obtain pixel height values for a particular font and font size, the fields of this structure must be multiplied by *FontSize* and divided by *designUnitsPerEm*.

This is what the LookAtFontMetrics program does in setting the *Y1* and *Y2* properties of all the *Line* elements. For some fonts, the results won't look quite right because those fonts are designed for non-Latin alphabets. But for the standard fonts used for languages based on Latin alphabets, the lines calculated from the font metrics are dead on:

The line on which the characters sit—the blue line if you're reading an electronic version of this book—is the baseline. In many fonts, rounded characters (such as 'e') dip a tad below that line. The next line up from the baseline is the x-height, which is the height of lowercase letters. Again, some rounded characters go slightly above that line. Next up is the caps height, which indicates the height of capital letters. The ascent line is even higher—at the very top of the rectangle that the *TextBlock* calculates for itself—and accounts for diacritical marks that might appear on some letters, such as the umlaut (Ü). Below the baseline is the area for descenders of those letters that go below the baseline. At the very bottom is a line gap, which is zero for many fonts. Here's a diagram using the names defined in the original DWRITE_FONT_METRICS structure:

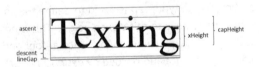

The height that *TextBlock* calculates for itself is based on the sum of the *ascent*, *descent*, and *lineGap* fields.

In Chapter 10, I showed a program that displayed a tilted shadow of a text string:

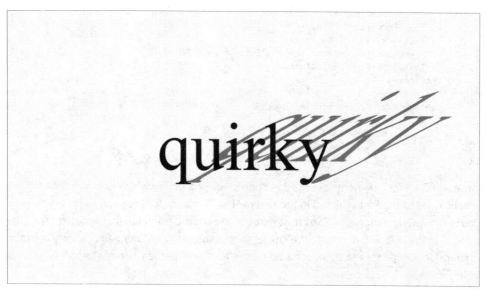

At the time I indicated that it's not possible to do something similar for an arbitrary font where the shadow tilts back from baseline. You need to know the font metrics, and now that we have those, let's try it.

Here's the XAML file for BaselineTiltedShadow. There's another *ListBox* for the system fonts, and there's some XAML for text and a shadow:

Project: BaselineTiltedShadow | File: MainPage.xaml (excerpt)

```
<Grid Background="{StaticResource ApplicationPageBackgroundThemeBrush}">
    <Grid.ColumnDefinitions>
        <ColumnDefinition Width="Auto" />
        <ColumnDefinition Width="*" />
    </Grid.ColumnDefinitions>

    <ListBox Name="lstbox"
            Grid.Column="0"
            Width="300"
            SelectionChanged="OnListBoxSelectionChanged">
        <ListBox.ItemTemplate>
            <DataTemplate>
                <TextBlock Text="{Binding}"
                           FontFamily="{Binding}"
                           FontSize="24" />
            </DataTemplate>
        </ListBox.ItemTemplate>
    </ListBox>

    <Grid Grid.Column="1"
          HorizontalAlignment="Center"
          VerticalAlignment="Center">
```

```
            <TextBlock Name="shadowTextBlock"
                       Text="shadow"
                       FontSize="192"
                       Foreground="Gray">
                <TextBlock.RenderTransform>
                    <CompositeTransform ScaleY="1.5" SkewX="-60" />
                </TextBlock.RenderTransform>
            </TextBlock>

            <TextBlock Name="foregroundTextBlock"
                       Text="shadow"
                       FontSize="192" />
        </Grid>
</Grid>
```

Those two *TextBlock* elements are missing *FontFamily* properties, which are set from the code-behind file to the font selected in the *ListBox*. The *TextBlock* for the shadow is also missing a *RenderTransformOrigin* property. The constructor of the code-behind file that initializes the *ListBox* is the same as in the previous program; the crucial part of the *SelectionChanged* property calculates this *RenderTransformOrigin* for the shadow based on the fractional percentage of the font height above the baseline:

Project: BaselineTiltedShadow | File: MainPage.xaml.cs (excerpt)

```
void OnListBoxSelectionChanged(object sender, SelectionChangedEventArgs args)
{
    string fontFamily = (sender as ListBox).SelectedItem as string;

    if (fontFamily == null)
        return;

    foregroundTextBlock.FontFamily = new FontFamily(fontFamily);
    shadowTextBlock.FontFamily = foregroundTextBlock.FontFamily;

    int index;
    if (writeFontCollection.FindFamilyName(fontFamily, out index))
    {
        WriteFontFamily writeFontFamily = writeFontCollection.GetFontFamily(index);
        WriteFont writeFont = writeFontFamily.GetFirstMatchingFont(FontWeights.Normal,
                                                                   FontStretch.Normal,
                                                                   FontStyle.Normal);

        WriteFontMetrics fontMetrics = writeFont.GetMetrics();

        double fractionAboveBaseline = (double)fontMetrics.Ascent /
                (fontMetrics.Ascent + fontMetrics.Descent + fontMetrics.LineGap);

        shadowTextBlock.RenderTransformOrigin = new Point(0, fractionAboveBaseline);
    }
}
```

And here it is:

Drawing on a *SurfaceImageSource*

There is only one other class in DirectXWrapper. I called it *SurfaceImageSourceRenderer*, and it takes a rather different architectural approach than the classes in the library that wrap the DirectWrite classes. The *SurfaceImageSourceRenderer* class instantiates a whole bunch of DirectX objects and uses those to provide a high-level interface to drawing lines on an object of type *SurfaceImageSource*.

SurfaceImageSource derives from *ImageSource* and hence can be set to the *Source* property of *Image* or to the *ImageSource* property of *ImageBrush*. It is basically a bitmap. However, you can use DirectX to draw graphics (or text) on this bitmap. The *SurfaceImageSourceRenderer* class performs all the necessary overhead and exposes three public methods: *Clear*, *DrawLine*, and *Update*. Obviously, it could be expanded to include a lot more.

Here's the header file:

Project: DirectXWrapper | File: SurfaceImageSourceRenderer.h

```
#pragma once

namespace DirectXWrapper
{
    public ref class SurfaceImageSourceRenderer sealed
    {
    private:
        int width, height;
        Microsoft::WRL::ComPtr<ID2D1Factory> pFactory;
        Microsoft::WRL::ComPtr<ID3D11Device> pd3dDevice;
        Microsoft::WRL::ComPtr<ID3D11DeviceContext> pd3dContext;
        Microsoft::WRL::ComPtr<ISurfaceImageSourceNative> sisNative;
```

```
        Microsoft::WRL::ComPtr<IDXGIDevice> pDxgiDevice;
        Microsoft::WRL::ComPtr<ID2D1BitmapRenderTarget> bitmapRenderTarget;
        Microsoft::WRL::ComPtr<ID2D1Bitmap> bitmap;
        Microsoft::WRL::ComPtr<ID2D1SolidColorBrush> solidColorBrush;
        Microsoft::WRL::ComPtr<ID2D1StrokeStyle> strokeStyle;
        bool needsUpdate;

    public:
        SurfaceImageSourceRenderer(
                Windows::UI::Xaml::Media::Imaging::SurfaceImageSource^ surfaceImageSource,
                int width, int height);
        void Clear(Windows::UI::Color color);
        void DrawLine(Windows::Foundation::Point pt1, Windows::Foundation::Point pt2,
                    Windows::UI::Color color, double thickness);

        void Update();

    private:
        ID2D1RenderTarget * CreateRenderTarget(Microsoft::WRL::ComPtr<IDXGISurface> pSurface);
        D2D1::ColorF ConvertColor(Windows::UI::Color color);
    };
}
```

The public constructor requires an instance of the *SurfaceImageSource* class. This is allowed in a public constructor because it's a Windows Runtime type defined in the *Windows.UI.Xaml.Media .Imaging* namespace. This constructor contains code that really can't be written from scratch by anyone who's not a DirectX wizard. I am certainly not, so I lifted much of this code from other sample projects intended to illustrate how to use *SurfaceImageSource*:

Project: DirectXWrapper | File: SurfaceImageSourceRenderer.cpp (excerpt)

```
SurfaceImageSourceRenderer::SurfaceImageSourceRenderer(SurfaceImageSource^ surfaceImageSource,
                                                       int width, int height)
{
    // Save the image width and height
    this->width = width;
    this->height = height;

    // Create Factory
    D2D1_FACTORY_OPTIONS options = { D2D1_DEBUG_LEVEL_NONE };

    HRESULT hr = D2D1CreateFactory(D2D1_FACTORY_TYPE_SINGLE_THREADED,
                                    __uuidof(ID2D1Factory),
                                    &options,
                                    &pFactory);
    if (!SUCCEEDED(hr))
        throw ref new COMException(hr);

    // Create ISurfaceImageSourceNative object
    IInspectable* sisInspectable = (IInspectable*)
                                    reinterpret_cast<IInspectable*>(surfaceImageSource);
    sisInspectable->QueryInterface(__uuidof(ISurfaceImageSourceNative), (void **)&sisNative);

    // Create Device and Device Context
    D3D_FEATURE_LEVEL featureLevels[] =
    {
        D3D_FEATURE_LEVEL_11_1,
```

```
        D3D_FEATURE_LEVEL_11_0,
        D3D_FEATURE_LEVEL_10_1,
        D3D_FEATURE_LEVEL_10_0,
        D3D_FEATURE_LEVEL_9_3,
        D3D_FEATURE_LEVEL_9_2,
        D3D_FEATURE_LEVEL_9_1,
};

hr = D3D11CreateDevice(nullptr,
                       D3D_DRIVER_TYPE_HARDWARE,
                       0,
                       D3D11_CREATE_DEVICE_SINGLETHREADED |
                               D3D11_CREATE_DEVICE_BGRA_SUPPORT,
                       featureLevels,
                       ARRAYSIZE(featureLevels),
                       D3D11_SDK_VERSION,
                       &pd3dDevice,
                       nullptr,
                       &pd3dContext);

if (!SUCCEEDED(hr))
    throw ref new COMException(hr);

// Get DXGIDevice
hr = pd3dDevice.As(&pDxgiDevice);

if (!SUCCEEDED(hr))
    throw ref new COMException(hr);

sisNative->SetDevice(pDxgiDevice.Get());

// Begin drawing
RECT update = { 0, 0, width, height };
POINT offset;
IDXGISurface * dxgiSurface;
hr = sisNative->BeginDraw(update, &dxgiSurface, &offset);

if (!SUCCEEDED(hr))
    throw ref new COMException(hr);

ID2D1RenderTarget * pRenderTarget = CreateRenderTarget(dxgiSurface);

// But only go far enough to create compatible BitmapRenderTarget
//      and get the Bitmap for updating the surface
pRenderTarget->CreateCompatibleRenderTarget(&bitmapRenderTarget);
bitmapRenderTarget->GetBitmap(&bitmap);

// End drawing
sisNative->EndDraw();
pRenderTarget->Release();
dxgiSurface->Release();

// Create a SolidColorBrush for drawing lines
bitmapRenderTarget->CreateSolidColorBrush(D2D1::ColorF(0, 0, 0, 0), &solidColorBrush);

// Create StrokeStyle for drawing lines
D2D1_STROKE_STYLE_PROPERTIES strokeStyleProperties =
```

```
    {
        D2D1_CAP_STYLE_ROUND,
        D2D1_CAP_STYLE_ROUND,
        D2D1_CAP_STYLE_ROUND,
        D2D1_LINE_JOIN_ROUND,
        10,
        D2D1_DASH_STYLE_SOLID,
        0
    };

    hr = pFactory->CreateStrokeStyle(&strokeStyleProperties, nullptr, 0, &strokeStyle);

    if (!SUCCEEDED(hr))
        throw ref new COMException(hr);
}
```

This constructor makes use of a private method that also comes into play during drawing operations. This method creates an object of type *ID2D1RenderTarget* on which the actual drawing takes place:

Project: DirectXWrapper | File: SurfaceImageSourceRenderer.cpp (excerpt)

```
ID2D1RenderTarget* SurfaceImageSourceRenderer::CreateRenderTarget(ComPtr<IDXGISurface> pSurface)
{
    D2D1_PIXEL_FORMAT format =
    {
        DXGI_FORMAT_UNKNOWN,
        D2D1_ALPHA_MODE_PREMULTIPLIED
    };

    float dpiX, dpiY;
    pFactory->GetDesktopDpi(&dpiX, &dpiY);

    D2D1_RENDER_TARGET_PROPERTIES properties =
    {
        D2D1_RENDER_TARGET_TYPE_DEFAULT,
        format,
        dpiX,
        dpiY,
        D2D1_RENDER_TARGET_USAGE_NONE,
        D2D1_FEATURE_LEVEL_DEFAULT
    };

    ID2D1RenderTarget * pRenderTarget;
    HRESULT hr = pFactory->CreateDxgiSurfaceRenderTarget(pSurface.Get(),
                                            &properties, &pRenderTarget);

    if (!SUCCEEDED(hr))
        throw ref new COMException(hr);

    return pRenderTarget;
}
```

Notice that in the constructor and this method I've defined two pointers to DirectX objects (named *dxgiSurface* and *pRenderTarget*) for which I did not use the *ComPtr* wrapper. This is because I was using these objects only for a very short period of time and released them "manually" with calls to the *Release* method.

The *Clear* method essentially calls the *Clear* method of the *ID2D1BitmapRenderTarget* object saved as a field:

Project: DirectXWrapper | File: SurfaceImageSourceRenderer.cpp (excerpt)

```cpp
void SurfaceImageSourceRenderer::Clear(Color color)
{
    bitmapRenderTarget->BeginDraw();
    bitmapRenderTarget->Clear(ConvertColor(color));
    bitmapRenderTarget->EndDraw();
    needsUpdate = true;
}
```

Because this is a public method, the argument must be a Windows Runtime type, and so it is. However, the *Color* structure defined in the Windows Runtime is the not the same as the various color structures in DirectX, which means that the color must be converted in this private method:

Project: DirectXWrapper | File: SurfaceImageSourceRenderer.cpp (excerpt)

```cpp
D2D1::ColorF SurfaceImageSourceRenderer::ConvertColor(Color color)
{
    D2D1::ColorF colorf(color.R / 255.0f,
                        color.G / 255.0f,
                        color.B / 255.0f,
                        color.A / 255.0f);
    return colorf;
}
```

Points must be converted as well. The public *DrawLine* method that I've defined renders a line between two points, but the method begins by converting those Windows Runtime *Point* values to DirectX D2D1_POINT_2F values for passing to the *DrawLine* method of the *ID2D1BitmapRenderTarget* object:

Project: DirectXWrapper | File: SurfaceImageSourceRenderer.cpp (excerpt)

```cpp
void SurfaceImageSourceRenderer::DrawLine(Point point1, Point point2,
                                          Color color, double thickness)
{
    // Convert the points
    D2D1_POINT_2F pt1 = { (float)point1.X, (float)point1.Y };
    D2D1_POINT_2F pt2 = { (float)point2.X, (float)point2.Y };

    // Convert the color for the SolidColorBrush
    solidColorBrush->SetColor(ConvertColor(color));
```

```
// Draw the line
bitmapRenderTarget->BeginDraw();
bitmapRenderTarget->DrawLine(pt1, pt2, solidColorBrush.Get(),
                                       (float)thickness,
                                       strokeStyle.Get());
bitmapRenderTarget->EndDraw();
needsUpdate = true;
}
```

Obviously, the *ID2D1BitmapRenderTarget* interface defines many other methods besides *DrawLine*, but if you're going to make extensive use of these other methods in your application, it might start making more sense to move at least some of the application into C++.

Both *Clear* and *DrawLine* draw on an *ID2D1BitmapRenderTarget*, and the *SurfaceImageSource* object must be updated from that. This occurs in the *Update* method:

Project: DirectXWrapper | File: SurfaceImageSourceRenderer.cpp (excerpt)

```
void SurfaceImageSourceRenderer::Update()
{
    // Check if needs update
    if (!needsUpdate)
        return;

    needsUpdate = false;

    // Begin drawing
    RECT update = { 0, 0, width, height };
    POINT offset;
    IDXGISurface * dxgiSurface;
    HRESULT hr = sisNative->BeginDraw(update, &dxgiSurface, &offset);

    if (!SUCCEEDED(hr))
        throw ref new COMException(hr);

    ID2D1RenderTarget * renderTarget = CreateRenderTarget(dxgiSurface);
    renderTarget->BeginDraw();

    // Draw the bitmap to the surface
    D2D1_RECT_F rect = { 0, 0, (float)width, (float)height };
    renderTarget->DrawBitmap(bitmap.Get(), &rect);

    // End drawing
    renderTarget->EndDraw();
    sisNative->EndDraw();

    // Release update resources
    renderTarget->Release();
    dxgiSurface->Release();
}
```

That concludes the *SurfaceImageSourceRenderer* source code. The class is demoed in the SpinPaint project. This program displays a spinning disk on which you can draw simply by holding your finger still on the screen or by moving it around. But what gets drawn is also drawn three additional times as mirror images, creating an interesting pattern with a minimum of effort:

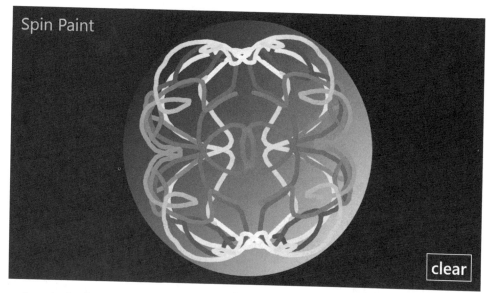

I wrote the first version of SpinPaint for the coffee-table-sized computers now known as Microsoft PixelSense. I then ported the program to Silverlight using *WriteableBitmap* and Windows Phone 7 using XNA.

In the Windows 8 version of SpinPaint, the XAML file defines a *Grid* called *referencePanel* that sits in the center of the page. During the *Loaded* event this *Grid* is given square dimensions the same size as the *SurfaceImageSource* that it also creates. Within this *Grid* is another *Grid* named *rotatingPanel* that (as the name implies) rotates. This inner *Grid* consists of some background shading simply to make it obvious that something is spinning prior to anything being drawn on it. On top of that is an *Image* element for displaying the *SurfaceImageSource* bitmap and a clipping circle:

Project: SpinPaint | File: MainPage.xaml (excerpt)

```
<Grid Background="{StaticResource ApplicationPageBackgroundThemeBrush}">
    <Grid Name="referencePanel"
          Margin="24"
          HorizontalAlignment="Center"
          VerticalAlignment="Center">

        <Grid Name="rotatingPanel">
            <Grid.RenderTransform>
                <RotateTransform x:Name="rotate" />
            </Grid.RenderTransform>

            <Ellipse>
                <Ellipse.Fill>
                    <LinearGradientBrush>
                        <GradientStop Offset="0" Color="Black" />
                        <GradientStop Offset="1" Color="White" />
                    </LinearGradientBrush>
```

```xml
                </Ellipse.Fill>
            </Ellipse>

            <Image Name="image"
                   Stretch="None" />

            <!-- Cover all but a circle (poor man's clipping) -->
            <Path Fill="{StaticResource ApplicationPageBackgroundThemeBrush}"
                  Stretch="Uniform">
                <Path.Data>
                    <GeometryGroup>
                        <RectangleGeometry Rect="0 0 100 100" />
                        <EllipseGeometry Center="50 50" RadiusX="50" RadiusY="50" />
                    </GeometryGroup>
                </Path.Data>
            </Path>
        </Grid>
    </Grid>

    <TextBlock x:Name="pageTitle"
               Text="Spin Paint"
               FontSize="48"
               Margin="24">
        <TextBlock.Foreground>
            <SolidColorBrush />
        </TextBlock.Foreground>
    </TextBlock>

    <Button Content="clear"
            HorizontalAlignment="Right"
            VerticalAlignment="Bottom"
            FontSize="48"
            Margin="24"
            Click="OnClearButtonClick" />
</Grid>
```

The *Loaded* handler determines a good size for the *SurfaceImageSource* object based on the dimensions of the screen and the view state. The *Loaded* handler also creates a *SurfaceImageSourceRenderer* from the DirectXWrapper library:

Project: SpinPaint | File: MainPage.xaml.cs (excerpt)

```csharp
public sealed partial class MainPage : Page
{

    ...

    int dimension;
    SurfaceImageSourceRenderer surfaceImageSourceRenderer;
    RotateTransform inverseRotate = new RotateTransform();

    public MainPage()
    {
        InitializeComponent();
        Loaded +=OnMainPageLoaded;
    }
```

```
void OnMainPageLoaded(object sender, RoutedEventArgs args)
{
    // Find the dimension of the square bitmap
    if (ApplicationView.Value == ApplicationViewState.FullScreenPortrait)
    {
        dimension = (int)(this.ActualWidth - referencePanel.Margin.Left
                                           - referencePanel.Margin.Right);
    }
    else
    {
        dimension = (int)(this.ActualHeight - referencePanel.Margin.Top
                                            - referencePanel.Margin.Bottom);
    }

    // Set this size to the reference panel so it doesn't get distorted in Snapped view
    referencePanel.Width = dimension;
    referencePanel.Height = dimension;

    // Create the SurfaceImageSource and renderer
    SurfaceImageSource surfaceImageSource = new SurfaceImageSource(dimension, dimension);
    surfaceImageSourceRenderer = new SurfaceImageSourceRenderer(surfaceImageSource,
                                                       dimension, dimension);

    image.Source = surfaceImageSource;

    // Set rotation centers
    rotate.CenterX = dimension / 2;
    rotate.CenterY = dimension / 2;

    inverseRotate.CenterX = dimension / 2;
    inverseRotate.CenterY = dimension / 2;

    // Start the event
    CompositionTarget.Rendering += OnCompositionTargetRendering;
}

...

void OnClearButtonClick(object sender, RoutedEventArgs e)
{
    SurfaceImageSource surfaceImageSource = new SurfaceImageSource(dimension, dimension);
    surfaceImageSourceRenderer = new SurfaceImageSourceRenderer(surfaceImageSource,
                                                       dimension, dimension);

    image.Source = surfaceImageSource;
}
}
```

The Clear button simply creates a new *SurfaceImageSource* and *SurfaceImageSourceRenderer* of that predetermined size.

Similar to the FingerPaint series of programs, you can draw on SpinPaint using multiple fingers. However, conceptually you're painting on a spinning disk, and you can simply hold your finger still on the screen and paint. In other words, your finger can paint without moving and without generating any *PointerMoved* events!

This requires a somewhat different approach to handling *Pointer* events. A dictionary is maintained, of course, and the *FingerInfo* values it contains have *LastPosition* and *ThisPosition* fields. However, in the *OnPointerPressed* override, *LastPosition* is initialized to infinite coordinates, and in both *OnPointerPressed* and *OnPointerMoved*, the *ThisPosition* field is set to the current finger position. Aside from the initialization of the *LastPosition* field, these overrides never set that field to anything else:

Project: SpinPaint | File: MainPage.xaml.cs (excerpt)

```
public sealed partial class MainPage : Page
{
    class FingerInfo
    {
        public Point LastPosition;
        public Point ThisPosition;
    }

    Dictionary<uint, FingerInfo> fingerTouches = new Dictionary<uint, FingerInfo>();
    ...
    protected override void OnPointerPressed(PointerRoutedEventArgs args)
    {
        uint id = args.Pointer.PointerId;
        Point pt = args.GetCurrentPoint(referencePanel).Position;

        if (fingerTouches.ContainsKey(id))
            fingerTouches.Remove(id);

        FingerInfo fingerInfo = new FingerInfo
        {
            LastPosition = new Point(Double.PositiveInfinity, Double.PositiveInfinity),
            ThisPosition = pt
        };

        fingerTouches.Add(id, fingerInfo);
        CapturePointer(args.Pointer);
        base.OnPointerPressed(args);
    }

    protected override void OnPointerMoved(PointerRoutedEventArgs args)
    {
        uint id = args.Pointer.PointerId;
        Point pt = args.GetCurrentPoint(referencePanel).Position;

        if (fingerTouches.ContainsKey(id))
            fingerTouches[id].ThisPosition = pt;

        base.OnPointerMoved(args);
    }

    protected override void OnPointerReleased(PointerRoutedEventArgs args)
    {
        uint id = args.Pointer.PointerId;
```

```
        if (fingerTouches.ContainsKey(id))
            fingerTouches.Remove(id);

        base.OnPointerReleased(args);
    }

    protected override void OnPointerCaptureLost(PointerRoutedEventArgs args)
    {
        uint id = args.Pointer.PointerId;

        if (fingerTouches.ContainsKey(id))
            fingerTouches.Remove(id);

        base.OnPointerCaptureLost(args);
    }
    ...
}
```

All the really interesting activity occurs in the *CompositionTarget.Rendering* event handler. Based on the current elapsed time of the application, a rotation angle is calculated to spin the *Grid* named *rotatingPanel* and to calculate a painting color. This color is also applied to the *TextBlock* displaying the name of the application at the upper-left corner of the page:

Project: SpinPaint | File: MainPage.xaml.cs (excerpt)

```
public sealed partial class MainPage : Page
{
void OnCompositionTargetRendering(object sender, object args)
{
    // Get elapsed seconds since app began
    TimeSpan timeSpan = (args as RenderingEventArgs).RenderingTime;
    double seconds = timeSpan.TotalSeconds;

    // Calculate rotation angle
    rotate.Angle = (360 * seconds / 5) % 360;

    // Calculate color and brush
    Color clr;
    double fraction = 6 * (seconds % 10) / 10;

    if (fraction < 1)
        clr = Color.FromArgb(255, 255, (byte)(fraction * 255), 0);
    else if (fraction < 2)
        clr = Color.FromArgb(255, (byte)(255 - (fraction - 1) * 255), 255, 0);
    else if (fraction < 3)
        clr = Color.FromArgb(255, 0, 255, (byte)((fraction - 2) * 255));
    else if (fraction < 4)
        clr = Color.FromArgb(255, 0, (byte)(255 - (fraction - 3) * 255), 255);
    else if (fraction < 5)
        clr = Color.FromArgb(255, (byte)((fraction - 4) * 255), 0, 255);
    else
        clr = Color.FromArgb(255, 255, 0, (byte)(255 - (fraction - 5) * 255));

    (pageTitle.Foreground as SolidColorBrush).Color = clr;
```

```
      // All done if nobody's touching
      if (fingerTouches.Count == 0)
          return;

      ...

}
```

Then, for each finger currently touching the screen, the *ThisPosition* field of *FingerInfo* is rotated so that the point is no longer in screen coordinates but relative to the rotated *Image* element. It is this point along with the *LastPosition* field of *FingerInfo* that is used for drawing. The four calls to the *DrawLine* method of *SurfaceImageSourceRenderer* draw four separate lines in the four quadrants of the bitmap:

Project: SpinPaint | File: MainPage.xaml.cs (excerpt)

```
public sealed partial class MainPage : Page
{
void OnCompositionTargetRendering(object sender, object args)
{
    ...

    bool bitmapNeedsUpdate = false;

    foreach (FingerInfo fingerInfo in fingerTouches.Values)
    {
        // Find point relative to rotated bitmap
        inverseRotate.Angle = -rotate.Angle;
        Point point1 = inverseRotate.TransformPoint(fingerInfo.ThisPosition);

        if (!Double.IsPositiveInfinity(fingerInfo.LastPosition.X))
        {
            Point point2 = fingerInfo.LastPosition;
            float thickness = 12;

            // Draw the lines
            surfaceImageSourceRenderer.DrawLine(point1, point2, clr, thickness);
            surfaceImageSourceRenderer.DrawLine(new Point(dimension - point1.X, point1.Y),
                                  new Point(dimension - point2.X, point2.Y),
                                  clr, thickness);
            surfaceImageSourceRenderer.DrawLine(new Point(point1.X, dimension - point1.Y),
                                  new Point(point2.X, dimension - point2.Y),
                                  clr, thickness);
            surfaceImageSourceRenderer.DrawLine(new Point(dimension - point1.X,
                                              dimension - point1.Y),
                                  new Point(dimension - point2.X,
                                              dimension - point2.Y),
                                  clr, thickness);

            bitmapNeedsUpdate = true;
        }
        fingerInfo.LastPosition = point1;
    }
```

```
    // Update bitmap
    if (bitmapNeedsUpdate)
    {
        surfaceImageSourceRenderer.Update();
    }
}
```

It is also this rotated finger position that is stored back into the *FingerInfo* object as *LastPosition*. This is how a finger sitting on the screen without moving can draw: Even if the finger hasn't moved at all, the current position of that finger was obtained in the *OnPointerPressed* override and remains stored in the *ThisPosition* field of *FingerInfo*. During every call to *CompositionTarget.Rendering*, the *ThisPosition* field is rotated with a new angle and a line is drawn from the *LastPosition* field. The rotated position value is then stored back into *FingerInfo* as *LastPosition* in preparation for the next iteration.

It's interesting that I first conceived the SpinPaint program for Microsoft PixelSense, where I could use a static *Contacts* class to obtain the current positions of all the fingers touching the screen without any touch event handling. Because I could treat finger touches as state rather than events, processing those fingers in a *CompositionTarget.Rendering* handler seemed very natural.

When porting the SpinPaint program to environments with only events for processing touch, I had to mimic the touch state of the *Contacts* class. The *ThisPosition* field of *FingerInfo* is precisely that: At any time, these *FingerInfo* objects in the dictionary indicate the current locations of all the fingers on the screen. But I'm not sure I would have even conceived of this program if I hadn't had experience with an environment in which touch was available as a state rather than just events.

This reinforces my belief that the more you know, the better you're able to think outside the box.

CHAPTER 16

Rich Text

The term "rich text" once meant text displayed with different fonts, sizes, and styling, but now that those features are commonplace, rich text has come to refer more vaguely to something somewhat beyond the ordinary. The bulk of this chapter focuses on the *RichTextBlock* element and the *RichEditBox* control, which (as their names suggest) are souped-up versions of *TextBlock* and *TextBox*. But this chapter also provides a few hints that might help get you started on more extensive text-processing jobs.

The terminology that surrounds fonts has changed somewhat over the years with the switch to digital typography. The word *typeface* traditionally indicated a particular design style of character glyphs. Common typefaces are Times New Roman and Helvetica. These typeface designs often have variations, most commonly italic and boldface, so a typeface family might include Times New Roman, Times New Roman Italic, and Times New Roman Bold.

A *font* is a physical implementation of a particular typeface with a particular style and a particular size: in predigital typography, for example, 10-point Helvetica Bold. Each character in a particular font was a unique chunk of metal type.

As people began working with text on computers, two trends resulted in the blurring of this terminology. First, users preferred thinking of italic or boldface as an attribute rather than an intrinsic part of a typeface. For example, rather than changing a particular word from Times New Roman to Times New Roman Italic, it was more convenient to apply an Italic attribute to the word regardless of the underlying typeface. Second, with the advent of digital outline font technologies such as TrueType, the size of font characters became a fairly trivial scaling process, so people no longer thought of size as constituting a crucial part of a font specification.

To help accommodate this different way of thinking, the term *font family* became common. A font family is much like a traditional typeface. It has a name such as Times New Roman or Helvetica. The font family is implemented in the Windows Runtime with a *FontFamily* class and in the *TextBlock* and *Control* classes with a *FontFamily* property. A Windows 8 program uses the *FontFamily* in connection with the other font-related properties (*FontSize*, *FontStyle*, *FontWeight*, and *FontStretch*) for a complete font specification.

The underlying technology, however, takes a more traditional approach. In Windows, fonts are implemented with font files, usually with the extension .TTF ("TrueType font"). These can be found in the /Windows/Fonts directory. Many of these files were probably installed along with Windows; some of them may have been added to the collection by various applications. Windows Explorer manages this directory a little differently from conventional directories, so you don't directly see the filenames. (Also in this directory are some bitmap fonts of particular sizes, but these are used for command-line windows.)

What's listed in the /Windows/Fonts directory instead of filenames are font family names, such as Georgia:

Georgia

Notice that this appears to be several documents. If you double-tap this stack, you'll see another screen that displays the individual font files that are members of this font family:

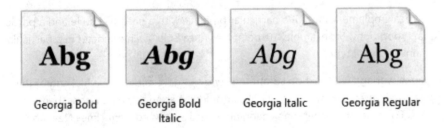

Georgia Bold   Georgia Bold   Georgia Italic   Georgia Regular
                  Italic

If you now right-click one of these and bring up a Properties screen, you'll see that these are each a separate file: in order, georgiab.ttf, georgiaz.ttf, georgiai.ttf, and georgia.ttf. Each file contains scalable outlines for many characters—not *all* Unicode characters but a substantial subset.

Some font families contain variations other than Italic and Bold, for example, Oblique or Light or Demibold, and some font families contain Compressed or Expanded variations. It is the responsibility of Windows to reference a suitable font file when a particular combination of *FontStyle*, *FontWeight*, and *FontStretch* properties are specified.

Some font families do not contain Italic or Bold variations. For those font families, these styles can be simulated: by tilting the characters toward the right or making the character strokes a bit wider.

Private Fonts

Your Windows Store program can use any of the outline fonts in the /Windows/Fonts directory, but as I discussed in Chapter 15, "Going Native," DirectWrite is required to actually enumerate the available font family names.

Sometimes programs need to use fonts that might not be installed under Windows. One traditional solution is to provide the fonts along with the application and have the user install them, but in some cases the program might want the fonts to remain private. Perhaps the fonts have been licensed by the font manufacturer strictly for use by the particular application. In this case, the fonts should remain private for the application's exclusive use.

In such cases, these private font files can be treated as application content and effectively embedded in the application executable. The PrivateFonts project demonstrates how this is done. I created a folder named Fonts in this project, and then I added eight TrueType files, as shown here:

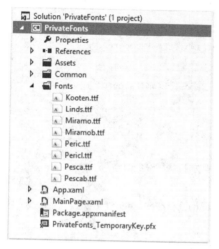

Each of these font files has its Build Action set to the default value of Content.

If you are creating such a program in Visual Studio for other people to run, you cannot simply add arbitrary font files to the project. Because these font files will be distributed to a user as part of the application, you must have permission to distribute them. For many font files—including many of the fonts that come with Windows and Windows applications—distributing the files with your application requires that you license the fonts for this purpose from the font manufacturer.

However, the particular font files I added to my PrivateFonts project have no such restrictions. If you're an XNA programmer, you might recognize these font files as the ones that Microsoft licensed from the Ascender Corporation for purposes of free distribution with applications.

A *TextBlock* element in a XAML file can access these fonts with a little different format of the *FontFamily* attribute. Normally, you set *FontFamily* to a font family name such as "Times New Roman" or "Segoe UI." To use a private font, you must specify a URI indicating the location of the font file, followed by a hash (or number) sign, followed by the font family name, as shown here:

Project: PrivateFonts | File: MainPage.xaml (excerpt)

```
<Page ... FontSize="36">
    <Grid Background="{StaticResource ApplicationPageBackgroundThemeBrush}">
        <Grid.ColumnDefinitions>
            <ColumnDefinition Width="*" />
            <ColumnDefinition Width="*" />
            <ColumnDefinition Width="*" />
            <ColumnDefinition Width="*" />
        </Grid.ColumnDefinitions>

        <StackPanel Grid.Column="0">
            <TextBlock Text="Kootenay"
                    FontFamily="ms-appx:///Fonts/Kooten.ttf#Kootenay" />

            <TextBlock Text="Lindsey"
                    FontFamily="ms-appx:///Fonts/Linds.ttf#Lindsey" />

            <TextBlock Text="Miramonte"
                    FontFamily="ms-appx:///Fonts/Miramo.ttf#Miramonte" />

            <TextBlock Text="Miramonte Bold"
                    FontFamily="ms-appx:///Fonts/Miramob.ttf#Miramonte" />

            <TextBlock Text="Pericles"
                    FontFamily="ms-appx:///Fonts/Peric.ttf#Pericles" />

            <TextBlock Text="Pericles Light"
                    FontFamily="ms-appx:///Fonts/Pericl.ttf#Pericles" />

            <TextBlock Text="Pescadero"
                    FontFamily="ms-appx:///Fonts/Pesca.ttf#Pescadero" />

            <TextBlock Text="Pescadero Bold"
                    FontFamily="ms-appx:///Fonts/Pescab.ttf#Pescadero" />

            <TextBlock Text="Pescadero Bold*"
                    FontFamily="ms-appx:///Fonts/Pesca.ttf#Pescadero"
                    FontWeight="Bold" />

            <TextBlock Text="Pescadero Italic*"
                    FontFamily="ms-appx:///Fonts/Pesca.ttf#Pescadero"
                    FontStyle="Italic" />
        </StackPanel>
        ...
    </Grid>
</Page>
```

These *FontFamily* strings include the ms-appx prefix for referencing embedded content of the application file, followed by the *Fonts* folder and the filename within the *Fonts* folder. Here's the URI of the Kooten.ttf file:

```
ms-appx:///Fonts/Kooten.ttf
```

It's possible to remove the "ms-appx:///" prefix and the program will work the same.

The URI is followed by a hash sign, and the family name of the font in this font file:

```
FontFamily="ms-appx:///Fonts/Kooten.ttf#Kootenay"
```

Obviously, this font family name is not the name of the file (but it could be). To obtain the font family name of an arbitrary TrueType font file not stored in the /Windows/Fonts directory, you can right-click the font file in Windows Explorer and choose Properties or Preview.

The Miramo.ttf file is the regular version of Miramonte; the bold version is in the Miramob.ttf file. Notice that in both cases the font family name specified in the markup is "Miramonte." If these two font files were installed under Windows, you'd reference either of them by setting the *FontFamily* attribute to "Miramonte", and you'd get the bold version by setting *FontWeight* to *Bold*. When you're using the syntax that includes the font file, the font family name is the same but you don't need to set *FontWeight*.

Similarly, the Peric.ttf file has the regular Pericles font and Pericl.ttf file contains the Light version; the regular Pescadero font is in Pesca.ttf, while the Bold version is in Pescab.ttf.

Notice that the last two *TextBlock* elements both reference the file containing the regular version of Pescadero, but the *FontWeight* and *FontStyle* attributes are set to *Bold* and *Italic*, respectively. Because these attributes are applied to a regular font, these styles are simulated, as I indicate with an asterisk and footnote.

The PrivateFonts program actually displays four columns of text. Here's only the first column generated from the XAML you've just seen:

Notice how the actual boldface font is different from the simulated boldface. (Also, notice how the Pericles font displays lowercase letters with small capitals!)

To reference a private font in code, you create a *FontFamily* object by using the same string you use in XAML:

```
txtblk.FontFamily = new FontFamily("ms-appx:///Fonts/Linds.ttf#Lindsey");
```

The PrivateFonts program displays four columns of very similar text, and you've seen only the first, so we're not quite finished with this program.

A Taste of *Glyphs*

An alternative to the *TextBlock* element is an element called *Glyphs*. It is harder to use than *TextBlock*, but it includes a facility to space individual characters.

The second column of text in PrivateFonts is displayed with the following markup:

Project: PrivateFonts | File: MainPage.xaml (excerpt)

```
<Grid Grid.Column="1">
    <Glyphs UnicodeString="Kootenay"
            FontUri="ms-appx:///Fonts/Kooten.ttf"
            FontRenderingEmSize="36"
            Fill="Black"
            OriginX="0"
            OriginY="45" />

    <Glyphs UnicodeString="Lindsey"
            FontUri="ms-appx:///Fonts/Linds.ttf"
            FontRenderingEmSize="36"
            Fill="Black"
            OriginX="0"
            OriginY="90" />

    <Glyphs UnicodeString="Miramonte"
            FontUri="ms-appx:///Fonts/Miramo.ttf"
            FontRenderingEmSize="36"
            Fill="Black"
            OriginX="0"
            OriginY="135" />

    <Glyphs UnicodeString="Miramonte Bold"
            FontUri="ms-appx:///Fonts/Miramob.ttf"
            FontRenderingEmSize="36"
            Fill="Black"
            OriginX="0"
            OriginY="180" />

    <Glyphs UnicodeString="Pericles"
            FontUri="ms-appx:///Fonts/Peric.ttf"
            FontRenderingEmSize="36"
            Fill="Black"
            OriginX="0"
            OriginY="225" />
```

```
<Glyphs UnicodeString="Pericles Light"
        FontUri="ms-appx:///Fonts/Pericl.ttf"
        FontRenderingEmSize="36"
        Fill="Black"
        OriginX="0"
        OriginY="270" />

<Glyphs UnicodeString="Pescadero"
        FontUri="ms-appx:///Fonts/Pesca.ttf"
        FontRenderingEmSize="36"
        Fill="Black"
        OriginX="0"
        OriginY="315" />

<Glyphs UnicodeString="Pescadero Bold"
        FontUri="ms-appx:///Fonts/Pescab.ttf"
        FontRenderingEmSize="36"
        Fill="Black"
        OriginX="0"
        OriginY="360" />

<Glyphs UnicodeString="Pescadero Bold*"
        FontUri="ms-appx:///Fonts/Pesca.ttf"
        StyleSimulations="BoldSimulation"
        FontRenderingEmSize="36"
        Fill="Black"
        OriginX="0"
        OriginY="405" />

<Glyphs UnicodeString="Pescadero Italic*"
        FontUri="ms-appx:///Fonts/Pesca.ttf"
        StyleSimulations="ItalicSimulation"
        FontRenderingEmSize="36"
        Fill="Black"
        OriginX="0"
        OriginY="450" />
</Grid>
```

Rather than a *Text* property, *Glyphs* defines a *UnicodeString* property. Three other properties are required: The *FontUri* property is (as the name suggests) a URI of the font file. Notice that it's *only* the URI; there is no need to supply the font family name. *Glyphs* works at a low level with the font file; it doesn't know about family names. The *FontRenderingEmSize* is equivalent to the *FontSize* property, but there is no default. Nor is there a default for the *Fill* property.

Notice that the last two items reference the regular Pescadero font file but set *StyleSimulations* to *BoldSimulation* and *ItalicSimulation*, respectively. The *StyleSimulations* enumeration also includes a *BoldItalicSimulation* member.

The *OriginX* and *OriginY* properties indicate the location of the text relative to its parent—or, more precisely, relative to where the parent places the element. The parent here is simply a single-cell *Grid* rather than a *StackPanel* as I used for the first column. (Very often the parent of a collection of *Glyphs* elements is a *Canvas*.) The origin specifies the left of the *baseline*, not the top of the text. I've simply set the first *OriginY* to 45 and incremented each by 45, which is approximately correct, as you can see with a visual comparison of the first two columns displayed by PrivateFonts:

```
Kootenay              Kootenay
Lindsey               Lindsey
Miramonte             Miramonte
Miramonte Bold        Miramonte Bold
PERICLES              PERICLES
PERICLES LIGHT        PERICLES LIGHT
Pescadero             Pescadero
Pescadero Bold        Pescadero Bold
Pescadero Bold*       Pescadero Bold*
Pescadero Italic*     Pescadero Italic*




                      *simulated
```

In a real program, you would be using font metrics to position each *Glyphs* element.

If you need to set the *FontUri* property in code, just create a *Uri* object and use the same string that you've seen in the XAML file:

```
glyphs.FontUri = new Uri("ms-appx:///Fonts/Linds.ttf");
```

The *Glyphs* element does not automatically wrap text in multiple lines. However, there is a property not shown in my examples called *Indices* that lets you provide additional offsets to space the individual characters with great precision. You can also use the *Indices* string to indicate substitute characters, such as ligatures, which are stylistic combinations of two or more letters in a single glyph.

Font Files in Local Storage

The *Glyphs* element is found most commonly in documents created using the XML Paper Specification (XPS) that Microsoft developed in connection with WPF. XPS is a fixed-page document format. That is, all the pages of the document are fixed in size and layout, much like Adobe Portable Document Format (PDF).

A file containing an XPS document is a "package," which is basically a ZIP file containing font files, bitmaps, and separate files for each page of the document. Each page of the document is a XAML file with a root element of *FixedPage* (a class not defined in the Windows Runtime), generally containing some *Path* elements for displaying graphics and bitmaps in the form of *ImageBrush* objects and containing *Glyphs* elements for displaying text. The *Glyphs* elements have their *FontUri* attributes set to a URI referencing a font file in the XPS package. These *Glyphs* elements already have all their properties set to correctly position the text within the page.

A WPF program can render an XPS file without too much bother. A Windows 8 program would have considerably more work to do. The program would need to open up the XPS package and parse the individual *FixedPage* files. For each page, the program would need to instantiate the various *Path*, *ImageBrush*, and *Glyphs* objects in code—all the time taking care to compensate for any XPS features not supported under the Windows Runtime.

Within the XPS package, the URIs of the *ImageBrush* and *Glyphs* elements reference bitmap files and font file within the package. These bitmaps and font files would need to be copied to application local storage, and the URIs modified to point to that storage.

The PrivateFonts program demonstrates the feasibility of this process. The first time you run the program, the third column displays text using the Windows 8 default font rather than any of the private fonts and the fourth column is absent:

Kootenay	Kootenay	Kootenay
Lindsey	Lindsey	Lindsey
Miramonte	Miramonte	Miramonte
Miramonte Bold	**Miramonte Bold**	Miramonte Bold
PERICLES	PERICLES	Pericles
PERICLES LIGHT	PERICLES LIGHT	Pericles Light
Pescadero	Pescadero	Pescadero
Pescadero Bold	**Pescadero Bold**	Pescadero Bold
Pescadero Bold*	**Pescadero Bold***	**Pescadero Bold***
Pescadero Italic*	*Pescadero Italic**	*Pescadero Italic**

*simulated

The subsequent times you run the program, the third and fourth columns match the first two:

Kootenay	Kootenay	Kootenay	Kootenay
Lindsey	Lindsey	Lindsey	Lindsey
Miramonte	Miramonte	Miramonte	Miramonte
Miramonte Bold	**Miramonte Bold**	**Miramonte Bold**	**Miramonte Bold**
PERICLES	PERICLES	PERICLES	PERICLES
PERICLES LIGHT	PERICLES LIGHT	PERICLES LIGHT	PERICLES LIGHT
Pescadero	Pescadero	Pescadero	Pescadero
Pescadero Bold	**Pescadero Bold**	**Pescadero Bold**	**Pescadero Bold**
Pescadero Bold*	**Pescadero Bold***	**Pescadero Bold***	**Pescadero Bold***
Pescadero Italic*	*Pescadero Italic**	*Pescadero Italic**	*Pescadero Italic**

*simulated

This difference is a fluke based on the structuring of the program. What happens when you first run the program is that the font files are copied to application local storage:

Project: PrivateFonts | File: MainPage.xaml.cs (excerpt)

```
public sealed partial class MainPage : Page
{
    public MainPage()
    {
        this.InitializeComponent();
        Loaded += OnLoaded;
    }

    async void OnLoaded(object sender, RoutedEventArgs args)
    {
        StorageFolder localFolder = ApplicationData.Current.LocalFolder;
        bool folderExists = false;

        try
        {
            StorageFolder fontsFolder = await localFolder.GetFolderAsync("Fonts");
            folderExists = true;
        }
        catch (Exception)
        {
        }

        if (!folderExists)
        {
            StorageFolder fontsFolder = await localFolder.CreateFolderAsync("Fonts");

            string[] fonts = { "Kooten.ttf", "Linds.ttf", "Miramo.ttf", "Miramob.ttf",
                               "Peric.ttf", "pericl.ttf", "Pesca.ttf", "Pescab.ttf" };
```

```
            foreach (string font in fonts)
            {
                // Copy from application content to IBuffer
                string uri = "ms-appx:///Fonts/" + font;
                IBuffer buffer = await PathIO.ReadBufferAsync(uri);

                // Copy from IBuffer to local storage
                StorageFile fontFile = await fontsFolder.CreateFileAsync(font);
                await FileIO.WriteBufferAsync(fontFile, buffer);
            }
        }
    }
}
```

The *Loaded* handler checks if a directory named *Fonts* exists in local storage. If not, it creates one and then copies all the font files into that directory with the same names. (If this job could be performed synchronously, I would have done it in the constructor prior to *InitializeComponent* so that the files would be available to the XAML parser the first time the program is run.)

The markup for referencing the files in local storage is pretty much the same as referencing program content except the prefix is *ms-appdata* and the *Fonts* directory needs to be preceded with *local*. I'm sure you don't need to see them all to get the general idea:

Project: PrivateFonts | File: MainPage.xaml (excerpt)

```
<Page ...  FontSize="36">
    <Grid Background="{StaticResource ApplicationPageBackgroundThemeBrush}">
        <Grid.ColumnDefinitions>
            <ColumnDefinition Width="*" />
            <ColumnDefinition Width="*" />
            <ColumnDefinition Width="*" />
            <ColumnDefinition Width="*" />
        </Grid.ColumnDefinitions>

        ...

        <StackPanel Grid.Column="2">
            <TextBlock Text="Kootenay"
                    FontFamily="ms-appdata:///local/Fonts/Kooten.ttf#Kootenay" />

            ...

            <TextBlock Text="Pescadero Italic*"
                    FontFamily="ms-appdata:///local/Fonts/Pesca.ttf#Pescadero"
                    FontStyle="Italic" />
        </StackPanel>

        <Grid Grid.Column="3">
            <Glyphs UnicodeString="Kootenay"
                    FontUri="ms-appdata:///local/Fonts/Kooten.ttf"
                    FontRenderingEmSize="36"
                    Fill="Black"
                    OriginX="0"
                    OriginY="45" />
```

```
            ...

        <Glyphs UnicodeString="Pescadero Italic*"
                FontUri="ms-appdata:///local/Fonts/Pesca.ttf"
                StyleSimulations="ItalicSimulation"
                FontRenderingEmSize="36"
                Fill="Black"
                OriginX="0"
                OriginY="450" />
    </Grid>

    <TextBlock Text="*simulated"
               Grid.ColumnSpan="4"
               VerticalAlignment="Bottom"
               HorizontalAlignment="Center" />
    </Grid>
</Page>
```

Again, if you need to do this in code, you'll be using the same strings you've seen in the XAML file:

```
txtblk.FontFamily = new FontFamily("ms-appdata:///local/Fonts/Linds.ttf#Lindsey");

glyphs.FontUri = new Uri("ms-appdata:///local/Fonts/Linds.ttf");
```

Of all the sophisticated document formats in existence that might be rendered under Windows 8, XPS is almost certainly the easiest because the contents are similar to elements found in the Windows Runtime, all the pages have already been constructed, and all the graphics and *Glyphs* elements have been positioned precisely within those pages. Much more challenging would be a reflow-page format like EPUB, where the job of positioning words on the page is the responsibility of the program. This job requires a more intimate familiarity with font metrics.

The simple approach to font metrics involves subjecting a *TextBlock* to a *Measure* call and obtaining its width and height. This would allow you to determine the placement of individual words in a paragraph, where lines break within a paragraph, and where paragraphs break between pages. However, if you ever need to align separate *TextBlock* elements of different font sizes or font families on the baseline, you'll need more information.

At that point, you'll need to either examine the internals of the font files themselves to extract font metrics or begin using DirectWrite. Once you start using DirectWrite for font metrics, quite possibly you'll also see that it's the best tool for laying out pages as well.

Typographical Enhancements

The *Typography* class in the *Windows.UI.Xaml.Documents* namespace contains nothing but a collection of attached properties for enhancing text. You can insert these attached properties in the root element of a page or in a *TextBlock* or *Run* element to control various aspects of how text is displayed. The catch is: You can't guarantee that these features work for all fonts. Indeed, you might find yourself searching a long time for a font that responds to some of these attached properties!

In the following examples, I've relied heavily on the documentation of the WPF version of the *Typography* class, which matches up some of these attached properties with particular fonts. Some of these examples involve the Lindsey, Miramonte, Pescadero, and Pericles fonts, which are included as program content:

Project: TypographyDemo | **File:** MainPage.xaml (excerpt)

```xaml
<Page ... >
    <Page.Resources>
        <Style TargetType="TextBlock">
            <Setter Property="FontSize" Value="48" />
            <Setter Property="Margin" Value="6 6 6 0" />
        </Style>
    </Page.Resources>

    <Grid Background="{StaticResource ApplicationPageBackgroundThemeBrush}">
        <StackPanel>
            <TextBlock Text="Small Caps are Nice for Titles"
                    Typography.Capitals="SmallCaps" />

            <TextBlock Text="Some random contextual alternates make script look more natural"
                    FontFamily="ms-appx:///Fonts/Linds.ttf#Lindsey"
                    Typography.ContextualAlternates="True" />

            <TextBlock Text="Stacked fractions: 1/2 1/4 1/8 1/3 2/3"
                    FontFamily="Palatino Linotype"
                    Typography.Fraction="Stacked" />

            <TextBlock Text="Historical forms: Four score and seven years ago"
                    FontFamily="Palatino Linotype"
                    Typography.HistoricalForms="True" />

            <TextBlock Text="Numeral alignment for tables: 0123456789"
                    FontFamily="ms-appx:///Fonts/Miramo.ttf#Miramonte"
                    Typography.NumeralAlignment="Tabular" />

            <TextBlock Text="Old-style numbers: 0123456789"
                    FontFamily="Palatino Linotype"
                    Typography.NumeralStyle="OldStyle" />

            <TextBlock Text="Standard Swashes With The Pescadero Font"
                    FontFamily="ms-appx:///Fonts/Pesca.ttf#Pescadero"
                    Typography.StandardSwashes="1" />

            <TextBlock Text="Slashed Zero: 0"
                    FontFamily="ms-appx:///Fonts/Miramo.ttf#Miramonte"
                    Typography.SlashedZero="True" />

            <TextBlock Text="STYLISTIC ALTERNATES WITH THE PERICLES FONT"
                    FontFamily="ms-appx:///Fonts/Peric.ttf#Pericles"
                    Typography.StylisticAlternates="1" />
```

```
<TextBlock FontFamily="Palatino Linotype">
        Sucrose is C<Run Typography.Variants="Inferior">12</Run
                   >H<Run Typography.Variants="Inferior">22</Run
                   >O<Run Typography.Variants="Inferior">11</Run>
    </TextBlock>
  </StackPanel>
 </Grid>
</Page>
```

And here's the result:

SMALL CAPS ARE NICE FOR TITLES

Some random contextual alternates make script look more natural

Stacked fractions: $\frac{1}{2}$ $\frac{1}{4}$ $\frac{1}{8}$ $\frac{1}{3}$ $\frac{2}{3}$

Historical forms: Four score and seven years ago

Numeral alignment for tables: 0123456789

Old-style numbers: 0123456789

Standard Swashes With The Pescadero Font

Slashed Zero: 0

STYLISTIC ALTERNATES WITH THE PERICLES FONT

Sucrose is $C_{12}H_{22}O_{11}$

RichTextBlock and **Paragraphs**

Although *TextBlock* continues to be preferred for text up to a paragraph in length, the *RichTextBlock* offers several enhancements. *RichTextBlock* does not have a *Text* property; nor does it have an *Inlines* property for specifying text in the form of *Inline* derivatives. What *RichTextBlock* defines instead is a property named *Blocks*, which is a collection of *Block* derivatives. Like *Inline*, *Block* derives from *TextElement*, from which it acquires a bunch of text-related properties. In addition, *Block* defines these properties:

- *LineHeight*

- *LineStackingStrategy*

- *Margin*

- *TextAlignment*

Also, like *Inline*, *Block* itself is not instantiable. The only class that currently derives from *Block* is *Paragraph*, which defines two properties:

- *Inlines*, a collection of *Inline* derivatives, and

- *TextIndent*, for setting an indentation of the first line of the paragraph.

So, basically, a *RichTextBlock* is a collection of paragraphs. The *Margin* property is useful for defining space between the paragraphs, and *TextIndent* can indent the first line.

The MadTeaParty project uses a *RichTextBlock* inside a *ScrollViewer* to let you peruse Chapter 7 of Lewis Carroll's *Alice's Adventures in Wonderland*, including three of John Tenniel's illustrations. Here's an excerpt of the XAML file:

Project: MadTeaParty | **File:** MainPage.xaml (excerpt)

```
<Page ... >
    <Grid Background="{StaticResource ApplicationPageBackgroundThemeBrush}">
        <ScrollViewer Width="720"
                      Padding="40 20">

            <!-- Text and images from http://ebooks.adelaide.edu.au/c/carroll/lewis/alice/ -->

            <RichTextBlock FontFamily="Cambria"
                           FontSize="24">
                <Paragraph Margin="0 12" TextAlignment="Center" FontSize="40">
                    <Italic>Alice's Adventures in Wonderland</Italic>
                    <LineBreak/>
                    by
                    <LineBreak/>
                    Lewis Carroll
                </Paragraph>

                <Paragraph Margin="0 24 0 36" TextAlignment="Center" FontSize="30">
                    Chapter VII
                    <LineBreak />
                    A Mad Tea-Party
                </Paragraph>

                <Paragraph Margin="0 6">
                    There was a table set out under a tree in front of the
                    house, and the March Hare and the Hatter were having tea at
                    it: a Dormouse was sitting between them, fast asleep, and
                    the other two were using it as a cushion, resting their
                    elbows on it, and talking over its head. 'Very uncomfortable
                    for the Dormouse,' thought Alice; 'only, as it's asleep, I
                    suppose it doesn't mind.'
                </Paragraph>

                <Paragraph Margin="0 6" TextIndent="48">
                    The table was a large one, but the three were all crowded
                    together at one corner of it: 'No room! No room!' they
                    cried out when they saw Alice coming. 'There's
                    <Italic>plenty</Italic> of room!' said Alice indignantly,
                    and she sat down in a large arm-chair at one end of the table.
                </Paragraph>
```

```
<Paragraph Margin="0 6" TextIndent="48">
    'Have some wine,' the March Hare said in an encouraging tone.
</Paragraph>

<Paragraph Margin="0 6" TextIndent="48">
    Alice looked all round the table, but there was nothing on it
    but tea. 'I don't see any wine,' she remarked.
</Paragraph>

<Paragraph Margin="0 6" TextIndent="48">
    'There isn't any,' said the March Hare.
</Paragraph>

...

<Paragraph Margin="0 6" TextIndent="48">
    'It
    <Italic>is</Italic> the same thing with you,' said the
    Hatter, and here the conversation dropped, and the party sat
    silent for a minute, while Alice thought over all she could
    remember about ravens and writing-desks, which wasn't much.
</Paragraph>

<Paragraph Margin="0 6" TextAlignment="Center">
    <InlineUIContainer>
        <Image Source="Images/ChapterVII-1.png" Stretch="None" />
    </InlineUIContainer>
</Paragraph>

<Paragraph Margin="0 6" TextIndent="48">
    The Hatter was the first to break the silence. 'What day of
    the month is it?' he said, turning to Alice: he had taken
    his watch out of his pocket, and was looking at it uneasily,
    shaking it every now and then, and holding it to his ear.
</Paragraph>

...

<Paragraph Margin="0 6" TextIndent="48">
    Just as she said this, she noticed that one of the trees
    had a door leading right into it. 'That's very curious!'
    she thought. 'But everything's curious today. I think I
    may as well go in at once.' And in she went.
</Paragraph>

<Paragraph Margin="0 6" TextIndent="48">
    Once more she found herself in the long hall, and close to
    the little glass table. 'Now, I'll manage better this time,'
    she said to herself, and began by taking the little golden
    key, and unlocking the door that led into the garden. Then
    she went to work nibbling at the mushroom (she had kept a
    piece of it in her pocket) till she was about a foot high:
    then she walked down the little passage: and
    <Italic>then</Italic> – she found herself at last in the
    beautiful garden, among the bright flower-beds and the cool
    fountains.
```

```
            </Paragraph>
        </RichTextBlock>
      </ScrollViewer>
    </Grid>
</Page>
```

Paragraph doesn't derive from *FrameworkElement*, so it doesn't have a *Style* property. If you want to set the same properties on a bunch of *Paragraph* objects, they need to be explicit. Most of the paragraphs in "A Mad Tea-Party" have a *Margin* property for a 12-pixel interparagraph spacing and a *TextIndent* property to indent the first line 48 pixels.

The *InlineUIContainer* doesn't work with *TextBlock*, but it does with *RichTextBlock*. This allows you to embed a *UIElement* derivative in text. The possibilities include *TextBlock*, so this facility provides a way to embed text in a paragraph that contains a binding on its *Text* property. However, this embedded *TextBlock* element can't itself wrap text.

In the MadTeaParty program, the *Image* elements become part of the *RichTextBlock*. This requires that they go inside an *InlineUIContainer* object, which then needs to be inside a *Paragraph*. There is no facility to wrap the text of a paragraph around an image. If you want to do something like that with C# and XAML, you'll need to start measuring individual words of text and positioning them yourself.

Here's the chapter scrolled down to a point where you can see the third of the three images:

she got up in great disgust, and walked off; the Dormouse fell asleep instantly, and neither of the others took the least notice of her going, though she looked back once or twice, half hoping that they would call after her: the last time she saw them, they were trying to put the Dormouse into the teapot.

'At any rate I'll never go *there* again!' said Alice as she picked her way through the wood. 'It's the stupidest tea-party I ever was at in all my life!'

RichTextBlock Selection

When the MadTeaParty program is running, tap a word with your finger. The word is selected with two circular handles at each end. You can then grab those handles and extend the selection. Tap the selection and a little menu comes up to copy the selection to the clipboard.

Or, if you don't have a touch screen, use the mouse with the button pressed to select some text. Then right-click to bring up the context menu with the Copy item.

RichTextBlock implements a *SelectionChanged* event, a *SelectedText* property to obtain the selected text—but not to replace it or delete it—and *SelectionStart* and *SelectionEnd* properties. These latter two properties are of type *TextPointer*, which not only provides an offset of the selected text within the *TextBlock* but also indicates the pixel location of the selection relative to the *TextBlock*.

There is also a *ContextMenuOpening* event that occurs right before the context menu is displayed. If you set the *Handled* property of the event arguments to *true*, the menu is not displayed, which means that you can display your own context menu.

If you'd prefer that the *RichTextBlock* not allow text to be selected, set *IsTextSelectionEnabled* to *false*.

RichTextBlock and Overflow

Throughout the history of books and reading, there have been two basic ways of presenting extended text: a scroll of continuous text—common in ancient Egypt, China, and the Mediterranean cultures of Greece and Rome—or a collection of individual pages, a form that began emerging in Europe during the first several centuries of the common era.

These two formats are also common on the computer: Most webpages use scrolling, but most e-book readers separate the text into pages.

I've just demonstrated that *RichTextBlock* can present text that is scrolled, but *RichTextBlock* takes a giant step beyond previous text-display elements by its ability to paginate a document. These pages can then be displayed sequentially, as in an e-book reader, or displayed in adjacent columns.

Here's how it works: You put all the text you want to display in a *RichTextBlock* and then give it a finite size, which means to subject it to a *Measure* pass, either manually or as part of normal page layout. If the *RichTextBlock* contains more text than it can display in the space allotted for it, its *HasOverflowContent* property becomes *true*. To display the second page of text beyond the *RichTextBlock*, create an instance of the *RichTextBlockOverflow* class and set that instance to the *OverflowContentTarget* property of the *RichTextBlock*.

RichTextBlockOverflow also defines *HasOverflowContent* and *OverflowContentTarget* properties, so you can create additional *RichTextBlockOverflow* objects for each additional page and string them in a chain. The *RichTextBlockOverflow* elements inherit all the text-related properties—*FontFamily*, *FontSize*, and so forth—from the parent *RichTextBlock*.

If you can estimate the maximum number of pages you'll need to display a document, you can do this chaining job entirely in XAML by using data bindings. The YoungGoodmanBrown project demonstrates how it's done. The text is Nathaniel Hawthorne's unnerving short story "Young Goodman Brown" that I lifted from Project Gutenberg. Just as for "A Mad Tea-Party," I put the entire text in a single *RichTextBlock*, but I gave the *OverflowContentTarget* property of that *RichTextBlock* to a *RichTextBlockOverflow* element, and so on down the chain:

Project: YoungGoodmanBrown | **File:** MainPage.xaml (excerpt)

```
<Page ... >
    <Page.Resources>
        <local:BooleanToVisibilityConverter x:Key="booleanToVisibility" />

        <Style TargetType="RichTextBlock">
            <Setter Property="Width" Value="480" />
            <Setter Property="Margin" Value="24 0 24 0" />
            <Setter Property="FontSize" Value="18" />
            <Setter Property="TextAlignment" Value="Justify" />
        </Style>

        <Style TargetType="RichTextBlockOverflow">
            <Setter Property="Width" Value="480" />
            <Setter Property="Margin" Value="24 0 24 0" />
        </Style>
    </Page.Resources>

    <Grid Background="{StaticResource ApplicationPageBackgroundThemeBrush}">
        <ScrollViewer HorizontalScrollBarVisibility="Hidden"
                      VerticalScrollBarVisibility="Disabled">
            <StackPanel Orientation="Horizontal">

                <!-- Text from http://www.gutenberg.org/files/512/512-h/512-h.htm -->

                <RichTextBlock Name="richTextBlock"
                               OverflowContentTarget="{Binding ElementName=overflow1}">
                    <Paragraph TextAlignment="Center">
                        YOUNG GOODMAN BROWN
                    </Paragraph>

                    <Paragraph TextAlignment="Center" Margin="0 12">
                        by
                        <LineBreak />
                        Nathaniel Hawthorne
                    </Paragraph>

                    <Paragraph Margin="0 6" TextIndent="48">
                        Young Goodman Brown came forth at sunset into the street at Salem
                        village; but put his head back, after crossing the threshold, to
                        exchange a parting kiss with his young wife. And Faith, as the wife was
                        aptly named, thrust her own pretty head into the street, letting the
                        wind play with the pink ribbons of her cap while she called to Goodman
                        Brown.
                    </Paragraph>
```

```
        <Paragraph Margin="0 6" TextIndent="48">
            "Dearest heart," whispered she, softly and rather sadly, when her lips
            were close to his ear, "prithee put off your journey until sunrise and
            sleep in your own bed to-night. A lone woman is troubled with such
            dreams and such thoughts that she's afeard of herself sometimes. Pray
            tarry with me this night, dear husband, of all nights in the year."
        </Paragraph>
        ...
    </RichTextBlock>

    <RichTextBlockOverflow Name="overflow1"
            Visibility="{Binding ElementName=richTextBlock,
                            Path=HasOverflowContent,
                            Converter={StaticResource booleanToVisibility}}"
            OverflowContentTarget="{Binding ElementName=overflow2}" />

    <RichTextBlockOverflow Name="overflow2"
            Visibility="{Binding ElementName=overflow1,
                            Path=HasOverflowContent,
                            Converter={StaticResource booleanToVisibility}}"
            OverflowContentTarget="{Binding ElementName=overflow3}" />

    <RichTextBlockOverflow Name="overflow3"
            Visibility="{Binding ElementName=overflow2,
                            Path=HasOverflowContent,
                            Converter={StaticResource booleanToVisibility}}"
            OverflowContentTarget="{Binding ElementName=overflow4}" />

    <RichTextBlockOverflow Name="overflow4"
            Visibility="{Binding ElementName=overflow3,
                            Path=HasOverflowContent,
                            Converter={StaticResource booleanToVisibility}}"
            OverflowContentTarget="{Binding ElementName=overflow5}" />

    <RichTextBlockOverflow Name="overflow5"
            Visibility="{Binding ElementName=overflow4,
                            Path=HasOverflowContent,
                            Converter={StaticResource booleanToVisibility}}"
            OverflowContentTarget="{Binding ElementName=overflow6}" />

    <RichTextBlockOverflow Name="overflow6"
            Visibility="{Binding ElementName=overflow5,
                            Path=HasOverflowContent,
                            Converter={StaticResource booleanToVisibility}}"
            OverflowContentTarget="{Binding ElementName=overflow7}" />

    <RichTextBlockOverflow Name="overflow7"
            Visibility="{Binding ElementName=overflow6,
                            Path=HasOverflowContent,
                            Converter={StaticResource booleanToVisibility}}"
            OverflowContentTarget="{Binding ElementName=overflow8}" />

    <RichTextBlockOverflow Name="overflow8"
            Visibility="{Binding ElementName=overflow7,
                            Path=HasOverflowContent,
                            Converter={StaticResource booleanToVisibility}}"
            OverflowContentTarget="{Binding ElementName=overflow9}" />
```

```
<RichTextBlockOverflow Name="overflow9"
        Visibility="{Binding ElementName=overflow8,
                      Path=HasOverflowContent,
                      Converter={StaticResource booleanToVisibility}}"
        OverflowContentTarget="{Binding ElementName=overflow10}" />

<RichTextBlockOverflow Name="overflow10"
        Visibility="{Binding ElementName=overflow9,
                      Path=HasOverflowContent,
                      Converter={StaticResource booleanToVisibility}}"
        OverflowContentTarget="{Binding ElementName=overflow11}" />

<RichTextBlockOverflow Name="overflow11"
        Visibility="{Binding ElementName=overflow10,
                      Path=HasOverflowContent,
                      Converter={StaticResource booleanToVisibility}}"
        OverflowContentTarget="{Binding ElementName=overflow12}" />

<RichTextBlockOverflow Name="overflow12"
        Visibility="{Binding ElementName=overflow11,
                      Path=HasOverflowContent,
                      Converter={StaticResource booleanToVisibility}}"
        OverflowContentTarget="{Binding ElementName=overflow13}" />

<RichTextBlockOverflow Name="overflow13"
        Visibility="{Binding ElementName=overflow12,
                      Path=HasOverflowContent,
                      Converter={StaticResource booleanToVisibility}}"
        OverflowContentTarget="{Binding ElementName=overflow14}" />

<RichTextBlockOverflow Name="overflow14"
        Visibility="{Binding ElementName=overflow13,
                      Path=HasOverflowContent,
                      Converter={StaticResource booleanToVisibility}}"
        OverflowContentTarget="{Binding ElementName=overflow15}" />

<RichTextBlockOverflow Name="overflow15"
        Visibility="{Binding ElementName=overflow14,
                      Path=HasOverflowContent,
                      Converter={StaticResource booleanToVisibility}}"
        OverflowContentTarget="{Binding ElementName=overflow16}" />

<RichTextBlockOverflow Name="overflow16"
        Visibility="{Binding ElementName=overflow15,
                      Path=HasOverflowContent,
                      Converter={StaticResource booleanToVisibility}}"
        OverflowContentTarget="{Binding ElementName=overflow17}" />

<RichTextBlockOverflow Name="overflow17"
        Visibility="{Binding ElementName=overflow16,
                      Path=HasOverflowContent,
                      Converter={StaticResource booleanToVisibility}}"
        OverflowContentTarget="{Binding ElementName=overflow18}" />
```

```
        <RichTextBlockOverflow Name="overflow18"
                Visibility="{Binding ElementName=overflow17,
                                Path=HasOverflowContent,
                                Converter={StaticResource booleanToVisibility}}"
                OverflowContentTarget="{Binding ElementName=overflow19}" />

        <RichTextBlockOverflow Name="overflow19"
                Visibility="{Binding ElementName=overflow18,
                                Path=HasOverflowContent,
                                Converter={StaticResource booleanToVisibility}}"
                OverflowContentTarget="{Binding ElementName=overflow20}" />

        <RichTextBlockOverflow Name="overflow20"
                Visibility="{Binding ElementName=overflow19,
                                Path=HasOverflowContent,
                                Converter={StaticResource booleanToVisibility}}"
                OverflowContentTarget="{Binding ElementName=overflow21}" />

        <RichTextBlockOverflow Name="overflow21"
                Visibility="{Binding ElementName=overflow20,
                                Path=HasOverflowContent,
                                Converter={StaticResource booleanToVisibility}}" />

        </StackPanel>
      </ScrollViewer>
    </Grid>
</Page>
```

Each *RichTextBlockOverflow* is hidden if the previous one doesn't have any overflow content, and each except the very last spills its overflow content into the next one through a binding. All the *RichTextBlockOverflow* elements share a horizontal *StackPanel* in a *ScrollViewer* with the original *RichTextBlock*, so the text forms columns that can be horizontally scrolled:

YOUNG GOODMAN BROWN

by
Nathaniel Hawthorne

Young Goodman Brown came forth at sunset into the street at Salem village; but put his head back, after crossing the threshold, to exchange a parting kiss with his young wife. And Faith, as the wife was aptly named, thrust her own pretty head into the street, letting the wind play with the pink ribbons of her cap while she called to Goodman Brown.

"Dearest heart," whispered she, softly and rather sadly, when her lips were close to his ear, "prithee put off your journey until sunrise and sleep in your own bed to-night. A lone woman is troubled with such dreams and such thoughts that she's afeard of herself sometimes. Pray tarry with me this night, dear husband, of all nights in the year."

"My love and my Faith," replied young Goodman Brown, "of all nights in the year, this one night must I tarry away from thee. My journey, as thou callest it, forth and back again, must needs be done 'twixt now and sunrise. What, my sweet, pretty wife, dost thou doubt me already, and we but three months married?"

"Then God bless you!" said Faith, with the pink ribbons; "and may you find all well when you come back."

"Amen!" cried Goodman Brown. "Say thy prayers, dear Faith, and go to bed at dusk, and no harm will come to thee."

So they parted; and the young man pursued his way until, being about to turn the corner by the meeting-house, he looked back and saw the head of Faith still peeping after him with a melancholy air, in spite of her pink ribbons.

"Poor little Faith!" thought he, for his heart smote him. "What a wretch am I to leave her on such an errand! She

talks of dreams, too. Methought as she spoke there was trouble in her face, as if a dream had warned her what work is to be done tonight. But no, no; 't would kill her to think it. Well, she's a blessed angel on earth; and after this one night I'll cling to her skirts and follow her to heaven."

With this excellent resolve for the future, Goodman Brown felt himself justified in making more haste on his present evil purpose. He had taken a dreary road, darkened by all the gloomiest trees of the forest, which barely stood aside to let the narrow path creep through, and closed immediately behind. It was all as lonely as could be; and there is this peculiarity in such a solitude, that the traveller knows not who may be concealed by the innumerable trunks and the thick boughs overhead; so that with lonely footsteps he may yet be passing through an unseen multitude.

"There may be a devilish Indian behind every tree," said Goodman Brown to himself; and he glanced fearfully behind him as he added, "What if the devil himself should be at my very elbow!"

His head being turned back, he passed a crook of the road, and, looking forward again, beheld the figure of a man, in grave and decent attire, seated at the foot of an old tree. He arose at Goodman Brown's approach and walked onward side by side with him.

"You are late, Goodman Brown," said he. "The clock of the Old South was striking as I came through Boston, and that is full fifteen minutes agone."

"Faith kept me back a while," replied the young man, with a tremor in his voice, caused by the sudden appearance of his companion, though not wholly unexpected.

It was now deep dusk in the forest, and deepest in that part of it where these two were journeying. As nearly as

could be discerned, the second t years old, apparently in the same r Brown, and bearing a considerab though perhaps more in expression might have been taken for father a the elder person was as simply clad simple in manner too, he had an who knew the world, and who wou at the governor's dinner table or were it possible that his affairs sho the only thing about him that c remarkable was his staff, which bor black snake, so curiously wrought seen to twist and wriggle itself like course, must have been an ocular d uncertain light.

"Come, Goodman Brown," c "this is a dull pace for the beginnir staff, if you are so soon weary."

"Friend," said the other, excha a full stop, "having kept covenant by my purpose now to return whence touching the matter thou wot'st of."

"Sayest thou so?" replied he apart. "Let us walk on, nevertheless, if I convince thee not thou shalt t little way in the forest yet."

"Too far! too far!" excl unconsciously resuming his walk. "M the woods on such an errand, nor h have been a race of honest men ar the days of the martyrs; and shall I of Brown that ever took this path an

"Such company, thou wouldst

These columns are more readable than text that extends to the full width of the landscape screen.

Of course, if you don't provide a sufficient number of *RichTextBlockOverflow* elements, the text will be truncated and you'll never be able to read the end of the story. For that reason, it's probably better to generate the *RichTextBlockOverflow* elements in code.

When you create a project of type Grid App or Split App in Visual Studio, you get a *RichTextColumns* class in the Common folder. This class derives from *Panel* and generates *RichTextBlockOverflow* elements in its *MeasureOverride* method.

I'll show you another approach. Like the two previous projects, the MainPage.xaml file in the next project contains a complete text in a *RichTextBlock* element. This time it's F. Scott Fitzgerald's tale of Jazz Age teenagers in "Bernice Bobs Her Hair":

Project: BerniceBobsHerHair | File: MainPage.xaml (excerpt)

```
<Page ... >
    <Page.Resources>
        <Style TargetType="RichTextBlock">
            <Setter Property="Width" Value="480" />
            <Setter Property="Margin" Value="24 0 24 0" />
            <Setter Property="FontSize" Value="18" />
            <Setter Property="TextAlignment" Value="Justify" />
        </Style>

        <Style TargetType="RichTextBlockOverflow">
            <Setter Property="Width" Value="480" />
            <Setter Property="Margin" Value="24 0 24 0" />
        </Style>
    </Page.Resources>

    <Grid Background="{StaticResource ApplicationPageBackgroundThemeBrush}">
        <ScrollViewer HorizontalScrollBarVisibility="Hidden"
                      VerticalScrollBarVisibility="Disabled">
            <StackPanel Name="stackPanel"
                        Orientation="Horizontal">
                <RichTextBlock SizeChanged="OnRichTextBlockSizeChanged">
                    <Paragraph TextAlignment="Center" FontSize="36" Margin="0 0 0 12">
                        "Bernice Bobs Her Hair"
                        <LineBreak />
                        by
                        <LineBreak />
                        F. Scott Fitzgerald
                    </Paragraph>
```

```
            <Paragraph Margin="0 6">
                After dark on Saturday night one could stand on the first tee of
                the golf-course and see the country-club windows as a yellow
                expanse over a very black and wavy ocean. The waves of this
                ocean, so to speak, were the heads of many curious caddies, a few
                of the more ingenious chauffeurs, the golf professional's deaf
                sister&#x2014;and there were usually several stray, diffident waves who
                might have rolled inside had they so desired. This was the
                gallery.
            </Paragraph>
            ...
            <Paragraph TextIndent="48" Margin="0 6">
                Then picking up her staircase she set off at a half-run down the
                moonlit street.
            </Paragraph>
        </RichTextBlock>
    </StackPanel>
</ScrollViewer>
    </Grid>
</Page>
```

Notice the *SizeChanged* handler set on the *RichTextBlock*. That handler begins by getting rid of all the previous *RichTextBlockOverflow* elements it might have created during previous size changes, and then it creates a whole new batch:

Project: BerniceBobsHerHair | File: MainPage.xaml.cs (excerpt)

```
void OnRichTextBlockSizeChanged(object sender, SizeChangedEventArgs args)
{
    RichTextBlock richTextBlock = sender as RichTextBlock;

    if (richTextBlock.ActualHeight == 0)
        return;

    // Get rid of all previous RichTextBlockOverflow objects
    while (stackPanel.Children.Count > 1)
        stackPanel.Children.RemoveAt(1);

    if (!richTextBlock.HasOverflowContent)
        return;

    // Create first RichTextBlockOverflow
    RichTextBlockOverflow richTextBlockOverflow = new RichTextBlockOverflow();
    richTextBlock.OverflowContentTarget = richTextBlockOverflow;
    stackPanel.Children.Add(richTextBlockOverflow);

    // Measure it
    richTextBlockOverflow.Measure(new Size(richTextBlockOverflow.Width, this.ActualHeight));
```

```
    // If it has overflow content, repeat the process
    while (richTextBlockOverflow.HasOverflowContent)
    {
        RichTextBlockOverflow newRichTextBlockOverflow = new RichTextBlockOverflow();
        richTextBlockOverflow.OverflowContentTarget = newRichTextBlockOverflow;
        richTextBlockOverflow = newRichTextBlockOverflow;
        stackPanel.Children.Add(richTextBlockOverflow);
        richTextBlockOverflow.Measure(new Size(richTextBlockOverflow.Width, this.ActualHeight));
    }
}
```

Notice the calls to the *Measure* method of *RichTextBlock* and *RichTextBlockOverflow*. This is necessary to force the element to determine how much text can fit within that rectangle, and to set the *HasOverflowContent* property appropriately. Here's the result:

"Bernice Bobs Her Hair"
by
F. Scott Fitzgerald

After dark on Saturday night one could stand on the first tee of the golf-course and see the country-club windows as a yellow expanse over a very black and wavy ocean. The waves of this ocean, so to speak, were the heads of many curious caddies, a few of the more ingenious chauffeurs, the golf professional's deaf sister—and there were usually several stray, diffident waves who might have rolled inside had they so desired. This was the gallery.

The balcony was inside. It consisted of the circle of wicker chairs that lined the wall of the combination clubroom and ballroom. At these Saturday-night dances it was largely feminine; a great babel of middle-aged ladies with sharp eyes and icy hearts behind lorgnettes and large bosoms. The main function of the balcony was critical, it occasionally showed grudging admiration, but never approval, for it is well known among ladies over thirty-five that when the younger set dance in the summer-time it is with the very worst intentions in the world, and if they are not bombarded with stony eyes stray couples will dance weird barbaric interludes in the corners, and the more popular, more dangerous, girls will sometimes be kissed in the parked limousines of unsuspecting dowagers.

But, after all, this critical circle is not close enough to the stage to see the actors' faces and catch the subtler byplay. It can only frown and lean, ask questions and make satisfactory deductions from its set of postulates, such as the one which states that every young man with a large income leads the life of a hunted partridge. It never really appreciates the drama of the shifting, semi-cruel world of adolescence. No; boxes, orchestra-circle, principals, and chorus be represented by the medley of faces and voices that sway to the plaintive African rhythm of Dyer's dance orchestra.

From sixteen-year-old Otis Ormonde, who has two more years at Hill School, to G. Reece Stoddard, over whose bureau at home hangs a Harvard law diploma; from little Madeleine Hogue, whose hair still feels strange and uncomfortable on top of her head, to Bessie MacRae, who has been the life of the party a little too long—more than ten years—the medley is not only the centre of the stage but contains the only people capable of getting an unobstructed view of it.

With a flourish and a bang the music stops. The couples exchange artificial, effortless smiles, facetiously repeat "la-de-da-dadum-dum," and then the clatter of young feminine voices soars over the burst of clapping.

A few disappointed stags caught in midfloor as they had been about to cut in subsided listlessly back to the walls, because this was not like the riotous Christmas dances —these summer hops were considered just pleasantly warm and exciting, where even the younger marrieds rose and performed ancient waltzes and terrifying fox trots to the tolerant amusement of their younger brothers and sisters.

Warren McIntyre, who casually attended Yale, being one of the unfortunate stags, felt in his dinner-coat pocket for a cigarette and strolled out onto the wide, semidark veranda, where couples were scattered at tables, filling the lantern-hung night with vague words and hazy laughter. He nodded here and there at the less absorbed and as he passed each couple some half-forgotten fragment of a story played in his mind, for it was not a large city and every one was Who's Who to every one else's past. There, for example,

were Jim Strain and Ethel Demorest, engaged for three years. Every one managed to hold a job for more would marry him. Yet how bored the wearily Ethel regarded Jim sometin why she had trained the vines of wind-shaken poplar.

Warren was nineteen and rath his friends who hadn't gone East to boys, he bragged tremendously ab when he was away from it. There w who regularly made the rounds o and football games at Princeton, Ya there was black-eyed Roberta Dil famous to her own generation a Cobb; and, of course, there was besides having a fairylike face and tongue was already justly celebrate cart-wheels in succession during th dance at New Haven.

Warren, who had grown up Marjorie, had long been "crazy abo seemed to reciprocate his feeling w she had tried him by her infallible gravely that she did not love him. she was away from him she forgot other boys. Warren found this dis Marjorie had been making little trips first two or three days after each a heaps of mail on the Harveys' hall t various masculine handwritings. To during the month of August she F cousin Bernice from Eau Claire, and see her alone. It was always neces

The Perils of Pagination

Now that we've seen *RichTextBlock* and *RichTextBlockOverflow* take on a couple of short stories, the question naturally poses itself: Can this same technique work for a whole novel?

Let's try it. But let's try it for a reasonably *short* novel, for example, George Eliot's *Silas Marner*. Rather than displaying columns of text, the SilasMarner program displays actual pages, and it uses a *FlipView* for displaying the *RichTextBlock* and *RichTextBlockOverflow* elements.

It's amazing how nicely *FlipView* gives the program the look and feel of an authentic e-book reader. Each page can occupy the whole screen (or nearly the whole screen) and you can navigate back and forth among the pages with swipes of your finger. In addition, I've put a *Slider* at the bottom of the page that provides a visual representation of your progress through the book, and lets you navigate to any page very quickly.

Perhaps more than any other program in this book, SilasMarner is much more suited for portrait mode rather than landscape. In landscape, the line lengths are simply too wide to read comfortably, as you can see:

"Silas Marner" by George Eliot — Page 36 of 163

more numerous than usual; several personages, who would otherwise have been admitted into the parlour and enlarged the opportunity of hectoring and condescension for their betters, being content this evening to vary their enjoyment by taking their spirits-and-water where they could themselves hector and condescend in company that called for beer.

CHAPTER VI

The conversation, which was at a high pitch of animation when Silas approached the door of the Rainbow, had, as usual, been slow and intermittent when the company first assembled. The pipes began to be puffed in a silence which had an air of severity; the more important customers, who drank spirits and sat nearest the fire, staring at each other as if a bet were depending on the first man who winked; while the beer-drinkers, chiefly men in fustian jackets and smock-frocks, kept their eyelids down and rubbed their hands across their mouths, as if their draughts of beer were a funereal duty attended with embarrassing sadness. At last Mr. Snell, the landlord, a man of a neutral disposition, accustomed to stand aloof from human differences as those of beings who were all alike in need of liquor, broke silence, by saying in a doubtful tone to his cousin the butcher--

"Some folks 'ud say that was a fine beast you druv in yesterday, Bob?"

The butcher, a jolly, smiling, red-haired man, was not disposed to answer rashly. He gave a few puffs before he spat and replied, "And they wouldn't be fur wrong, John."

After this feeble delusive thaw, the silence set in as severely as before.

"Was it a red Durham?" said the farrier, taking up the thread of discourse after the lapse of a few minutes.

The farrier looked at the landlord, and the landlord looked at the butcher, as the person who must take the responsibility of answering.

"Red it was," said the butcher, in his good-humoured husky treble--"and a Durham it was."

Turn it sideways, and the reading experience is rather better:

leave off skulking i' the dark and i' lone places--let 'em come where there's company and candles."

"As if ghos'es 'ud want to be believed in by anybody so ignirant!" said Mr. Macey, in deep disgust at the farrier's crass incompetence to apprehend the conditions of ghostly phenomena.

CHAPTER VII

Yet the next moment there seemed to be some evidence that ghosts had a more condescending disposition than Mr. Macey attributed to them; for the pale thin figure of Silas Marner was suddenly seen standing in the warm light, uttering no word, but looking round at the company with his strange unearthly eyes. The long pipes gave a simultaneous movement, like the antennae of startled insects, and every man present, not excepting even the sceptical farrier, had an impression that he saw, not Silas Marner in the flesh, but an apparition; for the door by which Silas had entered was hidden by the high-screened seats, and no one had noticed his approach. Mr. Macey, sitting a long way off the ghost, might be supposed to have felt an argumentative triumph, which would tend to neutralize his share of the general alarm. Had he not always said that when Silas Marner was in that strange trance of his, his soul went loose from his body? Here was the demonstration: nevertheless, on the whole, he would have been as well contented without it. For a few moments there was a dead silence, Marner's want of breath and agitation not allowing him to speak. The landlord, under the habitual sense that he was bound to keep his house open to all company, and confident in the protection of his unbroken neutrality, at last took on himself the task of adjuring the ghost.

"Master Marner," he said, in a conciliatory tone, "what's lacking to you? What's your business here?"

"Robbed!" said Silas, gaspingly. "I've been robbed! I want the constable-- and the Justice--and Squire Cass--and Mr. Crackenthorp."

"Lay hold on him, Jem Rodney," said the landlord, the idea of a ghost subsiding; "he's off his head, I doubt. He's wet through."

Jem Rodney was the outermost man, and sat conveniently near Marner's standing-place; but he declined to give his services.

"Come and lay hold on him yourself, Mr. Snell, if you've a mind," said Jem, rather sullenly. "He's been robbed, and murdered too, for what I know," he added, in a muttering tone.

"Jem Rodney!" said Silas, turning and fixing his strange eyes on the suspected man.

"Aye, Master Marner, what do you want wi' me?" said Jem, trembling a little, and seizing his drinking-can as a defensive weapon.

However, I have resisted giving the program a programmatic preference for portrait mode. In a real e-book reader—and I'm using the term broadly to describe any facility in a program for reading a large chunk of text—efficient pagination is crucial. Even if the user can't change the size of the screen, most e-book readers allow the user to change fonts or font sizes, and that affects the pagination of the book.

When running SilasMarner on a tablet, you can rotate it, try out snap views, and observe firsthand how long it takes for the *RichTextBlock* and *RichTextBlockOverflow* elements to repaginate the document.

One of the notorious problems of e-book readers involves maintaining and displaying a meaningful page number. Any time a document is repaginated, it has a different number of pages. The SilasMarner program saves information in local storage that lets you continue reading where you last left off, but it doesn't save a page number for that purpose. Instead, it maintains a fraction calculated by dividing the current page by the total number of pages. This is the only value that is maintained between launchings of the program:

Project: SilasMarner | File: MainPage.xaml.cs (excerpt)

```
public sealed partial class MainPage : Page
{
    double fractionRead;

    public MainPage()
    {
        this.InitializeComponent();

        // Save and reload fraction read
        IPropertySet propertySet = ApplicationData.Current.LocalSettings.Values;

        Application.Current.Suspending += (sender, args) =>
            {
                propertySet["FractionRead"] = fractionRead;
            };

        if (propertySet.ContainsKey("FractionRead"))
            fractionRead = (double)propertySet["FractionRead"];
    }
    ...
}
```

If the new page size isn't exactly the same as it was when the program last saved this value, you won't end up on exactly the same page, of course, but at least you'll be close.

A real e-book reader would probably download books. For this demonstration program, I've included the Project Gutenberg file as a program resource. Separating this book into paragraphs is the responsibility of the code-behind file.

Thus, there's no book text in the XAML file. Instead, the XAML file has a *FlipView* in the center and also displays a heading with the book's title, current page, and page count. This header isn't strictly necessary, of course, but I wanted a clear indication of the number of pages and current page. A *Slider* sits at the bottom:

Project: SilasMarner | File: MainPage.xaml (excerpt)

```
<Page ... >
    <Grid Background="{StaticResource ApplicationPageBackgroundThemeBrush}">
        <Grid.RowDefinitions>
            <RowDefinition Height="Auto" />
            <RowDefinition Height="*" />
            <RowDefinition Height="Auto" />
        </Grid.RowDefinitions>

        <StackPanel Grid.Row="0"
                    Orientation="Horizontal"
                    HorizontalAlignment="Center">
            <StackPanel.Resources>
                <Style TargetType="TextBlock">
                    <Setter Property="FontSize" Value="24" />
                </Style>
            </StackPanel.Resources>
```

```
        <TextBlock Text="&#x201C;Silas Marner&#x201D; by George Eliot" />
        <TextBlock Text="&#x00A0;&#x2014; Page&#x00A0;" />
        <TextBlock Name="pageNumber" />
        <TextBlock Text="&#x00A0;of&#x00A0;" />
        <TextBlock Name="pageCount" />
    </StackPanel>

    <FlipView Name="flipView"
              Grid.Row="1"
              Background="White"
              SizeChanged="OnFlipViewSizeChanged"
              SelectionChanged="OnFlipViewSelectionChanged">
        <FlipView.ItemsPanel>
            <ItemsPanelTemplate>
                <StackPanel Orientation="Horizontal" />
            </ItemsPanelTemplate>
        </FlipView.ItemsPanel>
    </FlipView>

    <Slider Name="pageSlider"
            Grid.Row="2"
            Margin="24 12 24 0"
            ValueChanged="OnPageSliderValueChanged" />
    </Grid>
</Page>
```

The crucial processing in this program is the *SizeChanged* handler for the *FlipView*. Based on the size of the *FlipView*, the program must generate the proper number of *RichTextBlockOverflow* elements.

The first time this *SizeChanged* event is fired after the program is launched, the handler must access the book file and divide it into paragraphs. In Project Gutenberg plain-text files, each paragraph consists of a sequence of lines with hard carriage returns. Paragraphs are delimited by blank lines. The handler must process this text in creating *Paragraph* objects that it adds to the *RichTextBlock* element:

Project: SilasMarner | File: MainPage.xaml.cs (excerpt)

```
async void OnFlipViewSizeChanged(object sender, SizeChangedEventArgs args)
{
    // Get the size of the FlipView
    Size containerSize = args.NewSize;

    // Actual value gets modified during processing here, so save it
    double saveFractionRead = fractionRead;

    // First time through after program is launched
    if (flipView.Items.Count == 0)
    {
        // Load book resource
        IList<string> bookLines =
            await PathIO.ReadLinesAsync("ms-appx:///Books/pg550.txt",
                                        UnicodeEncoding.Utf8);
```

```csharp
// Create RichTextBlock
RichTextBlock richTextBlock = new RichTextBlock
{
    FontSize = 22,
    Foreground = new SolidColorBrush(Colors.Black)
};

// Create paragraphs
Paragraph paragraph = new Paragraph();
paragraph.Margin = new Thickness(12);
richTextBlock.Blocks.Add(paragraph);

foreach (string line in bookLines)
{
    // End of paragraph, make new Paragraph
    if (line.Length == 0)
    {
        paragraph = new Paragraph();
        paragraph.Margin = new Thickness(12);
        richTextBlock.Blocks.Add(paragraph);
    }
    // Continue the paragraph
    else
    {
        string textLine = line;
        char lastChar = line[line.Length - 1];

        if (lastChar != ' ')
            textLine += ' ';

        if (line[0] == ' ')
            paragraph.Inlines.Add(new LineBreak());

        paragraph.Inlines.Add(new Run { Text = textLine });
    }
}

// Make RichTextBlock the same size as the FlipView
flipView.Items.Add(richTextBlock);
richTextBlock.Measure(containerSize);

// Generate RichTextBlockOverflow elements
if (richTextBlock.HasOverflowContent)
{
    // Add the first one
    RichTextBlockOverflow richTextBlockOverflow = new RichTextBlockOverflow();
    richTextBlock.OverflowContentTarget = richTextBlockOverflow;
    flipView.Items.Add(richTextBlockOverflow);
    richTextBlockOverflow.Measure(containerSize);
```

```
                    // Add subsequent ones
                    while (richTextBlockOverflow.HasOverflowContent)
                    {
                        RichTextBlockOverflow newRichTextBlockOverflow = new RichTextBlockOverflow();
                        richTextBlockOverflow.OverflowContentTarget = newRichTextBlockOverflow;
                        richTextBlockOverflow = newRichTextBlockOverflow;
                        flipView.Items.Add(richTextBlockOverflow);
                        richTextBlockOverflow.Measure(containerSize);
                    }
                }
            }
            ...
        }
```

In subsequent firings of the *SizeChanged* handler, the program could just clear out the *FlipView* and start over again, but I decided to attempt a little more efficiency by adding new *RichTextBlockOverflow* elements if some are needed or removing any that are no longer required:

Project: SilasMarner | File: MainPage.xaml.cs (excerpt)

```
async void OnFlipViewSizeChanged(object sender, SizeChangedEventArgs args)
{
    ...
    // Subsequent SizeChanged events
    else
    {
        // Resize all the items in the FlipView
        foreach (object obj in flipView.Items)
        {
            (obj as FrameworkElement).Measure(containerSize);
        }

        // Generate new RichTextBlockOverflow elements if needed
        while ((flipView.Items[flipView.Items.Count - 1]
                        as RichTextBlockOverflow).HasOverflowContent)
        {
            RichTextBlockOverflow richTextBlockOverflow =
                    flipView.Items[flipView.Items.Count - 1] as RichTextBlockOverflow;
            RichTextBlockOverflow newRichTextBlockOverflow = new RichTextBlockOverflow();
            richTextBlockOverflow.OverflowContentTarget = newRichTextBlockOverflow;
            richTextBlockOverflow = newRichTextBlockOverflow;
            flipView.Items.Add(richTextBlockOverflow);
            richTextBlockOverflow.Measure(args.NewSize);
        }
        // Remove superfluous RichTextBlockOverflow elements
        while (!(flipView.Items[flipView.Items.Count - 2]
                        as RichTextBlockOverflow).HasOverflowContent)
        {
            flipView.Items.RemoveAt(flipView.Items.Count - 1);
        }
    }
    ...
}
```

However, I discovered (as you'll probably discover) that this logic seems to calculate an insufficient number of *RichTextBlockOverflow* elements. The whole novel is preserved, but some of the licensing information toward the end of the file is truncated. I do not know why this happens.

The *SizeChanged* processing concludes with initializing the heading text and the *Slider* and then setting the *SelectedIndex* property of the *FlipView* to a value based on the *fractionRead* value:

Project: SilasMarner | File: MainPage.xaml.cs (excerpt)

```
async void OnFlipViewSizeChanged(object sender, SizeChangedEventArgs args)
{
    ...
    // Initialize the header and Slider
    int count = flipView.Items.Count;
    pageNumber.Text = "1";                      // probably modified soon
    pageCount.Text = count.ToString();
    pageSlider.Minimum = 1;
    pageSlider.Maximum = flipView.Items.Count;
    pageSlider.Value = 1;                       // probably modified soon

    // Go to approximate page
    fractionRead = saveFractionRead;
    flipView.SelectedIndex = (int)Math.Min(count - 1, fractionRead * count);
}
```

That's the bulk of the program. The *SelectionChanged* handler for the *FlipView* changes the heading and *Slider*, and the *ValueChanged* handler for the *Slider* changes the *SelectedIndex* property of the *FlipView*:

Project: SilasMarner | File: MainPage.xaml.cs (excerpt)

```
public sealed partial class MainPage : Page
{
    ...
    void OnFlipViewSelectionChanged(object sender, SelectionChangedEventArgs args)
    {
        int pageNum = flipView.SelectedIndex + 1;
        pageNumber.Text = pageNum.ToString();
        fractionRead = (pageNum - 1.0) / flipView.Items.Count;
        pageSlider.Value = pageNum;
    }

    void OnPageSliderValueChanged(object sender, RangeBaseValueChangedEventArgs args)
    {
        flipView.SelectedIndex = Math.Min(flipView.Items.Count, (int)args.NewValue) - 1;
    }
}
```

Now that the program is finished, how does it work?

Not very well, I think. A few seconds are required every time the *SizeChanged* handler executes, and this is code that cannot be moved to a secondary thread because virtually all of it involves user interface objects. Moreover, I've experienced some shifting around of the text contents of the elements, indicating to me that I'm pushing the envelope of *RichTextBlock* pagination.

What these problems imply is that *RichTextBlock* must be abandoned for performing pagination for larger documents. The program itself must take on these tasks, most efficiently based on text metric information. If you're interested in exploring some of the issues—and possible solutions— check out a series of articles I wrote for the June through November 2011 issues of *MSDN Magazine* (*http://msdn.microsoft.com/en-us/magazine*, and select Issues and Downloads). These articles describe code for Windows Phone 7, but the principles are very similar to working with Windows 8.

In particular, it's extremely helpful to divide a large document into chapters. In traditional typesetting as well as e-book readers, chapters represent points where pagination can begin anew. Within a particular chapter, pagination can be performed "on demand" as the need arises for each new page.

Rich Editing with *RichEditBox*

Just as there is an enhanced version of *TextBlock* called *RichTextBlock*, there is an enhanced version of *TextBox* called...no, it's not called *RichTextBox*. It's actually *RichEditBox*.

If you think of *TextBox* as the "engine" of the traditional Windows Notepad program, *RichEditBox* might be regarded as the engine of the Windows WordPad program. *RichEditBox* lets you program-matically select ranges of text—or (more commonly) allow the user to select ranges of text—and apply unique character and paragraph formatting to that selection. *RichEditBox* also has a built-in file loading and saving option, but unfortunately this option supports only the rather quaint Rich Text Format (RTF).

The following discussion just scratches the surface of *RichEditBox*. You'll want to begin exploring the unique features of this class through the portal of the *Document* property. This *Document* property is set internally to an object that implements the *ITextDocument* interface, defined in the *Windows.UI.Text* namespace. That interface supports loading and saving to streams, as well as methods to set and obtain default character and paragraph formatting, and to set the formatting for ranges of text within the document.

ITextDocument also supports a *Selection* property that refers to the area of the document selected by the user. This *Selection* property is of type *ITextSelection*, which also implements the *ITextRange* interface. The *ITextRange* interface supports clipboard copies and pastes, as well as defining *CharacterFormat* and *ParagraphFormat* properties, which reference objects that implement the *ITextCharacterFormat* and *ITextParagraphFormat* interfaces, respectively.

Let's use *RichEditBox* to construct a rudimentary rich-text editor called RichTextEditor. This program has an application bar at the top to apply character formatting (at the left) and paragraph formatting (at the right) and an application bar at the bottom for loading and saving files:

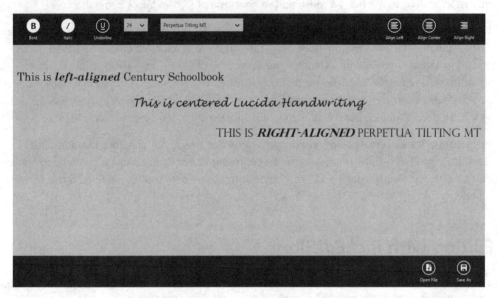

As soon as you start putting together a program of this sort, you start realizing that the hard part is not the *RichEditBox* programming interface—it's figuring out how to organize the user interface. I've used eight button styles from StandardStyles.xaml, but StandardStyles.xaml contains styles for buttons for font, font color, and font size. If you use those buttons, however, they'll need to invoke popup dialog boxes, and I wanted to avoid that in this program. For that reason, the size and font family are implemented as *ComboBox* controls right on the application bar, and there is no color selection. Like I said, I'm only scratching the surface here.

Here's the XAML file. As you can see, the markup for the *RichEditBox* is dwarfed by the two *AppBar* definitions:

Project: RichTextEditor | **File:** MainPage.xaml (excerpt)

```
<Page
    x:Class="RichTextEditor.MainPage"
    xmlns="http://schemas.microsoft.com/winfx/2006/xaml/presentation"
    xmlns:x="http://schemas.microsoft.com/winfx/2006/xaml"
    xmlns:local="using:RichTextEditor"
    xmlns:d="http://schemas.microsoft.com/expression/blend/2008"
    xmlns:mc="http://schemas.openxmlformats.org/markup-compatibility/2006"
    mc:Ignorable="d">

    <Grid Background="{StaticResource ApplicationPageBackgroundThemeBrush}">
        <RichEditBox Name="richEditBox" />
    </Grid>
```

```xaml
<Page.TopAppBar>
    <AppBar Opened="OnTopAppBarOpened">
        <Grid>
            <StackPanel Orientation="Horizontal"
                        HorizontalAlignment="Left">
                <!-- For CheckBox's, need to comment out BackgroundCheckedGlyph in
                     AppBarButtonStyle in StandardStyles.xaml -->
                <CheckBox Name="boldAppBarCheckBox"
                          Style="{StaticResource BoldAppBarButtonStyle}"
                          Checked="OnBoldAppBarCheckBoxChecked"
                          Unchecked="OnBoldAppBarCheckBoxChecked" />

                <CheckBox Name="italicAppBarCheckBox"
                          Style="{StaticResource ItalicAppBarButtonStyle}"
                          Checked="OnItalicAppBarCheckBoxChecked"
                          Unchecked="OnItalicAppBarCheckBoxChecked" />

                <CheckBox Name="underlineAppBarCheckBox"
                          Style="{StaticResource UnderlineAppBarButtonStyle}"
                          Checked="OnUnderlineAppBarCheckBoxChecked"
                          Unchecked="OnUnderlineAppBarCheckBoxChecked" />

                <ComboBox Name="fontSizeComboBox"
                          Width="72"
                          Margin="12 12 24 36"
                          SelectionChanged="OnFontSizeComboBoxSelectionChanged">
                    <x:Int32>8</x:Int32>
                    <x:Int32>9</x:Int32>
                    <x:Int32>10</x:Int32>
                    <x:Int32>11</x:Int32>
                    <x:Int32>12</x:Int32>
                    <x:Int32>14</x:Int32>
                    <x:Int32>16</x:Int32>
                    <x:Int32>18</x:Int32>
                    <x:Int32>20</x:Int32>
                    <x:Int32>22</x:Int32>
                    <x:Int32>24</x:Int32>
                    <x:Int32>26</x:Int32>
                    <x:Int32>28</x:Int32>
                    <x:Int32>36</x:Int32>
                    <x:Int32>48</x:Int32>
                    <x:Int32>72</x:Int32>
                </ComboBox>

                <ComboBox Name="fontFamilyComboBox"
                          Width="240"
                          Margin="12 12 24 36"
                          SelectionChanged="OnFontFamilyComboBoxSelectionChanged" />
            </StackPanel>
            <StackPanel Orientation="Horizontal"
                        HorizontalAlignment="Right">

                <StackPanel Name="alignmentPanel"
                            Orientation="Horizontal">
                    <RadioButton Name="alignLeftAppBarRadioButton"
                                 Style="{StaticResource AlignLeftAppBarButtonStyle}"
                                 Checked="OnAlignAppBarRadioButtonChecked" />
```

```
                    <RadioButton Name="alignCenterAppBarRadioButton"
                                 Style="{StaticResource AlignCenterAppBarButtonStyle}"
                                 Checked="OnAlignAppBarRadioButtonChecked" />

                    <RadioButton Name="alignRightAppBarRadioButton"
                                 Style="{StaticResource AlignRightAppBarButtonStyle}"
                                 Checked="OnAlignAppBarRadioButtonChecked" />
                </StackPanel>
            </StackPanel>
        </Grid>
    </AppBar>
</Page.TopAppBar>
<Page.BottomAppBar>
    <AppBar>
        <Grid>
            <StackPanel Orientation="Horizontal"
                        HorizontalAlignment="Left" />

            <StackPanel Orientation="Horizontal"
                        HorizontalAlignment="Right">
                <Button Style="{StaticResource OpenFileAppBarButtonStyle}"
                        Click="OnOpenAppBarButtonClick" />

                <Button Style="{StaticResource SaveAppBarButtonStyle}"
                        AutomationProperties.Name="Save As"
                        Click="OnSaveAsAppBarButtonClick" />
            </StackPanel>
        </Grid>
    </AppBar>
</Page.BottomAppBar>
</Page>
```

A *CheckBox* is used for the three buttons labeled Bold, Italic, and Underline. These items can be either off or on. The *ComboBox* for the font size is initialized with explicit values. Usually text editors provide a facility to enter a custom value, but for reasons of simplicity I eliminated that. The *ComboBox* for the font family is initialized in the code-behind file. The three buttons for the text alignment are a group of *RadioButton* controls.

Because this project wants to fill up the second *ComboBox* with a list of fonts installed on the system, it includes the DirectXWrapper project from Chapter 15, "Going Native." That *ComboBox* is initialized in the *Loaded* handler. The *Loaded* handler also loads a document-in-progress from local storage and two settings involving the selection the user last made of that document. That document and those settings are saved in the *Suspending* handler:

Project: RichTextEditor | **File:** MainPage.xaml.cs (excerpt)

```
public sealed partial class MainPage : Page
{
    public MainPage()
    {
        this.InitializeComponent();
        Loaded += OnLoaded;
        Application.Current.Suspending += OnAppSuspending;
    }
```

```
async void OnLoaded(object sender, RoutedEventArgs args)
{
    // Get fonts from DirectXWrapper library
    WriteFactory writeFactory = new WriteFactory();
    WriteFontCollection writeFontCollection =
                writeFactory.GetSystemFontCollection();

    int count = writeFontCollection.GetFontFamilyCount();
    string[] fonts = new string[count];

    for (int i = 0; i < count; i++)
    {
        WriteFontFamily writeFontFamily =
                          writeFontCollection.GetFontFamily(i);

        WriteLocalizedStrings writeLocalizedStrings =
                          writeFontFamily.GetFamilyNames();
        int index;

        if (writeLocalizedStrings.FindLocaleName("en-us", out index))
            fonts[i] = writeLocalizedStrings.GetString(index);
        else
            fonts[i] = writeLocalizedStrings.GetString(0);
    }

    Array.Sort<string>(fonts);
    fontFamilyComboBox.ItemsSource = fonts;

    // Load current document
    StorageFolder localFolder = ApplicationData.Current.LocalFolder;

    try
    {
        StorageFile storageFile = await localFolder.CreateFileAsync("RichTextEditor.rtf","
                                        CreationCollisionOption.OpenIfExists);
        IRandomAccessStream stream = await storageFile.OpenAsync(FileAccessMode.Read);
        richEditBox.Document.LoadFromStream(TextSetOptions.FormatRtf, stream);
    }
    catch
    {
        // Ignore exceptions here
    }

    // Load selection settings
    IPropertySet propertySet = ApplicationData.Current.LocalSettings.Values;

    if (propertySet.ContainsKey("SelectionStart"))
        richEditBox.Document.Selection.StartPosition = (int)propertySet["SelectionStart"];

    if (propertySet.ContainsKey("SelectionEnd"))
        richEditBox.Document.Selection.EndPosition = (int)propertySet["SelectionEnd"];
}

async void OnAppSuspending(object sender, SuspendingEventArgs args)
{
    SuspendingDeferral deferral = args.SuspendingOperation.GetDeferral();
```

```
        // Save current document
        StorageFolder localFolder = ApplicationData.Current.LocalFolder;

        try
        {
            StorageFile storageFile = await localFolder.CreateFileAsync("RichTextEditor.rtf",
                                            CreationCollisionOption.ReplaceExisting);
            IRandomAccessStream stream = await storageFile.OpenAsync(FileAccessMode.ReadWrite);
            richEditBox.Document.SaveToStream(TextGetOptions.FormatRtf, stream);
        }
        catch
        {
            // Ignore exceptions here
        }

        // Save selection settings
        IPropertySet propertySet = ApplicationData.Current.LocalSettings.Values;
        propertySet["SelectionStart"] = richEditBox.Document.Selection.StartPosition;
        propertySet["SelectionEnd"] = richEditBox.Document.Selection.EndPosition;

        deferral.Complete();
    }
    ...
}
```

The *LoadFromStream* and *SaveToStream* methods defined by the *ITextDocument* interface require the *FormatRtf* enumeration member to load and save RTF files. Otherwise, the methods just load and save plain text.

The *Suspending* handler saves only the *StartPosition* and *EndPosition* properties of the *ITextSelection* object exposed as the *Selection* property of *ITextDocument*. If no text is actually selected, these values are the same and indicate the current cursor position in the document—the current insertion point where typed text is next inserted.

The program does not save any formatting information because the program doesn't maintain any default formatting that is applicable to new documents or to plain-text files. Those formatting items on the application bar are applicable only to a particular selection (or insertion point) of a document. All those formatting specifications are internal to the document that *RichEditBox* maintains. (Of course, it's possible for a program to allow a user to select default formatting for an entire document, but that's another user interface problem.)

Because the program does not maintain any formatting information, it must initialize all the text-formatting items on the top application bar when that application bar appears, which it signals with the *Opened* event. These items are initialized based on the current selection or insertion point in the document. The current settings are available from the *CharacterFormat* and *ParagraphFormat* properties of the *ITextSelection* object exposed as the *Selection* property of *ITextDocument*:

Project: RichTextEditor | **File:** MainPage.xaml.cs (excerpt)

```
void OnTopAppBarOpened(object sender, object args)
{
    // Get the character formatting at the current selection
    ITextCharacterFormat charFormat = richEditBox.Document.Selection.CharacterFormat;

    // Set the CheckBox app bar buttons
    boldAppBarCheckBox.IsChecked = charFormat.Bold == FormatEffect.On;
    italicAppBarCheckBox.IsChecked = charFormat.Italic == FormatEffect.On;
    underlineAppBarCheckBox.IsChecked = charFormat.Underline == UnderlineType.Single;

    // Set the two ComboBox's
    fontSizeComboBox.SelectedItem = (int)charFormat.Size;
    fontFamilyComboBox.SelectedItem = charFormat.Name;

    // Get the paragraph alignment and set the RadioButton's
    ParagraphAlignment paragraphAlign =
                        richEditBox.Document.Selection.ParagraphFormat.Alignment;
    alignLeftAppBarRadioButton.IsChecked = paragraphAlign == ParagraphAlignment.Left;
    alignCenterAppBarRadioButton.IsChecked = paragraphAlign == ParagraphAlignment.Center;
    alignRightAppBarRadioButton.IsChecked = paragraphAlign == ParagraphAlignment.Right;
}
```

The *ITextCharacterFormat* object defines *Bold*, *Italic*, and *Underline* properties (as you can see) but also supplements those with a familiar *FontStyle* property and a *Weight* property that is a numeric value corresponding to properties of the *FontWeights* class.

FormatEffect is an enumeration with values *On*, *Off*, *Toggle*, and *Undefined*. If the current selection contains some italicized and nonitalicized text, the value of the *Italic* property is *FormatEffect* .*Undefined* and the corresponding application bar button should probably be set to an indeterminate state, but with the standard application bar style, that state looks the same as the unchecked state, so I didn't bother.

Notice that the font family applicable to the selection is provided by the string *Name* property of the *ITextCharacterFormat* object. The property has such an innocuous name that it's easy to overlook.

The Bold, Italic, and Underline buttons are all handled similarly. The *Bold*, *Italic*, and *Underline* properties of the *ITextCharacterFormat* object are set based on the *CheckBox* state, so these settings apply to the current selection or insertion point:

Project: RichTextEditor | **File:** MainPage.xaml.cs (excerpt)

```
void OnBoldAppBarCheckBoxChecked(object sender, RoutedEventArgs args)
{
    richEditBox.Document.Selection.CharacterFormat.Bold =
        (sender as CheckBox).IsChecked.Value ? FormatEffect.On : FormatEffect.Off;
}
```

```
void OnItalicAppBarCheckBoxChecked(object sender, RoutedEventArgs args)
{
    richEditBox.Document.Selection.CharacterFormat.Italic =
        (sender as CheckBox).IsChecked.Value ? FormatEffect.On : FormatEffect.Off;
}

void OnUnderlineAppBarCheckBoxChecked(object sender, RoutedEventArgs args)
{
    richEditBox.Document.Selection.CharacterFormat.Underline =
        (sender as CheckBox).IsChecked.Value ? UnderlineType.Single : UnderlineType.None;
}
```

The handlers of the two *ComboBox* controls are just about as simple:

Project: RichTextEditor | File: MainPage.xaml.cs (excerpt)

```
void OnFontSizeComboBoxSelectionChanged(object sender, SelectionChangedEventArgs args)
{
    ComboBox comboBox = sender as ComboBox;
    if (comboBox.SelectedItem != null)
    {
        richEditBox.Document.Selection.CharacterFormat.Size = (int)comboBox.SelectedItem;
    }
}

void OnFontFamilyComboBoxSelectionChanged(object sender, SelectionChangedEventArgs args)
{
    ComboBox comboBox = sender as ComboBox;
    if (comboBox.SelectedItem != null)
    {
        richEditBox.Document.Selection.CharacterFormat.Name = (string)comboBox.SelectedItem;
    }
}
```

The final formatting item on the application bar applies to paragraphs. The *Alignment* property of the *ITextParagraphFormat* object is set to one of the *ParagraphAlignment* enumeration members based on the checked *RadioButton*:

Project: RichTextEditor | File: MainPage.xaml.cs (excerpt)

```
void OnAlignAppBarRadioButtonChecked(object sender, RoutedEventArgs args)
{
    ParagraphAlignment paragraphAlign = ParagraphAlignment.Undefined;

    if (sender == alignLeftAppBarRadioButton)
        paragraphAlign = ParagraphAlignment.Left;

    else if (sender == alignCenterAppBarRadioButton)
        paragraphAlign = ParagraphAlignment.Center;

    else if (sender == alignRightAppBarRadioButton)
        paragraphAlign = ParagraphAlignment.Right;

    richEditBox.Document.Selection.ParagraphFormat.Alignment = paragraphAlign;
}
```

The only remaining code in *MainPage* handles the Open File and Save As buttons in the bottom application bar. The program allows loading and saving files with both .txt and .rtf extensions. This code should be fairly clear after the similar code in the *Loaded* and *Suspending* handlers that pertain to the current document:

Project: RichTextEditor | File: MainPage.xaml.cs (excerpt)

```
async void OnOpenAppBarButtonClick(object sender, RoutedEventArgs args)
{
    FileOpenPicker picker = new FileOpenPicker();
    picker.FileTypeFilter.Add(".txt");
    picker.FileTypeFilter.Add(".rtf");
    StorageFile storageFile = await picker.PickSingleFileAsync();

    // If user presses Cancel, result is null
    if (storageFile == null)
        return;

    TextSetOptions textOptions = TextSetOptions.None;

    if (storageFile.ContentType != "text/plain")
        textOptions = TextSetOptions.FormatRtf;

    string message = null;

    try
    {
        IRandomAccessStream stream = await storageFile.OpenAsync(FileAccessMode.Read);
        richEditBox.Document.LoadFromStream(textOptions, stream);
    }
    catch (Exception exc)
    {
        message = exc.Message;
    }

    if (message != null)
    {
        MessageDialog msgdlg = new MessageDialog("The file could not be opened. " +
                                  "Windows reports the following error: " +
                                  message, "RichTextEditor");
        await msgdlg.ShowAsync();
    }
}

async void OnSaveAsAppBarButtonClick(object sender, RoutedEventArgs args)
{
    FileSavePicker picker = new FileSavePicker();
    picker.DefaultFileExtension = ".rtf";
    picker.FileTypeChoices.Add("Rich Text Document", new List<string> { ".rtf" });
    picker.FileTypeChoices.Add("Text Document", new List<string> { ".txt" });
    StorageFile storageFile = await picker.PickSaveFileAsync();

    // If user presses Cancel, result is null
    if (storageFile == null)
        return;
```

```
        TextGetOptions textOptions = TextGetOptions.None;

        if (storageFile.ContentType != "text/plain")
            textOptions = TextGetOptions.FormatRtf;

        string message = null;

        try
        {
            IRandomAccessStream stream = await storageFile.OpenAsync(FileAccessMode.ReadWrite);
            richEditBox.Document.SaveToStream(textOptions, stream);
        }
        catch (Exception exc)
        {
            message = exc.Message;
        }

        if (message != null)
        {
            MessageDialog msgdlg = new MessageDialog("The file could not be saved. " +
                                        "Windows reports the following error: " +
                                        message, "RichTextEditor");

            await msgdlg.ShowAsync();
        }
    }
```

The two methods determine whether to use the *TextSetOptions.FormatRtf* and *TextGetOptions* *.FormatRtf* flags based on the MIME type of the *StorageFile* returned from the file picker. My experience reveals that these file pickers indicate that the MIME type of the selected file is either "text/plain" for files with the .txt extensions or "application/msword" for files with .rtf extensions, but I was somewhat wary of hard-coding that latter MIME type into the program given that MIME types of "text/rtf" and "application/rtf" are also associated with RTF files.

If the *FormatRtf* flag is not specified, the *RichEditBox* methods save and load plain-text files. However, the *SaveToStream* method saves plain text using the Unicode (or UTF-16) encoding, where each character in the file occupies two bytes. This encoding is rather uncommon for plain-text files, and the files contain no Byte-Order Mark (BOM) at the beginning to indicate the encoding. Windows Notepad can load these files—apparently it determines the encoding from an examination of the file content—but the PrimitivePad program in Chapter 7, "Asynchronicity," cannot. It stops reading at the first zero encountered in the stream.

Files saved from PrimitivePad have UTF-8 encoding, but they have no BOM either, so the *LoadFromStream* method of *RichEditBox* assumes that the encoding is UTF-16. This means that RichTextEditor cannot properly load files saved from PrimitivePad. Each pair of bytes in the file is treated as comprising a single Unicode character, and hence pairs of characters of the Latin alphabet are displayed mostly as Chinese ideograms.

Perhaps a better solution to saving and loading plain-text files with *RichEditBox* is making use of the *GetText* and *SetText* methods and the regular Windows Runtime file I/O facilities.

Your Own Text Input

Certainly, the *TextBox* and *RichEditBox* controls provide the best ways for your program to get text input from the computer's keyboard. But what if you wanted to implement your own text input?

The *UIElement* class defines *KeyDown* and *KeyUp* events, and the *Control* class supplements these with *OnKeyDown* and *OnKeyUp* virtual methods. However, the information is delivered to your program in the form of *VirtualKey* values. *VirtualKey* is a large enumeration with members for all the possible keys on your keyboard. This information is fine for obtaining activity involving the function keys or cursor movement keys, but it's not so great for alphanumeric input. It's difficult to derive characters from keys in a language-independent and device-independent manner.

A better event for obtaining character input is called *CharacterReceived*, but this event is not defined by *UIElement*. It is instead defined by *CoreWindow*, which you can easily obtain from the *Window* object associated with your application.

The GettingCharacterInput project has a simple demonstration of this technique. The XAML file contains a *TextBlock* for displaying the typed characters:

Project: GettingCharacterInput | **File:** MainPage.xaml (excerpt)

```
<Page ... >
    <Grid Background="{StaticResource ApplicationPageBackgroundThemeBrush}">
        <TextBlock Name="txtblk"
                   FontSize="24"
                   TextWrapping="Wrap" />
    </Grid>
</Page>
```

The code-behind file attaches a handler for the *CharacterReceived* event defined by *CoreWindow* and gets all the character input to that window. Characters are unsigned integer values that are cast to *char* values. The only special processing involves the Backspace key:

Project: GettingCharacterInput | **File:** MainPage.xaml.cs

```
using Windows.UI.Core;
using Windows.UI.Xaml;
using Windows.UI.Xaml.Controls;

namespace GettingCharacterInput
{
    public sealed partial class MainPage : Page
    {
        public MainPage()
        {
            this.InitializeComponent();

            Window.Current.CoreWindow.CharacterReceived += OnCoreWindowCharacterReceived;
        }

        void OnCoreWindowCharacterReceived(CoreWindow sender, CharacterReceivedEventArgs args)
        {
```

```
        // Process Backspace key
        if (args.KeyCode == 8 && txtblk.Text.Length > 0)
        {
            txtblk.Text = txtblk.Text.Substring(0, txtblk.Text.Length - 1);
        }
        // All other keys
        else
        {
            txtblk.Text += (char)args.KeyCode;
        }
    }
  }
}
```

That Backspace key is the only "editing" facility I've provided. The *KeyUp* and *KeyDown* events would need to be handled for implementing the use of cursor movement keys to go back and forth within the typed text string. You'd probably also want to add a way to select text involving the keyboard or pointer. For a more professional implementation, you'd need to draw a cursor and independently color text characters and backgrounds to indicate selection. This means you'll probably be displaying typed text by using individual *TextBlock* elements for each character (and I bet *TextBox* and *RichEditBox* are looking mighty fine about now).

The big problem with the GettingCharacterInput project is that it obtains input only from physical keyboards. If you need to get input from the touch keyboard that pops up on the screen for *TextBox* and *RichEditBox*, the process is more involved. Here are the basics:

The MainPage.xaml file in the BetterCharacterInput project instantiates a custom control named *RudimentaryTextBox*:

Project: BetterCharacterInput | File: MainPage.xaml (excerpt)

```
<Grid Background="{StaticResource ApplicationPageBackgroundThemeBrush}">
    <local:RudimentaryTextBox Background="DarkBlue"
                              Width="320"
                              Height="320" />
</Grid>
```

The *RudimentaryTextBox* class derives from *UserControl*, and the visuals consist mostly of a *TextBlock* that will display the typed text:

Project: BetterCharacterInput | File: RudimentaryTextBox.xaml

```
<UserControl
    x:Class="BetterCharacterInput.RudimentaryTextBox"
    xmlns="http://schemas.microsoft.com/winfx/2006/xaml/presentation"
    xmlns:x="http://schemas.microsoft.com/winfx/2006/xaml">
    <Grid Background="DarkBlue">
        <TextBlock Name="txtblk"
                   Foreground="Yellow"
                   FontSize="24"
                   TextWrapping="Wrap" />
    </Grid>
</UserControl>
```

The *CharacterReceived* event handler in the *RudimentaryTextBox* code-behind file is identical to the one in the previous project, except that the handler is attached only when the control has input focus. The class defines a simple *Text* property for the typed input:

Project: BetterCharacterInput | **File:** RudimentaryTextBox.xaml.cs

```
using Windows.UI.Core;
using Windows.UI.Xaml;
using Windows.UI.Xaml.Automation.Peers;
using Windows.UI.Xaml.Controls;
using Windows.UI.Xaml.Input;

namespace BetterCharacterInput
{
    public sealed partial class RudimentaryTextBox : UserControl
    {
        public RudimentaryTextBox()
        {
            this.InitializeComponent();
            this.IsTabStop = true;
            this.Text = "";
        }

        public string Text { set; get; }

        protected override void OnTapped(TappedRoutedEventArgs args)
        {
            this.Focus(FocusState.Programmatic);
            base.OnTapped(args);
        }

        protected override void OnGotFocus(RoutedEventArgs args)
        {
            Window.Current.CoreWindow.CharacterReceived += OnCoreWindowCharacterReceived;
            base.OnGotFocus(args);
        }

        protected override void OnLostFocus(RoutedEventArgs args)
        {
            Window.Current.CoreWindow.CharacterReceived -= OnCoreWindowCharacterReceived;
            base.OnLostFocus(args);
        }

        protected override AutomationPeer OnCreateAutomationPeer()
        {
            return new RudimentaryTextBoxPeer(this);
        }

        void OnCoreWindowCharacterReceived(CoreWindow sender, CharacterReceivedEventArgs args)
        {
            // Process Backspace key
            if (args.KeyCode == 8 && txtblk.Text.Length > 0)
            {
                txtblk.Text = txtblk.Text.Substring(0, txtblk.Text.Length - 1);
            }
```

```
            // All other keys
            else
            {
                txtblk.Text += (char)args.KeyCode;
            }
        }
    }
}
```

In a real application with multiple custom controls that obtain keyboard input, you might want the page rather than the controls themselves to determine when they get keyboard input.

The only really peculiar part of *RudimentaryTextBox* is the override of the *OnCreateAutomationPeer* method. Automation peers provide programmatic control to the user input functions of controls, and they are generally used to implement assistive technologies and application testing. For a control to be able to invoke the on-screen touch keyboard when it obtains input focus, it must have a custom automation peer that derives from *FrameworkElementAutomationPeer* and implements the *IValueProvider* and *ITextProvider* interfaces.

This custom automation peer class must also override the *FrameworkElementAutomationPeer* constructor and the *GetPatternCore* method. Implementing *IValueProvider* requires two properties and one method. Implementing *ITextProvider* requires two more properties and four methods, but if you're doing this only to provide your custom control with input from the touch keyboard, you can define these methods and properties in very simple ways.

This example code is not quite as simple as possible, but it's close:

Project: BetterCharacterInput | File: RudimentaryTextBoxPeer.cs

```
using Windows.Foundation;
using Windows.UI.Xaml.Automation;
using Windows.UI.Xaml.Automation.Peers;
using Windows.UI.Xaml.Automation.Provider;

namespace BetterCharacterInput
{
    public sealed class RudimentaryTextBoxPeer : FrameworkElementAutomationPeer,
                                                 IValueProvider, ITextProvider
    {
        RudimentaryTextBox rudimentaryTextBox;

        public RudimentaryTextBoxPeer(RudimentaryTextBox owner)
            : base(owner)
        {
            this.rudimentaryTextBox = owner;
        }
```

```csharp
    // Override
    protected override object GetPatternCore(PatternInterface patternInterface)
    {
        if (patternInterface == PatternInterface.Value ||
            patternInterface == PatternInterface.Text)
        {
            return this;
        }
        return base.GetPatternCore(patternInterface);
    }

    // Required for IValueProvider
    public string Value
    {
        get { return rudimentaryTextBox.Text; }
    }

    public bool IsReadOnly
    {
        get { return false; }
    }

    public void SetValue(string value)
    {
        rudimentaryTextBox.Text = value;
    }

    // Required for ITextProvider
    public SupportedTextSelection SupportedTextSelection
    {
        get { return SupportedTextSelection.None; }
    }

    public ITextRangeProvider DocumentRange
    {
        get { return null; }
    }

    public ITextRangeProvider RangeFromPoint(Point pt)
    {
        return null;
    }

    public ITextRangeProvider RangeFromChild(IRawElementProviderSimple child)
    {
        return null;
    }

    public ITextRangeProvider[] GetVisibleRanges()
    {
        return null;
    }
```

```
        public ITextRangeProvider[] GetSelection()
        {
            return null;
        }
    }
}
```

You can simplify this even further by returning *null* from the *Value* property and removing the body from the *SetValue* property.

Now when you tap the dark blue *RudimentaryTextBox* control, the virtual keyboard pops up (although getting a screen shot of that momentous event is a whole other story).

CHAPTER 17

Share and Print

Sweep your finger into the right edge of the Windows 8 screen (or press Windows+C), and you'll see not only the current date and time pop up but also the column of five icons known as *charms*:

The charm in the center navigates straight to the start screen, but the others are intended to provide services for your application. Each of them is associated with a "pane" that appears when the user taps the charm. When your application is on the screen—except when it's in the thin Snapped state—it can support functionality that is associated with these other four charms.

This chapter first examines how you can handle the Settings and Share charms before focusing more extensively on the Devices charm, which is primarily intended to give your programs access to printers.

Settings and Popups

Press the Settings charms for any program shown so far in this book, and you'll see only one item. This Permissions item is provided by Windows and lists the permissions your application has requested in the Capabilities section of the Package.appxmanifest file. At run time, your application can add items to this Settings list, and the items you add push the Permissions item down to the bottom. Commonly, these additional items are intended to provide information about your program and might have labels like About, Credits, Terms of Use, or Privacy Statement. Other items can obtain input from the user and might be labeled Options or Feedback.

Usually you implement each of the items you add to the Settings list in a very familiar manner: a *Popup* with a *UserControl* child. By convention, this is positioned on the right edge of the application and extends to the entire height of the screen.

Let me demonstrate by adding a traditional About box to the FingerPaint project. Because I intend to submit this program to the Windows Store, I'd like this About box to display a cover of this book with a link to buy the book from the website of Microsoft Press's distributor. I first added a new *UserControl* item to the FingerPaint project and called the class *AboutBox*. Here's the XAML file:

Project: FingerPaint | File: AboutBox.xaml (excerpt)

```
<UserControl ... Width="400">
    <UserControl.Transitions>
        <TransitionCollection>
            <EntranceThemeTransition FromHorizontalOffset="400" />
        </TransitionCollection>
    </UserControl.Transitions>

    <Grid>
        <Border BorderBrush="Black"
                BorderThickness="1"
                Background="#404040"
                Margin="0 12"
                Padding="0 24">
            <StackPanel>
                <StackPanel Orientation="Horizontal">
                    <Button Style="{StaticResource PortraitBackButtonStyle}"
                            Foreground="Black"
                            Click="OnBackButtonClick" />

                    <TextBlock Text="About"
                               Style="{StaticResource HeaderTextStyle}" />
                </StackPanel>
```

```
            <TextBlock FontSize="24"
                       FontWeight="Light"
                       TextWrapping="Wrap"
                       Margin="24">
                This program was written by Charles Petzold
                and is just one of many example programs in
                his book
                <Italic>Programming Windows</Italic>,
                6th edition.
                <LineBreak />
                <LineBreak />
                You can purchase a copy at many bookstores
                or directly from the O'Reilly website.
            </TextBlock>

            <HyperlinkButton HorizontalAlignment="Center"
                             NavigateUri="http://shop.oreilly.com/product/0790145369079.do">
                <StackPanel>
                    <Image Source="Assets/BookCover.gif"
                           Stretch="None" />
                    <TextBlock TextAlignment="Center">
                        <Italic>Programming Windows</Italic>,
                        6th edition
                    </TextBlock>
                </StackPanel>
            </HyperlinkButton>
        </StackPanel>
    </Border>
  </Grid>
</UserControl>
```

I have given this control a specific width but not a specific height because it will be stretched to the height of the window in which it's displayed. I've left a little margin on the top and bottom and supplied a transition so that it seems to slide in from the right. It has a Back button with a *Click* handler and a *HyperlinkButton* with the URL of the catalog page for this book at the O'Reilly website. The content of that *HyperlinkButton* includes an *Image* element that references a bitmap I added to the Assets folder.

The *Click* handler for the Back button is pretty sure that the parent of this control is a *Popup*, so it sets the *IsOpen* property of that *Popup* to *false*:

Project: FingerPaint | File: AboutBox.xaml.cs (excerpt)

```
void OnBackButtonClick(object sender, RoutedEventArgs args)
{
    // Dismiss Popup
    Popup popup = this.Parent as Popup;

    if (popup != null)
        popup.IsOpen = false;
}
```

This is one way of dismissing the popup.

The impact to the FingerPaint program of implementing this About box is very slight. The *MainPage* constructor obtains a *SettingsPane* object and attaches a handler for the *CommandsRequested* event:

Project: FingerPaint | File: MainPage.xaml.cs (excerpt)

```
public MainPage()
{
    ...
    // Install a handler for the Settings pane
    SettingsPane settingsPane = SettingsPane.GetForCurrentView();
    settingsPane.CommandsRequested += OnSettingsPaneCommandsRequested;
    ...
}
```

SettingsPane and related classes and enumeration are the occupants of the *Windows .UI.ApplicationSettings* namespace. Conceptually, the *SettingsPane* object refers to the pane that Windows displays when the user presses the Settings charm. That's why you obtain the *SettingsPane* object rather than creating it. When it displays itself, the pane requests the application to add additional items. That's what the *CommandsRequested* handler does.

Hooking into the other charms is similar. *SettingsPane* also has a *Show* method that displays the settings pane programmatically, but for most purposes you'll just want to install a handler for the *CommandsRequested* event. You don't need to retain the *SettingsPane* object, so you can combine the two statements in the *MainPage* constructor into one:

```
SettingsPane.GetForCurrentView().CommandsRequested += OnSettingsPaneCommandsRequested;
```

The *CommandsRequested* event is fired when your program is active and the user presses the Settings charm. This is your opportunity to add additional commands to the Settings pane. Because you're doing this every time the Settings charm is pressed, you can tailor these additional commands for the current application state.

FingerPaint processes this *CommandsRequested* event by adding one *SettingsCommand* object to the list:

Project: FingerPaint | File: MainPage.xaml.cs (excerpt)

```
void OnSettingsPaneCommandsRequested(SettingsPane sender,
                              SettingsPaneCommandsRequestedEventArgs args)
{
    SettingsCommand aboutCommand = new SettingsCommand(0, "About", OnAboutInvoked);
    args.Request.ApplicationCommands.Add(aboutCommand);
}
```

This command has an ID (which I've set to 0 because I'm not using it), a text label, and a method that's called when the user selects that command. After the program returns from the *CommandsRequested* handler, the pane is displayed with that new "About" item.

Here's the method that processes that command:

Project: FingerPaint | **File:** MainPage.xaml.cs (excerpt)

```
void OnAboutInvoked(IUICommand command)
{
    AboutBox aboutBox = new AboutBox();
    aboutBox.Height = this.ActualHeight;

    Popup popup = new Popup
    {
        IsLightDismissEnabled = true,
        Child = aboutBox,
        IsOpen = true,
        HorizontalOffset = this.ActualWidth - aboutBox.Width
    };
}
```

Because the *Popup* appears at a fixed location on the right side of the page, the code to set the *Height* of the *AboutBox* and the *HorizontalOffset* of the *Popup* is very simple, and here it is:

The *IsLightDismissEnabled* property setting ensures that the *Popup* is dismissed when the user presses anywhere outside the *Popup*, and the Back button within *AboutBox* provides dismissal as well. If the user presses the *Hyperlink* button, the *Popup* is dismissed as Internet Explorer is launched.

Sharing Through the Clipboard

Sharing data through the Share charm involves classes in the *Windows.ApplicationModel.DataTransfer* and *Windows.ApplicationModel.DataTransfer.ShareTarget* namespaces. That first namespace also includes a very traditional mechanism for transferring data among Windows applications: the clipboard.

I want to first add clipboard support to FingerPaint before tackling the Share charm. Adding this support to a program that works with bitmaps is potentially complex. You might want to implement a selection API that allows the user to carve out a rectangular area of the painting and copy that to the clipboard. You might also want to implement a paste API that allows an incoming bitmap to be positioned somewhere on the current image.

But I'm going to take the simple route: The Copy command will copy the entire artwork to the clipboard, and the Paste command will treat the incoming bitmap as a new image, just as if it had been loaded from a file but without a filename.

The first job is to add Copy and Paste buttons to the application bar:

Project: FingerPaint | **File:** MainPage.xaml (excerpt)

```
<Page.BottomAppBar>
    <AppBar>
        <Grid>
            <StackPanel Orientation="Horizontal"
                        HorizontalAlignment="Left">
                ...
                <Button Style="{StaticResource CopyAppBarButtonStyle}"
                        Click="OnCopyAppBarButtonClick" />

                <Button Name="pasteAppBarButton"
                        Style="{StaticResource PasteAppBarButtonStyle}"
                        Click="OnPasteAppBarButtonClick" />
            </StackPanel>
            ...
        </Grid>
    </AppBar>
</Page.BottomAppBar>
```

The Paste button needs a name because it must be enabled and disabled from code based on the presence of actual bitmap data in the clipboard.

I decided to implement all the data-sharing code in another partial class implementation of *MainPage* with a filename of MainPage.Share.cs. The *MainPage* constructor calls a method in that class:

Project: FingerPaint | **File:** MainPage.xaml.cs (excerpt)

```
public MainPage()
{
    ...
    // Call a method in MainPage.Share.cs
    InitializeSharing();
    ...
}
```

In part, that method checks if the Paste button should be initially enabled and then sets an event handler that's called when the content of the clipboard changes:

Project: FingerPaint | File: MainPage.Share.cs (excerpt)

```
public sealed partial class MainPage : Page
{
    void InitializeSharing()
    {
        // Initialize the Paste button and provide for updates
        CheckForPasteEnable();
        Clipboard.ContentChanged += OnClipboardContentChanged;
        ...
    }
    ...
    void OnClipboardContentChanged(object sender, object args)
    {
        CheckForPasteEnable();
    }

    void CheckForPasteEnable()
    {
        pasteAppBarButton.IsEnabled = CheckClipboardForBitmap();
    }

    bool CheckClipboardForBitmap()
    {
        DataPackageView dataView = Clipboard.GetContent();
        return dataView.Contains(StandardDataFormats.Bitmap);
    }
    ...
}
```

Clipboard is a small static class with only four methods and one event. The two most crucial methods are *GetContent* and *SetContent*. *GetContent* returns a *DataPackageView* object that provides a convenient way to check the current contents of the clipboard to determine whether a bitmap is present.

SetContent requires a *DataPackage* object, which has a bunch of methods to put various forms of data into the clipboard, including one named *SetBitmap*. The handler for the clipboard Copy button creates a *DataPackage* and sets the operation to Move, meaning that the program is not interested in any further involvement with the bitmap that it's putting into the clipboard:

Project: FingerPaint | File: MainPage.Share.cs (excerpt)

```
async void OnCopyAppBarButtonClick(object sender, RoutedEventArgs args)
{
    DataPackage dataPackage = new DataPackage
    {
        RequestedOperation = DataPackageOperation.Move,
    };
    dataPackage.SetBitmap(await GetBitmapStream(bitmap));

    Clipboard.SetContent(dataPackage);
    this.BottomAppBar.IsOpen = false;
}
```

However, that *SetBitmap* method does not want something as mundane as a *BitmapSource*. Instead, it wants a *RandomAccessStreamReference* that references an encoded bitmap image. You can create a *RandomAccessStreamReference* from an *InMemoryRandomAccessStream*. That's the job of the *GetBitmapStream* method referenced in the call to *SetBitmap*.

Notice that the argument to the *GetBitmapStream* call is the *WriteableBitmap* stored as a field in *MainPage*. I made the *GetBitmapStream* somewhat generalized in that it creates its own *pixels* array from that argument, but there's no reason why it couldn't access the existing *pixels* array also stored as a field in MainPage:

Project: FingerPaint | File: MainPage.Share.cs (excerpt)

```
async Task<RandomAccessStreamReference> GetBitmapStream(WriteableBitmap bitmap)
{
    // Get a pixels array for this bitmap
    byte[] pixels = new byte[4 * bitmap.PixelWidth * bitmap.PixelHeight];
    Stream stream = bitmap.PixelBuffer.AsStream();
    await stream.ReadAsync(pixels, 0, pixels.Length);

    // Create a BitmapEncoder associated with a memory stream
    InMemoryRandomAccessStream memoryStream = new InMemoryRandomAccessStream();
    BitmapEncoder encoder = await BitmapEncoder.CreateAsync(BitmapEncoder.PngEncoderId,
                                                            memoryStream);

    // Set the pixels into that encoder
    encoder.SetPixelData(BitmapPixelFormat.Bgra8, BitmapAlphaMode.Premultiplied,
                         (uint)bitmap.PixelWidth, (uint)bitmap.PixelHeight, 96, 96, pixels);
    await encoder.FlushAsync();

    // Return a RandomAccessStreamReference
    return RandomAccessStreamReference.CreateFromStream(memoryStream);
}
```

The Paste logic is a bit more complex, and not only because the button must be enabled based on the existence of bitmap content in the clipboard. If the current painting hasn't been saved and the user presses the Paste button, the program should request whether that artwork should be saved or abandoned, just as if the user had elected to load a new file.

That means that the handler for the Paste button should call the *CheckIfOkToTrashFile* method in MainPage.File.cs, passing to it a method that should be executed if the Paste operation should proceed. It was unclear to me how much processing of the incoming bitmap I should do before calling *CheckIfOkToTrashFile*. I was worried that the user might elect to save the existing picture and somehow the contents of the clipboard would change during that time. I avoid that problem by getting the pixels array right away. However, the code doesn't create the *WriteableBitmap* just yet. Delaying that job required that several items associated with the new bitmap be saved as fields:

Project: FingerPaint | File: MainPage.Share.cs (excerpt)

```
public sealed partial class MainPage : Page
{
    int pastedPixelWidth, pastedPixelHeight;
    byte[] pastedPixels;
    ...
```

```
async void OnPasteAppBarButtonClick(object sender, RoutedEventArgs args)
{
    // Temporarily disable the Paste button
    Button button = sender as Button;
    button.IsEnabled = false;

    // Get the Clipboard contents and check for a bitmap
    DataPackageView dataView = Clipboard.GetContent();

    if (dataView.Contains(StandardDataFormats.Bitmap))
    {
        // Get the stream reference and a stream
        RandomAccessStreamReference streamRef = await dataView.GetBitmapAsync();
        IRandomAccessStreamWithContentType stream = await streamRef.OpenReadAsync();

        // Create a BitmapDecoder for reading the bitmap
        BitmapDecoder decoder = await BitmapDecoder.CreateAsync(stream);
        BitmapFrame bitmapFrame = await decoder.GetFrameAsync(0);
        PixelDataProvider pixelProvider =
            await bitmapFrame.GetPixelDataAsync(BitmapPixelFormat.Bgra8,
                                                BitmapAlphaMode.Premultiplied,
                                                new BitmapTransform(),
                                                ExifOrientationMode.RespectExifOrientation,
                                                ColorManagementMode.ColorManageToSRgb);

        // Save information sufficient for creating WriteableBitmap
        pastedPixelWidth = (int)bitmapFrame.PixelWidth;
        pastedPixelHeight = (int)bitmapFrame.PixelHeight;
        pastedPixels = pixelProvider.DetachPixelData();

         // Check if it's OK to replace the current painting
        await CheckIfOkToTrashFile(FinishPasteBitmapAndPixelArray);
    }

    // Re-enable the button and close the app bar
    button.IsEnabled = true;
    this.BottomAppBar.IsOpen = false;
}

async Task FinishPasteBitmapAndPixelArray()
{
    bitmap = new WriteableBitmap(pastedPixelWidth, pastedPixelHeight);
    pixels = pastedPixels;

    // Transfer pixels to bitmap, among other chores
    await InitializeBitmap();

    // Set AppSettings properties for new image
    appSettings.LoadedFilePath = null;
    appSettings.LoadedFilename = null;
    appSettings.IsImageModified = false;
}
...
}
```

There's just one more job that needs to be done to implement this clipboard support: Many users are familiar with using Ctrl+C and Ctrl+V for performing Copy and Paste operations, so I added that support to MainPage.Share.cs as well, piggy-backing off the existing button handlers.

Project: FingerPaint | File: MainPage.Share.cs (excerpt)

```
public sealed partial class MainPage : Page
{
    ...
    void InitializeSharing()
    {
        ...
        // Watch for accelerator keys for Copy and Paste
        Window.Current.CoreWindow.Dispatcher.AcceleratorKeyActivated +=
                                                    OnAcceleratorKeyActivated;
        ...
    }
    ...
    void OnAcceleratorKeyActivated(CoreDispatcher sender, AcceleratorKeyEventArgs args)
    {
        if ((args.EventType == CoreAcceleratorKeyEventType.SystemKeyDown ||
             args.EventType == CoreAcceleratorKeyEventType.KeyDown) &&
            (args.VirtualKey == VirtualKey.C || args.VirtualKey == VirtualKey.V))
        {
            CoreWindow window = Window.Current.CoreWindow;
            CoreVirtualKeyStates down = CoreVirtualKeyStates.Down;

            // Only want case where Ctrl is down
            if ((window.GetKeyState(VirtualKey.Shift) & down) == down ||
                (window.GetKeyState(VirtualKey.Control) & down) != down ||
                (window.GetKeyState(VirtualKey.Menu) & down) == down)
            {
                return;
            }

            if (args.VirtualKey == VirtualKey.C)
            {
                OnCopyAppBarButtonClick(null, null);
            }
            else if (args.VirtualKey == VirtualKey.V)
            {
                OnPasteAppBarButtonClick(pasteAppBarButton, null);
            }
        }
    }
}
```

The Share Charm

A program can use the Share charm in two ways. What I'll be showing you here is how a program can provide data to other applications. It is rather more difficult for an application to function as a target for data from other applications. This second job requires that an application assert itself as a Share Target in the Declarations section of Package.appxmanifest, be activated in a unique state, and provide a special user interface for that purpose.

A program can be a Share provider by setting an event handler for a *DataTransferManager* instance, and a program that provides a bitmap to another application does so with the same *RandomAccessStreamReference* used to copy a bitmap to the clipboard. With the *GetBitmapStream* method already defined in MainPage.Share.cs, the additional code to support the Share charm is nearly trivial:

Project: FingerPaint | **File:** MainPage.Share.cs (excerpt)

```
public sealed partial class MainPage : Page
{
    ...
    void InitializeSharing()
    {
        ...
        // Hook into the Share pane for providing data
        DataTransferManager.GetForCurrentView().DataRequested += OnDataTransferDataRequested;
    }

    async void OnDataTransferDataRequested(DataTransferManager sender,
                                           DataRequestedEventArgs args)
    {
        DataRequestDeferral deferral = args.Request.GetDeferral();

        // Get a stream reference and hand it over
        RandomAccessStreamReference reference = await GetBitmapStream(bitmap);
        args.Request.Data.SetBitmap(reference);
        args.Request.Data.Properties.Title = "Finger Paint";
        args.Request.Data.Properties.Description = "Share this painting with another app";

        deferral.Complete();
    }
}
```

Now when the user selects the Share charm when FingerPaint is running, instead of the pane derisively reporting that "This app can't share," it says "Finger Paint" and "Share this painting with another app." Obviously, the *DataRequested* event handler has already been called and Windows has the *RandomAccessStreamReference*, so what follows in the Share pane is a list of those applications that can accept bitmap data. There is no further interaction required of the program because it has already provided the bitmap.

Basic Printing

For any program shown so far in this book, if you invoke the charms and press the Devices charm, you'll get a Devices pane that won't mention anything about printers. Your application needs to register with Windows 8 that it is capable of printing.

Three namespaces play a role in printing:

- The *Windows.UI.Xaml.Printing* namespace has the *PrintDocument* class and support for its events. As the name suggests, a *PrintDocument* represents something that the user of your program wishes to print.

- The *Windows.Graphics.Printing* namespace has *PrintManager*, which is the interface to the pane that Windows 8 provides that lists printers and printer options; and the *PrintTask*, *PrintTaskRequest*, and *PrintTaskOptions* classes. A print "task" is the same thing as a print "job"—a particular use of the printer to print a particular document.

- The *Windows.Graphics.Printing.OptionDetails* namespace contains classes you'll use for customizing printing options.

Much of the printer API involves overhead rather than the process of actually defining text and graphics for the printer page. Indeed, a Windows 8 application prints on a printer page in the same way that it draws on the screen: with a visual tree of instances of classes that derive from *UIElement*. Generally, the root element is a *Border* or a *Panel* of some sort with children. This visual tree can be defined in XAML but is probably more often constructed in code.

When defining elements to be displayed on the screen, one useful guideline is to treat the video display as if it has a resolution of 96 pixels per inch. For the printer, you do the same except that the equivalence is exact. Regardless of the actual resolution of the printer, you always treat it as a 96 DPI device.

To persuade Windows 8 to list printers when the user taps the Devices charm, the first task is to set an event handler:

```
PrintManager printManager = PrintManager.GetForCurrentView();
printManager.PrintTaskRequested += OnPrintManagerPrintTaskRequested;
```

Those two lines can be combined into one:

```
PrintManager.GetForCurrentView().PrintTaskRequested += OnPrintManagerPrintTaskRequested;
```

The static *GetForCurrentView* method obtains a *PrintManager* instance that is associated with your program's window. By setting a handler for the *PrintTaskRequested* event, your program is announcing its availability for printing. The handler looks like this:

```
void OnPrintManagerPrintTaskRequested(PrintManager sender, PrintTaskRequestedEventArgs args)
{
    ...
}
```

That handler is called when the user clicks the Devices charm (or presses Windows+K), but (as you'll see shortly) it needs to call another method with a callback function in order for Windows to display the list of printers.

This *PrintTaskRequested* handler should be attached only when the application is in a position to actually print something. If the application requires some preliminary information from the user or needs to load a document before it can legitimately print, the handler should not be attached to the *PrintTaskRequested* event. The handler should be detached when the program finds itself again in a position where it doesn't make any sense to print anything:

```
PrintManager.GetForCurrentView().PrintTaskRequested -= OnPrintManagerPrintTaskRequested;
```

In the sample programs in this chapter, I mostly attach and detach this event handler in the *OnNavigatedTo* and *OnNavigatedFrom* overrides as a symbolic representation of this process.

The handler for the *PrintTaskRequested* event is one of five callback methods and event handlers required of a program that performs simple printing. All five are required. Moreover, before the *PrintTaskRequested* event is even fired, your program needs to have prepared itself for printing by creating a *PrintDocument* object and attaching three event handlers to it.

So, let's look at a complete program that prints a one-page document consisting of a single *TextBlock* announcing "Hello, Printer!" The XAML file in the HelloPrinter project doesn't play a role in the program logic and simply informs a new user how to print something:

Project: HelloPrinter | **File:** MainPage.xaml (excerpt)

```
<Grid Background="{StaticResource ApplicationPageBackgroundThemeBrush}">
    <TextBlock FontSize="48"
               HorizontalAlignment="Center"
               VerticalAlignment="Center"
               TextAlignment="Center">
        Hello, Printer!
        <LineBreak />
        <Run FontSize="24">
            (Invoke charms, select Devices and a printer)
        </Run>
    </TextBlock>
</Grid>
```

The code-behind file defines three fields, one of which is the *TextBlock* that the program prints:

Project: HelloPrinter | **File:** MainPage.xaml.cs (excerpt)

```
public sealed partial class MainPage : Page
{
    PrintDocument printDocument;
    IPrintDocumentSource printDocumentSource;
```

```
    // UIElement to print
    TextBlock txtblk = new TextBlock
    {
        Text = "Hello, Printer!",
        FontFamily = new FontFamily("Times New Roman"),
        FontSize = 48,
        Foreground = new SolidColorBrush(Colors.Black)
    };
    ...
}
```

The *PrintDocument* object represents what your application prints. Generally, a program will create just one *PrintDocument* object and use it for every print task. In some cases, it might make sense for a program to maintain multiple *PrintDocument* objects—perhaps one to print the whole document, another to print a document outline, and a third to print thumbnails—but you shouldn't be creating new *PrintDocument* objects for every print task. (As you'll see, by the time a print task is requested, it's actually too late to create the *PrintDocument*!) If it's convenient, you can derive a class from *PrintDocument* to encapsulate some printing logic, but there's nothing in *PrintDocument* to override.

For a program that deals with a single type of document, you'll probably define the *PrintDocument* and *IPrintDocumentSource* as fields as I've done and create the *PrintDocument* object during program initialization:

Project: HelloPrinter | File: MainPage.xaml.cs (excerpt)

```
public sealed partial class MainPage : Page
{
    ...
    public MainPage()
    {
        this.InitializeComponent();

        // Create PrintDocument and attach handlers
        printDocument = new PrintDocument();
        printDocumentSource = printDocument.DocumentSource;
        printDocument.Paginate += OnPrintDocumentPaginate;
        printDocument.GetPreviewPage += OnPrintDocumentGetPreviewPage;
        printDocument.AddPages += OnPrintDocumentAddPages;
    }
    ...
}
```

The second field—the object of type *IPrintDocumentSource*—is obtained from the *PrintDocument* object. In addition, three events defined by *PrintDocument* require handlers. These event handlers are responsible for supplying a page count as well as the actual pages for print preview and actual printing.

The HelloPrinter program attaches a handler for the *PrintTaskRequested* event of the *PrintManager* during *OnNavigatedTo* and detaches it during *OnNavigatedFrom*, using two statements in the first case and one statement in the second just for a little variety.

Project: HelloPrinter | File: MainPage.xaml.cs (excerpt)

```
public sealed partial class MainPage : Page
{
    ...

    protected override void OnNavigatedTo(NavigationEventArgs args)
    {
        // Attach PrintManager handler
        PrintManager printManager = PrintManager.GetForCurrentView();
        printManager.PrintTaskRequested += OnPrintManagerPrintTaskRequested;

        base.OnNavigatedTo(args);
    }

    protected override void OnNavigatedFrom(NavigationEventArgs e)
    {
        // Detach PrintManager handler
        PrintManager.GetForCurrentView().PrintTaskRequested -= OnPrintManagerPrintTaskRequested;

        base.OnNavigatedFrom(e);
    }
    ...
}
```

In a real-life program, you'll be attaching this handler when your program is capable of printing, and detaching it when it has nothing to print.

When your program has this handler attached and the user sweeps a finger on the right side of the screen and then selects Devices, the *PrintTaskRequested* event handler is called. Here's the standard way to respond to that event:

Project: HelloPrinter | File: MainPage.xaml.cs (excerpt)

```
void OnPrintManagerPrintTaskRequested(PrintManager sender, PrintTaskRequestedEventArgs args)
{
    args.Request.CreatePrintTask("Hello Printer", OnPrintTaskSourceRequested);
}
```

The event arguments to the *PrintTaskRequested* event include a property of type *Request*, and the program usually responds by calling the *CreatePrintTask* method of that *Request* object, passing to it the name of the printer task—this could be the name of the application or the name of a document being printed by the application—and a callback function. The *CreatePrintTask* method returns a *PrintTask* object, but it's not usually necessary to retain that object here.

Windows 8 then displays a list of printers. Here's what comes up on my screen (your mileage may vary):

The only real printer here is the first one on the list. The second two items cause printing output to be saved in files. The last item isn't a printer at all and instead configures the second monitor attached to my tablet.

The callback I've named *OnPrintTaskSourceRequested* is called when the user selects one of the printers on the list. In the simplest case, the handler can respond by calling *SetSource* on the event arguments, passing to it the *IPrintDocumentSource* object obtained earlier from the *PrintDocument* object:

Project: HelloPrinter | File: MainPage.xaml.cs (excerpt)

```
void OnPrintTaskSourceRequested(PrintTaskSourceRequestedArgs args)
{
    args.SetSource(printDocumentSource);
}
```

When this method returns control back to Windows, a printer-specific pane is displayed:

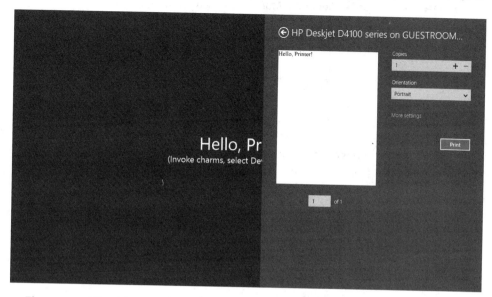

The name of the printer at the top of the screen might look a little odd. This particular printer isn't actually attached to the tablet on which I'm working but is instead on a computer in the guest room of the house where I'm writing this chapter, and what you're seeing there is part of that computer's name.

Over at the right is a box to specify the number of copies and a drop-down to select Portrait or Landscape. These are standard settings for printers. (For the "Send To OneNote 2010" and "Microsoft XPS Document Writer" options, only the Orientation option is shown in this area.) Pressing "More settings" makes available an option to select page size as well as some printer-specific options.

At the left of this pane is a preview of the page to be printed. If the document has more than one page, you can select the page to view by using the little box below it. But the page preview is a *FlipView* control, and it's easiest just to sweep it from side to side.

The total number of pages comes from the handler for the *Paginate* event, which is one of the three events defined by *PrintDocument*. Handlers for all three of these events were attached in the *MainPage* constructor. In HelloPrinter the *Paginate* handler is implemented simply like this:

Project: HelloPrinter | **File:** MainPage.xaml.cs (excerpt)

```
void OnPrintDocumentPaginate(object sender, PaginateEventArgs args)
{
    printDocument.SetPreviewPageCount(1, PreviewPageCountType.Final);
}
```

This *Paginate* handler is the application's opportunity to prepare all the pages for printing and then call a *PrintDocument* method indicating the number of pages available and whether this is a preliminary or final count. (If it's not possible or convenient to do all that work in one shot, things get a little more complex.)

The preview of the print page is supplied by the handler for the *GetPreviewPage* event also defined by *PrintDocument* and also set earlier in the *MainPage* constructor:

Project: HelloPrinter | File: MainPage.xaml.cs (excerpt)

```
void OnPrintDocumentGetPreviewPage(object sender, GetPreviewPageEventArgs args)
{
    printDocument.SetPreviewPage(args.PageNumber, txtblk);
}
```

The *PageNumber* property of the event arguments is one-based and can range from 1 to the number specified in the *SetPreviewPageCount* call. For this particular program, it will always equal 1. The program responds to this event by calling the *SetPreviewPage* method of *PrintDocument*, passing to it the page number and the *TextBlock* that I defined as a field. That's what's displayed in the print preview.

When the Print button is pressed, the final event handler is called:

Project: HelloPrinter | File: MainPage.xaml.cs (excerpt)

```
void OnPrintDocumentAddPages(object sender, AddPagesEventArgs args)
{
    printDocument.AddPage(txtblk);
    printDocument.AddPagesComplete();
}
```

The handler for the *AddPages* event is responsible for calling *AddPage* for every page in the document. In the usual case, these are the same objects passed to the *SetPreviewPage* method, but you do have an opportunity to make them different if you wish. It concludes with a call to *AddPagesComplete*. The printing pane disappears, and (with any luck) you'll hear the familiar sound of a printer kicking into action.

Watch out! The *Paginate* handler can be called more than once, particularly if the user starts playing around with various printer options. If your program is actually performing a lot of work to paginate the document, you'll probably want to avoid repeating it when the actual layout of the page doesn't change. In a real-life program generally you'll assemble all your pages in a *List* object during the *Paginate* handler and then deliver them up in the *GetPreviewPage* and *AddPages* handlers.

The *TextBlock* that HelloPrinter prints is given a *FontSize* of 48. That *TextBlock* might appear to have somewhat different sizes when it's seen on video displays of different sizes and resolutions. But when it's printed, that *FontSize* of 48 is an exact measurement and means 48/96 inch, which is half an inch or 36 points.

You'll notice I specified that the *Foreground* property of that printable *TextBlock* is black. Because this program uses a dark theme, the default *Foreground* property is white, and without an explicit *Foreground* setting, this *TextBlock* gets the default and would be invisible on white paper. This is the type of thing that can have you baffled for days! When experimenting with printer code, it might be helpful to get in the habit of using colors such as Red and Blue so that there's less of a chance of printing white text.

As you look over the code in HelloPrinter, you might think you see a couple ways to simplify it. For example, you might think you don't need to create a *PrintDocument* initially and save it as a field. You could simply create it in the *OnPrintTaskSourceRequested* method, set the three event handlers, and extract the *IPrintDocumentSource* object. The various *PrintDocument* event handlers can get access to the *PrintDocument* from the *sender* argument.

But this will not work. The *PrintDocument* needs to be created and accessed in the user-interface thread, and the *PrintTaskRequested* handler and the callback I've named *OnPrintTaskSourceRequested* do *not* run in the user-interface thread. If you wait until the *PrintTaskRequested* event is fired to create the *PrintDocument*, it's too late.

Printable and Unprintable Margins

Even with the caution of printing the *TextBlock* in black, it's not printed correctly on my printer, and it's probably not printed correctly on your printer either. The *TextBlock* is aligned smack against the upper-left corner of the page, and most printing mechanisms simply can't reach to the edge of the paper, which means that part of the text is sheared off.

If you try to solve this problem by setting the *HorizontalAlignment* and *VerticalAlignment* properties of the *TextBlock* to *Center*, you'll discover these properties don't work in this case. The alignment values are relative to a parent element, and this *TextBlock* has no parent because it's the top-level element on the printer page. *Margin* won't work either for the same reason. Setting the *Padding* property on the *TextBlock* will work, however, because that's something the *TextBlock* handles itself.

A much better general-purpose solution is for every printer page to be a visual tree that begins with a top-level *Border* object. When printed, this *Border* will occupy the entire size of the paper, but the *Border* can include a nonzero *Padding* property that effectively provides a margin for the entire page.

Both *PaginateEventArgs* and *AddPagesEventArgs* include a property named *PrintTaskOptions* of type *PrintTaskOptions*. Most of the properties of this object correspond to the printer properties that the user can set manually. These properties have names like *Collation*, *NumberOfCopies*, *Orientation*, and *PrintQuality*. A program can access these properties to customize printing, but this is generally not necessary. I'll show you later in this chapter how a program can initialize these properties and add some custom options.

PrintTaskOptions also has a method named *GetPageDescription*. The argument is a zero-based page number under the assumption that each page can be a different size. The *PrintPageDescription* structure returned from this method has *DpiX* and *DpiY* properties, which report the actual resolution of the printer (very often values like 600 or 1200) and a *PageSize* of type *Size* in units of 1/96 inch. For American standard letter size 8½ × 11" paper in portrait mode, the *PageSize* properties are 816 and 1056.

The *PrintPageDescription* structure also includes an *ImageableRect* property of type *Rect* that indicates the rectangular area of the page where the printer can actually print. For letter size paper on my printer, this rectangle has an upper-left corner at (12.48, 11.35748) and a size of (791.04, 988.1575), all in units of 1/96 inch. Compare this with the *PageSize* of 816 by 1056. Perform a few subtractions and you'll conclude that the printer can't print on the 12.48 units on the left and right edges, 11.35748 units on the top, and 56.48502 units (over ½ inch) on the bottom. In landscape mode, both *PageSize* and *ImageableRect* reflect the particular orientation of the page.

Let's examine how accurate these numbers are. The PrintPrintableArea program announces the name of itself in its XAML file:

Project: PrintPrintableArea | File: MainPage.xaml (excerpt)

```xaml
<Grid Background="{StaticResource ApplicationPageBackgroundThemeBrush}">
    <TextBlock Text="Print Printable Area"
               FontSize="24"
               HorizontalAlignment="Center"
               VerticalAlignment="Center" />
</Grid>
```

The code-behind file is structured very much like HelloPrinter except that the element to be printed by the program is rather more extensive, consisting of a *Border* with a red background, a nested *Border* with a white background and a black outline, and a centered *TextBlock*.

You'll notice also that instead of a separate callback method passed to the *CreatePrintTask* method, I've defined it as an anonymous lambda function. This is a common practice, but I've become less enamored of it for more complex printing logic:

Project: PrintPrintableArea | File: MainPage.xaml.cs (excerpt)

```csharp
public sealed partial class MainPage : Page
{
    PrintDocument printDocument;
    IPrintDocumentSource printDocumentSource;

    // Element to print
    Border border = new Border
    {
        Background = new SolidColorBrush(Colors.Red),

        Child = new Border
        {
            Background = new SolidColorBrush(Colors.White),
            BorderBrush = new SolidColorBrush(Colors.Black),
            BorderThickness = new Thickness(1),
            Child = new TextBlock
            {
                Text = "Print Printable Area",
                FontFamily = new FontFamily("Times New Roman"),
                FontSize = 24,
                Foreground = new SolidColorBrush(Colors.Black),
                HorizontalAlignment = HorizontalAlignment.Center,
                VerticalAlignment = VerticalAlignment.Center
            }
        }
    };

    public MainPage()
    {
        this.InitializeComponent();
```

```
    // Create PrintDocument and attach handlers
    printDocument = new PrintDocument();
    printDocumentSource = printDocument.DocumentSource;
    printDocument.Paginate += OnPrintDocumentPaginate;
    printDocument.GetPreviewPage += OnPrintDocumentGetPreviewPage;
    printDocument.AddPages += OnPrintDocumentAddPages;
}

protected override void OnNavigatedTo(NavigationEventArgs args)
{
    // Attach PrintManager handler
    PrintManager.GetForCurrentView().PrintTaskRequested += OnPrintManagerPrintTaskRequested;

    base.OnNavigatedTo(args);
}

protected override void OnNavigatedFrom(NavigationEventArgs e)
{
    // Detach PrintManager handler
    PrintManager.GetForCurrentView().PrintTaskRequested -= OnPrintManagerPrintTaskRequested;

    base.OnNavigatedFrom(e);
}

void OnPrintManagerPrintTaskRequested(PrintManager sender, PrintTaskRequestedEventArgs args)
{
    args.Request.CreatePrintTask("Print Printable Area", (requestArgs) =>
    {
        requestArgs.SetSource(printDocumentSource);
    });
}

void OnPrintDocumentPaginate(object sender, PaginateEventArgs args)
{
    PrintPageDescription printPageDescription = args.PrintTaskOptions.GetPageDescription(0);

    // Set Padding on outer Border
    double left = printPageDescription.ImageableRect.Left;
    double top = printPageDescription.ImageableRect.Top;
    double right = printPageDescription.PageSize.Width
                            - left - printPageDescription.ImageableRect.Width;
    double bottom = printPageDescription.PageSize.Height
                            - top - printPageDescription.ImageableRect.Height;
    border.Padding = new Thickness(left, top, right, bottom);

    printDocument.SetPreviewPageCount(1, PreviewPageCountType.Final);
}

void OnPrintDocumentGetPreviewPage(object sender, GetPreviewPageEventArgs args)
{
    printDocument.SetPreviewPage(args.PageNumber, border);
}

void OnPrintDocumentAddPages(object sender, AddPagesEventArgs args)
{
    printDocument.AddPage(border);
```

```
        printDocument.AddPagesComplete();
    }
}
```

The other big difference is the handler for the *Paginate* event of *PrintDocument*. The handler obtains the *PrintPageDescription* structure and calculates a *Padding* value that it applies to the outer *Border* of the element to be printed. As you can see, the preview displays the red background of the outer border to the edge of the paper:

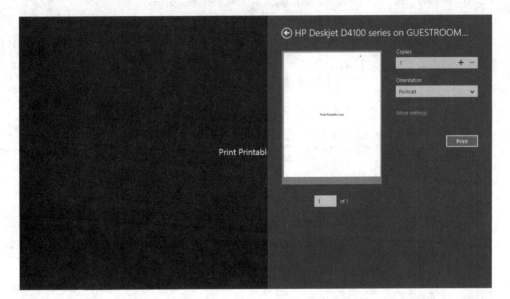

When the preview is displayed, try switching between Portrait and Landscape. Each change causes another call to the *Paginate* handler and a recalculation of the *Padding* value for the outer *Border*.

The preview obviously doesn't reflect the limitations of the printer in printing to the paper's edge. Otherwise, that red area wouldn't be visible at all. I was pleased to discover that the page that actually came out of the printer displayed the black inner *Border* just fine with only a tiny trace of the red background of the outer *Border*, indicating that the *ImageableRect* values for this printer are accurate.

Although a program that prints pictures and other bitmaps might want to print as large as possible on the page, most printing applications prefer to set a larger margin—perhaps an inch, more or less—either of a fixed size or customizable by the user. In these cases it's usually not necessary for the *ImageableRect* property to be accessed at all.

I'll have an example of user-supplied margins coming up.

The Pagination Process

In the general case, a Windows application prints more than a single page, and the number of pages might depend on many factors, for example, the length of a document, font sizes, paper size, page margins, and whether the page is in portrait or landscape mode.

It is the purpose of the *Paginate* event handler not only to prepare these pages for preview and printing, but to report the number of pages in the document. In some cases pagination might require some time, and there are ways to avoid doing it all at once, but it's easiest if you can do it in one shot.

Let's examine a fairly short pagination job by resurrecting the DependencyObjectClassHierarchy program from Chapter 4, "Presentation with Panels," and adding a print option to it. As you might recall, DependencyObjectClassHierarchy created a *TextBlock* for every class that derived from *DependencyObject* and put them all in a *StackPanel* in a *ScrollViewer*. The XAML file for the PrintableClassHierarchy program is the same as in the previous version:

Project: PrintableClassHierarchy | File: MainPage.xaml (excerpt)

```
<Grid Background="{StaticResource ApplicationPageBackgroundThemeBrush}">
    <ScrollViewer>
        <StackPanel Name="stackPanel" />
    </ScrollViewer>
</Grid>
```

I also decided to use a *StackPanel* containing *TextBlock* children for printing as well, but with a profound difference: For the screen, there's only one *StackPanel* because it's in a *ScrollViewer*. For printing, there must be a *StackPanel* for each page containing only the *TextBlock* elements for that page.

It is tempting to use the same *TextBlock* elements for the screen and the printer. In theory you can print elements already displayed on the screen, but it is my experience that this technique never really works as well as might be hoped. One major restriction is that a particular element cannot have two parents. In this example, a printed *TextBlock* must be a child of a *StackPanel* for the printer page, so it can't also be a child of a *StackPanel* on the screen.

For that reason, the revised version of the class hierarchy program creates a whole separate collection of *TextBlock* elements that it stores in a field named *printerTextBlocks*. This portion of the *MainPage* class is very similar to the code-behind file in DependencyObjectClassHierarchy except that the *TextBlock* creation code has been split into a separate method for the convenience of creating two parallel sets of *TextBlock* elements. Notice that the printer *TextBlock* elements are given an explicit *Foreground* of black in the *DisplayAndPrinterPrep* method (renamed from the earlier *Display* method). Most of the printing support is not shown in this excerpt:

Project: PrintableClassHierarchy | File: MainPage.xaml.cs (excerpt)

```
public sealed partial class MainPage : Page
{
    Type rootType = typeof(DependencyObject);
    TypeInfo rootTypeInfo = typeof(DependencyObject).GetTypeInfo();
    List<Type> classes = new List<Type>();
    Brush highlightBrush;

    // Printing support
    List<TextBlock> printerTextBlocks = new List<TextBlock>();
    Brush blackBrush = new SolidColorBrush(Colors.Black);
    ...
    public MainPage()
    {
```

```
            this.InitializeComponent();
            highlightBrush =
                new SolidColorBrush(new UISettings().UIElementColor(UIElementType.Highlight));

            // Accumulate all the classes that derive from DependencyObject
            AddToClassList(typeof(Windows.UI.Xaml.DependencyObject));

            // Sort them alphabetically by name
            classes.Sort((t1, t2) =>
            {
                return String.Compare(t1.GetTypeInfo().Name, t2.GetTypeInfo().Name);
            });

            // Put all these sorted classes into a tree structure
            ClassAndSubclasses rootClass = new ClassAndSubclasses(rootType);
            AddToTree(rootClass, classes);

            // Display the tree using TextBlocks added to StackPanel
            DisplayAndPrinterPrep(rootClass, 0);
            ...
        }
        ...
        void AddToClassList(Type sampleType)
        {
            Assembly assembly = sampleType.GetTypeInfo().Assembly;

            foreach (Type type in assembly.ExportedTypes)
            {
                TypeInfo typeInfo = type.GetTypeInfo();

                if (typeInfo.IsPublic && rootTypeInfo.IsAssignableFrom(typeInfo))
                    classes.Add(type);
            }
        }

        void AddToTree(ClassAndSubclasses parentClass, List<Type> classes)
        {
            foreach (Type type in classes)
            {
                Type baseType = type.GetTypeInfo().BaseType;

                if (baseType == parentClass.Type)
                {
                    ClassAndSubclasses subClass = new ClassAndSubclasses(type);
                    parentClass.Subclasses.Add(subClass);
                    AddToTree(subClass, classes);
                }
            }
        }

        void DisplayAndPrinterPrep(ClassAndSubclasses parentClass, int indent)
        {
            TypeInfo typeInfo = parentClass.Type.GetTypeInfo();

            // Create TextBlock and add to StackPanel
            TextBlock txtblk = CreateTextBlock(typeInfo, indent);
            stackPanel.Children.Add(txtblk);
```

```
        // Create TextBlock and add to printer list
        txtblk = CreateTextBlock(typeInfo, indent);
        txtblk.Foreground = blackBrush;
        printerTextBlocks.Add(txtblk);

        // Call this method recursively for all subclasses
        foreach (ClassAndSubclasses subclass in parentClass.Subclasses)
            DisplayAndPrinterPrep(subclass, indent + 1);
    }

    TextBlock CreateTextBlock(TypeInfo typeInfo, int indent)
    {
        // Create TextBlock with type name
        TextBlock txtblk = new TextBlock();
        txtblk.Inlines.Add(new Run { Text = new string(' ', 8 * indent) });
        txtblk.Inlines.Add(new Run { Text = typeInfo.Name });

        // Indicate if the class is sealed
        if (typeInfo.IsSealed)
            txtblk.Inlines.Add(new Run
            {
                Text = " (sealed)",
                Foreground = highlightBrush
            });

        // Indicate if the class can't be instantiated
        IEnumerable<ConstructorInfo> constructorInfos = typeInfo.DeclaredConstructors;
        int publicConstructorCount = 0;

        foreach (ConstructorInfo constructorInfo in constructorInfos)
            if (constructorInfo.IsPublic)
                publicConstructorCount += 1;

        if (publicConstructorCount == 0)
            txtblk.Inlines.Add(new Run
            {
                Text = " (non-instantiable)",
                Foreground = highlightBrush
            });

        return txtblk;
    }
    ...
}
```

The remainder of the printing support is very similar to what you've seen before, except that there's more than one page to print. The *Paginate* method takes on the brunt of the work and stores the formatted pages in the *printerPages* field. Each of these objects is a *Border* with *Padding* set to 96 (one inch) and a child *StackPanel* with a page worth of the *TextBlock* elements created earlier.

Keep in mind that the *Paginate* handler might be called multiple times as the user waffles between Portrait or Landscape mode, and letter or legal page sizes. Because the program is working with a fixed collection of *TextBlock* elements, and because elements are prohibited from having multiple parents, it's essential for the *Paginate* method to begin by ensuring that none of these *TextBlock* elements is still a child of a previously created *StackPanel*.

Project: PrintableClassHierarchy | **File:** MainPage.xaml.cs (excerpt)

```
public sealed partial class MainPage : Page
{
    ...
    PrintDocument printDocument;
    IPrintDocumentSource printDocumentSource;
    List<UIElement> printerPages = new List<UIElement>();

    public MainPage()
    {
        ...
        // Create PrintDocument and attach handlers
        printDocument = new PrintDocument();
        printDocumentSource = printDocument.DocumentSource;
        printDocument.Paginate += OnPrintDocumentPaginate;
        printDocument.GetPreviewPage += OnPrintDocumentGetPreviewPage;
        printDocument.AddPages += OnPrintDocumentAddPages;
    }

    protected override void OnNavigatedTo(NavigationEventArgs args)
    {
        // Attach PrintManager handler
        PrintManager.GetForCurrentView().PrintTaskRequested += OnPrintManagerPrintTaskRequested;

        base.OnNavigatedTo(args);
    }

    protected override void OnNavigatedFrom(NavigationEventArgs e)
    {
        // Detach PrintManager handler
        PrintManager.GetForCurrentView().PrintTaskRequested -= OnPrintManagerPrintTaskRequested;

        base.OnNavigatedFrom(e);
    }
    ...
    void OnPrintManagerPrintTaskRequested(PrintManager sender, PrintTaskRequestedEventArgs args)
    {
        args.Request.CreatePrintTask("Dependency Property Class Hierarchy", (requestArgs) =>
        {
            requestArgs.SetSource(printDocumentSource);
        });
    }

    void OnPrintDocumentPaginate(object sender, PaginateEventArgs args)
    {
        // Verbosely set some variables for the page margin
        double leftMargin = 96;
        double topMargin = 96;
        double rightMargin = 96;
        double bottomMargin = 96;
```

```
// Clear out previous printerPage collection
foreach (UIElement printerPage in printerPages)
    ((printerPage as Border).Child as Panel).Children.Clear();

printerPages.Clear();

// Initialize page construction
Border border = null;
StackPanel stackPanel = null;
double maxPageHeight = 0;
double pageHeight = 0;

// Look through the list of TextBlocks
for (int index = 0; index < printerTextBlocks.Count; index++)
{
    // A null Border object signals a new page
    if (border == null)
    {
        // Calculate the height available for text
        uint pageNumber = (uint)printerPages.Count;
        maxPageHeight =
            args.PrintTaskOptions.GetPageDescription(pageNumber).PageSize.Height;
        maxPageHeight -= topMargin + bottomMargin;
        pageHeight = 0;

        // Create StackPanel and Border
        stackPanel = new StackPanel();
        border = new Border
        {
            Padding = new Thickness(leftMargin, topMargin, rightMargin, bottomMargin),
            Child = stackPanel
        };

        // Add to the list of pages
        printerPages.Add(border);
    }

    // Get the TextBlock and measure it
    TextBlock txtblk = printerTextBlocks[index];
    txtblk.Measure(Size.Empty);

    // Check if OK to add TextBlock to this page
    if (stackPanel.Children.Count == 0 ||
        pageHeight + txtblk.ActualHeight < maxPageHeight)
    {
        stackPanel.Children.Add(txtblk);
        pageHeight += Math.Ceiling(txtblk.ActualHeight);
    }
```

```
            // Otherwise, it's the end of the page
            else
            {
                // No longer working with this Border object
                border = null;

                // Reprocess this TextBlock
                index--;
            }
        }
    }

    // Notify about the final page count
    printDocument.SetPreviewPageCount(printerPages.Count, PreviewPageCountType.Final);
}

void OnPrintDocumentGetPreviewPage(object sender, GetPreviewPageEventArgs args)
{
    printDocument.SetPreviewPage(args.PageNumber, printerPages[args.PageNumber - 1]);
}

void OnPrintDocumentAddPages(object sender, AddPagesEventArgs args)
{
    foreach (UIElement printerPage in printerPages)
        printDocument.AddPage(printerPage);

    printDocument.AddPagesComplete();
}
}
```

The strategy for pagination involves calculating a *maxPageHeight* number from the height of the paper page minus one-inch margins on the top and bottom. Another variable named *pageHeight* is increased for every *TextBlock* added to the *StackPanel* for that page. The method calls the *Measure* method on each *TextBlock* to calculate its size, and if the height of the *TextBlock* added to *pageHeight* exceeds *maxPageHeight*, a new page is required.

The *GetPreviewPage* handler uses the one-based *PageNumber* property in the event arguments to access the corresponding element in the *printerPages* list. The *AddPages* handler calls *AddPage* on all the pages.

In the preview, you can examine different pages before printing the whole list:

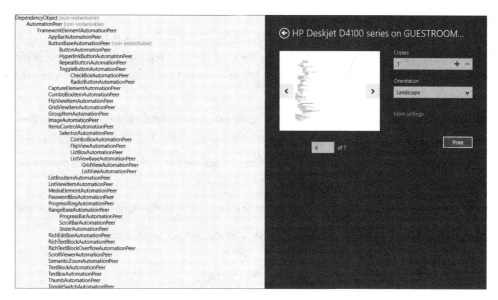

You might have noticed that the pagination logic increases the *pageHeight* based on each *Text-Block* height with the following code:

```
pageHeight += Math.Ceiling(txtblk.ActualHeight);
```

I originally wasn't using the *Math.Ceiling* call. The default *FontSize* is 11, and *ActualHeight* was reporting 13.2, and with that my program was giving each *StackPanel* 65 lines of text to display in the 9 inches available in portrait mode. However, in the preview, and coming out of the printer, only 62 lines were visible. The line spacing used to stack the text in the *StackPanel* was obviously greater than 13.2, resulting in three *TextBlock* elements per page being clipped because the resultant *StackPanel* was larger than the space allocated for it.

Using *Math.Ceiling* in this case resulted in 61 lines of text per page, which is a little off in the other direction, but at least none of the text disappears.

Still, it's a little odd. On a video display, of course, it makes perfect sense to align text with pixel boundaries for purposes of readability and that's why coordinates are rounded up to the next highest pixel. On a printer, however, there are 600 pixels (or so) to the inch, so the rounding doesn't need to be based on a 96 DPI device.

Pagination can be very complex, particularly when text is involved. If you encounter chronic problems with elements not appearing precisely where you want them on the printer page, you might want to switch to using a *Canvas*. The use of *Glyphs* rather than *TextBlock* is popular for sophisticated text layout needs, and if you run into a wall using *Glyphs*, you'll probably want to explore DirectWrite to render to both the screen and the printer page.

If you prefer going in the other direction—having the Windows Runtime do more of the work in determining how text is displayed—then using *RichTextBlock* (which I discussed in Chapter 16, "Rich Text") might be useful.

Custom Printing Properties

The one-inch margins in PrintableClassHierarchy are hard coded. Suppose you want to allow the user to select the margins. While we're at it, let's give the user the option of setting the font size used for printing.

It is possible without too much trouble to customize the printer setup pane, and to have the Windows Runtime do most of the work in creating the appropriate controls and managing input.

The place to perform this customization is in the handler for the *PrintTaskRequested* event of the *PrintManager*. So far, this handler has looked like this:

```
void OnPrintManagerPrintTaskRequested(PrintManager sender, PrintTaskRequestedEventArgs args)
{
    args.Request.CreatePrintTask("My Print Task Title", OnPrintTaskSourceRequested);
}
```

Or, it's used an anonymous lambda function for the callback:

```
void OnPrintManagerPrintTaskRequested(PrintManager sender, PrintTaskRequestedEventArgs args)
{
    args.Request.CreatePrintTask("My Print Task Title", (requestArgs) =>
    {
        requestArgs.SetSource(printDocumentSource);
    });
}
```

Whichever way you do it, the *CreatePrintTask* call actually returns an object of type *PrintTask*, so that object can be saved in a local variable:

```
void OnPrintManagerPrintTaskRequested(PrintManager sender, PrintTaskRequestedEventArgs args)
{
    PrintTask printTask = args.Request.CreatePrintTask("My Print Task Title", ... );
}
```

From that *PrintTask* object you can get an object of type *PrintTaskOptionDetails* via a roundabout static call that will probably resist becoming habitual:

```
PrintTaskOptionDetails optionDetails =
            PrintTaskOptionDetails.GetFromPrintTaskOptions(printTask.Options);
```

PrintTaskOptionDetails and related classes are defined in the *Windows.Graphics.Printing.OptionDetails* namespace.

If you want, you can then remove all the options from the first page of the printer setup pane:

```
optionDetails.DisplayedOptions.Clear();
```

Now you won't see the option to change the number of copies or the orientation. You could optionally put these back in, perhaps in reverse order:

```
optionDetails.DisplayedOptions.Add(StandardPrintTaskOptions.Orientation);
optionDetails.DisplayedOptions.Add(StandardPrintTaskOptions.Copies);
```

StandardPrintTaskOptions is a static class, and the properties represent standard printer options identified with string IDs. *StandardPrintTaskOptions.Orientation* is actually the string "PageOrientation" and *StandardPrintTaskOptions.Copies* is the string "JobCopiesAllDocuments". You can initialize these options if that is appropriate for your program:

```
optionDetails.Options[StandardPrintTaskOptions.Orientation].TrySetValue(
                                        PrintOrientation.Landscape);
```

PrintOrientation is one of eleven similar enumerations in *Windows.Graphics.Printing*.

You can add a less common option if you think it might be appropriate for your application:

```
optionDetails.DisplayedOptions.Add(StandardPrintTaskOptions.Collation);
```

You can also add your own items. You're limited to two types of custom options: a text field, or an expanding list of items like the *Orientation* option.

Let's create a new project named CustomizableClassHierarchy. This program is mostly the same as PrintableClassHierarchy but defines some customizable values as fields initialized with values that the program considers appropriate:

Project: CustomizableClassHierarchy | **File:** MainPage.xaml.cs (excerpt)

```
public sealed partial class MainPage : Page
{
    ...
    // Initial values of custom printer settings
    double fontSize = new TextBlock().FontSize;
    double leftMargin = 96;      // 1 inch
    double topMargin = 72;       // 3/4 inch
    double rightMargin = 96;
    double bottomMargin = 72;
    ...
}
```

These fields are accessed in the handler for the *PrintTaskRequested* event of the *PrintManager*. You'll recall that this event is fired when the user taps the Devices charm, probably in the process of selecting a printer:

Project: CustomizableClassHierarchy | File: MainPage.xaml.cs (excerpt)

```
void OnPrintManagerPrintTaskRequested(PrintManager sender, PrintTaskRequestedEventArgs args)
{
    PrintTask printTask = args.Request.CreatePrintTask("Dependency Property Class Hierarchy",
                                                       (requestArgs) =>
    {
        requestArgs.SetSource(printDocumentSource);
    });

    PrintTaskOptionDetails optionDetails =
                PrintTaskOptionDetails.GetFromPrintTaskOptions(printTask.Options);

    // Add item for font size
    optionDetails.CreateTextOption("idFontSize", "Font size (in points)");
    optionDetails.DisplayedOptions.Add("idFontSize");
    optionDetails.Options["idFontSize"].TrySetValue((72 * fontSize / 96).ToString());

    // Add items for page margins
    optionDetails.CreateTextOption("idLeftMargin", "Left margin (in inches)");
    optionDetails.DisplayedOptions.Add("idLeftMargin");
    optionDetails.Options["idLeftMargin"].TrySetValue((leftMargin / 96).ToString());

    optionDetails.CreateTextOption("idTopMargin", "Top margin (in inches)");
    optionDetails.DisplayedOptions.Add("idTopMargin");
    optionDetails.Options["idTopMargin"].TrySetValue((topMargin / 96).ToString());

    optionDetails.CreateTextOption("idRightMargin", "Right margin (in inches)");
    optionDetails.DisplayedOptions.Add("idRightMargin");
    optionDetails.Options["idRightMargin"].TrySetValue((rightMargin / 96).ToString());

    optionDetails.CreateTextOption("idBottomMargin", "Bottom margin (in inches)");
    optionDetails.DisplayedOptions.Add("idBottomMargin");
    optionDetails.Options["idBottomMargin"].TrySetValue((bottomMargin / 96).ToString());

    // Set handler for the option changing
    optionDetails.OptionChanged += OnOptionDetailsOptionChanged;
}
```

Each custom option requires at least two steps and possibly three. First the option must be created, in the process giving it an ID string and a label that appears on the printer settings pane. The custom option is then added to the *DisplayedOptions* collection. The third step is optional but sets an initial value. In my code, the fields storing these values are converted from pixels into points (for the font size) and inches (for the margin values).

The method concludes by setting an event handler for the *OptionChanged* event. This event will be fired for changes to all the printer options, not just the custom options. For text items like these, the event is not fired with every keystroke but only with a press of the Enter key, loss of input focus, or a press of the Print button. Here's what the customized settings pane looks like:

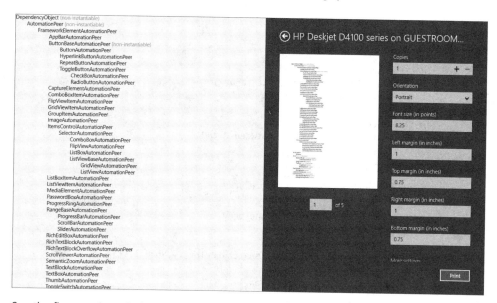

See the five new items? I know it looks like we've gone beyond the limit of the size available for custom options, but the list is scrollable.

Here's the implementation of the *OptionChanged* event handler. This is where validation occurs, and where you signal that the preview needs to be refreshed with new values, which forces your *Paginate* handler to be called again. The *PrintTaskOptionChangedEventArgs* class defines just one property—named *OptionId* of type *object* (but it's really a string) indicating the option that's changed—but you'll need to make use of the *sender* argument as well. That's the *PrintTaskOptionDetails* object you used during the customization in the *PrintTaskRequested* handler:

Project: CustomizableClassHierarchy | File: MainPage.xaml.cs (excerpt)

```
async void OnOptionDetailsOptionChanged(PrintTaskOptionDetails sender,
                                        PrintTaskOptionChangedEventArgs args)
{
    if (args.OptionId == null)
        return;

    string optionId = args.OptionId.ToString();
    string strValue = sender.Options[optionId].Value.ToString();
    string errorText = String.Empty;
    double value = 0;

    switch (optionId)
    {
        case "idFontSize":
            if (!Double.TryParse(strValue, out value))
                errorText = "Value must be numeric";
```

```
        else if (value < 4 || value > 36)
            errorText = "Value must be between 4 and 36";
        break;

    case "idLeftMargin":
    case "idTopMargin":
    case "idRightMargin":
    case "idBottomMargin":
        if (!Double.TryParse(strValue, out value))
            errorText = "Value must be numeric";

        else if (value < 0 || value > 2)
            errorText = "Value must be between 0 and 2";
        break;
}

sender.Options[optionId].ErrorText = errorText;

// If there's no error, then invalidate the preview
if (String.IsNullOrEmpty(errorText))
{
    await this.Dispatcher.RunAsync(CoreDispatcherPriority.Normal, () =>
        {
            printDocument.InvalidatePreview();
        });
}
}
```

If there's a problem with the input on one of the options, this method needs to set the *ErrorText* property for that option to a short but helpful text string. That string is displayed in red to the user. If the *ErrorText* of any option is set, the Print button also becomes disabled. Here's what it looks like:

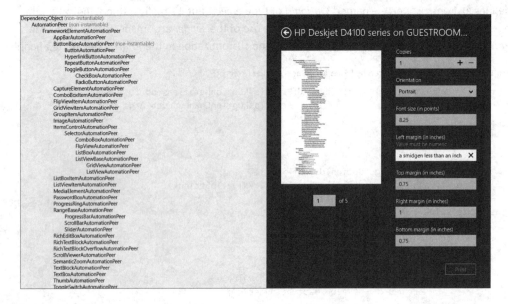

Notice how everything below the error message has been shifted down. If the error message you supply is longer than a line, it will be wrapped.

If there's no error, the *InvalidatePreview* method of the *PrintDocument* object should be called. Notice that a *CoreDispatcher* is required to force that call to occur in the user-interface thread. This *OptionChanged* handler runs in a secondary thread.

The *InvalidatePreview* call causes a new *Paginate* event to be fired on the *PrintDocument*. This new version of the *Paginate* handler begins by obtaining all the custom values and converting them into numbers that it can use. The font size is applied to all the *TextBlock* elements stored for printing, and the margin values are used as in the previous version of this method:

Project: CustomizableClassHierarchy | **File:** MainPage.xaml.cs (excerpt)

```
void OnPrintDocumentPaginate(object sender, PaginateEventArgs args)
{
    // Get values of custom settings
    PrintTaskOptionDetails optionDetails =
                PrintTaskOptionDetails.GetFromPrintTaskOptions(args.PrintTaskOptions);
    fontSize = 96 * Double.Parse(optionDetails.Options["idFontSize"].Value.ToString()) / 72;
    leftMargin = 96 * Double.Parse(optionDetails.Options["idLeftMargin"].Value.ToString());
    topMargin = 96 * Double.Parse(optionDetails.Options["idTopMargin"].Value.ToString());
    rightMargin = 96 * Double.Parse(optionDetails.Options["idRightMargin"].Value.ToString());
    bottomMargin = 96 * Double.Parse(optionDetails.Options["idBottomMargin"].Value.ToString());

    // Set FontSize of stored TextBlocks
    foreach (TextBlock txtblk in printerTextBlocks)
        txtblk.FontSize = fontSize;
    ...
}
```

With a little more work, you can check that the margin values entered by the user are high enough to avoid text appearing in the unprintable area of the page. In the *OptionChanged* handler you can easily access the page description from the *PrintTaskOptionDetails* object:

```
Rect imageableRect = sender.GetPageDescription(0).ImageableRect;
```

Printing a Monthly Planner

Sometimes when I'm working on a long project I like to use printed monthly calendars taped up to the wall. These calendars don't need any fancy features—just a lot of white space to write stuff in for each day.

The sole purpose of the PrintMonthlyPlanner program is to print a bunch of monthly calendars in a range specified by the user. The main page looks like this:

Each month and year is selectable via a *FlipView* control. The button is enabled only if the start month is less than or equal to the end month. The *Click* handler for the button is implemented with just a single line of code:

```
await PrintManager.ShowPrintUIAsync();
```

Although the user normally invokes the charms and Devices pane, a program can do so as well. Generally, this option is reserved for programs that print only on special occasions, for example, "Print

Ticket Confirmation." Interestingly, calling *ShowPrintUIAsync* brings up a slightly different pane than the Devices charm:

Because the PrintMonthlyPlanner program is dedicated to printing, the pages that it prints are not otherwise displayed by the program and are only visible on screen in the printing pane:

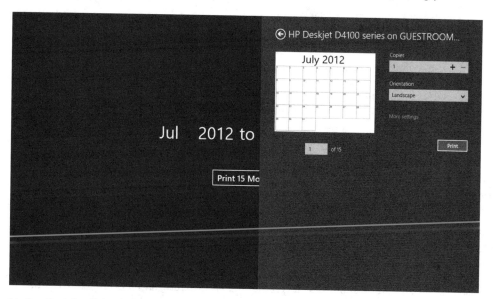

Notice that the Orientation is set to Landscape. The program sets that initial value under the assumption that the calendar pages are better formatted in landscape. Each page is printed to the very edge of the printable margins.

I created a custom control for the user to pick a month and year. This is called *MonthYearSelect*, and the XAML file reveals two templated *FlipView* controls, both with a horizontal *StackPanel* as the *ItemsPanel*:

Project: PrintMonthlyPlanner | File: MonthYearSelect.xaml (excerpt)

```
<UserControl ... >
    <UserControl.Resources>
        <Style TargetType="FlipView">
            <Setter Property="ItemsPanel">
                <Setter.Value>
                    <ItemsPanelTemplate>
                        <StackPanel Orientation="Vertical" />
                    </ItemsPanelTemplate>
                </Setter.Value>
            </Setter>

            <Setter Property="ItemTemplate">
                <Setter.Value>
                    <DataTemplate>
                        <TextBlock Text="{Binding}" VerticalAlignment="Center" />
                    </DataTemplate>
                </Setter.Value>
            </Setter>
        </Style>
    </UserControl.Resources>

    <Grid>
        <StackPanel Orientation="Horizontal">
            <FlipView x:Name="monthFlipView"
                    SelectionChanged="OnMonthYearSelectionChanged" />

            <TextBlock Text="&#x00A0;" />

            <FlipView x:Name="yearFlipView"
                    SelectionChanged="OnMonthYearSelectionChanged" />
        </StackPanel>
    </Grid>
</UserControl>
```

Partially to make use of new features in the Windows Runtime, I decided to make the public interface to this class a *Calendar* object rather than a traditional .NET *DateTime*. I was hoping to make the program generalized for any type of calendar, but the *Calendar* class doesn't seem to be documented sufficiently to go beyond the standard Gregorian. I couldn't even discover a way to determine if the day of the week should begin on a Sunday (the standard in most places) or Monday (used in France, for example).

I also discovered that *Calendar* is a class rather than a structure, and it bothered me to be generating new *Calendar* objects with every spin of the *FlipView*. I decided that the control would create just one *Calendar* object and change the *Month* and *Year* properties of that single object. But in that case it made no sense for *Calendar* to be exposed as a dependency property, which is customary with controls, so that's why the property of type *Calendar* is a plain old property named *MonthYear* supplemented with a *MonthYearChanged* event to indicate new values of *Month* or *Year*:

Project: PrintMonthlyPlanner | File: MonthYearSelect.xaml.cs (excerpt)

```
public sealed partial class MonthYearSelect : UserControl
{
    public event EventHandler MonthYearChanged;

    public MonthYearSelect()
    {
        this.InitializeComponent();

        // Create Calendar with current date
        Calendar calendar = new Calendar();
        calendar.SetToNow();

        // Fill the first FlipView with the abbreviated month names
        DateTimeFormatter monthFormatter =
            new DateTimeFormatter(YearFormat.None, MonthFormat.Abbreviated,
                                  DayFormat.None, DayOfWeekFormat.None);

        for (int month = 1; month <= 12; month++)
        {
            string strMonth = monthFormatter.Format(
                            new DateTimeOffset(2000, month, 15, 0, 0, 0, TimeSpan.Zero));
            monthFlipView.Items.Add(strMonth);
        }

        // Fill the second FlipView with years (5 years before current, 25 after)
        for (int year = calendar.Year - 5; year <= calendar.Year + 25; year++)
        {
            yearFlipView.Items.Add(year);
        }

        // Set the FlipViews to the current month and year
        monthFlipView.SelectedIndex = calendar.Month - 1;
        yearFlipView.SelectedItem = calendar.Year;
        this.MonthYear = calendar;
    }

    public Calendar MonthYear { private set; get; }

    void OnMonthYearSelectionChanged(object sender, SelectionChangedEventArgs args)
    {
        if (this.MonthYear == null)
            return;

        if (monthFlipView.SelectedIndex != -1)
            this.MonthYear.Month = (int)monthFlipView.SelectedIndex + 1;

        if (yearFlipView.SelectedIndex != -1)
            this.MonthYear.Year = (int)yearFlipView.SelectedItem;
```

```
            // Fire the event
        if (MonthYearChanged != null)
            MonthYearChanged(this, EventArgs.Empty);
    }
}
```

The MainPage.xaml file instantiates two of these *MonthYearSelect* controls:

Project: PrintMonthlyPlanner | File: MainPage.xaml (excerpt)

```
<Page ...
    FontSize="48">

    <Grid Background="{StaticResource ApplicationPageBackgroundThemeBrush}">
        <Grid HorizontalAlignment="Center"
              VerticalAlignment="Center">
            <Grid.ColumnDefinitions>
                <ColumnDefinition Width="Auto" />
                <ColumnDefinition Width="*" />
                <ColumnDefinition Width="Auto" />
            </Grid.ColumnDefinitions>

            <Grid.RowDefinitions>
                <RowDefinition Height="Auto" />
                <RowDefinition Height="Auto" />
            </Grid.RowDefinitions>

            <local:MonthYearSelect x:Name="monthYearSelect1"
                                   Grid.Row="0" Grid.Column="0"
                                   Height="144"
                                   VerticalAlignment="Center"
                                   MonthYearChanged="OnMonthYearChanged" />

            <TextBlock Text=" to&#x00A0;"
                       Grid.Row="0" Grid.Column="1"
                       VerticalAlignment="Center" />

            <local:MonthYearSelect x:Name="monthYearSelect2"
                                   Grid.Row="0" Grid.Column="2"
                                   Height="144"
                                   VerticalAlignment="Center"
                                   MonthYearChanged="OnMonthYearChanged" />

            <Button Name="printButton"
                    Content="Print 1 Month"
                    Grid.Row="1" Grid.Column="0" Grid.ColumnSpan="3"
                    FontSize="24"
                    HorizontalAlignment="Center"
                    Margin="0 24"
                    Click="OnPrintButtonClick" />
        </Grid>
    </Grid>
</Page>
```

This program is a little different from the others in this chapter in that printing is not enabled for the duration of the application. Printing is enabled only if the two *MonthYearSelect* controls are dialed in to an actual range of months. With each change of these two controls, the program needs to generate a new label for the *Button*, determine whether the button should be enabled or disabled, and determine whether to attach or detach the *PrintTaskRequested* event. That logic is much of what's going on in this initial section of the *MainPage* class:

Project: PrintMonthlyPlanner | File: MainPage.xaml.cs (excerpt)

```
public sealed partial class MainPage : Page
{
    PrintDocument printDocument;
    IPrintDocumentSource printDocumentSource;
    List<UIElement> calendarPages = new List<UIElement>();
    bool printingEnabled;

    public MainPage()
    {
        this.InitializeComponent();

        // Create PrintDocument and attach handlers
        printDocument = new PrintDocument();
        printDocumentSource = printDocument.DocumentSource;
        printDocument.Paginate += OnPrintDocumentPaginate;
        printDocument.GetPreviewPage += OnPrintDocumentGetPreviewPage;
        printDocument.AddPages += OnPrintDocumentAddPages;
    }

    void OnMonthYearChanged(object sender, EventArgs args)
    {
        // Calculate number of months and check if it's non-negative
        int printableMonths = GetPrintableMonthCount();
        printButton.Content = String.Format("Print {0} Month{1}", printableMonths,
                                            printableMonths > 1 ? "s" : "");
        printButton.IsEnabled = printableMonths > 0;

        // Attach or detach PrintManager handler
        if (printingEnabled != printableMonths > 0)
        {
            PrintManager printManager = PrintManager.GetForCurrentView();

            if (printableMonths > 0)
                printManager.PrintTaskRequested += OnPrintManagerPrintTaskRequested;
            else
                printManager.PrintTaskRequested -= OnPrintManagerPrintTaskRequested;

            printingEnabled = printableMonths > 0;
        }
    }

    int GetPrintableMonthCount()
    {
        Calendar cal1 = monthYearSelect1.MonthYear;
        Calendar cal2 = monthYearSelect2.MonthYear;
        return cal2.Month - cal1.Month + 1 + 12 * (cal2.Year - cal1.Year);
    }
```

```
async void OnPrintButtonClick(object sender, RoutedEventArgs args)
{
    await PrintManager.ShowPrintUIAsync();
}

void OnPrintManagerPrintTaskRequested(PrintManager sender, PrintTaskRequestedEventArgs args)
{
    // Create PrintTask
    PrintTask printTask = args.Request.CreatePrintTask("Monthly Planner",
                                                OnPrintTaskSourceRequested);

    // Set orientation to landscape
    PrintTaskOptionDetails optionDetails =
        PrintTaskOptionDetails.GetFromPrintTaskOptions(printTask.Options);

    PrintOrientationOptionDetails orientation =
        optionDetails.Options[StandardPrintTaskOptions.Orientation] as
                                                PrintOrientationOptionDetails;

    orientation.TrySetValue(PrintOrientation.Landscape);
}

void OnPrintTaskSourceRequested(PrintTaskSourceRequestedArgs args)
{
    args.SetSource(printDocumentSource);
}
...
}
```

Notice also that the *PrintTaskRequested* handler accesses the Orientation option and initializes it to Landscape. This will happen every time the user opens the printer pane. It could be that the user really doesn't want to print these calendar months in landscape mode. You might want to keep track of what setting the user ultimately uses by obtaining it, saving it in a field during the *Paginate* handler, and then using that the next time the printer pane comes up. The user's preference could even be saved in user settings for the next time the program is run.

Creating the pages is the responsibility of the *Paginate* handler, which saves them in a field for the *GetPreviewPage* and *AddPages* handlers. These pages are built around a *Grid* with seven columns for the seven days of the week, a number of rows based on the number of weeks in the particular month (which could range from four in February to six in other months), and one more row for the month and year title at the top:

Project: PrintMonthlyPlanner | File: MainPage.xaml.cs (excerpt)

```
public sealed partial class MainPage : Page
{
    ...
    void OnPrintDocumentPaginate(object sender, PaginateEventArgs args)
    {
        // Prepare to generate pages
        uint pageNumbers = 0;
        calendarPages.Clear();
        Calendar calendar = monthYearSelect1.MonthYear.Clone();
        calendar.Day = 1;
        Brush black = new SolidColorBrush(Colors.Black);
```

```
// For each month
do
{
    PrintPageDescription printPageDescription =
                        args.PrintTaskOptions.GetPageDescription(pageNumber);

    // Set Padding on outer Border
    double left = printPageDescription.ImageableRect.Left;
    double top = printPageDescription.ImageableRect.Top;
    double right = printPageDescription.PageSize.Width
                        - left - printPageDescription.ImageableRect.Width;
    double bottom = printPageDescription.PageSize.Height
                        - top - printPageDescription.ImageableRect.Height;
    Border border = new Border { Padding = new Thickness(left, top, right, bottom) };

    // Use Grid for calendar cells
    Grid grid = new Grid();
    border.Child = grid;
    int numberOfWeeks = (6 + (int)calendar.DayOfWeek + calendar.LastDayInThisMonth) / 7;

    for (int row = 0; row < numberOfWeeks + 1; row++)
        grid.RowDefinitions.Add(new RowDefinition
        {
            Height = new GridLength(1, GridUnitType.Star)
        });

    for (int col = 0; col < 7; col++)
        grid.ColumnDefinitions.Add(new ColumnDefinition
        {
            Width = new GridLength(1, GridUnitType.Star)
        });

    // Month and year display at top
    Viewbox viewbox = new Viewbox
    {
        Child = new TextBlock
        {
            Text = calendar.MonthAsSoloString() + " " + calendar.YearAsString(),
            Foreground = black,
            FontSize = 96,
            HorizontalAlignment = HorizontalAlignment.Center
        }
    };
    Grid.SetRow(viewbox, 0);
    Grid.SetColumn(viewbox, 0);
    Grid.SetColumnSpan(viewbox, 7);
    grid.Children.Add(viewbox);

    // Now loop through the days of the month
    for (int day = 1, row = 1, col = (int)calendar.DayOfWeek;
         day <= calendar.LastDayInThisMonth; day++)
    {
        Border dayBorder = new Border
        {
            BorderBrush = black,
```

```
                    // Avoid double line drawing
                    BorderThickness = new Thickness
                    {
                        Left = day == 1 || col == 0 ? 1 : 0,
                        Top = day - 7 < 1 ? 1 : 0,
                        Right = 1,
                        Bottom = 1
                    },

                    // Put day of month in upper-left corner
                    Child = new TextBlock
                    {
                        Text = day.ToString(),
                        Foreground = black,
                        FontSize = 24,
                        HorizontalAlignment = HorizontalAlignment.Left,
                        VerticalAlignment = VerticalAlignment.Top
                    }
                };
                Grid.SetRow(dayBorder, row);
                Grid.SetColumn(dayBorder, col);
                grid.Children.Add(dayBorder);

                if (0 == (col = (col + 1) % 7))
                    row += 1;
            }
            calendarPages.Add(border);
            calendar.AddMonths(1);
            pageNumber += 1;
        }
        while (calendar.Year < monthYearSelect2.MonthYear.Year ||
               calendar.Month <= monthYearSelect2.MonthYear.Month);

        printDocument.SetPreviewPageCount(calendarPages.Count, PreviewPageCountType.Final);
    }

    void OnPrintDocumentGetPreviewPage(object sender, GetPreviewPageEventArgs args)
    {
        printDocument.SetPreviewPage(args.PageNumber, calendarPages[args.PageNumber - 1]);
    }

    void OnPrintDocumentAddPages(object sender, AddPagesEventArgs args)
    {
        foreach (UIElement calendarPage in calendarPages)
            printDocument.AddPage(calendarPage);

        printDocument.AddPagesComplete();
    }
}
```

Printing a Range of Pages

The next program in this chapter is an experiment that got completely out of control. I wanted to demonstrate how to add an option to the printing pane to allow the user to select a variable range of pages to print. At the same time, I wanted to show how to share *UIElement* instances between the screen and the printer.

For this demonstration I chose to revamp the program from Chapter 4 that presented Beatrix Potter's *The Tale of Tom Kitten*. To allow the pages of this book to be easily printed, I decided that each book page should be a separate *UserControl* derivative. For the on-screen rendition, these separate *UserControl* pages could simply be assembled in a single scrollable *StackPanel*.

There's nothing really wrong with this scheme except that I ended up with 57 *UserControl* derivatives named *TomKitten03* through *TomKitten59*, the number indicating the page from the original book. But it turned out I really couldn't use the same instances of these controls on the screen and the printer unless I wanted the text or image from each page of the book to be printed in the upper-left corner of the printer page, and that was unacceptable.

Elements that are displayed on the screen are subjected to a layout process that defines their relationship to their parent, and in the general case you simply can't lift these elements out of a visual tree and expect that they will render satisfactorily on the printer. And you can't mess around with these elements either. You can't set new properties on them just for the printer because those properties will affect how they're displayed on the screen. And you can't put them into another container because that violates the rule that an element can have only one parent.

I finally realized that I could use the same 57 *UserControl* derivatives for the screen and printer, but only if they were separate instances, which means that each of these controls is instantiated twice: one in MainPage.xaml for the screen, and again in MainPage.xaml.cs for the printer.

So, in one sense the experiment was a failure because I couldn't simply reuse the instances, but the experiment also illuminated the awkwardness of a Visual Studio project that contains 57 *UserControl* derivatives! Visual Studio shakes in its boots loading and compiling all these XAML files, and we programmers should be nervous as well. This is not the way to make an e-book!

On the other hand, the program *does* demonstrate how to add a facility to the printer options to select a range of pages to print.

To allow a uniform set of styles to be applied to the *UserControl* derivatives in MainPage.xaml and as well as the *UserControl* derivatives instantiated in MainPage.xaml.cs, I moved all the *Style* definitions to App.xaml. This makes them available throughout the application.

Project: PrintableTomKitten | File: App.xaml

```
<Application
    x:Class="PrintableTomKitten.App"
    xmlns="http://schemas.microsoft.com/winfx/2006/xaml/presentation"
    xmlns:x="http://schemas.microsoft.com/winfx/2006/xaml"
    xmlns:local="using:PrintableTomKitten">
```

```
<Application.Resources>
    <ResourceDictionary>
        <ResourceDictionary.MergedDictionaries>
            <ResourceDictionary Source="Common/StandardStyles.xaml"/>
        </ResourceDictionary.MergedDictionaries>

        <Style x:Key="commonTextStyle" TargetType="TextBlock">
            <Setter Property="FontFamily" Value="Century Schoolbook" />
            <Setter Property="FontSize" Value="36" />
            <Setter Property="Foreground" Value="Black" />
            <Setter Property="Margin" Value="0 12" />
        </Style>

        <Style x:Key="paragraphTextStyle" TargetType="TextBlock"
            BasedOn="{StaticResource commonTextStyle}">
            <Setter Property="TextWrapping" Value="Wrap" />
        </Style>

        <Style x:Key="frontMatterTextStyle" TargetType="TextBlock"
            BasedOn="{StaticResource commonTextStyle}">
            <Setter Property="TextAlignment" Value="Center" />
        </Style>

        <Style x:Key="imageStyle" TargetType="Image">
            <Setter Property="Stretch" Value="None" />
            <Setter Property="HorizontalAlignment" Value="Center" />
        </Style>
    </ResourceDictionary>
</Application.Resources>
</Application>
```

The MainPage.xaml file does little more than list all the individual pages of the book in a *StackPanel*. The following listing leaves out the middle section:

Project: PrintableTomKitten | **File:** MainPage.xaml (excerpt)

```
<Page
    x:Class="PrintableTomKitten.MainPage"
    xmlns="http://schemas.microsoft.com/winfx/2006/xaml/presentation"
    xmlns:x="http://schemas.microsoft.com/winfx/2006/xaml"
    xmlns:local="using:PrintableTomKitten">

    <Grid Background="White">
        <ScrollViewer>
            <StackPanel Name="bookPageStackPanel"
                        MaxWidth="640"
                        HorizontalAlignment="Center">

                <local:TomKitten03 />
                <local:TomKitten04 />
                <local:TomKitten05 />
                <local:TomKitten06 />
                <local:TomKitten07 />
                <local:TomKitten08 />
                <local:TomKitten09 />

                <local:TomKitten10 />
```

```
                <local:TomKitten11 />
                <local:TomKitten13 />
                <local:TomKitten12 />

                <local:TomKitten14 />
                <local:TomKitten15 />
                <local:TomKitten17 />
                <local:TomKitten16 />
                ...
                <local:TomKitten50 />
                <local:TomKitten51 />
                <local:TomKitten53 />
                <local:TomKitten52 />

                <local:TomKitten54 />
                <local:TomKitten55 />
                <local:TomKitten56 />
                <local:TomKitten57 />

                <local:TomKitten59 />
                <local:TomKitten58 />
            </StackPanel>
        </ScrollViewer>
    </Grid>
</Page>
```

Some of these are seemingly out of sequence. As I discussed in Chapter 4, I found it necessary to swap some of the text and picture pages to provide a more coherent reading experience.

The pages containing only an image are quite small:

Project: PrintableTomKitten | File: TomKitten20.xaml

```
<UserControl
    x:Class="PrintableTomKitten.TomKitten20"
    xmlns="http://schemas.microsoft.com/winfx/2006/xaml/presentation"
    xmlns:x="http://schemas.microsoft.com/winfx/2006/xaml">

    <Image Source="Images/tom20.jpg" Style="{StaticResource imageStyle}" />
</UserControl>
```

Many pages have only one paragraph of text, like the following:

Project: PrintableTomKitten | File: TomKitten21.xaml

```
<UserControl
    x:Class="PrintableTomKitten.TomKitten21"
    xmlns="http://schemas.microsoft.com/winfx/2006/xaml/presentation"
    xmlns:x="http://schemas.microsoft.com/winfx/2006/xaml">

    <Grid VerticalAlignment="Center"
          MaxWidth="640">
        <TextBlock Style="{StaticResource paragraphTextStyle}">
              Tom Kitten was very fat, and he had grown;
            several buttons burst off. His mother sewed them on again.
        </TextBlock>
    </Grid>
</UserControl>
```

Notice the *VerticalAlignment* and *MaxWidth* settings on the *Grid*. These settings are for the benefit of the printer. The *VerticalAlignment* setting has no effect when the control is displayed on the screen because it's a child of a *StackPanel* with a vertical orientation, and the *StackPanel* itself has a *MaxWidth* setting of 640.

Those pages with more than a paragraph of text require a *StackPanel*:

Project: PrintableTomKitten | File: TomKitten21.xaml

```xml
<UserControl
    x:Class="PrintableTomKitten.TomKitten22"
    xmlns="http://schemas.microsoft.com/winfx/2006/xaml/presentation"
    xmlns:x="http://schemas.microsoft.com/winfx/2006/xaml">

    <Grid VerticalAlignment="Center"
          MaxWidth="640">
        <StackPanel>
            <TextBlock Style="{StaticResource paragraphTextStyle}">
                  When the three kittens were ready, Mrs.
                Tabitha unwisely turned them out into the garden, to be
                out of the way while she made hot buttered toast.
            </TextBlock>

            <TextBlock Style="{StaticResource paragraphTextStyle}">
                  "Now keep your frocks clean, children! You
                must walk on your hind legs. Keep away from the dirty
                ash-pit, and from Sally Henny Penny, and from the
                pig-stye and the Puddle-Ducks."
            </TextBlock>
        </StackPanel>
    </Grid>
</UserControl>
```

That's all the XAML you'll see from this project.

As you know, it's very common these days for programs to offer options to print all or part of a document. These options are often labeled something like All, Selection, and Custom Range. Because I have no concept of selection in the PrintableTomKitten project, my options are limited to "Print all pages" and "Print custom range."

It's also become common for this custom range to contain both individual pages and continuous page ranges separated by commas, such as 2-4, 7, 9-11. The constructor of the following *CustomPageRange* class accepts a string with such a custom page range and resolves the information into a list of consecutive pages. For the string "2-4, 7, 9-11", the *PageMapping* property is set to the list of integers 2, 3, 4, 7, 9, 10, 11. If the string is invalid in some way, then *PageMapping* is *null* and *IsValid* returns *false*:

Project: PrintableTomKitten | File: CustomPrintRange.cs

```csharp
using System;
using System.Collections.Generic;

namespace PrintableTomKitten
{
```

```
public class CustomPageRange
{
    // Structure used internally
    struct PageRange
    {
        public PageRange(int from, int to) : this()
        {
            this.From = from;
            this.To = to;
        }

        public int From { private set; get; }
        public int To { private set; get; }
    }

    public CustomPageRange(string str, int maxPageNumber)
    {
        List<PageRange> pageRanges = new List<PageRange>();
        string[] strRanges = str.Split(',');

        foreach (string strRange in strRanges)
        {
            int dashIndex = strRange.IndexOf('-');

            // Just one page number
            if (dashIndex == -1)
            {
                int page;

                if (Int32.TryParse(strRange.Trim(), out page) &&
                    page > 0 && page <= maxPageNumber)
                {
                    pageRanges.Add(new PageRange(page, page));
                }
                else
                {
                    return;
                }
            }
            // Two page numbers separated by a dash
            else
            {
                string strFrom = strRange.Substring(0, dashIndex);
                string strTo = strRange.Substring(dashIndex + 1);
                int from, to;

                if (Int32.TryParse(strFrom.Trim(), out from) &&
                    Int32.TryParse(strTo.Trim(), out to) &&
                    from > 0 && from <= maxPageNumber &&
                    to > 0 && to <= maxPageNumber &&
                    from <= to)
                {
                    pageRanges.Add(new PageRange(from, to));
                }
                else
                {
                    return;
```

```
                    }
                }
            }

            // If we made it to this, the input string is valid
            this.PageMapping = new List<int>();

            // Define a mapping to page numbers
            foreach (PageRange pageRange in pageRanges)
                for (int page = pageRange.From; page <= pageRange.To; page++)
                    this.PageMapping.Add(page);
        }

        // Zero-based in, one-based out
        public IList<int> PageMapping { private set; get; }

        public bool IsValid
        {
            get { return this.PageMapping != null; }
        }
    }
}
```

The PrintableTomKitten program uses this class in two places: when it's validating input that the user has entered in the printer options pane, and later in the *Paginate* event handler. In the second case, the *CustomPageRange* object is stored as a field for use by the *GetPreviewPage* and *AddPages* handlers.

Here's the MainPage.xaml.cs file through the *OnPrintTaskSourceRequested* override. Notice the big array at the top containing additional instances of all the book pages solely for printing:

Project: PrintableTomKitten | File: MainPage.xaml.cs (excerpt)

```
public sealed partial class MainPage : Page
{
    PrintDocument printDocument;
    IPrintDocumentSource printDocumentSource;
    CustomPageRange customPageRange;
    UIElement[] bookPages =
    {
        new TomKitten03(), new TomKitten04(), new TomKitten05(), new TomKitten06(),
        new TomKitten07(), new TomKitten08(), new TomKitten09(), new TomKitten10(),
        new TomKitten11(), new TomKitten12(), new TomKitten13(), new TomKitten14(),
        new TomKitten15(), new TomKitten16(), new TomKitten17(), new TomKitten18(),
        new TomKitten19(), new TomKitten20(), new TomKitten21(), new TomKitten22(),
        new TomKitten23(), new TomKitten24(), new TomKitten25(), new TomKitten26(),
        new TomKitten27(), new TomKitten28(), new TomKitten29(), new TomKitten30(),
        new TomKitten31(), new TomKitten32(), new TomKitten33(), new TomKitten34(),
        new TomKitten35(), new TomKitten36(), new TomKitten37(), new TomKitten38(),
        new TomKitten39(), new TomKitten40(), new TomKitten41(), new TomKitten42(),
        new TomKitten43(), new TomKitten44(), new TomKitten45(), new TomKitten46(),
        new TomKitten47(), new TomKitten48(), new TomKitten49(), new TomKitten50(),
        new TomKitten51(), new TomKitten52(), new TomKitten53(), new TomKitten54(),
        new TomKitten55(), new TomKitten56(), new TomKitten57(), new TomKitten58(),
        new TomKitten59()
    };
```

```
public MainPage()
{
    this.InitializeComponent();

    // Create PrintDocument and attach handlers
    printDocument = new PrintDocument();
    printDocumentSource = printDocument.DocumentSource;
    printDocument.Paginate += OnPrintDocumentPaginate;
    printDocument.GetPreviewPage += OnPrintDocumentGetPreviewPage;
    printDocument.AddPages += OnPrintDocumentAddPages;
}

protected override void OnNavigatedTo(NavigationEventArgs args)
{
    // Attach PrintManager handler
    PrintManager.GetForCurrentView().PrintTaskRequested += OnPrintManagerPrintTaskRequested;

    base.OnNavigatedTo(args);
}

protected override void OnNavigatedFrom(NavigationEventArgs e)
{
    // Detach PrintManager handler
    PrintManager.GetForCurrentView().PrintTaskRequested -= OnPrintManagerPrintTaskRequested;

    base.OnNavigatedFrom(e);
}

void OnPrintManagerPrintTaskRequested(PrintManager sender, PrintTaskRequestedEventArgs args)
{
    PrintTask printTask = args.Request.CreatePrintTask("The Tale of Tom Kitten",
                                            OnPrintTaskSourceRequested);

    // Get PrintTaskOptionDetails for making changes to options
    PrintTaskOptionDetails optionDetails =
        PrintTaskOptionDetails.GetFromPrintTaskOptions(printTask.Options);

    // Create the custom item
    PrintCustomItemListOptionDetails pageRange =
                        optionDetails.CreateItemListOption("idPrintRange", "Print range");
    pageRange.AddItem("idPrintAll", "Print all pages");
    pageRange.AddItem("idPrintCustom", "Print custom range");

    // Add it to the options
    optionDetails.DisplayedOptions.Add("idPrintRange");

    // Create a page-range edit item also, but this only
    //      comes into play when user selects "Print custom range"
    optionDetails.CreateTextOption("idCustomRangeEdit", "Custom Range");
```

```
        // Set a handler for the OptionChanged event
        optionDetails.OptionChanged += OnOptionDetailsOptionChanged;
    }

    void OnPrintTaskSourceRequested(PrintTaskSourceRequestedArgs args)
    {
        args.SetSource(printDocumentSource);
    }
    ...
}
```

Earlier you saw how to create custom text-entry fields using the *CreateTextOption* method of *PrintTaskOptionDetails*. The only alternative to a text-entry field involves the *CreateItemListOption* method shown here. This results in a list of mutually exclusive options similar to the Orientation option. Give the method a string ID and a label. The method returns an object of type *PrintCustomItemListOptionDetails*. To that you'll need to add the individual items with ID strings and labels and then add those same IDs to the *DisplayedOptions* collection. Here's what it looks like initially:

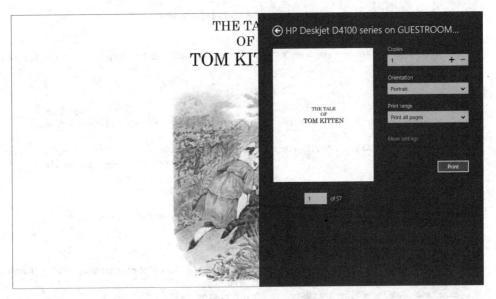

But notice also that the *PrintTaskRequested* handler also calls *CreateTextOption* to create a text-entry field for the custom page range:

```
optionDetails.CreateTextOption("idCustomRangeEdit", "Custom Range");
```

This is created but it's not added to the *DisplayedOptions* collection yet. You want this item displayed only when the user selects "Print custom range."

This logic occurs in the *OptionChanged* handler. If the option ID string is "idPrintCustom", you then want to add the text-entry field identified by the string "idCustomRangeEdit" to the *DisplayedOptions* collection, and if the ID string is "idPrintAll", it must be removed from *DisplayedOptions*:

Project: PrintableTomKitten | **File:** MainPage.xaml.cs (excerpt)

```
public sealed partial class MainPage : Page
{
    ...
    async void OnOptionDetailsOptionChanged(PrintTaskOptionDetails sender,
                                    PrintTaskOptionChangedEventArgs args)
    {
        if (args.OptionId == null)
            return;

        string optionId = args.OptionId.ToString();
        string strValue = sender.Options[optionId].Value.ToString();
        string errorText = String.Empty;

        switch (optionId)
        {
            case "idPrintRange":
                switch (strValue)
                {
                    case "idPrintAll":
                        if (sender.DisplayedOptions.Contains("idCustomRangeEdit"))
                            sender.DisplayedOptions.Remove("idCustomRangeEdit");
                        break;

                    case "idPrintCustom":
                        sender.DisplayedOptions.Add("idCustomRangeEdit");
                        break;
                }
                break;

            case "idCustomRangeEdit":
                // Check to see if CustomPageRange accepts this
                if (!new CustomPageRange(strValue, bookPages.Length).IsValid)
                {
                    errorText = "Use the form 2-4, 7, 9-11";
                }
                break;
        }

        sender.Options[optionId].ErrorText = errorText;

        // If no error, then invalidate the preview
        if (String.IsNullOrEmpty(errorText))
        {
            await this.Dispatcher.RunAsync(CoreDispatcherPriority.Normal, () =>
            {
                printDocument.InvalidatePreview();
            });
        }
    }
    ...
}
```

If the "idCustomRangeEdit" control is visible, you can also receive notifications from that. To determine whether the range is valid, the *CustomPageRange* constructor is called and a possible error text is set. Here's a page range that is successfully parsed:

Notice that the page numbers underneath the preview indicate the number of pages that should be printed but don't indicate the actual page numbers the user has selected. I'm not sure that problem can really be fixed unless a page range selection is moved into the standard options, and that's something beyond our control.

Also, notice that the *OptionChanged* handler does not save the *CustomPageRange* object as a field. You don't need to save it in this handler, and you should probably avoid doing so. As the user bounces back and forth among the options, it can be tricky to keep track of what's actually selected and visible and what's not.

Instead, you can obtain the final settings of the options in the three handlers for the *PrintDocument* events. In this example, the *Paginate* handler obtains the settings and saves a *CustomPageRange* object as a field, which is then accessed by the other two methods:

Project: PrintableTomKitten | File: MainPage.xaml.cs (excerpt)

```
public sealed partial class MainPage : Page
{
    ...
    void OnPrintDocumentPaginate(object sender, PaginateEventArgs args)
    {
        // Obtain the print range option
        PrintTaskOptionDetails optionDetails =
                PrintTaskOptionDetails.GetFromPrintTaskOptions(args.PrintTaskOptions);

        string strValue = optionDetails.Options["idPrintRange"].Value as string;

        if (strValue == "idPrintCustom")
        {
```

```
        // Parse the print range for GetPreviewPage and AddPages
        string strPageRange = optionDetails.Options["idCustomRangeEdit"].Value as string;
        customPageRange = new CustomPageRange(strPageRange, bookPages.Length);
    }
    else
    {
        // Make sure field is null if printing all pages
        customPageRange = null;
    }

    int pageCount = bookPages.Length;

    if (customPageRange != null && customPageRange.IsValid)
        pageCount = customPageRange.PageMapping.Count;

    printDocument.SetPreviewPageCount(pageCount, PreviewPageCountType.Final);
}

void OnPrintDocumentGetPreviewPage(object sender, GetPreviewPageEventArgs args)
{
    int oneBasedIndex = args.PageNumber;

    if (customPageRange != null && customPageRange.IsValid)
        oneBasedIndex = customPageRange.PageMapping[args.PageNumber - 1];

    printDocument.SetPreviewPage(args.PageNumber, bookPages[oneBasedIndex - 1]);
}

void OnPrintDocumentAddPages(object sender, AddPagesEventArgs args)
{
    if (customPageRange != null && customPageRange.IsValid)
    {
        foreach (int oneBasedIndex in customPageRange.PageMapping)
            printDocument.AddPage(bookPages[oneBasedIndex - 1]);
    }
    else
    {
        foreach (UIElement bookPage in bookPages)
            printDocument.AddPage(bookPage);
    }

    printDocument.AddPagesComplete();
}
}
```

I mentioned that I started this printable version of *The Tale of Tom Kitten* to determine whether I could share elements between the screen and printer. If you'd like to see what happens when you print those instances of the *UserControl* derivatives displayed from *MainPage*, simply replace *bookPages* with *bookPageStackPanel.Children* in the *OnPrintDocumentGetPreviewPage* and *OnPrintDocumentAddPages* methods.

Where to Do the Big Jobs?

A program that has the potential of printing many pages might encounter nontrivial pagination issues. Perhaps it takes some time to determine exactly how many pages are to be printed.

In the callback method that you pass to *CreatePrintTask* (this is the method I've been calling *OnPrintTaskSourceRequested*), after calling *SetSource* on the event arguments, you can use the event arguments to obtain a deferral for performing an asynchronous job:

```
PrintTaskSourceRequestedDeferral deferral = args.GetDeferral();
await BigJobInvolvingPrintingAsync();
deferral.Complete();
```

In this case, the printing pane with the name of the selected printer is displayed, but under that printer name spins a progress ring accompanied by the text "App preparing to print." The user might not enjoy the experience, but it's a valid way for the application to gain a little time without hanging the user-interface thread.

Also keep in mind that the second argument of the *SetPreviewPageCount* method of *PrintDocument* is a member of the *PreviewPageCountType* enumeration, either *Intermediate* or *Final*. You don't need to restrict calls of this method to the body of the *Paginate* handler. You can call it initially with a preliminary page count and then have a background task continuing with the pagination. A *Dispatcher* to the user-interface thread can make additional calls to *SetPreviewPageCount* to keep the count updated.

To assist your application in keeping the user informed of the progress of a long print job, *PrintTask* defines events named *Previewing*, *Submitting*, *Progressing*, and *Completed*.

Printing FingerPaint Art

Ever since you first started using the various FingerPaint programs in this book, I'm sure you've been eager to print out your artwork and display it on the refrigerator door. Of course, you can always make a screen shot of the FingerPaint screen and print that, but let's incorporate printing support right into FingerPaint itself.

To have as small an impact as possible on existing FingerPaint code, I decided to derive a class from *PrintDocument* called *BitmapPrintDocument*. I mentioned earlier that you can do such a thing, and although the resultant class has no overridable methods, it does make some object references a bit easier.

The *BitmapPrintDocument* class is instantiated in the *MainPage* constructor:

Project: FingerPaint | File: MainPage.xaml.cs (excerpt)

```
public MainPage()
{
    ...
    // Create a PrintDocument derivative for handling printing
    new BitmapPrintDocument(() => { return bitmap; });
}
```

Notice that odd argument to the *BitmapPrintDocument* constructor! The problem is that the *BitmapPrintDocument* class definitely requires a reference to the *WriteableBitmap* field named *bitmap* if it is to print that bitmap, but it can't simply be passed to the *BitmapPrintDocument* constructor. That *bitmap* field changes whenever the program loads an image from a file or the clipboard or when it creates a new canvas. For that reason, I've defined the constructor of *BitmapPrintDocument* with a parameter of type *Func<BitmapSource>* so that whenever the *BitmapPrintDocument* needs the current bitmap, it can simply call back into *MainPage*.

BitmapPrintDocument saves that argument in a field and performs the standard initialization:

Project: FingerPaint | File: BitmapPrintDocument.cs (excerpt)

```
public class BitmapPrintDocument : PrintDocument
{
    Func<BitmapSource> getBitmap;
    IPrintDocumentSource printDocumentSource;

    // Element to print
    Border border = new Border
    {
        Child = new Image()
    };

    public BitmapPrintDocument(Func<BitmapSource> getBitmap)
    {
        this.getBitmap = getBitmap;

        // Get IPrintDocumentSource and attach event handlers
        printDocumentSource = this.DocumentSource;
        this.Paginate += OnPaginate;
        this.GetPreviewPage += OnGetPreviewPage;
        this.AddPages += OnAddPages;

        // Attach PrintManager handler
        PrintManager.GetForCurrentView().PrintTaskRequested +=
                                    OnPrintDocumentPrintTaskRequested;
    }
    ...
}
```

The *PrintTaskRequested* handler is the first place where the bitmap is required because it sets the initial orientation of the printer page to be consistent with the orientation of the bitmap:

Project: FingerPaint | File: BitmapPrintDocument.cs (excerpt)

```
async void OnPrintDocumentPrintTaskRequested(PrintManager sender,
                                      PrintTaskRequestedEventArgs args)
{
    PrintTaskRequestedDeferral deferral = args.Request.GetDeferral();

    // Obtain PrintTask
    PrintTask printTask = args.Request.CreatePrintTask("Finger Paint",
                                      OnPrintTaskSourceRequested);

    // Probably set orientation to landscape
    PrintTaskOptionDetails optionDetails =
        PrintTaskOptionDetails.GetFromPrintTaskOptions(printTask.Options);

    PrintOrientationOptionDetails orientation =
        optionDetails.Options[StandardPrintTaskOptions.Orientation] as
                                      PrintOrientationOptionDetails;

    bool bitmapIsLandscape = false;

    await border.Dispatcher.RunAsync(CoreDispatcherPriority.Normal, () =>
        {
            BitmapSource bitmapSource = getBitmap();
            bitmapIsLandscape = bitmapSource.PixelWidth > bitmapSource.PixelHeight;
        });

    orientation.TrySetValue(bitmapIsLandscape ? PrintOrientation.Landscape :
                                      PrintOrientation.Portrait);

    deferral.Complete();
}
```

Notice that a *CoreDispatcher* object must be used to access the bitmap in the user-interface thread. The other event handlers should look familiar at this point, except that references to the *PrintDocument* methods are simply references to methods of *this*:

Project: FingerPaint | File: BitmapPrintDocument.cs (excerpt)

```
void OnPrintTaskSourceRequested(PrintTaskSourceRequestedArgs args)
{
    args.SetSource(printDocumentSource);
}

void OnPaginate(object sender, PaginateEventArgs args)
{
    PrintPageDescription pageDesc = args.PrintTaskOptions.GetPageDescription(0);
```

```
        // Get the Bitmap
        (border.Child as Image).Source = getBitmap();

        // Set Padding on the Border
        double left = pageDesc.ImageableRect.Left;
        double top = pageDesc.ImageableRect.Top;
        double right = pageDesc.PageSize.Width - left - pageDesc.ImageableRect.Width;
        double bottom = pageDesc.PageSize.Height - top - pageDesc.ImageableRect.Height;
        border.Padding = new Thickness(left, top, right, bottom);

        this.SetPreviewPageCount(1, PreviewPageCountType.Final);
    }

    void OnGetPreviewPage(object sender, GetPreviewPageEventArgs args)
    {
        this.SetPreviewPage(args.PageNumber, border);
    }

    void OnAddPages(object sender, AddPagesEventArgs args)
    {
        this.AddPage(border);
        this.AddPagesComplete();
    }
```

The *Image* element has its default *Stretch* mode of *Uniform*, which lets the bitmap be displayed as large as possible while still respecting the aspect ratio. In addition, the *OnPaginate* method sets the *Padding* property of the *Border* to avoid only the unprintable area of the page because of course you want your finger paintings printed as large as the printer will allow.

CHAPTER 18

Sensors and GPS

In recent years, computers have evolved to develop new sensory organs. This isn't the plot of a new movie! Many of our computers—and particularly tablets and other mobile devices—contain hardware that lets the machine know its orientation in 3D space, its location on the face of the Earth, the amount of ambient light in the vicinity, and even the speed that the computer is turning in the user's hands.

These pieces of hardware are referred to collectively as *sensors*, and the software interface to them can be found largely in the *Windows.Devices.Sensors* namespace, while the classes that help a program determine its geographical location are in the *Windows.Devices.Geolocation* namespace. The hardware that facilities this latter job is often referred to informally as GPS (after the Global Positioning System implemented with satellites), but a computer can also often determine its geographic location through a network connection.

This chapter focuses on the information available from the *SimpleOrientationSensor*, *Accelerometer*, *Compass*, *Inclinometer*, *OrientationSensor*, and *Geolocator* classes, but I'm afraid I'll be skipping the less commonly used *LightSensor* and *Gyrometer* classes, the latter of which measures the angular velocity of the computer.

To get the full benefit from this chapter, you'll need to grab the computer running these sample programs and move it around in space, even holding it over your head. If your Windows 8 development machine is pretty much anchored to a desk like mine is, you'll want to get a tablet such as the Microsoft Surface and deploy programs on it remotely, as Tim Heuer discusses in his blog entry, *http://timheuer.com/blog/archive/2012/10/26/remote-debugging-windows-store-apps-on-surface-arm-devices.aspx*.

Some of the sample programs in this chapter are adapted from articles I wrote about Windows Phone 7.5 sensors in the June through December 2012 issues of *MSDN Magazine*.

Orientation and Orientation

As its name declares, the simplest of the sensors that I'll be discussing is *SimpleOrientationSensor*, which gives your program a rough idea how the computer is oriented in 3D space but without details. To instantiate the *SimpleOrientationSensor* class, you call a static method:

```
SimpleOrientationSensor simpleOrientationSensor = SimpleOrientationSensor.GetDefault();
```

You'll only do this once in an application, so this code can appear as a field definition to allow access to that object within the whole class. If the *SimpleOrientationSensor.GetDefault* method returns *null*, the computer doesn't have a facility to determine its orientation.

At any time, you can obtain a value indicating the current orientation from the *SimpleOrientationSensor* object:

```
SimpleOrientation simpleOrientation = simpleOrientationSensor.GetCurrentOrientation();
```

SimpleOrientation is an enumeration with six members:

- *NotRotated*
- *Rotated90DegreesCounterclockwise*
- *Rotated180DegreesCounterclockwise*
- *Rotated270DegreesCounterclockwise*
- *Faceup*
- *Facedown*

The limitation of the information to these six members is the "simple" part of the *SimpleOrientationSensor.*

You can also be notified through an event when the orientation changes. Set a handler for the *OrientationChanged* event like so:

```
simpleOrientationSensor.OrientationChanged += OnSimpleOrientationChanged;
```

This event fires only when the orientation changes, which won't happen if the computer remains relatively still. If you need an initial value, call the *GetCurrentOrientation* method in addition to setting the event handler.

This event handler runs in its own thread, so to interact with the user-interface thread you'll need to use a *CoreDispatcher* object:

```
async void OnSimpleOrientationChanged(SimpleOrientationSensor sender,
                             SimpleOrientationSensorOrientationChangedEventArgs args)
{
    await this.Dispatcher.RunAsync(CoreDispatcherPriority.Normal, () =>
        {
            ...
        });
}
```

The event argument with the excessively long name has an *Orientation* property of the *SimpleOrientation* enumeration type and a *Timestamp* property of type *DateTimeOffset*.

You might be asking: Don't I already have this orientation information? Isn't it provided by the *Windows.Graphics.Display* namespace? Don't I use the *DisplayProperties* class and its *NativeOrientation* and *CurrentOrientation* static properties and the *OrientationChanged* event for orientation information? You'll recall that those two static properties return members of the *DisplayOrientations* enumeration type:

- *Landscape*

- *Portrait*

- *LandscapeFlipped*

- *PortraitFlipped*

The *SimpleOrientationSensor* and *DisplayProperties* classes are certainly related, but it's important to understand how: The *SimpleOrientationSensor* class indicates how the computer is oriented in 3D space. The *DisplayProperties.CurrentOrientation* property indicates how Windows has compensated for this computer orientation by automatically reorienting your program's window. In other words, *SimpleOrientationSensor* reports a hardware orientation, and *DisplayProperties.CurrentOrientation* reports a software orientation that has occurred in response to the hardware orientation.

The OrientationAndOrientation project is intended to help differentiate between the two types of orientation. The XAML file defines just a few *TextBlock* elements for labels and to display some information:

Project: OrientationAndOrientation | **Project:** MainPage.xaml (excerpt)

```
<Page ... FontSize="24">
    <Grid Background="{StaticResource ApplicationPageBackgroundThemeBrush}">
        <Grid HorizontalAlignment="Center"
                VerticalAlignment="Center">
            <Grid.RowDefinitions>
                <RowDefinition Height="Auto" />
                <RowDefinition Height="Auto" />
            </Grid.RowDefinitions>

            <Grid.ColumnDefinitions>
                <ColumnDefinition Width="Auto" />
                <ColumnDefinition Width="Auto" />
            </Grid.ColumnDefinitions>

            <TextBlock Text="SimpleOrientationSensor:&#x00A0;"
                    Grid.Row="0"
                    Grid.Column="0" />

            <TextBlock Name="orientationSensorTextBlock"
                    Grid.Row="0"
                    Grid.Column="1"
                    TextAlignment="Right" />

            <TextBlock Text="DisplayProperties.CurrentOrientation:&#x00A0;"
                    Grid.Row="1"
                    Grid.Column="0" />

            <TextBlock Name="displayOrientationTextBlock"
                    Grid.Row="1"
                    Grid.Column="1"
                    TextAlignment="Right" />
        </Grid>
    </Grid>
</Page>
```

The code-behind file defines two methods for the sole purpose of setting the two *TextBlock* elements in the second column of the *Grid*. These two methods are called both from the constructor to set initial values and from two event handlers:

Project: OrientationAndOrientation | File: MainPage.xaml.cs (excerpt)

```
public sealed partial class MainPage : Page
{
    SimpleOrientationSensor simpleOrientationSensor = SimpleOrientationSensor.GetDefault();

    public MainPage()
    {
        this.InitializeComponent();

        // SimpleOrientationSensor initialization
        if (simpleOrientationSensor != null)
        {
            SetOrientationSensorText(simpleOrientationSensor.GetCurrentOrientation());
            simpleOrientationSensor.OrientationChanged += OnSimpleOrientationChanged;
        }

        // DisplayProperties initialization
        SetDisplayOrientationText(DisplayProperties.CurrentOrientation);
        DisplayProperties.OrientationChanged += OnDisplayPropertiesOrientationChanged;
    }

    // SimpleOrientationSensor handler
    async void OnSimpleOrientationChanged(SimpleOrientationSensor sender,
                                    SimpleOrientationSensorOrientationChangedEventArgs args)
    {
        await this.Dispatcher.RunAsync(CoreDispatcherPriority.Normal, () =>
            {
                SetOrientationSensorText(args.Orientation);
            });
    }

    void SetOrientationSensorText(SimpleOrientation simpleOrientation)
    {
        orientationSensorTextBlock.Text = simpleOrientation.ToString();
    }

    // DisplayProperties handler
    void OnDisplayPropertiesOrientationChanged(object sender)
    {
        SetDisplayOrientationText(DisplayProperties.CurrentOrientation);
    }

    void SetDisplayOrientationText(DisplayOrientations displayOrientation)
    {
        displayOrientationTextBlock.Text = displayOrientation.ToString();
    }
}
```

Notice that the *SimpleOrientationSensor* is instantiated as a field but the constructor checks for a non-*null* value before accessing the object.

If you run this program on a tablet that has a native landscape orientation—that is, the *DisplayProperties.NativeOrientation* property returns *DisplayOrientations.Landscape*—and if you haven't done anything to prohibit Windows 8 from making orientation changes (such as putting the tablet in a docking station), then you'll *generally* find the following correspondence between the two orientation indicators as you progressively rotate the tablet in a clockwise direction:

SimpleOrientationSensor	DisplayProperties.CurrentOrientation
NotRotated	Landscape
Rotated270DegreesCounterClockwise	Portrait
Rotated180DegreesCounterClockwise	LandscapeFlipped
Rotated90DegreesCounterClockwise	PortraitFlipped

The *SimpleOrientationSensor* also reports *Faceup* and *Facedown* values, which have no correspondences in the *DisplayOrientations* enumeration.

While the preceding table is roughly true for a tablet that has a native landscape orientation, a mobile device that has a native portrait orientation will have the following correspondences:

SimpleOrientationSensor	DisplayProperties.CurrentOrientation
NotRotated	Portrait
Rotated270DegreesCounterClockwise	LandscapeFlipped
Rotated180DegreesCounterClockwise	PortraitFlipped
Rotated90DegreesCounterClockwise	Landscape

Moreover, an application can request that Windows not make any compensation for the orientation of the computer, either in the Package.appxmanifest file or in software by setting the *DisplayProperties.AutoRotationPreferences* property. In that case it's likely that *DisplayProperties.CurrentOrientation* will never change while the application is running. Some tablets also have a hardware switch that users can toggle to stop Windows from automatically rotating the display. In such cases, you might even see something like this:

SimpleOrientationSensor	DisplayProperties.CurrentOrientation
NotRotated	PortraitFlipped
Rotated270DegreesCounterClockwise	PortraitFlipped
Rotated180DegreesCounterClockwise	PortraitFlipped
Rotated90DegreesCounterClockwise	PortraitFlipped

If you want to perform your own compensation for orientation, you can do so. You can instruct Windows not to perform any orientation changes, and then use the *SimpleOrientationSensor* to determine how the computer is really oriented. However, keep in mind that what you are giving Windows in the Package.appxmanifest file and the *DisplayProperties.AutoRotationPreferences* is only what you prefer and not what Windows will actually do, so you might need to make a further adjustment if Windows has oriented the display contrary to your preferences.

Probably the safest approach to prevent auto-rotation is to set *DisplayProperties.AutoRotationPreferences* to *DisplayProperties.NativeOrientation*, as I'll begin doing later in this chapter.

Acceleration, Force, Gravity, and Vectors

Internally, the *SimpleOrientationSensor* undoubtedly has access to a piece of hardware called an *accelerometer*. An accelerometer is a device that measures acceleration, and at first it might seem as if knowing the acceleration of the computer is not very useful. However, we know from basic physics—specifically, Isaac Newton's second law of motion—that

$$F = ma$$

Force equals mass times acceleration, and one force that is very hard to escape is the force of gravity. Most of the time the computer's accelerometer measures gravity and answers the basic question, "Which way is down?"

You can get at the accelerometer hardware more directly through the *Accelerometer* class. To instantiate the *Accelerometer* class, you'll use a static method with the same name as the one in *SimpleOrientationSensor*:

```
Accelerometer accelerometer = Accelerometer.GetDefault();
```

If the *Accelerometer.GetDefault* method returns *null*, the computer doesn't have an accelerometer or Windows 8 doesn't know about it. If your application can't run right without an accelerometer, you'll need to notify the user that it's missing.

At any time, you can obtain a current value of the *Accelerometer*:

```
AccelerometerReading accelerometerReading = accelerometer.GetCurrentReading();
```

The similar method in *SimpleOrientationSensor* is named *GetCurrentOrientation*.

It's probably a good idea to check if the value returned from *GetCurrentReading* is *null*. *AccelerometerReading* defines four properties:

- *AccelerationX* of type *double*

- *AccelerationY* of type *double*

- *AccelerationZ* of type *double*

- *Timestamp* of type *DateTimeOffset*

The three *double* values together constitute a 3D vector that points toward the Earth relative to the device. More on this shortly.

You can also attach an event handler to the *Accelerometer* object:

```
accelerometer.ReadingChanged += OnAccelerometerReadingChanged;
```

The similar event in *SimpleOrientationSensor* is named *OrientationChanged*. Like *OrientationChanged*, the *ReadingChanged* handler runs in a separate thread, so it's likely you'll be handling it like so:

```
async void OnAccelerometerReadingChanged(Accelerometer sender,
                                AccelerometerReadingChangedEventArgs args)
{
    await this.Dispatcher.RunAsync(CoreDispatcherPriority.Normal, () =>
        {
            ...
        });
}
```

The *AccelerometerReadingChangedEventArgs* defines a property named *Reading* of type *AccelerometerReading*, the same as the object returned from *GetCurrentReading*.

How often can you expect the *ReadingChanged* handler to be called? If the computer is still, it might not be called at all! For that reason, if you need an initial *Accelerometer* reading, you should call *GetCurrentReading* at the outset.

If the computer is being moved and changing orientation in space, the *ReadingChanged* handler is called when the value changes (within certain criteria) but no more frequently than an interval in milliseconds that you can obtain from the *ReportInterval* property of *Accelerometer*. I see a default value of 112, which means that the *ReadingChanged* method is called no faster than about nine times a second.

You can set *ReportInterval* to another value if you'd like, but no lower than the value returned from the *MinimumReportInterval* property, which I've found is 16 milliseconds, or about 60 times per second. Set *ReportInterval* to *MinimumReportInterval* to get the maximum amount of data; set *ReportInterval* to zero to return to the default setting.

All the other sensor classes in *Windows.Devices.Sensors* have the same software interface as *Accelerometer*. They all have the following members:

- static *GetDefault* method

- *GetCurrentReading* instance method

- *ReportInterval* property

- get-only *MinimumReportInterval* property

- *ReadingChanged* event

Only *SimpleOrientationSensor* is different from the others.

If the computer is still, the *AccelerationX*, *AccelerationY*, and *AccelerationZ* properties of the *AccelerometerReading* class define a vector that points toward the center of the Earth. Vectors are generally notated with boldface coordinates such as **(x, y, z)** to differentiate them from points (*x, y, z*) in 3D space. A point is a location in space; a vector is a direction and a magnitude. Vectors and points are related, of course: The direction of the vector **(x, y, z)** is the direction from the point (0, 0, 0) to the point (x, y, z), and the magnitude of the vector is the length of that line. But the vector is not the line itself and has no location.

The magnitude of a vector can be calculated with the three-dimensional form of the Pythagorean Theorem:

$$Magnitude = \sqrt{x^2 + y^2 + z^2}$$

Any three-dimensional vector must be relative to a particular three-dimensional coordinate system, and the vector obtained from the *AccelerometerReading* object is no exception. For a tablet with a native landscape orientation, that coordinate system is imposed on the hardware of the device, as shown here:

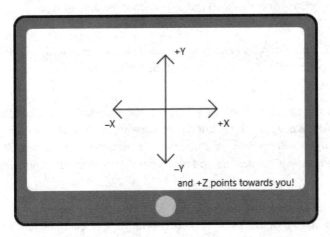

Notice that the direction of increasing Y is up, which is opposite of the convention when working with two-dimensional graphics. The positive Z axis points out of the screen. This convention is often referred to as a "right-hand" coordinate system. If you point the index finger of your right hand in the direction of positive X and your middle finger in the direction of positive Y, your thumb points toward positive Z.

Or, if you curl the fingers of your right hand in the direction necessary to rotate the positive X axis into the positive Y axis, your thumb points in the direction of the positive Z axis. This works with any pair of axes in the order X, Y, Z: Curl your right-hand fingers to rotate the positive Y axis into the positive Z axis, and your thumb points toward positive X. Or curl your right-hand fingers to rotate the positive Z axis into the positive X axis, and your thumb points toward positive Y.

The right-hand rule can also be used to determine the direction of rotations around the axis. For rotations around the X axis (for example), point your right-hand thumb in the direction of positive X, and your fingers curl in the direction of positive rotation angles around that axis.

For devices with a native portrait orientation, the coordinate system is the same from the user's perspective:

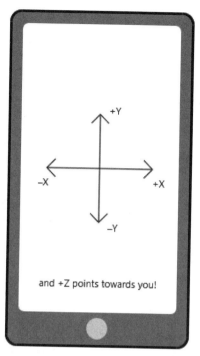

Although I haven't been able to confirm this, the coordinate system for conventional laptops is documented as being based on the keyboard rather than the screen. The X axis is along the width of the keyboard, the Y axis is along the height of the keyboard, and the Z axis points out of the keyboard.

This coordinate system is fixed to the hardware of the device, and the *Accelerometer* vector points toward the center of the Earth relative to that coordinate system. For example, when a tablet is held upright in its native orientation, the acceleration vector points in the −Y direction. The magnitude of the vector is approximately 1, so the vector is somewhere in the region **(0, −1, 0)**. When the device is lying on a flat surface like a table with the screen pointing up, the vector is somewhere in the region of **(0, 0, −1)**.

The magnitude of 1 indicates that the vector is in units of *g*, which is the acceleration caused by the force of gravity on the surface of the Earth, or about 32 feet per second squared. Take your tablet to the moon, and the magnitude will instead be in the vicinity of 0.17. Put your tablet into free fall (if you dare), and the magnitude of the acceleration vector will drop to zero until it hits the ground.

Here's a program called AccelerometerAndSimpleOrientation that displays values from the *Accelerometer* and the *SimpleOrientationSensor*. The XAML file contains a bunch of *TextBlock* elements for labels and awaiting values from the code-behind file:

Project: AccelerometerAndSimpleOrientation | File: MainPage.xaml (excerpt)

```xml
<Page ... >
    <Page.Resources>
        <Style TargetType="TextBlock">
            <Setter Property="FontSize" Value="24" />
            <Setter Property="Margin" Value="24 12 24 12" />
        </Style>
    </Page.Resources>

    <Grid Background="{StaticResource ApplicationPageBackgroundThemeBrush}">

        <Grid HorizontalAlignment="Center"
              VerticalAlignment="Center">
            <Grid.RowDefinitions>
                <RowDefinition Height="Auto" />
                <RowDefinition Height="Auto" />
                <RowDefinition Height="Auto" />
                <RowDefinition Height="Auto" />
                <RowDefinition Height="Auto" />
            </Grid.RowDefinitions>

            <Grid.ColumnDefinitions>
                <ColumnDefinition Width="Auto" />
                <ColumnDefinition Width="Auto" />
            </Grid.ColumnDefinitions>

            <TextBlock Grid.Row="0" Grid.Column="0" Text="Accelerometer X:" />
            <TextBlock Grid.Row="1" Grid.Column="0" Text="Accelerometer Y:" />
            <TextBlock Grid.Row="2" Grid.Column="0" Text="Accelerometer Z:" />
            <TextBlock Grid.Row="3" Grid.Column="0" Text="Magnitude:"
                       Margin="24 24" />
            <TextBlock Grid.Row="4" Grid.Column="0" Text="Simple Orientation:" />

            <TextBlock Grid.Row="0" Grid.Column="1" Name="accelerometerX"
                       TextAlignment="Right" />
            <TextBlock Grid.Row="1" Grid.Column="1" Name="accelerometerY"
                       TextAlignment="Right"/>
            <TextBlock Grid.Row="2" Grid.Column="1" Name="accelerometerZ"
                       TextAlignment="Right"/>
            <TextBlock Grid.Row="3" Grid.Column="1" Name="magnitude"
                       TextAlignment="Right"
                       VerticalAlignment="Center" />
            <TextBlock Grid.Row="4" Grid.Column="1" Name="simpleOrientation"
                       TextAlignment="Right" />
        </Grid>
    </Grid>
</Page>
```

The code-behind file has a couple more amenities than the previous one. If the *Accelerometer* or *SimpleOrientationSensor* cannot be instantiated, the program reports that to the user. Also, it's a good idea not to have an *Accelerometer* running when a program isn't using it because it could contribute to battery drain. To symbolize application politeness, this program attaches the handlers in the *OnNavigatedTo* override and detaches them in *OnNavigatedFrom*. Otherwise, it's structurally quite similar to the previous program:

Project: AccelerometerAndSimpleOrientation | File: MainPage.xaml.cs (excerpt)

```
public sealed partial class MainPage : Page
{
    Accelerometer accelerometer = Accelerometer.GetDefault();
    SimpleOrientationSensor simpleOrientationSensor = SimpleOrientationSensor.GetDefault();

    public MainPage()
    {
        this.InitializeComponent();
        this.Loaded += OnMainPageLoaded;
    }

    async void OnMainPageLoaded(object sender, RoutedEventArgs args)
    {
        if (accelerometer == null)
            await new MessageDialog("Cannot start Accelerometer").ShowAsync();

        if (simpleOrientationSensor == null)
            await new MessageDialog("Cannot start SimpleOrientationSensor").ShowAsync();
    }

    // Attach event handlers
    protected override void OnNavigatedTo(NavigationEventArgs args)
    {
        if (accelerometer != null)
        {
            SetAccelerometerText(accelerometer.GetCurrentReading());
            accelerometer.ReadingChanged += OnAccelerometerReadingChanged;
        }

        if (simpleOrientationSensor != null)
        {
            SetSimpleOrientationText(simpleOrientationSensor.GetCurrentOrientation());
            simpleOrientationSensor.OrientationChanged += OnSimpleOrientationChanged;
        }
        base.OnNavigatedTo(args);
    }
```

```csharp
// Detach event handlers
protected override void OnNavigatedFrom(NavigationEventArgs args)
{
    if (accelerometer != null)
        accelerometer.ReadingChanged -= OnAccelerometerReadingChanged;

    if (simpleOrientationSensor != null)
        simpleOrientationSensor.OrientationChanged -= OnSimpleOrientationChanged;

    base.OnNavigatedFrom(args);
}

// Accelerometer handler
async void OnAccelerometerReadingChanged(Accelerometer sender,
                                         AccelerometerReadingChangedEventArgs args)
{
    await this.Dispatcher.RunAsync(CoreDispatcherPriority.Normal, () =>
        {
            SetAccelerometerText(args.Reading);
        });
}

void SetAccelerometerText(AccelerometerReading accelerometerReading)
{
    if (accelerometerReading == null)
        return;

    accelerometerX.Text = accelerometerReading.AccelerationX.ToString("F2");
    accelerometerY.Text = accelerometerReading.AccelerationY.ToString("F2");
    accelerometerZ.Text = accelerometerReading.AccelerationZ.ToString("F2");
    magnitude.Text =
        Math.Sqrt(Math.Pow(accelerometerReading.AccelerationX, 2) +
                  Math.Pow(accelerometerReading.AccelerationY, 2) +
                  Math.Pow(accelerometerReading.AccelerationZ, 2)).ToString("F2");
}

// SimpleOrientationSensor handler
async void OnSimpleOrientationChanged(SimpleOrientationSensor sender,
                                      SimpleOrientationSensorOrientationChangedEventArgs args)
{
    await this.Dispatcher.RunAsync(CoreDispatcherPriority.Normal, () =>
        {
            SetSimpleOrientationText(args.Orientation);
        });
}

void SetSimpleOrientationText(SimpleOrientation simpleOrientation)
{
    this.simpleOrientation.Text = simpleOrientation.ToString();
}
}
```

Here's the program running on the tablet I'm using to write this book while the tablet sits in its docking station:

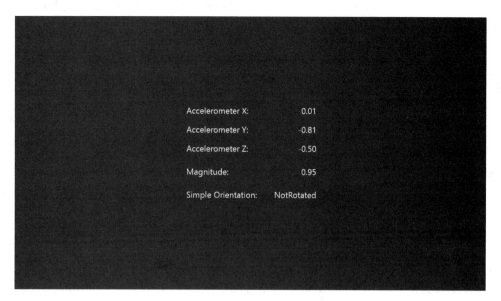

Accelerometer X:	0.01
Accelerometer Y:	-0.81
Accelerometer Z:	-0.50
Magnitude:	0.95
Simple Orientation:	NotRotated

Don't be alarmed at seeing magnitudes that are not precisely equal to 1. It doesn't mean that you've unknowingly drifted away from the surface of the Earth but only that accelerometer hardware is not always as precise as we'd prefer.

Both the *Y* and *Z* components are negative, indicating that the tablet is tilted back somewhat. As I mentioned earlier, if the tablet is sitting straight up, the vector is theoretically **(0, –1, 0)**, and if it's sitting on the desk with the screen pointing straight up, the vector is theoretically **(0, 0, –1)**. Between those two positions, the tablet is being rotated around its *X* axis. Pass the *Y* and *Z* values to the *Math.Atan2* method, and you'll get that angle of rotation.

If you run this program on a handheld device, you can twist the device around in different orientations to see the effect. Generally, you'll see the following correspondence between the *SimpleOrientationSensor* and the *Accelerometer*:

SimpleOrientationSensor	*Accelerometer* Vector
NotRotated	~ **(0, –1, 0)**
Rotated90DegreesCounterClockwise	~ **(–1, 0, 0)**
Rotated180DegreesCounterClockwise	~ **(0, 1, 0)**
Rotated270DegreesCounterClockwise	~ **(1, 0, 0)**
Faceup	~ **(0, 0, –1)**
Facedown	~ **(0, 0, 1)**

That "approximately equal to" symbol (~) should be interpreted very liberally. The *Accelerometer* vectors obviously show quite a bit of variation before they reach a value that precipitates a change to *SimpleOrientationSensor*.

This AccelerometerAndSimpleOrientation program doesn't indicate any preferred orientations, so as you're moving the tablet around in space, Windows automatically changes the display orientation under the assumption that you don't want to read numbers that are upside down. You should see a correspondence between the *SimpleOrientationSensor* values and the orientation of the screen, but this is only because Windows changes the display orientation based on these values! If you inhibit Windows from changing the screen orientation (by whatever means), the information displayed by this program is not affected.

In fact, you might find the continual display orientation changes to be rather annoying. As each one occurs, the updating of the screen pauses for a moment and the contents contract to signal this change. Think about it for a little while, and you'll probably come to the conclusion that programs that use the *Accelerometer* to alter screen content probably should also inhibit automatic display orientation changes.

For this reason, all of the programs in the remainder of this chapter include a simple statement in the program's constructor to set the preferred orientation to the native orientation:

```
DisplayProperties.AutoRotationPreferences = DisplayProperties.NativeOrientation;
```

You'll discover that if you run the AccelerometerAndSimpleOrientation program on a handheld device and move it rapidly, the direction and magnitude of the acceleration vector also change to no longer indicate 1g force coming from the center of the Earth. For example, if you jerk the device to the left, the acceleration vector points right—but only when the device is accelerating. If you manage to keep moving it at a steady velocity, the acceleration vector will settle down and resume pointing to the Earth. Suddenly stop the device from moving, and the acceleration vector also indicates that change in velocity.

The *Accelerometer* class also defines an event named *Shaken* with no other information. This event is useful for a program that needs to "throw" a pair of dice, or propose another restaurant recommendation, or perhaps erase a drawing or undo an accidental erasure.

One common application of an *Accelerometer* is a bubble level. This XAML file instantiates four *Ellipse* elements. Three are drawn as concentric outlines, and the fourth is the bubble itself:

Project: BubbleLevel | File: MainPage.xaml (excerpt)

```
<Grid Background="{StaticResource ApplicationPageBackgroundThemeBrush}">
    <Grid Name="centeredGrid"
          HorizontalAlignment="Center"
          VerticalAlignment="Center">
        <Ellipse Name="outerCircle"
                 Stroke="{StaticResource ApplicationForegroundThemeBrush}" />

        <Ellipse Name="halfCircle"
                 Stroke="{StaticResource ApplicationForegroundThemeBrush}" />

        <Ellipse Width="24"
                 Height="24"
                 Stroke="{StaticResource ApplicationForegroundThemeBrush}" />
```

```xml
        <Ellipse Fill="Red"
                Width="24"
                Height="24"
                HorizontalAlignment="Center"
                VerticalAlignment="Center">
            <Ellipse.RenderTransform>
                <TranslateTransform x:Name="bubbleTranslate" />
            </Ellipse.RenderTransform>
        </Ellipse>
    </Grid>
</Grid>
```

The code-behind file sets *DisplayProperties.AutoRotationPreferences* to *DisplayProperties.NativeOrientation*. There is simply no reason for Windows to be automatically changing the display orientation of this program. The program also processes the *SizeChanged* handler to set the dimensions of *outerCircle* and *halfCircle*:

Project: BubbleLevel | File: MainPage.xaml.cs (excerpt)

```csharp
public sealed partial class MainPage : Page
{
    Accelerometer accelerometer = Accelerometer.GetDefault();

    public MainPage()
    {
        this.InitializeComponent();
        DisplayProperties.AutoRotationPreferences = DisplayProperties.NativeOrientation;
        Loaded += OnMainPageLoaded;
        SizeChanged += OnMainPageSizeChanged;
    }

    async void OnMainPageLoaded(object sender, RoutedEventArgs args)
    {
        if (accelerometer != null)
        {
            accelerometer.ReportInterval = accelerometer.MinimumReportInterval;
            SetBubble(accelerometer.GetCurrentReading());
            accelerometer.ReadingChanged += OnAccelerometerReadingChanged;
        }
        else
        {
            await new MessageDialog("Accelerometer is not available").ShowAsync();
        }
    }

    void OnMainPageSizeChanged(object sender, SizeChangedEventArgs args)
    {
        double size = Math.Min(args.NewSize.Width, args.NewSize.Height);
        outerCircle.Width = size;
        outerCircle.Height = size;
        halfCircle.Width = size / 2;
        halfCircle.Height = size / 2;
    }
```

```
async void OnAccelerometerReadingChanged(Accelerometer sender,
                                         AccelerometerReadingChangedEventArgs args)
{
    await this.Dispatcher.RunAsync(CoreDispatcherPriority.Normal, () =>
    {
        SetBubble(args.Reading);
    });
}

void SetBubble(AccelerometerReading accelerometerReading)
{
    if (accelerometerReading == null)
        return;

    double x = accelerometerReading.AccelerationX;
    double y = accelerometerReading.AccelerationY;

    bubbleTranslate.X = -x * centeredGrid.ActualWidth / 2;
    bubbleTranslate.Y = y * centeredGrid.ActualHeight / 2;
}
}
```

The *SetBubble* method looks too simple: It just takes the X and Y components of the acceleration vector and uses those to set the *X* and *Y* coordinates of that center bubble, scaled to the radius of the outer circle. But consider a tablet sitting face up or face down on a table. The Z component of the acceleration vector is 1 or –1, and the X and Y components are both zero, meaning the bubble sits in the center of the screen. That's correct.

Now hold the tablet so that the screen is perpendicular to the Earth. The Z component becomes zero. This means that the magnitude of the acceleration vector results entirely from the X and Y components. In other words:

$$x^2 + y^2 = 1^2$$

That's the equation for a circle in two dimensions, so the bubble sits somewhere on that outer circle. Where exactly it sits is based on the current rotation of the tablet around its *Z* axis.

The acceleration vector points down toward the center of the Earth, and bubbles travel up, which means we need to swap the signs of the X and Y components of the acceleration vector to convert to two-dimensional screen coordinates. But recall that the *Y* axis of the acceleration vector is reversed from screen coordinates anyway, so only the X component needs to have its sign swapped, as you can see in the last two lines of code in the program.

Here's the program running on a Microsoft Surface tablet:

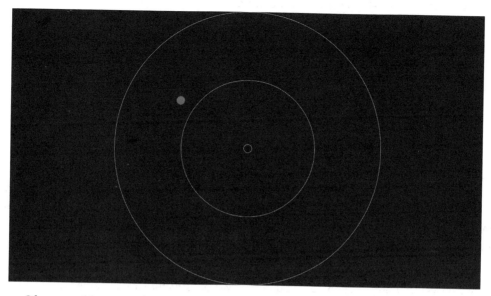

Of course, this screen shot doesn't quite capture how jittery the bubble is in real life. The *Accelerometer* values are rather raw, and in a real-life application you'll want to smooth them out a bit. I do this in the next two programs.

Follow the Rolling Ball

Using the *Accelerometer* is common in games for handheld devices. For example, if you have a game that simulates the driving of a car, the user might steer the car by tilting the computer to the left or right.

The following two programs simulate a ball rolling around the screen. If you hold the screen of your tablet parallel to the Earth and balance a real ball on top, you can make that ball roll around by tilting the screen. The greater the tilt, the greater the acceleration of the ball. The virtual ball in the next two programs moves in a similar way. Like the bubble level program, these programs ignore the Z component of the *Accelerometer* vector and use only the X and Y components to govern acceleration on the two-dimensional surface of the screen.

In the TiltAndRoll program, when the ball strikes one of the edges, it loses all its velocity in the direction perpendicular to the edge, continuing to roll along the edge if it still has velocity in that direction. The XAML file defines the ball. An *EllipseGeometry* allows the ball to be positioned at a particular coordinate by setting the *Center* property:

Project: TiltAndRoll | File: MainPage.xaml (excerpt)

```xaml
<Grid Background="{StaticResource ApplicationPageBackgroundThemeBrush}">
    <Path Fill="Red">
        <Path.Data>
            <EllipseGeometry x:Name="ball" />
        </Path.Data>
    </Path>
</Grid>
```

The code-behind file begins by defining a constant for GRAVITY in units of pixels per second squared. Theoretically, a sliding ball without friction is subject to the full force of gravity, but the acceleration of a rolling ball is 2/3 of gravitational acceleration. (See A. P. French, *Newtonian Mechanics*, W. W. Norton, 1971, pages 652–3, for the gory details.) This means you can calculate a value for GRAVITY by multiplying 32 feet per second squared by 12 inches per foot and 96 pixels per inch and 2/3 and get a value about 25,000, but I slowed it down considerably.

A two-dimensional vector value is very useful in calculations involving two-dimensional acceleration, velocity, and position, so I included the *Vector2* structure from Chapter 13, "Touch, Etc."

Because the ball needs to keep rolling regardless of the firing of the *ReadingChanged* event of the *Accelerometer*, the program doesn't install a handler for that event and instead uses *CompositionTarget.Rendering* to obtain the current value and apply it to the ball. Notice that the X and Y components of the *Accelerometer* readings are used to create a *Vector2* value, which is then averaged with the previous value, which itself is an average of its previous value, and so forth. This is an extremely simple form of smoothing:

Project: TiltAndRoll | File: MainPage.xaml.cs (excerpt)

```csharp
public sealed partial class MainPage : Page
{
    const double GRAVITY = 5000;     // pixels per second squared
    const double BALL_RADIUS = 32;

    Accelerometer accelerometer = Accelerometer.GetDefault();
    TimeSpan timeSpan;
    Vector2 acceleration;
    Vector2 ballPosition;
    Vector2 ballVelocity;

    public MainPage()
    {
        this.InitializeComponent();
        DisplayProperties.AutoRotationPreferences = DisplayProperties.NativeOrientation;

        ball.RadiusX = BALL_RADIUS;
        ball.RadiusY = BALL_RADIUS;

        Loaded += OnMainPageLoaded;
    }
```

```
async void OnMainPageLoaded(object sender, RoutedEventArgs args)
{
    if (accelerometer == null)
    {
        await new MessageDialog("Accelerometer is not available").ShowAsync();
    }
    else
    {
        CompositionTarget.Rendering += OnCompositionTargetRendering;
    }
}

void OnCompositionTargetRendering(object sender, object args)
{
    AccelerometerReading reading = accelerometer.GetCurrentReading();

    if (reading == null)
        return;

    // Get elapsed time since last event
    TimeSpan timeSpan = (args as RenderingEventArgs).RenderingTime;
    double elapsedSeconds = (timeSpan - this.timeSpan).TotalSeconds;
    this.timeSpan = timeSpan;

    // Convert accelerometer reading to display coordinates
    double x = reading.AccelerationX;
    double y = -reading.AccelerationY;

    // Get current X-Y acceleration and smooth it
    acceleration = 0.5 * (acceleration + new Vector2(x, y));

    // Calculate new velocity and position
    ballVelocity += GRAVITY * acceleration * elapsedSeconds;
    ballPosition += ballVelocity * elapsedSeconds;

    // Check for hitting edge
    if (ballPosition.X - BALL_RADIUS < 0)
    {
        ballPosition = new Vector2(BALL_RADIUS, ballPosition.Y);
        ballVelocity = new Vector2(0, ballVelocity.Y);
    }
    if (ballPosition.X + BALL_RADIUS > this.ActualWidth)
    {
        ballPosition = new Vector2(this.ActualWidth - BALL_RADIUS, ballPosition.Y);
        ballVelocity = new Vector2(0, ballVelocity.Y);
    }
    if (ballPosition.Y - BALL_RADIUS < 0)
    {
        ballPosition = new Vector2(ballPosition.X, BALL_RADIUS);
        ballVelocity = new Vector2(ballVelocity.X, 0);
    }
    if (ballPosition.Y + BALL_RADIUS > this.ActualHeight)
    {
        ballPosition = new Vector2(ballPosition.X, this.ActualHeight - BALL_RADIUS);
        ballVelocity = new Vector2(ballVelocity.X, 0);
    }
    ball.Center = new Point(ballPosition.X, ballPosition.Y);
}
}
```

The two crucial calculations are these:

```
ballVelocity += GRAVITY * acceleration * elapsedSeconds;
ballPosition += ballVelocity * elapsedSeconds;
```

Keep in mind that *acceleration*, *ballVelocity*, and *ballPosition* are all *Vector2* values, so they all have X and Y components. The velocity is increased by the *acceleration* times elapsed time, and the position is increased by the velocity times elapsed time. Then it's only a matter of checking whether the new position is outside the bounds of the page. If so, it's moved back within the page and one of the components of the velocity is set to zero.

The physics are fairly realistic. As you increase and decrease the tilt, the magnitude of the acceleration of the ball increases and decreases. Moreover, because the program is dealing with actual formulas for velocity and position, it becomes fairly easy to add some bounce. One easy way is to not set the velocity component to zero when the ball hits the edge but to make that velocity component the negative of its previous value. However, that means the ball has the same velocity magnitude after the bounce, and that's unrealistic. It makes more sense to include an attenuation factor that I called BOUNCE. Everything in this TiltAndBounce program is the same as TiltAndRoll except for that BOUNCE constant and different ball-moving logic in the *CompositionTarget.Rendering* handler:

Project: TiltAndBounce | **File:** MainPage.xaml.cs (excerpt)

```
public sealed partial class MainPage : Page
{
    ...
    const double BOUNCE = -2.0 / 3; // fraction of velocity
    ...
    void OnCompositionTargetRendering(object sender, object args)
    {
        AccelerometerReading reading = accelerometer.GetCurrentReading();

        if (reading == null)
            return;

        // Get elapsed time
        TimeSpan timeSpan = (args as RenderingEventArgs).RenderingTime;
        double elapsedSeconds = (timeSpan - this.timeSpan).TotalSeconds;
        this.timeSpan = timeSpan;

        // Convert accelerometer reading to display coordinates
        double x = reading.AccelerationX;
        double y = -reading.AccelerationY;

        // Get current X-Y acceleration and smooth it
        acceleration = 0.5 * (acceleration + new Vector2(x, y));

        // Calculate new velocity and position
        ballVelocity += GRAVITY * acceleration * elapsedSeconds;
        ballPosition += ballVelocity * elapsedSeconds;

        // Check for bouncing off edge
        bool needAnotherLoop = true;
```

```
        while (needAnotherLoop)
        {
            needAnotherLoop = false;

            if (ballPosition.X - BALL_RADIUS < 0)
            {
                ballPosition = new Vector2(-ballPosition.X + 2 * BALL_RADIUS, ballPosition.Y);
                ballVelocity = new Vector2(BOUNCE * ballVelocity.X, ballVelocity.Y);
                needAnotherLoop = true;
            }
            else if (ballPosition.X + BALL_RADIUS > this.ActualWidth)
            {
                ballPosition = new Vector2(-ballPosition.X + 2 *
                    (this.ActualWidth - BALL_RADIUS),
                                        ballPosition.Y);
                ballVelocity = new Vector2(BOUNCE * ballVelocity.X, ballVelocity.Y);
                needAnotherLoop = true;
            }
            else if (ballPosition.Y - BALL_RADIUS < 0)
            {
                ballPosition = new Vector2(ballPosition.X, -ballPosition.Y + 2 * BALL_RADIUS);
                ballVelocity = new Vector2(ballVelocity.X, BOUNCE * ballVelocity.Y);
                needAnotherLoop = true;
            }
            else if (ballPosition.Y + BALL_RADIUS > this.ActualHeight)
            {
                ballPosition = new Vector2(ballPosition.X,
                                        -ballPosition.Y + 2 *
                                            (this.ActualHeight - BALL_RADIUS));
                ballVelocity = new Vector2(ballVelocity.X, BOUNCE * ballVelocity.Y);
                needAnotherLoop = true;
            }
        }
        ball.Center = new Point(ballPosition.X, ballPosition.Y);
    }
}
```

In the TiltAndRoll program, it was possible for the ball to go beyond two adjacent edges during the same event, but those cases were handled with a series of *if* statements. In this program, bouncing the ball off one edge could make it go beyond another edge, which means that a loop is necessary to test the position of the ball repeatedly until there are no more bounces.

The Two Norths

Although the *Accelerometer* tells you which way is down, it doesn't reveal the complete orientation of the device in 3D space. To see what I mean, run the AccelerometerAndSimpleOrientation program on a handheld device. Stand up, and hold the device in some odd configuration. The *Accelerometer* tells you which way is down. Now turn your whole body around in a circle. The tablet has rotated 360 degrees in space, but the *Accelerometer* has reported pretty much the same value because the direction of down has remained the same relative to the device.

When you turn the tablet in a circle around the acceleration vector, what changes? One answer is: The direction of north relative to the tablet. This is why a *Compass* sensor is so important: It provides a missing factor in determining the tablet's orientation. By combining the *Compass* and the *Accelerometer*, you can derive a complete orientation of the tablet in 3D space. Or you can let Windows do it for you.

The *Compass* class is structured much like *Accelerometer*, and the *CompassReading* class has two properties: *HeadingMagneticNorth* and *HeadingTrueNorth*. These are both angles in degrees, and they indicate the angle of the computer relative to north. The angles should be close to zero if you hold your tablet screen parallel to the Earth and point the top of the screen toward north. (By "top" I'm referring to the direction of the positive *Y* axis in the diagrams shown earlier in this chapter.) As you turn the tablet screen toward the east, the angles increase.

Of course, these angles shouldn't be the same except in certain locations around the world. The tablet contains a magnetometer that responds to magnetic north (which is aligned with the Earth's magnetic field); true north refers to the axis around which the Earth rotates. Interestingly, the *HeadingMagneticNorth* property is of type *double*, but *HeadingTrueNorth* is of type nullable *double*, which ominously suggests that the value might not be available.

Let's try it. The XAML file for the SimpleCompass project defines two graphical arrows that have origins in the center of the screen and point straight up:

Project: SimpleCompass | File: MainPage.xaml (excerpt)

```xaml
<Grid Background="{StaticResource ApplicationPageBackgroundThemeBrush}">
    <Canvas HorizontalAlignment="Center"
            VerticalAlignment="Center">
        <Path Fill="Magenta"
              Data="M -10 0 L 10 0, 10 -300, 0 -350, -10 -300 Z">
            <Path.RenderTransform>
                <RotateTransform x:Name="magNorthRotate" />
            </Path.RenderTransform>
        </Path>

        <Path Name="trueNorthPath"
              Fill="Blue"
              Data="M -10 0 L 10 0, 10 -300, 0 -350, -10 -300 Z">
            <Path.RenderTransform>
                <RotateTransform x:Name="trueNorthRotate" />
            </Path.RenderTransform>
        </Path>
    </Canvas>
</Grid>
```

The two mnemonic colors are Magenta for Magnetic north and Blue for True north.

The code-behind file hides the second *Path* if the value of *HeadingTrueNorth* is *null*:

Project: SimpleCompass | **File:** MainPage.xaml.cs (excerpt)

```
public sealed partial class MainPage : Page
{
    Compass compass = Compass.GetDefault();

    public MainPage()
    {
        this.InitializeComponent();
        DisplayProperties.AutoRotationPreferences = DisplayProperties.NativeOrientation;
        Loaded += OnMainPageLoaded;
    }

    async void OnMainPageLoaded(object sender, RoutedEventArgs args)
    {
        if (compass != null)
        {
            ShowCompassValues(compass.GetCurrentReading());
            compass.ReportInterval = compass.MinimumReportInterval;
            compass.ReadingChanged += OnCompassReadingChanged;
        }
        else
        {
            await new MessageDialog("Compass is not available").ShowAsync();
        }
    }

    async void OnCompassReadingChanged(Compass sender, CompassReadingChangedEventArgs args)
    {
        await this.Dispatcher.RunAsync(CoreDispatcherPriority.Normal, () =>
            {
                ShowCompassValues(args.Reading);
            });
    }

    void ShowCompassValues(CompassReading compassReading)
    {
        if (compassReading == null)
            return;

        magNorthRotate.Angle = -compassReading.HeadingMagneticNorth;

        if (compassReading.HeadingTrueNorth.HasValue)
        {
            trueNorthPath.Visibility = Visibility.Visible;
            trueNorthRotate.Angle = -compassReading.HeadingTrueNorth.Value;
        }
        else
        {
            trueNorthPath.Visibility = Visibility.Collapsed;
        }
    }
}
```

Notice that the rotation angles of the two arrows are set to the negatives of the *HeadingMagneticNorth* and *HeadingTrueNorth* properties. These values indicate the rotation of the computer relative to north, so the arrows need to be rotated oppositely and show the direction of north relative to the computer.

On both tablets I've been using for this book—including a Microsoft Surface machine—the results are disappointing. The *HeadingTrueNorth* value is always *null* on both machines. On the Microsoft Surface, the value for magnetic north is quite erratic. On the Samsung tablet, values only range from 0 to 180 degrees! On my Technical Editor's tablet, *HeadingMagneticNorth* is always 0.

In theory, true north can be calculated from magnetic north knowing the location of the computer, but enabling Location capabilities in Package.appxmanifest doesn't help.

Nevertheless, we can cross our fingers and hope that the compass hardware works sufficiently well to be combined with accelerometer data and provide complete orientation information.

Inclinometer = Accelerometer + Compass

The *Inclinometer* sensor is one of two classes that internally combines accelerometer and compass data and smooths the result somewhat. This class provides information in the form of *yaw*, *pitch*, and *roll* angles, which are terms used in flight dynamics.

The yaw, pitch, and roll angles are often referred to as Euler angles, after 18th-century mathematician Leonhard Euler, who explored the mathematics of three-dimensional rotation. If you're flying a plane, yaw indicates the compass direction that the nose of the plane is facing. As the plane veers left or right, the yaw changes. Pitch indicates the angle of the nose of the plane. As the nose goes up for a climb and down for a dive, the pitch changes. Roll is achieved by banking left or right.

To understand how these apply to the computer, you might want to visualize yourself "flying" your tablet like a magic carpet. Assume a sitting position on the screen facing toward the top (in the tablet's native orientation, of course) and take off. In the coordinate system shown earlier in this chapter, yaw is rotation around the *Z* axis, pitch is rotation around the *X* axis, and roll is rotation around the *Y* axis.

The YawPitchRoll program also helps you visualize these angles. The XAML file contains some *Rectangle* elements used for lines, some *Ellipse* elements used as rolling balls, and some text:

Project: YawPitchRoll | File: MainPage.xaml (excerpt)

```
<Grid Background="{StaticResource ApplicationPageBackgroundThemeBrush}">
    <!-- Pitch -->
    <Rectangle Fill="Blue"
               Width="3"
               HorizontalAlignment="Center"
               VerticalAlignment="Stretch" />

    <Path Name="pitchPath"
          Stroke="Blue">
        <Path.Data>
```

```xml
            <EllipseGeometry x:Name="pitchEllipse" RadiusX="20" RadiusY="20" />
        </Path.Data>
    </Path>

    <!-- Roll -->
    <Rectangle Fill="Red"
               Height="3"
               HorizontalAlignment="Stretch"
               VerticalAlignment="Center" />

    <Path Name="rollPath"
          Stroke="Red"
          Fill="Red">
        <Path.Data>
            <EllipseGeometry x:Name="rollEllipse" RadiusX="20" RadiusY="20" />
        </Path.Data>
    </Path>

    <Grid>
        <Grid.RowDefinitions>
            <RowDefinition Height="*" />
            <RowDefinition Height="*" />
        </Grid.RowDefinitions>
        <Grid.ColumnDefinitions>
            <ColumnDefinition Width="*" />
            <ColumnDefinition Width="*" />
        </Grid.ColumnDefinitions>

        <!-- Pitch -->
        <TextBlock Text="PITCH"
                   Grid.Row="0"
                   Grid.Column="0"
                   Foreground="Blue"
                   HorizontalAlignment="Right"
                   Margin="0 0 24 0" />

        <TextBlock Name="pitchValue"
                   Grid.Row="0"
                   Grid.Column="1"
                   Foreground="Blue"
                   HorizontalAlignment="Left"
                   Margin="24 0 0 0" />

        <!-- Roll -->
        <TextBlock Text="ROLL"
                   Grid.Row="1"
                   Grid.Column="0"
                   Foreground="Red"
                   HorizontalAlignment="Left"
                   VerticalAlignment="Top"
                   Margin="0 108 0 0">
            <TextBlock.RenderTransform>
                <RotateTransform Angle="-90" />
            </TextBlock.RenderTransform>
        </TextBlock>
```

```xml
        <TextBlock Name="rollValue"
                   Grid.Row="0"
                   Grid.Column="0"
                   Foreground="Red"
                   HorizontalAlignment="Left"
                   VerticalAlignment="Bottom">
            <TextBlock.RenderTransform>
                <RotateTransform Angle="-90" />
            </TextBlock.RenderTransform>
        </TextBlock>

        <!-- Yaw -->
        <Grid Grid.Row="0"
              Grid.Column="1"
              HorizontalAlignment="Stretch"
              VerticalAlignment="Bottom"
              RenderTransformOrigin="0 1">
            <StackPanel Orientation="Horizontal"
                        HorizontalAlignment="Center">
                <TextBlock Text="YAW = " Foreground="Green" />
                <TextBlock Name="yawValue" Foreground="Green" />
            </StackPanel>

            <Rectangle Fill="Green"
                       Height="3"
                       HorizontalAlignment="Stretch"
                       VerticalAlignment="Bottom" />

            <Grid.RenderTransform>
                <TransformGroup>
                    <RotateTransform Angle="-90" />
                    <RotateTransform x:Name="yawRotate" />
                </TransformGroup>
            </Grid.RenderTransform>
        </Grid>
    </Grid>
</Grid>
```

As you can see from the code-behind file, the *Inclinometer* class is instantiated and used much like *Accelerometer* and *Compass*:

Project: YawPitchRoll | File: MainPage.xaml.cs (excerpt)

```csharp
public sealed partial class MainPage : Page
{
    Inclinometer inclinometer = Inclinometer.GetDefault();

    public MainPage()
    {
        this.InitializeComponent();
        DisplayProperties.AutoRotationPreferences = DisplayProperties.NativeOrientation;
        Loaded += OnMainPageLoaded;
    }

    async void OnMainPageLoaded(object sender, RoutedEventArgs args)
    {
```

```
        if (inclinometer == null)
        {
            await new MessageDialog("Cannot obtain Inclinometer").ShowAsync();
        }
        else
        {
            ShowYawPitchRoll(inclinometer.GetCurrentReading());
            inclinometer.ReportInterval = inclinometer.MinimumReportInterval;
            inclinometer.ReadingChanged += OnInclinometerReadingChanged;
        }
    }

    async void OnInclinometerReadingChanged(Inclinometer sender,
                                    InclinometerReadingChangedEventArgs args)
    {
        await this.Dispatcher.RunAsync(CoreDispatcherPriority.Normal, () =>
            {
                ShowYawPitchRoll(args.Reading);
            });
    }

    void ShowYawPitchRoll(InclinometerReading inclinometerReading)
    {
        if (inclinometerReading == null)
            return;

        double yaw = inclinometerReading.YawDegrees;
        double pitch = inclinometerReading.PitchDegrees;
        double roll = inclinometerReading.RollDegrees;

        yawValue.Text = yaw.ToString("F0") + "°";
        pitchValue.Text = pitch.ToString("F0") + "°";
        rollValue.Text = roll.ToString("F0") + "°";

        yawRotate.Angle = yaw;

        if (pitch <= 90 && pitch >= -90)
        {
            pitchPath.Fill = pitchPath.Stroke;
            pitchEllipse.Center = new Point(this.ActualWidth / 2,
                                    this.ActualHeight * (pitch + 90) / 180);
        }
        else
        {
            pitchPath.Fill = null;

            if (pitch > 90)
                pitchEllipse.Center = new Point(this.ActualWidth / 2,
                                        this.ActualHeight * (270 - pitch) / 180);
            else // pitch < -90
                pitchEllipse.Center = new Point(this.ActualWidth / 2,
                                        this.ActualHeight * (-90 - pitch) / 180);
        }
        rollEllipse.Center = new Point(this.ActualWidth * (roll + 90) / 180,
                                this.ActualHeight / 2);
    }
}
```

There's no secret source of compass data providing information for the Inclinometer. The *YawDegrees* property is just as erratic (or limited) as the *Compass* reading, except that they're complements: The sum of the *YawDegrees* and the *Compass* reading always approximately equals 360. When the tablet is lying with its screen up on a level surface, the yaw line points toward north (or thereabouts) and the balls for pitch and roll both sit in the center. As you tilt the top of the tablet up or down, *PitchDegrees* ranges from 90 degrees when the tablet is upright to –90 when the top of the tablet points down. *RollDegrees* ranges from 90 degrees to –90 degrees as the tablet is tilted right or left. Here's a view when the top and left sides of the tablet are elevated:

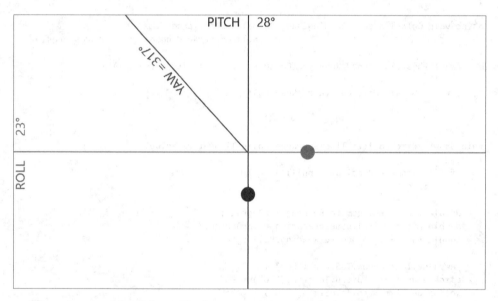

When the screen faces down, *YawDegrees* points south, and *PitchDegrees* takes on values ranging from 90 degrees to 180 degrees, and from –90 degrees to –180 degrees. The program symbolizes these values with a hollow red ball.

If you're working with a program where something is flying around the screen, these Euler angles might be exactly what you need. However, you might want something more mathematically oriented. That's the purpose of the next class.

OrientationSensor = Accelerometer + Compass

You can represent rotation in three-dimensional space several ways, all of which can be converted among each other. The *OrientationSensor* class is very similar to *Inclinometer* in the sense that it combines information from the accelerometer and compass to provide a complete orientation in 3D space. *OrientationSensor* provides this orientation in instances of two classes:

- *SensorQuaternion*
- *SensorRotationMatrix*

Quaternions are mathematically quite interesting. Just as an imaginary number can represent a rotation in two-dimensional space, a quaternion represents rotation in three-dimensional space. Game programmers particularly like representing rotations as quaternions because quaternions can be smoothly interpolated. (I discuss quaternions in Chapter 8 of my book *3D Programming for Windows* [Microsoft Press, 2007].)

A rotation matrix is a regular transform matrix missing the last row and last column. A regular three-dimensional transform matrix has 4 rows and 4 columns. The *SensorRotationMatrix* class defines 3 rows and 3 columns. Such a matrix is incapable of representing translation or perspective, and by convention it incorporates no scaling or skew. But it can easily be used to rotate objects in 3D space.

On the Samsung tablet I'm using to write this book, the *SensorRotationMatrix* contains all zeroes, so none of the programs in this book that use that matrix will work. Better results are available on the Microsoft Surface.

When you're working with this rotation matrix, a change in perspective might be helpful. I've been describing how the values from the *Accelerometer* and *Compass* are relative to the 3D coordinate system I presented in the early pages of this chapter. When working with the rotation matrix from the *OrientationSensor* class, it helps to visualize two 3D coordinate systems, one for the device and the other for the Earth:

- In the computer's 3D coordinate system, positive *Y* points to the top of the screen, positive *X* points to the right, and positive *Z* comes out of the screen, just as I showed earlier.

- In the Earth's coordinate system, positive *Y* points north, positive *X* points east, and positive *Z* comes out of the ground.

These two coordinate systems are aligned when the computer is lying on a level surface with its screen pointing up and the top pointing north. The *SensorRotationMatrix* becomes (theoretically) the identity matrix: 1s in the diagonal and 0s otherwise. Otherwise, the matrix describes how the Earth is rotated relative to the computer, which is the opposite of the rotation described by the Euler angles.

This difference is demonstrated by the AxisAngleRotation program, which computes yet another method of representing rotation in three-dimensional space—as a rotation around a 3D vector. The XAML file is a not-very-interesting assemblage of *TextBlock* elements, some functioning as labels and the others awaiting text:

Project: AxisAngleRotation | **File:** MainPage.xaml (excerpt)

```
<Page ... >
    <Page.Resources>
        <Style x:Key="DefaultTextBlockStyle" TargetType="TextBlock">
            <Setter Property="FontFamily" Value="Lucida Sans Unicode" />
            <Setter Property="FontSize" Value="36" />
            <Setter Property="Margin" Value="0 0 48 0" />
        </Style>

        <Style x:Key="rightText" TargetType="TextBlock"
                BasedOn="{StaticResource DefaultTextBlockStyle}">
            <Setter Property="TextAlignment" Value="Right" />
            <Setter Property="Margin" Value="48 0 0 0" />
        </Style>
    </Page.Resources>
```

```xml
<Grid Background="{StaticResource ApplicationPageBackgroundThemeBrush}">
    <StackPanel HorizontalAlignment="Center"
            VerticalAlignment="Center">

        <!-- Grid showing Pitch, Roll, and Yaw -->
        <Grid HorizontalAlignment="Center">
            <Grid.RowDefinitions>
                <RowDefinition Height="Auto" />
                <RowDefinition Height="Auto" />
                <RowDefinition Height="Auto" />
            </Grid.RowDefinitions>

            <Grid.ColumnDefinitions>
                <ColumnDefinition Width="Auto" />
                <ColumnDefinition Width="Auto" />
            </Grid.ColumnDefinitions>

            <Grid.Resources>
                <Style TargetType="TextBlock"
                        BasedOn="{StaticResource DefaultTextBlockStyle}" />
            </Grid.Resources>

            <TextBlock Text="Pitch: " Grid.Row="0" Grid.Column="0" />
            <TextBlock Name="pitchText" Grid.Row="0" Grid.Column="1"
                    Style="{StaticResource rightText}" />

            <TextBlock Text="Roll: " Grid.Row="1" Grid.Column="0" />
            <TextBlock Name="rollText" Grid.Row="1" Grid.Column="1"
                    Style="{StaticResource rightText}" />

            <TextBlock Text="Yaw: " Grid.Row="2" Grid.Column="0" />
            <TextBlock Name="yawText" Grid.Row="2" Grid.Column="1"
                    Style="{StaticResource rightText}" />
        </Grid>

        <!-- Grid for RotationMatrix -->
        <Grid HorizontalAlignment="Center"
            Margin="0 48">
            <Grid.RowDefinitions>
                <RowDefinition Height="Auto" />
                <RowDefinition Height="Auto" />
                <RowDefinition Height="Auto" />
            </Grid.RowDefinitions>

            <Grid.ColumnDefinitions>
                <ColumnDefinition Width="Auto" />
                <ColumnDefinition Width="Auto" />
                <ColumnDefinition Width="Auto" />
            </Grid.ColumnDefinitions>

            <Grid.Resources>
                <Style TargetType="TextBlock" BasedOn="{StaticResource rightText}" />
            </Grid.Resources>

            <TextBlock Name="m11Text" Grid.Row="0" Grid.Column="0" />
            <TextBlock Name="m12Text" Grid.Row="0" Grid.Column="1" />
            <TextBlock Name="m13Text" Grid.Row="0" Grid.Column="2" />
```

```
                    <TextBlock Name="m21Text" Grid.Row="1" Grid.Column="0" />
                    <TextBlock Name="m22Text" Grid.Row="1" Grid.Column="1" />
                    <TextBlock Name="m23Text" Grid.Row="1" Grid.Column="2" />

                    <TextBlock Name="m31Text" Grid.Row="2" Grid.Column="0" />
                    <TextBlock Name="m32Text" Grid.Row="2" Grid.Column="1" />
                    <TextBlock Name="m33Text" Grid.Row="2" Grid.Column="2" />
                </Grid>

                <!-- Axis/Angle rotation display -->
                <Grid HorizontalAlignment="Center">
                    <Grid.RowDefinitions>
                        <RowDefinition Height="Auto" />
                        <RowDefinition Height="Auto" />
                    </Grid.RowDefinitions>

                    <Grid.ColumnDefinitions>
                        <ColumnDefinition Width="Auto" />
                        <ColumnDefinition Width="Auto" />
                    </Grid.ColumnDefinitions>

                    <Grid.Resources>
                        <Style TargetType="TextBlock"
                                BasedOn="{StaticResource DefaultTextBlockStyle}" />
                    </Grid.Resources>

                    <TextBlock Text="Angle:" Grid.Row="0" Grid.Column="0" />
                    <TextBlock Name="angleText" Grid.Row="0" Grid.Column="1"
                            TextAlignment="Center"/>
                    <TextBlock Text="Axis:" Grid.Row="1" Grid.Column="0" />
                    <TextBlock Name="axisText" Grid.Row="1" Grid.Column="1"
                            TextAlignment="Center" />
                </Grid>
            </StackPanel>
        </Grid>
</Page>
```

The code-behind file instantiates both an *Inclinometer* to obtain the yaw, pitch, and roll angles, and an *OrientationSensor* to obtain (and display) the rotation matrix and convert it to an axis/angle rotation:

Project: AxisAngleRotation | File: MainPage.xaml.cs (excerpt)

```
public sealed partial class MainPage : Page
{
    Inclinometer inclinometer = Inclinometer.GetDefault();
    OrientationSensor orientationSensor = OrientationSensor.GetDefault();

    public MainPage()
    {
        this.InitializeComponent();
        DisplayProperties.AutoRotationPreferences = DisplayProperties.NativeOrientation;
        Loaded += OnMainPageLoaded;
    }
```

```
async void OnMainPageLoaded(object sender, RoutedEventArgs args)
{
    if (inclinometer == null)
    {
        await new MessageDialog("Inclinometer is not available").ShowAsync();
    }
    else
    {
        // Start the Inclinometer events
        ShowYawPitchRoll(inclinometer.GetCurrentReading());
        inclinometer.ReadingChanged += OnInclinometerReadingChanged;
    }

    if (orientationSensor == null)
    {
        await new MessageDialog("OrientationSensor is not available").ShowAsync();
    }
    else
    {
        // Start the OrientationSensor events
        ShowOrientation(orientationSensor.GetCurrentReading());
        orientationSensor.ReadingChanged += OrientationSensorChanged;
    }
}

async void OnInclinometerReadingChanged(Inclinometer sender,
                                        InclinometerReadingChangedEventArgs args)
{
    await this.Dispatcher.RunAsync(CoreDispatcherPriority.Normal, () =>
        {
            ShowYawPitchRoll(args.Reading);
        });
}

void ShowYawPitchRoll(InclinometerReading inclinometerReading)
{
    if (inclinometerReading == null)
        return;

    yawText.Text = inclinometerReading.YawDegrees.ToString("F0") + "°";
    pitchText.Text = inclinometerReading.PitchDegrees.ToString("F0") + "°";
    rollText.Text = inclinometerReading.RollDegrees.ToString("F0") + "°";
}

async void OrientationSensorChanged(OrientationSensor sender,
                                    OrientationSensorReadingChangedEventArgs args)
{
    await this.Dispatcher.RunAsync(CoreDispatcherPriority.Normal, () =>
        {
            ShowOrientation(args.Reading);
        });
}

void ShowOrientation(OrientationSensorReading orientationReading)
{
    if (orientationReading == null)
        return;
```

```
SensorRotationMatrix matrix = orientationReading.RotationMatrix;

if (matrix == null)
    return;

m11Text.Text = matrix.M11.ToString("F3");
m12Text.Text = matrix.M12.ToString("F3");
m13Text.Text = matrix.M13.ToString("F3");

m21Text.Text = matrix.M21.ToString("F3");
m22Text.Text = matrix.M22.ToString("F3");
m23Text.Text = matrix.M23.ToString("F3");

m31Text.Text = matrix.M31.ToString("F3");
m32Text.Text = matrix.M32.ToString("F3");
m33Text.Text = matrix.M33.ToString("F3");

// Convert rotation matrix to axis and angle
double angle = Math.Acos((matrix.M11 + matrix.M22 + matrix.M33 - 1) / 2);
angleText.Text = (180 * angle / Math.PI).ToString("F0");

if (angle != 0)
{
    double twoSine = 2 * Math.Sin(angle);
    double x = (matrix.M23 - matrix.M32) / twoSine;
    double y = (matrix.M31 - matrix.M13) / twoSine;
    double z = (matrix.M12 - matrix.M21) / twoSine;

    axisText.Text = String.Format("({0:F2} {1:F2} {2:F2})", x, y, z);
}
    }
}
}
```

Here's a screen shot from the Microsoft Surface showing the three Euler angles at the top, the rotation matrix in the middle, and a derived axis/angle rotation at the bottom:

For this screen shot, I'm holding the tablet roughly toward north so that the yaw angle is nearly zero. The tablet is tilted a tiny bit to the left, and that makes the roll angle a bit negative. But I have elevated the top of the tablet by a whopping 46 degrees. That same angle is displayed at the bottom as derived from the rotation matrix. But look at the axis: That's very nearly the vector **(–1, 0, 0)**, which is the negative *X* axis. Using the right-hand rule, point your thumb in the direction of the negative *X* axis. The curl of your fingers indicates the direction for rotations of positive angles (which this is), so it confirms what I said: The rotation matrix describes a rotation of the Earth relative to the computer.

This means that if you want a rotation matrix that represents a rotation of the computer relative to the Earth, you need to invert the matrix. The *SensorRotationMatrix* class has no facility to invert itself, but the *Matrix3D* structure does. (You'll recall that *Matrix3D* is defined in the *Windows.UI.Xaml.Media .Media3D* namespace and used in connection with *Matrix3DProjection*.) It's a simple matter to create a *Matrix3D* value from a *SensorRotationMatrix* object and then invert it.

I'm going to use that technique to create yet another representation of an orientation in 3D space.

Azimuth and Altitude

Conceptually, we live inside a celestial sphere. If you need to describe a location of an object in 3D space relative to yourself where distance doesn't matter, points relative to this celestial sphere are very convenient. This celestial sphere is particularly suitable for programs that let you use a computer screen for viewing a world of virtual reality or augmented reality. In such programs you hold a tablet as if you're using it to take a photograph from the camera on the back, but what you see on the screen is generated (in full or in part) by the program based on the screen's orientation. By panning the screen in arcs, you can view different parts of this world.

The celestial sphere has a familiar analogue in the terrestrial realm. When we need to identify a location on the Earth, we do so with longitude and latitude, both of which are angles with a vertex in the Earth's center. Conceptually, we divide the Earth's sphere in half at the equator. Lines of latitude are parallel to the equator and measured by positive angles north of the equator (to a maximum of 90 degrees at the North Pole) and negative angles south of the equator (to –90 degrees at the South Pole). Angles of longitude are based on great circles that pass through these two poles measured from the Prime Meridian, which is the longitude line that passes through Greenwich, England.

We can describe points on the celestial sphere in much the same way, but we're at the center of the sphere looking out and the terminology is different.

Point your outstretched arm in any direction. How can we identify that location? First, swing your arm up or down so that it becomes horizontal—that is, parallel to the surface of the Earth. The angle your arm has swung during this movement is called the *altitude*.

Positive altitude values are above the horizon; negative values are below the horizon. Straight up is the *zenith*, an altitude of 90 degrees. Straight down is the *nadir*, an altitude of –90 degrees.

You're still pointing your outstretched arm toward the horizon, right? Now swing your arm so that it's pointing north. The angle your arm has just swung this second time is called the *azimuth*.

Together, the altitude and azimuth constitute a *horizontal coordinate*, so named because the horizon divides the celestial sphere in half—similar to the equator in terrestrial coordinates.

The horizontal coordinate has no information about distance. During a solar eclipse, the sun and moon have the same horizontal coordinate. The horizontal coordinate is not a location in 3D space; it's a direction in 3D space from a viewer. In that sense the horizontal coordinate is like a 3D vector except that a vector is expressed in rectangular coordinates and the horizontal coordinate is spherical.

To make the job of deriving a horizontal coordinate a little easier, let's first define a *Vector3* structure for encapsulating a 3D vector:

Project: EarthlyDelights | **File:** Vector3.cs

```
using System;
using Windows.Foundation;
using Windows.UI.Xaml.Media;
using Windows.UI.Xaml.Media.Media3D;

namespace Petzold.Windows8.VectorDrawing
{
    public struct Vector3
    {
        // Constructors
        public Vector3(double x, double y, double z)
            : this()
        {
            X = x;
            Y = y;
            Z = z;
        }

        // Properties
        public double X { private set; get; }
        public double Y { private set; get; }
        public double Z { private set; get; }

        public double LengthSquared
        {
            get { return X * X + Y * Y + Z * Z; }
        }

        public double Length
        {
            get { return Math.Sqrt(LengthSquared); }
        }

        public Vector3 Normalized
        {
            get
            {
                double length = this.Length;

                if (length != 0)
```

```
            {
                return new Vector3(this.X / length,
                                   this.Y / length,
                                   this.Z / length);
            }
            return new Vector3();
        }
    }

    // Static properties
    public static Vector3 UnitX
    {
        get { return new Vector3(1, 0, 0); }
    }

    public static Vector3 UnitY
    {
        get { return new Vector3(0, 1, 0); }
    }

    public static Vector3 UnitZ
    {
        get { return new Vector3(0, 0, 1); }
    }

    // Static methods
    public static Vector3 Cross(Vector3 v1, Vector3 v2)
    {
        return new Vector3(v1.Y * v2.Z - v1.Z * v2.Y,
                           v1.Z * v2.X - v1.X * v2.Z,
                           v1.X * v2.Y - v1.Y * v2.X);
    }

    public static double Dot(Vector3 v1, Vector3 v2)
    {
        return v1.X * v2.X + v1.Y * v2.Y + v1.Z * v2.Z;
    }

    public static double AngleBetween(Vector3 v1, Vector3 v2)
    {
        return 180 / Math.PI * Math.Acos(Vector3.Dot(v1, v2) /
                                         v1.Length * v2.Length);
    }

    public static Vector3 Transform(Vector3 v, Matrix3D m)
    {
        double x = m.M11 * v.X + m.M21 * v.Y + m.M31 * v.Z + m.OffsetX;
        double y = m.M12 * v.X + m.M22 * v.Y + m.M32 * v.Z + m.OffsetY;
        double z = m.M13 * v.X + m.M23 * v.Y + m.M33 * v.Z + m.OffsetZ;
        double w = m.M14 * v.X + m.M24 * v.Y + m.M34 * v.Z + m.M44;
        return new Vector3(x / w, y / w, z / w);
    }
```

```
        // Operators
        public static Vector3 operator +(Vector3 v1, Vector3 v2)
        {
            return new Vector3(v1.X + v2.X, v1.Y + v2.Y, v1.Z + v2.Z);
        }

        public static Vector3 operator -(Vector3 v1, Vector3 v2)
        {
            return new Vector3(v1.X - v2.X, v1.Y - v2.Y, v1.Z - v2.Z);
        }

        public static Vector3 operator *(Vector3 v, double d)
        {
            return new Vector3(d * v.X, d * v.Y, d * v.Z);
        }

        public static Vector3 operator *(double d, Vector3 v)
        {
            return new Vector3(d * v.X, d * v.Y, d * v.Z);
        }

        public static Vector3 operator /(Vector3 v, double d)
        {
            return new Vector3(v.X / d, v.Y / d, v.Z / d);
        }

        public static Vector3 operator -(Vector3 v)
        {
            return new Vector3(-v.X, -v.Y, -v.Z);
        }

        // Overrides
        public override string ToString()
        {
            return String.Format("({0} {1} {2})", X, Y, Z);
        }
    }
}
```

This structure has lots of goodies, including a traditional dot product and cross product, as well as a *Transform* method that multiplies the *Vector3* value by a *Matrix3D* value. In practice, this *Matrix3D* value probably represents a rotation, so the multiplication effectively rotates the vector in 3D space.

When we hold our tablet up in the air and look at the screen, we are looking in a direction relative to the computer's coordinate system—specifically, in the direction of the vector coming out the back of the screen, which is the negative *Z* axis or **(0, 0, –1)**. We need to convert that to a horizontal coordinate.

Let's create a *Matrix3D* value called *matrix* based on the *SensorRotationMatrix* object that *OrientationSensor* provides. That value can be inverted to represent a transform from the computer's coordinate system to the Earth's coordinate system:

```
matrix.Invert();
```

Use that matrix to transform the **(0, 0, –1)** vector (which is the negative of the static *UnitZ* property provided by the *Vector3* structure) to Earth rectangular coordinates:

```
Vector3 vector = Vector3.Transform(-Vector3.UnitZ, matrix);
```

This vector is in rectangular coordinates, and we need to convert it to a horizontal coordinate. Recall that in the Earth's coordinate system, the Z coordinate points out of the Earth. If the tablet is held upright, the axis coming from the back of the device transformed to Earth coordinates has a Z component of zero. This means that the azimuth can be calculated with the well-known conversion from two-dimensional Cartesian coordinates to polar coordinates, and let's convert it from radians to angles as well:

```
double azimuth = 180 * Math.Atan2(vector.X, vector.Y) / Math.PI;
```

That formula is actually valid regardless of the Z component of the transformed vector. Because the altitude ranges only between negative and positive 90 degrees, it can be calculated with the inverse sine function:

```
double altitude = 180 * Math.Asin(vector.Z) / Math.PI;
```

But we're missing something. We've converted a three-dimensional rotation matrix into a coordinate that has only two components because it's confined to the interior surface of a sphere. What happens when you point your tablet at something on the celestial sphere and then rotate the tablet around that axis? It's the same altitude and azimuth, but the view on the computer's screen should definitely change through rotation. This missing component is sometimes called *tilt*. It's a little more difficult to compute, but the math is shown in this *HorizontalCoordinate* structure:

Project: EarthlyDelights | File: HorizontalCoordinate.cs

```
using System;
using Windows.UI.Xaml.Media.Media3D;

namespace Petzold.Windows8.VectorDrawing
{
    public struct HorizontalCoordinate
    {
        public HorizontalCoordinate(double azimuth, double altitude, double tilt)
            : this()
        {
            this.Azimuth = azimuth;
            this.Altitude = altitude;
            this.Tilt = tilt;
        }

        public HorizontalCoordinate(double azimuth, double altitude)
            : this(azimuth, altitude, 0)
        {
        }
```

```
// Eastward from north
public double Azimuth { private set; get; }

public double Altitude { private set; get; }

public double Tilt { private set; get; }

public static HorizontalCoordinate FromVector(Vector3 vector)
{
    double altitude = 180 * Math.Asin(vector.Z) / Math.PI;
    double azimuth = 180 * Math.Atan2(vector.X, vector.Y) / Math.PI;

    return new HorizontalCoordinate(azimuth, altitude);
}

public static HorizontalCoordinate FromMotionMatrix(Matrix3D matrix)
{
    // Invert the matrix
    matrix.Invert();

    // Transform (0, 0, -1) -- the vector extending from the lens
    Vector3 zAxisTransformed = Vector3.Transform(-Vector3.UnitZ, matrix);

    // Get the horizontal coordinates
    HorizontalCoordinate horzCoord = FromVector(zAxisTransformed);

    // Find the theoretical HorizontalCoordinate for the transformed +Y vector
    //     if the device is upright
    double yUprightAltitude = 0;
    double yUprightAzimuth = 0;

    if (horzCoord.Altitude > 0)
    {
        yUprightAltitude = 90 - horzCoord.Altitude;
        yUprightAzimuth = 180 + horzCoord.Azimuth;
    }
    else
    {
        yUprightAltitude = 90 + horzCoord.Altitude;
        yUprightAzimuth = horzCoord.Azimuth;
    }
    Vector3 yUprightVector =
        new HorizontalCoordinate(yUprightAzimuth, yUprightAltitude).ToVector();

    // Find the real transformed +Y vector
    Vector3 yAxisTransformed = Vector3.Transform(Vector3.UnitY, matrix);

    // Get the angle between the upright +Y vector and the real transformed +Y vector
    double dotProduct = Vector3.Dot(yUprightVector, yAxisTransformed);
    Vector3 crossProduct = Vector3.Cross(yUprightVector, yAxisTransformed);
    crossProduct = crossProduct.Normalized;
```

```
        // Sometimes dotProduct is slightly greater than 1, which
        // raises an exception in the angleBetween calculation, so....
        dotProduct = Math.Min(dotProduct, 1);
        double angleBetween = 180 * Vector3.Dot(zAxisTransformed, crossProduct)
                                * Math.Acos(dotProduct) / Math.PI;

        horzCoord.Tilt = angleBetween;

        return horzCoord;
    }

    public Vector3 ToVector()
    {
        double x = Math.Cos(Math.PI * this.Altitude / 180) *
                    Math.Sin(Math.PI * this.Azimuth / 180);
        double y = Math.Cos(Math.PI * this.Altitude / 180) *
                    Math.Cos(Math.PI * this.Azimuth / 180);
        double z = Math.Sin(Math.PI * this.Altitude / 180);

        return new Vector3((float)x, (float)y, (float)z);
    }

    public override string ToString()
    {
        return String.Format("Azi: {0} Alt: {1} Tilt: {2}",
                        this.Azimuth, this.Altitude, this.Tilt);
    }
  }
}
```

With this conversion, you're well on your way to making an astronomy program that displays a particular segment of the night sky depending how you orient the screen, much like I did for Windows Phone 7.5 in the October 2012 issue of *MSDN Magazine*. But let's do something here a bit less ambitious.

What if you wanted to look at a bitmap that was much larger than the computer screen, and you didn't want to shrink it to fit? One traditional solution involves scrollbars. A more modern solution allows you to move it around with your fingers.

But another approach involves putting this bitmap on the interior of the celestial sphere. You can then view this image by holding the tablet aloft and changing the orientation of the screen. Of course, we don't want to actually stretch a bitmap so that it conforms to the interior of a sphere! Instead, we'll simply use the azimuth for horizontal scrolling and the altitude for vertical scrolling.

The EarthlyDelights program lets you view a large (7,793 by 4,409 pixels) bitmap of Hieronymus Bosch's 500-year-old painting, *The Garden of Earthly Delights*. The program downloads the image from Wikipedia. Here's one part of it as displayed by the program running on Microsoft Surface:

The program has no touch interface for scanning or zooming the image. Everything is based on changing the orientation of the screen. However, if you tap the screen, the program applies scaling to bring the whole image into view with a rectangle showing the section viewed in regular mode:

This feature rather complicates the program, but I find it essential.

The most crucial part of the XAML file is obviously the *Image* element. Notice that the *Stretch* property of *Image* is set to *None*, and it contains a *BitmapImage* object with no URI source (as yet). The *Grid* containing that *Image* is in a *Canvas* so that it won't be clipped if it's larger than the screen (and it will be):

Project: EarthlyDelights | File: MainPage.xaml (excerpt)

```xaml
<Grid Background="{StaticResource ApplicationPageBackgroundThemeBrush}">
    <!-- Two items displayed only during downloading -->
    <ProgressBar Name="progressBar"
                 VerticalAlignment="Center"
                 Margin="96 0" />

    <TextBlock Name="statusText"
               Text="downloading image..."
               HorizontalAlignment="Center"
               VerticalAlignment="Center" />
    <Canvas>
        <Grid>
            <Image Stretch="None">
                <Image.Source>
                    <BitmapImage x:Name="bitmapImage"
                                 DownloadProgress="OnBitmapImageDownloadProgress"
                                 ImageFailed="OnBitmapImageFailed"
                                 ImageOpened="OnBitmapImageOpened" />
                </Image.Source>
            </Image>

            <Border Name="outlineBorder"
                    BorderBrush="White"
                    HorizontalAlignment="Left"
                    VerticalAlignment="Top">

                <Rectangle Name="outlineRectangle"
                           Stroke="Black" />

                <Border.RenderTransform>
                    <CompositeTransform x:Name="borderTransform" />
                </Border.RenderTransform>
            </Border>

            <Grid.RenderTransform>
                <CompositeTransform x:Name="imageTransform" />
            </Grid.RenderTransform>
        </Grid>
    </Canvas>

    <TextBlock Name="titleText"
               Margin="2 " />
</Grid>
```

The *Border* with the embedded *Rectangle* is used in the zoomed out view to show the part of the image that normally occupies the whole screen, but you can see that rectangle in the normal view as well. The outer *CompositeTransform* applies to both the *Image* and *Border*. In the normal view, this transform does nothing. The inner *CompositeTransform* orients the *Border* to the same area of the picture that's viewable in normal mode.

The *Loaded* handler checks whether the *OrientationSensor* is available and, if so, starts a download going by simply setting the *UriSource* property of the *BitmapImage* object. If the bitmap downloads OK, the pixel dimensions can be obtained, and these along with page dimensions are saved as fields:

Project: EarthlyDelights | **File:** MainPage.xaml.cs (excerpt)

```
public sealed partial class MainPage : Page
{
    ...
    OrientationSensor orientationSensor = OrientationSensor.GetDefault();
    double pageWidth, pageHeight, maxDimension;
    int imageWidth, imageHeight;
    string title = "The Garden of Earthly Delights by Hieronymus Bosch";
    double zoomInScale;
    double rotation;
    bool isZoomView;

    public MainPage()
    {
        this.InitializeComponent();
        DisplayProperties.AutoRotationPreferences = DisplayProperties.NativeOrientation;
        Loaded += OnMainPageLoaded;
        SizeChanged += OnMainPageSizeChanged;
    }
    ...
    async void OnMainPageLoaded(object sender, RoutedEventArgs args)
    {
        if (orientationSensor == null)
        {
            await new MessageDialog("OrientationSensor is not available",
                                    "Earthly Delights").ShowAsync();

            progressBar.Visibility = Visibility.Collapsed;
            statusText.Visibility = Visibility.Collapsed;
        }
        else
        {
            bitmapImage.UriSource =
                new Uri("http://upload.wikimedia.org/ ... Bosch_High_Resolution_2.jpg");
        }
    }

    void OnMainPageSizeChanged(object sender, SizeChangedEventArgs args)
    {
        // Save the page dimensions
        pageWidth = this.ActualWidth;
        pageHeight = this.ActualHeight;
        maxDimension = Math.Max(pageWidth, pageHeight);
```

```
        // Initialize some values
        outlineBorder.Width = pageWidth;
        outlineBorder.Height = pageHeight;
        borderTransform.CenterX = pageWidth / 2;
        borderTransform.CenterY = pageHeight / 2;
    }

    void OnBitmapImageDownloadProgress(object sender, DownloadProgressEventArgs args)
    {
        progressBar.Value = args.Progress;
    }

    async void OnBitmapImageFailed(object sender, ExceptionRoutedEventArgs args)
    {
        progressBar.Visibility = Visibility.Collapsed;
        statusText.Visibility = Visibility.Collapsed;

        await new MessageDialog("Could not download image: " + args.ErrorMessage,
                            "Earthly Delights").ShowAsync();
    }

    void OnBitmapImageOpened(object sender, RoutedEventArgs args)
    {
        progressBar.Visibility = Visibility.Collapsed;
        statusText.Visibility = Visibility.Collapsed;

        // Save image dimensions
        imageWidth = bitmapImage.PixelWidth;
        imageHeight = bitmapImage.PixelHeight;
        titleText.Text = String.Format("{0} ({1}\x00D7{2})", title, imageWidth, imageHeight);

        // Initialize image transforms
        zoomInScale = Math.Min(pageWidth / imageWidth, pageHeight / imageHeight);

        // Start OrientationSensor going
        if (orientationSensor != null)
        {
            ProcessNewOrientationReading(orientationSensor.GetCurrentReading());
            orientationSensor.ReportInterval = orientationSensor.MinimumReportInterval;
            orientationSensor.ReadingChanged += OnOrientationSensorReadingChanged;
        }
    }

    async void OnOrientationSensorReadingChanged(OrientationSensor sender,
                                    OrientationSensorReadingChangedEventArgs args)
    {
        await this.Dispatcher.RunAsync(CoreDispatcherPriority.Normal, () =>
            {
                ProcessNewOrientationReading(args.Reading);
            });
    }
    ...
}
```

The *ProcessNewOrientationReading* method creates a *Matrix3D* object from the *SensorRotationMatrix* and uses that to derive a *HorizontalCoordinate* value:

Project: EarthlyDelights | File: MainPage.xaml.cs (excerpt)

```
void ProcessNewOrientationReading(OrientationSensorReading orientationReading)
{
    if (orientationReading == null)
        return;

    // Get the rotation matrix & convert to horizontal coordinates
    SensorRotationMatrix m = orientationReading.RotationMatrix;

    if (m == null)
        return;

    Matrix3D matrix3d = new Matrix3D(m.M11, m.M12, m.M13, 0,
                                     m.M21, m.M22, m.M23, 0,
                                     m.M31, m.M32, m.M33, 0,
                                     0, 0, 0, 1);
    if (!matrix3d.HasInverse)
        return;

    HorizontalCoordinate horzCoord = HorizontalCoordinate.FromMotionMatrix(matrix3d);

    // Set the transform center on the Image element
    imageTransform.CenterX = (imageWidth + maxDimension) *
                            (180 + horzCoord.Azimuth) / 360 - maxDimension / 2;
    imageTransform.CenterY = (imageHeight + maxDimension) *
                            (90 - horzCoord.Altitude) / 180 - maxDimension / 2;

    // Set the translation on the Border element
    borderTransform.TranslateX = imageTransform.CenterX - pageWidth / 2;
    borderTransform.TranslateY = imageTransform.CenterY - pageHeight / 2;

    // Get rotation from Tilt
    rotation = -horzCoord.Tilt;
    UpdateImageTransforms();
}
```

That method is responsible for setting some of the transforms; the others are set in the *UpdateImageTransforms* method (a call to which you'll see right at the end of that method). When the azimuth is 0 (which occurs when the tablet is pointed north) and the altitude is 0 (when the tablet is upright), the *CenterX* and *CenterY* properties are set to the center of the bitmap. Otherwise, they are set to values along the whole width and height, including a margin so that there's a wrapping area where no part of the image can be seen. (Otherwise, the program would need to show both the right edge of the bitmap at the left of the screen and the left edge at the right of the screen.)

I wanted the zooming operation to be animated, so I gave *MainPage* a dependency property that is the target of an animation when the screen is tapped:

Project: EarthlyDelights | File: MainPage.xaml.cs (excerpt)

```csharp
public sealed partial class MainPage : Page
{
    // Dependency property for zoom-in transition animation
    static readonly DependencyProperty interpolationFactorProperty =
        DependencyProperty.Register("InterpolationFactor",
                                    typeof(double),
                                    typeof(MainPage),
                                    new PropertyMetadata(0.0, OnInterpolationFactorChanged));
    ...
    // Interpolation Factor property
    public static DependencyProperty InterpolationFactorProperty
    {
        get { return interpolationFactorProperty; }
    }

    public double InterpolationFactor
    {
        set { SetValue(InterpolationFactorProperty, value); }
        get { return (double)GetValue(InterpolationFactorProperty); }
    }
    ...
    protected override void OnTapped(TappedRoutedEventArgs e)
    {
        // Animate the InterpolationFactor property
        DoubleAnimation doubleAnimation = new DoubleAnimation
        {
            EnableDependentAnimation = true,
            To = isZoomView ? 0 : 1,
            Duration = new Duration(TimeSpan.FromSeconds(1))
        };
        Storyboard.SetTarget(doubleAnimation, this);
        Storyboard.SetTargetProperty(doubleAnimation, "InterpolationFactor");
        Storyboard storyboard = new Storyboard();
        storyboard.Children.Add(doubleAnimation);
        storyboard.Begin();
        isZoomView ^= true;
        base.OnTapped(e);
    }

    static void OnInterpolationFactorChanged(DependencyObject obj,
                                    DependencyPropertyChangedEventArgs args)
    {
        (obj as MainPage).UpdateImageTransforms();
    }
    ...
}
```

That *OnInterpolationFactorChanged* method also calls *UpdateImageTransforms*, which does the bulk of the heavy lifting:

Project: EarthlyDelights | File: MainPage.xaml.cs (excerpt)

```
void UpdateImageTransforms()
{
    // If being zoomed out, set scaling
    double interpolatedScale = 1 + InterpolationFactor * (zoomInScale - 1);
    imageTransform.ScaleX =
    imageTransform.ScaleY = interpolatedScale;

    // Move transform center to screen center
    imageTransform.TranslateX = pageWidth / 2 - imageTransform.CenterX;
    imageTransform.TranslateY = pageHeight / 2 - imageTransform.CenterY;

    // If being zoomed out, adjust for scaling
    imageTransform.TranslateX -= InterpolationFactor *
                        (pageWidth / 2 - zoomInScale * imageTransform.CenterX);
    imageTransform.TranslateY -= InterpolationFactor *
                            (pageHeight / 2 - zoomInScale * imageTransform.CenterY);

    // If being zoomed out, center image in screen
    imageTransform.TranslateX += InterpolationFactor *
                        (pageWidth - zoomInScale * imageWidth) / 2;
    imageTransform.TranslateY += InterpolationFactor *
                        (pageHeight - zoomInScale * imageHeight) / 2;

    // Set border thickness
    outlineBorder.BorderThickness = new Thickness(2 / interpolatedScale);
    outlineRectangle.StrokeThickness = 2 / interpolatedScale;

    // Set rotation on image and border
    imageTransform.Rotation = (1 - InterpolationFactor) * rotation;
    borderTransform.Rotation = -rotation;
}
```

This method is called when there's a new *OrientationSensor* value, or when the *InterpolationFactor* property changes for the zooming operation. If you're interested in understanding how this method works, you might want to clean it up by eliminating all the interpolation code. Set *InterpolationFactor* to 0 and then to 1, and you'll see that it's rather straightforward.

Bing Maps and Bing Map Tiles

The *Geolocator* class is not considered to be a sensor, and it's in another namespace entirely: *Windows.Devices.Geolocation*. Yet it's similar in that you start it going and it tells you when the computer has changed geographic location and what that location is.

You need to specifically indicate in the Capabilities section of the Package.appxmanifest file that your application requires Location information. Windows 8 then gets a confirmation from the user the first time the program runs.

Generally, you'll use the *Geolocator* location in connection with maps. A Bing Maps control is not built into Windows 8, but you can download a toolkit that lets you add it to your application. You'll need a credentials key that you can get from visiting *www.bingmapsportal.com*.

But I'm going to take a somewhat different approach for the last program in this chapter. I'm going to show you a map that rotates based on the orientation of the tablet. This rotation allows north on the map to be aligned with actual north (or whatever the tablet believes north to be). To do this, I don't use the Bing Maps control; instead, I'll use the Bing Maps SOAP service to download individual tiles and stitch them together into a composite map. A credentials key is still required.

When you run the RotatingMap program, you're going to want to use your fingers to scan and scale the map. It won't work. The program has no touch interface! To keep things simple, the program simply centers the map at the current location and reorients the map if the location changes. The program does provide application bar buttons for zooming in and zooming out, and for switching between road and aerial views, but that's it.

Here's the XAML file. All the tiles constituting the map go into the *Canvas* named *imageCanvas*. Notice the *RotateTransform* to rotate the *Canvas* around its center.

Project: RotatingMap | **File:** MainPage.xaml (excerpt)

```
<Page ... >
    <Grid Background="{StaticResource ApplicationPageBackgroundThemeBrush}">
        <Canvas Name="imageCanvas"
                HorizontalAlignment="Center"
                VerticalAlignment="Center">
            <Canvas.RenderTransform>
                <RotateTransform x:Name="imageCanvasRotate" />
            </Canvas.RenderTransform>
        </Canvas>

        <!-- Circle to show location -->
        <Ellipse Name="locationDisplay"
                 Width="24"
                 Height="24"
                 Stroke="Red"
                 StrokeThickness="6"
                 HorizontalAlignment="Center"
                 VerticalAlignment="Center"
                 Visibility="Collapsed" />

        <!-- Arrow to show north -->
        <Border HorizontalAlignment="Left"
                VerticalAlignment="Top"
                Margin="12"
                Background="Black"
                Width="36"
                Height="36"
                CornerRadius="18">
            <Path Stroke="White"
                  StrokeThickness="3"
                  Data="M 18 4 L 18 24 M 12 12 L 18 4 24 12">
                <Path.RenderTransform>
                    <RotateTransform x:Name="northArrowRotate"
```

```
                                    CenterX="18"
                                    CenterY="18" />
                        </Path.RenderTransform>
                    </Path>
                </Border>

                <!-- "powered by bing" display -->
                <Border Background="Black"
                        HorizontalAlignment="Center"
                        VerticalAlignment="Bottom"
                        Margin="12"
                        CornerRadius="12"
                        Padding="3">

                    <StackPanel Name="poweredByDisplay"
                                Orientation="Horizontal"
                                Visibility="Collapsed">
                        <TextBlock Text=" powered by "
                                Foreground="White"
                                VerticalAlignment="Center" />
                        <Image Stretch="None">
                            <Image.Source>
                                <BitmapImage x:Name="poweredByBitmap" />
                            </Image.Source>
                        </Image>
                    </StackPanel>
                </Border>
            </Grid>

        <Page.BottomAppBar>
            <AppBar Name="bottomAppBar"
                    IsEnabled="False">
                <StackPanel Orientation="Horizontal"
                            HorizontalAlignment="Right">

                    <!-- Must remove reference to BackgroundCheckedGlyph in
                         AppBarButtonStyle to use it for a CheckBox -->

                    <CheckBox Name="streetViewAppBarButton"
                            Style="{StaticResource StreetAppBarButtonStyle}"
                            AutomationProperties.Name="Street View"
                            Checked="OnStreetViewAppBarButtonChecked"
                            Unchecked="OnStreetViewAppBarButtonChecked" />

                    <Button Name="zoomInAppBarButton"
                            Style="{StaticResource ZoomInAppBarButtonStyle}"
                            Click="OnZoomInAppBarButtonClick" />

                    <Button Name="zoomOutAppBarButton"
                            Style="{StaticResource ZoomOutAppBarButtonStyle}"
                            Click="OnZoomOutAppBarButtonClick" />
                </StackPanel>
            </AppBar>
        </Page.BottomAppBar>
    </Page>
```

It's possible to use the Bing Maps SOAP service "manually" by transferring hairy XML files back and forth, but a much saner approach is using the Web service through a proxy class that Visual Studio generates. This proxy class makes the Web service appear to be a bunch of structures, enumerations, and asynchronous method calls. To add this proxy to the RotatingMap program, I right-clicked the project name in the Solution Explorer in Visual Studio and selected Add Service Reference from the menu. When the dialog box requested an address, I pasted in the URL for the Imagery Service (which you can find at *http://msdn.microsoft.com/en-us/library/cc966738.aspx* with URLs for three other Web services connected with Bing Maps). I gave it a name of ImageryService, which means that Visual Studio generates code using the namespace *RotatingMap.ImageryService*.

This service has two types of requests: *GetMapUriAsync* and *GetImageryMetadataAsync*. The first allows obtaining a static map of a particular location, but I gravitated toward the other, which allows you to obtain information necessary for downloading individual map tiles that you can then assemble into a complete map.

Let's begin looking at RotatingMap code with the *MainPage* constructor. You see that it saves only two values as application settings: the map style (a member of the *MapStyle* enumeration, which is among the code generated for the web service, indicating road or aerial view) and an integer zoom level:

Project: RotatingMap | **File:** MainPage.xaml.cs (excerpt)

```
public sealed partial class MainPage : Page
{
    ...
    // Saved as application settings
    MapStyle mapStyle = MapStyle.Aerial;
    int zoomLevel = 12;

    public MainPage()
    {
        this.InitializeComponent();
        DisplayProperties.AutoRotationPreferences = DisplayProperties.NativeOrientation;
        Loaded += OnMainPageLoaded;
        SizeChanged += OnMainPageSizeChanged;

        // Get application settings (and later save them)
        IPropertySet propertySet = ApplicationData.Current.LocalSettings.Values;

        if (propertySet.ContainsKey("ZoomLevel"))
            zoomLevel = (int)propertySet["ZoomLevel"];

        if (propertySet.ContainsKey("MapStyle"))
            mapStyle = (MapStyle)(int)propertySet["MapStyle"];

        Application.Current.Suspending += (sender, args) =>
        {
            propertySet["ZoomLevel"] = zoomLevel;
            propertySet["MapStyle"] = (int)mapStyle;
        };
    }
    ...
}
```

The Web service is accessed solely in the *Loaded* handler. Two calls must be made: one to get maps metadata for the road view, and the other for the aerial view. The information is saved in two instances of a local class named *ViewParams*. The most important part of this metadata is a URI template for downloading individual map tiles. The *ViewParams* class also has fields for the minimum and maximum zoom levels, but I know the zoom level ranges from 1 to 21 and you'll see that other parts of the code assume an upper limit of 21:

Project: RotatingMap | File: MainPage.xaml.cs (excerpt)

```
public sealed partial class MainPage : Page
{
    ...
    // Storage of parameters for two views
    class ViewParams
    {
        public string UriTemplate;
        public int MinimumLevel;
        public int MaximumLevel;
    }
    ViewParams aerialParams;
    ViewParams roadParams;

    Geolocator geolocator = new Geolocator();
    Inclinometer inclinometer = Inclinometer.GetDefault();
    ...
    async void OnMainPageLoaded(object sender, RoutedEventArgs args)
    {
        // Initialize the Bing Maps imagery service
        ImageryServiceClient imageryServiceClient =
            new ImageryServiceClient(
                ImageryServiceClient.EndpointConfiguration.BasicHttpBinding_IImageryService);

        // Make two requests for road and aerial views
        ImageryMetadataRequest request = new ImageryMetadataRequest
        {
            Credentials = new Credentials
            {
                ApplicationId = "put your own credentials string here"
            },
            Style = MapStyle.Road
        };
        Task<ImageryMetadataResponse> roadStyleTask =
                imageryServiceClient.GetImageryMetadataAsync(request);

        request = new ImageryMetadataRequest
        {
            Credentials = new Credentials
            {
                ApplicationId = "put your own credentials string here"
            },
            Style = MapStyle.Aerial
        };
        Task<ImageryMetadataResponse> aerialStyleTask =
                imageryServiceClient.GetImageryMetadataAsync(request);
```

```
// Wait for both tasks to complete
Task.WaitAll(roadStyleTask, aerialStyleTask);

// Check if everything is OK
if (!roadStyleTask.IsCanceled && !roadStyleTask.IsFaulted &&
    !aerialStyleTask.IsCanceled && !aerialStyleTask.IsCanceled)
{
    // Get the "powered by" bitmap
    poweredByBitmap.UriSource = roadStyleTask.Result.BrandLogoUri;
    poweredByDisplay.Visibility = Visibility.Visible;

    // Get the URIs and min/max zoom levels
    roadParams = CreateViewParams(roadStyleTask.Result.Results[0]);
    aerialParams = CreateViewParams(aerialStyleTask.Result.Results[0]);

    // Get the current location
    Geoposition geoPosition = await geolocator.GetGeopositionAsync();
    GetLongitudeAndLatitude(geoPosition.Coordinate);
    RefreshDisplay();

    // Get updated locations
    geolocator.PositionChanged += OnGeolocatorPositionChanged;

    // Enable the application bar
    bottomAppBar.IsEnabled = true;
    streetViewAppBarButton.IsChecked = mapStyle == MapStyle.Road;

    // Get the current yaw
    if (inclinometer != null)
    {
        SetRotation(inclinometer.GetCurrentReading());
        inclinometer.ReadingChanged += OnInclinometerReadingChanged;
    }
}
}

ViewParams CreateViewParams(ImageryMetadataResult result)
{
    string uri = result.ImageUri;
    uri = uri.Replace("{subdomain}", result.ImageUriSubdomains[0]);
    uri = uri.Replace("&token={token}", "");
    uri = uri.Replace("{culture}", "en-us");

    return new ViewParams
    {
        UriTemplate = uri,
        MinimumLevel = result.ZoomRange.From,
        MaximumLevel = result.ZoomRange.To
    };
}
...
}
```

Two asynchronous calls are required to obtain the metadata for the two views, yet the two calls aren't dependent on each other, so they can proceed at the same time. This seemed like a perfect application of the *Task.WaitAll* method, which waits until multiple *Task* items have completed.

When both Web service calls have completed successfully, the *Geolocator* and *Inclinometer* are started up. The *Inclinometer* is used solely to obtain a yaw value used for rotating the map and for rotating an arrow indicating north:

Project: RotatingMap | **File:** MainPage.xaml.cs (excerpt)

```
public sealed partial class MainPage : Page
{
    ...
    async void OnInclinometerReadingChanged(Inclinometer sender,
                                    InclinometerReadingChangedEventArgs args)
    {
        await this.Dispatcher.RunAsync(CoreDispatcherPriority.Normal, () =>
        {
            SetRotation(args.Reading);
        });
    }

    void SetRotation(InclinometerReading inclinometerReading)
    {
        if (inclinometerReading == null)
            return;

        imageCanvasRotate.Angle = inclinometerReading.YawDegrees;
        northArrowRotate.Angle = inclinometerReading.YawDegrees;
    }
    ...
}
```

Following completion of the *Loaded* handler, the program has two URI templates that it can use to download individual map tiles. The tiles that form the basis of Bing Maps are bitmaps that are always 256 pixels square. Each tile is associated with a particular longitude, latitude, and zoom level and contains an image of part of the world flattened using the common Mercator projection.

In Level 1, the entire Earth—or, rather, that part of the Earth with latitudes between positive and negative 85.05 degrees—is covered by four tiles:

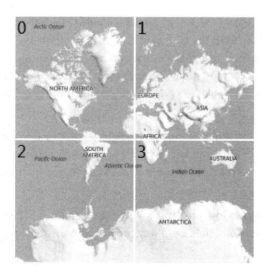

I'll discuss the numbers in these tiles shortly. The tiles are 256 pixels square, so at the equator each pixel covers about 49 miles.

In Level 2, 16 tiles cover the Earth:

These tiles are also 256 pixels square, so at the equator each pixel is about 24 miles.

Each tile in Level 1 covers the same area as four tiles in Level 2, and the trend continues in this way: Level 3 has 64 tiles, Level 4 has 256 tiles, and up and up to Level 21, which (in principle, anyway) covers the Earth with more than 4 trillion tiles—2 million horizontally and 2 million vertically for a resolution at the equator of 3 inches per pixel.

How can so many tiles possibly be organized in a coherent manner? Keep in mind that three dimensions are involved—longitude, latitude, and zoom level—and for maximum efficiency in providing these tiles through a Web service, tiles covering the same area should be stored near each other on the servers.

Obviously, a very clever numbering scheme is called for, and it's called a *quadkey*. Each tile has a unique quadkey. The URI templates just obtained from the Bing Maps Web service contain a placeholder "{quadkey}" that you replace to reference an actual tile. The two diagrams indicate the quadkeys for these particular tiles in the upper left corner. Leading zeroes are important! The number of digits in the quadkey is equal to the zoom level. The tiles in Level 21 are identified with 21-digit quadkeys.

The digits in a quadkey are always 0, 1, 2, or 3, which indicates that quadkeys are actually base-4 numbers. In binary, the digits 0, 1, 2, and 3 are 00, 01, 10, and 11. The first bit is a vertical coordinate, and the second bit is a horizontal coordinate. Thus, the bits correspond to an interleaved longitude and latitude.

As you've seen, each tile in Level 1 corresponds to four tiles in Level 2, so you can think of tiles as having parent and child relationships. The quadkey of a child tile always begins with the same digits as its parent but adds another digit, depending on its location relative to its parent. You can obtain a parent quadkey from a child quadkey by simply lopping off the last digit.

To use the Bing Maps Web service, it's necessary to derive a quadkey from a longitude and latitude. The code in the following *GetLongitudeAndLatitude* method shows the first step, which is to convert the longitude and latitude from the *Geolocator* into relative *double* values ranging from 0 to 1, and then into integer values:

Project: RotatingMap | File: MainPage.xaml.cs (excerpt)

```
public sealed partial class MainPage : Page
{
    const int BITRES = 29;
    ...
    int integerLongitude = -1;
    int integerLatitude = -1;
    ...
    async void OnGeolocatorPositionChanged(Geolocator sender, PositionChangedEventArgs args)
    {
        await this.Dispatcher.RunAsync(CoreDispatcherPriority.Normal, () =>
            {
                GetLongitudeAndLatitude(args.Position.Coordinate);
                RefreshDisplay();
            });
    }

    void GetLongitudeAndLatitude(Geocoordinate geoCoordinate)
    {
        locationDisplay.Visibility = Visibility.Visible;

        // Calculate integer longitude and latitude
        double relativeLongitude = (180 + geoCoordinate.Longitude) / 360;
        integerLongitude = (int)(relativeLongitude * (1 << BITRES));

        double sinTerm = Math.Sin(Math.PI * geoCoordinate.Latitude / 180);
        double relativeLatitude = 0.5 - Math.Log((1 + sinTerm) / (1 - sinTerm)) / (4 * Math.PI);
        integerLatitude = (int)(relativeLatitude * (1 << BITRES));
    }
    ...
}
```

The BITRES value is 29 to account for the 21 bits in a Level 21 quadkey plus 8 bits for the pixel size of the tile, which means that these integer values identify a longitude and latitude precise to the nearest pixel of a tile at the highest zoom level. The calculation of *integerLongitude* is trivial, but *integerLatitude* is more complex because the Mercator map projection compresses latitudes as you get farther from the equator.

An example: The center of Central Park in New York City has a longitude of –73.965368 and a latitude of 40.783271. The relative *double* values (to just a few decimal places) are 0.29454 and 0.37572. The 29-bit integer values (shown in binary and grouped in fours for easy readability) are:

```
0 1001 0110 1100 1110 0000 1000 0000
0 1100 0000 0101 1110 1011 0000 0000
```

Suppose you want a tile for this longitude and latitude in a Level 12 zoom. You need the top 12 bits of these integer longitudes and latitudes. (Watch out! The resultant digits are grouped a little differently.)

```
0100 1011 0110
0110 0000 0010
```

These are two binary numbers, but to form a quadkey they need to be combined into a base-4 number. You can't do this in code without actually looping through the bits, but for illustrative purposes, you can simply double all the bits in the latitude and add the two values as if they were base-4 values:

```
  0100 1011 0110
+ 0220 0000 0020
  --------------
  0320 1011 0130
```

And that's the quadkey you'll need to substitute for the "{quadkey}" placeholder in the URI templates obtained from the Web service. The resultant URI references a 256-pixel-square bitmap.

Here's the routine in RotatingMap that constructs a quadkey from the truncated integer longitudes and latitudes. For clarity, the logic has been separated to show first the derivation of a long integer and then a string:

Project: RotatingMap | File: MainPage.xaml.cs (excerpt)

```csharp
public sealed partial class MainPage : Page
{
    ...
    StringBuilder strBuilder = new StringBuilder();
    ...
    string ToQuadKey(int longitude, int latitude, int level)
    {
        long quadkey = 0;
        int mask = 1 << (level - 1);

        for (int i = 0; i < level; i++)
        {
            quadkey <<= 2;

            if ((longitude & mask) != 0)
                quadkey |= 1;

            if ((latitude & mask) != 0)
                quadkey |= 2;

            mask >>= 1;
        }

        strBuilder.Clear();
```

```
        for (int i = 0; i < level; i++)
        {
            strBuilder.Insert(0, (quadkey & 3).ToString());
            quadkey >>= 2;
        }

        return strBuilder.ToString();
    }
    ...
}
```

The quadkey references a tile containing the desired longitude and latitude, but the location of the precise longitude and latitude is actually somewhere within the tile. The pixel location within the tile can be determined by the next 8 digits of the integer longitude and latitude following the digits required for the quadkey.

We're in the home stretch now. Because the whole page must be covered with 256-pixel-square tiles, because this array of tiles is rotatable, and because the current location of the user is positioned in the center of the screen somewhere within the central tile, the *SizeChanged* handler determines how many tiles are required and hence how many *Image* elements need to be created. The field named *sqrtNumTiles* means "the square root of the number of tiles." For a 1366 by 768 pixel display, it's calculated as 9. The total number of tiles (and *Image* elements) is the square of that, or 81.

Project: RotatingMap | **File:** MainPage.xaml.cs (excerpt)

```
public sealed partial class MainPage : Page
{
    ...
    int sqrtNumTiles;          // always an odd number
    ...
    void OnMainPageSizeChanged(object sender, SizeChangedEventArgs args)
    {
        // Clear out the existing Image elements
        imageCanvas.Children.Clear();

        // Determine how many Image elements are needed
        double diagonal = Math.Sqrt(Math.Pow(args.NewSize.Width, 2) +
                                    Math.Pow(args.NewSize.Height, 2));

        sqrtNumTiles = 1 + 2 * (int)Math.Ceiling((diagonal / 2) / 256);

        // Create Image elements for a sqrtNumTiles x sqrtNumTiles array
        for (int i = 0; i < sqrtNumTiles * sqrtNumTiles; i++)
        {
            Image image = new Image
            {
                Source = new BitmapImage(),
                Stretch = Stretch.None
            };
            imageCanvas.Children.Add(image);
        }
        RefreshDisplay();
    }
    ...
}
```

The *RefreshDisplay* method does the real work. It loops through all the *Image* elements and determines the quadkey (and hence a URI) for each one:

Project: RotatingMap | File: MainPage.xaml.cs (excerpt)

```
public sealed partial class MainPage : Page
{
    ...
    void RefreshDisplay()
    {
        if (roadParams == null || aerialParams == null)
            return;

        if (integerLongitude == -1 || integerLatitude == -1)
            return;

        // Get coordinates and pixel offsets based on current zoom level
        int croppedLongitude = integerLongitude >> BITRES - zoomLevel;
        int croppedLatitude = integerLatitude >> BITRES - zoomLevel;
        int xPixelOffset = (integerLongitude >> BITRES - zoomLevel - 8) % 256;
        int yPixelOffset = (integerLatitude >> BITRES - zoomLevel - 8) % 256;

        // Prepare for the loop
        string uriTemplate = (mapStyle == MapStyle.Road ? roadParams : aerialParams).
            UriTemplate;
        int index = 0;
        int maxValue = (1 << zoomLevel) - 1;

        // Loop through the array of Image elements
        for (int row = -sqrtNumTiles / 2; row <= sqrtNumTiles / 2; row++)
            for (int col = -sqrtNumTiles / 2; col <= sqrtNumTiles / 2; col++)
            {
                // Get the Image and BitmapImage
                Image image = imageCanvas.Children[index] as Image;
                BitmapImage bitmap = image.Source as BitmapImage;
                index++;

                // Check if we've gone beyond the bounds
                if (croppedLongitude + col < 0 ||
                    croppedLongitude + col > maxValue ||
                    croppedLatitude + row < 0 ||
                    croppedLatitude + row > maxValue)
                {
                    bitmap.UriSource = null;
                }
                else
                {
                    // Calculate a quadkey and set URI to bitmap
                    int longitude = croppedLongitude + col;
                    int latitude = croppedLatitude + row;
                    string strQuadkey = ToQuadKey(longitude, latitude, zoomLevel);
                    string uri = uriTemplate.Replace("{quadkey}", strQuadkey);
                    bitmap.UriSource = new Uri(uri);
                }
```

```
            // Position the Image element
            Canvas.SetLeft(image, col * 256 - xPixelOffset);
            Canvas.SetTop(image, row * 256 - yPixelOffset);
        }
    }
    ...
}
```

The only part left involves the application bar buttons. The increase and decrease zoom buttons are carefully enabled and disabled based on the minimum and maximum zoom levels for the currently selected view although (as I've said) other parts of the program are apparently quite certain that the maximum zoom level is 21:

Project: RotatingMap | File: MainPage.xaml.cs (excerpt)

```
public sealed partial class MainPage : Page
{
    ...
    void OnStreetViewAppBarButtonChecked(object sender, RoutedEventArgs args)
    {
        ToggleButton btn = sender as ToggleButton;
        ViewParams viewParams = null;

        if (btn.IsChecked.Value)
        {
            mapStyle = MapStyle.Road;
            viewParams = roadParams;
        }
        else
        {
            mapStyle = MapStyle.Aerial;
            viewParams = aerialParams;
        }

        zoomLevel = Math.Max(viewParams.MinimumLevel,
                    Math.Min(viewParams.MaximumLevel, zoomLevel));

        RefreshDisplay();
        RefreshButtons();
    }

    void OnZoomInAppBarButtonClick(object sender, RoutedEventArgs args)
    {
        zoomLevel += 1;
        RefreshDisplay();
        RefreshButtons();
    }

    void OnZoomOutAppBarButtonClick(object sender, RoutedEventArgs args)
    {
        zoomLevel -= 1;
        RefreshDisplay();
        RefreshButtons();
    }

    void RefreshButtons()
```

```
        {
            ViewParams viewParams =
                            streetViewAppBarButton.IsChecked.Value ? roadParams : aerialParams;
            zoomInAppBarButton.IsEnabled = zoomLevel < viewParams.MaximumLevel;
            zoomOutAppBarButton.IsEnabled = zoomLevel > viewParams.MinimumLevel;
        }
}
```

We're not quite accustomed to seeing familiar regions of a map rotated, so the island of Manhattan looks a little odd in this view:

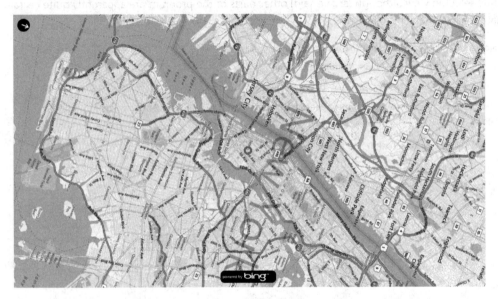

But if you're standing in a strange neighborhood with your tablet trying to figure out where you are, having the map rotate in accordance with reality can be very helpful. Maybe someday the labels showing cities and streets can be rotated as well.

CHAPTER 19

Pen (Also Known as Stylus)

An aura of controversy surrounds this chapter. The subject is an input device that has an uncertain future in computing, and passions are strong on each side of the issue: In 2010, Steve Jobs discussed the possibility of other tablets attempting to compete with the iPad and declared, "If you see a stylus, they blew it."[1]

Yet, anyone who's tried to use a traditional mouse-based application on a touch screen would certainly disagree. The stylus is not quite as convenient as a finger or as versatile as multiple fingers, but it's nearly as precise as a mouse and usually works much better than fingers for picking items from menus and selecting and erasing input. The Samsung 700T that I've been using for most of this book has a stylus, and I consider it essential for using Visual Studio on the machine when a mouse isn't attached.

I was therefore in great suspense awaiting the introduction of the first Microsoft Surface devices. Would a stylus be included? I was even contemplating that the answer to that question would govern whether a chapter on the stylus would be included in this book!

By Steve Jobs's criterion, the Microsoft Surface certainly did *not* "blow it." The first Surface computers do *not* include a stylus. I was disappointed, but I elected to include this chapter in the book regardless.

I personally prefer the word *stylus* for referring to these input devices, but from here on the terminology in this chapter will be consistent with the Windows Runtime programming interface, where it's called a *pen*. Often the pen input and rendered graphical output is referred to as *ink*.

By virtue of having read Chapter 13, "Touch, Etc.," you already know how to process and render pen input. However, the *Windows.UI.Input.Inking* namespace provides additional facilities when working with pens. These features include

- Erasure and selection modes in addition to inking

- Converting polyline input to Bézier curves for smoother rendition

- Handwriting recognition

---

[1] David Pogue, "On Touch Screens, Rest Your Finger by Using a Stylus," *New York Times*, August 1, 2012. *http://www.nytimes.com/2012/08/02/technology/personaltech/on-touch-screens-rest-your-finger-by-using-a-stylus-state-of-the-art.html*

- Saving ink to files and loading ink from files

I won't be exploring handwriting recognition in this chapter, however.

Interestingly, none of these facilities actually requires a pen! Theoretically, you can do everything in this chapter with touch or mouse input. However, touch or mouse input is awkward for handwriting because text drawn with fingers is often too large, while text drawn with the mouse is often too jittery. The pen is just right. That's to be expected from a device of a size and shape used for writing for at least two millennia.

The article from the *New York Times* that I cited earlier was all about *capacitance pens*. These are pens designed to supplement fingers on capacitance touch screens. They offer no real advantages over fingers except in precision and maneuverability.

Of much more versatility is an *electromagnetic pen*, sometimes referred to as a *digitizer* or *digital stylus*, but these pens require a screen that can respond to this type of pen input. Such is the case with the Samsung 700T tablet I'm using for this book. The pen has a small tip (about 1 mm in diameter), an "eraser" at the opposite end, and a button on the barrel. The *PointerPointProperties* class defines two properties, *IsEraser* and *IsInverted*, that are both *true* if the eraser is touching the screen rather than the pen tip. This is generally used for erasing earlier input. The *IsBarrelButtonPressed* property is *true* if the tip is being used and the barrel button is pressed. This is generally used for selection.

Unless you're writing a program specifically for electromagnetic pen users, you'll want to supplement the erase and selection facilities of the pen with software options, but to streamline the sample projects I'll skip that amenity in this chapter.

The *InkManager* Collections

The *Windows.UI.Input.Inking* namespace revolves around the *InkManager* class. This class is your application's portal into many of the features associated with pen use.

An *InkManager* instance maintains all the ink for a particular page of input. If your program implements a pad of sorts—as the last program in this chapter does—then each page of that pad will have its own *InkManager*.

An *InkManager* object maintains a collection of objects of type *InkStroke*. Each *InkStroke* is a continuous curve generally created by touching the pen to the screen, moving it, and lifting it. An *InkStroke* is associated with a particular *InkDrawingAttributes* object, the primary purpose of which is to indicate the color of the stroke and the shape and size of the pen tip, although (as you'll see) the *InkManager* and *InkStroke* don't really do anything with these drawing attributes.

Each *InkStroke* contains a collection of *InkStrokeRenderingSegment* objects. An *InkStrokeRenderingSegment* is a single Bézier curve with a particular pen pressure, tilt, and twist. The pressure is often used for computing a line thickness when rendering strokes. The value can range from 0 to 1 just like the *Pressure* property of *PointerPointProperties*. Pens that support tilt and twist are rather rare.

With help from your program, the *InkManager* can accumulate pen input and smooth it into Bézier curves, but it does no rendering on its own. Rendering is entirely your responsibility, and it's generally a two-step operation:

■ Render lines using *Polyline*, *Line*, or *Path* as the user is drawing or writing with the pen.

■ Replace these elements with Bézier curves as each stroke is completed.

You've already seen the first rendering step in connection with the FingerPaint programs. To clarify the basics of using *InkManager*, let me focus on the second rendering step in the first sample project, SimpleInking. The SimpleInking program is so simple that you don't see what you're actually drawing until you lift the pen from the screen!

Here's the XAML file. Notice that I've colored the *Grid* white, which is generally the convention for pen input:

Project: SimpleInking | File: MainPage.xaml (excerpt)

```
<Page ... >

    <Grid Name="contentGrid"
          Background="White" />
</Page>
```

By default, pen input is black.

I've used a single *InkManager* object for the duration of the program:

Project: SimpleInking | File: MainPage.xaml.cs (excerpt)

```
public sealed partial class MainPage : Page
{
    InkManager inkManager = new InkManager();
    bool hasPen;

    public MainPage()
    {
        this.InitializeComponent();

        // Check if there's a pen among the pointer input devices
        foreach (PointerDevice device in PointerDevice.GetPointerDevices())
            hasPen |= device.PointerDeviceType == PointerDeviceType.Pen;
    }
    ...
}
```

The constructor determines whether the machine supports a pen, and if it does, the *hasPen* field is set to *true*. For this program, I've decided to ignore all nonpen pointer input for computers that support a pen, but I'll accept all pointer input for computers that don't support a pen. This allows the program to be used on the Microsoft Surface.

The *InkManager* defines three methods that you use in conjunction with the *Pointer* events. These methods allow the *InkManager* object to accumulate pointer input. They are

- *ProcessPointerDown*, which you'll call from the *PointerPressed* event handler

- *ProcessPointerUpdate*, called multiple times from the *PointerMoved* event handler

- *ProcessPointerUp*, called from the *PointerReleased* event handler

The argument to each method is a *PointerPoint* object that you can obtain from *PointerRoutedEventArgs* by calling *GetCurrentPoint* or *GetIntermediatePoints*. As you'll recall, the *PointerPoint* object includes not only the position of the pointer but the pointer ID (which allows the *InkManager* to track multiple pointers) and *PointerPointProperties*, including pressure and tilt.

Here's the *OnPointerPressed* override in SimpleInking:

Project: SimpleInking | File: MainPage.xaml.cs (excerpt)

```
protected override void OnPointerPressed(PointerRoutedEventArgs args)
{
    if (args.Pointer.PointerDeviceType == PointerDeviceType.Pen || !hasPen)
    {
        PointerPoint pointerPoint = args.GetCurrentPoint(this);
        inkManager.ProcessPointerDown(pointerPoint);
    }
    base.OnPointerPressed(args);
}
```

The *if* statement checks for a device type of *Pen* but allows other pointer devices if the computer doesn't support a pen. You can remove the entire *if* statement if you want to support all pointer input devices regardless. In any case, simply pass the *PointerPoint* object to the *ProcessPointerDown* method of the *InkManager*. Processing *OnPointerMoved* is just a little more complex:

Project: SimpleInking | File: MainPage.xaml.cs (excerpt)

```
protected override void OnPointerMoved(PointerRoutedEventArgs args)
{
    if ((args.Pointer.PointerDeviceType == PointerDeviceType.Pen || !hasPen) &&
            args.Pointer.IsInContact)
    {
        IEnumerable<PointerPoint> points = args.GetIntermediatePoints(this).Reverse();

        foreach (PointerPoint point in points)
            inkManager.ProcessPointerUpdate(point);
    }
    base.OnPointerMoved(args);
}
```

Calls to *ProcessPointerUpdate* allow the *InkManager* to accumulate pieces of the total ink stroke. For maximum fidelity to pen input, the code uses *GetIntermediatePoints* rather than *GetCurrentPoint*, reversed with the LINQ *Reverse* operator.

Notice that the *if* statement for *OnPointerMoved* now also includes a check for the *IsInContact* property. As you'll recall, the pen begins generating *OnPointerMoved* events when the pen comes within the vicinity of the screen before actually touching the screen. If the *if* statement did not check *IsInContact*, it would call the *ProcessPointerUpdate* method of *InkManager* before first calling *ProcessPointerDown*, and that would raise an exception.

So far, the program hasn't been doing any drawing. Any reasonable program would have been drawing all along. This program reserves all the drawing for the *OnPointerReleased* method, but let's look at the *InkManager* overhead first:

Project: SimpleInking | File: MainPage.xaml.cs (excerpt)

```
protected override void OnPointerReleased(PointerRoutedEventArgs args)
{
    if (args.Pointer.PointerDeviceType != PointerDeviceType.Pen && hasPen)
        return;

    inkManager.ProcessPointerUp(args.GetCurrentPoint(this));

    // Render the most recent InkStroke
    ...

    base.OnPointerReleased(args);
}
```

Before rendering the new *InkStroke* object, you'll need to know about *InkDrawingAttributes*.

The Ink Drawing Attributes

Although *InkManager* doesn't perform any rendering on its own, it maintains information about attributes involved with rendering ink. This information is encapsulated in the *InkDrawingAttributes* class, which has the following properties and default values:

Property	Value
Color	Black (0xFF000000)
PenTip	Circle
Size	(2, 2)
FitToCurve	true
IgnorePressure	false

These are the default values when you create a new instance of *InkDrawingAttributes* on your own, and these are the default values for the *InkDrawingAttributes* that *InkManager* creates and retains internally.

These properties are strictly for the benefit of application programs that need to render ink strokes! They do not affect the operation of *InkManager* because the *InkManager* does no rendering on its own.

The only other option for *PenTip* is *Rectangle*, in which case the *Size* property (of type *Size*) describes the dimensions of the pen tip. For the default *Circle* tip, you can use the *Width* property of the *Size* value for determining the thickness of rendered lines.

The *FitToCurve* property indicates if ink should be rendered as Bézier curves; regardless of the setting, *InkManager* converts the pointer input to Bézier curves. The *IgnorePressure* property indicates that ink should be rendered without regard to pressure information, but the *InkManager* still includes this pressure information regardless of the setting.

The *InkManager* creates an *InkDrawingAttributes* object with these default properties and maintains it internally. However, your program can't get access to that object. If you want to set different default properties for the *InkManager* object, you must do so like this: .

```
InkDrawingAttributes inkDrawingAttributes = new InkDrawingAttributes();
inkDrawingAttributes.Color = Colors.Red;
inkDrawingAttributes.Size = new Size(6, 6);
inkManager.SetDefaultDrawingAttributes(inkDrawingAttributes);
```

When you create a new *InkDrawingAttributes* object and pass it to *InkManager*, don't assume that your program and *InkManager* now share this object and any changes to it by your application will be reflected in the internal object that *InkManager* maintains. If you make further changes to this *InkDrawingAttributes*, you must then call the *SetDefaultDrawingAttributes* method again for these changes to take effect.

As you've seen, a program using the *InkManager* processes a normal sequence of *PointerPressed*, multiple *PointerMoved*, and *PointerReleased* events by calling the *InkManager* methods *ProcessPointerDown*, *ProcessPointerUpdate* (multiple times), and *ProcessPointerUp*. When this sequence of calls has completed, the *InkManager* creates a new *InkStroke* and adds it to its collection.

This *InkStroke* object represents a continuous stroke of ink from the time the pointer touched the screen to the time it was lifted. *InkStroke* has a *DrawingAttributes* property of type *InkDrawingAttributes* that *InkManager* created based on its internal default *InkDrawingAttributes* object.

For example, suppose you create a new *InkManager* and handle pointer input by calling *ProcessPointerDown*, *ProcessPointerUpdate* multiple times, and *ProcessPointerUp*. The resultant *InkStroke* object has an *InkDrawingAttributes* object indicating a black pen with a size of (2, 2). Now your program creates a new *InkDrawingAttributes* object, sets a couple properties, and calls *SetDefaultDrawingAttributes* using the code I showed earlier. The next sequence of calls to *ProcessPointerDown*, *ProcessPointerUpdate*, and *ProcessPointerUp* results in a second *InkStroke* object, but this one has a *DrawingAttributes* property indicating a red pen with a size of (6, 6).

But none of this is set in stone. You can create new *InkDrawingAttributes* objects and set those to the individual *InkStroke* objects, and you can alter any of the properties of the existing *InkDrawingAttributes* object referenced from the *DrawingAttributes* property of an *InkStroke* object.

Following the call to the *ProcessPointerUp* method, the *InkManager* converts all the points accumulated internally for this new stroke into one or more Bézier curves that make up a new

InkStroke object. This new *InkStroke* is added to its internal collection, which is available from the *GetStrokes* method.

Because the SimpleInking program renders each stroke when the stroke is completed, it's only interested in the most recent *InkStroke* in this collection, which it can obtain like so:

```
IReadOnlyList<InkStroke> inkStrokes = inkManager.GetStrokes();
InkStroke inkStroke = inkStrokes[inkStrokes.Count - 1];
```

This *InkStroke* has a *DrawingAttributes* property and a collection of *InkStrokeRenderingSegment* objects that represent a series of connected Bézier splines. A program can obtain this collection of segments by calling *GetRenderingSegments*.

Each *InkStrokeRenderingSegment* contains three properties of type *Point*:

- *BezierControlPoint1*

- *BezierControlPoint2*

- *Position*

In the first *InkStrokeRenderingSegment* object in the collection, these three points are the same. This is the first point of the complete curve. Each subsequent *InkStrokeRenderingSegment* continues from that point with two control points and an end point.

In addition, each *InkStrokeRenderingSegment* also contains four properties of type *float*:

- *Pressure*

- *TiltX*

- *TiltY*

- *Twist*

These are obviously for much fancier pen systems than I've been using! When I use a pen on the Samsung 700T, I see *Pressure* values ranging from 0 to 1, but the other three properties have default values of 0.5. In theory, the *TiltX* and *TiltY* properties indicate how the body of the pen is tilted relative to the screen; the *Twist* property applies only to rectangular pen tips and indicates how the rectangular tip is rotated relative to the axes of the screen.

Throughout this chapter I will be taking *Pressure* values into account. As you'll recall in the FingerPaint programs, a *Polyline* was suitable for rendering a connected curve if pressure is ignored, but taking pressure into account requires individual *Line* elements, each with a potentially different line thickness, or individual *Path* elements to mimic a straight line with a varying thickness.

The code in SimpleInking draws each *InkStrokeRenderingSegment* (except the first) as a *Path* element with a *PathGeometry* consisting of a single *PathFigure* with a single *BezierSegment*. The *Stroke* property of that *Path* is a *SolidColorBrush* created from the *Color* property of the *DrawingAttributes* property of the *InkStroke*. The *StrokeThickness* property is the product of the *Size* property of the *DrawingAttributes* for the *InkStroke* and the *Pressure* property of the particular *Ink-StrokeRenderingSegment*:

Project: SimpleInking | File: MainPage.xaml.cs (excerpt)

```
protected override void OnPointerReleased(PointerRoutedEventArgs args)
{
    ...
    // Render the most recent InkStroke
    IReadOnlyList<InkStroke> inkStrokes = inkManager.GetStrokes();
    InkStroke inkStroke = inkStrokes[inkStrokes.Count - 1];

    // Create SolidColorBrush used for all segments in the stroke
    Brush brush = new SolidColorBrush(inkStroke.DrawingAttributes.Color);

    // Get the segments
    IReadOnlyList<InkStrokeRenderingSegment> inkSegments = inkStroke.GetRenderingSegments();

    // Notice loop starts at 1
    for (int i = 1; i < inkSegments.Count; i++)
    {
        InkStrokeRenderingSegment inkSegment = inkSegments[i];

        // Create a BezierSegment from the points
        BezierSegment bezierSegment = new BezierSegment
        {
            Point1 = inkSegment.BezierControlPoint1,
            Point2 = inkSegment.BezierControlPoint2,
            Point3 = inkSegment.Position
        };

        // Create a PathFigure that begins at the preceding Position
        PathFigure pathFigure = new PathFigure
        {
            StartPoint = inkSegments[i - 1].Position,
            IsClosed = false,
            IsFilled = false
        };
        pathFigure.Segments.Add(bezierSegment);

        // Create a PathGeometry with that PathFigure
        PathGeometry pathGeometry = new PathGeometry();
        pathGeometry.Figures.Add(pathFigure);

        // Create a Path with that PathGeometry
        Path path = new Path
        {
            Stroke = brush,
            StrokeThickness = inkStroke.DrawingAttributes.Size.Width *
                              inkSegment.Pressure,
            StrokeStartLineCap = PenLineCap.Round,
            StrokeEndLineCap = PenLineCap.Round,
            Data = pathGeometry
        };
```

```
        // Add it to the Grid
        contentGrid.Children.Add(path);
    }
    ...
}
```

The *for* loop starts at 1 in the collection of *InkStrokeRenderingSegment* objects because the first object represents only a start point, whereas each subsequent *InkStrokeRenderingSegment* is a single Bézier curve. In each *PathGeometry*, the *StartPoint* in the *PathFigure* is the *Position* property from the previous *InkStrokeRenderingSegment*.

Despite not being able to see what I'm drawing until I lift the pen, I managed this message:

InkManager converts a polyline to a series of Bézier curves not just to render a smoother line but also to reduce the quantity of data. This particular example consists of five *InkStroke* objects: two for the H, one for the rest of Hello, one for P, and the last for the rest of Pen. You might be interested in knowing the number of raw polyline segments *InkManager* was given and the number of *InkStrokeRenderingSegment* objects it created:

Stroke	Polyline Segments	Bézier Segments
0	44	9
1	75	14
2	213	29
3	96	16
4	105	16

Even considering that each polyline segment is one point and each Bézier segment (after the first) is three points, this is still a significant reduction in data.

If you want to ignore pressure, you can use a single *Path* element for the entire *InkStroke* and create the geometry with a single instance of *PolyBezierSegment*, filling the *Points* collection with the points from each *InkStrokeRenderingSegment* but using the first one only for setting the *StartPoint* property of *PathFigure*. This alternative approach looks like this:

```
// Render the most recent InkStroke
IReadOnlyList<InkStroke> inkStrokes = inkManager.GetStrokes();
InkStroke inkStroke = inkStrokes[inkStrokes.Count - 1];

// Create a PolyBezierSegment for all the segments in that stroke
IReadOnlyList<InkStrokeRenderingSegment> inkSegments = inkStroke.GetRenderingSegments();
PolyBezierSegment polyBezierSegment = new PolyBezierSegment();

for (int i = 1; i < inkSegments.Count; i++)
{
    InkStrokeRenderingSegment inkSegment = inkSegments[i];

    polyBezierSegment.Points.Add(inkSegment.BezierControlPoint1);
    polyBezierSegment.Points.Add(inkSegment.BezierControlPoint2);
    polyBezierSegment.Points.Add(inkSegment.Position);
}

// Create a PathFigure that begins at first point
PathFigure pathFigure = new PathFigure
{
    StartPoint = inkSegments[0].Position,
    IsClosed = false,
    IsFilled = false
};
pathFigure.Segments.Add(polyBezierSegment);

// Create a PathGeometry with that PathFigure
PathGeometry pathGeometry = new PathGeometry();
pathGeometry.Figures.Add(pathFigure);

// Create a Path with that PathGeometry
Path path = new Path
{
    Stroke = new SolidColorBrush(inkStroke.DrawingAttributes.Color),
    StrokeThickness = inkStroke.DrawingAttributes.Size.Width,
    StrokeStartLineCap = PenLineCap.Round,
    StrokeEndLineCap = PenLineCap.Round,
    Data = pathGeometry
};

// Add it to the Grid
contentGrid.Children.Add(path);
```

It's easy to confirm that *InkManager* does not attempt to capture the pointer. This is something you'll have to do on your own. However, if the pen drifts outside the control while you're accumulating pointer input and you lift the pen, *InkManager* graciously recovers. It doesn't raise an exception getting a call to *ProcessPointerDown* if it never finished up its last sequence with a call to *ProcessPointerUp*.

Erasing and Other Enhancements

One obvious enhancement to the SimpleInking program is to render a polyline as you're actually drawing with the pen. (That actually qualifies as a minimum standard rather than an enhancement!) This polyline is probably either an actual *Polyline* element if you're ignoring pen pressure or a collection of *Line* or *Path* elements if you're not. But once that logic is implemented, you have a choice: You can replace that polyline with the Bézier curves as the stroke is completed, or you can leave the polyline on the screen.

You might be inclined to leave the polyline on the screen if you've been experimenting with varying the pen pressure with the SimpleInking program. If you look closely at the rendered Bézier curves, you might not like what you see, and I don't blame you. Sometimes it's easy to see where one Bézier curve ends and the next begins because there's a discontinuity in the line thickness. This is particularly noticeable at the beginning and end of a stroke. (In the earlier screen shot, look at the ends of the two strokes for the word "Pen.")

As you start contemplating this problem, it becomes evident that these Bézier curves should *not* have uniform line thickness. For example, if a stroke consists of four *InkStrokeRenderingSegment* objects with *Pressure* values of 0.25, 0.5, 0.6, 0.4, the first Bézier curve should have a variable thickness starting with a thickness based on 0.25 and increasing to a thickness based on 0.5, the second Bézier curve should also have an increasing thickness based on a range from 0.5 to 0.6, and the final Bézier curve should decrease in thickness based on 0.6 to 0.4.

This means that you can't just set *BezierSegment* properties from the *InkStrokeRenderingSegment* objects. You probably want to use the Bézier curve points and pressure values to synthesize an *outline* of the stroke and then use *Path* to fill it, much like I did for lines in FingerPaint5. But, obviously, this job is much more algorithmically complex for a Bézier spline than for a straight line.

Another issue: The SimpleInking program renders each new stroke as it's completed and adds the *Path* elements to the *Grid* named *contentGrid*. If you're drawing polylines as the stroke is being created and then replacing them with the Bézier curves, those earlier elements need to be removed from the *Grid*. And, if you implement erasing, at some point you probably need to remove some Bézier curves from the *Grid*, but you won't be quite sure which ones need to come out unless you tag them in some way.

These two problems suggest that it might be easier just clearing the *Children* collection of the *Grid* during *OnPointerReleased* and rendering everything from scratch. It's usually necessary to do this if something has been erased, but you don't need to do it all the time, particularly if you define separate *Grid* elements for rendering the preliminary lines and rendering the final Bézier curves.

The *InkManager* has a *Mode* property of type *InkManipulationMode*, an enumeration with three members:

- *Inking*

- *Erasing*

- *Selecting*

The default value is obviously *Inking*. To enable erasing, you'll set the property to *Erasing* during *OnPointerPressed* and proceed normally but without rendering anything. Then, in subsequent calls to the *ProcessPointerUpdate* method of *InkManager*, whenever the movement of the pen crosses an existing stroke, the *InkManager* removes that stroke from its collection.

Although you can re-render all the remaining *InkStroke* objects during *OnPointerReleased*, the stroke is actually removed during *OnPointerMoved*, so you don't need to wait until *OnPointerReleased* to give the user feedback that a stroke has been erased.

The new project is called InkAndErase. To simplify the removal of preliminary *Line* elements created during the process of drawing a new stroke, the XAML file contains two sibling *Grid* elements:

Project: InkAndErase | File: MainPage.xaml (excerpt)

```
<Page ... >

    <Grid Background="White">
        <Grid Name="contentGrid" />
        <Grid Name="newLineGrid" />
    </Grid>
</Page>
```

The *contentGrid* is for the completed strokes rendered with Bézier splines, while the *newLineGrid* is for the *Line* elements created while a stroke is in progress. This separation makes it easy to get rid of those *Line* segments by just clearing the *Children* collection of *newLineGrid*.

The code-behind file creates an *InkDrawingAttributes* object and sets it to the *InkManager* with nondefault values (for the sake of variety), but it also maintains the *InkDrawingAttributes* object as a field for the benefit of the line-drawing code in the *OnPointerMoved* override. Because this program is performing some processing of pointer input on its own, it defines a *Dictionary* for storing information related to each pointer:

Project: InkAndErase | File: MainPage.xaml.cs (excerpt)

```
public sealed partial class MainPage : Page
{
    InkManager inkManager = new InkManager();
    InkDrawingAttributes inkDrawingAttributes = new InkDrawingAttributes();
    bool hasPen;

    Dictionary<uint, Point> pointerDictionary = new Dictionary<uint, Point>();

    public MainPage()
    {
        this.InitializeComponent();
```

```
            // Check if there's a pen among the pointer input devices
            foreach (PointerDevice device in PointerDevice.GetPointerDevices())
                hasPen |= device.PointerDeviceType == PointerDeviceType.Pen;

            // Default drawing attributes
            inkDrawingAttributes.Color = Colors.Blue;
            inkDrawingAttributes.Size = new Size(6, 6);
            inkManager.SetDefaultDrawingAttributes(inkDrawingAttributes);
        }
        ...
}
```

The Bézier rendering code in InkAndErase is virtually identical to that in the previous program, but I've separated it into two methods to allow the entire assemblage of ink to be redrawn or for individual *InkStroke* objects to be drawn:

Project: InkAndErase | File: MainPage.xaml.cs (excerpt)

```
public sealed partial class MainPage : Page
{
    ...
    void RenderAll()
    {
        contentGrid.Children.Clear();

        foreach (InkStroke inkStroke in inkManager.GetStrokes())
            RenderStroke(inkStroke);
    }

    void RenderStroke(InkStroke inkStroke)
    {
        Brush brush = new SolidColorBrush(inkStroke.DrawingAttributes.Color);
        IReadOnlyList<InkStrokeRenderingSegment> inkSegments = inkStroke.GetRenderingSegments();

        for (int i = 1; i < inkSegments.Count; i++)
        {
            InkStrokeRenderingSegment inkSegment = inkSegments[i];

            BezierSegment bezierSegment = new BezierSegment
            {
                Point1 = inkSegment.BezierControlPoint1,
                Point2 = inkSegment.BezierControlPoint2,
                Point3 = inkSegment.Position
            };

            PathFigure pathFigure = new PathFigure
            {
                StartPoint = inkSegments[i - 1].Position,
                IsClosed = false,
                IsFilled = false
            };
            pathFigure.Segments.Add(bezierSegment);

            PathGeometry pathGeometry = new PathGeometry();
            pathGeometry.Figures.Add(pathFigure);
```

```
        Path path = new Path
        {
            Stroke = brush,
            StrokeThickness = inkStroke.DrawingAttributes.Size.Width *
                            inkSegment.Pressure,
            StrokeStartLineCap = PenLineCap.Round,
            StrokeEndLineCap = PenLineCap.Round,
            Data = pathGeometry
        };
        contentGrid.Children.Add(path);
    }
    }
}
```

Aside from code to interact with the *InkManager* object, much of the *Pointer* event processing is very similar to the pressure-sensitive FingerPaint4 program in Chapter 13. The *OnPointerPressed* override is the only place the program checks that the pointer device is a pen. The subsequent *Pointer* overrides use the presence of the pointer ID key in *pointerDictionary* to determine if a drawing operation is in progress.

The *OnPointerPressed* override is where the *InkManager* is put into erasing mode based on the *IsEraser* property, which means that the user is touching the screen with the eraser end of the pen. A real program would probably have an application bar button to put the *InkManager* into erasing mode for those users who don't have quite so fancy pens:

Project: InkAndErase | File: MainPage.xaml.cs (excerpt)

```
protected override void OnPointerPressed(PointerRoutedEventArgs args)
{
    if (args.Pointer.PointerDeviceType == PointerDeviceType.Pen || !hasPen)
    {
        // Get information
        PointerPoint pointerPoint = args.GetCurrentPoint(this);
        uint id = pointerPoint.PointerId;

        // Initialize for inking or erasing
        if (!pointerPoint.Properties.IsEraser)
        {
            inkManager.Mode = InkManipulationMode.Inking;
        }
        else
        {
            inkManager.Mode = InkManipulationMode.Erasing;
        }

        // Give PointerPoint to InkManager
        inkManager.ProcessPointerDown(pointerPoint);

        // Add an entry to the dictionary
        pointerDictionary.Add(args.Pointer.PointerId, pointerPoint.Position);
```

```
        // Capture the pointer
        CapturePointer(args.Pointer);
    }
    base.OnPointerPressed(args);
}
```

The *OnPointerPressed* override concludes by capturing the pointer.

The *OnPointerMoved* override creates and renders a *Line* element just like the FingerPaint4 program, but only if we're not erasing. When erasing, the return value from *ProcessPointerUpdate* is checked. If a stroke has been deleted from the collection, this return value is a nonempty *Rect* object indicating the area of the screen that must be repainted. The method responds by re-rendering the entire collection of strokes, now missing the deleted stroke:

Project: InkAndErase | **File:** MainPage.xaml.cs (excerpt)

```
protected override void OnPointerMoved(PointerRoutedEventArgs args)
{
    // Get information
    PointerPoint pointerPoint = args.GetCurrentPoint(this);
    uint id = pointerPoint.PointerId;

    if (pointerDictionary.ContainsKey(id))
    {
        foreach (PointerPoint point in args.GetIntermediatePoints(this).Reverse())
        {
            // Give PointerPoint to InkManager
            object obj = inkManager.ProcessPointerUpdate(point);

            if (inkManager.Mode == InkManipulationMode.Erasing)
            {
                // See if something has actually been removed
                Rect rect = (Rect)obj;

                if (rect.Width != 0 && rect.Height != 0)
                {
                    RenderAll();
                }
            }
            else
            {
                // Render the line
                Point point1 = pointerDictionary[id];
                Point point2 = pointerPoint.Position;

                Line line = new Line
                {
                    X1 = point1.X,
                    Y1 = point1.Y,
                    X2 = point2.X,
                    Y2 = point2.Y,
                    Stroke = new SolidColorBrush(inkDrawingAttributes.Color),
                    StrokeThickness = inkDrawingAttributes.Size.Width *
```

```
                    pointerPoint.Properties.Pressure,
            StrokeStartLineCap = PenLineCap.Round,
            StrokeEndLineCap = PenLineCap.Round
        };
        newLineGrid.Children.Add(line);
        pointerDictionary[id] = point2;
      }
    }
  }
  base.OnPointerMoved(args);
}
```

Notice that the *Line* elements are put into the *newLineGrid* but the rendering of Bézier strokes involves the *contentGrid*.

By the time *OnPointerReleased* is called, all erasing should have been completed. However, any inking operation needs to be completed by rendering the new stroke in the *contentGrid* and removing the preliminary *Line* elements from the *newLineGrid*:

Project: InkAndErase | **File:** MainPage.xaml.cs (excerpt)

```
protected override void OnPointerReleased(PointerRoutedEventArgs args)
{
    // Get information
    PointerPoint pointerPoint = args.GetCurrentPoint(this);
    uint id = pointerPoint.PointerId;

    if (pointerDictionary.ContainsKey(id))
    {
        // Give PointerPoint to InkManager
        inkManager.ProcessPointerUp(pointerPoint);

        if (inkManager.Mode == InkManipulationMode.Inking)
        {
            // Get rid of the little Line segments
            newLineGrid.Children.Clear();

            // Render the new stroke
            IReadOnlyList<InkStroke> inkStrokes = inkManager.GetStrokes();
            InkStroke inkStroke = inkStrokes[inkStrokes.Count - 1];
            RenderStroke(inkStroke);
        }
        pointerDictionary.Remove(id);
    }
    base.OnPointerReleased(args);
}
```

Because this program has captured the pointer, it should also have a handler for the *PointerCaptureLost* event. It processes this event by deleting the preliminary lines from the *newLineGrid* and re-rendering everything else:

Project: InkAndErase | **File:** MainPage.xaml.cs (excerpt)

```
protected override void OnPointerCaptureLost(PointerRoutedEventArgs args)
{
    uint id = args.Pointer.PointerId;
```

```
    if (pointerDictionary.ContainsKey(id))
    {
        pointerDictionary.Remove(id);
        newLineGrid.Children.Clear();
        RenderAll();
    }
    base.OnPointerCaptureLost(args);
}
```

Selecting Strokes

The third of the *InkManipulationMode* members is *Selecting*. With an electromagnetic pen, you'll want to put the *InkManager* into selection mode during a *PointerPressed* event when the barrel button is pressed. The sample program coming up does that, but a real application should also have a program option so that the user can manually put the *InkManager* into selection mode.

In this mode, the points that you pass to the *ProcessPointerUpdate* method are interpreted as defining an enclosed area. You'll probably want to render this line but in a way that differentiates it from ink input. When this enclosure line has completed, *ProcessPointerUp* returns a nonempty *Rect* value that indicates the bounding rectangle of the selected strokes. If no strokes are selected, the *Rect* is empty. If strokes have been selected, the selected *InkStroke* objects in the collection have their *Selected* property set to *true*.

In actual use, selection using this enclosure line seems a little "cranky" to me. Often I have to try several times to get it to work.

It's also possible to select strokes programmatically using the *SelectWithLine* or *SelectWithPolyLine* methods of *InkManager* and to manually toggle the *Selected* property of *InkStroke*, but I won't be demonstrating these techniques. They allow you to implement your own selection protocol independent of *InkManager*, in which case you simply don't make any calls to *InkManager* methods while the selection operation is in progress.

After the user has selected one or more *InkStroke* objects, they should be highlighted in some way. You'll also need to provide program options to do something with these selected items. The *InkManager* class itself defines methods named *DeleteSelected*, *CopySelectedToClipboard*, and *MoveSelected*. This last method translates the strokes with a particular offset from their current position. You can also paste strokes from the clipboard into the *InkManager*.

You'll probably also want to define application bar controls to change the color or stroke width of the selected strokes. You might want these same application bar controls to set default colors and stroke widths when strokes are not selected. A lot of the hard stuff here is not the use of *InkManager*, but the design of the user interface surrounding *InkManager*.

The following project is named InkEraseSelect and demonstrates all three modes. Like InkAndErase, it contains two *Grid* elements for rendering ink and preliminary lines:

Project: InkEraseSelect | File: MainPage.xaml (excerpt)

```
<Page ... >
    <Grid Background="White">
        <Grid Name="contentGrid" />
        <Grid Name="newLineGrid" />
    </Grid>

    <Page.BottomAppBar>
        <AppBar Name="bottomAppBar"
                Opened="OnAppBarOpened">
            <StackPanel Orientation="Horizontal"
                        HorizontalAlignment="Left">

                <Button Name="copyAppBarButton"
                        Style="{StaticResource CopyAppBarButtonStyle}"
                        Click="OnCopyAppBarButtonClick" />

                <Button Name="cutAppBarButton"
                        Style="{StaticResource CutAppBarButtonStyle}"
                        Click="OnCutAppBarButtonClick" />

                <Button Name="pasteAppBarButton"
                        Style="{StaticResource PasteAppBarButtonStyle}"
                        Click="OnPasteAppBarButtonClick" />

                <Button Name="deleteAppBarButton"
                        Style="{StaticResource DeleteAppBarButtonStyle}"
                        Click="OnDeleteAppBarButtonClick" />
            </StackPanel>
        </AppBar>
    </Page.BottomAppBar>
</Page>
```

The XAML file also has an array of application bar buttons for the standard options Copy, Cut, Paste, and Delete.

The code-behind file starts off the same as in the previous program, except that a *Brush* is defined for coloring the enclosure line for selected items:

Project: InkEraseSelect | File: MainPage.xaml.cs (excerpt)

```
public sealed partial class MainPage : Page
{
    InkManager inkManager = new InkManager();
    InkDrawingAttributes inkDrawingAttributes = new InkDrawingAttributes();
    bool hasPen;

    Dictionary<uint, Point> pointerDictionary = new Dictionary<uint, Point>();
    Brush selectionBrush = new SolidColorBrush(Colors.Red);
```

```
public MainPage()
{
    this.InitializeComponent();

    // Check if there's a pen among the pointer input devices
    foreach (PointerDevice device in PointerDevice.GetPointerDevices())
        hasPen |= device.PointerDeviceType == PointerDeviceType.Pen;

    // Default drawing attributes
    inkDrawingAttributes.Color = Colors.Blue;
    inkDrawingAttributes.Size = new Size(6, 6);
    inkManager.SetDefaultDrawingAttributes(inkDrawingAttributes);
}
...
}
```

The *OnPointerPressed* override now also checks for the barrel button. If it's pressed, the selection mode is set. (In a real program, you'll want an option for setting this mode in the absence of a barrel button.) When in selection mode, the program draws a simple enclosure of uniform thickness, so it creates a *Polyline* for this purpose and adds it to *newLineGrid*:

Project: InkEraseSelect | File: MainPage.xaml.cs (excerpt)

```
protected override void OnPointerPressed(PointerRoutedEventArgs args)
{
    if (args.Pointer.PointerDeviceType == PointerDeviceType.Pen || !hasPen)
    {
        // Get information
        PointerPoint pointerPoint = args.GetCurrentPoint(this);
        uint id = pointerPoint.PointerId;

        // Initialize for erasing, selecting, or inking
        if (pointerPoint.Properties.IsEraser)
        {
            inkManager.Mode = InkManipulationMode.Erasing;
        }
        else if (pointerPoint.Properties.IsBarrelButtonPressed)
        {
            inkManager.Mode = InkManipulationMode.Selecting;

            // Create Polyline for showing enclosure
            Polyline polyline = new Polyline
            {
                Stroke = selectionBrush,
                StrokeThickness = 1
            };
            polyline.Points.Add(pointerPoint.Position);
            newLineGrid.Children.Add(polyline);
        }
        else
        {
            inkManager.Mode = InkManipulationMode.Inking;
        }
```

```
        // Give PointerPoint to InkManager
        inkManager.ProcessPointerDown(pointerPoint);

        // Add an entry to the dictionary
        pointerDictionary.Add(args.Pointer.PointerId, pointerPoint.Position);

        // Capture the pointer
        CapturePointer(args.Pointer);
    }
    base.OnPointerPressed(args);
}
```

In the *OnPointerMoved* override the erase and inking modes are the same as the previous program. For selection, the *Polyline* is simply continued as in the FingerPaint1 program in Chapter 13:

Project: InkEraseSelect | File: MainPage.xaml.cs (excerpt)

```
protected override void OnPointerMoved(PointerRoutedEventArgs args)
{
    // Get information
    PointerPoint pointerPoint = args.GetCurrentPoint(this);
    uint id = pointerPoint.PointerId;

    if (pointerDictionary.ContainsKey(id))
    {
        foreach (PointerPoint point in args.GetIntermediatePoints(this).Reverse())
        {
            Point point1 = pointerDictionary[id];
            Point point2 = pointerPoint.Position;

            // Give PointerPoint to InkManager
            object obj = inkManager.ProcessPointerUpdate(point);

            if (inkManager.Mode == InkManipulationMode.Erasing)
            {
                // See if something has actually been removed
                Rect rect = (Rect)obj;

                if (rect.Width != 0 && rect.Height != 0)
                {
                    RenderAll();
                }
            }
            else if (inkManager.Mode == InkManipulationMode.Selecting)
            {
                Polyline polyline = newLineGrid.Children[0] as Polyline;
                polyline.Points.Add(point2);
            }
            else // inkManager.Mode == InkManipulationMode.Inking
            {
                // Render the line
                Line line = new Line
                {
                    X1 = point1.X,
                    Y1 = point1.Y,
                    X2 = point2.X,
                    Y2 = point2.Y,
                    Stroke = new SolidColorBrush(inkDrawingAttributes.Color),
```

```
                StrokeThickness = inkDrawingAttributes.Size.Width *
                                        pointerPoint.Properties.Pressure,
                    StrokeStartLineCap = PenLineCap.Round,
                    StrokeEndLineCap = PenLineCap.Round
                };
                newLineGrid.Children.Add(line);
            }
            pointerDictionary[id] = point2;
        }
    }
    base.OnPointerMoved(args);
}
```

Of course, in the FingerPoint1 program there were potentially multiple *Polyline* elements associated with multiple fingers touching the screen, and these multiple *Polyline* elements are stored in a dictionary. Although the *InkManager* can handle multiple fingers, it cannot handle multiple pens, and because selection is enabled only for a pen in this program, it is not possible for multiple *Polyline* elements to exist. A program that allows alternate means of selection involving touch input might need to deal with multiple simultaneous selection areas being defined!

For selection, the *OnPointerReleased* override removes the *Polyline* defining an enclosure and calls *RenderAll*. The rendering logic is responsible for rendering selected strokes differently:

Project: InkEraseSelect | **File:** MainPage.xaml.cs (excerpt)

```
public sealed partial class MainPage : Page
{
    ...
    protected override void OnPointerReleased(PointerRoutedEventArgs args)
    {
        // Get information
        PointerPoint pointerPoint = args.GetCurrentPoint(this);
        uint id = pointerPoint.PointerId;

        if (pointerDictionary.ContainsKey(id))
        {
            // Give PointerPoint to InkManager
            inkManager.ProcessPointerUp(pointerPoint);

            if (inkManager.Mode == InkManipulationMode.Inking)
            {
                // Get rid of the little line segments
                newLineGrid.Children.Clear();

                // Render the new stroke
                IReadOnlyList<InkStroke> inkStrokes = inkManager.GetStrokes();
                InkStroke inkStroke = inkStrokes[inkStrokes.Count - 1];
                RenderStroke(inkStroke);
            }
            else if (inkManager.Mode == InkManipulationMode.Selecting)
            {
                // Get rid of the encircling line
                newLineGrid.Children.Clear();

                // Render everything so selected items are identified
                RenderAll();
```

```
        }
            pointerDictionary.Remove(id);
        }
        base.OnPointerReleased(args);
    }

    protected override void OnPointerCaptureLost(PointerRoutedEventArgs args)
    {
        uint id = args.Pointer.PointerId;

        if (pointerDictionary.ContainsKey(id))
        {
            pointerDictionary.Remove(id);
            newLineGrid.Children.Clear();
            RenderAll();
        }
        base.OnPointerCaptureLost(args);
    }
    . . .
}
```

Here's what it looks like right before the selection enclosure is completed and the pen lifts up, at which point the enclosure line is removed from the screen:

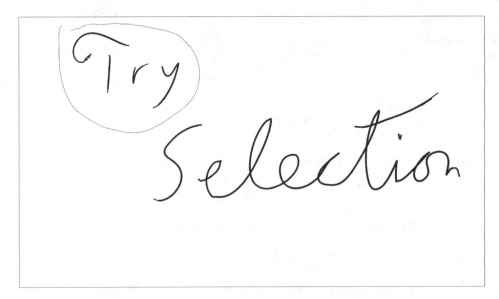

For this program I've separated the rendering logic into three methods. The *RenderStroke* method now calls *RenderBeziers*, but for selected strokes, it's done twice, the first time with a silver color and a thicker pen width so that it surrounds the real stroke:

Project: InkEraseSelect | **File:** MainPage.xaml.cs (excerpt)

```
public sealed partial class MainPage : Page
{
    . . .
    void RenderAll()
```

```
{
    contentGrid.Children.Clear();

    foreach (InkStroke inkStroke in inkManager.GetStrokes())
        RenderStroke(inkStroke);
}

public void RenderStroke(InkStroke inkStroke)
{
    Color color = inkStroke.DrawingAttributes.Color;
    double penSize = inkStroke.DrawingAttributes.Size.Width;

    if (inkStroke.Selected)
        RenderBeziers(contentGrid, inkStroke, Colors.Silver, penSize + 24);

    RenderBeziers(contentGrid, inkStroke, color, penSize);
}

static void RenderBeziers(Panel panel, InkStroke inkStroke, Color color, double penSize)
{
    Brush brush = new SolidColorBrush(color);
    IReadOnlyList<InkStrokeRenderingSegment> inkSegments = inkStroke.GetRenderingSegments();

    for (int i = 1; i < inkSegments.Count; i++)
    {
        InkStrokeRenderingSegment inkSegment = inkSegments[i];

        BezierSegment bezierSegment = new BezierSegment
        {
            Point1 = inkSegment.BezierControlPoint1,
            Point2 = inkSegment.BezierControlPoint2,
            Point3 = inkSegment.Position
        };

        PathFigure pathFigure = new PathFigure
        {
            StartPoint = inkSegments[i - 1].Position,
            IsClosed = false,
            IsFilled = false
        };
        pathFigure.Segments.Add(bezierSegment);

        PathGeometry pathGeometry = new PathGeometry();
        pathGeometry.Figures.Add(pathFigure);

        Path path = new Path
        {
            Stroke = brush,
            StrokeThickness = penSize * inkSegment.Pressure,
            StrokeStartLineCap = PenLineCap.Round,
```

```
            StrokeEndLineCap = PenLineCap.Round,
            Data = pathGeometry
        };
        panel.Children.Add(path);
    }
}
...
}
```

I made *RenderBeziers* static just to demonstrate exactly what parameters the method needs to render a single stroke.

Here are the selected strokes identified using this technique:

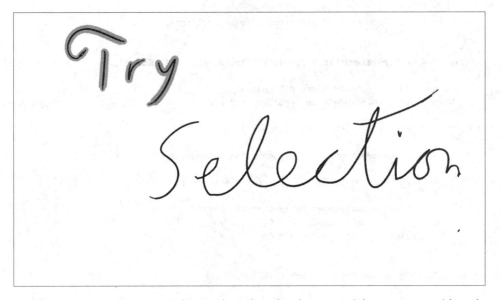

That's certainly one way to indicate selected strokes, but you might want to consider others.

When the application bar is opened, the *Opened* handler enables or disables the four buttons. Three of the buttons are enabled based on the presence of selected strokes in the *InkManager*; the Paste button is enabled based on the *CanPasteFromClipboard* property of *InkManager*:

Project: InkEraseSelect | File: MainPage.xaml.cs (excerpt)

```
public sealed partial class MainPage : Page
{
    ...
    void OnAppBarOpened(object sender, object args)
    {
        bool isAnythingSelected = false;

        foreach (InkStroke inkStroke in inkManager.GetStrokes())
            isAnythingSelected |= inkStroke.Selected;
```

```
        copyAppBarButton.IsEnabled = isAnythingSelected;
        cutAppBarButton.IsEnabled = isAnythingSelected;
        pasteAppBarButton.IsEnabled = inkManager.CanPasteFromClipboard();
        deleteAppBarButton.IsEnabled = isAnythingSelected;
    }

    void OnCopyAppBarButtonClick(object sender, RoutedEventArgs args)
    {
        inkManager.CopySelectedToClipboard();

        foreach (InkStroke inkStroke in inkManager.GetStrokes())
            inkStroke.Selected = false;

        RenderAll();
        bottomAppBar.IsOpen = false;
    }

    void OnCutAppBarButtonClick(object sender, RoutedEventArgs args)
    {
        inkManager.CopySelectedToClipboard();
        inkManager.DeleteSelected();
        RenderAll();
        bottomAppBar.IsOpen = false;
    }

    void OnPasteAppBarButtonClick(object sender, RoutedEventArgs args)
    {
        inkManager.PasteFromClipboard(new Point());
        RenderAll();
        bottomAppBar.IsOpen = false;
    }

    void OnDeleteAppBarButtonClick(object sender, RoutedEventArgs args)
    {
        inkManager.DeleteSelected();
        RenderAll();
        bottomAppBar.IsOpen = false;
    }
}
```

The Copy logic assumes that you don't want the strokes still selected after they've been copied to the clipboard. The Cut and Delete handlers don't need to do something similar because the selected strokes are now gone.

Interestingly, when copying ink to the clipboard, the *InkManager* also converts the ink to a bitmap and an enhanced metafile, so those clipboard formats are available as well for pasting. Some programs—most notably, Microsoft Word—can read ink from the clipboard directly, but programs that can paste bitmaps from the clipboard are very common.

All the coordinates in the ink that is copied to the clipboard are normalized to a minimum rendering coordinate of (0, 0). This is why the *PasteFromClipboard* method requires a *Point* argument. If no *Point* is specified (which is my approach here), the pasted ink appears in the upper-left corner. A real program that implements pasting would need to give the user some way to specify where the pasted ink should go on the page. Similar logic might also be used to implement the *MoveSelected* method supported by *InkManager*.

The Yellow Pad

I use a lot of narrow-ruled yellow legal pads when I'm writing a book. It's my favorite medium for taking notes, writing down ideas, sketching out code interrelationships, and figuring out the math problems. I'm not sure I'll ever move to an electronic yellow pad for this work, but I'll give the alternative a fair chance by coding an application that lets me try it out.

The YellowPad program is not commercial grade, but it does have a few more features than the programs presented so far in this chapter:

YellowPad supports multiple pages viewable in a *FlipView* control. Thus, you can go from page to page with a sweep of your finger. The program ensures that the *FlipView* never reaches the end of the collection by always creating a new page when that's about to happen.

YellowPad also demonstrates the *LoadAsync* and *SaveAsync* methods defined by *InkManager* by saving the contents of all pages in local application storage during the *Suspending* event and loading them the next time the program is run.

YellowPad has the application bar items you've just seen and adds items that let you set a pen width and color for the current page or for selected strokes.

To consolidate some of this logic away from the user interface, I defined a class named *InkFileManager*. If *InkManager* were not sealed, *InkFileManager* would derive from *InkManager*, but instead *InkFileManager* instantiates an *InkManager* as well as a default *InkDrawingAttributes* object and exposes those as public properties. It also includes a method to update the *InkManager* with new drawing attribute values:

Project: YellowPad | **File:** InkFileManager.cs (excerpt)

```
public class InkFileManager
{
    string id;
    ...

    public InkFileManager(string id)
    {
        this.id = id;
        this.InkManager = new InkManager();
        this.InkDrawingAttributes = new InkDrawingAttributes();
    }

    public InkManager InkManager
    {
        private set;
        get;
    }
```

```
public InkDrawingAttributes InkDrawingAttributes
{
    private set;
    get;
}

...

public void UpdateAttributes()
{
    this.InkManager.SetDefaultDrawingAttributes(this.InkDrawingAttributes);
}

...

}
```

InkFileManager also contains a couple small routines involving selection:

Project: YellowPad | **File:** InkFileManager.cs (excerpt)

```
public class InkFileManager
{
    ...
    public bool IsAnythingSelected
    {
        get
        {
            bool isAnythingSelected = false;

            foreach (InkStroke inkStroke in this.InkManager.GetStrokes())
                isAnythingSelected |= inkStroke.Selected;

            return isAnythingSelected;
        }
    }

    public void UnselectAll()
    {
        if (IsAnythingSelected)
        {
            foreach (InkStroke inkStroke in this.InkManager.GetStrokes())
                inkStroke.Selected = false;

            RenderAll();
        }
    }
    ...
}
```

I have also moved all the Bézier rendering logic into this file. Aside from the *InkManager* object itself, the only thing the rendering logic needs is a *Panel* to which to add *Path* elements. This vital information is provided through a public property named *RenderTarget*. The rendering of selected strokes is the same as in the previous program:

Project: YellowPad | **File:** InkFileManager.cs (excerpt)

```csharp
public class InkFileManager
{
    ...
    public Panel RenderTarget
    {
        set;
        get;
    }
    ...

    public void RenderAll()
    {
        this.RenderTarget.Children.Clear();

        foreach (InkStroke inkStroke in this.InkManager.GetStrokes())
            RenderStroke(inkStroke);
    }

    public void RenderStroke(InkStroke inkStroke)
    {
        Color color = inkStroke.DrawingAttributes.Color;
        double penSize = inkStroke.DrawingAttributes.Size.Width;

        if (inkStroke.Selected)
            RenderBeziers(this.RenderTarget, inkStroke, Colors.Silver, penSize + 24);

        RenderBeziers(this.RenderTarget, inkStroke, color, penSize);
    }

    static void RenderBeziers(Panel panel, InkStroke inkStroke, Color color, double penSize)
    {
        Brush brush = new SolidColorBrush(color);
        IReadOnlyList<InkStrokeRenderingSegment> inkSegments = inkStroke.GetRenderingSegments();

        for (int i = 1; i < inkSegments.Count; i++)
        {
            InkStrokeRenderingSegment inkSegment = inkSegments[i];

            BezierSegment bezierSegment = new BezierSegment
            {
                Point1 = inkSegment.BezierControlPoint1,
                Point2 = inkSegment.BezierControlPoint2,
                Point3 = inkSegment.Position
            };

            PathFigure pathFigure = new PathFigure
            {
                StartPoint = inkSegments[i - 1].Position,
                IsClosed = false,
                IsFilled = false
            };
            pathFigure.Segments.Add(bezierSegment);
```

```
            PathGeometry pathGeometry = new PathGeometry();
            pathGeometry.Figures.Add(pathFigure);

            Path path = new Path
            {
                Stroke = brush,
                StrokeThickness = penSize * inkSegment.Pressure,
                StrokeStartLineCap = PenLineCap.Round,
                StrokeEndLineCap = PenLineCap.Round,
                Data = pathGeometry
            };
            panel.Children.Add(path);
        }
    }
    ...
}
```

Finally, *InkFileManager* has two public methods that help justify the "File" part of its name. The *LoadAsync* method loads previously saved ink and settings, or it sets default values if the page is newly created. The *SaveAsync* method saves the current contents of the *InkManager* to local application storage, as well as the pen thickness and color currently associated with that *InkManager*. Both make use of an ID string originally passed to the constructor and saved as a field. This ID string is unique for every *InkFileManager* object the program maintains. As you'll see, it is simply an index (0, 1, 2, and so forth) converted to a string.

Project: YellowPad | **File:** InkFileManager.cs (excerpt)

```
public class InkFileManager
{
    ...
    bool isLoaded;
    ...

    public async Task LoadAsync()
    {
        if (isLoaded)
            return;

        // Load previously saved ink
        StorageFolder storageFolder = ApplicationData.Current.LocalFolder;

        try
        {
            StorageFile storageFile =
                await storageFolder.GetFileAsync("Page" + id + ".ink");

            using (IRandomAccessStream stream =
                        await storageFile.OpenAsync(FileAccessMode.Read))
            {
                await this.InkManager.LoadAsync(stream.GetInputStreamAt(0));
            }
        }
        catch
        {
```

```
        // Do nothing if an exception occurs
    }

    // Load saved settings
    IPropertySet appData = ApplicationData.Current.LocalSettings.Values;

    // Pen size setting
    double penSize = 4;

    if (appData.ContainsKey("PenSize" + id))
        penSize = (double)appData["PenSize" + id];

    this.InkDrawingAttributes.Size = new Size(penSize, penSize);

    // Color setting
    if (appData.ContainsKey("Color + id"))
    {
        byte[] argb = (byte[])appData["Color + id"];
        this.InkDrawingAttributes.Color =
            Color.FromArgb(argb[0], argb[1], argb[2], argb[3]);
    }

    // Set default drawing attributes
    UpdateAttributes();
    isLoaded = true;
}

public async Task SaveAsync()
{
    if (!isLoaded)
        return;

    // Save the ink
    StorageFolder storageFolder = ApplicationData.Current.LocalFolder;

    try
    {
        StorageFile storageFile =
            await storageFolder.CreateFileAsync("Page" + id + ".ink",
                                CreationCollisionOption.ReplaceExisting);

        using (IRandomAccessStream stream =
                await storageFile.OpenAsync(FileAccessMode.ReadWrite))
        {
            await this.InkManager.SaveAsync(stream.GetOutputStreamAt(0));
        }
    }
    catch
    {
        // Do nothing if an exception occurs
    }

    // Save settings
    IPropertySet appData = ApplicationData.Current.LocalSettings.Values;

    // Save pen size
    appData["PenSize" + id] = this.InkDrawingAttributes.Size.Width;
```

```
        // Save color
        Color color = this.InkDrawingAttributes.Color;
        byte[] argb = { color.A, color.R, color.G, color.B };
        appData["Color" + id] = argb;
    }
}
```

In the YellowPad program, each *InkFileManager* is associated with a *UserControl* derivative named *YellowPadPage*. Here's the XAML file for that class, including the visual mimicking of a legal pad with a yellow background and two red vertical lines toward the left of the page.

Project: YellowPad | File: YellowPadPage.xaml

```
<UserControl
    x:Class="YellowPad.YellowPadPage"
    xmlns="http://schemas.microsoft.com/winfx/2006/xaml/presentation"
    xmlns:x="http://schemas.microsoft.com/winfx/2006/xaml"
    xmlns:local="using:YellowPad">

    <Grid>
        <Viewbox>
            <Grid Name="sheetPanel"
                  Width="816" Height="1056"
                  Background="#FFFF80">

                <Line Stroke="Red" X1="132" Y1="0" X2="132" Y2="1056" />
                <Line Stroke="Red" X1="138" Y1="0" X2="138" Y2="1056" />

                <Grid Name="contentGrid" />
                <Grid Name="newLineGrid" />
            </Grid>
        </Viewbox>
    </Grid>
</UserControl>
```

The control incorporates a *Viewbox* so that it adapts to any size window.

As you can guess from seeing the names of the two inner *Grid* elements, the code-behind file handles all the pointer input. However, I discovered that trying to make this program run on a nonpen device was problematic. Keep in mind that instances of *YellowPadPage* are in a *FlipView*, and the *FlipView* wants its own touch input for changing the selected items. I decided to eliminate the logic that allows the program to run without a pen. YellowPad insists that you be using a real pen.

The *YellowPadPage* constructor is responsible for drawing the blue rule lines on the page:

Project: YellowPad | File: YellowPadPage.xaml.cs (excerpt)

```
public YellowPadPage()
{
    this.InitializeComponent();

    // Draw horizontal lines in blue
    Brush blueBrush = new SolidColorBrush(Colors.Blue);
```

```
    for (int y = 120; y < sheetPanel.Height; y += 24)
        sheetPanel.Children.Add(new Line
        {
            X1 = 0,
            Y1 = y,
            X2 = sheetPanel.Width,
            Y2 = y,
            Stroke = blueBrush
        });
}
```

The *YellowPadPage* control also defines a new dependency property of type *InkFileManager*.
Here's the overhead:

Project: YellowPad | File: YellowPadPage.xaml.cs (excerpt)

```
public sealed partial class YellowPadPage : UserControl
{
    static readonly DependencyProperty inkFileManagerProperty =
        DependencyProperty.Register("InkFileManager",
                        typeof(InkFileManager),
                        typeof(YellowPadPage),
                        new PropertyMetadata(null, OnInkFileManagerChanged));

    ...

    // Overhead for InkFileManager dependency property
    public static DependencyProperty InkFileManagerProperty
    {
        get { return inkFileManagerProperty; }
    }

    public InkFileManager InkFileManager
    {
        set { SetValue(InkFileManagerProperty, value); }
        get { return (InkFileManager)GetValue(InkFileManagerProperty); }
    }

    static void OnInkFileManagerChanged(DependencyObject obj,
                                        DependencyPropertyChangedEventArgs args)
    {
        (obj as YellowPadPage).OnInkFileManagerChanged(args);
    }

    async void OnInkFileManagerChanged(DependencyPropertyChangedEventArgs args)
    {
        contentGrid.Children.Clear();
        newLineGrid.Children.Clear();

        if (args.NewValue != null)
        {
            await this.InkFileManager.LoadAsync();
            this.InkFileManager.RenderTarget = contentGrid;
            this.InkFileManager.RenderAll();
        }
    }
    ...
}
```

When this *InkFileManager* property is set to a new *InkFileManager* instance, the property-changed handler calls *LoadAsync* to load any existing ink and settings, sets the *RenderTarget* to its own *contentGrid*, and then has the *InkFileManager* render all the ink that existed previously.

The remainder of *YellowPadPage* assumes this *InkFileManager* property has already been set and is dedicated to processing the *Pointer* events. This logic here is virtually the same as what you've seen in the previous program, except that it uses the *InkFileManager* property to obtain the *InkManager* and *InkDrawingAttributes* objects associated with this page and for rendering the strokes:

Project: YellowPad | File: YellowPadPage.xaml.cs (excerpt)

```
public sealed partial class YellowPadPage : UserControl
{
    ...
    Dictionary<uint, Point> pointerDictionary = new Dictionary<uint, Point>();
    Brush selectionBrush = new SolidColorBrush(Colors.Red);
    ...
    protected override void OnPointerPressed(PointerRoutedEventArgs args)
    {
        if (args.Pointer.PointerDeviceType == PointerDeviceType.Pen)
        {
            // Get information
            PointerPoint pointerPoint = args.GetCurrentPoint(sheetPanel);
            uint id = pointerPoint.PointerId;
            InkManager inkManager = this.InkFileManager.InkManager;

            // Initialize for inking, erasing, or selecting
            if (pointerPoint.Properties.IsEraser)
            {
                inkManager.Mode = InkManipulationMode.Erasing;
                this.InkFileManager.UnselectAll();
            }
            else if (pointerPoint.Properties.IsBarrelButtonPressed)
            {
                inkManager.Mode = InkManipulationMode.Selecting;

                // Create Polyline for showing enclosure
                Polyline polyline = new Polyline
                {
                    Stroke = selectionBrush,
                    StrokeThickness = 1
                };
                polyline.Points.Add(pointerPoint.Position);
                newLineGrid.Children.Add(polyline);
            }
            else
            {
                inkManager.Mode = InkManipulationMode.Inking;
                this.InkFileManager.UnselectAll();
            }

            // Give PointerPoint to InkManager
            inkManager.ProcessPointerDown(pointerPoint);

            // Add an entry to the dictionary
            pointerDictionary.Add(args.Pointer.PointerId, pointerPoint.Position);
```

```
            // Capture the pointer
            this.CapturePointer(args.Pointer);
        }
        base.OnPointerPressed(args);
    }

    protected override void OnPointerMoved(PointerRoutedEventArgs args)
    {
        // Get information
        PointerPoint pointerPoint = args.GetCurrentPoint(sheetPanel);
        uint id = pointerPoint.PointerId;
        InkManager inkManager = this.InkFileManager.InkManager;
        InkDrawingAttributes inkDrawingAttributes =
                            this.InkFileManager.InkDrawingAttributes;

        if (pointerDictionary.ContainsKey(id))
        {
            foreach (PointerPoint point in args.GetIntermediatePoints(sheetPanel).Reverse())
            {
                Point point1 = pointerDictionary[id];
                Point point2 = pointerPoint.Position;

                // Give PointerPoint to InkManager
                object obj = inkManager.ProcessPointerUpdate(point);

                if (inkManager.Mode == InkManipulationMode.Erasing)
                {
                    // See if something has actually been removed
                    Rect rect = (Rect)obj;

                    if (rect.Width != 0 && rect.Height != 0)
                    {
                        this.InkFileManager.RenderAll();
                    }
                }
                else if (inkManager.Mode == InkManipulationMode.Selecting)
                {
                    Polyline polyline = newLineGrid.Children[0] as Polyline;
                    polyline.Points.Add(point2);
                }
                else // inkManager.Mode == InkManipulationMode.Inking
                {
                    // Render the line
                    Line line = new Line
                    {
                        X1 = point1.X,
                        Y1 = point1.Y,
                        X2 = point2.X,
                        Y2 = point2.Y,
                        Stroke = new SolidColorBrush(inkDrawingAttributes.Color),
                        StrokeThickness = inkDrawingAttributes.Size.Width *
                                            pointerPoint.Properties.Pressure,
                        StrokeStartLineCap = PenLineCap.Round,
                        StrokeEndLineCap = PenLineCap.Round
                    };
                    newLineGrid.Children.Add(line);
```

```
                }
                pointerDictionary[id] = point2;
            }
        }
        base.OnPointerMoved(args);
    }


    protected override void OnPointerReleased(PointerRoutedEventArgs args)
    {
        // Get information
        PointerPoint pointerPoint = args.GetCurrentPoint(sheetPanel);
        uint id = pointerPoint.PointerId;
        InkManager inkManager = this.InkFileManager.InkManager;

        if (pointerDictionary.ContainsKey(id))
        {
            // Give PointerPoint to InkManager
            inkManager.ProcessPointerUp(pointerPoint);

            if (inkManager.Mode == InkManipulationMode.Inking)
            {
                // Get rid of the little line segments
                newLineGrid.Children.Clear();

                // Render the new stroke
                IReadOnlyList<InkStroke> inkStrokes = inkManager.GetStrokes();
                InkStroke inkStroke = inkStrokes[inkStrokes.Count - 1];
                this.InkFileManager.RenderStroke(inkStroke);
            }
            else if (inkManager.Mode == InkManipulationMode.Selecting)
            {
                // Get rid of the enclosure line
                newLineGrid.Children.Clear();

                // Render everything so selected items are identified
                this.InkFileManager.RenderAll();
            }
            pointerDictionary.Remove(id);
        }
        base.OnPointerReleased(args);
    }

    protected override void OnPointerCaptureLost(PointerRoutedEventArgs args)
    {
        uint id = args.Pointer.PointerId;

        if (pointerDictionary.ContainsKey(id))
        {
            pointerDictionary.Remove(id);
            newLineGrid.Children.Clear();
            this.InkFileManager.RenderAll();
        }
        base.OnPointerCaptureLost(args);
    }
}
```

YellowPadPage gets an instance of *InkFileManager* through a data binding. The *FlipView* control in *MainPage* contains a collection of *InkFileManager* objects—one for each page—so the *ItemTemplate* for the *FlipView* is dominated (in appearance though not markup) with a *YellowPadPage* with a binding to the item in the control's *ItemsSource* collection:

Project: YellowPad | File: MainPage.xaml (excerpt)

```
<Page ... >
    <Page.Resources>
        <local:IndexToPageNumberConverter x:Key="indexToPageNumber" />
    </Page.Resources>

    <Grid Background="{StaticResource ApplicationPageBackgroundThemeBrush}">
        <FlipView Name="flipView"
                  SelectionChanged="OnFlipViewSelectionChanged">
            <FlipView.ItemTemplate>
                <DataTemplate>
                    <Grid HorizontalAlignment="Center"
                          VerticalAlignment="Center">

                        <local:YellowPadPage InkFileManager="{Binding}" />

                        <TextBlock Name="pageNumTextBlock"
                                   HorizontalAlignment="Right"
                                   VerticalAlignment="Top"
                                   FontSize="12"
                                   Foreground="Black"
                                   Margin="6"
                                   Text="{Binding ElementName=flipView,
                                                  Path=SelectedIndex,
                                   Converter={StaticResource indexToPageNumber}}" />
                    </Grid>
                </DataTemplate>
            </FlipView.ItemTemplate>
        </FlipView>
    </Grid>

    <Page.BottomAppBar>
        ...
    </Page.BottomAppBar>
</Page>
```

The *TextBlock* defined in the *DataTemplate* along with *YellowPadPage* displays the current page number. This binding on the *Text* property references an ad hoc binding converter that converts a zero-based index to a text label:

Project: YellowPad | File: IndexToPageNumberConverter.cs

```
using System;
using Windows.UI.Xaml.Data;

namespace YellowPad
{
    public class IndexToPageNumberConverter : IValueConverter
    {
```

```
        public object Convert(object value, Type targetType, object parameter, string language)
        {
            return String.Format("Page {0}", (int)value + 1);
        }

        public object ConvertBack(object value, Type targetType, object parameter, string lang)
        {
            return value;
        }
    }
}
```

As you've seen, each *InkFileManager* instance saves and restores application settings associated with that page, including the ink content of that page. The *MainPage* code saves and restores settings associated with the application itself. This is just two integer items: the number of pages (which is the number of items in the collection of *InkFileManager* objects), and the current page index (which is the *SelectedIndex* property of the *FlipView*):

Project: YellowPad | **File:** MainPage.xaml.cs (excerpt)

```
public sealed partial class MainPage : Page
{
    ObservableCollection<InkFileManager> inkFileManagers =
                                new ObservableCollection<InkFileManager>();
    public MainPage()
    {
        this.InitializeComponent();
        Loaded += OnMainPageLoaded;
        Application.Current.Suspending += OnApplicationSuspending;
    }

    void OnMainPageLoaded(object sender, RoutedEventArgs args)
    {
        // Load application settings
        IPropertySet appData = ApplicationData.Current.LocalSettings.Values;

        // Get the page count
        int pageCount = 1;

        if (appData.ContainsKey("PageCount"))
            pageCount = (int)appData["PageCount"];

        // Create that many InkFileManager objects
        for (int i = 0; i < pageCount; i++)
            inkFileManagers.Add(new InkFileManager(i.ToString()));

        // Set the collection to the FlipView
        flipView.ItemsSource = inkFileManagers;

        // Set the SelectedIndex of the PageView
        if (appData.ContainsKey("PageIndex"))
            flipView.SelectedIndex = (int)appData["PageIndex"];
    }
```

```
async void OnApplicationSuspending(object sender, SuspendingEventArgs args)
{
    SuspendingDeferral deferral = args.SuspendingOperation.GetDeferral();

    // Save all the InkFileManager contents
    foreach (InkFileManager inkFileManager in inkFileManagers)
        await inkFileManager.SaveAsync();

    // Save the page count and current page index
    IPropertySet appData = ApplicationData.Current.LocalSettings.Values;
    appData["PageCount"] = inkFileManagers.Count;
    appData["PageIndex"] = flipView.SelectedIndex;

    deferral.Complete();
}

void OnFlipViewSelectionChanged(object sender, SelectionChangedEventArgs args)
{
    // If at the end of the FlipView, add another item!
    if (flipView.SelectedIndex == flipView.Items.Count - 1)
        inkFileManagers.Add(new InkFileManager(flipView.Items.Count.ToString()));
}
...
}
```

Notice that the *Loaded* handler creates all the *InkFileManager* objects for the current number of pages, but the *InkFileManager* constructor does nothing beyond creating *InkManager* and *InkDrawingAttributes* instances. In particular, it doesn't yet load in any previously saved ink. This happens later when the *InkFileManager* instance is actually bound to a *YellowPadPage*. Keep in mind that the items panel for the *FlipView* is a *VirtualizingStackPanel*, which creates visual trees for the items only as they're needed. This means that the loading of previously saved ink is spread out over a longer period of time and occurs as the user is actively flipping through the various pages. Some pages might not be loaded at all, and those that aren't loaded don't need to be saved again.

The remainder of the program is dedicated to handling buttons on the application bar, including the flawed Paste logic that you've already seen. In addition to the four clipboard-related buttons, the application bar also includes two very similarly templated *ComboBox* controls, one for the pen width and the other for the pen color:

Project: YellowPad | File: MainPage.xaml (excerpt)

```
<AppBar Name="bottomAppBar"
        Opened="OnAppBarOpened">
    <Grid>
        <StackPanel Orientation="Horizontal"
                    HorizontalAlignment="Left">

            <Button Name="copyAppBarButton"
                    Style="{StaticResource CopyAppBarButtonStyle}"
                    Click="OnCopyAppBarButtonClick" />
```

```
    <Button Name="cutAppBarButton"
            Style="{StaticResource CutAppBarButtonStyle}"
            Click="OnCutAppBarButtonClick" />

    <Button Name="pasteAppBarButton"
            Style="{StaticResource PasteAppBarButtonStyle}"
            Click="OnPasteAppBarButtonClick" />

    <Button Name="deleteAppBarButton"
            Style="{StaticResource DeleteAppBarButtonStyle}"
            Click="OnDeleteAppBarButtonClick" />
</StackPanel>

<StackPanel Orientation="Horizontal"
            HorizontalAlignment="Right">
    <ComboBox Name="penSizeComboBox"
              SelectionChanged="OnPenSizeComboBoxSelectionChanged"
              Width="200"
              Margin="20 0">
        <x:Double>2</x:Double>
        <x:Double>3</x:Double>
        <x:Double>4</x:Double>
        <x:Double>5</x:Double>
        <x:Double>7</x:Double>
        <x:Double>10</x:Double>

        <ComboBox.ItemTemplate>
            <DataTemplate>
                <Path StrokeThickness="{Binding}"
                      Stroke="Black"
                      StrokeStartLineCap="Round"
                      StrokeEndLineCap="Round"
                      Data="M 0 0 C 50 20 100 0 150 20" />
            </DataTemplate>
        </ComboBox.ItemTemplate>
    </ComboBox>

    <ComboBox Name="colorComboBox"
              SelectionChanged="OnColorComboBoxSelectionChanged"
              Width="200"
              Margin="20 0">
        <Color>#FF0000</Color>
        <Color>#800000</Color>
        <Color>#FFFF00</Color>
        <Color>#808000</Color>
        <Color>#00FF00</Color>
        <Color>#008000</Color>
        <Color>#00FFFF</Color>
        <Color>#008080</Color>
        <Color>#0000FF</Color>
        <Color>#000080</Color>
        <Color>#FF00FF</Color>
        <Color>#800080</Color>
        <Color>#C0C0C0</Color>
```

```
            <Color>#808080</Color>
            <Color>#404040</Color>
            <Color>#000000</Color>

            <ComboBox.ItemTemplate>
                <DataTemplate>
                    <Path StrokeThickness="6"
                          StrokeStartLineCap="Round"
                          StrokeEndLineCap="Round"
                          Data="M 0 0 C 50 20 100 0 150 20">
                        <Path.Stroke>
                            <SolidColorBrush Color="{Binding}" />
                        </Path.Stroke>
                    </Path>
                </DataTemplate>
            </ComboBox.ItemTemplate>
        </ComboBox>
    </StackPanel>
    </Grid>
</AppBar>
```

To keep the program simple, I have not implemented any adjustments for portrait or snapped modes. These modes result in overlapping buttons and combo boxes.

The application bar items are all applicable to the current page displayed in the *FlipView*. Moreover, the two *ComboBox* controls might be applicable to the page—that is, to the default *InkDrawingAttributes* object associated with the current *InkFileManager* for this page—or to selected items on the page. When the application bar is opened, these controls must be initialized appropriately:

Project: YellowPad | File: MainPage.xaml.cs (excerpt)

```
void OnAppBarOpened(object sender, object args)
{
    InkFileManager inkFileManager = (InkFileManager)flipView.SelectedItem;

    copyAppBarButton.IsEnabled = inkFileManager.IsAnythingSelected;
    cutAppBarButton.IsEnabled = inkFileManager.IsAnythingSelected;
    pasteAppBarButton.IsEnabled = inkFileManager.InkManager.CanPasteFromClipboard();
    deleteAppBarButton.IsEnabled = inkFileManager.IsAnythingSelected;

    if (!inkFileManager.IsAnythingSelected)
    {
        // Set initial selected item
        Size size = inkFileManager.InkDrawingAttributes.Size;
        penSizeComboBox.SelectedItem = (size.Width + size.Height) / 2;
        colorComboBox.SelectedItem = inkFileManager.InkDrawingAttributes.Color;
    }
    else
    {
        penSizeComboBox.SelectedItem = null;
        colorComboBox.SelectedItem = null;
    }
}
```

A more sophisticated version of this method would loop through the selected strokes and determine whether they all had the same color or width. If so, those values could be used to initialize the two *ComboBox* controls. As it is now, each *ComboBox* is given no selected value when strokes are selected.

The handling of the four clipboard items is very similar to the previous program except that the *InkManager* must be accessed through the *InkFileManager* available from the *SelectedItem* property of the *FlipView*:

Project: YellowPad | File: MainPage.xaml.cs (excerpt)

```
public sealed partial class MainPage : Page
{
    ...
    void OnCopyAppBarButtonClick(object sender, RoutedEventArgs args)
    {
        InkFileManager inkFileManager = (InkFileManager)flipView.SelectedItem;
        inkFileManager.InkManager.CopySelectedToClipboard();

        foreach (InkStroke inkStroke in inkFileManager.InkManager.GetStrokes())
            inkStroke.Selected = false;

        inkFileManager.RenderAll();
        bottomAppBar.IsOpen = false;
    }

    void OnCutAppBarButtonClick(object sender, RoutedEventArgs args)
    {
        InkFileManager inkFileManager = (InkFileManager)flipView.SelectedItem;
        inkFileManager.InkManager.CopySelectedToClipboard();
        inkFileManager.InkManager.DeleteSelected();
        inkFileManager.RenderAll();
        bottomAppBar.IsOpen = false;
    }

    void OnPasteAppBarButtonClick(object sender, RoutedEventArgs args)
    {
        InkFileManager inkFileManager = (InkFileManager)flipView.SelectedItem;
        inkFileManager.InkManager.PasteFromClipboard(new Point());
        inkFileManager.RenderAll();
        bottomAppBar.IsOpen = false;
    }

    void OnDeleteAppBarButtonClick(object sender, RoutedEventArgs args)
    {
        InkFileManager inkFileManager = (InkFileManager)flipView.SelectedItem;
        inkFileManager.InkManager.DeleteSelected();
        inkFileManager.RenderAll();
        bottomAppBar.IsOpen = false;
    }
    ...
}
```

The processing of the two *ComboBox* controls is very similar. In both cases, either the *InkDrawingAttributes* object of the *InkFileManager* is given new values for future drawing or the selected strokes are updated with new values:

Project: YellowPad | **File:** MainPage.xaml.cs (excerpt)

```
public sealed partial class MainPage : Page
{
    ...
    void OnPenSizeComboBoxSelectionChanged(object sender, SelectionChangedEventArgs args)
    {
        if (penSizeComboBox.SelectedItem == null)
            return;

        InkFileManager inkFileManager = (InkFileManager)flipView.SelectedItem;

        double penSize = (double)penSizeComboBox.SelectedItem;
        Size size = new Size(penSize, penSize);

        if (!inkFileManager.IsAnythingSelected)
        {
            inkFileManager.InkDrawingAttributes.Size = size;
            inkFileManager.UpdateAttributes();
        }
        else
        {
            foreach (InkStroke inkStroke in inkFileManager.InkManager.GetStrokes())
                if (inkStroke.Selected)
                {
                    InkDrawingAttributes drawingAttrs = inkStroke.DrawingAttributes;
                    drawingAttrs.Size = size;
                    inkStroke.DrawingAttributes = drawingAttrs;
                }
            inkFileManager.RenderAll();
        }
    }

    void OnColorComboBoxSelectionChanged(object sender, SelectionChangedEventArgs args)
    {
        if (colorComboBox.SelectedItem == null)
            return;

        InkFileManager inkFileManager = (InkFileManager)flipView.SelectedItem;

        Color color = (Color)colorComboBox.SelectedItem;

        if (!inkFileManager.IsAnythingSelected)
        {
            inkFileManager.InkDrawingAttributes.Color = color;
            inkFileManager.UpdateAttributes();
        }
        else
        {
```

```
        foreach (InkStroke inkStroke in inkFileManager.InkManager.GetStrokes())
            if (inkStroke.Selected)
            {
                InkDrawingAttributes drawingAttrs = inkStroke.DrawingAttributes;
                drawingAttrs.Color = color;
                inkStroke.DrawingAttributes = drawingAttrs;
            }
        inkFileManager.RenderAll();
    }
  }
}
```

This program certainly has some flaws. For example, you can set color and pen width attributes for the current page or for selected strokes, but you can't set values that apply to all new pages created in the future. Each new page starts out with defaults hard-coded in the *InkFileManager* class.

What the program really needs is a *GridView* control that displays all the pages as thumbnails and lets you move them around, or select them for deletion or printing, or even group them.

But that's the nature of software. It's never really finished because it never needs to be finished, and it's quite unlike books in that respect.

Index

A

C

D

M

N

R

About the Author

CHARLES PETZOLD began programming for Windows 28 years ago with beta versions of Windows 1. He wrote the first articles about Windows programming to appear in a magazine and wrote one of the first books on the subject, *Programming Windows*, first published in 1988. Over the past decade, he has written seven books on .NET programming, including the recent *Programming Windows Phone 7* (Microsoft Press, 2010), and he currently writes the DirectX Factor column for MSDN Magazine about DirectX programming in Windows 8. Petzold's books also include *Code: The Hidden Language of Computer Hardware and Software* (Microsoft Press, 1999), a unique exploration of digital technologies, and *The Annotated Turing: A Guided Tour through Alan Turing's Historic Paper on Computability and the Turing Machine* (Wiley, 2008). His website is *www.charlespetzold.com*.

What do you think of this book?

We want to hear from you!
To participate in a brief online survey, please visit:

microsoft.com/learning/booksurvey

Tell us how well this book meets your needs—what works effectively, and what we can do better. Your feedback will help us continually improve our books and learning resources for you.

Thank you in advance for your input!